THE MINSTER

GERMAN
DICTIONARY

THE MINSTER

GERMAN

DICTIONARY

MINSTER BOOKS

First published in 1976 by
The Hamlyn Publishing Group Limited
Published in 1983 by Newnes Books,
Michelin House, 81 Fulham Road,
London SW3 6RB

This 1992 edition reprinted exclusively for MINSTER BOOKS

© Copyright Reed International Books Limited 1976

ISBN 0 600 36564 6

Printed at Thomson Press (India) Ltd.
Faridabad (Haryana)

Foreword

This dictionary aims to give concise and accurate definitions of 24,000 of the most important words in use in the English and German languages today.

A pronunciation system based on the International Phonetic Alphabet is used (see *Key to symbols used in pronunciation*). Pronunciation is given for all headwords in both sections of the dictionary, and also for selected subentries in the German-English section.

Modern technical, commercial, and informal usage is given particular attention, in preference to outmoded terms or other expressions not in common contemporary use. Definitions are numbered in order to distinguish senses, and abbreviations are used to indicate use in specific technical, scientific, or commercial fields (see *Abbreviations used in the Dictionary*). An additional feature is the inclusion of idiomatic expressions and phrases, so necessary for the understanding and use of the foreign language.

This dictionary, with its emphasis on modernity, together with its compact form and clear typeface, should prove indispensable in the home, at school, in the office, and abroad.

Abbreviations used in the Dictionary

adj	adjective	indef art	indefinite article	pol	politics
adv	adverb	inf	informal	poss	possessive
anat	anatomy	infin	infinitive	pref	prefix
arch	architecture	interj	interjection	prep	preposition
aux	auxiliary	invar	invariable	pron	pronoun
aviat	aviation	lit	literature	rel	religion
bot	botany	m	masculine	s	singular
cap	capital	math	mathematics	sci	science
comm	commerce	med	medical	sl	slang
conj	conjunction	mil	military	suff	suffix
cul	culinary	min	minerals	tab	taboo
def art	definite article	mod	modal	Tdmk	trademark
derog	derogatory	mot	motoring	tech	technical
dom	domestic	mus	music	Th	theatre
educ	education	n	noun	US	United States
fam	familiar	naut	nautical	v	verb
fml	formal	neg	negative	vi	intransitive verb
game	cards, chess, etc.	neu	neuter	v imp	impersonal verb
gram	grammar	pers	person	vr	reflexive verb
geog	geography	phot	photography	vt	transitive verb
				zool	zoology

Key to symbols used in pronunciation

English

Vowels

iː	meet	u	put	ai	fly	
i	bit	uː	shoot	au	how	
e	get	ʌ	cut	ɔi	boy	
æ	hat	ə	ago	iə	here	
ɑː	heart	əː	sir	ɛə	air	
ɔ	hot	ei	late	uə	poor	
ɔː	ought	ou	go			

Consonants

θ	thin
ð	then
ŋ	sing
j	yes
ʃ	ship
ʒ	measure
tʃ	chin
dʒ	gin

' indicates that the following syllable is stressed, as in ago (ə'gou).

, placed under an n or l indicates that the n or l is pronounced as a syllable, as in button ('bʌtn̩) and flannel ('flænl̩).

However, a dash is used to indicate that a plural does not vary, or only takes an umlaut, as in the following examples:—

Kanzler . . . *nm* — (plural is *die Kanzler*)
Apfel . . . *nm* ⸚ (plural is *die Äpfel*)

Exceptions are nouns that cannot form a plural, such as *Kost* or *Unterrichtung*. To form the plural of compounds, the user should refer to the headword of the principal (final) component, which is always the part that takes the plural, e.g. for *Armbanduhr*, see *Uhr*.

Parentheses are used to show optional forms, particularly in the English-German section, thus:—

deliver . . . *vt* . . . (ab-, aus-)liefern . . . (indicates that *liefern* may be used alone or with the prefixes shown, as *abliefern* or *ausliefern*)
inoculation . . . *n* (Ein)Impfung *f* . . . (indicates that *Impfung* or *Einimpfung* may be used)
wash . . . (*vi*),*vt* . . . (sich) waschen . . . (indicates that *waschen* is transitive, but that the intransitive sense of *to wash* may be translated by *sich waschen*)

Adverbs: German adjectives can function as adverbs without modification. Therefore, in the German-English section, no translation of such adverbs is given where the adverbial form of the English adjective shown in the definition would be appropriate. In the English-German section, regular adverbial forms of English adjectives (i.e. those ending in -*ly*) are not shown where the given German translation could be used as an adverb, or where the English adverb has no special meaning requiring a separate translation.

English attributive adjectives can often be translated in German by using nouns to form compounds. This is shown by a dash as follows:—

manual . . . *adj* Hand—.

Thus, *manual worker* may be translated as *Handarbeiter*.

Feminine forms: Only the most common feminine forms of nouns have been selected for inclusion. However the feminine of agent nouns or nationalities ending in -*er* is formed by adding the suffix -*in* to the masculine; for example, *Arbeiterin* — female worker; *Dichterin* — poetess; *Italienerin* — Italian woman, etc. Weak nouns drop the final -*e* and add -*in*; thus *Chinese* becomes *Chinesin*. Adjectival nouns, shown with a final *r* in parentheses, behave as a masculine or feminine adjective. Thus the feminine nominative singular of *Abgeordnete(r)* is *die Abgeordnete*.

German

Vowels

							Consonants	
i	*ist*	a:	*Wagen*	y:	*fühlen*		ç	*ich*
i:	*wieder*	ɔ	*Holz*	œ	*Hölle*		ʒ	*Garage*
e	*General*	o	*Forelle*	œ:	*lösen*		ŋ	*lang*
e:	*gegen*	o:	*ohne*	ə	*besser*		ʃ	*Tisch*
ɛ	*setzen*	u	*rund*	ai	*frei*		j	*ja*
ɛ:	*Fähre*	u:	*Kugel*	au	*Haus*		x	*lachen*
a	*hat*	y	*Hütte*	ɔy	*treu*			

' indicates that the following syllable is stressed, as in *gegen* ('ge:gən).
In pronunciations of certain words borrowed from French, nasalization is indicated by
a tilde (~) over the appropriate vowel, as in *Pension* (pa'sjo:n).

Notes on the use of the Dictionary

An oblique stroke in a headword in the German-English section indicates that the part of
the word before the oblique may be combined with other words or word endings shown in
the text of the entry in heavy type after a dash, thus:—

   einwillig/en . . . *vi* agree, consent. **—ung** *nf* . . . agreement, consent.

In headwords with no oblique, the ending combines with the whole word. Since all German
nouns are spelt with a capital initial letter, the subentry above should be spelt *Einwilligung*.
Verbs, adjectives, or adverbs entered under a noun headword with an initial capital should
be written with a lower-case letter. Where a reflexive verb is the headword, subentries do not
take the pronoun *sich*.

A swung dash (~) before a change of part of speech indicates that the part of speech
refers to the headword, not the preceding subentry shown in heavy type.

Irregular verbs in the headword lists of both sections are marked with an asterisk. The
principal parts of these verbs are shown in the verb tables. For compounds with either
separable or inseparable prefixes, see the base form shown in the table, e.g. for *verstehen*,
see *stehen*.

Plurals of German nouns are shown after a hyphen immediately after the part of speech, as
follows:—

   Feind . . . *nm* **-e** (plural is *die Feinde*)
   Empfang . . . *nm* **-̈e** (plural is *die Empfänge*)
   Ablaß . . . *nm* **-lässe** (plural is *die Ablässe*)

Infinitive	Past Tense	Past Participle	Infinitive	Past Tense	Past Participle
abide	abode *or* abided	abode *or* abided	flee	fled	fled
			fling	flung	flung
arise	arose	arisen	fly	flew	flown
awake	awoke *or* awaked	awoke *or* awaked	forbid	forbade *or* forbad	forbidden *or* forbid
be	was	been	forget	forgot	forgotten *or* forgot
bear[1]	bore	borne *or* born			
beat	beat	beaten	forgive	forgave	forgiven
become	became	become	forsake	forsook	forsaken
begin	began	begun	freeze	froze	frozen
bend	bent	bent	get	got	got
bet	bet	bet	give	gave	given
beware[2]			go	went	gone
bid	bid	bidden *or* bid	grind	ground	ground
bind	bound	bound	grow	grew	grown
bite	bit	bitten *or* bit	hang[3]	hung *or* hanged	hung *or* hanged
bleed	bled	bled			
blow	blew	blown	have	had	had
break	broke	broken	hear	heard	heard
breed	bred	bred	hide	hid	hidden *or* hid
bring	brought	brought	hit	hit	hit
build	built	built	hold	held	held
burn	burnt *or* burned	burnt *or* burned	hurt	hurt	hurt
			keep	kept	kept
burst	burst	burst	kneel	knelt	knelt
buy	bought	bought	knit	knitted *or* knit	knitted *or* knit
can	could		know	knew	known
cast	cast	cast	lay	laid	laid
catch	caught	caught	lead	led	led
choose	chose	chose	lean	leant *or* leaned	leant *or* leaned
cling	clung	clung	leap	leapt *or* leaped	leapt *or* leaped
come	came	come	learn	learnt *or* learned	learnt *or* learned
cost	cost	cost	leave	left	left
creep	crept	crept	lend	lent	lent
crow	crowed *or* crew	crowed	let	let	let
cut	cut	cut	lie	lay	lain
deal	dealt	dealt	light	lit *or* lighted	lit *or* lighted
dig	dug *or* digged	dug *or* digged	lose	lost	lost
do	did	done	make	made	made
draw	drew	drawn	may	might	
dream	dreamed *or* dreamt	dreamed *or* dreamt	mean	meant	meant
			meet	met	met
drink	drank	drunk	mow	mowed	mown
drive	drove	driven	must		
dwell	dwelt	dwelt	ought		
eat	ate	eaten	panic	panicked	panicked
fall	fell	fallen	pay	paid	paid
feed	fed	fed	picnic	picnicked	picnicked
feel	felt	felt	put	put	put
fight	fought	fought	quit	quitted *or* quit	quitted *or* quit
find	found	found	read	read	read

English irregular verbs

Infinitive	Past Tense	Past Participle	Infinitive	Past Tense	Past Participle
rid	rid or ridded	rid or ridded	spill	spilt or spilled	spilt or spilled
ride	rode	ridden	spin	spun	spun
ring	rang	rung	spit	spat or spit	spat or spit
rise	rose	risen	split	split	split
run	ran	run	spread	spread	spread
saw	sawed	sawn or sawed	spring	sprang	sprung
say	said	said	stand	stood	stood
see	saw	seen	steal	stole	stolen
seek	sought	sought	stick	stuck	stuck
sell	sold	sold	sting	stung	stung
send	sent	sent	stink	stank or stunk	stunk
set	set	set	stride	strode	stridden
sew	sewed	sewn or sewed	strike	struck	struck
shake	shook	shaken	string	strung	strung
shall	should		strive	strove	striven
shear	sheared	sheared or shorn	swear	swore	sworn
			sweep	swept	swept
shed	shed	shed	swell	swelled	swollen or swelled
shine	shone	shone			
shoe	shod	shod	swim	swam	swum
shoot	shot	shot	swing	swung	swung
show	showed	shown	take	took	taken
shrink	shrank or shrunk	shrunk or shrunken	teach	taught	taught
			tear	tore	torn
shut	shut	shut	tell	told	told
sing	sang	sung	think	thought	thought
sink	sank	sunk	throw	threw	thrown
sit	sat	sat	thrust	thrust	thrust
sleep	slept	slept	traffic	trafficked	trafficked
slide	slid	slid	tread	trod	trodden or trod
sling	slung	slung			
slink	slunk	slunk	wake	woke	woken
slit	slit	slit	wear	wore	worn
smell	smelt or smelled	smelt or smelled	weave	wove	woven or wove
			weep	wept	wept
sow	sowed	sown or sowed	will	would	
speak	spoke	spoken	win	won	won
speed	sped or speeded	sped or speeded	wind	wound	wound
			wring	wrung	wrung
spell	spelt or spelled	spelt or spelled	write	wrote	written
spend	spent	spent			

[1] when bear means *give birth to*, the past participle is always *born*.

[2] used only in the infinitive or as an imperative.

[3] the preferred form of the past tense and past participle when referring to death by hanging is *hanged*.

Infinitive	Present Indicative	Imperfect Indicative	Past Participle	Infinitive	Present Indicative	Imperfect Indicative	Past Participle
backen	bäckt	backte	gebacken	halten	hält	hielt	gehalten
befehlen	befiehlt	befahl	befohlen	hangen	hängt	hing	gehangen
beginnen	beginnt	begann	begonnen	hauen	haut	haute or hieb	gehauen
beißen	beißt	biß	gebissen	heben	hebt	hob	gehoben
bergen	birgt	barg	geborgen	heißen	heißt	hieß	geheißen
bewegen[1]	bewegt	bewog	bewogen	helfen	hilft	half	geholfen
biegen	biegt	bog	gebogen	kennen	kennt	kannte	gekannt
bieten	bietet	bot	geboten	klingen	klingt	klang	geklungen
binden	bindet	band	gebunden	kneifen	kneift	kniff	gekniffen
bitten	bittet	bat	gebeten	kommen	kommt	kam	gekommen
blasen	bläst	blies	geblasen	können	kann	konnte	gekonnt[3]
bleiben	bleibt	blieb	geblieben	kriechen	kriecht	kroch	gekrochen
bleichen[2]	bleicht	blich	geblichen	laden	lädt	lud	geladen
braten	brät	briet	gebraten	lassen	läßt	ließ	gelassen
brechen	bricht	brach	gebrochen	laufen	läuft	lief	gelaufen
brennen	brennt	brannte	gebrannt	leiden	leidet	litt	gelitten
bringen	bringt	brachte	gebracht	leihen	leiht	lieh	geliehen
dreschen	drischt	drosch	gedroschen	liegen	liegt	lag	gelegen
dringen	dringt	drang	gedrungen	lügen	lügt	log	gelogen
dürfen	darf	durfte	gedurft[3]	mahlen	mahlt	mahlte	gemahlen
empfehlen	empfiehlt	empfahl	empfohlen	meiden	meidet	mied	gemieden
erschrecken[2]	erschrickt	erschrak	erschrocken	melken	melkt	melkte or molk	gemelkt or gemolken
essen	ißt	aß	gegessen	messen	mißt	maß	gemessen
fahren	fährt	fuhr	gefahren	mißlingen	mißlingt	mißlang	mißlungen
fallen	fällt	fiel	gefallen	mögen	mag	mochte	gemocht[3]
fangen	fängt	fing	gefangen	müssen	muß	mußte	gemußt[3]
fechten	ficht	focht	gefochten	nehmen	nimmt	nahm	genommen
finden	findet	fand	gefunden	nennen	nennt	nannte	genannt
flechten	flicht	flocht	geflochten	pfeifen	pfeift	pfiff	gepfiffen
fliegen	fliegt	flog	geflogen	preisen	preist	pries	gepriesen
fliehen	flieht	floh	geflohen	quellen[2]	quillt	quoll	gequollen
fließen	fließt	floß	geflossen	raten	rät	riet	geraten
fressen	frißt	fraß	gefressen	reiben	reibt	rieb	gerieben
frieren	friert	fror	gefroren	reißen	reißt	riß	gerissen
gären[4]	gärt	gor	gegoren	reiten	reitet	ritt	geritten
gebären	gebiert	gebar	geboren	rennen	rennt	rannte	gerannt
geben	gibt	gab	gegeben	riechen	riecht	roch	gerochen
gedeihen	gedeiht	gedieh	gediehen	ringen	ringt	rang	gerungen
gehen	geht	ging	gegangen	rufen	ruft	rief	gerufen
gelingen	gelingt	gelang	gelungen	saufen	säuft	soff	gesoffen
gelten	gilt	galt	gegolten	saugen	saugt	sog	gesogen
genesen	genest	genas	genesen	schaffen	schafft	schuf	geschaffen
genießen	genießt	genoß	genossen	scheiden	scheidet	schied	geschieden
gerinnen	gerinnt	gerann	geronnen	scheinen	scheint	schien	geschienen
geschehen	geschieht	geschah	geschehen	schieben	schiebt	schob	geschoben
gewinnen	gewinnt	gewann	gewonnen	schießen	schießt	schoß	geschossen
gießen	gießt	goß	gegossen	schinden	schindet	schund	geschunden
gleichen	gleicht	glich	geglichen	schlafen	schläft	schlief	geschlafen
gleiten	gleitet	glitt	geglitten	schleichen	schleicht	schlich	geschlichen
graben	gräbt	grub	gegraben	schleifen[5]	schleift	schliff	geschliffen
greifen	greift	griff	gegriffen	schleißen	schleißt	schliß	geschlissen
haben	hat	hatte	gehabt				

German irregular verbs

Infinitive	Present Indicative	Imperfect Indicative	Past Participle	Infinitive	Present Indicative	Imperfect Indicative	Past Participle
schließen	schließt	schloß	geschlossen	stoßen	stößt	stieß	gestoßen
schlingen	schlingt	schlang	geschlungen	streichen	streicht	strich	gestrichen
schmeißen	schmeißt	schmiß	geschmissen	streiten	streitet	stritt	gestritten
schmelzen	schmelzt	schmolz	geschmolzen	tragen	trägt	trug	getragen
schneiden	schneidet	schnitt	geschnitten	treffen	trifft	traf	getroffen
schreiben	schreibt	schrieb	geschrieben	treiben	treibt	trieb	getrieben
schreien	schreit	schrie	geschrie(e)n	treten	tritt	trat	getreten
schreiten	schreitet	schritt	geschritten	triefen	trieft	troff	getrieft
schweigen	schweigt	schwieg	geschwiegen	trinken	trinkt	trank	getrunken
schwellen	schwillt	schwoll	geschwollen	trügen	trügt	trog	getrogen
schwimmen	schwimmt	schwamm	geschwommen	tun	tut	tat	getan
schwingen	schwingt	schwang	geschwungen	verderben	verdirbt	verdarb	verdorben
schwören	schwört	schwur	geschworen	verdrießen	verdrießt	verdroß	verdrossen
sehen	sieht	sah	gesehen	vergessen	vergißt	vergaß	vergessen
sein	ist	war	gewesen	verlieren	verliert	verlor	verloren
senden	sendet	sandte	gesandt	verzeihen	verzeiht	verzieh	verziehen
singen	singt	sang	gesungen	wachsen	wächst	wuchs	gewachsen
sinken	sinkt	sank	gesunken	weben	webt	wob	gewoben
sinnen	sinnt	sann	gesonnen	weichen	weicht	wich	gewichen
sitzen	sitzt	saß	gesessen	weisen	weist	wies	gewiesen
sollen	soll	sollte	gesollt[3]	wenden	wendet	wandte or	gewandt or
spinnen	spinnt	spann	gesponnen			wendete	gewendet
sprechen	spricht	sprach	gesprochen	werben	wirbt	warb	geworben
sprießen	sprießt	sproß	gesprossen	werden	wird	wurde	geworden[3]
springen	springt	sprang	gesprungen	werfen	wirft	warf	geworfen
stechen	sticht	stoch	gestochen	wiegen	wiegt	wog	gewogen
stehen	steht	stand	gestanden	winden	windet	wand	gewunden
stehlen	stiehlt	stahl	gestohlen	wissen	weiß	wußte	gewußt
steigen	steigt	stieg	gestiegen	wollen	will	wollte	gewollt[3]
sterben	stirbt	starb	gestorben	ziehen	zieht	zog	gezogen
stinken	stinkt	stank	gestunken	zwingen	zwingt	zwang	gezwungen

[1] strong conjugation in the meaning *induce, persuade*, but weak in the meaning *move*.
[2] strong conjugation when intransitive, but weak when transitive.
[3] when used as an auxiliary verb, the past participle has the same form as the infinitive.
[4] weak conjugation when figurative.
[5] strong conjugation in the meaning *polish, sharpen*, but weak in the meaning *drag*.

A

Aal (a:l) *nm* -e eel.

ab (ap) *adv* 1 off. 2 away. 3 down. 4 from. **ab und zu** sometimes, now and then. **weit ab** far off. *prep* from.

abänder/lich ('apɛndərliç) *adj* 1 alterable. 2 variable. **—n** *vt* 1 alter, chánge. 2 *pol* amend. **—ung** *nf* -en alteration.

abarbeiten ('aparbaitən) *vt* work off. **sich abarbeiten** *vr* overwork oneself.

Abbau ('apbau) *nm* reduction, dismantling, cutting down. **—en** *vt* 1 demolish. 2 reduce.

abberufen ('apbəru:fən) *vt* recall.

abbestellen ('apbəʃtɛlən) *vt* cancel.

abbiegen ('apbi:gən) *vi* turn off. *vt* turn aside.

Abbild ('apbilt) *n neu* -er 1 image, copy. 2 likeness. **—en** *vt* 1 copy. 2 illustrate. 3 model. **—ung** ('apbildun) *nf* -en 1 copy(ing). 2 illustration. 3 picture.

abblenden ('apblɛndən) *vt* dim (one's headlights).

abbrechen ('apbrɛçən) *vt,vi* 1 break off. 2 stop. 4 tear down (houses).

abbremsen ('apbrɛmzən) *vi,vt* brake, slow down.

abbringen ('apbriŋən) *vt* 1 divert. 2 dissuade.

Abbruch ('apbrux) *nm* -̈e 1 sudden end. 2 damage. 3 demolition.

abdank/en ('apdaŋkən) *vi* resign, abdicate. **—ung** *nf* -en abdication, resignation.

abdecken ('apdɛkən) *vt* 1 uncover. 2 *sport* protect or cover. 3 clear, strip.

abdichten ('apdiçtən) *vt* seal.

abdrehen ('apdre:ən) *vt* turn off.

Abdruck ('apdruk) *nm* 1 *pl* -e copy, print. 2 *pl* -̈e cast, impression. **—en** ('apdrykən) *vt* squeeze. *vt,vi* shoot, fire (gun).

Abend ('a:bənt) *nm* -e evening, night. **gestern abend** last night. **heute abend** this evening. **abends** in the evening. **—brot** *n neu* supper. **—essen** *n neu* evening meal, supper.
—dämmerung *nf* dusk. **—kleid** *n neu* evening dress or gown. **—land** *n neu* Occident, West. **—mahl** *n neu* (Holy) Communion.

Abenteuer ('a:bəntɔyər) *n neu* adventure. **—er** *nm* — 1 adventurer. 2 crook. **—lich** *adj* 1 adventurous. 2 fantastic.

aber ('a:bər) *conj* 1 but. 2 however. *adv* 1 however. 2 again. **aber ja** yes indeed.

Aberglaub/e ('a:bərglaubə) *nm* superstition. **—isch** ('a:bərglɔybiʃ) *adj* superstitious.

Aberkennung ('apɛrkɛnuŋ) *nf* -en deprivation.

abermals ('a:bərma:ls) *adv* (once) again.

Abessin/ien (abɛ'si:niən) *n neu* Abyssinia. **—ier** *nm* — Abyssinian. **—isch** *adj* Abyssinian.

abfahr/en ('apfa:rən) *vi* depart, start. *vt* drive off. **—t** *nf* -en departure.

Abfall ('apfal) *nm* -̈e 1 waste, rubbish. 2 slope. 3 decrease. 4 defection. **—eimer** *nm* dustbin. **—en** *vi* 1 fall down or off. 2 desert. 3 decrease. **abfällig** ('apfɛliç) *adj* 1 disapproving, disparaging. 2 sloping.

abfassen ('apfasən) *vt* word, formulate.

abfertigen ('apfɛrtigən) *vt* 1 dispatch. 2 deal with.

Abfindung ('apfinduŋ) *nf* -en settlement, compensation.

abfliegen ('apfli:gən) *vi* fly away, take off.

abfließen ('apfli:sən) *vi* flow or drain away.

Abflug ('apfluk) *nm* -̈e take-off, departure.

Abfluß ('apflus) *nm* -flüsse 1 drain(ing). 2 discharge.

Abfuhr ('apfu:r) *nf* -en 1 removal. 2 *inf* rebuff. **—en** ('apfy:rən) *vt* lead off, take away. **—mittel** ('apfy:rmitəl) *n neu* laxative.

abfüllen ('apfylən) *vt* 1 fill. 2 bottle.

Abgabe ('apga:bə) *nf* -n 1 delivery. 2 duty, tax, levy. **—nfrei** *adj* duty-free. **—npflichtig** *adj* taxable, liable to duty.

Abgang ('apgaŋ) *nm* -̈e 1 departure, exit. 2 loss.

Abgas ('apgas) *n neu* -e exhaust (gas).

abgeben ('apge:bən) *vt* hand over, give up.

sich abgeben vr associate with, occupy oneself with.

abgegriffen ('apgəgrifən) adj 1 worn. 2 (of a book) well-thumbed.

abgehen* ('apge:ən) vi 1 go away or off, leave. 2 come or fall off. 3 branch off. **es ist alles gut abgegangen** everything went well.

Abgeordnete(r) ('apgəɔrdnətə) nm -n deputy, representative, Member of Parliament. **Abgeordnetenhaus** n neu Chamber of Deputies.

abgestanden ('apgəʃtandən) adj stale, flat.

abgestorben ('apgəʃtɔrbən) adj dead, numb.

abgezehrt ('apgətsɛ:rt) adj emaciated.

Abgott ('apgɔt) nm ̈er idol.

abgrenz/en ('apgrɛntsən) vt mark off, delimit. **—ung** nf -en demarcation, delimitation.

Abgrund ('apgrunt) nm ̈e 1 precipice. 2 abyss.

abhalten* ('aphaltən) vt 1 keep or hold off. 2 prevent.

Abhandlung ('aphandluŋ) nf -en essay, treatise.

Abhang nm ̈e slope, incline. ̈-en ('aphɛŋən) vt 1 take down or off. 2 unhook. 3 disconnect. vi 1 depend on. 2 slope. ̈-ig ('aphɛŋiç) adj 1 dependent. 2 sloping. 3 subject (to). ̈-igkeit nf dependence.

abhauen* ('aphauən) vt cut down or off. vi sl leave, go away.

Abhilfe ('aphilfə) nf -n remedy, relief.

abholen* ('aphoːlən) vt fetch (away), call for.

abhören ('aphœːrən) vt overhear, listen to.

Abitur (abi'tuːr) n neu -e school leaving examination or certificate.

abkanzeln ('apkantsəln) vt scold, rebuke.

abkehren ('apkeːrən) vi turn away.

abklingen* ('apkliŋən) vi (of sound) die out, fade away.

Abkommen ('apkɔmən) n neu — agreement, treaty. vi 1 deviate. 2 lose one's way.

abkühl/en ('apkyːlən) vt chill, cool. **—ung** nf cooling.

abkürz/en ('apkyrtsən) vt shorten, abbreviate. **—ung** nf -en abbreviation.

abladen* ('apla:dən) vt unload, dump.

Ablauf ('aplauf) nm ̈e 1 course of events. 2 end, expiry. 3 drain. **—en*** vi 1 run off or down. 2 expire. **gut ablaufen** pass off well, be a success.

Ablaut ('aplaut) nm -e gradation of vowels.

ablegen ('apleːgən) vt 1 take off (clothes). 2 lay down. 3 give up.

ablehn/en ('apleːnən) vt refuse, decline. **—ung** nf -en refusal, rejection.

ableit/en ('aplaitən) vt 1 divert. 2 derive. 3 draw off. **—ung** nf -en 1 diversion. 2 derivation.

ablenk/en ('aplɛŋkən) vt turn aside, divert. **—ung** nf -en diversion, distraction.

abliefer/n ('apliːfərn) vt deliver. **—ung** nf -en delivery.

ablös/en ('aplœːzən) vt 1 loosen, detach. 2 relieve (someone). **—ung** nf -en 1 loosening, detachment. 2 relief.

abmach/en ('apmaxən) vt settle, arrange. **abgemacht!** agreed! **—ung** nf -en agreement, arrangement.

sich abmeld/en ('apmɛldən) vr announce one's departure. **—ung** nf -en 1 notice of departure. 2 cancellation.

abmessen* ('apmɛsən) vt 1 measure off. 2 survey. 3 weigh (words).

Abnahme ('apnaːme) nf -n 1 removal, collection. 2 lessening, decrease. 3 acceptance.

abnehmen* ('apneːmən) vt take from or off. vi decrease.

Abneigung ('apnaigun) nf -en dislike, aversion.

abnutzen ('apnutsən) vt also **abnützen** wear out.

Abonn/ement (abɔn'mã) n neu -s subscription. **—ent** (abɔ'nɛnt) nm -en subscriber. **—ieren** vi subscribe.

Abort (a'bɔrt) nm -e lavatory.

abräumen ('aprɔymən) vt clear away.

abrechn/en ('aprɛçnən) vt 1 deduct. 2 reckon up. 3 settle (with someone). **—ung** nf -en deduction, settlement.

Abrede ('apreːdə) nf -n agreement. **in Abrede stellen** deny, dispute.

Abreise ('apraizə) nf -n departure. **—n** vi depart, set off.

abreißen* ('apraisən) vt 1 pull down. 2 tear off.

abrufen* ('apruːfən) vt 1 call back, recall. 2 cancel, call off.

Abrüstung ('aprystuŋ) nf -en disarmament.

Absage ('aoza:gə) nf -n 1 refusal. 2 cancellation. **—n** vi 1 refuse. 2 cancel. 3 renounce.

Absatz ('apzats) nm ̈e 1 sale. 2 heel (of a shoe). 3 paragraph. 4 pause, intermission.

abschaff/en* ('apʃafən) vt abolish. **—ung** nf abolition.

abschalten ('apʃaltən) vt switch off.

abschätz/en ('apʃɛtsən) vt estimate, assess. **—ung** nf -en assessment, valuation.

Abscheu ('apʃɔy) nm,f horror, loathing. **—lich** (ap'ʃɔyliç) adj loathsome, repugnant.

abschicken ('apʃikən) vt send off, dispatch.

Abschied ('apʃi:t) nm -e parting, departure. **Abschied nehmen** take one's leave.

abschießen* ('apʃi:sən) vt 1 fire (a gun), shoot (off). 2 launch (a rocket).

Abschlag ('apʃla:k) nm -̈e reduction. **auf Abschlag** on account.

abschließen* ('apʃli:sən) vt 1 lock up, close (up). 2 settle, conclude.

Abschluß ('apʃlus) nm -schlüsse 1 conclusion, end. 2 settlement, deal.

abschnallen ('apʃnalən) vt unbuckle.

abschneiden* ('apʃnaidən) vt cut off or out. **gut/schlecht abschneiden** do well/badly.

Abschnitt ('apʃnit) nm -e section, portion.

abschrauben ('apʃraubən) vt unscrew.

abschrecken ('apʃrɛkən) vt frighten (off).

abschreiben* ('apʃraibən) vt 1 copy, write out. 2 write off.

Abschrift ('apʃrift) nf -en copy.

Abschuß ('apʃus) nm -schüsse 1 discharge, firing. 2 launching. **—rampe** nf launching pad.

abschwächen ('apʃvɛçən) vt weaken.

abseh/bar ('apze:ba:r) adj 1 within sight. 2 foreseeable. **—en*** vt 1 foresee. 2 perceive. 3 aim at. 4 copy. **abgesehen von** apart from.

absend/en ('apzɛndən) vt send, dispatch. **—er** nm — sender. **—ung** nf -en dispatch(ing).

absetzen ('apzɛtsən) vt 1 put down. 2 remove, dismiss (someone). 3 sell.

Absicht ('apziçt) nf -en intention, purpose. **—lich** adj intentional.

absolut (apzo'lu:t) adj absolute.

absonder/n ('apzəndərn) vt separate, isolate. **—ung** nf -en separation.

Absorption (apzɔrptsi'o:n) nf -en absorption.

absperren ('apʃpɛrən) vt 1 cordon off, barricade. 2 shut off or away.

abspielen ('apʃpi:lən) vt perform (music). **sich abspielen** vr take place.

abspringen* ('apʃpriŋən) vi 1 jump off. 2 break off, shatter. 3 desert.

abspülen ('apʃpy:lən) vt 1 wash up. 2 rinse.

Abstammung ('apʃtamuŋ) nf -en descent, ancestry.

Abstand ('apʃtant) nm -̈e distance. **Abstand halten** keep one's distance.

abstatten ('apʃtatən) vt 1 give, render. 2 pay (a visit). 3 extend (thanks). 4 discharge (an obligation).

absteigen* ('apʃtaigən) vi 1 descend. 2 dismount, alight. 3 sport be relegated.

Abstieg ('apʃti:k) nm -e 1 descent. 2 sport relegation.

Abstimmung ('apʃtimuŋ) nf -en vote, poll.

Abstinenz (apsti'nɛnts) nf 1 abstinence. 2 teetotalism. **—ler** nm — 1 abstainer. 2 teetotaller.

abstoßen* ('apʃto:sən) vt push away, repel.

abstrakt (ap'strakt) adj abstract.

Abstufung ('apʃtu:fuŋ) nf -en graduation.

Absturz ('apʃturts) nm -̈e 1 fall. 2 aviat crash. **—en** ('apʃtyrtsən) vi 1 fall (down). 2 aviat crash.

absurd (ap'zurt) adj absurd.

Abszeß (aps'tsɛs) nm -zesse abcess.

Abt (apt) nm -̈e abbott. **Äbtissin** (ɛp'tisin) nf -nen abbess. **Abtei** (ap'tai) nf -en abbey.

Abteil (ap'tail) n neu -e compartment. **—en** ('aptailən) vt divide. **—ung** (ap'tailuŋ) nf -en division, department, group, section.

abtreib/en ('aptraibən) vt 1 drive off. 2 abort. vi drift off. **—ung** nf -en abortion.

abtreten ('aptre:tən) vt 1 cede. 2 wear out (shoes, etc). vi resign.

Abtritt ('aptrit) nm -e 1 withdrawal. 2 lavatory.

abtrocknen ('aptrɔknən) vt dry (up).

abtrünnig ('aptrynіç) adj disloyal, rebellious.

abtun* ('aptu:n) vt 1 abolish. 2 settle. 3 put aside. 4 take off (clothes).

abwägen* ('apvɛ:gən) vt consider, weigh.

abwand/eln ('apvandəln) vt 1 gram conjugate. 2 vary. **—lung** nf -en 1 gram inflection. 2 variation.

abwarten ('apvartən) vt wait for.

abwärts ('apvɛrts) adv 1 downwards. 2 aside.

abwaschen* ('apvaʃən) vt 1 wash off or away. 2 wash up.

abwechsel/n ('apvɛksəln) vi alternate. vt change. **—nd** adj alternating. **—ung** nf -en change, alternation.

Abwehr ('apve:r) nf -en defence, guard. **—en** vt ward off. **—stoff** nm antibody.

abweichen* ('apvaiçən) vi deviate, differ from. **—d** adj irregular, different.

abweisen* ('apvaisən) vt 1 turn away, dismiss. 2 reject.

abwenden* ('apvɛndən) vt 1 turn away. 2 prevent. **sich abwenden von** turn away from.

abwerfen* ('apvɛrfən) vt 1 throw off or away. 2 knock down. 3 yield. 4 drop (bombs).

abwert/en ('apvɛrtən) vt, vi devalue, devaluate. **—ung** nf -en devaluation.

3

abwesen/d ('apveːzənt) adj 1 absent. 2 absent-minded. **—heit** nf -en absence.

abwischen ('apviʃən) vt wipe off.

abzahlen ('aptsaːlən) vt pay off.

abzäunen ('aptsɔynən) vt fence off or in.

Abzeichen ('aptsaiçən) n neu badge, mark.

abziehen* ('aptsiːən) vt 1 draw off, remove. 2 subtract. 3 distract. vi go away.

Abzug ('aptsuːk) nm -̈e 1 deduction. 2 copy. 3 departure. 4 trigger. 5 outlet, vent. 6 (printing) proof. **—lich** ('aptsyːkliç) adv minus, less.

Abzweigung ('aptsvaiguŋ) nf -en branch.

ach (ax) interj oh!

Achse ('aksə) nf -n 1 axle. 2 axis.

Achsel ('aksəl) nf -n shoulder.

acht (axt) adj,nf eight. **—e** adj eighth. **heute in acht Tagen** today week.

Acht (axt) nf attention. **sich in Acht nehmen** look out, be on one's guard.

achten ('axtən) vt respect. **achten auf** pay attention to. **—sam** adj attentive. **—geben** vi pay attention. **—ung** nf respect. interj attention, look out! **—ungsvoll** adj respectful.

achtzehn ('axtseːn) adj,nf eighteen. **achtzehnte** adj eighteenth.

achtzig ('axtsiç) adj,nf eighty. **achtzigste** adj ʼhtieth.

ächzen ('ɛçtsən) vi groan.

Acker ('akər) nm -̈ 1 field, arable land. 2 (German) acre. **—bau** nm agriculture.

addier/en ('adiːrən) vt add. **—maschine** nf adding machine.

ade, adieu (a'deː, a'djøː) interj farewell.

Adel ('aːdəl) nm nobility, aristocracy. **adelig** adj also **adlig** noble. **Adlige(r)** ('aːdligə) nm -n nobleman, aristocrat. **Adelsstand** ('aːdəlʃtant) nm 1 nobility. 2 peerage.

Ader ('aːdər) nf -n 1 vein. 2 artery.

Adjektiv ('atjɛktiːf) n neu -e adjective.

Adjutant (atju'tant) nm -en adjutant, aide.

Adler ('aːdlər) nm — eagle.

Admiral (atmi'raːl) nm -e admiral.

adoptieren (adɔp'tiːrən) vt adopt. **Adoptivkind** (adɔp'tiːfkint) n neu adopted child.

Adrenalin (adreː'naliːn) n neu adrenaline.

Adress/e (a'drɛsə) nf -n address. **—ieren** (adrɛ'siːrən) vt address.

Adriatisches Meer (adri'aːtiʃəs) n neu Adriatic (Sea).

Advokat (atvo'kaːt) nm -en lawyer, advocate.

Affäre (a'fɛːrə) nf -n 1 affair. 2 love affair.

Affe ('afə) nm -n 1 ape, monkey. 2 inf silly ass. **—n** ('ɛfən) vt 1 deceive. 2 ape.

Afrika ('aːfrika) n neu Africa. **—ner** nm — African. **—nisch** adj African.

Ägäisches Meer (a'gɛiʃəs) n neu Aegean (Sea).

Agent (a'gɛnt) nm -en agent. **—ur** (agɛn'tuːr) nf agency.

Agitation (agitatsi'oːn) nf -en agitation.

Agnost/iker (a'gnɔstikər) nm — agnostic. **—isch** adj agnostic. **—izismus** (agnɔsti'tsismus) nm agnosticism.

Ägypt/en (ɛ'gyptən) n neu Egypt. **—isch** adj Egyptian.

Ahn (aːn) nm -en ancestor.

ähneln ('ɛːnəln) vi resemble.

ahn/en ('aːnən) vt 1 suspect, guess. 2 foresee. **—ung** nf -en 1 idea, suspicion. 2 presentiment.

ähnlich ('ɛːnliç) adj similar, like. **—keit** nf -en similarity, likeness.

Ahorn ('aːhɔrn) nm -e maple.

Akademie (akade'miː) nf -n academy, college. **Akademiker** (aka'deːmikər) nm — academic. **akademisch** (aka'deːmiʃ) adj academic.

Akkord (a'kɔrt) nm -e 1 arrangement, settlement. 2 mus chord. **im Akkord arbeiten** do piecework. **—arbeit** nf piecework.

Akrobat (akro'baːt) nm -en acrobat.

Akt (akt) nm -e 1 act, action. 2 nude study. 3 document.

Akte ('aktə) nf -n 1 document. 2 report. 3 file. **—nmappe** nf 1 folder. 2 portfolio. 3 briefcase. **—nschrank** nm filing-cabinet. **—ntasche** nf briefcase.

Aktie ('aktsiə) nf -n comm share. **—ngesellschaft** nf limited company.

Aktionär (aktsio'nɛːr) nm -e shareholder.

aktiv (ak'tiːf) adj 1 active. 2 effective.

aktuell (aktu'ɛl) adj 1 topical. 2 present-day.

Akzent (ak'tsɛnt) nm -e accent, stress.

akzeptieren (aktsɛp'tiːrən) vt accept.

Alabaster (ala'bastər) nm alabaster.

Alarm (a'larm) nm -e alarm. **—ieren** vt alarm.

Alaun (a'laun) nm -e alum.

Alban/ien (al'baːniən) n neu Albania. **—ier** nm — Albanian. **—isch** adj Albanian.

Albatros ('albatrɔs) nm -se albatross.

albern ('albərn) adj silly, foolish.

Alge (algə) nf -n seaweed.

Alger/ien (al'geːriən) n neu Algeria. **—ier** nm — Algerian. **—isch** adj Algerian.

Alimente (ali'mɛntə) n pl alimony.

Alkohol ('alkohol) *nm* -e alcohol. **—frei** *adj* non-alcoholic. **—verbot** *n neu* prohibition. **—isch** (alko'ho:liʃ) *adj* alcoholic. **—iker** (alko'ho:likər) *nm* alcoholic.

all (al) *pron* all everything. *adj* all, every. **alles in allem** on the whole. **—e** *adv inf* finished, all gone. **alledem** ('aləde:m) *pron* **bei** or **trotz alledem** in spite of all that.

All (al) *n neu* universe.

Allee (a'le:) *nf* -n avenue.

Allegorie (alego'ri:) *nf* -n allegory.

allein (a'lain) *adv, adj* alone, single. *conj* but. **—ig** *adj* 1 sole. 2 exclusive.

allemal ('aləma:l) *adv* always. **ein für allemal** once and for all.

allenfalls ('alənfals) *adv* if need be.

allerbest ('alərbɛst) *adj* best of all.

allerdings ('alərdiŋs) *adv* indeed, certainly.

allererst ('aləre:rst) *adj, adv* first of all.

allerhand ('alərhant) *adj* of all kinds, various.

allerhöchst ('alərhøːçst) *adj* supreme.

allerlei ('alərlai) *adj* of all kinds, various.

allerliebst ('alərli:pst) *adj* 1 dearest (of all). 2 most lovely.

allerwenigst ('alərve:niçst) *adj* the very least.

allezeit ('alətsait) *adv* always.

allgemein ('algəmain) *adj* general, common.

Alliierte(r) (a'li:rtə) *nm* -n ally.

alljährlich ('aljɛːrliç) *adj* annual, yearly.

Allmacht ('almaxt) *nf* omnipotence. **—ig** ('almɛçtiç) *adj* almighty.

allmählich ('almɛːliç) *adj* gradual.

allseitig ('alzaitiç) *adj* universal.

alltäglich ('altɛːkliç) *adj* daily, common(place).

allzu ('altsu:) *adv* much too, far too.

Almanach ('almanax) *nm* -e almanac.

Almosen ('almo:zən) *n neu* alms.

Alpen ('alpən) *n pl* Alps.

Alphabet (alfa'be:t) *n neu* -e alphabet.

Alptraum ('alptraum) *nm* -e *also* **Alpdrücken** *n neu* — nightmare.

als (als) *conj* 1 when. 2 as. 3 than. **als ob** *also* **als wenn** as if. **~prep** as. **nichts als** nothing but.

alsbald (als'balt) *adv* at once.

alsdann (als'dan) *adv* 1 then. 2 after.

also ('alzo:) *conj* therefore. *adv* so.

alt (alt) *adj* old, ancient. **—e(r)** ('altə) *nm* old one or man. **—klug** *adj* precocious. **—modisch** *adj* old-fashioned. **—papier** *n neu* wastepaper **—stadt** *nf* old part of a town. **—warenhändler** *nm* second-hand dealer.

Alt (alt) *nm* -e *also* **Altstimme** *nf* alto (voice).

Alter ('altər) *n neu* — (old) age. **im Alter von** at the age of. **—sheim** *n neu* old people's home. **—sversicherung** *nf* life insurance.

Altertum ('altərtu:m) *n neu* antiquity.

Aluminium (alu'mi:nium) *n neu* aluminium.

am (am) contraction of **an dem**

Amboß ('ambɔs) *nm* -bosse anvil.

Ameise ('a:maizə) *nf* -n ant.

Amerika (a'me:rika) *n neu* America. **—ner** (ameri'ka:nər) *nm* — American. **amerikanisch** (ameri'ka:niʃ) *adj* American.

Ampel ('ampəl) *nf* -n 1 (hanging) lamp. 2 traffic light.

Amsel ('amzəl) *nf* -n blackbird.

Amt (amt) *n neu* —er 1 office, (official) position. 2 charge, responsibility. **von Amts wegen** officially, ex officio. **—lich** *adj* official. **—mann** *nm* 1 official. 2 bailiff. **—sgeheimnis** *n neu* official secret. **—sgericht** *n neu* district court.

amüs/ant (amy'zant) *adj* amusing. **—ieren** (amy'zi:rən) *vt* amuse. **sich amüsieren** *vr* enjoy oneself.

an (an) *prep* 1 at. 2 on. 3 to. 4 against. 5 in. 6 by. **an (und für) sich** in itself. **von jetzt an** from now on.

analog (ana'lo:k) *adj* analogous. **—ie** (analo'gi:) *nf* -n analogy.

Analphabet (analfa'be:t) *nm* -en illiterate.

Analys/e (ana'ly:zə) *nf* -n analysis. **—ieren** (analy'zi:rən) *vt* analyse.

Ananas ('ananas) *nf* -se pineapple.

Anarchie (anar'çi:) *nf* -n anarchy.

Anatomie (anato'mi:) *nf* -n anatomy.

Anbau ('anbau) *nm* 1 *pl* -e cultivation. 2 *pl* -ten annexe, outbuilding. **—en** *vt* 1 cultivate. 2 build (an extension).

anbeißen* ('anbaisən) *vt* bite into. *vi* swallow the bait.

anbelangen ('anbəlaŋən) *vt* **was mich anbelangt** as for me.

anbet/en ('anbe:tən) *vt* worship, adore. **—ung** *vt* worship.

Anbetracht ('anbətraxt) *nf* **in Anbetracht** in view of.

anbetreffen* ('anbətrɛfən) *vt* concern.

anbieten* ('anbi:tən) *vt* offer.

Anblick ('anblik) *nm* -e view, sight. **—en** *vt* look at.

anbrechen* ('anbrɛçən) *vt* break into, open. *vi* dawn.

anbringen* ('anbriŋən) *vt* 1 attach. 2 place. 3 install. 4 bring (a complaint).

Anbruch ('anbrux) nm -̈e beginning, opening. **Anbruch des Tages** daybreak.

Andacht ('andaxt) nf -en devotion, prayers. **-̈ig** ('andɛçtiç) adj 1 devout. 2 attentive.

andauern ('andauərn) vi continue, last.

Anden ('andən) n pl Andes.

Andenken ('andɛŋkən) n neu — 1 remembrance, memory. 2 souvenir, keepsake.

ander ('andər) adj other, different. **am anderen Tag** the next day. **einmal über das andere** again and again. **ein andermal** ('andərma:l) sdv another time. **andernfalls** ('andərnfals) adv otherwise. **anderntags** ('andərnta:ks) adv the next day. **anderseits** ('andərzaits) adv or **andrerseits** ('andrərzaits) on the other hand. **anders** ('andərs) adv differently, otherwise. **anderswo** ('andərsvo) adv also **anderwärts** ('andərverts) elsewhere, in another place. **anderweit** ('andərvait) adv 1 in another place. 2 in another way.

änder/n ('ɛndərn) vt **sich ändern** vr change, alter. **-ung** nf -en change, alteration.

anderthalb ('andərthalp) adj one and a half.

andeut/en ('andɔytən) vt indicate, suggest. **-ung** nf -en indication, hint, suggestion.

Andrang ('andraŋ) nm press, rush, crowd.

andrehen ('andre:ən) vt turn or switch on.

aneignen ('anaignən) vt appropriate, acquire.

aneinander (anain'andər) adv 1 together. 2 to one another.

Anerbieten ('anɛrbi:tən) n neu — also **Anerbietung** nf -en offer, proposal.

anerkannt ('anɛrkant) adj recognized, acknowledged.

anerkenn/en* ('anɛrkrnən) vt recognize, acknowledge. **-ung** nf -en recognition, acknowledgment.

anfahr/en* ('anfa:rən) vt 1 carry. 2 collide with. vi 1 approach. 2 (of a vehicle) begin to move. **-t** nf -en 1 arrival. 2 drive(way).

Anfall ('anfal) nm -̈e 1 attack. 2 fit.

Anfang ('anfaŋ) nm -̈e 1 beginning, introduction. 2 basis. **am Anfang** at the beginning. **von Anfang an** from the outset. **-en*** vt,vi begin, start. **-̈er** ('anfɛŋər) nm — beginner, novice. **-̈lich** ('anfɛŋliç) adj initial. **-s** adv at first, at the beginning.

anfassen ('anfasən) vt 1 seize. 2 touch, handle.

anfecht/en* ('anfɛçtən) vt 1 contest, oppose. 2 trouble, bother. **-ung** nf -en 1 opposition. 2 temptation.

anfertig/en ('anfɛrtigən) vt manufacture, produce. **-ung** nf -en manufacture, fabrication.

Anforderung ('anfordəruŋ) nf -en 1 claim, demand. 2 requirement.

Anfrage ('anfra:gə) nf -n enquiry. **anfragen** ('anfra:gən) vi,vt enquire, ask.

anführ/en ('anfy:rən) vt 1 lead. 2 quote, state. 3 deceive. **-er** nm — 1 commander, leader. 2 agitator. **-ung** nf -en 1 lead(ership). 2 quotation. **-ungszeichen** n pl quotation marks inverted commas.

anfüllen ('anfylən) vt fill up.

Angabe ('anga:bə) nf -n 1 announcement, declaration. 2 information, details.

angeb/en* ('ange:bən) vt announce, state, give (reasons). vi 1 approach (a person). 2 game deal first, serve. **-er** nm — 1 informer. 2 showoff, poseur. **-lich** ('ange:pliç) adj supposed, alleged.

angeboren ('angəbo:rən) adj inborn.

Angebot ('angəbo:t) n neu -e 1 bid, offer. 2 supply.

angehen* ('ange:ən) vi begin. **das geht nicht an** that won't do. vt 1 approach (a person). 2 concern (a person). 3 tackle, attack. **das geht dich nichts an** that's none of your business.

angehör/en ('angəhø:rən) vi belong. **-ige(r)** nm -n 1 member. 2 relative.

Angeklagte(r) ('angəkla:ktə) nm -n accused, defendant.

Angelegenheit ('angəle:gənhait) nf -en matter, affair, business.

angeln ('aŋəln) vt,vi angle, fish (for). n neu fishing, angling.

Angelsachs/e ('aŋəlzaksə) nm -n Anglo-Saxon. **-̈isch** ('aŋəlzeksiʃ) adj Anglo-Saxon.

angemessen ('angəmesən) adj suitable.

angenehm ('angəne:m) adj pleasant, agreeable.

angenommen ('angənɔmən) adj 1 supposing, assuming. 2 approved.

angesehen ('angəze:ən) adj respected, distinguished.

Angesicht ('angəziçt) n neu -er face. **-s** prep in view of, considering.

Angestellte(r) ('angəʃtɛltə) nm -n 1 employee. 2 office worker.

angetan ('angəta:n) adj 1 dressed up. 2 likely.

angewandt ('angəvant) adj applied.

angewöhnen ('angəvœ:nən) vt accustom. **sich angewöhnen** vr grow accustomed to.

Angewohnheit ('angəvo:nhait) nf -en habit, custom.

Angler ('aŋlər) nm — angler.

anglikanisch (angli'ka:niʃ) adj Anglican.

angreif/en* ('angraifən) vt 1 attack, assault. 2

6

touch, grasp. **3** undertake. **—er** nm — aggressor, assailant.

angrenzen ('angrɛntsən) vi border on.

Angriff ('angrif) nm -e **1** attack. **2** undertaking. **—slustig** adj aggressive.

Angst (aŋst) nf -e fear, fright, anxiety. **Angst haben** be afraid. **jemandem Angst machen** frighten someone. **—igen** ('ɛŋstigən) vt frighten. **sich —igen** vr worry, be anxious. **—lich** ('ɛŋstliç) adj timid, anxious, cautious.

anhaben* ('anhɑːbən) vt wear, have on.

Anhalt ('anhalt) nm -e **1** support, hold. **2** clue, essential fact. **3** halt, stop. **—en*** vt check, stop. vi **1** stop. **2** continue, persist. **per Anhalter fahren** hitch-hike. **—spunkt** nm clue, lead.

Anhang ('anhaŋ) nm -e **1** appendix. **2** following. **—en** ('anhɛŋən) vt hang on, attach. **—er** ('anhɛŋər) nm — **1** follower, disciple. **2** (baggage) tag, label. **3** mot trailer.

anheimfallen* ('anhaimfalən) vi fall or come to (someone).

Anhöhe ('anhœːə) nf -n hill, rise.

anhören ('anhœːrən) vt listen to.

Ankauf ('ankauf) nm -e purchase. **—en** vt purchase.

Anker ('aŋkər) nm — anchor. **—n** vi anchor.

Anklage ('anklɑːgə) nf -n **1** accusation. **2** prosecution. **—n** vt accuse, charge.

Anklang ('anklaŋ) nm -e **1** approval. **2** reminiscence.

anknüpf/en ('anknypfən) vt **1** fasten. **2** begin.

ankommen* ('ankəmən) vi arrive. **es kommt darauf an 1** it depends (on). **2** it is important (to).

ankündigen ('ankyndigən) vt announce.

Ankunft ('ankunft) nf -e arrival.

Anlage ('anlɑːgə) nf -n **1** plan, lay-out. **2** park, gardens. **3** tendency. **4** talent, gift. **5** investment. **6** equipment, apparatus.

anlangen ('anlaŋən) vi arrive. vt concern (someone).

Anlaß ('anlas) nm **—lässe 1** cause, occasion. **anlassen*** vt **1** leave on (a machine, etc.). **2** start, begin. **3** mot start (engine). **4** scold. **anläßlich** ('anlɛsliç) prep on the occasion of.

Anlauf ('anlauf) nm -e start, take-off, run-up.

anlegen ('anleːgən) vt **1** lay or put on or against. **2** found. **3** invest. vi naut **1** berth. **2** land. **Feuer anlegen** start a fire.

Anleihe ('anlaiə) nf -n loan.

Anleitung ('anlaitun) nf -en instruction.

anlieg/en* ('anliːgən) vi **1** lie near. **2** fit well. n neu — request. **—end** adj adjacent.

anlocken ('anləkən) vt entice, attract.

Anmarsch ('anmarʃ) nm -e mil approach, advance.

Anmaßung ('anmɑːsun) nf -en **1** presumption. **2** insolence.

anmeld/en ('anmɛldən) vt **1** report. **2** declare, announce. **—ung** nf -en **1** registration (with the police). **2** application. **3** announcement.

Anmerk/en ('anmɛrkən) vt note, observe. **—ung** nf -en **1** remark, observation. **2** footnote.

Anmut ('anmuːt) nf grace, charm. **—ig** adj graceful, charming.

annähernd ('annɛːərnt) adj **1** approaching. **2** approximate.

Annahme ('annɑːmə) nf -n **1** supposition. **2** acceptance.

annehmen* ('anneːmən) vt **1** accept, receive. **2** assume, suppose.

anonym ('anoˈnyːm) adj anonymous.

anordn/en ('anərdnən) vt arrange, order. **—ung** nf -en **1** regulation. **2** direction, order.

anpacken ('anpakən) vt grasp, seize.

anpassen ('anpasən) vt **1** fit. **2** adapt, adjust. **sich anpassen** vr adapt, conform.

anrechn/en ('anrɛçnən) vt **1** think well of, value. **2** charge. **3** credit. **—ung** nf -en charge.

Anrede ('anreːdə) nf -n address, speech. **—n** vt address, speak to.

anreg/en ('anreːgən) vt stimulate, excite, stir up. **—end** adj stimulating, exciting. **—ung** nf -en **1** excitement. **2** inspiration. **3** suggestion.

anrichten ('anriçtən) vt **1** serve. **2** prepare. **3** cause.

Anruf ('anruːf) nm -e **1** shout, call. **2** (telephone) call. **—en*** vt **1** ring up. **2** call, hail.

anrühren ('anryːrən) vt **1** touch. **2** mix.

ans (ans) contraction of **an das.**

Ansag/e ('anzɑːgə) nf -n announcement. **—er** nm — (radio) announcer.

ansammeln ('anzaməln) vt collect, amass. **sich ansammeln** vr gather, assemble.

ansässig ('anzɛsiç) adj **1** resident. **2** settled.

Ansatz ('anzats) nm -e start, onset.

anschaffen* ('anʃafən) vt procure, buy.

anschalten ('anʃaltən) vt switch on, plug in.

anschau/en ('anʃauən) vt look at, view. **—lich** adj **1** vivid. **2** evident. **—ung** nf -en **1** opinion, view. **2** conception, idea.

7

Anschein (ˈanʃain) *nm* -e appearance. **allem Anschein nach** to all appearances. —**end** *adj* apparent.

Anschlag (ˈanʃlaːk) *nm* -̈e 1 striking, stroke. 2 poster. 3 plan, plot. 4 estimate. 5 (bomb) attack. —**en**° (ˈanʃlaːgən) *vt* 1 strike at. 2 affix. value. *vi* 1 take effect. 2 attack, strike.

anschließen° (ˈanʃliːsən) *vt* connect, add, chain (up). **sich anschließen** *vr* join.

Anschluß (ˈanʃlus) *nm* -**schlüsse** connection, addition. **im Anschluß an** following.

anschnallen (ˈanʃnalən) *vt* fasten, buckle (on).

Anschovis (anˈʃoːvis) *nf* — anchovy.

Anschrift (ˈanʃrift) *nf* -en address.

anschuldigen (ˈanʃuldigən) *vt* accuse, charge.

anseh/en° (ˈanzeːən) *vt* 1 look at or upon. 2 consider. **ansehen für** take for. —**nlich** (ˈanzeːnliç) *adj* 1 good-looking. 2 considerable, important.

ansetzen (ˈanzetsən) *vt* 1 set or put on. 2 fasten. 3 add. 4 apply. *vi* begin.

Ansicht (ˈanziçt) *nf* -en 1 view, sight. 2 opinion. **meiner Ansicht nach** in my opinion. **zur Ansicht** on approval. —**s(post)karte** *nf* picture postcard.

ansiedeln (ˈanziːdəln) *vt* settle, colonize.

anspiel/en (ˈanʃpiːlən) *vi* allude, insinuate. —**ung** *nf* -en reference, allusion.

Anspruch (ˈanʃprux) *nm* -̈e 1 claim, demand. 2 right, entitlement. —**slos** *adj* unassuming. —**svoll** *adj* 1 demanding. 2 sophisticated. 3 fastidious.

Anstalt (ˈanʃtalt) *nf* -en 1 institution. 2 *pl* arrangements.

Anstand (ˈanʃtant) *nm* -̈e 1 decency, decorum. 2 hesitation. -̈**ig** (ˈanʃtendiç) *adj* decent, respectable. -̈**igkeit** *nf* decency, respectability.

anstatt (anˈʃtat) *prep* instead of.

ansteck/en (ˈanʃtekən) *vt* 1 fasten or pin on. 2 set fire to, light. 3 infect. —**end** *adj* infectious, contagious..

anstell/en (ˈanʃtelən) *vt* 1 employ, appoint. 2 turn on, start. 3 place near. 4 carry out, implement. *vi* 1 queue up. 2 behave, act. —**ung** *nf* -en appointment, post.

anstiften (ˈanʃtiftən) *vt* 1 cause. 2 instigate, incite.

Anstoß (ˈanʃtoːs) *nm* -**stösse** 1 impulse, stimulus. 2 knock, collision. 3 offence. 4 kickoff. **Anstoß nehmen** take offence. —**en**° *vt* 1 push (on or against). 2 knock. *vi* offend.

8

anstreng/en (ˈanʃtrɛŋən) *vt* 1 exert. 2 strain. 3 tire. —**ung** *nf* -en 1 exertion. 2 strain.

Antarktis (antˈarktis) *nf* Antarctic. **antarktisch** (antˈarktiʃ) *adj* Antarctic.

antasten (ˈantastən) *vt* 1 touch. 2 damage.

Anteil (ˈantail) *nm* -e 1 share. 2 interest. 3 sympathy.

Antenne (anˈtɛnə) *nf* -n antenna, aerial.

Anthropologie (antropoloˈgiː) *nf* anthropology.

Antibiotikum (antibiˈoːtikum) *n neu* -**ka** antibiotic.

antik (anˈtiːk) *adj* 1 classical, ancient. 2 antique. **Antike** (anˈtiːkə) *nf* antiquity.

Antiquar (antiˈkvaːr) *nm* -e 1 second-hand bookseller. 2 antique dealer. **Antiquariat** (antikvariˈaːt) *n neu* -e second-hand bookshop. **Antiquität** (antikviˈtɛːt) *nf* -en antique.

antisemitisch (antizeˈmiːtiʃ) *adj* anti-Semitic.

antiseptisch (antiˈzɛptiʃ) *adj* antiseptic.

Antonym (antoˈnyːm) *n neu* -e antonym.

Antrag (ˈantraːk) *nm* -̈e 1 application. 2 proposal. —**steller** *nm* — 1 applicant. 2 mover (of a proposal).

antreffen° (ˈantrɛfən) *vt* meet (with).

antreiben° (ˈantraibən) *vt* push or drive on. *vi* drift ashore.

antreten° (ˈantreːtən) *vt* 1 begin. 2 take up. 3 enter into. 4 approach.

Antrieb (ˈantriːp) *nm* -e 1 impulse. 2 power. 3 motive force.

Antritt (ˈantrit) *nm* -e 1 beginning. 2 taking up, assumption.

antun° (ˈantuːn) *vt* 1 put on. 2 do to.

Antwerpen (antˈvɛːrpən) *n neu* Antwerp.

Antwort (ˈantvɔrt) *nf* -en answer, reply. **in Antwort auf** in reply to. —**en** *vi* answer, reply.

anvertrauen (ˈanfɛrtrauən) *vt* entrust.

Anwalt (ˈanvalt) *nm* -̈e lawyer, advocate.

anwärmen (ˈanvɛrmən) *vt* warm (gently).

anweis/en° (ˈanvaizən) *vt* 1 assign. 2 instruct. 3 *comm* remit. —**ung** *nf* -en 1 money order, remittance. 2 instruction.

anwend/bar (ˈanvɛntbaːr) *adj* 1 applicable. 2 practicable. —**en**° (ˈanvɛndən) *vt* use, apply. —**ung** (ˈanvɛnduŋ) *nf* -en application, use.

anwesen/d (ˈanveːzənt) *adj* present. —**heit** *nf* -en presence.

Anzahl (ˈantsaːl) *nf* 1 number. 2 quantity.

Anzeichen (ˈantsaiçən) *n neu* sign, symptom.

Anzeig/e (ˈantsaigə) *nf* -n 1 advertisement, notice, announcement. 2 denunciation. 3 notification, indication. —**en** *vt* 1 announce, advertise. 2 denounce. **—er** nm 1 indicator. 2 informer. 3 advertiser. 4 newspaper.

anzieh/en⁰ ('antsi:ən) vt 1 put on (clothes). 2 attract. 3 pull or draw on. 4 tighten. **sich anziehen** vr dress. **—ungskraft** nf 1 attractive force, gravitation. 2 attractiveness.

Anzug ('antsu:k) nm ⸗e 1 suit. 2 clothing, dress. 3 approach.

anzünden ('antsyndən) vt light, set fire to.

Apennin (ape'ni:n) nm also **Apenninen** n pl Apennines.

Apfel ('apfəl) nm ⸗ apple.

Apfelsine ('apfəlzi:nə) nf -n orange.

Apostel (a'pɔstəl) nm — apostle.

Apotheke (apo'te:kə) nf -n chemist's shop, pharmacy. **—r** nm — chemist, pharmacist.

Apparat (apə'ra:t) nm -e 1 apparatus, equipment. 2 device. 3 telephone. **am Apparat bleiben** hold the line.

appellieren (apɛ'li:rən) vi appeal.

Appetit (apə'ti:t) nm -e appetite. **—lich** adj appetizing.

Aprikose (apri'ko:zə) nf -n apricot.

April (a'pril) nm -e April.

Aquarell (akva'rɛl) n neu -e watercolour.

Aquarium (a'kva:rium) n neu -rien aquarium.

Äquator (ɛ'kva:tɔr) nm Equator.

Äquivalent (ɛkviva'lɛnt) n neu -e equivalent.

Arab/er ('arabər) nm — Arab. **—ien** (a'ra:biən) n neu Arabia. **—isch** (a'ra:biʃ) adj Arabian, Arabic. n neu Arabic (language).

Arbeit ('arbait) nf -en 1 work, labour. 2 job. 3 effort. **—en** vi,vt work, labour. **—er** nm — worker, workman, labourer. **—erklasse** nf also **—erschaft** nf -en working class(es). **—geber** nm — employer. **—nehmer** nm — employee. **—sgemeinschaft** nf 1 syndicate. 2 partnership (employers and employees). 3 working party, study group. **—skräfte** nf pl personnel, staff, workforce. **—slos** adj unemployed. **—slosigkeit** nf unemployment.

Archäologie (arçɛolo'gi:) nf archaeology.

Architekt (arçi'tɛkt) nm -en architect. **—ur** (arçitɛk'tu:r) nf -en architecture.

Archiv (ar'çi:f) n neu -e archives, records.

arg (ark) adj 1 bad, evil. 2 serious. n neu evil, malice. **—los** adj unsuspecting, innocent. **—wohn** ('arkvo:n) nm suspicion, distrust.

Argentin/ien (argɛn'ti:niən) n neu Argentina. **—ier** nm — Argentine. **—isch** adj Argentinian.

Ärger ('ɛrgər) nm 1 anger. 2 irritation, annoyance. **—lich** adj 1 angry. 2 annoying.

troublesome. **—n** vt annoy, irritate, bother. **—nis** n neu -se 1 nuisance. 2 offence.

Argument (argu'mɛnt) n neu -e argument, case.

Aristokrat (aristo'kra:t) nm -en aristocrat. **—ie** nf -n aristocracy. **—isch** adj aristocratic.

Arithmetik (arit'me:tik) nf arithmetic.

Arktis ('arktis) nf Arctic. **arktisch** ('arktiʃ) adj arctic.

arm (arm) adj poor. **—e(r)** nf,m poor man. **⸗lich** ('ɛrmliç) adj poor, lowly (of clothes, a house, etc.). **—selig** adj miserable, wretched (of persons). **—ut** ('armu:t) nf poverty.

Arm (arm) nm -e 1 arm. 2 (of rivers, etc.) branch. **—band** n neu bracelet. **—banduhr** nf wrist-watch. **—stuhl** nm arm-chair.

Armee (ar'me:) nf -n army. **—korps** n neu army corps.

Ärmel ('ɛrmal) nm — sleeve. **—kanal** nm (English) Channel.

Arrest (a'rɛst) nm -e 1 arrest, seizure. 2 detention, imprisonment.

Art (a:rt) nf -en 1 sort, type, kind. 2 way, manner. 3 nature. 4 species. **—en nach** vi take after. **—ig** adj 1 well-behaved, polite. 2 kind. 3 good. **—igkeit** nf -en 1 politeness, good behaviour. 2 compliment. **—artig** ('a:rtiç) suff -like.

Artikel (ar'ti:kəl) nm — article.

Artillerie (artilə'ri:) nf -n artillery.

Artischocke (a:ti'ʃɔkə) nf -n artichoke.

Arznei (arts'nai) nf -en, also **Arzneimittel** n neu medicine, drug.

Arzt (a:rtst) nm ⸗e doctor, physician. **⸗in** ('ɛ:rtstin) nf -nen (woman) doctor. **⸗lich** ('ɛ:rtstliç) adj medical.

As (a:s) n neu -se ace.

Asbest (as'bɛst) nm asbestos.

Asche ('aʃə) nf -n ash, ashes, cinders. **—nbahn** nf cinder-track, dirt-track. **—nbecher** nm ashtray. **—rmittwoch** (aʃər'mitvɔx) nm Ash Wednesday.

aß (a:s) v see **essen.**

Assistent (asis'tɛnt) nm -en assistant.

Ast (ast) nm ⸗e 1 bough, branch. 2 knot (in wood).

ästhetisch (ɛs'te:tiʃ) adj aesthetic.

Astronaut (astro'naut) nm -en astronaut.

Astronom (astro'no:m) nm -en astronomer. **—ie** (astrono'mi:) nf astronomy.

Asyl (a'zy:l) n neu -e asylum, sanctuary.

Atelier (atə'lje:) n neu -s studio.

Atem ('a:təm) nm breath. **außer Atem**

breathless. —**raubend** adj 1 breath-taking, terrifying. 2 fascinating. —**los** adj breathless.

Athe/ismus (ate'ismus) nm atheism. —**ist** (ate'ist) nm -**en** atheist.

Athen (a'te:n) n neu Athens.

Äther ('ε:tər) nm ether. —**isch** (ε'te:riʃ) adj ethereal.

Äthiop/ien (εti'o:piən) n neu Ethiopia. —**ier** nm — Ethiopian. —**isch** adj Ethiopian.

Athletik (at'le:tik) nf athletics.

Atlantik (at'lantik) nm also **Atlantischer Ozean** (at'lantiʃər) Atlantic.

Atlas[1] ('atlas) nm **-lasse** satin.

Atlas[2] ('atlas) nm **-lanten** atlas.

atmen ('a:tmən) vi,vt breathe, respire.

Atmosphäre (atmos'fε:rə) nf -**n** atmosphere. **atmosphärisch** (atmos'fε:riʃ) adj atmospheric.

Atom (a'to:m) n neu -**e** atom. —**bombe** nf atom(ic) bomb. —**energie** nf atomic energy. —**kern** nm atomic nucleus. —**kraftanlage** nf nuclear power station. —**waffen** nf pl nuclear weapons.

Atten/tat (atɛn'ta:t) n neu -**e** murderous attack, assault, (attempted) assassination. —**täter** (atɛn'tε:tər) nm — assassin, assailant.

ätzen ('ɛtsən) vt corrode, etch.

Aubergine (obɛr'ʒi:nə) nf -**n** aubergine.

auch (aux) adv, conj 1 also, as well, too. 2 even. 3 indeed. **auch wenn** also **wenn auch** even if. **nicht nur...sondern auch** not only...but also. **wer auch** whoever.

Audienz (audi'ɛnts) nf -**en** audience, hearing.

auf (auf) prep 1 (up)on. 2 in. 3 to. 4 at. 5 up. 6 against. **auf einmal** all at once. ~adv open, up(wards). interj (get) up!

Aufbau ('aufbau) nm -**e** or -**ten** 1 construction, erection. 2 composition, organization. 3 superstructure. —**en** vt construct, build up.

Aufbesserung ('aufbɛsəruŋ) nf -**en** 1 improvement. 2 increase (of salary etc.).

aufbewahren ('aufbəva:rən) vt store, keep.

aufbleiben* ('aufblaibən) vi 1 stay up. 2 remain open.

aufblicken ('aufblikən) vi look up.

aufbrauchen ('aufbrauxən) vt use up, consume.

aufbrechen* ('aufbrɛçən) vt break open. vi 1 burst open. 2 set off.

aufbringen* ('aufbriŋən) vt 1 bring up, raise. 2 irritate, anger.

aufdrehen ('aufdre:ən) vt 1 unscrew. 2 turn on.

aufdring/en* ('aufdriŋən) vt force on (someone). —**lich** adj intrusive, importunate.

aufeinander (aufain'andər) adv 1 successively. 2 one on or against the other.

Aufenthalt ('aufɛnthalt) nm -**e** 1 stop, halt, delay. 2 stay, period (of residence).

auferlegen ('auferle:gən) vt impose.

aufersteh/en* ('auferʃte:ən) vi rise from the dead. —**ung** nf -**en** resurrection.

auffahren* ('auffa:rən) vi 1 rise (up). 2 drive up. 3 start, jump. 4 become angry.

auffallen* ('auffalən) vi 1 fall upon. 2 be noticeable, evident. **es fiel mir auf, daß** it struck me that. **auffallend** ('auffalənt) adj also **auffällig** ('auffɛliç) striking, remarkable.

auffangen* ('auffaŋən) vt catch up, intercept.

auffass/en ('auffasən) vt 1 understand, interpret. 2 pick up. —**ung** nf -**en** 1 comprehension. 2 opinion. 3 conception.

auffinden* ('auffindən) vt find (out), discover.

auffliegen* ('auffli:gən) vi 1 fly up. 2 explode. 3 (of a door) fly open.

aufforder/n ('auffordərn) vt 1 challenge, invite. 2 summon. —**ung** nf -**en** 1 challenge, invitation. 2 summons.

auffressen* ('auffrɛsən) vt devour.

aufführ/en ('auffy:rən) vt 1 build. 2 perform. 3 specify. 4 list. 5 bring forward, introduce. —**ung** nf -**en** performance, presentation.

Aufgabe ('aufga:bə) nf -**n** 1 task, duty. 2 problem. 3 giving up. 4 delivery.

Aufgang ('aufgaŋ) nm -**e** 1 ascent, rise. 2 staircase.

aufgeben* ('aufge:bən) vt 1 give up or in. 2 deliver, surrender. 3 post (mail, etc.).

Aufgebot ('aufgəbo:t) n neu -**e** public notice.

aufgehen* ('aufge:ən) vi 1 rise. 2 open. 3 math divide exactly, work out correctly.

aufgeklärt ('aufgəklɛ:rt) adj enlightened.

aufgelegt ('aufgəle:kt) adj disposed, inclined. **gut/schlecht aufgelegt** in a good/bad mood.

aufhalten* ('aufhaltən) vt 1 hold open. 2 delay. **sich aufhalten** vr stay.

aufhängen* ('aufhɛŋən) vt hang (up).

aufheb/en* ('aufhe:bən) vt 1 pick up, raise. 2 keep, store. 3 annul, cancel. 4 suspend. 5 reverse. n neu — 1 lifting up. 2 fuss, ado. —**ung** nf -**en** 1 abolition, repeal. 2 suspension.

aufhören ('aufhœ:rən) vi cease, stop, discontinue.

aufklappen ('aufklapən) vt open.

aufklär/en ('aufklɛ:rən) vt,vi 1 clear up. 2

enlighten. 3 correct. **—ung** nf **-en** 1 clearing up. 2 enlightenment. 3 explanation.

aufkleben ('aufklɛːbən) vt paste on, affix.

aufknüpfen ('aufknypfən) vt 1 tie or hang up. 2 untie.

aufkommen* ('aufkɔmən) vi 1 rise. 2 recover. 3 make good. n neu — 1 yield (of taxes). 2 recovery, rise.

aufladen* ('auflaːdən) vt load.

Auflage ('auflaːgə) nf **-n** 1 edition, impression. 2 circulation. 3 tax, duty.

auflassen* ('auflasən) vt leave open.

Auflauf ('euflauf) nm ⁼e 1 riot. 2 soufflé.

auflös/en ('auflœːzən) vt 1 untie, loosen. 2 dissolve. 3 break up. **—ung** nf **-en** 1 dissolution. 2 decomposition.

aufmachen ('aufmaxən) vt 1 open, undo. 2 put up (an umbrella). **sich aufmachen** vr set out.

Aufmarsch ('aufmarʃ) nm ⁼e mil 1 approach, marching up (of troops). 2 deployment. 3 parade.

aufmerk/sam ('aufmɛrkzaːm) adj attentive. **—samkeit** nf attentiveness.

aufmuntern ('aufmuntərn) vt 1 rouse, encourage. 2 cheer up.

Aufnahme ('aufnaːmə) nf **-n** 1 acceptance, reception, admission. 2 recording. 3 photograph.

aufnehmen* ('aufneːmən) vt 1 take or pick up. 2 receive, admit. 3 record. 4 photograph.

aufopfer/n ('aufɔpfərn) vt sacrifice. **—ung** nf **-en** 1 sacrifice. 2 devotion.

aufpassen ('aufpasən) vi 1 watch. 2 pay attention.

Aufputz ('aufputs) nm finery, ornament.

aufräumen ('aufrɔymən) vt 1 tidy up. 2 clear away or out.

aufrecht ('aufrɛçt) adj 1 upright, erect. 2 honourable. **—erhalten*** vt maintain, support. **—erhaltung** nf maintenance.

aufreg/en ('aufreːgən) vt 1 excite. 2 irritate. 3 alarm. **sich aufregen** vr get excited. **—ung** nf **-en** excitement, agitation.

aufreiben* ('aufraibən) vt 1 chafe. 2 exhaust. 3 harass. 4 destroy, wipe out (an enemy).

aufricht/en ('aufriçtən) vt 1 erect, set up. 2 establish. **sich aufrichten** vr get or sit up. **—ig** adj honest, sincere. **—igkeit** nf sincerity.

Aufriß ('aufris) nm 1 sketch. 2 section. 3 plan.

aufrücken ('aufrykən) vi move up(wards).

Aufruf ('aufruːf) nm **-e** 1 call. 2 summons. 3 appeal.

Aufruhr ('aufruːr) nm **-e** 1 riot, uproar. 2 revolt. **⁼erisch** ('aufryːrarɪʃ) adj mutinous.

aufrüsten ('aufrystən) vt (re)arm.

aufs (aufs) contraction of **auf das.**

aufsagen ('aufzaːgən) vt recite.

Aufsatz ('aufzats) nm ⁼e 1 essay, article. 2 top piece. 3 centrepiece.

aufschieben* ('aufʃiːbən) vt 1 push open. 2 delay, postpone.

Aufschlag ('aufʃlaːk) nm ⁼e 1 hit, impact. 2 rise (of prices). 3 cuff, lapel, facing (of clothes). 4 sport service. **—en*** ('aufʃlaːgən) vt 1 break open, open. 2 put up, erect. 3 look or glance up.

aufschließen* ('aufʃliːsən) vt 1 unlock. 2 open up.

Aufschluß ('aufʃlus) nm 1 information. 2 explanation. **—reich** adj informative.

aufschneiden* ('aufʃnaidən) vt cut open or up. vi brag, exaggerate.

Aufschnitt ('aufʃnit) nm **-e** slices of cold meats.

Aufschrei ('aufʃrai) nm **-e** 1 scream. 2 outcry.

aufschreiben* ('aufʃraibən) vt write down.

Aufschrift ('aufʃrift) nf **-en** 1 inscription. 2 address.

Aufschub ('aufʃup) nm ⁼e delay, postponement.

Aufschwung ('aufʃvuŋ) nm ⁼e 1 rise, upward impetus. 2 comm boom. 3 enthusiasm. **einen neuen Aufschwung nehmen** revive.

aufseh/en* ('aufzeːən) vi look up. n neu — sensation, stir. **—er** nm 1 inspector, overseer, superintendant.

aufsetzen ('aufzɛtsən) vt 1 set up. 2 put on. **sich aufsetzen** vr sit up.

Aufsicht ('aufziçt) nf **-en** 1 supervision. 2 charge, care. **—sbehörde** nf controlling authority. **—srat** nm board of directors.

aufspringen* ('aufʃpriŋən) vi 1 jump up. 2 fly open. 3 crack.

Aufstand ('aufʃtant) nm ⁼e revolt, riot. **⁼isch** ('aufʃtɛndɪʃ) adj rebellious.

aufstapeln ('aufʃtaːpəln) vt 1 heap up. 2 store.

aufstehen* ('aufʃteːən) vi 1 get or stand up. 2 rebel. 3 stand open.

aufsteigen* ('aufʃtaigən) vi 1 climb (up), mount. 2 rise.

aufstell/en ('aufʃtɛlən) vt 1 put or set up. 2 draw up. 3 nominate. 4 display. 5 state. **—ung** nf **-en** 1 erection. 2 position. 3 arrangement. 4 list, table. 5 nomination.

Aufstieg ('aufʃtiːk) nm **-e** 1 ascent. 2 rise.

aufstützen ('aufʃtytsən) *vt* prop up.

aufsuchen ('aufzu:xən) *vt* seek (out). **jemanden aufsuchen** look up or visit someone.

auftanken ('auftaŋkən) *vt* fuel, fill up (with fuel).

auftauchen ('auftauxən) *vi* 1 emerge. 2 surface. 3 appear, crop up.

aufteilen ('auftailən) *vt* distribute, divide up.

Auftrag ('auftra:k) *nm* ⁼e 1 instructions, order. 2 task. 3 contract. 4 mandate. **im Auftrag von** by order of. **—geber** *nm* — *comm* customer.

auftreiben* ('auftraibən) *vt* 1 procure, obtain. 2 startle, rouse. 3 swell.

auftreten* ('auftre:tən) *vi* 1 come forward. 2 occur, appear. *vt* kick open. *n neu* — 1 appearance. 2 behaviour, manner.

Auftritt ('auftrit) *nm* -e 1 appearance. 2 *Th* scene.

auftun* ('auftu:n) *vt* 1 open. 2 start (up).

aufwachen* ('aufvaxən) *vi* wake up.

aufwachsen* ('aufvaksən) *vi* grow up.

Aufwand ('aufvant) *nm* ⁼e 1 expenditure. 2 extravagance.

aufwärmen ('aufvɛrmən) *vt* 1 warm up. 2 rake up, revive (a dispute, story, etc.).

aufwärts ('aufvɛrts) *adv* upward(s).

aufwecken ('aufvɛkən) *vt* wake, rouse.

aufweisen* ('aufvaizən) *vt* present, show.

aufwend/en* ('aufvɛndən) *vt* spend, expend. **—ung** *nf* -en expenditure.

aufwerfen* ('aufvɛrfən) *vt* 1 cast up. 2 throw open. 3 raise (a question).

aufwert/en ('aufvɛrtən) *vt* revalue (upwards). **—ung** *nf* -en revaluation.

aufwischen ('aufviʃən) *vt* wipe up.

aufwühlen ('aufvy:lən) *vt* 1 dig up, turn up. 2 stir up.

aufzählen ('auftsɛ:lən) *vt* count (up), enumerate.

aufzeichn/en ('auftsaiçnən) *vt* 1 draw, sketch. 2 note, record. **—ung** *nf* -en note, record.

aufziehen* ('auftsi:ən) *vt* 1 pull or draw up, raise. 2 open. 3 bring up, rear.

Aufzug ('auftsu:k) *nm* ⁼e 1 lift, elevator, hoist. 2 parade. 3 act (of a play). 4 attire.

Augapfel ('aukapfəl) *nm* eyeball.

Auge ('augə) *n neu* -n 1 eye. 2 bud. **blaues Auge** black eye. **ein Auge zudrücken** wink at. 2 shut one's eyes to. **unter vier Augen** face to face (in private). **—nblick** *nm* instant, moment. **—nfällig** *adj* conspicuous, obvious.

August (au'gust) *nm* August.

Aula ('aula) *nf* -len (great) hall.

au pair (o'pe:r) *adj* au pair.

aus (aus) *prep* 1 out (of). 2 from. 3 of. 4 by. *adv* 1 out. 2 over, finished.

ausarbeiten ('ausarbaitən) *vt* 1 work out. 2 prepare.

Ausbau ('ausbau) *nm* -e 1 completion. 2 extension (of a building).

ausbessern ('ausbesərn) *vt* 1 repair, refit. 2 rectify.

Ausbeut/e ('ausbɔytə) *nf* -n 1 profit, gain. 2 output. **—en** *vt* exploit, profit from. **—ung** *nf* -en exploitation.

ausbild/en ('ausbildən) *vt* 1 educate, train. 2 form, develop. **—ung** *nf* 1 education, training. 2 development.

ausbleiben* ('ausblaibən) *vi* stay away or out, be absent. *n neu* — absence, default.

Ausblick ('ausblik) *nm* -e view, outlook.

ausbrechen* ('ausbrɛçən) *vi* break out. *vt* vomit.

ausbreit/en ('ausbraitən) *vt* 1 spread (out). 2 stretch, extend. 3 spread. **—ung** *nf* -en spread, increase.

ausbringen* ('ausbriŋən) *vt* bring out. **eine Gesundheit ausbringen** propose a toast.

Ausbruch ('ausbrux) *nm* ⁼e 1 burst. 2 outbreak. 3 eruption. 4 escape.

ausbrüten ('ausbry:tən) *vt* 1 hatch. 2 plot.

Ausdauer ('ausdauər) *nf* 1 endurance. 2 perseverance.

ausdehn/en ('ausde:nən) *vt* extend, stretch, expand. **—ung** *nf* 1 expansion. 2 range, extent.

ausdenken* ('ausdɛŋkən) *vt* 1 think out, work out. **sich ausdenken** *vr* think up, invent.

ausdrehen ('ausdre:ən) *vt* turn or switch off.

Ausdruck ('ausdruk) *nm* ⁼e 1 expression, look. 2 expression, term. **—en** ('ausdrykən) *vt* 1 express. 2 press or squeeze out. **—lich** ('ausdryklic) *adj* explicit.

auseinander (ausain'andər) *adv* separately, apart (from one another). **—gehen*** 1 disperse. 2 separate. 3 differ. **—setzen** *vt* explain, expound. **—setzung** *nf* -en 1 discussion. 2 conflict. 3 arrangement. **—treiben*** *vt* disperse.

ausersehen* ('ausɛrze:ən) *vt* 1 select, choose. 2 destine. *adj* (pre)destined.

auserwählen ('ausɛrvɛ:lən) *vt* choose, select.

ausfahr/en* ('ausfa:rən) *vi* go for a drive. *vt* take (someone) for a drive. **—t** *nf* 1 drive, excursion. 2 way out, gateway. 3 departure.

Ausfall ('ausfal) *nm* ⁻e 1 loss. 2 falling out. 3 result. 4 attack, sortie.

ausfertigen ('ausfɛrtigən) *vt* 1 complete. 2 draw up. 3 issue. 4 execute.

ausfind/en ('ausfindən) *vt* find out. **ausfindig machen** 1 trace. 2 find out.

Ausflug ('ausflu:k) *nm* ⁻e excursion.

Ausfluß ('ausflus) *nm* 1 outflow, discharge. 2 outlet. 3 result.

ausfragen ('ausfra:gən) *vt* interrogate, question.

Ausfuhr ('ausfu:r) *nf* -en export(ing). —**handel** *nm* export trade.

ausführ/bar ('ausfy:rba:r) *adj* 1 practicable. 2 exportable. —**en** *vt* 1 lead out. 2 carry out, perform. 3 export. —**lich** *adj* detailed, full.

ausfüllen ('ausfylən) *vt* fill up or in.

Ausgabe ('ausga:bə) *nf* -n 1 delivery. 2 issue. 3 edition. 4 expense, expenditure.

Ausgang ('ausgaŋ) *nm* ⁻e 1 door, exit. 2 result, end. 3 going out.

ausgeben ('ausge:bən) *vt* 1 give out. 2 spend. **sich ausgeben für** pose as.

ausgeglichen ('ausgəgliçən) *adj* balanced.

ausgeh/en ('ausge:ən) *vi* 1 go out, depart. 2 proceed. 3 end, run out. 4 fade. —**verbot** *n neu* curfew.

ausgelassen ('ausgəlasən) *adj* boisterous, unrestrained.

ausgemacht ('ausgəmaxt) *adj* settled, agreed.

ausgenommen ('ausgənɔmən) *prep* except.

ausgeprägt ('ausgəprɛ:kt) *adj* distinct, marked.

ausgerechnet ('ausgərɛçnət) *adv* just, precisely. **ausgerechnet ich** I of all people.

ausgeschlossen ('ausgəʃlɔsən) *adj* impossible, out of the question.

ausgesprochen ('ausgəʃprɔçən) *adj* marked, pronounced.

ausgezeichnet ('ausgətsaiçnət) *adj* excellent.

ausgießen ('ausgi:sən) *vt* pour out.

Ausgleich ('ausglaiç) *nm* -e 1 balance. 2 agreement, settlement. 3 compromise. 4 compensation. 5 adjustment. —**en** *vt* 1 equalize, balance. 2 settle. 3 adjust.

Ausguß ('ausgus) *nm* -güsse 1 pouring out. 2 spout. 3 gutter. 4 sink.

aushalten ('aushaltən) *vi* 1 hold out. 2 persevere. *vt* endure, bear.

Aushang ('aushaŋ) *nm* ⁻e poster, notice. —**en** ('aushɛŋən) *vt,vi* hang out.

ausharren ('ausharən) *vi* persevere.

ausheben ('aushe:bən) *vt* 1 lift out. 2 enlist, recruit. 3 raid.

aushelfen ('aushɛlfən) *vi* help out.

Aushilfe ('aushilfə) *nf* -n assistance, help, (temporary) aid.

sich auskennen ('auskɛnən) *vr* know thoroughly.

auskleiden ('ausklaidən) *vt* 1 undress. 2 *tech* coat, line. **sich auskleiden** *vr* undress.

auskommen ('auskɔmən) *vi* 1 come out. 2 escape. 3 manage, make do. **mit jemandem gut auskommen** get on well with someone. *n neu* — livelihood.

Auskunft ('auskunft) *nf* -künfte information. —**sbüro** *n neu* information bureau. —**smittel** *n neu* 1 escape. 2 expedient.

auslachen ('auslaxən) *vt* laugh at.

ausladen ('ausla:dən) *vt* 1 unload.

Auslage ('ausla:gə) *nf* -n 1 outlay. 2 expense. 3 display.

Ausland ('auslant) *n neu* foreign countries. **im/ins Ausland** abroad. ⁻**er** ('auslɛndər) *nm* — foreigner, alien. ⁻**isch** ('auslɛndiʃ) *adj* foreign.

auslass/en ('auslasən) *vt* 1 let out. 2 leave out, omit. **sich auslassen** *vr* express one's opinion. —**ung** *nf* -en 1 omission. 2 remark. —**ungszeichen** *n neu* apostrophe.

Auslauf ('auslauf) *nm* ⁻e 1 flowing out. 2 outlet. 3 departure (of a ship). 4 *aviat* landing run. 5 (gradual) finish, run-out. —**en** *vi* 1 run out. 2 leak. 3 come to an end.

ausleg/en ('ausle:gən) *vt* 1 lay out. 2 spend. 3 explain, interpret. —**ung** *nf* -en interpretation, explanation.

Auslese ('ausle:zə) *nf* -n 1 selection. 2 choice wine.

auslliefer/n ('ausli:fərn) *vt* hand over, deliver (up). —**ung** *nf* 1 delivery. 2 extradition.

auslöschen ('ausloeʃən) *vt* 1 extinguish. 2 erase. 3 switch off.

auslös/en ('ausloe:zən) *vt* 1 release. 2 loosen. 3 ransom, redeem. 4 cause. 5 arouse. —**er** *nm* — 1 trigger. 2 release.

ausmachen ('ausmaxən) *vt* 1 put out (fire, lights). 2 constitute, make up. 3 make out, discern. 4 arrange. 5 agree. **es macht nichts aus** it doesn't matter.

Ausnahm/e ('ausna:mə) *nf* -n exception. —**efall** *nm* exceptional case. —**ezustand** *nm* state of emergency. —**slos** *adj* without exception. —**sweise** *adv* exceptionally, for once.

ausnehmen ('ausne:mən) *vt* 1 take out. 2 except, exempt.

13

ausnutzen ('ausnytsən) vt also **ausnützen** exploit, utilize.

auspacken ('auspakən) vt unpack.

auspräg/en ('aⁿusprɛːgən) vt 1 stamp, mark. 2 coin. —**ung** nf 1 coinage. 2 stamp(ing).

ausprobieren ('ausprobiːrən) vt try, sample.

Auspuff ('auspuf) nm -e exhaust. —**rohr** n neu exhaust pipe. —**topf** nm silencer.

ausradieren ('ausradiːrən) vt erase.

ausräumen ('ausrɔymən) vt 1 clear (out). 2 empty.

ausrechnen ('ausrɛçnən) vt calculate.

Ausrede ('ausreːdə) nf -n (false) excuse.

ausreichen ('ausraiçən) vi suffice. —**d** adj sufficient.

Ausreise ('ausraizə) nf -n departure.

ausrichten ('ausriçtən) vt 1 carry out, accomplish. 2 deliver. 3 adjust. 4 straighten.

ausrotten ('ausrɔtən) vt 1 root out. 2 destroy (utterly), eradicate.

Ausruf ('ausruːf) nm -e 1 cry. 2 proclamation. —**en** vt, vi cry out, exclaim. —**ewort** n neu interjection. —**ung** nf -en 1 exclamation. 2 proclamation. —**ungszeichen** n neu exclamation mark.

ausruhen ('ausruːən) vi rest.

ausrüst/en ('ausrystən) vt 1 provide with, equip. 2 arm. —**ung** nf -en 1 equipment. 2 armament.

aussäen ('auszɛːən) vt sow.

Aussag/e ('auszaːgə) nf -n 1 declaration, deposition. 2 evidence. —**en** vt 1 declare, state. 2 give evidence.

Aussatz ('auszats) nm leprosy. —**ig** ('auszɛtsiç) adj leprous.

ausschalten ('ausʃaltən) vt 1 switch off, disconnect, break. 2 eliminate, exclude.

ausscheid/en* ('ausʃaidən) vt 1 eliminate. 2 separate. vi withdraw, retire.

ausschicken ('ausʃikən) vt send out, dispatch.

ausschießen* ('ausʃiːsən) vt shoot or cast out.

ausschiffen ('ausʃifən) vt 1 disembark. 2 set sail.

ausschimpfen ('ausʃimpfən) vt scold.

ausschlafen* ('ausʃlaːfən) vi sleep late, lie in.

Ausschlag ('ausʃlaːk) nm -e 1 deflection. 2 rash, eruption. **den Ausschlag geben** tip the scales. —**en*** ('ausʃlaːgən) vt 1 beat or knock out. 2 refuse, reject. 3 line or trim with. vi 1 lash out. 2 sprout, break into leaf. 3 turn out, develop. —**gebend** adj decisive.

ausschließ/en* ('ausʃliːsən) vt shut out, exclude, bar. —**lich** adj exclusive. prep excluding, exclusive of. **Ausschluß** ('ausʃlus) nm exclusion.

ausschneiden* ('ausʃnaidən) vt cut out.

ausschöpfen ('ausʃœpfən) vt 1 scoop out. 2 drain (off). 3 exhaust.

ausschreiben* ('ausʃraibən) vt 1 write out, copy. 2 announce, advertise.

Ausschreitung ('ausʃraitun) nf -en 1 excess. 2 transgression.

Ausschuß ('ausʃus) nm 1 committee, commission. 2 scrap. 3 rejects.

ausschweif/en ('ausʃvaifən) vi lead an immoral or dissolute life. —**ung** nf debauchery.

aussehen* ('auszeːən) vi appear, look. **gut aussehend** good looking. n neu — 1 appearance. 2 exterior.

außen ('ausən) adv 1 out(side), out of doors. 2 outwards. —**bordmotor** nm outboard motor. —**handel** nm foreign trade. —**minister** nm foreign minister. —**politik** nf foreign policy, foreign affairs. —**seite** nf outside. —**stände** nm pl arrears, outstanding debts or accounts. —**welt** nf 1 external world. 2 visible world.

aussenden* ('auszɛndən) vt 1 send out. 2 emit, transmit.

außer ('ausər) prep 1 outside. 2 out of. 3 besides. 4 except for. **außer Betrieb** out of order. **außer Dienst** off duty. **außer Fassung** disconcerted. **außer Kraft setzen** annul, cancel. ~conj except, but. **außer daß** except that. —**dem** adv, conj besides, moreover. —**gewöhnlich** adj extraordinary. —**halb** prep outside, beyond. —**ordentlich** (ausər'ɔrdəntliç) adj extraordinary, uncommon.

äußer/e ('ɔysərə) adj external. n neu -n exterior, appearance. —**st** ('ɔysərst) adj 1 outermost. 2 utmost. 3 extreme.

äußerlich ('ɔysərliç) adj 1 external. 2 superficial.

äußer/n ('ɔysərn) vt utter, express. —**ung** nf -en remark.

aussetzen ('auszɛtsən) vt 1 set or put out. 2 suspend. 3 expose. 4 offer (money). 5 lower (a boat). vi stop, stall.

Aussicht ('ausziçt) nf -en outlook, prospect. —**slos** adj hopeless. —**spunkt** nm viewpoint.

aussondern ('auszɔndərn) vt single out, separate.

ausspannen ('ausʃpanən) vt stretch, extend. vi rest, relax.

ausspeien* ('ausʃpaiən) vt spit out.

Aussprache ('aus∫pra:xə) nf -n 1 pronunciation. 2 discussion.

aussprechen* ('aus∫prɛçən) vt 1 pronounce. 2 express, say.

Ausspruch ('aus∫prux) nm saying, utterance.

ausspülen ('aus∫py:lən) vt 1 wash or rinse out. 2 clean.

Ausstand ('aus∫tant) nm strike.

ausstatt/en ('aus∫tatən) vt 1 equip. 2 furnish. —ung nf -en 1 equipment. 2 fittings.

ausstehen* ('aus∫te:ən) vt endure, bear.

ausstell/en ('aus∫tɛlən) vt 1 exhibit. 2 issue. —ung nf exhibition.

aussterben* ('aus∫tɛrbən) vi die out.

Aussteuer ('aus∫tɔyər) nf -n 1 dowry. 2 trousseau.

ausstoßen* ('aus∫to:sən) vt 1 push or drive out, expel. 2 utter.

ausstrahlen ('aus∫tra:lən) vt,vi radiate.

ausstrecken ('aus∫trɛkən) vt extend.

ausstreichen* ('aus∫traiçən) vt cross out.

ausströmen ('aus∫trœ:mən) vi 1 stream out. 2 escape.

aussuchen ('auszu:xən) vt select, pick.

Austausch ('austau∫) nm -e exchange, barter. —en vt exchange.

austeilen ('austailən) vt distribute, hand out.

Auster ('austər) nf -n oyster.

austragen* ('austra:gən) vt 1 distribute. 2 deliver. 3 decide (a contest).

Austral/ien (au'stra:liən) n neu Australia. —ier nm Australian. —isch adj Australian.

austreiben* ('austraibən) vt 1 drive out, expel. 2 exorcize.

austreten* ('austre:tən) vi 1 go or step out. 2 withdraw. 3 resign from. vt tread out, stamp out. **Austritt** ('austrit) nm -e 1 departure, exit. 2 resignation. 3 withdrawal.

ausüb/en ('ausy:bən) vt 1 practise. 2 carry out. —ung nf practice, execution.

Ausverkauf ('ausfɛrkauf) nm (clearance) sale.

Auswahl ('ausva:l) nf -en 1 selection. 2 variety. —en ('ausvɛ:lən) vt choose, select.

Auswander/er ('ausvandərər) nm — emigrant. —n vi emigrate. —ung nf -en emigration.

auswärtig ('ausvɛrtiç) adj foreign. **das auswärtige Amt** foreign office.

auswärts ('ausvɛrts) adv 1 outward(s). 2 abroad. 3 outside.

Ausweg ('ausve:k) nm way out, expedient.

ausweich/en* ('ausvaiçən) vi 1 make way for. 2 avoid.

ausweiden ('ausvaidən) vt gut, disembowel.

Ausweis ('ausvais) nm -e 1 ticket. 2 identity card. 3 passport. 4 statement. —en* ('ausvaizən) vt turn out, expel, banish. **sich —en** vr prove one's identity. —**karte** nf identity card. —**papiere** n neu pl identification papers. —**ung** ('ausvaizuŋ) nf expulsion, deportation.

auswendig ('ausvɛndiç) adj external. **auswendig lernen** learn by heart, memorize.

auswerfen* ('ausvɛrfən) vt throw out, cast out.

auswerten ('ausvɛrtən) vt evaluate, analyse.

auswirken ('ausvirkən) vt 1 work out. 2 effect, bring about.

auswischen ('ausvi∫ən) vt wipe out, obliterate.

Auswuchs ('ausvuks) nm growth, deformity.

auszahlen ('austsa:lən) vt pay out or off.

auszeichn/en ('austsaiçnən) vt 1 mark out. 2 honour. 3 label. —ung nf 1 distinction, honour. 2 mark.

ausziehen* ('austsi:ən) vt 1 draw or pull out. 2 make out (a bill). 3 take off (clothes). vi 1 move (out). 2 set forth. **sich ausziehen** vr undress.

Auszug ('austsu:k) nm 1 departure. 2 extract, abstract. 3 move, removal. 4 statement of account.

Auto ('auto) n neu -s (motor) car, automobile. —**bahn** nf motorway. —**bus** nm -se bus. —**fahrer** nm motorist, driver. —**heber** nm jack. —**rennen** n neu motor racing. —**stop** nm hitchhiking. **per Autostop fahren** hitchhike. —**unfall** nm motoring accident.

Autogramm (auto'gram) n neu -e autograph.

Auto/mat (auto'ma:t) nm -en automat, vending machine. —**matisch** adj automatic. —**nom** (auto'no:m) adj autonomous.

Autor ('autor) nm -en writer, author.

Autorität (autori'tɛ:t) nf -en authority.

Axt (akst) nf -e axe.

Azoren (a'tso:rən) n pl Azores.

B

Baby ('be:bi) n neu -s baby.

Bach (bax) nm -e stream, brook.

Backbord ('bakbort) n neu naut port (side).

Backe ('bakə) nf -n also **Backen** ('bakən) nm — cheek.

back/en* ('bakən) vt 1 bake. 2 fry. —**er** ('bɛkər) nm — baker. —**erei** (bɛkə'rai) nf -en bakery. —**pulver** n neu baking powder.

Bad (ba:t) n neu -er 1 bath. 2 spa. —**ehose**

('ba:dəho:zə) nf bathing trunks. **—ekappe** ('ba:dəkapə) nf bathing cap. **—en** ('ba:dən) vi,vt bathe. **—etuch** ('ba:dətu:x) n neu bath towel. **—ewanne** ('ba:dəvanə) nf bath tub. **—ezimmer** ('ba:dətsimər) n neu bathroom.

Bagger ('bagə) nm — excavator.

Bahn (ba:n) nf **-en** 1 way, path, track. 2 railway. **—hof** nm (railway) station. **—steig** ·nm -e platform. **—übergang** nm level crossing.

Bahre ('ba:rə) nf -n stretcher, bier.

Bai (bai) nf -en bay.

Bajonett (bajo'nɛt) n neu -e bayonet.

Bakterium (bak'te:rium) n neu -rien also **Bakterie** (bak'te:riə) nf -n bacterium.

balancieren (balã'si:rən) vt balance.

bald (balt) adv 1 soon, shortly. 2 almost. **bald...bald** now...now. **—ig** ('baldiç) adj 1 early. 2 quick, speedy. **—möglichst** adv as soon as possible. ·

Balken ('balkən) nm — beam, rafter, girder.

Balkon (bal'kõ:) nm -s balcony.

Ball[1] (bal) nm -"e 1 ball. 2 globe.

Ball[2] (bal) nm -"e dance, ball.

Ballade (ba'la:də) nf -n ballad.

Ballast ('balast) nm -e ballast.

Ballen ('balən) nm — 1 bale. 2 package.

Ballett (ba'lɛt) n neu -e ballet.

Ballon (ba'lõ:) nm -e balloon.

Balsam ('balza:m) nm -e balsam, balm.

baltisch ('baltiʃ) adj baltic. **baltisches Meer** n neu Baltic (sea).

Bambus ('bambus) nm -se bamboo.

Banane (ba'na:nə) nf -n banana.

Band[1] (bant) n neu 1 pl -"er band, tape, ribbon. 2 pl -"er ligament. 3 pl -e bond, tie. **—aufnahme** nf tape-recording.

Band[2] (bant) nm -"e volume, tome.

Bandage (ban'da:ʒə) nf -n bandage.

Bande ('bandə) nf -n band, gang.

bändigen ('bɛndigən) vt tame, subdue.

Bandit (ban'di:t) nm -en bandit.

bang(e) (baŋ) adj afraid, anxious.

Bank[1] (baŋk) nf -"e bench, seat.

Bank[2] (baŋk) nf -en comm bank. **—ier** (baŋk-'je:) nm -s banker. **—konto** n neu bank account. **—note** nf bank note. **—wesen** n neu banking.

Bankett (baŋ'kɛt) n neu -e banquet.

bankrott (baŋ'krɔt) adj bankrupt. nm -e bankruptcy.

Bann (ban) nm -e 1 ban, proscription. 2 excom-

munication. 3 spell. **—en** vt 1 banish. 2 excommunicate. 3 enchant.

bar (ba:r) adj (of money) ready, in cash. **—fuß** adj barefoot. **—geld** n neu cash, ready money.

Bar (ba:r) nf -s tavern, bar.

Bär (bɛ:r) nm -en bear.

Barbar (bar'ba:r) nm -en barbarian. **—ei** (barba'rai) nf -en barbarism. **—isch** adj barbarous.

Barbiturat (barbitu'ra:t) n neu barbiturate.

Bariton ('bariton) nm -e baritone.

Barmädchen ('barmɛ:dçən) n neu — barmaid.

barmherzig (barm'hɛrtsiç) adj merciful.

Barock (ba'rɔk) nm,neu baroque.

Barometer (ba'rome:tər) n neu — barometer.

Baron (ba'ro:n) nm -e baron. **—in** nf -nen baroness.

Barre ('barə) nf -n bar.

Barriere (bari'ɛ:rə) nf -n barrier, gate.

barsch (barʃ) adj 1 harsh, rough. 2 rude.

Bart (ba:rt) nm -"e beard.

Base[1] ('ba:zə) nf -n female relative (especially a cousin).

Base[2] (be:s) nf -n base.

Basel ('ba:zəl) n neu Basle.

bas/ieren (ba'zi:rən) vi be based. **—is** ('ba:zis) nf -sen base, basis.

Baß (bas) nm **Bässe** bass. **—geige** nf double bass.

Bassist (ba'sist) nm -en bass singer, bass player.

Bastard ('bastart) nm -e 1 bastard. 2 hybrid.

bas/teln ('bastəln) vt tinker with, potter around with. **—tler** ('bastlər) nm — 1 dabbler. 2 handyman.

bat (ba:t) v see **bitten.**

Bataillon (batai'ljo:n) n neu -e battalion.

Batterie (batə'ri:) nf -n battery.

Bau (bau) nm -e, -ten 1 construction, building. 2 burrow. 3 mine. 4 cultivation. **—en** vt 1 build. 2 grow. **—fällig** adj in disrepair, dilapidated. **—herr** nm 1 builder. 2 person for whom a building is being constructed. **—kunst** nf architecture. **—meister** nm 1 builder. 2 architect. **—platz** nm also **—stelle** nf building site. **—sparkasse** nf building society. **—stein** nm building stone. **—werk** n neu building, structure.

Bauch (baux) nm -"e belly, stomach. **—schmerzen** nm pl stomach-ache. **—tanz** nm belly dance.

Bauer ('bauər) nm -n 1 farmer. 2 peasant.

Bäuerin (ˈbɔyərin) nf **-nen** farmer's wife, peasant woman. **Bauernhaus** (ˈbauərnhaus) n neu farmhouse. **Bauernhof** (ˈbauərnhoːf) nm farm(yard).

Baum (baum) nm **-e** 1 tree. 2 naut boom, mast. **—garten** nm orchard. **—wolle** nf cotton.

Bay/er (baiər) nm **-n** Bavarian. **—ern** (ˈbaiərn) n neu Bavaria. **—risch** (ˈbairiʃ) adj Bavarian.

Bazillus (baˈtsilus) nm **-illen** bacillus.

beabsichtigen (bəˈapziçtigən) vt intend.

beacht/en (bəˈaxtən) vt pay attention to. **—enswert** adj noteworthy, notable. **—ung** nf consideration, attention.

Beamte(r) (bəˈamtə) nm **-n, Beamtin** (bəˈamtin) nf **-nen** 1 official. 2 civil servant.

beängstigen (bəˈɛŋstigən) vt frighten.

beanspruchen (bəˈanʃpruxən) vt claim, require.

beanstand/en (bəˈanʃtandən) vt object to. **—ung** nf **-en** objection.

beantragen (bəˈantraːgən) vt 1 apply for. 2 propose.

beantwort/en (bəˈantvɔrtən) vt answer. **—ung** nf **-en** reply, answer.

bearbeit/en (bəˈarbaitən) vt 1 work. 2 revise, adapt. 3 cultivate. **—ung** nf **-en** 1 working. 2 treatment. 3 revision, adaptation.

beaufsichtig/en (bəˈaufziçtigən) vt 1 supervise. 2 inspect. **—ung** nf **-en** supervision, control.

beauftragen (bəˈauftraːgən) vt commission.

bebauen (bəˈbauən) vt 1 build on. 2 cultivate.

beben (ˈbeːbən) vi shake, tremble, shiver.

Becher (ˈbɛçər) nm **-** 1 cup. 2 beaker.

Becken (ˈbɛkən) n neu **-** 1 basin. 2 cymbal. 3 pelvis.

bedacht (bəˈdaxt) adj thoughtful. **bedacht auf** intent on. **~nm** 1 caution. 2 consideration. **mit Bedacht** deliberately. **~ig** (bəˈdɛçtiç) adj 1 deliberate. 2 cautious.

Bedarf (bəˈdarf) nm 1 need, want. 2 demand.

bedauer/lich (bəˈdauərliç) adj unfortunate, regrettable. **—n** vt 1 regret. 2 deplore. 3 pity. n neu **-** 1 regret. 2 pity.

bedeck/en (bəˈdɛkən) vt 1 cover. 2 protect. **—t** adj 1 covered. 2 (of the sky) overcast. **—ung** nf 1 covering. 2 protection. 3 escort.

bedenk/en* (bəˈdɛŋkən) vt consider, think about. **sich bedenken** vr deliberate. **~n** neu **-** 1 doubt, hesitation. 2 consideration. **—lich** adj 1 doubtful. 2 risky.

bedeut/en (bəˈdɔytən) vt 1 mean. 2 signify. **—end** adj also **—sam** (bəˈdɔytzaːm) sig-

nificant, important. **—ung** nf **-en** 1 meaning. 2 importance. **—ungslos** adj 1 meaningless. 2 insignificant. **—ungsvoll** adj significant.

bedien/en (bəˈdiːnən) vt 1 wait on, serve. 2 operate (a machine). **sich bedien/en** vr make use of. **bedienen Sie sich!** help yourself! **—te(r)** (bəˈdiːntə) nm **-n** servant. **—ung** nf **-en** service, attendance.

beding/t (bəˈdiŋkt) adj 1 conditional. 2 determined (by something). **—ung** nf **-en** condition, term. **—ungslos** adj unconditional.

Bedrängnis (bəˈdrɛŋnis) nf **-se** 1 distress. 2 oppression.

bedrohen (bəˈdroːən) vt threaten.

bedürf/en* (bəˈdyrfən) vi need, require. **—nis** n neu **-se** need, want, requirement.

sich beeilen (bəˈailən) vr hurry, hasten.

beeinflussen (bəˈainflusən) vt influence.

beeinträchtigen (bəˈaintrɛçtigən) vt 1 injure. 2 wrong. 3 interfere with. 4 impair.

beenden (bəˈɛndən) vt 1 conclude, end, finish.

Beerdigung (bəˈeːrdiguŋ) nf **-en** burial.

Beere (ˈbeːrə) nf **-n** berry.

Beet (beːt) n neu **-e** flower bed.

befähig/en (bəˈfɛːigən) vt enable. **—ung** nf **-en** 1 ability. 2 qualification.

befahl (baˈfaːl) v see **befehlen.**

befahr/bar (bəˈfaːrbaːr) adj 1 passable, navigable. 2 practicable. **—en*** vt 1 drive over. 2 navigate.

befallen* (bəˈfalən) vt 1 befall. 2 strike.

befangen (bəˈfaŋən) adj 1 embarrassed. 2 confused. 3 biased.

befassen (bəˈfasən) vt touch. **sich befassen mit** be occupied with.

Befehl (bəˈfeːl) nm **-e** command, order. **—en*** vt command, order. **—shaber** (bəˈfeːlshaːbər) nm **-** commander, commanding officer.

befestig/en (bəˈfɛstigən) vt 1 fasten. 2 fortify, strengthen. **—ung** nf **-en** 1 fortification. 2 strengthening. 3 fastening.

Befind/en (bəˈfindən) n neu **-** 1 health. 2 opinion. **sich befinden*** vr 1 be, be present. 2 feel. **—lich** (bəˈfintliç) adj situated, present, existing.

beflecken (bəˈflɛkən) vt stain, soil, dishonour.

beflissen (bəˈflisən) adj 1 studious. 2 assiduous.

befohlen (bəˈfoːlən) v see **befehlen.**

befolgen (bəˈfɔlgən) vt 1 follow. 2 obey.

beförder/n (bəˈfœrdərn) vt 1 transport, convey. 2 promote. 3 support. **—ung** nf **-en** 1 for-

befragen

warding. **2** transport. **3** advancement, promotion.

befragen (bəˈfraːgən) *vt* question.

befrei/en (bəˈfraiən) *vt* free, liberate. **—ung** *nf* **-en 1** liberation. **2** exemption.

sich befreunden (bəˈfrɔyndən) *vr* **sich mit jemandem befreunden** befriend someone.

befriedig/en (bəˈfriːdigən) *vt* **1** satisfy. **2** pacify. **—end** *adj* satisfactory. **—ung** *nf* **1** satisfaction. **2** pacification.

befruchten (bəˈfruxtən) *vt* **1** fertilize. **2** impregnate. **3** stimulate.

befug/en (bəˈfuːgən) *vt* empower, authorize. **—nis** (bəˈfuːknis) *nf* **-se** authority, right.

befürcht/en (bəˈfyrçtən) *vt* fear. **—ung** *nf* **-en** anxiety, fear.

befürworten (bəˈfyːrvɔrtən) *vt* advocate.

begab/t (bəˈgeːpt) *adj* talented, gifted. **—ung** (bəˈgaːbuŋ) *nf* **-en** talent, ability.

begann (bəˈgan) *v see* **beginnen**.

begeben* (bəˈgeːbən) *vt comm* **1** endorse. **2** negotiate. **sich begeben** *vr* **1** go, proceed. **2** surrender, give up. **—heit** *nf* **-en** occurrence, event.

begegn/en (bəˈgeːgnən) *vi* meet, encounter. **—ung** *nf* **-en** meeting, encounter.

begehen* (bəˈgeːən) *vt* **1** walk (on), go (along). **2** commit (a crime, error, etc.).

begehr/en (bəˈgeːrən) *vt* desire, long for. *n neu* **— desire, longing. **—enswert** *adj* desirable.

begeister/n (bəˈgaistərn) *vt* inspire. **—t** *adj* enthusiastic. **—ung** *nf* enthusiasm.

Begier (bəˈgiːr) *nf* **— also Begierde** (bəˈgiːrdə) *nf* **-n 1** desire, longing. **2** lust. **—ig** *adj* **1** covetous. **2** eager.

Beginn (bəˈgin) *nm* **-e** beginning. **—en*** *vt,vi* begin, start.

beglaubigen (bəˈglaubigən) *vt* certify, authenticate.

begleit/en* (bəˈglaitən) *vt* accompany. **—er** *nm* **1** companion, attendant. **2** accompanist. **—ung** *nf* **-en 1** escort, retinue. **2** accompaniment.

beglück/en (bəˈglykən) *vt* make happy. **—wünschen** *vt* congratulate.

begnadig/en (bəˈgnaːdigən) *vt* pardon, reprieve. **—ung** *nf* **-en** pardon, reprieve, amnesty.

sich begnügen (bəˈgnyːgən) *vr* be satisfied.

begonnen (bəˈgɔnən) *v see* **beginnen**.

begrab/en* (bəˈgraːbən) *vt* bury, inter. **—nis** (bəˈgrɛːpnis) *n neu* **-se 1** burial, funeral. **2** tomb.

begreif/en* (bəˈgraifən) *vt* understand, grasp. **—lich** *adj* understandable.

begrenzt (bəˈgrɛntst) *adj* limited, restricted.

Begriff (bəˈgrif) *nm* **-e 1** idea, concept. **2** understanding. **—en** *adj* engaged or occupied (in).

begründ/en (bəˈgryndən) *vt* **1** found, establish. **2** base. **3** substantiate. **—er** *nm* **—** founder. **—et** (bəˈgryndət) *adj* established. **—ung** *nf* **-en 1** foundation. **2** reason, substantiation.

begrüßen (bəˈgryːsən) *vt* greet, welcome.

begünstig/en (bəˈgynstigən) *vt* **1** favour. **2** further, promote. **—ung** *nf* **-en 1** favour. **2** encouragement.

begütert (bəˈgyːtərt) *adj* wealthy, well-off.

behäbig (bəˈhɛːbiç) *adj* **1** comfortable. **2** stout.

behaftet (bəˈhaftət) *adj* **1** burdened. **2** afflicted.

behag/en (bəˈhaːgən) *vi* please, suit. *n neu* **— 1** pleasure. **2** comfort. **—lich** (bəˈhaːkliç) *adj* comfortable, snug.

behalt/en* (bəˈhaltən) *vt* **1** keep. **2** remember. **3** retain. **—er** (bəˈhɛltər) *nm* **— also —nis** (bəˈhɛltnis) *n neu* **-se 1** container, holder. **2** case. **3** tank.

behand/eln (bəˈhandəln) *vt* treat, handle, manage. **—lung** *nf* treatment, handling, management.

beharr/en (bəˈharən) *vi* **1** insist, remain firm. **2** endure. **—lich** *adj* persistent, stubborn. **—lichkeit** *nf* perseverance, determination.

behaupt/en (bəˈhauptən) *vt* maintain, affirm, assert. **sich behaupten** *vr* be firm, hold one's own. **—ung** *nf* **-en** statement, assertion.

behend/(e) (bəˈhɛnt) *adj* **1** agile. **2** dexterous. **—igkeit** (bəˈhɛndiçkait) *nf* **1** agility. **2** dexterity.

beherbergen (bəˈhɛrbɛrgən) *vt* lodge, put up, house, shelter.

beherrschen (bəˈhɛrʃən) *vt* **1** rule, govern, reign over. **2** master (a language). **3** control.

beherzigen (bəˈhɛrtsigən) *vt* take to heart.

behilflich (bəˈhilfliç) *adj* helpful.

behinder/n (bəˈhindərn) *vt* hinder, obstruct. **—ung** *nf* **-en** hindrance, obstruction.

Behörd/e (bəˈhœːrdə) *nf* **-n 1** authority. **2** administrative or governing body. **3** *comm* board. **—lich** *adj* official.

behüten (bəˈhyːtən) *vt* **1** preserve. **2** guard.

behutsam (bəˈhuːtzaːm) *adj* careful, cautious.

bei (bai) *prep* **1** by. **2** at. **3** near. **4** beside. **5** with. **bei mir 1** at my house or home. **2** with or on me.

beibehalt/en° ('baibəhaltən) vt retain, maintain. **—ung** nf -en retention.

beibringen° ('baibriŋən) vt 1 bring forward, produce. 2 teach, impart.

Beicht/e ('baiçtə) nf confession. **—en** vi,vt confess. **—stuhl** nm confessional.

beide ('baidə) adj,pron both. **—rseitig** ('baidərzaitiç) adj joint, mutual, on both sides. **—rseits** ('baidərzaits) adv on both sides, mutually.

Beifahrer ('baifa:rər) nm 1 passenger. 2 co-driver.

Beifall ('baifal) nm 1 applause. 2 approval.

beifügen ('baify:gən) vt 1 add. 2 enclose.

beigeben° ('baige:bən) vt add. **klein beigeben** give in, knuckle under.

Beigeschmack ('baigəʃmak) nm 1 flavour. (after)taste. 2 tang, savour. 3 tinge, hint.

Beiheft ('baiheft) n neu supplement.

Beihilfe ('baihilfə) nf 1 aid, subsidy. 2 assistance, abetting.

Beil (bail) n neu -e hatchet, axe.

Beilage ('baila:gə) nf 1 supplement, insert, enclosure. 2 garnish.

beiläufig ('bailɔyfiç) adj 1 incidental. 2 casual. adv by the way.

Beileid ('bailait) n neu condolence.

beiliegend ('baili:gənt) adj enclosed.

beim (baim) contraction of **bei dem.**

Bein (bain) n neu -e 1 leg. 2 bone. **—bruch** nm fractured leg.

beinah(e) ('baina:) adv almost, nearly.

Beiname ('baina:mə) nm 1 nickname. 2 surname.

beirren (bə'irən) vt 1 mislead. 2 dissuade.

beisammen (bai'zamən) adv together.

beiseite (bai'zaitə) adv aside, apart.

beisetz/en ('baizetsən) vt 1 add. 2 put on or beside. 3 bury. **—ung** nf -en burial.

Beispiel ('baiʃpi:l) n neu example. **zum/als Beispiel** for example. **—haft** adj exemplary, model. **—los** adj unprecedented. **—sweise** adv for example, for instance.

beiß/en° ('baisən) vt,vi 1 bite. 2 burn. 3 itch.

Beistand ('baiʃtant) nm help, assistance.

beistehen° ('baiʃte:ən) vi aid, assist.

beistimmen ('baiʃtimən) vi agree (with).

Beitrag ('baitra:k) nm -"e 1 contribution. 2 fee. **—en°** ('baitra:gən) vt contribute. vi help.

beitreten° ('baitre:tən) vi 1 join. 2 assent (to).

Beiwagen ('baiva:gən) nm 1 side-car. 2 extra carriage.

beiwohnen ('baivo:nən) vi be present, attend.

beizeiten (bai'tsaitən) adv early, on time.

beizen ('baitsən) vt 1 corrode. 2 cauterize. 3 tan. 4 marinate. 5 stain (wood).

bejahen (bə'ja:ən) vt 1 affirm. 2 accept.

bekämpf/en (bə'kɛmpfən) vt 1 fight, combat. 2 oppose. **—ung** nf -en 1 fight, struggle. 2 opposition.

bekannt (bə'kant) adj (well-)known. **—e(r)** nm acquaintance, friend. **—lich** adv as is well known. **—machen** vt announce, make known. **—machung** nf -en 1 publication. 2 announcement. **—schaft** nf -en acquaintance.

bekehr/en (bə'ke:rən) vt convert (to a religion, etc.). **—ung** nf -en (religious) conversion.

bekenn/en° (bə'kɛnən) vt confess, acknowledge. **Farbe bekennen** 1 be frank. 2 game follow suit. **—tnis** (bə'kɛntnis) n neu -se 1 confession. 2 denomination.

beklag/en (bə'kla:gən) vt 1 mourn. 2 deplore. **sich beklagen** vr complain. **—te(r)** (bə'kla:ktə) nm -n accused, defendant.

bekleid/en (bə'klaidən) vt 1 clothe, dress. 2 cover. 3 occupy (a position, office). **—ung** nf clothing.

beklemmen (bə'klɛmən) vt stifle, oppress.

bekommen° (bə'kɔmən) vt 1 get, obtain. 2 receive. vi agree with (one's health).

bekräftigen (bə'krɛftigən) vt 1 confirm. 2 strengthen.

bekreuz(ig)en (bə'krɔytsigən) vt make the sign of the cross over.

bekümmern (bə'kymərn) vt trouble, distress. **sich bekümmern um** 1 care for. 2 worry about.

bekunden (bə'kundən) vt 1 state. 2 show.

beladen° (bə'la:dən) vt load, burden.

Belag (bə'la:k) nm -e coat(ing), cover(ing).

belager/n (bə'la:gərn) vt besiege. **—ung** nf -en siege.

Belang (bə'laŋ) nm -e 1 importance. 2 interest. **—los** adj unimportant, insignificant.

belast/en (bə'lastən) vt 1 load. 2 weigh down (on), burden. 3 accuse. **—ung** nf -en 1 burden, load. 2 charge.

belästig/en (bə'lɛstigən) vt molest, bother. **—ung** nf en 1 molestation. 2 inconvenience.

sich belaufen° (bə'laufən) vr **sich belaufen auf** total, amount to.

belauschen (bə'laufən) vt eavesdrop on.

beleb/en (bə'le:bən) vt 1 enliven, animate. 2 revive. **—t** adj 1 lively. 2 alive. 3 (of streets) crowded.

Beleg (bə'le:k) n -e 1 proof. 2 record. 3 evidence. 4 document. —en (bə'le:gən) vt 1 cover, lay (on). 2 reserve. —schaft nf -en 1 personnel, staff. 2 shift.

belehr/en (bə'le:rən) vt teach, instruct. —ung nf -en instruction.

beleidig/en (bə'laidigən) vt 1 insult. 2 offend. —ung nf -en 1 insult. 2 offence.

beleucht/en (bə'lɔyçtən) vt 1 light (up), illuminate. 2 elucidate. —ung nf -en 1 lighting. 2 elucidation.

Belg/ien ('bɛlgiən) n neu Belgium. —ier nm — Belgian. —isch adj Belgian.

Belgrad ('bɛlgra:t) n neu Belgrade.

belicht/en (bə'liçtən) vt phot expose. —ung nf -en exposure. —ungsmesser nm exposure or light meter.

belieb/en (bə'li:bən) vt like. vi please. n neu -1 liking. 2 pleasure. 3 wish. **nach Belieben** according to one's liking or taste. —ig adj any, whatever. —t (bə'li:pt) adj 1 beloved. 2 favourite. —theit (bə'li:pthait) nf -en popularity.

bellen ('bɛlən) vi bark, bay.

belohn/en (bə'lo:nən) vt reward, remunerate. —ung nf -en reward, remuneration.

sich bemächtigen (bə'mɛçtigən) vr seize, take possession of.

bemerk/bar (bə'mɛrkba:r) adj noticeable, perceptible. —en vt perceive, notice, observe. —enswert adj remarkable, notable. —ung nf -en remark.

bemessen* (bə'mɛsən) vt 1 measure, judge. 2 adjust. 3 regulate.

bemitleiden (bə'mitlaidən) vt pity, sympathize with.

sich bemüh/en (bə'my:ən) vr 1 strive, endeavour. 2 take pains. —ung nf -en effort, trouble, pains.

benachbart (bə'naxba:rt) adj neighbouring.

benachrichtig/en (bə'naxriçtigən) vt 1 inform. 2 report. —ung nf -en 1 notification. 2 information.

Benehmen (bə'ne:mən) n neu — behaviour. **sich benehmen** vr act, behave.

beneiden (bə'naidən) vt envy. —swert adj enviable.

Benennung (bə'nɛnuŋ) nf -en name, term.

Bengel ('bɛŋəl) nm — 1 club, cudgel. 2 brat, urchin. 3 rascal. 4 lout.

benutz/en (bə'nutsən) vt use, make use of. —ung nf utilization.

Benzin (bɛn'tsi:n) n neu -e mot petrol. —motor nm petrol engine.

beobacht/en (bə'o:baxtən) vt 1 observe, watch. 2 keep (silence, etc.). —er nm — observer. —ung nf -en observation.

bepflanzen (bə'pflantsən) vt plant.

bequem (bə'kve:m) adj 1 comfortable. 2 convenient. —lichkeit nf -en 1 comfort. 2 convenience.

berat/en* (bə'ra:tən) vt advise, counsel. —er nm — adviser. —ung nf -en 1 consultation. 2 deliberation. —ungsstelle nf advisory board or office.

berauben (bə'raubən) vt 1 rob. 2 deprive.

berauschen (bə'rauʃən) vt intoxicate. **sich berauschen** vr become enchanted (with).

berechn/en (bə'rɛçnən) vt calculate, reckon. —ung nf calculation, estimate.

berechtig/en (bə'rɛçtigən) vt empower, authorize. —ung nf -en authorization, right, title.

bered/en (bə're:dən) vt 1 talk over. 2 persuade. —sam (bə're:tza:m) adj also —t (bə're:t) eloquent. —samkeit nf eloquence.

Bereich (bə'raiç) nm -e 1 region, area, district. 2 range, scope.

bereichern (bə'raiçərn) vt enrich.

bereit (bə'rait) adj ready, prepared. —en vt prepare, make (ready). —halten* vt keep or hold in readiness. —s adv already. —schaft nf -en 1 readiness. 2 (police) squad. —stehen* vi be prepared, stand by. —ung nf -en preparation. —willig adj willing, ready.

bereuen (bə'rɔyən) vt regret, repent of.

Berg (bɛrk) nm -e mountain, hill. **über Berg und Tal** over hill and dale. —ab (bɛrk'ap) adv downhill. —auf (bɛrk'auf) adv also —an uphill, upwards. —arbeiter nm miner. —bau nm mining. —kette nf mountain range. —mann nm -leute miner. —rutsch nm also —sturz landslide. —steiger nm mountaineer, climber. —werk n neu mine.

bergen* ('bɛrgən) vt 1 save. 2 protect. 3 rescue. 4 conceal.

Bericht (bə'riçt) nm -e report, account. —en vt,vi report. —erstatter nm — reporter, informant.

berichtig/en (bə'riçtigən) vt correct, rectify. —ung nf -en correction, adjustment.

beritten (bə'ritən) adj mounted.

Bernstein ('bɛrnʃtain) nm amber.

berüchtigt (bə'ryçtiçt) adj notorious.

berücksichtig/en (bə'rykziçtigən) vt 1 consider. 2 take into account. —**ung** nf -**en** regard, consideration.

Beruf (bə'ru:f) nm -**e** 1 occupation, profession, trade. 2 vocation. —**en*** vt 1 call. 2 summon. 3 appoint. adj competent. **sich** —**en** vr 1 appeal. 2 refer to. —**lich** adj professional. —**sberatung** nf career guidance. —**smäßig** adj professional. —**sschule** nf 1 vocational school. 2 training college. —**ung** nf -**en** 1 call(ing). 2 nomination. 3 appointment. 4 (law) appeal.

beruhen (bə'ru:ən) vi rest on, be based on.

beruhig/en (bə'ru:igən) vt quieten, calm, pacify. —**ung** nf calming (down).

berühmt (bə'ry:mt) adj famous. —**heit** nf -**en** 1 fame. 2 famous person, celebrity.

berühr/en (bə'ry:rən) vt 1 touch, affect. 2 mention. —**ung** nf -**en** contact, touch(ing).

besäen (bə'zɛ:ən) vt sow. **besät** (bə'zɛ:t) adj strewn, covered.

besänftig/en (bə'zɛnftigən) vt calm, soothe.

Besatz/ung (bə'zatsuŋ) nf -**en** 1 mil occupation. 2 garrison. 3 crew. —**ungsbehörde** nf military adminstration (in occupied territory).

beschädig/en (bə'ʃɛ:digən) vt damage, injure. —**ung** nf -**en** damage, injury.

beschaffen (bə'ʃafən) vt 1 obtain, procure. 2 provide. adj constituted. **gut beschaffen sein** be in good condition. —**heit** nf -**en** condition, character, nature.

beschäftig/en (bə'ʃɛftigən) vt employ. **sich beschäftig/en** vr busy oneself (with). -**ung** nf -**en** occupation, employment.

beschämen (bə'ʃɛ:mən) vt shame.

beschatten (bə'ʃatən) vt 1 shade, overshadow. 2 shadow, tail.

Beschau/er (bə'ʃauər) nm — 1 observer. 2 inspector (of food, goods, etc.). —**lich** adj contemplative.

Bescheid (bə'ʃait) nm -**e** 1 answer. 2 information. 3 (law) decision. **Bescheid wissen** be well-informed, know. —**en** (bə'ʃaidən) adj modest, moderate, unassuming. —**enheit** nf modesty, moderation, discretion.

bescheinig/en (bə'ʃainigən) vt certify, attest. —**ung** nf -**en** certificate, acknowledgment.

beschenken (bə'ʃɛnkən) vt give a present to.

Bescherung (bə'ʃe:ruŋ) nf -**en** presentation.

beschieß/en* (bə'ʃi:sən) vt shoot at, bombard.

beschimpf/en (bə'ʃimpfən) vt insult. —**ung** nf -**en** abuse, insult.

Beschlag (bə'ʃla:k) nm -**e** 1 metal-work,

fittings. 2 moisture. **in Beschlag nehmen** seize. —**nahme** nf -**n** confiscation.

beschleunig/en (bə'ʃɔynigən) vt accelerate, hasten. —**er** nm — accelerator. —**ung** nf acceleration.

beschließen* (bə'ʃli:sən) vt 1 enclose. 2 decide, resolve, conclude.

Beschluß (bə'ʃlus) nm -**schlüsse** 1 resolution, decision. 2 conclusion. —**fassung** nf decision, resolution.

beschmutzen (bə'ʃmutsən) vt soil, blemish.

beschneid/en* (bə'ʃnaidən) vt 1 cut, clip, trim. 2 circumcise.

beschränk/en (bə'ʃrɛnkən) vt limit, restrict. —**t** adj 1 limited. 2 narrow(-minded). —**ung** nf -**en** restriction, limitation.

beschreib/en* (bə'ʃraibən) vt 1 describe. 2 write, draw on. —**ung** nf -**en** description.

beschuldig/en (bə'ʃuldigən) vt accuse, charge. —**ung** nf -**en** accusation.

beschützen (bə'ʃytsən) vt protect.

Beschwer/de (bə'ʃve:rdə) nf -**n** 1 complaint. 2 trouble, difficulty. —**en** vt burden, weigh down. **sich** —**en** vr complain. —**lich** adj 1 troublesome. 2 tiresome.

beschwichtigen (bə'ʃviçtigən) vt calm, pacify.

beschwipst (bə'ʃvipst) adj inf tipsy, merry.

beschwören (bə'ʃvœ:rən) vt 1 swear, take an oath (on). 2 implore, beg of. 3 summon, invoke or exorcize (spirits).

beseelen (bə'ze:lən) vt 1 inspire. 2 enliven.

besehen* (bə'ze:ən) vt look at, inspect.

beseitig/en (bə'zaitigən) vt 1 remove, do away with. 2 overcome. —**ung** nf -**en** removal.

Besen ('be:zən) nm — broom.

besessen (bə'zɛsən) adj 1 possessed (of the devil, etc.). 2 obsessed.

besetz/en (bə'zɛtsən) vt 1 occupy. 2 man. 3 fill. 4 trim, decorate. —**t** adj 1 occupied. 2 full, crowded. 3 (telephone) engaged. —**ung** nf -**en** 1 mil occupation. 2 Th cast(ing).

besichtig/en (bə'ziçtigən) vt 1 inspect, look at. 2 go sight-seeing (in). —**ung** nf -**en** 1 inspection. 2 sight-seeing.

besieg/en (bə'zi:gən) vt conquer, defeat. —**er** nm conqueror.

sich besinn/en* (bə'zinən) vr 1 consider, reflect. 2 remember, recall. —**ung** nf 1 consciousness. 2 contemplation.

Besitz (bə'zits) nm -**e** possession, property. —**en*** vt possess. —**er** nm — owner, proprietor. —**tum** n neu -**er** property, possession. —**ung** nf -**en** 1 possession. 2 estate.

besoffen (bə'zɔfən) adj inf drunk.

Besoldung (bə'zɔlduŋ) nf -en pay, salary.

besonder/e (bə'zɔndərə) adj special, particular, peculiar. —**s** adv 1 especially. 2 separately.

besonnen (bə'zɔnən) adj 1 prudent, cautious. 2 thoughtful. —**heit** nf 1 prudence. 2 thoughtfulness.

besorg/en (bə'zɔrgən) vt 1 take care of, attend to. 2 provide, procure. 3 fear. —**nis** (bə'zɔrknis) nf -**se** fear, worry, anxiety. —**t** (bə'zɔrkt) adj anxious, apprehensive. —**ung** nf -en 1 care. 2 matter (to attend to).

bespannen (bə'ʃpanən) vt 1 harness. 2 stretch over (covering). 3 (re)string (a guitar, etc.).

besprech/en (bə'ʃprɛçən) vt 1 discuss, debate, talk over. 2 review (a book, etc.). —**ung** nf -en 1 discussion. 2 conference. 3 review.

bespritzen (bə'ʃpritsən) vt splash, sprinkle.

besser ('bɛsər) adj better. **desto besser** so much the better. **um so besser** all the better. —**n** vt improve, better. —**ung** nf -en 1 improvement. 2 recovery. —**wisser** ('bɛsərvisər) nm — know-all.

Bestand (bə'ʃtant) nm ²e-1 continuance, duration. 2 comm stock, supply. 3 comm reserves, (cash-)balance. —**ig** (bə'ʃtɛndiç) adj continuous, constant. —**teil** nm constituent, part.

bestärken (bə'ʃtɛrkən) vt 1 strengthen. 2 confirm.

bestätig/en (bə'ʃtɛ:tigən) vt 1 confirm, verify. 2 acknowledge. —**ung** nf -en confirmation, verification.

bestatten (bə'ʃtatən) vt 1 bury. 2 cremate.

beste ('bɛstə) adj best. **aufs beste** in the best way possible. —**n** neu -**n** best.

bestech/en (bə'ʃtɛçən) vt 1 bribe. 2 corrupt. —**lich** adj corrupt(ible). —**ung** nf -en 1 bribery. 2 corruption.

Besteck (bə'ʃtɛk) n neu -**e** 1 set of cutlery, place-setting. 2 set of instruments.

bestehen* (bə'ʃte:ən) vi 1 be, exist. 2 last, endure. vt pass (a test, etc.). **bestehen auf** insist on. **bestehen aus/in** consist of/in.

besteigen* (bə'ʃtaigən) vt 1 ascend. 2 mount (a horse). 3 board (a ship).

bestell/en (bə'ʃtɛlən) vt 1 order. 2 appoint. 3 till (fields). 4 deliver (a message). —**ung** nf 1 order. 2 message. 3 cultivation. 4 arrangement.

bestenfalls ('bɛstənfals) adv at best. **bestens** ('bɛstəns) adv 1 at best. 2 in the best way.

besteuer/n (bə'ʃtɔyərn) vt tax. —**ung** nf -en taxation.

Bestie ('bɛstiə) nf -n beast, brute.

bestimm/en (bə'ʃtimən) vt 1 determine, fix. 2 assign, intend. —**t** adj 1 certain, definite. 2 assigned. 3 intended. —**theit** nf -en certainty. —**ung** nf -en 1 determination. 2 destination. 3 regulation. 4 destiny.

bestrafen (bə'ʃtra:fən) vt punish.

Bestrahlung (bə'ʃtra:luŋ) nf 1 irradiation. 2 radiotherapy.

sich bestreben (bə'ʃtre:bən) vr strive. **Bestrebung** nf -en attempt, endeavour.

bestreiten* (bə'ʃtraitən) vt 1 contest. 2 deny. 3 meet, defray (expenses).

bestürmen (bə'ʃtyrmən) vt 1 attack, storm. 2 implore.

bestürz/t (bə'ʃtyrtst) adj 1 upset. 2 dismayed. —**ung** nf dismay.

Besuch (bə'zu:x) nm -**e** 1 visit. 2 visitors, company. —**en** vt 1 visit. 2 attend (a school). —**er** nm — visitor, guest.

betagt (bə'ta:kt) adj aged, elderly.

betätigen (bə'tɛ:tigən) vt operate, set in action. **sich betätigen** vr busy oneself, participate (in).

betäub/en (bə'tɔybən) vt 1 stun. 2 deafen. 3 deaden. 4 anaesthetize. —**ungsmittel** n neu 1 anaesthetic. 2 narcotic.

beteilig/en (bə'tailigən) vt give a share to. **sich beteiligen** vr take part (in). —**ung** nf 1 participation. 2 share.

Bete ('be:tə) nf -n beetroot.

bet/en ('be:tən) vi,vt pray.

beteuern (bə'tɔyərn) vt 1 protest. 2 declare, aver.

Beton (be'tõ:) nm -e concrete.

betonen (bə'tonən) vt emphasize, stress.

Betracht (bə'traxt) nm **in Betracht kommen** come into question. **außer Betracht stehen** be out of the question. —**en** vt look at, view, regard. —**lich** (bə'trɛçtliç) adj considerable. —**ung** nf -en 1 view, consideration. 2 reflection. 3 meditation.

Betrag (bə'tra:k) nm ²e sum, amount. —**en*** (bə'tra:gən) vt amount to. n neu behaviour. **sich** vr behave.

betrauen (bə'trauən) vt entrust (someone).

Betreff (bə'trɛf) nm **in Betreff** also **betreffs** with regard to, concerning. —**en*** (bə'trɛfən) vt 1 affect, concern. 2 catch (in the act). —**end** adj concerned, in question. prep concerning.

betreiben* (bə'traibən) vt operate, carry on (a business, etc.).

betreten* (bə'tre:tən) vt 1 step on. 2 enter, set foot in. adj 1 embarrassed. 2 disconcerted.

Betrieb (bə'tri:p) nm -e 1 works, factory. 2 business. 3 working, operation, running. 4 bustle. **außer Betrieb** out of order. **in Betrieb** in operation, working. —**sfähig** adj in working order. —**skapital** n neu working capital. —**skosten** nf pl working costs or expenses. —**sleiter** nm (works) manager. —**sordnung** nf company rules. —**sstoff** nm mot fuel. —**sunfall** nm industrial accident, accident at work.

betroffen (bə'trɔfən) adj 1 affected. 2 perplexed.

betrüb/en (bə'try:bən) vt grieve, sadden. —**nis** nf -se sorrow, grief.

Betrug (bə'tru:k) nm deceit, fraud. **-̈en** (bə'try:gən) vt defraud, deceive, cheat. **-̈er** (bə'try:gər) nm — swindler, cheat, deceiver.

betrunken (bə'truŋkən) adj drunk. —**heit** nf drunkenness.

Bett (bɛt) n neu -en bed. —**decke** nf 1 bedspread. 2 blanket. —**en** vt put to bed. —**tuch** n neu sheet. —**wäsche** nf also —**zeug** n neu bedding.

betteln ('bɛtəln) vi beg. **Bettler** ('bɛtlər) nm — beggar.

beugen ('bɔygən) vt 1 bend. 2 gram inflect. **sich beugen** vr 1 bend down or over. 2 bow. 3 humble oneself.

Beule ('bɔylə) nf -n 1 swelling, boil. 2 dent.

beunruhigen (bə'unru:igən) vt disturb, upset.

beurkunden (bə'u:rkundən) vt prove, authenticate (by means of documents).

beurlauben (bə'u:rlaubən) vt give leave (of absence) to.

beurteil/en (bə'u:rtailən) vt judge, pass judgment on. —**ung** nf -en judgment.

Beute ('bɔytə) nf booty, spoil(s).

Beutel ('bɔytəl) nm — 1 bag. 2 purse.

bevölker/n (bə'fœlkərn) vt populate. —**ung** nf -en population. —**ungsdichte** nf population density.

bevollmächtig/en (bə'fɔlmɛçtigən) vt empower, authorize. —**te(r)** (bə'fɔlmɛçtiçtə) nm 1 (authorized) representative. 2 proxy. 3 deputy.

bevor (bə'fo:r) conj before. **bevor...nicht** until.

bevorstehen* (bə'fo:rʃte:ən) vi be near, be imminent.

bevorzugen (bə'fo:rtsu:gən) vt prefer.

bewachen (bə'vaxən) vt guard.

bewaffnen (bə'vafnən) vt arm.

bewahr/en (bə've:rən) vt preserve, keep. **sich —en** vr prove oneself (efficient, successful, etc.). —**ung** nf -en test, trial. —**ungsfrist** nf probation.

bewältigen (bə'vɛltigən) vt 1 overcome. 2 finish.

bewandert (bə'vandərt) adj knowledgeable, expert.

Bewandtnis (bə'vantnis) nf -se condition, circumstance.

bewässer/n (bə'vɛsərn) vt water, irrigate. —**ung** nf watering, irrigation.

beweg/en* (bə've:gən) vt 1 move. 2 induce, persuade. **sich —en** vr move. —**grund** nm motive. —**lich** (bə've:kliç) adj 1 movable, mobile, moving. 2 versatile. —**lichkeit** nf mobility. —**ung** nf en motion, movement.

Beweis (bə'vais) nm -e proof. —**aufnahme** nf hearing of evidence. —**en*** (bə'vaizən) vt prove, demonstrate, show. —**grund** nm argument. —**kraft** nf conclusiveness. —**mittel** n neu evidence. —**stück** n neu 1 exhibit. 2 evidence.

bewenden (bə'vɛndən) vi **es dabei bewenden lassen** let the matter rest (at that).

sich bewerb/en* (bə'vɛrbən) vr **sich bewerben um** 1 apply for. 2 seek. —**er** nm — 1 applicant. 2 competitor. 3 suitor.

bewerkstelligen (bə'vɛrkʃtɛligən) vt manage, accomplish.

bewillig/en (bə'viligən) vt 1 allow, grant. 2 approve. —**ung** nf -en 1 consent, approval. 2 grant, allowance.

bewirken (bə'virkən) vt cause, effect.

bewirten (bə'virtən) vt 1 entertain. 2 receive.

bewohn/en (bə'vo:nən) vt inhabit. —**er** nm — inhabitant.

bewölkt (bə'vœlkt) adj cloudy, overcast.

Bewunder/er (bə'vundərər) nm — admirer. —**n** vt admire. —**nswert** adj admirable. —**ung** nf admiration.

bewußt (bə'vust) adj 1 conscious, aware. 2 deliberate. adv knowingly. **die bewußten Personen** the people in question. —**heit** nf awareness, consciousness. —**los** adj unconscious. —**sein** n neu consciousness.

bezahl/en (bə'tsa:lən) vt pay (for). —**ung** nf -en payment.

bezaubern (bə'tsaubərn) vt bewitch, enchant, charm.

bezeichn/en (bə'tsaiçnən) vt 1 mark. 2 designate, indicate. —**end** adj characteristic.

—ung nf **-en 1** mark, sign. **2** marking. **3** designation.

bezeugen (bə'tsɔygən) vt bear witness to, certify.

bezieh/en* (bə'tsi:ən) vt **1** cover. **2** move into. **3** receive. **4** obtain. **sich beziehen auf** vr relate to, refer to. **—ung** nf **-en 1** reference. **2** relation(ship), connection. **—ungsweise** adv **1** or. **2** that is to say.

Bezirk (bə'tsirk) nm **-e** district, area.

Bezug (bə'tsu:k) nm **1** cover(ing). **2** comm supply, purchase. **3** pl income. **bezüglich** (auf) also **in Bezug auf** with regard to, concerning.

bezwecken (bə'tsvɛkən) vt aim at.

bezweifeln (bə'tsvaifəln) vt doubt, question.

bezwingen* (bə'tsviŋən) vt **1** overcome. **2** master.

Bibel ('bi:bəl) nf **-n** Bible.

Biber ('bi:bər) nm **—** beaver.

Bibliographie (bibliogra'fi:) nf **-n** bibliography.

Bibliothek (biblio'te:k) nf **-en** library. **—ar** (bibliote'ka:r) nm **-e** librarian.

biblisch ('bi:bliʃ) adj biblical.

bieder ('bi:dər) adj **1** upright, honest. **2** simpleminded. **—mann** nm honest fellow.

biegen* ('bi:gən) vt bend.

Biene ('bi:nə) nf **-n** bee. **—nkorb** nm beehive.

Bier (bi:r) n neu **-e** beer. **—garten** nm beer garden, (open air) cafe. **—krug** nm beermug.

bieten* ('bi:tən) vt offer.

Bigamie (biga'mi:) nf **-n** bigamy.

bigott (bi'gɔt) adj bigoted.

Bikini (bi'ki:ni:) nm **-s** bikini.

Bilanz (bi'lants) nf **-en** balance (sheet).

Bild (bilt) n neu **-er** picture, image. **—erbuch** ('bildərbu:x) n neu picture book. **—fläche** nf **1** field of vision. **2** television or cinema screen. **—hauer** nm **—** sculptor. **—nis** n neu **-se** likeness, portrait. **—säule** nf statue. **—schön** adj lovely, (most) beautiful.

bild/en ('bildən) vt **1** form. **2** educate. **—ung** nf **-en 1** education. **2** culture. **3** formation, creation.

Billard ('biljart) n neu **-s** billiards.

Billett (bil'jɛt) n neu **-e 1** note. **2** ticket.

billig ('biliç) adj **1** cheap. **2** reasonable, just. **—en** ('biligən) vt approve (of), sanction. **—keit** nf **-en 1** cheapness. **2** fairness. **—ung** ('biliguŋ) nf approval.

Bimsstein ('bimsʃtain) nm pumice-stone.

bin (bin) v see **sein²**.

Bind/e ('bində) nf **-n 1** band **2** bandage, sling. **3** sanitary towel. **—eglied** n neu connecting link. **—estrich** nm hyphen. **—ewort** n neu conjunction. **—faden** ('bintfa:dən) nm string, twine. **—ung** nf **-en 1** bond. **2** binding.

binden* ('bindən) vt bind, tie.

binnen ('binən) prep within. **—handel** nm domestic trade. **—land** n neu interior, inland.

Biographie (biogra'fi:) nf **-n** biography.

Biolog/e (bio'lo:gə) nm **-n** biologist. **—ie** (biolo'gi:) nf biology. **—isch** (bio'lo:giʃ) adj biological.

Birne ('birnə) nf **-n 1** pear. **2** (light) bulb.

bis (bis) prep **1** to. **2** up to. **3** until. conj **1** until. **2** by. **er wird bis morgen ankommen** he will arrive by tomorrow.

Bisam ('bi:zam) nm **-e** musk.

Bischof ('biʃɔf) nm **-e** bishop.

bisexuell (bizɛksu'ɛl) adj hermaphroditic, bisexual.

bisher (bis'he:r) adv until now, so far. **—ig** adj previous, until now.

biß (bis) v see **beißen**.

Biß (bis) nm **Bisse** bite. **—chen** ('bisçən) n neu,adj a little, a bit. **Bissen** ('bisən) nm **—** morsel, bite. **bissig** ('bisiç) adj **1** (of dogs) snappish. **2** cutting, biting.

bist (bist) v see **sein²**.

Bistum ('bistu:m) n neu **-er** bishopric.

bisweilen (bis'vailən) adv sometimes.

bitt/e ('bitə) interj please! nf **-n** request. **—en*** ('bitən) vt ask, beg, request. **—schreiben** n neu also **—schrift** nf petition.

bitter ('bitər) adj **1** bitter. **2** severe. **—keit** nf bitterness.

Biwak ('bi:vak) n neu **-s** bivouac.

Bizeps ('bi:tsɛps) nm **-e** biceps.

Blam/age (bla'ma:ʒə) nf **-n** disgrace, scandal. **—ieren** (bla'mi:rən) vt disgrace, compromise (someone). **sich —ieren** vr make a fool of oneself.

blank (blaŋk) adj **1** shiny, bright. **2** bare, naked.

blanko ('blaŋko) adj blank. **—scheck** nm blank cheque. **—vollmacht** nf full power of attorney.

Blas/e ('bla:zə) nf **-n 1** blister. **2** bubble. **3** bladder. **—en*** vi,vt blow. **—instrument** n neu wind instrument. **—kapelle** nf brass band.

blaß (blas) adj pale. **Blässe** ('blɛsə) nf pallor, paleness.

Blatt (blat) n neu **-er 1** leaf, blade. **2** page, sheet (of paper). **3** newspaper. **—ern**

('blɛtərn) vi 1 turn over the pages. 2 skim through a book. —**erteig** ('blɛtərtaik) nm puff-pastry.

blau (blau) adj 1 blue. 2 inf tipsy. n neu blue. —**beere** nf bilberry. —**e** ('blɔyə) nf blueness, azure. —**papier** n neu carbon paper.

Blech (blɛç) n neu —**e** 1 sheet metal. 2 tin.

Blei (blai) n neu —**e** lead.

bleiben° ('blaibən) vi remain, stay.

bleich (blaiç) adj pale, pallid. —**e** nf —**n** paleness, pallor. —**en**° vt bleach. vi turn white or pale. —**sucht** nf anaemia.

Bleistift ('blaiʃtift) nm —**e** pencil. —**spitzer** nm —**—** pencil-sharpener.

Blend/e ('blɛndə) nf —**n** 1 blind, shutter. 2 phot diaphragm. —**en** vt 1 blind, dazzle. 2 deceive.

Blick (blik) nm —**e** 1 look, glance. 2 gaze. —**en** vi look, glance.

blieb (bli:p) v see **bleiben**.

blind (blint) adj 1 blind. 2 false. 3 hidden. 4 tarnished. **blinder Passagier** nm stowaway. —**darm** nm anat appendix. —**darmentzündung** nf appendicitis. —**heit** nf blindness.

blinzeln ('blintsəln) vi 1 twinkle. 2 blink. 3 wink.

Blitz (blits) nm —**e** lightning. —**ableiter** nm —**—** lightning-conductor. —**en** vi flash, lighten. —**krieg** nm lightning war, blitzkrieg. —**licht** n neu (photographic) flash. —**schnell** adj as quick as lightning.

Block/ade (blɔ'ka:də) nf —**n** blockade. —**flöte** ('blɔkflø:tə) nf mus recorder. —**ieren** (blɔ'ki:rən) vt 1 obstruct, bar. 2 blockade. 3 jam.

blöd ('blø:t) adj 1 silly, stupid. 2 imbecile. 3 shy, timid. —**heit** ('blø:thait) nf —**en** stupidity. —**sinn** ('blø:tsin) nm 1 nonsense. 2 idiocy. —**sinnig** ('blø:tsiniç) adj idiotic, silly.

blond (blɔnt) adj blond, light-coloured, fair.

bloß (blo:s) adj 1 bare. 2 mere. adv only, simply. —**stellen** vt expose.

blühen ('bly:ən) vi 1 bloom, blossom. 2 flourish.

Blume ('blu:mə) nf —**n** 1 flower. 2 aroma. 3 (of wine) bouquet. —**nkohl** nm cauliflower. —**nstrauß** nm bouquet. —**nzwiebel** n bulb.

Bluse ('blu:zə) nf —**n** blouse.

Blut (blu:t) n neu blood. —**arm** adj 1 anaemic. 2 extremely poor. —**egel** nm —**—** leech. —**en** vi bleed. —**ig** adj 1 bloody. 2 complete, total. —**rünstig** adj bloody, blood-thirsty. —**schande** nf incest. —**spender** nm med blood-donor. —**sturz** nm bleeding, haemorrhage. —**übertragung** nf blood transfusion. —**wurst** nf black pudding.

Blüte ('bly:tə) nf —**n** 1 blossom, flower. 2 prime. —**zeit** nf 1 blossom-time. 2 prosperity, heyday.

Bö (bœ:) nf —**en** squall, gust.

Bock (bɔk) nm —**e** 1 ram, he-goat. 2 buck. 3 sport buck (for vaulting). 4 trestle. 5 strut. —**bier** n neu strong dark beer. —**wurst** nf (thick) frankfurter sausage.

Boden ('bo:dən) nm —**1** ground, soil. 2 bottom, bed. —**reform** nf land reform. —**schätze** nm pl mineral resources. —**tür** nf trap-door.

Bodensee ('bo:dənze:) nm Lake Constance.

Bogen ('bo:gən) nm —**1** curve, arch. 2 mus, sport bow. 3 sheet (of paper). —**gang** nm arcade, colonnade. —**linie** nf curve. —**schütze** nm archer.

Böhm/e ('bœ:mə) nm —**n** Bohemian. —**en** n neu Bohemia. —**isch** adj Bohemian.

Bohne ('bo:nə) nf —**n** bean.

Bohnenkaffee ('bo:nənkafe:) nm pure coffee.

bohr/en ('bo:rən) vt,vi bore, drill. —**er** nm —**—** borer, drill, gimlet.

Boje ('bo:jə) nf —**n** buoy.

Bollwerk ('bɔlvɛrk) n neu bulwark.

Bolzen ('bɔltsən) nm 1 bolt, peg. 2 bolt, arrow.

Bombe ('bɔmbə) nf —**n** bomb. —**nerfolg** nm huge success. —**r** nm —**—** bomber.

Bonbon (bõ'bõ) nm,neu —**s** sweet.

Bonze ('bɔntsə) nm —**n** sl boss, bigwig.

Boot (bo:t) n neu —**e** boat.

Bord (bɔrt) nm —**e** border, rim. **an Bord** on board.

Bordell (bɔr'dɛl) n neu —**e** brothel.

borgen ('bɔrgən) vt borrow.

Borke ('bɔrkə) nf —**n** bark, rind.

Börse ('bœ:rzə) nf —**n** 1 purse. 2 stock exchange. —**nkurs** nm market rate.

Borste ('bɔrstə) nf —**n** bristle.

bös/artig ('bœ:zartiç) adj 1 evil, malicious. 2 (illness) malignant. —**e** ('bœ:zə) adj 1 evil, bad. 2 angry. 3 (of disease) malignant. —**ewicht** ('bœ:zəviçt) nm —**e** villain, evil person.

bos/haft ('bo:shaft) adj spiteful, malicious. —**heit** ('bo:shait) nf —**en** 1 spite, malice. 2 wickedness.

Boß (bɔs) nm —**e** inf boss, manager.

bot (bo:t) v see **bieten**.

Botan/ik (boˈtaːnik) *nf* botany. **—iker** *nm* — botanist. **—isch** *adj* botanic(al).

Bot/e (ˈboːtə) *nm* -n messenger. **—schaft** *nf* -en 1 embassy. 2 message. **—schafter** *nm* — ambassador.

Bottich (ˈbɔtiç) *nm* -e vat, tub.

Bowle (ˈboːlə) *nf* -n 1 bowl. 2 fruit cup, punch.

box/en (ˈbɔksən) *vi* box. **—er** *nm* — boxer.

brach[1] (braix) *v see* **brechen.**

brach[2] (braix) *adj* fallow, uncultivated.

brechte (ˈbraxtə) *v see* **bringen.**

Branche (ˈbrãːʃə) *nf* -n 1 trade, line (of business). 2 department, branch.

Brand (brant) *nm* ⁼e 1 fire, burning. 2 gangrene. 3 mildew. **in Brand setzen** *or* **stecken** set on fire. **—bombe** *nf* incendiary bomb. **—sohle** *nf* inner sole, welt. **—stifter** *nm* incendiary, fire-raiser. **—stiftung** *nf* arson.

Brandung (ˈbranduŋ) *nf* -en surf, breakers.

Branntwein (ˈbrɛntvain) *nm* -e brandy.

Brasil/ianer (braziliˈaːnər) *nm* — Brazilian. **—ianisch** *adj* Brazilian. **—ien** (braˈziːliən) *n neu* Brazil.

brat/en[*] (ˈbraːtən) *vt,vi* 1 roast. 2 fry. 3 grill, broil. *n neu* — roast, joint. **—kartoffel** *nf* fried *or* roast potato. **—pfanne** *nf* frying pan. **—wurst** *nf* fried sausage.

Brauch (braux) *nm* ⁼e 1 custom. 2 usage. **—bar** *adj* 1 useful. 2 serviceable. **—en** *vt* 1 need, want. 2 use.

Braue (ˈbrauə) *nf* -n brow.

brau/en (ˈbrauən) *vt* brew. **—er** *nm* — brewer. **—erei** (brauəˈrai) *nf* -en brewery.

braun (braun) *adj* brown. **—en** (ˈbrɔynən) *vi,vt* brown, tan.

Braunschweig (ˈbraunʃvaik) *n neu* Brunswick.

Brause (ˈbrauzə) *nf* -n 1 shower. 2 nozzle, spray. 3 mineral water. 4 lemonade. **—n** *vi* 1 effervesce. 2 spray, shower. 3 roar, rage.

Braut (braut) *nf* ⁼e 1 bride. 2 fiancée. **—igam** (ˈbrɔytigam) *nm* -e 1 bridegroom. 2 fiancé. **—jungfer** *nf* bridesmaid. **—kleid** *n neu* wedding dress. **—paar** *n neu* 1 bridal pair. 2 engaged couple.

brav (braːf) *adj* 1 good. 2 honest. 3 brave.

brech/en[*] (ˈbrɛçən) *vt* 1 break, crush. 2 refract. **—bohne** *nf* French bean.

Brei (brai) *nm* -e 1 pap, pulp 2 porridge.

breit (brait) *adj* broad, wide. **—e** *nf* -n 1 breadth, width. 2 latitude. 3 verbosity. **—en** *vt* spread (out), broaden. **—engrad** *nm* degree of latitude.

Brems/e[1] (ˈbrɛmzə) *nf* -n brake. **—en** *vt,vi*

brake, apply the brakes. **—schuh** *nm* brake shoe.

Bremse[2] (ˈbrɛmzə) *nf* -n gadfly, horse-fly.

brenn/bar (ˈbrɛnbaːr) *adj* inflammable. **—en**[*] *vi* burn, sting. *vt* 1 burn. 2 roast. 3 distil. **—er** *nm* — 1 (gas) burner. 2 distiller. 3 fire-raiser. **—erei** (brɛnəˈrai) *nf* -en distillery, still. **—essel** (ˈbrɛnnɛsəl) *nf* -n stinging-nettle. **—holz** *n neu* firewood. **—material** *n neu* fuel. **—punkt** *nm* focus, focal point. **—stoff** *nm* fuel.

Brett (brɛt) *n neu* -er 1 board, plank. 2 shelf.

Brezel (ˈbreːtsəl) *nf* -n pretzel.

bricht (briçt) *v see* **brechen.**

Brief (briːf) *nm* -e letter. **—fach** *n neu* 1 pigeon-hole. 2 post-office box. **—kasten** *nm* letter box. **-lich** *adj* by letter. **—marke** *nf* (postage) stamp. **—tasche** *nf* wallet, pocket-book. **—träger** *nm* postman. **—umschlag** *nm* envelope. **—wechsel** *nm* correspondence.

Brigade (briˈgaːdə) *nf* -n brigade.

Brikett (briˈkɛt) *n neu* -s briquette.

brillant (brilˈjant) *adj* brilliant.

Brille (ˈbrilə) *nf* -n 1 spectacles. 2 goggles.

bringen[*] (ˈbriŋən) *vt* 1 bring. 2 take. 3 fetch. 4 lead. 5 carry. **jemanden um etwas bringen** deprive someone of something. **jemanden dazu bringen** induce someone to.

Brit/annien (briˈtaniən) *n neu* Britain. **—e** (ˈbritə) *nm* -n Briton. **—isch** (ˈbritiʃ) *adj* British.

bröckel/ig (ˈbrœkəliç) *adj* crumbly. **—n** *vt,vi* crumble.

Brokkoli (ˈbrɔkoli) *n pl* broccoli.

Brom (broːm) *n neu* bromine.

Brombeere (ˈbrɔmbeːrə) *nf* -n blackberry.

Bronze (ˈbrõːsə) *nf* -n bronze.

Brosche (ˈbrɔʃə) *nf* -n brooch.

Broschüre (brɔˈʃyːrə) *nf* -n pamphlet, booklet, brochure.

Brot (broːt) *n neu* -e 1 bread 2 loaf. **—chen** (ˈbroeːtçən) *n neu* — roll, bun.

Bruch (brux) *nm* ⁼e 1 break(ing), breach. 2 fracture. 3 rupture. 4 fraction. 5 crease, fold. **—ig** (ˈbryçiç) *adj* 1 fragile, brittle. 2 cracked. **—stück** *n neu* fragment. **—teil** *n neu* fraction.

Brücke (ˈbrykə) *nf* -n bridge.

Bruder (ˈbruːdər) *nm* ⁼ brother. **—lich** (ˈbryːdərliç) *adj* fraternal. **—schaft** *nf* -en fraternity, brotherhood. **⁼schaft** (ˈbryːdərʃaft) *nf* -en friendship.

Brühe ('bry:ə) nf -n broth, stock, soup.

brüllen ('brylən) vi 1 bellow. 2 roar.

Brumm/bär ('brumbɛ:r) nm,inf grumbler. **—en** vi 1 hum, buzz. 2 growl, grumble.

brünett (bry'nɛt) adj brunette.

Brunnen ('brunən) nm — 1 well. 2 fountain. 3 spring. **—kresse** nf watercress.

Brunst (brunst) nf ⁼e 1 zool rut, heat. 2 (sexual) lust. ⁼**ig** ('brynstiç) adj 1 in heat. 2 lustful.

Brüssel ('brysəl) n neu Brussels.

Brust (brust) nf ⁼e breast, chest. **—bild** n neu half-length portrait. **—kasten** nm chest, thorax.

brutal (bru'ta:l) adj brutal.

brüten ('bry:tən) vi,vt 1 brood. 2 incubate.

brutto (bruto) adj gross.

Bub(e) ('bu:bə) nm -(e)n 1 boy. 2 rogue. 3 game knave.

Buch (bu:x) n neu ⁼er book. ⁼**erei** (by:çə'rai) nf -en library. **—erschrank** ('by:çərʃraŋk) nm bookcase. **—fink** nm chaffinch. **—halter** nm comm bookkeeper. **—handel** nm 1 book trade. 2 bookselling. **—händler** nm bookseller. **—handlung** nf bookshop. ⁼**lein** ('by:çlain) n neu booklet.

Buche ('bu:xə) nf -n beech.

Büchse ('byksə) nf -n 1 box. 2 tin, can.

Buchstab/e ('bu:xʃta:bə) nm -n letter, character. **großer Buchstabe** capital letter. **—ieren** (bu:xʃta'bi:rən) vt spell. **—ierung** (bu:xʃta'bi:ruŋ) nf -en spelling. **—lich** ('bu:xʃtɛ:pliç) adj literal.

Bucht (buxt) nf -en 1 bay, inlet. 2 bight.

Buck/el ('bukəl) nm — 1 bulge, hump. 2 humpback. 3 stud, boss.

sich bücken ('bykən) vr 1 bow. 2 stoop.

Bude ('bu:də) nf -n 1 stall, booth. 2 inf digs, rooms.

Büfett (by'fɛt) n neu -s buffet.

Büffel ('byfəl) nm — buffalo, bison.

Bug (bu:k) nm -e 1 naut bow. 2 aviat nose. 3 (of animals) shoulder.

Bügel ('by:gəl) nm — 1 hanger. 2 grip. 3 stirrup. **—eisen** n neu (clothes) iron. **—n** vt iron, press.

Bühne ('by:nə) nf -n 1 stage. 2 theatre.

Bulgar/ien (bul'ga:riən) n neu Bulgaria. **—ier** nm — Bulgarian. **—isch** adj Bulgarian.

Bulle ('bulə) nm -n 1 bull. 2 sl policeman, copper.

Bumm/el ('buməl) nm — stroll. **—eln** vi 1 stroll. 2 loiter. **—ler** nm — idler, loafer.

bumsen ('bumzən) vi bump. vi,vt tab copulate, have sexual intercourse.

Bund (bunt) nm ⁼e 1 band. 2 league, (con)-federation. n neu -e bundle, bunch. **—esgenosse** nm ally, confederate. **—eskanzler** nm Federal Chancellor. **—espräsident** nm president (of a federal state). **—esrat** nm 1 Upper House of Parliament (in Austria and West Germany). 2 Executive Federal Council (in Switzerland). **—esrepublik** nf Federal Republic. **Bundesrepublik Deutschland, B.R.D.** nf Federal Republic of Germany, F.R.G. **—esstaat** nm 1 federal state. 2 member state of a federation. **—estag** nm (Lower House of) West German Parliament. **—eswehr** nf West German armed forces. ⁼**nis** ('byntnis) n neu -se alliance.

Bündel ('byndəl) n neu — bundle, bunch.

bunt (bunt) adj colourful, bright.

Bürde ('byrdə) nf -n burden.

Burg (burk) nf -en 1 castle. 2 fortress.

Bürg/e ('byrgə) nm -n surety, guarantor, bail. **—en** vi 1 vouch (for). 2 stand bail (for). **—schaft** ('byrkʃaft) nf surety, bond.

Bürger ('byrgər) nm —, **Bürger/in** nf -nen 1 citizen. 2 townsman or townswoman. 3 bourgeois. **—krieg** nm civil war. **—lich** adj 1 middle-class. 2 civil(ian). 3 unpretentious, simple. **—meister** nm mayor. **—recht** n neu 1 civic rights. 2 citizenship. **—schaft** nf -en citizens. **—stand** nm middle class(es). **—steig** nm pavement.

Büro (by'ro:) n neu -s office. **—krat** (byro-'kra:t) nm -en bureaucrat. **—kratie** (byrokra-'ti:) nf bureaucracy.

Bursche ('burʃə) nm -n 1 youth, lad. 2 student. 3 orderly. 4 servant. 5 apprentice.

Bürst/e ('byrstə) nf -n brush. **—en** vt brush.

Busch (buʃ) nm ⁼e 1 bush(land). 2 shrub(s). 3 thicket. 4 tuft. **—ig** adj bushy.

Busen ('bu:zən) nm — 1 breast, bosom. 2 gulf, bay.

Buß/e ('bu:sə) nf -n 1 penance. 2 fine. ⁼**en** -('by:sən) vt,vi atone for, pay (for), do penance (for). ⁼**er** ('by:sər) nm penitent.

Büste ('bystə) nf -n bust. **—nhalter** nm bra, brassiere.

Butter ('butər) nf butter. **—brot** n neu (slice of) bread and butter.

C

Café (ka'fe:) *n neu -s* cafe, coffee-house.
Camping ('kɛmpiŋ) *n neu* camping.
Cape (ke:p) *n neu -s* cape.
Cell/ist (tʃɛ'list) *nm -en* cellist. **—o** ('tʃɛlo) *n neu -s* cello.
Champagner (ʃamˈpanjər) *nm -s* champagne.
Champignon ('ʃampinjɔ) *nm -s* mushroom.
Chance ('ʃã:sə) *nf -n* chance.
Chao/s ('ka:ɔs) *n neu* chaos. **—tisch** (ka'o:tiʃ) *adj* chaotic.
Charakter ('karaktər) *nm -e* 1 character, nature. 2 letter, character. **—isieren** (karaktəri'zi:rən) *vt* characterize. **—istik** (karakˈteristik) *nf -en* characterization. **—istisch** (karaktəˈristiʃ) *adj* characteristic.
charmant (ʃarˈmant) *adj* charming.
Chauffeur (ʃɔˈfœːr) *nm -e* driver, chauffeur.
Chaussee (ʃoˈseː) *nf -n* main or high road.
Chef (ʃɛf) *nm -s* head, boss.
Chemi/e (çeˈmiː) *nf* chemistry. **—kalien** (çemiˈkaːliən) *nf pl* chemicals. **—ker** ('çeːmikər) *nm —* chemist (in science or industry). **—sch** ('çeːmiʃ) *adj* chemical. **chemische Reinigung** dry cleaning.
Chil/e ('tʃiːlə) *n neu* Chile. **—ene** (tʃiˈleːnə) *nm -n* Chilean. **—enisch** (tʃiˈleːniʃ) *adj* Chilean.
Chin/a ('çiːna) *n neu* China. **—ese** (çiˈneːzə) *nm -n* Chinaman, Chinese. **—esisch** (çiˈneː-ziʃ) *adj* Chinese.
Chirurg (çiˈrurk) *nm -en* surgeon. **—ie** (çirurˈgiː) *nf* surgery.
Chlor (kloːr) *n neu* chlorine.
Chloroform (kloroˈfɔrm) *n neu -e* chloroform.
Chor (koːr) *nm -e* choir, chorus.
Christ (krist) *nm -en* Christian. **—baum** *nm* Christmas tree. **—enheit** *nf* Christendom. **—entum** *n neu* Christianity. **—kind** *n neu* Christ-child. **—lich** *adj* Christian. **—us** ('kristus) *nm* Christ.
Chrom (kroːm) *n neu* chromium, chrome.
Chronik ('kroːnik) *nf -en* chronicle.
Computer (kɔmˈpjuːtər) *nm —* computer.
Creme (kreːm) *nf -s* 1 cream. 2 cream pudding.

D

da (da) *adv* 1 there. 2 here. 3 then. *conj* 1 as. 2 when. 3 since.
dabei (daˈbai) *adv* 1 by it. 2 nearby. 3 present. 4 at the same time. 5 thereby.
Dach (dax) *n neu -er* roof. **—boden** *nm* attic. **—fenster** *n neu also* **—luke** *nf -n* skylight. **—rinne** *also* **—traufe** *nf -n* 1 eaves. 2 gutter.
Dachs (daks) *nm -e* badger.
Dachshund ('dakshunt) *nm* dachshund.
dachte ('daxtə) *v see* **denken.**
dadurch (daˈdurç) *adv* 1 through there. 2 thus, in that way.
dafür (daˈfyːr) *adv* for that, in return.
dagegen (daˈgeːgən) *adv* 1 against it. 2 in comparison. *conj* on the other hand, but.
daher (daˈheːr) *adv* 1 from there. 2 therefore.
dahin (daˈhin) *adv* there, to that place. **bis dahin** until then. **dahin sein** be lost or gone.
dahinten (daˈhintən) *adv* behind (there).
dahinter (daˈhintər) *adv* behind it or that. **—kommen*** *vi* find out (about it).
damals ('daːmaːls) *adv* then, at that time.
Dame ('daːmə) *nf -n* 1 lady. 2 game queen. **—spiel** *n neu* draughts.
damit (daˈmit) *adv* 1 with or by it. 2 thereby. *conj* in order to, so (that).
Damm (dam) *nm -e* 1 dam, dyke, embankment. 2 roadway. **—en** ('dɛmən) *vt* dam, restrain.
Dämmerung ('dɛməruŋ) *nf -en* 1 dawn. 2 dusk, twilight.
Dampf (dampf) *nm -e* steam, vapour. **—en** *vi* 1 steam. 2 *inf* smoke. **—maschine** *nf* steam engine. **—schiff** *n neu* steamship.
dämpf/en ('dɛmpfən) *vt* 1 quieten, muffle. 2 steam. **—er** *nm —* 1 damper, silencer. 2 extinguisher.
danach (daˈnaːx) *adv* 1 after(wards). 2 accordingly.
Dän/e ('dɛːnə) *nm -n* Dane. **—emark** ('dɛː-nəmark) *n neu* Denmark. **—isch** ('dɛːniʃ) *adj* Danish. *n neu* Danish (language).
daneben (daˈneːbən) *adv* 1 near it. 2 nearby. 3 beside. *conj* moreover, as well.
Dank (daŋk) *nm* thanks. **vielen** or **schönen Dank!** many thanks! **—bar** *adj* thankful, grateful. **—barkeit** *nf* gratitude. **—e** *interj* thanks! thank you! **—en** *vi* thank.
dann (dan) *adv* then.

daran (da'ran) *adv also* **dran** at, on or by it or that. **daran gehen** set to work.

darauf (da'rauf) *adv also* **drauf** 1 on it or that, thereupon. 2 later.

daraus (da'raus) *adv also* **draus** 1 from or out of it or that. 2 from there.

darbieten ('da:rbi:tən) *vt* offer, tender.

darein (da'rain) *adv also* **drein** into it or that, therein.

darf (da:rf) *v see* **dürfen**.

darin (da'rin) *adv also* **drin** in it, that or there, within.

Darlegung ('da:rle:gun) *nf* **-en** statement, exposition.

Darlehen ('da:rle:ən) *n neu* —loan.

Darm (darm) *nm* **-e** intestine, bowel, gut.

darstell/en ('da:rʃtɛlən) *vt* 1 present, show. 2 represent, depict. **—ung** *nf* **-en** 1 presentation. 2 description, statement.

darüber (da'ry:bər) *adv* 1 about it or that. 2 over, above or beyond it or that. **darüber hinaus** 1 moreover. 2 over and above that, beyond that.

darum (da'rum) *adv* 1 about or around it or that. 2 therefore.

darunter (da'runtər) *adv* 1 under it or that, underneath. 2 among them.

das (das) *def art* the. *pron* that, which.

dasein* ('da:zain) *vi* exist, be present. *n neu* existence, being, presence.

daß (das) *conj* that. **daß nicht** lest. **so daß** so that.

datieren (da'ti:rən) *vt* date.

Datum ('da:tum) *n neu* **-ten** date.

Dauer ('dauər) *nf* duration, period. **auf die Dauer** in the long run. **—haft** *adj* durable, lasting. **—lauf** *nm* endurance run. **—n** *vi* last, continue, take (time). **lange dauern** take a long time. **—nd** *adj* lasting, constant, permanent.

Daumen ('daumən) *nm* — thumb.

Daunendecke ('daunəndɛkə) *nf* (continental) quilt, duvet, eiderdown.

davon (da'fɔn) *adv* of, from or about it or that. **—kommen*** *vi* get away. **—tragen*** *vt* carry off.

davor (da'fo:r) *adv* 1 before or in front of it or that. 2 of or from it or that.

dawider (da'vi:dər) *adv* against it or that.

dazu (da'tsu:) *adv* 1 to or for it or that. 2 for that purpose. 3 in addition. **—kommen*** *vi* arrive, happen. **—tun*** *vt* add.

dazwischen (da'tsviʃən) *adv* 1 between or among (them). 2 meanwhile. **—kommen*** *vi* 1 intervene, prevent. 2 come between. **—treten*** *vi* intervene.

Debatt/e (de'batə) *nf* **-n** debate, discussion.

Debet ('de:bɛt) *n neu* **-s** debit.

Deck (dɛk) *n neu* **-e** naut deck.

Deck/e ('dɛkə) *nf* **-n** 1 cover, blanket. 2 ceiling. **—el** *nm* — lid, cover. **—en** *vt* cover. **den Tisch decken** set or lay the table. **—mantel** *nm* 1 pretext. 2 cloak. 3 cover. **—name** *nm* assumed name. **—ung** *nf* **-en** 1 cover(ing), protection. 2 *mil* cover. 3 *comm* security.

defensiv (defɛn'zi:f) *adj* defensive. **—e** (defɛn'zi:və) *nf* **-n** 1 defensive. 2 defence.

defin/ieren (defi'ni:rən) *vt* define. **—ition** (definitsi'o:n) *nf* **-en** definition.

Defizit ('de:fitsit) *n neu* **-e** deficit.

Degen ('de:gən) *nm* — sword.

degenerieren (degene'ri:rən) *vi* degenerate.

dehnen ('de:nən) *vt* stretch, lengthen, expand.

Deich (daiç) *nm* **-e** dyke, embankment.

dein (dain) *poss adj,pron* 2nd pers *s fam* your, yours. **—er** *poss pron* 2nd pers *s fam also* **der —e** *or* **der —ige** yours. **—erseits** ('dainərzaits) *adv* on your part. **—esgleichen** *pron* people like you. **—ethalben** *also* **—etwegen** *or* **—etwillen** for your sake, on your account.

dekaden/t (deka'dɛnt) *adj* decadent. **—z** (deka'dɛnts) *nf* decadence.

Dekan (de'ka:n) *nm* **-e** dean.

Deklination (deklinatsi'o:n) *nf* **-en** *gram* declension.

Dekret (de'kre:t) *n neu* **-e** decree.

delikat (deli'ka:t) *adj* 1 delicate. 2 delicious.

Delikt (de'likt) *n neu* **-e** offence, crime.

Delphin (dɛl'fi:n) *nm* **-e** dolphin.

dem (de:m) *def art* to the. *pron* to it, that or whom.

dementieren (demɛn'ti:rən) *vt* deny.

demgemäß ('de:mgəmɛ:s) *adv* accordingly.

Demission (demisi'o:n) *nf* **-en** resignation.

demnach (de'mna:x) *adv* accordingly.

demnächst (de'mnɛ:çst) *adv* soon.

Demokrat (demo'kra:t) *nm* **-en** democrat. **—isch** *adj* democratic. **—ie** (demokra'ti:) *nf* **-n** democracy.

Demonstr/ation (demɔnstratsi'o:n) *nf* **-en** demonstration. **—ieren** (demɔn'stri:rən) *vt,vi* demonstrate.

Demut ('de:mu:t) *nf* humility. **—ig** ('de:my:tiç)

adj humble. **—igen** ('de:my:tigən) *vt* humble, humiliate.

demzufolge ('de:mtsufolgə) *adv* accordingly.

den (de:n) *def art* 1 the. 2 *pl* (to) the. *pron* 1 that, which, whom. 2 *pl* to these or those. **denen** *pron* to these or those.

denk/en* ('dɛŋkən) *vt,vi* think. **denken an** or **über** think of or about. **—bar** *adj* conceivable. **—er** *nm* thinker. **—mal** *n neu* **-er** monument, memorial. **—schrift** *nf* -**en** 1 inscription, memorial. 2 report. 3 memorandum. **—(ungs)art** *nf* -**en** way of thinking, mentality. **—würdig** *adj* notable, memorable.

denn (dɛn) *conj* for. *adv* then. **es sei denn, (daß)** unless.

dennoch ('dɛnɔx) *adv* yet, however.

Departement (departmã:) *n neu* -**s** department.

Depesche (de'pɛʃə) *nf* -**n** 1 dispatch. 2 telegram.

deponieren (depo'ni:rən) *vt* deposit.

Depression (depresi'o:n) *nf* -**en** depression.

deprimieren (depri'mi:rən) *vt* depress.

der (de:r) *def art* 1 the. 2 of the. *pron* that, which, who.

derart ('de:ra:rt) *adv* in such a way. **—ig** *adj* such, of that kind.

derb (dɛrp) *adj* 1 sturdy, sound. 2 rough, coarse, crude.

deren (de:rən) *pron* whose, of which.

dergestalt ('de:rgəʃtalt) *adv* in such a way.

dergleichen (de:r'glaiçən) *pron* such (a thing), the like, of the kind.

derjenige, diejenige, dasjenige ('de:rje:nigə, 'di:je:nigə, 'dasje:nigə) *pron m,f,neu* he or she who, that which, the one which.

dermaßen ('de:rma:sən) *adv* to such a degree.

derselbe, dieselbe, dasselbe (de:r'zɛlbə, di:-'zɛlbə, das'zɛlbə) *pron m,f,neu* the same.

derzeitig ('de:rtsaitiç) *adj* 1 present. 2 of or at that time.

des (dɛs) *def art* of the.

desgleichen (dɛs'glaiçən) *pron* such (a thing). *adv* likewise.

deshalb ('dɛshalp) *adv* therefore.

Desin/fektionsmittel (dezinfɛktsi'o:nzmitəl) *n neu* — disinfectant. **—fizieren** (dezinfi'tsi:-rən) *vt* disinfect.

dessen ('dɛsən) *pron* whose, of which. **—ungeachtet** (dɛsənunge'axtət) *adv* nevertheless.

desto ('dɛsto) *adv* so much, the. **je...desto**

the...the. **je mehr, desto besser** the more the better.

deswegen ('dɛsve:gən) *adv* therefore.

Detail (de'tai) *n neu* -**s** detail, item. **—handel** *nf* retail trade. **en detail** *adv* retail.

deut/en ('dɔytən) *vi* point (to). *vt* 1 explain. 2 show. **—lich** *adj* clear, distinct. **—lichkeit** *nf* distinctness. **—ung** *nf* -**en** explanation, interpretation.

deutsch (dɔytʃ) *adj* German. *n neu* German (language). **auf Deutsch** in German. **—(e)r** *nm* German. **—e Demokratische Republik, D.D.R.** *nf* German Democratic Republic, G.D.R. **—kunde** *nf* German studies. **—land** *n neu* Germany. **—sprachig** *adj* German-speaking. **—tum** *n neu* German nature or culture.

Devise (de'vi:zə) *nf* -**n** 1 *pl* foreign exchange. 2 motto, slogan.

Dezember (de'tsɛmbər) *nm* December.

Dialekt (dia'lɛkt) *nm* -**e** dialect.

Diamant (dia'mant) *nm* -**en** diamond.

Diapositiv (di:apozi'ti:f) *n neu* slide, transparency.

Diät (di'ɛ:t) *nf* — diet.

Diäten (di'ɛ:tən) *nf pl* allowance(s).

dich (diç) *pron* 2nd *pers s fam* you, yourself.

dicht (diçt) *adj* 1 dense, thick. 2 tight. 3 close (to). **—igkeit** *nf* -**en** also **—heit** 1 density, thickness. 2 imperviousness.

dicht/en ('diçtən) *vt* compose (poetry). **—er** *nm* — poet. **—ung** *nf* -**en** 1 poetry, poem. 2 fiction.

dick (dik) *adj* thick, fat, large. **—e** *nf* -**n** 1 thickness, fatness. 2 size. **—kopf** *nm* thickhead. **—icht** *n neu* -**e** thicket.

die *def art* the. *pron* that, which, who, whom.

Dieb (di:p) *nm* -**e** thief, robber. **—isch** ('di:biʃ) *adj* thieving, dishonest. **—stahl** *nm* -**e** theft.

Diele ('di:lə) *nf* -**n** 1 board, plank. 2 hall(way).

dien/en ('di:nən) *vi* serve. **—er** *nm* — man-servant. **—erin** *nf* -**nen** maid-servant. **—er-schaft** *nf* -**en** servants. **—st** (di:nst) *nm* -**e** 1 service. 2 duty. **außer Dienst** off duty. **—stbereit** *adj* ready for service. **—ststelle** *nf* place of work or service.

Dienstag ('di:nsta:k) *nm* Tuesday.

dieser, diese, dieses ('di:zər, 'di:zə, 'di:zəs) *pron,adj m,f,neu* this.

diesmal ('di:sma:l) *adv* this time.

diesseits ('di:szaits) *adv* on this side.

Dietrich ('di:triç) *nm* -**e** skeleton key.

Diktat (dik'ta:t) *n neu* -**e** 1 dictation. 2

command, decree. **—or** (dik'ta:tɔr) nm **-en** dictator. **—ur** (dikta'tu:r) nf **-en** dictatorship.

diktieren (dik'ti:rən) vt dictate.

Diner (di'ne:) n neu **-s** dinner.

Ding (diŋ) n neu **-e** thing, object.

Diplom (di'plo:m) n neu **-e** diploma, certificate.

dir (di:r) pron 2nd pers s fam (to) you, yourself.

Dirig/ent (diri'gɛnt) nm **-en** mus conductor. **—ieren** (diri'gi:rən) vt 1 direct. 2 mus conduct.

Dirne ('dirnə) nf **-n** 1 prostitute. 2 girl.

diskont/ieren (diskɔn'ti:rən) vt comm discount. **—satz** nm bank rate.

Diskothek (disko'te:k) nf **-en** discotheque.

Disku/ssion (diskusi'o:n) nf **-en** discussion. **—tieren** (disku'ti:rən) vt,vi discuss, debate.

disponieren (dispo'ni:rən) vt,vi arrange, dispose.

Distel ('distəl) nf **-n** thistle.

Disziplin (distsi'pli:n) nf **-en** discipline.

doch (dɔx) adv 1 nevertheless. 2 indeed, really. conj but, however, yet.

Docht (dɔxt) nm **-e** wick.

Dock (dɔk) n neu **-s** dock(yard). **—arbeiter** nm docker.

Dogge ('dɔgə) nf **-n** bulldog.

Dogma ('dɔgma) n neu **-s** dogma. **—tisch** (dɔg'ma:tiʃ) adj dogmatic.

Doktor ('dɔktɔr) nm **-e** doctor.

Dolch (dɔlç) nm **-e** dagger.

dolmetsch/en ('dɔlmɛtʃən) vt,vi interpret. **—er** nm **—** interpreter.

Dom (do:m) nm **-e** cathedral. **—herr** nm rel canon.

dominieren (domi'ni:rən) vi,vt dominate, domineer.

Donau ('do:nau) nf Danube.

Donner ('dɔnər) nm thunder. **—n** vi thunder, roar.

Donnerstag ('dɔnərsta:k) nm Thursday.

Doppel ('dɔpəl) n neu **—** 1 duplicate. 2 double. **—bett** n neu double bed. **—deckerbus** nm double-decker bus. **—ehe** nf bigamy. **—n** vt double. **—punkt** nm colon. **—sinn** nm ambiguity. **—t** adj double.

Dorf (dɔrf) n neu **-er** village, hamlet. **—bewohner** also **—ler** ('dɔrfbəvo:nər, 'doerflər) nm **—** villager.

Dorn (dɔrn) nm **-en** thorn. **—ig** adj thorny.

Dorsch (dɔrʃ) nm **-e** cod.

dort (dɔrt) adv there. **—her** adv from there. **—hin** adv to there or that place. **—ig** adj of that place or there.

Dose ('do:zə) nf **-n** 1 box. 2 tin, can.

dösen ('dø:zən) vi inf doze.

Dosis ('do:zis) nf **-sen** dose (of medicine etc.). **zu starke Dosis** overdose.

Dotter ('dɔtə) nm **—** yolk.

Dozent (do'tsɛnt) nm **-en** university or college lecturer.

Drache ('draxə) nm **-n** dragon.

Draht (dra:t) nm **-e** wire, cable. **—los** adj wireless. **—seilbahn** nf funicular, cable railway.

Drama ('dra:ma) n neu **-men** drama. **—tiker** (dra'ma:tikər) nm **—** playwright. **—tisch** (dra'ma:tiʃ) adj dramatic.

dran (dran) adv see **daran.**

Drang (draŋ) nm **-e** 1 drive, urge, stress. 2 pressure. **—en** ('drɛŋən) vi,vt 1 press, hurry, urge. 2 crowd.

drapieren (dra'pi:rən) vt drape.

drauf (drauf) adv see **darauf.**

draußen ('drausən) adv outside, out of doors.

Dreck (drɛk) nm 1 filth, dirt. 2 excrement. **—ig** adj filthy, dirty, muddy.

dreh/en ('dre:ən) vt,vi 1 turn, twist, wind. 2 shoot (a film). **—bank** nf **-e** lathe. **—buch** n neu (film) script. **—punkt** nm pivot. **—scheibe** nf turntable. **—ung** nf **-en** turn, rotation, revolution.

drei (drai) adj,nf three. **—bein** n neu tripod. **—eck** n neu triangle. **—eckig** adj triangular. **—einigkeit** nf also **—faltigkeit** Trinity. **—erlei** ('draiərlai) adj of three kinds. **—fach** adj triple, threefold. **—mal** adv three times. **—rad** n neu tricycle.

dreißig ('draisiç) adj,nf thirty. **dreißigste** adj thirtieth.

dreist (draist) adj 1 impudent. 2 bold.

dreizehn ('draitse:n) adj,nf thirteen. **dreizehnte** adj thirteenth.

dresch/en ('drɛʃən) vt thresh. **—flegel** nm flail.

dressieren (drɛ'si:rən) vt train (an animal).

drin (drin) adv see **darin.** **—nen** adv inside, indoors.

dring/en ('driŋən) vi 1 urge, force, press. 2 penetrate. **—end** adj also **—lich** urgent.

dritt(e) (drit) adj third. **—el** n neu **—** one third, third part. **—ens** adv thirdly.

Drog/e ('dro:gə) nf **-n** drug. **—erie** (drogə'ri:) nf **-n** chemist's shop.

droh/en ('dro:ən) vi threaten. **—ung** nf **-en** threat.

Drohne ('dro:nə) nf **-n** drone.

31

drollig ('drɔliç) adj droll, funny.

Drossel ('drɔsəl) nf -n 1 thrush. 2 tech throttle.

drüben ('dry:bən) adv on the other side, over there.

drüber ('dry:bər) adv see **darüber.**

Druck (druk) nm 1 -e print, printing. 2 -e pressure. —**en** vt print. —**er** nm — printer. —**erei** ('drukə'rai) nf -en printing works. —**fehler** nm misprint. —**knopf** nm 1 snap fastener. 2 push-button.

drück/en ('drykən) vt,vi 1 press (on), squeeze. 2 oppress. **sich drücken** vr dodge work, shirk.

drunten ('druntən) adv (there) below, down there.

drunter ('druntər) adv see **darunter.**

Drüse ('dry:zə) nf -n gland.

Dschungel ('dʒuŋəl) nm,f,neu -n jungle.

du (du:) pron 2nd pers s fam you.

ducken ('dukən) vt duck.

Dudelsack ('du:dəlzak) nm -e bagpipes.

Duell (du'ɛl) n neu -e duel. **sich —ieren** (due'li:rən) vr duel.

Duett (du'ɛt) n neu -e duet.

Duft (duft) nm -e aroma, scent. —**en** vi smell (sweet), be fragrant.

dulden ('duldən) vt suffer, bear, tolerate.

dumm (dum) adj 1 stupid, silly. —**heit** nf -en 1 stupidity. 2 foolish action. —**kopf** nm blockhead, fool.

dumpf (dumpf) adj 1 musty, close (atmosphere). 2 dull, hollow (sound).

Düne ('dy:nə) nf -n dune.

Dünger ('dyŋər) nm dung, manure.

dunkel ('duŋkəl) adj 1 dark, dim, gloomy. 2 obscure. —**kammer** nf darkroom.

dünn (dyn) adj 1 thin. 2 sparse.

Dunst (dunst) nm -e vapour, haze, smoke. —**en** ('dynstən) vt cul 1 steam. 2 stew.

Dur (du:r) n neu mus major.

durch (durç) prep through, during, by. adv completely, thoroughly.

durchaus (durç'aus) adv absolutely, completely.

durchblicken ('durçblikən) vt,vi look through, see through. **durchblicken lassen** give to understand.

durchbohren ('durçbo:rən) vt bore through, pierce.

durchbrechen* ('durçbreçən) vt,vi break through or out. (durç'breçən) vt break through.

durchdringen* (vi 'durçdriŋən; vt durç'driŋən)

vi press or get through. vt 1 permeate. 2 penetrate.

durcheinander (durçain'andər) adv 1 in confusion. 2 upset. n neu — disorder.

Durchfahrt ('durçfa:rt) nf -en 1 passage or journey through. 2 passageway. 3 gateway.

Durchfall ('durçfal) nm -e 1 failure. 2 diarrhoea.

durchforschen (durç'fɔrʃən) vt investigate.

durchführen ('durçfy:rən) vt 1 lead through. 2 carry out.

Durchgang ('durçgaŋ) nm -e passage. **durchgehen*** ('durçge:ən) vi 1 go or walk through. 2 run away. vt 1 examine. 2 wear out.

durch/lassen ('durçlasən) vt let through, pass. —**lässig** ('durçlɛsiç) adj permeable.

durchlaufen* ('durçlaufən) vi run through. vt wear out. (durç'laufən) vt run through.

durchleuchten (vi 'durçlɔyçtən; vt durç'lɔyçtən) vi shine through. vt 1 X-ray. 2 investigate. 3 search.

durchlöchern (durç'lœçərn) vt perforate, pierce.

durchmachen ('durçmaxən) vt go through, experience, endure.

Durchmesser ('durçmɛsər) nm — diameter.

durchqueren (durç'kve:rən) vt cross, traverse.

Durchreise ('durçraizə) nf -n passage, transit, journey through.

durchs (durçs) contraction of **durch das.**

durchschauen (vi 'durçʃauən; vt durç'ʃauən) vi look through. vt 1 see through. 2 penetrate.

Durchschlag ('durçʃla:k) nm -e 1 carbon (copy). 2 strainer. 3 tech punch. —**papier** n neu carbon paper.

Durchschnitt ('durçʃnit) nm -e 1 average. 2 cutting through. 3 (cross-)section. —**lich** adj average. —**mensch** nm man in the street.

durchsehen* ('durçze:ən) vt 1 look through. 2 examine.

durchsichtig ('durçziçtiç) adj transparent.

durchsuchen ('durçzu:xən) vt examine (closely).

durchtrieben (durç'tri:bən) adj cunning.

durchweg ('durçvɛk) adv throughout.

sich durchwinden* ('durçvindən) vr struggle through.

durchziehen* ('durçtsi:ən) vi march through. vt interlace. (durç'tsi:ən) vt draw or pass through.

dürfen* ('dyrfən) v mod aux be allowed, may.

dürftig ('dyrftiç) adj needy, poor.

dürr (dyr) adj 1 dry, arid. 2 thin. 3 barren.

Durst (durst) nm thirst. **—ig** adj thirsty.
Dusche ('duʃə) nf -n shower. **—n** vi shower.
Düse ('dy:zə) nf -n jet, nozzle. **—nflugzeug** n
neu jet (plane).
düster ('dy:stər) adj dark, dusky, gloomy.
Dutzend ('dutsənt) n neu -e dozen.
duzen ('du:tsən) vt address (someone) familiarly
with **du.**
Dynam/ik (dy'na:mik) nf dynamics. **—isch**
adj dynamic.
Dynamit (dyna'mi:t) n neu -e dynamite.
Dynast/ie (dynas'ti:) nf -n dynasty.
D-Zug ('de:tsu:k) nm -̈e express train.

E

Ebbe ('ɛbə) nf -n ebb, low-tide. **—n** vi ebb.
eben ('e:bən) adj 1 level, even. 2 smooth. adv
just, precisely. **—bild** n neu image. **—bürtig**
('e:bənbyrtiç) adj equal, of equal rank. **—e** nf
-n 1 plain. 2 math plane. **—falls** adv
likewise. **—heit** nf -en evenness, smoothness.
—holz n neu ebony. **—so** adv just as. **der
eine ist ebenso gut wie der andere** the one
is just as good as the other. **—soviel** adv just
as much.
Eber ('e:bər) nm — boar.
ebnen ('e:bnən) vt level, make smooth.
Echo ('ɛço) n neu -s echo.
echt (ɛçt) adj 1 genuine, real, authentic. 2 pure.
Eck (ɛk) n neu -e also **Ecke/e** ('ɛkə) nf -n 1
corner. 2 angle. **—ig** adj angular. **—stein**
nm 1 corner stone. 2 game diamonds.
edel ('e:dəl) adj noble, aristocratic. **—frau** nf
noblewoman. **—mann** nm, pl **-leute** nobleman. **—mütig** ('e:dəlmy:tiç) adj magnanimous, generous. **—stein** nm precious stone,
gem.
Edikt (e'dikt) n neu -e edict.
Edinburg ('e:dinburk) n neu Edinburgh.
Efeu ('e:fɔy) nm -s ivy.
Effekt/en (ɛ'fɛktən) n pl 1 comm securities,
bonds. 2 personal effects, belongings. **—iv**
(ɛfɛk'ti:v) adj 1 actual. 2 effective.
egal (e'ga:l) adv 1 even. 2 equal, the same.
Egoismus (ego'ismus) nm egoism.
ehe (e:) conj before. **—dem** (e:ə'de:m) adv
also **—mals** formerly. **—malig** (e:əma:liç)
adj former. **—r** adv 1 sooner, before. 2
rather.
Ehe ('e:ə) nf -n marriage. **—brecher** nm —
adulterer. **—brecherin** nf **-nen** adulteress.

—bruch nm adultery. **—frau** nf wife. **—lich**
adj 1 matrimonial. 2 (of a child) legitimate.
—mann nm husband. **—paar** n neu married
couple. **—stand** nm matrimony, married
state. **—scheidung** nf divorce.
Ehr/e ('e:rə) nf -n honour. **—en** vt honour.
—enwort n neu word of honour. **—erbietig**
adj respectful, deferential. **—furcht** nf reverence, awe, respect. **—geiz** nm ambition.
—geizig adj ambitious. **—lich** adj 1 honest.
2 sincere. 3 fair. **—lichkeit** nf honesty.
—würdig adj venerable.
Ei (ai) n neu -er egg.
Eich/e ('aiçə) nf -n oak. **—el** nf -n 1 acorn. 2
game clubs. **—hörnchen** ('aiçœrnçən) n
neu — squirrel.
Eid (ait) nm -e oath. **einen Eid abnehmen**
administer an oath. **unter Eid** on oath.
—bruch nm perjury. **—genosse** nm — 1
confederate. 2 Swiss. **—genossenschaft** nf
-en 1 confederation. 2 Swiss Confederation,
Switzerland. **—genössisch** ('aitgənœsiʃ) adj
1 federal. 2 Swiss.
Eidechse ('aidɛksə) nf -n lizard.
Eier/becher ('aiərbɛçər) nm eggcup. **—kuchen** nm 1 (sweet) omelette. 2 pancake.
—schale nf eggshell.
Eif/er ('aifər) nm zeal, fervour. **—ersucht** nf
jealousy. **—ersüchtig** adj jealous. **—rig** adj
zealous, eager.
Eigelb ('aigɛlp) n neu -e (egg) yolk.
eigen ('aigən) adj 1 own, proper. 2 characteristic. 3 strange. 4 particular, exact.
Eigenart ('aigəna:rt) nf -en 1 peculiarity. 2
character. **—ig** adj peculiar.
eigenhändig ('aigənhɛndiç) adj in or by one's
own hand, by oneself.
eigenmächtig ('aigənmɛçtiç) adj arbitrary.
Eigenname ('aigənna:mə) nm proper name.
Eigennutz ('aigənnuts) nm self-interest, selfishness. **-̈ig** adj selfish.
Eigenschaft ('aigənʃaft) nf -en characteristic,
trait, quality. **—swort** n neu adjective.
Eigensinn ('aigənzin) nm obstinacy. **—ig** adj
obstinate.
eigentlich ('aigəntliç) adj 1 real. 2 proper. 3
true. adv 1 actually. 2 just. 3 indeed.
Eigentum ('aigəntu:m) n neu -er property.
-̈er nm — owner. **-̈lich** adj 1 peculiar,
characteristic. 2 peculiar, strange.
sich eignen ('aignən) vr suit, be qualified.
Eil/bote ('ailbo:tə) nm express messenger.
—brief nm express letter. **—e** nf haste,

hurry, speed. **—en** vi also **sich —en** vr hurry, hasten. **—ig** adj hurried, hasty. **—zug** nm fast train.

Eimer (ˈaimər) nm — bucket, pail.

ein (ain) adv (ain, ˈainə) indef art m,f,neu a, an. adj one. **einer, eine, eins** (ˈainər, ˈainə, ains) pron one.

einander (aiˈnandər) pron each other, one another.

einatmen (ˈaina:tmən) vt,vi inhale, breathe in.

Einbahnstraße (ˈainba:nʃtra:sə) nf one-way street.

einbalsamieren (ainbalzaˈmiːrən) vt embalm.

Einband (ˈainbant) nm ⸚e binding, cover (of a book).

einbegreifen* (ˈainbəgraifən) vt comprise, include.

einbiegen* (ˈainbiːgən) vt bend in(wards). vi turn in(to).

sich einbild/en (ˈainbildən) vr imagine. **—ung** nf imagination. **—ungskraft** nf (power of) imagination.

Einblick (ˈainblik) nm 1 insight. 2 glimpse.

einbrech/en* (ˈainbreçən) vt,vi 1 break open, down or into. 2 burgle. **—er** nm — burglar.

einbürgern (ˈainbyrgərn) vt naturalize. **sich einbürgern** vr 1 settle. 2 (of a word, etc.) come into use.

einbüßen (ˈainbyːsən) vt 1 lose. 2 forfeit.

eindeutig (ˈaindɔytiç) adj unequivocal, clear.

eindring/en* (ˈaindriŋən) vi 1 enter by force, invade. 2 penetrate.

Eindruck (ˈaindruk) nm ⸚e impression. **—svoll** adj impressive.

einerlei (ˈainərlai) adj of one sort or kind.

einerseits (ˈainərzaits) adv on the one hand.

einfach (ˈainfax) adj 1 simple, plain. 2 single.

einfahr/en* (ˈainfa:rən) vi drive in. vt 1 bring in. 2 break in (horses). **—t** nf -en entrance, drive.

Einfall (ˈainfal) nm ⸚e 1 collapse, fall. 2 invasion. 3 brainwave, sudden idea. **—en*** vi collapse, fall. v imp occur (to someone). **es fiel mir ein** it (suddenly) occurred to me.

einfältig (ˈainfɛltiç) adj simple, stupid.

Einfassung (ˈainfasuŋ) nf -en 1 border (of a dress). 2 enclosure.

sich einfinden* (ˈainfindən) vr turn up, appear.

einflechten* (ˈainflɛçtən) vt 1 plait, interlace. 2 put in (a word, etc.).

Einfluß (ˈainflus) nm -flüsse 1 influx. 2 influence. **—reich** adj influential.

einförmig (ˈainfœrmiç) adj 1 uniform. 2 monotonous.

einfügen (ˈainfyːgən) vt 1 insert. 2 join. **sich einfügen** vr adapt, fit in.

Einfuhr (ˈainfuːr) nf — import(ation). **—en** (ˈainfyːrən) vt 1 bring in, introduce. 2 import. 3 install. **—er** (ˈainfyːrər) nm — importer. **—ung** (ˈainfyːruŋ) nf -en introduction. **—zoll** nm import duty.

Eingang (ˈaingaŋ) nm ⸚e 1 entrance. 2 arrival, receipt (of a letter, etc.). 3 introduction, beginning.

eingebildet (ˈaingəbildət) adj 1 imaginary. 2 conceited.

eingeboren (ˈaingəboːrən) adj 1 native. 2 innate. **—e(r)** nm native.

Eingebung (ˈaingəbuŋ) nf -en inspiration.

eingehen* (ˈaingeːən) vi 1 go or walk in(to), enter. 2 cease. 3 shrink, wither. 4 die. vt conclude (agreement, etc.). **ein Risiko eingehen** run a risk.

eingenommen (ˈaingənɔmən) adj biased, prejudiced.

Eingeweide (ˈaingəvaidə) n neu pl intestines, bowels.

eingießen* (ˈaingiːsən) vt pour in or out.

eingreifen* (ˈaingraifən) vi 1 intervene, interfere. 2 catch.

einhalten* (ˈainhaltən) vt 1 observe, respect (conditions). 2 restrain. vi stop.

einhändigen (ˈainhɛndigən) vt deliver, hand over.

einheimisch (ˈainhaimiʃ) adj native.

Einheit (ˈainhait) nf -en 1 unit. 2 unity. **—lich** adj uniform.

einholen (ˈainhoːlən) vt 1 gather (in). 2 shop. 3 catch up.

einig (ˈainiç) adj united, agreed. **—e** (ˈainigə) pron,adj a few, some. **—en** vt unite. **sich —en** vr agree. **—ermaßen** (ainigərˈmaːsən) adv to a certain extent, somewhat. **—keit** (ˈainiçkait) nf unity, concord. **—ung** (ˈainiguŋ) nf -en 1 unification. 2 agreement.

einkassieren (ˈainkasiːrən) vt cash.

Einkauf (ˈainkauf) nm ⸚e purchase. **—en** vt buy. **einkaufen gehen** go shopping. **—er** (ˈainkɔyfər) nm — purchaser. **—spreis** nm wholesale or trade price.

einkehren (ˈainkeːrən) vi stop or stay overnight.

Einklang (ˈainklaŋ) nm unison, harmony.

einkommen* (ˈainkɔmən) vi 1 come in. 2 apply. n neu — income, revenue. **—steuer** nf income tax.

einkreisen (ˈainkraizən) vt encircle.

Einkünfte (ˈainkynftə) nf pl revenue, income.

einlad/en* (ˈainlaːdən) vt 1 invite. 2 load. **—ung** nf -en 1 invitation. 2 loading.

Einlage (ˈainlaːgə) nf -n 1 insert, enclosure. 2 deposit, investment. 3 med arch-support. 4 cul meat or vegetables, etc., added to soup. **—n** vt store up.

Ein/laß (ˈainlas) nm -lässe entrance, admission. **—lassen*** vt admit, put or let in. **sich —lassen*** vr engage in.

einlaufen*. (ˈainlaufən) vi 1 enter, arrive. 2 shrink.

einleg/en (ˈainleːgən) vt 1 lay or put in, inlay. 2 insert, enclose. 3 deposit. 4 preserve, pickle. **—er** nm — depositor.

einleit/en (ˈainlaitən) vt 1 introduce. 2 begin. **—ung** nf -en introduction.

einlösen (ˈainløːzən) vt comm redeem.

einmachen (ˈainmaxən) vt preserve, pickle (food).

einmal (ˈainmaːl) adv 1 once, one time. 2 formerly, sometime. **noch einmal** once again. **—eins** n neu multiplication table. **—ig** adj unique.

Einmarsch (ˈainmarʃ) nm -e marching in, entry. **—ieren** (ainmarˈʃiːrən) vi march in.

sich einmischen (ˈainmiʃən) vr interfere.

einmünden (ˈainmyndən) vi 1 flow into. 2 join, run into.

Ein/nahme (ˈainnaːmə) nf -n 1 income. 2 takings. **—nehmen*** (ˈainneːmən) vt 1 take in (food etc.). 2 receive. 3 influence.

Einöde (ˈainøːdə) nf -n 1 desert. 2 isolated place.

einordnen (ˈainɔrdnən) vt 1 arrange, order. 2 file. 3 mot get in lane.

einpacken (ˈainpakən) vt pack or wrap up. vi pack or give up.

einprägen (ˈainprɛːgən) vt impress, imprint.

einrahmen (ˈainraːmən) vt frame.

einräumen (ˈainrɔymən) vt 1 give up, vacate. 2 clear away. 3 concede, admit.

einreden (ˈainreːdən) vt persuade. vi interrupt.

einreichen (ˈainraiçən) vt hand in, submit.

einreihen (ˈainraiən) vt 1 arrange, order. 2 insert. 3 enrol.

Einreise (ˈainraizə) nf -n entry (into a country). **—n** vi enter (a country).

einricht/en (ˈainriçtən) vt 1 arrange. 2 establish, set up. 3 fit out, furnish. **—ung** nf -en 1 arrangement. 2 institution. 3 furnishing, fittings.

einrücken (ˈainrykən) vi enter. vt insert.

eins (ains) 1 one. 2 ace. pron see **ein.**

einsam (ˈainzaːm) adj lonely. **—keit** nf loneliness, solitude.

Einsatz (ˈainzats) nm 1 insertion, putting in. 2 stake, deposit. 3 employment, engagement.

einschalten (ˈainʃaltən) vt 1 insert. 2 switch on. 3 tune in.

einschiffen (ˈainʃifən) vt load onto a ship.

einschlafen* (ˈainʃlaːfən) vi fall asleep.

Einschlag (ˈainʃlaːk) nm 1 impact. 2 jacket (of a book). 3 touch, hint. 4 woof, weft. **—en*** (ˈainʃlaːgən) vt 1 drive in. 2 strike. 3 wrap. vi shake hands (on a deal).

einschließ/en* (ˈainʃliːsən) vt 1 lock up or in, confine. 2 include. **—lich** adj inclusive of.

einschränk/en (ˈainʃrɛŋkən) vt 1 restrict, confine. 2 curb. **—ung** nf -en 1 restriction. 2 reduction.

Einschreib/ebrief (ˈainʃraibəbriːf) nm registered letter. **—en*** vt 1 write in. 2 take down. 3 register. **—ung** nf -en registration.

einschüchtern (ˈainʃyçtərn) vt intimidate.

einsehen* (ˈainzeːən) vt 1 understand. 2 look into.

einseitig (ˈainzaitiç) adj one-sided. **—keit** nf bias, one-sidedness.

einsetz/en (ˈainzɛtsən) vt 1 set or put in. 2 insert. 3 institute. 4 employ. vi begin. **—ung** nf -en 1 putting in. 2 institution. 3 appointment.

Einsicht (ˈainziçt) nf -en 1 insight, understanding. 2 judgment. 3 inspection.

Einsiedler (ˈainziːdlər) nm — hermit, recluse.

einspannen (ˈainʃpanən) vt 1 harness. 2 stretch. 3 clamp.

einsperren (ˈainʃpɛrən) vt lock up, imprison.

einspritzen (ˈainʃpritsən) vt inject.

Einspruch (ˈainʃprux) nm objection, protest. **—srecht** n neu veto.

einst (ainst) adv 1 once. 2 some day.

einsteigen* (ˈainʃtaigən) vi get or climb in.

einstell/en (ˈainʃtɛlən) vt 1 put in. 2 stop, cease, shut down. 3 employ. 4 strike. 5 adjust, tune in. **—ung** nf -en 1 attitude. 2 adjustment. 3 stoppage, suspension. 4 appointment, taking on.

einstig (ˈainstiç) adj former.

einstimm/en (ˈainʃtiman) vi 1 agree. 2 join in. **—ig** adj unanimous, in unison. **—igkeit** nf unanimity, unison.

einstmalig (ˈainstmaːliç) adj former.

einstoßen* ('ainʃto:sən) vt 1 push in. 2 knock down.

einströmen ('ainʃtrœ:mən) vi stream or flock in, pour in.

einstufen ('ainʃtu:fən) vt grade, classify.

einstürmen ('ainʃtyrmən) vi 1 rush in. 2 assault.

Einsturz ('ainʃturts) · nm 1 collapse. 2 fall. **—en** ('ainʃtyrtsən) vi fall in. vt demolish.

einstweilen ('ainʃtvailən) adv 1 meanwhile. 2 for now. **—ig** adj temporary.

eintägig ('aintɛ:giç) adj one-day.

Eintausch ('aintauʃ) nm -e exchange. **—en** vt barter, exchange.

Einteilung ('aintailuŋ) nf -en 1 division. 2 classification.

eintönig ('aintœ:niç) adj monotonous. **—keit** nf monotony.

Eintopf ('aintɔpf) nm stew, casserole.

Eintracht ('aintraxt) nf harmony, unity.

Eintrag ('aintra:k) nm -e 1 comm registration; entry. 2 damage, detriment. **—en*** ('aintra:gən) vt 1 bring in, yield. 2 register, enter.

eintreten* ('aintre:tən) vi 1 step or come in. 2 happen. 3 intercede. vt kick in.

Eintritt ('aintrit) nm 1 entry. 2 beginning. **—skarte** nf admission ticket.

einüben ('ainy:bən) vt 1 practise. 2 train.

einverleiben ('ainfɛrlaibən) vt 1 incorporate. 2 annex.

einverstanden ('ainfɛrʃtandən) adj 1 agreed. 2 agreeable.

Einwand ('ainvant) nm -e 1 objection. 2 pretext. **—frei** adj faultless.

Einwander/er ('ainvandərər) nm — immigrant. **—n** vi immigrate. **—ung** nf -en immigration.

einwärts ('ainvɛrts) adv inward(s).

einwechseln ('ainvɛksəln) vt (ex)change.

einweichen* ('ainvaiçən) vt soak, steep.

einweih/en ('ainvaiən) vt 1 inaugurate. 2 consecrate. 3 initiate. **—ung** nf -en 1 inauguration. 2 consecration. 3 initiation.

Einwendung ('ainvɛnduŋ) nf -en objection.

einwickel/n ('ainvikəln) vt 1 wrap (up). 2 entangle, implicate (someone). **—papier** n neu wrapping paper.

einwillig/en ('ainviligən) vi agree, consent. **—ung** nf -en consent.

Einwirkung ('ainvirkuŋ) nf -en 1 influence. 2 effect.

Einwohner ('ainvo:nər) nm — inhabitant.

Einzahl ('aintsa:l) nf gram singular. **—en** vt pay in. **—ung** nf -en 1 payment. 2 deposit.

Einzel/fall ('aintsəlfal) nm individual case. **—gänger** nm — outsider, loner. **—heit** nf **-en** detail, item. **—person** nf individual.

einziehen* ('aintsi:ən) vt 1 draw in. 2 collect. 3 call up. 4 seize. vi 1 march in. 2 enter.

einzig ('aintsiç) adj single, sole, unique. **—artig** adj unique, singular.

Einzug ('aintsu:k) nm entry.

Eis- (ais) n neu -e 1 ice. 2 ice cream. **—bahn** nf skating rink. **—bär** nm polar bear. **—bein** n neu knuckle of pork. **—berg** nm iceberg. **—ig** adj icy. **—kalt** adj ice-cold. **—schrank** nm refrigerator. **—zapfen** nm icicle. **—zeit** nf ice age.

Eisen ('aizən) n neu iron. **—bahn** nf 1 railway. 2 train. **—bahnwagen** nm railway carriage. **—beton** nm reinforced concrete. **—warenhändler** nm ironmonger.

eisern ('aizərn) adj 1 iron. 2 hard, inflexible. **Eiserner Vorhang** nm Iron Curtain.

eitel ('aitəl) adj 1 vain, conceited. 2 frivolous. 3 idle. **—keit** nf vanity.

Eiter ('aitər) nm pus. **—n** vi suppurate.

Eiweiß ('aivais) n neu -e egg white, albumen.

Ekel ('e:kəl) nm aversion, disgust. **—haft** adj loathsome, repulsive. **sich —n** vr feel disgust or loathing.

elastisch (e'la:stiʃ) adj elastic.

Elefant (ele'fant) nm -en elephant.

elegant (ele'gant) adj elegant.

elektr/ifizieren (elɛktrifi'tsi:rən) vt electrify (railway). **—iker** (e'lɛktrikər) nm — electrician. **—isch** (e'lɛktriʃ) adj electric(al). **—isieren** (elɛktri'zi:rən) vt electrify. **—izität** (elɛktritsi'tɛ:t) nf electricity. **—ode** (elɛk'tro:də) nf -n electrode. **—on** (e'lɛktron) n neu **-en** electron.

Element (ele'mɛnt) n neu -e 1 element. 2 battery, cell. **—ar** (elemɛn'ta:r) adj elementary, elemental.

elend ('e:lɛnt) adj miserable. n neu 1 misery. 2 poverty. **—sviertel** n neu slum(s).

elf (ɛlf) adj,nf eleven. **—te** adj eleventh.

Elf (ɛlf) nm -en also **Elfe** nf -n elf, fairy.

Elfenbein ('ɛlfənbain) n neu ivory.

Elite (e'li:tə) nf -n elite.

Ellbogen ('ɛlbo:gən) nm — elbow.

Ellipse (ɛ'lipsə) nf -n ellipse.

Ei/saß ('ɛlzas) n neu Alsace. **—sässisch** adj Alsatian. **—sässer** nm — Alsatian.

Elster ('ɛlstər) nf -n magpie.

elter/lich ('ɛltərliç) adj parental. **—n** n pl parents.

36

Email (e'ma:j) n neu -s enamel.
Emigr/ant (emi'grant) nm -en 1 emigrant. 2
   refugee. **—ieren** (emi'gri:rən) vi emigrate.
empfahl (ɛm'pfa:l) v see **empfehlen**.
Empfang (ɛm'pfaŋ) nm -e reception, welcome.
   in Empfang nehmen receive. **—en*** vt
   receive. vi conceive. **—er** (ɛm'pfɛŋər) nm —
   receiver. **—lich** (ɛm'pfɛŋliç) adj susceptible,
   impressionable.
empfehl/en* (ɛm'pfe:lən) vt recommend. **sich**
   empfehlen vr take one's leave. **—ung** nf -en
   recommendation.
empfind/en* (ɛm'pfindən) vt feel, sense.
   —lich (ɛm'pfintliç) adj 1 sensitive. 2 grievous,
   severe. **—lichkeit** nf sensitivity, touchiness.
   —ung nf -en 1 perception. 2 feeling. 3
   sentiment.
empfohlen (ɛm'pfo:lən) v see **empfehlen**. adj
   recommended.
empor (ɛm'po:r) adv up(wards). **—en** (ɛm-
   'pœ:rən) vt 1 rouse. 2 shock. **sich —en** vr
   revolt. **—end** (ɛm'pœ:rənt) adj revolting.
   —kommen* vi rise. **—kömmling** (ɛm'po:r-
   kœmliŋ) nm -e upstart. **—ung** (ɛm'pœ:ruŋ)
   nf -en 1 indignation. 2 rebellion.
emsig ('ɛmziç) adj busy, industrious.
End/e ('ɛndə) n neu -n end. **am Ende** in the
   end. **zu dem Ende** to that purpose. **zu Ende**
   over. **—en** vi,vt also **—igen** end, stop,
   finish. **—gültig** ('ɛntgy:ltiç) adj final, defini-
   tive. **—lich** ('ɛntliç) adj 1 final. 2 finite. adv
   at last. **—los** ('ɛntlo:s) adj endless. **—punkt**
   ('ɛntpuŋkt) nm end point, extremity. **—spiel**
   ('ɛntʃpi:l) n neu sport final. **—station**
   ('ɛntstatsio:n) nf -en terminus. **—ung** nf -en
   ending.
Energi/e (enɛr'gi:) nf -n energy. **—sch**
   (e'nɛrgiʃ) adj energetic.
eng (ɛŋ) adj 1 narrow. 2 tight. 3 close. **—e** nf
   -n 1 narrowness. 2 defile, straits. **—herzig**
   adj petty. **—paß** nm 1 narrow pass. 2
   bottle-neck. **—stirnig** adj narrow-minded.
Engel ('ɛŋəl) nm — angel. **—gleich** adj also
   —haft angelic.
Eng/land ('ɛŋlant) n neu England. **—länder**
   ('ɛŋlɛndər) nm — Englishman. **—länderin** nf
   -nen Englishwoman. **—lisch** adj, n neu
   English (language).
en gros (ã'gro:) adv wholesale.
Enkel ('ɛŋkəl) nm — grandson, grandchild.
   —in nf -nen granddaughter. **—kind** n neu
   grandchild.
enorm (e'nɔrm) adj enormous.

entart/en (ɛnt'artən) vi degenerate. **—ung** nf
   degeneration, degeneracy.
entbehrlich (ɛnt'be:rliç) adj superfluous.
entbinden* (ɛnt'bindən) vt 1 untie, release. 2
   med deliver.
entblößen (ɛnt'blœ:sən) vt 1 uncover, bare. 2
   denude, deprive.
entdeck/en (ɛnt'dɛkən) vt discover, disclose,
   invent. **—er** nm — discoverer, explorer.
   —ung nf -en 1 discovery. 2 disclosure. 3
   invention.
Ente ('ɛntə) nf -n 1 duck. 2 hoax.
entehren (ɛnt'e:rən) vt dishonour.
enteign/en (ɛnt'aignən) vt expropriate. **—ung**
   nf -en expropriation.
enterben (ɛnt'ɛrbən) vt disinherit.
entfallen* (ɛnt'falən) vi 1 escape the memory
   of. 2 fall out of. **entfällt** not applicable.
entfalt/en (ɛnt'faltən) vt 1 unfold. 2 exhibit,
   display. **—ung** nf -en 1 unfolding. 2 display.
entfern/en (ɛnt'fɛrnən) vt remove. **sich ent-**
   fernen vr go away, withdraw. **—t** adj
   distant. **—ung** nf -en 1 distance. 2 removal,
   departure.
entfliehen* (ɛnt'fli:ən) vi escape, flee.
entfremd/en (ɛnt'frɛmdən) vt alienate, antagonize. **—ung** nf alienation.
entführ/en (ɛnt'fy:rən) vt carry off, abduct,
   kidnap. **—ung** nf -en abduction, kidnapping.
entgegen (ɛnt'ge:gən) prep,adv 1 contrary (to),
   against. 2 towards. **—gehen*** vi go to meet.
   —gesetzt adj opposite, opposed. **—halten***
   vt 1 hold out (towards). 2 point out. 3
   contrast. **—kommen*** vi (come to) meet. n
   neu 1 cooperation. 2 kindness. **—laufen*** vi 1
   run to meet. 2 oppose. **—setzen** vt oppose.
   —stellen vt set against, contrast.
entgeg/nen (ɛnt'ge:gnən) vi answer. **—nung**
   nf -en answer.
entgehen* (ɛnt'ge:ən) vi 1 escape. 2 avoid.
Entgelt (ɛnt'gɛlt) n neu 1 compensation. 2
   remuneration. **—en*** vt 1 pay for. 2 compensate.
entgleisen (ɛnt'glaizən) vi run off the rails.
entgräten (ɛnt'grɛ:tən) vt bone (fish).
enthaaren (ɛnt'ha:rən) vt remove hair from,
   depilate.
enthalt/en* (ɛnt'haltən) vt contain, include.
   sich enthalten vr abstain. **—sam** adj ab-
   stemious. **—samkeit** nf moderation, abste-
   miousness.
enthaupten (ɛnt'haupten) vt behead.
enthüllen (ɛnt'hylən) vt reveal, disclose, unveil.

Enthusiasmus (ɛntuzi'asmus) *nm* enthusiasm.

entkernen (ɛnt'kɛrnən) *vt* stone (fruit, etc.).

entkommen* (ɛnt'kɔmən) *vi* escape.

entkuppeln (ɛnt'kupəln) *vt* 1 disconnect. 2 declutch.

entladen* (ɛnt'la:dən) *vt* 1 unload. 2 (of guns) fire. **sich entladen** *vr* get rid (of).

entlang (ɛnt'laŋ) *adv,prep* along.

entlarven (ɛnt'larfən) *vt* unmask.

entlass/en* (ɛnt'lasən) *vt* dismiss. **—ung** *nf* **-en** dismissal.

entlast/en (ɛnt'lastən) *vt* 1 unload. 2 relieve. 3 clear, exonerate. **—ung** *nf* 1 relief. 2 exoneration. **—sstraße** *nf* bypass.

sich entledigen (ɛnt'le:digən) *vr* rid oneself of.

entlegen (ɛnt'le:gən) *adj* remote, distant.

entmilitarisieren (ɛntmilitari'zi:rən) *vt* demilitarize.

entmutig/en (ɛnt'mu:tigən) *vt* discourage. **—ung** *nf* discouragement.

entnehmen* (ɛnt'ne:mən) *vt* 1 take out or away, remove. 2 infer. 3 learn.

entrahmen (ɛn'tra:mən) *vt* skim.

entrüst/en (ɛnt'rystən) *vt* anger, provoke. **sich entrüsten** *vr* grow angry. **—et** *adj* indignant, angry. **—ung** *nf* indignation, anger.

entsagen (ɛnt'za:gən) *vi* give up, renounce.

entschädig/en (ɛnt'ʃɛ:digən) *vt* 1 compensate. 2 indemnify. **—ung** *nf* **-en** 1 compensation. 2 indemnity.

Entscheid (ɛnt'ʃait) *nm* **-en** also **Entscheid/ung** (ɛnt'ʃaiduŋ) *nf* **-en** decision, verdict. **—en*** *vt,vi* decide, resolve. **sich —en** *vr* make up one's mind, decide (on). **—end** *adj* decisive.

entschieden (ɛnt'ʃi:dən) *adj* 1 decided. 2 determined. **—heit** *nf* determination.

sich entschließ/en* (ɛnt'ʃli:sən) *vr* decide. **—ung** *nf* **-en** resolution.

entschlossen (ɛnt'ʃlɔsən) *adj* determined. **—heit** *nf* resoluteness, determination.

Entschluß (ɛnt'ʃlus) *nm* **-schlüsse** decision.

entschlüsseln (ɛnt'ʃlysəln) *vt* decode, decipher.

entschuldig/en (ɛnt'ʃuldigən) *vt* 1 pardon. 2 justify. **sich entschuldigen** *vr* apologize. **—ung** *nf* **-en** excuse, apology. **Entschuldigung!** sorry! excuse me!

entsetz/en (ɛnt'zɛtsən) *vt* 1 frighten. 2 relieve. *n neu* terror. **—lich** *adj* terrible, dreadful.

entspann/en (ɛnt'ʃpanən) *vt* 1 release. 2 relax. **sich entspannen** *vr* relax, rest. **—ung** *nf* 1 relaxation. 2 recreation. 3 détente.

entsprechen* (ɛnt'ʃprɛçən) *vi* correspond (to), answer (to).

entspringen* (ɛnt'ʃpriŋən) *vi* 1 rise or spring from. 2 escape.

entstammen (ɛnt'ʃtamən) *vi* descend (from), spring (from).

entsteh/en* (ɛnt'ʃte:ən) *vi* arise. **—ung** *nf* **-en** origin.

enttäusch/en (ɛnt'tɔyʃən) *vt* disappoint, disillusion. **—ung** *nf* **-en** disappointment.

entvölkern (ɛnt'fœlkərn) *vt* depopulate.

entwaffnen (ɛnt'vafnən) *vt* disarm.

entwässer/n (ɛnt'vɛsərn) *vt* 1 drain. 2 dehydrate. **—ung** *nf* 1 drainage. 2 dehydration.

entweder (ɛnt've:dər) *conj* **entweder...oder** either...or.

entweichen* (ɛnt'vaiçən) *vi* 1 flee. 2 escape.

entweihen (ɛnt'vaiən) *vt* desecrate.

entwerf/en* (ɛnt'vɛrfən) *vt* 1 design, plan. 2 sketch, draw up. **—er** *nm* — designer, planner.

entwert/en (ɛnt'vɛrtən) *vt* 1 devalue. 2 cancel (postage stamps, etc.). **—ung** *nf* **-en** 1 devaluation. 2 cancellation.

entwick/eln (ɛnt'vikəln) *vt* 1 develop. 2 explain. 3 unfold. **—ler** *nm* — developer. **—lung** *nf* **-en** 1 development. 2 exposition. **—lungsländer** *n neu pl* developing countries.

entwirren (ɛnt'virən) *vt* unravel.

entwischen (ɛnt'viʃən) *vi* escape, slip away.

entwürdigen (ɛnt'wyrdigən) *vt* degrade.

Entwurf (ɛnt'vurf) *nm* **-̈e** plan, draft, outline.

entwurzeln (ɛnt'vurtsəln) *vt* uproot.

entzieh/en* (ɛnt'tsi:ən) *vt* 1 withdraw, take away. **sich entziehen** *vr* evade, shun.

entziffern (ɛnt'tsifərn) *vt* decipher.

entzück/en (ɛnt'tsykən) *vt* charm, delight. *n neu* — delight. **—end** *adj* charming, delightful.

entzünd/bar (ɛnt'tsyntba:r) *adj* inflammable. **—en** (ɛnt'tsyndən) *vt* 1 inflame. 2 ignite. **—ung** (ɛnt'tsynduŋ) *nf* **-en** 1 inflammation. 2 ignition.

entzwei (ɛnt'tsvai) *adj* in two, broken.

Enzyklopäd/ie (ɛntsyklopɛ'di:) *nf* **-n** encyclopedia. **-isch** (ɛntsyklo'pe:diʃ) *adj* encyclopedic.

Enzym (ɛn'tsym) *n neu* **-e** enzyme.

Epidem/ie (epide'mi:) *nf* **-n** epidemic. **—isch** (epi'de:miʃ) *adj* epidemic.

Epik ('e:pik) *nf* epic poetry.

Epilepsie (epilɛp'si:) *nf* epilepsy.

Episode (epi'zo:də) *nf* **-n** episode.

Epos ('e:pɔs) n neu **Epen** epic.
er (e:r, er) pron 3rd pers s he.
erachten (ɛr'axtən) vt think, deem. n neu — opinion. **meines Erachtens** in my opinion.
Erbarm/en (ɛr'barmən) n neu pity, mercy. **sich erbarmen** vr have pity. **—lich** (ɛr'bɛrmliç) adj pitiful. **—ungslos** adj merciless.
erbauen (ɛr'bauən) vt construct, build.
Erb/e ('ɛrbə) n neu **-n** inheritance. nm **-n** heir. **—en** ('ɛrbən) vt inherit. **—feind** ('ɛrpfaint) nm traditional enemy, sworn enemy. **—folge** ('ɛrpfɔlgə) nf hereditary succession. **—in** ('ɛrbin) nf **-nen** heiress. **—sünde** nf original sin. **—lich** ('ɛrpliç) adj hereditary. **—schaft** ('ɛrpʃaft) nf **-en** inheritance. **—stück** ('ɛrpʃtyk) n neu heirloom.
erbittern (ɛr'bitərn) vt embitter.
erblassen (ɛr'blasən) vi also **erbleichen*** 1 grow pale. 2 die.
erblinden (ɛr'blindən) vi grow or go blind.
Erbse ('ɛrpsə) nf **-n** pea.
Erd/beben ('e:rtbe:bən) n neu — earthquake. **—beere** nf strawberry. **—boden** nm soil, ground. **-e** ('e:rdə) nf **-n** 1 earth, world. 2 ground. 3 soil. **auf der Erde** on earth. **zu ebener Erde** at ground level. **—en** ('e:rdən) vt sci, tech earth. **—geschoß** n neu ground floor. **—kreis** nm globe. **—kunde** nf geography. **—nuß** nf peanut. **—öl** n neu petroleum. **—teil** nm continent.
erdenk/en* (ɛr'dɛŋkən) vt 1 invent, think up. 2 imagine. **—lich** adj conceivable.
Erdichtung (ɛr'diçtuŋ) nf **-en** figment, fiction.
erdrosseln (ɛr'drɔsəln) vt strangle, throttle.
sich ereign/en (ɛr'aignən) vr happen. **—is** n neu **-se** event.
erfahr/en* (ɛr'fa:rən) vt 1 experience. 2 learn. adj experienced. **—ung** nf **-en** experience.
erfassen (ɛr'fasən) vt 1 grasp. 2 include. 3 understand.
erfind/en* (ɛr'findən) vt 1 invent. 2 find out. **—er** nm — inventor. **—erisch** adj inventive. **—ung** nf **-en** invention, discovery.
Erfolg (ɛr'fɔlk) nm **-e** 1 success. 2 result. **—en** (ɛr'fɔlgən) vi follow, ensue. **—los** adj unsuccessful. **—reich** adj successful.
erforder/lich (ɛr'fɔrdərliç) adj necessary, required. **—n** vt call for, necessitate, require. **—nis** n neu **-se** requisite, requirement.
erforsch/en (ɛr'fɔrʃən) vt 1 investigate.. 2 explore. **—er** nm — investigator. 2 explorer. **—ung** nf **-en** 1 investigation. 2 exploration.

erfreu/en (ɛr'frɔyən) vt delight. **sich erfreuen** vr 1 enjoy. 2 be pleased. **—lich** adj delightful, pleasing.
erfrieren (ɛr'fri:rən) vi freeze to death.
erfrisch/en (ɛr'friʃən) vt refresh. **—ung** nf **-en** refreshment. **—ungsraum** nm snack bar.
erfüllen (ɛr'fylən) vt 1 fill (up). 2 fulfil.
ergänz/en (ɛr'gɛntsən) vt 1 complete. 2 supplement. 3 replenish. **—ung** nf **-en** completion.
ergeb/en* (ɛr'ge:bən) vt 1 yield, produce. 2 show, prove. **sich ergeben** vr surrender, yield. **sich ergeben aus** follow from. adj 1 devoted. 2 addicted. **—enheit** nf **-en** 1 devotion. 2 submission. 3 resignation. **—nis** (ɛr'ge:pnis) n neu **-se** result. **—nislos** adj without result, vain. **—ung** nf **-en** 1 surrender. 2 resignation.
ergehen* (ɛr'ge:ən) vi be published or issued. **sich ergehen** vr 1 (take a) walk. 2 indulge.
ergiebig (ɛr'gi:biç) adj productive, fertile.
ergreifen* (ɛr'graifən) vt 1 seize. 2 take up.
erhaben (ɛr'ha:bən) adj 1 raised. 2 sublime. 3 noble.
erhalt/en* (ɛr'haltən) vt 1 receive. 2 maintain, support. **—ung** nf 1 maintenance. 2 preservation.
erheb/en* (ɛr'he:bən) vt 1 raise (up). 2 demand. 3 levy. 4 praise. **sich erheben** vr 1 rise up. 2 rebel. **—lich** (ɛr'he:pliç) adj considerable.
erheitern (ɛr'haitərn) vt cheer (up).
erhöh/en (ɛr'hœ:ən) vt raise, increase. **—ung** nf **-en** 1 rise, increase. 2 elevation.
sich erhol/en (ɛr'ho:lən) vr 1 recover. 2 recuperate. **—ung** nf **-en** 1 recovery. 2 recreation.
erinner/n (ɛr'inərn) vt remind. **sich erinnern** vr remember. **—ung** nf **-en** 1 memory. 2 reminder.
erkält/en (ɛr'kɛltən) vt cool, chill. **sich erkälten** vr catch cold. **—ung** nf **-en** cold.
erkämpfen (ɛr'kɛmpfən) vt win or gain by fighting.
erkenn/bar (ɛr'kɛnba:r) adj recognizable. **—en*** vt 1 recognize. 2 perceive. 3 realize. **—ung** nf **-en** recognition. **—ungswort** n neu password.
Erkenntnis[1] (ɛr'kɛntnis) n neu **-se** judgment.
Erkenntnis[2] (ɛr'kɛntnis) nf **-se** recognition, realization.
erklär/en (ɛr'klɛ:rən) vt 1 explain. 2 declare. **—ung** nf **-en** 1 explanation. 2 declaration.

erkrank/en (ɛr'kraŋkən) *vi* fall ill. **—ung** *nf* **-en** illness.

sich erkund/igen (ɛr'kundigən) *vr* inquire. **—igung** *nf* **-en** enquiry.

erlahmen (ɛr'lɑːmən) *vi* become tired or lame.

erlangen (ɛr'laŋən) *vt* attain, obtain.

Erlaß (ɛr'las) *nm* **-lasse** 1 decree, ordinance. 2 remission. **erlassen*** (ɛr'lasən) *vt* 1 proclaim. 2 issue. 3 remit, pardon.

erlaub/en (ɛr'laubən) *vt* permit, allow. **—nis** (ɛr'laupnis) *nf* **-se** permission.

erläutern (ɛr'lɔytərn) *vt* explain, illustrate.

erleb/en (ɛr'leːbən) *vt* experience, live to see. **—nis** (ɛr'leːpnis) *n neu* **-se** 1 experience. 2 adventure.

erledig/en (ɛr'leːdigən) *vt* 1 settle. 2 finish (off). 3 deal with. **—ung** *nf* **-en** 1 completion. 2 execution.

erlegen (ɛr'leːgən) *vt* kill, shoot.

erleichter/n (ɛr'laiçtərn) *vt* lighten, relieve, ease. **—ung** *nf* relief.

erlernen (ɛr'lɛrnən) *vt* learn.

erleucht/en (ɛr'lɔyçtən) *vt* 1 illuminate. 2 enlighten. **—ung** *nf* **-en** 1 illumination. 2 enlightenment.

erliegen* (ɛr'liːgən) *vi* be defeated, succumb.

Erlös (ɛr'løːs) *nm* **-e** proceeds. **-en** (ɛr'løːzən) *vt* 1 release. 2 save. **—er** (ɛr'løːzər) *nm* — 1 liberator, deliverer. 2 saviour. **—ung** (ɛr'løːzuŋ) *nf* 1 deliverance. 2 salvation.

ermächtig/en (ɛr'mɛçtigən) *vt* empower. **—ung** *nf* **-en** authorization.

ermäßig/en (ɛr'mɛːsigən) *vt* reduce, moderate. **—ung** *nf* **-en** reduction, moderation.

ermitteln (ɛr'mitəln) *vt* find out, ascertain.

ermöglichen (ɛr'møːgliçən) *vt* render possible, enable.

ermorden (ɛr'mɔrdən) *vt* murder, assassinate.

ermüden (ɛr'myːdən) *vi,vt* tire.

ermuntern (ɛr'muntərn) *vt* rouse, cheer (up).

ermutig/en (ɛr'muːtigən) *vt* encourage, hearten. **—ung** *nf* **-en** encouragement.

ernähr/en (ɛr'nɛːrən) *vt* 1 feed. 2 maintain, support. **—er** *nm* — breadwinner. **—ung** *nf* 1 nourishment. 2 nutrition. 3 maintenance.

ernenn/en* (ɛr'nɛnən) *vt* 1 appoint. 2 nominate. **—ung** *nf* **-en** 1 appointment. 2 nomination.

erneuer/n (ɛr'nɔyərn) *vt* 1 renew. 2 restore. **—ung** *nf* **-en** 1 renewal. 2 restoration.

erniedrigen (ɛr'niːdrigən) *vt* 1 lower. 2 degrade, humiliate.

ernst (ɛrnst) *adj* serious, earnest. *nm* 1 serious-

ness. 2 severity. **—haft** *adj* earnest. **—lich** *adj* serious, earnest.

Ernte ('ɛrntə) *nf* **-n** harvest, crop. **—dankfest** *n neu* harvest festival. **—n** *vt,vi* harvest, gather in.

ernüchtern (ɛr'nyçtərn) *vt* 1 sober (up). 2 disillusion.

Erober/er (ɛr'oːbərər) *nm* — conqueror. **—n** *vt* conquer. **—ung** *nf* **-en** conquest.

eröffn/en (ɛr'œfnən) *vt* 1 open. 2 inaugurate, begin. **—ung** *nf* **-en** 1 opening. 2 inauguration, beginning.

erörter/n (ɛr'œrtərn) *vt* discuss. **—ung** *nf* **-en** discussion.

Eroti/k (e'roːtik) *nf* eroticism. **—sch** *adj* erotic.

erpress/en (ɛr'prɛsən) *vt* blackmail. **—er** *nm* — blackmailer. **—ung** *nf* **-en** blackmail.

erproben (ɛr'proːbən) *vt* try, test.

erraten* (ɛr'rɑːtən) *vt* 1 guess. 2 solve.

erreg/bar (ɛr'reːkbaːr) *adj* excitable. **—en** (ɛr'reːgən) *vt* 1 excite. 2 irritate. **—ung** (ɛr'reːguŋ) *nf* **-en** excitement.

erreich/bar (ɛr'raiçbaːr) *adj* attainable. **—en** *vt* reach, attain.

errricht/en (ɛr'riçtən) *vt* 1 erect. 2 establish. **—ung** *nf* **-en** 1 erection. 2 establishment.

erröten (ɛr'rœːtən) *vi* blush.

Errungenschaft (ɛr'ruŋənʃaft) *nf* **-en** 1 acquisition. 2 achievement.

Ersatz (ɛr'zats) *nm* 1 substitute, replacement. 2 reserve. 3 compensation. **—reifen** *nm* spare tyre. **—teil** *n neu* spare (part).

erschaff/en* (ɛr'ʃafən) *vt* create.

erschein/en* (ɛr'ʃainən) *vi* appear. **—ung** *nf* **-en** 1 appearance 2 vision, 3 phenomenon.

erschlagen* (ɛr'ʃlaːgən) *vt* kill.

erschließen* (ɛr'ʃliːsən) *vt* 1 open (up). 2 infer.

erschöpf/en (ɛr'ʃœpfən) *vt* exhaust. **—ung** *nf* exhaustion.

erschrak (ɛr'ʃraːk) *v see* **erschrecken.**

erschrecken* (ɛr'ʃrɛkən) *vt* frighten. *vi* be frightened.

erschrocken (ɛr'ʃrɔkən) *v see* **erschrecken.** *adj* frightened.

erschüttern (ɛr'ʃytərn) *vt* shake, upset.

ersehen* (ɛr'zeːən) *vt* 1 see, perceive. 2 observe.

ersetzen (ɛr'zɛtsən) *vt* replace, make good.

ersichtlich (ɛr'ziçtliç) *adj* evident.

erspar/en (ɛr'ʃpaːrən) *vt* spare, save. **—nis** *nf* **-se** 1 saving. 2 savings.

erst (ɛrst) *adj* first. *adv* 1 at first. 2 only, not

till. **der erste beste** the first that comes, anyone or anything. **erste Hilfe** first aid.

erstarren (ɛr'ʃtarən) vi grow stiff or rigid.

erstatten (ɛr'ʃtatən) vt 1 compensate, repay. 2 return. 3 give.

Erstaufführung ('ɛrstauffy:ruŋ) nf -**en** premiere, first night.

erstaun/en (ɛr'ʃtaunən) vt astonish. vi be astonished. n neu amazement. —**lich** adj astonishing.

erstens ('ɛ:rstəns) adv first(ly).

ersticken (ɛr'ʃtikən) vt,vi suffocate, choke.

erstklassig ('e:rstklasiç) adj first-class, prime.

ersuchen (ɛr'zu:xən) vt request.

ertappen (ɛr'tapən) vt 1 surprise. 2 catch. **auf frischer Tat ertappt** caught red-handed.

Ertrag (ɛr'tra:k) nm -**e** yield, return, profit. —**en** (ɛr'tra:gən) vt bear, endure. —**lich** (ɛr'tre:kliç) adj bearable, tolerable.

ertränken (ɛr'trɛŋkən) vt drown.

ertrinken (ɛr'triŋkən) vi drown.

erwachen (ɛr'vaxən) vi awake.

erwachsen (ɛr'vaksən) vi 1 grow up. 2 arise (from). adj adult. —**e(r)** nm adult.

erwäg/en (ɛr'vɛ:gən) vt 1 consider. 2 weigh. —**ung** nf —**en** consideration.

erwähnen (ɛr'vɛ:nən) vt mention.

erwärmen (ɛr'vɛrmən) vt warm.

erwart/en (ɛr'vartən) vt 1 await. 2 expect. —**ung** nf -**en** expectation.

erwecken (ɛr'vɛkən) vt awaken, (a)rouse.

erweisen (ɛr'vaizən) vt 1 render. 2 prove.

erweiter/n (ɛr'vaitərn) vt enlarge. —**ung** nf -**en** extension.

Erwerb (ɛr'vɛrp) nm -**e** 1 acquisition. 2 gain, profit. 3 livelihood. —**en** (ɛr'vɛrbən) vt 1 acquire. 2 earn. —**stätig** adj (gainfully) employed.

erwider/n (ɛr'vi:dərn) vt respond (to), reply (to). —**ung** nf -**en** reply, response.

erwischen (ɛr'viʃən) vt 1 catch. 2 surprise.

erwünscht (ɛr'vynʃt) adj desired.

erwürgen (ɛr'vyrgən) vt strangle.

Erz (e:rts) n neu -**e** ore.

erzähl/en (ɛr'tsɛ:lən) vt tell, report, relate. —**er** nm —1 narrator, story-teller. 2 reporter. —**ung** nf -**en** 1 narrative, story. 2 report.

Erz/bischof ('ɛrtsbiʃɔf) nm archbishop. —**engel** nm archangel. —**feind** nm archenemy.

erzeug/en (ɛr'tsɔygən) vt 1 beget, breed. 2 produce, manufacture. —**nis** (ɛr'tsɔyknis) n

neu -**se** 1 product. 2 produce. —**ung** nf 1 procreation. 2 production.

erzieh/en (ɛr'tsi:ən) vt 1 bring up. 2 educate. —**ung** nf education.

erzwingen (ɛr'tsviŋən) vt obtain by force.

es (ɛs) pron neu s it.

Esche ('ɛʃə) nf -**n** ash (tree).

Esel ('e:zəl) nm — ass, donkey.

esoterisch (ezo'te:riʃ) adj esoteric.

essen ('ɛsən) vt,vi eat. n neu — 1 food. 2 meal.

eß/bar ('ɛsbar) adj edible. —**löffel** nm tablespoon. —**tisch** nm dining table. —**zimmer** n neu dining room.

Essenz (ɛ'sɛnts) nf -**en** essence.

Essig ('ɛsiç) nm -**e** vinegar.

etablieren (eta'bli:rən) vt establish.

Etage (e'ta:ʒə) nf -**n** floor, storey.

Etat (e'ta:) nm -**s** 1 budget. 2 balance-sheet.

Eth/ik ('e:tik) nf ethics. —**isch** adj ethical.

ethnisch ('e:tniʃ) adj ethnic.

Etikett (eti'kɛt) n neu -**e** (price) label, tag.

Etikette (eti'kɛtə) nf -**n** etiquette.

etliche ('ɛtliçə) pron,adj pl some, a few.

Etui (et'vi:) n neu -**s** small case or box.

etwa ('ɛtva) adv 1 about, nearly 2 perhaps. —**ig** adj possible.

etwas ('ɛtvas) pron invar some(thing), anything. adj some. adv somewhat. n neu a something.

Etymologie (etymolo'gi:) nf -**n** etymology.

euch (ɔyç) pron 2nd pers pl fam you, to you.

euer ('ɔyər) poss adj 2nd pers pl fam your. poss pron 2nd pers pl also **eure, der** —**e**, or **der** —**ige** yours. —**ethalben** adv also —**etwegen** or —**etwillen** for your sake, on your account.

Eukalyptus (ɔyka'lyptus) nm -**ten** eucalyptus.

Eule ('ɔylə) nf -**n** owl.

Eunuch (ɔy'nu:x) nm -**en** eunuch.

Europa (ɔy'ro:pa) n neu Europe. —**er** (ɔyro-pɛ:ər) nm — European. —**isch** (ɔyro'pɛ:iʃ) adj European.

evakuieren (evaku'i:rən) vt 1 empty. 2 evacuate.

evangel/isch (evan'ge:liʃ) adj 1 Protestant. 2 evangelical. —**ist** (evange'list) nm -**en** evangelist. —**ium** (evan'ge:lium) n neu -**ien** gospel.

eventuell (eventu'ɛl) adj possible.

ewig ('e:viç) adj eternal. —**keit** nf eternity.

exakt (ɛ'ksakt) adj exact, accurate.

Examen (ɛ'ksa:mən) n neu — examination.

Exekutionskommando (ɛksekutsi'o:nskɔmando) n neu **—s** firing squad.

Exempel (ɛ'ksɛmpəl) n neu **—** example.

Exemplar (ɛksɛm'pla:r) n neu **-e 1** specimen. **2** copy. **—isch** adj model, exemplary.

Exil (ɛ'ksi:l) n neu **-e** exile.

Exist/enz (ɛksis'tɛnts) nf **-en 1** existence. **2** livelihood. **—ieren** (ɛksis'ti:rən) vi exist.

exklusiv (ɛksklu'zi:f) adj exclusive.

exotisch (ɛ'kso:tiʃ) adj exotic.

Expedition (ɛkspeditsi'o:n) nf **-en 1** expedition. **2** dispatching.

Experiment (ɛksperi'mɛnt) n neu **-e** experiment. **—ell** (ɛksperimɛn'tɛl) adj experimental. **—ieren** (ɛksperimɛn'ti:rən) vi experiment.

explodieren (ɛksplo'di:rən) vi explode.

explosiv (ɛksplo'zi:f) adj explosive.

Export (ɛks'pɔrt) nm **-e** export. **—ieren** (ɛkspɔr'ti:rən) vt export.

extrem (ɛks'tre:m) adj extreme.

exzentrisch (ɛks'tsɛntriʃ) adj eccentric.

F

Fabel ('fa:bəl) nf **-n 1** fable. **2** plot, story. **—haft** adj fabulous.

Fabrik (fa'bri:k) nf **-en** factory. **—at** (fabri'ka:t) n neu **-e** manufacture, product.

fabrizieren (fabri'tsi:rən) vt manufacture.

Fach (fax) n neu **-er 1** compartment, pigeonhole. **2** drawer. **3** subject, field. **4** department. **5** speciality. **—arbeiter** nm skilled worker. **—arzt** nm med specialist. **—berater** nm technical consultant. **—bildung** nf technical education. **—lehrer** nm specialist teacher. **—lich** adj **1** professional. **2** technical. **—mann** nm **-er** or **-leute** specialist, expert. **—schule** nf technical school. **—werk** n neu **1** half-timbered work. **2** framework.

fächeln ('fɛçəln) vt fan.

Fackel ('fakəl) nf **-n** torch.

fade ('fa:də) adj **1** dull. **2** insipid. **3** stale.

Faden ('fa:dən) nm **—** thread, string.

Fagott (fa'gɔt) n neu **-e** bassoon.

fähig ('fɛ:iç) adj **1** able, capable. **2** competent. **—keit** nf **-en** ability, capacity, capability.

fahl (fa:l) adj pale, faded.

fahnd/en ('fa:ndən) vi **nach jemandem fahnden** search for someone. **—ung** nf **-en** search.

Fahne ('fa:nə) nf **-n** flag, standard.

fahr/en ('fa:rən) vt,vi **1** go. **2** drive. **3** travel. **4** sail. **—bahn** nf roadway, carriageway. **—bar** adj **1** passable, negotiable, navigable. **2** mobile. **—er** nm **—** driver. **—gast** nm passenger. **—geld** n neu fare. **—karte** nf ticket. **—lässig** adj negligent. **—plan** nm timetable. **—rad** n neu bicycle. **—schein** nm ticket. **—schule** nf driving school. **—stuhl** nm lift, elevator. **—zeug** n neu **1** vehicle. **2** vessel.

Fähre ('fɛ:rə) nf **-n** ferry.

Fahrt (fa:rt) nf **-en 1** drive. **2** ride. **3** journey. **4** voyage.

Fährte ('fɛ:rtə) nf **-n 1** track, trail. **2** scent.

Faktur (fak'tu:r) nf **-en** invoice. **—ieren** (faktu'ri:rən) vt invoice.

Fakultät (fakul'tɛ:t) nf **-en** (university) faculty.

Falke ('falkə) nm **-n** falcon.

Fall (fal) nm **-e 1** fall, downfall. **2** case. **auf jeden Fall** in any case. **für diesen Fall, in diesem Fall** in this case. **—s** conj in case, if.

Fall/e ('falə) nf **-n 1** trap, snare. **2** catch, latch. **—en*** vi fall. **es fällt mir leicht/schwer** I find it easy/hard. **fallen lassen** drop, let fall. **—schirm** nm **-e** parachute. **—schirmjäger** nm paratrooper. **—schirmspringer** nm parachutist. **—sucht** nf epilepsy.

fäll/en ('fɛlən) vt **1** fell (a tree, etc.). **2** pass (judgment).

fällig ('fɛliç) adj payable, due.

falsch (falʃ) adj **1** false. **2** wrong. **—en** ('fɛlʃən) vt **1** falsify, forge. **2** adulterate. **—er** ('fɛlʃər) nm **—** falsifier, forger. **—heit** nf **-en 1** falsehood. **2** deceitfulness.

Falt/e ('faltə) nf **-n** fold, crease, wrinkle. **—en** vt fold, crease, wrinkle.

familiär (famil'jɛ:r) adj familiar.

Familie (fa'mi:liə) nf **-n** family. **—nname** nm surname.

Fanati/ker (fa'na:tikər) nm **—** fanatic. **—sch** adj fanatic(al).

Fanfare (fan'fa:rə) nf **-n** fanfare.

fand (fant) v see **finden**.

Fang (faŋ) nm **-e 1** catching, capture. **2** catch, prey. **3** pl fangs. **4** pl claws. **—en*** vt catch, capture. **sich —en** vr become entangled or ensnared.

Farb/e ('farbə) nf **-n 1** colour. **2** paint, dye. **3** game suit. **Farbe bekennen** show one's true colours. **—en** ('fɛrbən) vt dye, colour. **—enblind** ('farbənblint) adj colour-blind. **—er** ('fɛrbər) nm **—** dyer. **—film** nm colour film. **—ig** ('farbiç) adj coloured. **—ige(r)**

('farbigə) nm -n coloured man. **—los** adj colourless. **—stoff** nm pigment, dye.

Fasan (fa'zaːn) nm -e pheasant.

Fasching ('faʃiŋ) nm -e (Shrovetide) carnival.

Faschis/mus (fa'ʃismus) nm fascism. **—t** nm -en fascist.

Faser ('faːzər) nf -n fibre, strand.

Faß (fas) n neu **Fässer** barrel, cask, drum.

fass/en ('fasən) vt 1 take hold of, seize, catch. 2 contain, hold. 3 comprehend, grasp. **sich fassen** vr 1 pull oneself together. 2 control oneself. **sich kurz fassen** express oneself briefly, be brief. **—ung** nf **-en** 1 composure, self control. 2 setting (of gems). 3 wording, version.

fast (fast) adv almost, nearly.

fast/en ('fastən) vi fast. **—nacht** nf 1 the night of Shrove Tuesday. 2 carnival.

fatal (fa'taːl) adj 1 unfortunate. 2 disastrous. **—ist** (fata'list) nm -en fatalist.

faul (faul) adj 1 lazy. 2 rotten. **—enzen** vi idle, loaf about. **—heit** nf laziness. **—nis** ('fɔylnis) nf decay, rottenness.

Faust (faust) nf **¨-e** fist.

Februar ('feːbruaːr) nm February.

fechten ('fɛçtən) vi fence, fight.

Feder ('feːdər) nf -n 1 feather. 2 pen(-nib). 3 spring. **—ball** nm shuttlecock. **—n** vi 1 moult. 2 spring, be elastic. **—ung** nf 1 (spring) suspension. 2 elasticity.

Fee (feː) nf -n fairy.

fegen ('feːgən) vt,vi sweep.

fehl/bar ('feːlbaːr) adj fallible. **—betrag** nm deficit. **—druck** nm misprint. **—en** vi 1 be absent. 2 be wanting. 3 fail. 4 err. **—er** nm -1 fault, failing. 2 mistake. **—geburt** nf miscarriage. **—schlag** nm 1 failure. 2 miss. **—schlagen** vi 1 fail. 2 miss. **—schuß** nm bad shot, miss. **—zünden** vi misfire.

Feier ('faiər) nf -n celebration, festival. **—abend** nm 1 evening leisure. 2 (at work) finishing-time, knocking-off time. **—lich** adj 1 ceremonial. 2 festive. 3 solemn, dignified. **—lichkeit** nf 1 ceremony, pomp. 2 solemnity. **—n** vt,vi celebrate. vi rest (from work). **—tag** nm holiday.

feig/e ('faigə) adj cowardly. **—heit** ('faikhait) nf cowardice. **—ling** ('faikliŋ) nm -e coward.

Feige ('faigə) nf -n fig.

feil (fail) adj 1 for sale. 2 venal.

Feil/e ('failə) nf -n file. **—en** vt,vi 1 file. 2 polish.

feilschen ('failʃən) vi barter, haggle.

fein (fain) adj 1 fine. 2 delicate. 3 elegant. 4 distinguished. 5 acute. 6 sensitive. **—fühlig** adj sensitive, delicate. **—schmecker** nm — gourmet. **—sinnig** adj subtle, sensitive.

Feind (faint) nm -e enemy. **—schaft** nf enmity. **—selig** adj hostile.

Feld (fɛlt) n neu **¨-er** field. **—bett** n neu camp bed. **—herr** nm commander, general. **—messer** nm surveyor. **—stecher** nm field-glasses. **—wache** nf mil picket. **—webel** nm — sergeant. **—zug** nm 1 campaign. 2 expedition.

Fell (fɛl) n neu **-e** 1 hide, skin. 2 fur.

Fels (fɛls) nm **-en** also **Felsen** ('fɛlzən) nm — 1 cliff. 2 rock.

Fenster ('fɛnstər) n neu — window. **—brett** n neu window-sill. **—laden** nm shutter. **—scheibe** nf window-pane.

Ferien ('feːrjən) nm pl holidays.

Ferkel ('fɛrkəl) n neu — piglet.

fern (fɛrn) adj distant, far. **Ferne(r) Osten** nm Far East. **—e** nf -n distance, remoteness. **—er** adj farther. adv moreover. **—erhin** adv 1 in the future. 2 moreover. **—gespräch** n neu trunk call, long-distance call. **—meldung** nf 1 telecommunication. 2 remote signalling. **—rohr** n neu telescope. **—sehapparat** nm television set. **—sehen** vi watch television. n neu television. **—sprecher** nm telephone. **—sprechzelle** nf call-box.

Ferse ('fɛrzə) nf -n heel.

fertig ('fɛrtiç) adj 1 ready. 2 finished. **—en** ('fɛrtigən) vt manufacture, produce. **—keit** nf dexterity, proficiency. **—machen** vt finish.

Fessel ('fɛsəl) nf -n fetter, bond. **—n** vt 1 fetter. 2 captivate.

fest (fɛst) adj 1 solid, hard. 2 stable, fixed. **—halten** vt 1 seize. 2 hold tight. 3 record. 4 portray. vi hold fast, stick to (something). **—igen** vt make firm or stable. **—land** n neu mainland. **—machen** vt make fast, fasten. **—stehen** vi stand firm. **—stellen** vt establish, ascertain. **—ung** nf **-en** fortress.

Fest (fɛst) n neu **-e** festival, feast. **—lich** adj festive. **—lichkeit** nf **-en** festivity.

fett (fɛt) adj 1 fat. 2 greasy. 3 rich. **—en** ('fɛtən) vt 1 make greasy. 2 oil. **—arm** adj low in fat. **—en** vt oil. **—ig** adj 1 fatty. 2 oily.

Fetzen ('fɛtsən) nm — 1 scrap, piece. 2 rag.

feucht (fɔyçt) adj damp, moist. **—igkeit** nf damp, moisture, humidity.

Feuer ('fɔyər) n neu — fire. **—fest** adj fireproof. **—löscher** nm fire-extinguisher.

—melder nm fire-alarm. **—n** vi 1 fire (on). 2 make a fire. **—wehr** nf fire brigade. **—werk** n neu fireworks. **—zeug** n neu 'cigarette-lighter.

Feuilleton ('fœjɜtɔ̃) n neu -s cultural section of a newspaper.

feurig ('fɔyriç) adj fiery.

Fibel ('fi:bəl) nf -n 1 primer, spelling-book. 2 brooch.

Fichte ('fiçtə) nf -n pine, spruce.

ficken ('fikən) vi move to and fro. vt rub. vi,vt tab copulate.

Fieber ('fi:bər) n neu — fever. **—haft** adj feverish.

Fiedel ('fi:dəl) nf -n fiddle, violin. **—eln** vt fiddle. **—ler** nm — fiddler.

fiel (fi:l) v see **fallen.**

Figur (fi'gu:r) nf -en 1 figure. 2 chessman.

Filiale (fili'a:lə) nf -n comm branch.

Film (film) nm -e film. **—star** nm -s film star.

Filt/er ('filtər) nm,neu — filter. **—ern** vt also **—rieren** (fil'tri:rən) filter, strain.

Filz (filts) nm -e 1 felt. 2 miser, skin-flint. **—en** vt 1 line with felt. 2 sl search, frisk. **—ig** adj 1 felt. 2 miserly.

Finanz (fi'nants) nf -en finance. **—iell** (finan'tsjɛl) adj financial. **—ieren** (finan'tsi:rən) vt finance. **—mann** nm financier.

find/en ('findən) vt 1 find. 2 think, consider. **—igkeit** nf ingenuity.

fing (fiŋ) v see **fangen.**

Finger ('fiŋər) nm — finger. **—abdruck** nm fingerprint. **—hut** nm thimble. **—nagel** nm fingernail. **—spitze** nf fingertip.

Fink (fiŋk) nm -en finch.

Finn/e ('finə) nm -n also **Finn/länder** nm — Finn. **—isch** adj Finnish. n neu Finnish (language). **—land** n neu Finland.

finster ('finstər) adj 1 dark, gloomy. 2 ominous, sinister. **—nis** nf -se 1 darkness, gloom. 2 sci eclipse.

Firma ('firma) nf **Firmen** firm.

Firnis ('firnis) nm -e varnish. **—sen** vt varnish.

Fisch (fiʃ) nm -e 1 fish. 2 pl Pisces. **—en** vt fish (for), catch. **—er** nm — fisherman. **—erei** (fiʃə'rai) nf -en fishery, fishing. **—heber** nm fish-slice.

fix (fiks) adj 1 fixed. 2 quick, agile. **—ieren** (fi'ksi:rən) vt 1 fix. 2 stare at.

flach (flax) adj 1 flat. 2 shallow. **—e** ('flɛçə) nf -n 1 surface. 2 plain. 3 expanse. 4 (surface) area. **—enmaß** ('flɛçənmas) n neu square measure. **—land** n neu plain, lowland.

Flachs (flaks) nm flax.

flackern ('flakərn) vi (of light, flame) flicker.

Flagge ('flagə) nf -n flag, standard.

Flamme ('flamə) nf -n flame. **—n** vi flame, blaze.

Flanell (fla'nɛl) n neu -e flannel.

Flank/e ('flaŋkə) nf -n flank. **—ieren** (flaŋ-'ki:rən) vt (out)flank.

Flasche ('flaʃə) nf -n bottle, flask. **—nöffner** nm bottle opener.

flattern ('flatərn) vi flutter.

flau (flau) adj 1 weak. 2 slack. 3 dull. 4 stale.

Flaute ('flautə) nf -n lull, calm.

Flechte ('flɛçtə) nf -n 1 plait, braid. 2 lichen. **—n*** vt braid, plait.

Fleck (flɛk) nm -e 1 spot. 2 blemish. 3 patch. **—en** vt,vi spot, stain. nm — 1 spot. 2 blemish. 3 market town. **—ig** adj spotted, stained.

Fledermaus ('fle:dərmaus) nf -e bat.

flehen ('fle:ən) vi implore.

Fleisch (flaiʃ) n neu -e meat, flesh. **—er** nm — also **—hauer** butcher. **—erei** (flaiʃə'rai) nf -en butcher's shop. **—fressend** adj carnivorous. **—ig** adj fleshy, meaty. **—lich** adj 1 carnal, of the flesh. 2 sensual.

Fleiß (flais) nm industry, diligence. **—ig** adj industrious, diligent, hard-working.

flicken ('flikən) vt mend, patch. nm — patch.

Fliege ('fli:gə) nf -n fly. **—nklappe** nf fly-swatter.

flieg/en* ('fli:gən) vi fly. **—er** nm — flier, aviator.

fliehen* ('fli:ən) vi,vt flee (from).

Fließ/band ('fli:sbant) n neu 1 conveyor belt. 2 production line. **—en*** vi flow. **—end** adj 1 flowing. 2 fluent.

flimmern ('flimərn) vi glimmer, twinkle.

flink (fliŋk) adj nimble, quick. **—heit** nf nimbleness, quickness.

Flinte ('flintə) nf -n 1 rifle. 2 shotgun.

Flitterwochen ('flitərvɔxən) nf pl honeymoon.

Flocke ('flɔkə) nf -n 1 flake. 2 flock, tuft.

flog (flo:k) v see **fliegen.**

Floh (flo:) nm -e flea.

Florenz (flo'rɛnts) n neu Florence.

floß (flɔs) v see **fließen.**

Floß (flo:s) n neu -e 1 raft. 2 (fishing) float.

Flosse ('flɔsə) nf -n fin, flipper.

Flöt/e ('flœ:tə) nf -n flute. **—ist** nm -en flautist.

flott (flɔt) adj 1 afloat. 2 brisk. 3 stylish, gay. **—e** ('flɔtə) nf -n fleet, navy.

Fluch (flu:x) nm ⁻e curse, swear word. **—en** vi curse, swear.

Flucht (fluxt) nf **-en** 1 flight, escape. 2 row, line. **⁻ig** (ˈflyçtiç) adj 1 fleeing. 2 fugitive. 3 brief, fleeting. 4 superficial. **⁻ling** (ˈflyçtliŋ) nm **-e** 1 refugee. 2 fugitive.

Flug (flu:k) nm ⁻e 1 flight, flying. 2 flock, flight. **—abwehr** nf anti-aircraft defence. **—blatt** n neu leaflet, pamphlet. **—deck** n neu flight deck. **—hafen** nm airport. **—post** nf airmail. **—zeug** n neu aeroplane, aircraft.

Flügel (ˈfly:gəl) nm **-** wing.

Fluor (ˈflu:ɔr) n neu fluorine.

Flur (flu:r) nm **-e** (entrance) hall. nf **-en** field, meadow-land.

Fluß (flus) nm Flüsse 1 river, stream. 2 flow.

flüssig (ˈflysiç) adj liquid, fluid. **—keit** nf **-en** 1 liquid, fluid. 2 liquidity.

flüstern (ˈflystərn) vi,vt whisper.

Flut (flu:t) nf **-en** 1 flood. 2 (high) tide.

Fohlen (ˈfo:lən) n neu **—** foal.

Föhn (fœ:n) nm **-e** warm south wind.

Folg/e (ˈfɔlgə) nf **-n** 1 succession, series. 2 consequence, result. **—en** vi 1 follow. 2 ensue. 3 obey. **—endermaßen** adv in the following manner. **—ern** vt infer, conclude. **—erung** nf **-en** inference, conclusion. **—lich** (ˈfɔlkliç) conj consequently.

Folter (ˈfɔltər) nf **-n** torture. **—n** vt torture.

Fön (fœ:n) nm Tdmk **-e** hair-dryer.

Fonds (fɔ̃) nm comm fund(s), stock.

forcieren (fɔrˈsi:rən) vt 1 force, take by force. 2 overdo.

forder/n (ˈfɔrdərn) vt 1 demand, claim. 2 challenge, summon. **—ung** nf **-en** 1 demand. 2 challenge.

förder/n (ˈfœ:rdərn) vt 1 further, promote. 2 transport, convey. **—lich** adj 1 conducive. 2 advantageous. **—ung** nf **-en** advancement.

Forelle (fɔˈrɛlə) nf **-n** trout.

Form (fɔrm) nf **-en** 1 form, shape. 2 mould. **—el** nf **-n** formula. **—ell** (fɔrˈmɛl) adj also **⁻lich** (ˈfœrmliç) formal. **—en** vt form, mould. **—ieren** (fɔrˈmi:rən) vt 1 form. 2 arrange. **sich —ieren** vr mil fall in. **—ular** (fɔrmuˈlaːr) n neu **-e** 1 form. 2 schedule. **—ulieren** (fɔrmuˈliːrən) vt formulate.

forsch/en (ˈfɔrʃən) vi 1 search. 2 investigate. 3 research. **—er** nm **—** 1 researcher. 2 investigator. 3 explorer. **—ung** nf **-en** 1 research. 2 investigation.

Forst (fɔrst) nm **-e** forest, wood. **—er** (ˈfœrstər) nm **—** forester.

fort (fɔrt) adv 1 away. 2 off. 3 on. 4 forward.

fortan (fɔrtˈan) adv henceforth.

fortbestehen* (ˈfɔrtbəʃteːən) vi 1 continue (to exist). 2 persist.

Fortbildung (ˈfɔrtbilduŋ) nf further education or training.

fortdauern (ˈfɔrtdauərn) vi continue, last.

fortfahren* (ˈfɔrtfaːrən) vi 1 keep or go on or. 2 depart. vt 1 remove. 2 drive away.

fortgehen* (ˈfɔrtgeːən) vi go away or on.

fortkommen* (ˈfɔrtkɔmən) vi 1 get away. 2 make progress.

fortlaufend (ˈfɔrtlaufənt) adj continuous.

fortpflanzen (ˈfɔrtpflantsən) vt propagate. **sich fortpflanzen** vr multiply, propagate.

fortschreiten* (ˈfɔrtʃraitən) vi 1 proceed. 2 progress. **—d** adj 1 advancing. 2 progressive.

Fortschritt (ˈfɔrtʃrit) nm **-e** progress. **—lich** adj progressive.

fortsetz/en (ˈfɔrtzetsən) vt continue. **—ung** nf **-en** continuation.

fortwährend (ˈfɔrtvɛːrənt) adj perpetual, continual.

Fossil (fɔˈsiːl) n neu **-ien** fossil.

Fötus (ˈfœtus) nm **-usse** foetus.

Fracht (fraxt) nf **-en** freight, cargo. **—en** vt ship, freight. **—er** nm **—** freighter. **—gut** n neu freight, goods.

Frack (frak) nm **-e** dress coat, tails.

Frag/e (ˈfraːgə) nf **-n** question. **—ebogen** nm questionnaire. **—en** vt ask, question, inquire. **—ezeichen** n neu question mark. **—lich** (ˈfraːkliç) adj questionable. **—los** (ˈfraːkloːs) adv unquestionably. **—würdig** (ˈfraːkvyrdiç) adj doubtful.

Fragment (fragˈmɛnt) n neu **-e** fragment.

Fraktion (fraktsiˈoːn) nf **-en** 1 fraction. 2 parliamentary party.

Fraktur (frakˈtuːr) nf **-en** 1 fracture. 2 Gothic type or script.

Franken (ˈfraŋkən) nm **—** (Swiss) franc.

frankieren (fraŋˈkiːrən) vt frank, stamp.

Frankreich (ˈfraŋkraiç) n neu France.

Franse (ˈfranzə) nf **-n** fringe.

Franz/ose (franˈtsoːzə) nm **-n** Frenchman. **—ösin** (franˈtsøːzin) nf **-nen** Frenchwoman. **—ösisch** (franˈtsøːziʃ) adj French. n neu French (language).

Fratze (ˈfratsə) nf **-n** grimace. **Fratzen schneiden** pull faces.

Frau (frau) nf **-en** woman, wife. **—enarzt** nm gynaecologist. **—enzimmer** n neu 1 woman, female. 2 slut.

45

Fräulein ('frɔylain) n neu — 1 young or unmarried woman. 2 Miss.

frech (frɛç) adj impudent, cheeky. —**heit** nf impudence, cheek.

frei (frai) adj 1 free, at liberty, unconstrained. 2 free (of charge). 3 vacant. **freier Grundbesitz** freehold.

Freibad ('fraibat) n neu open-air swimming pool.

Freibrief ('fraibri:f) nm charter.

Freie ('fraiə) n neu open air. **im Freien** out of doors.

freigebig ('fraigə:biç) adj generous.

Freiheit ('fraihait) nf freedom. —**strafe** nf imprisonment.

Frei/herr ('fraihɛr) nm baron. —**herrin** nf baroness.

freilassen* ('frailasən) vt release.

freilich ('frailiç) adv certainly, of course.

freimütig ('fraimy:tiç) adj frank, candid.

freisprechen* ('fraiʃprɛçən) vt acquit.

Freitag ('fraita:k) nm Friday.

frei/willig ('fraiviliç) adj willing, voluntary. —**willige(r)** ('fraiviligə) nm volunteer.

Freizeit ('fraitsait) nf leisure, spare time.

fremd (frɛmt) adj 1 foreign. 2 strange. —**artig** adj strange, odd. —**e** ('frɛmdə) nf -n foreign country. —**e(r)** ('frɛmdə) nm 1 foreigner. 2 stranger. —**enführer** ('frɛmdənfy:rər) nm guide. —**enverkehr** ('frɛmdənferke:r) nm tourism. —**enzimmer** ('frɛmdəntsimər) n neu 1 guest-room. 2 room to let. —**sprache** nf foreign language. —**wort** n neu foreign word.

Frequenz (fre'kvɛnts) nf -en frequency.

fressen* ('frɛsən) vt (of animals) eat.

Freud/e ('frɔydə) nf -n joy, pleasure. —**ig** adj joyful. —**igkeit** nf joyfulness.

freuen ('frɔyən) vt please. **sich freuen** vr be glad. **sich freuen auf** look forward to.

Freund (frɔynt) nm -e friend, boyfriend. —**in** ('frɔyndin) nf -nen friend, girlfriend. —**lich** adj 1 friendly. 2 kind, pleasant. —**schaft** nf -en friendship.

Frevel ('fre:fəl) nm — crime, outrage.

Fried/e(n) ('fri:də) nm peace. —**ensstifter** nm peace-maker. —**ensvertrag** nm peace treaty. —**fertig** ('fri:tfɛrtiç) adj peaceable. —**hof** ('fri:tho:f) nm cemetery. —**lich** ('fri:tliç) adj peaceful, peaceable.

frieren* ('fri:rən) vi,vt freeze.

Fries (fri:s) nm -e frieze.

frigid (fri'gi:t) adj frigid. —**ität** (frigidi'tɛ:t) nf frigidity.

frisch (friʃ) adj 1 fresh. 2 cool. 3 new. —**e** nf freshness.

Fris/eur (fri'zœ:r) nm -e hairdresser, barber. —**iersalon** (fri'zi:rzalɔ̃) nm hairdresser's salon. —**ur** (fri'zu:r) nf -en hair style, hairdo.

Frist (frist) nf -en (period of) time, time-limit. —**los** adj without notice.

froh (fro:) adj happy, glad, merry. —**lich** ('frœ:liç) adj happy, merry. —**lichkeit** nf joyfulness, mirth. —**sinn** nm cheerfulness.

fromm (frɔm) adj 1 devout, pious. 2 docile. —**eln** ('frœməln) vi feign piety. —**igkeit** ('frœmiçkait) nf piety. —**ler** ('frœmlər) nm — bigot.

Fronleichnam (fro:n'laiçna:m) nm rel Corpus Christi Day.

Front (frɔnt) nf -en front, facade.

fror (fro:r) v see **frieren**.

Frosch (frɔʃ) nm -e frog.

Frost (frɔst) nm -e frost, chill. —**ig** adj frosty, chilly.

Frucht (fruxt) nf -e fruit. —**bar** adj fruitful, fertile. —**barkeit** nf fertility. —**los** adj fruitless.

früh (fry:) adj early. adv 1 early. 2 in the morning. —**e** nf early hour, morning. —**er** adj earlier, former, sooner. —**jahr** n neu also —**ling** nm -e spring. —**reif** adj precocious, premature, forward. —**stück** n neu breakfast. —**stücken** vi breakfast. —**zeitig** adj early, premature.

Fuchs (fuks) nm -e fox.

Fug/e ('fu:gə) nf -n 1 joint. 2 fugue. —**en** ('fy:gən) vt 1 add. 2 join. **sich —en** vr submit, acquiesce.

fühl/en ('fy:lən) vt 1 feel, touch. 2 sense. **sich fühlen** vr feel. **sich traurig fühlen** feel sad. —**er** nm — feeler.

führ/en ('fy:rən) vt 1 lead. 2 direct. 3 manage, control, carry on. 4 keep (books). —**er** nm — 1 leader. 2 manager. 3 guide(book). 4 driver. 5 pilot. —**erschein** nm driving licence. —**ung** nf 1 direction, control. 2 leadership. 3 administration.

Füll/e ('fylə) nf 1 fullness. 2 abundance. —**en** vt fill. —**feder** nf also —**er** nm — fountain pen.

Fundament (funda'mɛnt) n neu -e foundation.

fünf (fynf) adj,nf five. —**te** adj fifth. —**zehn** adj,nf fifteen. —**zehnte** adj fifteenth. —**zig** adj,nf fifty. —**zigste** adj fiftieth.

fungieren (fuŋ'gi:rən) vi **fungieren als** act as.

Funk (fuŋk) nm radio, wireless. **—eln** vi sparkle, twinkle. **—en** nm — spark. vi spark. vt 1 radio. 2 broadcast. **—er** nm — radio operator. **—gerät** n neu radio (set).

Funktion (fuŋktsio'o:n) nf **-en** function. **—är** (fuŋktsio'ne:r) nm **-e** functionary, official. **—ieren** (fuŋktsio'ni:rən) vi function.

für (fy:r) prep 1 for. 2 in place of. 3 in favour of. 4 on behalf of. **für sich 1** for oneself. 2 exceptional. **was für** what sort of. **—sorge** nf 1 care. 2 welfare. **—sorger** nm — social or welfare worker. **—wahr** adv truly, indeed. **—wort** n neu pronoun.

Furch/e (fUrçə) nf **-n** 1 furrow. 2 wrinkle. **—en** vt furrow.

Furcht (fUrçt) nf fear. **—bar** adj frightful, horrible. **—en** ('fYrçtən) vt fear. **sich —en** vr be afraid. **—los** adj fearless.

Furnier (fUr'ni:r) nm **-e** veneer.

Fürst (fYrst) nm **-en** prince. **—entum** ('fYrstən-tu:m) n neu **-er** principality. **—in** nf **-nen** princess. **—lich** adj princely.

Fuß (fu:s) nm **-e** foot. **zu Fuß gehen** walk, go on foot. **—ball** nm football. **—boden** nm floor. **—bremse** nf foot-brake. **—gänger** ('fu:sgɛŋər) nm — pedestrian. **—tritt** nm 1 kick. 2 footstep.

Futter (futar) n neu 1 feed, fodder. 2 lining. **—n** ('fytərn) vt 1 feed. 2 line.

G

gab (ga:p) v see **geben.**

Gabe ('ga:bə) nf **-n** gift.

Gabel ('ga:bəl) nf **-n** fork.

gackern ('gakərn) vi cackle.

gähnen ('gɛ:nən) vi yawn.

galant (ga'lant) adj gallant.

Galeere (ga'le:rə) nf **-n** galley.

Galerie (galə'ri:) nf **-n** gallery.

Galgen ('galgən) nm — gallows.

Galione (gali'o:nə) nf **-n** galleon.

Galopp (ga'lɔp) nm **-e** gallop. **—ieren** (galə-'pi:rən) vi gallop.

galvanisieren (galvani'zi:rən) vt galvanize.

Gang (gaŋ) nm **-e** 1 gait. 2 walking, progress. 3 functioning, operation. 4 corridor, aisle. 5 (of a meal) course. 6 mot gear. **im Gang** 1 going on. 2 working. **—art** nf walk, gait.

Gans (gans) nf **-e** goose. **—ebraten** ('gɛnzəbra:-tən) nm roast goose. **—efüßchen** ('gɛnzə-

fy:sçən) n neu pl inf quotation marks. **—emarsch** ('gɛnzəmarʃ) nm single file. **—erich** ('gɛnzəriç) nm **-e** gander.

ganz (gants) adj whole, all. adv 1 quite. 2 wholly, very. **im ganzen** on the whole. **—e(s)** n neu whole. **—lich** ('gɛntsliç) adj whole, entire.

gar (ga:r) adj 1 ready, finished. 2 cul tender, done. adv 1 quite. 2 about. 3 very. **gar nicht** not at all.

Garantie (garan'ti:) nf **-n** guarantee. **—ren** vt guarantee.

Garde ('gardə) nf **-n** guard(s).

Garderobe (gardə'ro:bə) nf **-n** 1 cloakroom. 2 wardrobe.

Gardine (gar'di:nə) nf **-n** curtain.

gär/en* ('gɛ:rən) vi ferment. **—ung** nf fermentation.

garnieren (gar'ni:rən) vt 1 garnish. 2 trim.

Garnison (garni'zo:n) nf **-en** garrison.

Gart/en ('gartən) nm — garden. **—ner** ('gɛrt-nər) nm — gardener.

Gas (ga:s) n neu **-e** gas. **—herd** nm gas cooker or stove. **—ofen** nm gas stove or oven, gas fire.

Gasse ('gasə) nf **-n** alley, lane.

Gast (gast) nm **-e** 1 guest, visitor. 2 stranger. 3 customer. **—arbeiter** nm immigrant worker. **—ebuch** ('gɛstəbu:x) n neu visitors' book. **—freundlich** adj hospitable. **—freundschaft** nf hospitality. **—geber** nm — host. **—geberin** nf **-nen** hostess. **—haus** n neu 1 inn. 2 restaurant. **—hof** nm 1 hotel. 2 restaurant. **—stätte** nf restaurant, cafe.

Gatt/e ('gatə) nm **-n** husband, spouse. **—in** nf **-nen** wife, spouse.

Gattung ('gatuŋ) nf **-en** 1 kind, sort. 2 species.

gaukeln ('gaukəln) vi 1 juggle. 2 conjure.

Gaul (gaul) nm **-e** horse, nag.

Gaumen ('gaumən) nm — palate.

Gauner ('gaunər) nm — swindler, rogue.

Gaze ('ga:zə) nf **-n** gauze.

Gazelle (ga'tsɛlə) nf **-n** gazelle.

Gebäck (gə'bɛk) n neu **-e** cakes, pastries.

Gebärde (gə'bɛ:rdə) nf **-n** gesture.

gebär/en* (gə'bɛ:rən) vt give birth to, bear. **—mutter** nf womb, uterus.

Gebäude (gə'bɔydə) n neu — building.

geben* ('ge:bən) vt give, present. **sich geben** vr 1 act, behave. 2 pass, abate. **es gibt** there is or are. **von sich geben** utter.

Gebet (gə'be:t) n neu **-e** prayer.

gebeten (gə'be:tən) v see **bitten.**

Gebiet (gə'bi:t) n neu -e territory, district, area. —**en*** vt,vi command. —**er** nm — commander, master. —**erisch** adj masterful, imperious.

Gebilde (gə'bildə) n neu — 1 creation, work. 2 form.

gebildet (gə'bildət) adj educated.

Gebirg/e (gə'birgə) n neu — mountains, mountain range. —**ig** adj mountainous.

Gebiß (gə'bis) n neu -**bisse** 1 teeth. 2 denture. 3 bit.

gebissen (gə'bisən) v see **beißen.**

Gebläse (gə'blɛ:zə) n neu — bellows.

geblieben (gə'bli:bən) v see **bleiben.**

Gebot (gə'bo:t) n neu -e command(ment).

gebracht (gə'braxt) v see **bringen.**

Gebrauch (gə'braux) nm -̈e 1 use. 2 custom. —**en** vt use. —**lich** (gə'brɔyçliç) adj customary, usual. —**sanweisung** nf directions for use. ⊢**t** adj used, second-hand.

gebrechlich (gə'brɛçliç) adj fragile, weak.

gebrochen (gə'brɔxən) v see **brechen.**

Gebrüder (gə'brydər) nm pl comm brothers, bros.

Gebühr (gə'by:r) nf -en 1 fee, charge. 2 tax, duty. —**lich** adj proper, appropriate.

gebunden (gə'bundən) adj 1 bound. 2 connected.

Geburt (gə'burt) nf -en birth. —**enbeschränkung** nf also —**enkontrolle** birth control. —**sort** nm birthplace. —**sschein** nm also —**surkunde** nf birth certificate. —**stag** nm birthday.

Gebüsch (gə'byʃ) n neu -e undergrowth, (clump of) bushes.

gedacht (gə'daxt) v see **denken.**

Gedächtnis (gə'dɛçtnis) n neu -se memory, remembrance.

Gedanke (gə'daŋkə) nm -n thought, idea.

Gedärm (gə'dɛrm) n neu -e bowels, intestines.

Gedeck (gə'dɛk) n neu -e 1 cover. 2 menu.

gedeih/en* (gə'daiən) vi prosper, flourish.

gedenk/en* (gə'dɛŋkən) vi 1 remember. 2 mention. 3 intend. —**stätte** nf memorial.

Gedicht (gə'diçt) n neu -e poem.

gediegen (gə'di:gən) adj 1 pure. 2 solid, reliable, good-quality.

Gedräng/e (gə'drɛŋə) n neu crowd, press.

Geduld (gə'dult) nf patience. —**ig** (gə'duldiç) adj patient.

geeignet (gə'aignət) adj suitable, appropriate.

Gefahr (gə'fa:r) nf -en danger. —**den** (gə-

'fɛ:rdən) vt endanger. —**lich** (gə'fɛ:rliç) adj dangerous.

Gefährte (gə'fɛ:rtə) nm -n companion.

gefall/en* (gə'falən) vi please. **dieses Bild gefällt mir** I like this picture, this picture pleases me. ~**n** neu — pleasure. nm — favour. —**ig** (gə'fɛliç) adj pleasing, agreeable. —**igkait** (gə'fɛliçkait) nf -en 1 kindness. 2 favour. —**igst** (gə'fɛliçst) adv please.

gefangen (gə'faŋən) adj captive. **gefangen nehmen** take prisoner. —**e(r)** nm prisoner, captive. —**schaft** nf imprisonment, captivity.

Gefängnis (gə'fɛŋnis) n neu -se 1 prison. 2 imprisonment. —**wärter** nm warder, jailer.

Gefäß (gə'fɛs) n neu -e vessel, container.

Gefecht (gə'fɛçt) n neu -e 1 fight. 2 action.

geflogen (gə'flo:gən) v see **fliegen.**

geflossen (gə'flosən) v see **fließen.**

Geflügel (gə'fly:gəl) n neu poultry.

Gefolge (gə'folgə) n neu retinue, followers.

gefräßig (gə'frɛ:siç) adj gluttonous, greedy.

Gefreite(r) (gə'fraitə) nm 1 lance corporal. 2 able seaman.

Gefrierpunkt (gə'fri:rpuŋkt) nm freezing point.

gefroren (gə'fro:rən) v see **frieren.**

gefügig (gə'fy:giç) adj pliant, compliant.

Gefühl (gə'fy:l) n neu -e 1 sense, touch. 2 feeling, emotion.

gefunden (gə'fundən) v see **finden.**

gegangen (gə'gaŋən) v see **gehen.**

gegebenenfalls (gə'ge:bənənfals) adv should the occasion or need arise.

gegen ('ge:gən) prep 1 against. 2 towards. 3 about. —**angriff** nm counter-attack. —**einander** (ge:gənain'andər) adv against one another. —**gewicht** n neu counterweight. —**gift** n neu antidote. —**satz** nm 1 contrast. 2 opposition. **im Gegensatz zu** 1 contrary to. 2 as opposed to. —**seitig** adj 1 mutual. 2 reciprocal. —**stand** nm object. —**teil** n neu 1 contrary. 2 reverse. **im Gegenteil** on the contrary. —**über** (ge:gən'y:bər) prep,adv opposite. ~**n** — person or object opposite. —**wart** nf -en 1 the present (time). 2 presence. —**wärtig** adj present, current. —**wehr** nf defence.

Gegend ('ge:gənt) nf -en district, area, neighbourhood.

gegessen (gə'gesən) v see **essen.**

Gegner ('ge:gnər) nm — opponent, enemy.

gegossen (gə'gosən) v see **gießen.**

gegriffen (gə'grifən) v see **greifen.**

gehabt (gə'ha:pt) v see **haben.**

Gehalt (gə'halt) *n neu* ̈-er salary. *nm* -e content, contents, capacity.

gehässig (gə'hɛsiç) *adj* 1 hateful. 2 spiteful.

geheim (gə'haim) *adj* secret. —**dienst** *nm* secret service. —**nis** *n neu* -**se** secret. —**nisvoll** *adj* mysterious.

gehen* ('ge:ən) *vi* 1 go, walk. 2 function, work. **es geht** it's all right. **wie geht es Ihnen?** how are you?

Gehilfe (gə'hilfə) *nm* -**n** assistant.

Gehirn (gə'hirn) *n neu* -e brain. —**erschütterung** *nf* concussion.

geholfen (gə'hɔlfən) *v see* **helfen.**

Gehör (gə'hœ:r) *n neu* hearing.

gehorchen (gə'hɔrçən) *vi* obey.

gehör/en (gə'hœ:rən) belong. **es gehört sich** it is proper. —**ig** *adj* 1 belonging. 2 suitable, proper.

gehorsam (gə'ho:rza:m) *adj* obedient. *nm* obedience.

Gehrock ('ge:rɔk) *nm* frock coat.

Gehsteig ('ge:ʃtaik) *nm* -e pavement.

Gehwerk ('ge:vɛrk) *n neu* clockwork.

Geier ('gaiər) *nm* — vulture.

Geifer ('gaifər) *nm* 1 spittle. 2 foam.

Geige ('gaigə) *nf* -**n** violin, fiddle. —**nspieler** *nm* violinist, fiddler.

Geisel ('gaizəl) *nm* —, *nf* -**n** hostage.

Geist (gaist) *nm* -er 1 spirit. 2 mind, intellect. 3 ghost. —**esabwesend** *adj* absent-minded. —**esgestört** *adj also* —**eskrank** insane, mentally ill. —**eswissenschaften** *nf pl* humanities, the Arts. —**ig** *adj* 1 spiritual. 2 intellectual, mental. 3 alcoholic (beverage, etc.). —**lich** *adj* 1 spiritual. 2 clerical. —**liche(r)** *nm* -n cleric. —**reich** *adj also* —**voll** 1 witty. 2 ingenious.

Geiz (gaits) *nm* 1 avarice. 2 miserliness. —**hals** *nm* miser. —**ig** *adj* miserly.

gekannt (gə'kant) *v see* **kennen.**

gekünstelt (gə'kynstəlt) *adj* 1 artificial. 2 affected. 3 feigned.

Gelächter (gə'lɛçtər) *n neu* laughter.

geladen (gə'la:dən) *adj* loaded.

Gelage (gə'la:gə) *n neu* — feast, drinking-bout.

Gelände (gə'lɛndə) *n neu* — ground, land.

Geländer (gə'lɛndər) *n neu* — railing, banisters.

gelang *v see* **gelingen.**

gelangen (gə'laŋən) *vi* arrive at, reach.

gelassen (gə'lasən) *adj* calm. —**heit** *nf* calmness, composure.

Gelatine (ʒɛla'ti:nə) *nf* gelatine. —**dynamit** *n neu* gelignite.

geläufig (gə'lɔyfiç) *adj* 1 common. 2 current. 3 familiar. 4 fluent.

gelb (gɛlp) *adj,n neu* yellow. —**sucht** *nf* jaundice.

Geld (gɛlt) *n neu* -er money. —**anweisung** *nf* money order. —**mittel** *n neu pl* funds, means. —**schrank** *nm* safe, strong-box. —**strafe** *nf* fine.

Gelee (ʒe'le:) *n neu* -s jelly.

gelegen (gə'le:gən) *adj* 1 situated. 2 convenient. —**heit** *nf* -en 1 opportunity. 2 occasion. —**tlich** *adj* 1 occasional. 2 incidental.

gelehr/t (gə'le:rt) *adj* learned. —**te(r)** *nm* scholar.

Geleit (gə'lait) *n neu* -e retinue, escort. —**en** *vt* escort.

Gelenk (gə'lɛŋk) *n neu* -e joint.

gelernt (gə'lɛrnt) *adj* trained, skilled.

Geliebte(r) (gə'li:ptə) *nm* sweetheart, lover.

gelinde (gə'lində) *adj* mild, soft.

gelingen* (gə'liŋən) *vi imp* succeed. **es gelingt mir, etwas zu tun** I am successful or I succeed in doing something.

gelitten (gə'litən) *v see* **leiden.**

geloben (gə'lo:bən) *vt* vow. **Gelübde** (gə'lypdə) *n neu* — vow.

gelogen (gə'lo:gən) *v see* **lügen.**

gelt/en* ('gɛltən) *vi* 1 be valid. 2 be worth. 3 pass for. 4 apply to. —**ung** *nf* -en 1 value. 2 validity.

gelungen (gə'luŋən) *v see* **gelingen.**

Gemach (gə'max) *n neu* ̈-er room, apartment. ̈-**lich** (gə'mɛçliç) *adj* 1 comfortable. 2 leisurely.

Gemahl (gə'ma:l) *nm* -e husband, consort. —**in** *nf* -**nen** wife, consort.

Gemälde (gə'mɛ:ldə) *n neu* — picture, painting.

gemäß (gə'mɛ:s) *prep* according to. *adj* conformable, appropriate. —**igt** *adj* moderate.

gemein (gə'main) *adj* 1 common, general. 2 vulgar. 3 mean. 4 nasty. —**e(r)** *nm mil* private. —**gut** *n neu* public property. —**heit** *nf* -en 1 vulgarity. 2 mean trick. —**hin** *adv* ordinarily, commonly. —**sam** *adj* common, joint. —**schaft** *nf* -en 1 community. 2 association, union.

Gemeinde (gə'maində) *nf* -**n** 1 community. 2 municipality. 3 parish. 4 congregation, communion. —**steuer** *nf* rates.

Gemenge (gə'mɛŋə) *n neu* — 1 mixture. 2 scuffle.

gemessen (gə'mɛsən) *adj* 1 measured, precise. 2 dignified, deliberate.

Gemisch (gə'miʃ) *n neu* -e mixture.

gemocht (gə'mɔxt) *v see* **mögen.**

Gemse ('gɛmzə) *nf* -n chamois.

Gemurmel (gə'murməl) *n neu* murmuring.

Gemüse (gə'my:zə) *n neu* — vegetable(s). —**händler** *nm* greengrocer.

Gemüt (gə'my:t) *n neu* -er 1 mind, soul. 2 temperament, disposition. —**lich** *adj* 1 good-natured, genial. 2 comfortable, cosy, agreeable. —**lichkeit** *nf* 1 geniality, kindliness. 2 comfort, cosiness.

Gen (gɛn) *n neu* -e gene.

genannt (gə'nant) *v see* **nennen.**

genau (gə'nau) *adj* exact, precise.

genehmig/en (gə'ne:migən) *vt* 1 approve. 2 ratify. —**ung** *nf* -en 1 approval. 2 permit. 3 ratification.

geneigt (gə'naikt) *adj* inclined or prone (to).

General (gene'ra:l) *nm* -e general. —**bevollmächtigte(r)** *nm* 1 chief representative. 2 commissioner. —**direktor** *nm* 1 general manager. 2 managing director. —**probe** *nf* dress rehearsal.

Generation (generatsi'o:n) *nf* -en generation.

genesen* (gə'ne:zən) *vi* recover, convalesce.

Genetik (ge'ne:tik) *nf* genetics.

Genf (gɛnf) *n neu* Geneva.

genial (geni'a:l) *adj* brilliant, inspired. —**ität** (geniali'tɛ:t) *nf* genius, brilliance.

Genick (gə'nik) *n neu* -e nape of the neck.

Genie (ʒe'ni:) *n neu* -s genius.

genieren (ʒe'ni:rən) *vt* 1 embarrass. 2 inconvenience. **sich genieren** *vr* feel embarrassed.

genieß/bar (gə'ni:sba:r) *adj* 1 enjoyable. 2 edible. 3 drinkable. —**en*** *vt* 1 enjoy. 2 eat. 3 drink.

Genitalien (geni'ta:liən) *n pl* genitals.

genommen (gə'nɔmən) *v see* **nehmen.**

genoß (gə'nɔs) *v see* **genießen.**

Genosse (gə'nɔsə) *nm* -n comrade, colleague. —**nschaft** *nf* -en 1 association. 2 company. 3 cooperative.

genossen (gə'nɔsən) *v see* **genießen.**

genug (gə'nu:k) *adj* enough, sufficient. —**e** (gə'ny:gə) *nf* sufficiency. —**en** (gə'ny:gən) *vi* suffice. —**end** (gə'ny:gənt) *adj* sufficient. —**sam** (gə'ny:kza:m) *adj* 1 easily satisfied. 2

unassuming. 3 frugal. —**tuung** (gə'nu:ktu:-uŋ) *nf* -en satisfaction.

Genuß (gə'nus) *nm* -nüsse 1 enjoyment, pleasure. 2 use. 3 consumption (of food, etc.).

Geograph (geo'gra:f) *nm* -en geographer. —**ie** (geogra'fi:) *nf* geography. —**isch** *adj* geographic(al).

Geolog/e (geo'lo:gə) *nm* -n geologist. —**ie** (geolo'gi:) *nf* geology. —**isch** *adj* geological.

Geometrie (geome'tri:) *nf* -n geometry.

Gepäck (gə'pɛk) *n neu* luggage. —**aufbewahrung** *nf* left-luggage office. —**netz** *n neu* luggage rack. —**träger** *nm* porter.

gepfiffen (gə'pfifən) *v see* **pfeifen.**

Gepflogenheit (gə'pflo:gənhait) *nf* -en habit, custom.

Geplapper (gə'plapər) *n neu* babble, prattle.

Geplauder (gə'plaudər) *n neu* chatter, talk.

Gepräge (gə'prɛ:gə) *n neu* — 1 impression, stamp. 2 character.

gerade (gə'ra:də) *adj* 1 straight. 2 even. 3 upright. 4 exact. *adv* 1 precisely. 2 just (now). 3 directly. —**aus** (gərada'aus) *adv* straight ahead or on. —**zu** (gəra:də'tsu:) *adv* directly, frankly.

Geradheit (gə'ra:thait) *nf* 1 straightness, evenness. 2 honesty.

Geranie (ge'ra:niə) *nf* -n *bot* geranium.

gerannt (gə'rant) *v see* **rennen.**

Gerät (gə'rɛ:t) *n neu* -e tool, implement, appliance.

geraten* (gə'ra:tən) *vi* 1 come or get into. 2 turn out. *adj* advisable.

geräumig (gə'rɔymiç) *adj* spacious, roomy.

Geräusch (gə'rɔyʃ) *n neu* -e noise.

gerben ('gɛrbən) *vt* tan (hides).

gerecht (gə'rɛçt) *adj* 1 straight. 2 just, fair. 3 suitable. 4 righteous. —**igkeit** *nf* 1 justice, fairness. 2 righteousness.

Gerede (gə're:də) *n neu* talk, gossip, rumour.

Gericht (gə'riçt) *n neu* -e 1 (law) court. 2 judgment. —**lich** *adj* judicial, legal. —**sbarkeit** *nf* jurisdiction. —**sdiener** *nm* bailiff. —**shof** *nm* (law) court.

gerieben (gə'ri:bən) *v see* **reiben.**

gering (gə'riŋ) *adj* 1 small, insignificant. 2 poor, inferior. —**fügig** *adj* insignificant, trivial. —**schätzung** *nf* disdain.

gerinnen* (gə'rinən) *vi* coagulate, congeal.

Gerippe (gə'ripə) *n neu* — skeleton.

gerissen (gə'risən) *v see* **reißen.** *adj* 1 torn. 2 clever, wily.

geritten (gə'ritən) *v see* **reiten.**

German/e (gɛrˈmaːnə) nm -n Teuton. **—isch** adj Germanic, Teutonic.

gern(e) (gɛrn) adv gladly, readily. **etwas gern haben** like something.

gerochen (gəˈrɔxən) v see **riechen**.

Gerste (ˈgɛrstə) nf barley.

Geruch (gəˈruːx) nm ⁺e smell, odour. **—sinn** nm sense of smell.

Gerücht (gəˈryçt) n neu -e rumour.

Gerüst (gəˈryst) n neu -e scaffold(ing), frame.

gesamt (gəˈzamt) adj total, whole, entire. **—ausgabe** nf complete edition. **—schule** nf comprehensive school.

gesandt (gəˈzant) v see **senden**.

Gesand/te(r) (gəˈzantə) nm envoy, diplomatic representative. **—schaft** nf -en legation, embassy.

Gesang (gəˈzaŋ) nm ⁺e 1 singing. 2 song.

Gesäß (gəˈzɛːs) n neu -e buttocks, seat.

Geschäft (gəˈʃɛft) n neu -e 1 business. 2 shop. **—lich** adj commercial. **—sführer** nm manager. **—smann** nm -leute businessman. **—sträger** nm 1 representative. 2 chargé d'affaires.

geschah (gəˈʃaː) v see **geschehen**.

gescheh/en' (gəˈʃeːən) vi happen, occur. n neu events, occurrences. **—nis** n neu -se event.

gescheit (gəˈʃait) adj intelligent, clever.

Geschenk (gəˈʃɛŋk) n neu -e present.

Geschicht/e (gəˈʃɪçtə) nf -n 1 history. 2 story. 3 affair. **—lich** adj historical. **—sschreiber** nm historian.

Geschick (gəˈʃɪk) n neu -e 1 skill, aptitude. 2 fate. **—lichkeit** nf -en skill, dexterity. **—t** adj skilful, dexterous.

geschieden (gəˈʃiːdən) v see **scheiden**. adj divorced.

geschienen (gəˈʃiːnən) v see **scheinen**.

Geschirr (gəˈʃɪr) n neu -e 1 dishes, crockery. 2 harness. **—tuch** n neu tea-towel.

Geschlecht (gəˈʃlɛçt) n neu -er 1 sex. 2 race. 3 species, kind. 4 family, blood. 5 gender. **—lich** adj sexual. **—skrankheit** nf venereal disease. **—sreife** nf puberty, sexual maturity. **—steile** nm pl genitals. **—sverkehr** nm sexual intercourse.

geschlossen (gəˈʃlɔsən) v see **schließen**.

Geschmack (gəˈʃmak) nm ⁺e 1 taste. 2 flavour. 3 liking, fancy. **—los** adj tasteless. **—sinn** nm sense of taste. **—voll** adj tasteful.

Geschnatter (gəˈʃnatər) n neu cackling.

geschnitten (gəˈʃnɪtən) v see **schneiden**.

geschoben (gəˈʃoːbən) v see **schieben**.

Geschöpf (gəˈʃœpf) n neu -e 1 creature. 2 creation.

Geschoß (gəˈʃɔs) n neu **-schosse** 1 missile. 2 bullet. 3 storey, floor.

geschossen (gəˈʃɔsən) v see **schießen**.

Geschrei (gəˈʃrai) n neu 1 shouting, clamour. 2 fuss.

geschrieben (gəˈʃriːbən) v see **schreiben**.

geschrie(e)n (gəˈʃriː(ə)n) v see **schreien**.

geschritten (gəˈʃrɪtən) v see **schreiten**.

Geschütz (gəˈʃyts) n neu -e gun, cannon.

geschwätzig (gəˈʃvɛtsɪç) adj talkative.

geschweige (gəˈʃvaigə) adv,conj also **geschweige denn** not to mention, let alone.

geschwiegen (gəˈʃviːgən) v see **schweigen**.

geschwind (gəˈʃvint) adj swift, quick. **—igkeit** (gəˈʃvindiçkait) nf -en speed. **—igkeitsmesser** nm speedometer. **—igkeitsbegrenzung** nf speed limit.

Geschwister (gəˈʃvistər) n pl brothers and sisters.

Geschworene(r) (gəˈʃvoːrənə) nm juror, juryman.

Geschwür (gəˈʃvyːr) n neu -e 1 ulcer. 2 abscess.

Gesell/e (gəˈzɛlə) nm -n 1 companion, fellow. 2 assistant. 3 journeyman. **—ig** adj sociable, companionable, gregarious. **—igkeit** nf sociability. **—schaft** nf -en 1 society. 2 company. 3 firm. 4 party, social gathering. **—schaftlich** adj 1 social. 2 sociable.

Gesetz (gəˈzɛts) n neu -e 1 law. 2 statute. **—gebend** adj legislative. **—geber** nm — legislator. **—gebung** nf -en legislation. **—lich** adj lawful, legal. **—los** adj lawless. **—mäßig** adj 1 legal. 2 legitimate. 3 regular. **—widrig** adj illegal.

gesetzt (gəˈzɛtst) adj 1 calm. 2 grave.

Gesicht (gəˈzɪçt) n neu -er face. **—skreis** nm horizon. **—spunkt** nm point of view.

Gesims (gəˈzɪms) n neu -e 1 moulding, cornice. 2 ledge.

gesinn/t (gəˈzɪnt) adj minded, disposed. **—ung** nf -en 1 convictions, beliefs. 2 attitude.

Gespann (gəˈʃpan) n neu -e team of (horses, oxen, etc.). **—t** adj 1 tense, strained. 2 curious. 3 anxious, agog.

Gespenst (gəˈʃpɛnst) n neu -er ghost, spectre.

Gespräch (gəˈʃprɛːç) n neu -e conversation, talk.

gesprochen (gəˈʃprɔxən) v see **sprechen**.

gesprungen (gəˈʃpruŋən) v see **springen**.

Gestalt (gə'ʃtalt) *nf* **-en 1** form, shape. **2** aspect. **3** figure. **4** stature. **—en** *vt* form. **sich —en** *vr* take shape.

gestanden (gə'ʃtandən) *v see* **stehen.**

Geständnis (gə'ʃtɛntnɪs) *n neu* **-nisse** confession.

Gestank (gə'ʃtaŋk) *nm* stench.

gestatten (gə'ʃtatən) *vt* permit, allow. **sich gestatten** *vr* **1** venture. **2** presume.

Geste ('gɛstə) *nf* **-n** gesture.

gestehen (gə'ʃte:ən) *vt* confess.

Gestein (gə'ʃtain) *n neu* **-e 1** stone. **2** mineral.

Gestell (gə'ʃtɛl) *n neu* **-e 1** stand. **2** frame. **3** trestle.

gest/ern ('gɛstərn) *adv* yesterday. **—rig** ('gɛstriç) *adj* yesterday's.

gestiegen (gə'ʃti:gən) *v see* **steigen.**

gestohlen (gə'ʃto:lən) *v see* **stehlen.**

Gesträuch (gə'ʃtrɔyç) *n neu* **-e** bush(es), shrubbery.

Gesuch (gə'zu:x) *n neu* **-e** petition, request.

gesund (gə'zunt) *adj* healthy, wholesome. **—heit** *nf* health, fitness.

gesungen (gə'zuŋən) *v see* **singen.**

gesunken (gə'zuŋkən) *v see* **sinken.**

getan (gə'ta:n) *v see* **tun.**

Getränk (gə'trɛŋk) *n neu* **-e** drink.

Getreide (gə'traidə) *n neu* cereals, grain, corn.

getreu (gə'trɔy) *adj* faithful, true, loyal.

getrieben (gə'tri:bən) *v see* **treiben.**

getroffen (gə'trɔfən) *v see* **treffen.**

getrost (gə'tro:st) *adj* confident.

getrunken (gə'truŋkən) *v see* **trinken.**

Getto ('geto:) *n neu* **-s** ghetto.

gewagt (gə'va:kt) *adj* risky, bold.

gewählt (gə'vɛ:lt) *adj* **1** selected. **2** refined.

Gewähr (gə'vɛ:r) *nf* guarantee, surety. **—en** *vt* allow, grant. **—leisten** *vt* guarantee.

Gewalt (gə'valt) *nf* **-en 1** violence, force. **2** power, might. **—ig** *adj* powerful, mighty. **—sam** *adj* violent, forcible.

Gewand (gə'vant) *n neu* **-̈er** gown, robe.

gewandt (gə'vant) *v see* **wenden.** *adj* agile, skilful.

gewann (gə'van) *v see* **gewinnen.**

Gewässer (gə'vɛsər) *n neu* waters, stretch of water.

Gewebe (gə've:bə) *n neu* **1** tissue. **2** textile, fabric.

geweckt (gə'vɛkt) *adj* alert, bright.

Gewehr (gə've:r) *n neu* **-e** gun, rifle.

Gewerb/e (gə'vɛrbə) *n neu* **-** trade, business, industry. **—lich** (gə'vɛrpliç) *adj* commercial.

Gewerkschaft (gə'vɛrkʃaft) *nf* **-en** trade union. **—ler** *nm* **-** trade-unionist.

gewesen (gə've:zən) *v see* **sein.**

Gewicht (gə'viçt) *n neu* **-e 1** weight. **2** importance. **—ig** *adj* important, weighty.

gewiesen (gə'vi:zən) *v see* **weisen.**

Gewimmel (gə'vimal) *n neu* swarms, throngs.

Gewinn (gə'vin) *nm* **-e 1** profit, gain. **3** winnings. **—en*** *vt* **1** win. **2** earn.

Gewirr (gə'vir) *n neu* confusion, tangle.

gewiß (gə'vis) *adj* sure, certain. **ein gewisser Herr** a certain gentleman. **~** *adv* indeed, certainly. **—ermaßen** *adv* to a certain extent. **—heit** *nf* **-en** certainty.

Gewissen (gə'visən) *n neu* conscience. **—los** *adj* unscrupulous.

Gewitter (gə'vitər) *n neu* **-** (thunder)storm. **—n** *vi* thunder.

gewogen (gə'vo:gən) *v see* **wiegen.** *adj* **1** affectionate. **2** well-disposed.

gewöhnen (gə'vø:nən) *vt* accustom. **sich gewöhnen** *vr* become accustomed or used (to).

Gewohnheit (gə'vo:nhait) *nf* **-en** habit. **—srecht** *n neu* common law.

gewöhnlich (gə'vø:nliç) *adj* usual, ordinary.

gewohnt (gə'vo:nt) *adj* accustomed.

Gewölbe (gə'vœlbə) *n neu* **-** arch, vault.

gewonnen (gə'vɔnən) *v see* **gewinnen.**

geworden (gə'vɔ:rdən) *v see* **werden.**

geworfen (gə'vɔ:rfən) *v see* **werfen.**

Gewürz (gə'vyrts) *n neu* **-e** seasoning, spice. **—ig** *adj* spicy.

gewußt (gə'vust) *v see* **wissen.**

gezogen (gə'tso:gən) *v see* **ziehen.**

gezwungen (gə'tsvuŋən) *v see* **zwingen.** *adj* **1** forced. **2** unnatural.

gibt (gi:bt) *v see* **geben.**

Gicht (giçt) *nf* **-en** gout.

Giebel ('gi:bəl) *nm* **-** gable.

Gier (gi:r) *nf* greed(iness). **—ig** *adj* greedy.

gießen* ('gi:sən) *vt* **1** pour. **2** water. **3** mould, found.

Gift (gift) *n neu* **-e** poison. **—ig** *adj* poisonous.

Gigue (ʒi:g) *nf* **-n** jig.

ging (giŋ) *v see* **gehen.**

Gipfel ('gipfəl) *nm* **-** peak, summit. **—höhe** *nf* aviat ceiling. **—n** *vi* culminate.

Gips (gips) *nm* **-e** plaster (of Paris), gypsum.

Giraffe (gi'rafə) *nf* **-n** giraffe.

Giro ('dʒi:ro:) *n neu* **-s 1** giro transfer. **2** endorsement.

Gischt (giʃt) *nm* **-e** spray, foam.

Gitarre (gi'tarə) *nf* **-n** guitar.

Gitter ('gitər) *n neu* — 1 grating, lattice. 2 railings, fence.

Glanz (glants) *nm* 1 brilliance, shine, lustre. 2 splendour. —**en** ('glɛntsən) *vi* shine, gleam.

Glas (gla:s) *n neu* ⁻**er** 1 glass. 2 drinking-glass. —**ern** ('glɛ:zərn) *adj* glass(y). —**ur** (gla'zu:r) *nf* -**en** 1 glaze. 2 enamel. 3 *cul* icing.

glatt (glat) *adj* 1 smooth, even. 2 slippery. 3 plain, downright. *adv* smoothly, easily. —**en** ('glɛtən) *vt* smooth, plane, polish.

Glaub/en ('glaubə) *nm* belief, faith. —**en** *vi* believe (in), trust. *vt* think. —**ig** ('glɔybiç) *adj* believing, faithful. —**iger** ('glɔybigə) *nm* believer. —**iger** ('glɔybigər) *nm* — creditor. —**würdig** ('glaupvyrdiç) *adj* credible, trustworthy.

gleich (glaiç) *adj* 1 same, like. 2 equal. 3 level, even. *adv* 1 equally, alike. 2 just. 3 at once, immediately.

gleichbedeutend ('glaiçbədɔytənt) *adj* 1 synonymous. 2 equivalent.

gleichberechtigt ('glaiçbərɛçtikt) *adj* having equal rights.

gleichen ('glaiçən) *vi* be like or equal.

gleichermaßen ('glaiçərmasən) *adv* in like manner, equally.

gleichfalls ('glaiçfals) *adv* likewise, equally.

Gleichgewicht ('glaiçgəviçt) *n neu* balance, equilibrium.

gleichgültig ('glaiçgyltiç) *adj* 1 indifferent. 2 unimportant.

Gleichheit (glaichait) *nf* -**en** 1 equality. 2 uniformity. **gleichmäßig** ('glaiçmɛsiç) *adj* 1 equal. 2 uniform. 3 symmetrical.

Gleichnis ('glaiçnis) *n neu* -**se** 1 parable. 2 simile. 3 image.

gleichschalten ('glaiçʃaltən) *vt* coordinate, synchronize.

Gleichschritt ('glaiçʃrit) *nm* marching in step.

Gleichstrom ('glaiçʃtro:m) *nm* direct current.

Gleichung ('glaiçuŋ) *nf* -**en** equation.

gleichviel ('glaiçvi:l) *adv* 1 no matter. 2 just as much.

gleichwohl ('glaiçvo:l) *adv* nevertheless.

gleichzeitig ('glaiçtsaitiç) *adj* simultaneous.

Gleis (glais) *n neu* -**e** 1 track. 2 rails.

gleiten ('glaitən) *vi* 1 glide. 2 slide.

Gletscher ('glɛtʃər) *nm* — glacier.

Glied (gli:t) *n neu* -**er** 1 member, limb. 2 row, rank. —**erung** ('gli:dəruŋ) *nf* -**en** 1 arrangement. 2 structure. 3 division. —**maßen** *n pl anat* extremities.

glimpflich ('glimpfliç) *adj* 1 gentle. 2 lenient.

Glocke ('glɔkə) *nf* -**n** bell. —**nblume** *nf* 1 bluebell. 2 harebell. —**nstuhl** *nm* belfry.

glor/ifizieren (glorifi'tsi:rən) *vt* glorify. —**reich** ('glo:raiç) *adj* glorious.

glotzen ('glɔtsən) *vi* stare, gape.

Glück (glyk) *n neu* 1 (good) luck. 2 fortune. 3 happiness. —**en** *vi* succeed, prosper. —**lich** *adj* 1 lucky. 2 happy. —**licherweise** *adv* fortunately —**wunsch** *nm* congratulation(s).

glüh/en ('gly:ən) *vi* glow, burn. —**birne** *nf* (light) bulb.

Glut (glu:t) *nf* -**en** 1 blaze, glow. 2 live coals, embers. 3 passion.

Gnad/e ('gna:də) *nf* -**n** 1 grace. 2 mercy. 3 favour. —**enfrist** *nf* reprieve, respite. —**ig** ('gnɛ:diç) *adj* 1 gracious. 2 merciful. **gnädige Frau** Madam.

Gold (gɔlt) *n neu* gold. —**en** ('gɔldən) *adj* gold(en). —**ig** ('gɔldiç) *adj* sweet, lovely, cute.

Golf [1] (gɔlf) *nm* -**e** gulf. —**strom** *nm* Gulf Stream.

Golf [2] (gɔlf) *n neu* golf.

gönn/en ('gœnən) *vt* grant, allow. —**er** *nm* — patron, benefactor.

goß (gɔs) *v* see **gießen**.

Gosse ('gɔsə) *nf* -**n** gutter.

Gott (gɔt) *nm* ⁻**er** god. —**esdienst** ('gɔtəsdi:nst) *nm* 1 church service. 2 worship. —**eslästerung** ('gɔtəslɛstəruŋ) *nf* blasphemy. —**in** ('gœtin) *nf* -**nen** goddess. —**lich** ('gœtliç) *adj* divine.

Götze ('gœtsə) *nm* -**n** idol.

Grab (gra:p) *n neu* ⁻**er** grave. —**en** ' ('gra:bən) *vt* dig. —**mal** *n neu* 1 tomb. 2 tombstone. —**schrift** *nf* epitaph. —**stätte** *nf* tomb, grave. —**stein** *nm* tombstone.

Grad (gra:t) *nm* -**e** 1 degree. 2 grade, rank.

Graf (gra:f) *nm* -**en** count, earl. —**in** ('grɛ:fin) *nf* -**nen** countess. —**schaft** *nf* -**en** county.

Gram (gra:m) *nm* grief, sorrow.

Gramm (gram) *n neu* -**e** gramme.

Grammat/ik (gra'matik) *nf* -**en** grammar. —**isch** *adj* grammatical.

Granatapfel (gra'na:tapfəl) *nm* pomegranate.

Granat/e (gra'na:tə) *nf* -**n** grenade, shell.

Granit (gra'ni:t) *nm* -**e** granite.

graphisch ('gra:fiʃ) *adj* graphic.

Gras (gra:s) *n neu* ⁻**er** grass. —**en** ('gra:zən) *vi* graze.

gräßlich ('grɛsliç) *adj* terrible, horrible.

Grat (gra:t) *nm* -**e** 1 edge. 2 ridge. 3 crest.

Gräte ('grɛ:tə) *nf* -**n** fishbone.

gratis ('gra:tis) *adj,adv* free (of charge).
gratulieren (gratu'li:rən) *vi* congratulate.
grau (grau) *adj* grey.
grauen[1] ('grauən) *vi* 1 become grey. 2 dawn.
grauen[2] ('grauən) *n neu* — horror, dread. **sich grauen** *vr* be afraid or horrified. **grauenhaft** *adj* horrible, dreadful.
grausam ('grauza:m) *adj* cruel, ferocious.
grausig ('grauziç) *adj* horrible, fearful.
gravieren (gra'vi:rən) *vt* engrave.
greifen* ('graifən) *vt* grasp, seize. *vi* 1 touch. 2 reach. 3 grope.
Greis (grais) *nm* -e old man. —**in** ('graisin) *nf* -nen old woman.
grell (grɛl) *adj* 1 harsh, sharp. 2 glaring.
Grenz/e (grɛnts) *nf* -n 1 frontier. 2 boundary, limit. —**en** *vi* border (on). —**enlos** *adj* limitless, boundless.
Greuel ('grɔyəl) *nm* — horror, abomination.
Griech/e ('gri:çə) *nm* -n Greek. —**enland** *n neu* Greece. —**isch** *adj* Greek. *n neu* Greek (language).
Grieß (gri:s) *nm* -e 1 gravel, grit. 2 semolina.
griff (grif) *v see* **greifen.**
Griff (grif) *nm* -e 1 grip, hold. 2 handle.
Grille ('grilə) *nf* -n 1 *zool* cricket. 2 whim.
grinsen ('grinzən) *vi* grin.
Grippe ('gripə) *nf* -n influenza, flu.
grob (gro:p) *adj* 1 coarse, crude. 2 gross.
Groll (grɔl) *nm* 1 grudge. 2 resentment.
Grönland ('grœ:nlant) *n neu* Greenland.
Gros (grɔs) *n neu* 1 gross. 2 main body. **en gros** wholesale.
Groschen ('grɔʃən) *nm* — ten-pfennig (piece).
groß (gro:s) *adj* 1 large, big. 2 tall. 3 great. **im großen** 1 in bulk. 2 wholesale. **im großen und ganzen** on the whole.
großartig ('gro:sa:rtiç) *adj* 1 grand, splendid. 2 lofty.
Großbritannien (gro:sbri'tanien) *n neu* Great Britain.
Größe ('grœ:sə) *nf* 1 size. 2 height. 3 greatness. 4 importance.
Großeltern ('gro:seltern) *n pl* grandparents.
großenteils ('gro:sentails) *adv* in large part, mostly.
Großhandel ('gro:shandəl) *nm* wholesale trade.
großherzig (gro:she:rtsik) *adj* magnanimous.
Großindustrie ('gro:sindustri:) *nf* heavy industry.
Großmacht ('gro:smaxt) *nf* great power.
Großmaul ('gro:smaul) *n neu* braggart, boaster.
Großmutter ('gro:smutər) *nf* grandmother.

Großstadt ('gro:sʃtat) *nf* (big) city.
größtenteils ('grœ:stəntails) *adv* for the most part, largely.
Großteil ('gro:stail) *nm* bulk.
Großvater ('gro:sfatə) *nm* grandfather.
großzügig ('gro:stsy:giç) *adj* 1 on a large scale. 2 generous.
grotesk (gro'tɛsk) *adj* grotesque.
Grube ('gru:bə) *nf* -n 1 hole, pit. 2 mine, quarry.
grübeln ('gry:bəln) *vi* brood, ponder.
grün (gry:n) *adj,n neu* green. —**kohl** *nm* kale.
Grund (grunt) *nm* -e 1 ground. 2 (plot of) land. 3 soil. 4 bottom, depth. 5 reason. 6 basis.
Grundbau ('gruntbau) *nm* foundation.
Grundbesitz ('gruntbazits) *nm* landed property.
gründ/en ('gryndən) *vt* 1 found. 2 ground. —**er** *nm* — founder.
Grundgesetz ('gruntgəzets) *n neu* 1 basic law. 2 constitution.
Grundlage ('gruntla:gə) *nf* foundation.
gründlich ('gryntliç) *adj* 1 thorough. 2 complete.
grundlos (gruntlo:s) *adj* baseless, groundless.
Grundriß ('gruntris) *nm* 1 outline. 2 plan.
Grundsatz ('gruntzats) *nm* 1 basic or fundamental principle. 2 axiom. —**lich** *adj* fundamental.
Grundstück ('gruntʃtyk) *n neu* piece of land.
Gründung ('grynduŋ) *nf* -en foundation, establishment.
grunzen ('gruntsən) *vi* grunt.
Grupp/e ('grupə) *nf* -n group. —**ieren** (gru'pi:rən) *vt* group, arrange.
gruselig (gru'za:liç) *adj* uncanny, creepy.
Gruß (gru:s) *nm* -e greeting. —**en** ('gry:sən) *vt* greet. **grüß Gott!** good day!
gucken ('gukən) *vi* look, peep.
Gulasch ('gu:laʃ) *nm,neu* -e goulash.
gültig ('gyltiç) *adj* 1 valid, good. 2 current. —**keit** *nf* 1 validity. 2 currency.
Gummi ('gumi) *nm,neu* -s 1 rubber. 2 gum. 3 eraser. —**band** *n neu* rubber band, elastic. —**schuh** *nm* overshoe, galosh.
Gunst (gunst) *nf* -e goodwill, favour. —**ig** ('gynstiç) *adj* favourable. —**ling** ('gynstliŋ) *nm* -e favourite.
gurgel/n ('gurgəln) *vi* 1 gargle. 2 gurgle. —**wasser** *n neu* gargle.
Gurke ('gurkə) *nf* -n cucumber.
Gürtel ('gyrtəl) *nm* — 1 belt. 2 zone.
Guß (gus) *nm* -üsse 1 pouring out, gush. 2 downpour. 3 casting. 4 *cul* icing.

gut (gu:t) adj good. adv well. —**achten** n neu — (expert) opinion. -̈**e** ('gy:tə) nf 1 goodness. 2 kindness. 3 excellence. —**heißen** vt approve (of). -̈**ig** ('gy:tiç) adj 1 kind. 2 good. 3 good-natured. —**willig** adj voluntary, willing.

Gut (gu:t) n neu -̈**er** 1 possession. 2 landed estate. 3 goods, wares. —**erbahnhof** ('gy:-tərba:nhof) nm goods yard. —**erzug** ('gy:-tərtsu:k) nm goods train. —**sherr** nm 1 lord of the manor. 2 landlord.

Gymnasium (gym'na:zium) n neu -**sien** grammar school.

H

Haag, Den (ha:k) nm The Hague.

Haar (ha:r) n neu -**e** hair. —**bürste** nf hairbrush. —**ig** adj hairy. —**schnitt** nm haircut. —**sträubend** adj hair-raising.

Hab/e ('ha:bə) nf — property, possessions. —**en**[*] vt have, possess. n neu credit. —**enichts** nm -**e** pauper. —**gier** ('ga:pgi:r) nf avarice, greed. —**seligkeiten** ('ha:pze:-liçkaitən) nf pl belongings, possessions.

Habicht ('ha:biçt) nm -**e** hawk.

hack/en ('hakən) vt 1 hash. 2 hack. 3 chop. —**fleisch** n neu minced meat, mince.

Hafen ('ha:fən) nm -̈ harbour, port. —**arbeiter** nm docker. —**damm** nm jetty. —**stadt** nf port.

Hafer ('ha:fər) nm — oat(s). —**brei** nm porridge. —**flocken** nf pl oat-flakes, rolled oats.

Haft (haft) nf 1 arrest. 2 imprisonment. —**befehl** nm warrant of arrest. —**en** vi 1 adhere, cling (to). 2 guarantee, answer (for). —**pflichtversicherung** nf -**en** third-party insurance. —**ung** nf -**en** liability.

Hagedorn ('ha:gədorn) nm -**e** hawthorn.

Hagel ('ha:gəl) nm — hail. —**n** vi hail.

hager ('ha:gər) adj gaunt.

Hahn (ha:n) nm -̈**e** 1 cock. 2 tap. -̈**chen** ('hɛ:nçən) n neu — 1 cockerel. 2 cul chicken.

Hai (hai) nm -**e** also **Haifisch** shark.

häkeln ('hɛ:kəln) vt crochet.

haken ('ha:kən) vi hook (on). nm — 1 hook. 2 difficulty, snag. —**kreuz** n neu swastika.

halb (halp) adj half. —**e(r)** ('halbə) nm half litre (of beer, wine, etc.). —**insel** nf peninsula. —**jährlich** adj half-yearly. —**kreis** nm semicircle. —**kugel** nf hemisphere. —**laut** adj (of a voice) low. adv in a low voice. —**messer** nm radius. —**mond** nm halfmoon, crescent. —**wegs** ('halpve:ks) adv 1 halfway. 2 to some or any extent.

half (half) v see **helfen**.

Hälfte ('hɛlftə) nf -**n** 1 half. 2 middle.

Halfter ('halftər) nm,neu —, nf -**n** halter.

Hall (hal) nm -**e** 1 clang. 2 peal. —**en** vi 1 resound. 2 clang.

Halle ('halə) nf -**n** 1 hall. 2 porch, lobby. 3 hangar. —**nbad** n neu indoor swimming pool.

Halm (halm) nm -**e** 1 blade (of grass). 2 stalk.

Hals (hals) nm -̈**e** 1 neck. 2 throat. —**starrig** ('halsʃtariç) adj obstinate, stubborn. —**tuch** n neu scarf. —**weh** n neu sore throat.

Halt (halt) nm -**e** 1 stop, halt. 2 support. —**bar** adj 1 tenable. 2 firm, lasting. **haltbar sein** (of foodstuffs) keep. —**los** adj 1 untenable. 2 unsteady.

halt/en[*] ('haltən) vt 1 hold. 2 keep. vi 1 stop, halt. 2 hold out. **halten fur** consider, deem. **sich halten** vr maintain oneself. —**estelle** nf (bus) stop.

hämisch ('hɛ:miʃ) adj malicious.

Hammelfleisch ('haməlflaiʃ) n neu mutton.

Hammer ('hamər) nm -̈ hammer. -̈**n** ('hɛmərn) vi,vt hammer.

Hamster ('hamstər) nm — hamster.

Hand (hant) nf -̈**e** hand. **an Hand von** with the aid of. **die Hand geben** shake hands. **in der Hand haben** have under one's control.

Handarbeit ('hanta:rbait) nf 1 manual work. 2 handwork, craft. 3 needlework.

Handbremse ('hantbremzə) nf handbrake.

Handbuch ('hantbux) n neu handbook.

Händedruck ('hɛndədruk) nm handshake.

Handel ('handəl) nm 1 trade, commerce. 2 transaction, deal. —**n** vi 1 act, do. 2 deal with. 3 haggle. 4 trade. **es handelt sich um** it is a question of. —**skammer** nf chamber of commerce. —**smarke** nf trademark, brand name. —**ssperre** nf embargo.

handfest ('hantfest) adj sturdy, strong.

Handfläche ('hantflɛçə) nf palm.

Handgelenk ('hantgəlɛŋk) n neu wrist.

Handgepäck ('hantgəpɛk) n neu hand luggage.

handhaben[*] ('hantha:bən) vt 1 handle. 2 manage.

Handschelle ('hantʃelə) nf -**n** handcuff.

Handschrift ('hantʃrift) nf 1 handwriting. 2 manuscript.

Handschuh ('hantʃu:) nm glove.

Handstreich ('hantʃtraiç) nm 1 raid. 2 surprise.

Handtasche ('hanttaʃə) nf handbag.

Handtuch ('hanttux) n neu towel.

Handwerk ('hantvɛrk) n neu craft, trade. **—er** nm artisan, craftsman.

Händler ('hɛndlər) nm — merchant, trader.

Handlung ('handluŋ) nf **-en** 1 act, action. 2 trade. 3 business, shop.

Hang (haŋ) nm **-̈e** 1 slope. 2 tendency. **-̈ebrücke** ('heŋəbrykə) nf suspension bridge. **-̈ematte** ('heŋəmatə) nf hammock. **—en** ('heŋən) vi 1 hang. 2 be attached. 3 depend (on). vt 1 hang. 2 attach.

Hannover (ha'noːfər) n neu Hanover.

Harfe ('harfə) nf **-n** harp.

harmlos ('harmloːs) adj harmless.

Harmon/ie (harmo'niː) nf — harmony. **—ika** (har'moːnika) nf **-s** 1 concertina. 2 harmonica. **—isch** (har'moːniʃ) adj harmonious, harmonic.

Harnisch ('harniʃ) nm **-e** armour.

Harpune (har'puːnə) nf **-n** harpoon.

harren ('harən) vi 1 wait for. 2 await. 3 hope for.

hart (hart) adj 1 hard. 2 rough. 3 severe. **-̈e** ('hɛrtə) nf 1 hardness. 2 roughness. 3 severity. **—en** ('hɛrtən) vt 1 harden, temper. **—näckig** ('hartnɛkiç) adj obstinate.

Harz (harts) n neu **-e** resin.

Haschisch ('haʃiʃ) n neu hashish.

Hase ('haːzə) nm **-n** hare.

Haselnuß ('haːzəlnus) nf hazelnut.

Haspe ('haspə) nf **-n** hasp, hinge.

Haß (has) nm hate, hatred. **-̈lich** ('hɛsliç) adj 1 ugly. 2 nasty, horrid.

hassen ('hasən) vt hate.

hast (hast) v see **haben**.

hasten ('hastən) vi hasten, hurry.

hat (hat) v see **haben**.

hätscheln ('hɛːtʃəln) vt 1 caress. 2 pamper, spoil.

hatte ('hatə) v see **haben**.

hätte ('hɛtə) v see **haben**.

Haube ('haubə) nf **-n** 1 cap, hood. 2 mot bonnet. 3 dome.

Hauch (haux) nm **-e** breath.

Haue ('hauə) nf **-n** 1 hoe. 2 thrashing, beating. **—n*** vt 1 chop. 2 fell. 3 thrash, spank.

Haufen ('haufən) nm — 1 heap, pile. 2 mass, large amount. **-̈en** ('hɔyfən) vt heap up, accumulate. **—enweise** ('haufənvaizə) adv in great quantities, in heaps.

häufig ('hɔyfiç) adj frequent. **—keit** nf **-en** frequency.

Haupt (haupt) n neu **-̈er** 1 head. 2 leader. **—bahnhof** nm main or central railway station. **—buch** n neu ledger. **—fach** n neu main subject. **—mann** nm captain. **—quartier** n neu headquarters. **—sache** nf main point or thing. **—sächlich** adj main, principal. **—stadt** nf capital. **—wort** n neu noun.

Haus (haus) n neu **-̈er** 1 house. 2 building. 3 home. **nach Hause gehen** go home. **zu Hause** at home. **—arbeit** nf 1 housework. 2 homework. **—en** ('hauzən) vi 1 live (economically). 2 play havoc. **—frau** nf housewife. **—halt** nm 1 housekeeping. 2 household. 3 budget. **—halten*** vi 1 keep house. 2 economize. **—herr** nm 1 head of the family. 2 landlord. **—ieren** (hau'ziːrən) vi peddle. **—meister** nm caretaker. **—tier** n neu domestic animal, pet.

Haut (haut) nf **-̈e** 1 skin, hide. 2 membrane, film. **-̈en** ('hɔytən) vt skin.

Hebamme ('heːpamə) nf **-n** midwife.

Heb/el ('heːbəl) nm — lever. **—en*** ('heːbən) vt lift, raise. **sich —en** vr 1 rise. 2 cancel. **—er** ('heːbər) nm — syphon. **—estange** ('heːbaʃtaŋə) nf crowbar. **—ung** ('heːbuŋ) nf **-en** 1 elevation 2 removal.

Hecht (hɛçt) nm **-e** pike.

Heck (hɛk) n neu stern, rear.

Hecke ('hɛkə) nf **-n** hedge. **—nschütze** nm sniper.

Heer (heːr) n neu **-e** army.

Hefe ('heːfə) nf **-n** 1 yeast. 2 dregs.

Heft (hɛft) n neu **-e** 1 handle. 2 exercise book. 3 (journal) volume, number. **—en** vt 1 fasten. 2 fix. 3 sew. **—klammer** nf paper clip. **—zwecke** nf drawing-pin.

heftig ('hɛftiç) adj 1 violent. 2 strong. 3 vehement. 4 fierce.

hegen ('heːgən) vt cherish, harbour.

Hehl (heːl) n neu 1 secret. 2 secrecy. **—en** vt 1 conceal. 2 receive (stolen property).

hehr (heːr) adj lofty, sublime.

Heide¹ ('haidə) nf **-n** heath. **—kraut** n neu heather. **—lbeere** nf bilberry.

Heid/e² ('haidə) nm **-n** heathen, pagan. **—nisch** adj heathen, pagan.

heikel ('haikəl) adj 1 critical. 2 delicate. 3 awkward.

heil (hail) adj 1 well. 2 unhurt. 3 whole. 4 sound, undamaged. n neu 1 welfare. 2

salvation. **—butt** ('hailbut) nm halibut. **—en** vt,vi heal. **—kraft** nf healing power. **—mittel** n neu remedy, cure. **—sam** adj 1 wholesome. 2 beneficial. **—sarmee** ('hailsarme:) nf Salvation Army. **—ung** nf **-en** 1 cure. 2 healing.

Heiland ('hailant) nm **-e** Saviour.

heilig ('hailiç) adj holy, sacred. **Heiliger Abend** Christmas Eve. **—e(r)** ('hailigə) nm saint. **—en** ('hailigən) vt sanctify. **—enschein** nm halo. **—keit** nf holiness, saintliness.

heim (haim) adv home(ward). n neu **-e** home. **—isch** adj domestic. **—kehr** nf homecoming. **—lich** adj secret. **—suchen** vt 1 visit. 2 punish. 3 afflict. **—tückisch** adj malicious. **—wärts** ('haimvɛrts) adv homeward(s). **—weh** n neu homesickness.

Heimat ('haima:t) nf 1 home. 2 homeland, native place. **—land** n neu homeland. **—los** adj homeless.

Heirat ('haira:t) nf **-en** marriage. **—en** vt marry. vi get married.

heiser ('haizər) adj hoarse.

heiß (hais) adj hot.

heißen* ('haisən) vi 1 be called. 2 mean. vt 1 name. 2 command. **das heißt, d.h.** that is, i.e.

heiter ('haitər) adj 1 cheerful. 2 serene, calm. 3 (of weather) bright, clear. **—keit** nf 1 cheerfulness. 2 brightness. 3 serenity.

Heiz/apparat ('haitsapara:t) nm heater. **—en** vt heat. **—körper** nm radiator. **—stoff** nm fuel. **—ung** nf **-en** heating.

Held (hɛlt) nm **-en** hero. **—enhaft** ('hɛldənhaft) adj heroic. **—in** ('hɛldin) nf **-nen** heroine.

helf/en* ('hɛlfən) vi 1 help, assist. **—er** nm **—** helper, assistant.

hell (hɛl) adj 1 bright. 2 light. 3 clear. **—e** nf 1 brightness. 2 daylight. 3 clearness.

Helm (hɛlm) nm **-e** helmet.

Hemd (hɛmt) n neu **-en** 1 shirt. 2 vest.

hemm/en ('hɛmən) vt 1 restrain, inhibit. 2 block. 3 hinder. 4 stop. **—ung** nf **-en** 1 restriction. 2 restraint. 3 check. 4 inhibition. **—ungslos** adj unrestrained, uninhibited.

Hengst (hɛŋst) nm **-e** stallion.

Henker ('hɛŋkər) nm**—** hangman, executioner.

her (he:r) adv 1 here, hither. 2 ago. 3 from.

herab (hɛ'rap) adv down(ward). **—lassen*** vt lower. **sich —lassen** vr condescend. **—setzen** vt 1 lower. 2 reduce. 3 degrade. **—setzung** nf **-en** 1 reduction. 2 degradation.

heran (hɛ'ran) adv 1 on (here). 2 up to. 3 along. **—kommen** vi draw near. **—treten*** vi step up (to), approach. **—ziehen*** vt 1 pull or draw up. 2 grow, raise. 3 make use of, call on. vi approach.

herauf (hɛ'rauf) adv 1 up (here). 2 upwards.

heraus (hɛ'raus) adv 1 out. 2 forth. **—finden*** vt find out. **—fordern** vt 1 challenge. 2 provoke. **—gabe** nf 1 publication, publishing. 2 delivering (up). **—geben*** vt 1 publish. 2 deliver up. 3 restore, give back. **—geber** nm publisher. **—stellen** vt put or bring out. **sich —stellen** vr turn out, prove to be.

herb (hɛrp) adj 1 (of taste, etc.) sharp, tart. 2 (of wine) dry.

herbei (hɛr'bai) adv 1 here, hither. 2 on. **—führen** vt 1 lead, bring (on). 2 cause, induce.

Herberge ('hɛrbɛrgə) nf **-n** 1 hostel. 2 lodging. **—n** vt,vi lodge, shelter.

Herbst (hɛrpst) nm **-e** autumn.

Herd (he:rt) nm **-e** 1 hearth, fireplace. 2 cooker, stove.

Herde ('he:rdə) nf **-n** herd, flock.

herein (hɛ'rain) adv 1 in (here). interj come in! **—lassen*** vt admit, allow in.

hergeben* ('he:rge:bən) vt hand over.

hergebracht ('he:rgəbraxt) adj 1 traditional, handed down. 2 established.

Hering ('he:riŋ) nm **-e** herring.

her/kommen* ('he:rkɔmən) vi 1 come from. 2 approach. n neu **—** 1 custom. 2 descent. **—kömmlich** ('he:rkœmliç) adj traditional. **—kunft** ('he:rkunft) nf 1 descent, origin.

hernach (hɛr'na:x) adv after(wards).

Heroin (hero'i:n) n neu heroin.

Herr (hɛr) nm **-en** 1 gentleman. 2 master, lord. 3 Mr. **—enhaus** n neu manor-house. **—gott** nm the Lord God. **—in** nf **-nen** mistress, lady. **—lich** adj 1 wonderful. 2 grand. 3 glorious. **—schaft** nf **-en** 1 rule, dominion. 2 power. 3 distinguished people. 4 manor. 5 estate. **—schen** ('hɛrʃən) vi 1 rule, govern. 2 dominate. 3 exist. 4 prevail. **—scher** ('hɛrʃər) nm **—** ruler. **—schsucht** ('hɛrʃzu:xt) nf 1 love of power. 2 ambition.

herstell/en ('he:rʃtɛlən) vt manufacture, produce. **—ung** nf **-en** manufacture, production.

herüber (hɛ'ry:bər) adv 1 over, across. 2 to this side or place.

herum (hɛ'rum) adv (a)round, about. **—führen** vt show or take (a)round. **—ziehen*** vi wander about.

57

herunter (hɛ'runtər) *adv* down, downwards. **—kommen*** *vi* 1 come down. 2 decay.

hervor (hɛr'fo:r) *adv* 1 forth, out. 2 forward. **—bringen*** *vt* produce. **—gehen*** *vi* 1 arise. 2 result. **—heben*** *vt* 1 stress. 2 highlight. **—ragend** *adj* 1 eminent. 2 projecting. 3 outstanding, excellent. **—rufen*** *vt* 1 call forth. 2 cause. **—treten*** *vi* come forward or out.

Herz (hɛrts) *n neu* **-en** heart. **—anfall** *nm* heart attack. **—lich** *adj* hearty, cordial. **—los** *adj* heartless. **—schlag** *nm med* stroke.

Herzog ('hɛrtso:k) *nm* **-e** duke. **—in** ('hɛrtso:gin) *nf* **-nen** duchess. **—tum** *n neu* -**tümer** duchy, dukedom.

herzu (hɛr'tsu:) *adv* 1 (to) here. 2 near. 3 up (to).

Hessen ('hɛsən) *n neu* Hesse.

Hetze ('hɛtsə) *nf* **-n** 1 hurry. 2 hunt. 3 agitation. **—n** *vt* 1 hunt. 2 set (dogs) on. 3 incite.

Heu (hɔy) *n neu* hay. **—gabel** *nf* pitchfork. **—schnupfen** *nm* hayfever. **—schrecke** *nf* **-n** 1 grasshopper. 2 locust.

Heuch/elei (hɔyçə'lai) *nf* **-en** hypocrisy. **—ler** ('hɔyçlər) *nm* hypocrite.

heulen ('hɔylən) *vi* howl, cry, scream.

heut/e ('hɔytə) *adv* today. **—ig** *adj* 1 of today. 2 modern, present. **—zutage** ('hɔyttsuta:gə) *adv* these days, nowadays.

Hexe ('hɛksə) *nf* **-n** 1 witch. 2 hag. **—rei** (hɛksə'rai) *nf* witchcraft.

Hieb (hi:p) *nm* **-e** 1 blow, stroke. 2 cut.

hielt (hi:lt) *v* see **halten**.

hier (hi:r) *adv* here. **—auf** (hi:'rauf) *adv* hereupon. **—bei** (hi:r'bai) *adv* 1 at this. 2 enclosed. **—durch** (hi:r'durç) *adv* hereby. **—her** (hi:r'he:r) *adv* 1 this way. 2 here. **—in** (hi:'rin) *adv* in this. **—von** (hi:r'fɔn) *adv* of this. **—zu** (hi:r'tsu:) *adv* in addition, moreover. **—zulande** ('hi:rtsulandə) *adv* in this country, in these parts, around here.

hiesig ('hi:ziç) *adj* of this place, local.

Hilf/e ('hilfə) *nf* **-n** help, assistance. **erste Hilfe** first aid. **—eleistung** *nf* assistance. **—los** *adj* helpless. **—reich** *adj* helpful. **—sarbeiter** *nm* unskilled or temporary worker. **—smittel** *n neu* 1 remedy. 2 resource.

Himbeere ('himbe:rə) *nf* **-n** raspberry.

Himmel ('himəl) *nm* **—** 1 sky. 2 heaven. **—fahrt** *nf* Ascension. **—reich** *n neu* (kingdom of) heaven.

himmlisch ('himliʃ) *adj* heavenly.

hin (hin) *adv* 1 (to) there. 2 gone, lost. 3 ruined. **hin und her** to and fro.

hinab (hi'nap) *adv* down(wards).

hinan (hi'nan) *adv* up (to), upward(s).

hinauf (hi'nauf) *adv* 1 up (to). 2 on high.

hinaus (hi'naus) *adv* out. **—gehen*** *vi* 1 go out. 2 result (in). **—gehen über** go beyond, exceed. **—wollen*** *vi* 1 want to go out. 2 aim at.

Hinblick ('hinblik) *nm* **im Hinblick auf** with regard to.

hinder/lich ('hindərliç) *adj* 1 in the way. 2 inconvenient. **—n** *vt* 1 prevent. 2 hinder. **—nis** *n neu* **-se** obstacle.

hindeuten ('hindɔytən) *vi* point (to or at).

hindurch (hin'durç) *adv* 1 through(out). 2 across.

hinein (hi'nain) *adv* in(to). **—gehen*** *vi* 1 go in(to). 2 contain. **—ziehen*** *vt* draw or pull in.

Hinfahrt ('hinfa:rt) *nf* outward journey.

hinfall/en* ('hinfalən) *vi* fall (down). **—ig** ('hinfɛliç) *adj* 1 obsolete. 2 decaying. 3 weak.

Hin/gabe ('hinga:bə) *nf* 1 delivery. 2 devotion. 3 surrender. **—geben*** ('hinge:bən) *vt* give away or up.

hingegen ('hinge:gən) *adv* on the other hand.

hingehen* ('hinge:ən) *vi* 1 go there or to. 2 pass away or over.

hinken ('hiŋkən) *vi* limp.

hinlegen ('hinle:gən) *vt* lay down. **sich hinlegen** *vr* lie down.

hinnehmen* ('hinne:mən) *vt* 1 receive, accept. 2 put up with.

hinreichend ('hinraiçənt) *adj* sufficient.

Hinreise ('hinraizə) *nf* outward journey or voyage.

hinricht/en ('hinriçtən) *vt* execute, put to death. **—ung** *nf* **-en** execution.

Hinsicht ('hinziçt) *nf* **in dieser Hinsicht** in this respect. **—lich** *prep* with regard to, as for.

hinten ('hintən) *adv* behind, at the back.

hinter ('hintər) *prep* behind, after. *adj* posterior, back. **—backe** *nf* buttock. **—einander** (hintərain'andər) *adv* one after another. **—gehen*** *vt* deceive. **—grund** *nm* background. **—halt** *nm* ambush, trap. **—her** (hintər'he:r) *adv* after(wards), behind. **—lassen*** *vt* 1 leave (behind). 2 bequeath. **—list** *nf* 1 cunning. 2 fraud. **—teil** *n neu* 1 back part or side. 2 *inf* bottom, bum, backside. **—tür** *nf* backdoor.

hinüber (hi'ny:bər) *adv* 1 over (there). 2 across. 3 beyond.

hinunter (hi'nuntər) *adv* down (there).

hinweg (hin'vɛk) *adv* 1 away. 2 off. *nm* outward journey.

Hinweis ('hinvais) *nm* -e 1 indication. 2 direction. —**en** ('hinvaizən) *vi* 1 point to. 2 allude to. *vt* 1 show. 2 direct (someone).

hinwerfen* ('hinvɛrfən) *vt* 1 throw down. 2 sketch. 3 note.

hinziehen* ('hintsi:ən) *vt* draw out or along. *vi* move (house). **sich hinziehen** *vr* drag or stretch out.

hinzu (hin'tsu:) *adv* 1 in addition. 2 near. —**fügen** *vt* 1 add. 2 enclose.

Hirn (hirn) *n neu* -e brain(s). —**schale** *nf* skull, cranium.

Hirsch (hirʃ) *nm* -e deer, stag.

Hirt (hirt) *nm* -en shepherd, herdsman. —**in** *nf* -nen shepherdess.

hissen ('hisən) *vt* hoist (up).

Histor/iker (hi'sto:rikər) *nm* — historian. —**isch** *adj* historic(al).

Hitz/e ('hitsə) *nf* heat. —**ig** *adj* hot, heated, fiery. —**kopf** *nm* hothead.

hoch (ho:x) *adj* 1 high, tall. *adv* up. *n neu* -e 1 cheer. 2 high (pressure).

Hochachtung ('ho:xaxtuŋ) *nf* respect, esteem. —**svoll** *adj* respectful. *adv* yours respectfully or sincerely.

Hochdruck ('ho:xdruk) *nm* high pressure.

Hochebene ('ho:xe:bənə) *nf* plateau.

hochfahrend ('ho:xfa:rənt) *adj* haughty.

Hochflut ('ho:xflu:t) *nf* high tide.

hochhalten* ('ho:xhaltən) *vt* 1 raise. 2 cherish.

Hochhaus ('ho:xhaus) *n neu* high-rise building.

Hochland ('ho:xlant) *n neu* highland, upland.

Hochmut ('ho:xmu:t) *nm* pride. —**tig** ('ho:x-my:tiç) *adj* proud.

hochnäsig ('ho:xnɛ:ziç) *adj inf* stuck-up, pretentious.

Hochschätzung ('ho:xʃɛtsuŋ) *nf* esteem.

Hochschule ('ho:xʃu:lə) *nf* college, university.

höchst (hœ:xst) *adj* 1 highest. 2 extreme. *adv* 1 most. 2 highly. —**ens** ('hœ:xstəns) *adv* at most or best. —**geschwindigkeit** ('ho:xst-gəʃvindiçkait) *nf* maximum speed.

Hochstapler ('ho:xʃta:plər) *nm* — swindler, confidence trickster.

Hochverrat ('ho:xfɛra:t) *nm* high treason.

Hochwasser ('ho:xvasə) *n neu* high water or tide.

Hochzeit ('hɔxtsait) *nf* -en wedding.

hock/en ('hɔkən) *vi* squat, crouch. —**er** *nm* — stool.

Hoden ('ho:dən) *nm* — *also* **Hode** *nf* -n testicle.

Hof (ho:f) *nm* -e 1 court. 2 yard. 3 farm. 4 halo. **jemandem den Hof machen** court or woo someone. —**rat** *nm* privy councillor.

hoff/en ('hɔfən) *vt,vi* hope (for). —**entlich** *adv* 1 hopefully. 2 it is to be hoped that. —**nung** *nf* -en hope. —**nungslos** *adj* hopeless. —**nungsvoll** *adj* hopeful.

höflich ('hœfliç) *adj* polite, courteous. —**keit** *nf* -en courtesy, politeness.

Höhe ('hœ:ə) *nf* -n 1 height, altitude. 2 hill. 3 top. —**punkt** *nm* 1 summit. 2 climax. —**r** *adj* higher, upper.

Hoheit ('ho:hait) *nf* — en grandeur, majesty.

hohl (ho:l) *adj* 1 empty, hollow. 2 concave. —**e** ('ho:lə) *nf* -n 1 cave. 2 den. —**maß** *neu* 1 capacity. 2 volume. —**ung** ('ho:luŋ) *nf* -en 1 excavation. 2 cavity.

Hohn (ho:n) *nm* scorn. —**isch** ('hoe:niʃ) *adj* scornful.

hold (hɔlt) *adj* charming, lovely.

holen ('ho:lən) *vt* 1 fetch. 2 call for.

Hölle ('hœlə) *nf* -n hell.

Holunder (ho'lundər) *nm* — *bot* elder.

Holz (hɔlts) *n neu* -er wood. —**ern** ('hœltsərn) *adj* wooden. —**kohle** *nf* charcoal. —**schnitt** *nm* woodcut.

Honig ('ho:niç) *nm* honey.

Honorar (hono'ra:r) *n neu* -e 1 honorarium. 2 royalty (payment).

Hopfen ('hɔpfən) *nm* — *bot* hop(s).

hör/bar ('hœ:rba:r) *adj* audible. —**en** *vt,vi* hear, listen (to). *n neu* hearing. —**er** *nm* — 1 hearer, listener. 2 student. 3 receiver. 4 headset. —**gerät** *n neu* hearing aid. —**saal** *nm* 1 auditorium. 2 lecture room. —**spiel** *n neu* radio play. —**weite** *nf* earshot.

horchen ('hɔrçən) *vi* listen (secretly).

Horde ('hɔrdə) *nf* -n 1 horde. 2 gang.

Horizont (hori'tsɔnt) *nm* -e horizon.

Hormon (hɔr'mo:n) *n neu* -e hormone.

Horn (hɔrn) *n neu* -er horn.

Horoskop (horo'sko:p) *n neu* -e horoscope.

Hose ('ho:zə) *nf* -n trousers. —**nbandorden** *nm* Order of the Garter. —**nträger** *nm pl* braces.

Hotel (ho'tɛl) *n neu* -s hotel.

Hub (hu:p) *nm* -e 1 *tech* stroke. 2 lift(ing). —**schrauber** *nm* — helicopter.

hübsch (hypʃ) *adj* 1 pretty. 2 nice, fine.

Huf (hu:f) *nm* -e hoof.

Hüfte ('hyftə) *nf* -n hip.

Hügel ('hy:gəl) *nm* — hill, knoll.
Huhn (hu:n) *n neu* ⸚er 1 chicken. 2 hen. **—erauge** ('hy:nɔraugə) *n neu med* corn.
Huldigung ('huldiguŋ) *nf* -en homage.
Hülle ('hylə) *nf* -n 1 cover(ing), wrapping. 2 case. **—n** *vt* wrap, cover.
Hülse ('hylzə) *nf* -n husk, shell, case.
human (hu'ma:n) *adj* humane. **—itär** (humani-'tɛːr) *adj* humanitarian.
Hummel ('huməl) *nf* -n bumblebee.
Hummer ('humər) *nm* — lobster.
Humor (hu'mo:r) *nm* -e (sense of) humour.
humpeln ('humpəln) *vi* hobble.
Hund (hunt) *nm* -e dog. ⸚in ('hyndin) *nf* -nen bitch.
hundert ('hundərt) *adj,n neu* -s hundred. **—jahrfeier** (hundərt'jaːrfaiər) *nf* centenary.
Hung/er ('huŋər) *nm* hunger. **—ersnot** *nf* famine. **—rig** *adj* hungry.
Hupe ('hu:pə) *nf* -n mot horn, hooter. **—n** *vi* sound the horn.
hüpfen ('hypfən) *vi* hop, skip.
Hürde ('hyrdə) *nf* -n 1 hurdle. 2 pen, fold.
Hure ('hu:rə) *nf* -n whore, prostitute.
husten ('hu:stən) *vi* cough. *nm* — cough.
Hut[1] (hu:t) *nm* ⸚e hat.
Hut[2] (hu:t) *nf* care, charge, protection.
hüten ('hy:tən) *vt* guard, watch over. **sich hüten** *vr* take care, be on one's guard.
Hütte ('hytə) *nf* -n 1 hut, cabin. 2 cottage. 3 forge.
Hyäne (hy'ɛ:nə) *nf* -n hyena.
Hygien/e (hygi'e:nə) *nf* hygiene. **—isch** *adj* hygienic.
Hymne ('hymnə) *nf* -n hymn.
Hypno/se (hyp'no:zə) *nf* -n hypnosis. **—tisch** *adj* hypnotic.
Hypothek (hypo'te:k) *nf* -en mortgage.
Hypothe/se (hypo'te:zə) *nf* -n hypothesis. **—tisch** *adj* hypothetical.
Hysterie (hyste'ri:) *nf* -n hysteria.

I

ich (iç) *pron 1st pers* s I. *n neu* self, ego.
ideal (ide'a:l) *adj* ideal. *n neu* -e ideal. **—ismus** (idea'lismus) *nm* idealism.
Idee (i'de:) *nf* -n idea.
identisch (i'dɛntiʃ) *adj* identical.
idiomatisch (idio'ma:tiʃ) *adj* idiomatic. **idiomatischer Ausdruck** *nm* idiom.

Idiot (idi'o:t) *nm* -en idiot. **—isch** *adj* idiotic, stupid.
ignorieren (igno'ri:rən) *vt* ignore, disregard.
ihm (i:m) *pron 3rd pers* s (to) him or it.
ihn (i:n) *pron 3rd pers* s him, it.
ihnen ('i:nən) *pron 1 3rd pers pl* (to) them. 2 *cap 2nd pers* s,pl fml (to) you.
ihr (i:r) *pron 1 3rd pers* s (to) her or it. 2 *2nd pers pl fam* you. *poss adj 1 3rd pers* s her. 2 *3rd pers pl* their. 3 *cap 3rd pers* s,pl your. **—er** *poss pron also* **der —e** or **der —ige** 1 *3rd pers* s hers. 2 *cap 3rd pers* s,pl fml yours. 3 *3rd pers pl* theirs. **—erseits** ('i:rarzaits) *adv* 1 on her or their part. 2 *cap* on your part. **—ethalben** *adv also* **—etwegen** or **—etwillen** 1 for her or their sake. 2 *cap* for your sake.
Illusion (iluzi'o:n) *nf* -en illusion.
illustrier/en (ilu'stri:rən) *vt* illustrate. **—te** *nf* -n (illustrated or colour) magazine.
im (im) contraction of **in dem**.
Imbiß ('imbis) *nm* -bisse snack, light meal. **Imbiß-Stube** *nf* snack bar.
Immatrikulation (imatrikulatsi'o:n) *nf* -en matriculation.
immer ('imər) *adv* always, ever. **—grün** *adj* evergreen. *n neu* -e evergreen. **—hin** *adv* nevertheless, yet, still.
Immigrant (imi'grant) *nm* -en immigrant.
Immobilien (imo'bi:liən) *nm pl* real estate.
imperfekt ('impɛrfɛkt) *n neu* -e *gram* imperfect.
impf/en ('impfən) *vt* vaccinate, inoculate. **—stoff** *nm* vaccine, serum.
imponieren (impo'ni:rən) *vt* impress.
Import (im'pɔrt) *nm* -e import(ation). **—ieren** (impor'ti:rən) *vt* import.
impotent ('impotɛnt) *adj* impotent.
improvisieren (improvi'zi:rən) *vt,vi* improvise, ad-lib.
imstande (im'ʃtandə) *adv* **imstande sein** be able or capable, be in a position (to).
in (in) *prep* 1 in(to). 2 at. 3 to. 4 during.
Inbegriff ('inbəgrif) *nm* 1 embodiment. 2 contents.
Inbrunst ('inbrunst) *nf* ardour, fervour.
indem (in'de:m) *conj* 1 while. 2 as, because. *adv* meanwhile.
Inder ('indər) *nm* — (Asian) Indian.
indes (in'dɛs) *adv also* **indessen** (in'dɛsən) 1 meanwhile. 2 however. 3 nevertheless. *conj* yet.
Indian/er (indi'a:nər) *nm* — (American) Indian. **—isch** *adj* Indian.

Indi/en ('indiən) n neu India. **—sch** ('indiʃ) adj Indian.

Indikativ ('indikati:f) nm -e gram indicative.

indirekt ('indirɛkt) adj indirect.

individu/ell (individu'ɛl) adj individual. **—um** (indi'vi:duum) n neu **-uen** individual, person.

Indones/ien (indo'ne:zian) n neu Indonesia. **—ier** nm — Indonesian. **—isch** adj Indonesian.

Industrie (indus'tri:) nf -n industry. **—ll** (industri'ɛl) adj industrial. **—lle(r)** (industri'ɛlə) nm industrialist.

ineinander (inain'andər) adv into one another.

Infanterie (infantə'ri:) nf -n infantry, foot.

infizieren (infi'tsi:rən) vt infect.

Inflation (inflatsi'o:n) nf -en comm inflation.

infolge (in'fɔlgə) prep in consequence of, due to. **—dessen** (infɔlgə'dɛsən) adv 1 accordingly, then. 2 as a result of this, due to which.

Inform/ation (infɔrmatsi'o:n) nf -en (item of) information. **—ationsbüro** n neu information bureau or centre. **—ieren** (infɔr'mi:rən) vt 1 inform. 2 instruct.

Ingenieur (inʒe'njœ:r) nm -e engineer. **—wesen** n neu engineering.

Inhaber ('inha:bər) nm — possessor, holder.

Inhalt ('inhalt) nm -e 1 contents. 2 volume. 3 meaning. **—sverzeichnis** n neu 1 table of contents. 2 index.

Initiative (initsia'ti:və) nf initiative.

inklusive (inklu'zi:və) adv inclusive, including.

Inkrafttreten (in'kraftre:tən) n neu coming into force or effect.

Inland ('inlant) n neu 1 native country. 2 inland.

inmitten (in'mitən) prep amid(st).

inne ('inə) adv within. **—halten*** vi stop. vt keep to.

innen ('inən) adv within, inside.

inner ('inər) adj inner, interior. **—halb** prep,adv within, inside. **—lich** adj inward, inner. **—st** adj inmost.

innig ('iniç) adj heartfelt, sincere.

ins (ins) contraction of **in das. —besondere** (insbə'zɔndərə) adv in particular. **—geheim** (insgə'haim) adv secretly. **—gesamt** (insgə'zamt) adv altogether.

Insasse ('inzasə) nm -n inmate, occupant.

Inschrift ('inʃrift) nf -en inscription.

Insekt (in'zɛkt) n neu -en insect. **—engift** n neu insecticide.

Insel ('inzəl) nf -n island, isle.

Inserat (inzə'ra:t) n neu -e advertisement, announcement.

insofern (inzo'fɛrn) adv also **insoweit** (inzo'vait) in this respect, to that extent. conj in so far as, inasmuch as.

instand halten* (in'ʃtanthaltən) vt maintain (in good order).

Instanz (in'stants) nf -en 1 law court. 2 authority.

Instinkt (in'stiŋkt) nm -e instinct.

Institut (insti'tu:t) n neu -e institute.

Instrument (instru'mɛnt) n neu -e instrument.

inszenieren (instse'ni:rən) vt stage, produce.

intelligen/t (intɛli'gɛnt) adj intelligent. **—z** (intɛli'gɛnts) nf 1 intelligence. 2 intelligentsia.

interess/ant (intərɛ'sant) adj interesting. **—e** (intə'rɛsə) n neu -n interest. **—ieren** (intərɛ'si:rən) vt interest. **sich —ieren** vr be interested.

international (intɛrnatsio'na:l) adj international. **—e** nf pol International.

intim (in'ti:m) adj intimate.

Intrige (in'tri:gə) nf -n intrigue, plot.

inwendig ('invɛndiç) adj interior, inside.

inwiefern (invi'fɛrn) adv also **inwieweit** (invi:'vait) to what extent, how far.

inzwischen (in'tsviʃən) adv meanwhile.

Irak (i'ra:k) nm Iraq. **—er** nm Iraqi. **—isch** adj Iraqi.

irdisch ('irdiʃ) adj 1 worldly, earthly. 2 mortal.

irgend ('irgənt) pron,adv some, any. **irgend etwas** something (or other). **irgend jemand** anybody, somebody or other. **—ein** (irgənt'ain) pron,adj some(one), any(one). **—wann** (irgənt'van) adv at some time. **—was** (irgənt'vas) pron something (or other). **—wie** (irgənt'vi:) adv somehow. **—wo** (irgənt'vo:) adv somewhere.

Iris ('i:ris) nf — anat iris.

Ir/land ('irlant) n neu Ireland. **—e** ('i:rə) nm -n also **—länder** — Irishman. **—in** nf -nen also **—länderin** Irishwoman. **—isch** adj Irish.

Iron/ie (iro'ni:) nf -n irony. **—isch** (i'ro:niʃ) adj ironical.

irr/e ('irə) adj 1 stray. 2 mad. 3 unsettled. 4 confused. **—e(r)** nm lunatic. **—eführen** vt 1 mislead. 2 deceive. **—en** vi wander, stray. **sich —en** vr 1 err. 2 be mistaken. **—ig** adj also **—tümlich** erroneous, false. **—tum** nm "er error, fault.

isolieren (izo'li:rən) vt 1 isolate. 2 insulate.

ißt (ist) v see **essen.**

ist (ist) v see **sein**[2].

Italien (i'ta:liən) n neu Italy. **—er** (itali'e:nər)

nm — Italian. **—isch** (itali'e:nɪʃ) *adj* Italian. *n neu* Italian (language).

J

ja (ja) *adv* yes, indeed. *n neu* **-s** assent. **mit Ja antworten** reply in the affirmative.

Jacht (jaxt) *nf* **-en** yacht.

Jacke ('jakə) *nf* **-n** jacket.

Jagd (ja:kt) *nf* **-en** hunt, hunting.

jag/en ('ja:gən) *vt* 1 hunt. 2 shoot. 3 drive. *vi* 1 hunt. 2 rush. **—er** ('jɛ:gər) *nm* — 1 hunter. 2 rifleman. 3 fighter pilot. 4 fighter plane.

jäh (jɛ:) *adj* 1 sudden. 2 steep.

Jahr (ja:r) *n neu* **-e** year. **—elang** *adj* lasting for one or several years. *adv* for years. **—eswechsel** *nm* turn of the year, New Year. **—eszeit** *nf* season. **—hundert** (ja:r-'hundərt) *n neu* **-e** century. **—lich** ('jɛ:rlɪç) *adj* annual. **—tausend** (ja:r'tauzənt) *n neu* **-e** millennium. **—zehnt** (ja:r'tse:nt) *n neu* **-e** decade.

Jammer ('jamər) *nm* 1 misery, sorrow. 2 lamentation. **—lich** ('jɛ:mərlɪç) *adj* pitiful. **—n** *vi* lament, bewail.

Januar ('janua:r) *nm* January.

Japan ('ja:pan) *n neu* Japan. **—er** (ja'pa:nər) *nm* — Japanese. **—isch** (ja'pa:nɪʃ) *adj* Japanese. *n neu* Japanese (language).

jauchzen ('jauxtsən) *vi* rejoice, shout with joy.

jawohl (ja'vo:l) *adv* yes indeed, certainly.

Jazz (dʒɛs) *nm* jazz.

je (je:) *adv* 1 ever. 2 each, apiece. **je...desto** the...the. **je nachdem** according as or to.

jedenfalls ('je:dənfals) *adv* in any case.

jeder, jede, jedes ('je:dər, 'je:də, 'je:dəs) *pron,adj m,f,neu* every, each.

jedermann ('je:dərman) *pron* everyone.

jederzeit ('je:dərtsait) *adv* at any time.

jedesmal ('je:dəsma:l) *adv* every time, each time.

jedoch (je'dɔx) *adv* however, yet.

jeglicher ('je:klɪçər) *pron,adj* every, each.

jemals ('je:ma:ls) *adv* at any time, ever.

jemand ('je:mant) *pron* someone, anyone.

jener, jene, jenes ('je:nər, 'je:nə, 'je:nəs) *pron,adj m,f,neu* 1 that. 2 the former.

jenseits ('jɛnzaits) *adv* on the other side. *prep* beyond. *n neu* the other world, the life to come.

jetz/ig ('jɛtsɪç) *adj* present, actual, current. **—t** *adv* at present, now.

62

Joch (jɔx) *n neu* **-e** yoke.

Jockei ('dʒɔki) *nm* **-s** jockey.

Jod (jo:t) *n neu* iodine.

jodeln ('jo:dəln) *vi* yodel.

Joghurt ('jo:gurt) *n neu* **-s** yoghurt.

Johannisbeere (jo'hanisbe:rə) *nf* redcurrant. **schwarze Johannisbeere** blackcurrant.

Journalist (ʒurna'list) *nm* **-en** journalist.

Jubel ('ju:bəl) *nm* rejoicing. **—n** *vi* rejoice.

jucken (jukən) *vt,vi* itch.

Jud/e ('ju:də) *nm* **-n** Jew. **—entum** *n neu* Judaism, Jewry. **—in** ('jy:din) *nf* **-nen** Jewess. **—isch** ('jy:dɪʃ) *adj* Jewish.

Judo ('ju:do) *n neu* judo.

Jugend ('ju:gənt) *nf* youth. **—lich** *adj* youthful, juvenile. **—herberge** *nf* youth hostel.

Jugoslaw/e (jugo'sla:və) *nm* **-n** Yugoslav. **—ien** *n neu* Yugoslavia. **—isch** *adj* Yugoslav(ian).

Juli ('ju:li) *nm* July.

jung (juŋ) *adj* young. **—e** *nm* **-n** youth, boy, lad. **—er** ('jyŋər) *adj* 1 younger. 2 junior. *nm* — disciple. **—fer** *nf* **-n** maid, virgin. **alte Jungfer** old maid, spinster. **—frau** *nf* 1 virgin, maiden. 2 Virgo. **—geselle** *nm* bachelor. **—ling** ('jyŋlɪŋ) *nm* **-e** youth, young man. **—st** (jyŋst) *adj* 1 youngest. 2 latest. **das Jüngste Gericht** the Last Judgment.

Juni ('ju:ni) *nm* June.

Junker ('juŋkər) *nm* — (young) nobleman, squire.

Jur/a[1] ('ju:ra) *n pl* (study of) law. **—ist** (ju'rist) *nm* **-en** lawyer.

Jura[2] ('ju:ra) *nm* **-s** the Juras.

just (just) *adv* 1 exactly. 2 just (now). 3 only just.

Justiz (jus'ti:ts) *nf* 1 legal administration. 2 justice.

Juwel (ju've:l) *n neu* **-en** jewel. **—ier** (juvə'li:r) *nm* **-e** jeweller.

Jux (juks) *nm* **-e** joke, prank.

K

Kabarett (kaba'rɛt) *n neu* **-e** cabaret.

Kabel ('ka:bəl) *n neu* — cable.

Kabine (ka'bi:nə) *nf* **-n** 1 cabin. 2 cubicle.

Kabinett (kabi'nɛt) *n neu* **-e** 1 *pol* cabinet. 2 closet.

Kadett (ka'dɛt) *nm* **-en** cadet.

Käfer ('kɛ:fər) *nm* --- beetle.

Kaffee ('kafe) *nm* **-s** coffee.

Käfig (ˈkɛːfiç) nm -e cage.

kahl (kaːl) adj 1 bald. 2 bare. **—kopf** nm bald head.

Kahn (kaːn) nm ⸚e 1 boat, skiff. 2 barge.

Kai (kai) nm -e quay, wharf.

Kaiser (ˈkaizər) nm — emperor. **—in** nf -nen empress. **—lich** adj imperial. **—reich** n neu empire.

Kakao (kaˈkaːo) nm cocoa.

Kaktus (ˈkaktus) nm -teen cactus.

Kalb (kalp) n neu ⸚er calf. **—fleisch** n neu veal. **—sbraten** nm roast veal.

Kalender (kaˈlɛndər) nm — calendar.

Kali (ˈkaːli) n neu potash.

Kalk (kalk) nm -e lime. **—stein** nm limestone.

kalt (kalt) adj 1 cold. 2 frigid. **—blütig** (ˈkaltblyːtiç) adj cold-blooded. ⸚e (ˈkɛltə) nf cold, coldness.

kam (kaːm) v see **kommen**.

Kamel (kaˈmeːl) n neu -e camel.

Kamera (ˈkamera) nf -s camera.

Kamerad (kaməˈraːt) nm -en, **—in** (kaməˈraːdin) nf -nen comrade, companion.

Kamin (kaˈmiːn) nm -e 1 chimney. 2 fireplace.

Kamm (kam) nm ⸚e 1 comb. 2 crest. 3 ridge. **—en** (ˈkɛmən) vt comb.

Kammer (ˈkamər) nf -n 1 small room, chamber. 2 pol,comm chamber. **—diener** nm valet. **—musik** nf chamber music.

Kampf (kampf) nm ⸚e fight, struggle, battle. **—en** (ˈkɛmpfən) vi fight, struggle. **—er** (ˈkɛmpfər) nm — fighter, combatant.

Kanad/a (ˈkanada) n neu Canada. **—ier** (kaˈnaːdiər) nm — Canadian. **—isch** (kaˈnaːdiʃ) adj Canadian.

Kanal (kaˈnaːl) nm -e 1 channel. 2 canal. 3 drain. 4 pipe. **Ärmelkanal** English Channel.

Kanarienvogel (kaˈnaːriənfoːgəl) nm canary.

Kandid/at (kandiˈdaːt) nm -en candidate. **—ieren** (kandiˈdiːrən) vi be a candidate, stand.

Känguruh (ˈkɛŋguruː) n neu -s kangaroo.

Kaninchen (kaˈniːnçən) n neu — rabbit.

kann (kan) v see **können**.

Kannabis (ˈkanabis) n neu cannabis.

Kanne (ˈkanə) nf -n 1 can. 2 jug. 3 pot.

kannte (ˈkantə) v see **kennen**.

Kanon (kaˈnoːn) nm -s canon.

Kanone (kaˈnoːnə) nf -n 1 cannon. 2 gun. 3 inf wizard, ace.

Kante (ˈkantə) nf -n 1 edge. 2 brim, rim.

Kantine (kanˈtiːnə) nf -n canteen.

Kanton (kanˈtoːn) nm -e canton.

Kanzel (ˈkantsəl) nf -n 1 pulpit. 2 aviat cockpit.

Kanzler (ˈkantslər) nm — chancellor.

Kap (kap) n neu -s cape, headland.

Kapazität (kapatsiˈtɛːt) nf -en 1 capacity. 2 authority.

Kapelle (kaˈpɛlə) nf -n 1 chapel. 2 band. 3 choir.

Kaper (ˈkaːpər) nf -n bot caper.

Kapital (kapiˈtaːl) n neu -ien capital. **—anlage** nf investment. **—ismus** (kapitaˈlismus) nm capitalism. **—ist** (kapitaˈlist) nm -en capitalist.

Kapitän (kapiˈtɛːn) nm -e captain, skipper.

Kapitel (kaˈpitəl) n neu — chapter.

Kappe (ˈkapə) nf -n 1 cap. 2 hood. 3 top. 4 dome.

kaputt (kaˈput) adj inf 1 bust, broken. 2 exhausted.

Kapuze (kaˈpuːtsə) nf -n 1 hood. 2 cowl.

Karat (kaˈraːt) n neu -e carat.

Karate (kaˈraːtə) n neu karate.

Karawane (karaˈvaːnə) nf -n caravan.

Kardinal (kardiˈnaːl) nm ⸚e cardinal.

Karfreitag (kaːrˈfraitaːk) nm Good Friday.

karg (kark) adj 1 thrifty. 2 sparing. 3 poor. 4 meagre. 5 barren. **—lich** (ˈkɛrkliç) adj 1 scanty. 2 poor.

kariert (kaˈriːrt) adj 1 checked. 2 chequered.

Karies (ˈkaːries) nf med caries.

Karikatur (karikaˈtuːr) nf -en caricature.

Karneval (ˈkarnevaːl) nm -e carnival.

Karo (ˈkaːro) n neu -s game diamonds.

Karosserie (karɔsəˈriː) nf -n mot bodywork.

Karotte (kaˈrɔtə) nf -n carrot.

Karpfen (ˈkarpfən) nm — carp.

Karre (ˈkarə) nf -n also **Karren** nm — cart, (wheel-)barrow.

Karriere (kaˈrjɛːrə) nf -n 1 career. 2 gallop.

Karte (ˈkartə) nf -n 1 card. 2 map. 3 ticket. 4 menu.

Kartell (karˈtɛl) n neu -e cartel.

Kartoffel (karˈtɔfəl) nf -n potato. **—brei** nm also **—püree** n neu mashed or creamed potatoes.

Karton (karˈtɔn) nm -e, -s cardboard (box), carton.

Kartusche (karˈtuʃə) nf -n cartridge.

Karussell (karuˈsɛl) n neu -e merry-go-round.

Kaschmir (ˈkaʃmir) n neu Cashmere.

Käse (ˈkɛːzə) nm — cheese.

Kaserne (kaˈzɛrnə) nf -n barracks.

Kasino (ka'zi:no) *n neu* **-s 1** casino. **2** officers' mess.

Kasse ('kasə) *nf* **-n 1** till, cash register. **2** cash-desk. **3** booking office. **4** cash. **5** cash-box. **6** strongbox.

Kassette (ka'sɛtə) *nf* **-n 1** casket, box. **2** film spool. **3** cassette (tape). **—nrecorder** *nm* — cassette-recorder.

kassier/en (ka'si:rən) *vt* **1** cash. **2** cashier. **3** cancel. **4** annul. **—er** *nm* — **1** cashier. **2** treasurer.

Kastanie (ka'sta:niə) *nf* **-n** chestnut.

Kasten ('kastən) *nm* $\div$ box, chest.

kastrieren (ka'stri:rən) *vt* castrate.

Kasus ('ka:zus) *nm* — *gram* case.

Katalog (kata'lo:k) *nm* **-e** catalogue.

Katarrh (ka'tar) *nm* **-e** catarrh.

katastroph/al (katastro'fa:l) *adj* catastrophic. **—e** (kata'stro:fə) *nf* **-n** catastrophe.

Kategorie (katego'ri:) *nf* **-n** category.

Kater ('ka:tər) *nm* — **1** tomcat. **2** *inf* hangover.

Kathedrale (kate'dra:lə) *nf* **-n** cathedral.

Kathol/ik (kato'li:k) *nm* **-en, —kin** *nf* **-nen** Catholic. **—isch** (ka'to:liʃ) *adj* Catholic.

Katze ('katsə) *nf* **-n** cat.

Kauderwelsch ('kaudərvɛlʃ) *n neu* double-dutch.

kauen ('kauən) *vt* chew.

kauern ('kauərn) *vi* cower.

Kauf (kauf) *nm* $\div$e **1** purchase, buy(ing). **2** bargain. **in Kauf nehmen** I accept. **2** put up with. **—en** *vt* buy, purchase. **—er** ('kɔyfər) *nm* — buyer, purchaser. **—haus** *n neu* department store. **—kraft** *nf* purchasing power. **—laden** *nm* shop. **—lich** ('kɔyflic) *adj* **1** purchasable, for sale. **2** venal, corrupt. **—mann** *nm* **-leute 1** shopkeeper. **2** merchant. **3** businessman.

Kaugummi ('kaugumi) *nm* chewing gum.

Kaukasus ('kaukazus) *nm* Caucasus.

kaum (kaum) *adv* hardly, scarcely, barely.

Kaution (kau'tsjo:n) *nf* **-en 1** security. **2** bail.

Kauz (kauts) *nm* $\div$e **1** owl. **2** odd fellow.

Kavallerie (kavalə'ri:) *nf* cavalry.

Kaviar ('ka:viar) *nm* **-e** caviar.

keck (kɛk) *adj* **1** bold, daring. **2** cheeky.

Kegel ('ke:gəl) *nm* — **1** skittle(s), ninepin(s). **2** cone. **—bahn** *nf* bowling alley.

Kehl/e ('ke:lə) *nf* **-n 1** throat. **—kopf** *nm* larynx. **—kopfentzündung** *nf* laryngitis.

kehren[1] ('ke:rən) *vt* turn.

kehr/en[2] ('ke:rən) *vt* sweep. **—icht** ('ke:rict) *nm* **1** sweepings. **2** rubbish.

Keil (kail) *nm* **-e** wedge. **—en** *vt* **1** (fix or split with a) wedge. **2** thrash. **sich —en** *vr* fight. **—er** *nm* — boar.

Keim (kaim) *nm* **-e 1** germ. **2** bud. **3** embryo. **—en** *vi* **1** germinate. **2** sprout.

kein/e, kein (kain, 'kainə, kain) *adj* no, not any. **es war kein Mensch zu sehen** there was not a soul to be seen. **—er, -e, -es** ('kainər, 'kainə, 'kainəs) *pron* **1** none. **2** no one. **—erlei** ('kainərlai) *adj* of no sort, not any. **—esfalls** ('kainəsfals) *adv* on no account. **—eswegs** ('kainəsve:ks) *adv* not at all, by no means.

Keks (ke:ks) *nm,neu* **-e** biscuit.

Keller ('kɛlər) *nm* — cellar.

Kellner ('kɛlnər) *nm* — **1** waiter. **2** barman. **—in** *nf* **-nen 1** waitress. **2** barmaid.

kenn/en[*] ('kɛnən) *vt* know, be acquainted with. **—er** *nm* — expert, connoisseur. **—enlernen** *vt* become acquainted with, get to know. **—tnis** *nf* **-se** knowledge. **—zeichen** *n neu* characteristic, (distinguishing) feature. **—zeichnen** *vt* **1** mark. **2** distinguish.

Kerbe ('kɛrbə) *nf* **-n 1** notch. **2** slot.

Kerker ('kɛrkər) *nm* — prison, jail.

Kerl (kɛrl) *nm* **-e 1** fellow, man. **2** *inf* bloke.

Kern (kɛrn) *nm* **-e 1** core. **2** kernel, pip, stone. **3** nucleus. **—energie** *nf* nuclear energy. **—gesund** *adj* thoroughly healthy. **—physik** *nf* nuclear physics. **—waffen** *nf pl* nuclear weapons.

Kerze ('kɛrtsə) *nf* **-n** candle.

Kessel ('kɛsəl) *nm* — **1** kettle. **2** boiler. **3** basin. **4** hollow.

Kette ('kɛtə) *nf* **-n** chain. **—nbrücke** *nf* suspension bridge. **—reaktion** *nf* chain reaction.

Ketzer ('kɛtsər) *nm* — heretic. **—ei** (kɛtsə'rai) *nf* **-en** heresy.

keuchen ('kɔyçən) *vi* pant, gasp.

Keule ('kɔylə) *nf* **-n 1** club, cudgel. **2** thigh (of an animal). **3** *cul* leg.

keusch (kɔyʃ) *adj* chaste.

kichern ('kiçərn) *vi* giggle.

Kiefer[1] ('ki:fər) *nm* — jaw.

Kiefer[2] ('ki:fər) *nf* **-n** pine, fir.

Kiel (ki:l) *nm* **-e 1** keel. **2** quill.

Kieme ('ki:mə) *nf* **-n** *zool* gill.

Kies (ki:s) *nm* **-e** gravel.

Kieselstein ('ki:zəlʃtain) *nm* pebble.

Kilo ('ki:lo) *n neu* kilo. **—gramm** (ki:lo'gram) *n neu* kilogram.

Kind (kint) *n neu* **-er** child. **—erei** (kində'rai) *nf* **-en** childishness. **—erspiel** ('kindərʃpi:l) *n* *neu* child's play. **—erstube** ('kindərʃtuːbə) *nf* nursery. **—erwagen** ('kindərvaːgən) *nm* pram. **—heit** ('kinthait) *nf* childhood. **—isch** ('kindiʃ) *adj* childish. **—lich** ('kintliç) *adj* childlike.

Kinn (kin) *n neu* -e chin.

Kino ('kiːno) *n neu* -s cinema.

Kiosk (ki'ɔsk) *nm* -e 1 kiosk. 2 newsstand.

Kirch/e ('kirçə) *nf* -n church. **—hof** *nm* 1 churchyard. 2 cemetery. **—lich** *adj* ecclesiastical, church. **-spiel** *n neu* parish **—turm** *nm* steeple, church tower.

Kirsch (kirʃ) *nm also* **Kirschwasser** ('kirʃvasər) *n neu* kirsch.

Kirsche ('kirʃə) *nf* -n cherry.

Kissen ('kisən) *n neu* — cushion, pillow.

Kiste ('kistə) *nf* -n box, case, crate.

Kitsch (kitʃ) *nm* tasteless rubbish, trash.

kitzeln ('kitsəln) *vt* tickle.

klaffen ('klafən) *vi* gape, yawn.

Klag/e ('klaːgə) *nf* -n 1 complaint. 2 *law* action. 3 lament. **—en** *vi* 1 complain. 2 *law* bring an action. 3 lament. **—er** ('klɛːgər) *nm* — plaintiff. **—lich** ('klɛːkliç) *adj* wretched, plaintive.

Klammer ('klamər) *nf* -n 1 clip, clamp. 2 peg. 3 bracket. **—n** *vt* fasten.

Klang (klaŋ) *nm* -e (ringing) sound. **—farbe** *nf* timbre, tone.

Klapp/e ('klapə) *nf* -n 1 flap. 2 lid. 3 stop. 4 valve. 5 *sl* mouth. **—en** *vi* clap. *vi* 1 flap. 2 collapse, fold. **es klappt** it works (well).

Klapper ('klapər) *nf* -n rattle. **—n** *vi* rattle.

klar (klaːr) *adj* 1 clear. 2 bright. 3 distinct. 4 evident. 5 pure. **—en** ('klɛːrən) *vt* 1 clarify. 2 purify. **—heit** *nf* clarity, clearness. **—legen** *vt also* **—machen** clear up, explain, point out.

Klarinette (klari'nɛtə) *nf* -n clarinet.

Klasse ('klasə) *nf* -n 1 class. 2 category. **—nzimmer** *n neu* classroom.

Klass/iker ('klasikər) *nm* — classic (author). **—isch** *adj* classic(al).

Klatsch (klatʃ) *nm* -e 1 clap. 2 gossip. 3 smack. **—en** *vi* 1 clap. 2 gossip. 3 slap, smack.

Klaue ('klauə) *nf* -n 1 hoof. 2 claw. 3 *sl* scrawl, handwriting. **—n** *vt* 1 claw. 2 *sl* pinch, steal.

Klausel ('klauzəl) *nf* -n clause.

Klavier (kla'viːr) *n neu* -e piano.

kleb/en ('kleːbən) *vt* glue, stick. *vi* 1 stick. 2 cling. **—(e)rig** *adj* sticky. **—estreifen** *nm* adhesive tape. **—stoff** *nm* adhesive, glue.

kleck/ern ('klɛkərn) *vi* dribble, slobber. **—s** (klɛks) *nm* -e 1 blot. 2 stain.

Klee (kleː) *nm* clover.

Kleid (klait) *n neu* -er 1 dress. 2 garment. 3 *pl* clothes. **—en** ('klaidən) *vt* clothe, dress. **—erschrank** ('klaidərʃraŋk) *nm* wardrobe. **—ung** ('klaiduŋ) *nf* clothing.

klein (klain) *adj* 1 small, little. 2 short. 3 petty, mean. **—asien** (klain'aːziən) *n neu* Asia Minor. **—geld** *n neu* (small) change. **—handel** *nm* retail trade. **—heit** *nf* smallness. **—igkeit** *nf* -en trifle, petty detail. **—laut** *adj* subdued, quiet. **—lich** *adj* petty, mean. **—stadt** *nf* small city or town.

Kleinod ('klainoːt) *n neu* -ien gem.

Kleister ('klaistər) *nm* — paste.

Klemme ('klɛmə) *nf* -n 1 clamp. 2 (electrical) terminal. 3 dilemma, difficulty.

Klempner ('klɛmpnər) *nm* — plumber.

Klerus ('kleːrus) *nm* clergy.

klettern ('klɛtərn) *vi* climb.

Klima ('kliːma) *n neu* -te climate. **—anlage** *nf* 1 air-conditioner. 2 air-conditioning.

Klinge ('kliŋə) *nf* -n blade. **—n** *vi* 1 sound. 2 ring, chink.

Klingel ('kliŋəl) *nf* -n 1 bell. 2 door-bell. **—n** *vi* ring, tinkle.

Klinik ('kliːnik) *nf* -en clinic, hospital.

Klinke ('kliŋkə) *nf* -n 1 latch. 2 handle.

Klippe ('klipə) *nf* -n reef, rocks.

klirren ('kliːrən) *vi* 1 clink. 2 clash, jangle.

Klo (kloː) *n neu* -s *inf* toilet, loo.

Kloben ('kloːbən) *nm* — 1 pulley, block. 2 vice. 3 pincers. 4 log.

klopfen ('klɔpfən) *vi,vt* beat, knock.

Klosett (klo'zɛt) *n neu* -e toilet, lavatory. **—papier** *n neu* toilet paper.

Kloster ('kloːstər) *n neu* -- 1 convent. 2 monastery.

Klotz (klɔts) *nm* -e 1 log. 2 block.

Klub (klup) *nm* -s club, society.

Kluft (kluft) *nf* -e 1 gap. 2 chasm. 3 cleft.

klug (kluːk) *adj* 1 clever, intelligent. 2 prudent. **—heit** *nf* 1 cleverness, intelligence. 2 prudence.

Klumpen ('klumpən) *nm* — 1 lump, clod. 2 heap.

knabbern ('knabərn) *vi,vt* gnaw, nibble.

Knabe ('knaːbə) *nm* -n boy, lad.

knacken ('knakən) *vt,vi* crack, snap.

Knall (knal) *nm* -e 1 crack. 2 bang, report. **—en** *vi* 1 crack, snap. 2 bang.

knapp (knap) adj 1 tight, close-fitting. 2 scarce, meagre. 3 bare, barely sufficient.

knarren ('knarən) vi 1 creak. 2 rattle.

Knecht (kneçt) nm -e 1 servant. 2 farmhand. **—schaft** nf servitude.

kneif/en* ('knaifən) vt pinch. vi 1 flinch. 2 retreat. **—zange** nf pliers, pincers.

Kneipe ('knaipə) nf -n public house, tavern.

kneten ('kne:tən) vt 1 knead, massage.

Knicks (kniks) nm -e curtsey.

Knie (kni:) n neu — knee. **—(e)n** ('kni:ən) vi kneel. **—hose** nf kneebreeches.

Kniff (knif) nm -e 1 crease. 2 pinch. 3 trick, knack.

knipsen ('knipsən) vt 1 clip. 2 snap (a photograph). vi snap one's fingers.

knirschen ('knirʃən) vt 1 grate. 2 grind.

Knoblauch ('kno:plaux) nm garlic.

Knöchel ('knœçəl) nm — 1 ankle. 2 knuckle.

Knoch/en ('knɔxən) nm — bone. **—ig** adj bony.

Knödel ('knœ:dəl) nm — dumpling.

Knopf (knɔpf) nm -̈e button. **—en** ('knœpfən) vt button.

Knorpel ('knɔrpəl) nm — cartilage.

Knospe ('knɔspə) nf -n bud. **—n** vi 1 bud. 2 sprout.

Knoten ('kno:tən) nm — 1 knot. 2 node. 3 difficulty. **—punkt** nm junction.

knüpfen ('knypfən) vt tie, bind.

knusprig ('knuspriç) adj crisp.

Koalition (koalitsi'o:n) nf -en coalition.

Kobra ('ko:bra) nf -s cobra.

Koch (kɔx) nm -̈e, **Köchin** ('kœçin) nf -nen cook. **—buch** n neu cookery book. **—en** vt,vi 1 cook. 2 boil.

Kodex ('ko:deks) nm — code.

Koexistenz (kɔeksis'tɛnts) nf co-existence.

Koffer ('kɔfər) nm — 1 suitcase. 2 trunk. **—radio** n neu portable radio. **—raum** nm mot boot.

Kohl (ko:l) nm -e cabbage.

Kohle ('ko:lə) nf -n 1 coal. 2 charcoal. 3 carbon. **—nbergwerk** n neu coalmine. **—nsäure** nf 1 carbonic acid. 2 carbon dioxide. **—nstoff** nm carbon. **—papier** n neu carbon paper.

Koje ('ko:jə) nf -n 1 cabin. 2 bunk.

kokettieren (kɔkɛ'ti:rən) vi flirt.

Kokosnuß ('ko:kɔsnus) nf coconut.

Koks (ko:ks) nm -e coke.

Kolben ('kɔlbən) nm — 1 butt(-end). 2 club. 3 piston. 4 sci retort, flask.

Kollege (kɔ'le:gə) nm -n, **Kollegin** nf -nen colleague.

kollektiv (kɔlɛk'ti:f) adj collective.

Köln (kœln) n neu Cologne.

kolon/ial (koloni'a:l) adj colonial. **—ie** (kolo'ni:) nf -n colony. **—ist** (kolo'nist) nm -en colonist, settler.

Kolonne (ko'lɔnə) nf -n column.

kolossal (kɔlɔ'sa:l) adj huge, immense.

Kombination (kɔmbinatsi'o:n) nf -en 1 combination. 2 conjecture, deduction.

Komet (ko'me:t) nm -en comet.

Komfort (kɔm'fo:r) nm 1 luxury. 2 comfort.

komisch ('ko:miʃ) adj 1 funny. 2 strange.

Komitee (komi'te:) n neu -s committee.

Komma ('kɔma) n neu -s comma.

Kommand/ant (kɔman'dant) nm -e commander. **—ieren** (kɔman'di:rən) vi,vt command.

kommen* ('kɔmən) vi 1 come, approach. 2 arrive. 3 happen. **auf etwas kommen** think of, hit upon something. **zu etwas kommen** come to, obtain something.

Kommiss/ar (kɔmi'sa:r) nm -e 1 commissioner. 2 (police) inspector. 3 commissar. **—ion** (kɔmisi'o:n) nf -en commission.

Kommode (kɔ'mo:də) nf -n chest of drawers.

kommun (kɔ'mu:n) adj common. **—al** (kɔmu'na:l) adj 1 communal. 2 municipal. **—e** (kɔ'mu:nə) nf -n 1 commune. 2 community.

Kommunikation (kɔmu:nikatsi'o:n) nf -en communication.

Kommunismus (kɔmu'nismus) nm communism. **—ist** (kɔmu'nist) nm -en communist. **—istisch** (kɔmu'nistiʃ) adj communist.

Komödie (ko'mœ:diə) nf -n comedy, farce.

Kompaß ('kɔmpas) nm -passe compass.

kompetent (kɔmpe'tɛnt) adj competent.

Kompliment (kɔmpli'mɛnt) n neu -e compliment.

kompliziert (kɔmpli'tsi:rt) adj complicated.

kompo/nieren (kɔmpo'ni:rən) vt compose. **—nist** (kɔmpo'nist) nm -en composer. **—sition** (kɔmpozitsi'o:n) nf -en composition.

Kompott (kɔm'pɔt) n neu -e stewed fruit.

Kompromiß (kɔmpro'mis) nm -misse compromise.

Konditorei (kɔndito'rai) nf -en coffee-shop, cake-shop.

Kondom (kɔn'do:m) nm -e condom.

Konferenz (kɔnfe'rɛnts) nf -en conference, meeting.

Konflikt (kɔn'flikt) nm -e 1 conflict. 2 dispute.

konfus (kɔn'fu:s) adj confused.

Kongreß (kɔnˈɡrɛs) nm **-gresse** congress.
König (ˈkœːnɪç) nm **-e** king. **—in** (ˈkœːnɪɡɪn) nf **-nen** queen. **—lich** adj royal, regal. **—reich** n neu kingdom.
Konjugation (kɔnjugatsiˈoːn) nf **-en** conjugation.
Konjunktiv (ˈkɔnjunktiːf) nm **-e** subjunctive.
Konjunktur (kɔnjunkˈtuːr) nf **-en** economic or commercial situation.
Konkurrenz (kɔnkuˈrɛnts) nf **-en** competition.
Konkurs (kɔnˈkurs) nm **-e** bankruptcy.
können¹ (ˈkœnən) v mod aux 1 be able. 2 be allowed. vi,vt know (how to do something).
konsequen/t (kɔnzeˈkvɛnt) adj consistent. **—z** (kɔnzeˈkvɛnts) nf **-en** 1 consistency. 2 consequence. **Konsequenzen ziehen** draw conclusions.
konservativ (kɔnzɛrvaˈtiːf) adj conservative.
Konserve (kɔnˈzɛrvə) nf **-n** tinned food, preserve.
Konsonant (kɔnzoˈnant) nm **-en** consonant.
Konstruktion (kɔnstruktsiˈoːn) nf **-en** 1 construction. 2 design.
Konsul (ˈkɔnzul) nm **-n** consul. **—at** (kɔnzuˈlaːt) n neu **-e** consulate.
Konsum (kɔnˈzuːm) nm consumption. **—ent** (kɔnzuˈmɛnt) nm **-en** consumer. **—verein** nm cooperative society.
Kontakt (kɔnˈtakt) nm **-e** contact.
Kontinent (ˈkɔntinɛnt) nm **-e** continent.
kontinuierlich (kɔntinuˈiːrlɪç) adj continuous.
Konto (ˈkɔnto) n neu **-ten** account.
Kontrast (kɔnˈtrast) nm **-e** contrast.
Kontroll/e (kɔnˈtrɔlə) nf **-n** 1 control. 2 supervision. **—ieren** (kɔntrɔˈliːrən) vt 1 control. 2 supervise. 3 check. 4 audit. **—punkt** nm checkpoint.
konventionell (kɔnvɛntsioˈnɛl) adj conventional.
Konversation (kɔnvɛrzatsiˈoːn) nf **-en** conversation. **—slexikon** n neu encyclopaedia.
Konzentr/ation (kɔntsɛntratsiˈoːn) nf **-en** concentration. **—ieren** (kɔntsɛnˈtriːrən) vt concentrate.
Konzept (kɔnˈtsɛpt) n neu **-e** 1 (rough) draft, sketch. 2 design.
Konzert (kɔnˈtsɛrt) n neu **-e** 1 concert. 2 concerto.
Kopf (kɔpf) nm **-̈e** head. **—haut** nf scalp. **—hörer** nm headphone(s). **—kissen** n neu pillow. **—schmerz** nm also **—weh** n neu headache.
Kopie (koˈpiː) nf **-n** copy.

Koralle (koˈralə) nf **-n** coral.
Korb (kɔrp) nm **-̈e** 1 basket. 2 refusal.
Korinthe (koˈrɪntə) nf **-n** currant.
Kork (kɔrk) nm **-e** cork. **—enzieher** nm corkscrew.
Korn (kɔrn) n neu **-̈er** 1 grain, corn. 2 seed. 3 whisky. 4 schnaps.
Koronarthrombose (kɔrɔˈnartrɔmboːzə) nf **-n** coronary thrombosis.
Körper (ˈkœrpər) nm **—** 1 body. 2 substance. **—haltung** nf bearing, deportment. **—lich** adj 1 physical, corporeal. 2 material. **—schaft** nf **-en** corporation, body. **—übung** nf physical exercise.
korrekt (kɔˈrɛkt) adj correct. **-ur** (kɔrɛkˈtuːr) nf **-en** 1 correction. 2 (printing) proof.
Korresponden/t (kɔrɛspɔnˈdɛnt) nm **-en** correspondent. **—z** (kɔrɛspɔnˈdɛnts) nf **-en** correspondence.
Korridor (ˈkɔridoːr) nm **-e** corridor.
korrigieren (kɔriˈgiːrən) vt correct.
Kosename (ˈkoːzənaːmə) nm pet name.
Kosmetik (kɔsˈmeːtik) nf **-en** cosmetics.
Kost (kɔst) nf 1 food, fare. 2 diet.
kostbar (ˈkɔstbaːr) adj 1 expensive. 2 precious.
kosten¹ (ˈkɔstən) vt cost. n pl cost(s). **—los** adj free (of charge).
kosten² (ˈkɔstən) vt taste, sample.
köstlich (ˈkœstlɪç) adj 1 delightful. 2 delicious.
Kostüm (kɔsˈtyːm) n neu **-e** 1 costume, dress. 2 suit.
Kot (kɔt) nm 1 mud, dirt. 2 excrement.
Kotelett (kɔtəˈlɛt) nm neu **-e** cutlet, chop. **—en** n pl sideburns.
kotzen (ˈkɔtsən) vi inf spew up, vomit.
Krabbe (ˈkrabə) nf **-n** 1 crab. 2 shrimp.
Krach (krax) nm **-e** 1 noise. 2 crash. 3 quarrel.
kraft (kraft) prep by virtue of. nf **-̈e** 1 strength, force, power. 2 efficacy. 3 worker. **außer Kraft setzen** annul. **in Kraft sein** be in force. **in Kraft treten** come into force. **—fahrzeug** n neu motor vehicle. **—ig** (ˈkrɛftɪç) adj strong, powerful. **—igen** (ˈkrɛftigən) vt strengthen. **—wagen** n 1 motor vehicle. 2 car. 3 lorry. **—werk** n neu power station.
Kragen (ˈkraːgən) nm **—** collar.
Krähe (ˈkrɛːə) nf **-n** crow.
Kralle (ˈkralə) nf **-n** claw, talon.
Kram (kraːm) nm **-̈e** inf 1 junk, rubbish. 2 things, stuff. 3 affair, business.
Krampf (krampf) nm **-e** 1 cramp. 2 convulsion.
Kran (kraːn) nm **-̈e** crane, hoist.

67

Kranich

Kranich ('kra:nıç) nm -e zool crane.

krank (kraŋk) adj sick, ill. **—e(r)** nm patient. **—en** ('krɛŋkən) vt 1 hurt. 2 offend. **sich —en** vr worry. **—enhaus** n neu hospital. **—enkasse** nf health insurance (company). **—enschwester** nf nurse. **—enversicherung** nf health insurance. **—enwagen** nm ambulance. **—haft** adj 1 morbid. 2 diseased. **—heit** nf -en 1 illness. 2 disease.

Kranz (krants) nm ⸚e wreath, garland.

Kratzbürste ('kratsbʏrstə) nf -n 1 wire brush. 2 shrew, bad-tempered woman.

kratzen ('kratsən) vt,vi scratch, scrape.

Kraul (kraul) n neu crawl (swimming stroke).

Kraut (kraut) n neu ⸚er 1 plant. 2 herb. 3 cabbage.

Krawall (kra'val) nm -e 1 row. 2 riot. 3 noise.

Krawatte (kra'vatə) nf -n (neck)tie.

Krebs (kre:ps) nm -e 1 crayfish. 2 crab. 3 med cancer. 4 Cancer.

Kredit (kre'di:t) nm -e credit.

Kreide ('kraidə) nf -n chalk.

Kreis (krais) nm -e 1 circle. 2 district. 3 sphere, field. **—en** ('kraizən) vi 1 circle. 2 circulate. **—förmig** ('kraisfœrmıç) adj circular, round. **—lauf** nm -en 1 circulation. 2 cycle, circuit.

kreischen ('kraiʃən) vi shriek, screech.

Krematorium (krema'to:rjum) n neu -rien crematorium.

Kreml ('kre:məl) nm Kremlin.

Krempe ('krɛmpə) nf -n brim.

krepieren (kre'pi:rən) vi 1 (of an animal) die. 2 explode.

Kresse ('krɛsə) nf -n cress.

Kreuz (krɔyts) n neu -e 1 cross. 2 mus sharp (symbol). 3 game club. 4 (small of the back, rump. **kreuz und quer** crisscross. **—en** vt cross. vi cruise. **—er** nm — cruiser. **—fahrt** nf 1 cruise. 2 crusade. **—gang** nm cloister(s). **—igen** ('krɔytsigən) vt crucify. **—igung** nf -en crucifixion. **—otter** nf -n adder. **—ung** nf -en crossing. **—zug** nm crusade.

kriech/en* ('kri:çən) vi 1 creep. 2 crawl. 3 cringe. 4 grovel. **—tier** n neu reptile.

Krieg (kri:k) nm -e war. **—er** ('kri:gər) nm — warrior. **—sgefangene(r)** nm prisoner of war. **—sgericht** n neu mil court martial. **—srecht** n neu martial law. **—sverbrechen** n neu war crime.

Krimi ('kri:mi) n neu -s inf detective story.

kriminal (krimi'na:l) adj criminal. **—beamte(r)** nm detective. **—roman** nm detective novel.

Krippe ('krıpə) nf -n 1 crib. 2 crèche.

Krise ('kri:zə) nf -n crisis.

Kristall (kri'stal) nm -e crystal.

Krit/ik (kri'ti:k) nf -en 1 criticism. 2 review. **—iker** ('kri:tikər) nm — critic. **—isch** ('kri:tiʃ) adj critical.

Krokodil (kroko'di:l) n neu -e crocodile.

Kron/e ('kro:nə) nf -n crown. **—leuchter** nm chandelier. **⸚en** ('krø:nən) vt crown. **—ung** ('krø:nuŋ) nf -en coronation.

Kröte ('krø:tə) nf -n toad.

Krücke ('krʏkə) nf -n crutch.

Krug (kru:k) nm ⸚e 1 jug. 2 mug.

krumm (krum) adj 1 crooked. 2 bent. 3 curved. **⸚en** ('krʏmən) vt 1 bend. 2 curve.

Krüppel ('krʏpəl) nm — cripple.

Kruste ('krustə) nf -n crust.

Kruzifix (krutsi'fiks) n neu -e crucifix.

Küche ('kʏçə) nf -n 1 kitchen. 2 cookery. **—nschabe** nf -n cockroach.

Kuchen ('ku:xən) nm — cake.

Kuckuck ('kukuk) nm -e cuckoo.

Kugel ('ku:gəl) nf -n 1 ball. 2 sphere, globe. 3 bullet. **—förmig** ('ku:gəlfœrmıç) adj spherical. **—schreiber** nm — ballpoint pen.

Kuh (ku:) nf ⸚e cow.

kühl (ky:l) adj cool, chilly. **—e** nf coolness, cool. **—en** vt,vi 1 cool. 2 refrigerate. **—schrank** nm refrigerator.

kühn (ky:n) adj bold, daring. **—heit** nf -en boldness, daring.

Kulissen (ku'lisən) nf pl Th 1 scenery. 2 wings. **hinter den Kulissen** backstage.

Kult (kult) nm -e 1 cult. 2 worship.

Kultur (kul'tu:r) nf -en 1 culture. 2 cultivation. **—ell** (kultu'rɛl) adj cultural.

Kummer ('kumər) nm 1 grief. 2 distress. 3 worry. **⸚lich** ('kʏmərlıç) adj miserable. **⸚n** ('kʏmərn) vt worry, be anxious. **sich kümmern um** care about, concern oneself with.

kund (kunt) adj known

Kund/e¹ ('kundə) nf information, knowledge. **—geben*** ('kuntge:bən) vt make known, declare. **—igen** ('kʏndigən) vt,vi 1 give notice. 2 cancel.

Kund/e² ('kundə) nm -n customer, client. **—schaft** ('kuntʃaft) nf customers, clientele.

künftig ('kʏnftıç) adj future.

Kunst (kunst) nf ⸚e 1 art. 2 skill. **—griff** nm trick, knack. **—ler** ('kʏnstlər) nm — artist. **⸚lerisch** ('kʏnstləriʃ) adj artistic. **—lich** ('kʏnstlıç) adj artificial, synthetic. **—stück** n neu 1 trick. 2 feat. 3 stunt. **—werk** n neu work of art.

Kupfer ('kupfər) n neu copper. **—stich** nm etching.

Kupp/el ('kupəl) nf -n dome, cupola. **—eln** vt 1 couple, pair. 2 join. vi pimp, procure. **—ler** ('kuplər) nm — 1 matchmaker. 2 pimp. **—lung** nf -en 1 coupling. 2 clutch.

Kur (kur) nf -en cure, treatment. **—ort** nm spa, health resort.

Kurbel ('kurbəl) nf -n 1 crank. 2 winch.

Kürbis ('kyrbis) nm -se 1 pumpkin. 2 marrow.

Kurs (kurs) nm -e 1 course. 2 rate (of exchange). **—buch** n neu timetable.

Kurve ('kurvə) nf -n 1 curve. 2 bend. 3 turn.

kurz (kurts) adj 1 short, brief. 2 abrupt, brusque. **in kurzem** soon, shortly. **kurz gesagt, um es kurz zu sagen** in a word, to cut a long story short. **vor kurzem** a short time ago. **—arbeit** nf short-time work. **—e** ('kyrtsə) nf -n shortness. **—en** ('kyrtsən) vt 1 shorten. 2 reduce. **—erhand** adv 1 without hesitation. 2 briefly. **—fristig** adj short-term. **—lich** ('kyrtsliç) adv lately, recently. **—schrift** nf shorthand.

Kusine (ku'zi:nə) nf -n cousin.

Kuß (kus) nm **Küsse** kiss. **küssen** vt kiss.

Küste ('kystə) nf -n coast, shore.

L

Laboratorium (labora'to:rium) n neu **-rien** laboratory.

lächeln ('lɛçəln) vi smile. n neu — smile.

lach/en ('laxən) vi laugh. n neu — laugh, laughter. **—erlich** ('lɛçərliç) adj ridiculous.

Lachs (laks) nm -e salmon.

Lack (lak) nm -e varnish, lacquer.

lad/en* ('la:dən) vt load. **—eraum** nm hold. **—ung** nf -en lo: d(ing), freight.

Laden ('la:dən) nm — 1 shop, store. 2 shutter. **—diebstahl** nm shoplifting.

lag (la:k) v see **liegen.**

Lage ('la:gə) nf -n 1 situation, position. 2 site, location. 3 layer. 4 mus pitch.

Lager ('la:gər) n neu — 1 camp. 2 warehouse, store. 3 couch, bed. 4 tech bearing. 5 (geological) layer. **—haus** n neu warehouse. **—n** vt store. vi lie down. **sich lagern** vr camp.

Lagune (la'gu:nə) nf -n lagoon.

lahm (la:m) adj lame. **lahm legen** paralyse. **—en** ('lɛ:mən) vt 1 paralyse. 2 lame.

Laib (laip) nm -e loaf.

Laie ('laiə) nm -n layman.

Lakritze (la'kritsə) nf -n liquorice.

Lamm (lam) n neu "er lamb.

Lampe ('lampə) nf -n lamp.

Land (lant) n neu "er 1 land. 2 ground, earth. 3 country. 4 state, province. **auf dem Lande** in the country(side).

Landarbeiter ('lanta:rbaitə) nm farm worker.

landen ('landən) vt,vi land.

Landenge ('lantɛŋə) nf isthmus.

Landgut ('lantgu:t) n neu estate.

Landhaus ('lanthaus) n neu country house.

Landkarte ('lantka:rtə) nf map.

ländlich ('lɛntliç) adj rural, rustic.

Landmann ('lantman) nm **-leute** 1 countryman. 2 farmer.

Landschaft ('lantʃaft) nf -en 1 landscape, countryside, scenery. 2 district.

Landsmann ('lantsman) nm **-sleute** fellow countryman.

Landstraße ('lantʃtra:sə) nf highway, main road.

Landstreicher ('lantʃtraiçə) nm — tramp.

Landtag ('lantta:g) nm 1 provincial assembly. 2 state parliament.

Landung ('landuŋ) nf -en landing (of ships, aeroplanes, etc.). **—sbrücke** nf jetty.

Landwirtschaft ('lantvirtʃaft) nf agriculture.

lang (laŋ) adj,adv long, tall. **ein Jahr lang** for a year. **lang und breit** at length.

lange ('laŋə) adv long, a long time.

Länge ('lɛŋə) nf -n 1 length, tallness. 2 duration. 3 size. 4 longitude. **—ngrad** ('lɛŋəngra:t) nm degree of longitude.

Lang(e)weile ('laŋ(ə)vailə) nf boredom.

langjährig ('laŋjɛriç) adj of long standing.

längs (lɛŋs) adv lengthways. prep along(side).

langsam ('laŋza:m) adj slow.

längst (lɛŋst) adj longest. adv for a long time, long ago. **längst nicht** not nearly.

längstens ('lɛŋstəns) adv at the latest or most.

langweil/en ('laŋvailən) vt 1 bore. 2 tire. **—ig** adj boring.

Lanze ('lantsə) nf -n lance.

Lappen ('lapən) nm — 1 rag, cloth. 2 lobe.

Lärche ('lɛrçə) nf -n larch.

Lärm (lɛrm) nm noise, din.

las (la:z) v see **lesen.**

Laser-Strahlen ('la:zərʃtra:lən) nm pl laser beams.

lassen* ('lasən) vt,vi 1 allow, let, permit. 2 cause. 3 have (done). 4 leave.

lässig ('lɛsiç) adj 1 careless. 2 idle.

Last (last) nf -en 1 burden, load. 2 cargo. 3 change. —**auto** n neu lorry, van. —**en** vi weigh (upon). =**ig** ('lɛstiç) adj 1 troublesome, annoying. 2 burdensome. —**kahn** nm barge. —**kraftwagen** nm lorry, truck, van.

Laster ('lastər) n neu — vice. =**lich** ('lɛstərliç) adj 1 scandalous. 2 slanderous. —**n** ('lɛstərn) vt slander. —**ung** ('lɛstəruŋ) nf -en defamation, slander.

Latein (la'tain) n neu Latin.

Laterne (la'tɛrnə) nf -n 1 lantern. 2 (street) lamp.

Latte ('latə) nf -n 1 slat. 2 board.

lau (lau) adj 1 lukewarm. 2 half-hearted.

Laub (laup) n neu foliage, leaves. —**baum** nm deciduous tree. —**säge** nf fretsaw.

Lauch (laux) nm -e leek.

lauern ('lauərn) vi lie in wait, lurk.

Lauf (lauf) nm =e 1 run(ning). 2 course. 3 race. 4 path, passage. 5 (gun) barrel. —**bahn** nf 1 career. 2 course. —**en** vi 1 run. 2 walk. 3 go, move. 4 flow. —**end** adj 1 running. 2 current. 3 regular, routine. =**er** ('ɔyfər) nm — 1 runner. 2 game bishop.

Laun/e ('launə) nf -n 1 mood. 2 whim. —**enhaft** adj moody, capricious. —**isch** adj 1 bad-tempered. 2 moody. 3 capricious.

Laus (laus) nf =e louse. —**bube** nm (young) rascal. —**ig** adj sl lousy.

lauschen ('lauʃən) vi listen, eavesdrop.

laut (laut) adj loud. adv loudly, aloud. prep according to. nm -e sound. —**en** vi 1 sound. 2 (of a text, letter, etc.) read, run. —**los** adj silent, mute. —**sprecher** nm (loud)speaker. —**stärke** nf loudness, volume.

läuten ('lɔytən) vi ring, sound.

lauter ('lautər) adj invar 1 only, nothing but. 2 pure. 3 genuine.

lauwarm ('lauvarm) adj lukewarm, tepid.

Lawine (la'vi:nə) nf -n avalanche.

lax (laks) adj 1 lax. 2 licentious.

leb/en ('le:bən) vi 1 live. n neu — life. —**end** ('le:bənt) adj living, alive. —**endig** (le'bɛndiç) adj 1 alive. 2 lively.

Lebensart ('le:bənsa:rt) nf way of life.

Lebensgefahr ('le:bənsgəfa:r) nf danger to (one's) life.

Lebenskraft ('le:bənskraft) nf vitality.

Lebenslänglich ('le:bənslɛŋliç) adj lifelong.

Lebenslauf ('le:bənslauf) nm curriculum vitae.

Lebensmittel ('le:bənsmitəl) n neu pl food.

Lebensstandard ('le:bənsstanda:rt) nm standard of living.

Lebensunterhalt ('le:bənsuntərhalt) nm livelihood.

Lebensversicherung ('le:bənsvɛrziçəruŋ) nf life insurance.

Lebensweise ('le:bənsvaizə) nf way of life.

Leber ('le:bər) nf -n liver. —**wurst** nf liver sausage.

Lebewesen ('le:bəve:zən) n neu creature.

Lebewohl ('le:bəvo:l) n neu, interj farewell.

Lebhaft ('le:phaft) adj lively, vivid.

Lebkuchen ('le:pku:xən) nm gingerbread.

leblos ('le:plo:s) adj 1 lifeless. 2 dull.

leck (lɛk) adj leaky, leaking. n neu -e leak.

lecken ('lɛkən) vt lick.

lecker ('lɛkər) adj 1 delicious. 2 delicate. —**bissen** nm delicacy, titbit.

Leder ('le:dər) n neu — leather.

ledig ('le:diç) adj 1 unmarried, single. 2 unrestrained, free. —**lich** ('le:dikliç) adv merely, only.

Lee (le:) nf lee(side).

leer (le:r) adj 1 empty. 2 vacant. —**e** nf -en 1 vacuum. 2 emptiness. —**en** vt empty.

legal (le'ga:l) adj legal.

legen ('le:gən) vt lay, place, put. **sich legen** vr lie down.

Legende (le'gɛndə) nf -n legend.

legieren (le'gi:rən) vt 1 alloy (metals). 2 thicken (soup).

legitim (legi'ti:m) adj legitimate.

Lehm (le:m) nm -e loam, clay.

Lehn/e ('le:nə) nf -n 1 support. 2 back or arm (of a chair). —**en** vt,vi, lean. —**sessel** nm also —**stuhl** armchair.

lehr/en ('le:rən) vt teach, instruct. —**buch** n neu textbook. —**e** nf -n 1 teaching, lesson. 2 theory, doctrine. 3 apprenticeship. 4 gauge. —**er** nm —, —**erin** nf teacher, instructor. —**gang** nm course, syllabus. —**ling** nm -e apprentice. —**reich** adj instructive. —**stuhl** nm professorial chair.

Leib (laip) nm -er body. —**chen** ('laipçən) n neu — bodice. —**esübung** ('laibəsy:buŋ) nf physical exercise. —**wache** nf bodyguard.

Leich/e ('laiçə) nf -n corpse. —**enhemd** n neu shroud. —**enschau** nf 1 inquest. 2 autopsy. —**schauhaus** n neu morgue. —**enwagen** nm hearse. —**nam** ('laiçna:m) nm -e corpse.

leicht (laiçt) adj 1 light. 2 easy. 3 slight. 4 unimportant. 5 superficial. —**athletik** nf athletics. —**fertig** adj 1 frivolous. 2 thoughtless. —**hin** adv lightly, casually. —**igkeit** nf

1 lightness. 2 ease. **—sinn** nm 1 careless-ness, thoughtlessness. 2 frivolity.

leid (lait) adv **es tut mir leid** I am sorry, I regret. n neu — 1 sorrow. 2 harm, pain. **—en°** ('laidən) vt 1 suffer. 2 permit. 3 tolerate. vi suffer. n neu — 1 suffering, pain, illness. 2 misfortune.

Leidenschaft ('laidənʃaft) nf **-en** passion. **—lich** adj passionate.

leider ('laidər) adv unfortunately.

leihen° ('laiən) vt lend, loan.

Leim (laim) nm **-e** glue, size.

Lein (lain) nm **-e** flax. **—en** adj linen. n neu — linen. **—wand** nf 1 (cinema) screen. 2 linen. 3 canvas.

Leine ('lainə) nf **-n** 1 rope, line. 2 lead.

leise ('laizə) adj quiet, low, soft.

leist/en ('laistən) vt 1 achieve, do. 2 perform. 3 give. 4 offer. **ich kann es mir nicht leisten** I can't afford it. **—ung** nf **-en** 1 achievement. 2 work. 3 performance. 4 sci power. **—ungs-fähig** adj 1 capable (of work). 2 productive.

leit/en ('laitən) vt 1 lead, guide. 2 manage. 3 direct. 4 conduct (electricity). **—artikel** nm leader, editorial. **—faden** nm 1 clue. 2 manual. **—gedanke** nm main thought or idea. **—ung** nf **-en** 1 direction. 2 manage-ment. 3 lead. 4 circuit.

Leiter¹ ('laitər) nm — 1 leader. 2 head. 3 director. 4 conductor (of electricity, etc.).

Leiter² ('laitər) nf **-n** 1 ladder. 2 mus scale.

Lektüre (lɛk'tyːrə) nf **-n** reading (material).

Lende ('lɛndə) nf **-n** 1 loin. 2 haunch, hip.

lenk/en ('lɛŋkən) vt 1 steer. 2 direct. 3 lead. **—rad** n neu steering wheel. **—stange** nf handlebars. **—ung** nf **-en** 1 steering. 2 direc-tion.

Leopard (leo'part) nm **-en** leopard.

Lepra ('le:pra) nf leprosy.

Lerche ('lɛrçə) nf **-n** lark.

lernen ('lɛrnən) vt learn.

les/bar ('le:sbaːr) adj 1 legible, readable. **—e** ('le:zə) nf **-n** 1 harvest. 2 vintage. **—en°** vt 1 read. 2 lecture on. 3 gather, pick. 4 select. vi read. **—er** nm — 1 reader. 2 picker.

letzt (lɛtst) adj 1 last. 2 latest, newest. **zum letzten Mal** for the last time. **—ens** adv lastly. **—ere** adj latter. **—hin** adv lately, recently.

Leucht/e ('lɔyçtə) nf **-n** light, lamp, lantern. **—en** vi give light, shine. **—er** nm — 1 candlestick. 2 chandelier. **—turm** nm light-house.

leugnen ('lɔygnən) vt 1 deny. 2 contradict.

Leukämie (lɔykɛ'miː) nf leukaemia.

Leukoplast (lɔyko'plast) n neu Tdmk (sticking) plaster.

Leumund ('lɔymunt) nm **-e** reputation.

Leute ('lɔytə) n pl people, persons.

Leutnant ('lɔytnant) nm **-e** lieutenant.

leutselig ('lɔytzeːlɪç) adj affable.

Lexikon ('lɛksikɔn) n neu **-ka** dictionary.

Liban/on ('liːbanɔn) nm Lebanon. **—ese** (liː-ba'neːzə) nm **-n** Lebanese. **—esisch** adj Leba-nese.

Libelle (li'bɛlə) nf **-n** dragon-fly.

liberal (libe'raːl) adj liberal.

licht (lɪçt) adj 1 bright. 2 light. n neu **-er** 1 light. 2 candle. 3 lamp. **—bild** n neu photograph. **—en** vt 1 clear. 2 thin (out). 3 weigh (anchor). **sich —en** vr 1 grow thinner. 2 grow brighter. **—ung** nf **-en** clearing glade.

Lid (liːt) n neu **-er** eyelid.

lieb (liːp) adj 1 dear, beloved. 2 pleasant, nice. 3 kind. 4 sweet.

liebäugeln ('liːbɔygəln) vi 1 ogle. 2 flirt.

Liebchen ('liːpçən) n neu — sweetheart, love.

Liebe ('liːbə) nf **-n** love.

Liebelei (liːbə'lai) nf **-en** flirtation.

lieben ('liːbən) vt love, like.

liebenswert ('liːbənzveːrt) adj lovely.

liebenswürdig ('liːbənzvyrdɪç) adj 1 amiable. 2 kindly.

lieber ('liːbər) adj dearer. adv rather.

Liebesaffäre ('liːbəsafɛːrə) nf **-n** also **Liebschaft** nf **-en** affair.

liebhab/en° ('liːphaːbən) vt love (a person). **—er** nm — 1 lover. 2 amateur. 3 con-noisseur.

liebkosen ('liːpkoːzən) vt cuddle, caress.

lieblich ('liːplɪç) adj charming, lovely.

Liebling ('liːplɪŋ) nm **-e** darling.

Liebreiz ('liːpraits) nm charm, attraction.

Lied (liːt) n neu **-er** 1 song. 2 hymn. 3 tune.

liederlich ('liːdərlɪç) adj 1 disorderly, slovenly. 2 dissolute.

lief (liːf) v see **laufen**.

Liefer/ant (liːfə'rant) nm **-en** supplier. **—n** vt 1 deliver. 2 supply. 3 produce. 4 submit. **—ung** nf **-en** 1 delivery. 2 supply(ing).

Liege ('liːgə) nf **-n** 1 couch. 2 be (situated), stuhl nm deckchair.

ließ (liːs) v see **lassen**.

Liga ('liːga) nf **-gen** league.

Likör (li'køːr) nm **-e** liqueur.

lila ('liːla) adj 1 lilac. 2 violet.

71

Lilie ('li:liə) nf -n lily.

Limonade (limo'na:də) nf -n lemonade.

Linde ('lində) nf -n linden or lime tree.

Lineal (line'a:l) n neu -e rule(r).

Linie ('li:niə) nf -n line.

link (liŋk) adj left. — nf -n 1 left (side). 2 pol Left. —**isch** adj awkward, clumsy. —**s** adv on the left. —**shändig** adj left-handed.

Linse ('linzə) nf -n 1 lentil. 2 lens.

Lippe ('lipə) nf -n lip. —**nstift** nm lipstick.

lispeln ('lispəln) vi 1 lisp. 2 whisper. 3 rustle.

List (list) nf -en 1 trick, ruse. 2 cunning. —**ig** adj cunning, artful.

Liste ('listə) nf -n 1 list. 2 register.

Litanei (lita'nai) nf -en litany.

Liter ('li:tər) n neu or m -- litre.

litera/risch (lite'ra:riʃ) adj literary. —**tur** (litəra'tu:r) nf -en literature.

litt (lit) v see **leiden**.

Lizenz (li'tsɛnts) nf -en licence.

Lob (lo:p) n neu -e praise. —**en** ('lo:bən) vt praise. —**enswert** adj praiseworthy. —**rede** nf eulogy.

Loch (lɔx) n neu ⸚er 1 hole. 2 sl prison. —**en** vt puncture, perforate.

Lock/e ('lɔkə) nf -n curl, lock (of hair). —**ig** adj curly.

lock/en ('lɔkən) vt lure, entice. —**mittel** n neu bait.

locker ('lɔkər) adj 1 loose, slack. 2 light. 3 spongy. 4 lax. 5 dissolute. —**n** vt loosen.

lodern ('lo:dərn) vi flame, blaze.

Löffel ('lœfəl) nm -- spoon. —**n** vt 1 spoon, ladle. 2 eat with a spoon.

log (lo:g) v see **lügen**.

Loge ('lo:ʒə) nf -n Th box.

Log/ik ('lo:gik) nf logic. —**isch** adj logical.

Lohn (lo:n) nm ⸚e 1 wages, pay. 2 reward, desert. —**arbeiter** nm labourer, workman. —**en** vt pay, reward. **sich —en** vr be worthwhile. —**steuer** nf income tax. —**tag** nm pay day. —**tüte** nf pay-packet.

lokal (lo'ka:l) adj local. n neu -e 1 restaurant. 2 pub.

Lokomotive (lokomo'ti:və) nf -n locomotive.

Lorbeer ('lɔrbe:r) nm -en laurel, bay.

los (lo:s) adj,adv free, loose. adv off, away. **es ist heute nicht viel los** there is not much happening or going on today. **was ist los?** what is the matter? ~**suff** without, free of. **arbeitslos** adj unemployed. **mühelos** adj effortless.

Los (lo:s) n neu -e 1 fate, destiny. 2 lot, share. 3 lottery ticket. —**en** ('lo:zən) vi draw lots. —**ung** ('lo:zuŋ) nf -en password.

lösbar ('lœ:sba:r) adj soluble.

losbinden (lo:sbindən) vt untie.

lösch/en ('lœʃən) vt 1 extinguish, quench. 2 turn off or out. 3 erase. 4 cancel. —**er** nm — 1 (fire) extinguisher. 2 blotter. —**papier** n neu blotting paper.

lose ('lo:zə) adj loose, loose.

Lösegeld ('lœ:zəgɛlt) n neu ransom.

lösen ('lœ:zən) vt 1 loosen, free. 2 solve. 3 dissolve.

losgeben* ('lo:sge:bən) vt set free.

loslassen* ('lo:slasən) vt let go, release.

losmachen ('lo:smaxən) vt unfasten, free.

losreißen* ('lo:sraisən) vt tear off or away.

lossprechen* ('lo:sʃprɛxən) vt 1 acquit. 2 free.

Lösung ('lœ:zuŋ) nf -en 1 solution. 2 loosening.

losziehen* ('lo:stsi:ən) vi 1 set out. 2 insult, abuse. 3 denounce.

löten ('lœ:tən) vt solder.

Lothringen ('lo:triŋən) n neu Lorraine.

Lotse ('lo:tsə) nm -n pilot. —**n** vt naut pilot.

Lotterie (lɔtə'ri:) nf -n lottery.

Löw/e ('lœ:və) nm -n 1 lion. 2 Leo. —**in** nf -nen lioness.

Luchs (luks) nm -e lynx.

Lücke ('lykə) nf -n 1 gap, chink. 2 omission.

lud (lu:d) v see **laden**.

Luft (luft) nf ⸚e 1 air. 2 draught, breeze. **in der freien Luft** in the open air. —**dicht** adj airtight. —**druck** nm air pressure. —**en** ('lyftən) vt 1 air, ventilate. 2 disclose. 3 lift, raise. —**fahrt** nf aviation. —**hafen** nm airport. —**ig** adj airy. —**post** nf airmail. —**ung** ('lyftuŋ) nf ventilation. —**verkehrslinie** nf also —**gesellschaft** -en airline. —**waffe** nf air force.

Lüg/e ('ly:gə) nf -n lie. —**en*** vi lie, tell a lie. —**ner** ('ly:gnər) nm — liar.

Luke ('lu:kə) nf -n 1 skylight. 2 trapdoor.

Lump (lump) nm -en rascal, lout.

Lumpen ('lumpən) nm — rag(s).

Lunge ('luŋə) nf -n lung. —**nentzündung** nf pneumonia.

Lupe ('lu:pə) nf -n magnifying glass.

Lust (lust) nf ⸚e 1 pleasure. 2 joy. 3 desire. **keine Lust haben** have no desire. **Lust auf etwas haben** want or be in the mood for something. —**en** ('lystən) adj 1 longing. 2 lustful. —**ig** adj 1 funny, amusing. 2 merry, jolly.

Luxus ('luksus) nm luxury.

Luzern (lu'tsɛrn) n neu Lucerne.

M

Maat (ma:t) nm -e petty officer, mate.

machen ('maxən) vt 1 make. 2 do. 3 produce, manufacture. 4 cause to. 5 amount or come to. **das macht nichts** it doesn't matter.

Macht (maxt) nf ¨e power, force, might. **¨ig** ('mɛçtiç) adj 1 powerful, mighty. 2 thick. 3 immense. **—los** adj powerless.

Mädchen ('mɛ:tçən) n neu — girl.

Made ('ma:də) nf -n maggot, grub.

mag (ma:k) v see mögen.

Magazin (maga'tsi:n) n neu -e 1 storehouse. 2 magazine.

Magen ('ma:gən) nm — stomach.

mager ('ma:gər) adj 1 thin, lean. 2 meagre. 3 poor. 4 scanty.

Magnet (mag'ne:t) nm -en magnet. **—isch** adj magnetic.

Mahagoni (maha'go:ni) n neu mahogany.

mäh/en ('mɛ:ən) vt mow, reap. **—maschine** nf reaping or mowing machine.

Mahl (ma:l) n neu -e meal. **—zeit** nf meal.

mahlen ('ma:lən) vt mill, grind.

Mähne ('mɛ:nə) nf -n mane.

mahn/en ('ma:nən) vt 1 warn. 2 remind. **—ung** nf -en 1 warning. 2 reminder.

Mai (mai) nm -e May. **—glöckchen** n neu lily of the valley.

Mais (mais) nm maize, corn. **—kolben** nm com cob.

Majestät (majɛs'tɛ:t) nf -en majesty.

Makel ('ma:kəl) nm — 1 blemish. 2 stain.

Makler ('ma:klər) nm — broker, middleman.

Makrele (ma'kre:lə) nf -n mackerel.

mal (ma:l) adv 1 just. 2 times, multiplied by.

Mal[1] (ma:l) n neu -e time. **zum ersten/letzten Mal** for the first/last time.

Mal[2] (ma:l) n neu -e, ¨er 1 sign, mark. 2 spot. 3 boundary. 4 monument.

mal/en ('ma:lən) vt paint. **—er** nm — painter, artist. **—erei** (ma:lə'rai) nf -en painting.

Malz (malts) n neu malt.

Mama ('ma:ma:, 'mama) nf -s mummy.

man (man) pron 3rd pers s 1 one. 2 you. 3 they. **man sagt** it is said, people say.

Manager ('mɛnidʒər) nm — manager.

manch (manç) adj,pron 1 many a. 2 pl some, many, several. **—erlei** (mançər'lai) adj

various, different (sorts of). **—mal** adv sometimes.

Mandat (man'da:t) n neu -e 1 mandate. 2 brief.

Mandel ('mandəl) nf -n 1 almond. 2 tonsil.

Mangel ('maŋəl) nm ¨ 1 lack, deficiency. 2 defect. **—haft** adj 1 incomplete. 2 faulty. **—n** vi be wanting, lacking.

Mani/e (ma'ni:) nf mania. **—sch** ('ma:niʃ) adj manic.

Manier (ma'ni:r) nf -en 1 style. 2 pl manners.

Manifest (mani'fɛst) n neu -e manifesto.

Mann (man) nm ¨er 1 man. 2 husband. **—esalter** n neu manhood. **—eskraft** nf virility. **—lich** ('mɛnliç) adj masculine, male. **—schaft** nf -en 1 team. 2 crew.

Mannequin (manə'kɛ̃) n neu -s (fashion) model.

mannigfaltig ('maniçfaltiç) adj manifold.

Manöver (ma'nœ:vər) n neu — manoeuvre.

Manschette (man'ʃɛtə) nf -n cuff.

Mantel ('mantəl) nm ¨ 1 (over)coat, cloak. 2 case. 3 cover(ing).

Manuskript (manu'skript) n neu -e manuscript.

Mappe ('mapə) nf -n 1 briefcase. 2 file, folder.

Märchen ('mɛ:rçən) n neu — fairytale.

Margarine (marga'ri:nə) nf -n margarine.

Marihuana (mariu'a:nə) n neu marijuana.

Marine (ma'ri:nə) nf -n navy.

marinieren (mari'ni:rən) vt marinate.

Marionette (mario'nɛtə) nf -n marionette, puppet.

Mark[1] (mark) nf — mark (coin or currency).

Mark[2] (mark) n neu 1 (bone) marrow. 2 pith.

Marke ('markə) nf -n 1 mark, sign. 2 trademark, brand. 3 postage stamp. 4 ticket.

Markt (markt) nm ¨e market.

Marmelade (marmə'la:də) nf -n 1 jam. 2 marmalade.

Marmor ('marmɔr) nm -e marble.

Marokko (ma'rɔko) n neu Morocco.

Marsch[1] (marʃ) nm ¨e march. **—ieren** (mar'ʃi:rən) vi march.

Marsch[2] (marʃ) nf -en marsh.

Marschall ('marʃal) nm ¨e marshal.

Märtyrer ('mɛrtyrər) nm — martyr.

März (mɛrts) nm -e March.

Masche ('maʃə) nf -n 1 stitch. 2 mesh.

Maschine (ma'ʃi:nə) nf -n machine, engine. **—nbau** nm mechanical engineering. **—ngewehr** n neu machine gun. **—npistole** nf submachine gun.

Maske ('maskə) nf -n mask.

maß (ma:s) v see messen.

Maß (ma:s) *n neu* **-e 1** measure. **2** size. **3** moderation. **—gebend** *adj* **1** authoritative. **2** standard. **-̈ig** (ˈmɛːsiç) *adj* moderate. **-̈igen** (ˈmɛːsigən) *vt* moderate. **—igung** (ˈmɛːsigʊŋ) *nf* moderation. **—nahme** *nf* **-n** measure, step. **—stab** *nm* **1** measure. **2** standard.

Masse (ˈmasə) *nf* **-n 1** mass, bulk, substance. **2** quantity, mass. **3** crowd. **4** assets. **—nhaft** *adj* **1** enormous. **2** in great quantities, in a mass. **—nmedien** *n neu pl* mass media.

massiv (maˈsiːf) *adj* **1** massive. **2** solid.

Mast (mast) *nm* **-e(n)** mast, pole.

mästen (ˈmɛstən) *vt* fatten.

Material (materiˈaːl) *n neu* **-ien 1** material, matter. **2** stores. **—ismus** (materiaˈlismus) *nm* materialism.

Materie (maˈteːriə) *nf* **-n** matter, substance. **—ll** (materiˈɛl) *adj* material.

Mathemat/ik (matemaˈtiːk) *nf* mathematics. **—iker** (mateˈmaːtikər) *nm* **—** mathematician. **—isch** (mateˈmaːtiʃ) *adj* mathematical.

Matratze (maˈtratsə) *nf* **-n** mattress.

Mätresse (mɛˈtrɛsə) *nf* **-n** mistress, lover.

Matrize (maˈtriːtsə) *nf* **-n 1** stencil. **2** mould.

Matrose (maˈtroːzə) *nm* **-n** sailor.

matschig (ˈmatʃiç) *adj* slushy, muddy.

matt (mat) *adj* **1** tired. **2** faint. **3** matt, dull. **4** checkmate. *n neu* **-s** checkmate.

Matte (ˈmatə) *nf* **-n** mat.

Mau/er (ˈmauər) *nf* **-n** wall. **—rer** (ˈmaurər) *nm* **—** bricklayer, mason.

Maul (maul) *n neu* -̈er mouth (of an animal). **—esel** *nm* mule. **—held** *nm* boaster, loudmouth. **—korb** *nm* muzzle. **—tier** *n neu* mule. **—wurf** *nm* -̈e mole.

Maus (maus) *nf* -̈e mouse. **—efalle** (ˈmauzəfalə) *nf* mousetrap. **—eloch** (ˈmauzəlɔx) *n neu* mousehole.

maximal (maksiˈmaːl) *adj* maximum.

Mechan/ik (meˈçaːnik) *nf* **-en 1** mechanics. **2** mechanism. **—iker** *nm* **—** mechanic. **—isch** *adj* mechanical. **—ismus** (meçaˈnismus) *nm* **-men** mechanism.

meckern (ˈmɛkərn) *vi* **1** grumble. **2** bleat.

Medaille (maˈdaijə) *nf* **-n** medal.

Medikament (medikaˈmɛnt) *n neu* **-e** medicine, drug.

Medizin (mediˈtsiːn) *nf* **-en** medicine.

Meer (meːr) *n neu* **-e** sea. **—enge** *nf* **-n** straits. **—rettich** *nm* horseradish.

Mehl (meːl) *n neu* **-e** flour, meal.

mehr (meːr) *adv,adj* more. **immer mehr** more

and more. **—deutig** *adj* ambiguous. **—ere** *adj pl* several. **—fach** *adj* **1** repeated. **2** multiple. **—heit** *nf* **-en** majority. **—mals** *adv* several times, repeatedly. **—wertsteuer** *nf* value added tax. **—zahl** *nf* **1** majority. **2** plural.

meiden* (ˈmaidən) *vt* **1** avoid. **2** shun.

Meile (ˈmailə) *nf* **-n** mile.

mein (main) *poss adj 1st pers s* my. **—er** *poss pron 1st pers s* also **der —e** or **der —ige** mine. **—erseits** (ˈmainərzaits) *adv* on or for my part. **—esgleichen** (ˈmainəsglaiçən) *pron* people like me. **—ethalben** (ˈmainəthalbən) *adv also* **—etwegen** or **'—etwillen** for my sake, on my account.

Meineid (ˈmainait) *nm* **-e** perjury. **meineidig werden** commit perjury.

mein/en (ˈmainən) *vt,vi* **1** mean. **2** think. **—ung** *nf* **-en 1** opinion. **2** meaning. **—ungsforschung** *nf* opinion poll.

Meißel (ˈmaisəl) *nm* **—** chisel.

meist (maist) *adj* most. **am meisten** most (of all). **—ens** *adv* mostly.

Meister (ˈmaistər) *nm* **—** **1** master. **2** champion. **—haft** *adj* masterly. **—n** *vt* master. **—schaft** *nf* **-en 1** mastery. **2** championship. **—stück** *n neu* masterpiece.

meld/en (ˈmɛldən) *vt* **1** inform of, report. **2** mention. **3** announce. **sich melden** *vr* report, present oneself. **—eamt** *n neu* registration office. **—ung** *nf* **-en 1** announcement. **2** report. **3** application. **4** message.

melken* (ˈmɛlkən) *vt* milk.

Melone (meˈloːnə) *nf* **-n 1** melon. **2** bowler hat.

Membran (memˈbraːn) *nf* **-en** also **Membrane** **-n** membrane, diaphragm.

Menge (ˈmɛŋə) *nf* **-n 1** crowd. **2** quantity.

Mensch (mɛnʃ) *nm* **-en** human being, person. **—enfreundlich** *adj* philanthropic, humanitarian. **—enliebe** *nf* philanthropy. **—enskind!** *interj* good gracious! **—heit** *nf* humanity, mankind. **—lich** *adj* **1** human. **2** humane. **—lichkeit** *nf* humaneness, humanity.

Menstruation (mɛnstruatsiˈoːn) *nf* **-en** menstruation.

merk/bar (ˈmɛrkbaːr) *adj* noticeable. **—en** *vt* **1** observe, notice. **2** note, mark. **sich —en** *vr* remember, make a note of. **—mal** *n neu* **-e 1** characteristic. **2** mark. **—würdig** *adj* remarkable, strange.

Messe (ˈmɛsə) *nf* **-n 1** *rel* mass. **2** fair, market. **3** *mil* mess.

messen* ('mɛsən) vt **1** measure. **2** survey (land). **sich messen** vr compete (with).

Messer ('mɛsər) n neu — knife.

Meßgewand ('mɛsgəvant) n neu ¨er vestment.

Messing ('mɛsiŋ) n neu brass.

Metall (me'tal) n neu -e metal. **—isch** adj metallic, metal.

Metaphysik (metafy'zi:k) nf metaphysics.

Meteor (mete'o:r) nm,neu -e meteor.

Meter ('me:tər) nm,neu — metre.

Method/e (me'to:də) nf -n method. **—isch** adj methodical.

metrisch (me'triʃ) adj metric(al).

Mettwurst ('mɛtvurst) nf type of lean pork sausage.

metz/eln ('mɛtsəln) vt **1** slaughter. **2** massacre. **—ger** ('mɛtsgər) nm — butcher.

Meuchelmord ('mɔyçəlmɔrt) nm assassination.

Meuter/ei (mɔytə'rai) nf -en mutiny. **—er** ('mɔytərər) nm — mutineer. **—n** ('mɔytərn) vi mutiny, rebel.

mich (miç) pron 1st pers s me, myself.

Mieder ('mi:dər) n neu — bodice.

Miene ('mi:nə) nf -n **1** air. **2** expression.

mies (mi:s) adj miserable, wretched.

Miet/auto ('mi:tauto) n neu -s **1** hire car. **2** taxi. **—e** nf -n **1** rent. **2** lease. **—en** vt **1** rent. **2** hire. **3** lease. **—er** nm — tenant.

Mikrophon (mikro'fo:n) n neu -e microphone.

Mikroskop (mikro'sko:p) n neu -e microscope.

Milbe ('milbə) nf -n mite.

Milch (milç) nf milk. **—straße** nf Milky Way.

mild (milt) adj **1** mild, gentle. **2** charitable. **—e** ('mildə) nf mildness, gentleness. **—ern** ('mildərn) vt mitigate, soften.

Militär (mili'tɛ:r) n neu army, military. nm -s soldier. **—isch** adj military.

Milliarde (mil'jardə) nf -n **1** thousand million. **2** US billion.

Million (mil'jo:n) nf -en million. **—är** (miljo-'nɛ:r) nm -e millionaire. **—ste** adj millionth.

Mimik ('mi:mik) nf -en **1** mimicry. **2** mime.

minder ('mindər) adj **1** less. **2** lower. **3** inferior. **—heit** nf -en minority. **—jährig** adj under age, minor. **—n** vt diminish, reduce. **—wertig** adj inferior.

mindest ('mindəst) adj least. **—ens** adv at least.

Mine ('mi:nə) nf -n mine.

Mineral (mine'ra:l) n neu -ien mineral. **—wasser** n neu mineral water.

Miniatur (minia'tu:r) nf -en miniature.

Minimum ('mi:nimum) n neu -ima minimum.

Minister (mi'nistər) nm — pol minister. **—iell** (ministeri'ɛl) adj ministerial. **—ium** (mini-'ste:rium) n neu -ien ministry. **—präsident** nm prime minister.

minus ('mi:nus) adv minus, less.

Minute (mi'nu:tə) nf -n minute.

mir (mi:r) pron 1st pers s to or for me, myself.

misch/en ('miʃən) vt **1** mix, blend. **2** shuffle (cards). **—ehe** nf mixed marriage. **—masch** ('miʃmaʃ) nm -e medley, hotchpotch. **—ung** nf -en mixture, blend.

mißachten (mis'axtən) vt **1** despise. **2** disregard.

Mißbilligung ('misbiliguŋ) nf disapproval.

Mißbrauch ('misbraux) nm misuse, abuse. **—en** (mis'brauxən) vt misuse, abuse.

mißdeuten (mis'dɔytən) vt misinterpret.

Mißerfolg ('misɛrfɔlk) nm failure.

Missetat ('misəta:t) nf misdeed, crime.

mißfallen* (mis'falən) vi displease.

Mißgeschick (misgə'ʃik) n neu misfortune.

mißglücken (mis'glykən) vi fail.

Mißgriff ('misgrif) nm mistake.

mißhandeln (mis'handəln) vt maltreat, abuse.

Mission (misi'o:n) nf -en mission. **—ar** (misio'na:r) nm -e missionary.

mißlich ('misliç) adj awkward, difficult.

mißlingen* (v mis'liŋən, n 'misliŋən) vi fail. n neu — failure.

mißtrau/en (mis'trauən) vi distrust. n neu distrust. **—ensvotum** n neu vote of no confidence. **—isch** ('mistrauiʃ) adj distrustful, suspicious.

Mißverständnis ('misfɛrʃtɛntnis) n neu misunderstanding.

Mist (mist) nm -e **1** manure, dung. **2** trash. **—haufen** nm dung heap.

mit (mit) prep **1** with. **2** by. **3** at. **4** upon. adv also, as well.

Mitarbeiter ('mita:rbaitər) nm fellow worker.

miteinander (mitain'andər) adv together, with one another, jointly.

Mitgefühl ('mitgəfy:l) n neu sympathy.

Mitglied ('mitgli:t) n neu member. **—schaft** nf membership.

mithin (mit'hin) adv consequently, therefore.

Mitlaut ('mitlaut) nm consonant.

Mitleid ('mitlait) n neu compassion, sympathy.

mitmachen ('mitmaxən) vt,vi join in, be involved in, be in on.

mitnehmen* ('mitne:mən) vt **1** take with one, take away. **2** wear out, tire.

mitnichten (mit'niçtən) *adv* by no means, on no account.

Mittag ('mita:k) *nm* -e midday, noon. —**essen** *n neu* lunch, dinner. —**s** *adv* (at) noon or midday.

Mitte ('mitə) *nf* -n **1** middle. **2** centre. **3** mean.

mitteil/en ('mittailən) *vt* inform of, communicate. —**ung** *nf* -en communication, information.

Mittel ('mitəl) *n neu* — **1** means. **2** average, mean. **3** remedy. —**alter** *n neu* Middle Ages. —**alterlich** *adj* medieval. —**bar** *adj* indirect. —**mäßig** *adj* mediocre. —**meer** *n neu* Mediterranean (Sea). —**punkt** *nm* centre, focus. —**s** *prep* by means of, with the help of. —**schule** *nf* middle school. —**stand** *nm* middle classes.

mitten ('mitən) *adv* in the middle. —**drin** (mitən'drin) *adv* in the middle (of it).

Mitternacht ('mitərnaxt) *nf* midnight.

mittler ('mitlər) *adj* **1** middle. **2** central. **im mittleren Alter** middle-aged. **Mittlere(r) Osten** Middle East. ~*nm* — mediator.

Mittwoch ('mitvɔx) *nm* Wednesday. —**s** *adv* on Wednesdays.

mitwirken ('mitvirkən) *vi* **1** cooperate. **2** contribute.

Möbel ('mœ:bəl) *n neu* — (piece of) furniture.

mobil (mo'bi:l) *adj* movable, mobile. —**isieren** (mobili'zi:rən) *vt* mobilize. —**machung** *nf* mobilization.

möblieren (mœ'bli:rən) *vt* furnish.

mochte ('mɔxtə) *v* see **mögen**.

Mod/e ('mo:də) *nf* -n fashion, vogue. —**isch** ('mo:diʃ) *adj* fashionable, stylish.

Modell (mo'dɛl) *n neu* -e model, pattern.

Moder ('mo:dər) *nm* mould, decay.

modern (mo'dɛrn) *adj* modern, up-to-date. —**isieren** (modɛrni'zi:rən) *vt* modernize.

modifizieren (modifi'tsi:rən) *vt* modify, alter.

mogeln ('mo:gəln) *vi* cheat.

mögen* ('mœ:gən) *vt,vi* like, wish. *v mod aux* may, might. **er mag kommen** he may or might come. **das mag sein** that may be, that's as may be. **ich möchte etwas** I would like or I desire something. **ich möchte etwas tun** I would like to do something.

möglich ('mœ:gliç) *adj* possible, feasible. —**erweise** *adv* possibly. —**keit** *nf* -en possibility. —**st** *adv* **möglichst bald/schnell** as soon/quickly as possible.

Mohammedaner (mohame'da:nər) *nm* — Muslim.

Mohn (mo:n) *nm* -e poppy.

Mohrrübe ('mo:rry:bə) *nf* -n carrot.

Molekül (mole'ky:l) *n neu* -e molecule.

Molkerei (mɔlkə'rai) *nf* -en dairy.

Moll (mɔl) *n neu mus* minor.

Moment (mo'mɛnt) *nm* -e moment, instant. *n neu* -e **1** momentum. **2** motive. **3** impulse. **4** element. —**an** (momɛn'ta:n) *adj* momentary, passing.

Monarch (mo'narç) *nm* -en monarch.

Monat ('mo:nat) *nm* -e month. —**lich** *adj* monthly.

Mönch (mœnç) *nm* -e monk.

Mond (mo:nt) *nm* -e moon. —**schein** *nm* moonlight.

Monopol (mono'po:l) *n neu* -e monopoly. —**isieren** (monopoli'zi:rən) *vt* monopolize.

Montag ('mo:nta:k) *nm* Monday. —**s** *adv* on Mondays.

Moor (mo:r) *n neu* -e **1** moor. **2** fen. **3** swamp.

Moos (mo:s) *n neu* -e **1** moss. **2** *sl* money.

Moral (mo'ra:l) *nf* -en **1** moral. **2** morality, morals. **3** morale. —**isch** *adj* moral. —**isieren** (morali'zi:rən) *vi* moralize. —**ität** (morali'tɛ:t) *nf* morality.

Mord (mɔrt) *nm* -e murder. —**anschlag** *nm* **1** murderous attack. **2** attempted murder. —**er** ('mœrdər) *nm* — murderer.

morgen ('mɔrgən) *adv* **1** tomorrow. **2** in the morning. *nm* — morning. *n neu* — following day. **(guten) Morgen** *interj* (good) morning! **morgen früh** (early) tomorrow morning. —**dämmerung** *nf also* —**grauen** *n neu* daybreak, dawn. —**land** *n neu* East, Orient. —**ländisch** *adj* oriental. —**rot** *n neu* dawn, (red) morning sky. —**s** *adv* in the morning.

Morphium ('mɔrfium) *n neu* morphine.

morsch (mɔrʃ) *adj* decayed, rotten.

Mosaik (moza'i:k) *n neu* -en mosaic.

Moschee (mɔ'ʃe:) *nf* -n mosque.

Mosel ('mo:zəl) *nf* Moselle.

Moskau ('mɔskau) *n neu* Moscow.

Most (mɔst) *nm* -e **1** fruit-juice or wine. **2** must, new wine. **3** cider.

Motiv (mo'ti:f) *n neu* -e **1** motive. **2** theme.

Motor ('mo:tɔr) *nm* -en motor, engine. —**boot** *n neu* motor boat. —**isieren** (motori'zi:rən) *vt* motorize. —**rad** *n neu* motorcycle.

Motte ('mɔtə) *nf* -n moth.

Möwe ('mœ:və) *nf* -n seagull.

Mücke ('mykə) *nf* -n gnat, mosquito.

müde ('my:də) *adj* tired, exhausted, weary.

Muff (muf) *nm* ⸚e 1 muff. 2 musty smell. —**ig** *adj* 1 surly. 2 musty.

Muff/el ('mufəl) *nm* — grumbler, surly person. —**elig** *adj* surly, grumpy.

Müh/e ('my:ə) *nf* -**n** trouble, effort. **sich Mühe geben** 1 take pains. 2 make great efforts.

Mühle ('my:lə) *nf* -**n** 1 mill. 2 grinder.

Mulde ('muldə) *nf* -**n** 1 trough. 2 valley.

Mull (mul) *nm* muslin.

Müll (myl) *nm* rubbish, refuse. —**eimer** *nm* dustbin. —**wagen** *nm* dust cart.

Müller ('mylər) *nm* — miller.

multiplizieren (multipli'tsi:rən) *vt* multiply.

Mummenschanz ('mumənʃants) *nm* masquerade.

München ('mynçən) *n neu* Munich.

Mund (munt) *nm* ⸚er mouth. —**art** *nf* -**en** dialect. ⸚**en** ('mundən) *vi* flow (into). —**harmonika** *nf* -**s** mouth organ. —**lich** ('myntliç) *adj* oral, verbal. ⸚**ung** ('mynduŋ) *nf* -**en** 1 mouth. 2 estuary. 3 (gun) muzzle.

mündig ('myndiç) *adj* of age, major.

Munition (munitsi'o:n) *nf* -**en** ammunition.

munter ('muntər) *adj* 1 lively, cheerful, merry. 2 awake.

Münze ('myntsə) *nf* -**n** 1 coin. 2 mint.

mürbe ('myrbə) *adj* 1 (of wood, stone, etc.) brittle, fragile. 2 (of food) soft, tender. 3 unnerved. 4 worn out.

murmeln ('murməln) 1 murmur. 2 mutter.

mürrisch ('myriʃ) *adj* surly, morose.

Muschel ('muʃəl) *nf* -**n** 1 mussel. 2 shell. 3 earpiece (of a telephone).

Museum (mu'ze:um) *n neu* -**seen** museum.

Musik (mu'zi:k) *nf* 1 music. 2 (military) band. —**alisch** (muzi'ka:liʃ) *adj* of music, musical. —**antenknochen** (muzi'kantənknɔxən) *nm* funny bone. —**er** ('mu:zikər) *nm* — musician.

Muskat (mɔs'ka:t) *nm* -**e** nutmeg.

Muskel ('muskəl) *nm* -**n** muscle.

Muß/e ('mu:sə) *nf* leisure (time), spare time. ⸚**ig** ('my:siç) *adj* 1 idle, lazy. 2 useless, superfluous.

müssen* ('mysən) *v mod aux* have to, be obliged to, must.

Muster ('mustər) *n neu* — 1 model, pattern. 2 paragon. 3 sample. —**n** *vt* 1 inspect, examine. 2 decorate with a pattern.

Mut (mu:t) *nm* courage. —**ig** *adj* brave, courageous. —**maßen** ('mu:tma:sən) *vt* guess, suppose.

Mutter ('mutər) *nf* ⸚ mother. —**leib** *nm* womb. ⸚**lich** ('mytərliç) *adj* maternal, motherly. —**schaf** *n neu* ewe. —**schaft** *nf* maternity, motherhood. —**sprache** *nf* mother tongue.

Mütze ('mytsə) *nf* -**n** cap.

mysteriös (mysteri'œ:s) *adj* mysterious.

mystifizieren (mystifi'tsi:rən) *vt* mystify.

Mystik ('mystik) *nf* mysticism. —**er** *nm* — mystic.

Mythos ('my:tos) *nm* -**then** *also* **Mythus** ('my:tus) myth.

N

Nabe ('na:bə) *nf* -**n** (wheel) hub.

Nabel ('na:bəl) *nm* — navel.

nach (na:x) *prep* 1 after, behind. 2 according to. 3 by. 4 to(wards). **nach London, nach Frankreich** to London, to France. ~*adv* after, behind. **nach und nach** gradually. **nach wie vor** as usual.

nachahmen ('na:xa:mən) *vt* imitate.

Nachbar ('na:xba:r) *nm* -**n** neighbour. —**schaft** *nf* -**en** neighbourhood.

nachdem (na:x'de:m) *conj* after. *adv* afterwards.

nachdenk/en* ('na:xdɛŋkən) *vi* reflect, consider, ponder. *n neu* — reflection, consideration. —**lich** *adj* thoughtful, pensive.

Nachdruck ('na:xdruk) *nm* -**e** 1 reproduction, reprint. 2 emphasis. 3 energy. ⸚**lich** ('na:xdrykliç) *adj* 1 emphatic. 2 energetic. —**srecht** *n neu* copyright.

nacheifern ('na:xaifərn) *vi* emulate.

nacheinander (na:xain'andər) *adv* one after the other.

Nachfolge ('na:xfɔlgə) *nf* succession. —**n** *vi* succeed, follow. —**r** *nm* — successor.

Nachfrage ('na:xfra:gə) *nf* 1 demand. 2 enquiry. **Angebot und Nachfrage** supply and demand.

nachgeben* ('na:xge:bən) *vi* give in, yield, give way.

nachgehen* ('na:xge:ən) *vi* 1 follow. 2 investigate. 3 (of a clock) be slow.

Nachgeschmack ('na:xgəʃmak) *nm* aftertaste.

nachgiebig ('na:xgi:biç) *adj* indulgent.

nachher (na:x'he:r) *adv* afterwards. **bis nachher!** see you later!

Nachhilfe ('na:xhilfə) *nf* assistance.

nachholen ('na:xho:lən) *vi* catch up, make up.

Nachhut ('na:xhu:t) *nf* -**en** rearguard.

Nachklang ('naːxklaŋ) nm resonance, echo.

Nachkomm/e ('naːxkɔmə) nm -n descendant. —**en*** vi 1 follow. 2 comply (with), fulfil. —**enschaft** nf posterity, descendants.

Nachkriegszeit ('naːxkriːkstsait) nf post-war period.

Nachlaß ('naːxlas) nm -lässe 1 inheritance. 2 estate. 3 reduction.

nachlassen* ('naːxlasən) vt 1 leave behind. 2 reduce. 3 temper. vi 1 slacken. 2 stop. 3 subside. 4 diminish.

nachmachen ('naːxmaxən) vt 1 imitate, copy. 2 counterfeit.

Nachmittag ('naːxmitaːk) nm -e afternoon. —**s** adv in the afternoon.

Nachnahme ('naːxnaːmə) nf -n cash on delivery, C.O.D.

nachprüfen ('naːxpryːfən) vt 1 check. 2 control. 3 verify.

Nachricht ('naːxriçt) nf -en 1 report, information. 2 pl news.

Nachruf ('naːxruːf) nm -e obituary.

nachschlag/en* ('naːxʃlaːgən) vt 1 look up, consult (books). 2 take after (a person). —**ewerk** n neu reference book.

Nachschrift ('naːxʃrift) nf 1 transcript. 2 notes. 3 postscript.

Nachschub ('naːxʃuːp) nm 1 reinforcement. 2 supplies.

nachsehen* ('naːxzeːən) vt 1 examine, inspect. 2 consult, look up. 3 excuse, overlook. vi watch, follow (with one's gaze).

nachsenden* ('naːxzɛndən) vt forward, send on.

Nachspeise ('naːxʃpaizə) nf -n dessert, sweet.

nachsprechen* ('naːxʃprɛçən) vt repeat.

nächst (nɛːçst) adj nearest, next. prep next to. —**e(r)** nm fellow, man, neighbour. —**enliebe** nf love for one's fellow men or one's neighbour. —**ens** adv shortly.

nachstellen ('naːxʃtɛlən) vt 1 place behind. 2 adjust. vi 1 pursue. 2 persecute.

nachstreben ('naːxʃtreːbən) vi 1 strive (for). 2 emulate.

Nacht (naxt) nf -e night. —**essen** n neu supper. —**hemd** n neu nightdress, nightshirt. —**lich** ('nɛçtliç) adj nocturnal, nightly. —**s** adv at night. —**wächter** nm night watchman. —**wandeln** vi sleepwalk.

Nachteil ('naːxtail) nm -e 1 disadvantage. 2 loss. —**ig** adj detrimental, disadvantageous.

Nachtigall ('naxtigal) nf -en nightingale.

Nachtisch ('naxtiʃ) nm -e dessert, sweet.

Nachtrag ('naːxtraːk) nm -e supplement. —**lich** ('naːxtrɛːkliç) adj supplementary.

Nachwahl ('naːxvaːl) nf by-election.

Nachweis ('naːxvais) nm -e 1 proof. 2 information. —**en*** ('naːxvaizən) vt 1 prove. 2 point out.

Nachwelt ('naːxvɛlt) nf posterity.

Nachwirkung ('naːxvirkuŋ) nf after-effect.

Nachwuchs ('naːxvuks) nm new or rising generation.

nachziehen* ('naːxtsiːən) vt 1 draw along or after, drag. 2 trace. vi follow.

Nachzügler ('naːxtsyːklər) nm — straggler.

Nacken ('nakən) nm — (nape of the) neck.

nackt (nakt) adj naked. —**kultur** nf nudism.

Nadel ('naːdəl) nf -n needle, pin. —**baum** nm,pl **Nadelhölzer** conifer.

Nagel ('naːgəl) nm -e 1 nail, pin. 2 (finger)-nail. —**feile** nf nail file. —**lack** nm nail polish or varnish. —**n** vt nail. —**neu** adj brand-new.

nag/en ('naːgən) vi,vt 1 gnaw. 2 erode. —**etier** n neu rodent.

nah/(e) ('naːə) adj near, close. **Nahe(r) Osten** nm Middle or Near East. —**e** ('nɛːə) nf 1 proximity, vicinity. 2 neighbourhood. **in der Nähe** nearby, in the vicinity. —**elegen** vt suggest. —**eliegen*** vi 1 lie near. 2 be obvious. —**er** ('nɛːər) adj 1 nearer. 2 more detailed. —**eres** ('nɛːərəs) n neu details. —**ern** ('nɛːərn) vt bring near. **sich —ern** vr approach. —**estehen*** vi 1 be connected (with). 2 be friendly or sympathize (with). —**ezu** ('naːə'tsuː) adv nearly, almost.

näh/en ('nɛːən) vt,vi sew. —**maschine** nf sewing machine.

nahm (naːm) v see **nehmen**.

nähren ('nɛːrən) vt feed, nourish. vi be nourishing. **sich nähren** vr live (on).

nahr/haft ('naːrhaft) adj 1 nutritious. 2 productive. —**ung** nf nourishment, food, sustenance. —**ungsmittel** n neu pl food(stuffs).

Naht (naːt) nf -e 1 seam. 2 med stitch(es).

naiv (naˈiːf) adj naive, simple.

Nam/e ('naːmə) nm -n name. —**enlos** adj nameless. —**ens** prep 1 named. 2 in the name of. —**entlich** adj by name. adv especially. —**lich** ('nɛːmliç) adv that is to say, namely. adj same.

nannte ('nantə) v see **nennen**.

Napf (napf) nm -e bowl, basin.

Narbe ('narbə) nf -n scar.

Narko/se (nar'ko:zə) *nf* **-n** anaesthesia. **—tisch** (nar'ko:tiʃ) *adj* narcotic.

Narr (nar) *nm* **-en** fool. **—enhaus** *n neu* madhouse. **—heit** *nf* **-en** folly, madness.

Nase ('na:zə) *nf* **-n** nose. **die Nase voll haben von** be fed up with. **—weis** *adj* cheeky.

naß (nas) *adj* wet, moist.

Nässe ('nɛsə) *nf* **-n** 1 moisture. 2 humidity. **—n** *vt* wet, moisten.

Nation (natsi'o:n) *nf* **-en** nation. **—al** (natsio-'na:l) *adj* national. **—alhymne** *nf* national anthem. **—alismus** (natsiona'lismus) *nm* nationalism. **—alität** (natsionali'tɛ:t) *nf* -en nationality. **—alsozialismus** *nm* national socialism, Nazism. **—alsozialist** *nm* Nazi.

Natter ('natər) *nf* **-n** adder.

Natur (na'tu:r) *nf* **-en** 1 nature. 2 disposition, temper. **—alien** (natu'ra:liən) *n pl* natural produce. **—erscheinung** *nf* natural phenomenon. **—gemäß** *adj* natural. **—geschichte** *nf* natural history. **—gesetz** *n neu* law of nature, natural law. **—lich** (na'ty:rliç) *adj* natural. *adv* of course, naturally. **—wissenschaft** *nf* (natural) science.

Navigation (navigatsi'o:n) *nf* **-en** navigation.

Nazi ('na:tsi) *nm* **-s** Nazi.

Nebel ('ne:bəl) *nm* **-** fog, mist.

neben ('ne:bən) *prep* 1 beside, near, next to. 2 in addition to. **—an** (ne:bən'an) *adv* 1 close or near by. 2 next door. **—bei** (ne:bən'bai) *adv* 1 incidentally. 2 besides, moreover. **—einander** (ne:bənain'andər) *adv* side by side, next to one another. **—fach** *n neu* subsidiary subject. **—fluß** *nm* tributary. **—gebäude** *n neu* annexe. **—her** (ne:bən-'he:r) *adv* 1 incidentally. 2 alongside. **—kosten** *n pl* incidental costs, extras. **—sächlich** *adj* incidental.

nebst (ne:pst) *prep* together with.

neck/en ('nɛkən) *vt* tease. **—isch** *adj* 1 teasing. 2 comical.

Neffe ('nɛfə) *nm* **-n** nephew.

negativ (nega'ti:f) *adj* negative. *n neu* **-e** negative.

Neger ('ne:gər) *nm* **—** Negro. **—in** *nf* **-nen** Negress.

nehmen* ('ne:mən) *vt* 1 take. 2 receive.

Neid (nait) *nm* envy. **—en** ('naidən) *vi* envy. **—isch** ('naidiʃ) *adj* envious.

Neig/e ('naigə) *nf* -n slope, decline. 2 remnant, dregs. **—en** *vt* 1 lean. 2 lower. *vi* incline (to), tend (to). **sich —en** *vr* 1 incline (to), tend (to). 2 dip. 3 bow. **—ung** *nf* **-en** 1

inclination, tendency, preference. 2 slope, incline.

nein (nain) *adv* no. **mit Nein antworten** reply in the negative.

Nelke ('nɛlkə) *nf* **-n** 1 carnation. 2 clove.

nenn/en* ('nɛnən) *vt* name, call. **—enswert** *adj* worth mentioning. **—ung** *nf* **-en** 1 naming. 2 *sport* entry.

Neon ('ne:ɔn) *n neu* neon.

Nerv (nɛrf) *nm* **-en** nerve. **—enzusammenbruch** *nm* nervous breakdown. **—ös** (nɛr-'vœ:s) *adj* nervous.

Nessel ('nɛsəl) *nf* **-n** nettle.

Nest (nɛst) *n neu* **-er** nest.

nett (nɛt) *adj* 1 nice. 2 neat. 3 pretty.

netto ('nɛto) *adv* net, clear.

Netz (nɛts) *n neu* **-e** 1 net, netting. 2 mains. 3 network, grid. **—haut** *nf* retina.

neu (nɔy) *adj* 1 new. 2 modern, recent. 3 fresh. **Neubau** ('nɔybau) *nm* 1 new building. 2 building under construction.

neuerdings ('nɔyərdiŋs) *adv* lately, recently.

Neuerung ('nɔyəruŋ) *nf* **-en** innovation.

neu(e)stens ('nɔystəns) *adv* lately, of late.

Neugier ('nɔygi:r) *nf also* **Neugier/de** ('nɔygi:-rdə) curiosity. **—ig** *adj* curious.

Neuheit ('nɔyhait) *nf* **-en** 1 novelty. 2 newness.

Neuigkeit ('nɔyiçkait) *nf* -en news.

Neujahr ('nɔyja:r) *n neu* New Year.

neulich ('nɔyliç) *adv* recently.

Neuphilologie ('nɔyfilɔlɔgi:) *nf* (study of) modern languages.

Neureiche(r) ('nɔyraiçə) *nm* new rich, nouveau riche.

Neuzeit ('nɔytsait) *nf* modern age or times. **—lich** *adj* modern.

neun (nɔyn) *adj,nf* nine. **—te** *adj* ninth. **—zehn** *adj,nf* nineteen. **—zehnte** *adj* nineteenth. **—zig** ('nɔyntsiç) *adj,nf* ninety. **—zigste** *adj* ninetieth.

Neurose (nɔy'ro:zə) *nf* **-n** neurosis.

Neuseeland (nɔy'ze:lant) *n neu* New Zealand.

neutr/al (nɔy'tra:l) *adj* neutral, impartial. **—alität** (nɔytrali'tɛ:t) *nf* neutrality. **—um** ('nɔytrum) *n neu* neuter.

nicht (niçt) *adv* not. *pref* non-. **nicht wahr?** is that not so? isn't it? **—raucher** *nm* nonsmoker. **—wissen** *n neu* ignorance. **—zutreffend** *adj* not applicable.

Nichte ('niçtə) *nf* **-n** niece.

Nichtigkeit ('niçtiçkait) *nf* **-en** 1 invalidity. 2 worthlessness.

nichts (niçts) *pron* nothing. *n neu* nothing-

(ness). —**destoweniger** (niçtsdɛsto've:nigər) adv nevertheless. —**sagend** adj meaningless. —**tuer** ('niçtstu:ər) nm — idler, slacker.

Nickel ('nikəl) n neu nickel.

nick/en ('nikən) vi 1 nod. 2 doze. —**erchen** ('nikərçən) n neu — doze, nap.

nie (ni:) adv never.

nieder ('ni:dər) adv down. adj 1 low. 2 inferior.

niederdrücken (ni:dər'drykən) vt 1 press down, weigh down. 2 depress.

Niedergang ('ni:dərgaŋ) nm 1 decline. 2 descent.

niedergehen* ('ni:dərge:ən) vi 1 go down. 2 alight, land.

niedergeschlagen ('ni:dərgəʃla:gən) adj downcast, depressed.

Niederlage ('ni:dərla:gə) nf 1 defeat. 2 warehouse. 3 comm branch.

Niederland/e ('ni:dərlandə) n pl Netherlands. —**er** nm — Dutchman. —**isch** adj Dutch.

Niederlassung ('ni:dərlasuŋ) nf **-en** settlement.

niederlegen ('ni:dərle:gən) vt 1 lay down. 2 demolish. 3 resign, stop. **sich niederlegen** vr lie down.

Niedersachsen ('ni:dɔzaksən) n neu Lower Saxony.

Niederschlag ('ni:dərʃla:k) nm 1 precipitation. 2 knock-out. 3 sediment. —**en*** vt 1 knock down. 2 defeat. 3 kill. 4 press or move down(wards). 5 calm down. 6 depress. 7 precipitate.

niederträchtig (ni:dətreçtiç) adj base, mean.

niedlich ('ni:dliç) adj nice, dainty, pretty.

niedrig ('ni:driç) adj 1 low. 2 humble.

niemals ('ni:ma:ls) adv never.

niemand ('ni:mant) pron nobody, no one.

Niere ('ni:rə) nf **-n** kidney.

nieseln ('ni:zəln) vi drizzle.

niesen ('ni:zən) vi sneeze.

Niet (ni:t) nm **-e** rivet. —**en** vt rivet.

Nikotin (niko'ti:n) n neu nicotine.

Nil (ni:l) nm Nile. —**pferd** n neu hippopotamus.

nimmer ('nimər) adv never. —**mehr** adv never again.

nimmt (nimt) v see **nehmen**.

nippen ('nipən) vi sip.

nirgends ('nirgənts) adv also **nirgendwo** ('nirgəntvo:) nowhere.

Nische ('ni:ʃə) nf **-n** niche.

nisten ('nistən) vi (build a) nest.

Niveau (ni:'vo:) n neu **-s** 1 standard. 2 level.

noch (nɔx) adv 1 still. 2 yet. 3 besides. **noch**

nicht not yet. **weder...noch** neither...nor. —**mal** adv also —**mals** once more, again.

Nomade (no'ma:də) nm **-n** nomad.

Nominativ ('no:minati:f) nm **-e** nominative.

nominell (nomi'nɛl) adj nominal.

Nonne ('nɔnə) nf **-n** nun.

Nord (nɔrt) nm also **Norden** ('nɔrdən) north.

Nordamerika ('nɔrdame:rika) n neu North America.

nordisch ('nɔrdiʃ) adj 1 Norse, Nordic. 2 northern.

nördlich ('nœrtliç) adj northern.

Nordost (nɔrd'ɔst) nm also **Nordosten** (nɔrd'ɔst'ən) north-east. —**lich** adj north-eastern.

Nordpol ('nɔrdpo:l) nm North Pole.

Nordrhein-Westfalen (nɔrdrainvɛst'fa:lən) n neu North Rhine-Westphalia.

Nordsee ('nɔrdze:) nf North Sea.

nordwärts ('nɔrtvɛrts) adv northward(s), north.

Nordwest (nɔrd'vɛst) nm also **Nordwesten** (nɔrd'vɛstən) north-west. —**lich** adj north-western.

normal (nɔr'ma:l) adj normal.

Normann/e (nɔr'manə) nm **-n** Norman. —**isch** adj Norman.

Norweg/en ('nɔrve:gən) n neu Norway. —**er** nm — Norwegian. —**isch** adj Norwegian. n neu Norwegian (language).

Not (no:t) nf **-e** 1 need, necessity. 2 emergency. 3 danger. 4 trouble. 5 poverty, misery, distress.

Notar (no'ta:r) nm **-e** notary.

Notbremse ('no:tbrɛmzə) nf emergency brake.

Notfall ('no:tfal) nm case of emergency or need. —**s** adv if necessary, in an emergency.

Nothilfe ('no:thilfə) nf emergency or relief service.

notieren (no'ti:rən) vt make a note of, take down.

nötig ('nœ:tiç) adj necessary. —**en** ('nœ:tigən) vt compel, urge.

Notiz (no'ti:ts) nf **-en** 1 notice. 2 note. —**buch** n neu notebook.

Notlage ('no:tla:gə) nf 1 crisis, emergency. 2 distress.

Notruf ('no:tru:f) nm emergency (telephone) call.

Notstand ('no:tʃtand) nm (state of) emergency.

notwendig ('no:tvɛndiç) adj necessary, requisite. —**keit** nf **-en** necessity.

Notzucht ('no:ttsuxt) nf rape.

Novelle (no'vɛlə) nf **-n** short novel or story.

November (no'vɛmbər) nm November.

Novize (no'vi:tsə) nm,f -n novice.

nüchtern ('nyçtərn) adj 1 sober. 2 prosaic, dull.

Nudeln ('nu:dəln) nf pl noodles.

null (nul) adj 1 nil. 2 null. nf -en nought, zero.

numerieren (nume'ri:rən) vt number.

Nummer ('numər) nf -n 1 issue, edition (of a magazine, etc.). 3 number, piece, song. **—nschild** n neu mot number plate.

nun (nu:n) adv now. interj well, well now. **—mehr** adv 1 (by) now. 2 from now on.

nur (nu:r) adv 1 only, solely. 2 merely. conj but.

Nürnberg ('nyrnberk) n neu Nuremberg.

Nuß (nus) n Nüsse nut. **—baum** nm walnut tree.

nutz/bar ('nutsba:r) adj useful. **—en** ('nutsən) n neu 1 use. 2 advantage. 3 gain. vt also **–en** ('nytsən) make use of. vi be useful, help. **–lich** ('nytsliç) adj useful. **—los** adj useless.

Nylon ('nailən) n neu nylon. **—strümpfe** nm pl nylon stockings, nylons.

Nymphe ('nymfə) nf -n nymph.

O

Oase (o'a:zə) nf -n oasis.

ob (ɔp) conj whether. prep 1 above. 2 beyond. 3 on account of. **als ob** conj as if, as though.

Obdach ('ɔpdax) n neu shelter. **—los** adj homeless.

oben ('o:bən) adv 1 above. 2 (high) up. 3 upstairs. **nach oben gehen** go upstairs. **—an** (o:bən'an) adv 1 at the top. 2 at the beginning. 3 at the head. **—drein** (o:bən'drain) adv in addition, into the bargain.

ober ('o:bər) adj 1 upper, higher. 2 superior. 3 senior. nm — (head) waiter.

Oberarm ('o:bərarm) nm upper arm.

Oberbefehlshaber (o:bərbə'fɛ:lshabər) nm commander-in-chief.

Oberfläch/e ('o:bərflɛçə) nf 1 surface. 2 area. **—lich** ('o:bərflɛçliç) adj superficial.

oberhalb ('o:bərhalp) adv,prep above.

Oberhand ('o:bərhant) nf upper hand.

Oberhaupt ('o:bərhaupt) nm leader, head.

Oberhemd ('o:bərhɛmt) n neu shirt.

Oberin ('o:bərin) nf -nen matron.

oberirdisch (o:bər'irdiʃ) adj 1 above ground. 2 overhead.

Oberkellner ('o:bərkɛlnər) nm head waiter.

Oberlicht ('o:bərliçt) n neu skylight.

Oberschicht ('o:bəʃiçt) nf 1 top layer. 2 upper classes, elite.

Oberschule ('o:bərʃu:lə) nf secondary school.

Oberst ('o:bərst) nm -en colonel. **—leutnant** nm mil lieutenant colonel.

obgleich (ɔp'glaiç) conj although.

Obhut ('ɔphu:t) nf protection, care.

obig ('o:biç) adj above(-mentioned).

Objekt (ɔp'jɛkt) n neu -e object. **—iv** (ɔpjɛk-'ti:f) adj objective.

obliegen* ('ɔpli:gən) vi **einem obliegen** be one's duty.

obligat (obli'ga:t) adj 1 obligatory. 2 necessary. **—orisch** (obliga'to:riʃ) adj compulsory.

Obmann ('ɔpman) nm 1 leader. 2 chairman. 3 spokesman.

Obo/e (o'bo:ə) nf -n oboe. **—ist** (obo'ist) nm -en oboe player.

Obrigkeit ('o:briçkait) nf -en 1 authorities. 2 pl government.

obschon (ɔp'ʃo:n) conj although.

Obst (o:pst) n neu fruit. **—garten** nm orchard.

obszön (ɔps'tsœ:n) adj obscene, indecent. **—ität** (ɔpstsœni'tɛ:t) nf -en obscenity.

obwohl (ɔp'vo:l) conj although.

Ochse ('ɔksə) nm -n ox.

Ode ('o:də) nf -n ode.

öde ('œ:də) adj 1 bleak, barren. 2 deserted. 3 dull. nf -n 1 desert. 2 dullness.

oder ('o:dər) conj or. **entweder...oder** either ...or.

Ofen ('o:fən) nm **–** 1 stove, oven. 2 heater. 3 furnace.

offen ('ɔfən) adj 1 open. 2 public. 3 frank, candid. 4 vacant. **—bar** (ɔfən'ba:r) adj obvious. **—baren** (ɔfən'ba:rən) vt disclose, reveal. **—barung** (ɔfən'ba:ruŋ) nf -en revelation, disclosure. **—heit** nf openness, frankness. **—sichtlich** adv obvious. **–tlichkeit** ('œfəntliçkait) nf 1 public. 2 publicity.

offensiv (ɔfɛn'zi:f) adj offensive. **—e** (ɔfɛn-'zi:və) nf -n offensive.

offiziell (ɔfi'tsjɛl) adj official.

Offizier (ɔfi'tsi:r) nm -e officer.

öffn/en ('œfnən) vt 1 open. 2 unlock. **—er** nm — opener. **—ung** nf -en opening, hole.

oft (ɔft) adv also **öfters** ('œftərs) or **oftmals** ('ɔftma:ls) often, frequently. **—er** ('œftər) adv (more) often. **—malig** ('ɔftma:liç) adj frequent.

Oheim ('o:haim) nm -e uncle.

ohn/e ('o:nə) prep without. **—edies** (o:nə'di:s) adv also **—ehin** (o:nə'hin) 1 in any case. 2

besides. —**macht** nf 1 unconsciousness. 2 powerlessness, impotence. —**mächtig** adj 1 unconscious. 2 powerless.

Ohr (o:r) n neu -en ear. —**feige** nf box on the ear. —**ring** nm -e earring.

Öhr (œ:r) n neu -e eye (of a needle).

Ökonom (œko'no:m) nm -en 1 farmer. 2 steward. 3 economist. —**ie** (œkono'mi:) nf -n 1 economics. 2 economy. 3 agriculture. —**isch** (œko'no:nıʃ) adj economical.

Oktave (ɔk'ta:və) nf -n octave.

Oktober (ɔk'to:bər) nm October.

Okzident ('ɔktsident) nm Occident.

Öl (ø:l) n neu -e oil. —**bild** n neu oil painting. —**en** vt 1 oil. 2 anoint. —**feld** n neu oil field. —**ig** adj oily. —**ung** nf -en 1 lubrication. 2 anointment.

Olive (ɔ'li:və) nf -n olive.

Oma ('o:ma) nf -s inf grandma.

Omelett (ɔmə'lɛt) n neu -s also **Omelette** nf -n omelette.

Omnibus ('ɔmnibus) nm -busse bus, coach.

ondulieren (ɔndu'li:rən) vt wave (hair).

Onkel ('ɔŋkəl) nm — uncle.

Opa ('o:pa) nm -s inf grandpa.

Opal (o'pa:l) nm -e opal.

Oper ('o:pər) nf -n opera. —**ette** (opə'rɛtə) nf -n operetta. —**nhaus** n neu opera house.

Oper/ation (operatsi'o:n) nf -en operation. —**ationssaal** nm operating theatre. —**ieren** (ope'ri:rən) vt,vi operate (on).

Opfer ('ɔpfər) n neu — 1 victim. 2 sacrifice. —**n** vt sacrifice.

Opium ('o:pium) n neu opium.

opportun (ɔpɔr'tu:n) adj opportune.

Opposition (ɔpozitsi'o:n) nf -en opposition.

Opt/ik ('ɔptik) nf optics. —**iker** nm — optician. —**isch** ('ɔptiʃ) adj optical.

Optimist (ɔpti'mist) nm -en optimist. —**isch** adj optimistic.

Orange (o'rã:ʒə) nf -n orange. —**nmarmelade** nf marmelade.

Orchester (ɔr'kɛstər) n neu — 1 orchestra. 2 band.

Orchidee (ɔrçi'de:ə) nf -n orchid.

Orden ('ɔrdən) nm — 1 order. 2 decoration. —**sbruder** nm member of an order, monk. —**sschwester** nf sister, nun.

ordentlich ('ɔrdəntliç) adj 1 orderly, tidy. 2 decent, proper. 3 regular. —**keit** nf 1 orderliness. 2 respectability. 3 regularity.

Order ('ɔrdər) nf -n command, order.

ordinär (ɔrdi'nɛ:r) adj ordinary, vulgar.

Ordinarius (ɔrdi'na:rius) nm -rien 1 professor. 2 class teacher.

ordn/en ('ɔrdnən) vt 1 (put in) order. 2 sort. 3 regulate. —**er** nm — 1 organizer. 2 steward. 3 file, folder. —**ung** nf -en 1 order. 2 regulation. 3 arrangement.

Organ (ɔr'ga:n) n neu -e organ. —**isation** (ɔrganizatsi'o:n) nf -en organization. —**isieren** (ɔrgani'zi:rən) vt organize. —**isch** (ɔr'ga:nıʃ) adj organic. —**ismus** (ɔrga'nısmus) nm -ismen organism.

Orgel ('ɔrgəl) nf -n mus organ.

Orgie ('ɔrgiə) nf -n orgy.

Orient ('o:rient) nm Orient. —**alisch** (orien'ta:liʃ) adj oriental.

orientieren (orien'ti:rən) vt 1 orientate. 2 inform. **sich orientieren** vr take one's bearings.

origin/al (origi'na:l) adj original, first. n neu -e original. —**ell** (origi'nɛl) adj 1 original. 2 unusual. 3 clever.

Orkan (ɔr'ka:n) nm -e hurricane.

Ornat (ɔr'na:t) nm -e (official) robes.

Ornithologie (ɔrnitolo'gi:) nf ornithology.

Ort (ɔrt) nm -e 1 place, spot. 2 point. 3 town. —**lich** ('œrtliç) adj local. —**schaft** nf -en 1 (small) town, village. 2 place.

Orthopädie (ɔrtopɛ'di:) nf orthopaedics.

Ost (ɔst) nm also **Ost/en** east. —**deutschland** n neu East Germany. —**lich** ('œstliç) adj eastern. —**see** nf Baltic Sea. —**wärts** ('ɔstverts) adv eastward(s), east.

Oster/n ('o:stərn) n neu pl Easter. —**ei** n neu Easter egg.

Österreich ('œ:stərraiç) n neu Austria. —**er** nm — Austrian. —**isch** adj Austrian.

Otter [1] ('ɔtər) nm — otter.

Otter [2] ('ɔtər) nf -n adder.

Ouvertüre (uvɛr'ty:rə) nf -n overture.

oval (o'va:l) adj oval.

Oxyd (ɔ'ksy:t) n neu -e oxide.

Ozean ('o:tsea:n) nm -e ocean. —**isch** (o:tse'a:nıʃ) adj oceanic.

Ozon (o'tso:n) n neu -e ozone.

P

Paar (pa:r) n neu -e pair, couple. **ein paar** a few. —**en** vt pair, couple. **sich** —**en** vr mate.

Pacht (paxt) nf -en 1 lease, tenure. 2 rent.

—en vt lease, rent. **—er** ('pɛçtər) nm — tenant, leaseholder. **—vertrag** nm lease.

Peck (pak) nm **-e** 1 packet, parcel. 2 pack. n neu mob, rabble. **—chen** ('pɛkçən) n neu — small parcel, packet. **—en** vt 1 grasp, seize. 2 pack. 3 thrill. **—papier** n neu wrapping paper. **—ung** nf-en packing.

Pädagog/ik (pɛda'goːgik) nf (theory of) education. **—isch** adj educational. **pädagogische Hochschule** nf teacher training college.

Paddel ('padəl) n neu — paddle. **—boot** n neu canoe. **—n** vi paddle.

Page ('paːʒə) nm **-n** page (boy).

Paket (pa'keːt) n neu **-e** packet, package.

Pakt (pakt) nm **-e** pact, agreement.

Palast (pa'last) nm **ᵉe** palace.

Palästin/a (palɛ'stiːna) n neu Palestine. **—ense(r)** nm Palestinian. **—isch** adj Palestinian.

Palm/e ('palmə) nf **-n** palm. **—sonntag** nm Palm Sunday.

Pampelmuse ('pampəlmuːzə) nf **-n** grapefruit.

panieren (pa'niːrən) vt coat with breadcrumbs.

Panik ('paːnik) nf **-en** panic.

Panne ('panə) nf **-n** mot breakdown.

Panther ('pantər) nm — panther.

Pantoffel (pan'tɔfəl) nm **-n** slipper.

Pantomime (panto'miːmə) nf **-n** pantomime.

Panzer ('pantsər) nm armour. **—(kampf)wagen** nm mil tank. **—n** vt 1 armour. 2 arm.

Papa (pa'paː, 'papa) nm **-s** dad, daddy.

Papagei (papa'gai) nm **-e** parrot.

Papier (pa'piːr) n neu **-e** paper. **—en** adj paper. **—geld** n neu paper money. **—korb** nm wastepaper basket.

Papp/e ('papə) nf **-n** cardboard. **—schachtel** nf cardboard box, carton.

Pappel ('papəl) nf **-n** poplar.

Paprika ('paprika) nm paprika, capsicum.

Papst (paːpst) nm **ᵉe** pope. **—lich** ('pɛːpstliç) adj papal.

Parabel (pa'raːbəl) nf **-n** 1 parable. 2 parabola.

Parad/e (pa'raːdə) nf **-n** 1 parade. 2 parry. **—ieren** (para'diːrən) vi parade.

Paradies (para'diːs) n neu **-e** paradise.

paradox (para'dɔks) adj paradoxical. **—on** (para'dɔksɔn) n neu **-oxa** paradox.

Paragraph (para'graːf) nm **-en** paragraph, article, section.

parallel (para'leːl) adj parallel. **—e** nf **-n** parallel.

Paralyse (para'lyːzə) nf **-n** paralysis.

Parasit (para'ziːt) nm **-en** parasite.

Parenthese (parɛn'teːzə) nf **-n** parenthesis.

Parfüm (par'fyːm) n neu **-e** or **-s** perfume.

parieren (pa'riːrən) vt 1 parry. 2 rein in (a horse). vi obey.

Parität (pari'tɛːt) nf **-en** parity.

Park (park) nm **-s** park. **—anlage** nf park, grounds. **—en** vt park. **—platz** nm car park. **—uhr** nf parking meter.

Parkett (par'kɛt) n neu **-s** 1 parquet (floor). 2 Th stalls.

Parlament (parla'mɛnt) n neu **-e** parliament. **—arisch** (parlamɛn'taːriʃ) adj parliamentary.

Parodie (paro'diː) nf **-n** parody.

Parole (pa'roːlə) nf **-n** 1 password. 2 pol slogan.

Partei (par'tai) nf **-en** pol party. **—gänger** (par'taigɛŋər) nm party man, partisan. **—isch** adj also **—lich** partial, partisan, biased. **—los** adj impartial, independent.

Parterre (par'tɛr) n neu **-s** 1 ground floor. 2 Th pit.

Partie (par'tiː) nf **-n** 1 part. 2 party, excursion. 3 match. 4 comm lot.

Partikel (par'tiːkəl) nf **-n** particle.

Partisan (parti'zaːn) nm **-e** partisan, guerrilla.

Partitur (parti'tuːr) nf **-en** mus score.

Partizip (parti'tsiːp) n neu **-ien** participle.

Party ('paːrti) nf **-ties** party.

Parzell/e (par'tsɛlə) nf **-n** allotment. **—ieren** (partse'liːrən) vt divide into lots.

Paß (pas) nm **Pässe** 1 passport. 2 pass. 3 passage. **—kontrolle** nf passport control.

Passag/e (pa'saːʒə) nf **-n** passage. **—ier** (pasa'ʒiːr) nm **-e** passenger.

Passant (pa'sant) nm **-en** passer-by.

passen ('pasən) vi 1 fit, suit. 2 sport,game pass. **sich passen** vr be proper or fitting. **—d** adj suitable, fit(ting).

passier/en (pa'siːrən) vt 1 pass (through), cross. 2 sieve, strain. vi happen, occur. **—schein** nm pass, permit.

Passion (pasi'oːn) nf **-en** passion. **—sspiel** n neu Passion Play.

passiv ('pasiːf) adj passive. n neu **-e** gram passive. **—ität** (pasivi'tɛːt) nf passivity.

Pastete (pa'steːtə) nf **-n** (meat) pie, pasty.

pasteurisieren (pastœri'ziːrən) vt pasteurize.

Pastor ('pastor) nm **-en** pastor, vicar. **—al** (pasto'raːl) adj pastoral.

Pate ('paːtə) nm **-n** godfather. **—nkind** n neu godchild.

patent (pa'tɛnt) adj splendid. n neu **-e** 1 patent.

2 commission. **—ieren** (patɛn'tiːrən) vt patent. **—inhaber** nm patent-holder.
pathetisch (pa'teːtiʃ) adj pathetic.
Pathologie (patoloːgiː) nf -n pathology.
Patient (patsi'ɛnt) nm -en patient.
Patin ('paːtin) nf -nen godmother.
Patriot (patri'oːt) nm -en patriot. **—isch** adj patriotic. **—ismus** (patrio'tismus) nm patriotism.
Patrizier (pa'triːtsiər) nm — patrician.
Patron (pa'troːn) nm -e patron. **—in** nf -nen patroness.
Patrone (pa'troːnə) nf -n 1 cartridge. 2 pattern.
Patrouille (pa'truljə) nf -n patrol.
Patt (pat) n neu -s stalemate.
Pauke ('paukə) nf -n kettledrum. **—n** vi 1 play the kettledrum 2 inf study, swot.
pauschal (pau'ʃaːl) adj inclusive. **—e** nf -n 1 lump sum. 2 all-in price. **—reise** nf package tour.
Pause ('pauzə) nf -n pause, interval.
Pavian ('paːviaːn) nm -e baboon.
Pazifik (pa'tsiːfik) nm Pacific (Ocean).
Pazifismus (patsi'fismus) nm pacifism.
Pech (pɛç) n neu -e 1 pitch. 2 inf hard luck.
Pedal (pe'daːl) n neu -e pedal.
Pedant (pe'dant) nm -en pedant.
Pegel ('peːgəl) nm -e water-gauge.
peilen ('pailən) vt naut 1 sound. 2 take the bearings of.
Pein (pain) nf pain, torture. **—lich** adj 1 embarrassing. 2 painful. 3 meticulous.
Peitsche ('paitʃə) nf -n whip. **—n** vt whip.
Pelikan ('peːlikaːn) nm -e pelican.
Pell/e ('pɛlə) nf -n 1 skin. 2 peel. **—en** vt 1 skin. 2 peel. **—kartoffeln** nf pl potatoes boiled in their skins.
Pelz (pɛlts) nm -e pelt, fur. **—ig** adj furry. **—mantel** nm fur coat.
Pend/el ('pɛndəl) n neu — pendulum. **—elverkehr** nm 1 commuter traffic. 2 shuttle service. **—ler** nm — commuter.
penibel (pe'niːbəl) adj meticulous.
Pension (pã'sjoːn) nf -en 1 guest house. 2 pension. **—är** (pãsjo'nɛːr) nm -e 1 paying guest. 2 pensioner. **—ieren** (pãsjo'niːrən) vt pension (off).
per (pɛr) prep by, per.
perfekt (pɛr'fɛkt) adj perfect. n neu -e gram perfect.
Pergament (pɛrgaˈmɛnt) n neu -e parchment.
Period/e (peri'oːdə) nf -n period, cycle. **—isch** adj periodic(al).

Perl/e ('pɛrlə) nf -n pearl. **—mutter** nf mother-of-pearl.
Pers/ien ('pɛrziən) n neu Persia. **—er** nm Persian. **—isch** adj Persian. n neu Persian (language).
Person (pɛr'zoːn) nf -en 1 person. 2 Th character. **—al** (pɛrzo'naːl) n neu -e personnel, staff. adj personal. **—alien** (pɛrzo'naːliən) n pl personal particulars. **—ell** (pɛrzo'nɛl) adj personal. **—lich** ('pɛr'zoːnliç) adj personal, private. **—lichkeit** nf -en personality.
Perspektive (pɛrspɛk'tiːvə) nf -n perspective.
Perücke (pe'rykə) nf -n wig.
pervers (pɛr'vɛrs) adj perverse.
Pessimis/mus (pɛsi'mismus) nm pessimism. **—t** (pɛsi'mist) nm -en pessimist. **—tisch** adj pessimistic.
Pest (pɛst) nf -en pestilence, plague.
Petersilie (petarˈziːliə) nf -n parsley.
Petroleum (pe'troːleum) n neu 1 petroleum. 2 paraffin.
Pfad (pfaːt) nm -e path. **—finder** nm Boy Scout. **—finderin** nf Girl Guide.
Pfahl (pfaːl) nm -e stake, post.
Pfalz (pfalts) nf -en the Palatinate.
Pfand (pfant) n neu -er 1 pledge, security. 2 deposit. 3 mortgage. **—brief** nm mortgage deed. **—en** ('pfɛndən) vt law seize, take possession of. **—haus** n neu pawnshop. **—leiher** nm pawnbroker.
Pfann/e ('pfanə) nf -n pan. **—kuchen** nm pancake.
Pfarr/er ('pfarər) nm — parson, rector, minister. **—haus** n neu parsonage, rectory. **—kirche** nf parish church.
Pfau (pfau) nm -en peacock.
Pfeffer ('pfɛfər) nm pepper. **—dose** nf pepper-pot. **—korn** n neu -er peppercorn. **—minze** nf -n peppermint. **—n** vt pepper.
Pfeife ('pfaifə) nf -n 1 pipe. 2 whistle. **—n** vi whistle.
Pfeil (pfail) nm -e arrow.
Pfeiler ('pfailər) nm — 1 pillar. 2 pier.
Pfennig ('pfɛniç) nm -e 1 a coin, one hundredth of a mark. 2 penny.
Pferch (pfɛrç) nm -e fold, pen.
Pferd (pfeːrt) n neu -e horse. **—ebremse** ('pfeːrdəbrɛmzə) nf horsefly. **—erennen** ('pfeːrdərɛnən) n neu 1 horse-race. 2 horse-racing. **—estall** ('pfeːrdəʃtal) nm stable. **—estärke** ('pfeːrdəʃtɛrkə) nf horse-power.
pfiff (pfif) v see pfeifen.

Pfiff (pfif) nm -e whistle. **—ig** adj cunning.

Pfifferling ('pfifərliç) nm -e type of mushroom.

Pfingst/en ('pfiŋstən) n neu or nf pl Whitsun-(tide). **—rose** nf peony.

Pfirsich ('pfirziç) nm -e peach.

Pflanze ('pflantsə) nf -n plant. **—en** vt plant. **—ung** nf -en plantation.

Pflaster ('pflastər) n neu — 1 pavement, road-surface. 2 (sticking-)plaster. **—n** vt pave. **—stein** nm paving stone.

Pflaume ('pflaumə) nf -n plum.

Pflege ('pfle:gə) nf -n 1 care. 2 cultivation. **—eltern** n pl foster-parents. **—kind** n neu 1 foster-child. 2 nurseling. **—mutter** nf foster-mother **—vater** nm foster-father. **—n** vt 1 care for, tend, foster. 2 cultivate. vi be accustomed to, be in the habit of. **—er** nm —, **—erin** nf -nen 1 nurse. 2 guardian.

Pflicht (pfliçt) nf -en duty, obligation. **—gefühl** n neu sense of duty. **—gemäß** adv according to duty, dutifully. **—treu** adj dutiful. **—vergessen** adj disloyal.

Pflock (pflɔk) nm ⁻e 1 peg. 2 plug.

pflücken ('pflykən) vt pluck, gather.

Pflug (pflu:k) nm ⁻e plough. **⁻en** ('pfly:gən) vt plough.

Pfort/e ('pfɔrtə) nf -n 1 door, gate. 2 porthole. **⁻ner** ('pfœrtnər) nm — porter, gate-keeper.

Pfosten ('pfɔstən) nm — 1 post. 2 door-post.

Pfote ('pfo:tə) nf -n paw.

Pfropf (pfrɔpf) nm -e plug, wad. **—en** vt 1 stop, plug. 2 fill, cram. 3 bot graft. nm — stopper, cork.

pfui (pfui) interj 1 shame! 2 ugh! pooh!

Pfund (Pfunt) n neu -e 1 pound, half-kilogram. 2 pound (sterling).

pfusch/en ('pfuʃən) vi,vt bungle, blunder. **—erei** (pfuʃə'rai) nf -en 1 bungling. 2 mess.

Pfütze ('pfytsə) nf -n puddle.

Phänomen (fɛno'me:n) n neu -e phenomenon.

Phantas/ie (fanta'zi:) nf -n 1 imagination, fancy. 2 fantasy. **—ieren** (fanta'zi:rən) vi 1 daydream. 2 mus improvise. 3 talk feverishly. **—tisch** (fan'tastiʃ) adj fantastic, fanciful.

Phantom (fan'to:m) n neu -e phantom, vision.

Phase ('fa:zə) nf -n phase.

Philist/er (fi'listər) nm — Philistine. **—erhaft** adj also **—rös** philistine.

Philosoph (filo'zo:f) nm -en philosopher. **—ie** (filozo'fi:) nf philosophy. **—isch** adj philosophical.

Phonet/ik (fo'ne:tik) nf phonetics. **—isch** adj phonetic.

Phosphor ('fɔsfɔr) nm phosphorus.

Photo ('fo:to) n neu -s photo(graph). **—apparat** nm camera. **—graph** (foto'gra:f) nm -en photographer. **—graphie** (fotogra'fi:) nf photography. **—graphieren** (fotogra'fi:rən) vt photograph. **—graphisch** (foto'gra:tiʃ) adj photographic. **—kopie** (fotoko'pi:) nf photocopy.

Phrase ('fra:zə) nf -n 1 phrase. 2 empty words, cliché. 3 mus phrase, theme.

Physik (fy'zi:k) nf physics. **—alisch** (fyzi'ka:liʃ) adj physical. **—er** ('fy:zikər) nm — physicist.

Physiologie (fyziolo'gi:) nf physiology.

physisch ('fy:ziʃ) adj physical, material, corporeal.

Pianist (pia'nist) nm -en pianist.

Picke ('pikə) nf -n pickaxe. **—l** nm — 1 pimple. 2 pickaxe. 3 ice-axe. **—n** vi pick, peck.

Piep (pi:p) nm -e chirp. **—en** vi chirp.

Pietät (pie'tɛ:t) nf piety.

pikant (pi'kant) adj spicy.

Pikkoloflöte ('pikoloflø:tə) nf -n piccolo.

Pilger ('pilgər) nm — pilgrim. **—n** vi go on a pilgrimage.

Pille ('pilə) nf -n pill.

Pilot (pi'lo:t) nm -en pilot.

Pilz (pilts) nm -e 1 fungus. 2 mushroom.

Pinguin (piŋgu'i:n) nm -e penguin.

Pinne ('pinə) nf -n 1 pin, peg. 2 tiller.

Pinsel ('pinzəl) nm — 1 brush. 2 simpleton.

Pionier (pio'ni:r) nm -e 1 pioneer. 2 mil engineer.

Pistole (pi'sto:lə) nf -n pistol.

Plackerei (plakə'rai) nf drudgery.

plädieren (plɛ'di:rən) vt plead (a case).

Plage ('pla:gə) nf -n 1 nuisance. 2 irony. **—n** vt plague, worry. **sich —n** vr toil.

Plakat (pla'ka:t) n neu -e poster.

Plan (pla:n) nm ⁻e 1 plan. 2 design, draft. 3 project. 4 schedule. **—en** vt,vi 1 plan. 2 design, draft. **—gemäß** adj also **—mäßig** according to plan. **—ung** nf planning.

Plane ('pla:nə)) nf -n 1 awning. 2 tarpaulin.

Planet (pla'ne:t) nm -en planet.

planieren (pla'ni:rən) vt plane, level.

Planke ('plaŋkə) nf -n plank.

Plänkelei (plɛŋkə'lai) nf -en skirmish(ing).

Plantage (plan'ta:ʒə) nf -n plantation.

plappern ('plapərn) vi,vt babble, chatter.

Plasti/k ('plastik) nf -en sculpture, plastic art. **—sch** adj plastic.

Plastilin

Plastilin (plasti'li:n) *n neu* **-s** *Tdmk* Plasticine *Tdmk*.

Platin (pla'ti:n) *n neu* platinum.

platt (plat) *adj* 1 flat, even. 2 insipid. 3 silly. **—deutsch** *n neu* Low German.

Platte ('platə) *nf* **-n** 1 record, disc. 2 plate. 3 tray. **—nspieler** *nm* record-player.

Platz (plats) *nm* **-e** 1 place. 2 square. 3 seat. 4 space. 5 locality. **—karte** *nf* (seat) reservation ticket.

platz/en ('platsən) *vi* burst, explode. **—regen** *nm* 1 heavy shower. 2 downpour.

plaudern ('plaudərn) *vi* chat, talk.

plausibel (plau'zi:bəl) *adj* plausible.

plombieren (plɔm'bi:rən) *vt* fill (a tooth).

plötzlich ('plœtsliç) *adj* sudden.

plump (plump) *adj* 1 coarse, crude. 2 awkward, clumsy.

plündern ('plyndərn) *vt,vi* plunder, pillage.

Plural ('plu:ra:l) *nm* **-e** plural.

Plusquamperfekt ('pluskvamperfekt) *n neu* **-e** pluperfect.

pneumatisch (pnɔy'ma:tiʃ) *adj* pneumatic.

Pöbel ('pœ:bəl) *nm* rabble, mob.

pochen ('pɔxən) *vi* knock, beat.

Pocken ('pɔkən) *nf pl* smallpox.

Poesie (poe'zi:) *nf* **-n** poetry.

Pokal (po'ka:l) *nm* **-e** 1 goblet. 2 *sport* cup.

Pökel ('pœ:kəl) *nm* — brine. **—n** *vt* pickle, salt.

Pol (po:l) *nm* **-e** pole (of the earth or of a magnet). **—ar** (po'la:r) *adj* polar. **—arisieren** (polari'zi:rən) *vt* polarize. **—arkreis** (po'la:rkrais) *nm* Arctic Circle.

Polem/ik (po'le:mik) *nf* **-en** polemic. **—isch** *adj* polemic.

Pol/en (po:lən) *n neu* Poland. **—e** *nm* Pole.

Police (po'li:s, po'li:sə) *nf* **-n** (insurance) policy.

polieren (po'li:rən) *vt* polish.

Polit/ik (poli'ti:k) *nf* 1 politics. 2 policy. **—iker** (po'li:tikər) *nm* — politician. **—isch** (po'li:tiʃ) *adj* political. **—isieren** (politi'zi:rən) *vt* politicize. *vi* talk politics.

Poliz/ei (poli'tsai) *nf* **-en** police. **—eibeamte(r)** *nm* police officer. **—eilich** *adj* (of, by or with the) police. **—eiwache** *nf* police station. **—ist** (poli'tsist) *nm* **-en** policeman.

polnisch ('pɔlniʃ) *adj* Polish. *n neu* Polish (language).

Polster ('pɔlstər) *n neu* 1 cushion. 2 stuffing. **—n** *vt* 1 stuff, pad. 2 upholster.

Poltergeist ('pɔltərgaist) *nm* **-er** poltergeist.

Polypen (po'ly:pən) *nm pl med* adenoids.

Polytechnikum (poly'tɛçnikum) *n neu* **—ken** technical college.

Pommern ('pɔmərn) *n neu* Pomerania.

Pommes frites (pɔm'frit) *n pl* chips, chipped potatoes.

populär (popu'lɛ:r) *adj* popular.

Pore ('po:rə) *nf* **-n** pore.

Pornographie (pɔrnogra'fi:) *nf* pornography. **—isch** (pɔrno'gra:fiʃ) *adj* pornographic.

Portion (pɔrtsi'o:n) *nf* **-en** portion, helping.

Porto ('pɔrto) *n neu* **-s** postage, carriage. **—frei** *adj* postage paid, post-free.

Porträt (pɔr'trɛ:, pɔr'trɛ:t) *n neu* **-s** portrait, picture.

Porzellan (pɔrtsɛ'la:n) *n neu* **-e** porcelain, china.

Posaune (po'zaunə) *nf* **-n** trombone.

Pose ('po:zə) *nf* **-n** pose.

Position (pozitsi'o:n) *nf* **-en** position.

positiv ('po:ziti:f) *adj* positive.

Poss/e ('pɔsə) *nf* **-n** 1 *Th* farce. 2 trick. **—ierlich** (pɔ'si:rliç) *adj* comic, funny.

possessiv ('pɔsesi:f) *adj* possessive.

Post (pɔst) *nf* 1 post, mail. 2 (the) Post Office.

Postamt ('pɔstamt) *n neu* post office.

Postanweisung ('pɔstanvaizuŋ) *nf* postal order.

Postbote ('pɔstbo:tə) *nm* postman.

Posten ('pɔstən) *nm* — 1 post, station. 2 *comm* entry, item. 3 lot. 4 picket. 5 guard.

Postfach ('pɔstfax) *n neu also* **Postschließfach** post-office box, P.O. box.

Postkarte ('pɔstkartə) *nf* postcard.

postlagernd ('pɔstla:gərnt) *adj* poste restante.

Postleitzahl ('pɔstlaitsa:l) *nf* postal code.

Poststempel ('pɔststɛmpəl) *nm* postmark.

Postulat (pɔstu'la:t) *n neu* **-e** postulate.

postwendend ('pɔstvɛndənt) *adv* by return of post.

Postwertzeichen ('pɔstvɛrtsaiçən) *n neu* postage stamp.

potent (po'tɛnt) *adj* potent, capable.

poten/tial (potɛntsi'a:l) *adj also* **poten/tiell** (potɛntsi'ɛl) potential. *n neu* **-e** potential. **—z** (po'tɛnts) *nf* **-en** 1 potency. 2 *math* power.

Pottasche ('pɔtaʃə) *nf* potash.

Pracht (praxt) *nf* 1 splendour, pomp. 2 luxury. **—ig** ('prɛçtiç) *adj* 1 splendid, magnificent. 2 pompous. **—voll** *adj* splendid, magnificent.

Prädikat (prɛdi'ka:t) *n neu* **-e** 1 predicate. 2 title.

Präfix (prɛ'fiks) *n neu* **-e** prefix.

Prag (pra:k) *n neu* Prague.

prägen ('prɛːgən) vt 1 stamp. 2 coin.

pragmatisch (prag'maːtiʃ) adj pragmatic.

prägnant (prɛg'nant) adj 1 precise. 2 meaningful.

prahl/en ('praːlən) vi boast. **—erei** (praːlə'rai) nf boasting. **—erisch** ('praːləriʃ) adj boastful.

Prakt/iker ('praktikər) nm — practical or experienced man. **—isch** adj 1 practical. 2 experienced. 3 handy.

Praline (praˈliːnə) nf -n chocolate cream.

prall (pral) adj 1 taut, tight. 2 stuffed, full. 3 plump. 4 (of the sun) blazing. nm -e collision, impact. **—en** vi 1 bump (into), crash. 2 (of the sun) glare.

Prämie ('prɛmiə) nf -n 1 premium. 2 prize, bonus.

Präparat (prɛpa'raːt) n neu -e preparation (of medicine, etc.).

Präposition (prɛpozitsi'oːn) nf -en preposition.

Präsens ('prɛːzɛns) n neu gram present.

präsentieren (prɛzɛn'tiːrən) vt present.

Präsid/ent (prɛziˈdɛnt) nm -en 1 president. 2 chairman. **—ieren** (prɛziˈdiːrən) vi act as president. vt preside over. **—ium** (prɛˈziːdium) n neu -ien 1 presidium. 2 presidency. 3 chair.

prasseln ('prasəln) vi patter, drum, crackle.

Präteritum (prɛ'teːritum) n neu -ita past tense.

Praxis ('praksis) nf -xen 1 practice. 2 (doctor's) surgery. 3 (lawyer's) office.

Präzedenzfall (prɛtse'dɛntsfal) nm precedent.

präzis (prɛ'tsiːs) adj 1 precise. 2 punctual.

predig/en ('preːdigən) vi,vt preach. **—er** nm — preacher. **—t** ('preːdiçt) nf -en sermon.

Preis (prais) nm -e 1 price. 2 prize. 3 praise. **—beaufsichtigung** nf -en price control. **—en*** ('praizən) vt praise. **—geben*** vt 1 give up, sacrifice. 2 expose. **—richter** nm umpire, judge. **—stopp** nm -s price freeze. **—wert** adj cheap, good value.

Preiselbeere ('praizəlbeːrə) nf -n cranberry.

prellen ('prɛlən) vt 1 deceive. 2 bang.

Premiere (prem'jeːrə) nf -n premiere, first night.

Premierminister (prem'jeːrministər) nm prime minister.

Presse ('prɛsə) nf -n 1 press, journalism. 2 tech press. **—ausweis** nm press card. **—freiheit** nf freedom of the press. **—n** vt 1 (com)press. 2 urge.

Preßkohle ('prɛskoːlə) nf briquette.

Preßluftbohrer ('prɛsluftboːrər) nm pneumatic drill.

Preuß/en ('prɔysən) n neu Prussia. **-e** nm -n Prussian. **—isch** adj Prussian.

prickeln ('prikəln) vi prickle, itch.

Priester ('priːstər) nm — priest. **—in** nf priestess.

prima ('priːma) adj,interj first class. nf -men sixth form.

primär (priˈmɛːr) adj primary.

Primel ('priːməl) nf -n primrose.

primitiv (primiˈtiːf) adj primitive.

Prinz (prints) nm -en prince. **—essin** (prin'tsɛsin) nf -nen princess.

Prinzip (prin'tsiːp) n neu -ien principle. **—iell** (printsipi'ɛl) adj principle. adv on or in principle.

Prise ('priːzə) nf -n 1 pinch (of salt, etc.). 2 naut prize, spoils.

Prisma ('prisma) n neu -men prism.

privat (pri'vaːt) adj private. **—eigentum** n neu private property. **—recht** n neu civil law.

Privileg (privi'leːk) n neu -ien privilege. **—iert** (privili'giːrt) adj privileged.

Prob/e ('proːbə) nf -n 1 experiment. 2 test. 3 rehearsal. 4 sample. **—en** vt,vi 1 test. 2 rehearse. **—ezeit** nf probation, trial period. **—ieren** (pro'biːrən) vt 1 try (out), attempt. 2 sample.

Problem (pro'bleːm) n neu -e problem. **—atisch** (proble'maːtiʃ) adj problematic.

Produkt (pro'dukt) n neu -e 1 product. 2 result. **—ion** (produktsi'oːn) nf production. **—ionsmittel** n neu pl means of production. **—iv** (produk'tiːf) adj productive. **—ivität** (produktivi'tɛːt) nf productivity.

Produz/ent (produ'tsɛnt) nm -en producer. **—ieren** (produ'tsiːrən) vt produce.

Profess/or (pro'fɛsɔr) nm -en professor. **—ur** (profɛ'suːr) nf -en professorship.

Profil (pro'fiːl) n neu -e profile.

Profit (pro'fiːt) nm -e profit. **—ieren** (profi'tiːrən) vi profit.

Prognose (pro'gnoːzə) nf -n forecast, prognosis.

Programm (pro'gram) n neu -e programme. **—ieren** vt program.

Projekt (pro'jɛkt) n neu -e project. **—ion** (projɛktsi'oːn) nf -en projection.

projizieren (proji'tsiːrən) vt project.

Prolet (pro'leːt) nm -en also **Prolet/arier** (prole'taːriər) — proletarian. **—ariat** (proletari'aːt) n neu proletariat.

Prolog (pro'loːk) nm -e prologue.

Promenade (promə'naːdə) nf -n promenade.

Promotion[1] (promotsi'oːn) nf comm promotion.

87

Promo/tion[2] (promotsi'o:n) *nf* **-en** award of a doctorate. **—vieren** (promo'vi:rən) *vt,vi* award or be awarded a doctorate.

Pronomen (pro'no:mɛn) *n neu* **-mina** pronoun.

Propaganda (propa'ganda) *nf* propaganda.

Propeller (pro'pɛlər) *nm* — propeller.

Proph/et (pro'fe:t) *nm* **-en** prophet. **—ezeien** (profe'tsaiən) *vt,vi* prophesy.

Proportion (proportsi'o:n) *nf* **-en** proportion.

Prosa ('pro:za) *nf* **-sen** prose. **—isch** (pro-'za:iʃ) *adj* prosaic.

prosit ('pro:zit) *interj* cheers! good health!

Prospekt (pro'spɛkt) *nm* **-e** 1 prospect, view. 2 prospectus.

prostituier/en (prostitu'i:rən) *vt* prostitute. **—te** *nf* **-n** prostitute.

Protektorat (protɛkto'ra:t) *n neu* **-e** 1 protectorate. 2 patronage.

Protest (pro'tɛst) *nm* **-e** protest. **—ant** (protɛ'stant) *nm* **-en** Protestant. **—antisch** (protɛ'stantiʃ) *adj* Protestant. **—ieren** (protɛ'sti:-rən) *vi* protest.

Protokoll (proto'kɔl) *n neu* **-e** 1 minutes, record. 2 protocol.

Proton ('pro:tɔn) *neu* **-en** proton.

Protz (prɔts) *nm* **-en** snob. **—en** *vi* show off (one's wealth), be ostentatious. **—ig** *adj* 1 snobbish, ostentatious. 2 gaudy.

Proviant (provi'ant) *nm* **-e** provisions, food.

Provinz (pro'vints) *nf* **-en** province. **—ial** (provintsi'a:l) *adj* provincial. **—iell** (provintsi'ɛl) *adj* provincial, narrow-minded, petty.

provisorisch (provi'zo:riʃ) *adj* provisional.

provozieren (provo'tsi:rən) *vt* provoke.

Prozedur (protse'du:r) *nf* **-en** 1 procedure. 2 law proceedings.

Prozent (pro'tsɛnt) *n neu* **-e** percent. **—satz** *nm* percentage.

Prozeß (pro'tsɛs) *nm* **-zesse** 1 lawsuit, case, trial. 2 process.

prüde (pry:də) *adj* prudish.

prüf/en ('pry:fən) *vt* 1 examine. 2 test. 3 inspect. **—er** *nm* — examiner, auditor. **—stein** *nm* yardstick. **—ung** *nf* **-en** 1 examination. 2 test, inspection.

Prügel ('pry:gəl) *nm* 1 stick. 2 beating. **—ei** (pry:gə'lai) *nf* **-en** brawl. **—n** *vt* beat.

Prunk (prʊŋk) *nm* splendour, pomp. **—en** *vi* make a show. **—voll** *adj* showy, ornate.

Psalm (psalm) *nm* **-en** psalm.

Psych/iatrie (psyçia'tri:) *nf* psychiatry. **—isch** ('psy:çiʃ) *adj* psychic. **—oanalyse** (psyçoana-'ly:za) *nf* psychoanalysis. **—ologie** (psyçolo-

'gi:) *nf* psychology. **—osomatisch** (psyçoso-'ma:tiʃ) *adj* psychosomatic.

Pubertät (pubɛr'tɛ:t) *nf* puberty.

Publikum ('pu:blikum) *n neu* public.

publizieren (publi'tsi:rən) *vt* publish.

Pudding ('pudiŋ) *nm* **-e** pudding.

Pudel ('pu:dəl) *nm* — poodle.

Puder ('pu:dər) *nm* powder. **—n** *vt* powder.

Puff (puf) *nm* **-e** 1 push. 2 thump. 3 bang, crash. 4 *inf* brothel. **—er** *nm* — buffer. **—spiel** *n neu* backgammon.

Puls (puls) *nm* **-e** pulse. **—ieren** (pul'zi:rən) *vi* pulsate, throb.

Pult (pult) *n neu* **-e** desk.

Pulver ('pulvər) *n neu* powder. **—isieren** (pul-vəri'zi:rən) *vt* pulverize.

Pumpe ('pumpa) *nf* **-n** pump. **—n** *vt* 1 pump. 2 *inf* borrow or lend.

Punkt (puŋkt) *nm* **-e** 1 point. 2 dot, spot. 3 full stop. 4 item. **—ieren** (puŋk'ti:rən) *vt* 1 punctuate. 2 *med* puncture. **—lich** ('pʏnktliç) *adj* 1 punctual. 2 exact. **—lichkeit** *nf* punctuality.

Pupille (pu'pilə) *nf* **-n** *anat* pupil.

Puppe ('pupə) *nf* **-n** 1 doll, puppet. 2 chrysalis, pupa. **—nspiel** *n neu* puppet show.

pur (pu:r) *adj* pure.

Purpur ('purpur) *nm* purple.

Purzel/baum ('purtsəlbaum) *nm* somersault. **—n** *vi* fall over, tumble down.

Pustel ('pustəl) *nf* **-n** pimple.

Pute ('pu:tə) *nf* **-n** turkey-hen. **—r** *nm* — turkey-cock.

Putsch (putʃ) *nm* **-e** 1 putsch, coup. 2 uprising.

putz/en ('putsən) *vt* 1 clean(se). 2 polish. 3 wipe. 4 sweep. 5 adorn. **sich putzen** *vr* dress up. **—frau** *nf* charwoman, cleaner. **—lappen** *nm* cleaning rag, duster.

Pyjama (pi'dʒa:ma) *nm,neu* **-s** pyjamas.

Pyramide (pyra'mi:də) *nf* **-n** pyramid.

Pyrenäen (pyre'nɛ:ən) *n pl* Pyrenees.

Q

quabbelig ('kvabəliç) *adj* flabby, wobbly.

Quadrat (kva'dra:t) *n neu* **-e** square. **—meter** *nm,neu* square metre.

quadrieren (kva'dri:rən) *vt* math square.

quäken ('kvɛ:kən) *vi* (óf a child, etc.) whine, squeal.

Qual (kva:l) *nf* **-en** pain, torment. **—en** ('kvɛ:-

lən) vt torment, torture. **—erei** (kvɛːləˈrai) nf torment, torture.

qualifizieren (kvalifiˈtsiːrən) vt qualify.

Qualität (kvaliˈtɛːt) nf -en quality.

Quelle (ˈkvalə) nf -n jelly-fish.

Quantität (kvantiˈtɛːt) nf -en quantity.

Quarantäne (kvaranˈtɛːnə) nf -n quarantine.

Quark (kvark) nm -e 1 curds. 2 sl rubbish, trash. **—käse** nm 1 curd cheese. 2 cream cheese.

Quart (kvart) n neu -e 1 quarto. 2 quart. **—al** (kvarˈtaːl) n neu -e quarter (of a year).

Quartett (kvarˈtɛt) n neu -e quartet.

Quarz (kvarts) nm -e quartz.

Quatsch (kvatʃ) nm nonsense. **—en** vi talk nonsense.

Quecksilber (ˈkvɛkzilbər) n neu mercury.

Quelle (ˈkvɛlə) nf -n 1 source. 2 spring, fountain. **—n*** vi 1 well, flow. 2 swell. vt soak.

quer (kveːr) adj cross, diagonal. adv crosswise, obliquely. **—en** vt traverse, cross. **—schiff** n neu transept. **—schnitt** nm cross-section **—straße** nf crossroad.

quetschen (ˈkvɛtʃən) vt 1 press, crush. 2 squeeze, pinch.

quietschen (ˈkviːtʃən) vi squeak.

Quintett (kvinˈtɛt) n neu —e quintet.

Quirl (kvirl) nm -e whisk. **—en** vt whisk.

quitt (kvit) adj even, quits.

Quitte (ˈkvitə) nf -n quince.

Quittung (ˈkvituŋ) nf -en receipt.

R

Rabatt (raˈbat) nm -e discount.

Rabbiner (raˈbiːnər) nm — rabbi.

Rabe (ˈraːbə) nm -n raven.

rabiat (rabiˈaːt) adj rabid, raging, furious.

Rach/e (ˈraxə) nf revenge, vengeance. **—durstig** adj vengeful. **—en** (ˈrɛçən) vt avenge, revenge. **sich —en** vr take revenge (on).

Rachen (ˈraxən) nm — 1 throat. 2 jaws.

Rad (raːt) n neu **-er** 1 wheel. 2 (bi)cycle. **—fahren*** vi cycle. **—fahrer** nm cyclist.

Radar (raˈdaːr) n neu radar.

Rädelsführer (ˈrɛːdəlsfyːrar) nm ringleader.

radier/en (raˈdiːrən) vt 1 erase. 2 etch. **—gummi** (raˈdiːrən) rubber, eraser. **—ung** nf 1 etching. 2 erasure.

Radieschen (raˈdiːsçən) n neu — radish.

radikal (radiˈkaːl) adj radical.

Radio (ˈraːdio) n neu -s radio.

radioaktiv (radioakˈtiːf) adj radioactive.

Radium (ˈraːdium) n neu radium.

raffen (ˈrafən) vt 1 snatch (up), grab. 2 gather up (cloth).

raffinier/en (rafiˈniːrən) vt refine. **—t** adj cunning, clever, artful.

ragen (ˈraːgən) vi tower (up), project.

Rahm (raːm) nm cream. **—käse** nm cream cheese.

Rahmen (ˈraːmən) nm — 1 frame, framework. 2 setting. v frame.

Rakete (raˈkeːtə) nf -n rocket.

Rakett (raˈkɛt) n neu -s sport racket.

Ramme (ˈramə) nf -n pile-driver. **—n** vt ram (in).

Rampe (ˈrampə) nf -n ramp.

'ran (ran) contraction of **heran.**

Rand (rant) nm **-er** 1 edge. 2 brink. 3 border. **—ern** (ˈrɛndərn) vt 1 border. 2 mill (coins).

Rang (raŋ) nm **-e** 1 rank, order. 2 row. **—erhöhung** nf promotion.

rangieren (rãˈʒiːrən) vt 1 arrange, classify. 2 shunt. vi 1 be classified. 2 rank.

Ranke (ˈraŋkə) nf -n 1 shoot. 2 branch.

rannte (ˈrantə) v see **rennen.**

ranzig (ˈrantsiç) adj rancid.

Rapier (raˈpiːr) n neu -e rapier.

rar (raːr) adj 1 rare. 2 exquisite. **sich rar machen** make oneself scarce.

rasch (raʃ) adj hasty, swift.

rascheln (ˈraʃəln) vi rustle.

rasen (ˈraːzən) vi 1 rage. 2 rush. **—d** adj mad, raving.

Rasen (ˈraːzən) nm — grass, lawn, turf.

rasier/en (raˈziːrən) vt,vi shave. **—apparat** nm shaver, safety razor. **—klinge** nf razor blade. **—krem** nm shaving cream. **—messer** n neu razor **—wasser** n neu after-shave lotion.

Raspel (ˈraspəl) nf -n 1 rasp, file. 2 grater. **—n** vt 1 file. 2 grate.

Rass/e (ˈrasə) nf -n 1 race. 2 breed. **—enhaß** nm racialism. **—entrennung** nf racial segregation. **—ig** adj 1 thoroughbred. 2 fiery.

rasseln (ˈrasəln) vi rattle.

Rast (rast) nf -en rest(ing). **—en** vi rest. **—los** adj restless. **—platz** nm layby.

Rasur (raˈzuːr) nf -en shave.

Rat (raːt) nm **-e** 1 advice, counsel. 2 council. 3 councillor. **mit Rat und Tat** by word and deed. **—en*** vt 1 advise. 2 guess. **—geber** nm adviser. **—haus** n neu town hall. **—los**

adj at a loss. **—sam** *adj* advisable. **—schlag** *nm* (piece of) advice, recommendation.

Rate ('ra:tə) *nf* -n 1 instalment. 2 rate.

Ratif/¹' ation (ratifikatsi'o:n) *nf* -en 1 ratification. ⊰ confirmation. **—izieren** (ratifi'tsi:rən) *vt* ratify.

Ration (ratsi'o:n) *nf* -en ration. **—al** (ratsio'na:l) *adj* rational, sensible. **—alisieren** (ratsionali'zi:rən) *vt* rationalize. **—ell** (ratsio'nɛl) *adj* 1 rational, logical. 2 economical. **—ieren** (ratsio'ni:rən) *vt* ration.

Rätsel ('rɛ:tsəl) *n neu* — 1 puzzle, riddle. 2 mystery. 3 enigma. **—haft** *adj* mysterious, puzzling.

Ratte ('ratə) *nf* -n rat.

raub/en ('rauban) *vt* rob. **—er** (rɔybər) *nm* — robber. **—tier** ('raupti:r) *n neu* beast of prey. **—überfall** ('raupy:bərfal) *nm* armed robbery, robbery with violence.

Rauch (raux) *nm* smoke. **—en** *vt,vi* smoke. *n neu* smoking. **—er** *nm* — smoker. **—ern** ('rɔyçərn) *vt* smoke, cure (meat, etc.). **—fang** *nm* -*e* chimney, flue. **—ig** *adj* smoky.

'rauf (rauf) contraction of **herauf.**

Raufbold ('raufbɔlt) *nm* -e bully, rowdy.

rauh (rau) *adj* 1 rough. 2 coarse. 3 hoarse. **—eit** ('rauhait) *nf* roughness, coarseness.

Raum (raum) *nm* -*e* 1 space. 2 room. 3 area. **—en** ('rɔymən) *vt* 1 remove. 2 clear away. 3 clear, evacuate. **—fahrt** *nf* space travel. **—lich** ('rɔymlıç) *adj* spatial. **—schiff** *n neu* space ship.

Raupe ('raupə) *nf* -n 1 caterpillar. 2 caterpillar track.

Rausch (rauʃ) *nm* -*e* intoxication. **—en** *vi* 1 rustle. 2 rush. **—gift** *n neu* narcotic, drug. **—giftsüchtige(r)** *nm* (drug) addict. **—mittel** *n neu* drug, intoxicant.

Reagenzglas (reaʹgɛntsglɑ:s) *n neu* test tube.

reagieren (rea'gi:rən) *vi* react.

Reakt/ion (reaktsi'o:n) *nf* -en reaction. **—ionär** (reaktsio'nɛ:r) *nm* -e reactionary. **—or** (re'aktɔr) *nm* -en reactor.

real (re'a:l) *adj* real. **—isieren** (reali'zi:rən) *vt* 1 realize. 2 perform. 3 convert into money. **—ismus** (rea'lismus) *nm* realism. **—ität** (reali'tɛ:t) *nf* -en reality. **—schule** *nf* (technical) secondary school.

Reb/e ('re:bə) *nf* -n vine. **—stock** ('rɛpstɔk) *nm* -e vine.

Rebell (re'bɛl) *nm* -en rebel. **—ion** (rebɛli'o:n) *nf* -en rebellion.

Rebhuhn ('rɛphu:n) *n neu* -*er* partridge.

rechen ('rɛçən) *vt* rake. *nm* — rake.

Rechen/maschine ('rɛçənmaʃi:nə) *nf* calculating machine, calculator. **—schaft** *nf* account. **Rechenschaft ablegen** account for.

rechn/en ('rɛçnən) *vt,vi* calculate, reckon, count. **—er** *nm* — calculator. **—ung** *nf* -en 1 bill. 2 calculation.

recht (rɛçt) *adj* 1 right, correct. 2 right, right-hand. 3 correct, suitable. 4 real. 5 just. **recht haben** be right or correct. *adv* 1 correctly. 2 very. 3 really. 4 justly. *n neu* -e 1 right, privilege. 2 law.

Rechteck (rɛçtɛk) *n neu* -e rectangle.

rechtfertigen ('rɛçtfɛrtigən) *vt* justify, vindicate.

rechtgläubig ('rɛçtglɔybıç) *adj* orthodox.

rechthaberisch ('rɛçtha:barıʃ) *adj* dogmatic, obstinate.

rechtmäßig ('rɛçtmɛsıç) *adj* legal, lawful.

rechts (rɛçts) *adv* on or to the right.

Rechtsanwalt ('rɛçtsanvalt) *nm* lawyer, solicitor, barrister.

rechtschaffen ('rɛçtʃafən) *adj* upright, just.

Rechtschreibung ('rɛçtʃraibuŋ) *nf* -en spelling.

Rechtsfall ('rɛçtsfal) *nm* lawsuit.

Rechtsprechung ('rɛçtʃprɛxuŋ) *nf* -en 1 administration of justice. 2 jurisdiction.

Rechtsstaat ('rɛçtsʃta:t) *nm* constitutional state.

rechtzeitig ('rɛçttsaitıç) *adj* timely.

recken ('rɛkən) *vt* stretch (one's arms, legs, etc.). **sich recken** *vr* stretch oneself.

Redakt/eur (redak'tœ:r) *nm* -e editor. **—ion** (redaktsi'o:n) *nf* -en 1 editorial staff. 2 editing.

Red/e ('re:də) *nf* -n 1 talk. 2 speech. **nicht der Rede wert** not worth mentioning. **—efreiheit** *nf* freedom of speech. **—egewandt** *adj* eloquent. **—en** *vi* speak, talk. **—ensart** *nf* 1 phrase, expression. 2 empty phrase, cliché. **—ewendung** *nf* -en idiom, expression.

redigieren (redi'gi:rən) *vt* edit, revise.

redlich ('re:tlıç) *adj* honest, fair.

Redner ('re:dnər) *nm* — speaker, orator.

redselig ('re:tze:lıç) *adj* talkative.

reduzieren (redu'tsi:rən) *vt* reduce, decrease.

Reeder ('re:dər) *nm* — shipowner.

reell (re'ɛl) *adj* 1 honest. 2 (of business, etc.) fair. 3 respectable.

Referat (refe'ra:t) *n neu* -e 1 report. 2 lecture.

Referent (refe'rɛnt) *nm* -en 1 expert adviser. 2 lecturer, speaker.

reflektieren (reflɛk'ti:rən) *vt,vi* reflect.

reflexiv (reflɛk'si:f) *adj* reflexive.

Reform (re'fɔrm) nf **-en** reform. **—ieren** (refɔr-'miːrən) vt reform.

Refrain (rə'frɛː) nm **-s** refrain.

Regal (re'gaːl) n neu **-e** shelf, book-shelf.

rege ('reːgə) adj lively, active. **—n** vt move, stir.

Regel ('reːgəl) nf **-n** 1 rule. 2 regulation. 3 menstruation, menses, period. **—n** vt regulate. **—mäßig** adj regular, periodic. **—recht** adj regular, proper. **—ung** nf **-en** regulation, rule.

Regen ('reːgən) nm rain. **—bogen** nm rainbow. **—mantel** nm raincoat. **—schirm** nm umbrella.

Regent (re'gɛnt) nm **-en** regent.

Regie (re'ʒiː) nf **-n** 1 Th production, direction. 2 administration. 3 state monopoly.

regier/en (re'giːrən) vt,vi govern, reign (over). **—ung** nf **-en** government, administration.

Regiment (regi'mɛnt) n neu **-er** 1 regiment. 2 rule, authority.

Regisseur (reʒi'sœːr) nm **-e** Th producer, director.

Regist/er (re'gistər) n neu **—** 1 register. 2 table of contents. 3 index. **—rieren** (regi-'striːrən) vt 1 register. 2 index.

regn/en ('reːgnən) vi rain. **—erisch** ('reː-gnəriʃ) adj rainy.

regulär (regu'lɛːr) adj regular.

regulieren (regu'liːrən) vt regulate, adjust.

Regung ('reːguŋ) nf **-en** 1 movement. 2 emotion. 3 impulse. **—slos** adj motionless.

Reh (reː) n neu **-e** roe (deer). **—bock** nm **-e** roebuck. **—kalb** n neu fawn.

reib/en ('raibən) vt 1 rub. 2 grate. **—erei** (raibə'rai) nf **-en** 1 friction. 2 conflict. **—ung** nf **-en** 1 rubbing, friction. 2 clash, conflict. **—ungslos** adj frictionless, smooth.

reich (raiç) adj wealthy, rich. **—haltig** adj copious, ample. **—lich** adj plentiful, abundant. **—tum** nm **-er** wealth, abundance.

Reich (raiç) n neu **-e** empire, realm.

reich/en ('raiçən) vt hand, offer, pass. vi 1 suffice. 2 reach. **—weite** nf 1 reach. 2 range.

reif (raif) adj mature, ripe. **—e** nf maturity, ripeness. **—ezeugnis** n neu school-leaving certificate.

Reif[1] (raif) nm hoarfrost.

Reif[2] (raif) nm **-e** 1 band. 2 ring.

Reifen ('raifən) nm **—** 1 tyre. 2 hoop. 3 collar. **—panne** nf mot puncture.

Reihe ('raiə) nf **-n** 1 file, row, rank. 2 series. 3

queue. **—n** vt 1 place in a row. 2 arrange. **—nfolge** nf sequence, order. **—nhäuser** n neu pl terraced houses.

Reiher ('raiər) nm **—** heron.

Reim (raim) nm **-e** rhyme. **—en** vt,vi rhyme.

rein[1] (rain) adj 1 clean. 2 pure. 3 absolute. **—machefrau** nf cleaner, charwoman. **—heit** nf cleanliness, purity. **—igen** vt 1 clean(se). 2 purify, refine. **—igung** nf **-en** 1 cleaning. 2 cleansing, purification. **—lich** adj 1 clean. 2 neat.

'rein[2] (rain) contraction of **herein**.

Reis (rais) nm rice.

Reise ('raizə) nf **-n** journey, trip, tour. **—büro** n neu 1 tourist office. 2 travel agency. **—führer** nm 1 guide(book). 2 nm vi travel. **—nde(r)** nm 1 traveller. 2 passenger. **—scheck** nm traveller's cheque.

reiß/en* ('raisən) vt 1 tear. 2 drag. vi tear, split. **sich reißen um** fight for or over, scramble for. **~n** neu inf rheumatism. **—er** nm **—** 1 thriller. 2 (box-office) success. **—verschluß** nm zip(-fastener).

reit/en* ('raitən) vt,vi ride. **—er** nm **—** rider. **—erei** (raitə'rai) nf **-en** cavalry.

Reiz (raits) nm **-e** 1 attraction, charm. 2 irritation, annoyance. **—bar** adj 1 sensitive. 2 irritable. **—en** vt 1 attract, charm. 2 irritate. 3 excite. vi game bid. **—end** adj charming, enchanting. **—mittel** n neu stimulant. **—ung** nf **-en** 1 irritation. 2 provocation. 3 enticement, charm.

Reklame (re'klaːmə) nf **-n** 1 advertising, publicity. 2 advertisement.

Rekord (re'kɔrt) nm **-e** record.

Rekrut (re'kruːt) nm **-en** recruit. **—ieren** (rekru'tiːrən) vt recruit. **sich —ieren** vr pick or take on recruits.

Rektor ('rɛktɔr) nm **-en** rector, vice-chancellor, principal.

relativ (rela'tiːf) adj relative.

Relief (reli'ɛf) n neu Art,geog relief.

Religi/on (religi'oːn) nf **-en** religion. **—ös** (religi'œːs) adj religious, pious.

Ren (rɛn) n neu **-s** reindeer.

Renn/bahn ('rɛnbaːn) nf **-en** racecourse or racetrack. **—en*** vi 1 run. 2 race. vt run. n neu **—** 1 running. 2 race. 3 racing. **—pferd** n neu racehorse. **—wagen** nm racing car.

Renomm/ee (reno'meː) n neu **-s** reputation. **—iert** (reno'miːrt) adj widely respected.

renovieren (reno'viːrən) vt renovate.

rentabel (rɛn'taːbəl) adj profitable.

Rent/e ('rɛntə) nf -n 1 pension. 2 annuity, (unearned) income. 3 interest. **—ner** nm — pensioner.

Repar/ation (reparatsi'o:n) nf -en reparation. **—stur** (repara'tu:r) nf -en repair. **—ieren** (repa'ri:rən) vt repair.

Report/age (repɔr'ta:ʒə) nf -n 1 news report. 2 commentary. **—er** (re'pɔrtər) nm — reporter.

Repressalien (reprɛ'sa:liən) n pl reprisals.

Reproduktion (reproduktsi'o:n) nf -en reproduction.

Reptil (rɛp'ti:l) n neu -ien reptile.

Republik (repu'bli:k) nf -en republic.

Reserv/e (re'zɛrvə) nf -n reserve. **—ereifen** n neu mot spare tyre. **—ieren** vt reserve.

Residenz (rezi'dɛnts) nf -en 1 residence (of a government, court, prince, etc.). 2 capital.

Resonanz (rezo'nants) nf -en resonance, echo.

Respekt (re'spɛkt) nm respect. **—ieren** (respɛk-'ti:rən) vt respect. **—ive** (respɛk'ti:və) adv respectively. **—voll** adj respectful.

Rest (rɛst) nm -e rest, remainder. **—lich** adj remaining.

Restaurant (rɛsto'rã:) n neu -s restaurant.

Restauration (rɛstauratsi'o:n) nf -en 1 restoration. 2 restaurant.

Resultat (rezul'ta:t) n neu -e result, outcome.

Retorte (re'tɔrtə) nf -n sci retort.

rett/en ('rɛtən) vt save, rescue. **—ung** nf -en 1 rescue. 2 escape. **—ungsboot** n neu lifeboat.

Reue ('rɔyə) nf 1 remorse, regret. 2 repentance. **—n** v imp **es reut mich** I regret.

Revanche (re'vã:ʃə) nf -n revenge.

Revers[1] (re'vɛrs) nm -e bond.

Revers[2] (re'vɛrs) nm -e back, reverse (side).

Revers[3] (re've:r) nm,neu -s lapel.

revidieren (revi'di:rən) vt 1 revise. 2 audit.

Revier (re'vi:r) n neu -e 1 district. 2 (policeman's) beat. 3 (delivery) round.

Revision (revizi'o:n) nf -en 1 revision. 2 audit, auditing. 3 law appeal.

Revolte (re'vɔltə) nf -n revolt.

Revolution (revolutsi'o:n) nf -en revolution. **—är** (revolutsio'nɛ:r) nm -e revolutionary. adj revolutionary.

Revolver (re'vɔlvər) nm — revolver.

rezens/ieren (retsɛn'zi:rən) vt Th,lit review. **—ion** (retsɛnzi'o:n) nf -en review.

Rezept (re'tsɛpt) n neu -e 1 prescription. 2 recipe.

Rhabarber (ra'barbər) nm — rhubarb.

Rhein (rain) nm Rhine. **—land** n neu Rhineland. **—land-Pfalz** nf Rhineland-Palatinate.

Rhetor/ik (re'to:rik) nf rhetoric. **—isch** adj rhetorical.

Rheumatismus (rɔyma'tismus) nm rheumatism.

Rhythmus ('rytmus) nm -men rhythm.

richt/en ('riçtən) vt 1 set. 2 direct, aim. 3 prepare. 4 arrange. 5 adjust. 6 judge. vi judge. **sich richten** vr 1 prepare. 2 comply. **—er** nm — 1 judge. 2 umpire. **—maß** n neu gauge. **—ung** nf -en direction.

richtig ('riçtiç) adj 1 correct, right. 2 real. 3 just. **—keit** nf 1 correctness. 2 accuracy.

rieb (ri:p) v see **reiben**.

riechen* ('ri:çən) vt,vi smell.

rief (ri:f) v see **rufen**.

Riegel ('ri:gəl) nm — bolt, bar. **—n** vt bolt, bar.

Riemen ('ri:mən) nm — 1 strap, band. 2 belt.

Ries/e ('ri:zə) nm -n giant. **—enhaft** adj gigantic, huge. **—ig** adj giant, enormous.

riet (ri:t) v see **raten**.

Riff (rif) n neu -e reef.

Rille ('rilə) nf -n groove, furrow.

Rind (rint) n neu -er 1 ox, cow. 2 pl cattle. **—fleisch** n neu beef. **—vieh** n neu cattle.

Rinde ('rində) nf -n 1 rind. 2 crust. 3 bark.

Ring (riŋ) nm -e 1 ring. 2 comm combine, syndicate. **—förmig** ('riŋfœrmiç) adj ring-shaped. **—straße** nf ring-road.

ring/en* ('riŋən) vi 1 wrestle, struggle. 2 fight (for), strive (after). vt wring (one's hands, etc.). **—kampf** nm wrestling match.

rings (riŋs) adv (a)round. **—um** (riŋs'um) adv also **—umher** or **—herum** all about or around.

Rinn/e ('rinə) nf -n 1 gutter, drain. 2 groove, channel. **—stein** nm gutter, drain.

Ripp/e ('ripə) nf -n 1 rib. 2 cul cutlet, chop. **—chen** n neu — cutlet.

Ris/iko ('ri:ziko) n neu -s, -ken risk. **—kant** (ris'kant) adj risky. **—kieren** (ris'ki:rən) vt risk.

riß (ris) v see **reißen**.

Riß (ris) nm **Risse** 1 tear. 2 crack, crevice. 3 tech drawing, design. 4 fracture.

ritt (rit) v see **reiten**.

Ritt (rit) nm -e ride.

Ritter ('ritər) nm — knight. **—gut** n neu manor, estate. **—lich** adj chivalrous.

rittlings ('ritliŋs) adv astride.

Ritus ('ri:tus) *nm* -ten rite.
Ritz (rits) *nm* -e also **Ritze** ('ritsə) *nf* -n 1 cleft, fissure. 2 scratch.
Rizinusöl ('ri:tsinusœ:l) *n neu* castor oil.
roch (rōx) *v* see **riechen**.
Rock (rɔk) *nm* ̈e 1 skirt. 2 jacket, coat.
rod/en ('ro:dən) *vt* clear (woodland for cultivation). **—ung** *nf* -en cleared woodland.
Roggen ('rɔgən) *nm* rye. **—brot** *n neu* ryebread.
roh (ro:) *adj* 1 raw. 2 crude. 3 rough, brutal. **—eit** ('ro:hait) *nf* -en 1 rawness. 2 roughness, brutality. **—stoff** *nm* raw material.
Rohr (ro:r) *n neu* -e 1 tube, pipe. 2 reed, cane. 3 barrel (of a gun). **— ̈e** ('roe:rə) *nf* -n 1 tube, pipe. 2 (radio) valve. 3 oven. **—geflecht** *n neu* wickerwork. **—weite** *nf tech* bore.
Roll/aden ('rɔlladən) *nm* roller blind. **—bahn** *nf aviat* runway. **—en** ('rɔlən) *vt,vi* roll. **—er** *nm* — 1 (motor) scooter. 2 roller, breaker. **—holz** *n neu* rolling pin. **—schuh** *nm* roller skate. **—stuhl** *nm* wheelchair. **—treppe** *nf* escalator.
Rolle ('rɔlə) *nf* -n 1 roll. 2 *Th* role. 3 pulley. 4 castor. 5 mangle. **das spielt keine Rolle** that doesn't matter.
Rom (ro:m) *n neu* Rome.
Roman (ro'ma:n) *nm* -e novel.
Roman/tik (ro'mantik) *nf* romantic poetry, romanticism. **—tiker** *nm* — romanticist. **—tisch** *adj* romantic.
röntgen ('rœntgən) *vt* X-ray. **—aufnahme** *nf* also **—bild** *n neu* X-ray (photograph). **—strahlen** *nm pl* X-rays.
rosa ('ro:za) *adj* pink.
Ros/e ('ro:zə) *nf* -n rose. **—enkohl** *nm* Brussels sprout. **—enkranz** *nm* rosary.
Rosine (ro'zi:nə) *nf* -n raisin.
Rosmarin (rɔsma'ri:n) *nm* -e rosemary.
Roß (rɔs) *n neu* **Rosse** horse, steed.
Rost[1] (rɔst) *nm* —e 1 grating. 2 *cul* grill. **—braten** *nm* roast (meat). **— ̈n** ('rœ:stən) *vt* 1 roast. 2 toast. 3 grill.
Rost[2] (rɔst) *nm* rust. **—en** *vi* rust.
rot (ro:t) *adj,n. neu* red. **— ̈e** ('rœ:tə) *nf* red, redness.
Röteln ('rœtəln) *n pl* German measles.
Rotor ('ro:tɔr) *nm* -en rotor, armature.
Rübe ('ry:bə) *nf* **gelbe Rübe** carrot. **weiße Rübe** turnip. **—nzucker** *nm* beet sugar.
Rubin (ru'bi:n) *nm* -e ruby.
Rubrik (ru'bri:k) *nf* -en 1 rubric. 2 heading.

ruch/bar ('ru:xba:r) *adj* notorious. **—los** *adj* wicked, impious.
rückbezüglich ('rykbətsy:kliç) *adj* reflexive
Rückblende ('rykblendə) *nf* flashback.
Rückblick ('rykblik) *nm* 1 retrospect. 2 backward glance.
rücken ('rykən) *vt,vi* move, shift.
Rücken ('rykən) *nm* — back.
Rückfahrkarte ('rykfa:rkartə) *nf* return ticket.
Rückfahrt ('rykfa:rt) *nf* return voyage or trip.
Rückfall ('rykfal) *nm* 1 relapse. 2 reversion.
Rückgang ('rykgaŋ) *nm* decline, decrease.
rückgängig ('rykgeŋiç) *adj* retrograde. **rückgängig machen** cancel, revoke.
Rückgrat ('rykgra:t) *n neu* -e backbone, spine.
Rückhalt ('rykhalt) *nm* support.
Rückkehr ('rykke:r) *nf* return.
Rucksack ('rukzak) *nm* 1 rucksack. 2 sack.
Rückschlag ('rykʃlak) *nm* 1 setback. 2 recoil.
Rücksicht ('rykziçt) *nf* respect, consideration. **—slos** *adj* inconsiderate.
Rückspiegel ('rykʃpi:gəl) *nm* rear-view mirror
rückständig ('rykʃtendiç) *adj* 1 backward. 2 in arrears.
Rückstoß ('rykʃtos) *nm* recoil.
Rücktritt ('ryktrit) *nm* 1 resignation. 2 withdrawal.
rückwärts ('rykverts) *adv* backwards.
Rückzug ('ryktsu:k) *nm* retreat.
Rudel ('ru:dəl) *n neu* — pack, herd, band.
Ruder ('ru:dar) *n neu* — 1 oar. 2 rudder. **—boot** *n neu* rowing boat. **—n** *vi,vt* row.
Ruf (ru:f) *nm* -e 1 cry, call. 2 reputation. 3 summons. **—en** *vt* 1 cry, call. 2 summon. *vi* cry, call. **—nummer** *nf* telephone number.
Rüge ('ry:gə) *nf* -n reprimand, reproach. **—n** *vt* 1 reproach, admonish. 2 blame.
Ruh/e ('ru:ə) *nf* 1 quiet. 2 stillness, calm. 3 rest, relaxation. **—elos** *adj* restless. **—en** *vi* 1 rest, sleep. 2 be still. 3 be based (on). **—estand** *nm* retirement. **—ig** ('ru:iç) *adj* 1 quiet, still. 2 calm, peaceful.
Ruhm (ru:m) *nm* fame, glory. **—en** ('ry:mən) *vt* praise. **sich ̈en** *vr* boast. **— ̈lich** ('ry:mliç) *adj* glorious.
Ruhr (ru:r) *nf* dysentery.
rühr/en ('ry:rən) *vt,vi* 1 move. 2 stir. 3 touch. **—ei** *n neu* scrambled eggs. **—selig** *adj* sentimental, emotional. **—ung** *nf* emotion.
Ruhrgebiet ('ru:rgəbi:t) *n neu* Ruhr region.
Ruin/e (ru'i:nə) *nf* -n ruin(s). **—ieren** (rui-'ni:rən) *vt* ruin.
Rülps (rylps) *nm* -e belch. **—en** *vi* belch.

Rum (rum) *nm* -s rum.

Rumän/ien (ru'mɛ:niən) *n neu* Rumania. —**e** *nm* Rumanian. —**isch** *adj* Rumanian. *n neu* Rumanian (language).

Rummel ('ruməl) *nm* 1 uproar, din. 2 bustle. —**platz** *nm* fairground, fun-fair.

Rumpf (rumpf) *nm* -e trunk, torso. 2 hull. 3 fuselage.

rümpfen ('rympfən) *vt* turn up (one's nose).

rund (runt) *adj* 1 round. 2 plump. *adv* about, approximately. —**e** ('rundə) *nf* -n 1 round. 2 lap. 3 circuit. 4 circle. —**fahrt** *nf* round trip. —**funk** *nm* 1 radio, wireless. 2 broadcasting. —**gang** *nm* 1 round. 2 circuit. —**heraus** (runthɛ'raus) *adv* in plain terms. —**herum** (runthɛ'rum) *adv* round about. —**schau** *nf* panorama, review. —**schreiben** *n neu* circular.

Runzel ('runtsəl) *nf* -n wrinkle. —**n** *vt* wrinkle, fold.

rupfen ('rupfən) *vt* 1 pluck. 2 *inf* fleece.

Ruß (ru:s) *nm* soot. —**ig** *adj* sooty.

Russ/e ('rusə) *nm* -n Russian. —**isch** *adj* Russian. *n neu* Russian (language). —**land** *n neu* Russia.

rüst/en ('rystən) *vt* 1 prepare. 2 equip. 3 arm. —**ig** *adj* vigorous. —**ung** *nf* -en 1 preparation(s). 2 equipment. 3 armament. 4 armour.

Rute ('ru:tə) *nf* -n rod.

Rutsch (rutʃ) *nm* -e slide, slip. —**bahn** *nf* 1 slide. 2 chute. —**en** *vi* slide, slip, skid. —**ig** *adj* slippery.

rütteln ('rytəln) *vt, vi* shake (up), jolt.

S

Saal (za:l) *nm* **Säle** large room, hall.

Saat (za:t) *nf* -en 1 seed(s). 2 sowing.

Sabbat ('zabat) *nm* -e sabbath.

sabbern ('zabərn) *vi inf* 1 slobber. 2 drivel.

Säbel ('zɛ:bəl) *nm* — sabre.

Saccharin (zaxa'ri:n) *n neu* saccharin.

Sach/e ('zaxə) *nf* -n 1 matter. 2 thing. 3 affair, business. 4 *law* case, issue. —**bearbeiter** *nm* official or expert (with responsibility for a particular case or field). —**lage** *nf* state of affairs, situation. —**lich** *adj* 1 to the point. 2 real. 3 factual. 4 objective, impartial. —**lich** ('zɛçliç) *adj* neuter.

Sachs/e ('zaksə) *nm* Saxon. —**en** *n neu* Saxony. —**isch** ('zɛksiʃ) *adj* Saxon.

sacht (zaxt) *adj* gentle, soft. *adv* 1 gradually. 2 cautiously.

Sack (zak) *nm* -e 1 sack, bag. 2 pocket, pouch. —**en** *vi* 1 sink. 2 sag. —**gasse** *nf* 1 blind alley, cul-de-sac. 2 deadlock.

Sadismus (za'dismus) *nm* sadism.

säen ('zɛ:ən) *vt* sow.

Saft (zaft) *nm* -e 1 juice. 2 sap. 3 gravy. —**ig** *adj* juicy.

Sage ('za:gə) *nf* -n legend, myth. —**nhaft** *adj* 1 legendary. 2 *inf* fabulous.

Säge ('zɛ:gə) *nf* -n saw. —**n** *vt, vi* saw.

sagen ('za:gən) *vt, vi* 1 say, tell. 2 express, declare. 3 mean.

sah (za:) *v* see **sehen.**

Sahn/e ('za:nə) *nf* cream. —**ig** *adj* creamy.

Saison (zɛ'zõ:) *nf* -s (high) season.

Saite ('zaitə) *nf* -n string, chord. —**ninstrument** *n neu* stringed instrument.

Sakrament (zakra'mɛnt) *n neu* -e sacrament.

Salat (za'la:t) *nm* -e 1 salad. 2 lettuce. —**soße** *nf* salad dressing.

Salbe ('zalbə) *nf* -n ointment, salve.

Salbei (zal'bai) *nm, f cul* sage.

Salut (za'lu:t) *nm* -e salute. —**ieren** (zalu-'ti:rən) *vt, vi* salute.

Salve ('zalvə) *nf* -n *mil* volley.

Salz (zalts) *n neu* -e salt. —**en** *vt* salt. —**faß** *n neu* saltcellar. —**ig** *adj* salty.

Sam/en ('za:mən) *nm* — 1 seed. 2 sperm, semen. —**ling** ('zɛmliŋ) *nm* -e seedling.

Sämischleder ('zɛmiʃle:dər) *n neu* chamois (leather).

samm/eln ('zaməln) *vt, vi* collect, gather. **sich sammeln** *vr* 1 assemble. 2 compose oneself. —**ler** *nm* — 1 collector, gatherer. 2 *tech* accumulator. —**lung** *nf* -en 1 collection. 2 concentration.

Samstag ('zamsta:k) *nm* -e Saturday. —**s** *adv* on Saturdays.

samt (zamt) *prep* together with. —**lich** ('zɛmt-liç) *adj* 1 all. 2 complete, entire.

Sand (zant) *nm* -e sand. —**uhr** *nf* hourglass.

Sandale (zan'da:lə) *nf* -n sandal.

sandte ('zantə) *v* see **senden.**

sanft (zanft) *adj* 1 gentle, mild. 2 smooth, soft. —**mut** *nf* gentleness, sweetness.

sang (zaŋ) *v* see **singen.**

Sang (zaŋ) *nm* -e song. —**er** ('zɛŋər) *nm* —, —**erin** ('zɛŋərin) *nf* -nen singer.

sanier/en (za'ni:rən) *vt* 1 *comm* restore, reorganize. 2 heal. —**ung** *nf* -en 1 restoration, reconstruction. 2 sanitation.

sanit/är (zani'tɛ:r) *adj* sanitary. **—äter** (zani'tɛ:tər) *nm* — 1 ambulance man. 2 *med* orderly.

sank (zaŋk) *v* see **sinken**.

Sankt (zaŋkt) *adj* Saint, St.

Sanktion (zaŋktsi'o:n) *nf* **-en** sanction.

Saphir ('za:fir) *nm* **-e** sapphire.

Sardine (zar'di:nə) *nf* **-n** sardine.

Sarg (zark) *nm* ⁼e coffin.

sarkastisch (zar'kastiʃ) *adj* 1 sarcastic. 2 ironic.

saß (za:s) *v* see **sitzen**.

Satan ('za:tan) *nm* Satan.

Satellit (zatɛ'li:t) *nm* **-en** satellite. **—enstaat** *nm* satellite state.

Satin (sa'tɛ̃) *nm* satin.

Satir/e (za'ti:rə) *nf* **-n** satire. **—isch** *adj* satirical.

satt (zat) *adj* 1 satisfied. 2 full. 3 tired (of), sick (of). 4 (of colour) deep. ⁼**igen** ('zɛtigən) *vt* 1 satisfy, satiate. 2 saturate.

Sattel ('zatəl) *nm* ⁼ saddle.

Satz (zats) *nm* ⁼e 1 sentence, clause. 2 leap, bound. 3 theorem, thesis. 4 *mus* movement. 5 dregs. **—lehre** *nf* syntax.

Satzung ('zatsuŋ) *nf* **-en** statute, regulation.

Sau (zau) *nf* ⁼e sow. **—arbeit** *nf sl* drudgery. **—erei** (zauə'rai) *nf* **-en** dirty business.

sauber ('zaubər) *adj* 1 clean. 2 neat, tidy. 3 *inf* pretty, fine. ⁼**n** ('zoybərn) *vt* 1 clean. 2 purge. **—ung** ('zoybəruŋ) *nf* **-en** 1 cleaning, clearing. 2 purge.

Saudi-Arabien ('zaudiara:biən) *n neu* Saudi-Arabia.

sauer ('zauər) *adj* 1 sour, acid. 2 (of work, etc.) hard. 3 sulky. **—stoff** *nm* oxygen.

sauf/en ('zaufən) *vt,vi* 1 *inf* booze, drink (excessively). 2 (of animals) drink. **—er** ('zoyfər) *nm* drunkard.

saug/en ('zaugən) *vt,vi* suck. **—er** *nm* — 1 sucker. 2 teat (of a baby's bottle). **—etier** *n neu* mammal. **—heber** *nm* siphon.

säug/en ('zoygən) *vt* suckle. **—etier** *n neu* mammal. **—ling** ('zoyklıŋ) *nm* **-e** baby, suckling.

Säule ('zoylə) *nf* **-n** column, pillar.

Saum (zaum) *nm* ⁼e 1 seam. 2 hem. 3 border.

säumen¹ ('zoymən) *vt* 1 hem. 2 border.

säumen² ('zoymən) *vi* 1 delay. 2 hesitate.

Saumtier ('zaumti:r) *n neu* **-e** beast of burden.

Sauna ('zauna) *nf* **-s** sauna (bath).

Säure ('zoyrə) *nf* **-n** 1 acid. 2 sourness.

Saxophon (zakso'fo:n) *n neu* **-e** saxophone.

schab/en ('ʃa:bən) *vt* 1 scrape. 2 grate. **—er** *nm* — scraper.

schäbig ('ʃɛ:biç) *adj* 1 shabby. 2 mean.

Schablone (ʃa'blo:nə) *nf* **-n** stencil, pattern.

Schach (ʃax) *n neu* chess. **—matt** *adj* checkmate.

Schacher ('ʃaxər) *nm* bargaining, haggling. **—n** *vi* haggle, barter.

Schacht (ʃaxt) *nm* ⁼e 1 pit, shaft. 2 tunnel. 3 mine.

Schachtel ('ʃaxtəl) *nf* **-n** box.

schad/e ('ʃa:də) *interj* what a pity or shame! *adj* **es/das ist schade** it's/that's a pity or shame. **—en** *vi* 1 harm. 2 damage. *nm* ⁼ 1 damage. 2 harm. 3 loss, damages. **—enersatz** *nm* compensation. **—enfreude** *nf* malicious pleasure (in the misfortunes of others). **—igen** ('ʃɛ:digən) *vt* 1 harm. 2 damage. ⁼**lich** ('ʃɛ:tlıç) *adj* harmful, injurious.

Schädel ('ʃɛ:dəl) *nm* — skull.

Schaf (ʃa:f) *n neu* **-e** sheep. ⁼**er** ('ʃɛ:fər) *nm* shepherd. ⁼**erhund** ('ʃɛ:farhunt) *nm* sheep dog. **deutscher** ⁼**erhund** Alsatian.

schaffen¹ ('ʃafən) *vt* 1 remove, shift. 2 accomplish, manage. *vi* work.

schaffen² ('ʃafən) *vt* create, make.

Schaffner ('ʃafnər) *nm* — 1 conductor. 2 ticket-collector. 3 guard. 4 steward.

Schaft (ʃaft) *nm* ⁼e 1 shaft. 2 stalk. 3 gunstock. 4 handle.

Schale ('ʃa:lə) *nf* **-n** 1 peel. 2 shell. 3 skin. 4 bowl, dish. **—n** ('ʃɛ:lən) *vt* 1 peel. 2 skin. 3 shell.

Schalk (ʃalk) *nm* **-e** rogue, joker.

Schall (ʃal) *nm* **-e** 1 sound. 2 noise. 3 ring. **—dämpfer** *nm* silencer. **—dicht** *adj* soundproof. **—en** *vi* (re)sound. **—(geschwindigkeits)grenze** *nf* sound barrier. **—platte** *nf* (gramophone) record.

Schalt/brett ('ʃaltbrɛt) *n neu* **-er** 1 switchboard. 2 dashboard. **—en** *vi* 1 switch. 2 *mot* change gear. *vt* switch. **—er** *nm* — 1 switch. 2 ticket office. 3 counter. **—hebel** *nm mot* gear lever. **—jahr** *n neu* leap year. **—ung** *nf* **-en** 1 *mot* gear change. 2 (electric) circuit.

Scham (ʃa:m) *nf* 1 shame, embarrassment. **sich** ⁼**en** ('ʃɛ:mən) *vr* be ashamed.

Schampun (ʃam'pu:n) *n neu* shampoo.

Schand/e ('ʃandə) *nf* shame, disgrace. **—en** ('ʃɛndən) *vt* 1 dishonour, disgrace. 2 rape. 3 desecrate. 4 disfigure. 5 soil. **—lich** ('ʃɛntlıç) *adj* shameful, base, dishonourable. **—tat**

('ʃantta:t) nf shameful deed, crime. —ung ('ʃenduŋ) nf -en 1 shaming, dishonouring. 2 disfigurement. 3 violation, rape.

Schanze ('ʃantsə) nf -n 1 fortification, earthwork. 2 naut quarterdeck.

Schar (ʃa:r) nf -en troop, host. **sich scharen** vr assemble, crowd together.

scharf (ʃarf) adj 1 sharp. 2 caustic. 3 pungent. 4 severe. 5 shrewd. 6 strong. 7 (of explosives, etc.) live. —e ('ʃerfə) nf -n 1 sharpness. 2 shrewdness. 3 severity. —en ('ʃerfən) vt 1 sharpen. 2 intensify. —richter nm executioner. —schütze nm sniper.

Scharlachfieber ('ʃarlaxfi:bər) n neu scarlet fever.

scharmant (ʃar'mant) adj charming.

Scharmützel (ʃar'mytsəl) n neu — skirmish. —n vi skirmish.

Scharnier (ʃar'ni:r) n neu -e hinge.

Schatten ('ʃatən) nm — shadow, shade. —bild n neu silhouette. —haft adj shadowy. —seite nf 1 dark side. 2 drawback, snag.

Schatz (ʃats) nm –e 1 treasure. 2 darling, sweetheart. —amt n neu treasury. —en ('ʃetsən) vt 1 estimate, assess. 2 esteem, regard (highly). —meister nm treasurer. —ung nf -en 1 estimate. 2 approximation. 3 esteem. —ungsweise ('ʃetsuŋsvaizə) adv approximately.

Schau (ʃau) nf -en 1 show. 2 exhibition. 3 view. —bühne nf stage, theatre. —en vt,vi 1 see. 2 look (at). —fenster n neu shop window. —spiel n neu play, drama. —spieler nm actor. —spielerin nf actress.

schauder/haft ('ʃaudərhaft) adj horrible. —n vi shudder.

Schauer ('ʃauər) nm — 1 shower. 2 shiver, shudder. 3 terror, awe.

Schaufel ('ʃaufəl) nf -n 1 shovel. 2 paddle, blade.

Schaukel ('ʃaukəl) nf -n swing. —n vt,vi swing, rock.

Schaum (ʃaum) nm –e foam, froth. —en ('ʃɔymən) vi foam, effervesce.

Scheck (ʃɛk) nm -s cheque.

Scheibe ('ʃaibə) nf -n 1 slice. 2 disc. 3 pane. 4 target. —nwischer nm — windscreen-wiper.

Scheid/e ('ʃaidə) nf -n 1 border. 2 sheath. 3 vagina. —en* vt 1 separate, divide. 2 divorce. **sich scheiden lassen** get divorced. vi depart, retire. —ung nf -en 1 separation. 2 divorce.

Schein (ʃain) nm -e 1 appearance, semblance.

2 shine. 3 light. 4 banknote. 5 certificate. 6 licence. 7 receipt. —bar adj apparent. —en* vi 1 seem. 2 shine. —heilig adj hypocritical. —werfer nm 1 searchlight, spotlight. 2 mot headlight. 3 reflector.

Scheiße ('ʃaisə) nf tab excrement.

Scheitel ('ʃaitəl) nm — 1 crown (of the head). 2 apex. 3 parting (of the hair). —punkt nm zenith, highest point.

scheitern ('ʃaitərn) vi 1 fail. 2 be wrecked.

Schellfisch ('ʃelfiʃ) nm -e haddock.

Schelm (ʃɛlm) nm -e 1 rogue, rascal. 2 joker.

Schemel ('ʃe:məl) nm — (foot)stool.

schenk/en ('ʃeŋkən) vt 1 give (as a present). 2 endow. 3 pour (out). —ung nf -en donation.

Scherbe ('ʃɛrbə) nf -n 1 fragment. 2 chip. 3 splinter (of glass, pottery, etc.).

Scher/e ('ʃe:rə) nf -n 1 scissors, shears. 2 zool pincer, claw.

Scherz (ʃɛrts) nm -e 1 joke, jest. 2 prank, lark. —en vi 1 joke. 2 lark about. —haft adj playful, joking.

scheu (ʃɔy) adj shy, bashful. nf shyness. —en vt avoid. **sich —en** vr 1 be afraid (to). 2 be shy (of).

Scheuche ('ʃɔyçə) nf -n scarecrow.

Scheune ('ʃɔynə) nf -n barn.

Scheusal ('ʃɔyza:l) n neu -e monster.

scheußlich ('ʃɔysliç) adj hideous.

Schi (ʃi:) nm -er ski. **Schi laufen** ski.

Schicht (ʃiçt) nf -en 1 layer. 2 coat(ing). 3 (social) class. 4 shift. —arbeit nf shift work. —en vt pile, stack.

schick (ʃik) adj chic, elegant. nm elegance.

schicken ('ʃikən) vt send. **sich schicken** vr 1 happen. 2 be proper, fitting, or decent.

schicklich ('ʃikliç) adj decent, proper.

Schicksal ('ʃikza:l) n neu -e fate, destiny.

schieb/en ('ʃi:bən) vt push, shove. vi profiteer. —er nm — 1 slide. 2 bolt (of a door, etc.). 3 profiteer. —ung nf -en 1 pushing. 2 profiteering. 3 underhand dealings, corrupt practice.

schied (ʃi:t) v see **scheiden**.

Schieds/gericht ('ʃi:tsgəriçt) n neu -e arbitration court. —richter nm 1 sport referee. 2 arbitrator

schief (ʃi:f) adj 1 slanting, oblique. 2 sloping, inclined. 3 wrong, false.

schielen ('ʃi:lən) vi squint.

schien (ʃi:n) v see **scheinen**.

Schien/e ('ʃi:nə) nf -n 1 rail (of a railway

track). **2** *med* splint. **—bein** *n* neu -e shin-bone.

schieß/en (ˈʃiːsən) *vt* shoot. *vi* **1** shoot. **2** rush. **—pulver** *n* neu gunpowder.

Schiff (ʃif) *n* neu -e **1** ship, vessel. **2** nave. **—ahrt** (ˈʃiffaːrt) *nf* shipping, navigation. **—bruch** *nm* shipwreck.

Schikan/e (ʃiˈkaːnə) *nf* -n **1** annoyance. **2** chicanery. **—ieren** (ʃikaˈniːrən) *vt* annoy.

Schild (ʃilt) *n* neu -er **1** name plate. **2** signboard. **3** badge. **4** label. *nm* -e **1** shield. **2** coat-of-arms. **3** shell (of a tortoise or crab). **—ern** (ˈʃildərn) *vt* describe, portray. **—kröte** (ˈʃiltkrœːtə) *nf* **1** turtle. **2** tortoise.

Schilf (ʃilf) *n* neu -e **1** reed, rush.

Schilling (ˈʃiliŋ) *nm* -e **1** Austrian unit of currency. **2** shilling.

Schimmel (ˈʃiməl) *nm* **1** mould, mildew. **2** *pl* — white horse. **—ig** *adj* mouldy.

Schimmer (ˈʃimər) *nm* gleam, glimmer. **—n** *vi* gleam, glimmer.

Schimpanse (ʃimˈpanzə) *nm* -n chimpanzee.

Schimpf (ʃimpf) *nm* -e **1** insult. **2** disgrace. **—en** *vt* abuse, insult. *vi* grumble, scold. **—wort** *n* neu **1** insult. **2** swear word.

schind/en (ˈʃindən) *vt* **1** torment. **2** exploit. **3** skin (an animal). **sich schinden** *vr* toil, slave. **—er** *nm* **1** exploiter. **2** tormentor.

Schinken (ˈʃiŋkən) *nm* ham.

Schirm (ʃirm) *nm* -e **1** umbrella. **2** shade. **3** screen. **4** protection, shelter. **—en** *vt* shelter, protect. **—herr** *nm* patron.

Schlacht (ʃlaxt) *nf* -en battle. **—en** *vt* slaughter, butcher. **—erei** (ʃlɛçtaˈrai) *nf* -en **1** butcher's shop. **2** massacre. **—feld** *n* neu battlefield. **—haus** *n* neu slaughterhouse, abattoir. **—schiff** *n* neu battleship.

Schlaf (ʃlaːf) *nm* sleep. **—en** *vi* sleep. **—anzug** *nm* pyjamas. **—tablette** *nf* sleeping pill. **—rig** (ˈʃlɛːfriç) *adj* **1** sleepy. **2** dozy. **—sack** *nm* sleeping bag. **—wagen** *nm* sleeping car. **—zimmer** *n* neu bedroom.

schlaff (ʃlaf) *adj* **1** slack. **2** soft. **3** lax. **4** weak.

Schlag (ʃlaːk) *nm* -e **1** blow, stroke. **2** punch, slap. **3** (electric) shock. **4** peal, clap. **5** kind, sort. **—ader** *nf* artery. **—anfall** *nm* neu stroke, fit. **—en** (ˈʃlaːgən) *vt* strike, beat. **2** defeat. **3** fell. *vi* **1** beat, strike. **2** ring. **sich —en** *vr* **1** fight (with). **2** side (with). **—fertig** *adj* quick-witted, ready. **—sahne** *nf* whipped cream. **—wort** *n* neu slogan. **—zeile** *nf* headline.

Schlager (ˈʃlaːgər) *nm* — **1** pop song, dance tune. **2** (smash) hit, great success.

Schläger (ˈʃlɛːgər) *nm* — **1** thug. **2** *cul* beater. **3** rapier. **4** *sport* racket, club, stick.

Schlamm (ʃlam) *nm* -e mud, sludge.

Schlamp/e (ˈʃlampə) *nf* -n slut. **—erei** (ʃlampəˈrai) *nf* -en slovenliness. **—ig** *adj* slovenly, sluttish.

Schlange (ˈʃlaŋə) *nf* -n **1** snake, serpent. **2** queue.

schlank (ʃlaŋk) *adj* slender, slim.

schlapp (ʃlap) *adj* **1** slack. **2** flabby.

schlau (ʃlau) *adj* **1** sly, cunning. **2** shrewd.

Schlauch (ʃlaux) *nm* -e **1** tube. **2** hose. **3** *mot* inner tube.

schlecht (ʃlɛçt) *adj* **1** bad, wicked. **2** inferior. **—hin** *adv* simply, perfectly.

Schlegel (ˈʃleːgəl) *nm* — **1** mallet. **2** club. **3** drumstick.

schleichen (ˈʃlaiçən) *vi* sneak, creep.

Schleier (ˈʃlaiər) *nm* — veil. **—n** *vt* veil.

Schleif/e (ˈʃlaifə) *nf* -n **1** bow, slipknot. **2** slide, chute. **3** curve, loop. **—en** *vt,vi* drag. *vt* **1** polish. **2** sharpen.

Schleim (ʃlaim) *nm* -e mucus, phlegm.

schleißen (ˈʃlaisən) *vt* **1** wear out. **2** slit, split.

schlendern (ˈʃlɛndərn) *vi* stroll, dawdle.

schlepp/en (ˈʃlɛpən) *vt* **1** drag, haul. **2** carry. **—er** *nm* — also **—dampfer** tug(boat).

Sohlesien (ˈʃleːziən) *n* neu Silesia.

Schleuder (ˈʃlɔydər) *nf* -n **1** sling, catapult. **2** spin-drier. **—n** *vt* **1** hurl, sling. **2** spin-dry. *vi* *mot* skid.

schleunig (ˈʃlɔyniç) *adj* quick, prompt. **—st** *adv* in all haste, as quickly as possible.

Schleuse (ˈʃlɔyzə) *nf* -n **1** sluice. **2** lock (of a canal).

schlicht (ʃliçt) *adj* **1** plain, simple. **2** smooth. **—en** *vt* **1** settle (a quarrel). **2** smooth.

schlief (ʃliːf) *v* see **schlafen.**

schließ/en (ˈʃliːsən) *vi,vt* close, shut. *vt* **1** lock. **2** end, finish. **3** infer, conclude. **—fach** *n* neu **1** locker. **2** safe-deposit box. **—lich** (ˈʃliːsliç) *adj* final. *adv* **1** finally. **2** after all.

schlimm (ʃlim) *adj* **1** bad, serious. **2** sick, ill. **—stenfalls** (ˈʃlimstənfals) *adv* at (the) worst.

Schlinge (ˈʃliŋə) *nf* -n **1** loop, noose. **2** *med* sling. **3** snare.

schlingen [1] (ˈʃliŋən) *vt* **1** wind, coil. **2** weave, plait. **3** tie, knot. **4** fling.

schlingen [2] (ˈʃliŋən) *vi* gulp, eat greedily.

Schlitt/en (ˈʃlitən) *nm* — sledge, sleigh.
—schuh *nm* skate. **—schuhlaufen** *vi* skate.

Schlitz (ʃlits) *nm* -e slit, slot.

schloß (ʃlɔs) *v* see **schließen**.

Schloß (ʃlɔs) *n neu* **Schlösser** 1 castle, palace.
2 lock, clasp.

Schlosser (ˈʃlɔsər) *nm* — 1 locksmith. 2 metal
worker, fitter.

schlotterig (ˈʃlɔtəriç) *adj* shaky, tottery.

Schluck (ʃluk) *nm* -e 1 gulp, swig. 2 sip. **—en**
vt gulp (down), swallow. *nm* hiccup(s).

schlug (ʃluːk) *v* see **schlagen**.

Schlund (ʃlunt) *nm* -e 1 throat, gullet. 2 gulf,
chasm.

schlüpf/en (ˈʃlypfən) *vi* slip. **—er** *nm* (ladies')
knickers, panties. **—rig** *adj* 1 slippery. 2 (of a
joke, remark, etc.) obscene.

Schlupfloch (ˈʃlupflɔx) *n neu* **-1** loophole. 2
hiding place.

Schluß (ʃlus) *nm* **Schlüsse** 1 end, close. 2
conclusion, deduction. **—folgerung** *nf* conclusion. **—licht** *n neu* tail-light. **—stein** *nm*
keystone.

Schlüssel (ˈʃlysəl) *nm* — 1 key. 2 spanner. 3
mus clef. **—bein** *n neu* collarbone.

schmächtig (ˈʃmɛçtiç) *adj* slender, slim.

schmackhaft (ˈʃmakhaft) *adj* appetizing, tasty.

schmal (ʃmaːl) *adj* 1 narrow, thin. 2 meagre.

Schmalz (ʃmalts) *n neu* 1 dripping, fat. 2
(exaggerated) sentimentality.

schmarotz/en (ʃmaˈrɔtsən) *vi* scrounge,
sponge. **—er** *nm* — sponger, parasite.

Schmarren (ˈʃmarən) *nm* — 1 pancake. 2
trash.

schmatzen (ˈʃmatsən) *vi* smack (one's lips).

schmecken (ˈʃmɛkən) *vt* 1 taste. 2 sample. *vi*
taste (good).

Schmeich/elei (ʃmaiçəˈlai) *nf* -en flattery.
—eln (ˈʃmaiçəln) *vi* flatter. **—ler** (ˈʃmaiçlər)
nm — flatterer.

schmeißen* (ˈʃmaisən) *vt inf* throw, chuck.

schmelzen* (ˈʃmɛltsən) *vt,vi* melt.

Schmerz (ʃmɛrts) *nm* -en 1 pain. 2 grief.
—haft *adj* also **—lich** painful.

Schmetterling (ˈʃmɛtərliŋ) *nm* -e butterfly.

Schmied (ʃmiːt) *nm* -e blacksmith. **—e** (ˈʃmiː-
də) *nf* -n (blacksmith's) forge. **—en** (ˈʃmiː-
dən) *vt* 1 forge. 2 construct.

Schmier/e (ˈʃmiːrə) *nf* -n 1 grease. 2 ointment.
—en *vt* 1 grease, lubricate. 2 smear. 3 spread
(butter, etc.). **—ig** *adj* 1 greasy. 2 dirty. 3
sordid.

Schmink/e (ˈʃmiŋkə) *nf* -n make-up. **—en** *vt*
make up.

Schmor/en (ˈʃmoːrən) *vt* 1 stew. 2 braise.
—braten *nm* — stewed or braised meat.

Schmuck (ʃmuk) *nm* -e 1 ornament(s), jewellery. 2 decoration. **—en** (ˈʃmykən) *vt* decorate, adorn.

schmugg/eln (ˈʃmugəln) *vt,vi* smuggle. **—ler**
(ˈʃmuglər) *nm* — smuggler.

Schmutz (ʃmuts) *nm* dirt. **—ig** *adj* dirty.

Schnabel (ˈʃnaːbəl) *nm* -1 beak. 2 nozzle.

Schnall/e (ˈʃnalə) *nf* -n buckle, fastener. **—en**
vt buckle, fasten.

Schnaps (ʃnaps) *nm* -e spirit, liquor.

schnarchen (ˈʃnarçən) *vi* snore.

schnattern (ˈʃnatərn) *vi* cackle.

schnaufen (ˈʃnaufən) *vi* wheeze, gasp, pant.

Schnauz/e (ˈʃnautsə) *nf* -n 1 muzzle. 2 snout.
—en *vi* shout, bellow.

Schneck/e (ˈʃnɛkə) *nf* -n snail. **—engang** *nm*
snail's pace.

Schnee (ʃneː) *nm* snow. **—ball** *nm* snowball.
—flocke *nf* snowflake. **—glöckchen** *n neu*
snowdrop.

Schneid/e (ˈʃnaidə) *nf* -n edge, blade. **—en***
vt 1 cut, carve. 2 reap, mow. **—er** *nm* —
tailor.

schneien (ˈʃnaiən) *vi* snow.

schnell (ʃnɛl) *adj* fast, quick, rapid. **—en** *vt* 1
jerk. 2 flick. *vi* spring. **—igkeit** *nf* speed,
rapidity. **—zug** *nm* express train.

schnippisch (ˈʃnipiʃ) *adj* saucy, cheeky.

schnitt (ʃnit) *v* see **schneiden**.

Schnitt (ʃnit) *nm* -e 1 cut. 2 slice. 3 pattern. 4
cut, fashion. 5 woodcut. 6 crop. **—lauch** *nm*
chive(s).

Schnitz/el (ˈʃnitsəl) *nm* — 1 cutlet. 2 chip.
—eln *vt,vi* chip, shred.

Schnitzer (ˈʃnitsər) *nm* — 1 carver, cutter. 2
blunder, (bad) mistake.

Schnörkel (ˈʃnœrkəl) *nm* — 1 flourish, scroll.
2 squiggle.

schnüffeln (ˈʃnyfəln) *vi* 1 sniff. 2 snoop.

Schnupfen (ˈʃnupfən) *nm* — cold, chill.

Schnur (ʃnuːr) *nf* -e 1 string, cord. 2 flex,
(electrical) lead. **—gerade** *adv* straight as a
die.

Schnür/band (ˈʃnyːrbant) *n neu* -er lace.
—en *vt* lace or tie (up). **—senkel** *nm* shoelace.

Schnurrbart (ˈʃnurbaːrt) *nm* moustache.

schob (ʃoːp) *v* see **schieben**.

Schock (ʃɔk) nm -s shock. —**ieren** (ʃɔ'ki:rən) vt shock.

Schokolade (ʃoko'la:də) nf -n chocolate.

Scholle (ʃɔlə) nf -n 1 clod, lump. 2 plaice.

schon (ʃo:n) adv 1 already. 2 yet.

schön (ʃœ:n) adj 1 beautiful, handsome. 2 nice, fine. —**heit** nf beauty. —**heitskönigin** nf beauty queen.

schon/en ('ʃo:nən) vt spare, preserve. —**ung** nf -en 1 clemency, mercy. 2 consideration, care.

Schopf (ʃɔpf) nm -ͤe 1 tuft, lock (of hair). 2 crest (of birds).

schöpf/en ('ʃœpfən) vt 1 scoop, ladle. 2 get, obtain. —**kelle** nf -n scoop, ladle.

Schöpf/er nm — creator. —**erisch** adj creative. —**ung** nf -en creation.

Schornstein ('ʃɔrnʃtain) nm -e chimney, funnel. —**feger** nm chimney-sweep.

schoß (ʃɔs) v see **schießen**.

Schoß[1] (ʃo:s) nm -ͤe 1 lap. 2 womb.

Schoß[2] (ʃɔs) nm **Schosse** bot shoot, sprout.

Schote ('ʃo:tə) nf -n pod, shell.

Schott/e ('ʃɔtə) nm -n Scot, Scotsman. —**isch** adj Scottish. —**land** n neu Scotland.

schräg (ʃrɛ:k) adj oblique, slanting.

Schrank (ʃraŋk) nm -ͤe cupboard, wardrobe.

Schranke ('ʃraŋkə) nf -n 1 barrier. 2 enclosure, arena. —**nlos** adj boundless.

Schraub/e ('ʃraubə) nf -n screw. —**en** vt screw, twist. —**enschlüssel** nm spanner, wrench. —**enzieher** nm screwdriver.

Schrebergarten ('ʃre:bargartən) nm allotment.

Schreck (ʃrɛk) nm -e also **Schrecken** — 1 fright. 2 terror, horror. —**en** vt frighten. —**lich** adj terrible, dreadful, horrible.

Schrei (ʃrai) nm -e cry, scream. —**en*** vi cry, scream.

schreib/en ('ʃraibən) vt,vi 1 write. 2 spell. —**n** neu — letter. —**maschine** ('ʃraipmaʃi:nə) nf typewriter. —**papier** ('ʃraippapi:r) n neu notepaper. —**tisch** ('ʃraiptiʃ) nm desk.

Schrein (ʃrain) nm -e chest, cabinet. —**er** nm — cabinet-maker, carpenter.

schreiten* ('ʃraitən) vi step, stride.

schrie (ʃri:) v see **schreien**.

schrieb (ʃri:p) v see **schreiben**.

Schrift (ʃrift) nf -en 1 writing, work. 2 handwriting. 3 type, script. 4 scripture(s). —**lich** ·adj written, in writing. —**sprache** nf written language. —**steller** nm — writer, author.

schritt (ʃrit) v see **schreiten**.

Schritt (ʃrit) nm -e 1 step. 2 pace. —**macher** nm pacemaker.

schroff (ʃrɔf) adj 1 brusque, abrupt. 2 steep, rugged.

Schrot (ʃro:t) nm,neu -e (lead) shot. —**flinte** nf shotgun.

Schrott (ʃrɔt) nm -e scrap metal. —**haufen** nm scrap heap.

schrubben ('ʃrubən) vt scrub.

schrumpfen ('ʃrumpfən) vi 1 shrink. 2 become wrinkled.

Schub (ʃu:p) nm -ͤe 1 push, thrust. 2 batch. —**karren** nm wheelbarrow. —**fach** n neu also —**lade** nf drawer.

schüchtern ('ʃyçtərn) adj shy, bashful, timid. —**heit** nf shyness.

Schuft (ʃuft) nm -e scoundrel.

Schuh (ʃu:) nm -e shoe, boot. —**löffel** nm shoehorn. —**macher** nm shoemaker.

Schul/e ('ʃu:lə) nf -n school, college. —**arbeit** nf 1 homework. 2 lesson. —**en** vt school, train. —**er** ('ʃy:lər) nm — schoolboy. —**erin** ('ʃy:lərin) nf -nen schoolgirl. —**rat** nm school inspector. —**ung** nf schooling.

Schuld (ʃult) nf -en 1 debt. 2 guilt. 3 offence. —**en** ('ʃuldən) vt owe. —**ig** ('ʃuldiç) adj 1 guilty. 2 indebted. —**los** ('ʃultlo:s) adj innocent.

Schulter ('ʃultər) nf -n shoulder.

Schund (ʃunt) nm trash, rubbish.

Schuppe ('ʃupə) nf -n 1 zool scale. 2 pl dandruff.

schüren ('ʃy:rən) vt stir up.

Schurke ('ʃurkə) nm -n villain, scoundrel.

Schürze ('ʃyrtsə) nf -n apron, pinafore.

Schuß (ʃus) nm **Schüsse** shot. —**waffe** nf firearm.

Schüssel ('ʃysəl) nf -n 1 bowl, dish. 2 dish, course.

Schuster ('ʃu:stər) nm — shoemaker, cobbler.

Schutt (ʃut) nm 1 rubbish. 2 rubble. —**haufen** nm rubbish or rubble heap.

schütteln ('ʃytəln) vt shake.

schütten ('ʃytən) vt,vi pour.

Schutz (ʃuts) nm 1 protection, defence. 2 shelter. —**brille** nf goggles. —**e** ('ʃytsə) nm -n 1 marksman, rifleman. 2 Sagittarius. —**en** ('ʃytsən) vt 1 protect, defend. 2 shelter. —**er** ('ʃytsər) nm — protector, patron. —**heilige(r)** nm patron saint. —**ling** ('ʃytsliŋ) —e protégé. —**mann** nm policeman. —**mittel** n neu preservative. —**polizei** nf police.

Schwabe ('ʃvaːbə) nm -n Swabian. —n n neu Swabia.

schwach (ʃvax) adj weak. ⁼e (ʃvɛçə) nf -n also -heit weakness. —lich (ʃvɛçliç) adj sickly, feeble. —sinn nm imbecility.

Schwadron (ʃvaˈdroːn) nf -en squadron.

Schwager ('ʃvaːgər) nm ⁼ brother-in-law. ⁼in (ʃvɛˈgɛrin) nf -nen sister-in-law.

Schwalbe ('ʃvalbə) nf -n swallow.

Schwall (ʃval) nm -e swell, torrent.

Schwamm (ʃvam) nm -e 1 sponge. 2 fungus.

Schwan (ʃvaːn) nm ⁼e swan. —engesang nm swan song.

schwanger ('ʃvaŋər) adj pregnant. —schaft nf -en pregnancy. —sverhütung nf contraception.

schwanken ('ʃvaŋkən) vi 1 rock, sway. 2 hesitate, waver.

Schwanz (ʃvants) nm ⁼e 1 tail. 2 trail, train.

schwärm/en ('ʃvɛrmən) vi 1 swarm. 2 be enthusiastic, rave (about). —erisch adj wildly enthusiastic.

schwarz (ʃvarts) adj,n neu black. —brot n neu black bread. —e(r) nm Black, Negro. ⁼e ('ʃvɛrtsə) nf black(ness). —en ('ʃvɛrtsən) vt 1 blacken. 2 slander, defame. 3 inf smuggle. —markt nm black market. —wald nm Black Forest. —weiß adj black and white.

schwatzen ('ʃvatsən) vi prattle, chatter.

Schweb/ebahn ('ʃveːbəbaːn) nf -en cable railway. —en vi 1 hover, soar. 2 hang. 3 waver.

Schwed/en ('ʃveːdən) n neu Sweden. —e nm -n Swede. —isch adj Swedish. n neu Swedish (language).

Schwefel ('ʃveːfəl) nm sulphur.

schweig/en* ('ʃvaigən) vi fall or be silent. —sam ('ʃvaikzaːm) adj silent, taciturn.

Schwein (ʃvain) n neu -e pig, swine. **Schwein haben** inf be in luck. —efleisch n neu pork. —ehund nm inf swine. —erei (ʃvaiˈnaˈrai) nf mean trick. —estall nm pigsty.

Schweiß (ʃvais) nm sweat. —en vt weld.

Schweiz (ʃvaits) nf Switzerland. —er nm — Swiss. —erisch adj Swiss.

Schwelle ('ʃvɛlə) nf -n 1 threshold. 2 sill. 3 beam. 4 (railway) sleeper.

schwellen* ('ʃvɛlən) vi,vt swell. vi expand, increase.

schwemmen ('ʃvɛmən) vt 1 water. 2 rinse. 3 float, drift.

Schwengel ('ʃvɛŋəl) nm — 1 clapper (of a bell). 2 handle (of a pump).

schwenk/en ('ʃvɛŋkən) vi 1 swivel, swing. 2 tilt. vt 1 swing. 2 shake, flourish. 3 cul toss. 4 rinse.

schwer (ʃveːr) adj 1 heavy. 2 difficult. 3 serious, grave. 4 clumsy. 5 (of food) stodgy. —e nf -n 1 weight. 2 sci gravity. 3 seriousness. 4 difficulty. 5 severity. —beschädigt adj 1 disabled, crippled. 2 badly damaged. —fällig adj clumsy, ponderous. —hörig adj hard of hearing. —industrie nf heavy industry. —lich adv with difficulty, scarcely. —punkt nm 1 centre of gravity. 2 main point. —verletzt adj 1 disabled. 2 badly wounded, seriously injured. —wiegend adj grave, weighty.

Schwert (ʃveːrt) n neu -er 1 sword. 2 naut centre-board, keel. —lilie nf bot iris.

Schwester ('ʃvɛstər) nf -n sister.

schwieg (ʃviːk) v see **schweigen.**

Schwieger/mutter ('ʃviːgərmutər) nf ⁼ mother-in-law. —sohn nm son-in-law. —tochter nf daughter-in-law. —vater nm father-in-law.

schwierig ('ʃviːriç) adj difficult, hard. —keit nf -en difficulty, trouble.

Schwimm/bad ('ʃvimbaːt) n neu also **Schwimm/becken** swimming pool. —en* vi 1 swim. 2 float. —er nm — 1 swimmer. 2 float. —weste nf life jacket.

Schwind/el ('ʃvindəl) nm — 1 dizziness, vertigo. 2 swindle. 3 lie, fib. —(e)lig adj dizzy. —eln vi 1 swindle, cheat. 2 lie. 3 be dizzy. **mir schwindelt** I feel dizzy. —ler ('ʃvindlər) nm — swindler, fraud.

Schwindsucht ('ʃvintzuxt) nf med consumption, tuberculosis.

schwingen* ('ʃviŋən) vt,vi 1 swing. 2 vibrate.

schwitzen ('ʃvitsən) vi sweat, perspire.

schwören* ('ʃvœːrən) vi,vt swear, take (an oath).

schwul (ʃvuːl) adj sl queer, homosexual.

schwül (ʃvyːl) adj sultry, humid. —e nf sultriness, oppressive heat.

Schwulst (ʃvulst) nm ⁼e bombast.

Schwung (ʃvuŋ) nm 1 swing. 2 impetus. 3 enthusiasm, verve. 4 flair.

Schwur (ʃvuːr) nm ⁼e oath. —gericht n neu assize court.

sechs (zɛks) adj,nf six. —te adj sixth.

sechzehn ('zɛçtseːn) adj,nf sixteen. —te adj sixteenth.

sechzig ('zɛçtsiç) adj,nf sixty. —**ste** adj sixtieth.

See (se:) nm -n lake. nf -n sea. —**bad** n neu
seaside resort. —**fahrt** nf 1 voyage. 2
navigation. —**krank** adj seasick. —**mann**
nm -leute sailor, marine. —**meile** nf nautical
mile, knot. —**räuber** nm — pirate. —**zunge**
nf zool sole.

Seel/e ('ze:lə) nf -n soul, mind. —**sorger** nm
— clergyman.

Segel ('ze:gəl) n neu — sail. —**boot** n neu
sailing boat. —**fliegen** n neu gliding. —**n** vi
1 sail. 2 soar, glide. —**tuch** n neu canvas.

Seg/en ('ze:gən) nm — 1 blessing. 2 prayer(s).
3 grace. —**nen** ('ze:gnən) vt bless. —**nung**
('ze:gnuŋ) nf -en blessing.

seh/en ('ze:ən) vt,vi see, look. —**enswert** adj
worth seeing. —**enswürdigkeit** nf -en object
of interest, sight. —**er** nm — prophet.

Sehn/e ('ze:nə) nf -n 1 tendon, sinew. 2 math
chord. 3 (bow) string. **sich** —**en** vr long
(for). —**sucht** nf longing.

sehr (ze:r) adv very, much.

sei (zai) v see **sein**[2].

seicht (zaiçt) adj 1 shallow. 2 insipid. 3 superficial.

seid (zait) v see **sein**[2].

Seide ('zaidə) nf -n silk.

Seidel ('zaidəl) n neu — (beer) mug.

Seif/e ('zaifə) nf -n soap. —**en** vt soap.

Seil (zail) n neu -e rope, cable. —**bahn** nf
cable railway.

sein[1] (zain) poss adj 3rd pers s his, its. —**er**
poss pron 3rd pers s also **der** —**e** or **der**
—**ige** his. —**erseits** ('zainərzaits) adv for his
part. —**esgleichen** ('zainəsglaiçən) pron people like him. —**ethalben** ('zainəthalbən) adv
also —**etwegen** ('zainətve:gən) or —**etwillen** ('zainətvilən) for his sake.

sein[2] (zain) vi be, exist. n neu being, existence.

seit (zait) prep,conj since. —**dem** (zait'de:m)
conj since. adv since then. —**her** (zait'he:r)
adv 1 since then. 2 till now.

Seit/e ('zaitə) nf -n 1 side. 2 page. —**engasse**
nf (small) side street. —**ens** adv on the part
or side of. —**lich** adj lateral, side. —**wärts**
('zaitvɛrts) adv sideways.

Sekretär (zekre'tɛ:r) nm -e, **Sekretärin** nf -nen
secretary.

Sekt (zɛkt) nm -e champagne.

Sekte ('zɛktə) nf -n sect.

Sekunde (ze'kundə) nf -n second.

selber ('zɛlbər) pron self.

selbst (zɛlpst) pron 1 self. 2 unaided, alone.
ich selbst I myself. ~**n** neu self. adv even.

Selbstachtung ('zɛlpstaxtuŋ) nf self-respect.

selbständig ('zɛlpstɛndiç) adj independent,
autonomous. —**keit** nf independence.

Selbstbedienung ('zɛlpstbədi:nuŋ) nf self-
service. —**srestaurant** n neu cafeteria.

Selbstbeherrschung ('zɛlpstbəhɛrʃuŋ) nf self-
control.

selbstbewußt ('zɛlpstbəvust) adj self-confident.

Selbstgefühl ('zɛlpstgəfy:l) n neu self-respect,
self-reliance, self-confidence.

selbstlos ('zɛlpstlo:s) adj selfless.

Selbstmord ('zɛlpstmɔrt) nm suicide. —**er**
(person) suicide.

selbstsicher ('zɛlpstziçər) adj self-confident.

Selbstsucht ('zɛlpstzuxt) nf selfishness. —**ig**
('zɛlpstzyçtiç) adj selfish.

selbstverständlich ('zɛlpstfɛrʃtɛntliç) adj
obvious. adv naturally, of course, obviously.

Selbstvertrauen ('zɛlpstfɛrtrauən) n neu self-
confidence.

selig ('ze:liç) adj 1 blessed. 2 happy. 3 deceased, late. —**keit** nf -en bliss.

Sellerie ('zɛlari:) nm,f celery.

selten ('zɛltən) adj rare. adv seldom, rarely.
—**heit** ('zɛltənhait) nf -en 1 rarity. 2 scarcity.

seltsam ('zɛltza:m) adj strange, singular.

Semester (ze'mɛstər) n neu — semester.

Seminar (zemi'na:r) n neu -e 1 seminar. 2
teacher-training college. 3 (academic) department.

Semmel ('zɛməl) nf -n roll, bun.

Senat (ze'na:t) nm -e senate.

send/en[*] ('zɛndən) vt 1 send. 2 broadcast.
—**er** nm — 1 sender. 2 transmitter. —**ung**
nf -en 1 shipment. 2 transmission. 3 mission.

Senf (zɛnf) nm -e mustard.

Senkel ('zɛŋkəl) nm — (shoe)lace.

senk/en ('zɛŋkən) vt sink, lower. **sich senken**
vr 1 sink. 2 slope. —**recht** adj vertical,
perpendicular.

Sensation (zɛnzatsi'o:n) nf -en 1 sensation. 2
thrill. —**ell** (zɛnzatsio'nɛl) adj sensational.

Sense ('zɛnzə) nf -n scythe.

sensuell (zɛnzu'ɛl) adj sensual.

sentimental (zɛntimɛn'ta:l) adj sentimental.

September (zɛp'tɛmbər) nm September.

Serie ('ze:riə) nf -n series. —**nbau** nm also
—**nherstellung** nf mass production.

seriös (zeri'œ:s) adj 1 serious. 2 reliable.

Serv/ice (zɛr'vi:s) n neu — 1 (dinner) service.

2 service. **—ieren** (zɛr'viːrən) vt, vi serve (food).

Serviette (zɛrvi'ɛtə) nf **-n** napkin, serviette.

Sessel ('zɛsəl) nm **—** armchair. **—lift** nm chair-lift.

seßhaft ('zɛshaft) adj 1 resident. 2 settled.

setzen ('zɛtsən) vt 1 set, put, place, lay. 2 erect. 3 wager. 4 compose. vi leap. **sich setzen** vr 1 sit down. 2 subside.

Seuche ('zɔʏçə) nf **-n** epidemic.

seufz/en ('zɔʏftsən) vi 1 sigh. 2 groan. **—er** nm **—** 1 sigh. 2 groan.

Sex (zɛks) nm 1 sex, sexual intercourse. 2 sexuality. **—uell** (zɛksu'ɛl) adj sexual.

sezieren (ze'tsiːrən) vt dissect.

Sibir/ien (zi'biːriən) n neu Siberia. **—ier** — Siberian. **—isch** adj Siberian.

sich (ziç) pron 1 himself, herself, itself. 2 oneself. 3 themselves. 4 one another, each other.

Sichel ('ziçəl) nf **-n** 1 sickle. 2 crescent.

sicher ('ziçər) adj 1 safe, secure. 2 certain. 3 reliable. **—heit** nf **-en** 1 certainty. 2 security. 3 safety. **—heitsdienst** nm security service. **—lich** adv certainly, surely. **—n** vt 1 protect. 2 secure. 3 fasten. 4 guarantee. **—stellen** vt safeguard, secure. **—ung** nf **-en** 1 safety mechanism. 2 protection. 3 comm security, guarantee. 4 fuse.

Sicht (ziçt) nf 1 sight. 2 visibility. **auf lange** or **weite Sicht** on a long-term basis. **—bar** adj visible. **—lich** adj obvious.

sie (ziː) pron 3rd pers 1 s she, her, it. 2 pl they, them. **Sie** pron 2nd pers fml s, pl you.

Sieb[1] ('ziːp) n neu **-e** sieve.

sieben[1] ('ziːbən) vt 1 sieve, sift. 2 select.

sieb/en[2] ('ziːbən) adj, nf seven. **—ente** adj also **—te** ('ziːptə) seventh.

siebzehn ('ziːptseːn) adj, nf seventeen. **—te** adj seventeenth.

siebzig ('ziːptsiç) adj, nf seventy. **—ste** adj seventieth.

sied/eln ('ziːdəln) vi settle, colonize. **—ler** ('ziːdlər) nm **—** settler. **—lung** ('ziːdluŋ) nf **-en** 1 settlement. 2 housing estate.

Siedepunkt ('ziːdəpuŋkt) nm boiling point.

Sieg (ziːk) nm 1 victory. 2 conquest. **—en** ('ziːgən) vi be victorious, win. **—er** ('ziːgər) nm **—** victor. **—reich** adj victorious.

Siegel ('ziːgəl) n neu **—** seal. **—n** vt seal.

sieht (ziːt) v see **sehen**.

Signal (zig'naːl) n neu **-e** signal. **—wärter** nm signalman.

Signatur (zigna'tuːr) nf **-en** 1 sign. 2 mark, stamp. 3 signature.

Silbe ('zilbə) nf **-n** syllable.

Silber ('zilbər) n neu silver.

Silvester (zil'vɛstər) nm New Year's Eve.

simpel ('zimpəl) adj 1 simple. 2 foolish.

Sims (zims) nm, neu **-e** 1 ledge, sill. 2 shelf.

simulieren (zimu'liːrən) vt simulate, feign. vi 1 malinger. 2 feign.

sind (zint) v see **sein**[2].

Sinfonie (zinfo'niː) nf **-n** symphony.

singen* ('ziŋən) vt, vi sing.

sinken* ('ziŋkən) vi 1 sink. 2 drop, slump.

Sinn (zin) nm **-e** 1 sense. 2 faculty. 3 meaning. 4 mind, consciousness. **—bild** n neu symbol. **—en*** vt, vi 1 think, reflect. 2 plan, scheme. **—lich** adj sensual, sensuous. **—los** adj senseless. **—voll** adj meaningful.

Sintflut ('zintfluːt) nf **-en** deluge.

Sipp/e ('zipə) nf **-n** 1 clan, tribe. 2 kin.

Sirup ('ziːrup) nm **-e** syrup.

Sitt/e ('zitə) nf **-n** 1 custom. 2 pl manners. 3 pl morals. **—lich** adj 1 moral. 2 decent, respectable. **—lichkeit** nf morality, morals.

Situation (zituatsi'oːn) nf **-en** situation.

Sitz (zits) nm **-e** 1 seat. 2 residence. 3 fit. **—en*** ('zitsən) vi 1 sit. 2 fit. **—ung** nf **-en** 1 sitting, session. 2 meeting.

Sizil/ien (zi'tsiːliən) n neu Sicily. **—ianer** (zitsili'aːnər) nm **—** Sicilian. **—ianisch** (zitsili'aːniʃ) adj Sicilian.

Skala ('skaːla) nf **Skalen** scale.

Skandal (skan'daːl) nm **-e** 1 scandal. 2 row, noise. **—ös** (skanda'løːs) adj scandalous.

Skandinav/ien (skandi'naːviən) n neu Scandinavia. **—ier** nm **—** Scandinavian. **—isch** adj Scandinavian.

Skelett (ske'lɛt) n neu **-e** skeleton.

skeptisch ('skɛptiʃ) adj sceptical.

Ski (ʃiː) nm see **Schi**.

Skizz/e ('skitsə) nf **-n** sketch. **—ieren** (ski'tsiːrən) vt sketch.

Sklav/e ('sklaːvə) nm **-n** slave. **—erei** (sklaːvə'rai) nf slavery. **—isch** ('sklaːviʃ) adj 1 slavish. 2 servile.

Skorpion ('skɔrpiən) nm **-e** 1 scorpion. 2 Scorpio.

Skrupel ('skruːpəl) nm **—** scruple. **—los** adj unscrupulous.

Smaragd (sma'rakt) nm **-e** emerald.

Smoking ('smoːkiŋ) nm **-s** dinner-jacket.

so (zoː) adv so, thus. **so daß** conj so that. **—bald** (zoˈbalt) conj as soon as.

Socke ('zɔkə) *nf* **-n** sock. **—nhalter** *nm* garter.

Sockel ('zɔkəl) *nm* — pedestal, base.

sodann (zo'dan) *conj* then.

Sodawasser ('zo:davasər) *n neu* soda water.

Sodbrennen ('zo:tbrɛnən) *n neu* heartburn.

soeben (zo'e:bən) *adv* just (now).

Sofa ('zo:fa) *n neu* **-s** sofa, couch.

sofern (zo'fɛrn) *conj* 1 as far as, so far as. 2 provided that.

sofort (zo'fɔrt) *adv* immediately, at once.

Sog (zo:k) *nm* **-e** 1 suction. 2 wake.

sogar (zo'ga:r) *adv* even.

sogenannt ('zo:gənant) *adj* so-called.

Sohle ('zo:lə) *nf* **-n** sole (of a shoe). **—n** *vt* sole.

Sohn (zo:n) *nm* **⁻e** son.

solang (zo'laŋ) *conj* while, so long as.

solch (zɔlç) *adj,pron* such.

Soldat (zɔl'da:t) *nm* **-en** soldier.

Söldner ('zœldnər) *nm* — mercenary.

solid (zo'li:t) *adj* 1 solid. 2 reliable.

Solist (zo'list) *nm* **-en** soloist.

sollen* ('zɔlən) *v mod aux* 1 should, ought (to). 2 be said, be supposed (to).

Solo ('zo:lo) *n neu* **-s** solo.

Sommer ('zɔmər) *nm* — summer. **—sprosse** *nf* freckle.

Sonate (zo'na:tə) *nf* **-n** sonata.

Sonde ('zɔndə) *nf* **-n** probe.

Sonder/angebot ('zɔndərangəbo:t) *n neu* — special offer. **—ausgabe** *nf* special edition. **—bar** ('zɔndərba:r) *adj* strange, singular.

sondern[1] ('zɔndərn) *vt* separate.

sondern[2] ('zɔndərn) *conj* but. **nicht nur ...sondern auch** not only...but also.

Sonett (zo'nɛt) *n neu* **-e** sonnet.

Sonnabend ('zɔna:bənt) *nm* **-e** Saturday. **-s** *adv* on Saturdays.

Sonn/e ('zɔnə) *nf* **-n** sun. **—aufgang** *nm* sunrise. **—nbrand** *nm* sunburn. **—nfinsternis** *nf* solar eclipse. **—nschein** *nm* sunshine. **—nstich** *nm* sunstroke. **—nuhr** *nf* sundial. **—nuntergang** *nm* sunset. **—ig** *adj* sunny.

Sonntag ('zɔnta:k) *nm* **-e** Sunday. **-s** *adv* on Sundays.

sonst (zɔnst) *adv* 1 otherwise. 2 else. 3 besides. **—ig** *adj* 1 other. 2 former. **—wo** ('zɔnstvo) *adv* elsewhere.

Sopran (zo'pra:n) *nm* **-e** soprano, treble. **—istin** (zopra'nistin) *nf* **-nen** soprano (singer)

Sorg/e ('zɔrgə) *nf* **-n** 1 care. 2 trouble, worry. 3 grief. **—en** *vi* care, take care. **—en für** care or provide for, take care of, look after. **sich —en** *vr* worry. **—falt** ('zɔrkfalt) *nf* care, carefulness.

Sort/e ('zɔrtə) *nf* **-n** sort, type. **—ieren** (zɔr'ti:rən) *vt* sort, arrange.

soso (zo'zo:) *adv inf* passably, so-so.

Soße ('zo:sə) *nf* **-n** 1 sauce. 2 gravy.

soweit (zo'vait) *conj* so far as.

sowie (zo'vi:) *conj* 1 as soon as. 2 just as.

sowieso (zovi'zo:) *adv* anyhow, anyway.

Sowjet (zɔ'vjɛt) *nm* **-s** Soviet. **—isch** *adj* Soviet. **—union** *nf* Soviet Union.

sowohl (zo'vo:l) *conj* **sowohl...als auch** both...and.

sozial (zotsi'a:l) *adj* social. **—demokrat** *nm* social democrat. **—ismus** (zotsia'lismus) *nm* socialism. **—ist** (zotsia'list) *nm* **-en** socialist. **—produkt** *n neu pol* national product.

Soziolog/e (zotsio'lo:gə) *nm* **-n** sociologist. **—ie** (zotsiolo'gi:) *nf* sociology. **—isch** (zotsio'lo:giʃ) *adj* sociological.

sozusagen (zotsu'za:gən) *adv* so to speak.

Spachtel ('ʃpaxtəl) *nm,f* **-n** 1 scraper. 2 spatula.

spähen ('ʃpɛ:ən) *vi* look out, watch.

Spalt (ʃpalt) *nm* **-e** crack, split. **—e** *nf* **-n** 1 crack, split. 2 column (of print, etc.). 3 rift. **—en** *vt* split, divide. **—pilz** *nm* bacteria.

Span (ʃpa:n) *nm* **⁻e** chip, splinter.

Span/ien ('ʃpa:niən) *n* Spain. **—ier** ('ʃpa:niər) *nm* — Spaniard. **—isch** ('ʃpa:niʃ) *adj* Spanish. *n neu* Spanish (language).

Spann (ʃpan) *nm* **-e** instep.

Spann/e ('ʃpanə) *nf* **-n** span. **—en** *vt* 1 stretch. 2 tighten. 3 harness. 4 excite. **—ung** *nf* **-en** 1 tension. 2 suspense. 3 voltage.

spar/en ('ʃpa:rən) *vt,vi* save. *vt* spare. **—kasse** *nf* savings bank. **—lich** ('ʃpɛ:rliç) *adj* meagre, scanty. **—sam** *adj* thrifty.

Spargel ('ʃpargəl) *nm* asparagus.

Spaß (ʃpa:s) *nm* **⁻e** 1 fun, amusement. 2 joke.

spät (ʃpɛ:t) *adj* late. **—estens** *adv* at the latest.

Spaten ('ʃpa:tən) *nm* — spade.

Spatz (ʃpats) *nm* **-en** sparrow.

spazier/en (ʃpa'tsi:rən) *vi* (take a) walk, stroll. **—engehen*** *vi* go for a walk. **—gang** *nm* walk.

Speck (ʃpɛk) *nm* 1 bacon. 2 fat.

spedieren (ʃpe'di:rən) *vt* dispatch, forward.

Speer (ʃpe:r) *nm* **-e** spear, lance.

Speichel ('ʃpaiçəl) *nm* saliva, spittle.

Speicher (ˈʃpaiçər) nm **-e 1** storeroom. **2** loft. **3** granary. **4** reservoir. **—n** vt store (up).

Speise (ˈʃpaizə) nf **-n 1** food. **2** meal. **3** dish. **—eis** n neu ice cream. **—kammer** nf pantry, larder. **—karte** nf menu. **—n** vi eat, dine. **—saal** nm dining room or hall. **—wagen** nm dining car.

Spektakel (ʃpɛkˈtaːkəl) nm **—** uproar, row.

spekulieren (ʃpekuˈliːrən) vi speculate.

Sperr/e (ˈʃpɛrə) nf **-n 1** closing. **2** barrier. **3** block. **4** blockade, embargo. **—en** vt **1** close, block (off). **2** shut (out). **3** cut off, stop.

Spesen (ˈʃpeːzən) n pl expenses, charges.

spez/ialisieren (ʃpetsiaˈliːziˌrən) vt specialize. **sich spezialisieren auf** specialize in. **—ialität** (ʃpetsialiˈtɛːt) nf **-en** speciality. **—iell** (ʃpetsiˈɛl) adj special.

spezifisch (ʃpeˈtsiːfiʃ) adj specific.

Sphäre (ˈsfɛːrə) nf **-n** sphere.

Spiegel (ˈʃpiːɡəl) nm **—** mirror. **—ei** n neu fried egg. **—n** vt reflect. vi shine. **—ung** nf **-en** reflection.

Spiel (ʃpiːl) n neu **-e 1** game. **2** play. **3** pack (of cards). **—en** vt,vi **1** play. **2** perform. **3** gamble. **—karte** nf playing card. **—platz** nm playground. **—zeug** n neu toy.

Spieß (ʃpiːs) nm **-e 1** spear. **2** cul spit. **—bürger** nm Philistine, (petit) bourgeois. **—ig** adj narrow-minded, Philistine.

Spinat (ʃpiˈnaːt) nm **-e** spinach.

Spinne (ˈʃpinə) nf **-n** spider. **—n*** (ˈʃpinən) vt **1** spin. **2** plot, think. vi inf **1** spin yarns, fib. **2** be crazy. **—r** nm **—** inf idiot.

Spion (ʃpiˈoːn) nm **-e** spy.

Spirale (ʃpiˈraːlə) nf **-n** spiral.

Spital (ʃpiˈtaːl) n neu ̈er hospital.

spitz (ʃpits) adj pointed, sharp. **—bube** nm rogue, rascal. **—e** nf **-n 1** point. **2** peak, top. **3** lace. **—en** vt point, sharpen. **—findig** adj subtle. **—ig** adj pointed, sharp. **—name** nm nickname.

Splitter (ˈʃplitər) nm **—** splinter. **—nackt** adj stark naked.

spontan (ʃpɔnˈtaːn) adj spontaneous.

Sporn (ʃpɔrn) nm **Sporen** spur.

Sport (ʃpɔrt) nm **-e** sport, games. **—ler** (ˈʃpɔrtlər) nm **—** sportsman, athlete. **—platz** nm sports field. **—wagen** nm sports car.

Spott (ʃpɔt) nm **—** mockery, ridicule. **—en** vi mock, ridicule.

sprach (ʃpraːx) v see **sprechen**.

Sprach/e (ˈʃpraːxə) nf **-n 1** speech. **2** language.

—lehre nf grammar. **—lich** adj linguistic. **—los** adj speechless.

sprang (ʃpraŋ) v see **springen**.

sprech/en* (ˈʃprɛçən) vi,vt speak, talk. **—stunde** nf consulting hours, surgery.

spreng/en (ˈʃprɛŋən) vt **1** explode, blast. **2** sprinkle. vi gallop. **—körper** nm explosive (charge). **—stoff** nm explosive.

spricht (ʃpriçt) v see **sprechen**.

Sprichwort (ˈʃpriçvɔrt) n neu ̈er proverb, saying.

sprießen* (ˈʃpriːsən) vi sprout, bud.

spring/en* (ˈʃpriŋən) vi **1** leap, jump. **2** dive. **—brett** n neu **1** diving board. **2** stepping stone. **—feder** nf spring.

Sprit (ʃprit) nm **-e 1** spirit, alcohol. **2** inf petrol.

Spritze (ˈʃpritsə) nf **-n 1** syringe. **2** spray. **3** injection. **4** fire engine. **—n** vt **1** spray, squirt. **2** inject. vi squirt.

Sproß (ʃprɔs) nm **-e** also **SpRößling** (ˈʃprœsliŋ) shoot, sprout.

Spruch (ʃprux) nm ̈e **1** saying. **2** judgment, sentence.

Sprudel (ˈʃpruːdəl) nm **—e 1** mineral water. **2** spring.

Sprung (ʃpruŋ) nm ̈e **1** leap, spring. **2** dive. **3** short distance, stone's throw. **4** crack. **—brett** n neu **1** diving board. **2** stepping stone. **—feder** nf spring.

spucken (ˈʃpukən) vi,vt spit.

Spuk (ʃpuːk) nm **-e** ghost. **—en** vi haunt.

Spule (ˈʃpuːlə) nf **-n 1** spool, reel. **2** coil.

spül/en (ˈʃpyːlən) vt **1** rinse, wash (up). **2** flush. **—mittel** n neu washing-up liquid.

Spur (ʃpuːr) nf **-en 1** track, trail. **2** trace, vestige, mark. **3** footprint.

Staat (ʃtaːt) nm **-en 1** state. **2** pomp. **—lich** adj state. **—sangehörigkeit** nf nationality. **—sanwalt** nm public prosecutor. **—smann** nm statesman. **—sstreich** nm coup d'état.

Stab (ʃtaːp) nm ̈e **1** staff. **2** rod, bar. **—springen*** vi pole-vault.

stabil (ʃtaˈbiːl) adj stable.

Stachel (ˈʃtaxəl) nm **-n 1** prickle. **2** sting. **3** quill, spine. **4** spike. **—beere** nf gooseberry. **—draht** nm barbed wire. **—schwein** n neu porcupine.

Stadt (ʃtat) nf ̈e city, town. **—isch** (ˈʃtɛːtiʃ) adj municipal, town. **—viertel** n neu quarter, district.

Staffel (ˈʃtafəl) nf **-n 1** step, rung. **2** stage, degree. **3** aviat squadron. **4** sport relay. **—ei** (ʃtafəˈlai) nf **-en** easel.

stahl (ʃtaːl) v see **stehlen**.

Stahl (ʃtɑːl) nm -e steel. **—ern** (ʃtɛːlərn) adj steel.

Stall (ʃtal) nm ⁼e 1 stable. 2 cowshed. 3 pigsty. 4 (dog-)kennel.

Stamm (ʃtam) nm ⁼e 1 trunk. 2 stem. 3 family. 4 race. **—baum** nm 1 family tree. 2 pedigree. **—en** vi originate, be descended. **—tisch** nm (table for) regular customers.

stampfen (ʃtampfən) vt,vi 1 stamp. 2 pound.

stand (ʃtant) v see **stehen**.

Stand (ʃtant) nm ⁼e 1 stand. 2 situation. 3 location. 4 class, rank. 5 position. **—bild** n neu statue. **—esamt** (ʃtandəsamt) n neu registry office. **—haft** adj steadfast, constant. **—halten** vi stand firm. **—ort** nm 1 location. 2 garrison. **—punkt** nm point of view, standpoint.

ständig (ʃtɛndiç) adj permanent, continuous. adv constantly, continually.

Stange (ʃtaŋə) nf -n pole, stick. **—nbohne** nf runner bean.

Stänker (ʃtɛŋkər) nm — inf trouble-maker. **—n** vi inf cause trouble, stir things up.

Stanniol (ʃtani'oːl) n neu -e tinfoil.

Stapel (ʃtaːpəl) nm — 1 pile. 2 stocks. **—lauf** nm launch(ing). **—n** vt pile up.

stark (ʃtark) adj 1 strong. 2 stout. 3 large. adv 1 strongly. 2 very, greatly. **—e** (ʃtɛrkə) nf -n 1 strength. 2 starch. **—en** (ʃtɛrkən) vt 1 strengthen. 2 starch.

starr (ʃtar) adj 1 stiff, rigid. **—köpfig** (ʃtarkœpfiç) adj stubborn.

Start (ʃtart) nm -e 1 start. 2 aviat take-off. **—en** vi 1 start. 2 aviat take off. **—erklappe** nf mot choke.

Station (ʃtatsi'oːn) nf -en 1 station, stop. 2 (hospital) ward.

Statist/ik (ʃta'tistik) nf -en statistics. **—isch** adj statistical.

statt (ʃtat) prep instead of. nf place, stead. **—finden** vi take place, occur. **—haft** adj 1 permissible. 2 legal.

Stätte (ʃtɛtə) nf -n 1 place, spot. 2 abode. 3 scene (of an accident, etc.).

Statut (ʃta'tuːt) n neu -en statute.

Staub (ʃtaup) nm 1 dust. 2 pollen. **—ig** (ʃtaubiç) adj dusty. **—sauger** nm — vacuum cleaner.

Stau/damm (ʃtaudam) nm ⁼e dam. **—en** vt dam up.

staunen (ʃtaunən) vi be amazed, wonder. n neu — amazement.

Steak (steːk) n neu steak.

stechen (ʃtɛçən) vt 1 stab, pierce. 2 cut. 3 game trump. vi 1 sting. 2 burn. **—d** adj stinging.

steck/en (ʃtɛkən) vt 1 put, stick. 2 insert. vi be (found). nm — stick. **—brief** nm (arrest) warrant. **—dose** nf (electric) socket. **—enpferd** (ʃtɛkənpfɛrt) n neu -e hobby-horse. **—er** nm — (electric) plug.

Steg (ʃteːk) nm -e 1 footpath. 2 footbridge. 3 mus bridge.

stehen (ʃteːən) vi 1 stand. 2 be. **—bleiben** vi stand still, stop.

stehlen (ʃteːlən) vt steal.

steif (ʃtaif) adj stiff.

steig/en (ʃtaigən) vi 1 climb. 2 rise. 3 mount. **—bügel** nm stirrup.

steiger/n (ʃtaigərn) vt 1 increase. 2 raise. **—ung** nf -en 1 rise. 2 increase. 3 intensification.

steil (ʃtail) adj steep.

Stein (ʃtain) nm -e stone, rock. **—alt** adj ancient, as old as the hills. **—bock** nm 1 ibex. 2 Capricorn. **—bruch** nm quarry. **—ern** (ʃtainərn) adj stone. **—ig** adj stony. **—schlag** nm rockfall, avalanche.

Stell/e (ʃtɛlə) nf -n 1 place, site, spot. 2 job, position. 3 office, authority. **—en** vt 1 place, put. 2 arrange. 3 adjust, set. 4 provide, supply. **sich —en** vr 1 present oneself. 2 sham, pretend to be. **—enlos** adj unemployed. **—envermittlung** nf employment agency. **—vertreter** nm deputy, representative.

Stellung (ʃtɛluŋ) nf -en 1 situation. 2 post, job. **—nahme** nf 1 attitude. 2 opinion.

Stelze (ʃtɛltsə) nf -n stilt.

Stempel (ʃtɛmpəl) nm — stamp. **—n** vt stamp, frank.

Stengel (ʃtɛŋəl) nm — stalk, stem.

Stenographie (ʃtenogra'fiː) nf -n shorthand.

Steppe (ʃtɛpə) nf -n steppe.

sterb/en (ʃtɛrbən) vi die. **—lich** (ʃtɛrpliç) adj mortal.

steril (ʃte'riːl) adj sterile.

Stern (ʃtɛrn) nm -e star. **—bild** n neu constellation. **—chen** (ʃtɛrnçən) n neu — asterisk. **—deuterei** nf astrology. **—kunde** nf astronomy. **—warte** nf -n observatory.

stet (ʃteːt) adj also **stetig** constant, steady. **—s** adv always, constantly.

Steuer[1] (ʃtɔyər) n neu — helm, rudder. **—bord** nm,neu starboard. **—mann** nm helmsman. **—n** vt,vi steer.

Steuer

Steuer[2] (ˈʃtɔyər) *nf* -n tax.

Stich (ʃtiç) *nm* -e 1 prick, sting. 2 stitch. 3 game trick. 4 engraving. 5 taunt. **—wort** *n neu* 1 key-word. 2 cue.

sticken (ˈʃtikən) *vt,vi* embroider.

Stickstoff (ˈʃtikʃtɔf) *nm* nitrogen.

Stief/bruder (ˈʃtiːfbruːdər) *nm* stepbrother. **—mutter** *nf* stepmother. **—mütterchen** *n neu* — pansy. **—schwester** *nf* stepsister. **—sohn** *nm* stepson. **—tochter** *nf* step-daughter. **—vater** *nm* stepfather.

Stiefel (ˈʃtiːfəl) *nm* -boot.

stieg (ʃtiːk) *v see* **steigen.**

Stiel (ʃtiːl) *nm* -e 1 handle. 2 stalk.

Stier (ʃtiːr) *nm* -e 1 bull. 2 Taurus.

stieß (ʃtiːs) *v see* **stoßen.**

Stift[1] (ʃtift) *n neu* -e (charitable) institution.

Stift[2] (ʃtift) *nm* -e 1 peg, pin. 2 pencil.

stift/en (ˈʃtiftən) *vt* 1 give, donate. 2 found. 3 cause. **—ung** *nf* -en 1 institution. 2 donation.

Stil (ʃtiːl) *nm* -e style.

still (ʃtil) *adj* 1 still, calm. 2 quiet. 3 silent. **Stiller Ozean** Pacific Ocean. **—e** *nf* -n 1 peace, stillness. 2 quiet, silence. **—en** (ˈʃtilləgən) *vt* shut down, stop. **—en** *vt* 1 still. 2 appease. 3 suckle (a child). 4 quench. 5 quieten. **—schweigend** (ˈʃtilʃvaigənt) *adj* 1 silent, taciturn. 2 tacit. **—stand** *nm* standstill.

Stimm/e (ˈʃtimə) *nf* -n 1 voice. 2 vote. **—en** *vi* 1 be correct. 2 agree. 3 vote. *vt* tune. **—ung** *nf* -en 1 mood, feeling. 2 tuning.

stinken[*] (ˈʃtiŋkən) *vi* stink.

Stipendium (ʃtiˈpɛndium) *n neu* -ien scholarship, grant.

Stirn (ʃtirn) *nf* -en forehead, brow.

stöbern (ˈʃtøːbərn) *vi* rummage (around).

Stock (ʃtɔk) *nm* -e 1 stick, cane. 2 storey, floor. **—en** *vi* 1 stop, pause. 2 rot. 3 curdle. 4 thicken. **—werk** *n neu* storey, floor.

Stoff (ʃtɔf) *nm* -e 1 matter, substance. 2 material, fabric, cloth. 3 topic.

stöhnen (ˈʃtøːnən) *vi* groan.

Stoi/ker (ˈʃtɔːikər) *nm* — Stoic. **—sch** (ˈʃtɔːiʃ) *adj* stoical.

stolpern (ˈʃtɔlpərn) *vi* stumble.

stolz (ʃtɔlts) *adj* 1 proud. 2 noble. 3 vain. *nm* pride.

stopfen (ˈʃtɔpfən) *vt* 1 stuff, fill. 2 darn. 3 constipate.

Stoppel (ˈʃtɔpəl) *nf* -n stubble.

stoppen (ˈʃtɔpən) *vt,vi* stop, halt.

Stör (ʃtøːr) *nm* -e sturgeon.

Storch (ʃtɔrç) *nm* -e stork.

stör/en (ˈʃtøːrən) *vt* bother, trouble, disturb. **—ung** *nf* -en 1 disturbance. 2 inconvenience. 3 interference (on a radio, etc.).

Stoß (ʃtoːs) *nm* -e 1 push, thrust. 2 punch, kick, blow. 3 impact. 4 pile (of books, etc.). **—dämpfer** *nm* shock-absorber. **—en**[*] *vt* 1 push. 2 stab. 3 thrust. 4 thrust. *vi* 1 bump, hit. 2 run (into). **sich —en** *vr* 1 bump. 2 take offence. **—stange** *nf* mot bumper.

stottern (ˈʃtɔtərn) *vt,vi* stammer, stutter.

Straf/anstalt (ˈʃtraːfanʃtalt) *nf* -en prison, penal institution. **—bar** *adj* punishable. **—e** *nf* -n 1 punishment, penalty. 2 fine. **—en** *vt* punish. **—ling** (ˈʃtrɛːfliŋ) *nm* -e convict. **—recht** *n neu* criminal law.

Strahl (ʃtraːl) *nm* -en 1 ray, beam. 2 jet. 3 flash. **—en** *vt,vi* 1 radiate. 2 beam. **—ung** *nf* -en radiation.

stramm (ʃtram) *adj* 1 taut. 2 robust.

Strand (ʃtrant) *nm* -e shore, coast, beach. **—gutjäger** *nm* beachcomber.

strapazieren (ʃtrapaˈtsiːrən) *vt* 1 tire, exhaust. 2 wear out.

Straße (ˈʃtraːsə) *nf* -n 1 street, road. 2 straits. **—nbahn** *nf* tram.

sträuben (ˈʃtrɔybən) *vt* ruffle (up). **sich sträuben** *vr* oppose, refuse.

Strauch (ʃtraux) *nm* -er bush, shrub.

Strauß[1] (ʃtraus) *nm* -e bouquet, bunch.

Strauß[2] (ʃtraus) *nm* -e ostrich.

streb/en (ˈʃtreːbən) *vi* strive (for). **—epfeiler** *nm* buttress. **—er** *nm* — climber, pusher.

Strecke (ˈʃtrɛkə) *nf* -n 1 stretch, section. 2 distance.

Streich (ʃtraiç) *nm* -e 1 stroke, blow. 2 trick. **—eln** *vt* stroke, caress. **—en**[*] *vt* 1 stroke. 2 strike (out). 3 spread. *vi* rush, run. **—holz** *n neu* match. **—instrument** *n neu* stringed instrument.

Streif (ʃtraif) *nm* -e also **Streifen** *nm* — stripe, streak.

Streife (ˈʃtraifə) *nf* -n 1 patrol. 2 raid.

streifen (ˈʃtraifən) *vt* 1 streak, stripe. 2 graze. 3 touch. 4 strip off. *vi* rove, ramble.

Streik (ʃtraik) *nm* -e (industrial) strike. **—brecher** *nm* strikebreaker, blackleg. **—en** *vi* strike. **—posten** *nm* picket.

Streit (ʃtrait) *nm* -e 1 dispute, quarrel. 2 brawl, struggle. **—en**[*] *vi* 1 quarrel, argue. 2 fight. **—frage** *nf* matter in dispute. **—ig** *adj* in dispute. **—kräfte** *nf pl* armed forces.

106

streng (ʃtrɛŋ) *adj* 1 harsh. 2 rigorous. —**e** *nf* 1 harshness. 2 rigour. —**gläubig** *adj* orthodox.

streuen (ʃtrɔyən) *vt* 1 scatter, sprinkle. 2 sow.

Strich (ʃtriç) *nm* -**e** 1 stroke. 2 line. 3 district. 4 touch. 5 (compass) point. 6 (wood) grain. —**punkt** *nm* semicolon.

Strick (ʃtrik) *nm* -**e** cord, rope. —**en** *vt, vi* knit.

strittig (ʃtritiç) *adj* in dispute.

Stroh (ʃtro:) *n neu* straw. —**halm** *nm* (blade of) straw.

Strolch (ʃtrɔlç) *nm* -**e** tramp.

Strom (ʃtro:m) *nm* ⁼**e** 1 (large) river. 2 current. 3 electricity, electric current. 4 flood, torrent. —**abwärts** (ʃtro:m'apvɛrts) *adv* downstream. —**aufwärts** (ʃtro:m'aufvɛrts) *adv* upstream. ⁼**en** (ʃtroe:mən) *vi* 1 stream, flow. 2 flock. ⁼**ung** (ʃtroe:muŋ) *nf* -**en** 1 current. 2 trend. 3 flow.

Struktur (ʃtruk'tu:r) *nf* -**en** structure.

Strumpf (ʃtrumpf) *nm* ⁼**e** stocking. —**band** *n neu* garter. —**halter** *nm* — suspender. —**hose** *nf* tights.

Stube (ʃtu:bə) *nf* -**n** room, chamber. —**nrein** *adj* house-trained.

Stück (ʃtyk) *n neu* -**e** 1 piece. 2 head, item. 3 play. —**arbeit** *nf* piecework. —**chen** (ʃtykçən) *n neu* — scrap, bit.

Student (ʃtu'dɛnt) *nm* -**en**, —**in** *nf* -**nen** student.

Stud/ie (ʃtu:diə) *nf* -**n** 1 study. 2 sketch. —**ienrat** *nm* secondary-school teacher. —**ieren** (ʃtu'di:rən) *vt, vi* study. —**ium** (ʃtu:-dium) *n neu* -**ien** 1 studies. 2 university education or course.

Stufe (ʃtu:fə) *nf* -**n** 1 step, stair. 2 rung. 3 stage. 4 *mus* interval. —**nweise** *adv* gradually, in stages.

Stuhl (ʃtu:l) *nm* ⁼**e** chair, seat.

stumm (ʃtum) *adj* 1 dumb, mute. 2 silent.

stumpf (ʃtumpf) *adj* 1 blunt. 2 dull. *nm* ⁼**e** stump. —**sinn** *nm* dullness, stupidity.

Stund/e (ʃtundə) *nf* -**n** 1 hour. 2 lesson. —**enplan** *nm* (school) timetable. ⁼**lich** (ʃtyntliç) *adj* hourly.

stur (ʃtu:r) *adj inf* obstinate.

Sturm (ʃturm) *nm* ⁼**e** 1 storm, gale. 2 attack. ⁼**isch** (ʃtyrmiʃ) *adj* stormy.

Sturz (ʃturts) *nm* ⁼**e** 1 fall. 2 downfall. 3 overthrow. 4 collapse. ⁼**en** (ʃtyrtsən) *vt* 1 overthrow. 2 throw down. *vi* 1 fall. 2 rush. 3 crash. **sich** —**en** *vr* rush, plunge.

Stute (ʃtu:tə) *nf* -**n** mare. —**nfüllen** *n neu* filly.

Stütze (ʃtytsə) *nf* -**n** 1 support, prop. 2 buttress. 3 help. —**n** *vt* prop (up), support.

Subjekt (zup'jɛkt) *n neu* -**e** subject.

Substantiv (zupstan'ti:f) *n neu* -**e** noun, substantive.

subtil (zup'ti:l) *adj* subtle.

Such/e ('zu:xə) *nf* -**n** search. —**en** *vt, vi* seek, search (for).

süchtig ('zyçtiç) *adj* 1 addicted (to). 2 sickly.

Süd (zy:t) *nm also* **Süden** ('zy:dən) south.

Südafrika (zy:t'afrika) *n neu* South Africa.

Südamerika (zyda'mɛrika) *n neu* South America.

südlich ('zy:tliç) *adj* south(ern).

Südost (zyd'ɔst) *nm also* **Südost/en** (zyd'ɔstən) south-east. —**lich** *adj* south-eastern.

Südpol ('zy:tpo:l) *nm* South Pole.

südwärts ('zy:tvɛrts) *adv* southward(s), south.

Südwest (zyd'vɛst) *nm also* **Südwest/en** (zyd-'vɛstən) south-west. —**lich** *adj* south-western.

Sultanine (zulta'ninə) *nf* -**n** *cul* sultana.

Sülze ('zyltsə) *nf* -**n** 1 jellied meat. 2 brine.

Summe ('zumə) *nf* -**n** sum, total.

summen ('zumən) *vt, vi* hum, buzz.

Sumpf (zumpf) *nm* ⁼**e** 1 swamp, marsh, bog. 2 *tech* sump. —**ig** *adj* swampy.

Sund (zunt) *nm* -**e** *naut* straits.

Sünd/e ('zyndə) *nf* -**n** sin. —**enbock** *nm* scapegoat. —**er** *nm* — sinner.

Suppe ('zupə) *nf* -**n** soup.

süß (zy:s) *adj* sweet. —**e** *nf* sweetness. —**igkeit** *nf* -**en** 1 sweetness. 2 *pl* sweets.

Sylvester (zyl'vɛstər) *nm see* **Silvester**.

Symbol (zym'bo:l) *n neu* -**e** symbol. —**isch** *adj* symbolic.

Synagoge (zyna'go:gə) *nf* -**n** synagogue.

Synonym (zyno'ny:m) *n neu* -**e** synonym.

Syphilis ('zy:filis) *nf* syphilis.

Syr/ien ('zy:riən) *n neu* Syria. —**ier** *nm* — Syrian. —**isch** *adj* Syrian.

System (zys'te:m) *n neu* -**e** 1 system. 2 method. 3 doctrine. —**atisch** (zyste'ma:tiʃ) *adj* systematic.

Szene ('stse:nə) *nf* -**n** 1 scene. 2 stage, set. 3 row, argument.

T

Tabak ('ta:bak) *nm* -**e** tobacco. —**händler** *nm* tobacconist.

Tabelle (ta'bɛlə) *nf* -**n** 1 table. 2 index.

Tadel ('ta:dəl) *nm* — 1 blame. 2 reprimand,

reproach. **3** fault. **—los** *adj* blameless, flawless. **—n** *vt* **1** blame. **2** scold, reproach.

Tafel ('taːfəl) *nf* **-n 1** board, panel. **2** blackboard. **3** tablet, bar. **4** index. **5** table. **—n** ('taːfəln) *vt* panel.

Taffet ('tafət) *nm* **-e** *also* **Taft** (taft) taffeta.

Tag (taːk) *nm* **-e 1** day. **2** daylight. **—ebuch** ('taːgəbuːx) *n neu* diary. **—en** ('taːgən) *vi* **1** dawn. **2** meet. **—esordnung** ('taːgəsɔrdnuŋ) *nf* agenda. **—esanbruch** ('taːgəsanbrux) *nm* daybreak. **—lich** ('tɛːkliç) *adj* daily. **—undnachtgleiche** *nf* **-n** equinox. **—ung** ('taːguŋ) *nf* **-en 1** meeting. **2** conference.

Taille ('taljə) *nf* **-n** waist.

Takelwerk ('taːkəlvɛrk) *n neu* rigging.

Takt (takt) *nm* **-e 1** mus time, beat. **2** tact. **—gefühl** *n neu* tact. **—los** *adj* tactless. **—stock** *nm* mus baton. **—voll** *adj* tactful.

Taktik ('taktik) *nf* **-en** tactics.

Tal (taːl) *n neu* **-er** valley.

Talent (ta'lɛnt) *n neu* **-e** talent, gift.

Talg (talk) *nm* **-e 1** suet. **2** tallow.

Talk (talk) *nm* **-e** talc, talcum powder.

tändeln ('tɛndəln) *vi* **1** dawdle. **2** flirt.

Tang (taŋ) *nm* **-e** seaweed.

Tanger ('taŋər) *n neu* Tangier(s).

Tank (taŋk) *nm* **-s 1** (fuel) tank. **2** *mil* tank. **—en** *vi* fill up, refuel. **—stelle** *nf* petrol or filling station.

Tanne ('tanə) *nf* **-n** fir, pine. **—nbaum** *nm* fir, pine tree.

Tante ('tantə) *nf* **-n** aunt.

Tanz (tants) *nm* **-e** dance. **—en** *vt,vi* dance. **—er** ('tɛntsər) *nm* **—, —erin** ('tɛntsarin) *nf* **-nen** dancer. **—gesellschaft** *nf* dance, ball.

Tap/ete (ta'peːtə) *nf* **-n** wallpaper. **—ezieren** (tape'tsiːrən) *vt* paper.

tapfer ('tapfər) *adj* brave, bold. **—keit** *nf* courage.

tappen ('tapən) *vi* grope, fumble.

Tarif (ta'riːf) *nm* **-e 1** price list, tariff. **2** list of fares. **3** wage scale.

tarn/en ('tarnən) *vt* camouflage. **—ung** *nf* **-en** camouflage.

Tasch/e ('taʃə) *nf* **-n 1** pocket. **2** wallet. **3** handbag. **—enbuch** *n neu* pocketbook. **—endieb** *nm* pickpocket. **—engeld** *n neu* pocket money. **—enmesser** *n neu* pocket knife. **—entuch** *n neu* handkerchief.

Tasse ('tasə) *nf* **-n** cup.

Tast/e ('tastə) *nf* **-n** key. **—atur** (tasta'tuːr) *nf*

-en keyboard. **—en** ('tastən) *vi* feel, grope. *vt* touch. **sich —en** *vr* feel one's way.

tat (taːt) *v* see **tun.**

Tat (taːt) *nf* **-en** deed, action, act. **in der Tat** in fact. **—bestand** *nm* **1** facts. **2** state of affairs. **—er** ('tɛːtər) *nm* **—** perpetrator, doer. **—ig** ('tɛːtiç) *adj* **1** active. **2** working, at work. **—igen** ('tɛːtigən) *vt* **1** carry out. **2** *comm* conclude, execute. **—kraft** *nf* energy. **—sache** *nf* fact. **—sächlich** ('tɛːtzɛçliç) *adj* **1** real. **2** factual. **3** effective. *adv* really, indeed.

tätowieren (tɛto'viːrən) *vt* tattoo.

Tatze ('tatsə) *nf* **-n 1** paw. **2** claw.

Tau[1] (tau) *n neu* **-e** cable, rope. **—en** ('tauən) *vt* tow.

Tau[2] (tau) *nm* dew. **—en** ('tauən) *vi* melt. **es taut** dew is falling.

taub (taup) *adj* **1** deaf. **2** empty. **3** numb.

Taube ('taubə) *nf* **-n** pigeon, dove.

tauch/en ('tauxən) *vi* dive, plunge. *vt* plunge, dip. **—sieder** *nm* **—** immersion heater.

Tauf/becken ('taufbɛkən) *n neu also* **Tauf/stein** *nm* (baptismal) font. **—e** *nf* **-n** baptism. **—en** *vt* baptize.

taug/en ('taugən) *vi* be worth, be of use. **—enichts** *nm* **-e** good-for-nothing. **—lich** ('taukliç) *adj* **1** useful. **2** suitable. **3** fit, capable.

Taumel ('taumɛl) *nm* **— 1** staggering. **2** dizziness. **3** frenzy. **—n** *vi* **1** stagger. **2** be giddy or dizzy.

Tausch (tauʃ) *nm* **-e** exchange, swap. **—en** *vt* exchange, swap. **—handel** *nm* barter.

täusch/en ('tɔyʃən) *vt* **1** deceive. **2** cheat. **—ung** *nf* **-en 1** deception. **2** cheating.

tausend ('tauzənt) *adj,nf* thousand. **—ste** *adj* thousandth.

Tauwerk ('tauvɛrk) *n neu* rigging, ropes.

Tax/e ('taksə) *nf* **-n 1** estimate. **2** rate, fee. **3** duty, tax. **—ieren** (ta'ksiːrən) *vt* evaluate, assess.

Taxi ('taksi) *n neu* **-s** taxi.

Techn/ik ('tɛçnik) *nf* **-en 1** skill, technique. **2** technical sciences. **—iker** *nm* **—** technician, engineer. **—isch** *adj* technical. **—ologie** (tɛçnolo'giː) *nf* technology.

Tee (teː) *nm* **-s** tea. **—beutel** *nm* teabag. **—kanne** *nf* teapot. **—löffel** *nm* teaspoon.

Teer (teːr) *nm* **-e** tar.

Teich (taiç) *nm* **-e** pond, pool.

Teig (taik) *nm* **-e 1** dough, batter. **2** paste. **—waren** *nf pl* pasta.

Teil (tail) *nm,neu* **-e 1** part. **2** share, portion. **3**

piece. **—bar** adj divisible. **—chen** ('tailçən) n neu — particle. **—en** vt divide. **—haber** nm — partner, associate. **—nahme** nf 1 participation. 2 interest. 3 sympathy. **—nehmen*** vi take part (in). **—nehmer** nm — participant, member. **—s** adv also **—weise** partly, in part. **—ung** nf -en 1 division. 2 scale.

Tele/gramm (tele'gram) n neu -e telegram. **—fon** see **—phon. —graph** (tele'gra:f) nm -en telegraph. **—graphieren** (telegra'fi:rən) vi,vt wire, telegraph. **—phon** (tele'fo:n) n neu -e telephone. **—phonanruf** nm telephone call. **—phonieren** (telefo'ni:rən) vi,vt telephone. **—phonisch** adj by telephone. **—phonzelle** nf callbox. **—skop** (tele'sko:p) n neu -e telescope.

Teller ('tɛlər) nm — plate.

Tempel ('tɛmpəl) nm — temple.

Temperament (tempəra'mɛnt) n neu -e temperament. 2 liveliness, vivacity. **—voll** adj temperamental.

Temperatur (tempəra'tu:r) nf -en temperature.

Tempo ('tɛmpo) n neu -pi tempo, pace.

Tendenz (tɛn'dɛnts) nf -en tendency.

Tender ('tɛndər) nm — (railway) tender.

Tennis ('tɛnis) n neu tennis. **—platz** nm tennis court.

Teppich ('tɛpiç) nm -e carpet, rug. **—kehrmaschine** nf carpet sweeper.

Termin (tɛr'mi:n) nm -e 1 deadline. 2 term. 3 (fixed) date.

Terminologie (tɛrminolo'gi:) nf -n terminology.

Terpentin (tɛrpɛn'ti:n) n neu turpentine.

Terrasse (tɛ'rasə) nf -n terrace.

Terror ('tɛrɔr) nm terror. **—isieren** (tɛrori'zi:rən) vt terrorize. **—ismus** (tɛro'rismus) nm terrorism. **—ist** (tɛro'rist) nm -en terrorist.

Terz (tɛrts) nf -en mus third. **—ett** (tɛr'tsɛt) n neu -e trio.

Testament (zɛsta'mɛnt) n neu -e 1 (last) will. 2 rel Testament.

testieren (tɛ'sti:rən) vt 1 bequeath. 2 testify.

teuer ('tɔyər) adj 1 expensive. 2 cherished, dear.

Teuf/el ('tɔyfəl) nm — devil. **—elei** (tɔyfə'lai) nf -en devilry. **—lisch** ('tɔyfliʃ) adj devilish, fiendish.

Text (tɛkst) nm -e text.

Textil/ien (tɛks'ti:liən) n pl textiles.

Theater (te'a:tər) n neu — theatre. **—stück** n neu play.

Thema (te:ma) n neu -men theme, topic.

Themse ('tɛmzə) nf Thames.

Theolog/e (teo'lo:gə) nm -n theologian. **—ie** (teolo'gi:) nf theology. **—isch** (teo'lo:giʃ) adj theological.

Theor/etiker (teo're:tikər) nm — theorist, theoretician. **—etisch** (teo're:tiʃ) adj theoretical. **—etisieren** (teoreti'zi:rən) vi theorize. **—ie** (teo'ri:) nf -n theory.

Therapie (tera'pi:) nf -n therapy.

therm/isch ('tɛrmiʃ) adj thermal, thermic. **—odynamik** (tɛrmody'na:mik) nf thermodynamics. **—ometer** (tɛrmo'me:tər) n neu thermometer. **—osflasche** ('tɛrmosflaʃə) nf Tdmk Thermos flask.

Thron (tro:n) nm -e throne. **—erbe** nm heir to the throne. **—folge** nf succession to the throne.

Thunfisch ('tu:nfiʃ) nm tunny (fish).

Thüringen ('ty:riŋən) n neu Thuringia.

Thymian ('ty:mia:n) nm -e thyme.

ticken ('tikən) vi tick, click.

tief (ti:f) adj 1 deep. 2 low. 3 profound. n neu -e (barometric) depression. **—druck** nm low pressure. **—e** nf -n depth. **—kühlen** vt deep-freeze. **—kühlkost** nf frozen food. **—kühltruhe** nf freezer.

Tiegel ('ti:gəl) nm -e 1 saucepan. 2 crucible.

Tier (ti:r) n neu -e animal, beast. **—arzt** nm veterinary surgeon, vet. **—isch** adj 1 animal. 2 brutal, brutish. **—kreis** nm zodiac.

Tiger ('ti:gər) nm — tiger.

tilg/en ('tilgən) vt 1 erase. 2 eradicate. 3 cancel. 4 repay. **—ung** nf -en 1 eradiction. 2 cancellation. 3 repayment.

Tint/e ('tintə) nf -n ink. **in der Tinte sitzen** be in a nice mess. **—enfaß** n neu inkwell.

tippen ('tipən) vt,vi 1 type. 2 tap.

Tirol (ti'ro:l) n neu Tyrol.

Tisch (tiʃ) nm -e 1 table. 2 board. **—decke** n also **—tuch** n neu tablecloth. **—ler** ('tiʃlər) nm — 1 joiner, cabinetmaker. 2 carpenter. **—tennis** n neu table tennis.

Titel ('ti:təl) nm — title.

titulieren (titu'li:rən) vt give a title to, entitle.

Toast (to:st) nm -e toast. **—brot** n neu toasting bread. **—er** nm — toaster.

tob/en ('to:bən) vi 1 rage. 2 roar.

Tochter ('tɔxtər) nf = daughter.

Tod (to:t) nm -e death. **—esanzeige** ('to:dəsantsaigə) nf obituary. **—esfall** ('to:dəsfal) nm death, casualty. **—eskampf** ('to:dəskampf) nm death agony. **—esstrafe** ('to:dəsʃtra:fə) nf death penalty. **—feind** ('to:tfaint) nm mortal enemy. **—lich** ('tœ:tliç) adj deadly, fatal. **—müde** ('to:tmy:də) *adj* dead tired.

Toilette (toa'lɛtə) *nf* **-n** 1 toilet. 2 dressing table. 3 toilette. **—npapier** *n neu* toilet paper.

toleran/t (tole'rant) *adj* tolerant. **—z** (tole'rants) *nf* 1 toleration. 2 tolerance.

toll (tɔl) *adj* 1 mad. 2 raving. 3 wild. 4 mad terrific. **—heit** *nf* **-en** 1 madness. 2 mad trick. **—kühn** *adj* foolhardy. **—wut** *nf* rabies.

Tölpel ('tœlpəl) *nm* — clumsy person, fool.

Tomate (to'ma:tə) *nf* **-n** tomato.

Ton [1] (ton) *nm* **-e** clay.

Ton [2] (to:n) *nm* =e 1 sound. 2 *mus* tone, note. 3 fashion. 4 stress, accent. **—art** *nf mus* key. **—band** *n neu* (magnetic) tape. **—bandgerät** *n neu* tape-recorder. **—en** ('tœ:nən) *vi* resound. *vt* shade, tint. **—fall** *nm* intonation. **—leiter** *nf mus* scale.

Tonne ('tɔnə) *nf* **-n** 1 ton. 2 barrel.

Topf (tɔpf) *nm* =e pot. **—er** ('tœpfər) *nm* — potter. **—erwaren** ('tœpfərvɛ:rən) *nf pl* pottery, earthenware.

Tor [1] (to:r) *n neu* **-e** 1 gate, door. 2 *sport* goal.

Tor [2] (to:r) *nm* **-en** fool. **—heit** *nf* **-en** folly. **—icht** ('tœ:riçt) *adj* foolish.

Torf (tɔrf) *nm* peat.

torkeln ('tɔrkəln) *vi* stagger.

Torpedo (tɔr'pe:do) *nm* **-s** torpedo.

Torte ('tɔrtə) *nf* **-n** tart, flan.

tot (to:t) *adj* dead. **Totes Meer** *n neu* Dead Sea.

total (to'ta:l) *adj* total, complete. **—itär** (totali'tɛ:r) *adj* totalitarian.

Tote(r) ('to:tə) *nm* 1 dead man. 2 corpse.

töten ('tœ:tən) *vt* kill.

Totenbett ('to:tənbɛt) *n neu* deathbed.

Totengräber ('to:təngrɛ:bər) *nm* — gravedigger.

Totenhemd ('to:tənhɛmt) *n neu* shroud.

totgeboren ('to:tgəbo:rən) *adj* still-born.

sich totlachen ('to:tlaxən) *vr* roar with laughter, kill oneself laughing.

totschießen* ('to:tʃi:sən) *vt* shoot dead.

Totschlag ('to:tʃlak) *nm* manslaughter.

totschweigen* ('to:tʃvaigən) *vt* hush up.

totsicher ('to:tziçər) *adj* dead certain.

Tour (tu:r) *nf* **-en** 1 tour, trip. 2 turn. **—ist** (tu'rist) *nm* **-en** tourist.

Trab (tra:p) *nm* trot. **—en** ('tra:bən) *vi* trot.

Tracht (traxt) *nf* **-en** 1 (national) costume. 2 dress. 3 load.

Tradition (traditsi'o:n) *nf* **-en** tradition. **—ell** (traditsio'nɛl) *adj* traditional.

traf (tra:f) *v see* **treffen.**

träg/e ('trɛ:gə) *adj* lazy, sluggish. **—heit** ('trɛ:khait) *nf* laziness, sluggishness.

trag/en* ('tra:gən) *vt* 1 carry. 2 wear. 3 bear, endure. 4 support. **—bahre** ('tra:kba:rə) *nf* **-n** stretcher. **—er** ('trɛ:gər) *nm* — 1 porter. 2 carrier. 3 support. 4 pillar, beam. **—weite** ('tra:kvaitə) *nf* 1 range. 2 importance.

trag/isch ('tra:giʃ) *adj* tragic. **—ödie** (tra-'gœ:diə) *nf* **-n** tragedy.

Train/er ('trɛ:nər) *nm* — *sport* trainer, coach. **—ing** *n neu* training.

Traktor ('traktɔr) *nm* **-en** tractor.

trampeln ('trampəln) *vi* trample, stamp.

Tran (tra:n) *nm* **-e** blubber, whale oil.

tranchieren (trã:'ʃi:rən) *vt* carve (up).

Träne ('trɛ:nə) *nf* **-n** tear. **—ngas** *n neu* tear-gas.

trank (traŋk) *v see* **trinken.**

transatlantisch (transat'lantiʃ) *adj* transatlantic.

transitiv ('tranziti:f) *adj* transitive.

Transmission (transmisi'o:n) *nf* **-en** transmission.

Transport (trans'pɔrt) *nm* **-e** transport. **—ieren** (transpɔr'ti:rən) *vt* transport.

trat (tra:t) *v see* **treten.**

Traube ('traubə) *nf* **-n** 1 grape. 2 bunch of grapes.

trau/en ('trauən) *vi* trust. *vt* (of a priest, etc.) marry (a man and a woman). **sich trauen** *vr* dare, venture. **—ring** *nm* wedding-ring. **—ung** *nf* **-en** wedding.

Trau/er ('trauər) *nf* 1 sorrow. 2 mourning. **—ern** *vi* mourn. **—erspiel** *n neu* tragedy. **—rig** ('trauriç) *adj* sad.

Trauf/e ('traufə) *nf* **-n** 1 eaves. 2 gutter. **—eln** ('trɔyfəln) *vi* drip, sprinkle. **—rinne** *nf* **-n** gutter (of a house).

traulich ('trauliç) *adj* cosy, familiar.

Traum (traum) *nm* =e dream. **—en** ('trɔymən) *vt,vi* dream (of). **—er** ('trɔymər) *nm* — dreamer. **—haft** *adj* dreamlike.

treff/en* ('trɛfən) *vt,vi* 1 hit, strike. 2 befall. 3 meet, encounter. **sich treffen** *vr* 1 meet. 2 happen. **eine Entscheidung treffen** come to a decision. **—en** *n neu* — meeting. **—er** *nm* — (direct or lucky) hit. **—lich** *adj* excellent. **—punkt** *nm* meeting place.

treib/en* ('traibən) *vt* 1 drive. 2 urge. 3 force. 4 carry on, do. 5 work (metal). *vi* drift. *n neu* activity. **—haus** ('traiphaus) n neu hothouse. **—stoff** ('traipʃtɔf) nm fuel.

trenn/bar ('trɛnbaːr) adj divisible. **—en** vt 1 divide, separate. 2 cut off (a telephone call). **—ung** nf -en separation.

Treppe ('trɛpə) nf -n stairs, staircase. **—enhaus** n neu stairwell.

tret/en* ('treːtən) vi 1 step, walk. 2 pedal. vt 1 kick. 2 tread on. **—mühle** nf treadmill.

treu (trɔy) adj 1 faithful, loyal. 2 accurate. **—bruch** nm breach of faith. **—e** nf loyalty. **—händer** ('trɔyhɛndər) nm — trustee. **—lich** adv faithfully. **—los** adj disloyal.

Tribut (tri'buːt) nm -e tribute.

Trichter ('trɪçtər) nm - 1 funnel. 2 crater.

Trick (trɪk) nm -s trick, dodge. **—film** nm animated cartoon.

trieb (triːp) v see **treiben**.

Trieb (triːp) nm -e 1 drive, force. 2 impulse. 3 bot shoot, sprout. 4 instinct. **—feder** nf (main)spring. **—haft** adj 1 instinctive. 2 unbridled. **—kraft** nf momentum. **—sand** nm quicksand.

triefen* ('triːfən) vi drip.

trifft (trɪft) v see **treffen**.

triftig ('trɪftɪç) adj 1 conclusive. 2 valid.

Trigonometrie (trigonome'triː) nf trigonometry.

Triller ('trɪlər) nm — mus trill.

trimmen ('trɪmən) vt trim.

trink/bar ('trɪŋkbaːr) adj drinkable. **—en*** vt, vi drink. **—geld** n neu tip.

Tripper ('trɪpər) nm gonorrhoea.

tritt (trɪt) v see **treten**.

Tritt (trɪt) nm -e 1 step. 2 kick.

Triumph (tri'umf) nm -e triumph. **—ieren** (trium'fiːrən) vi triumph.

trock/en* ('trɔkən) adj dry. **—nen** vt, vi dry.

Trog (troːk) nm ̈e trough.

Tromm/el ('trɔməl) nf -n drum. **—eln** vi drum. **—ler** ('trɔmlər) nm — drummer.

Trompete (trɔm'peːtə) nf -n trumpet.

Trop/en ('troːpən) n pl tropics. **—enhelm** nm sun-helmet. **—isch** adj tropical.

Tropf (trɔpf) nm -e simpleton. ̈**—eln** ('trœpfəln) vt, vi drip, trickle. **—en** ('trɔpfən) nm — drop. vt, vi drip, trickle.

Trost (troːst) nm consolation. **—los** adj 1 inconsolable. 2 bleak, desolate.

Trott (trɔt) nm -e trot.

Trottel ('trɔtəl) nm — idiot.

trotz (trɔts) prep in spite of, despite. nm 1 defiance. 2 obstinacy. **jemandem zum Trotz**

in defiance of someone. **—dem** ('trɔtsdeːm) adv nevertheless. conj notwithstanding. **—ig** adj defiant, obstinate.

trüb (tryːp) adj 1 gloomy, dismal. 2 cloudy, muddy. **—en** ('tryːbən) vt 1 make gloomy. 2 dull, tarnish. **—sal** nf -e distress, affliction. **—sinn** nm melancholy, depression.

Trug (truːk) nm 1 deceit, deception. 2 fraud. **—bild** n neu phantom, mirage. ̈**—en*** ('tryː-gən) vt deceive. vi be deceptive. **—erisch** ('tryːgərɪʃ) adj 1 deceptive. 2 deceitful.

Trümmer ('trymər) n neu pl 1 ruins. 2 rubble.

Trumpf (trumpf) nm ̈e trump. **—en** vt, vi trump.

Trunk (truŋk) nm ̈e drink. **—en** adj drunk, drunken. **—sucht** nf alcoholism.

Trupp (trup) nm -s band, party. **—e** nf -n 1 troop. 2 company, unit. 3 pl troops.

Truthahn ('truːthaːn) nm turkey(-cock).

Tschech/e ('tʃɛçə) nm -n Czech. **—isch** adj Czech. n neu Czech (language). **—oslowakei** (tʃɛçoslova'kai) nf Czechoslovakia. **—oslo-wakisch** adj Czechoslovakian.

Tuberkulose (tuberku'loːzə) nf tuberculosis.

Tuch (tuːx) n neu -e 1 cloth. 2 rag, duster. 3 scarf.

tüchtig ('tyçtɪç) adj 1 able. 2 efficient.

Tück/e ('tykə) nf -n malice, spite. **—isch** adj 1 malicious. 2 insidious.

Tugend ('tuːgənt) nf -en virtue. **—haft** adj virtuous.

Tulpe ('tulpə) nf -n tulip.

tun* (tuːn) vt, vi 1 do. 2 make. 3 act. 4 put. 5 pretend. n doings. **—lich** adj practicable.

Tünche ('tynçə) nf -n whitewash, distemper. **—n** vt whitewash, distemper.

Tunke ('tuŋkə) nf -n sauce, gravy. **—n** vt 1 dip. 2 steep.

Tunnel ('tunəl) nm — tunnel.

Tür (tyːr) nf -en door, doorway.

Türk/e ('tyrkə) nm Turk. **—ei** (tyr'kai) nf Turkey. **—isch** adj Turkish. n neu Turkish (language).

Türkis (tyr'kiːs) nm -e turquoise.

Turm (turm) nm ̈e 1 tower, steeple. 2 game rook, castle. ̈**—chen** ('tyrmçən) n neu — turret.

turn/en ('turnən) vi do gymnastics. n neu gymnastics. **—halle** nf gymnasium.

Turnier (tur'niːr) n neu -e tournament.

Tusch/e ('tuʃə) nf -n Indian ink. **—farbe** nf water-colour.

tuscheln ('tuʃəln) vi whisper.

Tüte ('ty:tə) *nf* -n 1 paper bag. 2 carrier bag.

Twen (tvɛn) *nm* -s man or woman in his or her twenties.

Typ (ty:p) *nm* -en 1 type. 2 model. **—isch** *adj* typical.

Typhus ('ty:fus) *nm* typhoid (fever).

Tyrann (ty'ran) *nm* -en tyrant. **—ei** (tyra'nai) *nf* tyranny.

U

U-Bahn ('u:ba:n) *nf* underground (railway).

übel ('y:bəl) *adj* 1 evil, wrong. 2 bad, nasty. 3 sick. *n neu* — 1 evil. 2 nuisance. 3 disease. **—keit** *nf* -en nausea, sickness. **—nehmen°** *vt* take amiss, take badly.

üben ('y:bən) *vt,vi* practise, exercise.

über ('y:bər) *prep* 1 over. 2 above. 3 (up)on. 4 beyond, across. 5 about.

überall (y:bər'al) *adv* everywhere.

überanstrengen (y:bər'anʃtrɛŋən) *vt* overexert.

überaus ('y:braus) *adv* exceedingly.

überbelichten ('y:bərbəliçtən) *vt* overexpose (a photograph).

überbieten (y:bər'bi:tən) *vt* outbid.

Überbleibsel ('y:bərblaipsəl) *n neu* — remainder, remnant.

Überblick ('y:bərblik) *nm* 1 survey. 2 summary. **—en** (y:bər'blikən) *vt* survey.

überbringen° (y:bər'briŋən) *vt* deliver, hand over.

überdies (y:bər'di:s) *adv* besides, moreover.

Überdruß ('y:bərdrus) *nm* 1 disgust. 2 boredom, weariness.

übereilen (y:bər'ailən) *vt* rush, hurry.

überein/ander (y:bərain'andər) *adv* one on top of another. **—kommen°** (y:bər'ainkɔmən) *vi* come to an agreement. *n neu* — agreement. **—kunft** (y:bər'ainkunft) *nf* -̈e agreement, compromise. **—stimmen** (y:bər'ainʃtimən) *vi* agree.

überfahr/en° ('y:bərfa:rən) *vt* 1 drive or pass over. 2 run over. **—t** *nf* passage, crossing.

Überfall ('y:bərfal) *nm* surprise attack, raid. **—en°** (y:bər'falən) *vt* attack suddenly. **—ig** ('y:bərfɛliç) *adj* overdue.

Über/fluß ('y:bərflus) *nm* abundance, excess. **—flüssig** ('y:bərflysiç) *adj* superfluous, excess.

überfordern (y:bər'fɔrdərn) *vt* overcharge.

überführ/en ('y:bərfy:rən) *vt* 1 transport. 2 convict. 3 convince. **—ung** (y:bər'fy:ruŋ) *nf* 1 transportation. 2 fly-over.

Übergabe ('y:bərga:bə) *nf* 1 surrender. 2 delivery.

Übergang ('y:bərgaŋ) *nm* 1 passage, crossing. 2 transition.

übergeben° ('y:bərge:bən) *vt* hand over, deliver. **sich übergeben** *vr* vomit.

übergehen° (*vi* 'y:bərge:ən; *vt* y:bər'ge:ən) *vi* 1 pass or cross over. 2 change. *vt* 1 omit. 2 pass or run over. 3 revise.

Übergewicht ('y:bərgeviçt) *n neu* -e 1 overweight. 2 preponderance.

überhandnehmen° (y:bər'hantne:mən) *vi* increase or spread rapidly.

überhäufen (y:bər'hɔyfən) *vt* overwhelm.

überhaupt (y:bər'haupt) *adv* 1 in general. 2 altogether. 3 at all.

überheblich (y:bər'he:pliç) *adj* presumptuous.

überholen ('y:bərho:lən) *vt* fetch or bring over. (y:bər'ho:lən) *vt* 1 overtake. 2 recondition.

überkochen ('y:bərkɔxən) *vi* boil over.

überkommen° (y:bər'kɔmən) *vt* 1 obtain, receive. 2 befall.

überlassen° (y:bər'lasən) *vt* **jemandem etwas überlassen** leave something to someone.

überlaufen° ('y:bərlaufən) *vi* run on or go over.

überleben° (y:bər'le:bən) *vt* survive, outlive.

überleg/en (y:bər'le:gən) *vt* consider. *adj* superior. **—ung** *nf* -en consideration.

überliefer/n (y:bər'li:fərn) *vt* 1 hand down. 2 deliver. 3 surrender. **—ung** *nf* -en 1 tradition. 2 delivery. 3 surrender.

überlisten (y:bər'listən) *vt* outwit.

Übermacht ('y:bərmaxt) *nf* superiority, superior strength.

übermäßig ('y:bərmɛsiç) *adj* excessive.

Übermensch ('y:bərmɛnʃ) *nm* superman.

übermitteln (y:bər'mitəln) *vt* 1 transmit. 2 convey.

übermorgen ('y:bərmɔrgən) *adv* the day after tomorrow.

Übermut ('y:bərmu:t) *nm* 1 high spirits. 2 insolence. 3 arrogance. **—ig** ('y:bərmy:tiç) *adj* 1 high-spirited. 2 insolent. 3 arrogant.

übernachten (y:bər'naxtən) *vi* spend the night.

übernehmen° (y:bər'ne:mən) *vt* 1 take over. 2 undertake.

überprüfen (y:bər'pry:fən) *vt* examine, check.

überqueren (y:bər'kve:rən) *vt* traverse, cross.

überragen (y:bər'ra:gən) *vt* surpass.

überrasch/en (y:bər'raʃən) *vt* surprise. **—ung** *nf* -en surprise.

überreden (y:bər're:dən) *vt* persuade.

überreichen (y:bər'raiçən) *vt* 1 hand over, present. 2 submit.

Überrest (y:bərrest) *nm* remains, remnant.

überrumpeln (y:bər'rumpəln) *vt* take unawares.

übers ('y:bərs) contraction of **über das.**

überschätzen (y:bər'ʃɛtsən) *vt* overrate, overestimate.

überschauen (y:bər'ʃauən) *vt* survey.

überschreiten (y:bər'ʃraitən) *vt* 1 step over. 2 exceed, transgress.

Überschrift ('y:bərʃrift) *nf* title, heading.

Überschuh ('y:bərʃu:) *nm* overshoe.

Überschuß ('y:bərʃus) *nm* surplus.

überschwemm/en (y:bər'ʃvɛmən) *vt* flood, swamp. **—ung** *nf* **-en** flood, inundation.

überschwenglich ('y:bərʃvɛŋliç) *adj* effusive, rapturous.

Übersee ('y:bərze:) *nf* overseas.

übersehen (y:bər'ze:ən) *vt* 1 overlook. 2 survey.

übersenden (y:bər'zɛndən) *vt* send, forward.

übersetz/en ('y:bərzɛtsən) *vt* ferry over. *vi* pass. (y:bər'zɛtsən) *vt* translate. **—ung** (y:bər'zɛtsuŋ) *nf* **-en** 1 translation. 2 *tech* gear.

Übersicht (y:bərziçt) *nf* **-en** survey, summary. **—lich** *adj* easily understood, clear.

übersiedeln ('y:bərzi:dəln) *vi* 1 (re)move. 2 emigrate.

übersinnlich ('y:bərzinliç) *adj* psychic, supernatural.

überspannen (y:bər'ʃpanən) *vt* 1 stretch over, cover. 2 overstrain. 3 exaggerate.

überspringen (vi 'y:bərʃpriŋən; vt y:bər'ʃpriŋən) *vi* leap or jump over. *vt* 1 leap or jump. 2 omit.

überstehen (y:bər'ʃte:ən) *vt* survive, overcome.

Überstunden (y:bərʃtundən) *nf pl* overtime.

überstürzen (y:bər'ʃtyrtsən) *vt* hurry, rush.

übertrag/en (y:bər'tra:gən) *vt* 1 carry over. 2 transport. 3 transmit, broadcast. 4 translate. **—ung** *nf* **-en** 1 transfer. 2 transportation. 3 transmission.

übertreffen (y:bər'trɛfən) *vt* surpass, excel, outdo.

übertreiben (y:bər'traibən) *vt* 1 overdo. 2 exaggerate.

übertreten (vi 'y:bərtre:tən; vt y:bər'tre:tən) *vi* go or change over. *vt* violate, infringe.

übertrieben (y:bər'tri:bən) *adj* overdone, exaggerated.

überwachen (y:bər'vaxən) *vt* supervise, control.

überwältigen (y:bər'vɛltigən) *vt* overpower.

überweis/en (y:bər'vaizən) *vt* 1 transfer. 2 remit. **—ung** *nf* **-en** 1 remittance. 2 transfer.

überwiegen (y:bər'vi:gən) *vt* outweigh, prevail.

überwinden (y:bər'vindən) *vt* overcome.

überzeug/en (y:bər'tsɔygən) *vt* convince. **—ung** *nf* **-en** conviction.

überzieh/en ('y:bərtsi:ən) *vt* put on. (y:bər'tsi:ən) *vt* 1 cover. 2 overdraw (an account).

Überzug (y:bərtsu:k) *nm* coating, cover.

üblich ('y:bliç) *adj* customary, usual.

U-Boot ('u:bo:t) *n neu* submarine.

übrig ('y:briç) *adj* left over, remaining. **—ens** ('y:brigəns) *adv* 1 by the way. 2 besides. 3 after all.

Übung ('y:buŋ) *nf* **-en** 1 exercise. 2 practice. 3 use.

Ufer ('u:fər) *n neu* — 1 bank. 2 shore.

Uhr (u:r) *nf* **-en** 1 clock, watch. 2 time, hour. **wieviel Uhr ist es?** what time is it? **—feder** *nf* watch spring.

ulkig ('ulkiç) *adj* funny, comical.

Ulme ('ulmə) *nf* **-n** elm.

um (um) *prep* 1 (a)round, about. 2 at, by, for. 3 on account of. *adv* 1 around, about. 2 over, up, finished. **um...zu** *conj* in order to.

umändern ('umɛndərn) *vt* alter, modify.

umarm/en (um'armən) *vt* embrace, hug. **—ung** *nf* embrace, hug.

umbauen ('umbauən) *vt* rebuild, remodel.

umbilden ('umbildən) *vt* 1 transform. 2 reform. 3 reconstruct.

umbinden ('umbindən) *vt* 1 put on. 2 tie round.

sich umblicken ('umblikən) *vr* look round or about.

umbringen ('umbriŋən) *vt* kill.

umdrehen ('umdre:ən) *vt* turn or twist round. **sich umdrehen** *vr* turn round.

umeinander (umain'andər) *adv* (a)round each other.

umfahren ('umfa:rən) *vt* knock down, run over. (um'fa:rən) *vt* drive round.

umfallen ('umfalən) *vi* 1 fall down or over. 2 collapse.

Umfang ('umfaŋ) *nm* 1 circumference. 2 girth. 3 extent, range.

umfassen (um'fasən) *vt* 1 include. 2 enclose. 3 embrace.

Umfrage ('umfra:gə) *nf* inquiry, poll.

Umgang ('umgaŋ) *nm* 1 relations, (social)

intercourse. 2 rotation, circuit. **—ssprache** *nf* colloquial or everyday speech.

umgeb/en* (um'ge:bən) *vt* surround. **—ung** *nf* **-en** surroundings, environment.

umgeh/en* (*vi* 'umge:ən; *vt* um'ge:ən) *vi* 1 go round. 2 associate (with). *vt* 1 go round. 2 avoid. **—ungsstraße** (um'ge:-uŋsʃtra:sə) *nf* by-pass.

umgekehrt ('umgəke:rt) *adj* 1 reversed. 2 contrary. *adv* vice versa.

umgraben* ('umgra:bən) *vt* dig up.

umher (um'he:r) *adv* about, around. **—gehen*** *vi* walk about. **—schweifen** *vi* wander, roam.

umhüllen (um'hylən) *vt* wrap (up), cover.

Umkehr (umke:r) *nf* return. **—en** *vi,vt* turn round.

umkippen ('umkipən) *vt,vi* turn or tip over.

umklammern (um'klamərn) *vt* clasp, cling (to).

sich umkleiden (um'klaidən) *vr* change (one's clothes).

umkommen* ('umkɔmən) *vi* 1 die, perish. 2 (of food) spoil.

Umkreis ('umkrais) *nm* 1 circumference. 2 surroundings.

Umlauf ('umlauf) *nm* 1 circulation. 2 rotation. **—en*** (*vt* um'laufən; *vi* 'umlaufən) *vt* move or run round. *vi* 1 circulate. 2 rotate.

Umlaut ('umlaut) *nm* **-e** vowel modification, umlaut.

umleit/en ('umlaitən) *vt* divert. **—ung** *nf* **-en** diversion.

umlernen ('umlɛrnən) *vt* relearn.

umrahmen (um'ra:mən) *vt* frame.

umrechn/en (um'rɛçnən) *vt* convert, exchange. **—ung** *nf* conversion, exchange.

umreißen (um'raisən) *vt* outline, sketch. ('umraisən) *vt* pull down.

umringen (um'riŋən) *vt* surround.

Umriß ('umris) *nm* outline, sketch.

umrühren (um'ry:rən) *vt* stir up or around.

ums (ums) contraction of **um das.**

Umsatz ('umzats) *nm comm* 1 turnover. 2 sale.

umschalten ('umʃaltən) *vt* 1 switch over. 2 change over.

umschauen ('umʃauən) *vi* look round.

Umschlag ('umʃla:k) *nm* 1 envelope. 2 cover, wrapper. 3 hem, cuff, turn-up. 4 (sudden) change, transformation. 5 poultice. 6 *comm* turnover. **—en*** (um'ʃla:gən) *vi* 1 turn or tip over. 2 change. ('umʃla:gən) *vt* 1 knock down or over. 2 turn over.

umschließen* (um'ʃli:sən) *vt* enclose, embrace.

umschulen ('umʃu:lən) *vt* 1 retrain, re-educate. 2 change (a child's) school.

Umschwung ('umʃvuŋ) *nm* 1 change. 2 *tech* revolution.

sich umsehen* ('umze:ən) *vr* 1 look round or back. 2 look out (for).

umsetzen ('umzɛtsən) *vt* 1 transpose. 2 transform. 3 sell, turn over.

umsichtig ('umziçtiç) *adj* cautious, prudent.

umsiedeln ('umzi:dəln) *vt,vi* resettle.

umsonst (um'zɔnst) *adv* 1 in vain. 2 free, for nothing.

Umstand ('umʃtant) *nm* 1 circumstance, condition. 2 *pl* ceremonies, fuss. **in anderen Umständen** *inf* pregnant, expecting. **—lich** ('umʃtɛntliç) *adj* 1 complicated, involved. 2 ceremonious.

umsteigen* ('umʃtaigən) *vi* change (trains or buses).

umstoßen* ('umʃto:sən) *vt* 1 overturn, overthrow. 2 invalidate. 3 reverse (a judgment).

Umsturz ('umʃturts) *nm* 1 overthrow, downfall. 2 revolution. **—en** ('umʃtyrtsən) *vt* overthrow. *vi* fall down.

umtauschen ('umtauʃən) *vt* exchange.

umwälzen ('umvɛltsən) *vt* 1 revolutionize. 2 roll round. **sich umwälzen** *vr* whirl round.

Umweg ('umve:k) *nm* roundabout way, detour.

Umwelt ('umvɛlt) *nf* environment.

umwenden* ('umvɛndən) *vt* turn over. **sich umwenden** *vr* turn back or round.

umwerben* (um'vɛrbən) *vt* seek the favour of, court.

umwerfen* ('umvɛrfən) *vt* 1 overturn. 2 put on.

umziehen* ('umtsi:ən) *vt* change (one's clothing). *vi* remove, move (house).

umzingeln (um'tsiŋəln) *vt* encircle, surround.

Umzug ('umtsu:k) *nm* 1 removal. 2 procession.

unabänderlich (unap'ɛndərliç) *adj* 1 unchangeable. 2 irrevocable.

unabhängig ('unaphɛŋiç) *adj* independent. **—keit** *nf* independence.

unachtsam ('unaxtza:m) *adj* inattentive.

unanfechtbar (unan'fɛçtba:r) *adj* incontestable.

unangemessen ('unangəmɛsən) *adj* 1 inadequate. 2 improper. 3 unsuitable.

unangenehm ('unangəne:m) *adj* unpleasant.

Unannehmlichkeit ('unanne:mliçkait) *nf* **-en** inconvenience, unpleasantness.

unanständig ('unanʃtɛndiç) *adj* indecent.

unartig ('una:rtiç) *adj* naughty, badly behaved.

unauffällig ('unauffɛliç) *adj* 1 inconspicuous. 2 unassuming.

unausstehlich (unaus'ʃteːliç) *adj* insufferable.

unbändig ('unbɛndiç) *adj* 1 unruly. 2 *inf* tremendous, excessive.

unbeachtet ('unbaaxtət) *adj* unnoticed.

unbedeutend ('unbədɔytənt) *adj* insignificant.

unbedingt ('unbədiŋt) *adj* 1 unconditional, absolute. 2 definite. *adv* definitely.

Unbehag/en ('unbəhaːgən) *n neu* 1 uneasiness. 2 discomfort. **—lich** (unbə'haːkliç) *adj* uneasy, uncomfortable.

unbeholfen ('unbəhɔlfən) *adj* clumsy, awkward.

unbekümmert (unbə'kymərt) *adj* 1 carefree, unconcerned. 2 careless.

unbemittelt ('unbəmitəlt) *adj* without means.

unbequem ('unbəkveːm) *adj* 1 uncomfortable. 2 inconvenient. **—lichkeit** *nf* 1 discomfort. 2 inconvenience.

unberufen (unbə'ruːfən) *adj* uncalled for. *interj* touch wood!

unbeschreiblich (unbə'ʃraipliç) *adj* indescribable.

unbesonnen ('unbəzɔnən) *adj* thoughtless, rash.

unbestimmt ('unbəʃtimt) *adj* indefinite.

unbestreitbar (unbə'ʃtraitbaːr) *adj* indisputable.

unbestritten ('unbəʃtritən) *adj* undisputed.

unbeweglich ('unbəveːkliç) *adj* 1 immovable. 2 motionless.

unbewußt ('unbəvust) *adj* 1 unconscious, unknowing. 2 instinctive, involuntary.

unbotmäßig ('unboːtmɛːsiç) *adj* unruly.

unbrauchbar ('unbrauxbaːr) *adj* useless, unserviceable.

und (unt) *conj* and. **na und?** so what?

undankbar ('undaŋkbaːr) *adj* ungrateful.

undenkbar (un'dɛŋkbaːr) *adj* unthinkable.

undeutlich ('undɔytliç) *adj* indistinct, blurred.

undurchdringlich ('undurçdriŋliç) *adj* impenetrable.

uneben ('uneːbən) *adj* 1 uneven. 2 rough.

unecht ('unɛçt) *adj* artificial, counterfeit.

unehelich ('uneːəliç) *adj* (of a child) illegitimate.

unehrlich ('uneːrliç) *adj* dishonest.

unendlich (un'ɛntliç) *adj* endless, infinite.

unentbehrlich (unɛnt'beːrliç) *adj* indispensable.

unerbittlich (unɛr'bitliç) *adj* relentless, unrelenting, unyielding.

unerfahren ('unɛrfaːrən) *adj* inexperienced.

unerhört (unɛr'høːrt) *adj* 1 unheard of. 2 outrageous.

unerläßlich (unɛr'lɛsliç) *adj* indispensable.

unerlaubt ('unɛrlaupt) *adj* 1 unauthorized. 2 illegal.

unermeßlich (unɛr'mɛsliç) *adj* immeasurable.

unermüdlich (unɛr'myːtliç) *adj* untiring.

unerreicht (unɛr'raiçt) *adj* unequalled.

unerschrocken ('unɛrʃrɔkən) *adj* undaunted.

unerwünscht ('unɛrvynʃt) *adj* undesirable, unwelcome.

unfähig ('unfɛːiç) *adj* 1 incapable. 2 incompetent. **—keit** *nf* 1 incapacity. 2 incompetence.

Unfall ('unfal) *nm* 1 accident. 2 disaster.

unfaßbar ('unfasbaːr) *adj* inconceivable.

unfehlbar (un'feːlbaːr) *adj* 1 unfailing. 2 infallible.

unfreundlich ('unfrɔyntliç) *adj* unfriendly.

Unfug ('unfuːk) *nm* 1 mischief. 2 offence. 3 disturbance. 4 (public) nuisance. **—sam** ('unfyːkzaːm) *adj* unruly, unmanageable.

Ungar ('uŋgar) *nm* **-n** Hungarian. **—isch** *adj* Hungarian. *n neu* Hungarian (language). **—n** *n neu* Hungary.

ungeachtet ('ungəaxtət) *prep* regardless of.

ungebührlich ('ungəbyːrliç) *adj* improper.

Ungeduld ('ungədult) *nf* impatience. **—ig** ('ungəduldiç) *adj* impatient.

ungefähr ('ungəfɛːr) *adv* about, approximately.

ungeheuer ('ungəhɔyər) *adj* huge, monstrous. *n neu* — monster. **—lich** (ungə'hɔyərliç) *adj* monstrous.

ungekürzt ('ungəkyrtst) *adj* unabridged.

ungelegen ('ungəleːgən) *adj* inconvenient.

Ungemach ('ungəmaːx) *n neu* **-e** 1 adversity. 2 discomfort.

ungemein ('ungəmain) *adj* uncommon, extraordinary.

ungemütlich ('ungəmyːtliç) *adj* unpleasant, uncomfortable.

ungeniert ('unʒəniːrt) *adj* unceremonious.

ungeraten ('ungəraːtən) *adj* 1 (of children) spoilt. 2 degenerate.

ungerecht ('ungərɛçt) *adj* unjust.

ungereimt ('ungəraimt) *adj* absurd.

ungern ('ungɛrn) *adv* reluctantly, unwillingly.

ungestüm ('ungəʃtyːm) *adj* 1 impetuous. 2 violent. *n neu* 1 impetuosity. 2 violence.

unge/wöhnlich ('ungəvœːnliç) *adj* unusual, uncommon, strange. **—wohnt** ('ungəvoːnt) *adj* unaccustomed.

Ungeziefer ('ungətsiːfər) *n neu* — vermin.

ungezogen ('ungətsoːgən) *adj* 1 ill-mannered, uncivil, rude. 2 naughty, disobedient.

115

ungezwungen ('ungətsvuŋən) adj natural, unconstrained, easy(-going).

ungläubig ('unglɔybiç) adj incredulous, unbelieving.

unglaublich ('unglauplíç) adj unbelievable, incredible.

ungleich ('unglaiç) adj unequal, unlike.

Unglimpf ('unglimpf) nm 1 insult. 2 harshness.

Unglück ('unglyk) n neu misfortune. —**lich** adj 1 unhappy. 2 unfortunate. —**licherweise** adv unfortunately. —**sfall** nm accident.

Ungnade (ungna:də) nf 1 disgrace. 2 displeasure.

ungünstig (ungynstiç) adj unfavourable.

unhaltbar ('unhaltba:r) adj untenable.

Unheil ('unhail) n neu 1 harm. 2 disaster, misfortune. —**bar** adj incurable.

unheimlich ('unhaimliç) adj 1 weird, sinister, uncanny. 2 inf tremendous, terrific.

universal (univɛr'za:l) adj universal.

Universität (univɛrzi'tɛ:t) nf -**en** university.

Universum (uni'vɛrzum) n neu universe.

unkennt/lich ('unkɛntliç) adj unrecognizable. —**nis** nf ignorance.

unklug (unklu:k) adj unwise, imprudent.

Unkosten ('unkɔstən) nf pl expenses, costs.

Unkraut ('unkraut) n neu weed(s).

unlängst (unlɛŋst) adv lately, recently.

unlauter ('unlautər) adj impure, unfair.

unlösbar ('unlœsba:r) adj insoluble.

unmäßig ('unmɛ:siç) adj immoderate.

Unmenge ('unmɛŋə) nf enormous number.

Unmensch ('unmɛnʃ) nm brute, barbarian. —**lich** adj brutal, inhuman, barbarous.

unmittelbar ('unmitəlba:r) adj direct.

unmöglich ('unmœ:kliç) adj impossible.

unmoralisch ('unmora:liʃ) adj immoral.

unnötig ('unnœ:tiç) adj unnecessary.

unnütz ('unnyts) adj useless, vain, idle.

unord/entlich ('unɔrdəntliç) adj untidy, disorderly. —**nung** ('unɔrdnuŋ) nf disorder, confusion.

unparteiisch ('unpartaiiʃ) adj impartial.

unpassend ('unpasənt) adj unsuitable.

Unrat ('unra:t) nm 1 dirt, filth. 2 rubbish.

unratsam ('unra:tza:m) adj inadvisable.

unrecht ('unrɛçt) adj 1 incorrect. 2 unjust. n neu injustice, wrong. —**mäßig** adj illegal.

unrein ('unrain) adj unclean, dirty.

Unruh/e ('unru:ə) nf 1 uneasiness, anxiety. 2 disturbance, riot. 3 unrest. —**ig** adj 1 restless, uneasy. 2 turbulent. —**stifter** nm agitator, troublemaker.

uns (uns) pron 1st pers pl 1 us. 2 ourselves.

unsagbar (un'za:kba:r) adj unspeakable.

unsauber ('unzaubər) adj dirty, untidy.

unscheinbar ('unʃainba:r) adj 1 insignificant. 2 unpretentious, plain.

unschlüssig ('unʃlysiç) adj irresolute, undecided.

Unschuld ('unʃult) nf innocence. —**ig** ('unʃuldiç) adj innocent.

unselig ('unze:liç) adj 1 unfortunate. 2 fatal.

unser ('unzər) poss adj 1st pers pl our. —**er** poss pron 1st pers pl also **der uns(e)re** or **der uns(e)rige** ours. —**(e)seits** ('unzər(ə)zaits) adv for our part. —**(e)sgleichen** ('unzər(ə)sglaiçən) pron people like us. —**thalben** ('unzərthalbən) adv also —**twegen** ('unzərtve:gən) or —**twillen** ('unzərtvilən) for our sake(s), on our account.

unsicher ('unziçər) adj 1 unsafe, insecure. 2 uncertain.

unsichtbar ('unziçtba:r) adj invisible.

Unsinn ('unzin) nm nonsense. —**ig** adj foolish, stupid.

Unsitt/e ('unzitə) nf bad habit. —**lich** adj immoral, indecent.

unsterblich ('unʃtɛrpliç) adj immortal. —**keit** nf immortality.

unstet ('unʃtɛ:t) adj unsteady, inconstant.

Untat ('unta:t) nf crime, outrage.

untätig ('untɛ:tiç) adj inactive.

untauglich ('untaukliç) adj unfit, useless.

unten ('untən) adv 1 below. 2 downstairs.

unter ('untər) prep 1 below, under. 2 among. 3 between. 4 of. 5 during. adj lower, inferior.

Unterarm ('untərarm) nm forearm.

Unterbau ('untərbau) nm -**ten** substructure, foundation.

unterbewußt ('untərbəvust) adj subconscious. —**sein** n neu subconscious.

unterbleiben* (untər'blaibən) vi not take place, be cancelled.

unterbrechen* (untər'brɛçən) vt interrupt.

unterbringen* ('untərbriŋən) vt 1 lodge, shelter. 2 place.

unterdes (untər'dɛs) adv also **unterdessen** meanwhile.

unterdrücken (untər'drykən) vt 1 suppress, repress. 2 oppress.

untereinander (untərain'andər) adv 1 among one another, mutually. 2 one beneath the other.

Unterführung (untər'fy:ruŋ) nf underpass.

Untergang ('untərgaŋ) nm 1 (of the sun) setting. 2 decline, (down)fall.

Untergebene(r) (untər'ge:bənə) nm subordinate.

untergehen* ('untərge:ən) vi 1 perish, die. 2 set, sink.

untergeordnet ('untərgəɔrdnət) adj subordinate.

Untergestell ('untərgəʃtɛl) n neu -e undercarriage, base.

untergraben* (untər'gra:bən) vt 1 undermine. 2 corrupt.

Untergrund ('untərgrunt) nm subsoil. **—bahn** nf underground (railway).

unterhalb ('untərhalp) prep below, under.

Unterhalt ('untərhalt) nm livelihood, subsistence. **—en*** (untər'haltən) vt 1 entertain. 2 maintain. 3 support. **sich —en** vr talk, converse. **—ung** nf -en 1 entertainment. 2 conversation.

unterhand/eln (untər'handəln) vi negotiate. **—lung** (untər'handluŋ) nf negotiation.

Unterhemd ('untərhɛmt) n neu vest.

Unterhosen ('untərho:zən) nf pl underpants.

unterirdisch ('untərirdiʃ) adj underground, subterranean.

unterkommen* ('untərkɔmən) vi 1 find work. 2 find accommodation or shelter. n neu also **Unterkunft** ('untərkunft) nf -ˀe 1 lodging(s), accommodation. 2 mil quarters.

Unterlage ('untərla:gə) nf 1 basis, foundation. 2 (documentary) proof, documents.

unterlassen* (untər'lasən) vt 1 omit. 2 abstain from.

unterlegen (v 'untərle:gən; adj untər'le:gən) vt put under. adj inferior.

Unterleib ('untərlaip) nm abdomen.

unterliegen* (untər'li:gən) vi be defeated.

unternehm/en* (untər'ne:mən) vt undertake, attempt. n neu — undertaking, enterprise. **—er** nm — 1 contractor 2 entrepreneur. 3 employer.

Unteroffizier ('untərɔfitsi:r) nm non-commissioned or petty officer.

Unterredung (untər're:duŋ) nf -en 1 conversation. 2 conference. 3 talk, interview.

Unterricht ('untərriçt) nm instruction, lessons. **—en** (untər'riçtən) vt instruct, teach, inform.

Unterrock ('untərrɔk) nm petticoat.

unters ('untərs) contraction of **unter das.**

untersagen (untər'za:gən) vt forbid, prohibit.

Untersatz ('untərzats) nm 1 support. 2 saucer.

unterscheid/en* (untər'ʃaidən) vt distinguish,

discriminate. **sich unterscheiden** vr differ. **—ung** nf -en distinction, difference.

unterschieben* (untər'ʃi:bən) vt attribute, impute.

Unterschied ('untərʃi:t) nm -e difference. **—lich** adj different.

unterschlagen* (untər'ʃla:gən) vt 1 embezzle. 2 suppress.

Unterschlupf ('untərʃlupf) nm -ˀe refuge.

unterschreiben* (untər'ʃraibən) vt 1 sign. 2 subscribe to.

Unterschrift ('untərʃrift) nf signature.

Untersee/boot ('untərze:bo:t) n neu submarine. **—isch** ('untərze:iʃ) adj submarine.

untersetzt (untər'zɛtst) adj thick-set, stocky.

Unterst ('untərst) adj lowest, last, bottom.

Unterstand ('untərʃtant) nm dugout, shelter.

unterstütz/en (untər'ʃtytsən) vt support, back. **—ung** nf -en support.

untersuch/en (untər'zu:xən) vt examine, inspect. **—ung** nf -en 1 examination. 2 inquiry.

Untertan ('untərta:n) nm -en subject. **—ig** ('untərtε:niç) adj 1 subject. 2 submissive.

Untertasse ('untərtasə) nf saucer.

Untertitel ('untərtitəl) nm subtitle, caption.

unterwärts ('untərvɛrts) adv downwards.

Unterwäsche ('untərvɛʃə) nf underwear.

unterwegs (untər've:ks) adv 1 on the way, en route. 2 bound (for).

unterweisen* (untər'vaizən) vt teach, instruct.

Unterwelt ('untərvɛlt) nf underworld.

unterwerfen* (untər'vɛrfən) vt subdue, subject. **sich unterwerfen** vr submit.

unterwürfig (untər'vyrfiç) adj submissive, servile.

unterzeichn/en (untər'tsaiçnən) vt sign. **—ung** nf signature.

unterziehen* (untər'tsi:ən) vt subject to. **sich unterziehen** vr undergo.

untreu ('untrɔy) adj 1 unfaithful. 2 disloyal.

untrüglich (un'try:kliç) adj infallible, unerring.

Untugend ('untu:gənt) nf vice, bad habit.

unumgänglich (unum'gɛŋliç) adj 1 indispensable. 2 unavoidable.

unumwunden ('unumvundən) adj 1 plain, blunt. 2 candid.

ununterbrochen ('ununtərbrɔxən) adj uninterrupted, continuous.

unverantwortlich (unfɛr'antvɔrtliç) adj 1 irresponsible. 2 inexcusable.

unverbesserlich (unfɛr'bɛsərliç) adj incorrigible.

117

unverbindlich ('unfɛrbintliç) *adj* **1** not binding, without obligation. **2** unkind.

unverdient ('unfɛrdi:nt) *adj* undeserved.

unverdorben ('unfɛrdɔrbən) *adj* unspoilt.

unverdrossen ('unfɛrdrɔsən) *adj* indefatigable.

unvereinbar (unfɛr'ainba:r) *adj* incompatible.

unvergeßlich (unfɛr'gɛsliç) *adj* unforgettable.

unvermeidlich (unfɛr'maitliç) *adj* unavoidable, inevitable.

unvermittelt ('unfɛrmitəlt) *adj* abrupt.

Unvermögen ('unfɛrmœ:gən) *n neu* impotence, inability.

unvermutet ('unfɛrmu:tət) *adj* unexpected.

unvernünftig ('unfɛrnynftiç) *adj* unreasonable.

unverschämt (unfɛr'ʃɛ:mt) *adj* **1** insolent, cheeky. **2** shameless.

unversehens ('unfɛrze:əns) *adv* unawares.

unversehrt ('unfɛrze:rt) *adj* uninjured.

unverständlich ('unfɛrʃtɛntliç) *adj* unintelligible.

unverträglich ('unfɛrtrɛ:kliç) *adj* **1** quarrelsome. **2** incompatible.

unverzüglich (unfɛr'tsy:kliç) *adj* immediate.

unwahr ('unva:r) *adj* untrue, false, wrong. **—scheinlich** *adj* **1** improbable. **2** *inf* incredible.

unweigerlich (un'vaigərliç) *adj* definite, certain. *adv* without fail.

unweit ('unvait) *adv* not far (off). *prep* near.

Unwetter ('unvɛtər) *n neu* storm, stormy weather.

unwichtig ('unviçtiç) *adj* unimportant.

unwiderruflich (unvi:dər'ru:fliç) *adj* irrevocable.

unwiderstehlich (unvi:dər'ʃte:liç) *adj* irresistible.

unwillig ('unviliç) *adj* indignant.

unwillkürlich ('unvilky:rliç) *adj* involuntary, instinctive.

unwirksam ('unvi:rkza:m) *adj* ineffective.

unwissen/d ('unvisənt) *adj* ignorant. **—heit** *nf* ignorance.

unwürdig ('unvyrdiç) *adj* unworthy.

Unzahl ('untsa:l) *nf* great or countless number. **—bar** (un'tsɛ:lba:r) *adj* also **—ig** (un'tsɛ:liç) innumerable, countless.

Unze ('untsə) *nf* **-n** ounce.

unzeitgemäß ('untsaitgəmɛ:s) *adj* inopportune.

unzerbrechlich (untsɛr'brɛçliç) *adj* unbreakable.

unzertrennlich (untsɛr'trɛnliç) *adj* inseparable.

unziemlich ('untsi:mliç) *adj* unseemly.

Unzucht ('untsuxt) *nf* indecent act, sexual offence.

unzufrieden ('untsufri:dən) *adj* dissatisfied.

unzugänglich ('untsu:gɛŋliç) *adj* inaccessible.

unzulänglich ('untsu:lɛŋliç) *adj* inadequate.

unzulässig ('untsu:lɛsiç) *adj* inadmissible.

üppig ('ypiç) *adj* **1** abundant, plentiful. **2** well-developed. **3** voluptuous. **4** presumptuous, cocky. **—keit** *nf* **1** abundance. **2** voluptuousness. **3** presumption.

uralt ('u:ralt) *adj* **1** very old, ancient. **2** prehistoric. **3** primeval.

Uran (u'ra:n) *n neu* uranium.

Uraufführung ('u:rauffy:ruŋ) *nf* first night or performance, premiere.

urbar ('u:rba:r) *adj* arable.

Ureinwohner ('u:rainvo:nər) *nm pl* original inhabitants, aborigines.

Ureltern ('u:rɛltərn) *n pl* ancestors.

Urgeschichte ('u:rgəʃiçtə) *nf* earliest history, earliest times.

Urheber ('u:rhe:bər) *nm* — author, originator.

Urin (u'ri:n) *nm* urine.

Urkund/e ('u:rkundə) *nf* **-n** document, deed. **—lich** ('u:rkuntliç) *adj* documentary.

Urlaub ('u:rlaup) *nm* **-e** holidays, leave.

Urmensch ('u:rmɛnʃ) *nm* primitive man.

Urne ('urnə) *nf* **-n** urn.

urplötzlich ('u:rplœtsliç) *adj* sudden, abrupt.

Ursache ('u:rzaxə) *nf* cause, reason.

Ursprung ('u:rʃpruŋ) *nm* origin, source, beginning. **—lich** ('u:rʃpryŋliç) *adj* original, primary.

Urteil ('urtail) *n neu* **1** judgment. **2** opinion. **—en** *vi* judge.

Urwald ('u:rvalt) *nm* primeval or virgin forest, jungle.

Urzeit ('u:rtsait) *nf* remotest antiquity, primitive times.

Utop/ie (uto'pi:) *nf* **-n** Utopia. **—isch** (u'to:piʃ) *adj* Utopian.

V

vag (va:k) *adj* also **vage** ('va:gə) vague.

Vagabund (vaga'bunt) *nm* **-en** vagabond, tramp.

vakant (va'kant) *adj* vacant.

Vakuum ('va:kuum) *n neu* **-kua** vacuum.

Valuta (va'lu:ta) *nf* **-ten** **1** rate of exchange. **2** currency. **3** value.

Vanille (va'niljə) *nf* vanilla.

Variation (variatsi'o:n) nf -en variation.

Vase ('va:zə) nf -n vase.

Vater ('fa:tər) nm ‑̈ father. **—land** n neu native country. **—ländisch** ('fa:tərlɛndiʃ) adj national, patriotic. ‑̈**lich** ('fɛ:tərliç) adj fatherly. **—unser** (fa:tər'unzər) n neu Lord's Prayer.

Vegetar/ier (vege'ta:riər) nm — vegetarian. **—isch** adj vegetarian.

Veilchen ('failçən) n neu — violet.

Vene ('ve:nə) nf -n vein.

Venedig (ve'ne:diç) n neu Venice.

Ventil (vɛn'ti:l) n neu -e valve.

verabred/en (fɛr'apre:dən) vt agree (upon), fix. **sich verabreden** vr make an appointment. **—ung** nf -en 1 agreement. 2 appointment.

verabschieden (fɛr'apʃi:dən) vt 1 dismiss. 2 pass (laws). **sich verabschieden** vr take one's leave.

veracht/en (fɛr'axtən) vt despise. ‑̈**lich** (fɛr-'ɛçtliç) adj 1 contemptuous, scornful. 2 contemptible, despicable.

verallgemeiner/n (fɛralgə'mainərn) vt generalize. **—ung** nf -en generalization.

veralten (fɛr'altən) vi become obsolete or out-of-date.

veränder/lich (fɛr'ɛndərliç) adj changeable, variable. **—n** vt change, alter.

veranlag/t (fɛr'anla:kt) adj talented. **—ung** (fɛr'anla:guŋ) nf -en 1 aptitude, talent. 2 assessment.

veranlassen (fɛr'anlasən) vt give rise to.

veranschaulichen (fɛr'anʃauliçən) vt 1 make clear. 2 illustrate.

veranstalt/en (fɛr'anʃtaltən) vt arrange, organize. **—ung** nf -en 1 arrangement. 2 entertainment, show. 3 sport event.

verantwort/en (fɛr'antvortən) vt answer for. **—lich** adj responsible. **—ung** nf -en responsibility.

verarbeiten (fɛr'arbaitən) vt work, process.

verargen (fɛr'argən) vt blame. **jemandem etwas verargen** blame someone for something.

verärgern (fɛr'ɛrgərn) vt annoy, vex.

veräußer/n (fɛr'ɔysərn) vt sell, dispose of. **—ung** nf -en 1 sale. 2 transfer.

Verb (vɛrp) n neu -en verb.

Verband (fɛr'bant) nm ‑̈e 1 bandage, dressing. 2 association, union.

verbannen (fɛr'banən) vt banish.

verbergen* (fɛr'bɛrgən) vt hide, conceal.

verbessern (fɛr'bɛsərn) vt 1 improve. 2 correct.

sich verbeugen (fɛr'bɔygən) vr bow.

verbieten* (fɛr'bi:tən) vt forbid, prohibit.

verbilligen (fɛr'biligən) vt 1 cheapen. 2 reduce (the price of).

verbind/en* (fɛr'bindən) vt 1 bandage. 2 bind, join. **—lich** (fɛr'bintliç) adj 1 obligatory, binding. 2 obliging. **—ung** (fɛr'binduŋ) nf -en 1 union. 2 bond. 3 connection. 4 relation.

verbissen (fɛr'bisən) adj grim, dogged.

verbittern (fɛr'bitərn) vt embitter.

verblassen (fɛr'blasən) vi grow pale, fade.

Verbleib (fɛr'blaip) nm whereabouts. **—en*** (fɛr'blaibən) vi 1 remain. 2 persist, stick (to).

verblenden (fɛr'blɛndən) vt 1 delude. 2 dazzle. 3 screen. 4 arch face.

verblüffen (fɛr'blyfən) vt 1 amaze, astonish. 2 confuse, bewilder.

verbluten (fɛr'blu:tən) vi bleed to death.

verbohrt (fɛr'bo:rt) adj stubborn.

verborgen (fɛr'bɔrgən) adj hidden, secret.

Verbot (fɛr'bo:t) n neu -e prohibition. **—en** adj forbidden.

Verbrauch (fɛr'braux) nm consumption, use. **—en** vt 1 consume. 2 wear out. **—er** nm — consumer, user.

verbrech/en* (fɛr'brɛçən) vt commit (a crime). n neu — crime. **—er** nm — criminal. **—erisch** adj criminal.

verbreiten (fɛr'braitən) vt spread.

verbrennen* (fɛr'brɛnən) vt 1 burn (up). 2 cremate. vi burn to death.

verbringen* (fɛr'briŋən) vt spend (time).

sich verbrüdern (fɛr'bry:dərn) vr fraternize.

Verbum ('vɛrbum) n neu **-ben** verb.

verbünd/en (fɛr'byndən) vt ally. **sich verbünden** vr ally oneself. **—ete(r)** nm ally, confederate.

Verdacht (fɛr'daxt) nm -e suspicion, distrust. **—ig** (fɛr'dɛçtiç) adj 1 suspicious. 2 suspect. ‑̈**igen** (fɛr'dɛçtigən) vt suspect.

verdamm/en (fɛr'damən) vt condemn, damn. **—nis** nf damnation.

verdampfen (fɛr'dampfən) vi evaporate.

verdanken (fɛr'daŋkən) vt be indebted for, owe.

verdauen (fɛr'dauən) vt digest.

Verdeck (fɛr'dɛk) n neu -e 1 naut deck. 2 mot hood, top. 3 covering. **—en** vt cover (up).

Verderb (fɛr'dɛrp) nm ruin, destruction. **—en*** (fɛr'dɛrbən) vt spoil, corrupt. vi spoil, decay. **—lich** (fɛr'dɛrpliç) adj 1 perishable. 2 contaminating. **—nis** (fɛr'dɛrpnis) nf corruption.

verdeutlichen (fɛr'dɔytliçən) vt make clear, explain.

verdichten (fɛr'diçtən) vt condense, compress.

verdicken (fɛr'dikən) vt thicken.

verdien/en (fɛr'di:nən) vt 1 deserve. 2 earn. **—st** n neu **-e** merit. **nm -e** earnings, gain.

verdingen (fɛr'diŋən) vt hire out.

verdoppeln (fɛr'dɔpəln) vt double.

verdorben (fɛr'dɔrbən) adj spoilt, damaged.

verdrängen (fɛr'drɛŋən) vt 1 thrust aside. 2 displace. 3 supplant. 4 suppress, repress.

verdrehen (fɛr'dre:ən) vt 1 distort. 2 twist.

verdrieß/en* (fɛr'dri:sən) vt annoy, vex. **—lich** adj 1 annoyed. 2 sulky. 3 annoying.

verdrossen (fɛr'drɔsən) adj 1 sulky. 2 annoyed.

verdummen (fɛr'dumən) vt make stupid, stupefy. vi become stupid.

verdunkeln (fɛr'duŋkəln) vt 1 darken, black out. 2 overshadow.

veredeln (fɛr'e:dəln) vt 1 ennoble. 2 improve. 3 bot graft.

verehr/en (fɛr'e:rən) vt honour, venerate, worship. **—ung** nf worship, veneration.

Verein (fɛr'ain) nm **-e** 1 association, union. 2 society, club. **—bar** adj consistent, compatible. **—baren** vt agree upon, arrange. **—barung** nf **-en** agreement. **—fachen** vt simplify. **—igen** vt also **—en** unite, join, combine. **die Vereinigten Staaten** the United States. **die Vereinten Nationen** the United Nations. **—igung** nf **-en** union, alliance.

vereiteln (fɛr'aitəln) vt frustrate, thwart.

vererben (fɛr'ɛrbən) vt 1 bequeath. 2 transmit. **sich vererben** vr be hereditary.

verewigen (fɛr'e:vigən) vt immortalize.

verfahren* (fɛr'fa:rən) vi act, deal. vt muddle. **sich verfahren** vr lose one's way. **~adj** bungled. n neu **— 1** method. 2 process. 3 law proceedings.

Verfall (fɛr'fal) nm 1 decay, decline. 2 comm maturity. 3 law forfeiture. **—en*** vi 1 decay, decline. 2 comm mature. 3 be forfeited.

verfälschen (fɛr'fɛlʃən) vt 1 falsify. 2 adulterate.

verfass/en (fɛr'fasən) vt compose, write. **—er** nm **—** author. **—ung** nf **-en** 1 pol constitution. 2 disposition, frame of mind. **—ungsgemäß** adj also **—ungsmäßig** constitutional. **—ungswidrig** adj unconstitutional.

verfechten (fɛr'fɛçtən) vt 1 defend. 2 advocate.

verfehl/en (fɛr'fe:lən) vt 1 miss. 2 fail (to do). **—t** adj unsuccessful.

verfeinern (fɛr'fainərn) vt 1 refine. 2 improve.

verfluchen (fɛr'flu:xən) vt curse.

verfolg/en (fɛr'fɔlgən) vt 1 pursue. 2 follow up.

3 persecute. 4 law prosecute. **—er** nm **— 1** pursuer. 2 persecutor. **—ung** nf **-en 1** pursuit. 2 persecution. 3 law prosecution.

verfüg/en (fɛr'fy:gən) vi 1 have at one's disposal. 2 dispose (of). vt order. **—ung** nf **-en** 1 disposal. 2 order, instruction.

verführ/en (fɛr'fy:rən) vt 1 lead astray. 2 seduce. 3 tempt, lure. **—er** nf **— 1** seducer. 2 tempter. **—erisch** adj seductive, alluring. **—ung** nf 1 seduction. 2 temptation.

vergang/en (fɛr'gaŋən) adj past, gone. **—enheit** nf past. **—lich** (fɛr'gɛŋliç) adj transitory, transient.

Vergaser (fɛr'ga:zər) nm **—** carburettor.

vergaß (fɛr'ga:s) v see **vergessen.**

vergeb/en* (fɛr'ge:bən) vt 1 forgive. 2 give away. **—ens** adv in vain. **—lich** (fɛr'ge:pliç) adj 1 fruitless. 2 futile.

vergegenwärtigen (fɛrge:gən'vɛrtigən) vt 1 bring to mind. 2 represent. **sich vergegenwärtigen** vr imagine, picture.

vergehen* (fɛr'ge:ən) vi 1 pass or fade (away). 2 cease. 3 perish. **sich vergehen** vr commit an offence. n neu **—** offence.

vergelten* (fɛr'gɛltən) vt repay, pay back.

vergessen* (fɛr'gɛsən) vt forget.

vergeuden (fɛr'gɔydən) vt squander.

vergewaltig/en (fɛrgə'valtigən) vt 1 rape. 2 violate. **—ung** nf **-en 1** rape. 2 violence.

sich vergewissern (fɛrgə'visərn) vr ascertain.

vergießen* (fɛr'gi:sən) vt 1 shed (blood or tears). 2 spill.

vergiften (fɛr'giftən) vt poison.

Vergißmeinnicht (fɛr'gismainniçt) n neu **-e** forget-me-not.

vergißt (fɛr'gist) v see **vergessen.**

verglasen (fɛr'gla:zən) vt glaze.

Vergleich (fɛr'glaiç) nm **-e** 1 comparison. 2 law arrangement, compromise. **—en*** vt 1 compare. 2 settle.

vergnüg/en (fɛr'gny:gən) vt entertain, amuse. **sich vergnügen** vr enjoy or amuse onself. **~n** neu **—** pleasure, enjoyment.

vergöttern (fɛr'gœtərn) vt 1 deify. 2 idolize.

vergraben* (fɛr'gra:bən) vt bury.

vergriffen (fɛr'grifən) adj 1 sold out. 2 out of print.

vergrößern (fɛr'grœ:sərn) vt enlarge, magnify.

Vergünstigung (fɛr'gynstiguŋ) nf **-en** concession, privilege.

vergüten (fɛr'gy:tən) vt compensate for, reimburse, make good.

verhaften (fɛr'haftən) vt arrest.

verhalt/en* (fɛr'haltən) *vt* keep back, suppress. **sich verhalten** *vr* behave. ~*n neu* behaviour. **≈nis** (fɛr'hɛltnɪs) *n neu* **-se** 1 relation(ship). 2 proportion. **≈nismäßig** (fɛr'hɛltnɪsmɛːsɪç) *adj* proportional. *adv* relatively.

verhand/eln (fɛr'handəln) *vi* 1 negotiate. 2 deal (with). *vt* 1 dispose of, sell. 2 discuss. 3 *law* plead. **—lung** (fɛr'handluŋ) *nf* 1 negotiation. 2 discussion.

verhäng/en (fɛr'hɛŋən) *vt* 1 impose, inflict. 2 drape. 3 cover. **—nis** *n neu* **-se** destiny, fate.

verhaßt (fɛr'hast) *adj* 1 hated, despised. 2 hateful, despicable.

Verhau (fɛr'hau) *nm,neu* **-e** entanglement. **—en** *vt inf* thrash.

verheimlichen (fɛr'haimlɪçən) *vt* conceal, keep secret.

verheiraten (fɛr'haira:tən) *vt* marry. **sich verheiraten** *vr* marry, get married.

verheißen* (fɛr'haisən) *vt* promise.

verhelfen* (fɛr'hɛlfən) *vi* jemandem zu etwas **verhelfen** help someone in (doing) something.

verherrlichen (fɛr'hɛrlɪçən) *vt* glorify.

verhindern (fɛr'hɪndərn) *vt* 1 prevent. 2 hamper.

Verhör (fɛr'høːr) *n neu* **-e** 1 examination. 2 interrogation. **—en** *vt* 1 examine. 2 question.

verhungern (fɛr'huŋərn) *vi* die of hunger, starve.

verhüten (fɛr'hyːtən) *vt* avert, prevent.

sich verirren (fɛr'irən) *vr* lose one's way.

verjüngen (fɛr'jyŋən) *vt* rejuvenate.

Verkauf (fɛr'kauf) *nm* **≈e** sale. **—en** *vt* sell. **≈er** (fɛr'kɔyfər) *nm* **—** 1 retailer. 2 salesman, shop assistant. **≈erin** *nf* **-nen** saleswoman, shop assistant.

Verkehr (fɛr'keːr) *nm* 1 traffic. 2 communication, intercourse. **—en** *vt* 1 reverse. 2 pervert. *vi* 1 associate (with). 2 (of a vehicle or transport service) run, operate. **—sampel** *nf* traffic light. **—t** *adj* 1 wrong. 2 inverted, reversed.

verkennen* (fɛr'kɛnən) *vt* 1 misjudge. 2 fail to recognize.

verklagen (fɛr'kla:gən) *vt* 1 accuse. 2 sue.

verklären (fɛr'klɛːrən) *vt* transfigure.

verkleiden (fɛr'klaidən) *vt* 1 disguise. 2 coat, face.

verkleinern (fɛr'klainərn) *vt* 1 diminish, reduce. 2 belittle.

verknüpfen (fɛr'knypfən) *vt* connect.

verkommen* (fɛr'kɔmən) *vi* 1 decay. 2 decline. *adj* 1 decayed. 2 depraved.

verkörpern (fɛr'kœrpərn) *vt* 1 embody. 2 represent.

verkrüppeln (fɛr'krypəln) *vt* cripple.

verkündig/en (fɛr'kyndigən) *vt* proclaim, announce. **—ung** *nf* **-en** proclamation or announcement.

verkürz/en (fɛr'kyrtsən) *vt* shorten. **—ung** *nf* **-en** 1 reduction. 2 abbreviation.

verladen* (fɛr'la:dən) *vt* load, ship.

Verlag (fɛr'la:k) *nm* **-e** publishing house.

verlangen (fɛr'laŋən) *vt* 1 demand. 2 require. **verlangen nach** long for. ~*n neu* **—** 1 desire. 2 demand.

verlängern (fɛr'lɛŋərn) *vt* 1 lengthen. 2 prolong.

verlangsamen (fɛr'laŋza:mən) *vt* slow down.

Verlaß (fɛr'las) *nm* 1 reliance. 2 dependability. **≈lich** (fɛr'lɛslɪç) *adj* reliable.

verlassen* (fɛr'lasən) *vt* 1 desert. 2 relinquish. **sich verlassen** *vr* rely.

Verlauf (fɛr'lauf) *nm* 1 course. 2 development. **—en*** *vi* 1 elapse. 2 develop. *adj* lost. **sich —en** *vr* lose one's way.

verlautbaren (fɛr'lautba:rən) *vt* divulge.

verleg/en (fɛr'le:gən) *vt* 1 misplace. 2 publish. 3 shift. 4 bar. *adj* embarrassed, confused. **—enheit** *nf* **-en** embarrassment, confusion. **—er** *nm* **—** publisher.

verleihen* (fɛr'laiən) *vt* 1 lend. 2 bestow.

verleiten (fɛr'laitən) *vt* 1 mislead. 2 seduce. 3 induce.

verlernen (fɛr'lɛrnən) *vt* forget.

verletzen (fɛr'lɛtsən) *vt* 1 wound. 2 violate.

verleugnen (fɛr'lɔygnən) *vt* 1 deny. 2 disavow. 3 renounce.

verleumd/en (fɛr'lɔymdən) *vt* slander. **—ung** *nf* **-en** slander, libel.

sich verlieben (fɛr'li:bən) *vr* fall in love.

verlieren* (fɛr'li:rən) *vt,vi* lose. **sich verlieren** *vr* 1 lose oneself or one's way. 2 disappear.

Verlob/te (fɛr'lo:ptə) *nf* fiancée. **—te(r)** *nm* fiancé. **—ung** (fɛr'lo:buŋ) *nf* **-en** engagement.

verlocken (fɛr'lɔkən) *vt* entice, tempt.

verlogen (fɛr'lo:gən) *adj* untruthful.

verlor (fɛr'lo:r) *v* see **verlieren**.

verloren (fɛr'lo:rən) *v* see **verlieren**. *adj* lost.

Verlust (fɛr'lust) *nm* **-e** 1 loss. 2 damage. 3 waste.

vermach/en (fɛr'maxən) *vt* bequeath. **≈tnis** (fɛr'mɛçtnɪs) *n neu* **-se** 1 legacy. 2 bequest.

vermähl/en (fɛr'mɛːlən) *vt* marry. **sich ver-**

mählen vr get married. **—ung** nf -en marriage.

vermehren (fɛr'me:rən) vt increase, multiply.

vermeid/en* (fɛr'maidən) vt avoid, elude. **—lich** (fɛr'maitlɪç) adj avoidable.

vermeintlich (fɛr'maintlɪç) adj supposed.

Vermerk (fɛr'mɛrk) nm -e note, notice. **—en** vt note (down).

vermess/en* (fɛr'mɛsən) vt 1 measure. 2 survey. **sich vermessen** vr dare. **— adj** bold, insolent. **—ung** nf -en 1 measuring. 2 survey.

vermiet/en (fɛr'mi:tən) vt let, lease. **—er** nm — landlord.

vermindern (fɛr'mindərn) vt diminish, decrease.

vermischen (fɛr'miʃən) vt mix, blend.

vermissen (fɛr'misən) vt miss.

vermitt/eln (fɛr'mitəln) vi,vt 1 mediate. 2 negotiate. vt obtain. **—lung** (fɛr'mitluŋ) nf -en 1 mediation. 2 intervention.

vermög/e (fɛr'mœ:gə) prep by virtue of. **—en*** vt be able. n neu 1 wealth, assets. 2 ability, power.

vermut/en (fɛr'mu:tən) vt suppose, presume. **—lich** adj likely, presumable. **—ung** nf -en 1 conjecture. 2 suspicion.

vernachlässigen (fɛr'na:xlɛsigən) vt neglect.

vernehmen* (fɛr'ne:mən) vt 1 perceive, hear. 2 learn. 3 interrogate.

verneinen (fɛr'nainən) vt deny.

vernicht/en (fɛr'niçtən) vt annihilate, destroy. **—ung** nf annihilation, destruction.

vernieten (fɛr'ni:tən) vt rivet.

Vernunft (fɛr'nunft) nf reason, (common) sense. **jemandem zur Vernunft bringen** bring someone to his senses. **—ig** (fɛr'nynftɪç) adj 1 sensible, reasonable. 2 rational.

veröden (fɛr'œ:dən) vt lay waste. vi become desolate.

veröffentlichen (fɛr'œfəntliçən) vt publish.

verpachten (fɛr'paxtən) vt 1 farm (out). 2 lease.

verpacken (fɛr'pakən) vt 1 pack (up or away). 2 wrap up.

verpassen (fɛr'pasən) vt 1 miss (a train, etc.). 2 fit (clothes).

verpfänden (fɛr'pfɛndən) vt pawn, pledge.

verpfleg/en (fɛr'pfle:gən) vt cater for, feed. **—ung** nf 1 catering. 2 board.

verpflicht/en (fɛr'pfliçtən) vt 1 oblige. 2 engage. **—ung** nf -en commitment, obligation.

verplempern (fɛr'plɛmpərn) vt inf fritter away.

verpönt (fɛr'pœ:nt) adj taboo.

verputzen (fɛr'putsən) vt 1 plaster. 2 inf squander.

verquicken (fɛr'kvikən) vt 1 amalgamate. 2 mix up.

Verrat (fɛr'ra:t) nm 1 treason. 2 betrayal. **—en*** vt betray. **—er** (fɛr'rɛ:tər) nm — traitor. **—erisch** (fɛr'rɛ:tariʃ) adj treacherous.

verrechnen (fɛr'rɛçnən) vt reckon up. **sich verrechnen** vr miscalculate.

verrenk/en (fɛr'rɛŋkən) vt med 1 sprain. 2 dislocate. **—ung** nf -en 1 sprain. 2 dislocation.

verrichten (fɛr'riçtən) vt perform, execute.

verringern (fɛr'riŋərn) vt diminish, lessen.

verrück/en (fɛr'rykən) vt shift, move. **—t** adj mad, crazy.

Verruf (fɛr'ru:f) nm ill repute, disrepute.

Vers (fɛrs) nm -e verse, stanza.

versag/en (fɛr'za:gən) vi fail. vt refuse. **—er** nm — failure.

versamm/eln (fɛr'zaməln) vt assemble, collect. **—lung** (fɛr'zamluŋ) nf assembly, meeting.

Versand (fɛr'zant) nm dispatch.

versäum/en (fɛr'zɔymən) vt 1 neglect, fail (to). 2 miss (a train, etc.). **—nis** nf,neu -se 1 neglect, omission. 2 delay.

verschaffen (fɛr'ʃafən) vt procure, provide.

verschämt (fɛr'ʃɛ:mt) adj 1 bashful, shy. 2 ashamed.

verschanzen (fɛr'ʃantsən) vt entrench.

verschärfen (fɛr'ʃɛrfən) vt 1 sharpen. 2 intensify.

verschieb/en* (fɛr'ʃi:bən) vt 1 postpone. 2 displace. 3 sell illegally. **—ung** nf -en 1 postponement. 2 displacement.

verschieden (fɛr'ʃi:dən) adj 1 different. 2 pl several, various. **—es** n neu miscellany, variety (of things). **—heit** nf -en 1 difference. 2 variety.

verschiffen (fɛr'ʃifən) vt ship.

verschimmeln (fɛr'ʃiməln) vi grow mouldy.

verschlafen* (fɛr'ʃla:fən) vt sleep through. vi oversleep.

Verschlag (fɛr'ʃla:k) nm 1 partition. 2 crate, box. 3 compartment. **—en*** (fɛr'ʃla:gən) vt 1 partition. 2 board up. adj cunning.

verschlechtern (fɛr'ʃlɛçtərn) vt make worse. **sich verschlechtern** vr deteriorate.

verschleiern (fɛr'ʃlaiərn) vt veil.

Verschleiß (fɛr'ʃlais) nm wear (and tear).

verschleudern (fɛr'ʃlɔydərn) vt 1 squander. 2 sell extremely cheaply or at a loss.

verschließen* (fɛrˈʃliːsən) vt 1 shut, close. 2 lock. 3 seal (a letter).

verschlimmern (fɛrˈʃlimərn) vt make worse. vi get worse.

verschlingen* (fɛrˈʃliŋən) vt 1 devour. 2 twist.

verschlucken (fɛrˈʃlukən) vt swallow.

Verschluß (fɛrˈʃlus) nm 1 fastening. 2 seal. 3 stopper.

verschmähen (fɛrˈʃmɛːən) vt disdain, despise.

verschmitzt (fɛrˈʃmitst) adj crafty, sly.

verschollen (fɛrˈʃɔlən) adj (of a person) missing.

verschönern (fɛrˈʃøːnərn) vt 1 adorn, embellish. 2 improve.

verschränken (fɛrˈʃrɛŋkən) vt cross, fold.

verschreiben* (fɛrˈʃraibən) vt 1 prescribe. 2 order.

verschulden (fɛrˈʃuldən) vt be guilty of. n neu — 1 wrong. 2 fault.

verschweigen* (fɛrˈʃvaigən) vt keep secret.

verschwend/en (fɛrˈʃvɛndən) vt squander, waste. **—erisch** adj wasteful, extravagant.

verschwiegen (fɛrˈʃviːgən) adj 1 discreet. 2 reserved, reticent. **—heit** nf 1 discretion. 2 reticence.

verschwinden* (fɛrˈʃvindən) vi disappear. n neu — disappearance.

verschwommen (fɛrˈʃvɔmən) adj vague, blurred.

verschwör/en (fɛrˈʃvøːrən) vt renounce. **sich verschwören** vr conspire, plot. **—er** nm — conspirator. **—ung** nf -en conspiracy, plot.

versehen* (fɛrˈzeːən) vt 1 furnish, provide, equip. 2 overlook. 3 fulfil, perform. **sich versehen** vr err, make a mistake. **~n** neu — mistake, error. **—tlich** (fɛrˈzeːəntliç) adv by mistake, mistakenly.

versenden* (fɛrˈzɛndən) vt 1 send. 2 ship.

versengen (fɛrˈzɛŋən) vt singe, scorch.

versenk/en (fɛrˈzɛŋkən) vt 1 submerge, sink, immerse. 2 countersink. **—ung** nf -en sinking, submersion, immersion.

versessen (fɛrˈzɛsən) adj **auf etwas versessen sein** 1 be bent on something. 2 be crazy about something.

versetzen (fɛrˈzɛtsən) vt 1 (re)move, transfer. 2 displace. 3 pawn.

verseuchen (fɛrˈzɔyçən) vt infect, contaminate.

versicher/n (fɛrˈziçərn) vt 1 insure. 2 affirm. **sich versichern** vr make sure of. **—ung** nf -en 1 insurance. 2 assurance. 3 confirmation. **—ungsstatistiker** nm actuary.

versiegeln (fɛrˈziːgəln) vt seal (up).

versöhnen (fɛrˈzøːnən) vt reconcile.

versorg/en (fɛrˈzɔrgən) vt 1 provide, supply. 2 look after. **—ung** nf -en 1 maintenance. 2 supply.

verspät/en (fɛrˈʃpɛːtən) vt delay. **sich verspäten** vr be late. **—ung** nf -en delay.

verspielen (fɛrˈʃpiːlən) vt gamble away.

verspotten (fɛrˈʃpɔtən) vt mock, deride.

versprech/en* (fɛrˈʃprɛçən) vt promise. n neu — promise. **—ung** nf -en promise.

versprengen (fɛrˈʃprɛŋən) vt disperse.

verstaatlichen (fɛrˈʃtaːtliçən) vt nationalize.

Verstand (fɛrˈʃtant) nm 1 reason. 2 understanding. 3 intellect. **—igen** (fɛrˈʃtɛndigən) vt inform. **sich —igen** vr 1 come to an understanding. 2 make oneself understood. **—igung** (fɛrˈʃtɛndiguŋ) nf -en 1 information. 2 understanding. **—lich** (fɛrˈʃtɛntliç) adj intelligible, clear. **—nis** (fɛrˈʃtɛntnis) n neu 1 comprehension. 2 appreciation.

verstärk/en (fɛrˈʃtɛrkən) vt strengthen. **—er** nm — amplifier. **—ung** nf -en 1 reinforcement(s). 2 strengthening 3 amplification.

verstauchen (fɛrˈʃtauxən) vt sprain.

Versteck (fɛrˈʃtɛk) n neu -e hiding-place. **—en** vt hide.

verstehen* (fɛrˈʃteːən) vt understand. **sich verstehen** vr 1 agree. 2 get on (with someone).

versteiger/n (fɛrˈʃtaigərn) vt auction, sell by auction. **—ung** nf -en auction.

versteinern (fɛrˈʃtainərn) vt petrify.

verstell/bar (fɛrˈʃtɛlbaːr) adj adjustable. **—en** vt 1 adjust. 2 shift. 3 disguise. 4 pretend, feign. 5 misplace. **—ung** nf 1 pretence. 2 disguise. 3 displacement. 4 adjustment.

verstimmt (fɛrˈʃtimt) adj 1 bad-tempered, annoyed. 2 out of tune.

verstockt (fɛrˈʃtɔkt) adj 1 stubborn. 2 callous.

verstohlen (fɛrˈʃtoːlən) adj furtive, stealthy.

Verstoß (fɛrˈʃtoːs) nm 1 offence. 2 error. **—en*** vt 1 repudiate. 2 reject. vi 1 offend. 2 violate.

verstricken (fɛrˈʃtrikən) vt entangle.

verstümmeln (fɛrˈʃtyməln) vt mutilate.

Versuch (fɛrˈzuːx) nm -e 1 attempt, trial. 2 experiment. **—en** vt 1 try, test. 2 tempt. **—ung** nf -en temptation.

vertagen (fɛrˈtaːgən) vt adjourn, postpone.

vertauschen (fɛrˈtauʃən) vt 1 exchange. 2 mistake for.

verteidig/en (fɛrˈtaidigən) vt defend. **—er** nm — defender, advocate. **—ung** nf -en defence.

verteil/en (fɛr'tailən) vt 1 distribute. 2 divide. **—ung** nf distribution. allocation.

vertiefen (fɛr'ti:fən) vt deepen. **sich vertiefen** vr be absorbed (in).

vertikal (vɛrti'ka:l) adj vertical.

vertilgen (fɛr'tilgən) vt exterminate, destroy.

Vertrag (fɛr'tra:k) nm -̈e 1 treaty. 2 agreement, contract. **—lich** adj stipulated, agreed.

vertrag/en (fɛr'tra:gən) vt 1 endure, stand, bear. 2 carry away. **sich vertragen** vr 1 get on (with someone). 2 agree. **—lich** (fɛr-'trɛ:kliç) adj 1 compatible. 2 sociable, good-natured.

vertrau/en (fɛr'trauən) vi trust, have confidence in. n neu confidence, trust. **—ensvoll** adj trustful. **—ensvotum** n neu vote of confidence. **—enswürdig** adj trustworthy. **—lich** adj 1 confidential. 2 intimate. **—t** adj intimate, familiar.

vertreiben* (fɛr'traibən) vt 1 expel, banish. 2 sell.

vertret/en* (fɛr'tre:tən) vt represent. **—er** nm **— 1** representative. 2 advocate.

vertrösten (fɛr'trœ:stən) vt 1 console. 2 put off.

vertun* (fɛr'tu:n) vt spend, squander.

vertuschen (fɛr'tuʃən) vt hush up.

verunglimpfen (fɛr'unglimpfən) vt disparage, slander.

verunglücken (fɛr'unglykən) vi 1 meet with or have an accident. 2 perish.

verursachen (fɛr'u:rzaxən) vt cause.

verurteilen (fɛr'u:rtailən) vt condemn, sentence.

vervielfältigen (fɛr'fi:lfɛltigən) vt 1 reproduce. 2 multiply.

vervollkommnen (fɛr'fɔlkɔmnən) vt perfect.

vervollständigen (fɛr'fɔlʃtɛndigən) vt complete.

verwachsen* (fɛr'vaksən) vi 1 grow out of (clothes). 2 grow deformed. 3 heal, close up. 4 become involved, be closely connected (with). adj 1 deformed, stunted. 2 healed. 3 overgrown.

verwahren (fɛr'va:rən) vt keep (safe).

verwahrlost (fɛr'va:rlo:st) adj 1 depraved. 2 neglected, unkempt.

verwalt/en (fɛr'valtən) vt 1 administer, administrate. 2 supervise, control. **—er** nm **— 1** administrator, controller. 2 steward. **—ung** nf **—en** administration. **—ungsbeamte(r)** nm Civil Servant.

verwandt (fɛr'vant) adj related. **—e(r)** nm

relative, relation. **—schaft** nf -en 1 relations. 2 relationship.

verwaschen (fɛr'vaʃən) adj faded.

verwechseln (fɛr'vɛksəln) vt mistake (for), confuse.

verwegen (fɛr've:gən) adj bold.

verweichlicht (fɛr'vaiçliçt) adj effeminate.

verweigern (fɛr'vaigərn) vt refuse, deny.

verweilen (fɛr'vailən) vi linger, stay.

Verweis (fɛr'vais) nm -e reprimand, reproach. **—en*** (fɛr'vaizən) vt 1 banish, expel. 2 reprimand.

verwenden (fɛr'vɛndən) vt use, apply.

verwerf/en* (fɛr'vɛrfən) vt refuse, reject. **—lich** adj objectionable.

verwesen (fɛr've:sən) vi decay, rot. vt administer.

verwickeln (fɛr'vikəln) vt entangle, involve.

verwirken (fɛr'virkən) vt 1 forfeit. 2 incur.

verwirklichen (fɛr'virkliçən) vt realize. vi be realized, materialize.

verwirren (fɛr'virən) vt 1 confuse. 2 entangle.

verwischen (fɛr'viʃən) vt 1 wipe or blot out. 2 blur.

verwöhnen (fɛr'vœ:nən) vt spoil, pamper.

verworfen (fɛr'vɔrfən) adj depraved.

verworren (fɛr'vɔrən) adj 1 confused. 2 tangled.

verwund/en[1] (fɛr'vundən) vt wound, hurt. **—ete(r)** nm injured person, casualty.

verwunden[2] (fɛr'vundən) adj twisted.

verwundern (fɛr'vundərn) vt astonish. **sich verwundern** vr wonder.

verwünschen (fɛr'vynʃən) vt curse.

verwüsten (fɛr'vy:stən) vt lay waste.

verzagt (fɛr'tsa:kt) adj despondent, depressed.

verzaubern (fɛr'tsaubərn) vt enchant, bewitch.

verzehren (fɛr'tse:rən) vt consume.

verzeichn/en (fɛr'tsaiçnən) vt catalogue, enter. **—is** n neu -se 1 list, register. 2 index.

verzeih/en* (fɛr'tsaiən) vt forgive, pardon. **—ung** nf pardon. interj excuse me! sorry!

verzerren (fɛr'tsɛrən) vt distort.

Verzicht (fɛr'tsiçt) nm -e renunciation. **—en** vi renounce.

verzögern (fɛr'tsœ:gərn) vt delay.

verzollen (fɛr'tsɔlən) vt pay duty on.

verzuckern (fɛr'tsukərn) vt sweeten, sugar.

verzückt (fɛr'tsykt) adj enraptured.

verzweif/eln (fɛr'tsvaifəln) vi despair. **—lung** nf despair, desperation.

sich verzweigen (fɛr'tsvaigən) vr branch out or off.

verzwickt (fɛr'tsvikt) adj complicated, involved, awkward.

Veterinär (veteri'nɛ:r) nm -e veterinary surgeon.

Vetter ('fɛtər) nm -n (male) cousin.

Vieh (fi:) n neu 1 cattle. 2 beast. **—isch** adj 1 bestial. 2 brutal.

viel (fi:l) adj,adv much. adj pl many. **—erlei** ('fi:lərlai) adj of many kinds. **—fach** ('fi:lfax) adj also **—fältig** ('fi:lfɛltiç) manifold, multiple. **—leicht** (fi:'laiçt) adv perhaps, maybe, possibly. **—mal(s)** adv many times, frequently, often. **—mehr** (fi:l'me:r) adv rather. **—seitig** ('fi:lzaitiç) adj many-sided.

vier (fi:r) adj,nf four. **—eck** ('fi:rɛk) n neu square. **—eckig** adj square. **—te** adj fourth. **—tel** n neu — quarter. **—teljährlich** ('fi:rtəljɛ:rliç) adj quarterly. **—telstunde** (fi:rtəl-'ʃtundə) nf quarter of an hour.

vierzehn ('fi:rtse:n) adj,nf fourteen. **—te** adj fourteenth.

vierzig ('fi:rtsiç) adj,nf forty. **—ste** adj fortieth.

Villa ('vila) nf **Villen** villa.

Vio/la (vi'o:la) nf **-len** viola. **—line** (vio'li:nə) nf -n violin.

Visum ('vi:zum) n neu **-sa** visa.

Vlies (fli:s) n neu -e fleece.

Vogel ('fo:gəl) nm — bird. **—scheuche** nf -en scarecrow.

Vogesen (vo'ge:zən) n pl Vosges.

Vokabel (vo'ka:bəl) nf -n word.

Vokal (vo'ka:l) nm -e vowel.

Volk (fɔlk) n neu —er 1 people, folk. 2 nation, race.

Völkerbund ('fœlkərbunt) nm League of Nations.

Völkerkunde ('fœlkərkundə) nf ethnology.

Völkerrecht ('fœlkərrɛçt) n neu international law.

volkreich ('fɔlkraiç) adj populous.

Volksabstimmung ('fɔlksapʃtimuŋ) nf plebiscite, referendum.

volkseigen ('fɔlksaigən) adj nationalized.

Volkskunde ('fɔlkskundə) nf folklore.

Volkslied ('fɔlksli:t) n neu folksong.

Volksschule ('fɔlksʃu:lə) nf primary school.

volkstümlich ('fɔlksty:mliç) adj 1 popular. 2 national.

Volkswirtschaft ('fɔlksvirtʃaft) nf economics.

voll (fɔl) adj 1 full. 2 complete. **—bringen** (fɔl'briŋən) vt accomplish. **—er·len** (fɔl-'ɛndən) vt 1 finish, end. 2 complete. **—ig** ('fœliç) adv fully, completely, totally. **—jährig** ('fɔljɛ:riç) adj of age. **—kommen** (fɔl'kɔmən)

adj perfect. **—macht** nf 1 power of attorney. 2 proxy. **—ständig** adj complete. **—strekken** vt carry out, execute. **—ziehen*** (fɔl-'tsi:ən) vt carry out, accomplish.

Volontär (volɔn'tɛ:r) nm -e volunteer, trainee.

vom (fɔm) contraction of **von dem**.

von (fɔn) prep 1 of. 2 from. 3 by. **von...an** from, since. **—nöten** (fɔn'nœ:tən) adj necessary.

vor (fo:r) prep before, in front of. **—ab** (fo:r'ap) adv 1 first (of all). 2 in advance.

Vorabend ('fo:ra:bənt) nm eve.

Vorahnung ('fo:ra:nuŋ) nf premonition.

voran (fo'ran) adv before, ahead. **—gehen*** vi go at the head, precede.

voraus (fo'raus) adv in advance, in front, ahead. **im voraus** in advance, beforehand. **—sage** nf prediction. **—sagen** vt predict, forecast. **—setzung** nf -en 1 (pre)condition, prerequisite. 2 assumption. **—sichtlich** adj probable.

Vorbau ('fo:rbau) nm **-ten** 1 front structure. 2 porch.

Vorbedacht ('fo:rbədaxt) nm forethought, premeditation.

Vorbedingung ('fo:rbədiŋuŋ) nf condition, prerequisite.

Vorbehalt ('fo:rbəhalt) nm -e 1 reservation. 2 proviso. **—en*** vt reserve.

vorbei (fo:r'bai) adv 1 by, along, past. 2 past, done, over. **—gehen*** vi go past, pass (by).

vorbereit/en ('fo:rbəraitən) vt prepare. **—ung** nf -en preparation.

vorbeug/en ('fo:rbɔygən) vi prevent. **—ung** nf prevention.

Vorbild ('fo:rbilt) n neu 1 model. 2 original. **—lich** adj 1 model. 2 typical.

vorbringen ('fo:rbriŋən) vt 1 bring forward or up. 2 propose. 3 argue.

vordem (fɔr'de:m) adv formerly.

vorder ('fɔrdər) adj front, fore. **—asien** (fɔrdər-'a:zən) n neu Near East. **—grund** nm foreground. **—hand** adv for the present.

vordring/en ('fo:rdriŋən) vi advance, press on or forward. **—lich** adj 1 urgent. 2 intrusive.

voreilig (fo:'railiç) adj hasty, premature.

voreingenommen ('fo:raiŋənɔmən) adj biased, prejudiced.

vorenthalten* ('fo:rɛnthaltən) vt withhold.

vorerst ('fo:rə:rst) adv 1 first of all. 2 for the present.

vorerwähnt ('fo:rɛrvɛ:nt) adj above-mentioned, aforesaid.

Vorfahr ('fo:rfa:r) nm -en ancestor.
Vorfahrt ('fo:rfa:rt) nf also **Vorfahrt(s)recht** n neu mot right-of-way, priority.
Vorfall ('fo:rfal) nm incident, occurrence.
vorführen ('fo:rfy:rən) vt 1 present, perform, display. 2 project (films).
Vorgang ('fo:rgaŋ) nm 1 proceedings. 2 event. 3 precedent. **—er** ('fo:rgɛŋər) nm — predecessor.
vorgeb/en* ('fo:rge:bən) vt pretend, feign. **—lich** ('fo:rgeplɪç) adj alleged, pretended.
vorgefaßt ('fo:rgəfast) adj preconceived.
vorgehen* ('fo:rge:ən) vi 1 go forward, first, or before. 2 (of a clock) be fast. 3 occur. n neu — 1 procedure. 2 law action.
vorgenannt ('fo:rgənant) adj aforementioned.
Vorgeschichte ('fo:rgəʃɪçtə) nf prehistory.
Vorgeschmack ('fo:rgəʃmak) nm foretaste.
Vorgesetzte(r) ('fo:rgəzɛtstə) nm superior, senior.
vorgestern ('fo:rgɛstərn) adv the day before yesterday.
vorhaben* ('fo:rha:bən) vt intend. n neu — plan, purpose.
Vorhalle ('fo:rhalə) nf entrance-hall, porch.
vorhanden ('fo:rhandən) adj 1 available. 2 existing.
Vorhang ('fo:rhaŋ) nm curtain.
vorher (fo:r'he:r) adv previously, before(hand). **—ig** adj previous.
vorhin (fo:r'hɪn) adv a little while ago.
Vorhut ('fo:rhu:t) nf -en vanguard.
vorig ('fo:rɪç) adj former, preceding, previous.
vorjährig ('fo:rjɛ:rɪç) adj last year's.
Vorkehrung ('fo:rke:ruŋ) nf -en 1 precaution. 2 provision.
Vorkenntnis ('fo:rkɛntnɪs) nf -se previous experience or knowledge.
vorkommen* ('fo:rkɔmən) vi 1 happen, occur. 2 be found.
vorlad/en* ('fo:rla:dən) vt law summon. **—ung** nf -en summons.
vorläufig ('fo:rlɔyfɪç) adj provisional, preliminary, tentative.
vorlaut ('fo:rlaut) adj presumptuous, impudent.
vorlegen ('fo:rle:gən) vt 1 propose. 2 display. 3 submit.
vorles/en* ('fo:rle:zən) vt read aloud. **—ung** nf -en 1 lecture. 2 reading.
vorletzt ('fo:rlɛtst) adj penultimate.
Vorliebe ('fo:rli:bə) nf preference, fondness.
vorliegen* ('fo:rli:gən) vi be present or at hand.
vormals ('fo:rma:ls) adv formerly.

vormerken ('fo:rmɛrkən) vt note (down).
Vormittag ('fo:rmɪta:k) nm morning. **—s** adv in the morning.
Vormund ('fo:rmunt) nm -er guardian.
vorn (fɔrn) adv in front, before, ahead. **von vornherein** from the first or start.
Vorname ('fo:rna:mə) nm first or Christian name.
vornehm ('fo:rne:m) adj 1 distinguished, noble. 2 elegant. **—en*** vt 1 put on (an apron). 2 undertake. **sich —en** vr resolve (to do something). **—lich** adj chiefly, especially.
Vorort ('fo:rɔrt) nm suburb.
Vorposten ('fo:rpɔstən) nm outpost.
Vorrang ('fo:rraŋ) nm precedence, priority.
Vorrat ('fo:rra:t) nm stock, store, supply.
Vorrede ('fo:rre:də) nf 1 preface. 2 introduction.
vorrücken ('fo:rrykən) vt,vi move forward.
Vorsatz ('fo:rzats) nm 1 purpose. 2 intention.
Vorschau ('fo:rʃau) nf 1 preview. 2 trailer (for a film).
Vorschein ('fo:rʃain) nm appearance.
vorschieben* ('fo:rʃi:bən) vt 1 push forward. 2 pretend. 3 plead.
Vorschlag ('fo:rʃla:k) nm suggestion, proposal. **—en*** ('fo:rʃla:gən) vt propose, suggest.
vorschreiben* ('fo:rʃraibən) vt prescribe, order.
Vorschrift ('fo:rʃrɪft) nf 1 decree. 2 regulation. 3 instructions. 4 prescription.
Vorschub ('fo:rʃu:p) nm aid, help, assistance.
Vorschuß ('fo:rʃus) nm advance (of money).
Vorsehung ('fo:rze:uŋ) nf -en providence.
vorsetzen ('fo:rzɛtsən) vt 1 set over. 2 put forward. 3 appoint. 4 prefix. 5 offer.
Vorsicht ('fo:rzɪçt) nf caution. **—ig** adj cautious.
Vorsilbe ('fo:rzɪlbə) nf prefix.
Vorsitz ('fo:rzɪts) nm chair(manship). **—ende(r)** nm chairman, president.
Vorsorg/e ('fo:rzɔrgə) nf 1 care. 2 provision. **—en** vi provide (for). **—lich** ('fo:rzɔrklɪç) adj provident.
Vorspeise ('fo:rʃpaizə) nf hors d'oeuvre.
vorspiegeln ('fo:rʃpi:gəln) vt simulate, pretend.
Vorspiel ('fo:rʃpi:l) n neu prelude.
vorspringen* ('fo:rʃprɪŋən) vi 1 project. 2 leap forward.
Vorsprung ('fo:rʃpruŋ) nm 1 projection. 2 advantage, start.
Vorstadt ('fo:rʃtat) nf suburb.
Vorstand ('fo:rʃtant) nm 1 board of directors. 2 executive, management.

vorsteh/en* ('fo:rʃteːən) vi 1 protrude. 2 head, manage. **—er** nm — superintendent, chief.

vorstell/en ('fo:rʃtɛlən) vt 1 introduce, present, put forward. 2 represent. **sich vorstellen** vr imagine. **—ung** nf 1 (re)presentation. 2 idea. 3 introduction. 4 performance.

Vorstoß ('fo:rʃtos) nm advance, attack. **—en*** vi,vt advance (suddenly).

vorstrecken ('fo:rʃtrɛkən) vt 1 stretch forward or out. 2 advance (money).

Vorstufe ('fo:rʃtuːfə) nf first step(s), preliminary or primary stage.

Vorteil ('fortail) nm 1 advantage. 2 profit. **—haft** adj advantageous, profitable.

Vortrag ('fo:rtraːk) nm ⁼e 1 lecture. 2 report. 3 delivery, performance. 4 comm balance carried forward. **—en*** ('fo:rtraːgən) vt 1 lecture (on). 2 comm carry forward. 3 perform.

vortrefflich (fo:r'trɛfliç) adj excellent, admirable.

Vortritt ('fo:rtrit) nm precedence.

vorüber (fo'ryːbər) adv past, gone (by). **—gehen*** vi pass (by or over). **—gehend** adj passing, transitory.

Vorurteil ('fo:rurtail) n neu prejudice.

Vorwand ('fo:rvant) nm pretext.

vorwärts ('fo:rvɛrts) adv forward, onward.

vorweg (for'vɛk) adv before, beforehand. **—nehmen*** vt anticipate.

vorwerfen* ('fo:rvɛrfən) vt 1 reproach with. 2 throw forward.

vorwiegend ('fo:rviːgənt) adj predominant.

Vorwissen ('fo:rvisən) n neu previous knowledge.

Vorwort ('fo:rvɔrt) n neu -e 1 preface, foreword. 2 gram preposition.

Vorwurf ('fo:rvurf) nm 1 reproach. 2 subject, theme. **—svoll** adj reproachful.

Vorzeichen ('fo:rtsaiçən) n neu omen.

vorzeigen ('fo:rtsaigən) vt exhibit, show.

vorzeitig ('fo:rtsaitiç) adj premature.

vorziehen* ('fo:rtsiːən) vt 1 prefer. 2 draw (forward).

Vorzug ('fo:rtsuːk) nm 1 preference. 2 advantage. 3 priority. 4 good quality, merit. **—lich** (for'tsyːkliç) adj excellent, superior.

vulgär (vul'gɛːr) adj vulgar.

Vulkan (vul'kaːn) nm -e volcano.

W

Waag/e ('vaːgə) nf -n 1 balance, scale. 2 Libra. **—recht** ('vaːkrɛçt) adj horizontal, level.

wabbelig ('vabəliç) adj flabby, wobbly.

Wabe ('vaːbə) nf -n honeycomb.

wach (vax) adj 1 awake. 2 alert, alive. **—e** nf -n guard, watch. **—en** vi 1 watch (over). 2 be awake. **—sam** adj watchful, alert.

Wachs (vaks) n neu -e wax.

wachs/en* ('vaksən) vi grow. **—tum** n neu growth.

Wacht (vaxt) nf -en guard. **⁼er** ('vɛçtər) nm — guard, keeper, warder. **—meister** nm 1 policeman. 2 cavalry sergeant.

Wachtel ('vaxtəl) nf -n quail.

wackel/ig ('vakəliç) adj shaky, wobbly. **—n** vi shake, totter.

wacker ('vakər) adj 1 valiant. 2 decent.

Wade ('vaːdə) nf -n anat calf.

Waff/e ('vafə) nf -n weapon. **—enstillstand** nm armistice, truce, cease-fire.

Waffel ('vafəl) nf -n 1 waffle. 2 wafer.

wag/en ('vaːgən) vt risk, dare. **—emut** ('vaːgəmuːt) nm daring. **—halsig** ('vaːkhalsiç) adj reckless. **—nis** ('vaːknis) n neu -se risk.

Wagen ('vaːgən) nm -1 car. 2 van, lorry. 3 carriage. 4 wagon, cart.

wägen* ('vɛːgən) vt weigh. **erst wägen, dann wagen** look before you leap.

Wahl (vaːl) nf -en 1 choice, selection. 2 election, vote. **⁼en** ('vɛːlən) vt 1 choose, select. 2 elect, vote. 3 dial. **—er** ('vɛːlər) nm — voter. **⁼erisch** ('vɛːləriʃ) adj fastidious. **⁼erschaft** ('vɛːlərʃaft) nf -en voters. **—recht** n neu franchise, vote. **⁼erscheibe** ('vɛːlərʃaibə) nf dial. **—stimme** nf vote. **—zettel** nm ballot paper.

Wahn (vaːn) nm 1 delusion, illusion. 2 madness, folly. **—bild** n neu 1 phantom. 2 hallucination. **—sinn** nm 1 madness, insanity. 2 frenzy. **—sinnig** adj mad, insane.

wahr (vaːr) adj true, real. **—haft** adj also **—haftig** adj 1 truthful, true. 2 genuine. **—haftigkeit** nf truthfulness. **—heit** nf -en truth. **—nehmen*** vt 1 perceive, notice. 2 protect (interests). **—sagen** vt prophesy. **—scheinlich** (vaːr'ʃainliç) adj probable, likely. **—scheinlichkeit** (vaːr'ʃainliçkait) nf

127

-en probability. **—zeichen** n neu 1 token. 2 emblem.

wahren ('va:rən) vt 1 defend. 2 maintain.

während ('vɛ:rənt) prep during. conj while. **—dem** (vɛ:rənt'de:m) adv also **—des** or **—dessen** meanwhile.

Währung ('vɛ:ruŋ) nf -en currency, standard.

Waise ('vaizə) nf -n also **Waisenkind** n neu orphan. **—nhaus** n neu orphanage.

Wal (va:l) nm -e also **Walfisch** ('va:lfiʃ) whale. **—fischspeck** nm blubber.

Wald (valt) nm ⸚er wood, forest.

Wall (val) nm -e 1 rampart. 2 dam, dike.

wall/en[1] ('valən) vi see **wallfahren.**

wall/en[2] ('valən) vi 1 boil (up). 2 flutter. **—ung** nf -en 1 agitation. 2 boiling.

wallfahr/en* ('valfa:rən) vi go on a pilgrimage. **—er** nm pilgrim. **—t** nf pilgrimage.

Walnuß ('valnus) nf walnut.

Walroß ('valrɔs) n neu -rosse walrus.

Walz/e ('valtsə) nf -n tech roller, drum. **—en** vi waltz. vt roll, crush. **—er** ('valtsər) nm — waltz.

Wand (vant) nf ⸚e wall. **—karte** nf wall map.

Wand/el ('vandəl) nm 1 change, transformation. 2 conduct. **—eln** vt change. vi wander. **—lung** nf -en change, transformation.

Wander/er ('vandərər) nm — wanderer, rambler. **—lust** nf love of rambling or travelling. **—n** vi 1 walk, hike. 2 migrate. **—ung** nf -en 1 hike, excursion. 2 migration.

wandte ('vantə) v see **wenden.**

Wange ('vaŋə) nf -n cheek.

wanken ('vaŋkən) vi 1 sway, shake. 2 waver.

wann (van) conj,adv when.

Wanne ('vanə) nf -n tub, bath.

Wanze ('vantsə) nf -n bug, bedbug.

Wappen ('vapən) n neu — (coat of) arms.

war (va:r) v see **sein**[2].

wäre ('vɛ:rə) v see **sein**[2].

Ware ('va:rə) nf -n 1 article, ware. 2 pl merchandise, goods. **—nhaus** n neu department store. **—nzeichen** n neu trademark.

warf (va:rf) v see **werfen.**

warm (varm) adj warm, hot. ⸚e ('vɛrmə) nf warmth. **—en** ('vɛrmən) vt warm. ⸚flasche ('vɛrmflaʃə) nf hot-water bottle.

warn/en ('varnən) vt warn. **—ung** nf -en warning.

Warschau ('varʃau) n neu Warsaw.

wart/en ('vartən) vi wait. vt look after. **—er** ('vɛrtər) nm — attendant, keeper. **—esaal** nm waiting room.

warum (va'rum) adv why.

Warze ('va:rtsə) nf -n wart.

was (vas) pron what, (that) which.

wasch/en ('vaʃən) vt,vi wash. **—automat** ('vaʃautoma:t) nm automatic washing machine. **—becken** n neu hand-basin, wash-basin. ⸚e ('vɛʃə) nf 1 wash(ing). 2 underwear. **—erei** (vɛʃə'rai) nf -en laundry. **—lappen** nm face cloth. **—maschine** nf washing machine. **—mittel** n neu soap powder, detergent.

Wasser ('vasər) n neu ⸚ water. **—dicht** adj watertight, waterproof. **—fall** nm waterfall. **—hahn** nm tap. ⸚ig ('vɛsəriç) adj watery. **—leitung** nf water supply. **—mann** nm Aquarius. ⸚n ('vɛsərn) vt 1 water, irrigate. 2 soak. **—stoff** nm hydrogen.

Watte ('vatə) nf -n 1 wadding. 2 cotton wool.

weben* ('ve:bən) vt weave. **—er** nm — weaver.

Wechsel ('vɛksəl) nm — 1 (ex)change. 2 bill of exchange. **—geld** n neu (small) change. **—n** vt,vi 1 change. 2 exchange. 3 vary.

weck/en ('vɛkən) vt wake, rouse. **—er** nm — alarm clock.

wedeln ('ve:dəln) vi 1 fan. 2 wag.

weder ('ve:dər) conj **weder...noch** neither ...nor.

weg (vɛk) adv 1 away. 2 gone. 3 off.

Weg (ve:k) nm -e 1 way, route. 2 path. 3 road. **—weiser** ('ve:kvaizər) nm — 1 signpost. 2 guide.

wegbleiben* ('vɛkblaibən) vi 1 stay away. 2 be omitted.

wegblicken ('vɛkblikən) vi look away.

wegen ('ve:gən) prep 1 because of. 2 for.

weggehen* ('vɛkge:ən) vi depart, leave.

weglassen* ('vɛklasən) vt 1 omit. 2 let go.

wegmüssen* ('vɛkmysən) vi have to go, be obliged to leave.

wegräumen ('vɛkrɔymən) vt clear away.

wegreißen* ('vɛkraisən) vt tear or snatch away.

wegschaffen* ('vɛkʃafən) vt get rid of.

wegtun* ('vɛktu:n) vt put away.

wegwerfen* ('vɛkvɛrfən) vt throw away or out.

weh (ve:) adj 1 sore, painful. 2 sad. interj woe! **weh tun** hurt, be painful. **—** n neu -e 1 pain. 2 grief. **—en** n pl labour pains. **—mut** nf melancholy.

Weh/e ('ve:ə) nf -n (snow)drift. **—en** vi blow.

Wehr[1] (ve:r) nf -en 1 defence. 2 weapon. 3 bulwark. **—dienst** nm military service. **—en**

vt 1 restrain. 2 forbid. **sich —en** *vr* resist. **—macht** *nf* armed forces. **—pflicht** *nf* compulsory service, conscription.

Wehr[2] (ve:r) *n neu* -e weir.

Weib (vaip) *n neu* -er *inf* 1 woman, female. 2 wife. **—isch** ('vaibiʃ) *adj* effeminate, womanish. **—lich** *adj* feminine, female.

weich (vaiç) *adj* 1 soft. 2 smooth. **—lich** *adj* soft, effeminate. **—ling** *nm* -e weakling.

Weiche ('vaiçə) *nf* -n 1 (railway) points. 2 *anat* flank.

weichen* ('vaiçən) *vi* 1 yield. 2 flinch.

Weichsel ('vaiksəl) *nf* Vistula.

Weide ('vaidə) *nf* -n 1 pasture. 2 willow. **—n** *vi* graze. **sich —n** *vr* gloat.

sich weigern ('vaigərn) *vr* refuse.

Weih/e ('vaiə) *nf* -n 1 consecration, dedication. 2 initiation. **—en** *vt* 1 consecrate, dedicate. 2 initiate. **—rauch** *nm* incense.

Weihnacht/en ('vainaxtən) *n pl* Christmas. **—slied** *n neu* carol.

weil (vail) *conj* because, since.

Weile ('vailə) *nf* -n 1 while. 2 time.

Wein (vain) *nm* -e 1 wine. 2 *also* **Weinstock** ('vainʃtɔk) *nm* vine. **—bau** *nm* vine-growing. **—lese** *nf* vintage, gathering, grape-harvest.

weinen ('vainən) *vi* cry, weep.

weis/e ('vaizə) *adj* wise, prudent. *nm* -n wise man, sage. **—heit** ('vaishait) *nf* wisdom. **—lich** (vaisliç) *adv* wisely.

Weise ('vaizə) *nf* -n 1 manner, way, method. 2 tune, melody.

weis/en* ('vaizən) *vt* indicate, show. **—ung** *nf* -en direction, instruction.

weiß[1] (vais) *adj,n neu* white. **—e(r)** *nm* white man. **—kohl** *nm* (white) cabbage.

weiß[2] (vais) *v see* **wissen**.

weit (vait) *adj* 1 distant. 2 wide. **—aus** (vait-'aus) *adv* by far. **—e** *nf* -n 1 distance. 2 width. 3 scope, size. **—läufig** ('vaitlɔyfiç) *adj* 1 distant. 2 extensive. 3 diffuse. **—reichend** ('vaitraiçənt) *adj* far-reaching. **—sichtig** *adj* 1 long-sighted. 2 far-sighted.

weiter ('vaitər) *adj* 1 further. 2 farther. 3 wider. *adv* 1 further on. 2 else.

Weizen ('vaitsən) *nm* wheat.

welch (vɛlç) *pron* who, which, what, that. *pron,adj* some, any.

welk (vɛlk) *adj* withered, limp.

Welle ('vɛlə) *nf* -n 1 wave. 2 axle. 3 shaft. **—nlänge** *nf* wavelength.

Welt (vɛlt) *nf* -en world. **—all** *n neu* universe. **—anschauung** *nf* philosophy of life, ideology.

—klug *adj* worldly-wise. **—lich** *adj* secular, worldly. **—macht** *nf* world power. **—männisch** ('vɛltmɛniʃ) *adj* sophisticated.

wem (ve:m) *pron* to whom.

wen (ve:n) *pron* whom.

Wend/e ('vɛndə) *nf* -n 1 turn, turning point. **—en*** *vi* turn. **—epunkt** *nm* turning point, crisis. **—ung** *nf* -en 1 turn(ing). 2 figure of speech.

wenig ('ve:niç) *adj,pron* 1 little. 2 *pl* few. **—st** *adj* least. **—stens** *adv* at least.

wer (ve:r) *pron* who, which.

werb/en* ('vɛrbən) *vi* 1 court. 2 advertise (for), *vt* recruit. **—ung** *nf* -en 1 advertising. 2 recruiting. 3 courting.

Werdegang ('verdəgaŋ) *nm* 1 career. 2 development.

werden* ('ve:rdən) *v mod aux* shall, will. *vi* 1 become. 2 happen. *n neu* 1 growth. 2 origin.

werfen* ('vɛrfən) *vt* throw. *vi* bring forth young.

Werft (vɛrft) *nf* -en 1 shipyard. 2 wharf.

Werk (vɛrk) *n neu* -e 1 work(s). 2 deed. 3 mechanism. **—statt** *nf* workshop. **—stoff** *nm* (raw) material. **—zeug** *n neu* tool.

Wermut ('ve:rmu:t) *nm* vermouth.

wert (vert) *adj* 1 worth. 2 worthy. *nm* -e worth, value. **—brief** *nm* registered money letter. **—en** *vt* value. **—sache** *nf* valuable. **—voll** *adj* valuable.

Wesen ('ve:zən) *n neu* — 1 being, creature. 2 essence, character. 3 way, manners. 4 fuss. **—tlich** *adj* 1 substantial. 2 essential.

weshalb (vɛs'halp) *adv,conj also* **weswegen** (vɛs've:gən) why, wherefore.

Wespe ('vɛspə) *nf* -n wasp.

wessen ('vɛsən) *pron* 1 of whom, whose. 2 of which, of what.

West (vɛst) *nm also* **West/en** ('vɛstən) west. **—deutschland** *n neu* West Germany. **—lich** *adj* west(ern), westerly. **—wärts** ('vɛstverts) *adv* westward(s), west.

Westfalen (vɛst'fa:lən) *n neu* Westphalia.

Westindien (vɛst'indiən) *n neu* West Indies.

wett (vɛt) *adj* even, quits.

Wett/e ('vɛtə) *nf* -n bet, wager. **—büro** *n neu* betting shop or office. **—en** *vt,vi* bet, wager. **—kampf** *nm* competition, contest, match. **—laufen*** *vi* (run a) race.

Wetter ('vɛtər) *n neu* — 1 weather. 2 storm. **—bericht** *nm* weather report or forecast.

wetzen ('vɛtsən) *vt* sharpen, whet.

wichtig ('viçtiç) *adj* important.

Widder ('vidər) *nm* — 1 ram. 2 Aries.

wider (ˈviːdər) *prep* against.

widerfahren* (viːdərˈfaːrən) *vi* happen (to).

Widerhaken (ˈviːdərhaːkən) *nm* barb, hook.

Widerhall (ˈviːdərhal) *nm* **-e 1** echo. **2** response.

widerleg/en (viːdərˈleːgən) *vt* refute. **—ung** *nf —en* refutation.

widerlich (ˈviːdərliç) *adj* repulsive.

widerrechtlich (ˈviːdərrɛçtliç) *adj* illegal.

Widerruf (ˈviːdərruːf) *nm* countermand, disavowal. **—en*** (viːdərˈruːfən) *vt* revoke.

sich widersetz/en (viːdərˈzɛtsən) *vr* oppose. **—lich** *adj* insubordinate. **—lichkeit** *nf* insubordination.

widerspenstig (ˈviːdərʃpɛnstiç) *adj* obstinate.

widersprechen* (viːdərˈʃprɛçən) *vi* contradict.

Widerspruch (ˈviːdərʃprux) *nm* **1** opposition. **2** contradiction.

Widerstand (ˈviːdərʃtant) *nm* **1** resistance. **2** opposition.

widerstehen* (viːdərˈʃteːən) *vi* withstand.

widerwärtig (ˈviːdərvɛrtiç) *adj* disagreeable, offensive.

widerwillig (ˈviːdərviliç) *adj* unwilling.

widmen (ˈvidmən) *vt* dedicate, devote.

widrig (ˈviːdriç) *adj* adverse, contrary. **—enfalls** (ˈviːdrigənfals) *adv* failing which.

wie (viː) *adv* how. *conj* **1** how. **2** as. **3** like.

wieder (ˈviːdər) *adv* **1** again. **2** back.

Wiederaufnahme (viːdərˈaufnaːmə) *nf* **-n** resumption.

wiederbringen* (ˈviːdərbriŋən) *vt* bring back, restore.

wiedererkennen* (ˈviːdərɛrkɛnən) *vt* recognize.

Wiedergabe (ˈviːdərgaːbə) *nf* **1** restitution. **2** reproduction.

wiedergeben* (ˈviːdərgeːbən) *vt* **1** return. **2** reproduce.

Wiedergeburt (ˈviːdərgəbuːrt) *nf* **1** rebirth, regeneration. **2** reincarnation.

wiedergutmachen (viːdərˈguːtmaxən) *vt* compensate for.

wiederhol/en (viːdərˈhoːlən) *vt* repeat. **—ung** *nf* repetition.

wiederhören (ˈviːdərhøːrən) *vt* hear again. **auf Wiederhören** (in a telephone conversation) goodbye.

wiederkäuen (ˈviːdərkɔyən) *vt* ruminate.

wiederkehren (ˈviːdərkeːrən) *vi* return.

wiederkommen* (ˈviːdərkɔmən) *vi* come back.

wiedersehen* (ˈviːdərzeːən) *vt* see again. **auf Wiedersehen** goodbye.

wiederum (ˈviːdərum) *adv* again, anew.

Wieg/e (ˈviːgə) *nf* **-n** cradle. **—enlied** *n neu* lullaby.

wiegen* (ˈviːgən) *vt,vi* weigh.

Wien (viːn) *n neu* Vienna.

wies (viːs) *v see* **weisen.**

Wiese (ˈviːzə) *nf* **-n** meadow.

Wiesel (ˈviːzəl) *n neu* — weasel.

wieso (viːˈzoː) *adv* why.

wieviel (viːˈfiːl) *adv* how much.

wild (vilt) *adj* **1** wild, savage. **2** fierce. **3** angry. *n neu* game. **—dieb** *nm* poacher. **—ern** (ˈvildərn) *vi* poach. **—hüter** *nm* gamekeeper. **—nis** *nf* **-se** wilderness.

will (vil) *v see* **wollen.**

Will/e (ˈvilə) *nm* will. **—enlos** *adj* irresolute, half-hearted. **—enskraft** *nf* will-power. **—kommen** (vilˈkɔmən) *adj,n neu,interj* welcome. **—kür** (ˈvilkyːr) *nf* discretion, choice. **—kürlich** (ˈvilkyːrliç) *adj* arbitrary.

wimmeln (ˈviməln) *vi* swarm (with).

Wimper (ˈvimpər) *nf* **-n** eyelash. **ohne mit der Wimper zu zucken** without batting an eyelid.

Wind (vint) *nm* **-e** wind. **—beutel** *nm* **1** eclair. **2** *sl* windbag. **—hund** *nm* greyhound. **—ig** (ˈvindiç) *adj* windy. **—schutzscheibe** *nf* windscreen. **—stille** *nf* calm, lull.

Winde (ˈvində) *nf* **-n** winch, reel.

Windel (ˈvindəl) *nf* **-n** nappy.

winden* (ˈvindən) *vt* wind.

Wink (viŋk) *nm* **-e 1** sign. **2** nod. **3** wave. **—en** *vi* **1** make a sign. **2** wink. **3** wave. **4** nod.

Wink/el (ˈviŋkəl) *nm* **1** angle. **2** corner. **3** nook. **—elmesser** *nm* protractor. **—lig** (ˈviŋkliç) *adj* angular.

winseln (ˈvinzəln) *vi* whimper, whine.

Winter (ˈvintər) *nm* — winter. **—lich** *adj* wintry.

Winzer (ˈvintsər) *nm* — vine-grower.

winzig (ˈvintsiç) *adj* tiny, minute.

Wipfel (ˈvipfəl) *nm* — treetop.

Wippe (ˈvipə) *nf* **-n** seesaw.

wir (viːr) *pron 1st pers pl* we.

Wirbel (ˈvirbəl) *nm* — **1** whirl, eddy. **2** vertebra. **3** peg. **—n** *vi* whirl, swirl. **—säule** *nf* spine, vertebral column.

wird (virt) *v see* **werden.**

wirk/en (ˈvirkən) *vi* work. *vt* **1** work. **2** effect. **3** weave. **—sam** *adj* effective. **—ung** *nf* **-en 1** effect, result. **2** action.

wirklich (ˈvirkliç) *adj* real, actual. **—keit** *nf* **-en** reality.

wirr (vir) *adj* confused, chaotic. **—warr** (ˈvirvar) *nm* muddle, disorder.

wirst (virst) v see **werden**.

Wirt (virt) nm **-e** 1 host. 2 innkeeper, landlord. **—in** nf **-nen** 1 hostess. 2 landlady. **—schaft** nf **-en** 1 economy. 2 housekeeping, household. 3 inn, pub. **—schaften** vi 1 keep house. 2 manage (well). **—schaft(l)er** nm — manager. **—schaftlich** adj 1 economic. 2 economical. **—schaftsprüfer** nm — chartered accountant. **—shaus** n neu inn, pub.

wisch/en ('viʃən) vt wipe, rub. **—lappen** nm — duster.

wispern ('vispərn) vi,vt whisper.

Wißbegier ('visbagiːr) nf also **Wißbegierde** nf craving for knowledge, curiosity. **—ig** adj eager to learn, inquisitive.

wissen* ('visən) vt,vi know. n neu knowledge, learning.

Wissenschaft ('visənʃaft) nf **-en** 1 science. 2 learning. **—ler** nm — 1 scientist. 2 scholar **—lich** adj 1 scientific. 2 learned, scholarly.

wittern ('vitərn) vt scent, smell.

Witwe ('vitvə) nf **-n** widow. **—r** (vitvər) nm — widower.

Witz (vits) nm **-e** 1 joke. 2 wit. **—eln** vi joke. **—ig** adj witty.

wo (voː) adv,conj where.

woanders (voːˈandərs) adv elsewhere.

wobei (voːˈbai) adv whereby. pron 1 in or at which. 2 in doing which.

Woche ('vɔxə) nf **-n** week. **—nblatt** n neu weekly (newspaper). **—nende** n neu weekend. **—ntlich** ('vœçəntliç) adj weekly.

wodurch (voːˈdurç) adv whereby. pron 1 by or through which. 2 in doing which.

wofür (voːˈfyːr) adv,pron for which.

wog (voːk) v see **wiegen**.

wogegen (voːˈgeːgən) adv in return for which. conj whereas.

woher (voːˈheːr) adv whence, wherefrom.

wohin (voːˈhin) adv whither, (to) where.

wohl (voːl) adv 1 well. 2 probably, presumably. n neu welfare, wellbeing.

wohlan (voːˈlan) interj come on! well!

wohlauf (voːˈlauf) adv well. interj well then!

Wohlbehagen (voːlbəˈhaːgən) n neu comfort.

Wohlfahrt ('voːlfaːrt) nf welfare. **—sstaat** nm welfare state. **—sgesellschaft** nf affluent society.

wohlfeil ('voːlfail) adj cheap.

wohlhabend ('voːlhaːbənt) adj well-off, prosperous.

Wohlklang ('voːlklaŋ) nm harmony.

Wohlstand ('voːlʃtant) nm prosperity.

Wohltat ('voːltaːt) nf benefit. **—er** ('voːltɛːtər) nm benefactor.

wohltun* ('voːltuːn) vi do good, benefit.

Wohlwollen ('voːlvɔlən) n neu goodwill, favour.

wohn/en ('voːnən) vi live, dwell. **—haft** adj resident. **—ung** nf **-en** 1 dwelling, residence. 2 flat, apartment. **—wagen** nm caravan. **—zimmer** n neu sitting room.

Wölbung ('vœlbuŋ) nf **-en** 1 vault. 2 dome. 3 arch.

Wolf (vɔlf) nm **-e** wolf.

Wolk/e ('vɔlkə) nf **-n** cloud. **—enkratzer** nm — skyscraper. **—ig** adj cloudy, clouded.

Woll/e ('vɔlə) nf **-n** wool. **—en** adj woollen. **—ig** adj woolly, fleecy. **—jacke** nf cardigan.

wollen* ('vɔlən) vi,vt want, desire. v mod aux 1 want or desire (to). 2 intend (to). 3 be about (to).

Wollust ('vɔlust) nf **-e** sensual pleasure, lust.

womit (voːˈmit) adv with or by which.

womöglich (voːˈmœːkliç) adv where or if possible.

wonach (voːˈnaːx) adv 1 according to which. 2 after which.

Wonne ('vɔnə) nf **-n** delight, joy, bliss.

woran (voːˈran) adv,pron at or about which or what.

worauf (voːˈrauf) adv,pron (up)on which or what.

woraus (voːˈraus) adv,pron of or from which or what.

worden ('vɔrdən) v see **werden**.

worin (voːˈrin) adv in(to) which or what.

Wort (vɔrt) n neu **-er** (written) word. n neu **-e** 1 (spoken) word, expression. 2 word, pledge. **—bruch** nm breach of one's word. **—erbuch** ('vœrtarbuːx) n neu dictionary. **—führer** nm 1 spokesman. 2 speaker. **—karg** adj taciturn. **—laut** nm wording, text. **—lich** ('vœrtliç) adj 1 literal. 2 verbal. 3 word-for-word. **—reich** adj verbose. **—schatz** nm vocabulary.

wovon (voːˈfɔn) adv,pron of or from which or what.

wozu (voːˈtsuː) adv,pron 1 to or for what, why. 2 in addition to which.

Wrack (vrak) n neu **-s** naut wreck.

wringen* ('vriŋən) vt wring.

Wucher ('vuːxər) nm 1 usury. 2 profiteering. **—er** nm — 1 usurer. 2 profiteer. **—isch** adj 1 usurious. 2 profiteering. **—n** vi 1 grow luxuriantly or abundantly. 2 profiteer.

Wuchs (vu:ks) *nm* 1 growth. 2 figure, size.

Wucht (vuxt) *nf* -en force, weight.

wühl/en ('vy:lən) *vt* stir up, agitate. *vi* burrow. —**er** *nm* — agitator.

Wulst (vulst) *nm* -̈e 1 roll, pad. 2 swelling.

wund (vunt) *adj* 1 sore. 2 wounded. —**e** ('vundə) *nf* -en wound.

Wunder ('vundər) *n neu* — 1 miracle. 2 wonder. —**bar** *adj* wonderful, marvellous. —**kind** *n neu* child prodigy. —**lich** *adj* strange, odd. —**n** *vt* astound, surprise. **sich** —**n** *vr* wonder (at). —**schön** *adj* beautiful, exquisite.

Wunsch (vunʃ) *nm* -̈e wish, desire. —**en** ('vynʃən) *vt* wish, desire. —**enswert** ('vynʃ-ənsve:rt) *adj* desirable.

wurde ('vu:rdə) *v* see **werden.**

würde ('vyrdə) *v* see **werden.**

Würd/e ('vyrdə) *nf* -n 1 dignity, honour. 2 rank. —**enträger** *nm* dignitary. —**ig** *adj* worthy.

Wurf (vurf) *nm* -̈e 1 throw, cast. 2 litter, brood. —**scheibe** *nf* discus.

Würfel ('vyrfəl) *nm* — 1 game die, dice. 2 cube. —**zucker** *nm* lump sugar.

würgen ('vyrgən) *vi,vt* choke.

Wurm (vurm) *nm* -̈er worm.

Wurst (vurst) *nf* -̈e sausage.

Württemberg ('vyrtəmbɛrk) *n neu* Wurtemberg.

Würz/e ('vyrtsə) *nf* -n 1 seasoning, spice. 2 flavour. —**en** *vt* season, spice. —**ig** *adj* spicy, seasoned.

Wurzel ('vurtsəl) *nf* -n root. —**n** *vi* take root.

wußte ('vustə) *v* see **wissen.**

wüst (vy:st) *adj* 1 desert, waste. 2 disorderly. 3 depraved. —**e** *nf* -n desert, wilderness. —**ling** *nm* -e libertine, depraved person.

Wut (vu:t) *nf* rage, fury. —**end** ('vy:tənt) *adj* furious.

X

Xenophobie (ksenofo'bi:) *nf* xenophobia.

x-mal ('iksma:l) *adv inf* umpteen times.

Xylophon (ksylo'fo:n) *n neu* -e xylophone.

Z

Zack/e ('tsakə) *nf* -n also **Zack/en** *nm* — 1 prong. 2 tooth. 3 peak. —**en** *vt* 1 notch. 2 indent. —**ig** *adj* 1 jagged. 2 spirited.

zaghaft ('tsa:khaft) *adj* timid.

zäh (tsɛ:) *adj* 1 tough. 2 resistant. —**igkeit** *nf* 1 toughness. 2 pertinacity.

Zahl (tsa:l) *nf* -en number, numeral. —**bar** *adj* payable. —**en** *vt,vi* pay. —**los** *adj* countless. —**reich** *adj* numerous. —**tag** *nm* payday. —**ung** *nf* -en payment. —**ungsfähig** *adj* solvent. —**wort** *n neu* numeral.

zähl/en ('tsɛ:lən) *vt,vi* count, number. —**ung** *nf* -en counting.

zahm (tsa:m) *adj* tame. —**en** ('tsɛ:mən) *vt* 1 tame. 2 break in (a horse).

Zahn (tsa:n) *nm* -̈e tooth. —**arzt** *nm* dentist. —**bürste** *nf* toothbrush. —**pasta** *nf* toothpaste. —**rad** *nm* cog wheel. —**schmerz** *nm* also —**weh** *n neu* toothache. —**stocher** *nm* toothpick.

Zange ('tsaŋə) *nf* -n 1 pincers, tweezers. 2 tongs.

Zank (tsaŋk) *nm* -̈e quarrel. —**en** *vi* quarrel. —**isch** ('tsɛŋkiʃ) *adj* quarrelsome.

zapfen ('tsapfən) *vt* tap. *nm* — 1 bung, plug. 2 pin. 3 pivot.

zappeln ('tsapəln) *vi* 1 wriggle. 2 fidget.

Zar (tsa:r) *nm* -en tsar.

zart (tsa:rt) *adj* 1 tender. 2 delicate. —**lich** ('tsɛ:rtliç) *adj* tender, affectionate.

Zauber ('tsaubər) *nm* — 1 magic. 2 spell, charm. —**ei** (tsaubə'rai) *nf* magic. —**er** *nm* — magician, sorcerer. —**haft** *adj* 1 magical. 2 enchanting. —**n** *vi,vt* conjure (up).

zaudern ('tsaudərn) *vi* hesitate, delay. *n neu* hesitation.

Zaum (tsaum) *nm* -̈e bridle, rein. —**en** ('tsɔymən) *vt* bridle.

Zaun (tsaun) *nm* -̈e fence.

Zeche ('tsɛçə) *nf* -n 1 bill. 2 mine.

Zehe ('tse:ə) *nf* -n toe.

zehn (tse:n) *adj,nf* ten. —**te** *adj* tenth.

zehren ('tse:rən) *vi* 1 feed. 2 waste (away).

Zeichen ('tsaiçən) *n neu* — 1 sign. 2 signal.

zeichn/en ('tsaiçnən) *vt* 1 draw. 2 mark. 3 design. 4 subscribe. —**er** *nm* — 1 designer. 2 draughtsman. 3 subscriber. —**ung** *nf* -en 1 drawing. 2 sketch. 3 design. 4 subscription.

Zeig/efinger ('tsaigəfiŋər) *nm* index finger.

—**en** vt show. **sich —en** vr appear. —**er**
nm — hand, pointer.

Zeile ('tsailə) nf -n line.

Zeit (tsait) nf -en time. **zur Zeit** at present.

Zeitalter ('tsaitaltər) n neu age, era.

Zeitfolge ('tsaitfɔlgə) nf chronological order.

Zeitgenoss/e ('tsaitgənɔsə) nm contemporary.
—**isch** ('tsaitgənœsiʃ) adj contemporary.

zeitig ('tsaitiç) adj 1 early. 2 timely. —**en** vt 1
ripen, mature. 2 cause, produce.

Zeitkarte ('tsaitkartə) nf season ticket.

Zeitlang ('tsaitlaŋ) nf **eine Zeitlang** for some
time.

zeitlich ('tsaitliç) adj temporal.

Zeitpunkt ('tsaitpuŋkt) nm 1 moment. 2 point.

Zeitraum ('tsaitraum) nm interval, period.

Zeitschrift ('tsaitʃrift) nf periodical, magazine.

Zeitung ('tsaituŋ) nf -en newspaper, journal.
—**swesen** n neu journalism.

zeitweilig ('tsaitvailiç) adj 1 temporary. 2
intermittent.

zeitweise ('tsaitvaizə) adv 1 for a time. 2 at
times.

Zeitwort ('tsaitvɔrt) n neu —er verb.

Zelle ('tsɛlə) nf -n 1 cell. 2 call-box.

Zelt (tsɛlt) n neu -e tent. —**en** vi camp. n neu
camping.

Zement (tse'mɛnt) nm -e cement.

Zensur (tsɛn'zu:r) nf -en 1 censorship. 2 educ
marks, report.

Zentimeter (tsɛnti'me:tər) nm,neu — centimetre.

Zentner ('tsɛntnər) nm — hundredweight, fifty
kilograms.

zentral (tsɛn'tra:l) adj central. —**e** nf -n 1 head
office, headquarters. 2 power station.
—**heizung** nf central heating. —**isieren**
(tsɛntrali'zi:rən) vt centralize.

zerbrech/en* (tsɛr'brɛçən) vt,vi break into
pieces, shatter. —**lich** adj fragile.

zerdrücken (tsɛr'drykən) vt crush, grind.

Zeremonie (tseremo'ni:) nf -n ceremony.

Zerfall (tsɛr'fal) nm decay, ruin. —**en*** vi fall
into ruin, decay.

zerfetzen (tsɛr'fɛtsən) vt shred.

zergliedern (tsɛr'gli:dərn) vt 1 dismember. 2
analyse. 3 anat dissect.

zerhauen (tsɛr'hauən) vt cut up, mince.

zerleg/en (tsɛr'le:gən) vt 1 take apart, divide,
dissect. 2 analyse. 3 carve. 4 dispense.

zerlumpt (tsɛr'lumpt) adj ragged, tattered.

zermürben (tsɛr'myrbən) vt wear down.

zerplatzen (tsɛr'platsən) vi burst.

zerquetschen (tsɛr'kvɛtʃən) vt squash, crush.

Zerr/bild ('tsɛrbilt) n neu caricature. —**en** vt 1
tug, pull. 2 strain.

zerreiben* (tsɛr'raibən) vt grind, pulverize.

zerreißen* (tsɛr'raisən) vt,vi tear or rip up.

zerrinnen* (tsɛr'rinən) vi melt away, vanish.

zerschellen (tsɛr'ʃɛlən) vt,vi shatter, smash.

zerschlagen* (tsɛr'ʃla:gən) vt break into pieces.
vi come to nothing.

zerschneiden* (tsɛr'ʃnaidən) vt cut up.

zersetz/en (tsɛr'zɛtsən) vt 1 decompose, disintegrate. 2 undermine. —**ung** nf decomposition.

zersplittern (tsɛr'ʃplitərn) vt split up, splinter.

zersprengen (tsɛr'ʃprɛŋən) vt blow up, burst.

zerstäub/en (tsɛr'ʃtɔybən) vt 1 spray. 2 disperse, scatter. —**er** nm — spray.

zerstör/en (tsɛr'ʃtœ:rən) vt destroy. —**er** nm
— destroyer. —**ung** nf destruction.

zerstreu/en (tsɛr'ʃtrɔyən) vt 1 disperse, scatter.
2 diffuse. 3 divert, entertain, amuse. —**t** adj
1 absent-minded. 2 dispersed. —**theit** nf
absent-mindedness. —**ung** nf -en 1 disper-
sion. 2 amusement.

zerteilen (tsɛr'tailən) vt cut up, divide.

zertreten* (tsɛr'tre:tən) vt trample underfoot,
stamp out.

zertrümmern (tsɛr'trymərn) vt lay waste, demolish, destroy, ruin.

zetern ('tse:tərn) vi 1 cry out (for help). 2 scold,
nag.

Zettel ('tsɛtəl) nm — 1 sheet or slip of paper,
note. 2 ticket. 3 label.

Zeug (tsɔyk) n neu -e 1 thing. 2 stuff. 3
material, cloth. —**haus** n neu arsenal.

Zeug/e ('tsɔygə) nm -n witness. —**nis** ('tsɔyknis) n neu -se 1 evidence, testimony. 2
certificate. 3 reference.

zeug/en[1] ('tsɔygən) vt produce, beget. —**ung**
nf -en procreation.

zeugen[2] ('tsɔygən) vi give testimony, testify.

Zickzack ('tsiktsak) nm -e zigzag.

Ziege ('tsi:gə) nf -n (she-)goat.

Ziegel ('tsi:gəl) nm — 1 brick. 2 tile. —**ofen**
nm brickkiln.

zieh/en* ('tsi:ən) vt 1 pull, draw (out). 2
cultivate, raise. 3 dig. vi 1 draw, pull. 2 move,
go. **es zieht** there is a draught, it is draughty.
sich ziehen vr 1 extend. 2 move. 3 withdraw.
—**harmonika** nf accordion.

Ziel (tsi:l) n neu -e 1 aim, end. 2 goal. 3
target. —**en** vi aim (at).

ziem/en ('tsi:mən) vi also **sich ziemen** vr 1

suit. 2 become. **—lich** *adv* quite, rather, moderately, fairly. *adj* suitable, fitting.

Zier (tsiːr) *nf* **-en** also **Zierat** *nm* **-e** ornament. **—en** *vt* decorate, adorn. **—lich** *adj* graceful, pretty, elegant.

Ziffer ('tsifər) *nf* **-n** figure, cipher.

Zigarette (tsiga'rɛta) *nf* **-n** cigarette.

Zigarre (tsi'garə) *nf* **-n** cigar.

Zigeuner (tsi'gɔynər) *nm* **-** gipsy.

Zimmer ('tsimər) *n neu* **-** room. **—mann** *nm* carpenter.

zimperlich ('tsimpərliç) *adj* **1** prim, prudish. **2** affected.

Zimt (tsimt) *nm* **-e** cinnamon.

Zink (tsiŋk) *n neu* zinc.

Zinke ('tsiŋka) *nf* **-n 1** prong. **2** dovetail.

Zinn (tsin) *n neu* tin.

Zins (tsins) *nm* **-en 1** interest. **2** rent. **—eszins** ('tsinzəstsins) *nm* compound interest. **—fuß** *nm* also **—satz** interest rate.

Zipfel ('tsipfəl) *nm* **—** tip, corner, edge.

Zirkus ('tsirkus) *nm* **-se** circus.

zirpen ('tsirpən) *vi* chirp.

Zitrone (tsi'troːna) *nf* **-n** lemon.

zittern ('tsitərn) *vi* tremble, quiver.

Zitze ('tsitsa) *nf* **-n** teat, nipple.

zivil (tsi'viːl) *adj* **1** civil. **2** civilian. **—ist** (tsivi'list) *nm* **-en** civilian.

Zivil/isation (tsiviliːzatsi'oːn) *nf* **-en** civilization, culture. **—isieren** (tsivili'zːran) *vt* civilize.

Zofe ('tsoːfə) *nf* **-n** lady's maid.

zog (tsoːk) *v* see **ziehen**.

zöger/n ('tsœːgərn) *vi* hesitate, linger. **—ung** *nf* **-en** delay, hesitation.

Zögling ('tsœːkliŋ) *nm* **-e** pupil.

Zoll[1] (tsɔl) *nm* **—** inch.

Zoll[2] (tsɔl) *nm* **-e** custom, duty, toll. **—amt** *n neu* customs office. **—beamte(r)** *nm* also **—ner** ('tsœlnər) *nm* **—** customs officer. **—en** *vt* pay. **—frei** *adj* duty-free. **—pflichtig** *adj* dutiable, liable to (customs) duty.

Zone ('tsoːna) *nf* **-n** zone.

Zoo (tsoː) *nm* **-s** zoo. **—loge** (tsoːo'loːgə) *nm* **-n** zoologist. **—logie** (tsoːolo'giː) *nf* zoology. **—logisch** (tsoːo'loːgiʃ) *adj* zoological.

Zopf (tsɔpf) *nm* **-e** plait, pigtail.

Zorn (tsɔrn) *nm* anger. **—ig** *adj* angry.

zu (tsuː) *prep* **1** in, into. **2** to. **3** at. **4** by, with. **5** along with, in addition to. *adv* **1** too. **2** to(wards). **3** closed, shut.

Zubehör ('tsuːbəhœːr) *n neu* **-e 1** accessories. **2** fittings.

zubereiten ('tsuːbəraitən) *vt* prepare.

zubringen* ('tsuːbriŋən) *vt* **1** bring to. **2** pass (the time).

Zucht (tsuxt) *nf* **1** discipline. **2** breed(ing). **3** decency. **4** culture. **5** training. **—en** ('tsuːçtən) *vt* **1** breed, rear. **2** grow, cultivate. **—er** ('tsyçtər) *nm* **—** breeder. **2** grower. **—ig** ('tsyçtiç) *adj* chaste, modest. **—igen** ('tsyçtigən) *vt* **1** punish, discipline. **2** flog, thrash.

zucken ('tsukən) *vi* **1** twitch. **2** flash. *vt* **1** shrug (one's shoulders). **2** bat (an eyelid).

Zucker ('tsukər) *nm* sugar. **—n** *vt* sugar. **—rohr** *n neu* sugar cane. **—rübe** *nf* sugar beet.

zudecken ('tsuːdɛkən) *vt* cover (up).

zudem (tsuː'deːm) *adv* besides.

Zudrang ('tsuːdraŋ) *nm* rush (towards).

zudrehen ('tsuːdreːən) *vt* turn or switch off.

zudringlich ('tsuːdriŋliç) *adj* importunate.

zueinander (tsuain'andər) *adv* to each other.

zuerst (tsuː'eːrst) *adv* (at) first, above all.

Zufahrt ('tsuːfaːrt) *nf* **1** approach, drive. **2** access (by road).

Zufall ('tsuːfal) *nm* chance, accident. **—en*** *vi* **1** fall to or on. **2** close. **—ig** ('tsuːfɛliç) *adj* accidental.

zufließen* ('tsuːfliːsən) *vi* flow (in)to.

Zuflucht ('tsuːfluxt) *nf* refuge, shelter.

zufolge (tsuː'fɔlgə) *prep* **1** according to. **2** owing to.

zufrieden (tsuː'friːdən) *adj* satisfied, content(ed). **—heit** *nf* satisfaction, contentment. **—stellen** *vt* satisfy.

zufügen ('tsuːfyːgən) *vt* **1** add (to). **2** cause, do.

Zufuhr ('tsuːfuːr) *nf* **-en** supply. **—en** ('tsuː-fyːrən) *vt* **1** lead or bring to. **2** supply.

Zug (tsuːk) *nm* **-e 1** train. **2** pull(ing), drawing. **3** draught. **4** procession. **5** trait, feature. **6** platoon, section. **—brücke** *nf* drawbridge.

Zugabe ('tsuːgaːbə) *nf* **-n 1** addition. **2** supplement.

Zugang ('tsuːgaŋ) *nm* **1** access, entry. **2** increase. **—lich** ('tsuːgɛŋliç) *adj* accessible.

zugeben* ('tsuːgeːbən) *vt* **1** admit, confess. **2** permit. **3** add.

zugegen (tsuː'geːgən) *adj* present.

zugehen* ('tsuːgeːən) *vi* **1** go on or to. **2** shut, close. **3** happen.

zugehör/en ('tsuːgəhœːrən) *vi* belong to. **—ig** *adj* belonging to.

Zügel ('tsyːgəl) *nm* **—** **1** rein, bridle. **2** restraint. **—los** *adj* unbridled. **—n** *vt* rein in, curb.

Zugeständnis ('tsuːgəʃtɛntnis) *n neu* **-se 1** concession. **2** admission.

zugestehen* ('tsu:gəʃte:ən) vt 1 admit. 2 concede.

Zugführer ('tsu:kfy:rər) nm (railway) guard.

zugig ('tsu:giç) adj draughty.

zugreifen* ('tsu:graifən) vi 1 grasp. 2 help oneself (at table).

zugrunde (tsu'grundə) adv **zugrunde gehen 1** perish, die. **2** be ruined.

zugunsten (tsu'gunstən) adv in favour of.

zugute (tsu'gu:tə) adv for the benefit of. **jemandem etwas zugute halten** give someone credit for something. **jemandem zugute kommen** stand someone in good stead.

zuhalt/en* ('tsu:haltən) vt keep shut. vi make for, go towards. **—er** ('tsu:hɛltər) nm — procurer, pimp.

zuhanden (tsu'handən) adv at or to hand.

zuhör/en ('tsu:hœ:rən) vi listen, attend (to). **—er** nm 1 listener. 2 pl audience.

zukommen* ('tsu:kɔmən) vi 1 come to, fall to. 2 be due to.

Zukunft ('tsu:kunft) nf future. **—ig** ('tsu:kynftiç) adj future.

Zulage ('tsu:la:gə) nf 1 increase. 2 extra pay or allowance.

zulänglich ('tsu:lɛŋliç) adj sufficient.

zulass/en* ('tsu:lasən) vt 1 leave shut. 2 admit (a person). 3 allow. 4 license (a car, etc.). **—ig** ('tsu:lɛsiç) adj admissible, allowable. **—ung** nf **-en** 1 admission. 2 permission. 3 (car) licence, registration.

Zulauf ('tsu:lauf) nm 1 rush. 2 crowd. 3 supply.

zuleide ('tsu:laidə) adv **jemandem etwas zuleide tun** hurt or harm someone.

zuleiten ('tsu:laitən) vt lead in or to.

zuletzt (tsu'lɛtst) adv (at) last, finally.

zuliebe (tsu'li:bə) adv **jemandem zuliebe 1** to please someone. **2** for someone's sake.

zum (tsum) contraction of **zu dem.**

zumachen ('tsu:maxən) vt shut, fasten.

zumal (tsu'ma:l) adv especially.

zumeist (tsu'maist) adv mostly.

zumindest (tsu'mindəst) adv at least.

zumute (tsu'mu:tə) adv **mir ist gut zumute** I feel well, I am in good spirits.

zumut/en ('tsu:mu:tən) vt expect or ask of (a person). **—ung** nf **-en** (unreasonable) demand, presumption.

zunächst (tsu'nɛ:çst) adv first (of all). prep next to.

Zunahme ('tsu:na:mə) nf **-n** increase, growth.

Zuname ('tsu:na:mə) nm surname.

zünd/en ('tsyndən) vi,vt ignite. **—er** nm — 1 fuse. 2 detonator. **—kerze** ('tsyntkɛrtsə) nf sparking plug. **—stoff** ('tsyntʃtɔf) nm 1 combustible matter. 2 fuel. **—ung** nf **-en** 1 mot ignition. 2 priming.

Zunder ('tsundər) nm — tinder.

zunehmen* ('tsu:ne:mən) vi grow, increase, put on (weight).

zuneig/en ('tsu:naigən) vi 1 lean. 2 incline. **—ung** nf **-en** 1 inclination. 2 sympathy.

Zunft (tsunft) nf **-e** 1 guild. 2 clique.

Zunge ('tsuŋə) nf **-n** 1 tongue. 2 zool sole.

zunichte (tsu'niçtə) adv ruined. **zunichte machen** ruin. **zunichte werden** come to nothing.

zunicken ('tsu:nikən) vi,vt nod (to).

zuoberst (tsu'o:bərst) adv at the top.

zupfen ('tsupfən) vt 1 pull. 2 pick.

zur (tsu:r) contraction of **zu der.**

zurechn/en ('tsu:rɛçnən) vt 1 add. 2 include. 3 ascribe. **—ung** nf 1 attribution. 2 addition.

zurecht (tsu'rɛçt) adv in order. **—legen** vt arrange. **—machen** vt prepare. **—setzen** vt set right. **—weisen*** vt 1 direct. 2 reprimand.

zureden ('tsu:re:dən) vi 1 urge, advise. 2 persuade.

zureichen ('tsu:raiçən) vt hand (over or to). vi suffice.

Zürich ('tsy:riç) n neu Zurich.

zurichten ('tsu:riçtən) vt 1 prepare. 2 tech dress.

zürnen ('tsyrnən) vi be angry.

zurück (tsu'ryk) adv back(wards), behind.

zurückbezahlen (tsu'rykbətsa:lən) vt repay.

zurückbleiben* (tsu'rykblaibən) vi remain or fall behind, be left behind.

zurückbringen* (tsu'rykbriŋən) vt bring back.

zurückeilen (tsu'rykailən) vi hurry back.

zurückfahren* (tsu'rykfa:rən) vi 1 drive or go back. 2 recoil. vt drive back.

sich zurückfinden* (tsu'rykfindən) vr find one's way back.

zurückführen (tsu'rykfy:rən) vt lead or trace back.

zurückgehen* (tsu'rykge:ən) vi 1 go or fall back. 2 decrease.

zurückgezogen (tsu'rykgətso:gən) adj retired, secluded.

zurückhalt/en* (tsu'rykhaltən) vt 1 hold back or in. 2 restrain. 3 detain. 4 repress. vi keep back. **—end** adj reserved. **—ung** nf reserve.

zurückkehren (tsu'rykke:rən) vi return.

zurückkommen* (tsuˈrykkɔmən) vi 1 return. 2 recur.

zurücklegen (tsuˈryklegən) vt 1 lay aside. 2 put by. 3 complete. 4 cover (distance). **sich zurücklegen** vr lie back.

zurücknehmen* (tsuˈryknemən) vt take back.

zurückrufen* (tsuˈrykrufən) vt 1 call back. 2 recall.

zurückschlagen* (tsuˈrykʃlagən) vt 1 repel. 2 throw off or open. 3 return. vi strike back.

zurücksetzen (tsuˈrykzɛtsən) vt 1 put back. 2 neglect (a person).

zurücktreten* (tsuˈryktretən) vi 1 step back. 2 resign. 3 retire.

zurückweichen* (tsuˈrykvaiçən) vi 1 fall back. 2 recede. 3 yield.

zurückweisen* (tsuˈrykvaizən) vt 1 send away or back. 2 decline, reject.

zurückziehen* (tsuˈryktsiən) vt withdraw.

Zuruf (ˈtsuːruf) nm shout, call.

Zusage (ˈtsuːzaɡə) nf 1 consent. 2 promise, word. **—n** vt promise. vi agree.

zusammen (tsuˈzamən) adv together.

Zusammenarbeit (tsuˈzamənarbait) nf cooperation, teamwork. **—en** vi cooperate, work together.

zusammenballen (tsuˈzamənbalən) vt 1 roll into a ball. 2 clench (one's fists).

zusammenbrechen* (tsuˈzamənbreçən) vi break down, collapse.

Zusammenbruch (tsuˈzamənbrux) nm breakdown, collapse.

zusammenfahren* (tsuˈzamənfaːrən) vi 1 collide. 2 wince, start.

zusammenfass/en (tsuˈzamənfasən) vt 1 comprise. 2 condense. 3 sum up. **—ung** nf summary.

zusammenfügen (tsuˈzamənfygən) vt combine.

zusammengesetzt (tsuˈzamənɡəzɛtst) adj composed, assembled.

Zusammenhang (tsuˈzamənhaŋ) nm 1 connection. 2 context. 3 continuity.

Zusammenkunft (tsuˈzamənkunft) nf assembly.

zusammenlegen (tsuˈzamənleɡən) vt 1 put together, combine. 2 fold (up). 3 pool.

zusammennehmen* (tsuˈzamənneːmən) vt gather up. **sich zusammennehmen** vr pull oneself together.

zusammenpassen (tsuˈzamənpasən) vi go well together. vt adjust.

zusammenrücken (tsuˈzamənrykən) vt,vi move closer together.

sich zusammenschließen* (tsuˈzamənʃliːsən) vr unite.

Zusammenschluß (tsuˈzamənʃlus) nm 1 union. 2 comm merger.

zusammensetz/en (tsuˈzamənzɛtsən) vt put together. **sich zusammensetzen** vr sit down together. **—ung** nf 1 composition. 2 construction.

zusammenstellen (tsuˈzamənʃtɛlən) vt 1 put together. 2 make up.

zusammenstimmen (tsuˈzamənʃtimən) vi agree, harmonize.

Zusammenstoß (tsuˈzamənʃtɔs) nm 1 collision. 2 conflict. **—en*** vt knock together. vi collide.

zusammentreffen* (tsuˈzaməntrɛfən) vi 1 meet. 2 coincide. n neu 1 meeting. 2 coincidence.

zusammentreten* (tsuˈzaməntretən) vi come together.

zusammenzieh/en* (tsuˈzaməntsiən) vt draw together. **—ung** nf contraction.

Zusatz (ˈtsuːzats) nm 1 addition. 2 appendix.

zuschau/en (ˈtsuːʃauən) vi look on. **—er** nm — spectator.

zuschicken (ˈtsuːʃikən) vt send on, forward.

zuschieben* (ˈtsuːʃiːbən) vt 1 push on. 2 shut.

zuschießen* (ˈtsuːʃiːsən) vt,vi 1 rush (at). 2 contribute (money). vt shoot (a glance, etc.) at.

Zuschlag (ˈtsuːʃlaːk) nm 1 surcharge. 2 increase. **—en*** (ˈtsuːʃlaɡən) vt slam. vi hit out. **—spflichtig** adj liable to surcharge.

zuschließen* (ˈtsuːʃliːsən) vt lock.

zuschneiden* (ˈtsuːʃnaidən) vt 1 cut out. 2 cut to size.

zuschreiben* (ˈtsuːʃraibən) vt ascribe to.

Zuschuß (ˈtsuːʃus) nm 1 extra allowance. 2 subsidy, grant.

zuschütten (ˈtsuːʃytən) vt 1 fill up with. 2 pour in or on.

zusehen* (ˈtsuːzeːən) vi 1 look on. 2 wait. **—ds** adv visibly.

zusenden* (ˈtsuːzɛndən) vt send on, forward.

zusetzen (ˈtsuːzɛtsən) vt 1 add. 2 lose (money). vi importune, pester.

Zuspruch (ˈtsuːʃprux) nm 1 encouragement. 2 consolation. 3 custom(ers).

Zustand (ˈtsuːʃtant) nm 1 condition. 2 situation. **—ig** (ˈtsuːʃtɛndiç) adj 1 appropriate. 2 competent, responsible.

zustatten (tsuˈʃtatən) adv **jemandem gut zu-**

statten kommen stand a person in good stead.
zustellen ('tsu:ʃtɛlən) vt deliver (letters, mail).
zustimm/en ('tsu:ʃtimən) vi agree, consent. **—ung** nf consent.
zustoßen* ('tsu:ʃto:sən) vt slam (shut). vi befall.
zustreben ('tsu:ʃtre:brən) vi strive (for).
zutage (tsu'ta:gə) adv **zutage bringen** bring to light.
Zutat ('tsu:ta:t) nf 1 cul ingredient. 2 seasoning. 3 trimming.
zuteil (tsu:'tail) adv **einem zuteil werden** fall to one's share.
zuteilen ('tsu:tailən) vt assign, allocate.
zutiefst (tsu:'ti:fst) adv deeply, intensely.
zutrag/en* ('tsu:tra:gən) vt carry (to). **sich zutragen** vi happen. **—er** ('tsu:tre:gər) nm — informer, gossipmonger. **—lich** ('tsu:-tre:kliç) adj 1 wholesome. 2 advantageous.
zutrau/en ('tsu:trauən) vt credit. n neu confidence. **—lich** adj trusting.
zutreffen* ('tsu:trɛfən) vi prove true.
Zutritt ('tsu:trit) nm access, admission.
zuverlässig ('tsu:fɛrlɛsiç) adj 1 reliable. 2 certain.
Zuversicht ('tsu:fɛrziçt) nf confidence. **—lich** adj confident.
zuviel (tsu'fi:l) adv too much.
zuvörderst (tsu'fœrdərst) adv first of all.
zuvorkommen* (tsu'fo:rkɔmən) vi anticipate.
zuvortun* (tsu'fo:rtu:n) vi outdo.
Zuwachs ('tsu:vaks) nm increase, growth.
zuweilen (tsu:vailən) adv at times, sometimes.
zuweisen* ('tsu:vaizən) vt allot.
zuwenden* ('tsu:vɛndən) vt 1 turn towards. 2 give. 3 procure.
zuwider (tsu'vi:dər) prep 1 contrary to. 2 distasteful to. **—handlung** nf violation, infringement. **—laufen*** vi run counter (to).
zuzeiten (tsu'tsaitən) adv at times.
zuziehen* (tsu:tsi:ən) vt 1 draw (together), tighten, shut. 2 invite. v 1 move in. 2 immigrate. **sich eine Krankheit zuziehen** catch or contract a disease. **sich Schwierigkeiten zuziehen** get into difficulties.
zwang (tsvaŋ) v see **zwingen**.
Zwang (tsvaŋ) nm -̈e 1 compulsion. 2 force. **—los** adj unconstrained. **—släufig** ('tsvaŋslɔyfiç) adj inevitable.
zwängen ('tsvɛŋən) vt press, squeeze.
zwanzig ('tsvantsiç) adj,nf twenty. **—ste** adj twentieth.

zwar (tsva:r) adv indeed. **und zwar** that is, namely, in fact.
Zweck (tsvɛk) nm -e 1 purpose. 2 design. **—los** adj useless, purposeless. **—mäßig** adj 1 suitable. 2 expedient. 3 practical.
Zwecke ('tsvɛkə) nf -n 1 drawing-pin. 2 tack. 3 peg.
zwei (tsvai) adj,nf two.
zweideutig ('tsvaidɔytiç) adj ambiguous.
zweierlei (tsvaiər'lai) adj of two kinds.
Zweifel ('tsvaifəl) nm — doubt. **—haft** adj doubtful. **—los** adj doubtless. **—n** vi doubt.
Zweig (tsvaik) nm -e branch, twig. **—stelle** nf branch office.
zweijährlich (tsvaije:rliç) adj every two years.
Zweikampf ('tsvaikampf) nm duel.
zweimal ('tsvaimal) adv twice.
zweisprachig ('tsvaiʃpra:xiç) adj bilingual.
zweistimmig ('tsvaiʃtimiç) adj mus for two voices.
zwei/te (tsvaitə) adj second. **zu Zweit** in twos, two by two. **—tens** ('tsvaitəns) adv secondly. **—tklassig** adj second-rate.
Zwerchfell ('tsvɛrçfɛl) n neu diaphragm.
Zwerg (tsvɛrk) nm -e dwarf.
zwicken ('tsvikən) vt pinch, tweak.
Zwieback ('tsvi:bak) nm -e biscuit, rusk.
Zwiebel ('tsvi:bəl) nf -n 1 onion. 2 bot bulb.
Zwiegespräch ('tsvi:gəʃprɛ:x) n neu dialogue.
Zwiespalt ('tsvi:ʃpalt) nm -e dissension.
Zwietracht ('tsvi:traxt) nf discord.
Zwilling ('tsviliŋ) nm -e 1 twin. 2 pl Gemini.
Zwinge ('tsviŋə) nf -n 1 clamp. 2 ferrule.
zwingen* ('tsviŋən) vt 1 force. 2 overcome.
zwischen ('tsviʃən) prep between, among. **—durch** adv 1 through. 2 in the midst. 3 **between**. **—fall** nm incident. **—raum** nm interval, gap, space. **—spiel** n neu interlude. **—wand** nf partition. **—zeit** nf interim, interval.
Zwist (tsvist) nm -e 1 discord. 2 quarrel. **—ig** adj 1 at variance. 2 in dispute.
zwitschern ('tsvitʃərn) vi chirp, twitter.
zwo (tsvo:) adj,nf see **zwei**.
zwölf (tsvœlf) adj,nf twelve. **—te** adj twelfth.
Zyklon (tsy'klo:n) nm -e cyclone.
Zyklus ('tsy:klus) nm -len 1 cycle. 2 series.
Zylinder (tsi'lindər) nm — 1 cylinder. 2 top-hat.
Zyn/iker ('tsy:nikər) nm — cynic. **—isch** ('tsy:niʃ) adj cynical.
Zyp/ern ('tsy:pərn) n neu Cyprus. **—riot** (tsypri:'o:t) nm -en Cypriot. **—riotisch** (tsypri:'o:tiʃ) adj Cypriot.

A

a, an (ǝ, ǝn; stressed ei, æn) indef art 1 ein, eine, ein m,f,neu. 2 pro, je.

aback (ǝ'bæk) adv nach hinten, zurück. **taken aback** bestürzt, verblüfft.

abandon (ǝ'bændǝn) n Ungezwungenheit, Hingabe f. vt 1 aufgeben, verlassen. 2 verzichten auf. 3 im Stich lassen.

abashed (ǝ'bæʃt) adj verlegen, sich schämend.

abate (ǝ'beit) vi (of wind) abnehmen, sich legen.

abattoir ('æbatwɑ:) n Schlachthaus neu.

abbess ('æbis) n Äbtissin f.

abbey ('æbi) n Abtei f.

abbot ('æbǝt) n Abt m.

abbreviate (ǝ'bri:vieit) vt abkürzen. **abbreviation** n Abkürzung f.

abdicate ('æbdikeit) vi abdanken. vt niederlegen. **abdication** n Abdankung f.

abdomen ('æbdǝmǝn) n Unterleib, Bauch m.

abduct (æb'dʌkt) vt entführen. **abduction** n Entführung f.

abet (ǝ'bet) vt 1 begünstigen. 2 anstiften. **aid and abet** law Vorschub leisten.

abhor (ǝb'hɔ:) vt verabscheuen. **abhorrence** n Abscheu m. **abhorrent** adj zuwider, verhaßt.

abide (ǝ'baid) vi bleiben, fortdauern. vt vertragen, ausstehen. **abide by** treu bleiben, sich halten an.

ability (ǝ'biliti) n 1 Fähigkeit f. 2 geistige Anlagen f pl.

abject ('æbdʒekt) adj gemein, verächtlich.

ablaze (ǝ'bleiz) adj,adv 1 in Flammen. 2 glänzend. 3 erregt.

able ('eibǝl) adj 1 fähig. 2 geschickt, tüchtig, begabt. **be able to** können.

abnormal (æb'nɔ:mǝl) adj 1 ungewöhnlich. 2 anormal, abnorm. **abnormality** n 1 Abnormität f. 2 Mißbildung f.

aboard (ǝ'bɔ:d) adv an Bord.

abode (ǝ'boud) n Wohnort m. Stätte f.

abolish (ǝ'boliʃ) vt abschaffen, aufheben. **abolition** n Abschaffung, Aufhebung f.

abominable (ǝ'bɔminǝbǝl) adj abscheulich.

Aborigine (æbǝ'ridʒini) n 1 Ureinwohner m. 2 pl Urbevölkerung f. **aboriginal** adj eingeboren.

abort (ǝ'bɔ:t) vi 1 fehlgebären. 2 fehlschlagen. **abortion** n 1 Abtreibung f. 2 Fehlgeburt f. **abortive** adj 1 vorzeitig. 2 fehlgeschlagen, mißlungen.

abound (ǝ'baund) vi reichlich vorhanden sein.

about (ǝ'baut) prep 1 wegen, über. 2 gegen. adv 1 herum, umher. 2 ungefähr, etwa. **be about to do something** eben etwas tun wollen.

above (ǝ'bʌv) prep über, oberhalb. adv oben, darüber. adj obig, oben erwähnt. **aboveboard** adj offen, ehrlich.

abrasion (ǝ'breiʒǝn) n Abschleifen, Abreiben neu. **abrasive** adj abreibend, abschleifend.

abreast (ǝ'brest) adv 1 nebeneinander. 2 auf dem laufenden. **keep abreast of** Schritt halten mit.

abridge (ǝ'bridʒ) vt (ab-, ver-)kürzen.

abroad (ǝ'brɔ:d) adv 1 ins or im Ausland. 2 draußen. 3 auswärts.

abrupt (ǝ'brʌpt) adj 1 abrupt, plötzlich. 2 schroff.

abscess ('æbses) n Abszeß m. Geschwür neu.

abscond (ǝb'skɔnd) vi sich heimlich davonmachen, flüchten.

absent (adj 'æbsǝnt; v ǝb'sent) adj 1 abwesend. 2 zerstreut. v absent oneself from sich entfernen von. **absence** n 1 Abwesenheit f. 2 Mangel m. **in the absence of** in Ermangelung von. **absentee** n Abwesende(r) m. **absenteeism** n (unerlaubtes) Fernbleiben neu. **absent-minded** adj zerstreut, geistesabwesend.

absinthe ('æbsinθ) n Absinth m.

absolute ('æbsǝlu:t) adj 1 absolut. 2 vollkommen. **absolutely** adv völlig, durchaus.

absolve (ǝb'zɔlv) vt freisprechen. **absolution** n rel Absolution f.

absorb (əb'zɔ:b) vt **1** absorbieren, aufsaugen. **2** aufnehmen. **be absorbed in** vertieft sein in. **absorbent** adj aufsaugend. **absorption** n Absorption, Aufsaugung f.

abstain (əb'stein) vi sich enthalten. **abstainer** n Abstinenzler m. **abstention** n Enthaltung f. **abstinence** n Enthaltsamkeit, Abstinenz f.

abstract (adj,n 'æbstrækt; v əb'strækt) adj abstrakt, theoretisch. n **1** Abstrakte neu. **2** Auszug m. vt ablenken, absondern. **abstraction** n **1** sci Absonderung f. **2** Abstraktion f. **3** Zerstreutheit f.

absurd (əb'sə:d) adj absurd, sinnwidrig, albern. **absurdity** n Albernheit f. Unsinn m.

abundance (ə'bʌndəns) n Überfluß m. Fülle f. **abundant** adj reichlich.

abuse (v ə'bju:z; n ə'bju:s) vt **1** mißbrauchen. **2** beschimpfen. n **1** Mißbrauch m. **2** Beschimpfung f. **abusive** adj beleidigend.

abyss (ə'bis) n Abgrund m. **abysmal** adj abgrundtief.

Abyssinia (æbi'siniə) n Abessinien neu. **Abyssinian** adj abessinisch. n Abessinier m.

academy (ə'kædəmi) n (Kunst)Akademie f. **academic** adj **1** akademisch. **2** rein theoretisch. n Akademiker m.

accelerate (ək'seləreit) vt **1** beschleunigen. **2** mot Gas geben. **acceleration** n Beschleunigung f. **accelerator** n Gaspedal neu.

accent (n 'æksənt; v æk'sent) n **1** Akzent m. **2** Betonung f. vt betonen. **accentuate** vt **1** betonen. **2** hervorheben.

accept (ək'sept) vt **1** (an-, entgegen-)nehmen, akzeptieren. **2** anerkennen, gelten lassen. vi annehmen, zusagen. **acceptable** adj **1** annehmbar. **2** angenehm. **acceptance** n **1** Annahme f. **2** Aufnahme f.

access ('ækses) n **1** Zugang, Zutritt m. **2** Zufahrt f. **accessible** adj zugänglich. **accession** n **1** Antritt m. **2** Thronbesteigung f. **accessory** n Zubehörteil m.

accident ('æksidnt) n **1** Zufall m. **2** Unfall m. Unglück neu. **accidental** adj zufällig.

acclaim (ə'kleim) vt **1** (mit Beifall) begrüßen, zujubeln. **2** anerkennen, begrüßen. **acclamation** n **1** Beifall m. **2** Zuruf m.

acclimatize (ə'klaimətaiz) (vi),vt (sich) akklimatisieren, (sich) eingewöhnen. **acclimatization** n Akklimatisierung, Eingewöhnung f.

accommodate (ə'kɔmədeit) vt **1** unterbringen. **2** anpassen. **3** aushelfen. **accommodating** adj **1** gefällig. **2** anpassungsfähig. **accommodation** n **1** Unterkunft f. **2** Anpassung f.

accompany (ə'kʌmpəni) vt begleiten. **accompaniment** n Begleitung f. **accompanist** n mus Begleiter m.

accomplice (ə'kʌmplis) n Mittäter m.

accomplish (ə'kʌmpliʃ) vt vollenden, zustande bringen. **accomplishment** n **1** Vollendung f. **2** Leistung f. **3** pl Talente neu pl.

accord (ə'kɔ:d) vt gewähren. vi übereinstimmen. n Übereinstimmung f. **of one's own accord** aus eigenem Antrieb. **accordance** n Übereinstimmung f. **in accordance with** in Übereinstimmung mit, gemäß. **according to** prep **1** gemäß. **2** laut, zufolge.

accordion (ə'kɔ:diən) n Ziehharmonika f.

accost (ə'kɔst) vt ansprechen.

account (ə'kaunt) vi Rechenschaft ablegen. vt ansehen als. n **1** Rechnung f. **2** Bericht m. **3** comm Konto neu. **on no account** auf keinen Fall. **accountable** adj verantwortlich. **accountancy** n Rechnungswesen neu. **accountant** n **1** Rechnungsführer m. **2** Bücherrevisor m.

accumulate (ə'kju:mjuleit) (vi),vt (sich) anhäufen. **accumulation** n Anhäufung f. **accumulative** adj (sich) anhäufend.

accurate ('ækjurət) adj **1** genau. **2** richtig. **accuracy** n Genauigkeit f.

accusative (ə'kju:zətiv) n Akkusativ m.

accuse (ə'kju:z) vt anklagen, beschuldigen. **accused** n Angeklagte(r) m. **accuser** n Kläger m.

accustom (ə'kʌstəm) vt gewöhnen. **become accustomed to** sich gewöhnen an.

ace (eis) n As neu.

ache (eik) vi schmerzen, weh tun. n Schmerz m. **aching** adj schmerzhaft.

achieve (ə'tʃi:v) vt **1** ausführen. **2** zustande bringen. **3** erreichen, erzielen. **achievement** n **1** Ausführung, Vollendung f. **2** Leistung f. Werk neu.

acid ('æsid) adj sauer. n Säure f.

acknowledge (ək'nɔlidʒ) vt **1** anerkennen, zugeben. **2** comm bestätigen. **acknowledgment** n **1** Anerkennung f. **2** Dank m. **3** comm Empfangsbestätigung f.

acne ('ækni) n Akne f. Hautausschlag m.

acorn ('eikɔ:n) n Eichel f.

acoustic (ə'ku:stik) adj akustisch. **acoustics** n Akustik f.

acquaint (ə'kweint) vt bekannt machen. **be acquainted with** kennen. **acquaintance** n **1**

Bekanntschaft f. 2 Bekannte(r) m. **make someone's acquaintance** jemanden kennenlernen.

acquiesce (ækwi'es) vi einwilligen, sich fügen. **acquiescent** adj ergeben, fügsam.

acquire (ə'kwaiə) vt erwerben, erlangen. **acquisition** n Erwerbung f. **acquisitive** adj gewinnsüchtig.

acquit (ə'kwit) vt freisprechen. **acquittal** n Freispruch m.

acre ('eikə) n Morgen m.

acrimony ('ækriməni) n Schärfe, Bitterkeit f. **acrimonious** adj scharf, beißend.

acrobat ('ækrəbæt) n Akrobat m. **acrobatic** adj akrobatisch. **acrobatics** n pl Akrobatik f.

across (ə'krɔs) adv 1 hinüber, herüber, (quer)durch. 2 kreuzweise. prep 1 über. 2 jenseits. **come across** stoßen auf.

acrylic (ə'krilik) n Polyacryl Tdmk neu.

act (ækt) vt darstellen, spielen. **act a part** eine Rolle spielen. vi handeln. **act as** fungieren als. act on wirken auf. n 1 Handlung, Tat f. 2 Th Aufzug m. 3 Gesetz neu. **acting** adj 1 handelnd. 2 amtierend. n Th Spielen neu.

action ('ækʃən) n 1 Handlung f. 2 Tat f. 3 Wirkung f. 4 law Klage f. 5 mil Gefecht neu.

active ('æktiv) adj tätig, wirksam, aktiv. n gram Aktiv neu. **activate** vt 1 in Tätigkeit setzen. 2 wirksam machen. **activity** n 1 Tätigkeit f. 2 Treiben neu. 3 pl Unternehmungen f pl.

actor ('æktə) n Schauspieler m.

actress ('æktris) n Schauspielerin f.

actual ('æktʃuəl) adj wirklich, tatsächlich, eigentlich.

acupuncture ('ækjupʌŋktʃə) n Akupunktur f.

acute (ə'kju:t) adj 1 akut, heftig. 2 scharf. **acute angle** spitzer Winkel m.

adamant ('ædəmənt) adj unerbittlich.

adapt (ə'dæpt) vt 1 anpassen, zurechtmachen. 2 bearbeiten. **adaptable** adj anpassungsfähig. **adaptation** n 1 Anpassung f. 2 Bearbeitung f. **adaptor** n Zwischenstecker m.

add (æd) vt 1 addieren. 2 hinzufügen. vi hinzukommen. **add up** zusammenzählen, addieren. **adding machine** n Addiermaschine f. **addition** n 1 Hinzufügung f. 2 Zusatz m. Zutat f. 3 Addition f. **in addition** außerdem, noch dazu. **in addition to which** wozu (kommt noch). **additional** adj zusätzlich. **additive** n Zusatz m.

addendum (ə'dendəm) n, pl **addenda** 1 Zusatz m. 2 Nachtrag m.

adder ('ædə) n Natter f.

addict ('ædikt) n Süchtige(r) m. **addicted** adj süchtig. **addiction** n Neigung, Sucht f.

addled ('ædld) adj 1 faul. 2 verwirrt.

address (ə'dres) vt 1 anreden, sprechen zu. 2 (a letter) adressieren. n 1 Adresse, Anschrift f. 2 Ansprache, Anrede f. **address book** n Adreßbuch neu.

adenoids ('ædinɔidz) n pl Polypen m pl.

adept ('ædept) adj geschickt.

adequate ('ædikwət) adj 1 ausreichend. 2 angemessen. **adequacy** n Angemessenheit f.

adhere (əd'hiə) vi 1 kleben, haften. 2 festhalten. **adherence** n Festhalten neu. **adherent** n Anhänger m. adj anhaftend. **adhesion** n 1 Anhaften neu. 2 Anhänglichkeit f. **adhesive** adj klebrig, gummiert. n Klebstoff m. **adhesive tape** n Klebestreifen m.

ad hoc (æd 'hɔk) adj,adv für diesen Fall bestimmt.

adjacent (ə'dʒeisənt) adj angrenzend.

adjective ('ædʒiktiv) n Adjektiv, Eigenschaftswort neu.

adjoin (ə'dʒɔin) vt angrenzen.

adjourn (ə'dʒə:n) vt aufschieben, vertagen. vi sich vertagen. **adjournment** n Vertagung f. Verschiebung f.

adjudicate (ə'dʒu:dikeit) vt gerichtlich entscheiden. vi als Schiedsrichter handeln. **adjudication** 1 richterliche Entscheidung f. 2 Zusprechung f. **adjudicator** n Schiedsrichter m.

adjust (ə'dʒʌst) vt 1 anpassen. 2 einstellen. vi sich anpassen. **adjustable** adj verstellbar. **adjustment** n 1 Anpassung f. 2 Einstellung f.

ad-lib (æd'lib) vt,vi inf improvisieren.

administer (əd'ministə) vt verwalten. vi als Verwalter fungieren. **administrate** vt verwalten. **administration** n 1 Verwaltung f. Verwaltungswesen neu. 2 Regierung f. **administration of justice** Rechtsprechung f. **administrative** adj Verwaltungs—, verwaltend. **administrator** n Verwalter m.

admiral ('ædmərəl) n Admiral m. **admiralty** n Admiralität f.

admire (əd'maiə) vt 1 bewundern. 2 hochschätzen. **admirable** adj bewundernswert, großartig. **admiration** n Bewunderung f. **admirer** n 1 Bewunderer m. 2 Verehrer m.

admit (əd'mit) vt 1 einlassen. 2 zugeben. 3 gelten lassen. **admission** n 1 Zulassung f. 2 Eintritt m. 3 Zugeständnis neu. **admittance** n Einlaß m. Zutritt m. **no admittance** Zutritt verboten.

ado (ə'du:) n Getue, Aufheben neu. **without further ado** ohne weitere Umstände.

adolescence (ædə'lesəns) n Jünglingsalter neu. **adolescent** n Jugendliche(r) m. adj jugendlich.

adopt (ə'dɔpt) vt 1 adoptieren. 2 annehmen, sich aneignen. **adoption** n Adoption, Annahme f. **adoptive** adj angenommen, Adoptiv—.

adore (ə'dɔ:) vt 1 anbeten, verehren. 2 lieben, sehr gern haben. **adorable** adj 1 verehrungswürdig. 2 entzückend. **adoration** n Anbetung, Verehrung f.

adorn (ə'dɔ:n) vt schmücken. **adornment** n Schmuck m.

adrenaline (ə'drenəlin) n Adrenalin neu.

Adriatic (eidri'ætik) adj adriatisch. **Adriatic (Sea)** n Adriatisches Meer neu.

adrift (ə'drift) adj,adv 1 (umher)treibend. 2 hilflos.

adroit (ə'drɔit) adj gewandt.

adulation (ædju'leiʃən) n Schmeichelei f.

adult ('ædʌlt) adj erwachsen. n Erwachsene(r) m.

adulterate (ə'dʌltəreit) vt 1 verfälschen. 2 verderben. **adulteration** n Verfälschung f.

adultery (ə'dʌltəri) n Ehebruch m. **adulterer** n Ehebrecher m. **adulteress** n Ehebrecherin f. **adulterous** adj ehebrecherisch.

advance (əd'va:ns) vt 1 vorrücken, vorwärtsbringen. 2 (money) vorschießen. 3 befördern. vi 1 vorrücken, vordringen. 2 Fortschritte machen. n 1 Vorrücken neu. 2 (money) Vorschuß m. 3 mil Vormarsch m. **in advance** im voraus. **advanced** adj fortgeschritten. **advancement** n 1 Beförderung f. 2 Fortschritt m.

advantage (əd'va:ntidʒ) n Vorteil m. **take advantage of** ausnutzen. **advantageous** adj vorteilhaft, günstig.

advent ('ædvent) n 1 Kommen neu. Ankunft f. 2 cap rel Advent m.

adventure (əd'ventʃə) n Abenteuer neu. **adventurer** n Abenteurer m. **adventurous** adj 1 abenteuerlich. 2 abenteuerlustig.

adverb ('ædvə:b) n Adverb, Umstandswort neu. **adverbial** adj adverbial.

adverse ('ædvə:s) adj 1 widrig. 2 feindlich. 3 ungünstig. **adversary** n Gegner m. **adversity** n Unglück neu. Not f.

advertise ('ædvətaiz) vt anzeigen. vi Reklame machen. **advertisement** n 1 Anzeige f. 2 Reklame f. **advertising** n Reklame, Werbung f.

advise (əd'vaiz) vt 1 raten, empfehlen. 2 beraten. 3 benachrichtigen, mitteilen. **advice** n 1 Rat m. 2 Ratschlag m. 3 comm Avis m. **advisable** adj ratsam. **adviser** n 1 Ratgeber m. 2 Berater m. **advisory** adj beratend, Beratungs—.

advocate (v 'ædvəkeit; n 'ædvəkət) vt 1 verteidigen. 2 befürworten. n 1 Advokat m. 2 Fürsprecher m. **advocacy** n Verteidigung f. Befürwortung f.

Aegean (i'dʒi:ən) adj ägäisch. **Aegean (Sea)** n Ägäisches Meer neu.

aerial ('ɛəriəl) adj 1 Luft—. 2 leicht, gasförmig. n tech Antenne f.

aerodynamics (ɛəroudai'næmiks) n pl Aerodynamik f. **aerodynamic** adj aerodynamisch.

aeronautics (ɛərə'nɔ:tiks) n pl Aeronautik f. Flugwesen neu. **aeronautical** adj aeronautisch.

aeroplane ('ɛərəplein) n Flugzeug neu.

aerosol ('ɛərəsɔl) n 1 Sprühdose f. Spray neu. 2 Aerosol neu.

aesthetic (is'θetik) adj ästhetisch, geschmackvoll.

afar (ə'fa:) adv fern. **from afar** aus weiter Ferne.

affable ('æfəbəl) adj leutselig.

affair (ə'fɛə) n 1 Angelegenheit, Sache, Affäre f. 2 (Liebes)Affäre, Liebschaft f.

affect[1] (ə'fekt) vt 1 berühren, angehen. 2 beeinflussen, einwirken auf. 3 beeinträchtigen.

affect[2] (ə'fekt) vt vortäuschen, vorgeben.

affection (ə'fekʃən) n Zuneigung, Liebe f. **affectionate** adj liebevoll, zärtlich.

affiliate (ə'filieit) vt 1 (als Mitglied) aufnehmen. 2 angliedern. **affiliated company** n Tochtergesellschaft f.

affinity (ə'finiti) n enge Beziehungen f pl.

affirm (ə'fə:m) vt behaupten, versichern. vi bestätigen, zustimmen. **affirmation** n Behauptung f. **affirmative** adj bejahend, bestimmt. **answer in the affirmative** bejahen, mit Ja antworten.

affix (ə'fiks) vt 1 aufkleben. 2 aufdrücken.

afflict (ə'flikt) vt 1 betrüben. 2 quälen. **afflicted** adj leidend. **affliction** n 1 Kummer m. 2 Leiden neu.

affluent ('æfluənt) adj 1 reich. 2 wohlhabend. **affluent society** n Wohlstandsgesellschaft f.

afford (ə'fɔ:d) vt 1 sich leisten (können). 2 gewähren.

affront (ə'frʌnt) *vt* beleidigen. *n* Beleidigung *f.*

Afghanistan (æf'gænista:n, -'stæn) *n* Afghanistan *neu.* **Afghanistani** *adj* afghanistanisch. *n* Afghanistaner *m.*

afield (ə'fi:ld) *adv* **far afield** weit weg.

afloat (ə'flout) *adv* **1** schwimmend. **2** auf dem Meere. **keep afloat** sich über Wasser halten.

afoot (ə'fut) *adv* **1** im Gang(e). **2** zu Fuß.

aforesaid (ə'fɔ:sed) *adj* vorerwähnt.

afraid (ə'freid) *adj* ängstlich, bange, erschrocken. **be afraid 1** Angst haben. **2** bedauern. **be afraid of** sich fürchten vor, Angst haben vor. **be afraid to do something** sich scheuen, etwas zu tun.

afresh (ə'freʃ) *adv* von neuem.

Africa ('æfrikə) Afrika *neu.* **African** *adj* afrikanisch. *n* Afrikaner *m.*

aft (ɑ:ft) *adv naut* achtern, hinten.

after ('ɑ:ftə) *prep* nach. *conj* nachdem. *adv* nachher. **shortly after** kurz darauf. **after-care** *n* Nachbehandlung *f.* **after-effect** *n* Nachwirkung *f.* **afterlife** *n* Leben nach dem Tode *neu.* **aftermath** *n* Nachwirkungen *f pl.* **afternoon** *n* Nachmittag *m.* **afterthought** nachträglicher Einfall *m.* **afterwards** *adv* später, nachher.

again (ə'gen) *adv* **1** wieder, nochmals. **2** ferner, außerdem. **once again** noch einmal.

against (ə'genst) *prep* **1** gegen, wider. **2** gegenüber.

age (eidʒ) *n* **1** Alter *neu.* **2** Zeitalter *neu.* **age-group** *n* Altersklasse *f.* **be of age** mündig sein. **old age** Alter *neu. vi* alt werden, altern. *vt* alt machen. **aged** *adj* **1** alt. **2** bejahrt, betagt.

agency ('eidʒənsi) *n* Agentur *f.*

agenda (ə'dʒendə) *n* Tagesordnung *f.*

agent ('eidʒənt) *n* **1** Agent, Vertreter *m.* **2** wirkende Kraft *f.* Mittel *neu.*

aggravate ('ægrəveit) *vt* **1** erschweren, verschlimmern. **2** *inf* ärgern. **aggravating** *adj* **1** erschwerend. **2** *inf* ärgerlich. **aggravation** *n* **1** Erschwerung *f.* **2** *inf* Verärgerung *f.*

aggregate (*adj,n* 'ægrigit; *v* 'ægrigeit) *adj* angehäuft, gesamt. *n* Anhäufung *f. vt* anhäufen.

aggression (ə'greʃən) *n* **1** Angriff *m.* **2** Aggression *f.* **aggressive** *adj* **1** angreifend. **2** streitsüchtig, aggressiv.

aggrieved (ə'gri:vd) *adj* betrübt, gekränkt.

aghast (ə'gɑ:st) *adj* entsetzt.

agile ('ædʒail) *adj* beweglich, behende, agil. **agility** *n* Beweglichkeit, Behendigkeit *f.*

agitate ('ædʒiteit) *vt* **1** bewegen, aufrühren. **2** erregen. *vi* agitieren. **agitation** *n* **1** Bewegung *f.* **2** Unruhe *f.* Aufruhr *m.* **agitator** *n* Agitator, Aufwiegler *m.*

aglow (ə'glou) *adj* glühend.

agnostic (æg'nɔstik) *n* Agnostiker *m. adj* agnostisch. **agnosticism** *n* Agnostizismus *m.*

ago (ə'gou) *adv* vor, her. **long ago** vor langer Zeit.

agog (ə'gɔg) *adv* gespannt.

agony ('ægəni) *n* Qual, Agonie *f.* **agonize** *vt* quälen. **agonizing** *adj* quälend.

agrarian (ə'grɛəriən) *adj* agrarisch.

agree (ə'gri:) *vi* übereinstimmen, einwilligen, einverstanden sein. **agree (on)** einig werden (über). **agreeable** *adj* **1** angenehm. **2** einverstanden. **agreed** *adj* **1** einig. **2** vereinbart. *interj* einverstanden! **agreement** *n* **1** Übereinstimmung *f.* **2** Abkommen *neu.* Vertrag *m.* **make an agreement** ein Abkommen treffen.

agriculture ('ægrikʌltʃə) *n* Landwirtschaft *f.* **agricultural** *adj* landwirtschaftlich.

aground (ə'graund) *adv* **run aground** stranden.

ahead (ə'hed) *adv* vorwärts, voran. **go ahead** fangen Sie an! **straight ahead** gerade aus.

aid (eid) *vt* helfen. *n* Hilfe *f.*

aide (eid) *n mil* Adjutant *m.*

ailment ('eilmənt) *n* Leiden *neu.* **ailing** *adj* kränklich, leidend.

aim (eim) *vt* **1** (a gun, etc.) richten. *vi* **1** zielen. **2** streben. *n* **1** Ziel *neu.* **2** Absicht *f.* Zweck *m.* **take aim** zielen. **aimless** *adj* ziellos.

air (ɛə) *n* **1** Luft *f.* **2** Miene *f.* Anschein *m.* **3** Melodie *f.* Lied *neu.* **go by air** fliegen. **put on the air** senden. *vt* **1** (aus)lüften, trocknen. **2** bekanntmachen.

airborne ('ɛəbɔ:n) *adj* im Flugzeug befördert. **be airborne** fliegen.

air-conditioning *n* Klimaanlage *f.*

aircraft ('ɛəkrɑ:ft) *n* Flugzeug *neu.*

airfield ('ɛəfi:ld) *n* Flugplatz *m.*

airforce ('ɛəfɔ:s) *n* Luftwaffe *f.*

air-hostess ('ɛəhoustis) *n* Stewardeß *f.*

air lift *n* Luftbrücke *f.*

airline ('ɛəlain) *n* Luftverkehrslinie, Luftgesellschaft *f.* **airline passenger** *n* Fluggast *m.*

airmail ('ɛəmeil) *n* Luftpost *f.*

airman ('ɛəmən) *n* Flieger *m.*

airport ('ɛəpɔ:t) *n* Flughafen *m.*

air-raid *n* Luftangriff *m.*

airtight ('ɛətait) *adj* luftdicht.

airy ('ɛəri) *adj* **1** luftig. **2** unbekümmert.

Alps

aisle (ail) n Seitenschiff neu.
ajar (ə'dʒɑ:) adv halb offen, angelehnt.
akin (ə'kin) adj 1 verwandt. 2 (sehr) ähnlich.
alabaster ('æləbɑ:stə) n Alabaster m.
alarm (ə'lɑ:m) vt 1 alarmieren. 2 beunruhigen. n
   1 Alarm m. 2 Angst f. alarm clock n Wecker
   m. alarming adj beunruhigend.
alas (ə'læs) interj ach! o weh! leider!
Albania (æl'beiniə) n Albanien neu. Albanian
   adj albanisch. n Albaner m.
albatross ('ælbətros) n Albatros m.
albeit (ɔ:l'bi:it) conj obgleich, wenn auch.
album ('ælbəm) n Album neu.
alchemy ('ælkəmi) n Alchimie f. alchemist n
   Alchimist m.
alcohol ('ælkəhol) n Alkohol m. alcoholic adj
   alkoholisch. n Alkoholiker m. alcoholism n
   Alkoholismus m.
alderman ('ɔ:ldəmən) n Ratsherr, Stadtrat m.
ale (eil) n Bier neu.
alert (ə'lə:t) adj 1 wachsam. 2 flink, munter. vt
   warnen. n Warnung f. be on the alert auf
   der Hut sein.
algebra ('ældʒibrə) n Algebra f.
Algeria (æl'dʒiəriə) n Algerien neu. Algerian
   adj algerisch. n Algerier m.
alias ('eiliəs) adv alias, sonst...genannt.
alibi ('ælibai) n 1 law Alibi neu. 2 inf Ausrede f.
alien ('eiliən) n Fremde(r) m. Ausländer m. adj
   fremd, ausländisch. alienate vt entfremden.
   alienation n Entfremdung f.
alight¹ (ə'lait) vi 1 absteigen. 2 landen.
alight² (ə'lait) adj 1 brennend, in Flammen. 2
   erleuchtet.
align (ə'lain) (vi),vt 1 (sich) in gerader Linie
   aufstellen. 2 (sich) ausrichten. align oneself
   sich anschließen.
alike (ə'laik) adj gleich, ähnlich. adv gleich, in
   gleicher Weise.
alimentary (æli'mentəri) adj Nahrungs—, nähr-
   haft. alimentary canal n Verdauungskanal m.
alimony ('æliməni) n Alimente neu pl.
alive (ə'laiv) adj 1 lebend, am Leben. 2 lebhaft.
   alive to empfänglich für.
alkali ('ælkəlai) n Alkali neu. alkaline adj
   alkalisch.
all (ɔ:l) adj 1 all, ganz. 2 jeder, jede, jedes
   m,f,neu. 3 pl alle, sämtliche. n Ganze neu. adv
   ganz. pron alles. above all vor allem. at all
   überhaupt. not at all durchaus nicht.
allay (ə'lei) vt 1 beruhigen. 2 stillen.
allege (ə'ledʒ) vt 1 behaupten. 2 angeben.
   allegation n Behauptung f. Aussage f.

allegiance (ə'li:dʒəns) n 1 Untertanenpflicht f.
   2 Treue f.
allegory ('æligəri) n Allegorie f.
allergy ('ælədʒi) n Allergie f. allergic adj aller-
   gisch.
alleviate (ə'li:vieit) vt erleichtern, mildern.
   alleviation n Erleichterung. Milderung f.
alley ('æli) n 1 Allee f. 2 Gasse f. 3 Durchgang
   m. bowling alley n Kegelbahn f.
alliance (ə'laiəns) n 1 Verbindung f. 2 Bund m.
   Bündnis neu. 3 Verwandtschaft f.
allied (ə'laid, 'ælaid) adj verbündet, alliiert.
alligator ('æligeitə) n Alligator m.
allocate ('æləkeit) vt zuteilen, zuweisen.
   allocation n Zuteilung, Zuweisung f.
allot (ə'lot) vt 1 verteilen. 2 bestimmen (für).
   allotment n 1 Verteilung f. 2 Parzelle f. 3
   Schrebergarten m.
allow (ə'lau) vt 1 erlauben, zulassen. 2 bewilligen. 3 zugeben. allow for berücksichtigen. be allowed to dürfen. allowable
   adj zulässig. allowance n 1 Erlaubnis f. 2
   Zuschuß m. 3 Nachsicht f. 4 comm Nachlaß
   m. make allowances for berücksichtigen.
alloy ('æloi) n Legierung f. vt legieren.
allude (ə'lu:d) vi allude to anspielen auf,
   andeuten. allusion n Andeutung, Anspielung
   f.
allure (ə'luə) vt (an-, ver-)locken.
ally (v ə'lai; n 'ælai) (vi),vt (sich) verbünden. n
   Verbündete(r) m.
almanac ('ɔ:lmənæk) n Almanach m.
almighty (ɔ:l'maiti) adj allmächtig. n Allmäch-
   tige(r) m.
almond ('ɑ:mənd) n Mandel f.
almost ('ɔ:lmoust) adv fast, beinahe.
alms (ɑ:mz) n Almosen neu.
aloft (ə'loft) adv 1 (hoch) oben. 2 nach oben.
alone (ə'loun) adj allein. adv allein, nur. leave
   alone in Ruhe lassen.
along (ə'loŋ) prep entlang. adv 1 entlang. 2
   vorwärts, weiter. get along with someone
   mit jemandem auskommen, sich mit jemandem verstehen. alongside prep neben. adv
   naut längsseits.
aloof (ə'lu:f) adv fern, abseits. keep aloof sich
   fernhalten. aloofness n Zurückhaltung f.
aloud (ə'laud) adv laut, mit lauter Stimme.
alphabet ('ælfəbet) n Alphabet neu. alphabeti-
   cal adj alphabetisch.
alpine ('ælpain) adj Alpen—. alpinist n Alpinist m.
Alps (ælps) n pl Alpen f pl.

143

already (ɔːlˈredi) *adv* schon, bereits.
Alsace (ˈælsæs) *n* Elsaß *neu*. **Alsatian** *adj* elsässich. *n* Elsässer *m*. **Alsatian (dog)** deutscher Schäferhund *m*.
also (ˈɔːlsou) *adv* auch, ferner.
altar (ˈɔːltə) *n* Altar *m*. **altarpiece** *n* Altarblatt *neu*. **altar-rail** *n* Altarschranke *f*.
alter (ˈɔːltə) *vt* (um-, ver-)ändern. *vi* sich ändern. **alterable** *adj* veränderlich. **alteration** *n* Veränderung, (Um)Änderung.
alternate (*v* ˈɔːltəneit; *adj* ɔːˈtəːnit) *vi* (*vt*) abwechseln (lassen). *adj* abwechselnd. **alternating** *adj* abwechselnd. **alternating current** *n* Wechselstrom *m*. **alternation** *n* **1** Abwechslung *f*. **2** Wechsel *m*. **alternative** *adj* **1** alternativ. **2** ander. *n* Alternative, Wahl *f*.
although (ˈɔːlðou) *conj* obgleich, obwohl.
altitude (ˈæltitjuːd) *n* Höhe *f*.
alto (ˈæltou) *n* Alt *m*. Altstimme *f*.
altogether (ɔːltəˈgeðə) *adv* **1** gänzlich, ganz und gar. **2** im ganzen (genommen).
aluminium (æljuˈminiəm) *n* Aluminium *neu*.
always (ˈɔːlweiz) *adv* immer, stets.
am (əm; *stressed* æm) *v see* **be**.
amalgamate (əˈmælgəmeit) *(vi,)vt* **1** (sich) amalgamieren. **2** (sich) vereinigen. **3** *comm* fusionieren.
amass (əˈmæs) *vt* anhäufen.
amateur (ˈæmətə) *n* Amateur, Liebhaber *m*.
amaze (əˈmeiz) *vt* erstaunen, verblüffen. **amazement** *n* (Er)Staunen *neu*. **amazing** *adj* **1** erstaunlich. **2** verblüffend.
ambassador (æmˈbæsədə) *n* Botschafter, Gesandte(r) *m*.
amber (ˈæmbə) *adj* **1** Bernstein—. **2** bernsteinfarben. *n* **1** Bernstein *m*. **2** *mot* Gelb, gelbes Licht *neu*.
ambidextrous (æmbiˈdekstrəs) *adj* **1** beidhändig. **2** ungewöhnlich geschickt.
ambiguous (æmˈbigjuəs) *adj* **1** zweideutig. **2** unklar. **ambiguity** *n* Zweideutigkeit *f*. Doppelsinn *m*.
ambition (æmˈbiʃən) *n* **1** Ehrgeiz *m*. **2** Ziel *neu*. **ambitious** *adj* ehrgeizig.
ambivalent (æmˈbivələnt) *adj* **1** ambivalent. **2** zwiespältig.
amble (ˈæmbəl) *vi* schlendern.
ambulance (ˈæmbjuləns) *n* Krankenwagen *m*.
ambush (ˈæmbuʃ) *n* Hinterhalt *m*. *vt* aus dem Hinterhalt überfallen.
amenable (əˈmiːnəbəl) *adj* **1** zugänglich. **2** gefügig.
amend (əˈmend) *vt* **1** verbessern. **2** abändern. **3** berichtigen. **amendment** *n* **1** Verbesserung *f*. **2** Abänderung *f*. **make amends for** wiedergutmachen.
amenity (əˈmiːniti) *n* **1** Annehmlichkeit *f*. **2** *pl* Vorzüge *m pl*.
America (əˈmerikə) *n* Amerika *neu*. **American** ~*adj* amerikanisch. *n* Amerikaner *m*.
amethyst (ˈæmiθist) *n* Amethyst *m*.
amiable (ˈeimiəbəl) *adj* freundlich.
amicable (ˈæmikəbəl) *adj* freundschaftlich.
amid (əˈmid) *prep* mitten in or unter.
amiss (əˈmis) *adj,adv* verkehrt, falsch. **take amiss** übel nehmen.
ammonia (əˈmouniə) *n* Ammoniak *neu*.
ammunition (æmjuˈniʃən) *n* Munition *f*.
amnesty (ˈæmnəsti) *n* Amnestie *f*. Straferlaß *m*.
amoeba (əˈmiːbə) *n* Amöbe *f*.
among (əˈmʌŋ) *prep also* **amongst** **1** unter. **2** inmitten, zwischen. **3** bei.
amoral (eiˈmɔrəl) *adj* amoralisch.
amorous (ˈæmərəs) *adj* **1** verliebt. **2** Liebes—.
amorphous (əˈmɔːfəs) *adj* **1** amorph. **2** formlos.
amount (əˈmaunt) *n* **1** Betrag *m*. Summe *f*. **2** Menge *f*. *vi* sich belaufen, betragen.
ampere (ˈæmpɛə) *n* Ampere *neu*.
amphetamine (æmˈfetəmiːn) *n* Benzedrin *neu*.
amphibian (æmˈfibiən) *n* Amphibie *f*. *adj* amphibisch. **amphibious** *adj* **1** *zool* amphibisch. **2** *tech* Amphibien—.
amphitheatre (ˈæmfiθiətə) *n* Amphitheater *neu*.
ample (ˈæmpəl) *adj* **1** reichlich. **2** weit, groß.
amplify (ˈæmplifai) *vt* **1** *tech* verstärken. **2** erweitern, ausdehnen. **amplifier** *n* Verstärker *m*.
amputate (ˈæmpjuteit) *vt* amputieren, abnehmen. **amputation** *n* Amputation *f*.
amuse (əˈmjuːz) *vt* amüsieren, unterhalten. **be amused** sich amüsieren *or* freuen. **amusement** *n* **1** Unterhaltung *f*. **2** Vergnügen *neu*. **amusing** *adj* amüsant, unterhaltend.
an (ən; *stressed* æn) *indef art see* **a.**
anachronism (əˈnækrənizəm) *n* Anachronismus *m*.
anaemia (əˈniːmiə) *n* Anämie, Blutarmut *f*. **anaemic** *adj* anämisch, bleichsüchtig.
anaesthetic (ænisˈθetik) *n* Betäubungsmittel *neu*. *adj* betäubend, narkotisch. **anaesthetist** *n* Narkotiseur *m*. **anaesthetize** *vt* betäuben, narkotisieren.
anal (ˈeinl) *adj* anal, After—.
analogy (əˈnælədʒi) *n* Analogie, Ähnlichkeit *f*. **analogous** *adj* analog, ähnlich.

analysis (ə'næləsis) n, pl **analyses 1** Analyse f. **2** Zergliederung f. **3** Untersuchung f. **analyse** vt **1** analysieren. **2** zergliedern, auswerten. **3** genau untersuchen. **analyst** n Analytiker m. **analytical** adj analytisch.

anarchy ('ænəki) n Anarchie, Gesetzlosigkeit f. **anarchist** n Anarchist m.

anatomy (ə'nætəmi) n Anatomie f. **anatomical** adj anatomisch.

ancestor ('ænsəstə) n Vorfahr, Ahn m.

anchor ('æŋkə) n Anker m. vt verankern. vi ankern.

anchovy ('æntʃəvi) n Anschovis f.

ancient ('einʃənt) adj alt, aus alter Zeit.

ancillary ('ænsiləri) adj **1** Hilfs—. Neben— **2** untergeordnet.

and (ən, ənd; stressed ænd) conj und.

anecdote ('ænikdout) n Anekdote f.

anemone (ə'neməni) n Anemone f.

anew (ə'njuː) adv von neuem.

angel ('eindʒəl) n Engel m. **angelic** adj engelhaft.

anger ('æŋgə) n Zorn, Ärger m. vt ärgern.

angle[1] ('æŋgəl) n **1** math Winkel m. **2** Ecke f. **3** Standpunkt m. **4** Seite f.

angle[2] ('æŋgəl) vi angeln. **angler** n Angler m. **angling** n Angeln neu.

Anglican ('æŋglikən) adj anglikanisch. n Anglikaner m.

angry ('æŋgri) adj zornig, ärgerlich, böse.

anguish ('æŋgwiʃ) n Qual, Angst f. Schmerz m.

angular ('æŋgjulə) adj winklig, eckig.

animal ('æniməl) n Tier neu. adj tierisch.

animate ('ænimeit) vt **1** beleben. **2** aufmuntern. **animated** adj lebhaft, munter. **animation** n Lebhaftigkeit, Munterkeit f.

animosity ('æni'mɔsiti) n Feindseligkeit f.

aniseed ('ænisiːd) n Anis m.

ankle ('æŋkəl) n (Fuß)Knöchel m.

annals ('ænlz) n pl Annalen f pl.

annex (ə'neks) vt **1** annektieren. **2** anhängen. **3** beifügen. **annexation** n Annexion f. **annexe** n **1** Anbau m. **2** Nebengebäude neu.

annihilate (ə'naiəleit) vt vernichten. **annihilation** n Vernichtung f.

anniversary (æni'vɔːsəri) n Jahrestag m. Jahresfeier f.

annotate ('ænəteit) vt mit Anmerkungen versehen.

announce (ə'nauns) vt **1** ankündigen, bekanntmachen. **2** anzeigen. **announcement** n **1** Ankündigung f. **2** Anzeige f. **announcer** n Ansager m.

annoy (ə'nɔi) vt ärgern, belästigen. **be annoyed** sich ärgern. **annoyance** n Belästigung f. Ärgernis neu. **annoying** adj ärgerlich.

annual ('ænjuəl) adj **1** jährlich, Jahres— **2** bot einjährig. n **1** Jahrbuch neu. **2** einjährige Pflanze f.

annul (ə'nʌl) vt für ungültig erklären.

anode ('ænoud) n Anode f.

anoint (ə'nɔint) vt salben.

anomaly (ə'nɔməli) n Anomalie, Unregelmäßigkeit f.

anonymous (ə'nɔniməs) adj anonym, namenlos. **anonymity** n Anonymität f.

another (ə'nʌðə) adj,pron **1** ein anderer. **2** ein zweiter or weiterer. **3** noch einer.

answer ('ɑːnsə) n Antwort f. vt **1** (a question) beantworten. **2** (a person) antworten. **answer for** verantwortlich sein für. **answerable** adj verantwortlich.

ant (ænt) n Ameise f.

antagonize (æn'tægənaiz) vt zum Gegner or Feind machen. **antagonism** n **1** Feindseligkeit f. **2** Widerstand m. **antagonist** n Gegner m. **antagonistic** adj feindlich, gegnerisch.

Antarctic (æn'tɑːktik) n Antarktis f. adj antarktisch, Südpol—. **Antarctic Ocean** n südliches Polarmeer neu.

antelope ('æntiloup) n Antelope f.

antenatal (ænti'neitl) adj vor der Geburt. **antenatal care** n Schwangerschaftsfürsorge f.

antenna (æn'tenə) n **1** pl **antennae** zool Fühler m. **2** pl **antennas** tech Antenne f.

anthem ('ænθəm) n **1** Hymne f. **2** Choral m. **national anthem** Nationalhymne f.

anthology (æn'θɔlədʒi) n Anthologie f.

anthropology (ænθrə'pɔlədʒi) n Anthropologie f. **anthropological** adj anthropologisch. **anthropologist** n Anthropologe m.

antibiotic (æntibai'ɔtik) n Antibiotikum neu. adj antibiotisch.

antibody ('æntibɔdi) n Antikörper m.

anticipate (æn'tisipeit) vt **1** voraussehen. **2** vorwegnehmen. **3** erwarten, erhoffen. **anticipation** n **1** Vorahnung f. **2** Vorwegnahme f. **3** Hoffnung, Erwartung f.

anticlimax (ænti'klaimæks) n Abfallen neu. Antiklimax m.

anticlockwise (ænti'klɔkwaiz) adv gegen den Uhrzeigersinn.

antics ('æntiks) n pl Posse, Fratze f.

anticyclone (ænti'saikloun) n Hochdruckgebiet neu.

antidote ('æntidout) n Gegengift neu.

145

antifreeze ('æntifri:z) n Frostschutzmittel neu.

antique (æn'ti:k) n Antike f. alter Kunstgegenstand m. adj 1 antik. 2 alt. **antique dealer** n Antiquitätenhändler m. **antique shop** n Antiquitätengeschäft neu. **antiquated** adj 1 altmodisch. 2 veraltet, überholt. **antiquity** n 1 Altertum neu. 2 pl Antiquitäten f pl.

anti-Semitic adj antisemitisch. **anti-Semitism** n Antisemitismus m.

antiseptic (ænti'septik) adj antiseptisch. n Antiseptikum neu.

antisocial (ænti'souʃəl) adj gesellschaftsfeindlich.

antithesis (æn'tiθəsis) n, pl -ses Antithese f. Gegensatz m.

antler ('æntlə) n 1 Geweihsprosse f. 2 pl Geweih neu.

antonym ('æntənim) n Antonym neu.

anus ('einəs) n After m.

anvil ('ænvil) n Amboß m.

anxious (æŋkʃəs) adj 1 ängstlich, besorgt. 2 begierig. **anxiety** n Angst, Sorge f.

any ('eni) adj 1 (irgend)einer, (irgend)welcher. 2 jeder. **in any case** auf jeden Fall. **not any** kein. ~pron irgendeiner, irgendwelcher. adv 1 etwas. 2 irgendwie. **anybody** pron (irgend) jemand, irgendeiner. **anyhow** adv 1 irgendwie. 2 jedenfalls. **anyone** pron (irgend) jemand, irgendeiner. **anything** pron 1 (irgend) etwas. 2 alles. **anything but** alles andere als. **if anything** wenn überhaupt. **anyway** adv 1 irgendwie. 2 jedenfalls, sowieso. **anywhere** adv 1 irgendwo(hin). 2 überall.

apart (ə'pɑ:t) adv 1 beiseite. 2 getrennt, abgesondert. **apart from** abgesehen von.

apartheid (ə'pɑ:tait) n Rassentrennung f.

apartment (ə'pɑ:tmənt) n 1 Zimmer neu. 2 US Wohnung f. 3 pl Wohnung f.

apathy ('æpəθi) n Apathie, Gleichgültigkeit f. **apathetic** adj apathisch.

ape (eip) n Affe m. vt (nach)äffen.

aperitive (ə'peritiv) n Aperitif m.

aperture ('æpətʃə) n 1 Öffnung f. 2 tech Blende f.

apex ('eipeks) n, pl apexes or apices Höhepunkt, Gipfel m. Spitze f.

apiece (ə'pi:s) adv 1 je, für jedes Stück. 2 pro Person.

apology (ə'pɔlədʒi) n 1 Entschuldigung f. 2 Rechtfertigung f. **apologetic** adj entschuldigend. **apologize** vi sich entschuldigen.

apostle (ə'pɔsəl) n Apostel m.

apostrophe (ə'pɔstrəfi) n Apostroph m.

appal (ə'pɔ:l) vt erschrecken, entsetzen. **appalling** adj entsetzlich, schrecklich.

apparatus (æpə'reitəs) n, pl -tus or -tuses Apparat m. Gerät neu.

apparent (ə'pærənt) adj 1 augenscheinlich, offenbar. 2 sichtbar. 3 scheinbar. **apparently** adv anscheinend.

appeal (ə'pi:l) vi 1 appellieren, sich wenden. 2 bitten. 3 gefallen, zusagen. 4 sich berufen auf. n 1 (dringende) Bitte f. 2 Appell m. 3 Anziehungskraft f.

appear (ə'piə) vi 1 erscheinen, sich zeigen. 2 scheinen, aussehen. 3 auftauchen. **appearance** n 1 Erscheinen neu. 2 Äußere neu. Erscheinung f. 3 Anschein m. **to all appearances** allem Anschein nach.

appease (ə'pi:z) vt 1 beruhigen. 2 befriedigen.

appendix (ə'pendiks) n, pl -dixes or -dices 1 Anhang m. 2 anat Blinddarm m. **appendicitis** n Blinddarmentzündung f.

appetite ('æpətait) n 1 Appetit m. 2 Verlangen neu.

applaud (ə'plɔ:d) vt 1 beklatschen, Beifall spenden. 2 billigen. vi applaudieren. **applause** n Beifall m.

apple ('æpəl) n Apfel m.

apply (ə'plai) vt 1 anwenden, verwenden. 2 auflegen. vi 1 sich bewerben. 2 sich wenden an. 3 sich anwenden lassen. **apply oneself** sich widmen. **appliance** n Gerät neu. Apparat m. **applicable** adj 1 anwendbar. 2 geeignet. **not applicable** nicht zutreffend. **applicant** n Bewerber, Antragsteller m. **application** n 1 Anwendung f. 2 Antrag m. Bewerbung f. 3 Eifer m. 4 Auflegen neu.

appoint (ə'pɔint) vt 1 ernennen, anstellen. 2 verabreden. 3 ausstatten. **appointment** n 1 Ernennung, Anstellung f. 2 Verabredung f.

appraise (ə'preiz) vt abschätzen, bewerten. **appraisal** n Abschätzung f.

appreciate (ə'pri:ʃieit) vt 1 (richtig) schätzen. 2 Gefallen finden. 3 dankbar sein (für). 4 wahrnehmen, erkennen. vi im Wert steigen. **appreciable** adj merklich, nennenswert. **appreciation** n 1 Schätzung f. 2 Verständnis neu. **appreciative** adj 1 anerkennend. 2 verständnisvoll.

apprehend (æpri'hend) vt 1 verhaften. 2 begreifen. 3 befürchten. **apprehension** n 1 Besorgnis, Befürchtung f. 2 Verstand m. 3 Verhaftung f. **apprehensive** adj besorgt, bedenklich, ängstlich.

apprentice (ə'prentis) n Lehrling m. **apprenticeship** n Lehrzeit f.
approach (ə'prəutʃ) vt,vi 1 sich nähern. 2 nahekommen. vt 1 sich wenden an. 2 herantreten an. n 1 (Heran)Nahen neu. Annäherung f. 2 Zugang m. Auffahrt, Zufahrt f. 3 Behandlung f. **approachable** adj zugänglich.
appropriate (adj ə'prəupriət; v ə'prəuprieit) adj 1 angemessen, geeignet. 2 entsprechend. vt sich aneignen.
approve (ə'pru:v) vt,vi billigen, anerkennen, genehmigen. vt annehmen, akzeptieren. **approval** n Billigung, Genehmigung, Anerkennung f. **on approval** auf Ansicht.
approximate (adj ə'prɔksimət; v ə'prɔksimeit) adj ungefähr. vt nahekommen. vi sich nähern.
apricot ('eiprikɔt) n Aprikose f.
April ('eiprəl) n April m.
apron ('eiprən) n Schürze f.
apt (æpt) adj 1 geeignet. 2 geschickt.
aptitude ('æptitju:d) n Begabung f. Geschick neu.
aquarium (ə'kwεəriəm) n, pl **-riums** or **-ria** Aquarium neu.
Aquarius (ə'kwεəriəs) n Wassermann m.
aquatic (ə'kwætik) adj Wasser—
aqueduct ('ækwədʌkt) n Aquädukt m.
Arabia (ə'reibiə) n Arabien neu. **Arab** adj arabisch. n Araber m. **Arabian** adj arabisch. n Araber m. **Arabic** adj arabisch. n (language) Arabisch neu.
arable ('ærəbəl) adj Acker—.
arbitrary ('ɑːbitrəri) adj willkürlich, eigenmächtig.
arbitrate ('ɑːbitreit) vt entscheiden, schlichten. vi Schiedsrichter sein. **arbitration** n Schiedsspruch m. **arbitrator** n Schiedsrichter m.
arc (ɑːk) n Bogen m.
arcade (ɑː'keid) n 1 Arkade f. 2 Durchgang m.
arch (ɑːtʃ) n 1 arch Bogen m. 2 Wölbung f. vi sich wölben.
archaeology (ɑːki'ɔlədʒi) n Archäologie f. **archaeological** adj archäologisch. **archaeologist** n Archäologe m.
archaic (ɑː'keiik) adj 1 veraltet. 2 altertümlich. **archaism** n veralteter Ausdruck m.
archbishop (ɑːtʃ'biʃəp) n Erzbischof m.
archduke (ɑːtʃ'djuːk) n Erzherzog m.
archery ('ɑːtʃəri) n Bogenschießen m. **archer** n Bogenschütze m.
archetype ('ɑːkitaip) n Archetyp m.
archipelago (ɑːki'peləgou) n Archipel m.
architect ('ɑːkitekt) n 1 Architekt m. 2 Schöp-

fer, Urheber m. **architecture** n 1 Architektur f. 2 Konstruktion f.
archives ('ɑːkaivz) n pl Archiv neu.
archway ('ɑːtʃwei) n Bogengang m.
Arctic ('ɑːktik) n Arktis f. Nordpolargebiet neu. adj arktisch. **Arctic Ocean** n Nördliches Polarmeer neu.
ardent ('ɑːdnt) adj 1 heiß, glühend. 2 eifrig, begeistert.
ardour ('ɑːdə) n 1 Hitze f. 2 Eifer m. Begeisterung f.
arduous ('ɑːdjuəs) adj schwierig, anstrengend.
are (ə; stressed ɑː) v see **be**.
area ('εəriə) n 1 Fläche f. Flächeninhalt m. 2 Gebiet neu. Gegend f. 3 Bereich m. Zone f.
arena (ə'riːnə) n Arena f.
Argentina (ɑːdʒən'tiːnə) n Argentinien neu. **Argentine** adj also **Argentinian** argentinisch. n Argentinier m.
argue ('ɑːgjuː) vt 1 erörtern, diskutieren. 2 behaupten. vi 1 streiten, argumentieren. 2 Einwände machen. **argument** n 1 Beweis m. Beweisführung f. 2 Streit m. 3 Argument neu. **argumentative** adj streitlustig.
arid ('ærid) adj trocken, dürr.
Aries ('εəriːz) n 1 Widder m.
arise* (ə'raiz) vi 1 entstehen. 2 aufstehen.
aristocracy (æri'stɔkrəsi) n Aristokratie f. Adel m. **aristocrat** n Aristokrat, Adlige(r) m. **aristocratic** adj aristokratisch.
arithmetic (ə'riθmətik) n Arithmetik f. Rechnen neu. **arithmetical** adj arithmetisch.
arm[1] (ɑːm) n 1 Arm m. 2 (of a chair) Armlehne f. **with open arms** mit offenen Armen. **armchair** n Lehnstuhl, Sessel m. **armful** n Armvoll m. **armhole** n Ärmelloch neu. **armpit** n Achselhöhle f.
arm[2] (ɑːm) n Waffe f. **arms race** Wettrüsten neu. **coat of arms** Wappen neu. **up in arms** in Aufruhr. ~(vi),vt (sich) bewaffnen, (sich) ausrüsten. **armed forces** n Streitkräfte f pl. **armament** n 1 Bewaffnung f. 2 (Kriegsaus)Rüstung f.
armour ('ɑːmə) n Panzer m. **armour-plated** adj also **armoured** gepanzert, Panzer—.
army ('ɑːmi) n 1 Armee f. Heer neu. 2 Menge f.
aroma (ə'roumə) n Aroma neu. Duft m. **aromatic** (ærə'mætik) adj aromatisch, würzig.
arose (ə'rouz) v see **arise**.
around (ə'raund) prep 1 um, um...herum. 2 ungefähr. adv 1 rundherum. 2 in der Nähe.
arouse (ə'rauz) vt 1 aufwecken. 2 erregen.
arrange (ə'reindʒ) vt 1 anordnen. 2 einrichten.

array

3 erledigen. 4 vereinbaren. 5 *mus* bearbeiten. *vi* 1 sich verständigen. 2 Vorkehrungen treffen. 3 sich einigen. **arrangement** *n* 1 Anordnung f. 2 Einrichtung f. 3 Vereinbarung f. Abkommen *neu*. 4 *mus* Bearbeitung f.

array (ə'rei) *vt* 1 ordnen. 2 kleiden, putzen. *n* 1 Ordnung f. 2 Kleidung, Aufmachung f.

arrears (ə'riəz) *n pl* Rückstände *m pl*. Schulden f *pl*. **in arrears** im Rückstand m.

arrest (ə'rest) *vt* 1 verhaften. 2 aufhalten, hindern. *n* Haft, Verhaftung f. **under arrest** verhaftet. **arresting** *adj* interessant, fesselnd.

arrive (ə'raiv) *vi* 1 ankommen. 2 erreichen, gelangen. 3 erscheinen. **arrival** *n* 1 Ankunft f. 2 Erscheinen *neu*.

arrogant ('ærəgənt) *adj* arrogant, anmaßend, überheblich. **arrogance** *n* Arroganz f. Anmaßung f.

arrow ('ærou) *n* 1 Pfeil m. 2 Pfeilzeichen *neu*.

arsenic ('a:snik) *n* Arsenik *neu*.

arson ('a:sən) *n* Brandstiftung f.

art (a:t) *n* 1 Kunst f. 2 Geschick *neu*. 3 List f. 4 *pl educ* Geisteswissenschaften f *pl*. **work of art** Kunstwerk *n*. ∼*adj* Kunst—. **art gallery** *n* Kunstgalerie, Bildergalerie f. **art school** *n* Kunstschule f. **artful** *adj* 1 listig, schlau. 2 geschickt.

artery ('a:təri) *n* Arterie, Pulsader f. **arterial** *adj* arteriell.

arthritis (a:'θraitis) *n* Arthritis f.

artichoke ('a:titʃouk) *n* Artischocke f.

article ('a:tikəl) *n* 1 Artikel m. 2 Ware f. Gegenstand m.

articulate (*v* a:'tikjuleit: *adj* a:'tikjulət) *vt* 1 aussprechen, artikulieren. 2 gliedern. *vi* deutlich sprechen. *adj* 1 deutlich. 2 sich gut ausdrückend.

artificial (a:ti'fiʃəl) *adj* 1 künstlich, Kunst—. 2 gekünstelt.

artillery (a:'tiləri) *n* Artillerie f.

artist ('a:tist) *n* 1 Künstler m. 2 Könner m. **artiste** *n* Artist m. **artistic** *adj* künstlerisch, Kunst—.

as (æz: *stressed* æz) *conj* 1 da, weil. 2 wie, sowie. 3 als, während. *adv* 1 so, wie, ebenso wie. 2 als. **as...as** (eben)so...wie. **as far as** soviel, sofern, soweit. **as if** als ob, als wenn. **as long as** solange. **as well** ebenfalls, auch.

asbestos (æs'bestəs) *n* Asbest m.

ascend (ə'send) *vi* (auf-, hinauf-)steigen. *vt* besteigen. **ascendant** *adj* 1 aufsteigend. 2 vorherrschend. **in the ascendant** im Auf-

steigen. **Ascension** *n rel* Himmelfahrt f. **ascent** *n* Aufstieg m.

ascertain (æsə'tein) *vt* feststellen.

ash[1] (æʃ) *n* Asche f. **ashtray** *n* Aschenbecher m.

ash[2] (æʃ) *n bot* Esche f.

ashamed (ə'ʃeimd) *adj* beschämt. **be ashamed** sich schämen.

ashore (ə'ʃɔ:) *adv* am or ans Ufer. **go ashore** an Land gehen.

Ash Wednesday *n* Aschermittwoch f.

Asia ('eiʃə) *n* Asien *neu*. **Asia Minor** Kleinasien *neu*. **Asian** *adj* asiatisch. *n* Asiat m. **Asiatic** *adj* asiatisch.

aside (ə'said) *adv* beiseite.

ask (a:sk) *vt* 1 fragen. 2 fragen nach. 3 bitten. 4 fordern, verlangen. **ask about** or **after** sich erkundigen nach or wegen.

askew (ə'skju:) *adv* schief, schräg.

asleep (ə'sli:p) *adv* schlafend. **be asleep** schlafen. **fall asleep** einschlafen.

asparagus (ə'spærəgəs) *n* Spargel m.

aspect ('æspekt) *n* 1 Aussehen *neu*. 2 Aspekt m. Hinsicht f. 3 Aussicht f.

asphalt ('æsfælt) *n* Asphalt m.

aspire (ə'spaiə) *vi* 1 streben. 2 sich erheben. **aspiring** *adj* hochstrebend.

aspirin ('æsprin) *n* Aspirin *neu*.

ass (æs) *n* Esel m.

assassinate (ə'sæsineit) *vt* ermorden. **assassin** *n* (politischer) Mörder m. **assassination** *n* Ermordung f.

assault (ə'sɔ:lt) *vt* angreifen, überfallen. *n* Angriff, Überfall m.

assemble (ə'sembəl) *vt* 1 versammeln. 2 zusammensetzen, montieren. *vi* sich versammeln. **assembly** *n* 1 Versammlung f. 2 Montage f. **assembly hall** *n educ* Aula f. **assembly line** *n* Fließband *neu*.

assent (ə'sent) *vi* 1 zustimmen. 2 genehmigen. *n* 1 Zustimmung f. 2 Genehmigung f.

assert (ə'sə:t) *vt* 1 behaupten, erklären. 2 bestehen auf. **assert oneself** sich durchsetzen. **assertion** *n* Behauptung f. **assertive** *adj* anmaßend.

assess (ə'ses) *vt* 1 zur Steuer einschätzen. 2 einschätzen. **assessment** *n* Einschätzung f.

asset ('æset) *n* 1 Vorteil m. 2 *pl comm* Vermögen *neu*.

assign (ə'sain) *vt* 1 anweisen. 2 bestimmen. **assignment** *n* 1 Anweisung f. 2 Aufgabe f.

assimilate (ə'simileit) *vt* 1 absorbieren, aufnehmen. 2 anpassen. **assimilation** n Aufnahme f.

assist (ə'sist) vt 1 helfen. 2 unterstützen. 3 fördern. vi 1 mithelfen. 2 teilnehmen. 2 beiwohnen. **assistance** n 1 Hilfe f. 2 Unterstützung f. **assistant** n 1 Assistent m. 2 Verkäufer m.

assizes (ə'saiziz) n pl Gerichtssitzungen f pl.

associate (v ə'souʃieit; adj,n ə'souʃiit) vt 1 vereinigen, anschließen. 2 verbinden, verknüpfen. vi verkehren. adj verbündet. n Kollege, Mitarbeiter m. **association** n 1 Vereinigung f. 2 Verein, Verband m. 3 Verkehr m. 4 Verbindung f.

assort (ə'sɔːt) vt assortieren. **assorted** adj gemischt. **assortment** n Sortiment neu.

assume (ə'sjuːm) vt 1 annehmen. 2 übernehmen. 3 sich aneignen. **assuming** adj anmaßend. **assumption** n 1 Annahme f. 2 Aneignung f.

assure (ə'ʃuə) vt 1 sichern, sicherstellen. 2 versichern. **assurance** n 1 Versicherung f. 2 Selbstsicherheit f.

asthma ('æsmə) n Asthma neu.

astonish (ə'stɔniʃ) vt erstaunen, überraschen. **be astonished** erstaunt sein **astonishing** adj erstaunlich. **astonishment** n Erstaunen neu.

astound (ə'staund) vt verblüffen.

astray (ə'strei) adv **go astray** sich verlaufen. **lead astray** irreführen.

astride (ə'straid) prep,adj,adv rittlings.

astrology (ə'strɔlədʒi) n Astrologie, Sterndeuterei f. **astrologer** n Astrologe m. **astrological** adj astrologisch.

astronaut ('æstrənɔːt) n Astronaut m.

astronomy (ə'strɔnəmi) n Astronomie, Sternkunde f. **astronomer** n Astronom m. **astronomical** adj 1 astronomisch, Stern— 2 riesengroß.

astute (ə'stjuːt) adj scharfsinnig.

asunder (ə'sʌndə) adv auseinander.

asylum (ə'sailəm) n 1 pol Asyl neu. Freistätte f 2 Heim neu. **lunatic asylum** Irrenanstalt f

at (ət; stressed æt) prep 1 an, auf. 2 in, zu 3 bei. 4 für. 5 um. 6 über. **at two o'clock** um zwei Uhr

ate (eit, et) v see **eat.**

atheism ('eiθiizəm) n Atheismus m. **atheist** n Atheist m.

Athens ('æθinz) n Athen neu.

athlete ('æθliːt) n (Leicht)Athlet, Sportler m. **athletic** adj athletisch, Sport—. **athletics** n pl Athletik f.

Atlantic (ət'læntik) adj atlantisch. **Atlantic (Ocean)** n Atlantik, Atlantischer Ozean m.

atlas ('ætləs) n Atlas m.

atmosphere ('ætməsfiə) n 1 Atmosphäre f. 2 Luft f. 3 Stimmung f.

atom ('ætəm) n Atom neu. **atom bomb** n Atombombe f. **atomic** adj atomisch, Atom—.

atone (ə'toun) vi 1 büßen. 2 wiedergutmachen. **atonement** n Buße f.

atrocious (ə'trouʃəs) adj scheußlich, gräßlich. **atrocity** n Scheußlichkeit, Greueltat f.

attach (ə'tætʃ) vt 1 befestigen 2 anheften. 3 verbinden. **attachment** n 1 Befestigung f. 2 Zusatzgerät neu. 3 Anhänglichkeit f.

attaché (ə'tæʃei) n Attaché m. **attaché case** n Aktentasche f

attack (ə'tæk) vt 1 angreifen, überfallen. 2 in Angriff nehmen. 3 kritisieren. n 1 Angriff, Überfall m. 2 Kritik f 3 med Anfall m. **attacker** n Angreifer m

attain (ə'tein) vt erreichen, erlangen. **attain to** gelangen zu. **attainable** adj erreichbar. **attainment** n Erreichung f.

attempt (ə'tempt) vt 1 versuchen. 2 sich wagen (an). n 1 Versuch m. 2 Attentat neu.

attend (ə'tend) vt 1 beiwohnen. 2 (a school) besuchen. 3 pflegen. vi 1 achten. 2 sich besorgen. 3 erledigen. 4 erscheinen. 5 bedienen. **attendance** n 1 Anwesenheit f. 2 Beteiligung f. 3 Pflege, Bedienung f. 4 Besuch m. **attendant** n 1 Diener m. 2 Begleiter m. 3 Bedienungsmann, Wärter m. **attention** n 1 Aufmerksamkeit, Beachtung f. 2 Erledigung f 3 pl Aufmerksamkeiten f pl. 4 Bedienung f. **pay attention** achtgeben. interj Achtung! **attentive** adj aufmerksam.

attic ('ætik) n Dachstube f.

attire (ə'taiə) vt ankleiden, schmücken. n Kleidung f Schmuck m.

attitude ('ætitjuːd) n 1 Stellung, Haltung f 2 Einstellung, Stellungnahme f

attract (ə'trækt) vt 1 anziehen 2 reizen, fesseln. **attract attention** Aufmerksamkeit erregen. **attraction** n 1 Anziehung, Attraktion f. 2 Anziehungskraft f. **attractive** adj 1 anziehend, reizvoll. 2 hübsch. **attractiveness** n Reiz m.

attribute (v ə'tribjuːt; n 'ætribjuːt) vt 1 zuschreiben. 2 zurückführen. n Eigenschaft f.

aubergine ('oubəʒiːn) n Aubergine f.

auburn ('ɔːbən) adj kastanienbraun.

auction ('ɔːkʃən) n Auktion, Versteigerung f. v **auction off** versteigern.

audacious (ɔ:'deiʃəs) *adj* 1 kühn. 2 frech. **audacity** *n* 1 Kühnheit f. 2 Frechheit f.

audible ('ɔ:dibəl) *adj* hörbar.

audience ('ɔ:diəns) *n* 1 Publikum *neu.* Zuhörer *m pl.* 2 Audienz f.

audit ('ɔ:dit) *vt* prüfen, revidieren. *n* Bücherrevision f. **auditing** *n* Bücherrevision f. **auditor** *n* Bücherrevisor m.

audition (ɔ:'diʃən) *n* Hörprobe f. *vt* einer Hörprobe unterziehen.

August ('ɔ:gəst) *n* August m.

aunt (ɑ:nt) *n* Tante f.

au pair (ou 'pɛə) *n also* **au pair girl** Aupair-Mädchen *neu.*

aura ('ɔ:rə) *n, pl* **auras** *or* **aurae** 1 Aura, Atmosphäre f. 2 Hauch, Duft m.

austere (ɔ:'stiə) *adj* 1 streng. 2 enthaltsam.

Australia (ɔ:'streiliə) *n* Australien *neu.* **Australian** *adj* australisch. *n* Australier m.

Austria ('ɔ:striə) *n* Österreich *neu.* **Austrian** *adj* österreichisch. *n* Österreicher m.

authentic (ɔ:'θentik) *adj* authentisch, echt.

author ('ɔ:θə) *n* 1 Verfasser m. 2 Autor, Schriftsteller m. 3 Urheber m.

authority (ɔ:'θɔriti) *n* 1 Autorität f. 2 Gewalt f. 3 Vollmacht f. 4 Quelle f. 5 Fachmann m. 6 pl Behörde f. **authoritarian** *adj* autoritär. **authoritative** *adj* 1 maßgebend. 2 herrisch.

authorize ('ɔ:θəraiz) *vt* 1 ermächtigen. 2 billigen, genehmigen. **authorization** *n* Genehmigung f.

autobiography (ɔ:təbai'ɔgrəfi) *n* Autobiographie f. **autobiographical** *adj* autobiographisch.

autograph ('ɔ:təgrɑ:f) *n* eigenhändige Unterschrift f. Autogramm *neu.* *vt* (eigenhändig) unterschreiben.

automatic (ɔ:tə'mætik) *adj* 1 automatisch, selbsttätig. 2 unwillkürlich. **automation** *n* Automation f.

autonomous (ɔ:'tɔnəməs) *adj* autonom. **autonomy** *n* Autonomie, Selbständigkeit f.

autumn ('ɔ:təm) *n* Herbst m.

auxiliary (ɔ:g'ziliəri) *adj* helfend, Hilfs—. *n* 1 Helfer m. 2 pl Hilfspersonal *neu.*

available (ə'veiləbəl) *adj* verfügbar, vorhanden. **availability** *n* Verfügbarkeit f. Vorhandensein *neu.*

avalanche ('ævəlɑ:nʃ) *n* Lawine f.

avenge (ə'vendʒ) *vt* rächen.

avenue ('ævənju:) *n* 1 Allee f. 2 Weg m.

average ('ævəridʒ) *adj* durchschnittlich. *n* Durchschnitt m. **on average** im Durchschnitt.

aversion (ə'və:ʃən) *n* Abneigung f.

aviary ('eiviəri) *n* Vogelhaus *neu.*

aviation (eivi'eiʃən) *n* Flugwesen *neu.*

avid ('ævid) *adj* gierig.

avocado (ævə'kɑ:dou) *n* Avocadobirne f.

avoid (ə'vɔid) *vt* 1 vermeiden. 2 ausweichen. 3 aus dem Wege gehen.

await (ə'weit) *vt* erwarten, warten auf.

awake* (ə'weik) *vt* 1 wecken. 2 erwecken. *vi* 1 aufwachen, erwachen. 2 bewußt werden. *adj* wach. **wide awake** munter. **awaken** *vt* 1 wecken. 2 erwecken. *vi* aufwachen, erwachen. **awakening** *n* Erwachen *neu.*

award (ə'wɔ:d) *vt* 1 zusprechen, verleihen. 2 gewähren. *n* Belohnung f. Preis m.

aware (ə'wɛə) *adj* bewußt. **awareness** *n* Bewußtsein *neu.* Kenntnis f.

away (ə'wei) *adv* 1 weg, fort, hinweg. 2 entfernt. 3 fort, verreist.

awe (ɔ:) *n* Ehrfurcht f. **awe-inspiring** *adj* ehrfurchtgebietend. **awe-struck** *adj* von Ehrfurcht ergriffen. **awful** *adj* 1 schrecklich, furchtbar. 2 inf furchtbar, scheußlich. **awfully** *adv* inf furchtbar, sehr.

awkward ('ɔ:kwəd) *adj* 1 ungeschickt, linkisch. 2 peinlich, unangenehm. 3 lästig, schwierig.

awoke (ə'wouk) *v see* **awake.**

axe (æks) *n* Axt f. Beil *neu.*

axis ('æksis) *n pl* **axes** Achse, Mittellinie f.

axle ('æksəl) *n* (Rad)Achse f.

B

babble ('bæbəl) *vt* 1 schwatzen, plappern. 2 plätschern, murmeln. *n* Geschwätz *neu.*

baboon (bə'bu:n) *n* Pavian m.

baby ('beibi) *n* Baby *neu.* Säugling m. Kleinkind *neu.* **baby-sit** *vi* Kinder beaufsichtigen, babysitten. **babyish** *adj* babyhaft.

bachelor ('bætʃələ) *n* Junggeselle m.

back (bæk) *n* 1 Rücken m. Kreuz *neu.* 2 Rückseite f. Hinterseite f. *adj* Nach—, Hinter—.' 1 zurück. 2 rückwärts. *vt* 1 wetten auf. 2 unterstützen. 3 rückwärts fahren.

backache ('bækeik) *n* Rückenschmerz m.

backbone ('bækboun) *n* Wirbelsäule f. Rückgrat *neu.*

backdate ('bækdeit) *vt* zurückdatieren.

backfire ('bækfaiə) *vi* 1 fehlzünden, frühzünden. 2 fehlschlagen. *n* Fehlzündung f.

backgammon ('bækgæmən) *n* Puffspiel *neu.*

background ('bækgraund) *n* Hintergrund m.

backhand ('bækhænd) n Rückhand f. **backhander** n 1 Rückhandschlag m. 2 geheime Belohnung f.
backlash ('bæklæʃ) n 1 tech Spielraum m. 2 (politische) Reaktion f. 3 Rückschlag m.
backlog ('bæklɔg) n Rückstand m. Rücklage f.
backside (bæk'said) n inf Hinterteil neu.
backstage (bæk'steidʒ) adj,adv hinter den Kulissen.
backstroke ('bækstrouk) n Gegenschlag m. Rückenschwimmen neu.
backward ('bækwəd) adj 1 (geistig) zurückgeblieben. 2 rückständig. 3 widerwillig.
backwards ('bækwədz) adv zurück, rückwärts.
backwater ('bækwɔtə) n Stauwasser neu.
bacon ('beikən) n Speck m.
bacteria (bæk'tiəriə) n pl Bakterie f.
bad (bæd) adj 1 schlecht, schlimm. 2 böse. **bad-tempered** adj mißgelaunt.
bade (beid) v see **bid**.
badge (bædʒ) n Abzeichen neu. Medaille f.
badger ('bædʒə) n Dachs m. vt belästigen.
badminton ('bædmintən) n Federballspiel neu.
baffle ('bæfəl) vt verwirren, täuschen.
bag (bæg) n 1 Beutel m. Tüte f. 2 Tasche f. 3 Sack m. vt 1 abschießen. 2 erlegen. **baggage** n Gepäck neu. **baggy** adj bauschig, sackartig, schlotterig. **bagpipes** n Dudelsack m.
bail (beil) n law Bürgschaft, Kaution f.
bailiff ('beilif) n 1 Gerichtsdiener m. 2 Gutsverwalter m.
bait (beit) n 1 Köder m. Lockspeise f. 2 Lockung f. Reiz m. vt 1 ködern. 2 hetzen, quälen.
bake (beik) vt backen. **baker** n Bäcker m. **bakery** n Bäckerei f.
balance ('bæləns) vt 1 balancieren. 2 erwägen. 3 saldieren. n 1 Waage f. 2 Gleichgewicht neu. 3 Saldo m. Guthaben neu. **balance sheet** n Bilanz f. Bilanzbogen m.
balcony ('bælkəni) n Balkon m.
bald (bɔːld) adj 1 kahl, haarlos. 2 nackt.
bale¹ (beil) n Ballen m.
bale² (beil) vt,vi ausschöpfen. **bale out** mit dem Fallschirm abspringen.
ball¹ (bɔːl) n 1 Ball m. 2 Kugel f. **ballpoint pen** n Kugelschreiber m.
ball² (bɔːl) n Ball m. Tanzgesellschaft f. **ballroom** n Tanzsaal, Ballsaal m.
ballad ('bæləd) n Ballade f. Lied neu.
ballast ('bæləst) n Ballast m.
ballet ('bælei) n Ballett neu. **ballet dancer** n Ballettänzer m. Ballettänzerin f.
ballistic (bə'listik) adj ballistisch.

balloon (bə'luːn) n Ballon m. Luftballon m.
ballot ('bælət) n Wahl f. Abstimmung f. **ballot paper** n Stimmzettel m.
Baltic ('bɔːltik) adj baltisch. **Baltic (Sea)** n Ostsee f.
bamboo (bæm'buː) n Bambus m.
ban (bæn) vt verbannen, ächten. n Bann m. Verbannung, Achtung f.
banal (bə'nɑːl) adj banal, alltäglich.
banana (bə'nɑːnə) n Banane f.
band¹ (bænd) n 1 mus Kapelle f. Orchester neu. 2 Gruppe, Bande f.
band² (bænd) n 1 Band neu. Binde, Schnur f. 2 Riemen m. **bandage** n Bandage, Binde f. Verband m. vt verbinden.
bandit ('bændit) n Bandit m.
bandy ('bændi) adj krummbeinig. v **bandy words** hin und herstreiten.
bang (bæŋ) n 1 Knall, schallender Schlag m. vi,(vt) knallen (lassen). **banger** n inf 1 Feuerwerkskörper m. 2 Wurst f.
bangle ('bæŋgəl) n Spange f. Armband neu.
banish ('bæniʃ) vt verbannen, vertreiben.
banister ('bænistə) n Treppengeländer neu.
banjo ('bændʒou) n Banjo neu.
bank¹ (bæŋk) n 1 Ufer neu. 2 Damm m.
bank² (bæŋk) n Bank, Sparkasse f. **bank account** n Bankkonto neu. **bankbook** n Bankbuch, Sparbuch neu. **bank holiday** n (amtlicher) Feiertag m. **banknote** n Banknote f. **banker** n Bankier m. **banker's card** n Scheckkarte, Bankkarte f.
bankrupt ('bæŋkrʌpt) adj bankrott, zahlungsunfähig. n Bankerotteur m.
banner ('bænə) n Banner m. Fahne f.
banquet ('bæŋkwit) n Bankett, Festessen neu.
baptize (bæp'taiz) vt taufen. **baptism** n Taufe f.
bar (bɑː) n 1 Stange f. Riegel, Stab m. 2 Bar, Schank f. vt 1 verriegeln, vergittern. 2 ausschließen, verbieten. **barmaid** n Kellnerin, Barmädchen neu. **barman** n Kellner m.
barbarian (bɑː'bɛəriən) n Barbar m. **barbaric** adj barbarisch, roh, grausam. **barbarism** n Barbarismus m. **barbarity** n Barbarei, Roheit, Grausamkeit f.
barbecue ('bɑːbikjuː) n Bratrost m. Barbecue neu.
barbed wire (bɑːbd) n Stacheldraht m.
barber ('bɑːbə) n Barbier m. (Herren)Friseur m.
barbiturate (bɑː'bitjurət) n Barbiturat neu.
bare (bɛə) adj 1 nackt, unbekleidet. 2 bloß, unbedeckt, kahl. 3 leer. vt 1 entblößen,

enthüllen. **2** (one's teeth) blecken. **barefoot** *adj,adv* barfuß. **barely** *adv* kaum.

bargain ('ba:gin) *n* (vorteilhaftes) Geschäft *neu.* Gelegenheitskauf *m.* **into the bargain** obendrein. — *vt,vi* feilschen, handeln. **bargain for** erwarten

barge (ba:dʒ) *n* Lastkahn *m.* v **barge into** *inf* stürzen in.

baritone ('bæritoun) *n* Bariton *m.*

bark[1] (ba:k) *vi* bellen. *n* Gebell *neu.*

bark[2] (ba:k) *n* (Baum)rinde, Borke *f.*

barley ('ba:li) *n* Gerste *f.*

barn (ba:n) *n* Scheune *f.*

barometer (bə'rɔmitə) *n* Barometer *neu.*

baron ('bæran) *n* Baron, Freiherr *m.* **baroness** *n* Baronin *f.*

baronet ('bærənit) *n* Baronet *m.*

barracks ('bærəks) *n pl* Kaserne *f.*

barrel ('bærəl) *n* **1** Faß *neu.* Tonne *f.* **2** (of a gun) Lauf *m.*

barren ('bæran) *adj* unfruchtbar, öde.

barricade ('bærikeid) *n* Barrikade, Sperre *f.* *vt* versperren.

barrier ('bæriə) *n* Barriere, Schranke *f.*

barrister ('bæristə) *n* Rechtsanwalt *m.*

barrow ('bærou) *n* Karren *m.*

barter ('ba:tə) *vt* (ein)tauschen. *vi* Tauschhandel treiben. *n* Tauschhandel *m.*

base[1] (beis) *n* **1** Grundfläche, Basis *f.* **2** Fuß, Stützpunkt *m.* *vi* **1** basieren. **2** stützen. **be based on** sich beruhen auf. **baseball** *n* Baseballspiel *neu.* **basement** *n* Kellergeschoß *neu.*

base[2] (beis) *adj* niedrig, gemein, verächtlich.

bash (bæʃ) *vt* heftig schlagen. **have a bash** versuchen.

bashful ('bæʃfəl) *adj* scheu, schüchtern.

basic ('beisik) *adj* **1** einfach. **2** grundliegend. **basically** *adv* im Grunde, grundsätzlich.

basil ('bæzəl) *n* Basilienkraut *neu.*

basin ('beisən) *n* Becken *neu.* Schüssel *f.*

basis ('beisis) *n pl* **-ses** Basis, Grundlage *f.*

bask (ba:sk) *vi* sich sonnen.

basket ('ba:skit) *n* Korb *m.* **basketball** *n* Basketballspiel *neu.*

Basle (ba:l) *n* Basel *neu.*

bass (beis) *mus adj* Baß—. *n* Baß *m.*

bassoon (bə'su:n) *n* Fagott *neu.*

bastard ('ba:stəd) *n* Bastard *m.*

baste (beist) *vt cul* (mit Fett) begießen.

bat[1] (bæt) *n* Schläger *m.* Schlagholz *neu.* *vt* **1** schlagen. **2** (eyelids, etc.) zucken, zwinkern. **batsman** *n* Schläger *m.*

bat[2] (bæt) *n zool* Fledermaus *f.*

batch (bætʃ) *n* Schub, Stoß *m.*

bath (ba:θ) *n* **1** Bad *neu.* **2** Badewanne *f.* **bathroom** *n* Badezimmer *neu.* **bathtub** *n* Badewanne *f.*

bathe (beiθ) (*vi*),*vt* (sich) baden. **bathing costume** *n* Badeanzug *m.* **bathing trunks** *n* Badehose *f.*

baton ('bætən) *mus* Taktstock *m.*

battalion (bə'tæljən) *n* Bataillon *neu.*

batter[1] ('bætə) *vt* schlagen, prügeln.

batter[2] ('bætə) *n cul* Eierteig *m.*

battery ('bætəri) *n* Batterie *f.*

battle ('bætl) *n* Schlacht *f.* Gefecht *neu.* *vi* kämpfen. **battlefield** *n* Schlachtfeld *neu.* **battleship** *n* Schlachtschiff *neu.*

Bavaria (bə'vɛəriə) *n* Bayern *neu.* **Bavarian** *adj* bayrisch. *n* Bayer *m.*

bawl (bɔ:l) *vi* schreien, brüllen.

bay[1] (bei) *n* **1** *geog* Bai, Bucht *f.* **2** Lücke, Nische *f.*

bay[2] (bei) *n* **1** Fach. *neu.* Abteilung *f.* **2** Fensternische *f.*

bay[3] (bei) *vi* (dumpf) bellen, kläffen. **keep at bay** in Schach halten.

bay[4] (bei) *n bot* Lorbeer *m.*

bayonet ('beiənit) *n* Bajonett *neu.*

be[*] (bi:) *vi* **1** sein. **2** existieren. **3** sich befinden. *v aux* sein, werden. **there is, there are** es gibt.

beach (bi:tʃ) *n* Strand *m.* *vt* stranden. **beachcomber** *n* Strandgutjäger *m.*

beacon ('bi:kən) *n* **1** Signalfeuer *neu.* **2** Blinklicht *neu.*

bead (bi:d) *n* Perle, Glasperle *f.*

beak (bi:k) *n* Schnabel *m.*

beaker ('bi:kə) *n* **1** Becher *m.* **2** *sci* Becherglas *neu.*

beam (bi:m) *n* **1** Balken *m.* **2** Strahl *m.* *vt,vi* strahlen. *vi* strahlend lächeln.

bean (bi:n) *n* Bohne *f.* **full of beans** lebhaft.

bear[*1] (bɛə) *vt* **1** tragen, stützen. **2** erleiden, aushalten. **3** gebären. **bearing** *n* **1** Haltung *f.* **2** Verhalten, Betragen *neu.* **3** Beziehung *f.* **4** Richtung *f.* **5** *tech* Lager *neu.*

bear[2] (bɛə) *n* Bär *m.*

beard (biəd) *n* Bart *m.*

beast (bi:st) *n* **1** Tier, Vieh *neu.* **2** Bestie *f.*

beat[*] (bi:t) *vt* **1** schlagen, prügeln, klopfen. **2** besiegen, schlagen. *n* **1** *mus* Rhythmus, Takt *m.* **2** Schlag *m.* **3** (of a policeman) Revier *neu.*

beauty ('bju:ti) *n* Schönheit *f.* **beauty queen** *n*

Schönheitskönigin f. **beautiful** adj schön, hübsch.

beaver ('bi:və) n Biber m.

became (bi'keim) v see **become**.

because (bi'kɔːz) conj weil. **because of** wegen.

beckon ('bekən) vt,vi heranwinken.

become* (bi'kʌm) vi werden. vt passen, geziemen. **becoming** adj passend, geziemend.

bed (bed) n Bett neu. **bed bug** n Wanze f. **bedclothes** n pl Bettwäsche f. **bedding** n 1 Bettzeug neu. 2 Streu f. **bedridden** adj bettlägerig. **bedroom** n Schlafzimmer, Schlafgemach neu. **bed-sitter** n Wohnschlafzimmer neu. **bedspread** n Bettdecke f.

bedraggled (bi'drægəld) adj beschmutzt, naß.

bee (bi:) n Biene f. **beehive** n Bienenstock m.

beech (bi:tʃ) n Buche f.

beef (bi:f) n Rindfleisch neu.

beer (biə) n Bier neu.

beet (bi:t) n Bete, Rübe f. **beetroot** n rote Rübe f.

beetle ('bi:tl) n Käfer m. Schabe f.

befall* (bi'fɔːl) vi sich ereignen. vt (jemandem) zustoßen.

before (bi'fɔː) conj bevor, ehe, bis. adv 1 voraus, voran. 2 vorher, früher, ehe. prep vor. **beforehand** adv zuvor, davor.

befriend (bi'frend) vt befreunden.

beg (beg) vt,vi 1 betteln, bitten. vi erbitten. **beggar** n Bettler m.

begin* (bi'gin) vt,vi anfangen, beginnen. **beginner** n Anfänger m. **beginning** n Anfang, Beginn m.

begrudge (bi'grʌdʒ) vt mißgönnen.

behalf (bi'hɑːf) n **on behalf of 1** im Namen or im Auftrag von. 2 zugunsten. **on my behalf** um meinetwillen.

behave (bi'heiv) vi sich verhalten, sich betragen, sich benehmen. **behave oneself** sich gut betragen. **behaviour** n Betragen, Verhalten, Benehmen neu.

behind (bi'haind) adv 1 hinten. 2 zurück prep hinter. n Hinterteil neu. **behindhand** adv verspätet, im Rückstand.

behold* (bi'hould) vt erblicken, sehen.

beige (beiʒ) adj beige. n Beige neu.

being ('bi:iŋ) n 1 (Da)Sein neu. Existenz f. 2 Geschöpf, Wesen neu.

belch (beltʃ) vi rülpsen. n Rülpsen neu.

belfry ('belfri) n Glockenturm m.

Belgium ('beldʒəm) n Belgien neu. **Belgian** adj belgisch. n Belgier m.

believe (bi'liːv) vt glauben. **belief** n 1 Glaube

m. 2 Überzeugung f. **believer** n Gläubige(r)

bell (bel) n 1 Glocke f. 2 Klingel f. **bellringer** n Glöckner m.

belligerent (bə'lidʒərənt) adj kriegführend.

bellow ('belou) vi brüllen, schreien. n Gebrüll, Geschrei neu.

bellows ('belouz) n pl Gebläse neu.

belly ('beli) n Bauch m.

belong (bi'lɔŋ) vi 1 gehören. 2 (to a club, etc.) angehören. **belongings** n pl Eigentum neu.

below (bi'lou) adv unter. prep unter(halb).

belt (belt) n 1 Gürtel, Riemen m. Binde f. 2 Bereich m. Gebiet neu.

bench (bentʃ) n 1 Bank f. 2 Arbeitstisch m.

bend* (bend) n Kurve, Krümmung f. vt biegen, krümmen. vi (sich) beugen.

beneath (bi'niːθ) prep unter(halb).

benefactor ('benifæktə) n Wohltäter, Gönner m.

benefit ('benifit) n 1 Nutzen, Vorteil m. 2 Wohltat f. vi nützen, Nutzen ziehen (aus). **beneficial** adj 1 wohltuend. 2 vorteilhaft, nützlich.

benevolent (bi'nevələnt) adj wohlwollend, gütig. **benevolence** n Wohlwollen neu. Güte f.

bent (bent) v see **bend**.

bereave* (bi'riːv) vt berauben. **bereavement** n Beraubung f. Verlust m.

berry ('beri) n Beere f.

berth (bəːθ) n 1 Ankerplatz m. 2 Liegeplatz m. Koje f.

beside (bi'said) prep neben, dicht bei. **besides** adv außerdem, ferner. prep außer.

besiege (bi'siːdʒ) vt belagern.

best (best) adj best. adv am besten. **at best** im besten Fall(e). n Beste(r) m. **best man** n die rechte Hand des Bräutigams bei der Hochzeit. **best-seller** n Verkaufsschlager, Bestseller m.

bestow (bi'stou) vt geben, schenken.

bet* (bet) n Wette f. vt,vi wetten. **betting shop** n Wettbüro neu.

betray (bi'trei) vt verraten. **betrayal** n Verrat m.

better ('betə) adj,adv besser. vt 1 (ver)bessern. 2 übertreffen. **better oneself** sich bessern.

between (bi'twiːn) prep zwischen. adv dazwischen.

beverage ('bevridʒ) n Getränk neu.

beware* (bi'weə) vi sich vorsehen, sich hüten.

bewilder (bi'wildə) vt verwirren, bestürzen.

153

beyond (bi'jɔnd) *prep* jenseits, außer. *adv* darüber hinaus, jenseits.

bias ('baiəs) *n* 1 Neigung f. 2 Vorurteil neu. **biased** *adj* voreingenommen.

bib (bib) *n* Lätzchen neu.

Bible ('baibəl) *n* Bibel f. **biblical** *adj* biblisch.

bibliography (bibli'ɔgrəfi) *n* Bibliographie f.

biceps ('baiseps) *n* Bizeps m.

bicker ('bikə) *vi* zanken, streiten.

bicycle ('baisikəl) *n* Fahrrad neu.

bid* (bid) *n* 2 Angebot neu. 2 Versuch m. *vi* 1 bieten. 2 *game* reizen.

biennial (bai'eniəl) *adj* zweijährig.

big (big) *adj* 1 groß. 2 dick.

bigamy ('bigəmi) *n* Bigamie, Doppelehe f.

bigot ('bigət) *n* Fanatiker, Frömmler m. **bigoted** *adj* bigott, blind ergeben.

bikini (bi'ki:ni) *n* Bikini m.

bilingual (bai'liŋgwəl) *adj* zweisprachig.

bilious ('biliəs) *adj* gallig.

bill[1] (bil) *n* 1 Rechnung f. 2 Gesetzesvorlage f.

bill[2] (bil) *n* (Vogel)Schnabel m.

billiards ('biliədz) *n* Billard(spiel) neu.

billion ('biljən) *n* 1 Billion f. 2 US Milliarde f.

bin (bin) *n* Behälter, Kasten m.

binary ('bainəri) *adj* binär.

bind* (baind) *vt* 1 binden, befestigen, festmachen. 2 verbinden, verpflichten. **binding** *adj* verbindlich. *n* 1 Bindung f. 2 Einband m.

binoculars (bi'nɔkjuləz) *n pl* Feldstecher m.

biography (bai'ɔgrəfi) *n* Biographie f.

biology (bai'ɔlədʒi) *n* Biologie f.

birch (bə:tʃ) *n* Birke f. *vt* züchtigen.

bird (bə:d) *n* Vogel m.

birth (bə:θ) *n* 1 Geburt f. 2 Entstehung f. **birth certificate** *n* Geburtsschein m. Geburtsurkunde f. **birth control** *n* Geburtenkontrolle, Geburtenbeschränkung f. **birthday** *n* Geburtstag m. **birthmark** *n* Muttermal neu. **birth rate** *n* Geburtenziffer f.

biscuit ('biskit) *n* Keks, Zwieback m.

bishop ('biʃəp) *n* Bischof m.

bit[1] (bit) *n* 1 Stück, Stückchen, Bißchen neu. 2 Gebiß neu.

bit[2] (bit) *v see* **bite**.

bitch (bitʃ) *n* 1 Hündin f. 2 *sl* gemeine Frau, Dirne f.

bite* (bait) *vt* beißen. *n* Biß, Bissen m.

bitter ('bitə) *adj* 1 bitter. 2 verbittert.

bizarre (bi'za:) *adj* bizarr, grotesk.

black (blæk) *adj* schwarz. *n* 1 Schwarz neu. 2 Schwarze(r), Farbige(r) m. **blacken** *vt* 1 schwärzen. 2 anschwärzen, verleumden. *vi*

schwarz *or* dunkel werden. **blackness** *n* Schwärze f.

blackberry ('blækbəri) *n* Brombeere f.

blackbird ('blækbə:d) *n* Amsel f.

blackboard ('blækbɔ:d) *n* (Wand)Tafel f.

blackcurrant (blæk'kʌrənt) *n* schwarze Johannisbeere f.

blackleg ('blækleg) *n* Streikbrecher m.

blackmail ('blækmeil) *n* Erpressung f. *vt* erpressen.

black market *n* Schwarzmarkt m.

blackout ('blækaut) *n* 1 Verdunkelung f. 2 Gedächtnisstörung f.

black pudding *n* Blutwurst f.

blacksmith ('blæksmiθ) *n* Schmied m.

bladder ('blædə) *n* Blase f.

blade (bleid) *n* 1 Klinge, Schneide f. 2 (of grass, etc.) Halm m.

blame (bleim) *n* Schuld, Verantwortung f. *vt* 1 tadeln. 2 beschuldigen.

blank (blæŋk) *adj* weiß, blank(o), leer, unausgefüllt.

blanket ('blæŋkit) *n* Wolldecke f. *vt* zudecken.

blare (blɛə) *vi* schmettern. *n* Geschmetter neu.

blaspheme (blæs'fi:m) *vi* lästern, fluchen. **blasphemy** *n* Gotteslästerung f.

blast (bla:st) *n* 1 Windstoß, Sturm m. 2 (of trumpets) Schall. m. 1 Sprengschuß m. Explosion f. *vt* sprengen.

blatant ('bleitnt) *adj* 1 lärmend. 2 offenkundig.

blaze (bleiz) *vi* brennen, lodern. *n* Feuer neu. Flammen f. **blazer** *n* Sportjacke f. Blazer m.

bleach (bli:tʃ) *n* Bleichmittel neu. *vt* bleichen.

bleak (bli:k) *adj* 1 kahl, öde. 2 trüb, freudlos.

bleat (bli:t) *vi* blöken, meckern. *n* Blöken neu.

bleed* (bli:d) *vi* bluten. *vt* 1 bluten lassen. 2 *inf* schröpfen. **bleeding** *n* Blutung f.

blemish ('blemiʃ) *n* 1 Flecken m. 2 Fehler m. *vt* verunstalten.

blend (blend) *vt* mischen, vermengen.˙ *vi* sich vermischen. *n* Mischung f. Gemisch neu.

bless (bles) *vt* 1 segnen. 2 preisen, loben. **blessed** *adj* gesegnet. **blessing** *n* Segen m. Segnung f.

blew (blu:) *v see* **blow**[1].

blind (blaind) *adj* blind. *adv* blindlings. *vt* (ver)blenden. *n* (of a window) Vorhang m. Jalousie f. **blind alley** *n* Sackgasse f. **blindfold** *adj* blindlings. *vt* die Augen verbinden.

blink (bliŋk) *vi* blinzeln. *n* Blinzeln neu.

bliss (blis) *n* Wonne, Seligkeit f.

blister ('blistə) *n* (Haut)Blase f. *vt* Blasen ziehen. *vi* Blasen bekommen.

blizzard ('blizəd) n (dichter) Schneesturm m.

blob (blɔb) n Tropfen m.

bloc (blɔk) n pol Block m. **en bloc** adv im ganzen, en bloc.

block (blɔk) n Block, Klotz m. vt blockieren, sperren, aufhalten, verhindern. **blockade** n Blockade, Sperre f. vt blockieren, sperren.

blond (blɔnd) adj blond, hell(farbig). **blonde** n Blondine f.

blood (blʌd) n Blut neu. **bloodcurdling** adj schrecklich, furchtbar, Mark und Bein durchdringend. **blood donor** n Blutspender m. **blood pressure** n Blutdruck m. **bloodstream** n Blutkreislauf m. **bloodthirsty** adj blutdürstig, blutrünstig. **blood transfusion** n Blutübertragung f. **bloody** adj 1 blutig. 2 sl verdammt.

bloom (blu:m) n Blüte, Blume f. vi blühen.

blossom ('blɔsəm) n Blüte f. vi blühen, Blüten treiben.

blot (blɔt) n 1 Fleck, Klecks m. 2 Makel m. vt beflecken, beklecksen. **blotting paper** n Löschpapier neu.

blotch (blɔtʃ) n Klecks m.

blouse (blauz) n Bluse f.

blow[1] (blou) n 1 Schlag, Stoß m. 2 Unglück neu. Nachteil m.

blow[2] (blou) vi 1 blasen. 2 (of wind) wehen. 3 keuchen, schnaufen.

blubber ('blʌbə) n Walfischspeck, Tran m. vi inf heulen, plärren.

blue (blu:) adj 1 blau. 2 inf traurig, deprimiert. n Blau neu. **bluebell** n Glockenblume f. **blueprint** n Blaudruck m. 2 Plan m.

bluff (blʌf) vi bluffen, täuschen. n Bluff m. Irreführung f. adj grob, derb.

blunder ('blʌndə) n Fehler, Schnitzer m. vi 1 stolpern. 2 irren, unbesonnen handeln.

blunt (blʌnt) adj 1 stumpf. 2 grob, offen. vt stumpfmachen.

blur (blə:) vt beflecken, verwischen. n Fleck m. Verschwommenheit f.

blush (blʌʃ) vi erröten. n Erröten neu.

boar (bɔ:) n Eber, Keiler m.

board (bɔ:d) n 1 Brett neu. 2 Tafel f. 3 Vorstand, Aufsichtsrat m. 4 Verpflegung f. **boarding house** n Pension f. **boarding school** n Internat neu.

boast (boust) vi prahlen, angeben. n Prahlerei f. **boaster** n Prahler, Angeber m.

boat (bout) n 1 Boot neu. 2 Dampfer m. Schiff neu.

bob (bɔb) vi sich auf und ab bewegen, baumeln.

bodice ('bɔdis) n Mieder neu.

body ('bɔdi) n 1 Körper m. 2 Leiche f. Leichnam m. 3 Gruppe f. 4 mot Karosserie f. **bodyguard** n Leibwächter m.

bog (bɔg) n Sumpf m. Moor neu.

bohemian (bə'hi:miən) adj leichtlebig, ungebunden, zigeunerhaft.

boil[1] (bɔil) vt kochen, sieden. **boiler** n 1 Kocher, Kessel m. 2 Dampfkessel m. **boiling point** n Siedepunkt m.

boil[2] (bɔil) n Geschwür neu.

boisterous ('bɔistərəs) adj ungestüm, heftig, laut.

bold (bould) adj 1 kühn, mutig. 2 frech, unverschämt. **boldness** n Kühnheit f. Mut m.

Bolivia (bə'liviə) n Bolivien neu. **Bolivian** adj bolivianisch. n Bolivianer m.

bolster ('boulstə) n Kissen, Polster neu. v **bolster up** unterstützen.

bolt (boult) n 1 Bolzen m. 2 Riegel m. 3 Bund m. Rolle f. vt 1 verriegeln. 2 (food) hinunterschlingen. vi hastig fliehen.

bomb (bɔm) n Bombe f. vt bombardieren. **bombard** vt bombardieren, beschießen. **bombardment** n Beschuß m.

bond (bɔnd) n 1 Verbindung f. 2 Fesseln f pl. 3 Bürgschaft f. vt verbinden, aufschichten, verkleben.

bone (boun) n 1 Knochen m. Bein neu. 2 (of fish) Gräte f. **bony** adj 1 knochig. 2 grätig.

bonfire ('bɔnfaiə) n (Garten)Feuer neu.

bonnet ('bɔnit) n 1 Haube, Damenmütze f. 2 Motorhaube f.

bonus ('bounəs) n Zulage, Extrazahlung f.

booby trap ('bu:bi) n (Spreng)Falle f.

book (buk) n 1 Buch neu. 2 Heft neu. vt aufschreiben, eintragen. **bookcase** n Bücherschrank m. Bücherregal neu. **booking office** n Fahrkartenschalter m. **bookkeeper** n Buchhalter m. **bookkeeping** n Buchhaltung, Buchführung f. **booklet** n Büchlein neu. Broschüre f. **bookmaker** n Buchmacher m. **bookshop** n Buchladen m. Buchhandlung f. **bookstall** n Bücherstand m.

boom (bu:m) n 1 comm Hochkonjunktur f. Aufschwung m. 2 naut Baum m. 3 Dröhnen neu. vi dröhnen, brummen.

boost (bu:st) vt 1 heben, unterstützen. 2 verstärken, aufladen. n Aufschwung m.

boot (bu:t) n 1 Stiefel m. 2 mot Kofferraum m. v **boot out** sl hinauswerfen.

booth (bu:θ) n 1 Bude f. 2 Zelle f.

booze (bu:z) n inf alkoholisches Getränk neu. vi inf saufen, trinken.

border ('bɔ:də) n 1 Rand, Saum m. 2 Grenze f. vt grenzen, begrenzen. **borderline** adj unsicher, zweifelhaft. n Grenze f.

bore[1] (bɔ:) vi,vt bohren, durchdringen. n 1 Bohrung, Höhlung f. 2 Kaliber neu.

bore[2] (bɔ:) vt langweilen. n langweiliger or lästiger Mensch m. **boredom** n Langeweile f. **boring** adj langweilig.

bore[3] (bɔ:) v see **bear**[1].

born (bɔ:n) adj geboren.

borne (bɔ:n) v see **bear**[1].

borough ('bʌrə) n Verwaltungsbezirk m.

borrow ('bɔrou) vt borgen, entleihen.

bosom ('buzəm) n Busen m. Brust f.

boss (bɔs) n 1 Chef, Boß m. 2 Arbeitgeber m. **bossy** adj herrisch, rechthaberisch.

botany ('bɔtəni) n Botanik, Pflanzenkunde f. **Botanist** n Botaniker, Pflanzenkenner m.

both (bouθ) pron,adj beide(s). **both...and** sowohl...als(auch).

bother ('bɔðə) n Belästigung, Störung f. vt belästigen, stören.

bottle ('bɔtl) n Flasche f. vt in Flaschen füllen. **bottleneck** Engpaß m.

bottom ('bɔtəm) n 1 Boden, Unterteil m. 2 Grund m. 3 inf Hintern m. adj 1 Grund—. 2 letzt.

bough (bau) n Ast, Hauptzweig m.

bought (bɔ:t) v see **buy.**

boulder ('bouldə) n Felsbrocken m.

bounce (bauns) vi springen, aufprallen. n Sprung, Aufprall m.

bound[1] (baund) v see **bind.** adj 1 verpflichtet. 2 bestimmt.

bound[2] (baund) n Sprung, Satz m. vi springen, hüpfen.

bound[3] (baund) n Grenze, Schranke f. **boundary** n Grenze f. **boundless** grenzenlos.

bound[4] (baund) adv bestimmt, unterwegs nach.

bouquet (bu'kei) n 1 Bukett neu. Blumenstrauß m. 2 (of wine) Blume f.

bourgeois ('buəʒwa:) n Bürger, Bourgeois m. ~ adj bürgerlich, bourgeois. **bourgeoisie** n Bürgertum neu. Bourgeoisie f.

bout (baut) n 1 Reihe, Tour f. 2 Kampf m. 3 med Anfall m.

bow[1] (bau) n Verbeugung, Verneigung f. vi sich verbeugen, sich verneigen.

bow[2] (bou) n 1 mil (Schieß)Bogen m. 2 mus Bogen m. 3 Schleife f. 4 Kurve f.

bow[3] (bau) n naut Bug m.

bowels ('bauəlz) n pl 1 Darm m. Eingeweide neu pl. 2 Innere neu.

bowl[1] (boul) n 1 Schüssel, Schale f. 2 Becken neu. 3 Pfeifenkopf m.

bowl[2] (boul) n Kugel f. vt werfen, kugeln, schieben, rollen.

box[1] (bɔks) n 1 Kasten m. Büchse, Schachtel f. 2 Th Loge f. vt einpacken, in Schachteln packen. **box number** n Postfachnummer f. **box office** n Theaterkasse f.

box[2] (bɔks) vi,vt (sich) boxen. n **box on the ear** Ohrfeige f. **boxer** Boxer m. **boxing match** n Boxkampf m.

Boxing Day n zweite Weihnachtsfeiertag m.

boy (bɔi) n Junge, Knabe, Bube m. **boyfriend** Freund m. **boyhood** n Jugend f. Knabenalter neu.

boycott ('bɔikɔt) vt boykottieren. n Boykott m.

brace (breis) n 1 Stütze f. 2 Bohrwinde f. 3 Paar neu. 4 pl Hosenträger m pl. vt spannen, stützen, festziehen. **brace oneself** sich zusammennehmen.

bracelet ('breislət) n Armband neu.

bracket ('brækit) n 1 Träger m. 2 Klammer f. 3 Klasse, Kategorie f.

brag (bræg) vi angeben, prahlen.

braille (breil) n Blindenschrift f.

brain (brein) n 1 (Ge)Hirn neu. 2 pl Verstand m. Intelligenz f. **brainwash** vt gehirnwaschen. **brainwashing** n Gehirnwäsche f. **brainwave** n Idee, Eingebung f. Einfall m.

braise (breiz) vt schmoren.

brake (breik) n Bremse f. vt,vi bremsen. vt aufhalten.

branch (bra:ntʃ) n 1 Ast, Zweig m. 2 comm Zweigstelle, Filiale f. vi (ab)zweigen.

brand (brænd) n 1 comm Marke f. Fabrikat neu. 2 (Feuer)Brand m. vt einbrennen, brandmarken. **brand-new** adj nagelneu.

brandy ('brændi) n Branntwein, Weinbrand m.

brass (bra:s) n 1 Messing neu. 2 Blasinstrumente neu pl. 3 sl Geld neu. **brass band** n Blasorchester neu. Blaskapelle f.

brassiere ('bræsiə) n Büstenhalter m.

brave (breiv) adj mutig, tapfer.

brawl (brɔ:l) n Streit m. Schlägerei f. vi streiten, zanken, raufen.

bray (brei) vi schreien. n Eselsgeschrei neu.

brazen ('breizən) adj 1 ehern. 2 unverschämt.

Brazil (brə'zil) n Brasilien neu. **Brazilian** adj brasilianisch. n Brasilianer m.

breach (bri:tʃ) n 1 Bruch m. Lücke f. 2

Vergehen *neu.* Verstoß *m. vt* **1** durchbrechen. **2** verstoßen gegen.

bread (bred) *n* **1** Brot *neu.* **2** Nahrung *f.* **breadcrumb** *n* Brotkrume *f.* **coated with breadcrumbs** paniert. **breadwinner** *n* Brotverdiener, Ernährer *m.*

breadth (bredθ) *n* Breite *f.*

break* (breik) *vt* brechen, zerbrechen, kaputtmachen. *n* **1** Riß, Bruch *m.* **2** Pause *f.* **breakdown** *n* **1** *med* Zusammenbruch *m.* **2** *mot* (Auto)Panne *f.* **breakthrough** *n* Durchbruch *m.*

breakfast ('brekfəst) *n* Frühstück *neu. vi* frühstücken.

breast (brest) *n* Brust *f.* Busen *m.* **breaststroke** *n* Brustschwimmen *neu.*

breath (breθ) *n* **1** Atem, Hauch *m.* **2** Atemzug *m.* **breathtaking** *adj* atemraubend.

breathe (bri:ð) *vi,vt* atmen.

breed* (bri:d) *vt* **1** erzeugen, hervorbringen. **2** aufziehen, züchten. *vi* sich fortpflanzen. *n* Rasse, Zucht *f.*

breeze (bri:z) *n* Brise *f.* Wind *m.*

brew (bru:) *n* Gebräu, Getränk *neu. vt* brauen. *vi* (of a storm) sich zusammenziehen. **brewery** *n* Brauerei *f.*

bribe (braib) *n* Bestechung *f. vt* bestechen.

brick (brik) *n* Ziegelstein, Mauerstein *m.*

bride (braid) *n* Braut *f.* **bridegroom** *n* Bräutigam *m.* **bridesmaid** *n* Brautjungfer *f.*

bridge¹ (bridʒ) *n* **1** Brücke *f.* **2** *mus* Steg *m. vt* überbrücken.

bridge² (bridʒ) *n* Bridgespiel *neu.*

bridle ('braidl) *n* Zaum, Zügel *m. vt* zügeln, bändigen. **bridlepath** *n* Reitweg *m.*

brief (bri:f) *adj* kurz, flüchtig. **in brief** *adv* kurz gesagt, kurz gefaßt. *~n law* Schriftsatz *m.* **briefcase** *n* Aktentasche, Mappe *f.* **briefing** *n* Anweisung, Instruktion *f.* **briefs** *n pl* (Herren) Unterhose *f.*

brigade (bri'geid) *n* Brigade *f.* **brigadier** *n* Brigadekommandeur *m.*

bright (brait) *adj* **1** hell, glänzend, leuchtend. **2** intelligent, klug. **brighten** *vt,vi* erhellen, aufleuchten, aufheitern.

brilliant ('briljənt) *adj* **1** brillant, strahlend, glänzend. **2** hochbegabt.

brim (brim) *n* **1** Rand *m.* **2** (of a hat) Krempe *f.*

bring* (briŋ) *vt* (her-, mit-)bringen. **bring about** zustande bringen. **bring up 1** (a child) erziehen, aufziehen. **2** (a question, etc.) aufwerfen.

brink (briŋk) *n* **1** Rand *m.* **2** Ufer *neu.*

brisk (brisk) *adj* frisch, lebhaft, munter.

bristle ('brisl) *n* Borste *f.*

Britain ('britn) *n* Großbritannien. **British** *adj* britisch. **Briton** *n* Brite *m.*

brittle ('britl) *adj* brüchig, zerbrechlich.

broad (brɔ:d) *adj* breit, ausgedehnt. **broad bean** *n* Saubohne *f.* **broadcast** *n* Radiosendung *f. vt* **1** senden, funken. **2** verbreiten. *adj* weit verstreut. **broadcasting** *n* Rundfunk *m.* **broaden** *vt* verbreitern, ausdehnen. **broadminded** *adj* tolerant.

broccoli ('brɔkəli) *n* Brokkoli *pl.* Spargelkohl *m.*

brochure ('brouʃə) *n* Broschüre *f.*

broke (brouk) *v see* **break**. *adj inf* pleite.

broken ('broukən) *v see* **break**. *adj* kaputt.

broker ('broukə) *n* Vermittler, Makler *m.*

bronchitis (brɔŋ'kaitis) *n* Bronchitis *f.*

bronze (brɔnz) *n* **1** Bronze *f.* **2** Bronzefigur *f.*

brooch (broutʃ) *n* Spange, Brosche *f.*

brood (bru:d) *vi* brüten. *n* Brut *f.*

brook (bruk) *n* Bach *m.*

broom (bru:m) *n* Besen *m.*

brothel ('brɔθəl) *n* Bordell *neu.*

brother ('brʌðə) *n* Bruder *m.* **brotherhood** *n* Bruderschaft *f.* **brother-in-law** *n* Schwager *m.* **brotherly** *adj* brüderlich.

brought (brɔ:t) *v see* **bring**.

brow (brau) *n* **1** Augenbraue *f.* **2** Stirn *f.* **3** (of a hill) Rand *m.*

brown (braun) *adj* braun. *n* Braun *neu. vt* bräunen.

browse (brauz) *vi* **1** grasen, (ab)weiden. **2** flüchtig lesen, durchblättern, schmökern.

bruise (bru:z) *n* Quetschung *f. vt* quetschen.

brunette (bru:'net) *n* Brünette *f. adj* brünett.

brush (brʌʃ) *n* **1** Bürste *f.* **2** Pinsel *m.* **3** Unterholz *m. vt* **1** bürsten, fegen. **2** berühren, streifen.

brusque (bru:sk) *adj* schroff, angebunden.

Brussels ('brʌsəlz) *n* Brüssel *neu.* **Brussels sprout** *n* Rosenkohl *m.*

brute (bru:t) *n* Unmensch *m. adj* roh. **brutal** *adj* brutal.

bubble ('bʌbəl) *n* Blase *f. vi* brodeln, aufwallen, sprudeln.

buck¹ (bʌk) *n* **1** (Reh)Bock *m.* **2** (of a rabbit) Männchen *neu.*

buck² (bʌk) *vi* bocken. **buck up** sich zusammenreißen, sich beeilen.

bucket ('bʌkit) *n* Eimer *m.*

buckle ('bʌkəl) *n* Schnalle, Spange *f. vt* anschnallen, (zu)schnallen.

bud (bʌd) *n* **1** Knospe *f.* **2** Keim *m.* **nip in the**

bud im Keime ersticken. ~vi knospen, keimen.

Buddhism ('budizəm) n Buddhismus m.

budget ('bʌdʒit) n Budget neu. Staatshaushalt, Etat m. vi sparen, Geld einteilen.

buffalo ('bʌfəlou) n Büffel m.

buffer ('bʌfə) n Puffer, Prellbock m.

buffet[1] ('bʌfit) n Stoß, Schlag m. vt schlagen, stoßen.

buffet[2] ('bufei) n Büfett neu.

bug (bʌg) n 1 Wanze f. 2 inf Bazillus m. 3 inf (microphone) Wanze f. vt sl stören.

bugger ('bʌgə) n 1 Sodomit m. 2 sl Kerl, Schuft m.

bugle ('bjuːgəl) n (Jagd)Horn neu.

build* (bild) vt 1 bauen, errichten. 2 zusammenstellen. **building** n Gebäude neu. **building society** n Bausparkasse f.

bulb (bʌlb) n 1 Glühbirne f. 2 bot Knolle, Zwiebel f.

Bulgaria (bʌl'gɛəriə) n Bulgarien neu. **Bulgarian** adj bulgarisch. n Bulgare m.

bulge (bʌldʒ) n (Aus)Bauchung, Ausbuchtung f. vi sich (aus)bauchen, vorstehen.

bulk (bʌlk) n 1 Maße, Größe f. 2 Großteil m.

bull (bul) n Bulle, Stier m. **bulldog** n Bulldogge f. **bulldozer** n Bulldozer m. **bullfight** n Stierkampf m.

bullet ('bulit) n Kugel f. Geschoß neu. **bulletproof** adj kugelsicher, gepanzert.

bulletin ('bulətin) n Bulletin neu.

bully ('buli) n Raufbold, Tyrann m. vt einschüchtern, tyrannisieren.

bum (bʌm) n inf Hintern m. Hinterteil neu.

bump (bʌmp) n 1 Stoß, Schlag m. 2 Beule f. vt stoßen, schlagen. **bumper** n mot Stoßstange f. adj ungewöhnlich gut or groß.

bun (bʌn) n 1 Semmel f. Brötchen neu. 2 (of hair) Kauz m.

bunch (bʌntʃ) n 1 Bund neu. 2 Strauß m. 3 Traube f. 4 Büschel m. 5 Gruppe f. vt,vi zusammenfügen, bündeln.

bundle ('bʌndj) n Bündel neu. vt einbündeln, (schnell) zusammenpacken.

bungalow ('bʌŋgəlou) n Bungalow, Landhaus neu.

bungle ('bʌŋgəl) vt pfuschen. vi verpfuschen.

bunk (bʌŋk) n Schlafkoje f.

bunker ('bʌŋkə) n 1 Bunker m. 2 Sandloch neu.

buoy (bɔi) n Boje f. **buoyant** adj 1 schwimmfähig. 2 tragfähig.

burden ('bəːdn) n Last, Bürde f. vt beladen, belasten.

bureau ('bjuərou) n 1 Schreibtisch m. 2 Büro neu.

bureaucracy (bju'rɔkrəsi) n Bürokratie f. **bureaucrat** n Bürokrat, Beamte(r) m.

burgle ('bəːgəl) vt einbrechen. **burglar** n Einbrecher m. **burglary** n Einbruch m.

burn* (bəːn) vt (ver)brennen, in Brand stecken. vi brennen. n Brandwunde f.

burrow ('barou) n Höhle f. Bau m. vi sich eingraben, wühlen. vt aufwühlen, graben.

burst* (bəːst) vi platzen, zerspringen. vt sprengen. **burst into tears/out laughing** in Tränen/Lachen ausbrechen. ~n Bruch m.

bury* ('beri) vt begraben. **burial** n Beerdigung f. Begräbnis neu. **burial ground** n Begräbnisplatz m.

bus (bʌs) n (Auto)Bus m. **bus-stop** n Bushaltestelle f.

bush (buʃ) n Busch, Strauch m. Gebüsch neu.

bushy ('buʃi:) adj buschig, dicht.

business ('biznis) n 1 Geschäft neu. 2 Gewerbe neu. 3 Angelegenheit f. 4 Beruf m. **businessman** n Geschäftsmann m.

bust[1] (bʌst) n 1 Büste f. 2 (Frauen)Brust f. Busen m.

bust[2] (bʌst) vt brechen, zerbrechen. adj sl 1 kaputt. 2 bankrott, pleite.

bustle ('bʌsəl) n Gewühl, Gedränge neu. vi herumrennen.

busy ('bizi) adj (viel)beschäftigt, fleißig.

but (bət; stressed bʌt) conj 1 aber, jedoch, sondern. 2 außer, als. adv nur, bloß. **all but** fast, beinahe. **not only...but also** nicht nur...sondern auch.

butcher ('butʃə) n Fleischer m. vt schlachten. **butcher's shop** n Fleischerei f.

butler ('bʌtlə) n Butler, Diener m.

butt[1] (bʌt) n 1 dickes Ende neu. 2 Stummel m. 3 Gegenstand m.

butt[2] (bʌt) vt stoßen, schlagen. **butt in** sich einmischen. ~n Stoß m.

butt[3] (bʌt) n Faß neu. Tonne f.

butter ('bʌtə) n Butter f. **buttercup** n Butterblume f. **butterfly** n Schmetterling m.

buttocks ('bʌtəks) n pl Gesäß neu.

button ('bʌtn) n Knopf m. **buttonhole** n Knopfloch neu. vt anhalten.

buttress ('bʌtrəs) n Strebepfeiler m. Stütze f.

buy* (bai) vt kaufen, erwerben, einkaufen. n Kauf m.

buzz (bʌz) n Summen neu. vi summen.

by (bai) prep bei, neben, an, nahe bei, von, durch. adv vorbei, dabei. **by (the time that)**

bis. **by the way** übrigens. **by and by** bald. **by bus** per Bus, mit dem Bus. **by-election** n Nachwahl f. **bylaw** n Ortsstatut neu. **bypass** n Umgehungsstraße f. vt umgehen, meiden.

C

cab (kæb) n 1 Droschke f. Taxi neu. 2 Fahrerhaus neu.

cabaret ('kæbərei) n Kabarett neu.

cabbage ('kæbidʒ) n 1 Kohl m. 2 Kohlkopf m.

cabin ('kæbin) n 1 Hütte f. Häuschen neu. 2 Kabine f. **cabin cruiser** n Kabinenboot neu.

cabinet ('kæbinət) n 1 Schrank m. 2 pol Kabinett neu. **cabinet maker** n Tischler m.

cable ('keibl) n Kabel neu. Draht m. vt,vi telegraphieren, kabeln.

cackle ('kækl) vi gackern, schnattern. n Geschnatter neu.

cactus ('kæktəs) n Kaktus m.

cadence ('keidns) n mus Tonfall m.

cadet (kə'det) n Kadett m.

cafe ('kæfei) n Café, Kaffeehaus neu.

cafeteria (kæfi'tiəriə) n Selbstbedienungsrestaurant neu.

caffeine ('kæfi:n) n Koffein neu.

cage (keidʒ) n 1 Käfig m. 2 Fahrkorb m. vt einsperren.

cake (keik) n 1 Kuchen m. 2 (of soap, etc.) Stück neu. vt überziehen, bedecken.

calamity (kə'læməti) n 1 Unheil neu. 2 Katastrophe f.

calcium ('kælsiəm) n Kalzium neu.

calculate ('kælkjuleit) vt kalkulieren, ausrechnen, berechnen. **calculator** n Rechenmaschine f.

calendar ('kælində) n Kalender m.

calf[1] (ka:f) n, pl **calves** Kalb neu.

calf[2] (ka:f) n, pl **calves** anat Wade f.

calibre ('kælibə) n 1 Kaliber neu. 2 Wert m.

call (kɔ:l) n 1 Ruf m. 2 Anruf m. 3 Besuch m. 4 comm Einforderung, Nachfrage f. vt 1 rufen. 2 anrufen. 3 benennen. vi 1 rufen. 2 besuchen. **be called** heißen. **call for** fordern. **callbox** n Telefonzelle f.

callous ('kæləs) adj gefühllos, hart.

calm (ka:m) adj ruhig, gelassen. n Ruhe, Stille f.

calorie ('kæləri) n Kalorie f.

Cambodia (kæm'boudiə) n Kambodscha neu. **Cambodian** n Kambodschaner m. adj kambodschanisch.

came (keim) v see **come**.

camel ('kæməl) n Kamel neu. **camelhair** n Kamelhaar neu.

camera ('kæmrə) n Kamera f. Photoapparat m. **cameraman** n Kameramann m.

camouflage ('kæməfla:ʒ) n Tarnung f. vt tarnen.

camp[1] (kæmp) n Lager neu. Lagerplatz m. vi lagern, zelten. **camp bed** n Feldbett neu. **camp fire** n Lagerfeuer neu. **camping** n Zelten, Camping neu. **camping site** n Zeltlager neu. Campingplatz m.

camp[2] (kæmp) adj 1 weiblich. 2 homosexuell.

campaign (kæm'pein) n 1 Feldzug m. 2 Kampagne f. vi kämpfen, Wahlpropaganda machen.

campus ('kæmpəs) n Universitätsgelände neu.

can[1] (kæn) v mod aux 1 können. 2 dürfen. 3 fähig sein.

can[2] (kæn) n Dose, Kanne, Büchse f.

Canada ('kænədə) n Kanada neu. **Canadian** adj kanadisch n Kanadier m.

canal (kə'næl) n Kanal m.

canary (kə'nɛəri) n Kanarienvogel m.

cancel ('kænsəl) vt 1 stornieren, abbestellen. 2 streichen, entwerten. 3 absagen.

cancer ('kænsə) n 1 med Krebs m. 2 cap Krebs m.

candid ('kændid) adj offen, ehrlich.

candidate ('kændidət) n Kandidat, Bewerber m.

candle ('kændl) n Kerze f. **candlelight** n Kerzenlicht neu. **candlestick** n Kerzenhalter m.

candour ('kændə) n Offenheit f.

cane ('kein) n 1 Zuckerrohr neu. 2 Spazierstock m. Rute f. vt mit der Rute schlagen.

canine ('keinain) adj Hunds—. **canine teeth** n Reißzähne m pl.

cannabis ('kænəbis) n Kannabis neu.

cannibal ('kænibəl) n Kannibale m.

cannon ('kænən) n Kanone f. Geschütz neu. vi stoßen gegen. **cannonball** n Kanonenkugel f.

cannot ('kænɔt) contraction of **can not**.

canoe (kə'nu:) n Kanu neu. vi paddeln.

canon[1] ('kænən) n Kanon m. **canonize** vt kanonisieren, heiligsprechen.

canon[2] ('kænən) n Domherr m.

canopy ('kænəpi) n Dach neu. Traghimmel m.

cant (kænt) n 1 Jargon m. 2 Heuchelei f.

canteen (kæn'ti:n) n Kantine f.

canter ('kæntə) n leichter Galopp m.

canton ('kæntɔn) n 1 Kanton m. 2 Bezirk m.

canvas ('kænvəs) n 1 Segeltuch neu. 2 Zeltleinwand f.

canvass

canvass ('kænvəs) *vi* 1 untersuchen, prüfen. 2 um Stimmen werben.

canyon ('kænjən) *n* Schlucht *f.*

cap (kæp) *n* 1 Mütze *f.* 2 Kappe *f. vt* 1 bedecken. 2 übertreffen.

capable ('keipəbəl) *adj* fähig. **capability** *n* Fähigkeit *f.*

capacity (kə'pæsiti) *n* 1 Fassungsvermögen *neu.* 2 Leistungsfähigkeit *f.*

cape¹ (keip) *n* Cape *neu.* Umhang *m.*

cape² (keip) *n* Kap, Vorgebirge *neu.*

caper ('keipə) *n* Kapriole *f. vi* hüpfen.

capital ('kæpitl) *n* 1 Hauptstadt *f.* 2 Kapital *neu. adj* 1 hauptsächlich. 2 todeswürdig, Todes—. 3 großartig. **capitalism** *n* Kapitalismus *m.* **capitalist** *n* Kapitalist *m.* **capitalize** *vt* kapitalisieren.

capricious (kə'priʃəs) *adj* launisch.

Capricorn ('kæprikɔ:n) *n* Steinbock *m.*

capsicum ('kæpsikəm) *n* spanischer Pfeffer *m.*

capsize ('kæpsaiz) *vi* kentern, umschlagen.

capsule ('kæpsju:l) *n* Kapsel, Hülle *f.*

captain ('kæptin) *n* 1 Kapitän *m.* 2 Hauptmann *m.* 3 Führer *m. vt* anführen, leiten.

caption ('kæpʃən) *n* Überschrift *f.* Titel *m.*

captive ('kæptiv) *n* Gefangene(r) *m. adj* gefangen, eingesperrt. **captivate** *vt* fesseln, bezaubern. **captivity** *n* Gefangenschaft *f.*

capture ('kæptʃə) *n* 1 Gefangennahme *f.* 2 Fang *m.* 3 Eroberung *f. vt* 1 fangen, gefangennehmen. 2 erobern. 3 gewinnen.

car (kɑ:) *n* 1 Wagen *m.* Auto(mobil) *neu.* **car park** *n* Parkplatz *m.*

caramel ('kærəməl) *n* Karamel *m.*

carat ('kærət) *n* Karat *neu.*

caravan ('kærəvæn) *n* 1 Karawane *f.* 2 Wohnwagen *m.*

caraway ('kærəwei) *n* Kümmel *m.*

carbohydrate (kɑ:bou'haidreit) *n* Kohlenhydrat *neu.*

carbon ('kɑ:bən) *n* Kohlenstoff *m.* **carbon dioxide** *n* Kohlensäure *f.* **carbon paper** *n* Kohlepapier *neu.*

carburettor (kɑ:bju'retə) *n* Vergaser *m.*

carcass ('kɑ:kəs) *n* Kadaver *m.*

card (kɑ:d) *n* 1 Karte *f.* 2 Spielkarte *f.* 3 Postkarte *f.* **cardboard** *n* Pappe *f.* **cardboard box** *n* Pappschachtel *f.*

cardigan ('kɑ:digən) *n* Wolljacke *f.*

cardinal ('kɑ:dinl) *n* Kardinal *m. adj* hauptsächlich.

care (kɛə) *n* 1 Sorge *f.* 2 Pflege *f.* 3 Sorgfalt, Vorsicht *f.* 4 Kummer *m.* **take care of 1**

aufpassen auf. 2 erledigen. ~*vi* sich sorgen. **care for 1** sorgen für. 2 sich kummern um. 3 gern haben. **carefree** *adj* sorgenlos. **careful** *adj* 1 sorgfältig. 2 vorsichtig. **careless** *adj* 1 sorglos. 2 unordentlich, nachlässig. 3 unüberlegt. **caretaker** *n* Hausmeister, Hauswart *m.*

career (kə'riə) *n* Karriere, Laufbahn *f. vi* rasen, jagen.

caress (kə'res) *n* Liebkosung *f. vt* liebkosen, streicheln.

cargo ('kɑ:gou) *n* Fracht *f.* Frachtgut *neu.*

Caribbean (kæri'bi:ən) *adj* karibisch. **Caribbean (Sea)** *n* Karibisches Meer *neu.*

caricature ('kærikətjuə) *n* Karikatur *f.*

carnal ('kɑ:nl) *adj* fleischlich, geschlechtlich.

carnation (kɑ:'neiʃən) *n* Nelke *f.*

carnival ('kɑ:nivəl) *n* Karneval, Fasching *m.*

carnivorous (kɑ:'nivərəs) *adj* fleischfressend.

carol ('kærəl) *n* Weihnachtslied *neu.*

carpenter ('kɑ:pintə) *n* Zimmermann, Tischler *m.*

carpet ('kɑ:pit) *n* Teppich *m.* **carpet-sweeper** *n* Teppichkehrmaschine *f.*

carriage ('kæridʒ) *n* 1 Wagen *m.* Kutsche *f.* 2 (Körper)Haltung *f.* **carriageway** *n* Fahrbahn *f.*

carrier ('kæriə) *n* 1 Träger *m.* 2 Spediteur *m.* **carrier bag** *n* Tragtasche *f.*

carrot ('kærət) *n* Karotte, Mohrrübe *f.*

carry ('kæri) *vt* 1 tragen. 2 befördern. **carrycot** *n* tragbares Babybett *neu.*

cart (kɑ:t) *n* Wagen, Karren *m.* Fuhrwerk *neu. vt* tragen, schleppen. **carthorse** *n* Zugpferd *neu.*

cartilage ('kɑ:tilidʒ) *n* Knorpel *m.*

carton ('kɑ:tn) *n* Pappschachtel *f.* Karton *m.*

cartoon (kɑ:'tu:n) *n* 1 Karikatur *f.* 2 Zeichentrickfilm *m.* 3 Musterzeichnung *f.*

cartridge ('kɑ:tridʒ) *n* Patrone *f.*

carve (kɑ:v) *vt* 1 schnitzen. 2 zerlegen, tranchieren. **carving-knife** *n* Vorlegemesser *neu.*

cascade (kæ'skeid) *n* Kaskade *f.* Wasserfall *m. vi* herabregnen.

case¹ (keis) *n* 1 Fall *m.* 2 *law* (Rechts)Fall *m.* 3 Sache *f.* **in case** falls. **in case of** im Falle von.

case² (keis) *n* 1 Gehäuse *neu.* 2 Tasche, Mappe *f.* 3 Etui *neu.*

cash (kæʃ) *n* Bargeld *neu.* **cash desk** *n* Kasse *f.* **cash register** *n* Registrierkasse *f.* ~*vt* einlösen.

cashier¹ (kæ'ʃiə) *n* Kassierer *m.*

cashier² (kæ'ʃiə) *vt* kassieren, entlassen.

160

cashmere (ˈkæʃˈmiə) n Kaschmir m.

casino (kəˈsiːnou) n Spiellokal, Kasino neu.

casket (ˈkɑːskit) n Kästchen neu.

casserole (ˈkæsəroul) n Schmorpfanne f.

cassette (kəˈset) n Kassette f.

cassock (ˈkæsək) n Soutane f.

cast* (kɑːst) n 1 Wurf m. 2 tech Guß m. Gußform f. 3 Th Besetzung f. 4 Typ m. Art f. vt 1 werfen. 2 tech gießen. 3 Th Rollen verteilen.

castanets (kæstəˈnets) n Kastagnetten f pl.

caste (kɑːst) n Kaste, Gesellschaftsklasse f.

castle (ˈkɑːsəl) n 1 Schloß neu. Burg, Festung f. 2 game Turm m.

castrate (kæˈstreit) vt kastrieren.

casual (ˈkæʒuəl) adj 1 zufällig, beiläufig. 2 gleichgültig, nachlässig. 3 salopp. 4 lässig.

casualty n 1 Verunglückte(r) m. 2 pl Verluste m pl.

cat (kæt) n Katze f. **cat's eye** n mot Katzenauge neu. **tom cat** n Kater m.

catalogue (ˈkætələg) n Katalog m.

catamaran (kætəməˈræn) n Katamaran, Auslegerboot neu.

catapult (ˈkætəpʌlt) n Katapult m. Wurfmaschine f. vt katapultieren, schleudern.

cataract (ˈkætərækt) n 1 Katarakt, Wasserfall m. 2 med Star m.

catarrh (kəˈtɑː) n Katarrh, Schnupfen m.

catastrophe (kəˈtæstrəfi) n Katastrophe f.

catch* (kætʃ) n Fang m. vt 1 fangen. 2 fassen. 3 (rechtzeitig) erreichen.

category (ˈkætigəri) n Kategorie, Klasse, Ordnung f. **categorical** adj kategorisch, unbedingt. **categorize** vt kategorisieren.

cater (ˈkeitə) vi Lebensmittel anschaffen or liefern. **cater for** sorgen für. **catering** (Lebensmittel)Versorgung f. Verpflegungswesen neu.

caterpillar (ˈkætəpilə) n Raupe f. **caterpillar track** n Raupe, Gleiskette f.

cathedral (kəˈθiːdrəl) n Dom m. Kathedrale f.

cathode (ˈkæθoud) n Kathode f.

catholic (ˈkæθlik) adj 1 allgemein, allumfassend. 2 katholisch.

catkin (ˈkætkin) n Kätzchen neu.

cattle (ˈkætl) n Vieh, Rindvieh neu.

caught (kɔːt) v see **catch**.

cauliflower (ˈkɔliflauə) n Blumenkohl m.

cause (kɔːz) n 1 Ursache f. Anlaß, Grund m. 2 Sache f. vt verursachen, bewirken, veranlassen.

causeway (ˈkɔːzwei) n Damm, Fußweg m.

caustic (ˈkɔːstik) adj 1 ätzend, brennend. 2 scharf, beißend, sarkastisch.

caution (ˈkɔːʃən) n 1 Vorsicht f. 2 (Ver)-Warnung f. vt verwarnen.

cavalry (ˈkævəlri) n Kavallerie, Reiterei f.

cave (keiv) n Höhle f.

caviar (ˈkæviɑː) n Kaviar m.

cavity (ˈkæviti) n Höhle m. Höhlung f.

cayenne (keiˈen) n Cayennepfeffer m.

cease (siːs) vi aufhören, unterlassen, einstellen. **cease-fire** n Waffenstillstand m. Feuereinstellung f.

cedar (ˈsiːdə) n Zeder f.

ceiling (ˈsiːliŋ) n Decke f.

celebrate (ˈseləbreit) vt feiern. **celebration** n Feier f. Fest neu. **celebrity** n Berühmtheit, prominente Person f.

celery (ˈseləri) n Sellerie m.

celestial (siˈlestiəl) adj himmlisch.

celibate (ˈselibət) adj unverheiratet.

cell (sel) n Zelle f.

cellar (ˈselə) n Keller(raum) m.

cello (ˈtʃelou) n Cello neu.

Cellophane (ˈseləfein) n Tdmk Cellophan neu.

cement (siˈment) n Zement m. vt zementieren.

cemetery (ˈsemətri) n Friedhof m.

censor (ˈsensə) n Zensor m. vt zensieren. **censorship** n Zensur f.

censure (ˈsenʃə) vt tadeln, verurteilen. n Tadel m. Rüge f. **vote of censure** Mißtrauensvotum neu.

census (ˈsensəs) n Zensus m. Volkszählung f.

cent (sent) n Cent m.

centenary (senˈtiːnəri) adj hundertjährig. n Hundertjahrfeier f.

centigrade (ˈsentigreid) adj Celsius.

centimetre (ˈsentimiːtə) n Zentimeter m.

centre (ˈsentə) n 1 Mittelpunkt m. Zentrum neu. Mitte f. 2 Zentrale, Zentralstelle f. vi sich konzentrieren auf. **central** adj zentral. **central heating** n Zentralheizung f. **centralize** vt zentralisieren. **centre-forward** n Mittelstürmer m. **centre-half** n Mittelläufer m.

centrifugal (senˈtrifjugəl) adj zentrifugal.

century (ˈsentʃəri) n Jahrhundert neu.

ceramic (siˈræmik) adj keramisch. **ceramics** n pl Keramik f.

cereal (ˈsiəriəl) n Getreidepflanze f. adj Getreide—.

ceremony (ˈserəməni) n 1 Zeremonie, Feier f. 2 Feierlichkeit f. **ceremonial** adj zeremoniell, feierlich. **ceremonious** adj steif, förmlich.

certain ('sɔ:tn) *adj* 1 sicher, überzeugt. 2 gewiß, bestimmt, sicher. 3 gewiß.

certificate (sə'tifikət) *n* Schein *m.* Urkunde, Bescheinigung *f.* **certify** *vi,vt* bescheinigen, bestätigen.

chaffinch ('tʃæfintʃ) *n* Buchfink *m.*

chain (tʃein) *n* 1 Kette *f.* 2 Reihe *f.* *vt* (an)ketten. **chain-smoke** *vi* kettenrauchen. **chain-store** *n* Filialgeschäft *neu.*

chair (tʃɛə) *n* 1 Stuhl *m.* 2 Lehrstuhl *m.* Professur *f.* *vt* den Vorsitz führen. **chair-lift** *n* Sessellift *m.* **chairman** *n* Vorsitzende(r) *m.*

chalet ('ʃælei) *n* Chalet, Landhaus *neu.*

chalk (tʃɔ:k) *n* 1 Kreide *f.* 2 Kreidestift *m.* *vt* ankreiden.

challenge ('tʃæləndʒ) *n* 1 Herausforderung *f.* 2 Aufforderung *f.* 3 Anfechtung *f.* *vt* 1 herausfordern. 2 auffordern. 3 anzweifeln.

chamber ('tʃeimbə) *n* 1 Kammer *f.* Zimmer *neu.* **chambermaid** *n* Zimmermädchen *neu.* **chamber music** *n* Kammermusik *f.*

chameleon (kə'mi:liən) *n* Chamäleon *neu.*

chamois *n* 1 ('ʃæmwa:) Gemse *f.* 2 ('ʃæmi) Sämischleder *neu.*

champagne (ʃæm'pein) *n* Champagner, Sekt *m.*

champion ('tʃæmpiən) *n* 1 Sieger, Meister *m.* 2 Verfechter *m.* *vt* unterstützen, verfechten, eintreten für. **championship** *n* Meisterschaft *f.*

chance (tʃa:ns) *n* 1 Zufall *m.* 2 Schicksal, Geschick *neu.* 3 Risiko *neu.* 4 Chance, Aussicht *f.* 5 Gelegenheit, Chance *f.* **by chance** zufällig. **take a chance** sein Glück versuchen. ~*vt* riskieren.

chancellor ('tʃa:nsələ) *n* Kanzler *m.*

chandelier (ʃændə'liə) *n* Kronleuchter *m.*

change (tʃeindʒ) *vi,vt* 1 (ab-, ver-)ändern. 2 (ver)wandeln. 3 (ab)wechseln. *vt* 1 (um-, aus-)tauschen. **change one's clothes** sich umziehen. **change trains** umsteigen. ~*n* 1 (Ab-, Ver-)Änderung *f.* 2 Wechsel *m.* Abwechselung *f.* 3 Wendung *f.* 4 Wandlung *f.* 5 (Aus)Tausch *m.* 6 Kleingeld, Wechselgeld *neu.*

channel ('tʃænl) *n* 1 Kanal *m.* 2 Fahrrinne *f.* 3 (radio, etc.) Station *f.* Sender *m.* *vt* leiten, lenken.

Channel Islands *n pl* Kanalinseln *f pl.*

chant (tʃa:nt) *n* (Kirchen)Gesang *m.* *vt* intonieren, singen.

chaos ('keiɔs) *n* Chaos, Durcheinander *neu.*

chap[1] (tʃæp) *vt* spalten, aufreißen. **chapped skin** aufgesprungene Haut.

chap[2] (tʃæp) *n* Junge, Kerl, Bursche *m.*

chapel ('tʃæpəl) *n* Kapelle *f.*

chaperon ('ʃæpəroun) *n* Anstandsdame *f.* *vt* (als Anstandsdame) begleiten.

chaplain ('tʃæplin) *n* 1 Kaplan, Geistliche(r) *m.* 2 *mil* Feldgeistliche(r) *m.*

chapter ('tʃæptə) *n* Kapitel *neu.*

char[1] (tʃa:) *vt* verkohlen, versengen.

char[2] (tʃa:) *vi* scheuern, putzen. *n* 1 Putzfrau *f.* 2 *inf* Tee *m.* **charwoman** *n* Scheuerfrau, Putzfrau *f.*

character ('kæriktə) *n* 1 Charakter *m.* Persönlichkeit *f.* Natur *f.* 2 (Schrift)Zeichen *neu.* 3 Figur, Gestalt *f.* **characteristic** *adj* 1 charakteristisch, bezeichnend. 2 typisch. **characterization** *n* Charakterisierung, Kennzeichnung *f.* **characterize** *vt* charakterisieren, kennzeichnen.

charcoal ('tʃa:koul) *n* (Holz)Kohle *f.*

charge (tʃa:dʒ) *vt* 1 anstürmen, angreifen. 2 (be)laden, belasten. 3 beauftragen. 4 berechnen. 5 *law* anklagen. 6 befehlen. *n* 1 Ladung *f.* 2 Preis *m.* 3 Sorge, Verantwortung *f.* 4 Anklage *f.* 5 *comm* Belastung *f.* 6 Befehl *m.* **charge hand** *n* Vorarbeiter *m.*

chariot ('tʃæriət) *n* Streitwagen *m.*

charisma (kə'rizmə) *n* Charisma *f.*

charity ('tʃæriti) *n* 1 Wohltätigkeit, Nächstenliebe, Güte *f.* 2 Stiftung *f.* Wohltätigkeitsverein *m.* **charitable** *adj* mild, wohltätig.

charm (tʃa:m) *n* 1 Zauber *m.* 2 Reiz, Charme *m.* 3 Amulett *neu.* *vt* entzücken, bezaubern.

chart (tʃa:t) *n* 1 Seekarte *f.* 2 Übersichtstafel, Tabelle *f.* *vt* entwerfen, verzeichnen.

charter ('tʃa:tə) *n* (Verfassungs)Urkunde *f.* Gnadenbrief *m.* *vt* chartern, mieten. **charter flight** *n* Charterflug *m.*

chase (tʃeis) *vt* jagen, verfolgen. *n* Jagd, Verfolgung *f.*

chasm ('kæzəm) *n* Spalte, Kluft *f.*

chassis ('ʃæsi) *n* Fahrgestell *neu.*

chaste (tʃeist) *adj* rein, anständig, keusch.

chastise (tʃæ'staiz) *vt* strafen, züchtigen.

chastity ('tʃæstiti) *n* Keuschheit, Reinheit *f.*

chat (tʃæt) *vi* schwatzen, plaudern. *n* Plauderei, Unterhaltung *f.*

chatter ('tʃætə) *vi* 1 plaudern, schwatzen, plappern. 2 (of teeth) klappern.

chauffeur ('ʃoufə) *n* Chauffeur, Fahrer *m.*

chauvinism ('ʃouvinizəm) *n* Chauvinismus *m.*

cheap (tʃiːp) adj **1** billig. **2** gemein, minderwertig.

cheat (tʃiːt) n Betrüger, Schwindler m. vi,vt betrügen, schwindeln.

check (tʃek) n **1** Prüfung, Untersuchung, Kontrolle f. **2** game Schach neu. **3** US Scheck m. vt **1** prüfen, untersuchen, kontrollieren. **2** hindern, aufhalten. **checkmate** n Schachmatt neu. vt in Schachmatt stellen neu. **checkpoint** n Grenzübergang m. **checkup** n Untersuchung f.

cheek (tʃiːk) n **1** Wange, Backe f. **2** Frechheit f. vt frech sein gegen. **cheekbone** n Backenknochen m. **cheeky** adj frech, dreist, keck.

cheer (tʃiə) n **1** Laune, Stimmung f. **2** Hoch, Hurra neu. vt aufheitern, erfreuen. vi hurra rufen. **cheer up** vt aufmuntern, aufheitern. **cheerful** adj fröhlich, heiter.

cheese (tʃiːz) n Käse m.

cheetah ('tʃiːtə) n Gepard m.

chef (ʃef) n Küchenchef m.

chemistry ('kemistri) n Chemie f. **chemical** n **1** chemisches Präparat neu. **2** pl Chemikalien f pl. adj chemisch. **chemist** n **1** sci Chemiker m. **2** med Apotheker m. **chemist's shop** n Apotheke f.

cheque (tʃek) n Scheck m. **chequebook** n Scheckbuch neu. **cheque card** n Scheckkarte f.

cherish ('tʃeriʃ) vt **1** (wert)schätzen. **2** (feelings) hegen. **3** (an idea) festhalten an.

cherry ('tʃeri) n Kirsche f.

cherub ('tʃerəb) n Cherub m.

chess (tʃes) n Schachspiel neu. **chessboard** n Schachbrett neu. **chessman** n Schachfigur f. **chess set** n Schachspiel neu.

chest (tʃest) n **1** Brust f. **2** Truhe, Kiste f. **chest of drawers** n Kommode f.

chestnut ('tʃesnʌt) n Kastanie f.

chew (tʃuː) vt kauen. **chewing gum** n Kaugummi m.

chicken ('tʃikən) n Hühnchen, Hähnchen neu. adj sl feig. **chick** n Küchlein, Kuken neu. **chickenpox** n Windpocken f pl.

chicory ('tʃikəri) n Zichorie f.

chief (tʃiːf) n Häuptling, Anführer m. Chef m. adj haupt, Haupt—, hauptsächlich.

chilblain ('tʃilblein) n Frostbeule f.

child (tʃaild) n, pl **children** Kind neu. **childbirth** n Geburt, Entbindung f. **childhood** n Kindheit f. **childish** adj kindisch. **childlike** adj kindlich.

Chile ('tʃili) n Chile neu. **Chilean** adj chilenisch. n Chilene m.

chill (tʃil) n **1** Kälte f. **2** Erkältung f. **3** Schauer m. adj kalt. vt kühlen. **chilly** adj kalt, kühl, frostig.

chilli ('tʃili) n spanischer Pfeffer m.

chime (tʃaim) n **1** Geläut neu. **2** Glockensatz m. vi klingen, tönen. **chime in** einstimmen.

chimney ('tʃimni) n Schornstein, Rauchfang, Schlot m. **chimneypot** n Schornsteinaufsatz m. **chimneysweep** n Schornsteinfeger m.

chimpanzee (tʃimpæn'ziː) n Schimpanse m.

chin (tʃin) n Kinn neu.

china ('tʃainə) n Porzellan neu.

China ('tʃainə) n China neu. **Chinese** adj chinesisch. n Chinese m.

chink[1] (tʃiŋk) n Spalt m. Lücke f.

chink[2] (tʃiŋk) n Geklimper, Klingen neu. vi klingen, klimpern.

chip (tʃip) n **1** Span, Splitter m. Holzstückchen neu. **2** pl cul Pommes frites pl. vt behauen, beschneiden.

chiropody (ki'rɔpədi) n Fußpflege f. **chiropodist** n Fußpfleger m.

chirp (tʃəːp) vi zwitschern, zirpen.

chisel ('tʃizəl) n Meißel m. Stemmeisen neu.

chivalry ('ʃivəlri) n Ritterlichkeit f.

chives (tʃaivz) pl n Schnittlauch m.

chlorine ('klɔːriːn) n Chlor neu.

chlorophyll ('klɔrəfil) n Blattgrün, Chlorophyll neu.

chocolate ('tʃɔklit) n Schokolade f.

choice (tʃɔis) n **1** Wahl f. **2** Auswahl f. adj auserlesen.

choir (kwaiə) n Chor m. **choirboy** n Chorknabe m. **choirmaster** n Chormeister m.

choke (tʃouk) vt würgen. vt,vi ersticken. n mot Starterklappe f.

cholera ('kɔlərə) n Cholera f.

choose[*] (tʃuːz) vt wählen, aussuchen, auslesen.

chop (tʃɔp) vt hacken, zerhacken. n Kotelett neu. **chopper** n Beil neu.

chopstick ('tʃɔpstik) n Eßstäbchen neu.

chord (kɔːd) n Akkord m.

chore (tʃɔː) n Hausarbeit f.

choreography (kɔri'ɔgrəfi) n Choreographie f.

chorus ('kɔːrəs) n **1** (Sänger)Chor m. **2** Refrain m. **choral** n Choral m. adj Chor —.

chose (tʃouz) v see **choose.**

chosen ('tʃouzən) v see **choose.** adj auserwählt.

Christ (kraist) n Christus m.

christen ('krisən) vt taufen. **christening** n Taufe f.

Christian ('kristʃən) n Christ m. **Christian name** n Vorname m. **Christianity** n Christentum neu.

Christmas ('krisməs) n Weihnachten f pl. **Christmas card** n Weihnachtskarte f. **Christmas tree** n Weihnachtsbaum m.

chromatic (krə'mætik) adj chromatisch.

chrome (kroum) adj 1 chromgelb. 2 aus Chrom.

chromium ('kroumiəm) n Chrom neu.

chronic ('krɔnik) adj 1 chronisch, (an)dauernd. 2 inf schlecht.

chronicle ('krɔnikəl) n Chronik, Zeitgeschichte f.

chronological (krɔnə'lɔdʒikəl) adj chronologisch.

chrysalis ('krisəlis) n Puppe f.

chrysanthemum (kri'zænθiməm) n Goldblume, Chrysantheme f.

chubby ('tʃʌbi) adj plump, pausbäckig.

chuck (tʃʌk) vt inf 1 werfen, schleudern. 2 aufgeben.

chuckle ('tʃʌkəl) n Kichern, Gekicher neu. vi kichern, vergnügt lachen.

chunk (tʃʌŋk) n Stück neu. Klotz m.

church (tʃəːtʃ) n Kirche f. **churchgoer** n Kirchengänger m. **churchyard** n Kirchhof m.

churn (tʃəːn) n Butterfaß neu. vt aufwühlen.

chute (ʃuːt) n Gleitbahn, Rinne f.

chutney ('tʃʌtni) n Chutney neu.

cider ('saidə) n Apfelwein m.

cigar (si'gaː) n Zigarre f. **cigarette** n Zigarette f. **cigarette lighter** n Feuerzeug neu.

cinder ('sində) n 1 ausgeglühte Kohle f. 2 pl Asche pl.

cinecamera ('sinikæmrə) n Filmkamera f.

cinema ('sinəmə) n Kino neu.

cinnamon ('sinəmən) n Zimt m.

circle ('səːkəl) n 1 Kreis m. Ring m. 2 Th Rang m. vt umkreisen, umringen. **circular** adj kreisförmig, rund. **circulate** vi kreisen. vt in Umlauf setzen. **circulation** n 1 Kreislauf m. 2 Umlauf m. Verkehr m. 3 Auflage f.

circuit ('səːkit) n 1 Kreisbewegung f. 2 Runde f. 3 Stromkreis m.

circumcise ('səːkəmsaiz) vt beschneiden.

circumference (sə'kʌmfərəns) n Kreisumfang, Umkreis m.

circumscribe ('səːkəmskraib) vt umschreiben.

circumstance ('səːkəmstæns) n 1 Umstand m. 2 Tatsache f. 3 Formalität f. **circumstantial** adj zufällig, indirekt, nebensächlich.

circus ('səːkəs) n Zirkus m.

cistern ('sistən) n Zisterne f.

cite (sait) vt 1 zitieren, anführen. 2 vorladen. **citation** n 1 Zitat neu. 2 Vorladung f.

citizen ('sitizən) n (Staats)Bürger m.

citrus ('sitrəs) n Zitrusfrucht f.

city ('siti) n Stadt, Großstadt f.

civic ('sivik) adj bürgerlich, städtisch.

civil ('sivəl) adj 1 bürgerlich, städtisch. 2 höflich. 3 Staats—. **civil engineering** n Ingenieurbau m. **civil servant** n Staatsbeamte(r) m. **civil service** n Staatsverwaltung f. **civil war** n Bürgerkrieg m.

civilian (si'viliən) n Zivilist m. adj Zivil—.

civilization (sivilai'zeiʃən) n Zivilisation f. **civilize** vt zivilisieren.

clad (klæd) adj bekleidet, bedeckt.

claim (kleim) n 1 Anspruch m. (An)Recht neu. 2 Forderung f. 3 Behauptung f. vt beanspruchen, fordern.

clam (klæm) n Venusmuschel f.

clamber ('klæmbə) vi klettern.

clammy ('klæmi) adj feuchtkalt, klebrig.

clamour ('klæmə) n Lärm m. Geschrei neu. vi schreien, lärmen.

clamp (klæmp) n Klammer, Schelle f. vt festklemmen, befestigen.

clan (klæn) n Stamm m. Sippe f.

clandestine (klæn'destin) adj heimlich.

clang (klæŋ) vi,(vt) klingen or schallen (lassen). n Klang, Schall m.

clank (klæŋk) vi,(vt) rasseln or klirren (mit). n Gerassel neu.

clap (klæp) vi,(vt) klatschen (mit). n 1 Donnerschlag m. 2 Knall m. **clapper** n Klöppel m.

claret ('klærət) n Klarett m.

clarify ('klærifai) vt klarmachen, erläutern, klären. **clarification** n (Er)Klärung f. **clarity** n Klarheit, Reinheit f.

clarinet (klæri'net) n Klarinette f.

clash (klæʃ) n 1 Geklirr neu. 2 Zusammenstoß m. 3 Konflikt m. vi 1 klirren, rasseln. 2 zusammenstoßen.

clasp (klaːsp) n Schnalle, Spange f. vt 1 schnallen. 2 festhalten, umklammern.

class (klaːs) n 1 Klasse, Kategorie f. 2 (Schul-)Klasse f. vt einstufen, einreihen. **classify** vt klassifizieren, einordnen, einteilen. **classification** n Klassifizierung, Einteilung f. **classroom** n Klassenzimmer neu.

classic ('klæsik) adj klassisch. n Klassiker m. **classical** adj klassisch.

clatter ('klætə) vi rasseln, klappern. n Geklapper neu.

clause (klɔːz) n 1 Satz m. 2 Klausel f.

claustrophobia (klɔstrəˈfoubiə) n Klaustrophobie f. **claustrophobic** adj eng, überfüllt.

claw (klɔː) n Klaue f. Kralle f.

clay (klei) n Ton m.

clean (kliːn) adj sauber, rein, gewaschen. vt 1 reinigen, säubern. vi,vt putzen.

cleanse (klenz) vt säubern, heilen.

clear (kliə) adj 1 klar, durchsichtig. 2 verständlich. 3 rein. 4 offen, frei. vi 1 leeren, räumen. 2 freisprechen. 3 (a cheque) einlösen. 4 verzollen. 5 springen über. vi sich (auf)klären. **clear away, out,** or **up** vi,vt ausräumen, aufräumen. **clear off** vi inf abhauen. **clearance** n 1 Aufräumen f. 2 Verzollung f. 3 tech Spielraum m. 4 Räumungsausverkauf m. **clear-headed** adj besonnen, klardenkend. **clearing** n Lichtung f.

clef (klef) n Notenschlüssel m.

clench (klentʃ) vt zusammenpressen, ballen.

clergy (ˈklɜːdʒi) n Klerus m. **clergyman** n Geistliche(r) m.

clerical (ˈklerikəl) adj 1 geistlich. 2 Büro—. **clerical work** n Büroarbeit f.

clerk (klɑːk) n Büroangestellte(r) m.

clever (ˈklevə) adj geschickt, klug, intelligent.

cliché (ˈkliːʃei) n Klischee neu.

click (klik) vi,vt knipsen, knacken, (zu)schnappen. n Schnappen neu. Schlag m.

client (ˈklaiənt) n Kunde m. **clientèle** n Kundschaft f.

cliff (klif) n Klippe f. Felsen m.

climate (ˈklaimit) n Klima neu.

climax (ˈklaimæks) n Höhepunkt m.

climb (klaim) n Aufstieg m. vt,vi klettern, steigen. **climber** n Kletterer, Bergsteiger m.

cling (kliŋ) vi sich klammern, sich halten, haften.

clinic (ˈklinik) n Klinik f.

clip¹ (klip) vt schneiden, stutzen, knipsen. n Schlag m. **clipping** n (Zeitungs)Ausschnitt m.

clip² (klip) n Klammer f. vt befestigen, zusammenheften.

cloak (klouk) n Gewand neu. Mantel m. vt ummanteln, umhüllen. **cloakroom** n Garderobe f.

clock (klɔk) n Uhr f. **three o'clock** drei Uhr. **clocktower** n Uhrturm m. **clockwise** adj,adv im Uhrzeigersinn. **clockwork** n Uhrwerk neu.

clog (klɔg) n Holzschuh m. (vi),vt (sich) verstopfen.

cloister (ˈklɔistə) n Kloster neu.

close vt,vi (klouz) zumachen, schließen. adj

(klous) 1 dicht, nahe. 2 intim, vertraut. 3 knapp. n 1 (klous) Sackgasse f. 2 (klouz) Schluß m.

closet (ˈklɔzit) n Schrank m.

clot (klɔt) n Klumpen m. vi gerinnen.

cloth (klɔθ) n 1 Stoff m. Gewebe, Tuch neu. 2 Lappen m.

clothe (klouð) vt bekleiden. **clothes** n pl Kleider neu pl. Kleidung f. **clothes brush** n Kleiderbürste f. **clothes line** n Wäscheleine f. **clothes peg** n Wäscheklammer f. **clothing** n Kleidung f.

cloud (klaud) n Wolke f. vi,vt bewölken, umnebeln. **cloudburst** n Wolkenbruch m. **cloudy** adj 1 wolkig, bewölkt. 2 trübe.

clove¹ (klouv) n Gewürznelke f.

clove² (klouv) n (Knoblauch)Zehe f.

clover (ˈklouvə) n Klee m.

clown (klaun) n Clown m.

club (klʌb) n 1 Klub m. Verein m. 2 sport Schläger m. 3 Keule f.

clue (kluː) n Hinweis, Anhaltspunkt m.

clump (klʌmp) n 1 Haufen m. 2 Gruppe f.

clumsy (ˈklʌmzi) adj ungeschickt, schwerfällig.

clung (klʌŋ) v see **cling**.

cluster (ˈklʌstə) n 1 Gruppe f. 2 bot Traube f. vi sich (ver)sammeln, sich gruppieren.

clutch (klʌtʃ) n 1 Kupplung f. 2 pl Klauen f pl. vt packen, greifen, fassen.

clutter (ˈklʌtə) n Unordnung f. Durcheinander neu. vt vollstopfen.

coach (koutʃ) n 1 Kutsche f. 2 Bus m. 3 sport Trainer m. vt 1 sport trainieren. 2 educ Nachhilfeunterricht geben.

coal (koul) n (Stein)Kohle f. **coalmine** n Kohlenbergwerk m.

coalition (kouəˈliʃən) n Koalition f.

coarse (kɔːs) adj 1 grob. 2 rauh, unhöflich.

coast (koust) n Küste f. **coastguard** n Küstenwacht f. **coastline** n Küstenlinie f.

coat (kout) n 1 Mantel m. 2 Pelz m. Fell neu. 3 Belag m. 4 (of paint) Anstrich m. vt bedecken, beschichten. **coat-hanger** n Kleiderbügel m. **coating** n Schicht f. Belag m.

coax (kouks) vt (geduldig) überreden.

cobbler (ˈkɔblə) n Schuster m.

cobra (ˈkoubrə) n Kobra f.

cobweb (ˈkɔbweb) n Spinngewebe neu.

cock (kɔk) n 1 Hahn m. 2 (Vogel)Männchen neu. 3 tab Penis m. **cockpit** n Kanzel, Kabine f. **cockroach** n Küchenschabe f. **cocktail** n Cocktail neu. **cocky** adj inf eingebildet, frech.

cock

cock[2] (kɔk) vt **1** (one's ears) spitzen. **2** (a hat, etc.) schiefmachen, schief aufsetzen.

cockle ('kɔkəl) n Herzmuschel f.

cocoa ('koukou) n Kakao m.

coconut ('koukənʌt) n Kokosnuß f.

cocoon (kə'ku:n) n Puppe f.

cod (kɔd) n Dorsch m.

code (koud) n **1** Kodex m. **2** Schlüssel m. Geheimschrift f. vt verschlüsseln.

codeine ('koudi:n) n Kodein neu.

coeducation (kouedju'keiʃən) n Gemeinschaftserziehung f.

coerce (kou'ə:s) vt zwingen.

coexist (kouig'zist) vi koexistieren, zusammenleben. **coexistence** n Koexistenz f.

coffee ('kɔfi) n Kaffee m. **coffee bar** n Kaffeehaus, Café neu. **coffee bean** n Kaffeebohne f.

coffin ('kɔfin) n Sarg m.

cog (kɔg) n Radzahn m.

cognac ('kɔnjæk) n Kognak m.

cohabit (kou'hæbit) vi zusammenleben.

cohere (kou'hiə) vi zusammenhängen, zusammenkleben. **coherence** n Zusammenhang m. **coherent** adj zusammenhängend, verständlich.

coil (kɔil) n Windung, Spule f. vt aufrollen, aufwinden, vi sich zusammenrollen.

coin (kɔin) n Münze f. vt prägen.

coincide (kouin'said) vi **1** zusammentreffen. **2** übereinstimmen. **coincidence** n Zufall m. Zusammentreffen neu.

colander ('kʌləndə) n Sieb neu.

cold (kould) adj kalt. n **1** Kälte f. **2** Erkältung f. Schnupfen m. **catch a cold** sich erkälten. **cold-blooded** adj kaltblütig.

collaborate (kə'læbəreit) vi **1** zusammenarbeiten, mitarbeiten. **2** mit dem Feind arbeiten, kollaborieren. **collaboration** n **1** Zusammenarbeit f. **2** Kollaboration f.

collapse (kə'læps) n Zusammenbruch, Einsturz m. vi zusammenbrechen, einstürzen.

collar ('kɔlə) n Kragen m. **collarbone** n Schlüsselbein neu.

colleague ('kɔli:g) n Kollege, Mitarbeiter m.

collect (kə'lekt) vt sammeln, auflesen. **collection** n **1** Sammlung f. **2** Ansammlung f. Anhäufung f. **3** (of mail) Abholung f. **collective** adj vereint, zusammengefaßt, gesamt. kollektiv—. n Kollektiv m.

college ('kɔlidʒ) n Kollegium neu. Hochschule f.

collide (kə'laid) vi zusammenstoßen. **collision** n Zusammenstoß m.

colloquial (kə'loukwiəl) adj familiär, umgangssprachlich.

Cologne (kə'loun) n Köln neu.

colon ('koulən) n **1** Doppelpunkt m. Kolon neu. **2** anat Dickdarm m.

colonel ('kə:nl) n Oberst m.

colony ('kɔləni) n Kolonie, Siedlung f. **colonial** adj kolonial.

colossal (kə'lɔsəl) adj kolossal, riesig.

colour ('kʌlə) n Farbe f. **colour-bar** n Farbschranke f. **colour-blind** adj farbenblind. **coloured** adj farbig, bunt. **coloured (man)** Farbige(r) m.

colt (koult) n Füllen, Fohlen neu.

column ('kɔləm) n **1** Säule f. Pfeiler m. **2** Kolonne f. **3** Rubrik f. **4** (Zeitungs)Spalte f. **columnist** n Kolumnist m.

coma ('koumə) n Koma, anhaltende Bewußtlosigkeit f.

comb (koum) n Kamm m. vt **1** kämmen. **2** durchsuchen.

combat ('kɔmbæt) n Kampf m. vt bekämpfen.

combine (v kəm'bain: n 'kɔmbain) vt vereinigen, verbinden. n **1** Verband m. **2** Kartell neu. **combine harvester** n Mähdrescher m.

combustion (kəm'bʌstʃən) n Verbrennung f.

come* (kʌm) vi kommen. **come about** geschehen. **come across** stoßen auf. **comeback** n Rückkehr f. Comeback neu.

comedy ('kɔmədi) n Lustspiel neu. Komödie f. **comedian** n Komiker m. **comic** n **1** Komiker m. **2** Witzblatt neu. adj witzig, komisch. **comical** adj witzig, spaßig.

comet ('kɔmit) n Komet m.

comfort ('kʌmfət) n **1** Trost m. **2** Komfort m. **3** Gemütlichkeit f. vt trösten. **comfortable** adj bequem, behaglich.

comma ('kɔmə) n Komma neu. Beistrich m.

command (kə'mɑ:nd) n **1** Befehl m. **2** Führung f. vt **1** befehlen. **2** kommandieren. **commander** n Kommandant, Befehlshaber, Führer m. **commandment** n Gebot neu.

commemorate (kə'meməreit) vt feiern, gedenken.

commence (kə'mens) vt,vi anfangen, beginnen. **commencement** n Anfang, Beginn m.

commend (kə'mend) vt empfehlen, loben.

comment ('kɔment) n **1** Bemerkung f. **2** Stellungnahme f. vi bemerken, kommentieren. **commentary** n Kommentar m. **commentator** n Kommentator, Berichterstatter m.

commerce ('kɔmə:s) n Handel(sverkehr) m. **commercial** adj kommerziell, kaufmännisch, geschäftlich. *n* Fernsehreklame *f*. **commercialize** *vt* marktfähig machen. **commercial vehicle** *n* Nutzfahrzeug *neu*.

commission (kə'miʃən) *n* 1 Auftrag *m*. 2 *mil* Offizierspatent *neu*. 3 Kommission *f*. Ausschuß *m*. *vt* 1 bestellen, beauftragen. 2 eine Bestellung geben. **commissioner** *n* Kommissionär *m*.

commit (kə'mit) *vt* 1 begehen. 2 übergeben. **commit oneself** sich verpflichten.

committee (kə'miti) *n* Ausschuß *m*. Komitee *neu*.

commodity (kə'mɔditi) *n* Handelsgut *neu*. Ware *f*.

common ('kɔmən) *adj* 1 allgemein, gemeinsam. 2 gewöhnlich, häufig. 3 alltäglich. *n* Allmende *f*. **Common Market** *n* Gemeinsamer Markt *m*. Europäische Wirtschaftsgemeinschaft *f*. **commonplace** *n* Gewöhnliche(s), Alltägliche(s) *neu*. Gemeinplatz *m*. *adj* gewöhnlich, alltäglich. **common sense** *n* gesunder Menschenverstand *m*. Vernunft *f*. **commonwealth** *n* 1 Staat *m*. Gemeinwesen *neu*. 2 Commonwealth *neu*.

commotion (kə'mouʃən) *n* Aufruhr *m*. Getue *neu*.

commune[1] (kə'mju:n) *vi* 1 sich unterhalten. 2 *rel* Kommunion empfangen. **communion** *n* Kommunion *f*.

commune[2] ('kɔmju:n) *n* Kommune, Gemeinde *f*. **communal** *adj* Kommunal—, Gemeinschafts—.

communicant (kəmju:nikənt) *n* Kommunikant *m*.

communicate (kə'mju:nikeit) *vt* 1 mitteilen. 2 übertragen. *vi* 1 in Verbindung stehen. 2 *rel* Kommunizieren. **communication** *n* 1 Mitteilung *f*. 2 Verbindung, Kommunikation *f*. Verkehr *m*.

communism ('kɔmjunizəm) *n* Kommunismus *m*. **communist** *n* Kommunist *m*. *adj* kommunistisch.

community (kə'mju:niti) *n* 1 Gemeinschaft, Gemeinde *f*. 2 Gemeinsamkeit *f*.

commute (kə'mju:t) *vt* 1 umwandeln, austauschen. *vi* zur Arbeit reisen, pendeln. **commuter** *n* Pendler *m*.

compact[1] (kəm'pækt) *adj* dicht, fest, kompakt. *vt* verdichten, verbinden.

compact[2] ('kɔmpækt) *n* Vertrag, Pakt *m*. Übereinkommen *neu*.

companion (kəm'pæniən) *n* Begleiter, Kamerad

m. **companionship** *n* Gesellschaft, Kameradschaft *f*.

company ('kʌmpəni) *n* 1 *comm* Firma, Gesellschaft *f*. 2 Gesellschaft *f*.

compare (kəm'pɛə) (*vi*),*vt* (sich) vergleichen. **comparable** *adj* vergleichbar. **comparative** *adj* 1 vergleichend. 2 verhältnismäßig. **comparison** *n* Vergleich *m*.

compartment (kəm'pɑ:tmənt) *n* 1 Abteilung *f*. 2 Fach *neu*. 3 Abteil *neu*.

compass ('kʌmpəs) *n* Kompaß *m*.

compassion (kəm'pæʃən) *n* Mitleid, Erbarmen *neu*. **compassionate** *adj* mitleidsvoll.

compatible (kəm'pætibəl) *adj* vereinbar.

compel (kəm'pel) *vt* zwingen, nötigen.

compensate ('kɔmpənseit) *vi* 1 ausgleichen. 2 wiedergutmachen, entschädigen. **compensation** *n* Entschädigung *f*. Schadenersatz *m*.

compete (kəm'pi:t) *vi* 1 teilnehmen. 2 konkurrieren. **competition** *n* 1 Wettbewerb *m*. 2 Konkurrenz *f*. **competitive** *adj* 1 konkurrenzfähig. 2 wetteifernd, konkurrierend. **competitor** *n* Konkurrent *m*.

competent ('kɔmpitənt) *adj* kompetent, fähig. **competence** *n* Kompetenz, Befähigung *f*.

compile (kəm'pail) *vt* aufstellen, zusammenstellen.

complacent (kəm'pleisənt) *adj* gleichgültig. **complacency** *n* Selbstgefälligkeit.

complain (kəm'plein) *vi* sich beklagen *or* beschweren. **complaint** *n* Klage, Beschwerde *f*.

complement ('kɔmplimənt) *n* 1 Ergänzung. 2 *math* Komplement *neu*. *vt* ergänzen.

complete (kəm'pli:t) *vt* vervollständigen, beenden, fertigstellen. *adj* ganz, vollständig.

complex ('kɔmpleks) *adj* komplex, kompliziert. *n* Komplex *m*. **complexity** *n* Kompliziertheit, Schwierigkeit *f*.

complexion (kəm'plekʃən) *n* Gesichtsfarbe *f*. Teint *m*.

complicate ('kɔmplikeit) *vt* komplizieren, erschweren. **complicated** *adj* kompliziert.

compliment ('kɔmplimənt) *n* Kompliment *neu*. *vt* loben, ein Kompliment machen. **complimentary** *adj* 1 höflich, schmeichelhaft. 2 Gratis—, Frei—.

comply (kəm'plai) *vi* einwilligen, nachgeben, sich fügen. **comply with** erfüllen, befolgen.

component (kəm'pounənt) *n* (Bestand)Teil *m*. *adj* teilbildend.

compose (kəm'pouz) *vt* 1 zusammensetzen. 2 dichten, verfassen. 3 *mus* komponieren. **com-**

pose oneself sich beruhigen, sich fassen.
composed adj ruhig, gelassen. **composition**
n 1 Zusammensetzung f. 2 Aufsatz m. 3 mus
Komposition f.
composure (kəm'pouʒə) n Gelassenheit f.
compound[1] (v kəm'paund; n 'kɔmpaund) vt 1
zusammensetzen, mischen. 2 verbinden. n 1
sci Verbindung f. 2 Gemisch neu. Mischung f.
compound[2] ('kɔmpaund) n eingezäuntes Gelände neu.
comprehend (kɔmpri'hend) vt 1 verstehen,
begreifen. 2 umfassen, einschließen. **comprehensive** adj umfassend, allgemein. **comprehensive school** n Gesamtschule f.
compress (v kəm'pres; n 'kɔmpres) vt kompri-
mieren, zusammendrücken. n Kompressions-
binde f. **compression** n tech Verdichtung f.
comprise (kəm'praiz) vt einschließen, umfassen.
compromise ('kɔmprəmaiz) n Kompromiß m. vi
übereinkommen, einen Kompromiß schließen.
vt kompromittieren, gefährden.
compulsion (kəm'pʌlʃən) n Zwang m. **com-
pulsive** adj zwingend, Zwangs—. **compulsory** adj zwangsläufig, obligatorisch.
compunction (kəm'pʌŋkʃən) n Gewissensbisse
m pl.
computer (kəm'pju:tə) n Rechenautomat neu.
Computer, Datenverarbeiter m.
comrade ('kɔmrəd, -reid) n 1 Kamerad, Gefährte m. 2 pol Genosse m.
concave ('kɔŋkeiv) adj konkav, hohl.
conceal (kən'si:l) vt 1 verstecken, verbergen. 2
verschweigen.
concede (kən'si:d) vt zugestehen, zugeben.
conceit (kən'si:t) n Eingebildetheit, Eitelkeit f.
conceive (kən'si:v) vt 1 (a child) empfangen. 2
begreifen, sich vorstellen, ersinnen.
concentrate ('kɔnsəntreit) (vi),vt (sich) konzentrieren. vt richten. **concentration** n Kon-
zentration f.
concentric (kən'sentrik) adj konzentrisch.
concept ('kɔnsept) n Konzept neu. Begriff
m. **conception** n 1 Empfängnis f. 2 Auf-
fassungsvermögen neu. 3 Vorstellung f.
concern (kən'sə:n) n 1 Teilnahme f. Belang m.
2 Interesse n. 3 Sorge f. 4 comm Unternehmen neu. vt angehen. **concern oneself**
sich beschäftigen.
concert ('kɔnsət) n Konzert neu.
concertina (kɔnsə'ti:nə) n Ziehharmonika f.
concerto (kən'tʃeətou) n (Solo)Konzert neu.
concession (kən'seʃən) n 1 Konzession f. 2
Zugeständnis neu.

conciliate (kən'silieit) vt aussöhnen.
concise (kən'sais) adj knapp, kurz.
conclude (kən'klu:d) vt,vi beenden, schließen.
conclusion n Schluß m. **draw conclusions
(from)** Schlüsse ziehen (aus).
concoct (kən'kɔkt) vt zusammenbrauen.
concrete ('kɔŋkri:t) n Beton m. adj 1 fest, dicht.
2 konkret, dinglich.
concussion (kən'kʌʃən) n Gehirnerschütterung
f.
condemn (kən'dem) vt verurteilen. **condemna-
tion** n Verurteilung f.
condense (kən'dens) vt 1 kondensieren. 2
abkürzen, zusammenfassen. **condensation** n
1 Kondensation f. 2 Abkürzung f.
condescend (kɔndi'send) vi sich herablassen.
condition (kən'diʃən) n 1 Zustand m. 2 Bedingung, Voraussetzung f. **conditional** adj
bedingt, abhängig.
condolence (kən'douləns) n Beileid neu.
condom ('kɔndəm) n Kondom neu.
condone (kən'doun) vt billigen.
conduct (n 'kɔndʌkt; v kən'dʌkt) n 1 Betragen,
Verhalten neu. 2 Führung f. vt 1 durchführen.
2 leiten, dirigieren. **conduct oneself** sich
verhalten.
conductor (kən'dʌktə) n 1 Schaffner m. 2 mus
Dirigent m.
cone (koun) n Kegel m.
confectioner (kən'fekʃənə) n Konditor m. **con-
fectionery** n Konditorwaren f pl.
confederate (n,adj kən'fedərət; v kən'fedəreit)
n 1 Verbündete(r) m. adj 2 Mitschuldige(r) m. adj
verbündet, Bundes—. (vi),vt (sich) verbünden.
confer (kən'fə:) vt verleihen, erteilen. **conference** n Konferenz, Tagung f.
confess (kən'fes) vt,vi 1 zugeben, bekennen,
gestehen. 2 rel beichten. **confession** n 1
Zugeständnis neu. 2 rel Beichte f. 3 law
Geständnis neu.
confide (kən'faid) vi vertrauen. vt anvertrauen.
confidence n Vertrauen neu. Zuversicht
f. **confidence trick** n Schwindel m. **confident** adj 1 zuversichtlich. 2 selbstsicher.
confidential adj geheim, vertraulich.
confine (kən'fain) vt begrenzen, einschränken.
confirm (kən'fə:m) vt bestätigen, bekräftigen.
confirmation n 1 Bestätigung f. 2 rel Konfir-
mation f.
confiscate ('kɔnfiskeit) vt konfiszieren, einziehen.

construct

conflict (v kənˈflikt; n ˈkɔnflikt) vi **1** streiten. **2** widersprechen. n Konflikt, Kampf m.

conform (kənˈfɔːm) (vi),vt (sich) anpassen.

confound (kənˈfaund) vt verwirren, verblüffen.

confront (kənˈfrʌnt) vt **1** gegenüberstehen, konfrontieren. **2** entgegenhalten. **confrontation** n Konfrontation f.

confuse (kənˈfjuːz) vt **1** verwirren, durcheinanderbringen. **2** verwechseln. **confusion** n Verwirrung f. Durcheinander neu.

congeal (kənˈdʒiːl) vi gerinnen, erstarren.

congenial (kənˈdʒiːniəl) adj kongenial, gleichartig, übereinstimmend.

congested (kənˈdʒestid) adj verstopft, überfüllt.

congratulate (kənˈgrætjuleit) vt beglückwünschen, gratulieren. **congratulation** n Glückwunsch m.

congregate (ˈkɔŋgrigeit) vi sich versammeln. **congregation** n **1** Versammlung f. **2** Kirchengemeinde f.

congress (ˈkɔŋgres) n Kongreß m.

conical (ˈkɔnikəl) adj kegelförmig.

conifer (ˈkɔnifə) n **1** Nadelbaum m. **2** pl Nadelhölzer neu pl.

conjugal (ˈkɔndʒugəl) adj ehelich.

conjugate (ˈkɔndʒugeit) vt gram konjugieren.

conjunction (kənˈdʒʌŋkʃən) n **1** gramm Konjunktion f. **2** Verbindung f.

conjure (ˈkʌndʒə) vi zaubern. **conjure up** vt **1** heraufbeschwören. **2** hervorrufen. **conjurer** n Zauberer m.

connect (kəˈnekt) vt verbinden, verknüpfen, anschließen. **connection** n **1** Verbindung, Verknüpfung f. **2** Anschluß m. **3** Zusammenhang m.

connoisseur (kɔnəˈsəː) n Kenner m.

connotation (kɔnəˈteiʃən) n Nebenbedeutung f.

conquer (ˈkɔŋkə) vt besiegen, erobern. **conqueror** n Sieger, Eroberer m. **conquest** n Eroberung f.

conscience (ˈkɔnʃəns) n Gewissen neu.

conscientious (kɔnʃiˈenʃəs) adj gewissenhaft.

conscious (ˈkɔnʃəs) adj **1** bei Bewußtsein. **2** bewußt. **3** wissentlich. **consciousness** n Bewußtsein neu.

conscript (n ˈkɔnskript; v kənˈskript) n Wehrdienstpflichtige(r) m. vt (zwangsweise) einziehen. **conscription** n Wehrpflicht f.

consecrate (ˈkɔnsikreit) vt weihen. **consecration** n Weihung f.

consecutive (kənˈsekjutiv) adj aufeinanderfolgend.

consent (kənˈsent) vi zustimmen, einwilligen. n Zustimmung f.

consequence (ˈkɔnsikwəns) n Folge f. Ergebnis neu. **consequent** adj folgend. **consequently** adv folglich, deshalb.

conserve (kənˈsəːv) vt **1** erhalten, bewahren. **2** einmachen. **conservation** n **1** Erhaltung f. **2** Schutz m. **conservative** adj konservativ. n Konservative(r) m. **conservatory** n Treibhaus neu.

consider (kənˈsidə) vt **1** betrachten (als). **2** bedenken, überlegen. **3** berücksichtigen. **considerable** adj beträchtlich, erheblich. **considerate** adj überlegt, rücksichtsvoll. **consideration** n **1** Betracht(ung), Überlegung, Berücksichtigung f. **2** Rücksicht f.

consign (kənˈsain) vt übergeben, überliefern. **consignment** n Lieferung f.

consist (kənˈsist) vi bestehen. **consistency** n **1** Dichtigkeit f. **2** Übereinstimmung f. **3** Konsequenz, Folgerichtigkeit f. **consistent** adj **1** konsequent, folgerichtig. **2** übereinstimmend.

console (kənˈsoul) vt trösten. **consolation** n Trost m.

consolidate (kənˈsɔlideit) vt stärken, festigen, konsolidieren.

consonant (ˈkɔnsənənt) n Konsonant, Mitlaut m.

conspicuous (kənˈspikjuəs) adj auffallend.

conspire (kənˈspaiə) vi sich verschwören.

constable (ˈkʌnstəbəl) n Polizist m.

Constance, Lake (ˈkɔnstəns) n Bodensee m.

constant (ˈkɔnstənt) adj **1** dauernd, beständig. **2** treu. **3** unveränderlich. **constantly** adv stets, ständig.

constellation (kɔnstəˈleiʃən) n Konstellation f.

constipation (kɔnstiˈpeiʃən) n (Darm)Verstopfung f.

constitute (ˈkɔnstitjuːt) vt **1** ausmachen, bilden. **2** gründen. **constituency** n Wahlkreis, Wahlbezirk m. **constituent** adj teilbildend. n **1** Bestandteil m. **2** Wähler m. **constitution** n **1** pol (Staats)Verfassung f. **2** Struktur, Konstitution f. **constitutional** adj verfassungsmäßig.

constraint (kənˈstreint) n **1** Zwang m. **2** Zurückhaltung f.

constrict (kənˈstrikt) vt **1** zusammenziehen. **2** hemmen, einengen.

construct (kənˈstrʌkt) vt bauen, errichten, konstruieren. **construction** n **1** Bau m. Errichtung f. **2** Bau m. Gebäude neu. **3** Konstruktion f. **constructive** adj konstruktiv.

169

consul ('kɔnsəl) n Konsul m. **consulate** n Konsulat neu.

consult (kən'sʌlt) vi,vt konsultieren, um Rat fragen. **consult a book** in einem Buch nachschlagen. **consultant** n 1 Berater m. 2 med Konsilarius m. **consultation** n 1 Beratung f. 2 Konsultation f.

consume (kən'sju:m) vt 1 konsumieren, essen. 2 verbrauchen. 3 vernichten. **consumer** n Verbraucher m. **consumption** n 1 Verbrauch m. 2 Genuß m.

contact ('kɔntækt) n 1 Kontakt m. Berührung f. 2 Anschluß m. vt sich in Verbindung setzen mit. **contact lenses** n Kontaktlinsen f pl.

contagious (kən'teidʒəs) adj ansteckend.

contain (kən'tein) vt 1 enthalten. 2 zurückhalten. **container** n Behälter m.

contaminate (kən'tæmineit) vt verseuchen, vergiften. **contamination** n Verseuchung f.

contemplate ('kɔntəmpleit) vt 1 betrachten, nachdenken, erwägen. 2 vorhaben. **contemplation** n 1 Betrachtung f. Nachdenken neu. 2 Meditation f.

contemporary (kən'tempərəri) adj zeitgenössisch. n Zeitgenosse m.

contempt (kən'tempt) n 1 Verachtung f. 2 law Mißachtung (des Gerichts) f. **contemptible** adj verächtlich. **contemptuous** adj verachtungsvoll.

content[1] ('kɔntent) n 1 Inhalt m. 2 Gehalt m.

content[2] (kən'tent) adj zufrieden, genügsam. vt zufriedenstellen. **contentment** n Zufriedenheit f.

contest (n 'kɔntest; v kən'test) n 1 Streit m. 2 Wettkampf m. vt bestreiten, anfechten. **contestant** n Teilnehmer, Bewerber m.

context ('kɔntekst) n Zusammenhang m.

continent ('kɔntinənt) n Kontinent m. adj mäßig, keusch. **continental** adj kontinental.

contingency (kən'tindʒənsi) n 1 Möglichkeit f. 2 Zufälligkeit f. **contingent** adj zufällig, nicht notwendig.

continue (kən'tinju:) vt fortsetzen, weitermachen. **continual** adj fortgesetzt. **continually** adv immer wieder, dauernd. **continuation** n Fortsetzung, Weiterführung f. **continuity** n Kontinuität, Stetigkeit f. **continuous** adj ununterbrochen, (fort)dauernd.

contour ('kɔntuə) n 1 Umriß m. Kontur f. 2 geog Höhenlinie f.

contraband ('kɔntrəbænd) n Schmuggelware f.

contraception (kɔntrə'sepʃən) n Empfängnisverhütung f. **contraceptive** n Empfängnisverhütungsmittel neu.

contract (n 'kɔntrækt; v kən'trækt) n Vertrag, Kontrakt m. vt 1 verkürzen, zusammenziehen. 2 (an illness) sich zuziehen. vi sich zusammenziehen, kleiner werden.

contradict (kɔntrə'dikt) vt widersprechen. **contradiction** n Widerspruch m.

contralto (kən'træltou) n Alt m. Altstimme f.

contraption (kən'træpʃən) n inf (neuartiges) Gerät neu. Kniff m.

contrary ('kɔntrəri) adj 1 entgegengesetzt, widrig. 2 widerspenstig.

contrast (v kən'tra:st; n 'kɔntra:st) vt kontrastieren, entgegensetzen, gegenüberstellen. vi sich unterscheiden. n Kontrast, Gegensatz m.

contravene (kɔntrə'vi:n) vt 1 übertreten. 2 zuwiderhandeln.

contribute (kən'tribju:t) vt,vi beitragen, beisteuern. **contribution** n Beitrag m.

contrive (kən'traiv) vt 1 erdenken, erfinden. 2 zustande bringen.

control (kən'troul) vt 1 lenken, steuern. 2 beaufsichtigen. 3 beherrschen. 4 kontrollieren. n 1 Macht, Gewalt f. 2 Aufsicht, Kontrolle f. **controller** n 1 Aufseher. 2 (Strom)Regler m.

controversy ('kɔntrəvə:si, kən'trɔvəsi) n Kontroverse f. Streit m. **controversial** adj umstritten.

convalesce (kɔnvə'les) vi genesen, gesund werden.

convenience (kən'vi:niəns) n 1 Bequemlichkeit, Annehmlichkeit f. 2 Gelegenheit f. **convenient** adj passend, geeignet, gelegen.

convent ('kɔnvənt) n Kloster neu.

convention (kən'venʃən) n 1 Tagung, Versammlung f. 2 Brauch m. Sitte, Regel f. **conventional** adj konventionell.

converge (kən'və:dʒ) vi zusammenlaufen, sich nähern.

converse (v kən'və:s; n 'kɔnvə:s) vi sich unterhalten, sprechen. n Umkehrung f. Gegenteil neu. **conversation** n Unterhaltung f. Gespräch neu. **conversational** adj Unterhaltungs—.

convert (v kən'və:t; n 'kɔnvə:t) vt 1 umwandeln, verwandeln. 2 umwechseln. 3 rel bekehren. n Bekehrte(r) m.

convex ('kɔnveks) adj konvex, gewölbt.

convey (kən'vei) vt 1 befördern, transportieren. 2 mitteilen, vermitteln. **conveyor belt** n Fließband neu.

convict (v kən'vikt; n 'kɔnvikt) vt law überführen. n Sträfling m.

conviction (kən'vikʃən) n 1 law Überführung, Verurteilung f. 2 Überzeugung f.

convince (kən'vins) vt überzeugen, überreden.

convoy ('kɔnvɔi) n 1 Geleitzug m. 2 mil Kolonne f.

cook (kuk) n Koch m. Köchin f. vt kochen. **cookery** n Kochen neu.

cool (ku:l) adj kühl. vt kühlen. vi sich abkühlen.

coop (ku:p) n Brutkorb m. vt einsperren.

cooperate (kou'ɔpəreit) vi zusammenarbeiten, kooperieren. **cooperation** f. 1 Zusammenarbeit f. 2 Hilfe f. **cooperative** adj 1 zusammenarbeitend. 2 hilfsbereit. 3 pol genossenschaftlich. n Arbeitsgenossenschaft f. **cooperative society** n Konsumverein m.

coordinate (adj, n kou'ɔ:dnət; v kou'ɔ:dineit) adj koordiniert. n Koordinate f. vt koordinieren, gleichstellen. **coordination** n Koordinierung, Gleichstellung f.

cope (koup) vi sich messen mit, meistern.

Copenhagen (koupən'heigən) n Kopenhagen neu.

copious ('koupiəs) adj reichlich.

copper[1] ('kɔpə) n Kupfer neu. adj Kupfer—.

copper[2] ('kɔpə) n inf Polyp, Polizist m.

copulate ('kɔpjuleit) vi sich paaren.

copy ('kɔpi) vt kopieren, nachmachen. n 1 Kopie, Abschrift f. 2 Exemplar neu. **copyright** n Verlagsrecht, Copyright neu.

coral ('kɔrəl) n Koralle f.

cord (kɔ:d) n Schnur f. Strick m.

cordial ('kɔ:diəl) adj freundlich, herzlich.

cordon ('kɔ:dn) n Kette f. Gürtel m. **cordon off** absperren.

corduroy ('kɔ:dərɔi) n Kord(samt) m.

core (kɔ:) n Kern m.

cork (kɔ:k) n Korken, Pfropfen m. **corkscrew** n Korkenzieher m.

corn[1] (kɔ:n) n Getreide, Korn neu. **cornflour** n Maismehl neu. **cornflower** n Kornblume f.

corn[2] (kɔ:n) n med Hühnerauge neu.

corner ('kɔ:nə) n Ecke f.

cornet ('kɔ:nit) n 1 mus (Ventil)kornett neu. 2 Eiswaffeltüte f.

coronary ('kɔrənəri) adj koronar. **coronary thrombosis** n Koronarthrombose f.

coronation (kɔrə'neiʃən) n Krönung f.

corporal[1] ('kɔ:prəl) adj körperlich, physisch.

corporal[2] ('kɔ:prəl) n Korporal, Gefreite(r) m.

corporation (kɔ:pə'reiʃən) n Körperschaft, Korporation f.

corps (kɔ:) n Armeekorps neu.

corpse (kɔ:ps) n Leiche f. Leichnam m.

correct (kə'rekt) adj 1 richtig. 2 korrekt. vt 1 berichtigen, richtigstellen. 2 korrigieren. **correction** n 1 Berichtigung, Verbesserung f. 2 Korrektur f.

correlate ('kɔrəleit) vi entsprechen. vt aufeinander beziehen.

correspond (kɔri'spɔnd) vi 1 übereinstimmen, entsprechen. 2 einen Briefwechsel führen, korrespondieren. **correspondence** n 1 Übereinstimmung f. 2 Briefwechsel m. 3 Briefe m pl. **correspondent** n Korrespondent m.

corridor ('kɔridɔ:) n Korridor, Gang m.

corrode (kə'roud) vt zerfressen. vi rosten.

corrupt (kə'rʌpt) vt 1 verderben. 2 verführen. adj 1 verdorben, verfault. 2 korrupt.

corset ('kɔ:sit) n Korsett neu.

cosmetic (kɔz'metik) adj kosmetisch. n Schönheitsmittel neu.

cosmopolitan (kɔzmə'pɔlitən) adj weltbürgerlich.

cost[1] (kɔst) n 1 Preis m. Kosten pl. 2 Schaden m. vi kosten. vt die Kosten berechnen von. **costly** adj teuer.

costume ('kɔstju:m) n Kostüm neu. Tracht f.

cosy ('kouzi) adj bequem, gemütlich.

cot (kɔt) n Kinderbett neu.

cottage ('kɔtidʒ) n Hütte f. Häuschen f.

cotton ('kɔtn) n Baumwolle f. **cotton-wool** n Watte f.

couch (kautʃ) n Couch f. Liegesofa neu.

cough (kɔf) n Husten m. vi husten.

could (kud; unstressed kəd) v see **can**.

council ('kaunsəl) n Rat m. **councillor** n Ratsherr m.

counsel ('kaunsəl) n Rat(schlag) m. vt beraten.

count[1] (kaunt) vt 1 zählen. 2 halten für. vi 1 zählen. 2 gelten. n Zählen neu. **countdown** n Startzählung f.

count[2] (kaunt) n Graf m.

counter[1] ('kauntə) n 1 Ladentisch m. 2 Spielmarke f. 3 Zähler m.

counter[2] ('kauntə) pref gegen, entgegen.

counterattack ('kauntərətæk) n Gegenangriff m.

counterfeit ('kauntəfit) adj falsch, unecht, verfälscht. vt fälschen.

counterfoil ('kauntəfɔil) n Quittung f. Kontrollabschnitt m.

counterpart ('kauntəpɑ:t) n Gegenstück neu.

countess ('kauntis) n Gräfin f.

country ('kʌntri) n 1 Land neu. 2 Staat

m. **country house** *n* Landhaus *neu.* **countryside** *n* Landschaft *f.*

county ('kaunti) *n* Grafschaft *f.*

coup (ku:) *n* Coup, Putsch *m.* **coup d'état** *n* Staatsstreich *m.*

couple ('kʌpəl) *n* Paar *neu.* **a couple of** ein Paar. *vt* 1 paaren, verbinden. 2 koppeln.

coupon ('ku:pɔn) *n* Gutschein, Kupon *m.*

courage ('kʌridʒ) *n* Mut *m.* Tapferkeit *f.*

courgette (kuəˈʒet) *n* Courgette *f.*

courier ('kuriə) *n* 1 Kurier, Eilbote *m.* 2 Reiseleiter *m.*

course (kɔ:s) *n* 1 Lauf, Gang *m.* 2 Kurs *m.* Richtung *f.* 3 Rennbahn *f.* · 4 *educ* Kursus, Lehrgang *m.* **of course** natürlich, selbstverständlich.

court (kɔ:t) *n* 1 Hof *m.* 2 Spielplatz *m.* *vt* werben um. **court martial** *n* Militärgericht, Kriegsgericht *neu.* **courtship** *n* Werbezeit, Werbung *f.* **courtyard** *n* Hof *m.*

courteous ('kə:tiəs) *adj* höflich, verbindlich. **courtesy** *n* Höflichkeit *f.*

cousin ('kʌzən) *n* Vetter, Cousin *m.* Kusine *f.*

cove (kouv) *n* Bucht *f.*

cover ('kʌvə) *n* 1 Decke *f.* 2 (Be)Deckung *f.* 3 Hülle *f.* *vt* decken, bedecken.

cow (kau) *n* Kuh *f.* **cowboy** *n* Cowboy *m.*

coward ('kauəd) *n* Feigling *m.*

cower ('kauə) *vi* sich ducken, kauern.

coy (kɔi) *adj* scheu, bescheiden.

crab (kræb) *n* Krebs *m.*

crack (kræk) *vi,vt* 1 knallen. 2 spalten, zerbrechen. *n* 1 Spalt, Riß *m.* 2 Knall *m.*

cracker ('krækə) *n* Keks *m.*

crackle ('krækəl) *vi* knistern. *n* Geknister *neu.*

cradle ('kreidl) *n* Wiege *f.* *vt* wiegen.

craft (krɑ:ft) *n* 1 Kunst, Fertigkeit *f.* 2 List, Schlauheit *f.* **craftsman** *n* Künstler, Handwerker *m.* **craftsmanship** *n* Kunstfertigkeit *f.* **crafty** *adj* listig, gerissen.

cram (kræm) *vt* vollstopfen, überladen.

cramp[1] (kræmp) *n* Krampf *m.* **cramped** *adj* beengt, zusammengepfercht.

cramp[2] (kræmp) *n* Klammer, Krampe *f.* *vt* mit Klammern befestigen.

crane (krein) *n* 1 *zool* Kranich *m.* 2 Kran *m.*

crash (kræʃ) *n* 1 Zusammenstoß, Aufprall *m.* 2 Absturz *m.* 3 Krachen *neu.* *vi* 1 zusammenstoßen. 2 abstürzen. **crash-helmet** *n* Sturzhelm *m.*

crate (kreit) *n* Kiste *f.* *vt* verpacken.

crater ('kreitə) *n* Krater, Trichter *m.*

crave (kreiv) *vt* sich sehnen nach, flehen um.

crawl (krɔ:l) *vi* kriechen, sich schleppen. *n* 1 Kriechen *neu.* 2 *sport* Kraulschwimmen *neu.*

crayfish ('kreifiʃ) *n* (Fluß)Krebs *m.*

crayon ('kreiən) *n* Buntstift *m.*

craze (kreiz) *n* Fimmel *m.* Manie, Mode *f.* **crazy** *adj* verrückt, toll.

creak (kri:k) *vi* knarren. *n* Knarren *neu.*

cream (kri:m) *n* 1 Sahne *f.* Rahm *m.* 2 Creme *f.*

crease (kri:s) *n* 1 Falte *f.* 2 Bügelfalte *f.* *vt* 1 falten. 2 bügeln. **crease-resistant** *adj* knitterfrei.

create (kriˈeit) *vt* 1 (er)schaffen, kreieren. 2 verursachen. 3 erheben (zu). **creation** *n* Erschaffung, Schöpfung *f.* **creative** *adj* kreativ, schöpferisch. **creator** *n* Schöpfer *m.* **creature** *n* Geschöpf, Wesen *neu.*

credentials (kriˈdenʃəlz) *n pl* 1 Ausweispapiere *neu pl.* 2 Beglaubigungsschreiben *neu.*

credible ('kredibəl) *adj* glaubwürdig.

credit ('kredit) *n* 1 Kredit *m.* Guthaben *neu.* 2 Anerkennung *f.* 3 Glaube *m.* *vt* 1 kreditieren, gutschreiben. 2 zutrauen. **credit card** *n* Kreditkarte *f.*

credulous ('kredjuləs) *adj* leichtgläubig.

creep* (kri:p) *vi* 1 kriechen, schleichen. 2 sich heimlich nähern. *n sl* Kriecher *m.*

cremate (kriˈmeit) *vt* einäschern, verbrennen. **crematorium** *n* Krematorium *neu.*

crept (krept) *v see* **creep.**

crescent ('kresənt) *n* Halbmond *m.*

cress (kres) *n* Kresse *f.*

crest (krest) *n* 1 Familienwappen *neu.* 2 Kamm *m.* 3 Gipfel *m.*

crevice ('krevis) *n* Spalte *f.* Riß *m.*

crew[1] (kru:) *n* Mannschaft, Besatzung *f.*

crew[2] (kru:) *v see* **crow**[2].

crib (krib) *n* Krippe *f.* *vi inf* abschreiben.

cricket[1] ('krikit) *n* Grille *f.*

cricket[2] ('krikit) *n* Kricketspiel *neu.*

crime (kraim) *n* Verbrechen *neu.* **criminal** *n* Verbrecher *m.* *adj* kriminell, verbrecherisch.

crimson ('krimzən) *adj* karmesinrot.

cringe (krindʒ) *vi* sich krümmen, kauern.

crinkle ('kriŋkəl) *vi* sich kräuseln. **crinkly** *adj* kraus.

cripple ('kripəl) *n* Krüppel *m.* *vt* lahmlegen, schwer schädigen.

crisis ('kraisis) *n, pl* **crises** Krise *f.*

crisp (krisp) *adj* 1 knusprig. 2 frisch. **crisps** *n pl* Kartoffelscheiben *f pl.*

criterion (kraiˈtiəriən) *n* Kriterium *neu.*

criticize ('kritisaiz) *vt* kritisieren, tadeln. **critic**

n Kritiker *m.* **critical** *adj* 1 kritisch. 2 entscheidend. **criticism** *n* Kritik *f.*
croak (krouk) *n* Quaken *neu.* *vi* quaken, krächzen.
crochet ('krouʃei) *vt* häkeln. *n* Häkelarbeit *f.*
crockery ('krɔkəri) Geschirr *neu.*
crocodile ('krɔkədail) *n* Krokodil *neu.*
crocus ('kroukəs) *n* Krokus *m.*
crook (kruk) *n* 1 Haken *m.* 2 Krummstab *m.* 3 Schwindler, Gauner *m.* *vt* krümmen.
crooked ('krukid) *adj* schief, gebogen, krumm.
crop (krɔp) *n* 1 Feldfrucht *f.* Getreide *neu.* 2 Ernte *f.* 3 Reitpeitsche *f.* *vi* 1 abgrasen, abweiden. 2 stutzen. **crop up** auftauchen.
croquet ('kroukei) *n* Krocketspiel *neu.*
cross (krɔs) *vt* 1 überqueren, hinübergehen. 2 kreuzen. *vi* sich kreuzen. *n* 1 Kreuz *neu.* 2 Querstrich *m.* *adj* 1 böse, verärgert. 2 Quer—, Kreuz—. **cross-examination** *n* Kreuzverhör *m.* **cross-eyed** *adj* schielend. **cross-fire** *n* Kreuzfeuer *neu.* **crossing** *n* 1 Übergang *m.* 2 Kreuzung *f.* **cross-reference** *vt* kreuzverweisen. *n* Kreuzverweis *m.* **crossroads** *n* 1 (Straßen)Kreuzung *f.* 2 Scheideweg *m.* **crossword** *n* Kreuzworträtsel *neu.*
crotchet ('krɔtʃit) *n* mus Viertelnote *f.*
crouch (krautʃ) *vi* sich bücken, hocken.
crow¹ (krou) *n* Krähe *f.*
crow²² (krou) *vi* krähen.
crowd (kraud) *n* 1 (Menschen)Menge *f.* 2 *inf* Clique *f.* *vi* sich drängen. *vt* überfüllen.
crown (kraun) *n* Krone *f.* *vt* krönen. **crowning** *adj* krönend, höchst. **crown prince** *n* Kronprinz *m.*
crucial ('kru:ʃəl) *adj* kritisch, entscheidend.
crucify ('kru:sifai) *vt* kreuzigen. **crucifix** *n* Kruzifix *neu.*
crude (kru:d) *adj* 1 roh, unreif. 2 grob, ungehobelt. **crude oil** *n* Rohöl *neu.*
cruel ('kruəl) *adj* grausam, unbarmherzig. **cruelty** *n* 1 Grausamkeit *f.* 2 Quälerei *f.*
cruise (kru:z) *n* Kreuzfahrt *f.* *vi* kreuzen.
crumb (krʌm) *n* Krume *f.* Brösel *m.*
crumble ('krʌmbəl) *vt* zerkrümeln, zerbröckeln. *vi* zerfallen.
crumple ('krʌmpəl) *vt* zerknittern, zusammenbrechen. *vi* faltig werden.
crunch (krʌntʃ) *vt* zerknirschen. *vi* knirschen. **crunchy** *adj* knusprig.
crusade (kru:'seid) *n* Kreuzzug *m.* **crusader** *n* Kreuzfahrer *m.*
crush (krʌʃ) *vt* zerdrücken, zerquetschen.
crust (krʌst) *n* Kruste, Rinde *f.*

crustacean (krʌs'teiʃən) *n* Krustentier *neu.*
crutch (krʌtʃ) *n* Krücke *f.*
cry (krai) *vi* 1 schreien, rufen. 2 weinen. *n* Schrei, Ruf *m.*
crypt (kript) *n* Gruft *f.* **cryptic** *adj* geheim.
crystal ('kristl) *n* Kristall *m.* **crystallize** *vt,vi* kristallisieren.
cub (kʌb) *n* Welpe *m.*
cube (kju:b) *n* Würfel, Kubus *m.* **cubic** *adj* 1 würfelförmig. 2 Kubik—. **cubicle** *n* Kabine *f.*
cuckoo ('kuku:) *n* Kuckuck *m.*
cucumber ('kju:kʌmbə) *n* (Salat)Gurke *f.*
cuddle ('kʌdl) *vt* umarmen, hätscheln. *vi* sich (zusammen)kuscheln. *n* Umarmung *f.*
cue¹ (kju:) *n* 1 Th Stichwort *neu.* 2 Wink *m.*
cue² (kju:) *n* Billardstock *m.*
cuff¹ (kʌf) *n* Manschette *f.* Ärmelaufschlag *m.* **cufflink** *n* Manschettenknopf *m.*
cuff² (kʌf) *vt* schlagen, knuffen. *n* Ohrfeige *f.*
culinary ('kʌlinri) *adj* kulinarisch, Koch—.
culminate ('kʌlmineit) *vi* kulminieren, gipfeln.
culprit ('kʌlprit) *n* Schuldige(r), Täter *m.*
cult (kʌlt) *n* Kult *m.*
cultivate ('kʌltiveit) *vt* 1 bebauen, kultivieren. 2 pflegen, hegen. **cultivation** *n* 1 Ackerbau *m.* 2 Bebauung, Kultivierung *f.*
culture ('kʌltʃə) *n* 1 Kultur *f.* 2 Zucht *f.* **cultural** *adj* kulturell.
cumbersome ('kʌmbəsəm) *adj* schwerfällig.
cunning ('kʌniŋ) *adj* listig, schlau.
cup (kʌp) *n* 1 Tasse *f.* 2 *sport* Pokal *m.* **cupful** *n* Tasse(voll) *f.*
cupboard ('kʌbəd) *n* Schrank *m.*
curate ('kjuəreit) *n* Unterpfarrer *m.*
curator (kju'reitə) *n* 1 Verwalter *m.* 2 Museumsdirektor *m.*
curb (kə:b) *vt* bändigen, zügeln. *n* 1 Kinnkette *f.* 2 Zügel *m.*
curdle ('kə:dl) *vi,(vt)* gerinnen (lassen).
cure (kjuə) *vt* 1 heilen. 2 *cul* räuchern. *n* 1 Heilung *f.* 2 Heilmittel *neu.* 3 Kur *f.*
curfew ('kə:fju:) *n* Ausgehverbot *m.*
curious ('kjuəriəs) *adj* 1 neugierig. 2 merkwürdig, seltsam. **curiosity** *n* Neugier *f.*
curl (kə:l) *(vi),vt* 1 (sich) locken, (sich) kräuseln. 2 (sich) zusammenrollen. *n* 1 Locke *f.* 2 Windung *f.*
currant ('kʌrənt) *n* Korinthe *f.*
current ('kʌrənt) *n* Strom *m.* *adj* 1 laufend. 2 gegenwärtig. **current account** *n* Kontokorrent *neu.* **currency** *n* 1 *comm* Währung *f.* 2 Umlauf *m.*
curry ('kʌri) *n* *cul* Curry *m.*

curse (kə:s) vi fluchen, schimpfen. vt (ver)-fluchen. n Fluch m.

curt (kə:t) adj knapp, barsch.

curtail (kə:'teil) vt 1 verkürzen. 2 beschneiden. 3 vermindern.

curtain ('kə:tn) n Gardine f. Vorhang m.

curtsy ('kə:tsi) vi einen Knicks machen. n Knicks m.

curve (kə:v) (vi),vt (sich) biegen, (sich) krümmen. n Kurve, Krümmung f.

cushion ('kuʃən) n Kissen, Polster neu. vt dämpfen.

custard ('kʌstəd) n Eierkrem f.

custody ('kʌstədi) n 1 Bewachung f. Schutz m. 2 law Haft f.

custom ('kʌstəm) n Brauch m. Gewohnheit, Sitte f. **customary** adj gebräuchlich, Gewohnheits—. **customer** n Kunde, Klient m.

cut[1] (kʌt) vt 1 schneiden. 2 vermindern, verkürzen. n Schnitt m. 2 Schlag m. 3 Anteil m. 4 Abzug m. 5 Kürzung f. **cut down** 1 fällen. 2 verringern. **cut off** abschneiden. **cut up** zerschneiden. **cut-price** adj herabgesetzt. **cutting** n Ausschnitt m. adj beißend, scharf.

cute (kju:t) adj süß, niedlich.

cuticle ('kju:tikəl) n Oberhaut f.

cutlery ('kʌtləri) n Besteck neu.

cutlet ('kʌtlit) n Kotelett neu.

cycle ('saikəl) n 1 Fahrrad neu. 2 Zyklus m. Kreislauf m. vi radfahren.

cyclone ('saikloun) n Wirbelsturm m.

cygnet ('signit) n junger Schwan m.

cylinder ('silində) n Zylinder m.

cymbal ('simbəl) n Zimbel f. Becken neu.

cynic ('sinik) n Zyniker m. **cynical** adj zynisch.

cypress ('saiprəs) n Zypresse f.

Cyprus ('saiprəs) n Zypern neu. **Cypriot** n Zypriot m. adj zypriotisch.

Czech (tʃek) n Tscheche m. adj tschechisch.

Czechoslovakia (tʃekəslə'vækiə) n Tschechoslowakei f. **Czechoslovakian** adj tschechoslowakisch. n Tschechoslowake m.

D

dab (dæb) vt (be)tupfen.

dabble ('dæbəl) vi 1 benetzen. 2 hineinpfuschen. **dabbler** n Dilettant m.

dad (dæd) n inf also **daddy** Vati m.

daffodil ('dæfədil) n Narzisse f.

daft (dɑ:ft) adj blöd, dumm.

dagger ('dægə) n Dolch m.

daily ('deili) adj täglich.

dainty ('deinti) adj zierlich.

dairy ('dɛəri) n Molkerei f. **dairy farm** n Meierei f.

daisy ('deizi) n Gänseblümchen neu.

dam (dæm) n Damm, Deich m. vt eindämmen.

damage ('dæmidʒ) n Schaden m. Beschädigung f. vt beschädigen.

damn (dæm) vt 1 verdammen. 2 verfluchen. 3 verurteilen. interj varflucht! **damnable** adj verdammt, verflucht. **damnation** n Verdammung f.

damp (dæmp) adj feucht. **dampen** vt 1 anfeuchten. 2 inf niederschlagen.

damson ('dæmzən) n Zwetschge f.

dance (dɑ:ns) n Tanz m. vi tanzen. **dancer** n Tänzer m. Tänzerin f.

dandelion ('dændilaiən) n Löwenzahn m.

dandruff ('dændrʌf) n Schuppen f pl.

Dane (dein) n Däne m. **Danish** adj dänisch. n (language) Dänisch neu.

danger ('deindʒə) n Gefahr f. **dangerous** adj gefährlich.

dangle ('dæŋgəl) vi,(vt) baumeln, schwenken (lassen).

Danube ('dænju:b) n Donau f.

dare (dɛə) vi wagen, sich getrauen. **daring** adj mutig, waghalsig.

dark (dɑ:k) adj dunkel, finster. **darken** vt verdunkeln. vi sich verdunkeln, trüben. **darkness** n Dunkelheit, Finsternis f.

darling ('dɑ:liŋ) n Liebling m.

darn (dɑ:n) vt stopfen.

dart (dɑ:t) n Wurfpfeil m. vi hervorschießen.

dash (dæʃ) vt 1 zerschlagen. 2 zerstören. vi eilen, stürzen. n Zusatz, Schuß m. **dashboard** n Armaturenbrett neu.

data ('deitə) n pl Daten neu pl. **data processing** n Datenverarbeitung f.

date[1] (deit) n 1 Datum neu. 2 Termin m. 3 Periode f. vt 1 datieren. 2 inf sich verabreden mit. **date line** n Datumsgrenze f.

date[2] (deit) n Dattel f.

dative ('deitiv) adj dativ. n Dativ m.

daughter ('dɔ:tə) n Tochter f. **daughter-in-law** n Schwiegertochter f.

dawdle ('dɔ:dl) vi bummeln, trödeln.

dawn (dɔ:n) n Morgendämmerung f. Tagesanbruch m.

day (dei) n Tag m. **daybreak** n Tagesanbruch m. **daydream** n Träumerei f. **daylight** n Tageslicht neu.

daze (deiz) n Verwirrung f. vt verwirren, betäuben.

dazzle ('dæzl) vt blenden.

dead (ded) adj tot, leblos. **deaden** vt abtöten, dämpfen. **deadline** n Frist f. Termin m. **deadlock** n Stillstand m.

deaf (def) adj taub, schwerhörig. **deaf-aid** n Hörgerät neu. **deafen** vt taub machen. **deafmute** n Taubstumme(r) m. adj taubstumm.

deal* (di:l) vi 1 handeln. 2 sich beschäftigen. vt game austeilen. n 1 Geschäft neu. 2 Abkommen neu. 3 Menge f. **a great** or **good deal** sehr viel, eine ganze Menge. **dealer** n 1 Händler m. 2 Verteiler m.

dean (di:n) n Dekan m.

dear (diə) adj 1 lieb, geschätzt. 2 teuer. 3 (in letters) Liebe(r), Sehr geehrte(r). n 1 Liebling neu. **oh dear!** ach je! **dearly** adv 1 herzlich. 2 teuer.

death (deθ) n Tod m. **death certificate** n Sterbeurkunde f.

debase (di'beis) vt verderben, in Wert mindern.

debate (di'beit) vt debattieren, besprechen.

debit ('debit) vt belasten. n Belastung f. Soll neu.

debris ('deibri) n Trümmer pl. Schutt m.

debt (det) n Schuld, Verpflichtung f. **debtor** n Schuldner m.

decade ('dekeid) n Jahrzehnt neu.

decadent ('dekədənt) adj dekadent. **decadence** n Dekadenz f.

decant (di'kænt) vt umfüllen. **decanter** n Karaffe f.

decay (di'kei) n Verfall m. vi verfallen, verfaulen.

decease (di'si:s) vi sterben. **deceased** n Verstorbene(r) m.

deceit (di'si:t) n Täuschung f. Betrug m.

deceive (di'si:v) vt irreführen, betrügen, täuschen.

December (di'sembə) n Dezember m.

decent ('di:sənt) adj dezent, anständig.

deceptive (di'septiv) adj täuschend, trügerisch.

decide (di'said) vi si sich entscheiden, sich entschließen. vt bestimmen, entscheiden.

deciduous (di'sidjuəs) adj Laub—.

decimal ('desiməl) adj dezimal.

decipher (di'saifə) vt entziffern.

decision (di'siʒən) n Entscheidung f. Entschluß m. **decisive** adj entscheidend.

deck (dek) n 1 Deck neu. 2 game Spielkarten f pl. Pack neu. **deckchair** n Liegestuhl m.

declare (di'kleə) vt erklären, bekanntgeben. vi erklären. **declaration** n Erklärung, Anmeldung f.

decline (di'klain) vi 1 verfallen, sich neigen. 2 ablehnen. 3 abnehmen. vt 1 ablehnen. 2 gram deklinieren. n Verfall m. **declension** n Deklination f.

decompose (di:kəm'pouz) vt 1 spalten. 2 scheiden. vi sich auflösen. 2 verfaulen.

decorate ('dekəreit) vt 1 schmücken, dekorieren. 2 tapezieren, streichen. 3 auszeichnen. **decoration** n 1 Schmuck m. Verzierung f. 2 Ausstattung f. 3 Auszeichnung f. Order m.

decoy (n 'di:kɔi; v di'kɔi) n Lockvogel, Köder m. vt locken, verleiten.

decrease (di'kri:s) n Abnahme f. Verminderung f. vt verringern, vermindern. vi abnehmen, sich vermindern.

decree (di'kri:) n Erlaß, Bescheid m.

decrepit (di:krepit) adj 1 hinfällig. 2 verfallen.

dedicate ('dedikeit) vt 1 (ein)weihen. 2 widmen. **dedicated** adj pflichtgetreu. **dedication** n Widmung, Hingabe f.

deduce (di'dju:s) vt folgern, schließen, ableiten.

deduct (di'dʌkt) vt abziehen, abrechnen. **deduction** n 1 Abzug m. 2 Schlußfolgerung f.

deed (di:d) n 1 Tat, Handlung f. 2 Urkunde f.

deep (di:p) adj tief. n Tiefe f. **deep-freeze** n Tiefkühltruhe f. vt tiefkühlen.

deer (diə) n invar Reh neu.

deface (di'feis) vt entstellen, verunstalten.

default (di'fɔ:lt) n Nichterfüllung, Unterlassung f. Versäumnis neu. vi in Verzug geraten.

defeat (di'fi:t) n Niederlage f. vt schlagen, überwinden, besiegen.

defect (n 'di:fekt; v di'fekt) n Mangel, Fehler m. vi übertreten. **defection** n Treubruch m. **defective** adj fehlerhaft, mangelhaft.

defend (di'fend) vt verteidigen. **defence** n Verteidigung f. **defender** n Verteidiger m.

defer (di'fə:) vt verschieben. vi nachgeben, sich beugen. **deference** n 1 Nachgiebigkeit f. 2 (Hoch)Achtung f. **deferential** adj rücksichtsvoll.

defiant (di'faiənt) adj trotzig, herausfordernd. **defiance** n Trotz, Widerstand m. Widerspenstigkeit f.

deficient (di'fiʃənt) adj mangelhaft, unzulänglich. **deficiency** n Mangel m. Unzulänglichkeit f.

deficit ('defisit) n Fehlbetrag, Ausfall m.

define (di'fain) vt 1 definieren, festlegen, bestimmen. 2 abgrenzen. **definition** n 1 Definition f. 2 Deutlichkeit f.

definite ('defənit) *adj* bestimmt, unbedingt.

deflate (di'fleit) *vt* entleeren, Luft ablassen aus.

deform (di'fɔːm) *vt* deformieren, verunstalten.

defraud (di'frɔːd) *vt* betrügen.

defrost (di'frɔst) *vt* entfrosten.

deft (deft) *adj* gewandt, geschickt.

defunct (di'fʌŋkt) *adj* **1** verstorben. **2** nicht mehr bestehend.

defy (di'fai) *vt* **1** trotzen. **2** herausfordern.

degenerate (di'dʒenəreit) *vi* entarten, degenerieren. **degeneration** *n* Entartung, Degeneration *f*.

degrade (di'greid) *vt* degradieren, erniedrigen.

degree (di'griː) *n* **1** Grad *m*. **2** Stufe *f*. **3** *educ* Grad *m*.

dehydrate (di'haidreit) *vt* trocknen, das Wasser entziehen.

deity ('deiiti) *n* Gott *m*. Gottheit *f*.

dejected (di'dʒektid) *adj* niedergeschlagen, traurig.

delay (di'lei) *n* Verzögerung, Verspätung *f*. *vt* verzögern, verschieben. *vi* zögern.

delegate (*n* 'deligət; *v* 'deligeit) *n* Delegierte(r), Abgeordnete(r) *m*. *vt* **1** bevollmächtigen, delegieren. **2** übertragen.

delete (di'liːt) *vt* (aus)streichen.

deliberate (*adj* di'libərət; *v* di'libəreit) *adj* absichtlich. *vi* nachdenken, überlegen. **deliberation** *n* Überlegung.

delicate ('delikət) *adj* **1** zart, fein. **2** empfindlich. **delicacy** *n* **1** Delikatesse *f*. **2** Feinheit *f*. **delicatessen** *n* Feinkostgeschäft *neu*.

delicious (di'liʃəs) *adj* köstlich, herrlich.

delight (di'lait) *n* Freude, Wonne *f*. *vt* erfreuen, entzücken. *vi* Freude haben, entzückt sein.

delinquency (di'liŋkwənsi) *n* Kriminalität *f*. **delinquent** *adj* kriminell. *n* Verbrecher *m*.

deliver (di'livə) *vt* **1** (ab-, aus-)liefern, austragen. **2** *med* entbinden. **3** befreien. **deliverance** *n* Befreiung *f*. **delivery** *n* **1** (Aus)Lieferung *f*. **2** *med* Entbindung *f*. **3** *sport* Wurf *m*.

delta ('deltə) *n* Delta *neu*.

delude (di'luːd) *vt* täuschen, irreführen. **delusion** *n* Wahn *m*. Täuschung *f*.

delve (delv) *vi* sich vertiefen.

demand (di'maːnd) *n* Forderung *f*. Verlangen *neu*. *vt* fordern, verlangen.

democracy (di'mɔkrəsi) *n* Demokratie *f*. **democratic** *adj* demokratisch.

demolish (di'mɔliʃ) *vt* abreißen, zerstören. **demolition** *n* Abreißen *neu*.

demon ('diːmən) *n* Dämon *m*.

demonstrate ('demənstreit) *vi,vt* demonstrieren, zeigen. **demonstration** *n* Demonstration *f*.

demoralize (di'mɔrəlaiz) *vt* entmutigen.

demure (di'mjuə) *adj* zurückhaltend, zimperlich.

den (den) *n* Höhle *f*. Loch *neu*.

denial (di'naiəl) *n* **1** Verweigerung *f*. **2** (Ab)Leugnung *f*.

denim ('denim) *n* Drillich *m*.

Denmark ('denmaːk) *n* Dänemark *neu*.

denomination (dinɔmi'neiʃən) *n* **1** *rel* Konfession *f*. **2** Einheit *f*. **3** Bezeichnung *f*.

denote (di'nout) *vt* kennzeichnen, bedeuten.

denounce (di'nauns) *vt* anzeigen, denunzieren.

dense (dens) *adj* **1** dicht. **2** beschränkt. **density** *n* Dichte *f*.

dent (dent) *vt* einbeulen. *n* Beule *f*.

dental ('dentl) *adj* zahnärztlich, Zahn—. **dentist** *n* Zahnarzt *m*. **denture** *n* Zahnprothese *f*.

denunciation (di'nʌnsiei ʃən) *n* Verurteilung, Denunziation *f*.

deny (di'nai) *vt* **1** leugnen, verneinen. **2** verweigern.

deodorant (diː'oudərənt) *n* Desodorans *neu*.

depart (di'paːt) *vi* **1** weggehen, abfahren. **2** abweichen. **departure** *n* Abfahrt *f*. Abflug *m*.

department (di'paːtmənt) *n* Abteilung *f*. **department store** *n* Warenhaus, Kaufhaus *neu*.

depend (di'pend) *vi* **1** abhängen. **2** ankommen. **dependant** *n* Abhängige(r), Angehörige(r) *m*. **dependence** *n* Abhängigkeit *f*. **dependent** *adj* abhängig.

depict (di'pikt) *vt* **1** zeichnen. **2** schildern.

deplete (di'pliːt) *vt* **1** (ent)leeren. **2** erschöpfen.

deplore (di'plɔː) *vt* bedauern, mißbilligen.

deport (di'pɔːt) *vt* deportieren, ausweisen. **deportation** *n* Deportation, Ausweisung *f*.

depose (di'pouz) *vt* absetzen.

deposit (di'pɔzit) *n* **1** Anzahlung *f*. **2** Niederschlag *m*. *vt* **1** niederlegen. **2** hinterlegen, anzahlen.

depot ('depou) *n* Depot, Lagerhaus *neu*.

deprave (di'preiv) *vt* (moralisch) verderben. **depraved** *adj* verdorben. **depravity** *n* Verdorbenheit *f*.

depreciate (di'priːʃieit) *vt* entwerten. *vi* im Wert sinken.

depress (di'pres) *vt* **1** bedrücken. **2** niederschlagen, deprimieren. **depression** *n* **1** Depression *f*. **2** Vertiefung *f*. **3** Tiefdruckgebiet *neu*.

deprive (di'praiv) *vt* berauben, vorenthalten. **deprivation** *n* Beraubung, Verlust *f*.

depth (depθ) n Tiefe f. **in depth** ausführlich, gründlich.

deputy ('depjuti) n Stellvertreter m.

derail (di'reil) vt entgleisen.

derelict ('derəlikt) adj verlassen, aufgegeben, verfallen.

deride (di'raid) vt verlachen, verhöhnen.

derive (di'raiv) vt ableiten, herleiten. vi abstammen. **derivation** n Ableitung, Abstammung f.

derogatory (di'rɔgətri) adj herabsetzend, abfällig.

descend (di'send) vi 1 herunterkommen. 2 absteigen. 3 aussteigen. 4 sinken. 5 herkommen. **descendant** n Nachkomme m. **descent** (di'sent) n 1 Abstieg m. 2 Niedergang m. 3 Herkunft f.

describe (di'skraib) vt beschreiben. **description** n Beschreibung f.

desert[1] ('dezət) n Wüste, Einöde f.

desert[2] (di'zə:t) vt verlassen. vi desertieren. **deserter** n mil Deserteur m.

desert[3] (di'zə:t) n Verdienst m.

deserve (di'zə:v) vt verdienen.

design (di'zain) n 1 Entwurf m. Zeichnung f. 2 Konstruktion f. 3 Muster neu. 4 Absicht f. Plan m. vt entwerfen, planen.

designate ('dezigneit) vt bezeichnen, vorsehen.

desire (di'zaiə) vt 1 wünschen. 2 begehren. n 1 Wunsch, Wille m. 2 Begierde f. Verlangen neu.

desk (desk) n Pult neu. Schreibtisch m.

desolate ('desələt) adj 1 wüst, öde. 2 traurig.

despair (di'spɛə) vi verzweifeln. n Verzweiflung f.

desperate ('despərət) adj verzweifelt, hoffnungslos.

despise (di'spaiz) vt verachten. **despicable** adj verächtlich.

despite (di'spait) prep trotz, ungeachtet.

despondent (di'spɔndənt) adj mutlos, verzweifelt.

dessert (di'zə:t) n Nachtisch m. **dessertspoon** n Dessertlöffel m.

destine ('destin) vt bestimmen, ausersehen. **destination** n Ziel neu. Bestimmungsort m. **destiny** n Schicksal neu.

destitute ('destitju:t) adj mittellos, verarmt.

destroy (di'strɔi) vt zerstören. **destroyer** n Zerstörer m. **destruction** n 1 Zerstörung f. 2 Verwüstung f.

detach (di'tætʃ) vt loslösen, abtrennen. **detached** adj 1 abgetrennt. 2 objektiv. **detachment** n 1 Abtrennung f. 2 Objektivität f.

detail ('di:teil) n Detail neu. Einzelheit f. **in detail** ausführlich. vt detaillieren. **detailed** adj ausführlich.

detain (di'tein) vt zurückhalten, festhalten.

detect (di'tekt) vt 1 entdecken, (heraus)finden. 2 spuren, empfinden. **detective** n Detektiv m.

détente (dei'tɑ:nt) n pol Entspannung f.

detention (di'tenʃən) n Haft f.

deter (di'tə:) vt abschrecken. **deterrent** n Abschreckmittel neu. Abschreckung f. adj abschreckend.

detergent (di'tə:dʒənt) n Waschmittel neu.

deteriorate (di'tiəriəreit) vi sich verschlechtern. **deterioration** n Verschlechterung f.

determine (di'tə:min) vt 1 entschließen, entscheiden. 2 bestimmen, feststellen. **determination** n Entschlossenheit f.

detest (di'test) vt hassen.

detonate ('detəneit) vi,(vt) explodieren (lassen).

detour ('di:tuə) n Umweg m.

detract (di'trækt) vi herabsetzen. vt entziehen.

devalue (di'vælju:) vt entwerten. **devaluation** n Entwertung f.

devastate ('devəsteit) vt verwüsten, verheeren. **devastation** n Verwüstung f.

develop (di'veləp) vt entwickeln. **development** n Entwicklung f.

deviate ('di:vieit) vi abweichen. **deviation** n Abweichung f. **devious** adj unaufrichtig.

device (di'vais) n 1 Plan m. 2 Apparat m. Gerät neu.

devil ('devəl) n Teufel m.

devise (di'vaiz) vt,vi ausdenken, erfinden.

devoid (di'vɔid) adj ohne, frei von.

devote (di'vout) vt widmen. **devote oneself** sich hingeben. **devotee** n 1 Verehrer m. 2 Anhänger m. **devotion** n Hingabe f.

devour (di'vauə) vt 1 fressen, verschlingen. 2 verzehren. 3 vernichten.

devout (di'vaut) adj fromm, andächtig.

dew (dju:) n Tau m.

dexterous ('dekstrəs) adj gewandt. **dexterity** n Gewandtheit f.

diabetes (daiə'bi:tiz) n Zuckerkrankheit f. **diabetic** adj zuckerkrank. n Zuckerkranke(r) m.

diagonal (dai'agənl) adj diagonal.

diagram ('daiəgræm) n Diagramm, Schema neu.

dial (dail) n 1 (telephone) Wählscheibe f. 2 Ziffernscheibe f. vt,vi wählen.

dialect ('daiəlekt) n Mundart f. Dialekt m.

dialogue

dialogue ('daɪəlɒg) n Dialog m. Zwiegespräch neu.

diameter (daɪ'æmɪtə) n Durchmesser m.

diamond ('daɪəmənd) n Diamant m.

diaphragm ('daɪəfræm) n 1 Membran f. 2 anat Zwerchfell neu. 3 phot Blende f.

diarrhoea (daɪə'rɪə) n Durchfall m.

diary ('daɪərɪ) n Tagebuch neu. Kalender m.

dice (daɪs) n pl or s Würfel m. vi würfeln. vt cul in Würfel schneiden.

dictate (v dɪk'teɪt; n 'dɪkteɪt) vt diktieren. n Gebot neu. **dictation** n 1 Vorschrift f. Diktieren neu. 2 Diktat neu. **dictator** n 1 Diktator m. **dictatorship** n Diktatur f.

dictionary ('dɪkʃənrɪ) n Wörterbuch neu.

did (dɪd) v see **do**.

die (daɪ) vi 1 sterben. 2 (of animals) eingehen.

diesel ('diːzəl) n tech Diesel m. **diesel engine** Dieselmotor m.

diet ('daɪət) n 1 Ernährung, Kost f. 2 Diät f.

differ ('dɪfə) vi 1 (sich) unterscheiden. 2 abweichen. **difference** n Unterschied m. Verschiedenheit f. **different** adj verschieden, ander(s).

difficult ('dɪfɪkəlt) adj schwierig, schwer, mühsam. **difficulty** n Schwierigkeit, Mühe f.

dig* (dɪg) vt,vi graben.

digest (v daɪ'dʒest; n 'daɪdʒest) vt verdauen. n Auslese f. **digestion** n Verdauung f.

digit ('dɪdʒɪt) n 1 Finger m. 2 math Stelle f.

dignified ('dɪgnɪfaɪd) adj würdevoll.

dignity ('dɪgnɪtɪ) n Würde, Ehre f.

dilapidated (dɪ'læpɪdeɪtɪd) adj verfallen, schäbig.

dilemma (dɪ'lemə) n Dilemma neu. Verlegenheit f.

diligent ('dɪlɪdʒənt) adj 1 sorgfältig. 2 fleißig.

dilute (daɪ'luːt) vt verdünnen, wässern.

dim (dɪm) adj 1 düster, trübe. 2 schwach. vt verdunkeln.

dimension (dɪ'menʃən) n Dimension f. Ausmaß neu.

diminish (dɪ'mɪnɪʃ) vt vermindern, verringern. vi sich vermindern, abnehmen.

diminutive (dɪ'mɪnjutɪv) adj klein, winzig.

dimple ('dɪmpəl) n Grübchen neu.

din (dɪn) n Lärm m. Getöse neu.

dine (daɪn) vi speisen, essen. **dining car** n Speisewagen m. **dining room** n Speisezimmer, Eßzimmer neu.

dinghy ('dɪŋɪ) n Beiboot neu.

dingy ('dɪndʒɪ) adj schmutzig, schäbig.

dinner ('dɪnə) n (Haupt)Mahlzeit f. Abendessen, Mittagessen neu.

diocese ('daɪəsɪs) n Diözese f.

dip (dɪp) vt 1 eintauchen. 2 (one's headlights) abblenden. vi untertauchen. n 1 Vertiefung f. 2 Eintauchen neu.

diphthong ('dɪfθɒŋ) n Doppellaut m.

diploma (dɪ'pləumə) n Diplom neu.

diplomacy (dɪ'pləuməsɪ) n Diplomatie f. **diplomat** n Diplomat m. **diplomatic** adj diplomatisch.

direct (dɪ'rekt) adj 1 direkt. 2 gerade, unmittelbar. vt 1 führen, leiten. 2 richten. 3 anweisen. **direction** n 1 Richtung f. 2 pl Vorschrift, Anweisung f. **direct object** n direktes Objekt neu. **director** n Direktor m. Leiter m. **directory** n Telephonbuch neu.

dirt (dəːt) n Dreck, Schmutz m. **dirty** adj schmutzig.

disability (dɪsə'bɪlɪtɪ) n Unfähigkeit, Behinderung f. **disabled** adj (körper)behindert.

disadvantage (dɪsəd'vɑːntɪdʒ) n Nachteil m. **disadvantageous** adj nachteilig.

disagree (dɪsə'griː) vi 1 nicht übereinstimmen, nicht einig sein. 2 sich widersprechen. 3 (sich) streiten. **disagreement** n 1 Uneinigkeit, Unstimmigkeit f. 2 (Meinungs)Verschiedenheit f. Streit m.

disappear (dɪsə'pɪə) vi verschwinden. **disappearance** n Verschwinden neu.

disappoint (dɪsə'pɔɪnt) vt enttäuschen. **disappointment** n Enttäuschung f.

disapprove (dɪsə'pruːv) vt,vi mißbilligen. **disapproval** n Mißbilligung f.

disarm (dɪs'ɑːm) vt,vi entwaffnen, abrüsten. **disarmament** n Abrüstung f.

disaster (dɪ'zɑːstə) n Unglück neu. Katastrophe f. **disastrous** adj unglücklich, schrecklich.

disc (dɪsk) n 1 Scheibe f. 2 Schallplatte f. **disc jockey** n Schallplattenansager m.

discard (dɪs'kɑːd) vt ablegen, aufgeben.

discern (dɪ'səːn) vt 1 unterscheiden. 2 wahrnehmen.

discharge (dɪs'tʃɑːdʒ) vt erfüllen. n 1 Entlassung f. 2 Erfüllung f. 3 med Absonderung f.

disciple (dɪ'saɪpəl) n Schüler, Jünger m.

discipline ('dɪsəplɪn) n 1 Disziplin f. 2 Wissenszweig m. vt bestrafen, zurechtweisen.

disclaim (dɪs'kleɪm) vt 1 verzichten auf. 2 nicht anerkennen, abstreiten.

disclose (dɪs'kləuz) vt offenbaren, enthüllen.

discomfort (dɪs'kʌmfət) n Unbehagen neu.

disconnect (diskə'nekt) *vt* trennen, unterbrechen.

disconsolate (dis'kɔnsələt) *adj* trostlos.

discontinue (diskən'tinju:) *vt* unterbrechen. *vi* aufhören.

discord ('diskɔ:d) *n* Uneinigkeit *f.* Mißklang *m.*

discotheque ('diskətek) *n* Diskothek *f.*

discount ('diskaunt) *n* Rabatt *m.*

discourage (dis'kʌridʒ) *vt* 1 abraten. 2 entmutigen.

discover (dis'kʌvə) *vt* 1 entdecken. 2 herausfinden, erkennen. **discovery** *n* Entdeckung *f.*

discredit (dis'kredit) *vt* 1 in Verruf bringen. 2 anzweifeln. *n* 1 schlechter Ruf *m.* 2 Zweifel *m.*

discreet (dis'kri:t) *adj* besonnen, diskret. **discretion** *n* 1 Belieben *neu.* 2 Takt *m.*

discrepancy (dis'krepənsi) *n* Widerspruch *m.* Unstimmigkeit *f.*

discriminate (dis'krimineit) *vi* unterschiedlich behandeln. *vt* unterscheiden, absondern. **discrimination** *n* Diskriminierung, Unterscheidung *f.*

discus ('diskəs) *n sport* Diskus *m.*

discuss (dis'kʌs) *vt* besprechen, diskutieren, erörtern. **discussion** *n* Erörterung, Diskussion *f.*

disease (di'zi:z) *n* Krankheit *f.*

disembark (disim'ba:k) *vi* ausschiffen.

disengage (disin'geidʒ) *vt* 1 (los)lösen, freimachen. 2 loskuppeln. *vi* sich freimachen.

disfigure (dis'figə) *vt* verunstalten.

disgrace (dis'greis) *n* 1 Schande *f.* 2 Ungnade *f. vt* schänden, entehren. **disgraceful** *adj* schändlich.

disgruntled (dis'grʌntəld) *adj* mürrisch.

disguise (dis'gaiz) *vt* 1 verkleiden. 2 verhüllen. *n* Verkleidung *f.* **in disguise** verkleidet.

disgust (dis'gʌst) *n* Ekel *m. vt* anekeln. **disgusting** *adj* ekelhaft, widerlich.

dish (diʃ) *n* 1 *cul* Gericht *neu.* 2 Schüssel *f.* **dishcloth** *n* Abwaschtuch *neu.*

dishearten (dis'ha:tn) *vt* entmutigen.

dishevelled (di'ʃevəld) *adj* zerzaust.

dishonest (dis'ɔnist) *adj* unehrlich. **dishonesty** *n* Unehrlichkeit *f.*

dishonour (dis'ɔnə) *vt* entehren. *n* Schande, Unehre *f.*

disillusion (disi'lu:ʒən) *n* Enttäuschung, Ernüchterung *f. vt* ernüchtern, enttäuschen. **disillusioned** *adj* enttäuscht, verbittert, ernüchtert.

disinfect (disin'fekt) *vt* desinfizieren. **disinfectant** *n* Desinfektionsmittel *neu.*

disinherit (disin'herit) *vt* enterben.

disintegrate (dis'intigreit) (*vi,*)*vt* (sich) auflösen, (sich) zersetzen. *vi* verfallen. **disintegration** *n* Auflösung, Zersetzung *f.*

disinterested (dis'intrəstid) *adj* unbeteiligt.

dislike (dis'laik) *vt* nicht mögen. *n* Abneigung *f.*

dislocate ('dislakeit) *vt med* verrenken. **dislocation** *n* Verrenkung *f.*

dislodge (dis'lɔdʒ) *vt* 1 entfernen. 2 vertreiben.

disloyal (dis'lɔiəl) *adj* untreu.

dismal ('dizməl) *adj* traurig, trübe.

dismantle (dis'mæntl) *vt* demontieren, auseinandernehmen.

dismay (dismei) *n* Bestürzung *f. vt* bestürzen.

dismiss (dis'mis) *vt* 1 entlassen. 2 gehen lassen. 3 abweisen. **dismissal** *n* Entlassung *f.*

dismount (dis'maunt) *vi* absteigen.

disobey (disə'bei) *vt* ungehorsam sein gegen, nicht gehorchen. **disobedience** *n* Ungehorsam *m.* **disobedient** *adj* ungehorsam.

disorder (dis'ɔ:də) *n* 1 Unordnung *f.* 2 Unruhe *f.* 3 *med* Störung *f.*

disorganized (dis'ɔ:gənaizd) *adj* in Unordnung, aufgelöst.

disown (dis'oun) *vt* nicht anerkennen, verleugnen.

disparage (dis'pæridʒ) *vt* verunglimpfen, herabsetzen.

dispassionate (dis'pæʃənət) *adj* 1 leidenschaftslos. 2 sachlich.

dispatch (dis'pætʃ) *n* Absendung, Abfertigung *f. vt* (eilig) wegschicken, absenden.

dispel (dis'pel) *vt* zerstreuen, vertreiben.

dispense (dis'pens) *vt* verteilen, ausgeben. **dispense with** entbehren, verzichten auf. **dispensary** *n* Arzneiausgabe, Apotheke *f.*

disperse (dis'pə:s) (*vi,*)*vt* (sich) zerstreuen, (sich) verteilen. **dispersal** *n* Zerstreuung, Vertreibung *f.*

displace (dis'pleis) *vt* 1 verschieben. 2 *naut* verdrängen. **displacement** *n* Verrückung, Verdrängung *f.*

display (dis'plei) *n* 1 Auslage *f.* 2 *mil* Vorführung *f. vt* 1 zur Schau stellen. 2 zeigen.

displease (dis'pli:z) *vt* mißfallen. **displeasure** *n* Mißfallen *neu.*

dispose (dis'pouz) *vt* anordnen. **dispose of** beseitigen, abschaffen. **disposal** *n* 1 Verfügung *f.* 2 Erledigung *f.* **disposition** *n* 1 Neigung *f.* 2 Veranlagung *f.*

disproportion (disprə'pɔ:ʃən) *n* Mißverhältnis *neu.* **disproportionate** *adj* 1 unverhältnismäßig. 2 übertrieben.

disprove (dis'pru:v) *vt* widerlegen.

dispute (dis'pju:t) *n* Streit *m*. Debatte *f*. *vi* (sich) streiten. *vt* bestreiten.

disqualify (dis'kwɔlifai) *vt* 1 ausschließen, disqualifizieren. 2 unfähig erklären.

disregard (disri'gɑ:d) *vt* 1 mißachten. 2 außer Acht lassen.

disreputable (dis'repjutəbəl) *adj* verrufen.

disrespect (disri'spekt) *n* Respektlosigkeit *f*.

disrupt (dis'rʌpt) *vt* 1 spalten, zerbrechen. 2 unterbrechen, stören.

dissatisfy (di'sætisfai) *vt* nicht zufriedenstellen, mißfallen.

dissect (di'sekt) *vt* sezieren, zergliedern.

dissent (di'sent) *n* abweichende Meinung. *vi* anderer Meinung sein.

dissimilar (di'similə) *adj* verschieden, unähnlich.

dissociate (di'souʃieit) *vt* trennen. **dissociate oneself** sich lossagen, abrücken.

dissolve (di'zɔlv) *vt* auflösen. *vi* sich auflösen, schmelzen.

dissuade (di'sweid) *vt* abraten.

distance ('distəns) *n* Entfernung *f*. Abstand *m*. **distant** *adj* weit, entfernt.

distaste (dis'teist) *n* Abneigung *f*. **distasteful** *adj* widerlich, unangenehm.

distil (dis'til) *vt* destillieren.

distinct (dis'tiŋkt) *adj* 1 verschieden. 2 deutlich. 3 ausgeprägt. **distinction** *n* 1 Unterschied *m*. 2 Auszeichnung *f*. 3 Würde *f*. **distinctive** *adj* deutlich, kennzeichnend.

distinguish (dis'tiŋgwiʃ) *vt,vi* unterscheiden. **distinguish oneself** sich auszeichnen.

distort (dis'tɔ:t) *vt* verzerren.

distract (dis'trækt) *vt* 1 ablenken. 2 beunruhigen.

distraught (dis'trɔ:t) *adj* 1 erregt, verwirrt. 2 wahnsinnig.

distress (dis'tres) *n* 1 Not *f*. Elend *neu*. 2 Leid *neu*. Schmerz *m*. *vt* beunruhigen, quälen.

distribute (dis'tribju:t) *vt* verteilen, ausgeben. **distribution** *n* Verteilung, Verbreitung *f*.

district ('distrikt) *n* Bezirk *m*. Gegend *f*.

distrust (dis'trʌst) *n* Mißtrauen. *vt* mißtrauen.

disturb (dis'tə:b) *vt* 1 stören. 2 beunruhigen. **disturbance** *n* 1 Störung *f*. 2 Unruhe *f*.

ditch (ditʃ) *n* Graben *m*. *vt inf* wegwerfen.

ditto ('ditou) *adv* dito, desgleichen.

divan (di'væn) *n* Diwan *m*.

dive (daiv) *n* 1 Kopfsprung *m*. 2 *aviat* Sturzflug *m*. *vi* 1 tauchen. 2 sich stürzen. 3 einen Kopfsprung machen. 4 einen Sturzflug machen. **diving board** *n* Sprungbrett *neu*.

diverge (dai'və:dʒ) *vi* 1 auseinanderlaufen, sich trennen. 2 abweichen.

diverse (dai'və:s) *adj* verschieden, vielfältig.

divert (dai'və:t) *vt* 1 ablenken. 2 umleiten. 3 unterhalten. **diversion** *n* 1 Umleitung *f*. 2 Zerstreuung *f*.

divide (di'vaid) *vt* 1 teilen. 2 verteilen. 3 zerteilen, spalten. **divisible** *adj* teilbar. **division** *n* 1 Teilung *f*. 2 Trennung *f*. 3 *mil,sport* Division *f*.

dividend ('dividend) *n* Dividende *f*. (Gewinn-) Anteil *m*.

divine (di'vain) *adj* 1 göttlich, Gottes— **divinity** *n* 1 Gottheit *f*. 2 Theologie *f*.

divorce (di'vɔ:s) *n* Scheidung *f*. *vi* scheiden, sich scheiden lassen.

divulge (di'vʌldʒ) *vt* enthüllen, bekanntmachen.

dizzy ('dizi) *adj* 1 schwindelig. 2 unbesonnen.

do [1] (du:) *vt* 1 tun, machen. 2 ausführen. *vi* tun, handeln. **do away with** abschaffen, beseitigen.

docile ('dousail) *adj* gelehrig, fügsam.

dock [1] (dɔk) *n* 1 Dock *neu*. 2 Hafenanlage *f*. **dockyard** *n* Werft *f*.

dock [2] (dɔk) *vt* 1 stutzen. 2 vermindern.

dock [3] (dɔk) *n law* Anklagebank *f*.

doctor ('dɔktə) *n* 1 *med* Doktor, Arzt *m*. 2 *educ* Doktor *m*.

doctrine ('dɔktrin) *n* Lehre, Doktrin *f*.

document ('dɔkjumənt) *n* Urkunde *f*. Dokument, Schriftstück *neu*. *vt* dokumentieren, beurkunden. **documentary** *n* Dokumentarfilm *m*. *adj* dokumentarisch, schriftlich.

dodge (dɔdʒ) *vi* ausweichen. *vt* vermeiden. *n* 1 Seitensprung *m*. 2 Trick, Kniff *m*.

does (dʌz) *v* see **do**.

dog (dɔg) *n* Hund *m*. *vt* nachspüren. **dogged** *adj* verbissen.

dogma ('dɔgmə) *n* Glaubenssatz *m*. Dogma *neu*. **dogmatic** *adj* dogmatisch.

dole (doul) *n* Arbeitslosenunterstützung *f*. *v* **dole out** austeilen, ausgeben.

doll (dɔl) *n* Puppe *f*.

dollar ('dɔlə) *n* Dollar *m*.

Dolomites ('dɔləmaits) *n* Dolomiten *pl*.

dolphin ('dɔlfin) *n* Delphin *m*.

domain (də'mein) *n* Bereich *m*.

dome (doum) *n* Kuppel *f*.

domestic (də'mestik) *adj* 1 häuslich. 2 inländisch. **domestic animal** *n* Haustier *neu*. **domesticate** *vt* 1 zähmen. 2 häuslich machen.

dominate ('dɔmineit) vt beherrschen, herrschen über, dominieren. **dominance** n (Vor)Herrschaft f. **dominant** adj (vor)herrschend. **domination** n Herrschaft f. **domineer** vi den Herrn spielen.

dominion (dɔ'miniən) n Herrschaft f.

donate (dou'neit) vt schenken. vi eine Schenkung machen.

done (dʌn) v see **do**. adj fertig. interj abgemacht!

donkey ('dɔŋki) n Esel m.

donor ('dounə) n Spender m.

doom (du:m) n 1 Schicksal, Verhängnis neu. 2 Verderben neu. vt verdammen. **doomed** adj verloren, verdammt.

door (dɔ:) n Tür f. **door to door** von Haus zu Haus. **out of doors** draußen, im Freien. **doorbell** n Türklingel f. **doorhandle** n Türgriff m. Türklinke f. **doorstep** n Türschwelle f. **doorway** n Türeingang m.

dope (doup) n sl Rauschgift neu.

dormant ('dɔ:mənt) adj schlafend, untätig.

dormitory ('dɔ:mitri) n Schlafsaal m.

dormouse ('dɔ:maus) n, pl **dormice** n Haselmaus f.

dose (dous) n Dosis f. vt dosieren. **dosage** n Dosierung f.

dot (dɔt) n Punkt m. vt 1 punktieren. 2 verstreuen.

dote (dout) vi **dote on** 1 schwärmen für. 2 (zärtlich) lieben.

double ('dʌbəl) adj doppelt, Doppel—. adv doppelt, zu zweien. n 1 Doppelte neu. 2 Doppelgänger m. (vi),vt (sich) verdoppeln. **double bass** n Kontrabaß m. **doublecross** vt inf hintergehen, betrügen.

doubt (daut) n Zweifel m. vi zweifeln. vt bezweifeln. **no doubt** zweifellos, ohne Zweifel, gewiß. **doubtful** adj zweifelhaft, ungewiß.

dough (dou) n Teig m. **doughnut** n Berliner Pfannkuchen m.

dove (dʌv) n Taube f.

dowdy ('daudi) adj nachlässig, schlampig.

down[1] (daun) adv hinunter, herab, abwärts, nieder.

down[2] (daun) n Daunen f pl.

downcast ('daunka:st) adj niedergeschlagen.

downfall ('daunfɔ:l) n 1 Fall m. 2 Niedergang m.

downhearted (daun'hɑ:tid) adj mutlos, niedergeschlagen.

downhill ('daunhil) adv bergab. adj Abwärts—.

downpour ('daunpɔ:) n Regenguß m.

downright ('daunrait) adj offen, völlig.

downstairs (daun'stɛəz) adv 1 nach unten, die Treppe hinunter. 2 unten. adj unter, im Erdgeschoß (liegend).

downstream (daun'stri:m) adv flußabwärts.

downtrodden ('dauntrɔdn) adj getreten, unterdrückt.

downward ('daunwəd) adj Abwärts—.

downwards ('daunwədz) adv abwärts.

dowry ('dauəri) n Mitgift f.

doze (douz) n Nickerchen neu. kurzer Schlaf m. vi dösen. **dozy** adj schläfrig.

dozen ('dʌzn) n Dutzend neu.

drab (dræb) adj 1 gelbgrau. 2 eintönig, farblos.

draft (drɑ:ft) n 1 Skizze f. Entwurf m. 2 comm Abhebung f. 3 mil Aushebung f. vt 1 entwerfen. 2 (zur Armee) einziehen.

drag (dræg) (vi),vt (sich) schleppen, (sich) ziehen. n sl langweilige Sache.

dragon ('drægən) n Drachen m. **dragonfly** n Libelle f.

drain (drein) n 1 Abfluß m. 2 Abflußrohr neu. Gosse f. vt 1 entwässern. 2 ableiten. vi abfliessen. **drainage** n Abfluß m. Entwässerung f. **draining-board** n Abtropfbrett neu. **drainpipe** n Abflußrohr neu.

drake (dreik) n Enterich m.

dram (dræm) n Schluck m. Gläschen neu.

drama ('drɑ:mə) n Drama neu. **dramatic** adj 1 dramatisch. 2 spannend. **dramatist** n Dramatiker m. **dramatize** vt dramatisieren.

drank (dræŋk) v see **drink**.

drape (dreip) vt behängen, drapieren. vi schön fallen.

draper ('dreipə) n Tuchhändler m. **drapery** n 1 Tuchwaren f pl. 2 Tuchhandel m.

drastic ('dræstik) adj drastisch, gründlich.

draught (drɑ:ft) n 1 Zug m. 2 Entwurf m. 3 pl Damespiel neu. **draught beer** n Faßbier neu. **draughtsman** n Zeichner m. **draughty** adj zugig.

draw* (drɔ:) vt 1 ziehen. 2 zeichnen. 3 anziehen. 4 dehnen. 5 (money) abheben. vi 1 ziehen. 2 zeichnen. 3 sport unentschieden spielen. **draw near** sich nähern. ~n 1 Ziehen neu. Zug m. 2 sport Unentschieden neu. **drawback** n Nachteil m. **drawbridge** n Zugbrücke f. **drawer** n 1 Zeichner m. 2 Schublade f. **drawing** n Zeichnung f. **drawing-board** n Zeichenbrett neu. **drawingpin** n Heftzwecke f. **drawing room** n Salon m.

181

drawl (drɔːl) n gedehnte Sprechweise f. vi gedehnt sprechen.

dread (dred) n Furcht f. Schrecken m. vt fürchten, sich fürchten vor. **dreadful** adj furchtbar, schrecklich.

dream* (driːm) vi,vt träumen. n Traum m. **dreamer** n Träumer m. **dreamlike** adj traumhaft.

dreary (ˈdriəri) adj öde, eintönig.

dredge (dredʒ) vt 1 mit dem Schleppnetz fangen. 2 ausbaggern. **dredger** n Bagger m.

dregs (dregz) n pl Bodensatz m.

drench (drentʃ) vt durchnässen.

dress (dres) n 1 Kleidung f. Anzug m. 2 (Damen)Kleid neu. 3 Gewand neu. vi sich anziehen. vt 1 ankleiden. 2 schmücken. 3 bearbeiten. **dress circle** n Th erster Rang m. **dressing** n 1 Ankleiden neu. 2 med Verband m. 3 cul Zutat, Soße f. **dressing-gown** n Morgenrock m. **dressing-room** n Ankleidezimmer neu. **dressing-table** n Toilettentisch m. **dressmaker** n Damenschneiderin f.

dresser[1] (ˈdresə) n Anrichter, Dekorateur m.

dresser[2] (ˈdresə) n Küchenschrank m.

drew (druː) v see **draw**.

dribble (ˈdribəl) vi 1 tröpfeln. 2 geifern.

drier (ˈdraiə) n Trockner m.

drift (drift) n 1 Treiben neu. 2 (Schnee)Wehe f. 3 Treibenlassen neu. 4 Tendenz f. vi 1 (dahin)treiben. 2 getrieben werden.

drill (dril) n 1 Bohrer m. 2 mil Exerzieren neu. vt,vi 1 bohren. 2 mil exerzieren.

drink* (driŋk) vi,vt trinken. n 1 Getränk neu. 2 Drink m. 3 Alkohol m. **drinking water** n Trinkwasser neu.

drip (drip) vi tröpfeln, triefen, tropfen. n Tröpfeln neu. **drip-dry** adj bügelfrei.

drive* (draiv) n 1 Fahrt f. 2 Auffahrt f. 3 Trieb, Drang m. 4 tech Antrieb m. vt,vi 1 fahren. 2 treiben. **driver** n 1 Fahrer, Chauffeur m. 2 Führer m. 3 Treiber m. **driving licence** n Führerschein m. **driving school** n Fahrschule f. **driving test** n Fahrprüfung f.

drivel (ˈdrivəl) vi sabbern, geifern. n inf Unsinn m.

drizzle (ˈdrizəl) vi nieseln, sprühen. n Sprühregen, Nieselregen m.

drone[1] (droun) n 1 zool Drohne f. 2 Faulenzer m.

drone[2] (droun) n Summen neu. vi summen.

droop (druːp) vi 1 schlaff werden, herabhängen. 2 verwelken.

drop (drɔp) n 1 Tropfen m. 2 Fall, Sturz m. 3 Bonbon m. vi 1 tropfen. 2 fallen. vt fallen lassen, niederlassen. **drop someone a line** jemandem ein paar Zeilen schreiben. **drop out** vi ausscheiden, aufgeben. **dropout** n inf Aussteiger, Drop-out n.

drought (draut) n Trockenheit, Dürre f.

drove (drouv) v see **drive**.

drown (draun) vi ertrinken. vt ertränken, überschwemmen.

drowsy (ˈdrauzi) adj schläfrig.

drudge (drʌdʒ) n Kuli, Sklave m. vi schuften. **drudgery** n mühsame Arbeit, Plackerei f.

drug (drʌg) n 1 Droge f. 2 Rauschgift neu. **drug-addict** n Rauschgiftsüchtige(r) m.

drum (drʌm) n 1 Trommel f. 2 Faß neu. vt,(vi) trommeln (auf).

drunk (drʌŋk) v see **drink**. adj betrunken. **get drunk** sich betrinken. ~n Betrunkene(r) m. **drunken** adj betrunken.

dry (drai) adj 1 trocken. 2 (of wine) herb. vt (ab-, aus-)trocknen. vi trocknen. **dry-clean** vt chemisch reinigen. **dry-cleaning** n chemische Reinigung f.

dual (ˈdjuəl) adj doppelt, zweifach. **dual carriageway** n Doppelfahrbahn f.

dubious (ˈdjuːbiəs) adj zweifelhaft.

duchess (ˈdʌtʃis) n Herzogin f.

duck[1] (dʌk) n Ente f. **duckling** n Entchen neu.

duck[2] (dʌk) vi untertauchen. 2 sich ducken. vt untertauchen.

duct (dʌkt) n Röhre f. Kanal m.

dud (dʌd) n mil Blindgänger m. adj falsch, verfälscht, wertlos.

due (djuː) adj 1 fällig. 2 erwartet. 3 angemessen, gebührend. **due to** infolge, wegen, zuzuschreiben. adv genau, gerade. n 1 Recht neu. Anteil m. 2 pl Gebühren f pl.

duel (ˈdjuəl) n Duell neu.

duet (djuˈet) n mus Duett neu.

dug (dʌg) v see **dig**.

duke (djuːk) n Herzog m.

dull (dʌl) adj 1 stumpfsinnig. 2 matt. 3 (of light) schwach. 4 langweilig. 5 stumpf. vi,vt abstumpfen.

dumb (dʌm) adj 1 stumm. 2 inf dumm. **dumbfound** vt sprachlos machen, verblüffen.

dummy (ˈdʌmi) n 1 Attrappe f. 2 Puppe f. 3 (for a baby) Schnuller m.

dump (dʌmp) n Müllablageplatz m. vt abladen, auskippen.

dumpling (ˈdʌmpliŋ) n Kloß, Knödel m.

dunce (dʌns) n Dummkopf m.

dune (dju:n) n Düne f.

dung (dʌŋ) n Dung, Mist m.

dungeon ('dʌndʒən) n Kerker m.

duplicate (adj,n 'dju:plikət; v 'dju:plikeit) adj 1 doppelt. 2 Duplikat—. n Duplikat neu. Kopie f. vt 1 duplizieren. 2 verdoppeln.

durable ('djuərəbəl) adj dauerhaft.

duration (djuə'reiʃən) n Dauer f.

during ('djuəriŋ) prep während.

dusk (dʌsk) n (Abend)Dämmerung f. **dusky** adj 1 dämmerig. 2 dunkel.

dust (dʌst) n Staub m. vt abstauben. **dustbin** n Mülleimer m. **duster** n Staubtuch neu. **dustman** n Müllmann m. **dustpan** n Kehrichtschaufel f.

Dutch (dʌtʃ) adj holländisch. n (language) Holländisch neu. **Dutchman** n Holländer m.

dutiful ('dju:tifəl) adj pflichtgetreu.

duty ('dju:ti) n 1 Pflicht f. 2 Aufgabe f. 3 Zoll m. Abgabe f. **dutiful** adj pflichtbewußt. **duty-free** adj zollfrei, abgabenfrei.

duvet ('dju:vei) n Federbett neu. Daunendecke f.

dwarf (dwɔ:f) n Zwerg m. vt in den Schatten stellen.

dwell (dwel) vi 1 wohnen. 2 verweilen. **dwelling** n Wohnung f. Wohnsitz m.

dwindle ('dwindl) vi schwinden, abnehmen.

dye (dai) n Färbemittel neu. Farbe f. vt färben.

dyke (daik) n Deich, Damm m.

dynamic (dai'næmik) adj dynamisch.

dynamite ('dainəmait) n Dynamit neu.

dynasty ('dinəsti) n Dynastie f.

dysentery ('disəntri) n med Ruhr f.

dyslexia (dis'leksiə) n Dyslexie, Wortblindheit f.

E

each (i:tʃ) pron, adj jeder, jede, jedes. adv je

eager ('i:gə) adj begierig, eifrig.

eagle ('i:gəl) n Adler m.

ear[1] (iə) n 1 Ohr neu. 2 Gehör neu. **earache** n Ohrenschmerzen m pl. **eardrum** n Trommelfell neu. **earmark** vt 1 kennzeichnen. 2 bestimmen. **earring** n Ohrring m.

ear[2] (iə) n (of corn) Ähre f.

earl (ə:l) n Graf m.

early ('ə:li) adj,adv 1 früh. 2 vorzeitig.

earn (ə:n) vt verdienen, erwerben.

earnest ('ə:nist) adj 1 ernst(haft). 2 aufrichtig. n Ernst m.

earth (ə:θ) n 1 Erde f. 2 (Erd)Boden m. **earth-enware** n Steingut neu. **earthquake** n Erdbeben neu.

ease (i:z) n 1 Leichtigkeit f. 2 Behagen neu. Ungezwungenheit f. vt erleichtern. **easy** adj 1 leicht, mühelos. 2 bequem. 3 ungezwungen. **easygoing** adj lässig, leichtlebig.

easel ('i:zəl) n Staffelei f.

east (i:st) n 1 Osten m. 2 Orient m. Morgenland neu. adj östlich, Ost—. adv nach Osten, ostwärts. **easterly** adj östlich. **eastern** adj 1 östlich. 2 oriental, morgenländisch. **eastward** adj ostwärts. **eastwards** adv ostwärts.

Easter ('i:stə) n Ostern neu.

eat (i:t) vt 1 essen. 2 (of animals) fressen.

eavesdrop ('i:vzdrɔp) vi lauschen, heimlich zuhören.

ebb (eb) n 1 Ebbe f. 2 Abnahme f. vi 1 verebben. 2 abnehmen.

ebony ('ebəni) n Ebenholz neu.

eccentric (ik'sentrik) adj exzentrisch. n Exzentriker, Sonderling m.

ecclesiastical (ikli:zi'æstikəl) adj kirchlich.

echo ('ekou) n, pl **echoes** Echo neu. vi widerhallen.

eclair (ei'klɛə) n Cremekuchen m.

eclipse (i'klips) n Verfinsterung, Finsternis f. vt 1 verfinstern. 2 in den Schatten stellen.

ecology (i'kɔlədʒi) n Ökologie f.

economy (i'kɔnəmi) n 1 Wirtschaft f. 2 Sparsamkeit f. 3 Sparmaßnahme f. **economic** adj wirtschaftlich, Wirtschafts—. **economical** adj wirtschaftlich, sparsam. **economics** n pl Ökonomie, (Volks)Wirtschaft f. **economize** vt (ein)sparen.

ecstasy ('ekstəsi) n Ekstase, Verzückung f. **ecstatic** adj ekstatisch, verzückt.

edge (edʒ) n 1 Rand m. 2 Schneide f. vt 1 schärfen. 2 umsäumen.

edible ('edibəl) adj eßbar.

Edinburgh ('edinbərə) n Edinburg neu.

edit ('edit) vt redigieren, druckfertig machen. **editor** n Redakteur m. **editorial** n Leitartikel m. adj Redaktions—.

edition (i'diʃən) n 1 Auflage f. 2 Ausgabe f.

educate ('edjukeit) vt erziehen, (aus)bilden. **education** n Erziehung, Bildung f. **educational** adj Erziehungs—, pädagogisch.

eel (i:l) n Aal m.

eerie ('iəri) adj unheimlich.

effect (i'fekt) n 1 Wirkung f. 2 Einfluß m. 3 Eindruck m. 4 Gültigkeit f. vt 1 bewirken. 2 einwirken auf. 3 ausführen. **effective** adj 1 wirksam. 2 eindrucksvoll.

effeminate (i'feminət) *adj* weibisch.

effervesce (efə'ves) *vi* aufbrausen, sprudeln.

efficient (i'fiʃənt) *adj* 1 leistungsfähig. 2 tüchtig. 3 wirksam. **efficiency** *n* 1 Leistungsfähigkeit *f*. 2 Tüchtigkeit *f*. 3 Wirksamkeit *f*.

effigy ('efidʒi) *n* Bildnis *neu*.

effort ('efət) *n* Anstrengung, Bemühung, Mühe *f*. **effortless** *adj* mühelos.

egg[1] (eg) *n* Ei *neu*. **eggcup** *n* Eierbecher *m*. **eggshell** *n* Eierschale *f*. **eggwhisk** *n* Schneebesen *m*.

egg[2] (eg) *vt* **egg on** aufreizen.

ego ('i:gou) *n* Ich *neu*. **egocentric** *adj* egozentrisch. **egoism** *n* Selbstsucht *f*. **egotism** *n* Selbstgefälligkeit *f*.

Egypt ('i:dʒipt) *n* Ägypten *neu*. **Egyptian** *adj* ägyptisch. *n* Ägypter *m*.

eiderdown ('aidədaun) *n* Daunendecke *f*.

eight (eit) *adj* acht. *n* Acht *f*. **eighth** *adj* achte.

eighteen (ei'ti:n) *adj* achtzehn. *n* Achtzehn *f*. **eighteenth** *adj* achtzehnte.

eighty ('eiti) *adj* achtzig. *n* Achtzig *f*. **eightieth** *adj* achtzigste.

either ('aiðə) *pron, adj* 1 einer (von zweien). 2 beide, jeder (von zweien). **either...or** entweder...oder.

ejaculate (i'dʒækjuleit) *vt* ausstoßen.

eject (i'dʒekt) *vt* ausstoßen, vertreiben.

eke (i:k) *vt* **eke out** ergänzen, verlängern.

elaborate (*adj* i'læbrət; *v* i'læbəreit) *adj* ausgearbeitet, kompliziert. *vt* ausarbeiten.

elapse (i'læps) *vi* vergehen, verstreichen.

elastic (i'læstik) *adj* dehnbar, elastisch. **elasticity** *n* Elastizität *f*.

elated (i'leitid) *adj* erfreut, erregt.

elbow ('elbou) *n* Ell(en)bogen *m*.

elder[1] ('eldə) *adj* älter. *n* 1 (Kirchen)Älteste(r) *m*. 2 Respektsperson *f*.

elder[2] ('eldə) *n bot* Holunder *m*. **elderberry** *n* Holunderbeere *f*.

eldest ('eldist) *adj* ältest.

elect (i'lekt) *vt* wählen, auserwählen. *vi* sich entschließen. **election** *n* Wahl *f*.

electorate (i'lektərət) *n* Wählerschaft *f*.

electricity (ilek'trisiti) *n* Elektrizität *f*. **electric** *adj also* **electrical** elektrisch. **electrician** *n* Elektriker *m*. **electrify** *vt* 1 elektrisieren. 2 elektrifizieren. **electrocute** *vt* durch elektrischen Strom töten. **electrode** *n* Elektrode *f*. **electron** *n* Elektron *neu*. **electronic** *adj* elektronisch.

elegant ('eligənt) *adj* elegant, geschmackvoll.

element ('eləmənt) *n* 1 Element *neu*. 2 Grund-

bestandteil *neu*. **elemental** *adj* wesentlich. **elementary** *adj* elementar, einfach.

elephant ('eləfənt) *n* Elefant *m*.

elevate ('eləveit) *vt* aufrichten, erheben, erhöhen. **elevation** *n* 1 Erhebung *f*. 2 *math* Aufriß *m*. **elevator** *n* Aufzug, Fahrstuhl *m*.

eleven (i'levən) *adj* elf. *n* Elf *f*. **eleventh** *adj* elfte.

elf (elf) *n, pl* **elves** Elf *m*. Elfe *f*.

eligible ('elidʒəbl) *adj* 1 annehmbar, wünschenswert. 2 berechtigt. 3 heiratsfähig.

eliminate (i'limineit) *vt* eliminieren, ausstoßen. **elimination** *n* Eliminierung, Ausstoßung *f*.

elite (ei'li:t) *n* Elite *f*.

ellipse (i'lips) *n* Ellipse *f*.

elm (elm) *n* Ulme *f*.

elocution (elə'kju:ʃən) *n* Vortragskunst *f*.

elope (i'loup) *vi* (mit ihrem *or* seiner Geliebten) entlaufen.

eloquent ('eləkwənt) *adj* redegewandt.

else (els) *adv* sonst. **anyone else** 1 sonst noch jemand? 2 irgend ein anderer. **something else** etwas anderes. **elsewhere** *adv* anderswo, anderswohin.

elucidate (i'lu:sideit) *vt* erläutern, aufklären.

elude (i'lu:d) *vt* umgehen, ausweichen.

emaciated (i'meiʃieitəd) *adj* abgemagert.

emanate ('eməneit) *vi* ausströmen, ausfließen.

emancipate (i'mænsipeit) *vt* emanzipieren, befreien. **emancipation** *n* Befreiung *f*.

embalm (im'ba:m) *vt* einbalsamieren.

embankment (im'bæŋkmənt) *n* 1 Deich, Damm *m*. 2 Uferstraße.

embargo (im'ba:gou) *n* Handelssperre *f*. *vt* sperren.

embark (im'ba:k) *(vi)*, *vt* (sich) einschiffen.

embarrass (im'bærəs) *vt* in Verlegenheit bringen. **embarrassed** *adj* verlegen.

embassy ('embəsi) *n* Botschaft *f*.

embellish (im'beliʃ) *vt* schmücken, verschönern.

ember ('embə) *n* glühende Asche *f*.

embezzle (im'bezəl) *vt* veruntreuen.

embitter (im'bitə) *vt* verbittern.

emblem ('embləm) *n* Abzeichen, Sinnbild *neu*.

embody (im'bɔdi) *vt* verkörpern.

emboss (im'bɔs) *vt* prägen, in Relief ausarbeiten.

embrace (im'breis) *vt* 1 umarmen. 2 umfassen. *n* Umarmung *f*.

embroider (im'brɔidə) *vt* besticken. **embroidery** *n* Stickerei *f*.

embryo ('embriou) *n* Embryo *m*.

emerald ('emrəld) n Smaragd m. adj smaragdgrün.

emerge (i'mɜːdʒ) vi 1 auftauchen. 2 hervorkommen. **emergence** n Auftauchen, Hervorkommen neu.

emergency (i'mɜːdʒənsi) n Notfall m.

emigrate ('emigreit) vi auswandern.

eminent ('eminənt) adj hervorragend, berühmt. **eminently** adv ganz besonders.

emit (i'mit) vt 1 ausstrahlen, aussenden. 2 von sich geben.

emotion (i'mouʃən) n Gemütsbewegung f. Gefühl neu. **emotional** adj 1 emotionell, gefühlvoll. 2 rührend.

empathy ('empəθi) n Einfühlung f.

emperor ('empərə) n Kaiser m.

emphasis ('emfəsis) n Betonung f. **emphasize** vt betonen, unterstreichen. **emphatic** adj nachdrücklich, betont.

empire ('empaiə) n Reich neu.

empirical (im'pirikəl) adj empirisch.

employ (im'plɔi) vt 1 verwenden. 2 beschäftigen. **employee** n Arbeitnehmer m. **employer** n Arbeitgeber m. **employment** n 1 Beschäftigung, Arbeit f. 2 Verwendung f.

empower (im'pauə) vt 1 bevollmächtigen, befähigen.

empress ('empras) n Kaiserin f.

empty ('empti) adj 1 leer. 2 unbeladen. 3 eitel. vt entleeren. **empty-handed** adj mit leeren Händen. **empty-headed** adj ohne Verstand.

emu ('iːmjuː) n Emu m.

emulate ('emjuleit) vt nacheifern.

emulsion (i'mʌlʃən) n Emulsion f.

enable (i'neibəl) vt befähigen, ermöglichen.

enact (i'nækt) vt 1 law erlassen. 2 Th aufführen, darstellen.

enamel (i'næməl) n Emaille f. vt glasieren, emaillieren.

encapsulate (in'kæpsjuleit) vt einkapseln.

enchant (in'tʃɑːnt) vt entzücken.

encircle (in'sɜːkəl) vt einkreisen, umkreisen.

enclose (in'klouz) vt 1 einschließen. 2 beifügen. **enclosure** n 1 Umzäunung f. 2 Anlage f.

encore ('ɔŋkɔː) interj noch einmal! n Zugabe f.

encounter (in'kauntə) n Begegnung f. vt begegnen, stoßen auf.

encourage (in'kʌridʒ) vt 1 ermutigen. 2 unterstützen, fördern. **encouragement** n Unterstützung, Ermutigung f.

encroach (in'kroutʃ) vi unbefugt eingreifen.

encumber (in'kʌmbə) vt belasten, beschweren.

encyclopedia (insaiklə'piːdiə) n Enzyklopädie f.

end (end) n 1 Ende neu. 2 Zweck m. Ziel neu. 3 Tod m. **be at an end** am Ende sein. ~vi enden, zu Ende kommen. vt beendigen, zu Ende führen. **endless** vt endlos, unendlich.

endanger (in'deindʒə) vt gefährden.

endeavour (in'devə) n Bestreben neu. vi streben, sich bemühen.

endemic (en'demik) adj endemisch.

endive ('endaiv) n bot Endivie f.

endorse (in'dɔːs) vt 1 vermerken. 2 bestätigen. **endorsement** n 1 Vermerk m. 2 Bestätigung f.

endow (in'dau) vt 1 schenken. 2 vermachen.

endure (in'djuə) vi (fort)dauern. vt ertragen.

enemy ('enəmi) n Feind, Gegner m. adj feindlich, Feind—.

energy ('enədʒi) n 1 Energie f. 2 Tatkraft f.

enfold (in'fould) vt einhüllen, einschlagen.

enforce (in'fɔːs) vt durchsetzen.

engage (in'geidʒ) vt 1 verpflichten. 2 anstellen. 3 tech einschalten. vi 1 sich verpflichten. 2 sich beschäftigen. **get engaged** sich verloben. **engagement** n 1 Verlobung f. 2 Beschäftigung f. 3 Verabredung f.

engine ('endʒin) n 1 Motor m. 2 Lokomotive f. 3 Maschine f.

engineer (endʒi'niə) n Ingenieur, Techniker m. vt konstruieren, bauen. **engineering** n 1 Ingenieurwesen neu. 2 Maschinenbaukunst f.

England ('iŋglənd) n England neu. **English** adj englisch. n (language) Englisch neu. **Englishman** n Engländer m.

English Channel n (Ärmel)Kanal m.

engrave (in'greiv) vt gravieren.

engrossed (in'groust) adj vertieft, versunken.

engulf (in'gʌlf) vt 1 versenken. 2 verschlingen.

enhance (in'hɑːns) vt erhöhen.

enigma (i'nigmə) n Rätsel neu.

enjoy (in'dʒɔi) vt genießen, Freude haben an. **enjoy oneself** sich (gut) unterhalten. **enjoyment** n Genuß m. Freude f.

enlarge (in'lɑːdʒ) (vi),vt (sich) vergrößern, (sich) erweitern.

enlighten (in'laitn) vt erleuchten, aufklären. **enlightenment** n Aufklärung f.

enlist (in'list) mil vt anwerben. vi sich anwerben lassen.

enormous (i'nɔːməs) adj enorm, ungeheuer.

enough (i'nʌf) adj,adv genug.

enquire (in'kwaiə) vi sich erkundigen. **enquiry** n 1 Erkundigung f. 2 Untersuchung f.

enrage (in'reidʒ) vt wütend machen.

enrich (in'ritʃ) vt bereichern, verzieren.

enrol (in'roul) vt 1 einschreiben. 2 anwerben. vi sich einschreiben lassen.

ensign ('ensain) n Fahne f. Abzeichen neu.

enslave (in'sleiv) vt versklaven.

ensure (in'ʃuə) vt 1 sicherstellen, sichern. 2 dafür sorgen.

entail (in'teil) vt mit sich bringen.

entangle (in'tæŋgəl) vt verwickeln, verwirren.

enter ('entə) vt 1 eintreten (in), betreten. 2 eintragen.

enterprise ('entəpraiz) n 1 Unternehmen neu. 2 Unternehmungslust f. **enterprising** adj unternehmungslustig.

entertain (entə'tein) vt 1 unterhalten. 2 bewirten. 3 eingehen auf. vi Gäste haben or einladen. **entertainment** n Unterhaltung f.

enthral (in'θrɔ:l) vt fesseln, bezaubern.

enthusiasm (in'θju:ziæzəm) n Begeisterung f. Enthusiasmus m. **enthusiastic** adj beigestert, enthusiastisch.

entice (in'tais) vt verlocken.

entire (in'taiə) adj vollständig, ganz.

entitle (in'tait|) vt berechtigen.

entity ('entiti) n Wesen, Dasein neu.

entrails ('entreilz) n pl Eingeweide neu pl.

entrance[1] ('entrəns) n 1 Eingang, Eintritt m. 2 Eintreten neu.

entrance[2] (in'tra:ns) vt entzücken, bezaubern.

entreat (in'tri:t) vt bitten, ersuchen.

entrench (in'trentʃ) vt mil verschanzen.

entrepreneur (ɔntrəprə'nə:) n Unternehmer m.

entrust (in'trʌst) vt anvertrauen.

entry ('entri) n 1 Eintritt m. 2 Einreise, Einfahrt f. 3 Eintragung f.

entwine (in'twain) vi verflechten.

enunciate (i'nʌnsieit) vt ausdrücken.

envelop (in'veləp) vt einwickeln, umhüllen.

envelope ('envəloup) n (Brief)Umschlag m.

environment (in'vaiərənmənt) n 1 Umwelt f. 2 Umgebung. **environmental** adj Umwelt—.

envisage (in'vizidʒ) vt ins Auge fassen, sich vorstellen.

envoy ('envɔi) n Gesandte(r) m.

envy ('envi) n Neid m. vt beneiden. **envious** adj neidisch.

enzyme ('enzaim) n Enzym neu.

epaulet ('epəlet) n Epaulette f.

ephemeral (i'femərəl) adj vergänglich, flüchtig.

epic ('epik) adj episch.

epicure ('epikjuə) n Genießer, Feinschmecker m.

epidemic (epi'demik) adj epidemisch. n Epidemie, Seuche f.

epilepsy ('epilepsi) n Epilepsie, Fallsucht f.

epilogue ('epilɔg) n Nachwort neu, Epilog m.

Epiphany (i'pifəni) n Dreikönigsfest neu.

episcopal (i'piskəpəl) adj bischöflich.

episode ('episoud) n Episode f.

epitaph ('epita:f) n Grabschrift f.

epitome (i'pitəmi) n Auszug, Abriß m.

epoch ('i:pɔk) n Epoche f.

equable ('ekwəbəl) adj ausgeglichen.

equal ('i:kwəl) adj 1 gleich. 2 entsprechend. 3 fähig, gewachsen. n 1 Gleiche(r) m. 2 Gleichgestellte(r) m. vt gleichen. **equality** n Gleichberechtigung f. **equalize** vt gleichstellen, ausgleichen. vi sport ausgleichen.

equate (i'kweit) vt gleichsetzen. **equation** n Gleichung f. **equator** n Äquator m.

equestrian (i'kwestriən) n Reiter m. adj Reiter—.

equilateral (i:kwi'lætərəl) adj gleichseitig.

equilibrium (i:kwi'libriəm) n Gleichgewicht neu.

equinox (i:kwinɔks) n Tagundnachtgleiche f.

equip (i'kwip) vt ausstatten, ausrüsten. **equipment** n Ausrüstung, Ausstattung f.

equity ('ekwiti) n 1 Gerechtigkeit f. 2 pl Wertpapiere neu pl.

equivalent (i'kwivələnt) adj 1 gleichwertig. 2 entsprechend.

era ('iərə) n Ära f.

eradicate (i'rædikeit) vt ausrotten, vernichten.

erase (i'reiz) vt 1 ausradieren. 2 auslöschen.

erect (i'rekt) adj aufrecht. vt 1 aufrichten. 2 bauen, errichten. **erection** n 1 Errichtung f. 2 Bau m.

ermine ('ə:min) n zool Hermelin neu.

erode (i'roud) vt 1 zerfressen. 2 erodieren. **erosion** n 1 Zerfressung f. 2 Erosion f.

erotic (i'rɔtik) adj erotisch.

err (ə:) vi 1 sich irren. 2 abweichen.

errand ('erənd) n Botengang, Auftrag m.

erratic (i'rætik) adj 1 unregelmäßig. 2 unberechenbar, nicht konstant.

error ('erə) n Irrtum, Fehler m.

erupt (i'rʌpt) vi ausbrechen. **eruption** n Ausbruch m.

escalate ('eskəleit) (vi),vt eskalieren, (sich) steigern. **escalator** n Rolltreppe f.

escalope (i'skæləp) n cul Schnitzel neu.

escape (i'skeip) n 1 Flucht f. Entkommen neu. 2 Befreiung f. vi 1 flüchten, entkommen. 2 ausfließen. vt 1 entgehen.

escort ('eskɔ:t) n 1 Begleitung f. 2 Begleiter m. 3 mil Eskorte f. vt 1 geleiten. 2 begleiten.

Eskimo ('eskimou) n Eskimo m.

esoteric (esǝ'terik) adj esoterisch.

especial (i'speʃǝl) adj besonder, speziell. **especially** adv besonders, hauptsächlich.

espionage ('espiǝnɑ:ʒ) n Spionage f.

essay ('esei) n Aufsatz m. Abhandlung f.

essence ('esǝns) n Essenz f. Kern m. **essential** adj 1 wesentlich. 2 unentbehrlich.

establish (i'stæbliʃ) vt 1 festlegen, aufstellen. 2 begründen, errichten. **establishment** n 1 Gründung, Errichtung f. 2 Firma f. 3 Anstalt m.

estate (i'steit) n 1 Besitz m. 2 Nachlaß m. **estate agent** n Häusermakler m. **estate car** n mot Kombiwagen m.

esteem (i'sti:m) n Achtung f. vt hochschätzen.

estimate (n 'estimat; v 'estimeit) n Schätzung f. vt schätzen. **estimation** n 1 Schätzung f. 2 Urteil neu.

estuary ('estʃuǝri) n Flußmündung f.

eternal (i'tǝ:nl) adj ewig. **eternity** n Ewigkeit f.

ethereal (i'θiǝriǝl) adj ätherisch.

ethical ('eθikǝl) adj ethisch, sittlich. **ethics** n pl 1 Sitten f pl. Moral f. 2 Sittenlehre f.

Ethiopia (i:'θi'oupiǝ) n Äthiopien neu. **Ethiopian** adj äthiopisch. n Äthiopier m.

ethnic ('eθnik) adj ethnisch, Volks—.

etiquette ('etikit) n Etikette f.

etymology (eti'mɔlǝdʒi) n Etymologie f.

Eucharist ('ju:kǝrist) n heiliges Abendmahl m.

eunuch ('ju:nǝk) n Eunuch m.

euphemism ('ju:fǝmizǝm) n Euphemismus m.

euphoria (ju:'fɔ:riǝ) n 1 Euphorie f. 2 (heftige) Begeisterung f.

Europe ('juǝrǝp) n Europe neu. **European** adj europäisch. n Europäer m.

European Economic Community n Europäische Wirtschaftsgemeinschaft, EWG f.

euthanasia (ju:θǝ'neiziǝ) n Sterbehilfe, Euthanasie f. Gnadentod m.

evacuate (i'vækjueit) vt 1 entleeren. 2 evakuieren. 3 räumen.

evade (i'veid) vt,vi ausweichen, umgehen, vermeiden. **evasive** adj ausweichend.

evaluate (i'væljueit) vt abschätzen, berechnen.

evangelical (i:væn'dʒelikǝl) adj evangelisch. **evangelist** n Evangelist m.

evaporate (i'væpǝreit) vi,(vt) verdampfen (lassen).

eve (i:v) n Vorabend m.

even ('i:vǝn) adj 1 glatt, eben. 2 gleich. 3 math gerade. 4 quitt. adv gerade, sogar. **even better** noch besser. **not even** nicht einmal. **even-tempered** adj gleichmütig, gelassen.

evening ('i:vǝniŋ) n Abend m. **evening dress** n 1 Abendkleid neu. 2 Smoking m.

event (i'vent) n 1 Ereignis neu. Vorfall m. 2 Veranstaltung f. **eventual** adj schließlich. **eventually** adv schließlich, endlich.

ever ('evǝ) adv 1 immer, stets. 2 je, jemals. 3 überhaupt. **ever so** inf besonders, sehr. **for ever** für immer, auf ewig, stets. **evergreen** n Immergrün neu. adj immergrün. **everlasting** adj 1 ewig. 2 dauerhaft. **evermore** adv immerfort.

every ('evri) pron jeder, jede, jedes m,f,neu. all. **everybody** pron also **everyone** jeder, jedermann. **everyday** adj Alltags— alltäglich. **everything** pron alles. **everywhere** adv überall, überallhin.

evict (i'vikt) vt law ausweisen.

evidence ('evidǝns) n 1 Zeugnis neu. 2 Nachweis, Beweis m. **evident** adj offenbar, klar.

evil ('i:vǝl) adj böse, übel. n Böse, Übel neu.

evoke (i'vouk) vt hervorrufen.

evolve (i'vɔlv) vi sich entwickeln, enstehen. vt entwickeln. **evolution** n Entwicklung, Evolution f.

ewe (ju:) n Mutterschaf neu.

exact (ig'zækt) adj 1 genau, exakt. 2 streng. vt verlangen, fordern.

exaggerate (ig'zædʒǝreit) vt,vi übertreiben.

exalt (ig'zɔ:lt) vt verherrlichen. **exaltation** n Verherrlichung f.

examine (ig'zæmin) vt 1 prüfen. 2 untersuchen. 3 verhören. **examination** n 1 Prüfung f. 2 Untersuchung f. 3 Verhör neu.

example (ig'zɑ:mpǝl) n 1 Beispiel neu. 2 Vorbild neu. **for example** zum Beispiel.

exasperate (ig'zɑ:spǝreit) vt ärgern, reizen.

excavate ('ekskǝveit) vt ausgraben, aushöhlen.

exceed (ik'si:d) vt 1 überschreiten. 2 hinausgehen über. **exceedingly** adv äußerst, höchst.

excel (ik'sel) vt übertreffen. **excel oneself** sich auszeichnen. **excellence** n Vorzüglichkeit f. **excellent** adj vorzüglich, ausgezeichnet.

Excellency ('eksǝlǝnsi) n Exzellenz f.

except (ik'sept) prep ausgenommen, außer. **except for** abgesehen von. **except that** nur daß, außer daß. vt ausnehmen, ausschließen. **exception** n Ausnahme f.

excerpt ('eksǝ:pt) n Auszug m. Szene f.

excess (ik'ses) n 1 Übermaß neu. Überfluß m. 2 pl Unmäßigkeiten f pl. **in excess of** mehr als. **excessive** adj übermäßig.

exchange (iks'tʃeindʒ) vt (aus-, um-)tauschen, wechseln. n 1 (Aus)Tausch m. 2 Wechsel m. 3

187

comm Börse *f.* **4** (Telephon)Zentrale *f.* **exchange rate** *n* Wechselkurs *m.*

exchequer (iks'tʃeka) *n* Staatskasse *f.* Finanzministerium *neu.* **chancellor of the exchequer** *n* Finanzminister *m.*

excise ('eksaiz) *n* (indirekte) Steuer *f.*

excite (ik'sait) *vt* erregen, anregen, aufregen. **excitement** *n* Aufregung *f.*

exclaim (ik'skleim) *vt,vi* ausrufen.

exclamation (eksklə'meiʃən) *n* Ausruf *m.* **exclamation mark** *n* Ausrufungszeichen *neu.*

exclude (ik'sklu:d) *vt* ausschließen. **exclusive** *adj* **1** exklusiv. **2** ausschließlich.

excommunicate (eskə'mju:nikeit) *vt* exkommunizieren.

excrete (ik'skri:t) *vi* ausscheiden, absondern. **excreta** *n pl* Auswurf, Kot *m.*

excruciating (ik'skru:ʃieitiŋ) *adj* qualvoll.

excursion (ik'skə:ʒən) *n* Ausflug *m.*

excuse (*n* ik'skju:s; *v* ik'skju:z) *n* Entschuldigung, Ausrede *f.* *vt* entschuldigen. **excuse me** entschuldigen Sie!

execute ('eksikju:t) *vt* **1** ausführen, vollziehen. **2** (a person) hinrichten. **executive** *n* **1** Verwaltung *f.* **2** (hoher) Angestellte(r). *adj* vollziehend.

exempt (ig'zempt) *adj* befreit, ausgenommen. *vt* ausnehmen, befreien.

exercise ('eksəsaiz) *n* **1** Übung *f.* **2** Ausübung *f.* **3** Schulaufgabe *f.* *vt* **1** üben, anwenden. **2** ausüben. **exercise book** *n* Schulheft *neu.*

exert (ig'zə:t) *vt* ausüben. **exert oneself** sich anstrengen. **exertion** *n* Anstrengung *f.*

exhale (eks'heil) *vt,vi* ausatmen.

exhaust (ig'zɔ:st) *n* **1** Abgas *neu.* **2** *mot* Auspuff *m.* *vt* **1** erschöpfen. **2** ermüden. **exhausted** *adj* erschöpft. **exhaust pipe** *n* Auspuffrohr *neu.*

exhibit (ig'zibit) *vt* **1** ausstellen. **2** zeigen, vorführen. *n* Ausstellungsstück *neu.* **exhibition** *n* **1** Ausstellung *f.* **2** Vorführung *f.* **exhibitionism** *n* Exhibitionismus, Öffentlichkeitsdrang *m.*

exhilarate (ig'zilareit) *vt* erheitern.

exile ('egzail) *n* **1** Verbannung *f.* Exil *neu.* **2** Verbannte(r) *m.* *vt* verbannen, vertreiben.

exist (ig'zist) *vi* **1** existieren, sein. **2** leben. **existence** *n* Dasein *neu.* Existenz *f.*

exit ('eksit) *n* **1** Ausgang *m.* **2** Abgang *m.* *vi Th* (geht) ab.

exonerate (eg'zɔnəreit) *vt* freisprechen.

exorbitant (ig'zɔ:bitənt) *adj* maßlos, übermäßig.

exorcize ('eksɔ:saiz) *vt* beschwören, austreiben.

exotic (ig'zɔtik) *adj* exotisch.

expand (ik'spænd) (*vi),vt* **1** (sich) ausdehnen, (sich) ausbreiten. **2** (sich) erweitern. **expansion** *n* **1** Ausdehnung, Ausbreitung *f.* **2** *pol* Expansion *f.*

expanse (ik'spæns) *n* Weite, weite Fläche *f.*

expatriate (eks'pætriit) *vt* ausbürgern. *adj* im Ausland lebend. *n* Ausgebürgerte(r) *m.*

expect (ik'spekt) *vt* **1** erwarten. **2** annehmen. **expectancy** *n* Erwartung *f.*

expedient (ik'spi:diənt) *adj* ratsam, zweckmäßig. *n* Ausweg *m.* Hilfsmittel *neu.*

expedition (ekspi'diʃən) *n* Expedition *f.*

expel (ik'spel) *vt* (hin)ausstoßen, vertreiben.

expenditure (ik'spenditʃə) *n* **1** (Geld)Ausgabe *f.* **2** Verbrauch *m.*

expense (ik'spens) *n* **1** Kosten *f pl.* Ausgabe *f.* **2** *pl* Unkosten *f pl.* **at the expense of** auf Kosten. **expensive** *adj* teuer.

experience (ik'spiəriəns) *n* **1** Erfahrung *f.* **2** Erlebnis *neu.* *vt* erleben, erfahren. **experienced** *adj* erfahren.

experiment (ik'speriment) *n* Versuch *m.* Experiment *neu.* *vi* experimentieren. **experimental** *adj* Experimental—.

expert ('ekspə:t) *n* Fachmann, Experte *m.* *adj* erfahren, fachmännisch. **expertise** (ekspə'ti:z) *n* Spezialwissen *neu.* Erfahrung *f.*

expire (ik'spaiə) *vi* **1** ablaufen. **2** sterben. **3** ausatmen. **expiry** *n* Ablauf *m.*

explain (ik'splein) *vt* erklären, erläutern. **explain oneself** sich rechtfertigen. **explanation** *n* Erklärung, Erläuterung *f.*

expletive (ik'spli:tiv) *adj* ausfüllend. *n* **1** Füllwort *neu.* **2** Fluchwort *neu.*

explicit (ik'splisit) *adj* verständlich, ausdrücklich, deutlich.

explode (ik'sploud) *vi* explodieren. *vt* sprengen. **explosion** *n* Explosion *f.* **explosive** *adj* explosiv. *n* Sprengstoff *m.*

exploit[1] ('eksplɔit) *n* Heldentat *f.* Abenteuer *neu.*

exploit[2] (ik'splɔit) *vt* **1** ausbeuten, ausnutzen. **2** auswerten. **exploitation** *n* **1** Ausbeutung *f.* **2** Ausnutzung *f.*

explore (ik'splɔ:) *vt* **1** erforschen. **2** untersuchen.

exponent (ik'spounənt) *n* Exponent, Vertreter *m.*

export (*v* ik'spɔ:t; *n* 'ekspɔ:t) *vt* exportieren, ausführen. *n* Ausfuhr *f.* Export(handel) *m.*

expose (ik'spouz) *vt* **1** aussetzen. **2** enthüllen. **3** bloßstellen. **4** *phot* belichten. **exposure** *n* **1**

Enthüllung f. 2 Aussetzung f. 3 med Entkräftung f. 4 phot Belichtung f.

express (ik'spres) vt ausdrücken, äußern. adj 1 ausdrücklich. 2 Expreß—. **expression** n Ausdruck m. **express letter** Eilbrief m. **express (train)** n Schnellzug m.

exquisite (ek'skwizit) adj vorzüglich, vornehm, auserlesen.

extend (ik'stend) vt 1 ausdehnen, erweitern. 2 ausbauen. 3 verlängern. 4 gewähren, verweisen. vi 1 sich ausdehnen, erstrecken. **extension** n 1 Erweiterung, Ausdehnung f. 2 Verlängerung f. 3 Anbau m. 4 (Telephon)-Nebenanschluß m. **extensive** adj umfassend, ausgedehnt.

extent (ik'stent) n 1 Ausdehnung f. 2 Größe f. 3 (Aus)Maß neu. **to some extent** gewissermaßen. **to that/what extent** insofern/inwiefern.

exterior (ek'stiəriə) adj außer, Außen—. n 1 Äußere neu. 2 Außenseite f.

exterminate (ik'stə:mineit) vt ausrotten, vertilgen.

external (ik'stə:nl) adj äußer(lich), Außen—.

extinct (ik'stiŋkt) adj 1 ausgestorben. 2 erloschen.

extinguish (ik'stiŋgwiʃ) vt auslöschen.

extra ('ekstrə) adj zusätzlich, Extra—, Sonder—.

extract (ik'strækt) vt (heraus)ziehen. n 1 Auszug m. 2 Extrakt m.

extramural (ekstrə'mjuərəl) adj educ außerhalb der Mauern (einer Universität).

extraordinary (ik'strɔ:dənri) adj außerordentlich, außergewöhnlich.

extravagant (ik'strævəgənt) adj verschwenderisch. **extravagance** n Verschwendung f.

extreme (ik'stri:m) adj 1 äußerst. 2 extrem, radikal. 3 höchst, außerordentlich. n Äußerste neu. **extremist** n Radikale(r), Fanatiker m. **extremity** n 1 Äußerste neu. 2 Spitze f. 3 pl Gliedmaßen pl.

extricate ('ekstrikeit) vt herausziehen, freimachen.

extrovert ('ekstrəvə:t) n Extravertierte(r), Extravert m.

exuberant (ig'zju:bərənt) adj 1 üppig. 2 überschwenglich.

eye (ai) n 1 Auge neu. 2 Blick m. 3 Ansicht f. vt ansehen.

eyeball ('aibɔ:l) n Augapfel m.

eyebrow ('aibrau) n Augenbraue f.

eye-catching adj auffällig.

eyelash ('ailæʃ) n Wimper f.

eyelid ('ailid) n Augenlid neu.

eye-opener n aufschlußreiche or überraschende Entdeckung f.

eye shadow n Lidschatten, Augenschatten m.

eyesight ('aisait) n Sehkraft f.

eyesore ('aisɔ:) n Dorn im Auge m.

eyestrain ('aistrein) n Überanstrengung des Auges f.

eyewitness (ai'witnis) n Augenzeuge m.

F

fable ('feibəl) n Fabel f. Märchen neu.

fabric ('fæbrik) n 1 Stoff m. Gewebe neu. 2 Struktur f. **fabricate** vt erfinden, fabrizieren.

fabulous ('fæbjuləs) adj 1 fabelhaft. 2 inf toll, fantastisch.

facade (fə'sɑ:d) n Fassade f.

face (feis) n 1 Gesicht neu. 2 Oberfläche f. 3 Vorderseite f. **in the face of** angesichts. **pull faces** Fratzen schneiden. ~vt 1 gegenüberstehen. 2 ansehen. **face up to** 1 entgegentreten. 2 hinnehmen. 3 gewachsen sein. **face value** n Nennwert m. **take at face value** für bare Münze nehmen.

facet ('fæsit) n Seite f. Aspekt m.

facetious (fə'si:ʃəs) adj witzig, spaßig.

facile ('fæsail) adj 1 leicht. 2 gefällig, nachgiebig. **facilitate** vt erleichtern, fördern. **facility** n 1 Möglichkeit f. 2 Leichtigkeit f. 3 pl Einrichtungen f pl.

facing ('feisiŋ) prep gegenüber.

facsimile (fæk'siməli) n Faksimile neu.

fact (fækt) n 1 Tatsache, Wahrheit f. 2 pl Tatbestand m. **in fact** tatsächlich, in der Tat. **factual** adj tatsächlich.

faction ('fækʃən) n 1 Partei, Splittergruppe f. 2 Zwietracht f.

factor ('fæktə) n Faktor, Umstand m.

factory ('fæktri) n Fabrik f. Betrieb m.

faculty ('fækəlti) n 1 Vermögen neu. Kraft f. 2 educ Fakultät f.

fad (fæd) n inf Liebhaberei, Mode f.

fade (feid) vi 1 verblassen. 2 verklingen. 3 verschwinden.

fag (fæg) n 1 sl Zigarette f. 2 Plackerei f.

fail (feil) vi 1 scheitern, versagen. 2 nachlassen. 3 versäumen. 4 educ durchfallen. vt 1 educ durchfallen lassen. 2 im Stich lassen. **without fail** unbedingt. **failing** prep in Ermangelung. n Schwäche f. **failure** n 1 Scheitern, Versagen *neu*. 2 Verfall *m*. 3 Versäumnis *neu*. 4 Mißerfolg *m*. 5 *educ* Durchfallen *neu*.

faint (feint) *adj* 1 schwach, matt. 2 leise. 3 ohnmächtig. *vi* ohnmächtig werden. **faint-hearted** *adj* zaghaft, verzagt.

fair[1] (fɛə) *adj* 1 hübsch, schön. 2 blond, hell. *adj,adv* gerecht, fair. **fairly** *adv* ziemlich, ganz schön. **fair-minded** *adj* gerecht, ehrlich. **fairness** *n* Gerechtigkeit *f*.

fair[2] (fɛə) *n* 1 Ausstellung, Messe *f*. 2 Jahrmarkt *m*. **fairground** *n* Rummelplatz *m*.

fairy ('fɛəri) *n* Fee *f*. Elf *m*. **fairytale** *n* Märchen *neu*.

faith (feiθ) *n* 1 Vertrauen *neu*. Glaube *m*. 2 Treue *f*. 3 Religion *f*. **faithful** *adj* 1 treu. 2 zuverlässig, genau. 3 gläubig. **yours faithfully** hochachtungsvoll.

fake (feik) *n* Fälschung *f*. *adj* verfälscht. *vt* fälschen, nachmachen.

falcon ('fɔ:lkən) *n* Falke *m*.

fall (fɔ:l) *n* 1 Fall, Sturz *m*. 2 Niedergang, Verfall *m*. 3 Sinken, Abnehmen *neu*. 3 *US* Herbst *m*. *vi* 1 fallen, stürzen. 2 sinken, abnehmen. **fall behind** zurückbleiben. **fall down** niederfallen. **fall through** durchfallen, scheitern.

fallacy ('fæləsi) *n* Täuschung *f*. Irrtum *m*.

fallible ('fæləbəl) *adj* fehlbar.

fallow ('fælou) *adj* **lie fallow** brachliegen.

false (fɔ:ls) *adj* 1 falsch. 2 trügerisch. 3 künstlich. **false alarm** *n* blinder Alarm *m*. **falsehood** *n* Falschheit, Unwahrheit *f*. **false pretences** *pl* Vorspiegelung falscher Tatsachen *f*. Betrug *m*. **false teeth** *n pl* künstliche Zähne *m pl*. **falsify** *vt* verfälschen, unrichtig darstellen.

falter ('fɔ:ltə) *vi* 1 stolpern. 2 zögern.

fame (feim) *n* Ruhm, Ruf *m*.

familiar (fə'miliə) *adj* 1 vertraut, bekannt. 2 gewohnt. **familiarity** *n* Vertrautheit *f*. **familiarize** *vt* vertraut machen.

family ('fæmili) *n* 1 Familie *f*. 2 Gruppe *f*.

famine ('fæmin) *n* Hungersnot *f*.

famous ('feiməs) *adj* berühmt.

fan[1] (fæn) *n* 1 Fächer *m*. 2 *tech* Ventilator *m*. **fanbelt** *n* mot Keilriemen *m*.

fan[2] (fæn) *n* Anhänger, Liebhaber *m*.

fanatic (fə'nætik) *n* Fanatiker *m*. *adj also* **fanatical** fanatisch.

fancy ('fænsi) *n* 1 Neigung, Vorliebe *f*. 2 Einbildung, Phantasie *f*. *adj* verziert, geschmückt. *vt* mögen, Lust haben auf. **fancy oneself** *inf* sich einbilden. **fancy someone**

inf auf jemanden ein Auge haben. **fancy dress** *n* Maskenkostüm *neu*. **fanciful** *adj* phantasievoll.

fanfare ('fænfɛə) *n* Fanfare *f*.

fang (fæŋ) *n* Reißzahn *m*.

fantastic (fæn'tæstik) *adj* 1 phantastisch. 2 eingebildet. 3 *inf* wunderbar, toll.

fantasy ('fæntəsi) *n* Phantasie *f*.

far (fɑ:) *adj* weit, entfernt. *adv* weit, fern. **by far** weitaus, bei weitem. **far and wide** weit und breit. **in so far as** insofern als. **faraway** *adj* 1 weit entfernt. 2 verträumt. **far-fetched** *adj* weit hergeholt, phantastisch. **far-off** *adj* entfernt, weit. **far-reaching** *adj* weitreichend.

farce (fɑ:s) *n* *Th* Posse, Farce *f*.

fare (fɛə) *n* 1 Fahrgeld *neu*. 2 Kost *f*. *vi* 1 (er)gehen.

Far East *n* Ferne(r) Osten *m*.

farewell (fɛə'wel) *n* Lebewohl *neu*. Abschied *m*. *interj* lebe wohl!

farinaceous (færi'neiʃəs) *adj* mehlig, Mehl—. **farinaceous food** *n* Teigwaren *f pl*.

farm (fɑ:m) *n* 1 Bauernhof *m*. 2 Farm *f*. *vt* bewirtschaften. **farmer** *n* Bauer *m*. **farmhouse** *n* Bauernhaus *neu*. **farming** *n* Landwirtschaft *f*. **farmland** *n* Ackerland *neu*. **farmyard** *n* Hofplatz *m*.

farther ('fɑ:ðə) *adv* weiter, ferner. *adj* entfernter.

farthest ('fɑ:ðist) *adj* weitest, fernst. *adv* am weitesten.

farthing ('fɑ:ðiŋ) *n* 1 Farthing *m*. 2 Kleinigkeit *f*.

fascinate ('fæsineit) *vt* faszinieren.

fascism ('fæʃizəm) *n* Faschismus *m*. **fascist** *adj* faschistisch. *n* Faschist *m*.

fashion ('fæʃən) *n* 1 Mode *f*. 2 Art, Weise *f*. *vt* bilden, gestalten.

fast[1] (fɑ:st) *adj,adv* 1 schnell. 2 fest, befestigt. 3 waschecht.

fast[2] (fɑ:st) *n* Fasten *neu*. *vi* fasten.

fasten ('fɑ:sən) *vt* 1 befestigen. 2 anschnallen. *vi* sich klammern an.

fastidious (fə'stidiəs) *adj* anspruchsvoll, penibel, wählerisch.

fat (fæt) *adj* fett, dick. *n* Fett *neu*. *vt* 1 fett machen. 2 (animals) mästen. *vi* fett werden.

fatal ('feitl) *adj* 1 tödlich. 2 verhängnisvoll, fatal. **fatality** *n* Todesfall *m*.

fate (feit) *n* Schicksal *neu*.

father ('fɑ:ðə) *n* Vater *m*. *vt* zeugen. **father-in-law** *n* Schwiegervater *m*. **fatherland** *n* Vaterland *neu*. Heimat *f*.

fathom ('fæðəm) n Faden m. vt 1 ergründen, begreifen. 2 sondieren.

fatigue (fə'ti:g) n Ermüdung f. vi ermüden.

fatuous ('fætjuəs) adj albern, blödsinnig.

fault (fɔ:lt) n 1 Fehler m. 2 Schuld f. 3 tech Störung f. Defekt m. **be at fault** sich irren. **find fault** tadeln.

fauna ('fɔ:nə) n Fauna, Tierwelt f.

favour ('feivə) n 1 Gefallen m. 2 Begünstigung f. vt 1 begünstigen. 2 vorziehen. **favourable** adj günstig, vorteilhaft, gelegen. **favourite** adj Lieblings—. n Liebling m. Favorit m.

fawn[1] (fɔ:n) n Rehkalb neu. adj rehbraun.

fawn[2] (fɔ:n) vi 1 kriechen. 2 schmeicheln.

fear (fiə) n Furcht, Angst f. vt (be)fürchten, sich fürchten vor. **fearless** adj furchtlos.

feasible ('fi:zibəl) adj möglich, ausführbar.

feast (fi:st) n Fest, Festmahl neu. vi sich ergötzen. **feast-day** rr Festtag m.

feat (fi:t) n 1 Kunststück neu. 2 Heldentat f.

feather ('feðə) n Feder f. **featherbed** n Federbett neu. **featherweight** n Federgewicht neu.

feature ('fi:tʃə) n 1 (Gesichts)Zug m. 2 Grundzug m. 3 Merkmal neu. 4 (in a newspaper) Feature neu. spezieller Artikel m. vt 1 charakterisieren. 2 in der Hauptrolle zeigen.

February ('februəri) n Februar m.

feckless ('fekləs) adj 1 hilflos. 2 wirkungslos.

fed (fed) v see **feed**.

federal ('fedərəl) adj 1 Bundes—, bundesstaatlich. 2 (in Switzerland) eidgenössisch. **federate** adj verbündet. **federation** n Vereinigung f. 2 pol Bundesstaat m.

fee (fi:) n Gebühr, Bezahlung f. Honorar neu.

feeble ('fi:bəl) adj schwach, lahm, kraftlos. **feeble-minded** adj geistesschwach. **feeblemindedness** n Schwachsinn m.

feed[*] (fi:d) vt 1 ernähren, 2 füttern. vi 1 sich (er)nähren. 2 weiden. n 1 Nahrung f. 2 Futter neu. **be fed up with** satt haben. **feedback** n Feedback m.

feel[*] (fi:l) vt 1 betasten, (be)fühlen. 2 spüren, wahrnehmen. 3 empfinden. vi 1 sich fühlen, sich vorkommen. 2 glauben. **feel like doing something** Lust haben, etwas zu tun. **feeler** n Fühler m. **feeling** n 1 Gefühl neu. 2 Empfindung f. 3 Ahnung f. **with feeling** adv gefühlvoll.

feign (fein) vi,vt vorgeben, simulieren. vt heucheln. **feigned** adj vorgeblich, heuchlerisch.

feint[1] (feint) n 1 Finte f. 2 Verstellung f.

feint[2] (feint) adj,adv schwach.

feline ('fi:lain) adj Katzen—, katzenartig.

fell[1] (fel) v see **fall**.

fell[2] (fel) vt 1 niederschlagen. 2 fällen.

fellow ('felou) n 1 Gefährte m. 2 Mitglied neu. 3 Kerl, Bursche m. **fellow passenger** Mitreisende(r) m. **fellowship** n Gemeinschaft f. Gesellschaft f.

felon ('felən) n Verbrecher m. **felonious** adj verbrecherisch. **felony** n schwere Verbrechen neu.

felt[1] (felt) v see **feel**.

felt[2] (felt) n Filz m.

female ('fi:meil) n 1 Weib neu. 2 (of animals) Weibchen neu. adj weiblich.

feminine ('feminin) adj weiblich. **femininity** n Weiblichkeit f. weibliches Wesen neu.

feminism ('feminizəm) n Frauenrechtlertum neu. **feminist** n Frauenrechtler m.

fence (fens) n 1 Einzäunung f. Zaun m. vi fechten. **fence** in einzäunen. **fencing** n 1 Fechtkunst f. 2 Einzäunung f.

fend (fend) vt **fend off** abwehren. vi **fend for** sorgen für.

fennel ('fenl) n bot Fenchel m.

ferment (n 'fə:ment; v fə'ment) n Gärungsmittel neu. vi gären, fermentieren. vt gären lassen. **fermentation** n Gärung f.

fern (fə:n) n Farn m. Farnkraut neu.

ferocious (fə'rouʃəs) adj 1 wild. 2 grausam. **ferocity** n Wildheit f. 2 Grausamkeit f.

ferret ('ferit) n Frettchen neu. v **ferret out** 1 herausjagen. 2 ausforschen.

ferry ('feri) n Fähre f. vt übersetzen.

fertile ('fə:tail) adj 1 fruchtbar. 2 ergiebig. **fertility** n Fruchtbarkeit f. **fertilize** vt 1 fruchtbar machen. 2 bot befruchten. 3 düngen. **fertilization** n · 1 Befruchtung f. 2 Düngung f. **fertilizer** n Düngemittel neu.

fervent ('fə:vənt) adj glühend, leidenschaftlich. **fervour** n Leidenschaft f. Eifer m.

fester ('festə) vi 1 eitern. 2 verfaulen.

festival ('festivəl) n Fest neu. Feier f. **festive** adj festlich. **festivity** n Festlichkeit f.

festoon (fes'tu:n) n Girlande f. vt schmücken.

fetch (fetʃ) vt 1 holen. 2 (in a sale) bringen. **fetching** adj inf reizend, anziehend.

fete (feit) n Fest neu. vt feiern.

fetid ('fetid) adj stinkend.

fetish ('fetiʃ) n Fetisch m.

fetter ('fetə) n Fessel f. vt fesseln.

feud (fju:d) n 1 Fehde f. 2 Lehen neu. **feudal** adj feudal. **feudalism** n Feudalismus m.

fever ('fi:və) n 1 med Fieber neu. 2 fieberhafte

Aufregung f. **feverish** adj 1 fiebrig. 2 aufgeregt, fieberhaft.

few (fju:) adj,pron wenige. **a few** ein paar.

fiance (fi'ɒnsei) n Verlobte(r) m. **fiancee** n Verlobte, Braut f.

fiasco (fi'æskou) n Fiasko neu.

fib (fib) n Schwindelei, (kleine) Lüge f.

fibre ('faibə) n Faser, Fiber f. **fibreglass** n Fiberglas neu. **fibrous** adj faserig.

fickle ('fikəl) adj wankelmutig, unbeständig. **fickleness** n Wankelmut m. Unbeständigkeit f.

fiction ('fikʃən) n 1 Romanliteratur f. 2 Erdichtung f. **fictional** adj erdichtet, erfunden. **fictitious** adj unwirklich, erfunden.

fiddle ('fidl) n 1 Geige, Fiedel f. 2 inf Schwindelei f. vi 1 fiedeln. 2 tändeln. 3 beschwindeln.

fidelity (fi'deliti) n Treue f.

fidget ('fidʒit) vi (herum)zappeln. **fidgety** adj zappelig.

field (fi:ld) n 1 Feld neu. 2 Gebiet, Fach neu. Bereich m. 3 sport Platz m. **fieldwork** n praktische (wissenschaftliche) Arbeit f.

fiend (fi:nd) n 1 Teufel m. 2 Unhold m. **fiendish** adj teuflisch, unmenschlich.

fierce (fiəs) adj 1 wild, grimmig. 2 heftig. 3 (of light) grell. **fierceness** n 1 Wildheit f. 2 Heftigkeit f.

fiery ('faiəri) adj feurig, leidenschaftlich.

fifteen (fif'ti:n) adj fünfzehn. n Fünfzehn f. **fifteenth** adj fünfzehnte.

fifth (fifθ) adj fünfte. **fifthly** adv fünftens.

fifty ('fifti) adj fünfzig. n Fünfzig f. **fifty-fifty** adv halb und halb. **fiftieth** adj fünfzigste.

fig (fig) n Feige f.

fight* (fait) n 1 Kampf m. 2 Konflikt m. 3 Schlägerei f. vt bekämpfen. vi kämpfen, sich schlagen. **fighter** n Kämpfer m.

figment ('figmənt) n (reine) Einbildung f.

figure ('figə) n 1 Ziffer f. 2 Gestalt, Figur f. 3 Persönlichkeit f. 4 Statue f. vi 1 erscheinen, auftreten. 2 meinen, denken. vt bildlich darstellen. **figure out** ausrechnen. **figurative** adj bildlich, symbolisch. **figurehead** n Repräsentationsfigur f. Strohmann m.

filament ('filəmənt) n 1 Faden m. Faser f. 2 (in an electric appliance) Glühfaden m.

file[1] (fail) n 1 Akte f. 2 Mappe f. Ordner m. 3 Reihe f. **in single file** hintereinander. vt (ein)ordnen, ablegen. **filing cabinet** n Aktenschrank m.

file[2] (fail) n Feile f. vt (zu)feilen, glätten.

filial ('filiəl) adj kindlich, Kindes—.

fill (fil) vt 1 (ab-, er-)füllen. 2 sättigen. 3 besetzen. 4 (a tooth) plombieren. vi sich füllen. **fill up (with petrol)** (auf)tanken.

filling ('filiŋ) n 1 Einlage f. 2 Füllung f. 3 med Zahnplombe f. adj sättigend. **filling station** n Tankstelle f.

fillet ('filit) n cul Filet neu.

filly ('fili) n weibliches Füllen or Fohlen neu.

film (film) n 1 Film m. 2 Haut, Membrane f. 3 med Schleier m. vt (ver)filmen, drehen. vi drehen. **film star** n Filmstar, Filmschauspieler m.

filter ('filtə) n Filter m. vt filtern, filtrieren.

filth (filθ) n Dreck, Schmutz m. **filthiness** n Schmutzigkeit f. **filthy** adj schmutzig, dreckig.

fin (fin) n Flosse, Finne f.

final ('fainl) adj 1 letzt. 2 End—, Schluß—. 3 endgültig. n sport Endspiel neu. **finale** n Finale neu. **finalize** vt 1 vollenden, abschließen. 2 endgültige Form geben. **finally** adv 1 endlich, schließlich. 2 zum Schluß.

finance ('fainæns) n Finanz f. Finanzwesen neu. vt finanzieren. **financial** adj finanziell, Finanz—. **financier** n Finanzier m.

finch (fintʃ) n Fink m.

find* (faind) vt 1 finden, entdecken. 2 halten für, denken. **find out** herausfinden. ~n Fund m.

fine[1] (fain) adj 1 fein. 2 schön. 3 scharf. **finery** n 1 Putz m. 2 Eleganz f.

fine[2] (fain) n 1 Geldstrafe f. vt zu einer Geldstrafe verurteilen.

finesse (fi'nes) n 1 Finesse f. 2 Schlauheit f.

finger ('fiŋgə) n Finger m. vt fingern, betasten. **fingermark** n Fingerabdruck m. **fingernail** n Fingernagel m. **fingerprint** n Fingerabdruck m. **fingertip** n Fingerspitze f.

finish ('finiʃ) vt 1 beenden. 2 vollenden. vi enden, aufhören. n 1 sport Ziel neu. 2 Ende neu.

finite ('fainait) adj begrenzt, endlich. **finite verb** n gram Verbum finitum neu.

Finland ('finlənd) n Finnland neu.

Finn (fin) n Finne f. **Finnish** adj finnisch. n (language) Finnisch neu.

fir (fə:) n Tanne f. **fircone** n Tannenzapfen m.

fire (faiə) n 1 Feuer neu. 2 Brand m. **on fire** in Flammen. ~vt 1 anzünden. 2 anfeuern. vi feuern. **fire away!** schieß los!

fire alarm n Feuermelder, Feueralarm m.

fire brigade n Feuerwehr f.

fire drill n Feueralarmübung f.

fire-engine n Motorspritze f. Feuerwehrauto neu.

fire-escape n Nottreppe f.

fire-extinguisher n Feuerlöscher m.

fireman ('faiəmən) n Feuerwehrmann m.

fireplace ('faiəpleis) n (offener) Kamin m.

fireproof ('faiəpruːf) adj feuerfest.

fireside ('faiəsaid) n Kamin m. adj häuslich.

fire station n Feuerwache f.

firework ('faiəwəːk) n Feuerwerk neu.

firing squad n Exekutionskommando neu.

firm[1] (fəːm) adj 1 fest. 2 standhaft. 3 entschlossen. **firmness** n 1 Festigkeit f. 2 Entschlossenheit f.

firm[2] (faim) n Firma f.

first (fəːst) adj 1 erste. 2 beste. adv 1 erstens. 2 zuerst. **at first** anfangs, zuerst. **first of all** zuallererst. ~n Erste(r) m. **first aid** n Nothilfe f. adj Unfalls—. **first class** n erste Klasse f. **first-class** adj prima, erstklassig, ausgezeichnet. **first-hand** adv aus erster Hand, direkt. **first name** n Vorname m. **first person** n gram erste Person f. **first-rate** adj ausgezeichnet.

fiscal ('fiskəl) adj fiskalisch, Finanz—.

fish (fiʃ) n, pl **fishes** or **fish** Fisch m. **queer fish** n komischer Kauz m. **a pretty kettle of fish** eine schöne Bescherung f. vi fischen, angeln. **fisherman** n Fischer m. **fish finger** n Fischstäbchen neu. **fishing** n Fischen, Angeln neu. **fishing rod** n Angelrute f. **fishmonger** n Fischhändler m. **fishslice** n Fischheber m. **fishy** adj 1 fischig. 2 verdächtig.

fission ('fiʃən) n Spaltung f.

fist (fist) n Faust f.

fit[1] (fit) adj 1 passend. 2 sport in Form, fit. 3 fähig. **fit as a fiddle** kerngesund. ~vt 1 passen. 2 passend machen, anpassen. vi 1 sich eignen. 2 (of clothes) sitzen. n (of clothes) Sitz m. **fitting** adj passend, schicklich.

fit[2] (fit) n 1 med Anfall m. 2 Ausbruch m. **fitful** adj 1 unbeständig. 2 launenhaft.

five (faiv) adj fünf. n Fünf f.

fix (fiks) vt 1 befestigen, anheften. 2 (one's eyes) richten, heften. 3 bestimmen, festsetzen. vi fest werden. **fix up** arrangieren. **fixation** n Fixierung f. **fixed** adj starr. 2 bestimmt. **fixture** n Zubehör(teil) m.

fizz (fiz) vi zischen, sprudeln. n Zischen neu. **fizzle** vi zischen. **fizzle out** verpuffen.

fjord (fjɔːd) n Fjord m.

flabbergast ('flæbəgaːst) vt verblüffen.

flabby ('flæbi) adj schlaff, schlapp.

flag[1] (flæg) n Fahne, Flagge f. vt beflaggen. **flagpole** n Fahnenstange f.

flag[2] (flæg) vi 1 ermatten. 2 mutlos werden.

flagon ('flægən) n (bauchige) Flasche f.

flagrant ('fleigrənt) adj 1 schamlos. 2 offenkundig.

flair ('flɛə) n Spürsinn, Flair m.

flake (fleik) n 1 Flocke f. 2 Schuppe f. Blatt neu. vi (sich) flocken. vi,vt abblättern. **flaky** adj flockig, schuppig.

flamboyant (flæm'bɔiənt) adj 1 auffallend. 2 überladen. 3 flammend.

flame (fleim) n 1 Flamme f. 2 Leidenschaft f. vi flammen, lodern.

flamingo (flə'miŋgou) n Flamingo m.

flan (flæn) n Torte f.

flank (flæŋk) n 1 mil Flanke f. 2 zool Weiche f. vt flankieren.

flannel ('flænl) n 1 Flanell m. 2 Waschlappen m.

flap (flæp) n 1 anat Lappen m. 2 Klappe f. 3 (Flügel)Schlag m. vi 1 flattern. 2 lose herabhängen.

flare (flɛə) vi 1 flackern. 2 sich bauschen. n 1 flackerndes Licht neu. 2 Lichtsignal neu. v **flare up** 1 aufflackern. 2 aufbrausen.

flash (flæʃ) n 1 Blitz m. 2 Aufblitzen neu. vi (auf)blitzen. vt werfen. **flashback** n Rückblende f. **flashbulb** n Blitzlichtlampe f. **flashlight** n 1 Blitzlicht neu. Taschenlampe f.

flask (flaːsk) n 1 (Taschen-, Reise-) Flasche f. 2 sci Kolben m.

flat[1] (flæt) adj 1 flach, platt. 2 eben. n 1 Fläche f. 2 Flachland neu. **flatfish** n Plattfisch m. **flat-footed** adj plattfüßig. **flatten** vt platt machen, (ein)ebnen. vi flach werden.

flat[2] (flæt) n Wohnung f.

flatter ('flætə) vt schmeicheln. **flatterer** n Schmeichler m. **flattering** adj schmeichelhaft. **flattery** n Schmeichelei f.

flaunt (flɔːnt) vt 1 prunken. 2 offen zeigen.

flautist ('flɔːtist) n Flötist m.

flavour ('fleivə) n Geschmack m. Aroma neu. **flavouring** n Würze f. Geschmackstoff m.

flaw (flɔː) n 1 Sprung m. 2 Makel m. **flawless** adj 1 makellos. 2 tadellos.

flax (flæks) n Flachs m.

flea (fliː) n Floh m.

fleck (flek) n Fleck m. vt sprenkeln.

fled (fled) v see **flee.**

flee* (fliː) vi fliehen. vt meiden.

fleece (fli:s) n Fell, Vlies neu. vt schröpfen. **fleecy** adj wollig.

fleet (fli:t) n Flotte f.

fleeting ('fli:tiŋ) adj flüchtig, vergänglich.

Flemish ('flemiʃ) adj flämisch. n (language) Flämisch neu.

flesh (fleʃ) n Fleisch neu. **fleshy** adj 1 fleischig. 2 fett.

flew (flu:) v see **fly**[1].

flex (fleks) n Kabel neu. vt biegen, beugen. **flexible** adj 1 biegsam. 2 flexibel. **flexibility** n Biegsamkeit f.

flick (flik) vt schnellen. n (leichter) Hieb m.

flicker ('flikə) n Flackern neu. vi flackern.

flight[1] (flait) n 1 Flug m. 2 Schwarm m. **flight deck** n Flugdeck neu. **flight of stairs** n Treppe f.

flight[2] (flait) n Flucht f. **flighty** adj flüchtig.

flimsy ('flimzi) adj 1 dünn. 2 schwach.

flinch (flintʃ) vi zurückschrecken, zucken.

fling* (fliŋ) vt werfen, schleudern. n Hieb m.

flint (flint) n Kiesel m. 2 Flint m.

flip (flip) n Klaps m. vt klapsen, schnellen. **flipper** n 1 zool Flosse f. 2 Schwimmflosse f.

flippant ('flipənt) adj leichtfertig. **flippancy** n Leichtfertigkeit, Frechheit f.

flirt (flə:t) vi flirten. **flirtation** n Liebelei f. Flirt m. **flirtatious** adj kokett.

flit (flit) vi 1 flitzen. 2 wegziehen, sich entfernen.

float (flout) vi 1 (obenauf) schwimmen. 2 schweben. vt 1 bewässern. 2 flottmachen. 3 flößen. n 1 tech Schwimmer m. 2 Floß neu.

flock[1] (flɔk) n 1 Herde f. 2 Schar f. vi 1 sich scharen. 2 zusammenströmen.

flock[2] (flɔk) n (Woll)Flocke f.

flog (flɔg) vt 1 (aus)peitschen. 2 prügeln, züchtigen. 3 sl verkaufen. **flogging** n 1 Prügelstrafe f. 2 (Aus)Peitschen neu.

flood (flʌd) n 1 Flut f. 2 Überschwemmung f. vt,vi 1 überfluten. 2 überschwemmen. **floodlight** n Scheinwerfer m. Flutlicht neu.

floor (flɔ:) n 1 Fußboden m. 2 Stock m. Stockwerk, Geschoß neu. Etage f. vt 1 einen Fußboden legen. 2 inf verblüffen. **floorboard** n Diele f. Fußbodenbrett neu.

flop (flɔp) vi 1 (hin)plumpsen. 2 flattern, schlottern. 3 Th durchfallen. n 1 Plumps m. 2 Versager, Durchfall m. **floppy** adj schlapp.

flora ('flɔ:rə) n Flora, Pflanzenwelt f. **floral** adj Blumen—, Blüte—. **florist** n Blumenhändler m.

flounce[1] (flauns) vi stürzen.

flounce[2] (flauns) n Volant m.

flounder[1] ('flaundə) vi taumeln, stolpern.

flounder[2] ('flaundə) n Flunder f.

flour ('flauə) n Mehl neu. vt mit Mehl bestreuen.

flourish ('flʌriʃ) n 1 Schnörkel m. 2 Schwingen neu. 3 mus Verzierung f. vi 1, blühen, gedeihen. 2 Schnörkel machen. vt schwingen.

flout (flaut) vt verspotten, verhöhnen.

flow (flou) vi 1 fließen. 2 wallen. n Fluß m.

flower ('flauə) n 1 Blume f. 2 Blüte f. vi blühen. **flowerbed** n Blumenbeet neu. **flowerpot** n Blumentopf m. **flowery** adj blumig.

flown v see **fly**[1].

fluctuate ('flʌktʃueit) vi schwanken, fluktuieren. **fluctuation** n 1 Schwanken neu. Schwankung f. 2 comm Fluktuieren neu.

flue (flu:) n Kaminrohr, Abzugsrohr neu.

fluent ('flu:ənt) adj fließend. **fluency** n Fluß m. Geläufigkeit f.

fluff (flʌf) n 1 Flaum m. 2 Staubflocke f. **fluffy** adj 1 flaumig. 2 flockig.

fluid ('flu:id) n Flüssigkeit f. adj 1 flüssig. 2 fließend. 3 veränderlich.

flung (flʌŋ) v see **fling**.

fluorescent (fluə'resənt) adj fluoreszierend. **fluorescence** n Fluoreszenz f.

fluoride ('fluəraid) n Fluor neu.

flush[1] (flʌʃ) vi erröten. vt (aus)spülen. n 1 Erröten neu. 2 Spülung f.

flush[2] (flʌʃ) adj eben, glatt. **be flush** inf gut bei Kasse sein.

fluster ('flʌstə) n Verwirrung f. vt verwirren.

flute (flu:t) n mus Flöte f.

flutter ('flʌtə) vi,(vt) flattern (lassen).

flux (flʌks) n 1 Fluß m. 2 beständiger Wechsel m.

fly*[1] (flai) vi 1 fliegen. 2 fliehen. vt fliegen (lassen). **flyover** n (Straßen)Überführung f.

fly[2] (flai) n Fliege f.

foal (foul) n Fohlen neu. vi fohlen.

foam (foum) n Schaum m. vi schäumen. **foamy** adj schaumig.

focal ('foukəl) adj im Brennpunkt stehend, fokal. **focus** n Fokus, Brennpunkt m. vt fokussieren, einstellen.

fodder ('fɔdə) n Futter neu. vt füttern.

foe (fou) n Feind m.

foetus ('fi:təs) n Fötus m. Leibesfrucht f.

fog (fɔg) n 1 (dicker) Nebel m. 2 Schleier, Dunst m. vt,vi verschleiern. **foggy** adj 1 nebelig. 2 verschleiert, unklar. **foghorn** n Nebelhorn neu.

foible ('fɔibəl) n Schwäche f.

foil¹ (fɔil) vt vereiteln.

foil² (fɔil) n Folie f. Blattmetall neu.

foil³ (fɔil) n sport Florett neu.

foist (fɔist) vt 1 aufhalsen. 2 unterschieben.

fold¹ (fould) vt 1 falten. 2 (one's arms) kreuzen. vi 1 sich falten. 2 sich zusammenklappen (lassen). n Falte f.

fold² (fould) n 1 (Schaf)Hürde f. 2 Herde f.

foliage ('fouliidʒ) n Laub neu.

folk (fouk) n pl Leute pl. adj Volks—. **folkdance** n Volkstanz m. **folklore** n Volkssagen f pl. **folksong** n Volkslied neu.

follicle ('folikəl) n 1 Follikel m. 2 Haarbalg m.

follow ('folou) vt,vi 1 folgen, nachgehen. **follower** n 1 Nachfolger m. 2 Anhänger m. **following** n Anhängerschaft f.

folly ('foli) n Torheit, Narrheit f.

fond (fond) adj 1 liebevoll. 2 (of a hope, etc.) töricht. **be fond of** gern haben.

fondle ('fondl) vt liebkosen, streicheln.

font (font) n Taufstein m.

food (fu:d) n Nahrung, Kost f. Essen neu. Lebensmittel neu pl. 2 Futter neu.

fool (fu:l) n Narr, Dumme(r) m. vt zum Narren haben. vi Spaß machen. **foolish** adj 1 närrisch, albern, dumm. 2 unklug. **foolishness** n Dummheit f.

foolscap ('fu:lzkæp) n 1 Kanzleipapier neu. 2 Aktenformat neu.

foot (fut) n, pl **feet** 1 Fuß m. 2 Fußende neu. **on foot** zu Fuß. ~vt (bill) bezahlen. **foot it** inf zu Fuß gehen. **football** n 1 Fußball m. 2 Fußballspiel neu. **footbridge** n Steg m. Fußgängerbrücke f. **foothold** n 1 fester Stand m. 2 Halt m. **footing** n 1 Halt m. 2 Grundlage f. 3 Verhältnis neu. **footlights** n pl Th 1 Rampenlichter neu pl. 2 Bühne f. **footnote** n Anmerkung, Fußnote f. **footprint** n Fußspur f. **footstep** n 1 Spur f. 2 Tritt m. **footwear** n Schuhwerk neu.

for (fə; stressed fɔ:) prep 1 für. 2 zu, nach. 3 aus, vor. 4 lang. conj denn.

forage ('foridʒ) n Futter neu. vi 1 Futter holen. 2 durchstöbern, herumsuchen.

forbear (fə'bɛə) vi 1 sich enthalten. 2 gedulden. vt sich enthalten, unterlassen. **forbearance** n 1 Geduld f. 2 Unterlassung f.

forbid* (fə'bid) vt verbieten, untersagen. **forbidding** adj 1 abstoßend. 2 gefährlich.

force (fɔ:s) n 1 Kraft, Stärke f. 2 Zwang m. 3 Gewalt f. 4 pl Streitkräfte f pl. vt 1 zwingen. 2 (a door) aufbrechen. **force-feed** vt zwangsweise ernähren. **forceful** adj 1 kräftig. 2 eindringlich. **forcible** adj gewaltsam.

forceps ('fɔ:seps) n s or pl Zange f.

ford (fɔ:d) n Furt f. vt durchwaten.

fore (fɔ:) adv vorn n. Vorderteil neu. adj vorder, Vorder—.

forearm¹ ('fɔ:ra:m) n Vorderarm m.

forearm² (fɔ:'ra:m) vt im voraus bewaffnen.

forebear (fə'bɛə) n Vorfahr m.

forecast ('fɔ:ka:st) n Vorhersage, Voraussage f. **weather forecast** n Wetterbericht m. ~vt vorhersagen, voraussagen.

forefather ('fɔ:fɑ:ðə) n Vorfahr m.

forefinger ('fɔ:fiŋgə) n Zeigefinger m.

forefront ('fɔ:frʌnt) n 1 Vorderseite f. 2 vorderste Reihe f.

foreground ('fɔ:graund) n Vordergrund m.

forehand ('fɔ:hænd) n Vorhand f. adj mit Vorhand gespielt.

forehead ('forid) n Stirn f.

foreign ('forin) adj 1 fremd. 2 ausländisch. **foreigner** n 1 Ausländer m. 2 Fremde(r) m. **foreign exchange** n Devisen f pl.

foreleg ('fɔ:leg) n Vorderbein neu.

forelock ('fɔ:lok) n Stirnlocke f.

foreman ('fɔ:mən) n Aufseher, Vorarbeiter m.

foremost ('fɔ:moust) adj vorderst, erst. adv zuerst.

forensic (fə'rensik) adj gerichtlich, Gerichts—.

forerunner (fɔ:rʌnə) n Vorläufer m.

foresee* (fɔ:'si:) vt voraussehen. **forseeable** adj absehbar.

foresight ('fɔ:sait) n Voraussicht f.

forest ('forist) n Wald, Forst m. adj Wald—, Forst—. vt beforsten. **forester** n Förster m. **forestry** n Forstwirtschaft f.

forestall (fɔ:'stɔ:l) vt vereiteln.

foretaste ('fɔ:teist) n Vorgeschmack m.

foretell* (fɔ:'tel) vt 1 voraussagen. 2 vorbedeuten.

forethought ('fɔ:θɔ:t) n Vorbedacht m.

forfeit ('fɔ:fit) n 1 Verwirkung f. 2 Buße f. 3 Pfand neu. vt 1 verwirken. 2 einbüßen. 3 verlieren. adj verwirkt.

forge¹ (fɔ:dʒ) n Schmiede f. vt 1 schmieden. 2 fälschen.

forge² (fɔ:dʒ) **forge ahead** sich vorwärtsdrängen, an die Spitze kommen.

forgery ('fɔ:dʒəri) n Fälschung f.

forget* (fə'get) vt 1 vergessen. 2 vernachlässigen. **forgetful** adj vergeßlich.

forgive* (fə'giv) vt verzeihen, vergeben. **for-**

giveness n Verzeihung, Vergebung f. **for-giving** adj versöhnlich.

forgo° (fɔ:'gou) vt verzichten auf.

fork (fɔ:k) n 1 Gabel f. 2 (in a road, etc.) Gabelung f. vi sich gabeln. **fork out** Geld herausrücken. **forked** adj gabelförmig.

forlorn (fə'lɔ:n) adj 1 verloren. 2 hoffnungslos. 3 hilflos.

form (fɔ:m) n 1 Form, Figur, Gestalt f. 2 Art, Weise, Methode f. 3 Förmlichkeit f. 4 Formular neu. 5 (Schul)Klasse f. 6 (Schul)Bank f. vt 1 formen, bilden, gestalten. 2 erdenken. 3 schließen. vi sich formen. **formal** adj 1 formal, förmlich. 2 formell, feierlich. **formality** n Formalität, Förmlichkeit f. **formation** n 1 Bildung, Gestaltung f. 2 Formation f. **formative** adj bildend, gestaltend. **formative years** n pl Entwicklungsjahre neu pl.

former ('fɔ:mə) adj 1 vorig. 2 ehemalig. 3 jene. **formerly** adv ehemals.

formidable ('fɔ:midəbəl) adj 1 furchtbar, erschreckend. 2 ungeheuer, gewaltig.

formula ('fɔ:mjulə) n Formel f. **formulate** vt formulieren.

forsake° (fə'seik) vt 1 aufgeben. 2 verlassen.

fort (fɔ:t) n Fort neu. Festung f.

forte ('fɔ:tei) n Stärke f. adv mus forte.

forth (fɔ:θ) adv hervor. **from this day forth** von heute an. **forthcoming** adj bevorstehend.

fortify ('fɔ:tifai) vt 1 befestigen. 2 stärken. **fortification** n 1 Befestigung f. 2 Stärkung f.

fortnight ('fɔ:tnait) n vierzehn Tage m pl.

fortress ('fɔ:trəs) n Festung f.

fortune ('fɔ:tʃən) n 1 Glück neu. 2 Schicksal neu. 3 Vermögen neu. **fortunate** adj glücklich. **fortunately** adv glücklicherweise.

forty ('fɔ:ti) adj vierzig. n Vierzig f. **fortieth** adj vierzigste.

forum ('fɔ:rəm) n 1 Forum neu. 2 Tribunal neu.

forward ('fɔ:wəd) adj 1 vorder, vornliegend. 2 fortschrittlich. 3 vorlaut. adv 1 vorwärts. 2 nach vorn. vt 1 befördern. 2 nachsenden. **forwards** adv vorwärts.

fossil ('fɔsəl) n Fossil neu. adj versteinert.

foster ('fɔstə) vt pflegen, aufziehen. adj Pflege—. **fosterchild** n Pflegekind neu. **fostermother** n Pflegemutter f.

fought (fɔ:t) v see **fight**.

foul (faul) adj schmutzig, ekelhaft, übel, widrig. vi schmutzig werden. vt verschmutzen. n sport Regelverstoß m. Foul neu.

found¹ (faund) v see **find**.

found² (faund) vt (be)gründen, stiften. **foundation** n Gründung, Stiftung f. adj Grund—.

founder ('faundə) vi 1 naut sinken, untergehen. 2 scheitern. vt zum Scheitern bringen.

foundry ('faundri) n Gießerei, Hütte f.

fountain ('fauntin) n 1 Springbrunnen m. 2 Quelle f. **fountain pen** n Füllfeder f.

four (fɔ:) adj vier. n Vier f. **four-poster** n Himmelbett neu. **foursome** n 1 sport Viererspiel neu. 2 Quartett neu. **fourth** adj vierte. **fourthly** adv viertens.

fourteen (fɔ:'ti:n) adj vierzehn. n Vierzehn f. **fourteenth** adj vierzehnte.

fowl (faul) n 1 Geflügel neu. 2 Huhn neu.

fox (fɔks) n Fuchs m. vt täuschen, betrügen, verwirren. **foxglove** n bot Fingerhut m. **fox-hunting** n Fuchsjagd f.

foyer ('fɔiei) n Foyer neu.

fraction ('frækʃən) n 1 math Bruch m. 2 Bruchteil m.

fracture ('fræktʃə) n med Knochenbruch m. vt brechen.

fragile ('frædʒail) adj zerbrechlich, zart.

fragment ('frægmənt) n Bruchstück neu. Splitter m. Scherbe f. **fragmentary** adj bruchstückhaft, unvollständig, fragmentarisch.

fragrant ('freigrənt) adj duftend.

frail (freil) adj 1 zerbrechlich. 2 schwach. **frailty** n Schwachheit f.

frame (freim) n 1 Rahmen m. 2 Gestell neu. vt 1 (ein)rahmen. 2 bilden, bauen. **framework** n 1 Gerippe neu. 2 Bau m. 3 Rahmen m.

franc (fræŋk) n 1 (französischer) Franc m. 2 (schweizerischer) Franken m.

France (frɑːns) n Frankreich neu.

franchise ('fræntʃaiz) n 1 Wahlrecht neu. 2 Bürgerrecht neu. 3 US Konzession f.

frank (fræŋk) adj offen, freimütig. vt (maschinell) frankieren.

frankfurter ('fræŋkfə:tə) n Frankfurter f.

frantic ('fræntik) adj 1 wahnsinnig. 2 verzweifelt, außer sich.

fraternal (frə'tə:nl) adj brüderlich. **fraternity** n 1 Brüderlichkeit f. 2 Bruderschaft f. **fraternize** vi sich verbrüdern. **fraternization** n Verbrüderung f.

fraud (frɔ:d) n 1 Betrug m. 2 Schwindel m. 3 Betrüger, Schwindler m. **fraudulence** n Betrügerei f. **fraudulent** adj betrügerisch.

fraught (frɔ:t) adj beladen, voll (von).

fray¹ (frei) n Streit m. Schlägerei f.

fray² (frei) (vt),vi (sich) ausfransen.

freak (fri:k) n 1 Laune f. Einfall m. 2 Abnormität, Mißbildung f. adj 1 launenhaft. 2 abnorm, grotesk.

freckle ('frekəl) n Sommersprosse f.

free (fri:) adj 1 frei. 2 ungebunden, unabhängig. 3 kostenlos, umsonst, gratis. 4 freigebig, großzügig. vt befreien. **freedom** n Freiheit f. **freehand** adj freihändig. **freehold** n eigener Grundbesitz m. **freelance** adj freischaffend, selbständig. **freely** adv 1 freiwillig. 2 reichlich. **Freemason** n Freimaurer m. **free will** n freier Wille m.

freeze (fri:z) vi 1 (ge)frieren. 2 erstarren. vt 1 frieren, tiefkühlen. 2 (credit) sperren. 3 (wages, prices) stoppen. n 1 (Ge)frieren neu. 2 Lohnstopp m. 3 Preisstopp m. **freezing** adj eisig. **freezing point** n Gefrierpunkt m.

freight (freit) n 1 Fracht f. 2 Frachtgeld neu. vt 1 beladen. 2 befrachten. **freight train** n Güterzug m.

French (frentʃ) adj französisch. n (language) Französisch neu. **French bean** n grüne Bohne f. **French horn** n Waldhorn neu. **Frenchman** n Franzose m. **French window** n Flügeltür f. **Frenchwoman** n Französin f.

frenzy ('frenzi) n Wahnsinn m. Raserei f. **frenzied** adj wahnsinnig, rasend.

frequency ('fri:kwənsi) n 1 Häufigkeit f. 2 sci Frequenz f. **frequent** adj häufig, öfters. vt häufig or öfters besuchen, frequentieren.

fresco ('freskou) n Fresko(gemälde) neu.

fresh (freʃ) adj 1 frisch. 2 unerfahren. 3 neu. 4 sl frech. **freshen up** vt,vi auffrischen. **freshwater** adj Süßwasser neu. adj Süßwasser—.

fret[1] (fret) vt zerfressen. vi sich ärgern. **fretful** adj ärgerlich, mürrisch.

fret[2] (fret) n Flechtband neu. **fretsaw** n Laubsäge f.

friar ('fraiə) n Mönch m. **friary** n Mönchskloster neu.

friction ('frikʃən) n Reibung f.

Friday ('fraidi) n Freitag m.

fridge (fridʒ) n inf Kühlschrank m.

fried (fraid) v see **fry**. adj gebraten, Brat—. **fried egg** n Spiegelei neu.

friend (frend) n 1 Freund m. 2 Bekannte(r) m. **make friends with** sich anfreunden mit. **friendliness** n Freundlichkeit f. **friendly** adj 1 freundlich. 2 befreundet 3 wohlwollend. **friendship** n Freundschaft f.

frieze (fri:z) n Fries m.

fright (frait) n Schreck, Schrecken m. **frighten** vt erschrecken. **be frightened of** Angst haben vor. **frightful** adj schrecklich.

frigid ('fridʒid) adj 1 kalt. 2 frigid. **frigidity** n 1 Kälte f. 2 Frigidität f.

frill (fril) n Krause f. vt kräuseln.

fringe ('frindʒ) n 1 Franse f. 2 Rand m. vt 1 mit Fransen besetzen. 2 säumen.

frisk (frisk) vi hüpfen. vt sl durchsuchen, filzen. **frisky** adj 1 hüpfend. 2 munter.

fritter[1] ('fritə) vt **fritter away** verzetteln, verschwenden, vergeuden.

fritter[2] ('fritə) n in Eierteig gebackene Obstscheiben f pl.

frivolity (fri'vɔliti) n Leichtfertigkeit f. **frivolous** adj leichtfertig.

frizz (friz) (vi),vt (sich) kräuseln. **frizzy** adj kraus, gekräuselt.

frizzle[1] ('frizəl) (vi),vt (sich) kräuseln.

frizzle[2] ('frizəl) vi zischen.

fro (frou) adv **to and fro** hin und her, auf und ab.

frock (frɔk) n 1 Damenkleid, Kinderkleid neu. 2 rel Kutte f. **frockcoat** n Gehrock m.

frog (frɔg) n Frosch m. **frogman** n Froschmann m.

frolic ('frɔlik) n 1 lustiger Streich, Spaß m. 2 Lustbarkeit f. vi scherzen. **frolicsome** adj lustig, vergnügt.

from (frəm; stressed frɔm) prep 1 von, aus, von...her. 2 seit. 3 nach.

front (frʌnt) n 1 Vorderseite f. Vorderteil m. 2 Front f. adj Vorder—. **in front** adv vorne. **in front of** gegenüber vor.

frontier ('frʌntiə) n Grenze f. adj Grenz—.

frost (frɔst) n Frost m. **frostbite** n Erfrierung f. **frosty** adj frostig.

froth (frɔθ) n Schaum m. vi schäumen. vt zu Schaum schlagen. **frothy** adj schaumig.

frown (fraun) n 1 Stirnrunzeln neu. 2 finsterer Blick m. vi 1 die Stirn runzeln. 2 finster blicken.

froze (frouz) v see **freeze**.

frozen ('frouzn) v see **freeze**. adj 1 gefroren. 2 cul Gefrier—. **frozen food** n tiefgekühlte Lebensmittel f pl.

frugal ('fru:gəl) adj 1 frugal, mäßig. 2 sparsam. **frugality** n 1 Mäßigkeit f. 2 Sparsamkeit f.

fruit (fru:t) n 1 Frucht f. 2 Früchte f pl. Obst neu. **fruitful** adj 1 fruchtbar. 2 ergiebig. **fruition** n 1 Genuß m. 2 Erfüllung f. **fruitless** adj 1 unfruchtbar. 2 vergeblich, fruchtlos. **fruit machine** n Spielautomat m. **fruit salad** n Obstsalat m. **fruity** adj fruchtig, saftig.

frustrate (frʌs'treit) vt vereiteln, verhindern. **frustration** n Vereitelung, Enttäuschung f.

fry (frai) vt braten, (in der Pfanne) backen.

frying pan n Bratpfanne f. **out of the frying pan into the fire** aus dem Regen in die Traufe.

fuchsia ('fju:ʃə) n Fuchsie f.

fuck (fʌk) vi,(vt) tab sich paaren (mit).

fudge (fʌdʒ) n Weichkaramelle f. vt inf (zurecht)pfuschen.

fuel ('fju:əl) n 1 Brennstoff m. 2 Treibstoff m. vt 1 mit Brennstoff versehen. 2 tanken.

fugitive ('fju:dʒitiv) n Flüchtling m. adj flüchtig.

fulcrum ('fʌlkrəm) n Drehpunkt m.

fulfil (ful'fil) vt erfüllen. **fulfilment** n Erfüllung f.

full (ful) adj 1 voll. 2 besetzt. 3 satt. adv direkt, gerade, völlig. **to the full** adv vollständig. **full-length** adj in Lebensgröße f. **full moon** n Vollmond m. **fullness** n Fülle f. **full stop** n Punkt m. **full-time** adj ganztägig, Vollzeit—. **fully** adv voll, ausführlich.

fumble ('fʌmbəl) vi umhertappen, fummeln. **fumbling** adj 1 tappend. 2 linkisch.

fume (fju:m) n 1 Dunst, Dampf, Rauch m. 2 pl Abgase neu. vi 1 dunsten, rauchen. 2 wütend sein, aufgebracht sein.

fun (fʌn) n Spaß, Scherz m. **make fun of** vi sich lustig machen über. **funfair** n Rummelplatz, Jahrmarkt m.

function ('fʌŋkʃən) n 1 Funktion, Aufgabe f. 2 Veranstaltung f. vi funktionieren. **functional** adj funktionell. **functionary** n Beamte(r) m.

fund (fʌnd) n 1 Kapital neu. Fonds m. 2 Vorrat, Schatz m. 3 pl Geldmittel neu pl.

fundamental (fʌndə'mentl) adj Grund—, wesentlich, grundsätzlich, fundamental.

funeral ('fju:nərəl) n Beerdigung. adj Trauer—.

fungus ('fʌŋgəs) n, pl fungi Schwamm, Pilz m.

funnel ('fʌnl) n 1 Trichter m. 2 Schornstein m.

funny ('fʌni) adj 1 komisch. 2 sonderbar. **funny bone** n inf Musikantenknochen m.

fur (fə:) n 1 Pelz m. 2 med Belag m. 3 pl Pelzwaren f pl. adj Pelz—.

furious ('fjuəriəs) adj wütend, rasend.

furnace ('fə:nis) n Schmelzofen m.

furnish ('fə:niʃ) vt 1 versehen. 2 möblieren. **furnished** adj möbliert. **furnishing** n Einrichtung f.

furniture ('fə:nitʃə) n Möbel neu pl.

furrow ('fʌrou) n Furche, Rinne f. vt (durch)furchen.

further ('fə:θə) adj weiter, ferner. vt fördern. **furthermore** adv überdies, weiter.

furthest ('fə:ðist) adj weitest. adv am weitesten.

furtive ('fə:tiv) adj verstohlen, heimlich.

fury ('fjuəri) n Wut f. Zorn m.

fuse[1] (fju:z) n 1 (Schmelz)Sicherung f. 2 Zünder m. vi durchbrennen.

fuse[2] (fju:z) vt schmelzen. vi verschmelzen.

fuselage ('fju:zəla:ʒ) n (Flugzeug)Rumpf m.

fusion ('fju:ʒən) n 1 Schmelzen neu. 2 Verschmelzung f. 3 comm Fusion f.

fuss (fʌs) n Getue neu. Aufregung f. vi sich aufregen über. **fussy** adj penibel.

futile ('fju:tail) adj unnütz, nutzlos, vergeblich. **futility** n Nutzlosigkeit, Sinnlosigkeit f.

future ('fju:tʃə) n 1 Zukunft f. 2 gram Futur neu. adj (zu)künftig.

fuzz (fʌz) n 1 Fussel f. Flaum m. 2 sl Polizei f. **fuzzy** adj 1 fusselig. 2 verschwommen. 3 kraus.

G

gabble ('gæbəl) n Geschnatter, Geplapper neu. vi,vt schnattern, plappern.

gable ('geibəl) n Giebel m.

gadget ('gædʒit) n Apparat m. Dings neu.

gag[1] (gæg) n Knebel m. vt knebeln.

gag[2] (gæg) n Gag m. Pointe f.

gaiety ('geiəti) n Heiterkeit, Fröhlichkeit f.

gaily ('geili) adv heiter, fröhlich.

gain (gein) n 1 Gewinn m. 2 Profit m. vt 1 gewinnen. 2 erlangen, erreichen. vi (of a clock) vorgehen.

gait (geit) n 1 Gangart f. 2 Haltung f.

gala ('ga:lə) n Fest neu. Festlichkeit f.

galaxy ('gæləksi) n Milchstraße f.

gale (geil) n Sturm m.

gallant ('gælənt) adj 1 tapfer, ritterlich. 2 galant, höflich.

galleon ('gæliən) n Galeone f.

gallery ('gæləri) n Galerie f.

galley ('gæli) n 1 Galeere f. 2 Schiffsküche f.

gallon ('gælən) n Gallone f.

gallop ('gæləp) n Galopp m. vi galoppieren.

gallows ('gælouz) n pl Galgen m.

galore (gə'lɔ:) adv in Hülle und Fülle.

galvanize ('gælvənaiz) vt 1 galvanisieren. 2 beleben, anspornen.

gamble ('gæmbəl) vi (um Geld) spielen. **gamble away** verspielen. ~n Risiko neu. **gambling** n Glücksspiel neu.

game (geim) n 1 Spiel neu. 2 Partie f. 3 (animals) Wild neu. adj inf bereit, aufgelegt (zu). **gamekeeper** n Wildhüter m.

gammon ('gæmən) n (geräucherter) Schinken m.

gander ('gændə) n Gänserich m.

gang (gæŋ) n 1 Arbeitskolonne f. 2 Gruppe, Bande f. v **gang up** sich zusammenrotten. **gangster** n Gangster, Verbrecher m.

gangrene ('gæŋgri:n) n Gangrän f.

gangway ('gæŋwei) n 1 Durchgang m. 2 naut Fallreep neu.

gap (gæp) n Lücke f.

gape (geip) vi 1 klaffen. 2 starren, glotzen. **gape at** angaffen.

garage ('gæra:ʒ) n 1 Garage f. 2 Reparaturwerkstatt f. vt einstellen, garagieren.

garble ('ga:bəl) vt verstümmeln, entstellen.

garden ('ga:dn) n Garten m. vi im Garten arbeiten. **gardner** n Gärtner m.

gargle ('ga:gəl) vi gurgeln. n Gurgelwasser neu.

garland ('ga:lənd) n Girlande f. Kranz m. vt bekränzen.

garlic ('ga:lik) n Knoblauch m.

garment ('ga:mənt) n Kleidungsstück, Gewand neu.

garnish ('ga:niʃ) vt 1 cul garnieren. 2 verzieren, schmücken. n 1 Garnierung f. 2 Schmuck m. Verzierung f.

garrison ('gærisən) n Garnison f.

garter ('ga:tə) n Strumpfband neu.

gas (gæs) n Gas neu. vt vergasen. **gas cooker** n Gasherd, Gasofen m. **gas fire** n Gasfeuer neu.

gash (gæʃ) n 1 (klaffende) Wunde f. 2 Riß m. vt tief schneiden in.

gasket ('gæskit) n tech Dichtung f.

gasp (ga:sp) vi keuchen. n Keuchen neu.

gastric ('gæstrik) adj gästrisch, Magen—. **gastronomic** adj gastronomisch. **gastronomy** n Gastronomie, Kochkunst f.

gate (geit) n 1 Tor neu. 2 Pforte f. **gatecrasher** n inf uneingeladener Gast, Eindringling m.

gateau ('gætou) n Torte f.

gather ('gæðə) vt 1 (ein-, ver-)sammeln. 2 ernten, lesen. 3 pflücken. 4 (cloth) raffen. vi sich versammeln. **gathering** n Versammlung f.

gauche (gouʃ) adj linkisch, taktlos.

gaudy ('go:di) adj bunt, grell, protzig.

gauge (geidʒ) n 1 Normalmaß neu. 2 Maßstab m. 3 Meßgerät neu. vt 1 eichen. 2 (aus-)messen. 3 abschätzen, beurteilen.

gaunt (go:nt) adj hager, mager.

gauze (go:z) n Gäze f.

gave (geiv) v see **give**.

gay (gei) adj 1 heiter. 2 bunt. 3 ausschweifend. 4 sl homosexuell.

gaze (geiz) vi starren. **gaze at** anstarren. ~n (starrer) Blick m.

gazelle (gə'zel) n Gazelle f.

gear (giə) n 1 Zeug neu. 2 Ausrüstung f. 3 Getriebe neu. 4 mot Gang m. 5 (Be)Kleidung f. **gearbox** n Getriebe neu. **gear lever** n Schalthebel m.

gelatine ('dʒeləti:n) n Gelatine f.

gelignite ('dʒelignait) n Gelatinedynamit neu.

gem (dʒem) n 1 Edelstein m. 2 Gemme f.

Gemini ('dʒeminai) n pl Zwillinge m pl.

gender ('dʒendə) n Geschlecht neu.

genealogy (dʒi:ni'ælədʒi) n Genealogie f.

general ('dʒenərəl) adj 1 allgemein. 2 gewöhnlich. 3 Allgemein—. **in general** im allgemeinen. ~n General m. **general election** n allgemeine Wahlen f pl. **general practitioner** n praktischer Arzt m. **generalize** vi verallgemeinern. **generalization** n Verallgemeinerung f.

generate ('dʒenəreit) vt 1 tech erzeugen, hervorbringen. 2 verursachen. 3 zeugen. **generation** n 1 Erzeugung f. 2 Menschenalter neu. Generation f. **generator** n 1 Erzeuger m. 2 tech Generator m.

generic (dʒi'nerik) adj 1 allgemein, generell. 2 generisch, Gattungs—.

generous ('dʒenərəs) adj 1 großzügig. 2 großmütig. 3 reichlich. **generosity** n 1 Großzügigkeit f. 2 Großmut f.

genetic (dʒi'netik) adj Entstehungs—, genetisch. **genetics** n pl Genetik, Vererbungslehre f.

Geneva (dʒi'ni:və) n Genf neu.

genial ('dʒi:niəl) adj 1 freundlich, herzlich. 2 mild. 3 heiter, jovial. **geniality** n 1 Freundlichkeit f. 2 Herzlichkeit f.

genital ('dʒenitl) adj 1 Zeugungs—. 2 Geschlechts—. **genitals** n pl Genitalien neu pl. Geschlechtsteile m pl.

genitive ('dʒenitiv) n gram Genitiv m.

genius ('dʒi:niəs) n Genie neu. Genius m.

genteel (dʒen'ti:l) adj 1 vornehm. 2 fein.

gentile ('dʒentail) n Heide m. adj heidnisch.

gentle ('dʒentl) adj 1 mild, sanft. 2 vornehm. **gentleman** n 1 Herr m. 2 Gentleman m.

genuflect ('dʒenjuflekt) vi die Knie beugen. **genuflection** n Kniebeugung f.

genuine ('dʒenjuin) adj 1 echt. 2 wirklich.

genus ('dʒi:nəs) n Gattung f.

geography (dʒi'ɔgrəfi) n Erdkunde, Geographie f.

geology (dʒi'ɔlədʒi) n Geologie f.

geometry (dʒi'ɔmɪtri) n Geometrie f.

geranium (dʒi'reiniəm) n Geranie f.

germ (dʒə:m) n Keim, Bazillus m. Bakterie f. **germinate** vi keimen.

Germany ('dʒə:məni) n Deutschland neu. **German** adj deutsch. n 1 Deutsche(r) m. 2 (language) Deutsch neu. **German measles** n pl Röteln pl. **Germanic** adj germanisch.

gerund ('dʒerənd) n Gerundium neu.

gesticulate (dʒis'tikjuleit) vi gestikulieren, sich lebhaft gebärden.

gesture ('dʒestʃə) n Gebärde, Geste f.

get* (get) vt 1 bekommen, erhalten. 2 inf kriegen. 3 gewinnen. 4 veranlassen. 5 besorgen. vi 1 gelangen, kommen. 2 werden. **get in** einsteigen. **get off** aussteigen. **get over** hinwegkommen über. **get ready** fertig machen. **get up** aufstehen.

geyser ('gi:zə) n 1 Geiser, Geysir m. 2 Durchlauferhitzer m.

ghastly ('gɑ:stli) adj gräßlich, schrecklich.

gherkin ('gə:kin) n Essiggurke f.

ghetto ('getou) n Getto neu.

ghost (goust) n Gespenst neu. Geist m.

giant ('dʒaiənt) n Riese m. adj riesig.

giddy ('gidi) adj 1 schwindlig. 2 leichtsinnig.

gift (gift) n 1 Geschenk neu. 2 Begabung f.

gigantic (dʒai'gæntik) adj riesenhaft, gigantisch.

giggle ('gigəl) vi kichern. n Gekicher neu.

gild (gild) vt vergolden.

gill (gil) n zool Kieme f.

gilt (gilt) adj vergoldet. n Vergoldung f.

gimmick ('gimik) n inf Trick, Kniff m.

gin (dʒin) n Gin, Wacholderschnaps m.

ginger ('dʒindʒə) n Ingwer m. **ginger beer** n Ingwerbier neu. **gingerbread** n Pfefferkuchen m.

gipsy ('dʒipsi) n Zigeuner m.

giraffe (dʒi'rɑ:f) n Giraffe f.

girder ('gə:də) n Tragbalken, Träger m.

girdle ('gə:dl) n (Hüft)Gürtel m.

girl (gə:l) n Mädchen neu. **girlfriend** n Freundin f.

Giro ('dʒairou) n Giro neu.

girth (gə:θ) n 1 (Sattel)Gurt m. 2 Umfang m.

give* (giv) vt 1 geben, schenken. 2 erteilen. **give away** verschenken. **give back** zurückgeben. **give in** nachgeben. **give out** 1 verteilen, ausgeben. 2 zu Ende gehen. **give up** aufgeben.

glacier ('glæsiə) n Gletscher m.

glad (glæd) adj 1 froh, erfreut. 2 fröhlich.

glamour ('glæmə) n Glanz, Zauber m. **glamorize** vt verherrlichen. **glamorous** adj bezaubernd, schön.

glance (glɑ:ns) n (flüchtiger) Blick, Schimmer m. vi flüchtig blicken.

gland (glænd) n Drüse f.

glare (glɛə) vi 1 (wütend) anblicken, starren. 2 hell glänzen. n 1 blendender Glanz m. 2 (wütender) Blick m.

glass (glɑ:s) n 1 Glas neu. 2 pl Brille f.

glaze (gleiz) n Glasur f. vt 1 verglasen. 2 glasieren.

gleam (gli:m) n Schimmer, Lichtstrahl m. vi strahlen, schimmern.

glean (gli:n) vt (auf-, nach-)lesen.

glee (gli:) n Fröhlichkeit f.

glib (glib) adj zungenfertig, glatt.

glide (glaid) vi 1 (vorüber)gleiten, fließen. 2 im Gleitflug fliegen. **glider** n Segelflugzeug neu.

glimmer ('glimə) n Schimmer m.

glimpse (glimps) n flüchtiger Blick m.

glisten ('glisən) vi glänzen, schimmern.

glitter ('glitə) vi glitzern. n Glanz m.

gloat (glout) vi sich weiden, sich hämisch freuen.

globe (gloub) n (Erd)Kugel f. Globus m.

gloom¹ (glu:m) n Dunkelheit, Düsternis f.

gloom² (glu:m) n Schwermut f. Trübsinn m.

glory ('glɔ:ri) n Ruhm, Glanz m. **glorify** vt verherrlichen. **glorious** adj glorreich, herrlich, prachtvoll.

gloss¹ (glɔs) n Glanz, Schein m. v **gloss over** vertuschen.

gloss² (glɔs) n Randbemerkung, Glosse f.

glossary ('glɔsəri) n (Spezial)Wörterverzeichnis neu.

glove (glʌv) n Handschuh m.

glow (glou) vi glühen. n Glühen neu. Glut f.

glucose ('glu:kous) n Traubenzucker m.

glue (glu:) n Klebstoff m. vt kleben.

glum (glʌm) adj mürrisch, verdrießlich.

glut (glʌt) n 1 Sättigung, Stillung f. 2 comm Überangebot neu.

glutton ('glʌtn) n 1 Vielfraß m. 2 unersättliche(r) Mensch m.

gnarled (nɑ:ld) adj knorrig.

gnash (næʃ) vt knirschen.

gnat (næt) n Mücke f.

gnaw (nɔ:) vt,vi nagen.

gnome (noum) n Zwerg, Erdgeist m. Gnom m.

go* (gou) vi 1 gehen, fahren, laufen. 2 funktionieren. 3 reichen. **go abroad** ins Ausland gehen. **go ahead 1** losgehen. **2** vorausgehen. **go away 1** weggehen. **2** verreisen. **go back** zurückkehren. **go down** hinuntergehen, untergehen. **go into** eintreten. **go off 1** weggehen. **2** (of food) schlecht werden. **go on** weitergehen. **go out** (hin)ausgehen. **go through 1** durchgehen. **2** durchmachen. **go up** (hinauf)steigen.

goad (goud) vt anspornen, anstacheln.

goal (goul) n 1 Ziel m. 2 sport Tor neu. **goalkeeper** n Torwart m. **goalpost** n/Torpfosten m.

goat (gout) n Ziege f.

gobble ('gɔbəl) vt (hinunter-, ver-)schlingen.

goblin ('gɔblin) n Kobold m.

god (gɔd) n Gott m. **godchild** n Patenkind neu. **goddaughter** n Patentochter f. **godfather** n Pate m. **godmother** n Patin f. **godson** n Patensohn m.

goddess ('gɔdis) n Göttin f.

goggles ('gɔgəlz) n pl Schutzbrille f.

going ('gouiŋ) adj laufend, im Gang. n Gehen neu. Abreise f.

gold (gould) n Gold neu. adj golden. **golden** adj golden. **goldfish** n Goldfisch m.

golf (gɔlf) n Golf(spiel) neu. **golfball** n Golfball m. **golfclub** n Golfschläger m. **golfcourse** n Golfplatz m.

gondola ('gɔndələ) n Gondel f. **gondolier** n Gondoliere m.

gone (gɔn) v see **go.** adj 1 vergangen. 2 fort. 3 tot.

gong (gɔŋ) n Gong m.

good (gud) adj 1 gut. 2 ordentlich. 3 artig, brav. 4 law gültig. n 1 Gut(e) neu. 2 Wohl neu. 3 pl Waren, Güter pl. **for good** auf immer. **good afternoon** interj guten Tag. **goodbye** interj auf Wiedersehen. n Lebewohl neu. **good evening** interj guten Abend. **good-looking** adj gut aussehend, schön, hübsch. **good morning** interj guten Morgen. **good night** interj gute Nacht. **goods train** n Güterzug m. **goodwill** n 1 Wohlwollen neu. guter Wille m. 2 Kundschaft f.

Good Friday n Karfreitag m.

goose (gu:s) n, pl **geese** Gans f. **gooseberry** n Stachelbeere f.

gore[1] (gɔ:) n (geronnenes) Blut neu.

gore[2] (gɔ:) vt durchbohren, aufspießen.

gorge (gɔ:dʒ) n Schlucht f. vt,vi gierig essen. **gorge oneself** sich vollstopfen.

gorgeous ('gɔ:dʒəs) adj 1 prächtig, großartig. 2 inf phantastisch. 3 inf sehr schmackhaft.

gorilla (gə'rilə) n Gorilla m.

gorse (gɔ:s) n Stechginster m.

gory ('gɔ:ri) adj blutig.

gosh (gɔʃ) interj Donnerwetter!

gosling ('gɔzliŋ) n Gänschen neu.

gospel ('gɔspəl) n Evangelium neu.

gossip ('gɔsip) n 1 Geschwätz neu. 2 Klatschbase f. vi schwatzen.

got (gɔt) v see **get.**

Gothic ('gɔθik) adj gotisch.

goulash ('gu:læʃ) n Gulasch neu.

gourd (guəd) n Kürbis m.

gourmet (guə'mei) n Gourmet, Feinschmecker m.

govern ('gʌvən) vt 1 regieren, beherrschen. 2 bestimmen. vi regieren, herrschen. **government** n Regierung f. **governor** n 1 Gouverneur, Statthalter m. 2 Direktor m.

gown (gaun) n 1 (Damen)Kleid neu. 2 Robe f.

grab (græb) vt schnappen, ergreifen. vi gierig greifen.

grace (greis) n 1 Gnade f. 2 Reiz m. 3 Tischgebet neu. 4 Gunst f. 5 Anmut f. **His/. Her/Your Grace** Sein/Ihr/Euer Gnaden. ~vt 1 schmücken. 2 ehren. **graceful** adj 1 anmutig. 2 taktvoll. **gracious** adj gütig, gnädig, anmutig.

grade (greid) n 1 Rang, Grad m. 2 Qualität f. vt ordnen, sortieren, einteilen. **gradient** n 1 Neigung f. 2 Hang m. 3 Steigerung f. **gradual** adj allmählich, stufenweise, schrittweise. **graduate** n Graduierte(r) m. vi ein Diplom erwerben. vt einteilen.

graffiti (grə'fi:ti) n pl Graffiti neu.

graft[1] (gra:ft) vt 1 bot (auf-, ein-)pfropfen. 2 med verpflanzen. n 1 Propfreis neu. 2 Verpflanzung f.

graft[2] (gra:ft) n inf 1 Schiebung, Bestechung f. 2 Gaunerei f. vt 1 schieben. 2 (er)gaunern.

grain (grein) n 1 Getreide neu. 2 Samenkorn neu. 3 (Holz)Faser f.

gram (græm) n Gramm neu.

grammar ('græmə) n Grammatik f. **grammar school** n Gymnasium neu. **grammatical** adj grammatisch, grammatikalisch.

gramophone ('græməfoun) n Plattenspieler m. Gramophon m.

granary ('grænəri) n Kornspeicher m.

grand (grænd) adj groß, erhaben, stattlich.

grand piano n Flügel. m. **grandeur** n Erhabenheit, Größe f. **grandiose** adj großartig, grandios.

grandad ('grændæd) n inf also **grandpa** Opa m.

grandchild ('græntʃaild) n Enkelkind neu.

grand-daughter ('grændɔːtə) n Enkelin f.

grandfather ('grænfɑːðə) n Großvater m.

grandma ('grænmɑː) n inf also **granny** Oma f.

grandmother ('grænmʌðə) n Großmutter f.

grandparents ('grænpɛərənts) n pl Großeltern pl.

grandson ('grænsʌn) n Enkel m.

grandstand ('grændstænd) n Zuschauertribüne f.

granite ('grænit) n Granit m.

grant (grɑːnt) n 1 Bewilligung f. 2 Verleihung f. 3 Zuschuß m. 4 educ Stipendium. vt 1 bewilligen. 2 verleihen. 3 zugestehen.

grape (greip) n Weintraube f. **grapefruit** n Grapefruit, Pampelmuse f.

graph (græf) n Diagramm neu. Kurve f. **graphic** adj 1 graphisch. 2 anschaulich.

grapple ('græpəl) vi ringen. vt 1 packen. 2 befestigen (an). **grapple with** in Angriff nehmen, sich auseinandersetzen mit.

grasp (grɑːsp) vt 1 greifen, fassen. 2 begreifen, verstehen. n Griff m.

grass (grɑːs) n 1 Gras neu. 2 Rasen m. **grassroots** n pl Wurzel f. adj volksnah, volkstümlich.

grate[1] (greit) n (Feuer)Rost m. Gitter neu.

grate[2] (greit) vt 1 cul reiben. 2 krächzen. 3 knirschen mit. vi kratzen, knirschen, knarren.

grateful ('greitfəl) adj dankbar. **gratify** vt erfreuen, befriedigen, zufriedenstellen.

gratitude ('grætitjuːd) n Dankbarkeit f.

grave[1] (greiv) n Grab neu. **gravestone** n Grabstein m. **graveyard** n Friedhof m.

grave[2] (greiv) adj ernst(haft).

gravel ('grævəl) n Kies m.

gravity ('græviti) n 1 sci Gravität, Schwerkraft f. 2 Schwere f. Ernst m.

gravy ('greivi) n (Braten)Soße f.

graze[1] (greiz) n 1 flüchtige Berührung f. 2 Abschürfung f. vt 1 streifen. 2 abschürfen.

graze[2] (greiz) vi weiden, grasen.

grease (griːs) n 1 Fett neu. 2 Schmiere f. vt schmieren, einfetten. **greasepaint** n Bühnenschminke f. **greaseproof** adj fettdicht.

great (greit) adj 1 groß. 2 beträchtlich. 3 bedeutend. 4 berühmt. 5 inf toll, sagenhaft, prima.

Great Britain n Großbritannien neu.

Greece (griːs) n Griechenland neu. **Greek** adj also **Grecian** griechisch. n 1 Grieche m. 2 (language) Griechisch neu.

greed (griːd) n (Hab)Gier f. **greedy** adj gierig.

green (griːn) adj 1 grün. 2 inf unerfahren. n 1 Grün neu. 2 Grünfläche f. 3 pl Grüngemüse neu pl. **greenery** n Laub(werk) neu. **greenfly** n grüne Blattlaus f. **greengage** n Reineclaude f. **greengrocer** n Obst- und Gemüsehändler m. **greenhouse** n Treibhaus neu.

Greenland ('griːnlənd) n Grönland neu. **Greenlander** n Grönländer m.

greet (griːt) vt (be)grüßen. **greeting** n Gruß m.

gregarious (griˈgɛəriəs) adj gesellig.

grenade (griˈneid) n Granate f.

grew (gruː) v see **grow**.

grey (grei) adj grau. n Grau neu. **greyhound** n Windhund m.

grid (grid) n 1 Gitter neu. 2 Netz neu.

grief (griːf) n Kummer, Schmerz m.

grieve (griːv) vi trauern, sich kränken über. **grievance** n Beschwerde f. Groll m.

grill (gril) n Bratrost m. vt grillen, rosten.

grille (gril) n Gitter neu.

grim (grim) adj 1 grimmig, finster. 2 hart.

grimace (griˈmeis) n Grimasse f. vi Grimassen schneiden.

grime (graim) n (fettiger) Schmutz m.

grin (grin) vi grinsen. n Grinsen neu.

grind[*] (graind) vt (zer)reiben, (zer)mahlen. n inf Plackerei f.

grip (grip) vt packen, (er)greifen. n Griff m.

gristle ('grisəl) n Knorpel m.

grit (grit) n grober Sand, Kies m.

groan (groun) vi stöhnen, seufzen. n Stöhnen neu.

grocer ('grousə) n Lebensmittelhändler m.

groin (grɔin) n Leiste f.

groom (gruːm) n 1 Stallknecht, Reitknecht m. 2 Bräutigam m. vt versorgen, pflegen.

groove (gruːv) n Rinne, Furche, Rille f.

grope (group) vi herumtasten, herumtappen.

gross (grous) adj 1 comm brutto. 2 dick. 3 grob, roh. n Gros neu.

grotesque (grouˈtesk) adj grotesk.

grotto ('grɔtou) n Grotte f.

ground[1] (graund) n 1 Grund, Boden m. 2 pl Gelände f. Anlagen f pl. 3 (Beweg)Grund m. vt 1 begründen. 2 heißen. **ground floor** n Erdgeschoß neu. **groundsheet** n Zeltbahn f. **groundsman** n (Sportplatz)Wärter m.

ground[2] (graund) v see **grind**.

group (gru:p) n Gruppe f. vt gruppieren.

grouse[1] (graus) n Rebhuhn neu.

grouse[2] (graus) vi inf murren, meckern.

grove (grouv) n Gehölz neu. Waldung f.

grovel (grɔvəl) vi (auf dem Bauch) kriechen.

grow* (grou) vi 1 wachsen. 2 werden. 3 zunehmen. vt (an)bauen, züchten, wachsen lassen. **growth** n 1 Wachstum neu. Entwicklung f. 2 Zunahme, Vergrößerung f.

growl (graul) vi,vt grollen, knurren, brummen. n Brummen, Knurren, Grollen neu.

grub (grʌb) n 1 Made f. 2 sl Futter neu. Fraß m. vi graben.

grubby (ˈgrʌbi) adj schmutzig, dreckig.

grudge (grʌdʒ) n Groll m. vt beneiden, mißgönnen.

gruelling (ˈgru:əliŋ) adj erschöpfend.

gruesome (ˈgru:səm) adj grausig.

gruff (grʌf) adj 1 schroff, barsch. 2 mürrisch.

grumble (ˈgrʌmbəl) vi murren, schimpfen.

grumpy (ˈgrʌmpi) adj verdrießlich, mürrisch.

grunt (grʌnt) vi grunzen. n Grunzen neu.

guarantee (gærənˈti:) n Garantie, Bürgschaft f. vt garantieren, gewährleisten. **guarantor** n Bürge, Garant m.

guard (gɑ:d) vt bewachen, (be)schützen. vi sich hüten. n 1 Wache f. 2 (railway) Schaffner m. **guardian** n 1 law Vormund m. 2 Wächter m. **guard's van** n Gepäckwagen m.

guerrilla (gəˈrilə) n Guerillakämpfer m.

guess (ges) vt erraten, vermuten. n Vermutung, Mutmaßung f. **guesswork** n Vermutungen f pl.

guest (gest) n Gast m. **guesthouse** n Pension f.

guide (gaid) n 1 Führer m. 2 Leitfaden m. 3 Ratgeber m. vt führen. **Girl Guide** n Pfadfinderin f. **guidebook** n Reiseführer m. **guidedog** n Blindenhund m. **guidance** n Führung, Anleitung f.

guild (gild) n Zunft f.

guillotine (giləˈti:n) n Guillotine f.

guilt (gilt) n Schuld f. **guilty** adj schuldig, schuldhaft.

guinea (ˈgini) n Guinee f. **guinea pig** n 1 zool Meerschweinchen neu. 2 Versuchskaninchen neu.

guitar (giˈtɑ:) n Gitarre f.

gulf (gʌlf) n 1 Golf m. 2 Abgrund m. 3 Kluft f.

gull (gʌl) n Möwe f.

gullet (ˈgʌlit) n Speiseröhre f. Schlund m.

gulp (gʌlp) n Schluck m. vt hinunterschlingen. vi schlucken.

gum[1] (gʌm) n Gummi neu. vt (an)kleben.

gum[2] (gʌm) n anat Zahnfleisch neu.

gun (gʌn) n 1 Gewehr, Geschütz neu. 2 Flinte f. 3 Revolver m. **gunboat** n Kanonenboot neu. **gunman** n bewaffneter Verbrecher m. **gunpowder** n Schießpulver neu. **gunrunning** n Waffenschmuggel m. **gunshot** n 1 Schuß m. 2 Schußweite f.

gurgle (ˈgə:gəl) vi glucksen, gurgeln.

gush (gʌʃ) vi 1 sich ergießen. 2 strömen. n 1 Erguß m. 2 Flut f.

gust (gʌst) n Windstoß m.

gut (gʌt) n 1 Darm m. 2 pl Eingeweide pl. 3 pl sl Mut f. vt ausweiden.

gutter (ˈgʌtə) n 1 Rinnstein m. 2 Dachrinne f. 3 Gosse f.

guy[1] (gai) n sl Kerl, Bursche m.

guy[2] (gai) n Spannschnur f.

gymnasium (dʒimˈneiziəm) n Turnhalle f. **gymnast** n Leichtathlet, Turner m. **gymnastic** adj gymnastisch, Turn—. **gymnastics** n pl Turnen neu. Gymnastik f.

gynaecology (gainiˈkɔlədʒi) n Gynäkologie f. **gynaecologist** n Frauenarzt, Gynäkologe m.

gypsum (ˈdʒipsəm) n Gips m.

gyrate (dʒaiˈreit) vi wirbeln, kreisen.

H

haberdasher (ˈhæbədæʃə) n Kurzwarenhändler m. **haberdashery** n Kurzwarenhandlung f.

habit (ˈhæbit) n Gewohnheit f. **get into the habit of** sich angewöhnen. **habitual** adj gewohnt, üblich.

habitable (ˈhæbitəbəl) adj bewohnbar.

hack[1] (hæk) vt (zer)hacken. **hacksaw** n Metallsäge f.

hack[2] (hæk) n 1 Mietpferd neu. 2 Gaul m. 3 Lohnschreiber m.

hackneyed (ˈhæknid) adj abgedroschen.

had (hæd) v see **have.**

haddock (ˈhædək) n Schellfisch m.

haemorrhage (ˈheməridʒ) n Blutung f.

hag (hæg) n häßliches altes Weib neu.

haggard (ˈhægəd) adj 1 verstört. 2 hager.

haggle (ˈhægəl) vi streiten, feilschen.

Hague, The (heig) n Den Haag m.

hail[1] (heil) n Hagel m. vi hageln. **hailstone** n Hagelkorn neu. **hailstorm** n Hagelschauer m.

hail[2] (heil) vt (be)grüßen, zurufen.

hair (hɛə) n Haar neu. **hairbrush** n Haarbürste

f. **haircut** *n* Haarschnitt *m.* **hairdresser** *n* Friseur *m.* Friseuse *f.* **hairpin** *n* Haarnadel *f.* **hair-raising** *adj* haarsträubend. **hairstyle** *n* Haartracht *f.*

half (hɑːf) *n, pl* **halves** Hälfte *f. adj,adv* halb.

half-dozen *n* halbes Dutzend *neu.*

half-and-half *adj,adv* halb und halb.

half-back *n sport* Läufer *m.*

half-breed *n also* **half-caste** Mischling *m.*

half-brother *n* Halbbruder *m.*

half-hearted *adj* lau, zaghaft.

half-hour *n* halbe Stunde *f.*

half-mast *n* Halbmast *m.* **at half-mast** halbmast.

half-sister *n* Halbschwester *f.*

half-term *n* Semesterhalbzeit *f.*

half-time *n* Halbzeit *f.*

halfway (hɑːf'wei) *adj,adv* auf halbem Wege, halbwegs.

halfwit ('hɑːfwit) *n* Schwachkopf, Idiot *m.*

halibut ('hælibət) *n* Heilbutt *m.*

hall (hɔːl) *n* **1** Halle *f.* **2** Saal *m.* **3** Diele *f.* Flur *m.*

hallelujah (hæli'luːjə) *interj* halleluja!

hallmark ('hɔːlmɑːk) *n* **1** Feingehaltsstempel *m.* **2** Kennzeichen *neu.*

hallo (hə'lou) *interj* **1** guten Tag! grüß Gott! **2** hallo!

hallowed ('hæloud) *adj* geheiligt.

Hallowe'en (hælou'iːn) *n* Abend vor Allerheiligen *m.*

hallucination (həluːsi'neiʃən) *n* Halluzination, Sinnestäuschung *f.*

halo ('heilou) *n pl* **-os** *or* **-oes** **1** Heiligenschein *m.* **2** *sci* Hof *m.*

halt (hɔːlt) *n* Halt *m.* Pause *f. vt,vi* (an)halten.

halter ('hɔːltə) *n* Halfter *neu.*

halve (hɑːv) *vt* halbieren.

ham (hæm) *n* Schinken *m.*

hamburger ('hæmbəːgə) *n* Frikadelle *f.*

hammer ('hæmə) *n* Hammer *m. vt,vi* hämmern.

hammock ('hæmək) *n* Hängematte *f.*

hamper[1] ('hæmpə) *vt* (be)hindern, hemmen.

hamper[2] ('hæmpə) *n* Packkorb *m.*

hamster ('hæmstə) *n* Hamster *m.*

hand (hænd) *n* Hand *f.* **give** *or* **lend a hand** behilflich sein. **on the one hand...on the other** einerseits...andererseits. **~vt** überreichen. **hand in** einreichen. **hand on** weitergeben. **hand out** verteilen. **hand over** übergeben.

handbag ('hændbæg) *n* Handtasche *f.*

handbook ('hændbuk) *n* Handbuch *neu.*

handbrake ('hændbreik) *n* Handbremse *f.*

handcart ('hændkɑːt) *n* Handwagen *m.*

handcuff ('hændkʌf) *vt* Handschellen anlegen. **handcuffs** *n pl* Handschellen *f pl.*

handful ('hændful) *n* Handvoll *f.*

handicap ('hændikæp) *n* **1** Nachteil *m.* **2** *sport* Vorgabe *f. vt* benachteiligen.

handicraft ('hændikrɑːft) *n* Handwerk *neu.*

handiwork ('hændiwəːk) *n* **1** Handarbeit *f.* **2** Werk *neu.*

handkerchief ('hæŋkətʃif) *n* Taschentuch *neu.*

handle ('hændl) *n* Griff *m. vt* **1** anfassen. **2** handhaben. **3** behandeln. **handlebars** *n pl* Lenkstange *f.*

handmade (hænd'meid) *adj* handgearbeitet, Hand—.

hand-out *n* **1** Almosen *neu.* **2** Werbezettel *m.*

hand-pick *vt* auslesen, auswählen.

handrail ('hændreil) *n* Geländer *neu.*

handshake ('hændʃeik) *n* Händedruck *m.*

handsome ('hænsəm) *adj* **1** hübsch, schön, gut aussehend. **2** beträchtlich.

handstand ('hændstænd) *n sport* Handstand *m.*

handwriting ('hændraitiŋ) *n* Handschrift *f.*

handy ('hændi) *adj* **1** handlich, zur Hand. **2** geschickt.

hang* (hæŋ) *vt* (auf-, ein-)hängen. *vi* hängen. **hanger** *n* Kleiderbügel *m.* **hangman** *n* Henker *m.* **hangover** *n inf* Kater *m.*

hanker ('hæŋkə) *vi* sich sehnen.

Hanover ('hænəvə) *n* Hannover *neu.*

haphazard (hæp'hæzəd) *adj* zufällig.

happen ('hæpən) *vi* geschehen, sich ereignen, vorkommen, passieren. **happen to do something** etwas zufällig tun.

happy ('hæpi) *adj* **1** glücklich, zufrieden. **2** erfreulich. **happily** *adv* glücklicherweise. **happiness** *n* Glück *neu.*

harass ('hærəs) *vt* belästigen, quälen.

harbour ('hɑːbə) *n* Hafen *m. vt* beherbergen.

hard (hɑːd) *adj* **1** hart. **2** schwer. **3** streng. **4** schlecht. *adv* **1** heftig. **2** mühsam. **3** fleißig. **hardback** *n* Buch mit steifem Einband *or* Leineneinband *neu.* **hardboard** *n* Hartfaserplatte *f.* **hard-boiled** *adj* hartgekocht. **harden** *vt* (ab)härten, hart machen. *vi* hart werden. **hard-headed** *adj* nüchtern, eigensinnig. **hard-hearted** *adj* hartherzig. **hardship** *n* Strapaze, Bedrängnis *f.* **hardware** *n* Eisenwaren *f pl.*

hardly ('hɑːdli) *adv* **1** kaum, schwerlich. **2** mit Mühe.

hardy ('hɑːdi) *adj* abgehärtet, zäh.

hare ('hɛə) n Hase m.

haricot ('hærikou) n weiße Bohne f.

hark (hɑːk) vi horchen.

harm (hɑːm) n Schaden m. vt Leid or Schaden zufügen, schaden. **harmful** adj schädlich.

harmonic (hɑːˈmɔnik) adj harmonisch. **harmonica** n Mundharmonika f. **harmonize** vt 1 mus harmonisieren. 2 in Einklang bringen. vi in Einklang sein. **harmony** n 1 mus Harmonie f. 2 Einklang m.

harness ('hɑːnis) n Geschirr neu. vt anschirren, anspannen.

harp (hɑːp) n Harfe f.

harpoon (hɑːˈpuːn) n Harpune f.

harpsichord ('hɑːpsikɔːd) n Spinett neu.

harsh (hɑːʃ) adj 1 rauh, hart. 2 streng.

harvest ('hɑːvist) n 1 Ernte f. 2 (Wein)Lese f. vt ernten, einbringen.

has (hæz) v see **have**.

haste (heist) n Eile, Hast f. **hasten** vi eilen, sich beeilen. vt beschleunigen.

hat (hæt) n Hut m.

hatch (hætʃ) vt ausbrüten. vi brüten. n Brut f.

hatch[2] (hætʃ) n Luke, Klapptür f.

hatchet ('hætʃit) n Beil neu.

hate (heit) vt hassen. n Haß m. **hateful** adj verhaßt.

haughty ('hɔːti) adj hochmütig.

haul (hɔːl) vt schleppen, zerren, transportieren. n Fang m.

haunch (hɔːntʃ) n Hüfte, Keule f.

haunt (hɔːnt) vt 1 häufig besuchen. 2 heimsuchen. vi spuken. n Aufenthalt m.

have* (hæv) vt haben. v aux haben, sein. **have something done** etwas tun lassen. **have to do something** etwas tun müssen.

haven ('heivən) n Hafen, Zufluchtsort m.

haversack ('hævəsæk) n Rucksack m.

havoc ('hævək) n 1 Verwüstung f. 2 Zerstörung f. **cause havoc** große Zerstörungen verursachen.

hawk (hɔːk) n Habicht, Falke m.

hawthorn ('hɔːθɔːn) n Hagedorn m.

hay (hei) n Heu neu. **hayfever** n Heuschnupfen m. **haystack** n Heuschober m. **go haywire** kaputt gehen.

hazard ('hæzəd) n 1 Risiko neu. Gefahr f. 2 Zufall m. vt wagen, riskieren.

haze (heiz) n 1 Dunst m. 2 Unklarheit f.

hazel ('heizəl) n Hasel f. Haselstrauch m. **hazelnut** n Haselnuß f.

he (hiː) pron 3rd pers s er.

head (hed) n 1 Kopf m. Haupt neu. 2 Leiter,

Chef m. 3 Spitze f. vorderes Ende neu. 4 Stück neu. 5 Höhepunkt m. vt führen, vorstehen.

headache ('hedeik) n Kopfweh neu. Kopfschmerzen m pl.

heading ('hediŋ) n Überschrift f.

headlight ('hedlait) n Scheinwerfer m.

headline ('hedlain) n Schlagzeile f.

headlong ('hedlɔŋ) adv kopfüber. adj ungestüm, unbesonnen.

headmaster (hedˈmɑːstə) n (Schul)Direktor m.

headphones ('hedfouns) n pl Kopfhörer m.

headquarters ('hedkwɔːtəz) n pl 1 Hauptquartier neu. 2 Hauptgeschäftsstelle f.

headscarf ('hedskɑːf) n Kopftuch neu.

headstrong ('hedstrɔŋ) adj starrköpfig, halsstarrig.

headway ('hedwei) n Fortschritte m pl.

heal (hiːl) vt,vi heilen.

health (helθ) n Gesundheit f. **your health** interj prosit! auf Ihr Wohl! **healthy** adj 1 gesund. 2 kräftig.

heap (hiːp) n 1 Haufen m. 2 inf Menge f. v **heap up** anhäufen.

hear* (hiə) vi,vt hören. **hearing** n 1 Hören neu. 2 Verhör neu. **hearing aid** n Hörgerät neu.

hearse (hɔːs) n Leichenwagen m.

heart (hɑːs) n 1 Herz neu. 2 Kern m. 3 Mut m. **heart attack** n Herzanfall m. **heartbeat** n Herzschlag, Puls m. **heartbroken** adj untröstlich. **heartless** adj herzlos. **hearty** adj herzhaft, herzlich.

hearth (hɑːθ) n Herd m.

heat (hiːt) n 1 Hitze f. 2 Eifer m. 3 sport Runde f. vt heizen. **heater** n Heizapparat m. **heating** n Heizung f. **heatwave** n Hitzewelle f.

heath (hiːθ) n Heide f.

heathen ('hiːðən) n Heide m. adj heidnisch.

heather ('heθə) n Heidekraut neu. Erika f.

heave (hiːv) vt (hoch)heben. vi sich heben und senken.

heaven ('hevən) n Himmel m. **heavenly** adj himmlisch.

heavy ('hevi) adj 1 schwer, gewichtig. 2 schwerfällig. **heavyweight** n Schwergewicht neu.

Hebrew ('hiːbruː) adj hebräisch. n 1 Hebräer m. 2 (language) Hebräisch neu.

heckle ('hekəl) vt (jemandem) Fangfragen stellen. **heckler** n Zwischenrufer m.

hectare ('hektɛə) n Hektar neu.

hectic ('hektik) adj hektisch, fieberhaft.

hedge (hedʒ) n Hecke f. **hedgehog** n Igel m.

heed (hiːd) vt achten auf.

heel (hi:l) n **1** Ferse f. **2** Absatz m.

hefty ('hefti) adj kräftig.

height (hait) n **1** Höhe f. **2** Höhepunkt m. **heighten** vt **1** erhöhen. **2** verstärken.

heir (ɛə) n Erbe m. **heirloom** n Erbstück neu.

held (held) v see **hold.**

helicopter ('helikɔptə) n Hubschrauber m.

hell (hel) n Hölle f. interj verdammt!

hello (hə'lou) interj **1** guten Tag! grüß Gott! **2** hallo!

helm (helm) n Ruder neu.

helmet ('helmit) n Helm m.

help (help) vt helfen, unterstützen. vi helfen. **help oneself** sich bedienen. ~n Hilfe f. **helpless** adj hilflos.

hem (hem) n Saum m. vt säumen.

hemisphere ('hemisfiə) n Halbkugel, Hemisphäre f.

hemp (hemp) n Hanf m.

hen (hen) n **1** Huhn neu. **2** Weibchen neu.

hence (hens) adv **1** hieraus, daher, daraus. **2** von hier.

henna ('henə) n Henna f.

her (hə:) pron 3rd pers s **1** sie. **2** ihr. poss adj 3rd pers s ihr.

herald ('herəld) n Herold m. vt ankündigen.

herb (hə:b) n Kraut neu.

herd (hə:d) n Herde f. vt weiden, hüten. **herdsman** n Hirt m.

here (hiə) adv **1** hier. **2** hierher.

hereditary (hi'reditri) adj erblich.

heredity (hi'rediti) n Vererbung f.

heresy ('herəsi) n Ketzerei f.

heritage ('heritidʒ) n **1** Erbschaft f. **2** Erbrecht neu.

hermit ('hə:mit) n Einsiedler m.

hero ('hiərou) n, pl **heroes** Held m. **heroine** n Heldin f.

heroin ('herouin) n Heroin neu.

heron ('herən) n Reiher m.

herring ('heriŋ) n Hering m.

hers (hə:z) poss pron 3rd pers s ihrer, der ihre or ihrige. **herself** pron 3rd pers s **1** sich. **2** sich selbst. **3** sie selbst. **by herself** allein, von selbst.

hesitate ('heziteit) vi zögern. **hesitation** n Zögern, Schwanken neu.

hexagon ('heksəgən) n Sechseck neu.

hibernate ('haibəneit) vi überwintern.

hiccup ('hikʌp) n Schluckauf m. vi den Schluckauf haben.

hide*1 (haid) vt **1** verstecken, verbergen. **2** verheimlichen. vi sich verbergen.

hide2 (haid) n Fell neu. Haut f.

hideous ('hidiəs) adj **1** scheußlich, gräßlich. **2** häßlich.

hiding1 ('haidiŋ) n Versteck neu. **hiding-place** n Schlupfwinkel m.

hiding2 ('haidiŋ) n Prügel f.

hierarchy ('haiərɑ:ki) n Hierarchie f.

high (hai) adj **1** hoch. **2** groß. **3** bedeutend. **4** vornehm. **highly** adv **1** in hohem Maße, äußerst, hoch. **2** lobend.

highbrow ('haibrau) adj inf intellektuell.

high-fidelity adj Hi-Fi.

high frequency n Hochfrequenz f.

high jump n Hochsprung m.

highland ('hailnd) n Hochland neu.

highlight ('hailait) n **1** Glanzlicht neu. **2** Höhepunkt m. vt hervorheben.

highness ('hainis) n **His/Her/Your Highness** Seine/Ihre/Eure Hoheit f.

highpitched ('haipitʃd) adj schrill, hoch.

high-rise adj vielstöckig. **high-rise building** n Hochhaus neu.

high-spirited adj übermütig, wagemutig.

highway ('haiwei) n Landstraße f.

hijack ('haidʒæk) vt **1** (be)rauben. **2** (an aeroplane) entführen.

hike (haik) vi wandern. n Wanderung f.

hilarious (hi'lɛəriəs) adj lustig, fröhlich.

hill (hil) n Hügel, Berg m. **hillside** n Abhang m. **hilltop** n Bergspitze f.

him (him) pron 3rd pers s **1** ihn. **2** ihm. **himself** pron 3rd pers s **1** sich. **2** sich selbst. **3** er selbst. **by himself** allein, von selbst.

hind (haind) adj hinter. **hindleg** n Hinterbein neu. **hindsight** n späte Einsicht, Nachsicht f.

hinder ('hində) vt (ver)hindern, hemmen.

Hindu ('hindu:) n Hindu m. **Hinduism** n Hinduismus m.

hinge (hindʒ) n Scharnier f. Gelenk neu. vi abhängen, ankommen.

hint (hint) n Hinweis, Wink m. vt andeuten.

hip (hip) n Hüfte f.

hippopotamus (hipə'pɔtəməs) n Nilpferd neu.

hire (haiə) vt mieten. n Miete f. **hire car** Mietauto neu.

his (hiz) poss adj 3rd pers s sein. poss pron 3rd pers s seiner, der seine or seinige.

hiss (his) vi zischen. n Zischen neu.

history ('histri) n Geschichte f. **historian** n Historiker m. **historical** adj geschichtlich, historisch.

hit* (hit) vt, vi **1** schlagen. **2** treffen. n **1** Treffer m. **2** Schlag m. **3** mus Schlager m.

hitch (hitʃ) vt **1** festmachen. **2** rücken. **hitch-hike** vi per Anhalter fahren, trampen.

hive (haiv) n Bienenstock m.

hoard (hɔːd) n Vorrat, Schatz m. vi,vt hamstern, horten.

hoarding ('hɔːdiŋ) n **1** Bauzaun m. **2** Reklamewand f.

hoarse (hɔːs) adj heiser.

hoax (houks) n Täuschung, Fopperei f. vt zum besten haben, anführen.

hobble ('hɔbəl) vi humpeln.

hobby ('hɔbi) n Hobby, Steckenpferd neu.

hock[1] (hɔk) n Sprunggelenk neu.

hock[2] (hɔk) n Rheinwein m.

hockey ('hɔki) n Hockey neu.

hoe (hou) n Haue, Hacke f. vt,vi hacken.

hog (hɔg) n Schwein neu. vt sl an sich reißen.

hoist (hoist) vt hochziehen. n Aufzug, Kran m. Winde f.

hold[1] (hould) vt **1** (fest)halten. **2** zurückhalten. **3** besitzen. **4** abhalten. **5** fassen, enthalten. **6** vertreten. vi **1** gelten. **2** sich halten. n Griff, Halt m. **holdall** n Reisetasche f. **holder** n **1** Behälter m. **2** Inhaber m.

hold[2] (hould) n Laderaum, Schiffsraum m.

hole (houl) n Loch neu. Höhle f.

holiday ('hɔlidi) n **1** Feiertag m. **2** pl Ferien pl. Urlaub m. **holiday camp** n Ferienlager neu. **holiday-maker** n Urlauber m.

Holland ('hɔlənd) n Holland neu.

hollow ('hɔlou) adj hohl. n Höhle, Aushöhlung f.

holly ('hɔli) n Stechpalme f.

holster ('houlstə) n Pistolenhalfter f.

holy ('houli) adj heilig.

homage ('hɔmidʒ) n Huldigung f.

home (houm) n **1** Heim neu. **2** Heimat f. adv heim, nach Hause. **at home** zu Hause. ~adj **1** einheimisch. **2** häuslich. **homecoming** n Heimkehr f. **homeland** n Heimatland neu. Heimat f. **homesick** adj **be homesick** Heimweh haben. **homework** n Schularbeit f. Schulaufgaben f pl.

homosexual (houmə'sekʃuəl) adj homosexuell. n Homosexuelle(r) m.

honest ('ɔnist) adj ehrlich.

honey ('hʌni) n Honig m. **honeymoon** n Flitterwochen f pl.

honour ('ɔnə) n **1** Ehre, Würde f. **2** Ruf m. **3** Auszeichnung f. **His/Her/Your Honour** Sein/Ihr/Euer Ehrwürden or Gnaden. ~vt (be)ehren, verehren. **honorary** adj Ehren—.

hood (hud) n **1** Kapuze f. **2** mot Verdeck neu.

hoof (huːf) n Huf m.

hook (huk) n Haken m. vt (an-, zu-)haken, fangen.

hooligan ('huːligən) n Rowdy m.

hoop (huːp) n Reifen, Ring m.

hoot (huːt) vi **1** mot hupen. **2** schreien.

Hoover ('huːvə) n Tdmk Staubsauger m. vt (ab)saugen.

hop[1] (hɔp) vi hüpfen, springen. n Hüpfer, Sprung m.

hop[2] (hɔp) n bot Hopfen m.

hope (houp) vt,vi (er)hoffen. n Hoffnung f.

horde (hɔːd) n Horde f.

horizon (hə'raizən) n Horizont m. **horizontal** adj waagerecht, horizontal.

horn (hɔːn) n **1** Horn neu. **2** mot Hupe f.

horoscope ('hɔrəskoup) n Horoskop neu.

horrible ('hɔrəbl) adj **1** schrecklich, entsetzlich. **2** gräßlich.

horrid ('hɔrid) adj gräßlich, scheußlich.

horrify ('hɔrifai) vt entsetzen, erschrecken.

horror ('hɔrə) n **1** Entsetzen neu. **2** Grausen neu. **3** Greuel m.

hors d'oeuvres (ɔː 'dɔːv) n pl Vorspeise f.

horse (hɔːs) n **1** Pferd neu. **2** mil Reiterei f. **on horseback** adv zu Pferde. **horse chestnut** n Roßkastanie f. **horseman** n Reiter m. **horsepower** n Pferdestärke f. **horseracing** n Pferderennen neu. **horseshoe** n Hufeisen neu.

horticulture ('hɔːtikʌltʃə) n Gartenbau m.

hose (houz) n **1** Schlauch m. **2** (lange) Strümpfe f pl.

hosiery ('houziəri) n Strumpfwaren f pl.

hospitable ('hɔspitəbl) adj gastfreundlich.

hospital ('hɔspitl) n Krankenhaus, Spital neu.

hospitality (hɔspi'tæliti) n Gastfreundschaft f.

host[1] (houst) n **1** Gastgeber m. **2** Wirt m.

host[2] (houst) n Menge f.

hostage ('hɔstidʒ) n Geisel m,f.

hostel ('hɔstl) n **1** Herberge f. **2** Wohnheim neu.

hostess ('houstis) n Gastgeberin f.

hostile ('hɔstail) adj feindlich.

hot (hɔt) adj **1** heiß. **2** scharf, pikant. **hotplate** n Kochplatte f. **hot-tempered** adj heißblütig, feurig. **hot-water bottle** n Wärmflasche f.

hotel (hou'tel) n Hotel neu.

hound (haund) n Jagdhund m.

hour (auə) n Stunde f.

house (n haus; v hauz) n Haus neu. vt unterbringen.

houseboat ('hausbout) n Hausboot neu.

housebound ('hausbaund) adj gezwungen, zu Hause zu bleiben.

household

household ('haushould) *n* Haushalt *m*.
housekeeper ('hauski:pə) *n* Haushälterin *f*.
housemaid ('hausmeid) *n* Hausmädchen *neu*.
House of Commons *n* Abgeordnetenhaus, Unterhaus *neu*.
House of Lords *n* Herrenhaus, Oberhaus *neu*.
houseproud ('hauspraud) *adj* penibel.
housewife ('hauswaif) *n* Hausfrau *f*.
housework ('hauswə:k) *n* Hausarbeit *f*.
housing ('hauziŋ) *n* Unterkunft, Unterbringung *f*.
hover ('hɔvə) *vi* schweben. **hovercraft** *n* Luftkissenfahrzeug *neu*.
how (hau) *adv* wie. **how do you do?** wie geht es (Ihnen)? **how much** wieviel. **however** *adv* wie auch (immer). *conj* dennoch, doch, jedoch, aber.
hub (hʌb) *n* **1** Nabe *f*. **2** Angelpunkt *m*.
huddle ('hʌdl) *vi* sich (zusammen)drängen.
huff (hʌf) *n* üble Laune *f*.
hug (hʌg) *vt* umarmen. *n* Umarmung *f*.
huge (hju:dʒ) *adj* ungeheuer, riesig.
hulk (hʌlk) *n* **1** Schiffsgerippe *f*. **2** unförmige Masse *f*.
hull (hʌl) *n* Schiffsrumpf *m*.
hullo (hə'lou) *interj* **1** guten Tag! grüß Gott! **2** hallo!
hum (hʌm) *vi,vt* summen.
human ('hju:mən) *adj* menschlich. *n* Mensch *m*. **humane** *adj* menschlich, human. **humanism** *n* Humanismus *m*. **human nature** *n* menschliche Natur *f*.
humanity (hju'mæniti) *n* **1** Menschheit *f*. **2** Menschlichkeit *f*. **humanitarian** *adj* menschenfreundlich. *n* Menschenfreund *m*.
humble ('hʌmbəl) *adj* bescheiden, demütig.
humdrum ('hʌmdrʌm) *adj* eintönig, fad, langweilig. *n* Eintönigkeit *f*.
humid ('hju:mid) *adj* feucht.
humiliate (hju'milieit) *vt* demütigen.
humility (hju'militi) *n* Demut, Bescheidenheit *f*.
humour ('hju:mə) *n* **1** Humor *m*. **2** Laune *f*. *vt* willfahren, aufheitern. **humorist** *n* Humorist *m*. **humorous** *adj* komisch, lustig.
hump (hʌmp) *n* Buckel *m*.
hunch (hʌntʃ) *vi* nach vorn rücken. *vt* krümmen. *n inf* Ahnung *f*. Verdacht *m*. **hunchback** *n* Bucklige(r) *m*.
hundred ('hʌndrəd) *adj* hundert. *n* Hundert *neu*. **hundredth** *adj* hundertste. **hundredweight** *n* Zentner *m*.
hung (hʌŋ) *v* see **hang.**
Hungary ('hʌŋgəri) *n* Ungarn *neu*. **Hungarian** *adj* ungarisch. *n* **1** Ungar *m*. **2** (language) Ungarisch *neu*.
hunger ('hʌŋgə) *n* Hunger *m*. *vi* hungern (nach). **hunger-strike** *n* Hungerstreik *m*. **hungry** *adj* hungrig. **be hungry** Hunger haben.
hunt (hʌnt) *vt,vi* jagen. *n* Jagd *f*. **hunting** *n* Jagen *neu*. **huntsman** *n* Jäger, Weidmann *m*.
hurdle ('hə:dl) *n* Hürde *f*.
hurl (hə:l) *vt* schleudern.
hurrah (hu'ra:) *interj* hurra!
hurricane ('hʌrikein) *n* Orkan *m*.
hurry ('hʌri) *vi* eilen, sich beeilen. *vt* beschleunigen, antreiben. *n* Eile, Hast *f*. **be in a hurry** Eile *or* es eilig haben.
hurt* (hə:t) *vt* **1** verletzen. **2** weh tun. *vi* weh tun. *n* **1** Schmerz *m*. **2** Verletzung *f*.
husband ('hʌzbənd) *n* Ehemann, Mann, Gatte *m*.
hush (hʌʃ) *interj* still! *n* Stille *f*. *v* **hush up** verschweigen.
husk (hʌsk) *n* Hülse, Schale *f*. *vt* schälen.
husky ('hʌski) *adj* heiser.
hussar (hu'za:) *n* Husar *m*.
hustle ('hʌsəl) *vi* eilen. *vt* drängen. *n* Drängen *neu*.
hut (hʌt) *n* Hütte *f*.
hutch (hʌtʃ) *n* **1** Kasten *m*. **2** Verschlag *m*.
hyacinth ('haiəsinθ) *n* Hyazinthe *f*.
hybrid ('haibrid) *n* Mischling *m*. Hybride *f*.
hydraulic (hai'drɔ:lik) *adj* hydraulisch.
hydro-electric *adj* hydroelektrisch.
hydrogen ('haidrədʒən) *n* Wasserstoff *m*.
hyena (hai'i:nə) *n* Hyäne *f*.
hygiene ('haidʒi:n) *n* Hygiene *f*. **hygienic** *adj* hygienisch.
hymn (him) *n* Hymne *f*. Kirchenlied *neu*. **hymnbook** *n* Gesangbuch *neu*.
hyphen ('haifən) *n* Bindestrich *m*.
hypnosis (hip'nousis) *n* Hypnose *f*. **hypnotism** *n* Hypnotismus *m*.
hypochondria (haipə'kɔndriə) *n* Hypochondrie *f*. **hypochondriac** *n* Hypochonder *m*.
hypocrisy (hi'pɔkrəsi) *n* Heuchelei *f*. **hypocrite** *n* Heuchler, Scheinheilige(r) *m*.
hypodermic (haipə'də:mik) *adj* **hypodermic syringe** Spritze *f*.
hypothesis (hai'pɔθəsis) *n pl* **-ses** Hypothese *f*.
hysterectomy (histə'rektəmi) *n* Hysterektomie *f*.
hysteria (his'tiəriə) *n* Hysterie *f*. **hysterical** *adj* hysterisch.

I

I (ai) *pron 1st pers sing* ich.

ice (ais) *n* Eis *neu*. **iceberg** *n* Eisberg *m*. **ice-cream** *n* Eiskrem f. (Speise)Eis *neu*. **icerink** *n* Eisbahn f. **ice skate** *n* Schlittschuh *m*. **icing** *n* Zuckerguß *m*. **icy** *adj* eisig.

Iceland ('aisland) *n* Island *neu*. **Icelander** *n* Isländer *m*. **Icelandic** (ais'lændik) *adj* isländisch. *n* (language) Isländisch *neu*.

idea (ai'dia) *n* Idee f. Begriff, Gedanke *m*.

ideal (ai'dial) *n* Ideal *neu. adj* ideal, vorbildlich. **idealistic** *adj* idealistisch. **idealize** *vt* idealisieren.

identify (ai'dentifai) *vt* identifizieren. **identification** *n* Identifizierung f.

identity (ai'dentiti) *n* 1 Identität, Gleichheit f. 2 Persönlichkeit f. **identical** *adj* 1 identisch. 2 derselbe. **identical twins** *n pl* eineiige Zwillinge *m pl*. **identity card** *n* (Personal)Ausweis *m*.

ideology (aidi'ɔlədʒi) *n* Ideologie f.

idiom ('idiəm) *n* 1 Idiom *neu*. 2 Mundart f.

idiosyncrasy (idiə'siŋkrəsi) *n* Eigenart f.

idiot ('idiət) *n* Idiot, Schwachsinnige(r) *m*.

idle ('aidl) *adj* 1 müßig. 2 faul. 3 unbenutzt.

idol ('aidl) *n* Idol *neu*. Abgott *m*. **idolatry** *n* Abgötterei f.

idyllic (i'dilik) *adj* idyllisch.

if (if) *conj* 1 wenn, falls. 2 ob. **as if** als ob.

igloo ('iglu:) *n* Iglu *m*.

ignite (ig'nait) (vi),vt (sich) entzünden. **ignition** *n* 1 Entzündung f. Anzünden *neu*. 2 mot Zündung f.

ignorant ('ignərənt) *adj* 1 unwissend, ungebildet. 2 nicht wissend.

ignore (ig'nɔ:) *vt* ignorieren, nicht beachten *or* berücksichtigen.

ill (il) *adj* krank. *adj,adv* übel, schlecht. **ill-bred** *adj* ungezogen, unhöflich, schlecht erzogen. **illness** *n* Krankheit f. **ill-treat** *vt* mißhandeln, mißbrauchen. **ill will** *n* Mißgunst f.

illegal (i'li:gəl) *adj* ungesetzlich, illegal.

illegible (i'ledʒəbl) *adj* unlesbar.

illegitimate (ili'dʒitimət) *adj* unehelich.

illicit (i'lisit) *adj* gesetzwidrig.

illiterate (i'litərət) *adj* analphabetisch. *n* Analphabet *m*.

illogical (i'lɔdʒikəl) *adj* unlogisch.

illuminate (i'lu:mineit) *vt* beleuchten.

illusion (i'lu:ʒən) *n* Illusion, Täuschung f.

illustrate ('iləstreit) *vt* 1 illustrieren. 2 erläutern. **illustration** *n* 1 Illustration f. Bild *neu*. 2 Erläuterung f. 3 Beispiel *neu*.

illustrious (i'lʌstriəs) *adj* berühmt.

image ('imidʒ) *n* 1 Bild, Abbild *neu*. 2 Sinnbild *neu*. **imagery** *n* Bildersprache f.

imagine (i'mædʒin) *vt* sich vorstellen. **imaginary** *adj* imaginär, eingebildet. **imagination** *n* Einbildung(skraft). Phantasie, Vorstellungskraft f. **imaginative** *adj* phantasievoll, einfallsreich.

imbalance (im'bæləns) *n* Unausgewogenheit f.

imbecile ('imbisi:l) *n* Schwachsinnige(r) *m*.

imitate ('imiteit) *vt* nachahmen. **imitation** *n* 1 Nachahmung f. 2 Nachbildung f. *adj* Kunst—.

immaculate (i'mækjulət) *adj* fleckenlos.

immature (imə'tjuə) *adj* unreif.

immediate (i'mi:diət) *adj* unmittelbar, sofortig. **immediately** *adv* sofort, gleich.

immense (i'mens) *adj* gewaltig, ungeheuer.

immerse (i'mə:s) *vt* eintauchen, vertiefen. **immersion** *n* Eintauchen, Vertieftsein *neu*. **immersion heater** *n* Tauchsieder *m*.

immigrate ('imigreit) *vi* einwandern. **immigrant** *n* Einwanderer *m*.

imminent ('iminənt) *adj* bevorstehend.

immobile (i'moubail) *adj* unbeweglich, bewegungslos. **immobilize** *vt* unbeweglich machen.

immoral (i'mɔrəl) *adj* unmoralisch, unsittlich.

immortal (i'mɔ:tl) *adj* unsterblich.

immovable (i'mu:vəbəl) *adj* 1 unbeweglich. 2 unerschütterlich.

immune (i'mju:n) *adj* 1 immun. 2 geschützt. **immunize** *vt med* immunisieren, impfen.

imp (imp) *n* 1 Kobold *m*. 2 Spitzbube *m*.

impact ('impækt) *n* 1 Zusammenstoß, Aufprall *m*. 2 Einfluß *m*. Wirkung f.

impair (im'pεə) *vt* beeinträchtigen.

impart (im'pa:t) *vt* 1 mitteilen. 2 geben.

impartial (im'pa:ʃəl) *adj* unparteiisch.

impassable (im'pa:səbəl) *adj* unbefahrbar.

impatient (im'peiʃənt) *adj* ungeduldig. **impatience** *n* Ungeduld f.

impeach (im'pi:tʃ) *vt* 1 anklagen. 2 zur Rechenschaft ziehen.

impeccable (im'pekəbəl) *adj* 1 sündlos. 2 einwandfrei.

impediment (im'pedimənt) *n* 1 Hindernis *neu*. 2 (of speech) Sprachfehler *m*.

imperative (im'perativ) *adj* 1 erforderlich. 2 befehlend. *n* Befehlsform f. Imperativ *m*.

imperfect (im'pə:fikt) adj 1 unvollkommen. 2 mangelhaft. n Imperfekt neu.

imperial (im'piəriəl) adj kaiserlich, Reichs—.

impersonal (im'pə:sənl) adj unpersönlich.

impersonate (im'pə:səneit) vt 1 verkörpern. 2 sich ausgeben als.

impertinent (im'pə:tinənt) adj unverschämt, frech.

impetuous (im'petʃuəs) adj ungestüm.

impetus ('impitəs) n Antrieb, Anstoß m.

impinge (im'pindʒ) vi 1 stoßen. 2 einwirken.

implement ('impləmənt) n Werkzeug, Gerät neu. vt durchführen.

implicate ('implikeit) vt 1 hineinziehen, verwickeln. 2 implizieren.

implicit (im'plisit) adj implizit, inbegriffen.

implore (im'plɔ:) vt anflehen.

imply (im'plai) vt 1 implizieren, in sich schließen. 2 andeuten, zu verstehen geben. **implication** n 1 Bedeutung f. 2 Folge f.

import (v im'pɔ:t; n 'impɔt) vt einführen, importieren. n 1 Einfuhr f. Import m. 2 pl Einfuhrwaren f pl. 3 Bedeutung f. **importation** n Einfuhr f. Import m.

importance (im'pɔ:tns) n 1 Wichtigkeit f. 2 Bedeutung f. **important** adj 1 wichtig. 2 bedeutend. 3 einflußreich.

impose (im'pouz) vt auferlegen, aufbürden. **impose upon** zu sehr beanspruchen. **imposing** adj imponierend, eindrucksvoll.

impossible (im'posəbəl) adj unmöglich.

impostor (im'postə) n Betrüger, Hochstapler m.

impotent ('impətənt) adj 1 unfähig. 2 med impotent.

impound (im'paund) vt beschlagnehmen.

impoverish (im'povəriʃ) vt arm machen.

impress (im'pres) vt 1 beeindrucken, Eindruck machen auf. 2 (ein)drücken, einprägen. **impression** n 1 Eindruck m. 2 Abdruck m. 3 (of a book) Auflage f.

imprint (n 'imprint; v im'print) n 1 Aufdruck m. 2 Eindruck m. vt aufdrücken, einprägen.

imprison (im'prizən) vt 1 einsperren, ins Gefängnis werfen. **imprisonment** n 1 Gefangenschaft f. 2 Gefängnisstrafe f.

improbable (im'probəbəl) adj 1 unwahrscheinlich. 2 unglaubhaft.

improper (im'propə) adj 1 unanständig. 2 ungeeignet.

improve (im'pru:v) vt (ver)bessern. vi sich (ver)bessern, besser werden.

improvise ('imprəvaiz) vt improvisieren.

impudent ('impjudənt) adj unverschämt, frech.

impulse ('impʌls) n 1 (An)Trieb, Stoß m. 2 Impuls, Drang m.

impure (im'pjuə) adj unrein, unsauber.

in (in) prep 1 in. 2 an. 3 auf. 4 nach. adv 1 hinein, herein. 2 innen.

inability (inə'biliti) n Unfähigkeit f.

inaccurate (in'ækjurət) adj 1 ungenau, unrichtig. 2 fehlerhaft.

inadequate (in'ædikwit) adj unangemessen, unzulänglich, ungenügend.

inadvertent (inəd'və:tnt) adj 1 unachtsam. 2 unabsichtlich. 3 nachlässig.

inane (i'nein) adj sinnlos, nichtig, geistlos.

inarticulate (ina:'tikjulət) adj 1 unartikuliert, undeutlich. 2 sich schlecht ausdrückend.

inasmuch (inəz'mʌtʃ) conj **inasmuch as** (in)sofern (als), da, weil.

inaugurate (i'nɔ:gjureit) vt einweihen.

incapable (in'keipəbəl) adj unfähig.

incendiary (in'sendiəri) n 1 Brandstifter m. 2 Brandbombe f.

incense[1] ('insens) n Weihrauch m.

incense[2] (in'sens) vt in Wut bringen, erzürnen.

incessant (in'sesənt) adj unaufhörlich.

incest ('insest) n Blutschande f. Inzest m.

inch (intʃ) n Zoll m.

incident ('insidənt) n 1 Zwischenfall m. 2 Zufall m. **incidental** adj 1 beiläufig. 2 gelegentlich. 3 zufällig. 4 Neben—.

incite (in'sait) vt aufregen, anstacheln.

incline (in'klain) vi sich neigen, geneigt sein zu. n Hang, Abhang m.

include (in'klu:d) vt einschließen, enthalten.

incoherent (inkou'hiərənt) adj unzusammenhängend.

income ('inkʌm) n Einkommen neu. Einkünfte f pl.

incompatible (inkəm'pætibəl) adj unvereinbar, nicht zusammenpassend.

incompetent (in'kompətənt) adj unfähig.

incomplete (inkəm'pli:t) adj unvollständig.

incomprehensible (inkɔmpri'hensibəl) adj 1 unverständlich. 2 unbegreiflich.

inconceivable (inkən'si:vəbəl) adj unbegreiflich.

incongruous (in'kɔŋgruəs) adj unvereinbar.

inconsiderate (inkən'sidərət) adj rücksichtslos.

inconsistent (inkən'sistənt) adj 1 widersprechend. 2 inkonsequent. 3 unbeständig.

inconvenient (inkən'vi:niənt) adj ungelegen, unbequem, lästig.

incorporate (in'kɔ:pəreit) vt einverleiben, aufnehmen, vereinigen.

incorrect (inkə'rekt) adj unrichtig, falsch.

increase (v in'kri:s; n 'inkri:s) vt 1 erhöhen, steigern. 2 vermehren. vi 1 sich vermehren. 2 sich vergrößern, zunehmen. n 1 Vergrößerung f. 2 Zunahme f. Wachstum neu.

incredible (in'kredəbəl) adj unglaublich.

incubate ('inkjubeit) vt ausbrüten.

incur (in'kə:) vt 1 sich zuziehen. 2 herbeiführen. 3 eingehen. 4 (debts) machen.

incurable (in'kjuərəbəl) adj unheilbar.

indecent (in'di:sənt) adj unanständig. **indecency** n Unanständigkeit f.

indeed (in'di:d) adv 1 in der Tat, tatsächlich. 2 zwar. 3 gewiß. interj 1 wirklich? 2 so!

indefinite (in'definit) adj unbestimmt.

indemnity (in'demniti) n Entschädigung f.

indent (in'dent) vt 1 auszacken, einschneiden. 2 bestellen. n 1 Einschnitt m. 2 Bestellung f.

independent (indi'pendənt) adj unabhängig, selbständig. **independence** n Unabhängigkeit, Selbständigkeit f.

index ('indeks) n 1 Zeiger m. 2 Inhaltsverzeichnis neu. **index finger** n Zeigefinger m.

India ('indiə) n Indien neu. **Indian** adj 1 indisch. 2 (of America) indianisch. n 1 Inder m. 2 (of America) Indianer m.

indicate ('indikeit) vt (an)zeigen, hinweisen. **indicator** n 1 Zeiger m. 2 mot Winker m.

indifferent (in'difrənt) adj 1 gleichgültig. 2 mittelmäßig.

indigenous (in'didʒənəs) adj eingeboren, einheimisch.

indigestion (indi'dʒestʃən) n Verdauungsstörung f.

indignant (in'dignənt) adj entrüstet, empört.

indirect (indi'rekt) adj indirekt.

indiscreet (indi'skri:t) adj indiskret.

indispensable (indi'spensəbəl) adj unentbehrlich.

individual (indi'vidʒuəl) adj 1 einzeln. 2 persönlich. 3 individuell. n Individuum neu.

indoctrinate (in'dɔktrineit) vt schulen, belehren. **indoctrination** n Schulung, Belehrung f.

indolent ('indələnt) adj lässig, träge.

Indonesia (ində'ni:ziə) n Indonesien neu. **Indonesian** adj indonesisch. n Indonesier m.

indoor ('indɔ:) adj 1 Innen—, Haus—, häuslich. 2 sport Hallen—. **indoors** adv innen, im Hause, drinnen.

induce (in'dju:s) vt 1 dazu bringen, bewegen. 2 herbeiführen.

indulge (in'dʌldʒ) vt 1 sich hingeben, nachgeben. 2 schwelgen. 3 verwöhnen. vi sich hingeben.

industry ('indəstri) n 1 Industrie f. 2 Fleiß m. **industrial** adj industriell, gewerblich. **industrialisation** n Industrialisierung f. **industrious** adj fleißig, arbeitsam.

inefficient (ini'fiʃənt) adj 1 unwirksam. 2 unwirtschaftlich. 3 untüchtig.

inept (i'nept) adj 1 unpassend. 2 ungeschickt.

inequality (ini'kwɔliti) n Ungleichheit f.

inert (i'nə:t) adj 1 träge. 2 sci wirkungslos. **inertia** n Trägheit, Untätigkeit f.

inevitable (in'evitəbəl) adj unvermeidlich.

inexpensive (inik'spensiv) adj preiswert, billig.

inexperienced (inik'spiəriənst) adj unerfahren.

infallible (in'fæləbəl) adj unfehlbar.

infamous ('infəməs) adj berüchtigt, ehrlos.

infancy ('infənsi) n (frühe) Kindheit f.

infant ('infənt) n (Klein)Kind neu.

infantry ('infəntri) n Infanterie f.

infatuate (in'fætʃueit) vt verblenden, betören. **be infatuated with** verliebt or vernarrt sein in. **infatuation** n Verblendung f.

infect (in'fekt) vt 1 infizieren, anstecken. **infection** n Ansteckung, Infektion f. **infectious** adj ansteckend.

infer (in'fə:) vt folgern, schließen.

inferior (in'fiəriə) adj 1 minderwertig. 2 niedriger. 3 untergeordnet. **inferiority** n Minderwertigkeit nf. **inferiority complex** n Minderwertigkeitskomplex m.

infernal (in'fə:nl) adj teuflisch, höllisch.

infest (in'fest) vt 1 (in Schwärmen) überlaufen, überschwemmen. 2 heimsuchen, plagen.

infidelity (infi'deliti) n Untreue f.

infiltrate ('infiltreit) vt durchsickern lassen, infiltrieren. vi eindringen.

infinite ('infinit) adj unendlich. **infinity** n Unendlichkeit f.

infinitive (in'finitiv) n Infinitiv m.

infirm (in'fə:m) adj schwach, gebrechlich.

inflame (in'fleim) vt 1 med entzünden. 2 entflammen, erregen.

inflammable (in'flæməbəl) adj 1 (leicht) entzündlich. 2 feuergefährlich.

inflate (in'fleit) vt aufblasen, aufpumpen. **inflation** n Inflation f.

inflection (in'flekʃən) n 1 gram Flexion, Abwandlung f. 2 Modulation f.

inflict (in'flikt) vt 1 zufügen. 2 auferlegen.

influence ('influəns) n 1 Einfluß m. 2 Wirkung f.

influenza (influ'enzə) n Grippe f.

211

influx ('inflʌks) n 1 Zustrom m. 2 Einfließen neu.

inform (in'fɔːm) vt informieren, mitteilen.

informal (in'fɔːməl) adj 1 zwanglos, nicht formell. 2 ungezwungen. **informality** n Ungezwungenheit, Zwanglosigkeit f.

information (infə'meiʃən) n 1 Auskunft f. 2 Information, Nachricht f.

infringe (in'frindʒ) vt,vi verletzen, übertreten.

infuriate (in'fjuərieit) vt rasend machen, aufbringen.

ingenious (in'dʒiːniəs) adj geistreich, erfinderisch, originell.

ingredient (in'griːdiənt) n Bestandteil m. Zutat f.

inhabit (in'hæbit) vt bewohnen. **inhabitant** n 1 Einwohner m. 2 Bewohner m.

inhale (in'heil) vt einatmen.

inherent (in'hiərənt) adj 1 innewohnend. 2 angeboren.

inherit (in'herit) vt erben. **inheritance** n Erbschaft f.

inhibit (in'hibit) vt 1 hemmen. 2 hindern. **inhibition** n 1 Hemmung f. 2 (Be)Hinderung f.

inhospitable (in'hospitəbəl) adj 1 nicht gastfreundlich. 2 ungastlich.

inhuman (in'hjuːmən) adj unmenschlich.

iniquity (i'nikwiti) n 1 Ungerechtigkeit f. 2 Schlechtigkeit f. 3 Schandtat f.

initial (i'niʃəl) adj ursprünglich, anfänglich. n Anfangsbuchstabe m.

initiate (i'niʃieit) vt einweihen. vt,vi anfangen, beginnen. vi die Initiative ergreifen.

initiative (i'niʃətiv) n Initiative f.

inject (in'dʒekt) vt 1 einspritzen. 2 ausspritzen. **injection** n 1 Einspritzung f. 2 med Injektion, Spritze f.

injure ('indʒə) vt 1 beschädigen. 2 verletzen. 3 schaden. 4 beleidigen. **injury** n 1 Verletzung f. 2 Unrecht neu. 3 Beleidigung f.

injustice (in'dʒʌstis) n Ungerechtigkeit f.

ink (iŋk) n 1 Tinte f. 2 Druckerschwärze f.

inkling ('iŋkliŋ) n Andeutung, Ahnung f.

inland ('inlənd) adj inländisch, Binnen—. n Binnenland neu. adv 1 landeinwärts. 2 im Inland. **Inland Revenue** n 1 Steuereinnahmen f pl. 2 (Einkommens)Steuerbehörde f.

inmate ('inmeit) n 1 Insasse m. 2 Mitbewohner m.

inn (in) n Wirtshaus, Gasthaus neu.

innate (i'neit) adj angeboren.

inner ('inə) adj inner, Innen—, innerlich.

innocent ('inəsənt) adj 1 unschuldig. 2 harmlos. 3 einfältig. **innocence** n 1 Unschuld f. 2 Harmlosigkeit f. 3 Einfalt f.

innocuous (i'nɔkjuəs) adj harmlos, unschädlich.

innovation (inə'veiʃən) n Neuerung f.

innuendo (inju'endou) n Anspielung f.

innumerable (i'njuːmərəbəl) adj unzählbar, zahllos.

inoculate (i'nɔkjuleit) vt (ein)impfen. **inoculation** n (Ein)Impfung f.

inquest ('inkwest) n gerichtliche Untersuchung f.

inquire (in'kwaiə) vi (nach)fragen, sich erkundigen. **inquiry** n 1 Nachfrage, Erkundigung f. 2 Untersuchung f. 3 pl Auskünfte f pl.

inquisition (inkwi'ziʃən) n 1 Untersuchung f. 2 Inquisition f.

inquisitive (in'kwizitiv) adj 1 neugierig. 2 wißbegierig. **inquisitiveness** n 1 Neugier f. 2 Wißbegierde f.

insane (in'sein) adj 1 wahnsinnig. 2 verrückt. **insanity** n 1 Wahnsinn m. 2 Verrücktheit f.

insatiable (in'seiʃəbəl) adj unersättlich.

inscribe (in'skraib) vt 1 einschreiben. 2 beschriften. 3 eintragen. **inscription** n 1 Inschrift f. 2 Eintragung f.

insect ('insekt) n Insekt neu. **insecticide** n Insektengift neu.

insecure (insi'kjuə) adj unsicher. **insecurity** n Unsicherheit f.

inseminate (in'semineit) vt 1 befruchten. 2 einpflanzen. **insemination** n Befruchtung f.

insensitive (in'sensitiv) adj unempfindlich.

inseparable (in'sepərəbəl) adj untrennbar.

insert (in'səːt) vt 1 einsetzen. 2 (a coin, etc.) einwerfen. 3 (an advertisement, etc.) aufgeben. **insertion** n 1 Einsetzung f. 2 Einwurf m. 3 Inserat neu.

inside (in'said) n Innere neu. Innenseite f. adj inner, Innen—. adv 1 drinnen. 2 hinein, herein. prep innerhalb.

insidious (in'sidiəs) adj heimtückisch.

insight (in'sait) n Einsicht f.

insignificant (insig'nifikənt) adj 1 unbedeutend. 2 bedeutungslos.

insincere (insin'siə) adj unaufrichtig. **insincerity** n Unaufrichtigkeit f.

insinuate (in'sinjueit) vt 1 anspielen auf. 2 unbemerkt hineinbringen. 3 zu verstehen geben. 4 sich einschmeicheln. **insinuation** n 1 Andeutung f. 2 Einschmeichelung f.

insist (in'sist) vi bestehen. **insistence** n Bestehen neu.

insolent ('insələnt) adj unverschämt, frech. **insolence** n Unverschämtheit, Frechheit f.

insomnia (in'somnia) n Schlaflosigkeit f.

inspect (in'spekt) vt 1 untersuchen. 2 inspizieren, besichtigen. **inspection** n 1 Untersuchung f. 2 Inspektion, Besichtigung f.

inspire (in'spaiə) vt,vi 1 inspirieren, eingeben, begeistern. 2 einatmen. **inspiration** n 1 Eingebung, Begeisterung f. 2 Einatmung f. **inspiring** adj begeisternd, belebend.

instability (instə'biliti) n Unbeständigkeit f.

install (in'stɔ:l) vt 1 einsetzen. 2 installieren, einrichten. **installation** n 1 Einsetzung f. 2 Installierung, Einrichtung f. Montage f.

instalment (in'stɔ:lmənt) n 1 Rate f. 2 (Teil)Lieferung f. **by instalments** adv ratenweise.

instance ('instəns) n 1 Beispiel neu. 2 (besonderer) Fall m. 3 Bitte f. 4 law Instanz f. **for instance** zum Beispiel. **instant** adj 1 sofortig, augenblicklich. 2 dringend. n Augenblick m. **instantaneous** adj sofortig, augenblicklich. **instantly** adv sogleich, sofort.

instead (in'sted) adv statt dessen. **instead of** (an)statt.

instep ('instep) n Rist, Spann m.

instigate ('instigeit) vt anstiften. **instigation** n Anstiftung f. **instigator** n Anstifter m.

instil (in'stil) vt 1 einträufeln. 2 einflößen. **instillation** n 1 Einträufeln neu. 2 Einflößung f.

instinct ('instiŋkt) n (Natur)Trieb, Instinkt m. **instinctive** adj unwillkürlich, instinktiv.

institute ('institju:t) vt einsetzen, einführen, gründen. n Institut neu. **institution** n 1 Institut neu. Anstalt f. 2 Stiftung f. 3 Einführung. 4 Institution, Einrichtung f.

instruct (in'strʌkt) vt 1 unterrichten. 2 unterweisen. 3 anweisen. **instruction** n 1 Unterricht m. 2 Unterweisung f. 3 Vorschrift, Anordnung. 4 Anweisung f. **instructive** adj instruktiv, lehrreich.

instrument ('instrumənt) n 1 Instrument neu. 2 Werkzeug neu. 3 Mittel neu. **instrumental** adj 1 behilflich, förderlich. 2 Instrumental—.

insubordinate (insə'bɔ:dinət) adj aufsässig, widersetzlich, ungehorsam. **insubordination** n Widersetzlichkeit f. Ungehorsam m.

insular ('insjulə) adj 1 insular, Insel—. 2 beschränkt.

insulate ('insjuleit) vt isolieren. **insulation** n Isolierung f.

insulin ('insjulin) n Insulin neu.

insult (v in'sʌlt; n 'insʌlt) vt beleidigen, beschimpfen. n Beleidigung, Beschimpfung f.

insure (in'ʃuə) vt versichern. **insurance** n Versicherung f. adj Versicherungs—.

intact (in'tækt) adj unberührt, intakt.

intake ('inteik) n 1 tech Einlaß m. 2 (Neu)Aufnahme f.

integral ('intigrəl) adj 1 integral, ganz, vollständig. 2 math Integral—.

integrate ('intigreit) vt 1 ergänzen. 2 integrieren. **integration** n pol Integration f.

integrity (in'tegriti) n 1 Vollständigkeit f. 2 Redlichkeit, Integrität f.

intellect ('intəlekt) n Intellekt, Verstand m. **intellectual** adj 1 Verstandes—, geistig. 2 intellektuell. n Intellektuelle(r) m.

intelligent (in'telidʒənt) adj 1 intelligent. 2 klug. **intelligence** n 1 Intelligenz f. 2 Verstand m. 3 pol (geheimer) Nachrichtendienst m. **intelligentsia** n Intelligenz, Intelligentsia f. **intelligible** adj verständlich.

intend (in'tend) vt 1 vorhaben, die Absicht haben zu. 2 meinen. 3 bestimmen. **intended** adj absichtlich.

intense (in'tens) adj 1 intensiv. 2 angespannt. 3 heftig. **intensify** (vi),vt (sich) verstärken. **intensity** n 1 Intensität f. 2 Anspannung f. 3 Heftigkeit f. **intensive** adj 1 intensiv, heftig. 2 verstärkend.

intent[1] (in'tent) n 1 Absicht f. 2 Plan m.

intent[2] (in'tent) adj 1 versessen. 2 gespannt.

intention (in'tenʃən) n 1 Absicht f. 2 Zweck m. **intentional** adj absichtlich.

inter (in'tə:) vt beerdigen.

interact (intə'rækt) vt sich gegenseitig beeinflussen. **interaction** n Wechselwirkung f.

intercept (intə'sept) vt 1 abfangen. 2 unterbrechen. **interception** n 1 Abfangen neu. 2 Unterbrechung f.

interchange (intə'tʃeindʒ) vt austauschen. vi abwechseln. n 1 Austausch m. 2 Abwechslung f. **interchangeable** adj austauschbar.

intercourse ('intəkɔ:s) n Verkehr, Umgang m.

interest ('intrəst) n 1 Interesse neu. Anteilnahme m. 2 Beteiligung f. 3 Nutzen m. 4 comm Zins m. vt 1 interessieren. 2 angehen. **take an interest in** sich interessieren für. **interesting** adj interessant.

interfere (intə'fiə) vi 1 sich einmischen. 2 stören. **interference** n 1 Einmischung f. 2 Störung f. 3 Dazwischentreten neu.

interim ('intərim) n Interim neu. Zwischenzeit f. adj vorläufig, Interims—.

interior (in'tiəriə) *adj* inner, Innen—, innerlich. *n* 1 Innere *neu.* 2 Binnenland *neu.*

interjection (intə'dʒekʃn) *n* Ausruf, Einwurf *m.* Interjektion *f.*

interlude ('intəlu:d) *n* Zwischenspiel *neu.*

intermediate (intə'mi:diət) *adj* 1 dazwischenliegend. 2 Mittel—, Zwischen—. **intermediary** *adj* 1 dazwischen befindlich. 2 vermittelnd. *n* Vermittler *m.*

interminable (in'tə:minəbəl) *adj* endlos, unendlich.

intermission (intə'miʃən) *n* 1 Aussetzen *neu.* 2 Unterbrechung *f.* 3 Pause *f.*

intermittent (intə'mitnt) *adj* aussetzend, mit Unterbrechungen.

intern (in'tə:n) *vt* internieren. **internment** *n* Internierung *f.*

internal (in'tə:nl) *adj* 1 inner(lich). 2 inländisch. **internal-combustion engine** *n* Verbrennungsmotor *m.*

international (intə'næʃnl) *adj* international. *n sport* internationaler Spieler *m.*

interpose (intə'pouz) *vt* 1 einlegen. 2 einwerfen. *vi* 1 dazwischenstellen. 2 vermitteln.

interpret (in'tə:prit) *vt* 1 interpretieren, auslegen, erklären. 2 dolmetschen. 3 darstellen. **interpretation** *n* 1 Interpretation, Auslegung, Erklärung *f.* 2 Darstellung *f.* **interpreter** *n* Dolmetscher *m.*

interrogate (in'terəgeit) *vt* 1 befragen. 2 verhören. **interrogation** *n* 1 Befragen *neu.* 2 Verhör *neu.*

interrogative (intə'rogətiv) *adj* fragend, Frage—.

interrupt (intə'rʌpt) *vt* unterbrechen. **interruption** *n* Unterbrechung *f.*

intersect (intə'sekt) *vt* durchschneiden. *vi* (sich) schneiden. **intersection** *n* 1 Durchschnitt *m.* 2 Schnittpunkt *m.* 3 *mot* Kreuzung *f.*

interval ('intəvəl) *n* 1 Zwischenraum *m.* 2 Pause *f.* 3 *mus* Intervall *neu.*

intervene (intə'vi:n) *vi* 1 dazwischenkommen. 2 dazwischenliegen. 3 intervenieren. **intervention** *n* 1 Dazwischenkommen *neu.* 2 Intervention *f.*

interview ('intəvju:) *n* 1 Unterredung *f.* 2 Interview *neu.* *vt* interviewen. **interviewer** *n* Interviewer *m.*

intestine (in'testin) *n* 1 Darm *m.* 2 *pl* Eingeweide *neu pl.*

intimate[1] ('intimeit) *adj* 1 vertraut, intim. 2 innig. **intimacy** *n* Vertraulichkeit, Intimität *f.*

intimate[2] ('intimit) *vt* 1 andeuten. 2 zu verstehen geben.

intimidate (in'timideit) *vt* einschüchtern. **intimidation** *n* Einschüchterung *f.*

into ('intə; *stressed* 'intu:) *prep* in, in...hinein.

intolerable (in'tolərəbəl) *adj* unerträglich. **intolerant** *adj* intolerant, unduldsam. **intolerance** *n* Intoleranz, Unduldsamkeit *f.*

intonation (intə'neiʃən) *n* 1 Anstimmung *f.* 2 Tonfall *m.* 3 *mus* Tongebung *f.*

intoxicate (in'toksikeit) *vt* berauschen. **intoxication** *n* 1 Berauschung *f.* 2 Rausch *m.*

intransitive (in'trænsitiv) *adj gram* intransitiv.

intricate ('intrikət) *adj* 1 kompliziert. 2 schwierig. **intricacy** *n* 1 Kompliziertheit *f.* 2 Schwierigkeit *f.*

intrigue (in'tri:g) *n* 1 Intrige *f.* 2 (Liebes)-Verhältnis *neu.* *vi* intrigieren. *vt* neugierig machen. **intriguing** *adj* interessant, faszinierend.

intrinsic (in'trinsik) *adj* 1 innerlich. 2 wahr, eigentlich, wesentlich.

introduce (intrə'dju:s) *vt* 1 einführen, einleiten. 2 (a person) vorstellen. **introduction** *n* 1 Einführung, Einleitung *f.* 2 Vorstellung *f.* **introductory** *adj* einführend, einleitend.

introspective (intrə'spektiv) *adj* beschaulich, nach innen gekehrt, introspektiv.

introvert ('introvə:t) *vt* einwärts kehren. *n* introvertierter Mensch *m.*

intrude (in'tru:d) *vt* einzwängen. *vi* 1 sich eindrängen. 2 stören. **intruder** *n* Eindringling *m.* **intrusion** *n* Eindringen *neu.*

intuition (intju'iʃən) *n* Intuition *f.* **intuitive** *adj* intuitiv.

inundate ('inʌndeit) *vt* überschwemmen. **inundation** *n* Überschwemmung *f.*

invade (in'veid) *vt* 1 einfallen in, eindringen in. 2 befallen. **invasion** *n* Einfall *m.* Invasion *f.*

invalid[1] ('invəli:d) *n* 1 Kranke(r) *m.* 2 Invalide *m.*

invalid[2] (in'vælid) *adj* ungültig. **invalidate** *vt* ungültig machen.

invaluable (in'væljubəl) *adj* unschätzbar.

invariable (in'vɛəriəbəl) *adj* unveränderlich. **invariably** *adv* immer, stets.

invent (in'vent) *vt* 1 erfinden. 2 erdichten. **invention** *n* 1 Erfindung *f.* 2 Erdichtung *f.* **inventive** *adj* erfinderisch. **inventor** *n* Erfinder *m.*

inventory ('invəntəri) *n* 1 Inventar *neu.* 2 *comm* Inventur *f.*

jaded

invert (in'vəːt) *vt* umkehren. **inverted commas** Anführungszeichen *neu pl.*

invertebrate (in'vəːtəbreit) *adj* 1 wirbellos. 2 rückgratlos. *n* wirbelloses Tier *neu.*

invest (in'vest) *vt* 1 *comm* anlegen, investieren. 2 bekleiden. **invest in** *inf* kaufen. **investor** *n* Geldanleger *m.* **investment** *n* Kapitalanlage *f.*

investigate (in'vestigeit) *vt* erforschen, untersuchen. **investigation** *n* Untersuchung *f.*

invincible (in'vinsəbl) *adj* unüberwindlich.

invisible (in'vizəbl) *adj* unsichtbar.

invite (in'vait) *vt* 1 einladen. 2 anlocken. **invitation** *n* Einladung *f.*

invoice ('invois) *n* Faktura, Rechnung *f.*

invoke (in'vouk) *vt* 1 anrufen. 2 (a spirit) beschwören. **invocation** *n* Anrufung, Beschwörung *f.*

involve (in'volv) *vt* verwickeln, hineinziehen. **involvement** *n* 1 Verwicklung *f.* 2 Schwierigkeit *f.*

inward ('inwəd) *adj* 1 innerlich. 2 nach innen gehend. **inwards** *adv* einwärts, nach innen.

iodine ('aiədiːn) *n* Jod *neu.*

Iran (i'rɑːn) *n* Iran *m.* **Iranian** *adj* iranisch. *n* Iranier *m.*

Iraq (i'rɑːk) *n* Irak *m.* **Iraqi** *adj* irakisch. *n* Iraker *m.*

Ireland ('aiələnd) *n* Irland *neu.* **Irish** *adj* irisch. **Irishman** *n* Ire, Irländer *m.* **Irishwoman** *n* Irin, Irländerin *f.*

iris ('airis) *n* 1 *anat* Iris *f.* 2 *bot* Schwertlilie *f.*

iron ('aiən) *n* 1 Eisen *neu.* 2 *dom* Bügeleisen *neu. adj* eisern, Eisen—. *vt* bügeln. **ironing board** *n* Bügelbrett *neu.* **ironmonger** *n* Eisenwarenhändler *m.*

Iron Curtain *n* Eiserner Vorhang *m.*

irony ('airəni) *n* Ironie *f.* **ironic** *adj* ironisch, spöttisch.

irrational (i'ræʃənl) *adj* irrational, unvernünftig. **irrationality** *n* Unvernunft *f.*

irregular (i'regjulə) *adj* unregelmäßig. **irregularity** *n* Unregelmäßigkeit *f.*

irrelevant (i'reləvənt) *adj* 1 irrelevant, nicht zur Sache gehörig. 2 belanglos. **irrelevance** *n* Belanglosigkeit *f.*

irresistible (iri'zistəbl) *adj* unwiderstehlich.

irrespective (iri'spektiv) *adj* **irrespective of** ohne Rücksicht auf, unabhängig von.

irresponsible (iri'sponsəbl) *adj* verantwortungslos. **irresponsibility** *n* Verantwortungslosigkeit *f.*

irrevocable (i'revəkəbl) *adj* unwiderruflich.

irrigate ('irigeit) *vt* bewässern. **irrigation** *n* Bewässerung *f.*

irritate ('iriteit) *vt* reizen. **irritable** *adj* reizbar. **irritating** *adj* aufreizend, ärgerlich.

is (iz) *v* see **be.**

Islam ('izlɑːm) *n* Islam *m.* **Islamic** *adj* islamisch.

island ('ailənd) *n* Insel *f.* **islander** *n* Inselbewohner *m.*

isle (ail) *n* Insel *f.*

isolate ('aisəleit) *vt* 1 absondern. 2 isolieren. **isolated** *adj* 1 abgesondert. 2 abgeschieden, isoliert. **isolation** *n* 1 Absonderung *f.* 2 Isolierung *f.*

Israel ('izreiəl) *n* Israel *neu.* **Israeli** *adj* israelisch. *n* Israeli *m.*

issue ('iʃuː) *n* 1 Herauskommen, Herausgeben *neu.* 2 Ausgabe *f.* 3 Nummer *f.* 4 Ergebnis *neu.* 5 Streitfrage *f. vi* herauskommen. *vt* 1 aussenden. 2 emittieren. 3 herausgeben.

isthmus ('isməs) *n* Landenge *f.* Isthmus *m.*

it (it) *pron 3rd pers s* 1 er *m.* sie *f.* es *neu.* 2 ihn *m.* sie *f.* es *neu.* 3 ihm *m,neu.* ihr *f.*

italic (i'tælik) *adj* kursiv. **italics** *n pl* Kursivdruck *m.*

Italy ('itəli) *n* Italien *neu.* **Italian** *adj* italienisch. *n* 1 Italiener *m.* 2 (language) Italienisch *neu.*

itch (itʃ) *n* Jucken *neu.* Krätze *f. vi* jucken. **itchy** *adj* juckend, krätzig.

item ('aitəm) *n* 1 Einzelheit *f.* 2 (Zeitungs)Notiz *f.* 3 (Rechnungs)Posten *m.*

itinerary (ai'tinərəri) *n* 1 Reiseroute *f.* 2 Reisebericht *m.* **itinerant** *adj* 1 (herum)reisend. 2 Wander—, Reise—.

its (its) *poss adj 3rd pers* sein *m. neu.* ihr *f.* **itself** *pron 3rd pers s* 1 selbst. 2 sich. 3 sich selbst. **by itself** allein, von selber.

ivory ('aivəri) *n* Elfenbein *neu. adj* Elfenbein—.

ivy ('aivi) *n* Efeu *m.*

J

jab (dʒæb) *n* 1 Stich *m.* 2 *inf med* Spritze *f. vt* stechen.

jack (dʒæk) *n* 1 *mot* Wagenheber *m.* 2 *game* Bube *m.* 3 *naut* Bugflagge *f. vt* heben.

jackdaw ('dʒækdɔː) *n* Dohle *f.*

jacket ('dʒækit) *n* 1 Jacke *f.* 2 (Schutz)Umschlag *m.*

jackpot ('dʒækpɔt) *n game* Jackpot *m.*

jade (dʒeid) *n* Jade, Nephrit *m.*

jaded ('dʒeidid) *adj* abgehetzt, ermüdet.

jagged

jagged ('dʒægid) *adj* zackig.

jaguar ('dʒægjuə) *n* Jaguar *m*.

jail (dʒeil) *n* Gefängnis *neu*. *vt* ins Gefängnis bringen, einsperren. **jailer** *n* Gefängniswärter *m*.

jam[1] (dʒæm) *vt* 1 (fest)klemmen. 2 versperren. *vi* sich (ver-, ein-)klemmen. *n* Gedränge *neu*.

jam[2] (dʒæm) *n* Marmelade *f*. **jam-jar** *n* Marmeladenglas *neu*.

Jamaica (dʒə'meikə) *n* Jamaika *neu*. **Jamaican** *adj* jamaikisch. *n* Jamaiker *m*.

January ('dʒænjuəri) *n* Januar *m*.

Japan (dʒə'pæn) *n* Japan *neu*. **Japanese** (dʒæpə'niːz) *adj* japanisch. *n*. 1 Japaner *m*. 2 (language) Japanisch *neu*.

jar[1] (dʒɑː) *n* 1 Glas *neu*. 2 Krug *m*.

jar[2] (dʒɑː) *n* Knarren *neu*. *vi* knarren.

jargon ('dʒɑːgən) *n* Jargon *m*. Fachsprache *f*.

jasmine ('dʒæzmin) *n* Jasmin *m*.

jaundice ('dʒɔːndis) *n med* Gelbsucht *f*. **jaundiced** *adj* 1 gelbsüchtig. 2 neidisch.

jaunt (dʒɔːnt) *n* Ausflug *m*. **jaunty** *adj* flott, munter.

javelin ('dʒævlin) *n* 1 Wurfspieß *m*. 2 *sport* Speer *m*.

jaw (dʒɔː) *n* 1 Kiefer *m*. 2 *pl* Rachen *m*. *vi sl* schwatzen. **jawbone** *n* Kieferknochen *m*.

jazz (dʒæz) *n* Jazz *m*. *v* **jazz up** *sl* Leben bringen in, aufmöbeln. **jazzy** *adj inf* grell, schreiend.

jealous ('dʒeləs) *adj* eifersüchtig, neidisch. **jealousy** *n* Eifersucht *f*. Neid *m*.

jeans (dʒiːnz) *n pl* Jeans *pl*.

jeep (dʒiːp) *n* Jeep *m*.

jeer (dʒiə) *vi* höhnen, spotten. *vt* verhöhnen. *n* Spott *m*. **jeering** *adj* spöttisch, höhnisch.

jelly ('dʒeli) *n* Gelee *neu*. **jellyfish** *n* Qualle *f*.

jeopardize ('dʒepədaiz) *vt* gefährden. **jeopardy** *n* Gefahr *f*.

jerk (dʒəːk) *vt* rucken. *vi* ziehen, schleudern. *n* 1 Ruck, plötzlicher Stoß *m*. **jerky** *adj* 1 ruckartig. 2 holperig.

jersey ('dʒəːzi) *n* (Woll)Pullover *m*.

Jersey ('dʒəːzi) *n* (Insel) Jersey *neu*.

jest (dʒest) *n* Scherz, Spaß, Witz *m*. *vi* scherzen. **jester** *n* (Hof)Narr *m*.

Jesus ('dʒiːzəs) *n* Jesus *m*.

jet (dʒet) *n* 1 (Wasser-, Gas-)Strahl *m*. 2 Düse *f*. **jet-plane** *n* Düsenflugzeug *neu*.

jetty ('dʒeti) *n* 1 Hafendamm *m*. 2 Landungsbrücke *f*.

Jew (dʒuː) *n* Jude *m*. **jewish** *adj* jüdisch. **Jewry** *n* Judentum *neu*.

jewel ('dʒuːəl) *n* Juwel *neu*,*m*. **jeweller** *n* Juwelier *m*. **jewellery** *n* Schmuck *m*.

jig (dʒig) *n* Gigue *f*. *vi* Gigue tanzen, (herum) hüpfen.

jiggle ('dʒigəl) *(vi)*,*vt* (umher)wackeln.

jigsaw ('dʒigsɔː) *n* Zusammensetzspiel *neu*.

jilt (dʒilt) *vt* sitzen lassen.

jingle ('dʒiŋgəl) *n* 1 Geklingel *neu*. 2 Wortgeklingel *neu*. *vi*,*vt* klingeln, klimpern.

job (dʒɔb) *n* 1 Arbeit *f*. 2 Stelle *f*. Job *m*. 3 Sache, Aufgabe *f*.

jockey ('dʒɔki) *n* Jockei *m*.

jodhpurs ('dʒɔdpəz) *n pl* Reithose *f*.

jog (dʒɔg) *vt* (an)stoßen, rütteln. *vi* (dahin)trotten. *n* 1 Stoß *m*. 2 Rütteln *neu*. 3 Trott *m*.

join (dʒɔin) *vt* 1 verbinden. 2 fügen. 3 zusammenbringen, vereinigen. 4 eintreten in, Mitglied werden. *vi* 1 sich verbinden. 2 angrenzen. **join in** mitmachen, teilnehmen. ~*n* 1 Verbindung(sstelle) *f*. 2 Fuge *f*. 3 Naht *f*. **joiner** *n* Tischler *m*. **joinery** *n* Tischlerarbeit *f*. **joint** *n* 1 Verbindung(sstelle) *f*. 2 *anat* Gelenk *neu*. 3 *cul* Braten *m*. 4 *sl* Lokal *neu*. Bude *f*. 5 *sl* Marihuana-Zigarette *f*. Joint *m*. *adj* 1 verbunden. 2 gemeinsam. *vt* 1 zusammenfügen. 2 verbinden. 3 mit Gelenken versehen.

joist (dʒɔist) *n* Querbalken *m*.

joke (dʒouk) *n* Scherz, Witz, Spaß *m*. *vi* scherzen. **joker** *n* 1 Spaßvogel *m*. 2 *game* Joker *m*. **practical joke** *n* Streich *m*.

jolly ('dʒɔli) *adj* lustig. *adv inf* ganz schön.

jolt (dʒoult) *vt*,*vi* rütteln. *vi* holpern. *n* Rütteln *neu*.

Jordan ('dʒɔːdn) *n* Jordanien *neu*. **Jordanian** *adj* jordanisch. *n* Jordanier *m*.

jostle ('dʒɔsəl) *vt* anstoßen. *vi* sich drängen. *n* (Zusammen)Stoß *m*. Gedränge *neu*.

journal ('dʒəːnl) *n* 1 Journal *neu*. 2 Tagebuch *neu*. 3 Zeitschrift *f*. **journalism** *n* Zeitungswesen *neu*. Journalismus *m*. **journalist** *n* Journalist *m*.

journey ('dʒəːni) *n* 1 Reise *f*. 2 Fahrt *f*. *vi* reisen, wandern.

jovial ('dʒouviəl) *adj* heiter, jovial. **joviality** *n* Heiterkeit, Jovialität *f*.

joy (dʒɔi) *n* Freude *f*. **joyful** *adj* 1 freudig. 2 froh. **joyfulness** *n* Fröhlichkeit *f*.

jubilee ('dʒuːbiliː) *n* Jubiläum *neu*.

Judaism ('dʒuːdeiizəm) *n* Judaismus *m*.

judge (dʒʌdʒ) *n* 1 *law* Richter *m*. 2 Schiedsrichter *m*. 3 Beurteiler *m*. *vi* 1 urteilen. *vt* 1 beurteilen. 2 ein Urteil fällen über. **judgment**

n **1** Urteil *neu.* **2** Meinung *f.* **3** Urteilvermögen *neu.*

judicial (dʒu:'diʃəl) *adj* **1** Gerichts—, gerichtlich. **2** richterlich. **3** kritisch.

judicious (dʒu:'diʃəs) *adj* einsichtsvoll.

judo ('dʒu:dou) *n* Judo *neu.*

jug (dʒʌg) *n* Krug *m.* Kanne *f.*

juggernaut ('dʒʌgənɔ:t) *n inf* Fernlaster *m.*

juggle ('dʒʌgəl) *vi.vt* jonglieren, Kunststücke machen. **juggler** *n* Jongleur *m.*

juice (dʒu:s) *n* **1** Saft *m.* **2** *mot sl* Sprit *m.* **juicy** *adj* **1** saftig. **2** *inf* pikant.

jukebox ('dʒu:kbɔks) *n* Musikautomat *m.*

July (dʒu'lai) *n* Juli *m.*

jumble ('dʒʌmbəl) *n* Mischmasch *m.* Durcheinander *neu. vt* durcheinanderwerfen. *vi* durcheinandergeraten. **jumble sale** *n* Wohltätigkeitsbasar *m.*

jump (dʒʌmp) *vi* **1** springen, hüpfen. **2** auffahren. *vt* hinwegspringen über. **jump the queue** sich vordrängen. ~*n* Sprung, Satz *m.*

jumper ('dʒʌmpə) *n* Pullover *m.*

junction ('dʒʌŋkʃən) *n* **1** Verbindung *f.* **2** Kreuzung *f.* **3** Knotenpunkt *m.*

June (dʒu:n) *n* Juni *m.*

jungle ('dʒʌŋgəl) *n* Dschungel *m.*

junior ('dʒu:niə) *adj* **1** jünger. **2** Unter—. *n* **1** Jüngere(r) *m.* **2** Junior *m.*

juniper ('dʒu:nipə) *n* Wachholder *m.*

junk[1] (dʒʌŋk) *n* Altwaren *f pl.* alter Kram *m.*

junk[2] (dʒʌŋk) *n* Dschunke *f.*

junta ('dʒʌntə) *n* Junta *f.*

Jupiter ('dʒu:pitə) *n* Jupiter *m.*

jurisdiction (dʒuəris'dikʃən) *n* **1** Rechtsprechung *f.* **2** Gerichtsbarkeit, Zuständigkeit *f.*

jury ('dʒuəri) *n* **1** die Geschworenen *pl.* **2** Jury *f.* **juror** *n* Geschworene(r) *m.*

just (dʒʌst) *adj* **1** gerecht. **2** richtig. **3** gehörig. *adv* **1** gerade, eben. **2** genau.

justice ('dʒʌstis) *n* **1** Gerechtigkeit *f.* **2** Recht *neu.* **3** Richter *m.*

justify ('dʒʌstifai) *vt* rechtfertigen.

jut (dʒʌt) *vi* hervorragen, vorspringen. *n* Vorsprung *m.*

jute (dʒu:t) *n bot* Jute *f.*

juvenile ('dʒu:vənail) *adj* jung, jugendlich, Jugend—. **juvenile delinquency** *n* Jugendkriminilität *f.* **juvenility** *n* **1** Jugendlichkeit *f.* **2** Kinderei *f.*

juxtapose (dʒʌkstə'pouz) *vt* nebeneinanderstellen.

K

kaftan ('kæftæn) *n* Kaftan *m.*

kaleidoscope (kə'laidəskoup) *n* Kaleidoskop *neu.*

kangaroo (kæŋgə'ru:) *n* Känguruh *neu.*

karate (kə'rɑ:ti) *n* Karate *neu.*

kebab (kə'bæb) *n* Kebab *m.*

keel (ki:l) *n* Kiel *m.* **on an even keel** *n* gleichmäßig, ausgeglichen.

keen (ki:n) *adj* **1** scharf. **2** eifrig. **3** heftig. **keen on** *inf* erpicht auf, scharf auf.

keep[*] (ki:p) *vt* **1** halten. **2** unterhalten. **3** (auf)bewahren. **4** (accounts, etc.) führen. *vi* sich halten. *n* **1** Unterhalt *m.* **2** Bergfried *m.* **keeper** *n* Wärter *m.* **keepsake** *n* Andenken *neu.*

keg (keg) *n* Fäßchen *neu.*

kennel ('kenl) *n* **1** Hundehütte *f.* **2** *pl* Hundezwinger *m.*

Kenya ('kenjə) *n* Kenya *f.* **Kenyan** *adj* Kenianisch. *n* Kenianer *m.*

kept (kept) *v see* **keep.**

kerb (kə:b) *n* Strassenkante *f.*

kernel ('kə:nl) *n* **1** Kern *m.* **2** Korn *neu.*

kettle ('ketl) *n* Kessel *m.* **kettledrum** *n* (Kessel)Pauke *f.*

key (ki:) *n* **1** Schlüssel *m.* **2** Taste *f.* **3** *mus* Tonart *f.* **keyboard** *n* Tastatur *f.*

khaki ('kɑ:ki) *n* Khaki *neu. adj* khakifarben.

kibbutz (ki'buts) *n* Kibbuz *m.*

kick (kik) *vt* mit dem Fuß stoßen *or* treten. *vi* **1** ausschlagen. **2** (zurück)stoßen. **kick off** anstoßen. **kick-off** *n* Anstoß *m.* **kick one's heels** *inf* wartend herumstehen. **kick the bucket** ins Gras beißen. ~*n* **1** Fußtritt *m.* **2** Rückstoß *m.* **3** *inf* Schwung *m.* Energie *f.* **get a kick out of** Spaß daran haben.

kid[1] (kid) *n* **1** *zool* Zicklein *neu.* **2** Ziegenleder *neu.* **3** *inf* Kind *neu.*

kid[2] (kid) *vt* foppen, aufziehen. *vi* scherzen.

kidnap ('kidnæp) *vt* entführen. **kidnapper** *n* Entführer, Kidnapper *m.*

kidney ('kidni) *n* Niere *f.* **kidney bean** *n* weiße Bohne *f.*

kill (kil) *vt* **1** töten. **2** umbringen, morden. **3** abschlachten. **kill time** die Zeit totschlagen.

kiln (kiln) *n* Ziegelofen, Brennofen *m.*

kilo ('ki:lou) *n* Kilo *neu.*

kilogram ('kiləgræm) *n* Kilogramm *neu.*

kilometre (ki'lɔmitə) *n* Kilometer *m.*

kilt

kilt (kilt) *n* Schottenrock, Kilt *m*.

kimono (ki'mounou) *n* Kimono *m*.

kin (kin) *n* 1 Geschlecht *neu*. Sippe *f*. 2 (Bluts)Verwandtschaft *f*. **the next of kin** die nächsten Verwandten.

kind[1] (kaind) *adj* freundlich, gütig, gut.

kind[2] (kaind) *n* 1 Art, Sorte *f*. 2 Geschlecht *neu*. **all kinds of** allerlei. **what kind of?** was für?

kindergarten ('kindəgɑːtn) *n* Kindergarten *m*.

kindle ('kindl) *vt* anzünden. *vi* (sich) entzünden, aufflammen.

kinetic (ki'netik) *adj* kinetisch, bewegend. **kinetics** *n pl* Kinetik *f*.

king (kiŋ) *n* König *m*. **kingdom** *n* Königreich *neu*. **kingfisher** *n* Eisvogel *m*.

kink (kiŋk) *n* 1 Schleife *f*. Knick *m*. 2 Fimmel *m*. *vt* knicken. *vi* (sich) verfilzen.

kiosk ('kiɔsk) *n* Kiosk *m*.

kipper ('kipə) *n* Räucherhering *m*.

kiss (kis) *vi,vt* küssen. *n* Kuß *m*.

kit (kit) *n* 1 Ausrüstung *f*. 2 Werkzeug *neu*. 3 Bausatz *m*.

kitchen ('kitʃin) *n* Küche *f*.

kite (kait) *n* (Papier)Drachen *m*.

kitten ('kitn) *n* Kätzchen *neu*. junge Katze *f*.

kitty ('kiti) *n* (gemeinsame) Kasse *f*.

kiwi ('kiːwi) *n* Kiwi *m*.

kleptomania (kleptə'meiniə) *n* Kleptomanie *f*. **kleptomaniac** *n* Kleptomane *m*.

knack (næk) *n* 1 Kniff, Trick *m*. 2 Geschicklichkeit *f*.

knapsack ('næpsæk) *n* Rucksack *m*.

knead (niːd) *vt* kneten.

knee (niː) *n* Knie *neu*. **kneecap** *n* Kniescheibe *f*.

kneel* (niːl) *vi* knien.

knew (nuː) *v* see **know**.

knickers ('nikəz) *n pl* (Damen)Schlüpfer *m*. **knickerbockers** *n pl* Kniehosen *f pl*.

knife (naif) *n, pl* **knives** Messer *neu*. *vt* (er)stechen.

knight (nait) *n* 1 Ritter *m*. 2 *game* Springer *m*. *vt* zum Ritter schlagen. **knighthood** *n* Ritterwürde *f*.

knit* (nit) *vt* 1 stricken. 2 (ver)knüpfen. **knit one's brows** die Stirn runzeln. **knitting** *n* 1 Stricken *neu*. 2 Strickzeug *neu*. **knitting needle** *n* Stricknadel *f*. **knitwear** *n* Strickwaren *f pl*.

knob (nɔb) *n* Knopf *m*.

knobbly ('nɔbli) *adj* knorrig.

knock (nɔk) *vi,vt* klopfen, schlagen, pochen.

knock down 1 niederschlagen. 2 überfahren. **knock off** 1 abschlagen, abziehen. 2 *inf* Feierabend machen. 3 *sl* stehlen. **knock out** k.o. schlagen. **knockout** *n* knockout *m*. ~*n* 1 Klopfen *neu* 2 Stoß, Schlag *m*.

knot (nɔt) *n* 1 Knoten *m*. 2 Ast *m*. 3 Schwierigkeit *f*. *vi,vt* (ver)knoten, (ver)knüpfen.

know* (nou) *vt* 1 wissen. 2 kennen. **get to know** kennenlernen. **know the ropes** sich auskennen. **knowing** *adj* 1 erfahren. 2 verständnisvoll.

knowledge ('nɔlidʒ) *n* 1 Wissen *neu*. 2 Kenntnis *f*. **to my knowledge** meines Wissens. **knowledgeable** *adj* 1 kenntnisreich. 2 gut informiert.

knuckle ('nʌkl) *n* Knöchel *m*. *v* **knuckle under** nachgeben.

Korea (kə'riə) *n* Korea *neu*. **Korean** *adj* koreanisch. ~*n* Koreaner *m*.

kosher ('kouʃə) *adj* koscher.

Kuwait (ku'weit) *n* Kuwait *neu*.

L

label ('leibəl) *n* 1 Zettel *neu*. 2 Bezeichnung *f*. *vt* beschriften, mit einem Zettel versehen.

laboratory (lə'bɔrətri) *n* Laboratorium, Labor *neu*. **laboratory assistant** *n* Laborant *m*.

labour ('leibə) *vi* 1 arbeiten. 2 sich anstrengen. 3 sich schwer bewegen. *vt* 1 ausarbeiten. 2 ausführlich eingehen. *n* 1 Arbeit *f*. 2 Mühe, Anstrengung *f*. 3 (Geburts)Wehen *f pl*. 4 Arbeitskräfte *f pl*. **hard labour** *n* Zwangsarbeit *f*. **labour force** *n* Arbeiterschaft *f*. **Labour Party** *n* Labour Party, Arbeiterpartei *f*. **labour-saving** *adj* arbeitssparend. **laborious** *adj* mühsam, anstrengend. **labourer** *n* Arbeiter *m*.

laburnum (lə'bəːnəm) *n* Goldregen *m*.

labyrinth ('læbərinθ) *n* Labyrinth *neu*.

lace (leis) *n* 1 Spitze *f*. 2 Schnur *f*. *vt* 1 mit Spitze besetzen. 2 (zu)schnüren.

lack (læk) *n* Mangel *m*. Fehlen *neu*. *vt* ermangeln. *vi* fehlen, mangeln.

lacquer ('lækə) *n* Lack *m*. *vt* lackieren. **lacquered** *adj* Lack—.

lad (læd) *n* Bursche, Junge *m*.

ladder ('lædə) *n* 1 Leiter *f*. 2 (in stockings) Laufmasche *f*. *vi* eine Laufmasche bekommen.

laden ('leidn) *adj* beladen.

ladle ('leidl) *n* Schöpflöffel *m*. Kelle *f*. *v* **ladle out** 1 schöpfen. 2 austeilen.

lady ('leidi) n 1 Dame f. 2 Herrin f. **Ladies and Gentlemen!** Meine Damen und Herren! **ladybird** n Marienkäfer m.

lag[1] (læg) vi sich verzögern, zurückbleiben. n 1 Rückstand m. 2 Zeitabstand m.

lag[2] (læg) vt verschalen, verkleiden.

lager ('lɑːgə) n Lagerbier neu.

laid (leid) v see **lay**[1]. **laid up** adj inf bettlägerig.

lain (lein) v see **lie**[1].

laity ('leiəti) n Laien m pl.

lake (leik) n See m.

lamb (læm) n 1 Lamm neu. 2 Lammfleisch neu.

lame (leim) adj lahm. vt lähmen. **lameness** n Lahmheit f.

lament (lə'ment) n 1 (Weh)Klage f. 2 Klagelied neu. vt beklagen. vi trauern.

lamp (læmp) n Lampe f. **lamppost** n Laternenpfahl m. **lampshade** n Lampenschirm m.

lance (lɑːns) n Lanze f.

land (lænd) n 1 (festes) Land neu. 2 Boden, Grund m. 3 Grundbesitz m. vi,vt landen. **landing** n 1 Landung f. 2 Treppenabsatz m. **landlady** n (Haus)Wirtin f. **landlord** n (Haus)Wirt m. **landmark** n 1 Grenzstein m. 2 Wendepunkt m. **landscape** n Landschaft f.

lane (lein) n 1 Feldweg m. 2 Gasse f. 3 (on motorways, etc.) Fahrbahn f.

language ('læŋgwidʒ) n 1 Sprache f. 2 pl Fremdsprachen pl. **bad language** Schimpfworte m pl. **language laboratory** n Sprachlabor neu.

lanky ('læŋki) adj schlaksig, schlank.

lantern ('læntən) n Laterne f.

lap[1] (læp) n Schoß m.

lap[2] (læp) vt 1 übereinanderlegen, umschlagen. 2 sport überrunden. vi (ein)hüllen. n sport Runde f.

lap[3] (læp) vt (auf)lecken. vi plätschern.

lapel (lə'pel) n Aufschlag m.

Lapland ('læplænd) n Lappland neu. **Lapp** adj lappisch. n 1 Lappländer, Lappe m. 2 (language) Lappisch neu.

lapse (læps) n 1 Verlauf m. 2 Verfallen neu. 3 Versehen neu. vi 1 verlaufen. 2 (ver)fallen.

larceny ('lɑːsəni) n Diebstahl m.

larch (lɑːtʃ) n Lärche f.

lard (lɑːd) n Schmalz, Schweinefett neu.

larder ('lɑːdə) n Speiseschrank m.

large (lɑːdʒ) adj 1 groß. 2 reichlich. 3 weitherzig. **largely** adv zum großen Teil.

lark[1] (lɑːk) n zool Lerche f.

lark[2] (lɑːk) n Streich m.

larva ('lɑːvə) n Larve, Puppe f.

larynx ('læriŋks) n Kehlkopf m. **laryngitis** n med Kehlkopfentzündung f.

laser ('leizə) n Laser m. **laser beams** n Laserstrahlen m pl.

lash (læʃ) n 1 Peitschenschnur f. 2 (Peitschen)-Hieb m. 3 anat Wimper f. vt peitschen, geißeln. **lash out** ausschlagen.

lass (læs) n inf Mädchen neu.

lasso (læ'suː) n Lasso m,neu. vt mit dem Lasso fangen.

last[1] (lɑːst) adj 1 letzt. 2 vorig. n 1 Letzte(r) m. 2 Ende neu. **at last** 1 schließlich. 2 zuletzt. **last but not least** nicht zuletzt.

last[2] (lɑːst) vi 1 dauern. 2 halten. 3 ausreichen.

latch (lætʃ) n 1 Klinke f. 2 Sicherheitsschloß neu. **on the latch** (nur) eingeklinkt. ~vt einklinken.

late (leit) adj 1 spät. 2 verspätet. 3 (jüngst) verstorben, selig. 4 ehemalig. **be late** 1 zu spät kommen. 2 Verspätung haben. **lately** adv vor kurzem, neulich, in letzter Zeit.

latent ('leitnt) adj 1 verborgen. 2 latent.

lateral ('lætərəl) adj seitlich, Seiten—. Quer—.

latest ('leitist) adj spätest, neuest, letzt. **at the latest** adv spätestens.

lathe (leið) n Drehbank f.

lather ('lɑːðə) n (Seifen)Schaum m. vt einseifen. vi schäumen.

Latin ('lætin) adj lateinisch. n 1 Latiner m. 2 (language) Latein neu. **Latin America** n Lateinamerika neu.

latitude ('lætitjuːd) n 1 geog Breite f. 2 Spielraum m. **latitudinal** adj Breiten—.

latter ('lætə) adj 1 letzter. 2 neuer.

lattice ('lætis) n Gitter neu.

laugh (lɑːf) vi lachen. **laugh at** auslachen. ~n Lachen neu. **laughable** adj lächerlich. **laughter** n Gelächter neu.

launch[1] (lɔːntʃ) vt 1 naut vom Stapel lassen. 2 loslassen. 3 (a rocket) abschießen. **launch into** sich stürzen in. **launching pad** n Raketenabschußrampe f.

launch[2] (lɔːntʃ) n 1 Barkasse f. 2 Ausflugsdampfer m.

launder ('lɔːndə) (vi),vt (sich) waschen. **launderette** n Schnellwäscherei f. **laundry** n 1 Wäscherei f. 2 Wäsche f.

laurel ('lɔrəl) n Lorbeer m.

lava ('lɑːvə) n Lava f.

lavatory ('lævətri) n Toilette f.

lavender ('lævində) n Lavendel m.

lavish ('læviʃ) adj 1 verschwenderisch, freige-

big. 2 reichlich. vt verschwenden. **lavishness**
n (verschwenderische) Freigebigkeit f.

law (lɔ:) n 1 Gesetz, Recht neu. 2 Jura neu
pl. **law-abiding** adj gesetzestreu, friedlich.
lawsuit n 1 Verfahren neu. 2 Klage f. **lawyer**
n 1 Rechtsanwalt m. 2 Jurist m.

lawn (lɔ:n) n 1 Rasen neu. **lawn-mower** n Rasen-
mäher m.

lax (læks) adj lax, locker, nachlässig.

laxative ('læksətiv) n Abführmittel neu.

lay[1] (lei) vt 1 legen. 2 (the table) decken. 3
setzen, (hin)stellen. **layer** n Schicht, Lage f.
vt überlagern. vi sich lagern.

lay[2] (lei) v see **lie**[1].

lay[3] (lei) adj 1 Laien—. laienhaft. **layman** n
Laie m.

laze (leiz) vi faulenzen. **laze away** vertrödeln.
laziness n Faulheit, Trägheit f. **lazy** adj faul,
träge. **lazy bones** n inf Faulenzer m.

lead[1] (li:d) vt,vi 1 führen, leiten. 2 vorangehen.
n 1 Führung f. 2 tech (Zu)Leitung f. 3
(Hunde)Leine f. 4 Th Hauptrolle f. 5 Hinweis
m. Beispiel neu. **leading** adj Haupt—, herr-
schend, führend, Leit—. **leader** n 1 Führer
m. 2 Leiter m. 3 (in a newspaper) Leitartikel
m. **leadership** n Führerschaft f.

lead[2] (led) n 1 Blei neu. 2 Bleistiftmine f. adj
bleiern.

leaf (li:f) n 1 Blatt neu. 2 Flügel m. 3 Klappe f. v
leaf through durchblättern. **leaflet** n 1
Blättchen neu. 2 Prospekt m.

league (li:g) n 1 Bund m. 2 sport Liga f.

leak (li:k) n 1 Leck neu. 2 pol Durchsickern neu.
vi 1 lecken. 2 durchsickern. **leakage** n 1
Durchsickern neu. 2 Schwund m.

lean[1] (li:n) vi sich lehnen, sich neigen. vt
lehnen, stützen. **lean on** sich stützen auf.

lean[2] (li:n) adj mager.

leap[*] (li:p) vi springen, hüpfen. vt überspringen.
n Sprung, Satz m. **look before you leap** erst
wägen, dann wagen. **leapfrog** n Bocksprin-
gen neu. **leap year** n Schaltjahr neu.

learn[*] (lə:n) vt 1 lernen. 2 erfahren, erlernen.
learned adj 1 gelehrt. 2 erfahren. **learner** n 1
Anfänger m. 2 mot Fahrschüler m.

lease (li:s) n 1 Pachtvertrag m. 2 Pacht f. vt
(ver)pachten. **leasehold** n 1 Pacht f. 2
Pachtbesitz m. adj Pacht—. **leaseholder** n
Pächter m.

leash (li:ʃ) n (Koppel)Leine f.

least (li:st) adj wenigst, mindest. adv am
wenigsten. n Wenigste, Mindeste neu. **at
least** wenigstens, mindestens, zumindest.

leather ('leðə) n Leder neu. adj ledern, Leder—.
leathery adj zäh.

leave[1] (li:v) vt 1 verlassen. 2 lassen. vi abfahren, (fort-, weg-)gehen.

leave[2] (li:v) n 1 Erlaubnis f. 2 Urlaub m. **take
one's leave** Abschied nehmen.

Lebanon ('lebənən) n Libanon m. **Lebanese**
adj libanesisch. n Libanese(r) m.

lecherous ('letʃərəs) adj wollüstig.

lectern ('lektən) n Lesepult neu.

lecture ('lektʃə) n 1 Vorlesung f. Vortrag m. 2
Strafpredigt f. vi eine Vorlesung halten. vt
abkanzeln. **lecturer** n Dozent m.

led (led) v see **lead**[1].

ledge (ledʒ) n 1 Sims m. 2 Felsbank f.

ledger ('ledʒə) n comm Hauptbuch neu.

lee (li:) n 1 Schutz m. 2 naut Leeseite f.

leech (li:tʃ) n Blutegel m.

leek (li:k) n Lauch m.

leer (liə) vi schielen. n lüsterner Seitenblick m.

left[1] (left) adj link. n linke Seite, Linke f. adv
(nach) links. **left-hand** adj link, linksseitig.
left-handed adj linkshändig. **left-wing** adj
pol Links—, linksradikal.

left[2] (left) v see **leave**[1]. adj übrig. **left-luggage
office** n Gepäckaufbewahrung f.

leg (leg) n 1 Bein neu. 2 cul Keule f. **pull
someone's leg** jemanden auf den Arm nehmen.

legacy ('legəsi) n Vermächtnis neu.

legal ('li:gəl) adj 1 gesetzlich. 2 juristisch. 3
Rechts—. **legality** n Gesetzlichkeit f. **le-
galize** vt rechtskräftig machen, legalisieren.

legend ('ledʒənd) n Legende f. Sage f.

legible ('ledʒibəl) adj leserlich, lesbar.

legion ('li:dʒən) n Legion f. **legionary** adj
Legions—. n Legionär m.

legislate ('ledʒisleit) vi Gesetze geben. **legislation** n Gesetzgebung f.

legitimate (li'dʒitimət) adj 1 legitim, rechtmäßig. 2 (of a child) ehelich. **legitimize** vt
legitimieren, für rechtmäßig erklären.

leisure ('leʒə) n Muße, freie Zeit f. **at your
leisure** wenn es Ihnen paßt. **be at leisure**
Muße haben. ~adj müßig, Muße—. **leisurely** adj,adv gemächlich, ohne Hast.

lemon ('lemən) n Zitrone f. **lemonade** n
(Zitronen)Limonade f.

lend[*] (lend) vt 1 (ver-, aus-)leihen. 2 leisten,
gewähren. **lend a hand** helfen.

length (leŋθ) n 1 Länge f. 2 Strecke f. 3 Dauer
f. **at length** adv 1 ausführlich. 2 endlich.

lengthen (vi),vt (sich) verlängern. **lengthy** adj 1 sehr lang. 2 weitschweifig.

lenient ('li:niənt) adj mild, nachsichtig.

lens (lenz) n Linse f.

lent (lent) v see **lend**.

Lent (lent) n Fastenzeit f. Fasten f pl.

lentil ('lentl) n Linse f.

Leo ('li:ou) n Löwe m.

leopard ('lepəd) n Leopard m.

leper ('lepə) n Aussätzige(r) m. **leprosy** n Aussatz m. Lepra f. **leprous** adj aussätzig.

lesbian ('lezbiən) n Lesbierin f. adj lesbisch.

less (les) adv weniger, adj kleiner, geringer. **lessen** (vi),vt (sich) vermindern.

lesson ('lesən) n 1 Lektion f. 2 educ Stunde f. 3 rel Lesung f. 4 pl Unterricht m. **teach someone a lesson** jemandem eine Lektion erteilen.

lest (lest) conj damit or daß nicht.

let* (let) vt 1 lassen. 2 vermieten. **let on** inf es verraten. **let someone down** jemanden im Stich lassen. **~n** sport Netzball m.

lethal ('li:θəl) adj tödlich.

lethargy ('leθədʒi) n Lethargie f. **lethargic** adj lethargisch.

letter ('letə) n 1 Brief m. 2 Buchstabe m. 3 Type f. **man of letters** Literat m. **to the letter** buchstäblich. **letterbox** n Briefkasten m.

lettuce ('letis) n Kopfsalat m.

leukaemia (lu:'ki:miə) n Leukämie f.

level ('levəl) adj 1 eben. 2 ausgeglichen. **level crossing** n Bahnübergang m. **level-headed** adj vernünftig. **~n** 1 ebene Fläche, Ebene f. 2 Niveau neu. Höhe f. vt 1 gleichmachen. 2 nivellieren. 3 ebnen, planieren.

lever ('li:və) n 1 Hebel m. 2 Hebestange f. vt mit einem Hebel bewegen. **leverage** n Hebelkraft f.

levy ('levi) n 1 Erhebung f. Beitrag m. 2 mil Aushebung f. vt 1 erheben. 2 ausheben.

lewd (lu:d) adj unzüchtig. **lewdness** n Unzucht f.

liable ('laiəbl) adj 1 verantwortlich. 2 haftpflichtig. 3 ausgesetzt. **be liable to** neigen zu. **liability** n 1 Verantwortlichkeit f. 2 Haftpflicht f. 3 Neigung f. 4 pl Verbindlichkeiten f pl.

liaison n 1 Verbindung f. 2 Liebschaft f.

liar ('laiə) n Lügner m.

libel ('laibəl) n 1 Schmähschrift f. 2 Verleumdung f. vt 1 schmähen. 2 (schriftlich) verleumden.

liberal ('libərəl) adj 1 liberal. 2 großzügig.

freigebig. 2 reichlich. 3 freisinnig. n Liberale(r) m.

liberate ('libəreit) vt befreien. **liberation** n Befreiung f.

liberty ('libəti) n Freiheit f.

Libra ('li:brə) n Waage f.

library ('laibrəri) n Bücherei, Bibliothek f. **lending library** Leihbücherei. **librarian** n Bibliothekar m.

libretto (li'bretou) n Libretto neu.

Libya ('libiə) n Libyen neu. **Libyan** adj libysch. n Libyer m.

licence ('laisəns) n 1 Lizenz f. 2 Erlaubnis f. 3 Konzession f. 4 Zügellosigkeit f. 5 Freiheit f. **driving licence** Führerschein m. **license** vt lizenzieren, genehmigen, zulassen. **licensing hours** n pl Ausschankstunden f pl. **licensee** n Lizenzinhaber m.

lick (lik) vt 1 lecken. 2 inf besiegen, übertreffen. vi (of flames) züngeln. n Lecken neu.

lid (lid) n 1 Deckel m. 2 anat Augenlid neu.

lie¹ (lai) vi liegen. **lie down** sich (hin-, nieder-) legen. **~n** Lage f.

lie² (lai) n Lüge f. **white lie** Notlüge f. vi lügen.

lieutenant (lef'tenənt) n Leutnant m. **lieutenant colonel** n Oberstleutnant m.

life (laif) n, pl **lives** î Leben neu. 2 Menschenleben neu. 3 Lebendigkeit f. **lifebelt** n Rettungsgürtel m. **lifeboat** n Rettungsboot neu. **lifebuoy** n Rettungsboje f. **lifeguard** n Bademeister m. **lifeline** n Rettungsleine f. **lifetime** n Lebenszeit f.

lift (lift) vt 1 (auf-, hoch-)heben. 2 erheben. vi sich heben. n 1 Aufzug, Fahrstuhl m. 2 (Auf)Heben neu. 3 Erhebung f. **give someone a lift** jemanden im Auto mitnehmen.

light¹ (lait) n 1 Licht. 2 Beleuchtung f. 3 Lampe f. 4 (for tobacco) Feuer neu. 5 Leuchte f. **lighthouse** n Leuchtturm m. ~vt 1 anzünden. 2 beleuchten. adj hell. **lighter** n 1 Anzünder m. 2 Feuerzeug neu. **lighting** n Beleuchtung f.

light² (lait) adj leicht. **light-headed** adj leichtsinnig. **light-hearted** adj leichtherzig, fröhlich. **lightweight** adj leicht. n Leichtgewichtler m.

light³ (lait) vi **light upon** stoßen auf.

lighten¹ ('laitn) vi 1 erleuchten. 2 sich erhellen. 3 blitzen.

lighten² ('laitn) (vi),vt (sich) erleichtern.

lightning ('laitniŋ) n Blitz m.

like¹ (laik) adj,adv gleich, ähnlich. prep wie. **like-minded** adj gleichgesinnt. **likeness** n 1

Ähnlichkeit f. 2 Abbild neu. **likewise** adv gleichfalls, auch, ebenso.

like² (laik) vt mögen, gern haben, lieben; gefallen. **like doing something** etwas gern tun. **I like this picture** dieses Bild gefällt mir.

likely ('laikli) adj,adv wahrscheinlich.

lilac ('lailək) adj lila. n 1 bot (spanischer) Flieder m. 2 Lila neu.

lily ('lili) n Lilie f. **lily-of-the-valley** n Maiglöckchen neu.

limb (lim) n 1 Glied neu. 2 Ast m. **artificial limb** n Prothese f.

limbo ('limbou) n 1 Vorhölle f. 2 Vergessenheit f. 3 Gefängnis, Kittchen neu.

lime¹ (laim) n Kalk m. vt mit Kalk düngen. **limelight** n 1 Kalklicht neu. 2 Scheinwerferlicht neu. 3 Rampenlicht neu. **limestone** n Kalkstein m.

lime² (laim) n 1 Limone f. 2 Linde f.

limerick ('limərik) n Limerick m.

limit ('limit) n Grenze f. Äußerste neu. **that is the limit!** das ist (doch wirklich) die Höhe! ~vt begrenzen, beschränken. **limitation** n 1 Begrenzung, Beschränkung f. 2 Grenze f.

limp¹ (limp) vi hinken. n Hinken neu.

limp² (limp) adj 1 schlaff. 2 kraftlos.

limpet ('limpit) n Napfschnecke f.

linden ('lindən) n Linde f. Lindenbaum m.

line¹ (lain) n 1 Linie f. 2 Reihe f. 3 Zeile f. Fach neu. vt 1 linieren. 2 aufstellen. 3 (um-)säumen. **lineage** n Abstammung f. **linear** adj linear, Linien—.

line² (lain) vt (a coat, etc.) füttern.

linen ('linin) n 1 Leinen neu. Leinwand f. 2 Wäsche f. **linen basket** n Wäschekorb m. ~adj leinen, Leinen—.

liner ('lainə) n Passagierdampfer m.

linger ('liŋgə) vi 1 zögern. 2 verweilen. 3 sich hinziehen. 4 schlendern.

lingerie ('lɔnʒəri:) n Damenunterwäsche f.

linguist ('liŋgwist) n Linguist, Sprachwissenschaftler m. **linguistic** adj linguistisch, sprachlich, Sprach—. **linguistics** n pl Linguistik, Sprachwissenschaft f.

lining ('lainiŋ) n 1 Futter neu. 2 Verkleidung f.

link (liŋk) n 1 Glied neu. 2 Verbindung f. vt (vi,vt) (sich) verketten, (sich) verbinden.

linoleum (li'nouliəm) n also **lino** Linoleum n.

linseed ('linsi:d) n Leinsamen m. **linseed oil** n Leinöl neu.

lion ('laiən) n Löwe m.

lip (lip) n 1 Lippe f. 2 Rand m. 3 inf Unver-

schämtheit f. **lip-read** von den Lippen ablesen. **lipstick** n Lippenstift m.

liqueur (li'kjuə) n Likör m.

liquid ('likwid) adj flüssig. n Flüssigkeit f. **liquidation** n 1 comm Liquidation f. 2 Beseitigung f. **go into liquidation** sich auflösen. **liquidize** (vi),vt (sich) verflüssigen.

liquor ('likə) n 1 Flüssigkeit f. 2 Alkohol m.

liquorice ('likəris) n Lakritze f.

lira ('liərə) n, pl **lire** or **liras** Lira f.

lisp (lisp) vi lispeln. n Lispeln neu.

list¹ (list) n Liste f. Verzeichnis neu. vt (in eine Liste) eintragen, verzeichnen.

list² (list) vi naut Schlagseite haben. n Schlagseite f.

listen ('lisən) vi 1 (an-, zu-)hören. 2 lauschen. **listener** n (Zu)Hörer m.

listless ('listləs) adj lustlos, träg. **listlessness** n Lustlosigkeit, Trägheit f.

lit (lit) v see **light¹**.

litany ('litəni) n Litanei f.

literal ('litərəl) adj 1 buchstäblich, wörtlich. 2 genau.

literary ('litərəri) adj 1 literarisch. 2 literarisch gebildet.

literate ('litərət) adj gebildet.

literature ('litrətʃə) n Literatur f.

litre ('li:tə) n Liter m,neu.

litter ('litə) n 1 Tragbahre f. 2 (of animals) Wurf m. 3 Abfall neu. **litter-bin** n Abfallkorb m. ~vt 1 verstreuen. 2 verunreinigen.

little ('litl) adj 1 klein. 2 kurz. 3 wenig. adv wenig. n Wenige neu. **a little** ein wenig, ein bißchen.

liturgy ('litədʒi) n Liturgie f.

live¹ (liv) vi 1 leben. 2 wohnen. vt (a life) führen.

live² (laiv) adj 1 lebend, lebendig. 2 Direkt—. 3 stromführend. **livestock** n Vieh neu.

livelihood ('laivlihud) n Lebensunterhalt m.

lively ('laivli) adj lebhaft.

liver ('livə) n Leber f.

livid ('livid) adj 1 bläulich. 2 inf wütend.

living ('liviŋ) adj lebend(ig), Lebens—. n Lebensunterhalt m. **living room** n Wohnzimmer neu.

lizard ('lizəd) n Eidechse f.

llama ('la:mə) n Lama neu.

load (loud) n 1 Last f. 2 Belastung f. 3 Ladung f. **loads of** inf sehr viel, eine ganze Menge. ~vt 1 (be-, auf-)laden. 2 überhäufen, überladen.

loaf¹ (louf) n Brotlaib m.

loaf[2] (louf) vi bummeln, gammeln. **loafer** n Bummler, Gammler m.

loan (loun) n 1 Anleihe f. 2 Leihgabe f. **on loan** leihweise.

loathe (louð) vt sich ekeln vor, verabscheuen. **loathsome** adj ekelhaft, widerlich.

lob (lɔb) n sport Hochschlag m. vt hochschlagen.

lobby ('lɔbi) n 1 Vorhalle f. 2 Interessengruppe f. 3 Lobby neu. vt beeinflussen.

lobe (loub) n 1 Lappen m. 2 (of the ear) (Ohr)Läppchen neu.

lobster ('lɔbstə) n Hummer m.

local ('loukəl) adj örtlich, Orts—. Lokal—. n Ortsbewohner m. **local authority** n Ortsbehörden f pl. **locality** n 1 Örtlichkeit f. Ort m. 2 Lage f. **localize** vt lokalisieren. **locate** vt 1 ausfindig machen. 2 unterbringen, errichten. **location** n 1 Standort m. 2 Lage f.

loch (lɔx) n See m. Bucht f.

lock[1] (lɔk) n 1 Schloß neu. 2 (on a canal, etc.) Schleuse f. vt (ver)schließen. vi sich schließen. **locksmith** n Schlosser m.

lock[2] (lɔk) n (of hair, etc.) Locke f.

locker ('lɔkə) n Kasten m.

locket ('lɔkit) n Medaillon neu.

locomotive (loukə'moutiv) n Lokomotive f.

locust ('loukəst) n Heuschrecke f.

lodge (lɔdʒ) n 1 (Jagd)Hütte f. 2 Forsthaus, Parkhaus neu. vt 1 aufnehmen. 2 unterbringen. 3 hinterlegen. 4 (a complaint) einreichen. vi 1 wohnen, logieren. 2 steckenbleiben. **lodger** n (Unter)Mieter m. **lodgings** n pl (Miets)Wohnung f.

loft (lɔft) n Dachboden m. **lofty** adj 1 (sehr) hoch. 2 hochmütig. 3 erhaben.

log (lɔg) n (Holz)Klotz m. **log-book** n 1 Logbuch neu. 2 mot Zulassungsbuch neu.

logarithm ('lɔgəriðəm) n Logarithmus m.

logic ('lɔdʒik) n Logik f. **logical** adj logisch.

loins (lɔinz) n pl Lenden f pl.

loiter ('lɔitə) vi bummeln, herumlungern.

lollipop ('lɔlipɔp) n Lutscher m.

London ('lʌndən) n London neu.

lonely ('lounli) adj einsam. **loneliness** n Einsamkeit f.

long[1] (lɔg) vi sich sehnen.

long[2] (lɔg) adj lang. **in the long run** auf die Dauer. **long-distance** adj Fern—, Weit—. **long jump** n Weitsprung m. **long-playing record** n Langspielplatte f. **long-range** adj weittragend, auf weite Sicht. **long-sighted** adj weitsichtig. **longstanding** adj seit langer

Zeit bestehend, alt. **long-term** adj langfristig.

long wave n Langwelle f. **longwinded** adj langatmig.

longevity (lɔn'dʒeviti) n Langlebigkeit f.

longitude ('lɔndʒitju:d) n Länge f.

loo (lu:) n inf Klo neu.

look (luk) n 1 Blick m. 2 Aussehen neu. vi 1 (an)blicken, sehen, schauen 2 zusehen. 3 nachsehen. 4 aussehen. **look for** suchen. **look up** (for reference) nachschlagen.

loom[1] (lu:m) n Webstuhl m.

loom[2] (lu:m) vi (drohend) aufragen.

loop (lu:p) n Schleife f. vt in Schleifen legen. vi eine Schleife machen.

loophole ('lu:phoul) n Schlupfloch neu.

loose (lu:s) adj 1 locker. 2 schlaff. 3 (of clothes) weit. 4 frei. 5 lose, nicht verpackt. **at a loose end** beschäftigungslos. **loosen** (vi),vt (sich) lösen, (sich) lockern.

loot (lu:t) n Beute f. vi,vt plündern.

lop (lɔp) vt beschneiden, stutzen.

lopsided (lɔp'saidid) adj 1 schief. 2 einseitig.

lord (lɔ:d) n 1 Herr m. 2 Edelmann m. 3 Lord m. **lordly** adj 1 edel. 2 herrisch. **lordship** n Herrlichkeit f.

lorry ('lɔri) n Lastkraftwagen, Lastwagen m.

lose* (lu:z) vt verlieren. vi 1 sich verlieren. 2 (of a clock) nachgehen. **lose weight** abnehmen.

loss (lɔs) n 1 Verlust m. 2 Schaden m. **at a loss** in Verlegenheit.

lost (lɔst) adj verloren.

lot (lɔt) n 1 Los neu. 2 Schicksal neu. 3 Menge f. **draw lots** losen.

lotion ('louʃən) n Schönheitswasser neu.

lottery ('lɔtəri) n Lotterie f.

lotus ('loutəs) n Lotos m.

loud (laud) adj 1 laut. 2 grell. **loud-mouth** n inf Maulheld m. **loudness** n Lautheit, Lautstärke f. **loudspeaker** n Lautsprecher m.

lounge (laundʒ) n 1 Wohnzimmer neu. 2 Salon m. vi faulenzen, herumlungern. **lounge suit** n Straßenanzug m.

louse (laus) n Laus f. **lousy** adj lausig.

love (lʌv) n 1 Liebe f. 2 Liebling m. 3 liebe Grüße m pl. 4 sport Null f. **be in love with** verliebt sein in. **fall in love with** sich verlieben in. ~adj Liebes—. vt 1 lieben. 2 gern haben. **love affair** n Liebschaft f. **lovesick** adj liebeskrank. **lovely** adj 1 lieblich, reizend. 2 inf wunderschön. **lover** n Liebhaber, Geliebte(r) m. **loving** adj liebevoll, liebend.

low[1] (lou) adj 1 niedrig. 2 tief. 3 niedergeschlagen. 4 gemein. **lowbrow** adj nicht intellektuel, geistig anspruchslos. **low frequency** n Niederfrequenz f. **low-grade** n Unterstufe f. **lowland** n Tiefland neu. **low-necked** adj tief ausgeschnitten. **low-pitched** adj tief.

low² (lou) vi muhen. n Muhen neu.

lower ('louə) adj 1 niedriger. 2 niedere, untere, Unter—. **lower class** n untere Klassen f pl. ~vt 1 niederlassen, herunterlassen. 2 senken. 3 (one's eyes) niederschlagen.

Lower Saxony ('sæksəni) n Niedersachsen neu.

loyal ('lɔiəl) adj treu. **loyalty** n Treue f.

lozenge ('lɔzindʒ) n Pastille f.

lubricate ('lu:brikeit) vt schmieren. **lubricant** n Schmiermittel neu. **lubrication** n Schmierung f. Ölen neu.

Lucerne (lu:'sə:n) n Luzerne f.

lucid ('lu:sid) adj 1 hell. 2 klar, deutlich.

luck (lʌk) n 1 Glück neu. 2 Geschick neu. **bad luck** n Unglück, Pech neu. **lucky** adj glücklich. **be lucky** Glück haben. **luckily** adv glücklicherweise.

lucrative ('lu:krətiv) adj lukrativ.

ludicrous ('lu:dikrəs) adj lächerlich.

lug (lʌg) vt schleppen, zerren.

luggage ('lʌgidʒ) n Gepäck neu.

lukewarm (lu:k'wɔ:m) adj lauwarm.

lull (lʌl) vt 1 einlullen. 2 beruhigen. vi sich legen. n Stille f. **lullaby** n Wiegenlied neu.

lumbago (lʌm'beigou) n Hexenschuß m.

lumber¹ ('lʌmbə) n 1 Gerümpel neu. 2 Bauholz neu. **lumberjack** n Holzfäller m. ~vt mit Gerümpel vollpacken.

lumber² ('lʌmbə) vi sich schwerfällig schleppen.

luminous ('lu:minəs) adj 1 leuchtend, Leuchter—. 2 hellerleuchtet. 3 klar, einleuchtend.

lump (lʌmp) n 1 Klumpen m. 2 Beule f. **lump sum** Pauschalsumme f. ~vt zusammenwerfen.

lunacy ('lu:nəsi) n Irrsinn, Wahnsinn m.

lunar ('lu:nə) adj Mond—.

lunatic ('lu:nətik) adj wahnsinnig. n Irre(r) m.

lunch (lʌntʃ) n Mittagessen neu. **lunch-hour** n Mittagspause f. ~vi zu Mittag essen.

lung (lʌŋ) n Lunge f.

lunge (lʌndʒ) n Ausfall, Stoß m. vi 1 ausfallen. 2 (dahin)stürmen.

lurch¹ (lə:tʃ) vi taumeln. n Taumeln neu.

lurch² (lə:tʃ) n **leave someone in the lurch** jemanden im Stich lassen.

lure (luə) n 1 Köder m. 2 Lockung f. vt 1 ködern. 2 (an)locken.

lurid ('luərid) adj unheimlich, düster.

lurk (lə:k) vi lauern.

luscious ('lʌʃəs) adj köstlich.

lush (lʌʃ) adj saftig, üppig.

lust (lʌst) n 1 (Wol)Lust f. 2 Sucht, Gier f. v **lust for** begehren, gelüsten (nach).

lustre ('lʌstə) n 1 Glanz m. 2 Lüster m.

Luxembourg ('lʌksəmbə:g) n Luxemburg neu.

luxury ('lʌkʃəri) n 1 Luxus m. 2 Luxusartikel m. **luxurious** adj luxuriös.

lynx (liŋks) n Luchs m.

lyre (laiə) n Leier, Lyra f.

lyrical ('lirikəl) adj lyrisch.

lyrics ('liriks) n pl Lyrik f.

M

mac (mæk) n inf Regenmantel m.

macabre (mə'ka:b) adj grausig, makaber.

mace¹ (meis) n 1 Keule f. 2 Amtsstab m.

mace² (meis) n bot Muskatblüte f.

machine (mə'ʃi:n) n 1 Maschine f. vt maschinell bearbeiten, herstellen. **machine-gun** n Maschinengewehr neu. **machinery** n 1 Mechanismus m. 2 Maschinerie f. 3 Maschinerie f.

mackerel ('mækrəl) n Makrele f.

mackintosh ('mækintɔʃ) n Regenmantel m.

mad (mæd) adj 1 wahnsinnig, verrückt. 2 toll, wild. 3 inf wütend. **madness** n Wahnsinn m.

madam ('mædəm) n gnädige Frau f.

made (meid) v see **make**.

Madonna (mə'dɔnə) n Madonna f.

magazine (mægə'zi:n) n 1 Magazin neu. 2 Illustrierte f.

maggot ('mægət) n Made f.

magic ('mædʒik) n 1 Magie f. 2 Zauber m. Zauberei f. adj 1 magisch. 2 zauberhaft. Zauber—. **magician** n Zauberer, Magier m.

magistrate ('mædʒistreit) n Friedensrichter m.

magnanimous (mæg'næniməs) adj großmütig.

magnate ('mægneit) n Magnat m.

magnet ('mægnit) n Magnet m. **magnetic** adj 1 magnetisch. 2 anziehend. **magnetic tape** n (Ton)Band neu. **magnetism** n 1 Magnetismus m. 2 Anziehungskraft f. **magnetize** vt 1 magnetisieren. 2 anziehen, fesseln.

magnificent (mæg'nifisənt) adj herrlich, prächtig, großartig. **magnificence** n Herrlichkeit, Pracht f.

magnify ('mægnifai) vt vergrößern. **magnifying glass** n Vergrößerungsglas neu. Lupe f.

magnitude ('mægnitjuːd) n 1 Größe f. 2 Bedeutung f.

magnolia (mæg'noulia) n Magnolie f.

magpie ('mægpai) n Elster f.

mahogany (ma'hogani) n Mahagoni(holz) neu.

maid (meid) n 1 Mädchen neu. 2 Dienstmädchen neu. **old maid** n alte Jungfer f. **maiden** n Jungfrau f. **maiden name** n Mädchenname m.

mail (meil) n Post f. vt (mit der Post) schicken. **mailbag** n Postsack m. **mail order firm** n Postversandhaus neu.

maim (meim) vt verstümmeln, zum Krüppel machen.

main (mein) adj Haupt—, hauptsächlich. n 1 Hauptleitung f. 2 pl Stromnetz neu. **mainland** n Festland neu. **mainsail** n Großsegel neu. **mainspring** n 1 Hauptfeder f. 2 treibende Kraft f. **mainstream** n Hauptstrom m.

maintain (mein'tein) vt 1 erhalten. 2 unterhalten. 3 behaupten. **maintenance** n 1 Erhaltung f. 2 Unterhalt m.

maize (meiz) n Mais m.

majesty ('mædʒisti) n Majestät f. **majestic** adj majestätisch.

major ('meidʒə) adj 1 größer. 2 bedeutend, wichtig. 3 law volljährig, mündig. n 1 law Volljährige(r). 2 mil Major m. 3 mus Dur neu. **major general** n Generalmajor m. **majority** n 1 Mehrheit f. größter Teil m. 2 law Volljährigkeit f.

make* (meik) vt 1 machen. 2 bauen. 3 herstellen. 4 zwingen. 5 sich belaufen auf. 6 inf erreichen. 7 inf schaffen. **make for** sich ergeben nach. **make good** wiedergutmachen. **make off** sich davonmachen. **make out** 1 ausmachen. 2 ausstellen. 3 vorgeben. **make up** 1 erdichten. 2 sich schminken. 3 sich versöhnen. 4 wiedergutmachen. 5 bilden. **makebelieve** n Verstellung f. Vorwand m. **makeshift** adj Behelfs—. n Notbehelf m. **make-up** n 1 Schminke f. Make-up neu. 2 Veranlagung, Natur f.

maladjusted (mælə'dʒʌstid) adj 1 schlecht angepaßt. 2 milieu gestört.

malaria (mə'lɛəriə) n Malaria f. Sumpffieber m.

male (meil) adj männlich, Männer—. n 1 Mann. 2 zool Männchen.

malfunction (mæl'fʌŋkʃən) vi schlecht funktionieren. n Funktionsstörung f.

malice ('malis) n 1 Böswilligkeit f. 2 law böse Absicht f. **malicious** adj 1 böswillig. 2 boshaft.

malignant (mə'lignənt) adj 1 med bösartig. 2 boshaft.

malinger (mə'liŋgə) vi simulieren, sich krank stellen. **malingerer** n Simulant m.

mallet ('mælət) n 1 Holzhammer m. 2 sport Schlagholz neu.

malnutrition (mælnjuː'triʃən) n Unterernährung f.

malt (mɔːlt) n Malz neu. vt mälzen.

Malta ('mɔːltə) n Malta neu. **Maltese** adj maltesisch. n Malteser m.

maltreat (mæl'triːt) vt mißhandeln, schlecht behandeln. **maltreatment** n Mißhandlung, schlechte Behandlung f.

mammal ('mæməl) n Säugetier neu.

mammoth ('mæməθ) n Mammut neu. adj riesig.

man (mæn) n 1 Mann m. 2 Mensch m. 3 Menschheit f. vt bemannen. **manhandle** vt 1 durch Menschenkraft bewegen. 2 rauh behandeln, mißhandeln. **manhole** n Einsteigeöffnung, Luke f. **manly** adj männlich. **manmade** adj künstlich, Kunst—. **manpower** n 1 Arbeitskräfte f pl. 2 Menschenkraft f. **manslaughter** n Totschlag m.

Man, Isle of (mæn) n (Insel) Man neu.

manage ('mænidʒ) vt 1 handhaben. 2 leiten, führen. 3 beaufsichtigen. vi 1 es schaffen. 2 auskommen. **management** n 1 Handhabung f. 2 (Geschäfts)Leitung f. Management neu. **manager** n (Betriebs)Leiter, Manager m.

mandarin ('mændərin) n 1 Mandarin m. 2 bot Mandarine f.

mandate ('mændeit) n 1 Mandat neu. Auftrag m. 2 Befehl m. **mandatory** adj 1 verbindlich, obligatorisch. 2 Mandats—.

mane (mein) n Mähne f.

mange (meindʒ) n Räude f.

mangle[1] ('mæŋgəl) vt zerstückeln, zerfleischen.

mangle[2] ('mæŋgəl) n Wäscherolle, Wringmaschine f. vt mangeln, rollen, wringen.

mango ('mæŋgou) n Mangopflaume f.

mania ('meinia) n 1 Manie f. 2 Wahnsinn m. 3 inf Fimmel m. **maniac** n Wahnsinnige(r), Verrückte(r) m. **manic** adj manisch.

manicure ('mænikjuə) n Maniküre, Nagelpflege f. vt maniküren. **manicurist** n Maniküre f.

manifest ('mænifest) adj offenbar, manifest, klar. vt 1 offenbaren. 2 zeigen. **manifestation** n 1 Offenbarung, Kundgebung f. 2 Erscheinung f.

manifesto (mæni'festou) n Manifest neu.

manifold ('mænifould) adj mannigfaltig.

manipulate (mə'nipjuleit) vt 1 (geschickt) handhaben. 2 manipulieren. **manipulation** n 1 Handhabung f. 2 Manipulation f.

mankind ('mænkaind) n Menschheit f.

manner ('mænə) n 1 Art, Weise f. 2 Manier f. 3 Benehmen neu. 4 pl Manieren pl. Betragen neu. **mannerism** n 1 Manieriertheit f. 2 (of style) Manierismus m.

manoeuvre (mə'nu:və) n Manöver neu. vi,(vt) manövrieren (lassen).

manor ('mænə) n Gut neu. **lord of the manor** n Gutsherr m. **manor house** n Herrensitz m.

mansion ('mænʃən) n 1 herrschaftliches Wohnhaus neu. 2 pl Mietshaus neu.

mantle ('mæntl) n 1 (Deck)Mantel m. 2 Hülle f. vt verhüllen. **mantlepiece** n Kaminsims m.

manual ('mænjuəl) adj 1 Hand—. 2 handgefertigt. 3 manuell. n 1 Handbuch neu. 2 mus Manual m.

manufacture (mænju'fæktʃə) n 1 Herstellung, Fabrikation, Erzeugung f. 2 Fabrikat neu. vt 1 herstellen, erzeugen, anfertigen. 2 erfinden, erdichten. **manufactured** adj Fabrik—, Fertig—.

manure (mə'njuə) n Dünger m. vt düngen.

manuscript ('mænjuskript) n 1 Manuskript neu. Handschrift f. 2 Druckvorlage f.

many ('meni) adj viele. **how many** wieviele. **many a** manche (ein). **many times** oft, häufig. **the many** die Masse f. die Vielen pl.

map (mæp) n 1 Landkarte, Seekarte f. 2 Stadtplan m. vt aufzeichnen, eintragen.

maple ('meipəl) n bot Ahorn m.

mar (ma:) vt 1 verderben. 2 verunstalten.

marathon ('mærəθən) adj Dauer—. **marathon race** n Langstreckenlauf, Marathonlauf m.

marble (ma:bəl) n 1 Marmor m. 2 Marmorkunstwerk n. 3 Murmel f. adj marmorn.

march (ma:tʃ) n Marsch m. **march past** n Vorbeimarsch m. ~vi,(vt) marschieren (lassen). **marching** adj Marsch—.

March (ma:tʃ) n März m.

marchioness ('ma:ʃənis) n Marquise f.

mare (mɛə) n Stute f.

margarine (ma:dʒə'ri:n) n Margarine f.

margin ('ma:dʒin) n 1 Rand m. 2 Grenze f.

marguerite (ma:gə'ri:t) n Gänseblümchen neu.

marigold ('mærigould) n Dotterblume f.

marijuana (mæri'wa:nə) n Marihuana neu.

marinade (n mæri'neid; v 'mærineid) n cul Marinade f. vt marinieren.

marine (mə'ri:n) adj 1 See—, Marine—. 2 Schiffs—. n 1 Marine f. 2 Marineinfantrist

m. **maritime** adj 1 See—. 2 Küsten—. 3 Schiffahrts—.

marital ('mæritl) adj ehelich.

marjoram ('ma:dʒərəm) n Marjoran m.

mark[1] (ma:k) n 1 Marke f. 2 Fleck m. 3 Kennzeichen neu. 4 educ Note f. 5 Ziel neu. vt 1 (aus)zeichnen. 2 educ zensieren, korrigieren. 3 beachten. 4 markieren. vi beflecken. **marked** adj auffällig, deutlich, gezeichnet. **marksman** n (guter) Schütze m.

mark[2] (ma:k) n Mark f.

market ('ma:kit) n Markt m. vt auf den Markt bringen. **market garden** n Handelsgärtnerei f. **market place** n Marktplatz m. **market research** n Marktforschung f.

marmalade ('ma:məleid) n Orangenmarmelade f.

maroon[1] (mə'ru:n) adj dunkelrot.

maroon[2] (mə'ru:n) vt 1 (auf einer öden Insel) aussetzen. 2 verlassen, im Stich lassen.

marquee (ma:'ki:) n großes Zelt neu.

marquess ('ma:kwis) n Marquis m.

marriage ('mæridʒ) n 1 Ehe f. 2 Ehestand m. 3 Hochzeit, Heirat f. **civil marriage** n standesamtliche Trauung f. **marriage certificate** n Trauschein m.

marrow ('mærou) n 1 (Knochen)Mark neu. 2 Kern m. 3 bot Kürbis m. **marrowbone** n Markknochen m.

marry ('mæri) vt 1 (ver)heiraten, trauen. 2 sich verheiraten mit. vi sich verheiraten, heiraten.

Mars (ma:z) n Mars m.

marsh (ma:ʃ) n Sumpfland neu.

marshal ('ma:ʃəl) n 1 (Feld)Marschall m. 2 Zeremonienmeister, Festordner m. vt 1 ordnen. 2 (feierlich) führen.

martial ('ma:ʃəl) adj 1 kriegerisch. 2 Kriegs—.

martin ('ma:tin) n zool Mauerschwalbe f.

martyr ('ma:tə) n Märtyrer m. vt zum Märtyrer machen. **martyrdom** n 1 Märtyrertum neu. 2 Martyrium neu.

marvel ('ma:vəl) n Wunder m. vi sich wundern.

marvellous ('ma:vələs) adj wunderbar, erstaunlich.

Marxism ('ma:ksizəm) n Marxismus m. **Marxist** adj marxistisch. n Marxist m.

marzipan ('ma:zipæn) n Marzipan neu.

mascara (mæ'ska:rə) n Wimperntusche f.

mascot ('mæskɔt) n Maskottchen neu.

masculine ('mæskjulin) adj männlich. n gram Maskulinum neu.

mash (mæʃ) n 1 Gemisch neu. 2 Brei m. 3 Mengfutter neu. vt 1 mischen. 2 zerquetschen, zerstampfen. **mashed potatoes** n pl Kartoffelpüree m.

mask (ma:sk) n Maske f. vt verbergen.

mason ('meisən) n Maurer m. **masonry** n Mauerwerk neu.

masquerade (mæskə'reid) 1 Maskenball m. 2 Maskerade f. vi sich maskieren.

mass[1] (mæs) n 1 Masse f. 2 Menge f. (vi),vt (sich) anhäufen, (sich) ansammeln. **mass media** n pl Massenmedien neu pl. **mass-produce** vt serienmäßig herstellen. **mass production** n Serienbau m. Serienproduktion f.

mass[2] (mæs) n rel Messe f.

massacre ('mæsəkə) n Gemetzel, Massaker neu. vt niedermetzeln.

massage ('mæsa:ʒ) n Massage f. vt massieren.

massive ('mæsiv) adj 1 massiv. 2 schwer. 3 massig. 4 fest.

mast (ma:st) n Mast m. **masthead** n Mastkorb m.

mastectomy (mæs'tektəmi) n med Brustamputation f.

master ('ma:stə) n 1 Meister m. 2 Herr m. 3 Lehrer m. vt beherrschen. **masterpiece** n Meisterstück neu. **masterful** adj 1 herrisch. 2 meisterhaft. **mastery** n 1 Herrschaft f. 2 Beherrschung f.

masturbate ('mæstəbeit) vi masturbieren.

mat (mæt) n Matte f.

match[1] (mætʃ) n Streichholz, Zündholz neu. **matchbox** n Streichholzschachtel f.

match[2] (mætʃ) n 1 Passende(r), Gleiche(r) m. 2 Wettspiel neu. (Wett)Kampf m. 3 Partie f. 4 Match neu. vt 1 anpassen. 2 passen zu. vi zusammenpassen, dazupassen.

mate (meit) n 1 Gefährte m. Gefährtin f. 2 Gatte m. Gattin f. 3 zool Männchen, Weibchen neu. 4 naut Maat m. (vi),vt (sich) paaren.

material (mə'tiəriəl) n Material neu. Stoff m. adj materiell, stofflich. **materialism** n Materialismus m. **materialist** n Materialist m. **materialize** vi sich verwirklichen.

maternal (mə'tə:nl) adj 1 mütterlich. 2 mütterlicherseits. **maternity** n Mutterschaft f. adj Schwangerschafts—, Umstands—.

mathematics (mæθə'mætiks) n Mathematik f.

matins ('mætinz) n pl Frühmesse f.

matinee ('mætinei) n Nachmittagsvorstellung f.

matriarchal ('meitria:kəl) adj matriarchalisch.

matrimony ('mætriməni) n Ehe f. Ehestand m.

matrix ('meitriks) n, pl -ices 1 Matrix f. 2 tech Matrize f. 3 Nährboden m.

matron ('meitrən) n 1 Matrone f. 2 Vorsteherin f.

matter ('mætə) n 1 Materie f. Stoff m. Substanz f. 2 Sache, Angelegenheit f. vi etwas bedeuten, etwas ausmachen. **it doesn't matter** es macht nichts. **what's the matter?** was ist los?

mattress ('mætrəs) n Matratze f.

mature (mə'tjuə) adj reif, entwickelt. vi reifen. **maturity** n Reife f.

maudlin ('mɔ:dlin) adj sentimental.

maul (mɔ:l) vt verprügeln, zerreißen.

mausoleum (mɔ:sə'liəm) n Mausoleum neu.

mauve (mouv) adj malvenfarbig. n Malvenfarbe f.

maxim ('mæksim) n Grundsatz m. Maxime f.

maximum ('mæksiməm) n Maximum, Höchstmaß neu. **maximize** vt vergrößern, verstärken.

may[*] (mei) v mod aux 1 mögen, können. 2 dürfen. **maybe** adv vielleicht.

May (mei) n Mai m. **May Day** n erster Mai m. **maypole** n Maibaum m.

mayonnaise (meiə'neiz) n Mayonnaise f.

mayor ('mɛə) n Bürgermeister m.

maze (meiz) n Irrgarten m.

me (mi:) pron 1st pers s 1 mich. 2 mir.

meadow ('medou) n Wiese f.

meagre ('mi:gə) adj mager, ärmlich.

meal[1] (mi:l) n Mahlzeit f. Mahl, Essen neu.

meal[2] (mi:l) n (grobes) Mehl neu.

mean[*][1] (mi:n) vt bedeuten, heißen, meinen. vi,vt beabsichtigen.

mean[2] (mi:n) adj 1 gering, niedrig. 2 geizig.

meander (mi'ændə) vi sich winden. n Windung f. Krümmung f.

meaning ('mi:niŋ) n Bedeutung f. Sinn m.

means (mi:nz) n pl Mittel neu pl. **by means of** mittels, durch.

meanwhile ('mi:nwail) adv inzwischen.

measles ('mi:zəlz) n Masern f pl.

measure ('meʒə) vt (ab-, aus-)messen. n 1 Maß neu. 2 Maßnahme f. **measurement** n 1 Messung f. 2 Maß neu.

meat (mi:t) n 1 Fleisch neu. 2 Kern m.

mechanic (mi'kænik) n Mechaniker, Autoschlosser m. **mechanical** adj mechanisch. **mechanical engineering** n Maschinenbau m. **mechanics** n pl 1 Mechanik f. Konstruktion f. **mechanism** n Mechanismus m. Arbeitsweise f. **mechanize** vt mechanisieren.

medal ('medl) n Orden m. Medaille f. **medallion** n Medaille f.

meddle ('medl) vi sich einmischen.

media ('mi:diə) n Nachrichtenmittel, Medien neu pl.

medial ('mi:diəl) adj durchschnittlich, Mittel—.

median ('mi:diən) adj in der Mitte liegend, mittler. n Mittelwert m.

mediate ('mi:dieit) vi vermitteln.

medical ('medikəl) adj medizinisch, ärztlich. **medication** n medizinische Behandlung, Verordnung f. **medicine** n 1 Medizin f. 2 Arzneimittel neu.

medieval (medi'i:vəl) adj mittelalterlich.

mediocre (mi:di'oukə) adj mittelmäßig. **mediocrity** n Mittelmäßigkeit f.

meditate ('mediteit) vi 1 meditieren. 2 überlegen. 3 nachdenken.

Mediterranean (meditə'reiniən) adj Mittelmeer—. **Mediterranean (Sea)** n Mittelmeer neu.

medium ('mi:diəm) n, pl **media** 1 Mitte f. 2 Mittel neu. 3 Medium neu. adj mittler.

meek (mi:k) adj sanft, demütig, mild.

meet (mi:t) vt 1 begegnen. 2 treffen. 3 erfüllen. **meeting** n 1 Begegnung f. 2 Zusammenkunft f. 3 Versammlung, Sitzung f.

megaphone ('megəfoun) n Megaphon neu.

melancholy ('melənkəli) n Schwermut, Melancholie f. adj schwermütig, melancholisch.

mellow ('melou) adj 1 ausgereift. 2 mild.

melodrama ('melədra:mə) n Melodrama neu.

melody ('melədi) n Melodie f. **melodic** adj melodisch.

melon ('melən) n Melone f.

melt (melt) vt,vi schmelzen. **melting point** n Schmelzpunkt m.

member ('membə) n 1 Mitglied neu. 2 anat Glied neu. **membership** n Mitgliedschaft f.

membrane ('membrein) n Membrane f.

memento (mə'mentou) n Memento neu.

memo ('memou) n inf Notiz, Mitteilung f.

memoirs ('memwa:z) n pl Memoiren, Lebenserinnerungen f pl.

memorandum (memə'rændəm) n, pl **-da** Notiz, Mitteilung f.

memory ('meməri) n 1 Gedächtnis neu. 2 Erinnerung f. **memorable** adj denkwürdig. **memorial** n Denkmal neu. adj Gedächtnis—. **memorize** vt auswendig lernen, im Gedächtnis behalten.

menace ('menəs) vt (be)drohen. n 1 Drohung f. 2 inf lästiger Mensch m. lästiges Kind neu.

menagerie (mə'nædʒəri) n Menagerie f.

mend (mend) vt reparieren, ausbessern.

menial ('mi:niəl) adj niedrig, gemein.

menopause ('menəpɔ:z) n Menopause f. Wechseljahre neu pl.

menstrual ('menstruəl) adj 1 monatlich, Monats—. 2 Menstruations—. **menstruate** vi menstruieren, die Regel haben. **menstruation** n Monatsblutung, Menstruation, Regel f.

mental ('mentl) adj 1 geistig. intellektuell, Geistes—. 2 sl verrückt. **mental hospital** n Nervenklinik f. **mental illness** n Geisteskrankheit f. **mentality** n Mentalität, Denkweise f.

menthol ('menθol) n Menthol neu.

mention ('menʃən) vt erwähnen. n Erwähnung f. **don't mention it!** bitte! gern geschehen! **not to mention** ganz zu schweigen von.

menu ('menju:) n Speisekarte f.

mercantile ('mə:kəntail) adj kaufmännisch.

mercenary ('mə:sənəri) adj 1 käuflich. 2 Gewinn—, Geld—. n Söldner m.

merchant ('mə:tʃənt) n 1 (Groß)Händler m. 2 (Groß)Kaufmann m. **merchant bank** n Handelsbank f. **merchant navy** n Handelsflotte f. **merchandise** n Güter neu pl. Waren f pl.

mercury ('mə:kjuri) n 1 sci Quecksilber neu. 2 cap Merkur m.

mercy ('mə:si) n Gnade, Barmherzigkeit f.

mere (miə) adj bloß.

merge (mə:dʒ) vi aufgehen, sich verschmelzen. vt verschmelzen, aufgehen lassen. vt,vi comm fusionieren. **merger** n comm Fusionierung f.

meridian (mə'ridiən) n Meridian m.

meringue (mə'ræŋ) n Meringe f. Baiser neu.

merit ('merit) n 1 Verdienst neu. 2 Wert m. vt verdienen.

mermaid ('mə:meid) n Meerjungfer, Seenixe f.

merry ('meri) adj 1 lustig, fröhlich. 2 inf beschwipst, leicht betrunken. **merry-go-round** n Karussell neu.

mesh (meʃ) n Masche f. Netz neu. vt verfangen. vi tech ineinandergreifen.

mesmerize ('mezməraiz) vt mesmerisieren.

mess (mes) n 1 Unordnung f. 2 Verwirrung f. Durcheinander neu. 3 Schmutz m. 4 mil Messe f.

message ('mesidʒ) n 1 Botschaft f. 2 Mitteilung f. **messenger** n Bote m.

met (met) v see **meet**.

metabolism (mi'tæbəlizəm) n Stoffwechsel m.

metal ('metl) n Metall neu. **metallurgy** n Metallurgie, Hüttenkunde f.

metamorphosis (metə'mɔ:fəsis) n Metamorphose, Verwandlung f.

metaphor ('metəfə) n Metapher f.
metaphysics (metə'fiziks) n Metaphysik f.
meteor ('mi:tiə) n Meteor neu. **meteorology** n Meteorologie, Wetterkunde f.
meter ('mi:tə) n Messer, Zähler m.
methane ('mi:θein) n Methan, Sumpfgas neu.
method ('meθəd) n 1 Methode f. 2 Weise f. 3 tech Verfahren neu. **methodical** adj methodisch. **methodology** n Methodologie f.
Methodist ('meθədist) n Methodist m.
meticulous (mi'tikjuləs) adj peinlich genau, penibel, übergenau.
metre ('mi:tə) n 1 Meter m,neu. 2 lit Versmaß neu. **metric** adj metrisch.
metropolis (mə'trɔpəlis) n Hauptstadt, Metropole f. **metropolitan** adj großstädtisch.
Mexico ('meksikou) n Mexiko neu. **Mexican** adj mexikanisch. n Mexikaner m.
miaow (mi'au) n Miauen neu. vi miauen.
microbe ('maikroub) n Mikrobe f.
microphone ('maikrəfoun) n Mikrophon neu.
microscope ('maikrəskoup) n Mikroskop neu.
mid (mid) adj in der Mitte, mittler. **midday** n Mittag m. **midland** n Mittelland neu. **midnight** n Mitternacht f. **midstream** n Strommitte f. **midsummer** n Hochsommer m. **midway** adj,adv auf halbem Wege. **midweek** n Mitte der Woche f.
middle ('midl) n Mitte f. Zentrum neu. **middle-aged** adj im mittleren Alter. **middle class** n Mittelstand m. Burgertum neu. **middle-class** adj Mittelstands—.
Middle Ages n Mittelalter neu.
Middle East n Nahe(r) Osten m.
midget ('midʒit) n Zwerg m.
midst (midst) n Mitte f. **in the midst of** mitten unter, inmitten.
midwife ('midwaif) n Hebamme f.
might[1] (mait) v see **may.**
might[2] (mait) n 1 Macht f. 2 Gewalt f. **mighty** adj mächtig.
migraine ('mi:grein) n Migräne f.
migrate (mai'greit) vi (aus)wandern.
mike (maik) n sl Mikrophon neu.
Milan (mi'læn) n Mailand neu.
mild (maild) adj 1 mild. 2 sanft.
mildew ('mildju:) n 1 Meltau m. 2 Moder m.
mile (mail) n Meile f. **mileage** n Meilenzahl f. **mileometer** n Meilenzähler, Kilometerzähler m. **milestone** n 1 Meilenstein m. 2 Markstein m.
militant ('militənt) adj militant, kämpferisch. n

Kämpfer m. **military** adj militärisch. n Militär neu.
milk (milk) n Milch f. **milkman** n Milchmann m. **Milky Way** n Milchstraße f.
mill (mil) n 1 Mühle f. 2 Fabrik f. vt mahlen. vi herumirren. **millstone** n Mühlstein m.
millennium (mi'leniəm) n Jahrtausend neu.
milligram ('miligræm) n Milligramm neu.
millilitre ('mililli:tə) n Milliliter m.
millimetre ('milimi:tə) n Millimeter m,neu.
million ('miliən) n Million f. **millionth** adj millionste. **millionaire** n Millionär m.
mime (maim) n Mime m. vt,vi mimen. **mimic** vt nachahmen. n Mimiker, Nachahmer m.
minaret (minə'ret) n Minarett neu.
mince (mins) vt zerhacken, zerstückeln. n Hackfleisch neu.
mind (maind) n 1 Geist, Verstand m. 2 Sinn m. 3 Meinung f. 4 Gedächtnis neu. vt 1 achten or aufpassen auf. 2 sorgen für. sehen nach. 3 sich kümmern um. 4 sich hüten vor. vt,vi etwas dagegen haben. **never mind!** macht nichts!
mine[1] (main) poss pron 1st pers s meiner, der meine or meinige.
mine[2] (main) n 1 min Mine f. Bergwerk neu. 2 mil Mine f. vi graben. vt 1 mil verminen. 2 abbauen.
mineral ('minərəl) n Mineral neu. Bodenschatz m. adj mineralisch. **mineral water** n Mineralwasser neu.
mingle ('mingl) (vi),vt (sich) vermischen.
miniature ('miniətʃə) n Miniatur f. adj Klein—. Miniatur—.
minim ('minim) n Halbnote f.
minimum ('miniməm) n, pl **-ma** Minimum neu. **minimal** adj Mindest—, minimal.
mining ('mainiŋ) n Bergbau m.
minister ('ministə) n Minister m. **ministry** n Ministerium neu.
mink (miŋk) n Nerz m.
minor ('mainə) adj 1 kleiner, geringer. 2 geringfügig. n 1 Minderjährige(r). 2 Moll neu. **minority** n Minderheit, Minorität f.
minstrel ('minstrəl) n 1 Minnesänger m. 2 Sänger m.
mint[1] (mint) n bot Minze f.
mint[2] (mint) n Münzanstalt f.
minuet (minju'et) n Menuett neu.
minus ('mainəs) prep weniger, minus.
minute[1] ('minit) n Minute f.
minute[2] (mai'nju:t) adj winzig.

miracle ('mirəkəl) n 1 Wunder neu. 2 Wundertat f. **miraculous** adj wunderbar.

mirage ('mira:ʒ) n Täuschung f.

mirror ('mirə) n Spiegel m. vt widerspiegeln.

mirth (mə:θ) n 1 Fröhlichkeit f. 2 Heiterkeit f.

misbehave (misbi'heiv) vi sich schlecht benehmen.

miscarriage (mis'kæridʒ) n Fehlgeburt f. **miscarriage of justice** n Rechtsbeugung f.

miscellaneous (misə'leiniəs) adj (newspaper column) Verschiedenes neu. **miscellany** n Gemisch neu. Sammlung f.

mischance (mis'tʃɑ:ns) n Mißgeschick neu.

mischief ('mistʃif) n 1 Unheil neu. Schaden m. 2 Unfug m. **mischievous** adj 1 schelmisch. 2 verderblich.

misconceive (miskən'si:v) vt mißverstehen, falsch begreifen. **misconception** n Mißverständnis neu.

misconduct (mis'kəndʌkt) n schlechtes or unangemessenes Verhalten neu.

misdeed (mis'di:d) n Missetat f.

miser ('maizə) n Geizhals m.

miserable ('mizərəbəl) adj 1 elend, erbärmlich. 2 unglücklich.

misery ('mizəri) n Elend neu.

misfire ('maizə) vi 1 mot fehlzünden. 2 mil versagen. 3 scheitern.

misfit ('misfit) n 1 schlechtpassendes Stück neu. 2 Mensch, der sich seiner Umwelt nicht anpassen kann m.

misfortune (mis'fɔ:tʃən) n Unglück, Mißgeschick neu.

misgiving (mis'giviŋ) n Befürchtung f. Zweifel m.

misguided (mis'gaidid) adj irregeführt.

mishap ('mishæp) n Unfall m. Unglück neu.

mislay* (mis'lei) vt verlegen.

mislead* (mis'li:d) vt irreführen.

misprint ('misprint) n Druckfehler m.

miss[1] (mis) vt 1 verfehlen. 2 vermissen. 3 versäumen, verpassen. n Fehlschuß m. **missing** adj fehlend, abwesend.

miss[2] (mis) n 1 Fräulein neu. 2 cap (title of address) Fräulein, Frl.

missile ('misail) n Geschoß neu.

mission (miʃən) n 1 Mission f. 2 Auftrag m. **missionary** n Missionar m.

mist (mist) n Nebel, Dunst m.

mistake* (mis'teik) n Fehler, Irrtum m. vt verwechseln, falsch verstehen.

mister ('mistə) n Herr m.

mistletoe ('misəltou) n Mistel f.

mistress ('mistrəs) n 1 Lehrerin f. 2 Geliebte f. 3 Herrin f. 4 Frau des Hauses f.

mistrust (mis'trʌst) vt mißtrauen. n Mißtrauen neu.

misunderstand* (misʌndə'stænd) vt mißverstehen. **misunderstanding** n Mißverständnis neu.

misuse (v mis'ju:z; n mis'ju:s) vt mißbrauchen. n Mißbrauch m.

mitre ('maitə) n Bischofsmütze f.

mitten ('mitn) n Fausthandschuh m.

mix (miks) vt (ver)mischen. **mix up** 1 verwechseln. 2 vermischen. ~n Mischung f. **mixture** n Mischung f.

moan (moun) vi 1 stöhnen. 2 jammern, meckern.

moat (mout) n Burggraben m.

mob (mɔb) n 1 Pöbel m. Gesindel neu. 2 Bande f.

mobile ('moubail) adj mobil, beweglich. **mobility** n Beweglichkeit f. **mobilize** vt mobilisieren.

mock (mɔk) vt verspotten, verhöhnen. adj nachgemacht, unecht, Pseudo—.

mode (moud) n 1 Weise, Methode f. 2 Form, Art f.

model ('mɔdl) n 1 Modell neu. 2 Vorbild neu. adj 1 Modell—. 2 vorbildlich.

moderate ('mɔdərət) adj mäßig. **moderation** n Maß neu. Mäßigung f.

modern ('mɔdən) adj modern. **modernize** vt modernisieren.

modest ('mɔdist) adj bescheiden. **modesty** n Bescheidenheit f.

modify ('mɔdifai) vt abändern, modifizieren. **modification** n Abänderung, Modifikation f.

modulate ('mɔdjuleit) vt 1 abstimmen, anpassen. 2 abstufen. 4 dämpfen. 4 modulieren.

module ('mɔdju:l) n Modul, Model m.

mohair ('mouhɛə) n Mohär m.

moist (mɔist) adj feucht. **moisten** vt (be-, an-)feuchten, nässen. **moisture** n Feuchtigkeit f. **moisturizing cream** n Feuchtigkeitscreme f.

mole[1] (moul) n Muttermal neu. Leberfleck m.

mole[2] (moul) n Maulwurf m.

molecule ('mɔlikju:l) n Molekül neu.

molest (mə'lest) vt belästigen.

mollusc ('mɔləsk) n Weichtier neu. Molluske f.

molten ('moultən) adj 1 geschmolzen. 2 (of metal) flüssig.

moment ('moumənt) n Moment, Augenblick m. **momentary** adj momentan, augenblicklich. **momentous** adj bedeutend, gewichtig.

momentum n Triebkraft, Schwungkraft f. Impuls m.

monarch ('mɔnək) n Monarch m.

monastery ('mɔnəstri) n (Mönchs)Kloster neu.

Monday ('mʌndi) n Montag m.

money ('mʌni) n Geld neu. **get one's money's worth** etwas für sein Geld bekommen. **moneybox** n Sparbüchse f. **money order** n Postanweisung f. **monetary** adj 1 Geld—. 2 finanziell.

mongrel ('mʌŋgrəl) n Mischling m. Kreuzung f. ⏸

monitor ('mɔnitə) n Monitor m. vt 1 abhören. 2 kontrollieren, überwachen.

monk (mʌŋk) n Mönch m.

monkey ('mʌŋki) n Affe m.

monogamy (mə'nɔgəmi) n Monogamie, Einehe f.

monologue ('mɔnəlɔg) n Monolog m.

monopolize (mə'nɔpəlaiz) vt monopolisieren. **monopoly** n Monopol neu.

monosyllable ('mɔnəsiləbəl) n einsilbiges Wort neu. **speak in monosyllables** einsilbige Antworten geben.

monotone ('mɔnətoun) n Eintönigkeit, Monotonie f. **monotonous** adj eintönig, monoton.

monsoon (mɔn'suːn) n Monsun m.

monster ('mɔnstə) n 1 Ungeheuer neu. 2 Scheusal neu. **monstrous** adj 1 ungeheuer, riesig. 2 ungeheuerlich. 3 scheußlich.

month (mʌnθ) n Monat m.

monument ('mɔnjumənt) n Denkmal, Monument neu.

moo (muː) vi muhen.

mood[1] (muːd) n Laune, Stimmung f. **be in a good/bad mood** guter/schlechter Laune sein. **moody** adj launisch.

mood[2] (muːd) n Modus m.

moon (muːn) n Mond m. **moonlight** n Mondlicht neu. Mondschein m.

moor[1] (muə) n Moor neu. **moorhen** n Teichhuhn neu. **moorland** n Moor(land) neu.

moor[2] (muə) vt festmachen, verankern.

Moor (muə) n Maure m. **Moorish** adj maurisch.

mop (mɔp) n Mop, Staubbesen m. vt (auf)wischen.

mope (moup) vi traurig sein.

moped ('moupd) n Moped neu.

moral ('mɔrəl) n 1 Moral, Lehre f. 2 pl Moral f. Sitten f pl. adj moralisch. **morale** n Moral f. **morality** n 1 Moral(ität) f. 2 Sittlichkeit f. **moralize** vi moralisieren.

morbid ('mɔːbid) adj krankhaft, morbid.

more (mɔː) adj 1 mehr. 2 mehr, noch (etwas). weiter. adv 1 mehr. 2 noch. **more and more** immer mehr. **more or less** mehr oder weniger. **moreover** adv außerdem, weiter, ferner.

morgue (mɔːg) n Leichenschauhaus neu.

morning ('mɔːniŋ) n 1 Morgen m. 2 Vormittag m. **in the mornings** morgens. **this morning** heute früh, heute morgen..

Morocco (mə'rɔkou) n Marokko neu. **Moroccan** adj marokkanisch. n Marokkaner m.

moron ('mɔːrɔn) n Schwachsinnige(r) m.

morose (mə'rous) adj mürrisch, verdrießlich.

morphine ('mɔːfiːn) n Morphium neu.

morse code (mɔːs) n Morsealphabet neu.

mortal ('mɔːtl) adj sterblich. **mortality** n Sterblichkeit f.

mortar[1] ('mɔːtə) n Mörser m.

mortar[2] ('mɔːtə) n (for building) Mörtel m.

mortgage ('mɔːgidʒ) n Hypothek f. vt 1 eine Hypothek nehmen auf. 2 verpfänden.

mortify ('mɔːtifai) vt 1 demütigen. 2 abtöten.

mortuary ('mɔːtjuəri) n Leichenhalle f.

mosaic (mou'zeiik) n Mosaik neu.

Moselle (mou'zel) n 1 Mosel f. 2 Moselwein m.

mosque (mɔsk) n Moschee f.

mosquito (mə'skiːtou) n pl **-oes** or **-os** Mücke f. Moskito m.

moss (mɔs) n Moos neu.

most (moust) adj 1 die meisten. 2 meist, höchst. adv am meisten, Meist—. n 1 das meiste, das Höchste neu. 2 der größte Teil m. **mostly** adv 1 hauptsächlich. 2 größtenteils.

motel (mou'tel) n Motel neu.

moth (mɔθ) n Motte f.

mother ('mʌðə) n Mutter f. vt bemuttern. **motherhood** n Mutterschaft f. **mother-in-law** n Schwiegermutter f. **mother superior** n Äbtissin f.

motion ('moufən) n 1 Bewegung f. Gang m. 3 Antrieb m. vt zuwinken.

motive ('moutiv) n Bewegrund m.

motor ('moutə) n Motor m. **motor car** n Auto(mobil) neu. Personenkraftwagen m. **motorcycle** n Motorrad neu. **motorcyclist** n Motorradfahrer m. **motorist** n Autofahrer m. **motorway** n Autobahn f.

mottled ('mɔtld) adj gefleckt.

motto ('mɔtou) n Motto m. Sinnspruch m.

mould[1] (mould) n 1 tech (Guß)Form f. 2 Art f. vt 1 tech gießen. 2 formen, bilden.

mould[2] (mould) n Schimmel m. **mouldy** adj schimm(e)lig.

moult

moult (moult) *vi* 1 (of birds) sich mausern. 2 (of animals) sich häuten.

mound (maund) *n* Hügel, Erdwall *m*.

mount[1] (maunt) *vt* 1 besteigen. 2 hinaufgehen. 3 einbauen. 4 aufkleben. 5 montieren.

mount[2] (maunt) *n* Berg *m*.

mountain ('mauntin) *n* Berg *m*. **mountaineer** *n* Alpinist, Bergsteiger *m*.

mourn (mɔ:n) *vt* betrauern. *vi* trauern. **mourning** *n* Trauer *f*. **go into mourning** Trauer anlegen.

mouse (maus) *n, pl* **mice** Maus *f*. **mousetrap** *n* Mausefalle *f*. **mousy** *adj* 1 mauseartig. 2 grau.

mousse (mu:s) *n* Kremeis *neu*.

moustache (mə'sta:ʃ) *n* Schnurrbart *m*.

mouth (mauθ) *n* 1 Mund *m*. 2 Öffnung *f*. 3 *geog* Mündung *f*. **mouthpiece** *n* Mundstück *neu*. **mouth-watering** *adj* schmackhaft.

move (mu:v) *(vi),vt* 1 (sich) bewegen. 2 (sich) rühren. 3 umziehen. 1 Bewegung *f*. 2 Umzug *m*. 3 Schritt *m*. 4 (taktischer) Zug *m*. **movable** *adj* beweglich. **movement** *n* 1 Bewegung *f*. 2 *mus* Satz *m*. 3 Lauf *m*. **moving** *adj* 1 (sich) bewegend. 2 rührend, packend.

mow* (mou) *vt* mähen.

Mr ('mistə) (title of address) Herr.

Mrs ('misiz) (title of address) Frau.

much (mʌtʃ) *adj* viel. *adv* 1 sehr. 2 viel. 3 bei weitem. **how much** wieviel.

muck (mʌk) *n* 1 Mist *m*. 2 Dreck, Schmutz *m*. **mucky** *adj* dreckig.

mud (mʌd) *n* Schlamm, Schmutz *m*. **muddy** *adj* schlammig. **mudguard** *n* Kotflügel *m*.

muddle ('mʌdl) *n* Durcheinander *neu*. Wirrwarr *m*. *vt* verwirren. **muddle up** durcheinanderbringen. **muddle through** sich durchwursteln.

muff (mʌf) *n* Muff *m*. *vt* *inf* verpfuschen.

muffle ('mʌfəl) *vt* dämpfen, unterdrücken.

mug (mʌg) *n* 1 Becher, Krug *m*. 2 *inf* Dumme(r) *m*.

mulberry ('mʌlbəri) *n* Maulbeere *f*.

mule[1] (mju:l) *n* Maultier *neu*.

mule[2] (mju:l) *n* Pantoffel *m*.

multiple ('mʌltipəl) *adj* mehrfach, vielfach.

multiply ('mʌltiplai) *vt* *math* multiplizieren. *(vi),vt* (sich) vermehren.

multitude ('mʌltitju:d) *n* Menge, große Zahl *f*.

mum (mʌm) *n* *inf* Mutti *f*.

mumble ('mʌmbəl) *vi,vt* murmeln.

mummy[1] ('mʌmi) *n* Mumie *f*.

mummy[2] ('mʌmi) *n* *inf* Mutti *f*.

mumps (mʌmps) *n* Mumps, Ziegenpeter *m*.

munch (mʌntʃ) *vt,vi* hörbar kauen, schmatzen.

mundane ('mʌndein) *adj* 1 alltäglich, banal. 2 weltlich, irdisch.

Munich ('mju:nik) *n* München *neu*.

municipal (mju'nisipəl) *adj* städtisch, Stadt—. **municipality** *n* Stadt *f*. Stadtbezirk *m*.

mural ('mjuərəl) *n* Wandgemälde *neu*.

murder ('mɜ:də) *n* Mord *m*. *vt* ermorden. **murderer** *n* Mörder *m*.

murmur ('mɜ:mə) *n* Murmeln *neu*. *vt* murmeln.

muscle ('mʌsəl) *n* Muskel *m*.

muse (mju:z) *n* Muse *f*. *vi* (nach)sinnen, (nach)denken.

museum (mju:'ziəm) *n* Museum *neu*.

mushroom ('mʌʃrum) *n* Pilz, Champignon *m*.

music ('mju:zik) *n* Musik *f*. **musical** *adj* musikalisch. **musician** *n* Musiker *m*.

musk (mʌsk) *n* 1 *zool* Moschus *m*. 2 *bot* Moschuspflanze *f*.

musket ('mʌskit) *n* Muskete, Flinte *f*.

Muslim ('muzlim) *n* Muselmann, Mohammedaner *m*. *adj* mohammedanisch.

muslin ('mʌzlin) *n* Musselin *m*.

mussel ('mʌsəl) *n* Muschel *f*.

must[1] (mʌst) *v mod aux* müssen.

must[2] (mʌst) *n* Most *m*.

mustard ('mʌstəd) *n* Senf *m*. *adj* senfgelb.

mute (mju:t) *adj* 1 stumm. 2 still, schweigend. *n* Stumme(r) *m*.

mutilate ('mju:tileit) *vt* verstümmeln, entstellen. **mutilation** *n* Verstümmelung *f*.

mutiny ('mju:tini) *n* Meuterei *f*.

mutter ('mʌtə) *vt,vi* murren, murmeln.

mutton ('mʌtn) *n* Hammelfleisch *neu*.

mutual ('mju:tjuəl) *adj* 1 gegenseitig. 2 gemeinsam.

muzzle ('mʌzəl) *n* 1 Maul *neu*. Schnauze *f*. 2 (of a gun) Mündung *f*. *vt* knebeln.

my (mai) *poss adj 1st pers s* mein. **myself** *pron 1st pers s* 1 mich. 2 mich selbst. 3 ich selbst. **by myself** allein.

myrrh (mɜ:) *n* Myrrhe *f*.

mystery ('mistəri) *n* 1 Geheimnis *neu*. 2 Rätsel *neu*. **mysterious** *adj* geheimnisvoll, mysteriös, rätselhaft.

mystic ('mistik) *n* Mystiker *m*. *adj* mystisch. **mysticism** *n* Mystizismus *m*.

mystify ('mistifai) *vt* 1 verwirren, irremachen. 2 täuschen. 3 in Dunkel hüllen.

mystique (mi'sti:k) *n* 1 Atmosphäre des Mysteriösen *f*. 2 Geheimnis *neu*.

myth (miθ) *n* Mythos *m*. **mythology** *n* Mythologie *f*.

N

nag[1] (næg) vt nörgeln.

nag[2] (næg) n Gaul m.

nail (neil) n Nagel m. **hit the nail on the head** den Nagel auf den Kopf treffen. **nailbrush** n Nagelbürste f. **nailfile** n Nagelfeile f. **nail varnish** n Nagellack m. ~vt nageln.

naive (nai'i:v) adj naiv.

naked ('neikid) adj 1 nackt. 2 bloß.

name (neim) n Name m. **namesake** n Namensvetter m. vt nennen. **nameless** adj 1 namenlos. 2 unbekannt. 3 unerwähnt. **namely** adv nämlich.

nanny ('næni) n Kinderpflegerin f.

nap (næp) n inf Schläfchen, Nickerchen neu.

napkin ('næpkin) n Serviette f.

Naples ('neipəlz) n Neapel neu.

nappy ('næpi) n Windel f.

narcotic (nɑː'kɔtik) n Betäubungsmittel, Narkotikum neu. adj betäubend, narkotisch.

narrate (nə'reit) vt erzählen. **narrative** n Erzählung f.

narrow ('nærou) adj eng, schmal. **narrow-minded** adj beschränkt, kleinlich, engstirnig.

nasal ('neizəl) adj nasal, Nasen—.

nasturtium (nə'stəːʃəm) n Kapuzinerkresse f.

nasty ('nɑːsti) adj 1 unangenehm, widerlich. 2 gemein. 3 schlimm, ernst.

nation ('neiʃən) n Nation f. Volk neu. **nationwide** adj allgemein, die Nation umfassend, weit verbreitet. **national** adj national. **national anthem** n Nationalhymne f. **national insurance** n Sozialversicherung f. **national service** n Militärdienst m. **nationalism** n Nationalismus m. **nationality** n Nationalität, Staatsangehörigkeit f. **nationalize** vt nationalisieren, verstaatlichen.

native ('neitiv) n 1 Eingeborene(r) m. 2 Einheimische(r) m. adj einheimisch.

nativity (nə'tiviti) n Geburt (Christi) f. **nativity play** Christfestspiel neu.

natural ('nætʃərəl) adj natürlich. **natural gas** n Erdgas neu. **natural history** n Naturgeschichte f. **natural science** n Naturwissenschaft f. **naturalize** vt naturalisieren, einbürgern.

nature ('neitʃə) n 1 Natur f. 2 Wesen neu. Art f. 3 Charakter m.

naughty ('nɔːti) adj unartig, schlimm.

nausea ('nɔːsiə, -ziə) n 1 Übelkeit f. 2 Ekel m. **nauseate** vt anekeln.

nautical ('nɔːtikəl) adj nautisch, See—.

naval ('neivəl) adj Marine—, See—, Flotten—.

nave (neiv) n Kirchenschiff neu.

navel ('neivəl) n Nabel m.

navigate ('nævigeit) vt steuern, befahren. vi navigieren. **navigation** n Nautik, Navigation f.

navy ('neivi) n Kriegsmarine, (Kriegs)Flotte f. **navy blue** adj marineblau. n Marineblau neu.

near (niə) prep nahe, in der Nähe von. adj,adv nahe. **nearby** adj nahe(gelegen). adv in der Nähe. **nearly** adv nahe, fast, beinahe. **nearside** n Fahrerseite f.

neat (niːt) adj sauber, nett, ordentlich.

nebulous ('nebjuləs) adj nebelhaft, unbestimmt, verschwommen.

necessary ('nesəsəri) adj notwendig, nötig, erforderlich. **necessarily** adv 1 notwendigerweise. 2 unbedingt. **necessity** n 1 Notwendigkeit f. 2 Bedürfnis neu.

neck (nek) n Hals, Nacken m. **neckband** n Halsband m. **necklace** n Halskette f.

nectar ('nektə) n Nektar m.

need (niːd) n 1 Notwendigkeit f. 2 Bedarf m. Bedürfnis neu. 3 Not, Armut f. vt 1 benötigen. 2 brauchen. **needless** adj unnötig. **needless to say** selbstverständlich.

needle ('niːdl) n Nadel f. **needlework** n Näherei f. ~vt sl stichen, reizen.

negate (ni'geit) vt verneinen, leugnen, negieren. **negation** n Verneinung, Negation f. **negative** adj negativ. n 1 (of a photograph) Negativ neu. 2 Negation f. **answer in the negative** mit Nein antworten, verneinen.

neglect (ni'glekt) n 1 Nachlässigkeit f. vt 1 vernachlässigen. 2 unterlassen. **negligent** adj nachlässig. **negligible** adj unbedeutend, geringfügig.

negotiate (ni'gouʃieit) vt 1 verhandeln. 2 überwinden. vi verhandeln. **negotiation** n 1 Verhandlung f. 2 Überwindung f.

Negro ('niːgrou) n, pl -oes Neger m. **Negress** n Negerin f.

neigh (nei) vi wiehern. n Wiehern neu.

neighbour ('neibə) n Nachbar m. **neighbourhood** n Nachbarschaft f. **neighbouring** adj angrenzend, benachbart.

neither ('naiðə) conj auch nicht. **neither...nor** weder...noch. adj,pron keiner (von beiden).

neon ('niːən) n Neon neu.

nephew ('nevju:) n Neffe m.

nepotism ('nepətizəm) n Nepotismus m.

Neptune ('neptju:n) n Neptun m.

233

nerve (nɜːv) n 1 Nerv m. 2 inf Frechheit f. Mut m. 3 pl Nervosität f. **nerve-racking** adj nervenaufreibend. **nervous** adj 1 nervös. 2 Nerven—. **nervous breakdown** n Nervenzusammenbruch m. **nervous system** n Nervensystem neu.

nest (nest) n Nest neu. vi nisten.

nestle ('nesəl) vi sich schmiegen an.

net[1] (net) n Netz neu. vt fangen. **netball** n Korbballspiel neu. **network** n Netz neu.

net[2] (net) adj netto.

Netherlands ('neðələndz) n pl Niederlande f pl. **Netherlander** n Niederländer m.

nettle ('netl) n Nessel f.

neurosis (njuə'rousis) n Neurose f. **neurotic** adj neurotisch.

neuter ('njuːtə) n Neutrum neu. adj 1 sächlich. 2 geschlechtslos. vt kastrieren.

neutral ('njuːtrəl) adj 1 neutral. 2 unparteiisch. **neutrality** n Neutralität f. **neutralize** vt neutralisieren.

never ('nevə) adv nie, niemals. **on the never-never** inf auf Abzahlung. **nevertheless** adv dennoch, nichtsdestoweniger.

new (njuː) adj neu. **newcomer** n Neuankömmling m. **newly** adv neulich, kürzlich. **news** n Nachrichten f pl. **a piece of news** Neuigkeit, Nachricht f. **newsagent** n Zeitungshändler m. **newspaper** n Zeitung f. **newsreel** n Wochenschau f.

newt (njuːt) n Wassermolch m.

New Testament n Neues Testament neu.

New Year n Neujahr neu. **New Year's Day** n Neujahrstag m. **New Year's Eve** n Silvester m.

New Zealand ('ziːlənd) n Neuseeland neu. adj neuseeländisch. **New Zealander** n Neuseeländer m.

next (nekst) adj 1 nächst. 2 folgend. **next door** nebenan. ~adv 1 nächstens. 2 das nächste Mal. n Nächste(r) m.

nib (nib) n (of a pen) Spitze f.

nibble ('nibəl) vi,(vt) knabbern or nagen (an).

nice (nais) adj 1 nett. 2 schön. 3 lieb, freundlich.

niche (nitʃ) n 1 Nische f. 2 passende Stelle f.

nick (nik) vt einkerben. n Kerbe f. **in the nick of time** gerade rechtzeitig.

nickel ('nikəl) n Nickel neu.

nickname ('nikneim) n Spitzname m.

nicotine ('nikətiːn) n Nikotin neu.

niece (niːs) n Nichte f.

Nigeria (nai'dʒiəriə) n Nigeria neu. **Nigerian** adj nigerianisch. n Nigerianer m.

nigger ('nigə) n derog Neger, Schwarze(r) m.

niggle ('nigəl) vi nörgeln, herumtüfteln.

night (nait) n 1 Nacht f. 2 Abend m. **last night** gestern Abend. **spend the night** übernachten. **nightclub** n Nachtklub m. **nightdress** n also **nightgown** Nachthemd neu. **nightmare** n Alptraum m.

nightingale ('naitiŋgeil) n Nachtigall f.

nil (nil) n Null f.

Nile (nail) n Nil m.

nimble ('nimbəl) adj flink, behend.

nine (nain) adj neun. n Neun f. **ninth** adj neunte.

nineteen (nain'tiːn) adj neunzehn. n Neunzehn f. **nineteenth** adj neunzehnte.

ninety ('nainti) adj neunzig. n Neunzig f. **ninetieth** adj neunzigste.

nip[1] (nip) n leichter Biß, Kniff m. vt beißen, kneifen. vi flitzen. **nippy** adj inf spritzig.

nip[2] (nip) n Schlückchen neu.

nipple ('nipəl) n Brustwarze f.

nitrogen ('naitrədʒən) n Stickstoff m. Nitrogen neu.

no[1] (nou) adv nein.

no[2] (nou) adj kein. **in no way** keineswegs.

noble ('noubəl) adj 1 vornehm, edel. 2 adlig. n Edelmann m. **nobleman** n Edelmann, Adlige(r) m. **nobility** n 1 Adel m. 2 Vornehmheit f.

nobody ('noubədi) pron also **no-one** niemand, keiner. n inf Null f. Niemand m.

nocturnal (nɔk'təːnl) adj nächtlich.

nod (nɔd) vt,vi (mit dem Kopf) nicken. n Kopfnicken neu.

node (noud) n Knoten m.

noise (nɔiz) n 1 Geräusch neu. Lärm m. 2 Krach m. **noisy** adj lärmend.

nomad ('noumæd) n Nomade m. **nomadic** adj nomadisch.

nominal ('nɔminl) adj nominell.

nominate ('nɔmineit) vt (er)nennen, nominieren.

nominative ('nɔminətiv) n Nominativ m.

non- pref nicht—.

nonchalant ('nɔnʃələnt) adj 1 gleichgültig. 2 unbekümmert. 3 nonchalant.

nondescript ('nɔndiskript) adj schwer zu beschreiben.

none (nʌn) pron 1 kein. 2 niemand. adv keineswegs.

nonentity (nɔn'entiti) n 1 inf unbedeutender Mensch, Null f. 2 Nichts neu.

nonsense ('nɔnsəns) n Unsinn m.

noodles ('nu:dlz) n pl Nudeln f pl.

noon (nu:n) n Mittag m.

noose (nu:s) n Schlinge f.

nor (nɔ:) conj noch, auch nicht. **neither...nor** weder...noch.

norm (nɔ:m) n Norm, Regel, Richtschnur f. **normal** adj normal.

Norman ('nɔ:mən) adj normannisch. n Normanne m.

Normandy ('nɔ:məndi) n Normandie f.

Norse (nɔ:s) adj altnorwegisch. n (language) Altnorwegisch neu.

north (nɔ:θ) n Nord(en) m. adj nördlich, Nord—. adv nördlich. **northeast** n Nordost(en) m. adj,adv nordöstlich. **northeasterly** adj,adv nordöstlich. **northeastern** adj nordöstlich. **northerly** adj nördlich. **northern** adj nördlich. **northwards** adv nordwärts. **northwest** n Nordwest(en) m. adj,adv nordwestlich. **northwesterly** adj,adv nordwestlich. **northwestern** adj nordwestlich.

North America n Nordamerika neu.

Northern Ireland n Nordirland neu.

North Pole n Nordpol m.

North Rhine-Westphalia (west'feiliə) n Nordrhein-Westfalen neu.

Norway ('nɔ:wei) n Norwegen neu. **Norwegian** adj norwegisch. n 1 Norweger m. 2 (language) Norwegisch neu.

nose (nouz) n Nase f. **nosy** adj inf neugierig.

nostalgia (nɔ'stældʒiə) n 1 Nostalgie, Sehnsucht f. 2 Heimweh neu. **nostalgic** adj wehmütig, voll Heimweh.

nostril ('nɔstril) n Nasenloch neu.

not (nɔt) adv nicht. **not a** kein.

notch (nɔtʃ) n Kerbe f. vt einkerben.

note (nout) n 1 Zettel m. 2 Notiz f. 3 Vermerk m. 4 Ton m. 5 Bedeutung f. **notebook** n Notizbuch neu. **notepaper** n Briefpapier neu. **noteworthy** adj bemerkenswert. ~vt 1 merken. 2 vermerken, aufschreiben. **notable** adj bemerkenswert, beträchtlich, hervorragend. **notation** n 1 Aufzeichnung f. 2 Schreibweise f.

nothing ('nʌθiŋ) pron nichts. n Nichts neu. **nothing of the kind** nichts dergleichen.

notice ('noutis) n 1 Notiz f. 2 Meldung f. Hinweis m. 3 Kündigung(sfrist) f. 4 Anschlag m. Plakat neu. **notice board** n Anschlagtafel

f. vt bemerken. **noticeable** adj 1 bemerkenswert. 2 merklich.

notify ('noutifai) vt benachrichtigen, bekanntgeben. **notification** n Benachrichtigung f.

notion ('nouʃən) n 1 Begriff, Gedanke m. 2 Idee f. 3 Vorstellung f.

notorious (nou'tɔ:riəs) adj berüchtigt, notorisch, allbekannt.

notwithstanding (nɔtwiθ'stændiŋ) prep ungeachtet, trotz.

nought (nɔ:t) n Null f. pron nichts.

noun (naun) n Hauptwort neu. Substantiv m.

nourish ('nʌriʃ) vt (er)nähren. **nourishing** adj nahrhaft.

novel[1] ('nɔvəl) n Roman m. **novelist** n Romanschriftsteller m.

novel[2] ('nɔvəl) adj neuartig. **novelty** n 1 Neuheit f. 2 Ungewöhnlichkeit f.

November (nou'vembə) n November m.

novice ('nɔvis) n 1 Anfänger m. 2 rel Novize m.

now (nau) adv 1 nun, jetzt. 2 sofort. 3 eben. conj nun. **nowadays** adv heutzutage.

nowhere ('nouwɛə) adv nirgends, nirgendwo.

noxious ('nɔkʃəs) adj schädlich.

nozzle ('nɔzəl) n 1 Schnauze. 2 Ausgußröhre f. 3 Düse f.

nuance ('nju:əns) n 1 Nuance f. 2 Abtönung f. 3 Schattierung f.

nucleus ('nju:kliəs) n 1 sci Kern m. 2 Mittelpunkt m. **nuclear** adj Kern—, Atom—, nuklear.

nude (nju:d) adj nackt. n 1 Nackte(r) m. 2 Art Akt m.

nudge (nʌdʒ) vt leicht anstoßen.

nugget ('nʌgit) n Goldklumpen, Nugget m.

nuisance ('nju:səns) n 1 Ärgernis neu. Belästigung f. 2 lästiger Mensch m.

null (nʌl) adj nichtig, ungültig, null.

numb (nʌm) adj starr, empfindungslos. vt starr machen, betäuben.

number ('nʌmbə) n 1 Nummer f. 2 Zahl, Ziffer f. 3 (An)Zahl f. **numberplate** n mot Nummernschild neu. **numeral** n 1 Zahlzeichen neu. 2 Zahlwort neu. **numerate** adj rechenkundig. **numerical** adj zahlenmäßig, numerisch. **numerous** adj zahlreich.

nun (nʌn) n Nonne f.

Nuremberg ('njuərəmbə:g) n Nürnberg neu.

nurse (nə:s) n 1 Krankenschwester f. vt 1 pflegen. 2 aufziehen. **nursing home** n (Privat)Klinik f. Sanatorium neu. **nursery** n 1 Kinderzimmer neu. 2 bot Pflanzschule f. **nursery rhyme** n

Kinderreim m. Kinderlied neu. **nursery school** n Kindergarten m.

nurture ('nɜ:tʃə) vt 1 ernähren. 2 hegen.

nut (nʌt) n 1 Nuß f. 2 tech (Schrauben)Mutter f. 3 inf Kopf m. **in a nutshell** kurz gefaßt. **nutcrackers** n Nußknacker m. **nutmeg** n Muskatnuß f. **nutshell** n Nußschale f.

nutrition (nju:'trɪʃən) n Nahrung, Ernährung f.

nuzzle ('nʌzəl) vi 1 schnüffeln. 2 sich anschmiegen.

nylon ('nailən) n Nylon neu. **nylon stockings** n pl also **nylons** Nylonstrümpfe m pl.

nymph (nimf) n Nymphe f.

O

oak (ouk) n Eiche f.

oar (ɔ:) n Ruder neu. **oarsman** n Ruderer m.

oasis (ou'eisis) n Oase f.

oath (ouθ) n Eid, Schwur m.

oats (outs) n pl 1 Hafer m pl. 2 Haferflocken f pl. **oatmeal** n Hafermehl m.

obedient (ə'bi:diənt) adj gehorsam. **obedience** n Gehorsam m.

obese (ou'bi:s) adj fettleibig.

obey (ə'bei) vt 1 gehorchen. 2 befolgen.

obituary (ə'bitjuəri) n Todesanzeige f.

object (n 'ɔbdʒikt; v əb'dʒekt) n 1 Gegenstand m. Objekt neu. 2 Ziel neu. Zweck m. vi 1 einwenden. 2 protestieren. **objection** n 1 Einwand m. 2 Abneigung f. **objective** n Ziel neu. Absicht f. adj sachlich, objektiv.

oblige (ə'blaidʒ) vt 1 binden, verpflichten. 2 nötigen. 3 gefällig sein. **be obliged to do something** etwas tun müssen. **be obliged to someone** jemandem dankbar sein. **obligation** n Verpflichtung f. **obligatory** adj verbindlich, verpflichtend.

oblique (ə'bli:k) adj schräg, schief.

obliterate (ə'blitəreit) vt 1 auslöschen, ausradieren. 2 unkenntlich machen.

oblivion (ə'bliviən) n Vergessenheit f. **oblivious** adj 1 vergeßlich. 2 nicht bewußt.

oblong ('ɔblɔŋ) n Rechteck neu. adj rechteckig, länglich.

obnoxious (əb'nɔkʃəs) adj anstößig, verhaßt.

oboe ('oubou) n Oboe f.

obscene (əb'si:n) adj obszön, unzüchtig.

obscure (əb'skjuə) adj 1 dunkel, finster. 2 unbekannt. vt verdecken, verdunkeln.

observe (əb'zə:v) vt 1 beobachten. 2 bemerken. **observance** n 1 Beobachtung f. 2 Befolgung

f. **observant** adj aufmerksam, wachsam. **observation** n 1 Beobachtung f. 2 Bemerkung f. **observatory** n Sternwarte f. Observatorium neu.

obsess (əb'ses) vt verfolgen, quälen. **obsession** n Besessenheit f.

obsolescent (ɔbsə'lesənt) adj veraltend.

obsolete ('ɔbsəli:t) adj veraltet, überholt.

obstacle ('ɔbstəkəl) n Hindernis neu.

obstinate ('ɔbstinət) adj hartnäckig, eigensinnig. **obstinacy** n Hartnäckigkeit f.

obstruct (əb'strʌkt) vt 1 verstopfen, blockieren. 2 (ver)hindern. **obstruction** n 1 Verstopfung f. 2 Hindernis neu.

obtain (əb'tein) vt erhalten, bekommen.

obtrusive (əb'tru:siv) adj aufdringlich.

obtuse (əb'tju:s) adj stumpf, stumpfwinkelig.

obverse ('ɔbvə:s) adj Vorder—. n Kehrseite f.

obvious ('ɔbviəs) adj offensichtlich, klar.

occasion (ə'keiʒən) n 1 Gelegenheit f. 2 Anlaß m. **on the occasion of** anläßlich.

Occident ('ɔksidənt) n Westen m. Abendland neu. **occidental** adj westlich, abendländisch.

occult (ɔ'kʌlt) adj okkult. **occultism** n Okkultismus m.

occupy ('ɔkjupai) vt 1 besetzen. 2 bewohnen. 3 beschäftigen. **occupy oneself** sich beschäftigen. **occupation** n 1 Beruf m. Beschäftigung f. 2 mil Besetzung, Besatzung f.

occur (ə'kə:) vi 1 vorkommen, sich ereignen. 2 einfallen. **occurrence** n 1 Ereignis neu. 2 Vorfall m.

ocean ('ouʃən) n Meer neu. Ozean m.

ochre ('oukə) n Ocker m. adj ockergelb.

octagon ('ɔktəgən) n Achteck neu. **octagonal** adj achteckig.

octane ('ɔktein) n Oktan neu.

octave ('ɔktiv) n Oktave f.

October (ɔk'toubə) n Oktober m.

octopus ('ɔktəpəs) n, pl **-puses** or **-pi** Krake m. Polyp m.

oculist ('ɔkjulist) n Augenarzt m.

odd (ɔd) adj 1 ungleich. 2 seltsam, sonderbar. 3 (of numbers) ungerade. **oddity** n Seltsamkeit, seltsame Sache f. **oddment** Überbleibsel neu. Rest m. **odds** n pl Gewinnchancen f pl.

ode (oud) n Ode f.

odious ('oudiəs) adj verhaßt.

odour ('oudə) n Geruch m.

oesophagus (i'sɔfəgəs) n, pl **-gi** Speiseröhre f.

of (əv; stressed ɔv) prep 1 von. 2 aus.

off (ɔf) adv 1 davon, fort, weg. 2 nicht frisch. **well/badly off** gut/schlecht daran.

236

offal ('ɔfəl) n Fleischabfall m.

offend (ə'fend) vt beleidigen. **offence** n 1 Beleidigung f. Anstoß m. 2 Vergehen neu. **take offence** Anstoß nehmen. **offensive** adj anstößig, beleidigend. n Offensive f. Angriff m.

offer ('ɔfə) vt anbieten. n Angebot neu.

offhand (ɔf'hænd) adj 1 kurz (angebunden). 2 improvisiert, spontan, aus dem Stegreif. adv spontan.

office ('ɔfis) n 1 Büro neu. 2 Dienst m. Amt neu. **officer** n 1 mil Offizier m. 2 Beamte(r) m. **official** adj offiziell. n Beamte(r) m.

officious (ə'fiʃəs) adj offiziös, aufdringlich.

offing ('ɔfiŋ) n offene See f. **in the offing** in (Aus)Sicht, im Werden.

off-licence n Ausschank über die Straße m.

off-peak adj außerhalb der Hauptverkehrszeit.

off-putting adj abstoßend.

off-season adj außer Saison.

offset ('ɔfset) vt ausgleichen.

offshore (ɔf'ʃɔ:) adj 1 von der Küste entfernt. 2 vom Land kommend, ablandig.

offside (ɔf'said) adj,adv sport abseits. n rechte Seite f.

offspring ('ɔfspriŋ) n 1 Nachkomme m. 2 Nachkommenschaft f.

offstage (ɔf'steidʒ) adj hinter der Bühne f.

often ('ɔfən) adv oft, häufig.

ogre ('ougə) n Unhold, Riese m.

oil (ɔil) n 1 Öl neu. 2 Erdöl neu. vt ölen, schmieren. **oilfield** n Ölfeld neu. **oil painting** n Ölgemälde neu. **oil rig** n 1 Ölplattform f. 2 Ölbohrturm m. **oilskin** n 1 Öltuch neu. 2 pl Ölkleidung f.

ointment ('ɔintmənt) n Salbe f.

old (ould) adj alt. **six years old** sechs Jahre alt. **old age** n Alter neu. **old-fashioned** adj altmodisch, veraltet.

Old Testament n Altes Testament neu.

olive ('ɔliv) n 1 Olive f. Ölbaum m. 2 Olive f. adj olivgrün. **olive oil** n Olivenöl neu.

omelette ('ɔmlət) n Omelett neu.

omen ('oumen) n Omen neu. Vorzeichen neu.

ominous ('ɔminəs) adj unheilvoll, drohend.

omit (ə'mit) vt auslassen, weglassen. **omission** n Auslassung f.

omnibus ('ɔmnibəs) n Omnibus, Bus m.

omnipotent (ɔm'nipətənt) adj allmächtig.

on (ɔn) prep 1 auf. 2 an. 3 über, zu. adv 1 auf. 2 an. 3 weiter. vorwärts. **be on** 1 an (geschaltet) sein. 2 los sein. **from...on** von...an.

once (wʌns) adv 1 einmal. 2 einst. **at once** 1

auf einmal. 2 sofort. **once and for all** ein für allemal.

one (wʌn) adj eins. n Eins f. pron 3rd pers s einer, man. **oneself** pron 3rd pers s sich (selbst). **by oneself** allein. **one-sided** adj einseitig. **one-way** adj Einweg—. **one-way street** Einbahnstraße f.

onion ('ʌniən) n Zwiebel f.

onlooker ('ɔnlukə) n Zuschauer m.

only ('ounli) adj einzig. adv 1 nur. 2 erst. **not only...but also** nicht nur...sondern auch. ~conj nur daß, jedoch.

onset ('ɔnset) n 1 Anfang m. 2 Angriff m.

onslaught ('ɔnslɔ:t) n (plötzlicher) Angriff m.

onus ('ounəs) n Last f.

onward ('ɔnwəd) adv vorwärts, weiter. adj weitergehend. **onwards** adv vorwärts, weiter.

ooze (u:z) vi (durch)sickern, triefen.

opal ('oupəl) n Opal m.

opaque (ou'peik) adj undurchsichtig.

open ('oupən) vt 1 (er)öffnen. 2 aufmachen. 3 anfangen. adj offen, offenstehend, auf. **open-air** adj Freiluft—. **in the open air** im Freien. **open-air swimming pool** Freibad neu. **open-ended** adj offenendig. **open-handed** adj großzügig, freigebig. **open-hearted** adj offenherzig. **open-minded** adj aufgeschlossen, unvoreingenommen. **open-mouthed** adj 1 mit offenem Mund. 2 verblüfft, erstaunt. **open-plan** adj Großraum—. **opening** 1 Öffnung, Lücke f. 2 Eröffnung f.

opera ('ɔprə) n Oper f. **opera house** n Opernhaus neu. **operetta** n Operette f.

operate ('ɔpəreit) vi 1 laufen, funktionieren. 2 handeln, Geschäft betreiben. 3 med operieren. vt betätigen. **operation** n 1 Arbeitslauf, Betrieb m. 2 Betätigung f. 3 med Operation. 4 mil Unternehmung, Operation f. **operative** adj tätig, wirksam. n Arbeiter, Handwerker m.

opinion (ə'piniən) n Meinung, Ansicht f. **opinion poll** n Meinungsumfrage f.

opium ('oupiəm) n Opium neu.

opponent (ə'pounənt) n Gegner m.

opportune (ɔpə'tju:n) adj 1 günstig. 2 rechtzeitig.

opportunity (ɔpə'tju:niti) n Gelegenheit, Möglichkeit f.

oppose (ə'pouz) vt 1 ablehnend gegenüberstehen, bekämpfen. 2 gegenüberstellen. vi Widerstand leisten, opponieren. **opposed** adj 1 entgegengesetzt. 2 feindlich. **as opposed to** im Vergleich zu.

opposite ('ɔpəzit) adj 1 gegenüberliegend. 2

237

gegensätzlich. *n* Gegensatz *m*. **opposition** *n* 1 Widerstand *m*. 2 *pol* Opposition *f*.

oppress (ə'pres) *vt* unterdrücken, tyrannisieren. **oppression** *n* Unterdrückung *f*.

opt (ɔpt) *vi* wählen. **opt for** sich entscheiden für.

optical ('ɔptikəl) *adj* optisch. **optician** *n* Optiker *m*.

optimism ('ɔptimizəm) *n* Optimismus *m*. **optimist** *n* Optimist *m*. **optimistic** *adj* optimistisch.

option ('ɔpʃən) *n* 1 Wahl, Alternative *f*. 2 Option *f*. Vorkaufsrecht *neu*.

opulent ('ɔpjulənt) *adj* reich, üppig.

or (ɔ:) *conj* oder.

oral ('ɔ:rəl) *adj* mündlich.

orange ('ɔrindʒ) *n* Apfelsine, Orange *f*. *adj* orangenfarbig.

orator ('ɔrətə) *n* Redner *m*.

orbit ('ɔ:bit) *n* Umlaufbahn *f*. *vt* umkreisen.

orchard ('ɔ:tʃəd) *n* Obstgarten *m*.

orchestra ('ɔ:kistrə) *n* Orchester *neu*. **orchestral** *adj* orchestral.

orchid ('ɔ:kid) *n* Orchidee *f*.

ordain (ɔ:'dein) *vt* 1 bestimmen. 2 *rel* weihen.

ordeal (ɔ:'di:l) *n* Qual, Plage, Nervenprobe *f*.

order ('ɔ:də) *n* 1 Befehl *m*. 2 Ordnung *f*. 3 *comm* Bestellung *f*. Auftrag *m*. 4 Stand *m*. **in order that** damit. **in order to** um...zu. *vt* 1 befehlen. 2 bestellen. 3 ordnen. **orderly** *n* Ordner *m*. *adj* ordentlich.

ordinal ('ɔ:dinl) *adj* Ordinal—. *n* Ordnungszahl *f*.

ordinary ('ɔ:dənri) *adj* 1 gewöhnlich, normal. 2 mittelmäßig, Durchschnitts—.

ore (ɔ:) *n* Erz *neu*.

oregano (ɔri'ga:nou) *n* Origanum *neu*.

organ ('ɔ:gən) *n* 1 Organ *neu*. 2 *mus* Orgel *f*.

organism ('ɔ:gənizəm) *n* Organismus *m*. **organic** *adj* 1 organisch. 2 geordnet.

organize ('ɔ:gənaiz) *vt* 1 organisieren. 2 einrichten. **organization** *n* 1 Organisation *f*. 2 systematischer Aufbau *m*. 3 Gesellschaft *f*.

orgasm ('ɔ:gæzəm) *n* Orgasmus *m*.

orgy ('ɔ:dʒi) *n* Orgie *f*.

Orient ('ɔ:riənt) *n* Orient, Osten *m*. Morgenland *neu*. **oriental** *adj* orientalisch, morgenländisch. *n* Orientale *m*.

orientate ('ɔ:rienteit) *vt* orientieren, richten. **orientation** *n* Orientierung *f*.

origin ('ɔridʒin) *n* 1 Ursprung *m*. 2 Herkunft *f*. **original** *adj* 1 original, ursprünglich. 2 originell, schöpferisch. **originate** *vi* entspringen, entstehen, ausgehen.

Orlon ('ɔ:lɔn) *n Tdmk* Orlon *neu*.

ornament ('ɔ:nəmənt) *n* Schmuck *m*. Ornament *neu*. **ornamental** *adj* ornamental. **ornamentation** *n* Verzierung *f*.

ornate (ɔ:'neit) *adj* geschmückt, verziert.

ornithology (ɔ:ni'θɔlədʒi) *n* Ornithologie, Vogelkunde *f*.

orphan ('ɔ:fən) *n* Waise *m*.

orthodox ('ɔ:θədɔks) *adj* 1 *rel* orthodox, rechtgläubig. 2 konventionell.

orthopaedic (ɔ:θə'pi:dik) *adj* orthopädisch.

oscillate ('ɔsəleit) *vi* 1 schwingen, oszillieren. 2 schwanken.

ostensible (ɔ'stensəbəl) *adj* 1 scheinbar. 2 angeblich.

ostentatious (ɔsten'teiʃəs) *adj* prahlerisch, prunkhaft.

osteopath ('ɔstiəpæθ) *n* Chiropraktiker *m*.

ostracize ('ɔstrəsaiz) *vt* verbannen, ausstoßen.

ostrich ('ɔstritʃ) *n* Strauß *m*.

other ('ʌðə) *adj* 1 ander. 2 weiter. 3 zweite. *adv* anders. *pron oder* **each other** einander. **otherwise** *adv* 1 sonst. 2 anders. 3 anderweitig.

otter ('ɔtə) *n* Otter *m*.

ought (ɔ:t) *v mod aux* sollen.

ounce (auns) *n* Unze *f*.

our (auə) *poss adj* 1st *pers pl* unser. **ours** *poss pron* 1st *pers pl* unser, der uns(e)re or uns(e)rige. **ourselves** *pron* 1st *pers pl* 1 uns. 2 uns selbst. 3 wir selbst.

oust (aust) *vt* vertreiben, verdrängen.

out (aut) *adv* 1 aus. 2 heraus, hinaus. 3 draußen. 4 fort. **out and out** durch und durch.

outboard ('autbɔ:d) *adj* Außenbord—.

outbreak ('autbreik) *n* Ausbruch *m*.

outburst ('autbə:st) *n* Ausbruch *m*.

outcast ('autka:st) *n* Ausgestoßene(r) *m*.

outcome ('autkʌm) *n* Resultat, Ergebnis *neu*.

outcry ('autkrai) *n* Aufschrei *m*.

outdo ('aut'du:) *vt* übertreffen.

outdoor ('autdɔ:) *adj* Außen—, im Freien. **outdoors** *adv* draußen, im Freien.

outer ('autə) *adj* äußere, Außen—.

outfit ('autfit) *n* 1 Ausstattung, Ausrüstung *f*. 2 Gruppe, Mannschaft *f*.

outgoing ('autgouin) *adj* 1 weggehend, abgehend. 2 gesellig. **outgoings** *n pl* Ausgaben *f pl*.

outgrow ('aut'grou) *vt* herauswachsen aus.

outhouse ('authaus) n Nebengebäude neu.

outing ('autiŋ) n Ausflug m.

outlandish (aut'lændiʃ) adj fremdartig.

outlaw ('autlɔ:) n 1 Geächtete(r) m. 2 Bandit m. vt ächten.

outlay ('autlei) n Auslage f.

outlet ('autlet) n 1 Abfluß, Auslauf m. 2 Absatzmarkt m.

outline ('autlain) n 1 Umriß m. 2 Überblick m. 3 Abriß m. vt umreißen.

outlive (aut'liv) vt überleben.

outlook ('autluk) n 1 Aussicht f. 2 Standpunkt m. Weltanschauung f.

outlying ('autlaiiŋ) adj abgelegen, abseits liegend.

outnumber (aut'nʌmbə) vt an Zahl übertreffen.

outpatient ('autpeiʃənt) n ambulanter Patient m.

outpost ('autpoust) n Vorposten m.

output ('autput) n Leistung, Produktion f.

outrage ('autreidʒ) n Gewalttat, Schandtat f. Exzeß m. vt schockieren, Gewalt antun.

outrageous (aut'reidʒəs) adj unerhört, empörend, schändlich.

outright ('autrait) adj,adv völlig, total.

outside (aut'said) n Außenseite f. adv 1 außen, draußen. 2 hinaus. **outsider** n Außenseiter m.

outsize ('autsaiz) adj übergroß.

outskirts ('autskə:ts) n pl Randgebiet neu. Vororte m pl.

outspoken (aut'spoukən) adj freimütig, offen.

outstanding (aut'stændiŋ) adj hervorragend.

outstrip (aut'strip) vt überholen, übertreffen.

outward ('autwəd) adj 1 äußere. 2 Auswärts—. adv auswärts, nach außen. **outwards** adv auswärts, nach außen.

outweigh (aut'wei) vt überwiegen.

outwit (aut'wit) vt überlisten.

oval ('ouvəl) adj oval. n Oval neu.

ovary ('ouvəri) n Eierstock m.

ovation (ou'veiʃən) n Huldigung, Ovation f.

oven ('ʌvən) n Ofen, Backofen m.

over ('ouvə) prep 1 über. 2 zu Ende, aus. 3 während. adv 1 (hin-, her-)über. 2 drüben. 3 übermäßig. **over again** nochmals.

overall ('ouvərɔ:l) adj gesamt, Gesamt—. n Arbeitsanzug, Schutzanzug m.

overbalance (ouvə'bæləns) vt,vi umkippen.

overboard ('ouvəbɔ:d) adv über Bord.

overcast ('ouvəkɑ:st) adj bewölkt.

overcharge (ouvə'tʃɑ:dʒ) vt 1 zu viel verlangen von. 2 überladen.

overcoat ('ouvəkout) n Mantel m.

overcome* (ouvə'kʌm) vt überwinden, überwältigen. adj überwältigt.

overdo* (ouvə'du:) vt übertreiben.

overdose ('ouvədous) n Überdosis f.

overdraft ('ouvədrɑ:ft) n Überziehung f.

overdraw* (ouvə'drɔ:) vt,vi überziehen.

overdue (ouvə'dju:) adj 1 überfällig. 2 verspätet.

overestimate (ouvər'estimeit) vt überschätzen.

overfill (ouvə'fil) vt überfüllen, überladen.

overflow (v ouvə'flou; n 'ouvəflou) vi überlaufen, überfließen. n Überlauf m. Überfließen neu.

overgrow* (ouvə'grou) vt überwachsen.

overhang (v ouvə'hæŋ; n 'ouvəhæŋ) vt überhängen über. n Überhang m.

overhaul (ouvə'hɔ:l) vt überholen. n Überholung f.

overhead (adv ouvə'hed; adj,n 'ouvəhed) adv oben, droben. adj oben liegend, Hoch—. **overheads** n pl (allgemeine) Unkosten f pl.

overhear* (ouvə'hiə) vt (zufällig) hören.

overheat (ouvə'hi:t) vi heißlaufen.

overjoyed (ouvə'dʒɔid) adj entzückt, überglücklich.

overland (adv ouvə'lænd; adj 'ouvəlænd) adv über Land. adj Überland—.

overlap (v ouvə'læp; n 'ouvəlæp) vi,(vt) sich überschneiden (mit). n Überschneidung f. Übergreifen neu.

overlay* (ouvə'lei) vt bedecken, überziehen.

overleaf (ouvə'li:f) adv umseitig.

overload (v ouvə'loud; n 'ouvəloud) vt überladen, überbelasten. n Überladung f.

overlook (ouvə'luk) vt übersehen.

overnight (adv ouvə'nait; adj 'ouvənait) adv über Nacht f. adj 1 Nacht—. 2 plötzlich.

overpower (ouvə'pauə) vt überwältigen.

overrate (ouvə'reit) vt überbewerten.

overreach (ouvə'ri:tʃ) vt (zu weit) hinausreichen über. **overreach oneself** sich übernehmen.

overrule (ouvə'ru:l) vt zurückweisen.

overrun* (ouvə'rʌn) vt,vi überrennen.

overseas (ouvə'si:z) adv in Übersee. adj Übersee—.

overshadow (ouvə'ʃædou) vt überschatten.

overshoot* (ouvə'ʃu:t) vt hinausschießen über, zu weit gehen.

oversight ('ouvəsait) n Versehen neu.

oversleep* (ouvə'sli:p) vi verschlafen.

overspill* ('ouvəspil) n Überschuß m.

239

overt ('ouvə:t) adj offen(bar), offensichtlich.

overtake* (ouvə'teik) vt überholen.

overthrow* (v ouvə'θrou; n 'ouvəθrou) vt umwerfen, umstürzen. n Umsturz m.

overtime ('ouvətaim) n 1 Überstunden f pl. **work overtime** Überstunden machen.

overtone ('ouvətoun) n 1 Unterton, Beiklang m. 2 pl Nebenbedeutungen, Assoziationen f pl.

overture ('ouvətʃə) n 1 Vorspiel neu. Einleitung f. 2 mus Ouvertüre f.

overturn (ouvə'tə:n) vt umstürzen, umstoßen, umkippen. vi umkippen, umschlagen, umfallen. n Umsturz m.

overweight (n 'ouvəweit; adj ouvə'weit) n Übergewicht neu. **be overweight** Übergewicht haben.

overwhelm (ouvə'welm) vt 1 überschütten, überhäufen. 2 überwältigen.

overwork (v ouvə'wə:k; n 'ouvəwə:k) vt 1 überanstrengen, mit Arbeit überlasten. vi sich überarbeiten. n Überarbeitung f.

overwrought (ouvə'rɔ:t) adj überarbeitet, überreizt.

ovulate ('ɔvjuleit) vi ovulieren. **ovulation** n Eiausstoßung, Ovulation f.

owe (ou) vt 1 schulden, schuldig sein. 2 verdanken. vi Schulden haben. **owing to** prep infolge.

owl (aul) n Eule f.

own (oun) adj eigen. **get one's own back** sich revanchieren. ~vt besitzen. vi sich bekennen. **own up** inf gestehen. **ownership** n 1 Eigentumsrecht neu. 2 Besitz m.

ox (ɔks) n, pl **oxen** Ochse m. Rind neu.

oxygen ('ɔksidʒən) n Sauerstoff m.

oyster ('ɔistə) n Auster f.

P

pace (peis) n 1 Schritt m. 2 Tempo neu. 3 Gangart f. vi 1 durchschreiten, überschreiten. 2 sport Schritt machen für. vi (einher)-schreiten.

Pacific (pə'sifik) adj pazifisch. **Pacific (Ocean)** n Pazifik, Stiller Ozean m.

pacify ('pæsifai) vt 1 befrieden, den Frieden bringen. 2 besänftigen. **pacifism** n Pazifismus m. **pacifist** n Pazifist m. adj pazifistisch.

pack (pæk) n 1 Paket, Bündel neu. 2 Menge f. Haufen m. 3 Pack neu. Bande f. 4 Päckchen neu. Packung f. vt 1 (ver)packen. 2 vollstopfen. vi 1 packen. 2 sich zusammen-

drängen. **package** n 1 Packung f. Paket neu. 2 Ballen m. vt 1 (in Pakete) (ver)packen. **packet** n Paket, Päckchen neu. **packing** n 1 Packen neu. 2 Packmaterial neu.

pact (pækt) n Pakt, Vertrag m.

pad¹ (pæd) n 1 Polster, Kissen neu. Bausch m. 2 Stempelkissen neu. 3 (Brief)Block m. **padding** n Wattierung, Polsterung f.

pad² (pæd) n (leises) Tappen, Trotten neu.

paddle¹ ('pædl) n Paddel neu. vi paddeln.

paddle² ('pædl) vi (im Wasser) spielen, herumpaddeln.

paddock ('pædɔk) n Pferdekoppel f.

paddyfield ('pædifi:ld) n Reisfeld neu.

padlock ('pædlɔk) n Vorhängeschloß neu.

paediatric (pi:di'ætrik) adj med pädiatrisch. **paediatrician** n Kinderarzt m.

pagan ('peigən) n Heide m. adj heidnisch.

page¹ (peidʒ) n Seite f. Blatt neu.

page² (peidʒ) n Page, Boy m.

pageant ('pædʒənt) n 1 (großartiges) Schauspiel neu. 2 Festspiel neu. **pageantry** n Prunk m. Gepränge neu.

paid (peid) v see **pay.**

pain (pein) n 1 Schmerz m. Pein f. 2 Leid m. 3 Strafe f. **be in pain** Schmerzen haben. **take pains** sich Mühe geben. ~vt weh tun. **painful** adj 1 schmerzhaft. 2 schmerzlich. 3 peinlich. **painstaking** adj sorgfältig, gewissenhaft.

paint (peint) vt 1 malen. 2 anstreichen. vi malen. n 1 Farbe f. 2 Anstrich m. 3 Lack m. **wet paint!** frisch gestrichen! **paintbrush** n Pinsel m. **painter** n 1 Maler m. 2 Anstreicher m. **painting** n 1 Malen neu. 2 Malerei f. 2 Gemälde, Bild neu.

pair (pɛə) n Paar neu. vi 1 sich paaren, verbinden. vt paarweise anordnen, paaren.

Pakistan (pɑ:ki'stɑ:n) n Pakistan neu. **Pakistani** adj pakistanisch. n Pakistaner m.

pal (pæl) n inf Kumpel, Freund, Kamerad m.

palace ('pælis) n Palast m. Schloß neu.

palate ('pælət) n 1 Gaumen m. 2 Geschmack m. **palatable** adj 1 wohlschmeckend. 2 annehmbar, angenehm.

pale (peil) adj blaß, bleich. vi blaß werden, erblassen. vt bleich machen.

Palestine ('pælistain) n Palästina neu. **Palestinian** adj palästinisch. n Palästiner m.

palette ('pælit) n Palette f. Farbenteller m.

palm¹ (pɑ:m) n Handfläche f. Handteller m. vt 1 berühren. 2 (in der Hand) verbergen. **palm off** abschieben. **palmistry** n Handlesekunst f.

palm² (pɑ:m) n bot Palme f. **palm tree** Palmenbaum m.

Palm Sunday n Palmsonntag m.

pamper ('pæmpə) vt verwöhnen, hätscheln.

pamphlet ('pæmflət) n 1 Flugschrift f. 2 Broschüre f. **pamphleteer** n Pamphletist m.

pan (pæn) n Pfanne f. **frying pan** Bratpfanne f. **pancake** n Pfannkuchen m. **flat as a pancake** flach wie ein Brett.

Panama ('pænəmɑ:) n Pānama neu.

pancreas ('pæŋkriəs) n Pankreas neu.

panda ('pændə) n Panda, Katzenbär m.

pander ('pændə) n Kuppler m. vt verkuppeln. vi 1 kuppeln. 2 Vorschub leisten.

pane (pein) n 1 (Fenster)Scheibe f.

panel ('pænl) 1 (Tür)Füllung, Täfelung f. 2 law Geschworene m pl. 3 Diskussionsteilnehmer m pl. Ausschuß m. **instrument panel** Armaturenbrett neu. ~vt täfeln, paneelieren. **panelling** n Täfelung f. Täfelwerk neu.

pang (pæŋ) n stechender Schmerz, Stich m.

panic ('pænik) adj panisch. n Panik f. vi Angst bekommen, in eine Panik ausbrechen. **panic-stricken** von panischem Schrecken ergriffen.

pannier ('pæniə) n (großer) Korb m.

panorama (pænə'rɑ:mə) n Panorama neu.

pansy ('pænzi) n bot Stiefmütterchen neu.

pant (pænt) vi keuchen, schnaufen. n Keuchen, Schnaufen neu.

panther ('pænθə) n Panther m.

pantomime ('pæntəmaim) n Pantomime f.

pantry ('pæntri) n Speisekammer f.

pants (pænts) n pl 1 Herrenunterhose f. 2 (lange) Hose f.

papal ('peipəl) adj päpstlich.

paper ('peipə) n 1 Papier neu. 2 pl (Ausweis)Papiere, Urkunden f. 3 Zeitung f. 4 educ schriftliche Prüfung f. adj Papier—. **paper money** Papiergeld neu. ~vt tapezieren. **paperback** n 1 Buch im Pappeinband neu. 2 Taschenbuch, Paperback neu. **paperclip** n Heftklammer, Büroklammer f. **paperwork** n Schreibarbeit, Büroarbeit f.

papier-mâché (pæpiei'mæʃei) n Papiermaché neu.

paprika ('pæprikə) n Paprika m.

par (pɑ:) n 1 Gleichheit f. Pari neu. 2 Nennwert m. 3 Normalmaß neu. **on a par with** auf derselben Ebene wie.

parable ('pærəbəl) n Parabel f. Gleichnis neu.

parachute ('pærəʃu:t) n Fallschirm m. **parachutist** n Fallschirmabspringer m.

parade (pə'reid) vt 1 mil vorführen, paradieren.
2 zur Schau stellen. vi 1 promenieren. 2 paradieren. n Parade, Vorführung f.

paradise ('pærədais) n Paradies neu.

paradox ('pærədɒks) n Paradoxon neu. widersprüchliche Aussage f. **paradoxical** adj paradox, widersinnig.

paraffin ('pærəfin) n Paraffin neu.

paragon ('pærəgɒn) n Muster, Vorbild neu.

paragraph ('pærəgrɑ:f) n Absatz, Paragraph m.

parallel ('pærəlel) adj 1 gleichlaufend, parallel. 2 entsprechend, Parallel—. n math Parallele f. 2 Parallelfall m. **draw a parallel** einen Vergleich anstellen. ~vt 1 gleich sein mit. 2 parallel laufen.

paralyse ('pærəlaiz) vt paralysieren, lähmen. **paralysis** n Lähmung, Paralyse f.

paramilitary (pærə'militəri) adj halbmilitärisch.

paramount ('pærəmaunt) adj höchst, oberst.

paranoia (pærə'nɔiə) n Paranoia f. **paranoiac** adj paranoisch.

parapet ('pærəpit) n 1 mil Brustwehr f. 2 Geländer neu. Brüstung f.

paraphernalia (pærəfə'neiliə) n pl 1 law Paraphernalgüter neu. 2 Ausstattung f. Zubehör neu. 3 Drum und Dran neu.

paraphrase ('pærəfreiz) n Paraphrase, Umschreibung f. vt umschreiben, paraphrasieren.

parasite ('pærəsait) n Schmarotzer, Parasit m. **parasitic** adj schmarotzend, parasitisch.

paratrooper ('pærətru:pə) n Fallschirmjäger m.

parcel ('pɑ:səl) n 1 Paket, Bündel neu. 2 Los neu. 3 Parzelle f. v **parcel out** austeilen, verteilen.

parch (pɑ:tʃ) vt (aus)dörren, austrocknen. **be parched** vor Durst verschmachten.

parchment ('pɑ:tʃmənt) n Pergament neu.

pardon ('pɑ:dn) n Verzeihung, Vergebung f. **I beg your pardon** ich bitte um Entschuldigung. ~vt verzeihen, entschuldigen. **pardon me** entschuldigen Sie! **pardonable** adj verzeihlich.

pare (pɛə) vt 1 (be)schneiden. 2 schälen.

parent ('pɛərənt) n 1 Vater m. Mutter f. 2 pl Eltern pl. 3 Elternteil m. **parental** adj 1 elterlich. 2 väterlich. 3 mütterlich. **parenthood** n Elternschaft f.

parenthesis (pə'renθəsis) n, pl **-ses** 1 Parenthese f. 2 pl Klammern f pl.

Paris ('pæris) n Paris neu.

parish ('pæriʃ) n Pfarrbezirk m. Kirchspiel neu adj Pfarr—, zum Kirchspiel gehörig.

parity ('pæriti) n Gleichheit, Parität f.

park (pɑ:k) n Park m. Parkanlagen f pl. car

241

park Parkplatz m. ~vt parken, abstellen. vi parken. **parking meter** n Parkuhr f.

parliament ('pɑ:ləmənt) n Parlament neu. **parliamentary** adj parlamentarisch.

parlour ('pɑ:lə) n Wohnzimmer neu. Salon m.

parochial (pə'roukiəl) adj 1 Pfarr—, Gemeinde—. 2 beschränkt, begrenzt.

parody ('pærədi) n Parodie f. vt parodieren.

parole (pə'roul) n 1 Ehrenwort neu. 2 mil Losungswort neu. Parole f. 3 bedingte Haftentlassung f. **on parole** auf Ehrenwort.

paroxysm (pærəksizm) n 1 (krankhafter) Anfall, Krampf m. 2 Steigerung (einer Krankheit) f.

parquet ('pɑ:kei) n Parkett neu.

parrot ('pærət) n Papagei m.

parsley ('pɑ:sli) n Petersilie f.

parsnip ('pɑ:snip) n Pastinak m. Pastinake f.

parson ('pɑ:sən) n Pastor, Pfarrer, Geistliche(r) m. **personage** n Pfarrhaus neu.

part (pɑ:t) n 1 Teil m. Stück neu. 2 Aufgabe, Pflicht f. 3 Th Rolle f. **play a part** eine Rolle spielen. ~vi 1 sich trennen, auseinandergehen. 2 Abschied nehmen. vt 1 teilen, trennen. 2 (the hair) scheiteln. adv teils, zum Teil. **parting** n 1 Scheiden neu. Abschied m. 2 (of the hair) Scheitel m. adj scheidend, Trennungs—. **part-time** adj teilzeitbeschäftigt. adv halbtags. **part-time job** Nebenbeschäftigung, Teilzeitbeschäftigung f.

partake* (pɑ:'teik) vi 1 teilnehmen, teilhaben. 2 etwas an sich haben. vt teilen.

partial ('pɑ:ʃəl) adj 1 einseitig, parteiisch. 2 Teil—, partiell. **be partial to** eine Vorliebe haben für.

participate (pɑ:'tisipeit) vi teilnehmen, sich beteiligen. **participation** n Teilnahme f.

participle ('pɑ:tisəpəl) n Partizip m.

particle ('pɑ:tikəl) n 1 Teilchen, Stückchen neu. 2 Partikel f.

particular (pə'tikjulə) adj 1 individuell, einzeln. 2 ungewöhnlich. 3 ausführlich. 4 peinlich, genau. **nothing particular** nichts Besonderes. ~n Einzelheit f. **in particular** besonders, insbesondere.

partisan (pɑ:ti'zæn) n 1 Anhänger, Parteigänger m. 2 mil Partisan m.

partition (pɑ:'tiʃən) n 1 (Auf)Teilung, Trennung f. 2 Trennwand f. 3 Abteilung f. vt (ver-, auf-)teilen. **partition off** abteilen, abtrennen.

partly ('pɑ:tli) adv teilweise, zum Teil.

partner ('pɑ:tnə) n 1 Teilhaber, Partner m. 2 Gatte m. Gattin f. vt sich zusammentun mit,

zusammenarbeiten mit. **partnership** n Teilhaberschaft, Partnerschaft f.

partridge ('pɑ:tridʒ) n Rebhuhn neu.

party ('pɑ:ti) n 1 Partei f. 2 Gesellschaft, Party f. 3 Gruppe f. 4 Beteiligte(r) m. adj Partei—. **party line** n festgelegte Parteipolitik, Parteilinie f. **follow the party line** linientreu sein.

pass (pɑ:s) vt 1 vorbeigehen. 2 übergehen, überschlagen. 3 bestehen. 4 passieren. 5 verbringen. 6 durchgehen lassen. vi 1 vorbeigehen. 2 gehen. **pass away** sterben. **pass off** ausgeben. **pass through** durchfahren. ~n 1 Engpaß, enger Weg m. 2 Paß m. 3 (in an exam) Bestehen neu. **password** n Losungswort neu. Parole f.

passage ('pæsidʒ) n 1 Durchgang m. Passage, Durchfahrt, Überfahrt f. 2 enger Gang, Weg m. Gasse f. 3 (in a book) Stelle f.

passenger ('pæsindʒə) n Fahrgast, Passagier m.

passion ('pæʃən) n 1 Leidenschaft f. 2 Zorn m. Wut f. 3 Liebhaberei f. **passionate** adj leidenschaftlich.

passive ('pæsiv) adj 1 passiv. 2 zurückhaltend, still, widerstandslos. n Passiv neu.

Passover ('pɑ:souvə) n Passahfest neu.

passport ('pɑ:spɔ:t) n (Reise)Paß, Ausweis m.

past (pɑ:st) adj 1 vergangen. 2 ehemalig. **past participle** n Partizip der Vergangenheit neu. n Vergangeheit f. Vergangene neu. adv vorbei, vorüber. prep 1 nach. 2 an...vorbei. 3 über...hinaus.

pasta ('pæstə) n Teigwaren f pl.

paste (peist) n 1 Kleister, Klebstoff m. 2 Teig m. Paste f. vt (fest)kleben, kleistern.

pastel ('pæstəl) n Pastellfarbe f.

pasteurize ('pæstəraiz) vt pasteurisieren.

pastime ('pɑ:staim) n 1 Zeitvertreib m. Erholung f. Belustigung f.

pastoral ('pæstərəl) adj Hirten—, Schäfer—.

pastry ('peistri) n 1 Gebäck, Backwerk neu. Torten f pl. 3 Blätterteig m.

pasture ('pɑ:stʃə) n Weide f. Weideland neu.

pasty[1] ('peisti) adj 1 teigig, teigartig. 2 bläßlich, kränklich.

pasty[2] ('pæsti) n (Fleisch)Pastete f.

pat[1] (pæt) n Klopfen neu. Klaps m. vt, vi klopfen, klapsen.

pat[2] (pæt) adj bereit, glatt. adv genau.

patch (pætʃ) n 1 Lappen, Flicken m. 2 Fleck m. 3 (of land) kleines Stück neu. vt flicken.

patchwork n 1 Flickarbeit f. 2 Buntgemustertes neu.

pâté ('pætei) n Pastete, Leberwurst f.
patent ('peitnt) adj 1 offen, offenkundig. 2 patentiert. 3 Patent—. n 1 Patent neu. Patentbrief m. vt patentieren. **patent leather** n Lackleder neu.
paternal (pə'tə:nļ) adj väterlich, Vater—. **paternity** n 1 Vaterschaft f.
path (pɑ:θ) n 1 Pfad, Weg m. 2 Bahn f.
pathetic (pə'θetik) adj 1 rührend, ergreifend, pathetisch. 2 inf jämmerlich, armselig.
pathology (pə'θɔlədʒi) n med Krankheitslehre, Pathologie f. **pathologist** n Pathologe m.
patience ('peiʃəns) n 1 Geduld f. 2 Ausdauer f. **patient** n Kranke(r), Patient m. adj geduldig.
patio ('pætiou) n Innenhof, Terasse, Veranda f.
patriarchal (peitri'ɑ:kəl) adj patriarchalisch.
patrician (pə'triʃən) n Patrizier m. adj 1 patrizisch. 2 aristokratisch.
patriot ('peitriət) n Patriot m. **patriotic** adj 1 patriotisch. 2 vaterländisch.
patrol (pə'troul) n 1 mil Patrouille f. 2 (Polizei)-Streife f. (vt,)vi (ab)patrouillieren.
patron ('peitrən) n 1 Patron, Schutzherr m. 2 Gönner m. 3 Kunde m. **patronage** n 1 Gönnerschaft, Protektion f. 2 law Patronatsrecht neu. 3 Schutz m 4 Kundschaft f. **patronize** vt 1 herablassend behandeln, 2 in Schutz nehmen, beschützen. 3 Kunde sein bei. **patronizing** adj gönnerhaft, herablassend.
patter[1] ('pætə) vi 1 klatschen, platschen. 2 trappeln. n 1 Platschen, Prasseln. neu. 2 Getrappel neu.
patter[2] ('pætə) n 1 Jargon m. 2 Geplapper neu. vi schwatzen, plappern.
pattern ('pætən) n 1 Muster neu. Schablone f. 2 Plan m. Anlage f.
paunch (pɔ:ntʃ) n 1 Bauch, Wanst m. 2 zool Pansen m.
pauper ('pɔ:pə) n Arme(r) m.
pause (pɔ:z) n Pause, Unterbrechung f. vi innehalten, pausieren, warten.
pave (peiv) vt pflastern. **pave the way** den Weg bahnen. **pavement** n 1 Gehsteig m. 2 Pflaster neu.
pavilion (pə'viliən) n Pavillon m.
paw (pɔ:) n Pfote, Tatze f. vt mit den Pfoten kratzen, scharren, stampfen. vi scharren, kratzen.
pawn[1] (pɔ:n) vt verpfänden, versetzen. n Pfand neu. **pawnbroker** n Pfandleiher m.
pawn[2] (pɔ:n) n game Bauer m.
pay* (pei) vi 1 zahlen, Zahlung leisten. 2 sich

lohnen, sich rentieren. vt 1 bezahlen. 2 schenken. 3 abstatten, machen. n 1 Bezahlung f. 2 Lohn m. 3 Belohnung f. **pay-packet** n Lohntüte f. **payroll** n Lohnliste f.
pea (pi:) n Erbse f.
peace (pi:s) n 1 Frieden m. 2 Ruhe f. **peaceful** adj friedlich, ruhig. **peacemaker** n Friedensstifter m.
peach (pi:tʃ) n Pfirsich m.
peacock ('pi:kɔk) n Pfau m.
peak (pi:k) n 1 Spitze, Bergspitze f. 2 Gipfel, Höhepunkt m. adj Hoch—, Spitzen—. **peak hours** n pl Hauptverkehrszeit f.
peal (pi:l) n 1 Geläute neu. 2 Getöse neu. Krach m. vi 1 läuten. 2 erschallen.
peanut ('pi:nʌt) n Erdnuß f.
pear (pɛə) n Birne f.
pearl (pə:l) n Perle f.
peasant ('pezənt) n Bauer, Landmann m. adj bäuerlich, ländlich.
peat (pi:t) n Torf m.
pebble ('pebəl) n Kieselstein m.
peck (pek) n 1 Picken, Hacken neu. 2 Küßchen neu. vt,vi picken, hacken.
peckish ('pekiʃ) adj inf hungrig.
peculiar (pi'kju:liə) adj 1 eigen(tümlich). 2 eigenartig. **peculiarity** n Eigentümlichkeit f.
pedal ('pedļ) n Pedal neu. Fußhebel m. vt fahren, treten. vi 1 das Pedal treten. 2 radfahren.
peddle ('pedļ) vt,vi hausieren.
pedestal ('pedistəl) n Postament neu. Ständer, Sockel m. **put on a pedestal** aufs Podest heben.
pedestrian (pi'destriən) n Fußgänger m. adj 1 Fuß—, zu Fuß (gehend). 2 prosaisch, alltäglich. **pedestrian crossing** n Fußgängerübergang m.
pedigree ('pedigri:) n Stammbaum m.
pedlar ('pedlə) n Hausierer m.
peel (pi:l) n Schale, Rinde, Haut f. vt 1 schälen, entrinden. 2 abstreifen. vi sich abschälen, sich abblättern.
peep (pi:p) n Gucken neu. neugieriger Blick m. vi neugierig gucken.
peer[1] (piə) n 1 Peer, Adlige(r) m. 2 Gleiche(r) m.
peer[2] (piə) vi 1 spähen, scharf blicken. 2 sich zeigen, erscheinen.
peevish ('pi:viʃ) adj verdrießlich, mürrisch.
peg (peg) n Pflock, Stift m. 2 (Wäsche)-Klammer f. vt 1 mit Pflocken befestigen, anpflocken. 2 (an)nageln.

pejorative (pi'dʒɔrətiv) adj verschlechternd, herabsetzend, pejorativ.

pelican ('pelikən) n Pelikan m.

pellet ('pelit) n 1 Kügelchen neu. 2 Schrotkugel f. vt mit Kugeln bewerfen.

pelmet ('pelmit) n Vorhangsfalbel f.

pelt[1] (pelt) vt (be)werfen. vi 1 niederprasseln, eilen. **pelting rain** n Platzregen m. ~n 1 Wurf, Schlag. 2 Prasseln, Klatschen neu. 3 Eile, Geschwindigkeit f.

pelt[2] (pelt) n Pelz, Fell m.

pelvis ('pelvis) n Becken neu.

pen[1] (pen) n 1 (Schreib)Feder f. vt 1 schreiben. 2 verfassen. **penfriend** n Brieffreund m. **penknife** n Taschenmesser neu.

pen[2] (pen) n Gehege neu. Pferch m. Koppel f. vt einpferchen, einschließen.

penal ('pi:nl) adj 1 Straf—. 2 strafbar. **penalize** vt 1 bestrafen. 2 belasten. **penalty** n Strafe, Buße f. **penalty (kick)** sport Strafstoß, Elfmeter m.

penance ('penəns) n Buße f.

pencil ('pensəl) n 1 Bleistift m. 2 Stift m. **pencil-sharpener** n Bleistiftspitzer m.

pendant ('pendənt) n 1 Anhänger m. 2 Hängeleuchter m. adj also **pendent** 1 herabhängend. 2 schwebend.

pending ('pendiŋ) adj 1 hängend. 2 schwebend, unentschieden. 3 bevorstehend. prep 1 bis zu. 2 während.

pendulum ('pendjuləm) n Pendel neu.

penetrate ('penitreit) vt 1 eindringen, durchdringen. 2 erforschen, ergründen. vi eindringen. **penetration** n 1 Eindringen neu. Eindringungsvermögen neu. 3 Ergründung f.

penguin ('peŋgwin) n Pinguin m.

penicillin (peni'silin) n Penicillin neu.

peninsula (pə'ninsjulə) n Halbinsel f.

penis ('pi:nis) n 1 Penis m. 2 zool Rute f.

penitent ('penitənt) adj reuig, bußfertig. n Büßer m.

pennant ('penənt) n Wimpel m. Fähnchen neu.

penny ('peni) n 1 pl **pence** British unit of currency. 2 pl **pennies** Pfennig, Penny neu. **penniless** adj ohne Geld, mittellos. **be penniless** keinen roten Heller haben.

pension ('penʃən) n Pension, Rente f. v **pension off** pensionieren, in den Ruhestand versetzen. **pensioner** n Rentner, Pensionist m.

pensive ('pensiv) adj gedankenvoll, nachdenklich.

pent (pent) adj **pent up** 1 eingepfercht. 2 (of feelings) verhalten.

pentagon ('pentəgən) n math Fünfeck neu.

Pentecost ('pentikɔst) n Pfingsten neu.

penthouse ('penthaus) n 1 Schutzdach neu. 2 Dachterassenwohnung f.

people ('pi:pəl) n pl 1 Leute pl. 2 Volk neu. 3 Bevölkerung f. vt bevölkern, besiedeln. **people say** man sagt.

pepper ('pepə) n Pfeffer m. vt 1 pfeffern. 2 bestreuen. **peppercorn** n Pfefferkorn neu. **peppermill** n Pfeffermühle f. **peppermint** n 1 Pfefferminze f. 2 Pfefferminzbonbon m,neu. **pepperpot** n Pfefferstreuer m.

per (pə:) pre 1 pro. 2 per, durch, mit. **as per** gemäß, laut.

perambulator (pə'ræmbjuleitə) n Kinderwagen m.

perceive (pə'si:v) vt,vi 1 wahrnehmen, empfinden. 2 erkennen, begreifen.

per cent (pə 'sent) n Prozent neu. adj —prozentig.

percentage (pə'sentidʒ) n 1 Prozentsatz m. 2 Gewinnanteil m. Provision f.

perception (pə'sepʃən) n 1 (geistige) Wahrnehmung f. 2 Empfindungsvermögen neu. 3 Vorstellung f. **perceptive** adj 1 wahrnehmend, empfindend. 2 auffassungsfähig.

perch (pə:tʃ) n (Sitz)Stange f. vi sich setzen.

percolate ('pə:kəleit) vt 1 filtern, perkolieren. 2 klären. vi durchsickern, durchlaufen.

percussion (pə'kʌʃən) n 1 Schlag, Stoß m. 2 mus Schlaginstrumente neu pl.

perennial (pə'reniəl) n perennierende Pflanze f. adj 1 fortdauernd, beständig. 2 perennierend.

perfect (adj,n 'pə:fikt; v pə'fekt) adj 1 vollkommen. 2 gründlich. 3 geschickt. 4 gänzlich, vollständig. n Perfekt neu. vt 1 vollenden. 2 vervollkommnen.

perforate ('pə:fəreit) vt durchbohren, durchlochen, perforieren.

perform (pə'fɔ:m) vi 1 eine Vorstellung geben. 2 seine Aufgabe erfüllen. 3 arbeiten, leisten. vt 1 verrichten, ausführen. 2 vollenden. 3 aufführen, vortragen. **performance** n 1 Ausführung, Vollziehung f. 2 Aufführung, Darstellung f. 3 Leistung f. 4 Benehmen neu. 5 inf Theater, Getue neu.

perfume ('pə:fju:m) n 1 Parfüm neu. 2 Duft m. vt parfümieren.

perhaps (pə'hæps) adv vielleicht.

peril ('perəl) n Gefahr f. Risiko neu. **at one's peril** auf eigene Gefahr.

perimeter (pə'rimitə) n 1 math Umkreis m. 2 Peripherie f.

period ('piəriəd) n 1 Periode f. Zeitabschnitt m. 2 Pause f. Absatz m. 3 Weile f. 4 med Periode, Menstruation f. 5 educ (Unterrichts)-Stunde f. **periodical** n Zeitschrift f. Magazin neu. adj regelmäßig wiederkehrend, periodisch.

peripheral (pə'rifərəl) adj peripherisch, Umfangs—.

periscope ('periskoup) n Periskop neu.

perish ('periʃ) vi 1 umkommen, sterben. 2 verfallen, vergehen. vt zerstören.

perjure ('pə:dʒə) vt **perjure oneself** eidbrüchig or meineidig werden. **perjurer** n Meineidige(r) m. **perjury** n Meineid m.

perk (pə:k) vi 1 sich brüsten, den Kopf hochtragen. 2 sich vorrecken. **perk up** munter werden or machen, in Stimmung kommen. **perky** adj keck, munter.

perm (pə:m) n inf Dauerwelle f.

permanent ('pə:mənənt) adj 1 beständig, (fort)-dauernd, permanent. 2 dauerhaft. **permanence** n Beständigkeit, Permanenz f.

permeate ('pə:mieit) vt durchdringen. vi eindringen.

permit (v pə'mit; n 'pə:mit) vt,vi erlauben, gestatten. n 1 Erlaubnis, Genehmigung f. 2 Passierschein m. **permissible** adj zulässig. **permission** n Erlaubnis, Zulassung, Bewilligung f. **permissive** adj gestattend, zulassend.

permutation (pə:mju'teiʃən) n Permutation f.

pernicious (pə:'niʃəs) adj verderblich, schädlich.

perpendicular (pə:pən'dikjulə) adj senkrecht, lotrecht. n Senkrechte f.

perpetrate ('pə:pətreit) vt verüben, begehen. **perpetrator** n Täter m.

perpetual (pə'petʃuəl) adj 1 unaufhörlich, beständig. 2 lebenslänglich.

perpetuate (pə'petʃueit) vt verewigen, immerwährend fortsetzen.

perplex (pə'pleks) vt verwirren, verblüffen.

persecute ('pə:sikju:t) vt 1 verfolgen. 2 plagen, belästigen.

persevere (pə:si'viə) vi beharren, nicht nachgeben.

Persia ('pə:ʃə) n Persien neu. **Persian** adj persich. n 1 Perser m. 2 (language) Persisch neu.

persist (pə'sist) vi beharren, hartnäckig bestehen.

person ('pə:sən) n 1 Person f. Individuum neu.

2 Persönlichkeit f. **personal** adj persönlich. **personality** n 1 Persönlichkeit f. 2 Ausstrahlung f.

personify (pə'sɔnifai) vt verkörpern, personifizieren.

personnel (pə:sə'nel) n Personal neu. Angestellte(n) pl. **personnel manager** n Personalchef m.

perspective (pə'spektiv) n 1 Perspektive f. 2 Aussicht, Fernsicht f. adj perspektivisch. **in perspective** in richtiger Perspektive.

Perspex ('pə:speks) n Tdmk Plexiglas Tdmk neu.

perspire (pə'spaiə) vi schwitzen, transpirieren. vt ausschwitzen. **perspiration** n Schweiß m.

persuade (pə'sweid) vt 1 überreden, verleiten. 2 überzeugen. **persuasion** n 1 Überredung f. 2 Überzeugung f. 3 Glaube m.

pert (pə:t) adj 1 keck, schnippisch. 2 munter, flink.

pertain (pə'tein) vi 1 (an)gehören. 2 sich ziemen. **pertinent** adj 1 angemessen, passend. 2 gehörig.

perturb (pə'tə:b) vt beunruhigen, ängstigen.

Peru (pə'ru:) n Peru neu. **Peruvian** adj peruanisch. n Peruaner m.

pervade (pə'veid) vt durchdringen, erfüllen.

perverse (pə'və:s) adj 1 schlecht, böse. 2 pervers, widernatürlich. 3 verstockt, störrisch. 4 verkehrt.

pervert (v pə'və:t; n 'pə:və:t) vt 1 verkehren, verdrehen. 2 verführen. n 1 perverser Mensch m. 2 Abtrünnige(r) m.

pessimism ('pesimizəm) n Pessimismus m. **pessimist** n Pessimist m. **pessimistic** adj pessimistisch.

pest (pest) n 1 Pest f. 2 Schädling m. **pesticide** n Schädlingsbekämpfungsmittel neu.

pester ('pestə) vt plagen, belästigen.

pet[1] (pet) n 1 (zahmes) Haustier neu. 2 Liebling m. adj Lieblings—. vt verhätscheln.

pet[2] (pet) n üble Laune f. vi übler Laune or mürrisch sein.

petal ('petl) n Blumenblatt neu.

peter ('pi:tə) vi **peter out** allmählich aufhören, sich totlaufen.

petition (pi'tiʃən) n 1 Bitte, Bittschrift, Petition f. vt bitten, petitionieren. vi ansuchen.

petrify ('petrifai) vt 1 versteinern. 2 bestürzen, erschrecken. vi sich versteinern, zu Stein werden.

petroleum (pi'trouliəm) n Petroleum, Erdöl neu. **petrol** n Benzin neu.

petticoat ('petikout) n (Frauen)Unterrock m.

petty ('peti) adj 1 klein, unbedeutend. 2 engstirnig, kleinlich, beschränkt. **petty cash** n kleine Summen f pl. geringe Beträge m pl. **petty officer** n Maat m.

petulant ('petjulənt) adj 1 reizbar, launisch. 2 mürrisch, eigensinnig.

pew (pju:) n Kirchenstuhl m.

pewter ('pju:tə) n (Hart)Zinn neu.

phallus ('fæləs) n Phallus m.

phantom ('fæntəm) n Phantom neu. Erscheinung f.

pharmacy ('fɑ:məsi) n 1 Pharmazie f. 2 Apotheke f. **pharmacist** n Apotheker m.

pharynx ('færiŋks) n Schlund, Rachen m.

phase (feiz) n 1 Phase f. 2 Entwicklungsstadium neu. 3 Aspekt m. v **phase out** abwickeln.

pheasant ('fezənt) n Fasan m.

phenomenon (fi'nɔminən) n Phänomen neu. Erscheinung f. **phenomenal** adj phänomenal, außerordentlich.

philanthropy (fi'lænθrəpi) n Menschenliebe f. **philanthropist** n Menschenfreund, Philanthrop m.

philately (fi'lætəli) n Philatelie, Briefmarkenkunde f.

Philippines ('filipi:nz) n pl Philippinen pl.

Philistine ('filistain) n 1 Philister m. 2 Spießbürger m. adj spießbürgerlich.

philosophy (fi'lɔsəfi) n Philosophie f. **philosopher** n Philosoph m. **philosophical** adj 1 philosophisch. 2 gleichmütig.

phlegm (flem) n 1 med Phlegma neu. Schleim m. 2 Gleichgültigkeit f.

phlegmatic (fleg'mætik) adj 1 phlegmatisch, schleimhaltig. 2 phlegmatisch, gleichgültig, träge.

phobia ('foubiə) n Phobie, krankhafte Angst f.

phoenix ('fi:niks) n Phoenix m.

phone (foun) inf n 1 Telefon neu. Fernsprecher m. vi,vt anrufen, telefonieren.

phonetic (fə'netik) adj phonetisch.

phoney ('founi) adj unecht, falsch, Schein—.

phosphate ('fɔsfeit) n Phosphat neu.

phosphorescence (fɔsfə'resəns) n Phosphoreszenz f. Nachleuchten neu.

phosphorous ('fɔsfərəs) n Phosphor m.

photo ('foutou) n Photo neu.

photocopy ('foutoukɔpi) n Photokopie f. vt photokopieren.

photogenic (foutə'dʒenik) adj photogen.

photograph ('foutəgrɑ:f) n Photographie f. Lichtbild neu. vt photographieren. **photog-**

rapher n Photograph m. **photography** n Photographie f.

phrase (freiz) n 1 Redensart, (Rede)Wendung f. 2 Phrase f. 3 Satz m. vt formulieren, ausdrücken. **phrasebook** n Konversations-Handbuch neu.

physical ('fizikəl) adj 1 physisch, körperlich. 2 physikalisch. **physical education** n Leibeserziehung f.

physician (fi'ziʃən) n Arzt m.

physics ('fiziks) n Physik f. **physicist** n Physiker m.

physiology (fizi'ɔlədʒi) n Physiologie f.

physiotherapy (fiziou'θerəpi) n Physiotherapie f.

physique (fi'zi:k) n Körperbau m.

piano (pi'ænou) n Klavier, Piano neu. **pianist** n Klavierspieler, Pianist m.

pick[1] (pik) vt 1 hacken, picken. 2 auswählen. 3 pflücken, lesen. vi hacken, picken. **pick out** auswählen. **pick up** 1 aufheben. 2 sl auflesen. 3 mot mitnehmen. 4 sich erholen. 5 (sound) abnehmen. ~n Auswahl, Auslese f. **pickpocket** n Taschendieb m. **pick-up** n 1 sl zufällige Bekanntschaft f. 2 kleiner Lieferwagen m.

pick[2] (pik) n Spitzhacke, Picke f.

picket ('pikit) n 1 Pfahl, Pflock m. 2 Streikposten m. vt einzäunen. vi (als) Streikposten stehen.

pickle ('pikəl) n 1 Eingepökeltes neu. 2 eingelegtes Gemüse neu. vt einpökeln, einsalzen, marinieren.

picnic ('piknik) n Mahlzeit im Freien f. Picknick neu.

pictorial (pik'tɔːriəl) adj bildlich, illustriert, Bild—. n Illustrierte f.

picture ('piktʃə) n 1 Bild neu. 2 Gemälde neu. Zeichnung f. 3 pl Kino neu. vt sich vorstellen, darstellen.

picturesque (piktʃə'resk) adj pittoresk, malerisch, anschaulich.

pidgin ('pidʒən) n Verkehrssprache f. **pidgin English** Pidgin-Englisch neu.

pie (pai) n 1 Pastete f. 2 Torte f. **have a finger in the pie** die Hand im Spiel haben.

piece (pi:s) n 1 Stück neu. 2 Teil m. 3 (Geld)Stück neu. 4 game Figur f. **piecemeal** adv stückweise, Stück für Stück. **piecework** n Akkordarbeit f. ~v **piece together** 1 zusammensetzen. 2 zusammenreimen.

pied (paid) adj buntscheckig.

pier (piə) n 1 Pier m. 2 Landungssteg m. 3 Hafendamm m. 4 Pfeiler m.

pierce (piəs) vt 1 durchstechen, durchbohren. 2 durchdringen. vi eindringen.

piety ('paiəti) n Frömmigkeit, Pietät f.

pig (pig) n Schwein, Ferkel neu. **pig-headed** adj dickschädelig, stur. **pig-iron** n Masseleisen, Roheisen neu. **piglet** n Schweinchen, Ferkel neu. **pigskin** n Schweinsleder neu. **pigsty** n Schweinestall m. **pigtail** n Zopf m.

pigeon ('pidʒən) n Taube f. **pigeonhole** n (Brief)Fach neu. vt einordnen.

piggyback ('pigibæk) adj,adv huckepack.

pigment ('pigmənt) n 1 Pigment neu. 2 Farbe f. Farbstoff m. vt pigmentieren, färben.

pike (paik) n Hecht m.

pilchard ('piltʃəd) n Sardine f.

pile[1] (pail) n Haufen, Stapel, Stoß m. vt anhäufen, stapeln. **pile up** sich ansammeln, anhäufen. **pile-up** n mot (Massen)Zusammenstoß m.

pile[2] (pail) n 1 zugespitzter Pfahl m. 2 Pfeiler m. **piledriver** n Ramme f.

pile[3] (pail) n 1 Flaum m. 2 Flor m. 3 Haar, Fell neu.

piles (pailz) n med Hämorrhoiden f pl.

pilfer ('pilfə) vt,vi 1 stehlen. 2 mausen, klauen.

pilgrim ('pilgrim) n Pilger, Wallfahrer m. adj pilgernd, Wallfahrts—. **pilgrimage** n Pilgerfahrt, Wallfahrt f. **go on a pilgrimage** pilgern, wallfahren.

pill (pil) n Pille f. **the pill** inf die Pille.

pillage ('pilidʒ) vt ausplündern, rauben.

pillar ('pilə) n 1 Pfeiler m. 2 Säule f. **pillar-box** n Briefkasten m.

pillion ('piliən) n 1 Damensattel m. 2 Soziussitz m.

pillow ('pilou) n Kopfkissen neu. **pillowcase** n Kissenbezug m.

pilot ('pailət) n Pilot, Flugzeugführer m. vt 1 steuern, lotsen. 2 leiten, führen. **pilot-light** n 1 Zündflamme f. 2 Kontrollampe f.

pimento (pi'mentou) n Piment m.

pimp (pimp) n Zuhälter, Kuppler m.

pimple ('pimpəl) n Pickel, Pustel f.

pin (pin) n 1 Nadel f. 2 Stift, Bolzen m. vt 1 mit einer Nadel festmachen. 2 festnageln, festhalten. **pinball** n Kugelspiel neu, Flipper m. **pincushion** n Nadelkissen neu. **pin-money** n 1 Geldbetrag für kleine Sonderausgaben m. 2 Nadelgeld neu. **pinpoint** vt genau feststellen. **pinstripe** n Nadelstreifen m.

pinafore ('pinəfɔ:) n (Kinder)Schürze f.

pincers ('pinsəz) n pl 1 (Kneif) Zange f. 2 zool Krebsschere f.

pinch (pintʃ) vt 1 kneifen, drücken. 2 inf klauen. 3 beschränken, einschränken. vi drücken, kneifen. n 1 Kneifen, Zwicken neu. 2 Druck m. 3 cul Prise f.

pine[1] (pain) n bot Kiefer, Föhre f.

pine[2] (pain) vi sich sehnen, schmachten.

pineapple ('painæpəl) n Ananas f.

ping-pong ('pinpɔn) n Tischtennis, Pingpong neu.

pinion ('piniən) n 1 Flügelspitze f. 2 Flügel m. vt 1 beschneiden, stutzen. 2 binden, fesseln.

pink (pink) adj rosa. n bot Nelke f.

pinnacle ('pinəkəl) n 1 Spitzturm m. 2 Gipfel m. Spitze f.

pint (paint) n 1 Pinte f. 2 Schoppen m.

pioneer (paiə'niə) n 1 Pionier m. 2 Wegbereiter m. vt den Weg bahnen für, bahnbrechende Arbeit leisten.

pious ('paiəs) adj fromm.

pip[1] (pip) n Obstkern m.

pip[2] (pip) n Ton m. vi piepsen.

pipe (paip) n 1 Pfeife f. 2 Röhre f. Rohr neu. 3 Rohrleitung f. 4 pl mus Dudelsack m. vt durch ein Rohr leiten. **pipedream** n Luftschloß neu. **pipeline** n Pipeline, Rohrleitung f. **pipette** n Pipette f.

piquant ('pi:kənt) adj pikant, würzig.

pique (pi:k) n Groll, Ärger m. vt ärgern.

pirate ('pairət) n Pirat, Seeräuber m. vi plündern.

pirouette (piru'et) n Pirouette, Kreiseldrehung f. vi pirouettieren.

Pisces ('pisi:z) n Fische m pl.

piss (pis) vi tab urinieren, harnen. **piss off!** interj schleich dich! verzieh dich!

pistol ('pistəl) n Pistole f.

piston ('pistən) n 1 tech Kolben m. 2 mus Ventil neu.

pit (pit) n 1 Grube, Höhle f. 2 Zeche f. 3 Abgrund m. 4 (Pocken)Narbe f. vt 1 mit Narben bedecken. 2 zerfressen. **pitfall** n 1 Falle, Fallgrube f. 2 Gefahr f.

pitch[1] (pitʃ) vt 1 werfen, schleudern. 2 errichten, aufstellen. 3 mus stimmen. 4 festsetzen. 5 gabeln. vi hinstürzen. n 1 Wurf m. 2 mus Tonhöhe f. 3 Stufe f. Grad m. **pitchfork** n Heugabel, Mistgabel f.

pitch[2] (pitʃ) n Pech neu. vt (ver)pechen.

pith (piθ) n 1 Mark neu. 2 Innere neu. Kern m. 3 Bedeutung f.

pittance ('pitns) n 1 Hungerlohn m. 2 kleiner Anteil m.

pituitary gland (pi'tjuətri) n Hypophyse f. Hirnanhang m.

pity ('piti) n 1 Mitleid, Erbarmen neu. 2 Jammer m. **what a pity!** wie schade! ~vt bemitleiden.

pivot ('pivət) n 1 Drehpunkt m. 2 (Tür)Angel f. vi sich drehen. vt 1 schwenken. 2 mit Angeln versehen.

pizza ('pi:tsə) n Pizza f.

placard ('plæka:d) n Plakat neu.

placate (plə'keit) vt besänftigen, beruhigen.

place (pleis) n 1 Ort m. 2 Stelle f. 3 Platz m. 4 Stand, Rang m. 5 Stadt f. 6 inf Wohnung f. Haus neu. **all over the place** inf überall. ~vt 1 stellen, legen, setzen. 2 unterbringen. 3 identifizieren. **placename** n Ortsname m.

placenta (plə'sentə) n Plazenta f.

placid ('plæsid) adj ruhig, gelassen.

plagiarize ('pleidʒəraiz) vt abschreiben, plagieren, nachahmen. vi ein Plagiat begehen.

plague (pleig) n 1 Plage f. 2 Seuche, Pest f. 3 Quälgeist m. vt quälen, verfolgen, belästigen.

plaice (pleis) n Scholle f.

plaid (plæd) n 1 Plaid m,neu Schottenmuster neu. adj buntkariert.

plain (plein) adj 1 klar. 2 offen. 3 einfach, schlicht. 4 schmucklos, ungemustert. 5 unschön. **plain sailing** n einfache Sache, reibungslose Affäre f. ~adv klar. n Ebene, Fläche f. **plain-clothes** n Zivilkleidung f.

plaintiff ('pleintif) n law Kläger m.

plaintive ('pleintiv) adj 1 klagend, kläglich. 2 traurig.

plait (plæt) n 1 Falte f. 2 Zopf m. vt 1 (zu einem Zopf) flechten. 2 falten.

plan (plæn) n 1 Plan m. Skizze f. Entwurf m. 3 Absicht f. vt 1 entwerfen, skizzieren. 2 planen, beabsichtigen.

plane [1] (plein) adj flach, eben. n 1 Ebene f. 2 Höhe f. Niveau neu. 3 Flugzeug neu. vi gleiten.

plane [2] (plein) Hobel m. vt ebnen, glätten, hobeln.

planet ('plænit) n Planet m.

plank (plæŋk) n Planke, Bohle f.

plankton ('plæŋktən) n Plankton neu.

plant (pla:nt) n 1 bot Pflanze f. 2 Fabrik f. Werk neu. vt 1 pflanzen. 2 bepflanzen. **plantation** n (An)Pflanzung f. Plantage f.

plaque (pla:k) n 1 (Schmuck)Platte f. 2 Brosche f. 3 Gedenktafel f.

plasma ('plæzmə) n Plasma neu.

plaster ('pla:stə) n 1 Pflaster neu. 2 Mörtel m. 3 Gips m. **plaster of Paris** n (gebrannter) Gips m. **sticking plaster** Heftpflaster neu. ~vt 1 (be)pflastern. 2 verputzen.

plastic ('plæstik) n Kunststoff m. adj 1 Plastik—, Kunststoff—. 2 bildend. 3 plastisch.

Plasticine ('plæstisi:n) n Tdmk Plastilin Tdmk neu.

plate (pleit) n 1 Tafel, Platte f. 2 Teller m. 3 Silbergeschirr neu. vt plattieren, überziehen. **platelayer** n Schienenleger, Streckenarbeiter m.

plateau ('plætou) n Plateau neu. Hochebene f.

platform ('plætfɔ:m) n 1 Rednerbühne f. 2 Bahnsteig m. 3 Plattform f.

platinum ('plætnəm) n Platin neu.

platonic (plə'tɔnik) adj platonisch.

plausible ('plɔ:zəbəl) adj 1 plausibel, einleuchtend. 2 überzeugend.

play (plei) n 1 Spiel neu. 2 Schauspiel, Theaterstück neu. 3 Verhalten neu. 4 Spielraum m. vi 1 spielen. 2 tändeln, flirten. 3 mus Musik machen. vt spielen. **playboy** n Playboy m. **playful** adj spielerisch, scherzhaft. **playground** n Spielplatz m. 2 Schulhof m. **playgroup** n Spielgruppe f. **playhouse** n 1 Schauspielhaus neu. 2 Puppenhaus neu. **playing card** n Spielkarte f. **playing field** n Sportplatz m. **playmate** n Spielkamerad m. **playschool** n Kindergarten m. **playwright** n Dramatiker m.

plea (pli:) n 1 Gesuch neu. Bitte f. 2 Vorwand m. 3 law Einspruch m.

plead (pli:d) vi law plädieren, sich verteidigen. vt 1 vertreten. 2 verteidigen. 3 vorbringen, geltend machen. **plead guilty** sich schuldig bekennen.

please (pli:z) vt 1 gefallen, Freude machen. 2 befriedigen. vi gefallen, angenehm sein. adv bitte. **please yourself** tun Sie, was Sie wollen. **pleasant** adj 1 angenehm. 2 freundlich, liebenswürdig. **pleasure** n 1 Vergnügen neu. Freude f. 2 Genuß m.

pleat (pli:t) n Falte f. vt in Falten legen, plissieren.

plectrum ('plektrəm) n Plektron neu.

pledge (pledʒ) n 1 Pfand neu. Bürgschaft f. 2 Versprechen neu. Zusage f. 3 Trinkspruch, Toast m. vt 1 verpfänden, als Pfand geben. 2 versprechen. 3 verpflichten.

plenty ('plenti) n Fülle f. Reichtum m. adj

reichlich. **in plenty** reichlich, im Überfluß.
plenty of viel, reichlich.

pliable ('plaiǝbl) adj 1 biegsam. 2 nachgiebig, fügsam.

pliers ('plaiǝz) n (Kneif)Zange f.

plight (plait) n Notlage, Zwangslage f.

plimsoll ('plimsǝl) n Turnschuh m.

plod (plɔd) vi 1 (mühsam) daherstampfen, sich hinschleppen. 2 sich abmühen, sich mühsam durcharbeiten.

plonk (plɔŋk) vt hinplumpsen.

plot[1] (plɔt) n 1 lit Handlung f. 2 Plan m. 3 Verschwörung f. vi sich verschwören. vt 1 (heimlich) planen. 2 entwerfen. 3 ersinnen. 4 graphisch darstellen, aufzeichnen.

plot[2] (plɔt) n Parzelle f. Grundstück neu.

plough (plau) n Pflug m. vt pflügen.

pluck (plʌk) vt 1 pflücken. 2 rupfen. 3 reißen, zerren. vi reißen, zerren. n 1 Ruck, Zug m. 2 Mut m. Beherztheit f.

plug (plʌg) n Stöpsel, Pfropf m. vt verstopfen.

plum (plʌm) n bot Pflaume f.

plumage ('plu:midʒ) n Gefieder neu.

plumb (plʌm) n Senkblei, Lot neu. adj senkrecht, lotrecht. vt 1 sondieren. 2 erforschen. vi klempnern. **plumber** n Klempner, Installateur m. **plumbing** n 1 Kempnerarbeit f. 2 Ausloten neu.

plume (plu:m) n 1 Feder f. 2 Federbusch m. vt mit Federn schmücken.

plump[1] (plʌmp) adj rundlich, dick.

plump[2] (plʌmp) vi plumpsen. **plump for** sich entscheiden für.

plunder ('plʌndǝ) vt n 1 Plünderung f. 2 Beute f.

plunge (plʌndʒ) vt 1 tauchen. 2 stürzen. vi 1 tauchen. 2 sich hineinstürzen. n 1 Tauchen neu. 2 Sturz m.

pluperfect (plu:'pǝ:fikt) n Plusquamperfekt neu.

plural ('pluǝrǝl) adj mehrfach, Plural—. n Plural m. Mehrzahl f.

plus (plʌs) prep plus, und. n Plus, Mehr neu. adj 1 positiv, Plus—. 2 mehr, Extra—.

plush (plʌʃ) n Plüsch m. adj Plüsch—.

Pluto ('plu:tou) n Pluto m.

ply[1] (plai) vt 1 ausüben. 2 handhaben. vi regelmässig fahren, verkehren.

ply[2] (plai) n 1 Schicht f. 2 Strähne f. 3 Neigung f. **plywood** n Sperrholz neu.

pneumatic (nju:'mætik) adj pneumatisch, Luft—. **pneumatic drill** n Preßluftbohrer m.

pneumonia (nju:'mouniǝ) n Lungenentzündung, Pneumonie f.

poach[1] (poutʃ) vi 1 wildern, unerlaubt jagen. 2 widerrechtlich betreten.

poach[2] (poutʃ) vt cul pochieren. **poached egg** n pochiertes or verlorenes Ei.

pocket ('pɔkit) n Tasche f. vt in die Tasche stecken. **pocket-money** n Taschengeld neu.

pod (pɔd) n Schote, Schale f. vt ausschoten.

poem ('pouim) n Gedicht neu.

poet ('pouit) n Dichter m. **poetic** adj dichterisch, poetisch. **poetry** n 1 Dichtung, Poesie f. 2 Gedichte neu.

poignant ('pɔinjǝnt) adj 1 scharf. 2 pikant. 3 rührend, ergreifend.

point (pɔint) n 1 Punkt m. 2 Spitze f. 3 Frage, Sache f. 4 Zweck m. Absicht f. 5 Stufe f. Zeitpunkt m. 6 Stelle f. **be on the point of doing** eben tun wollen. **beside the point** nicht zur Sache gehörig. **point-blank** adj, adv 1 (schnur)gerade. 2 direkt, offen. 3 mil Kern—, Kernschuß—. ~vt 1 richten. 2 spitzen. 3 deuten auf. **point out** aufmerksam machen auf. **point to** hinweisen auf. **pointed** adj 1 spitz. 2 scharf, treffend.

poise (pɔiz) n 1 Gleichgewicht neu. 2 Haltung f. 3 Ruhe, Gelassenheit f. vt 1 balancieren. 2 im Gleichgewicht halten. vi schweben.

poison ('pɔizǝn) n Gift neu. vt vergiften. **poisonous** adj giftig.

poke (pouk) n Stoß, Puff m. vi stoßen, stochern, tasten. vt 1 stoßen, knuffen. 2 (a fire) schüren.

poker[1] ('poukǝ) n Feuerhaken m.

poker[2] ('poukǝ) n Poker(spiel) neu.

Poland ('poulǝnd) n Polen neu.

polar ('poulǝ) adj polar, Polar—. **polar bear** n Eisbär m. **polarize** vt polarisieren.

pole[1] (poul) n 1 Pfahl m. 2 Stange f. Pfosten m. Stock m. vt staken. **pole-vault** n Stabhochsprung m.

pole[2] (poul) n Pol m. **Pole Star** n Polarstern m.

Pole (poul) n Pole m.

polemic (pǝ'lemik) adj 1 polemisch. 2 streitsüchtig. n Polemik f.

police (pǝ'li:s) n Polizei f. vt 1 polizeilich bewachen. 2 schützen. 3 kontrollieren. **policeman** n Polizist, Schutzmann m. **police station** n Polizeiwache f.

policy[1] ('pɔlisi) n 1 Politik, politische Linie f. 2 Taktik, Methode f.

policy[2] ('pɔlisi) n (Versicherungs)Police f.

polish ('pɔliʃ) vt 1 polieren, glätten. 2 bohnern. 3 verfeinern. vi glatt werden, Glanz annehmen. n 1 Glanz m. Politur f. 2 Putzmittel neu.

Polish ('pouliʃ) adj polnisch n (language) Polnisch neu.

polite (pə'laɪt) adj 1 höflich, zuvorkommend. 2 fein, schön.

politics ('politiks) n Politik f. **political** adj politisch. **politician** n Politiker m.

polka ('polkə) n Polka f.

poll (poul) n 1 Wahl, Abstimmung f. 2 Wählerliste f. 3 Umfrage. 4 Stimmabgabe f. **go to the polls** zur Wahl gehen. ~vt 1 (votes) erhalten. 2 stutzen, abschneiden. vi wählen, stimmen.

pollen ('polən) n Blütenstaub, Pollen m.

pollute (pə'luːt) vt 1 verschmutzen, verunreinigen. 2 schänden, entweihen. **pollution** n (Umwelts)Verschmutzung f.

polygamy (pə'lɪgəmi) n Polygamie f.

polygon ('poligən) n Vieleck neu.

polytechnic (poli'teknik) adj polytechnisch. n polytechnische Hochschule f.

polythene ('poliθiːn) n 1 sci Polyäthylen neu. 2 Plastik—.

pomegranate ('pomigrænət) n Granatapfel m.

pomp (pomp) n Pomp, Prunk m. Pracht f. **pompous** adj 1 pompös, prunkvoll. 2 hochtrabend, anmaßend.

pond (pond) n Teich m.

ponder ('pondə) vt erwägen, nachdenken über. vi tief nachdenken, nachsinnen.

pony ('pouni) n Pony neu. **ponytail** n Pferdeschwanz m.

poodle ('puːdl) n Pudel m.

pool[1] (puːl) n 1 Teich m. 2 Pfütze f.

pool[2] (puːl) n 1 Pool, Ring m. Interessengemeinschaft f. 2 gemeinsame Kasse f. vt zusammenlegen, vereinigen.

poor (puə, pɔː) adj 1 arm, bedürftig. 2 schlecht. 3 jämmerlich.

pop[1] (pop) n 1 Knall, Puff m. 2 inf Sprudel m. Limonade f. vt knallen lassen. vi puffen, knallen. **pop up** plötzlich auftauchen or erscheinen. interj paff! **popcorn** n Popcorn m. Puffmais m.

pop[2] (pop) adj inf populär, beliebt. **pop music** n Popmusik f. **pop song** n Schlager m.

pope (poup) n Papst m.

poplar ('poplə) n Pappel f.

poppy ('popi) n Mohn m. Mohnpflanze f.

popular ('popjulə) adj 1 populär. 2 beliebt. 3 volkstümlich.

population (popju'leiʃən) n Bevölkerung f.

porcelain ('pɔːslin) adj Porzellan—. n Porzellan neu.

porch (pɔːtʃ) n 1 Portal neu. 2 Vorhalle f. 3 Veranda f.

porcupine ('pɔːkjupain) n Stachelschwein neu.

pore[1] (pɔː) n anat Pore f.

pore[2] (pɔː) vi **pore over** eifrig studieren, aufmerksam untersuchen.

pork (pɔːk) n Schweinefleisch neu.

pornography (pɔː'nɔgrəfi) n Pornographie f. **pornographic** adj pornographisch.

porous ('pɔːrəs) adj porös, durchlässig.

porpoise ('pɔːpəs) n Tümmler m.

porridge ('pɔridʒ) n Hafer(flocken)brei m.

port[1] (pɔːt) n Hafen m.

port[2] (pɔːt) adj Backbord—. n Backbord neu.

port[3] (pɔːt) n Portwein m.

port[4] (pɔːt) n Tor neu. Pforte f.

portable ('pɔːtəbəl) adj tragbar, portabel.

portent ('pɔːtent) n 1 Vorbedeutung f. übles Vorzeichen neu. 2 Wunder neu.

porter[1] ('pɔːtə) n Gepäckträger m.

porter[2] ('pɔːtə) n Pförtner, Portier m.

portfolio (pɔːt'fouliou) n 1 (Brief)Mappe f. 2 Geschäftsbereich (eines Ministers) m.

porthole ('pɔːthoul) n Pfortluke f.

portion ('pɔːʃən) n 1 Portion f. 2 Anteil m. vt einteilen, zuteilen.

portrait ('pɔːtrit) n Porträt, Bildnis neu.

portray (pɔː'trei) vt 1 porträtieren, abmalen. 2 beschreiben, schildern.

Portugal ('pɔːtjugəl) n Portugal neu. **Portuguese** adj portugiesisch. n 1 Portugiese m. 2 (language) Portugiesisch neu.

pose (pouz) n Stellung, Pose f. vi posieren. vt 1 (questions) stellen. 2 aufstellen. **pose as** auftreten als.

posh (poʃ) adj inf elegant, schick, prima.

position (pə'ziʃən) n 1 Position, Stellung f. 2 Rang m. 3 Standpunkt m. Einstellung f. 4 Lage f. vt (richtig hin)stellen.

positive ('pozitiv) adj 1 positiv. 2 genau, exakt. 3 konstruktiv. 4 definitiv, eindeutig. n 1 Postivum neu. 2 phot Positiv neu.

possess (pə'zes) vt 1 besitzen, haben. 2 in Besitz nehmen. 3 beherrschen. **possession** n 1 Besitz m. 2 pl Habe f. Reichtum m. **be in possession of** besitzen. **possessive** adj 1 besitzgierig. 2 anhänglich. 3 gram Possessiv.

possible ('posəbəl) adj 1 möglich. 2 eventuell.

post[1] (poust) n Pfosten, Pfahl m. vt ankleben, anschlagen.

post[2] (poust) n 1 Stellung f. 2 Posten m. vt postieren, aufstellen.

post[3] (poust) n 1 Post f. 2 Postamt neu. vt (per Post) schicken. **postage** n Porto neu. Postgebühr f. **postal order** n Postanweisung f. **postbox** n Briefkasten m. **postcard** n Postkarte f. **postcode** n Postleitzahl f. **postman** n Briefträger m. **postmark** n Poststempel f. vt abstempeln. **post office** n Postamt neu.

poster ('pousta) n Plakat neu.

posterior (pos'tiaria) adj 1 später. 2 folgend, hinter. n Hinterteil neu.

posterity (pos'teriti) n 1 Nachkommenschaft f. 2 Nachwelt f.

postgraduate (poust'grædjuat) n Doktorand m. adj 1 vorgeschritten. 2 Forschungs—.

posthumous ('postjumas) adj 1 posthum. 2 nachträglich.

post-mortem (poust'mo:tam) adj nach dem Tode. **post mortem (examination)** n Autopsie f.

postpone (pas'poun) vt 1 verschieben. 2 unterordnen.

postscript ('pouskript) n Postskriptum neu. Nachschrift f. Nachtrag m.

postulate (v 'postjuleit; n 'postjulat) vt 1 postulieren. 2 fordern, verlangen. n 1 Postulat neu. 2 Forderung f.

posture ('postʃa) n 1 Stellung, Haltung f. 2 Lage f.

pot (pot) n 1 Topf m. 2 Krug m. vt 1 in einen Topf tun. 2 einmachen.

potassium (pa'tæsiam) n 1 Pottasche f. 2 Kalium neu.

potato (pa'teitou) n Kartoffel f.

potent ('poutnt) adj 1 stark, kräftig. 2 potent.

potential (pa'tenʃal) adj möglich, potentiell. n Potential neu.

pothole ('pothoul) n Schlagloch neu.

potion ('pouʃan) n Trank m.

potter ('pota) n Töpfer m.

pottery ('potari) n 1 Töpferwaren f pl. 2 Töpferei f.

pouch (pautʃ) n Tasche f. Beutel m. (vi), vt (sich) bauschen.

poultice ('poultis) n Umschlag m. Packung f.

poultry ('poultri) n Geflügel neu.

pounce (pauns) vi sich stürzen, herabstoßen. n Sprung, Satz m.

pound[1] (paund) vt 1 zerstoßen, zerstampfen. 2 schlagen, stoßen. vi schlagen, hämmern.

pound[2] (paund) n Pfund neu.

pour (po:) vt gießen, schütten. vi 1 fließen, strömen. 2 stark regnen. n 1 Guß m. 2 (Regen)Guß m.

pout (paut) vi 1 die Lippen spitzen. 2 schmollen. n Schmollen neu.

poverty ('povati) n 1 Armut f. 2 Elend neu. Not f. **poverty-stricken** adj verarmt, bedürftig.

powder ('pauda) n 1 Pulver neu. Puder m. vt 1 (ein)pudern, bestreuen. 2 pulverisieren. vi zu Pulver werden. **powder room** n Damentoilette f.

power ('paua) n 1 Kraft, Stärke f. 2 Macht, Autorität f. 3 Gewalt f. 4 math Potenz f. 5 Energie. vt antreiben. **powerful** adj mächtig, stark, kräftig.

practicable ('præktikabal) adj ausführbar, möglich.

practical ('præktikal) adj praktisch.

practice ('præktis) n 1 Praxis f. 2 Brauch m. Gewohnheit f. 3 Übung f. 4 Verfahren neu.

practise ('præktis) vt 1 ausüben, betreiben. 2 üben. vi 1 üben. 2 praktisch tätig sein. 3 sport trainieren.

practitioner (præk'tiʃana) n 1 med praktischer Arzt m. 2 law Rechtsanwalt m. 3 Praktiker m.

pragmatic (præg'mætik) adj pragmatisch.

Prague (pra:g) n Prag neu.

prairie ('preari) n Prärie, Steppe f.

praise (preiz) vt preisen, loben. n Lob neu. Preis m. Anerkennung f. **praiseworthy** adj lobenswert.

pram (præm) n Kinderwagen m.

prance (pra:ns) vi 1 sich bäumen. 2 umherspringen. 3 einherstolzieren.

prank (præŋk) n Streich, Ulk m.

prattle ('prætl) vi schwazen, plappern. n Geschwätz, Geplapper neu.

prawn (pro:n) n Garnele f.

pray (prei) vi beten. vt bitten, anflehen. **prayer** n Gebet neu. **prayerbook** n Gebetbuch neu.

preach (pri:tʃ) vi, vt predigen.

precarious (pri'kɛarias) adj 1 prekär, unsicher, riskant. 2 law widerruflich.

precaution (pri'ko:ʃan) n Vorsichtsmaßnahme f. **take precautions** Vorsichtsmaßnahmen treffen.

precede (pri'si:d) vi, vt vorausgehen, vorangehen. **precedence** n Vorrang m. Priorität f. **precedent** n Präzedenzfall m.

precinct ('pri:siŋkt) n 1 Bezirk m. 2 pl Umgebung f.

precious ('preʃas) adj kostbar, vertvoll. adv inf recht, sehr.

precipice ('presipis) n Abgrund m.

precipitate (prə'sipiteit) vt 1 hinabstürzen. 2 überstürzen, übereilen. vi 1 sich übereilen. 2 sich niederschlagen. adj voreilig, überstürzt. **precipitation** n 1 Niederschlag m. 2 Überstürzung f.

precis ('preisi) n Zusammenfassung f. vt zusammenfassen.

precise (pri'sais) adj 1 präzis, genau. 2 korrekt. **precision** n Präzision f.

preclude (pri'klu:d) vt 1 ausschließen. 2 (ver)hindern.

precocious (pri'kouʃəs) adj frühreif, altklug.

preconceive (pri:kən'si:v) vt sich vorher vorstellen, vorher ausdenken. **preconception** n Vorurteil m. vorgefaßte Meinung f.

predatory ('predətəri) adj räuberisch, Raub—.

predecessor ('pri:disesə) n Vorgänger m.

predestine (pri:'destin) vt vorherbestimmen, vorher festlegen. **predestination** n Prädestination, Vorherbestimmung f.

predicament (pri'dikəmənt) n heikle or mißliche Lage f.

predicate (n 'predikit; v 'predikeit) n Prädikat neu. vt 1 aussagen, feststellen. 2 begründen.

predict (pri'dikt) vt voraussagen, prophezeien.

predominate (pri'domineit) vi 1 vorherrschen. 2 überlegen sein.

pre-eminent adj hervorragend.

preen (pri:n) vt (of a bird) putzen.

prefabricate (pri'fæbrikeit) vt vorfabrizieren.

preface ('prefis) n Vorrede, Einleitung f. vt einleiten.

prefect ('pri:fekt) n 1 pol Präfekt m. 2 educ Aufsichtsschüler m.

prefer (pri'fə:) vt 1 vorziehen, lieber tun or haben. 2 einreichen. 3 begünstigen. **preference** n 1 Bevorzugung f. 2 Vorliebe f. 3 Vortritt, Vorrecht neu.

prefix ('pri:fiks) n Präfix neu. Vorsilbe f.

pregnant ('pregnant) adj 1 schwanger. 2 wichtig, gehaltvoll, bedeutsam. **pregnancy** n Schwangerschaft f.

prehistoric (pri:his'torik) adj vorgeschichtlich, urgeschichtlich, prähistorisch.

prejudice ('predʒədis) n 1 Vorurteil neu. 2 Beeinträchtigung f. Schaden m. vt ungünstig beeinflussen, beeinträchtigen. **prejudiced** adj voreingenommen.

preliminary (pri'liminəri) adj vorbereitend, einleitend, vorläufig.

prelude ('prelju:d) n 1 Einleitung f. 2 mus Vorspiel neu.

premarital (pri:'mæritl) adj vorehelich.

premature ('premətʃə) adj 1 frühreif. 2 vorzeitig, frühzeitig.

premeditate (pri:'mediteit) vt vorher überlegen. **premeditation** n Vorbedacht m.

premier ('premiə) n Premierminister m. adj 1 erst. 2 frühest.

premiere ('premiɛə) n Erstaufführung, Premiere f.

premise ('premis) n 1 Prämisse, Voraussetzung f. 2 pl Grundstück neu. 3 pl Haus neu.

premium ('pri:miəm) n Prämie f.

preoccupied (pri:'ɔkjupaid) adj vertieft, in Gedanken versunken.

prepare (pri'pɛə) vt 1 vorbereiten. 2 zubereiten. 3 präparieren. vi 1 Vorbereitungen treffen, sich vorbereiten. 2 mil sich rüsten. **preparation** n 1 Vorbereitung f. 2 pl Vorkehrungsmaßnahmen n pl. **preparatory** adj vorbereitend, Vorbereitungs—.

preposition (prepə'ziʃən) n Präposition f. Verhältniswort neu.

preposterous (pri'pɔstərəs) adj unnatürlich, unsinnig, grotesk, lächerlich.

prerogative (pri'rɔgətiv) n Vorrecht, Privileg neu. Prärogative f. adj bevorrechtet.

prescribe (pri'skraib) vt 1 vorschreiben. 2 med verordnen. vi Vorschriften machen, Anweisungen geben. **prescription** n 1 Vorschrift, Verordnung f. 2 med Rezept neu.

presence ('prezəns) n 1 Gegenwart f. 2 Anwesenheit. 3 Aussehen, Äußere neu.

present[1] ('prezənt) adj 1 gegenwärtig. 2 anwesend. 3 vorhanden. 4 augenblicklich. **present participle** n Partizip des Präsens neu. ~n Gegenwart f. at present im Augenblick. **presently** adv 1 bald. 2 kurz darauf.

present[2] (v pri'zent; n 'prezənt) vt 1 vorstellen. 2 schenken, überreichen. 3 darbieten, vorführen. n Geschenk neu.

preserve (pri'zə:v) vt 1 bewahren, schützen. 2 cul einmachen, konservieren. 3 beibehalten, aufrechterhalten. n Konserve f.

preside (pri'zaid) vi präsidieren, den Vorsitz führen.

president ('prezidənt) n 1 Präsident m. 2 Vorsitzende(r) m.

press (pres) vt 1 drücken, pressen. 2 bügeln. vi 1 Druck ausüben, drücken. 2 dringend bitten. 3 drängen. n 1 Druck m. 2 Presse f. 3 Gedränge neu. **press conference** n Pressekonferenz f. **press-gang** n Anwerbetrupp

m. **press-stud** n Druckknopf m. **press-up** n sport Liegestütz m.

pressure ('preʃə) n 1 Druck m. Druckkraft f. 2 Dringlichkeit f. 3 Druck, Zwang m. **pressure cooker** n Schnellkochtopf m. **pressurize** vt 1 unter Druck setzen. 2 Druck ausüben auf, zwingen.

prestige (pres'ti:ʒ) n Prestige, Ansehen neu.

presume (pri'zju:m) vt vermuten, annehmen. vi 1 vermuten. 2 wagen, sich erlauben. 3 mißbrauchen. **presumption** n 1 Vermutung f. 2 Anmaßung f. **presumptuous** adj anmaßend.

pretend (pri'tend) vt vorgeben, vorspiegeln. vi vorgeben. **pretend to** 1 tun, als ob. 2 Anspruch machen auf. **pretence** n Vorwand m. **pretension** n Anspruch m. **pretentious** adj anspruchsvoll, angeberisch.

pretext ('pri:tekst) n Vorwand m. Ausrede f.

pretty ('priti) adj hübsch, schön. adv inf ziemlich.

prevail (pri'veil) vi 1 die Oberhand gewinnen, sich durchsetzen. 2 vorherrschen. **prevalent** adj 1 vorherrschend. 2 überlegen.

prevent (pri'vent) vt abhalten, zurückhalten, verhindern, verhüten. **prevention** n Verhinderung f.

preview ('pri:vju:) n (private) Vorschau, Vorbesichtigung f. vt vorher sehen.

previous ('pri:viəs) adj vorhergehend, früher. **previously** adv vorher, früher.

prey (prei) n Raub m. Beute f. **bird of prey** Raubvogel m. v **prey on** Jagd machen auf.

price (prais) n 1 Preis m. 2 Wert m. vt 1 bewerten. 2 den Preis festsetzen von. **price-list** n Preisliste f.

prick (prik) n 1 Dorn m. 2 Stich m. vt stechen. vi stechen, prickeln. **prickle** n Stachel, Dorn m. vt stechen, prickeln.

pride (praid) n 1 Stolz m. 2 Hochmut m. v **pride oneself on** stolz sein auf.

priest (pri:st) n Priester, Geistliche(r) m. **priesthood** n Priesteramt neu.

prim (prim) adj gekünstelt, (über)korrekt, steif.

primary ('praiməri) adj 1 erst, ursprünglich, Grund—. 2 hauptsächlich, Haupt—. 3 elementar. **primary school** n Grundschule, Volksschule, Elementarschule f.

primate n 1 ('praimit) Erzbischof m. 2 ('praimeit) zool Primat m.

prime (praim) adj 1 erst, Haupt—, Ober—. 2 höchst. n Vollkommenheit, Blüte f. vt vorbereiten, fertigmachen. **prime minister** n Ministerpräsident, Premierminister m.

primitive ('primitiv) adj 1 ursprünglich, Ur—. 2 primitiv.

primrose ('primrouz) n Primel, Schlüsselblume f. adj blaßgelb.

prince (prins) n Fürst, Prinz m. **princess** n Fürstin, Prinzessin f.

principal ('prinsəpəl) adj 1 hauptsächlich, Haupt—. 2 wichtigst. n Chef, Vorsitzende(r) m. **principality** n Fürstentum neu.

principle ('prinsəpəl) n Prinzip neu. Grundsatz m. **in/on principle** im/aus Prinzip.

print (print) vt 1 drucken. 2 stempeln. 3 herausgeben, veröffentlichen. n 1 Druck m. 2 Abzug m. 3 Spur f.

prior ('praiə) adj eher, früher, vorausgehend. n Prior m. **priority** n Priorität f. Vorrang m.

prise (praiz) vt **prise open** aufbrechen.

prism ('prizəm) n Prisma neu.

prison ('prizən) n Gefängnis neu. **prisoner** n Gefangene(r) m.

private ('praivit) adj 1 privat. 2 persönlich. 3 nicht öffentlich, Privat—. 4 heimlich. n gemeiner Soldat m. **in private** im Vertrauen, unter vier Augen. **private eye** n Privatdetektiv m. **privacy** n 1 Geheimhaltung f. 2 Ruhe, Ungestörtheit f. 3 Privatleben neu.

privet ('privit) n Liguster m. Rainweide f.

privilege ('privilidʒ) n Privileg, Vorrecht neu. vt privilegieren, bevorrechten.

privy ('privi) adj 1 eingeweiht, mitwissend. 2 Privat—, Geheim—.

prize[1] (praiz) n Preis m.

prize[2] (praiz) vt hoch einschätzen.

probable ('probabl) adj wahrscheinlich.

probation (prə'beiʃən) n 1 Prüfung f. 2 Probezeit f. 3 law Bewährungsfrist f. **on probation** 1 auf Probe. 2 law auf Bewährung. **probation officer** n Bewährungshelfer m.

probe (proub) n 1 med Sonde f. 2 Untersuchung f. vt 1 sondieren. 2 untersuchen.

problem ('probləm) n 1 Problem neu. 2 Schwierigkeit f. 3 math Aufgabe f. adj Problem—, problematisch. **problematic** adj problematisch.

proceed (prə'si:d) vi 1 vorwärtsgehen. 2 weitermachen, fortfahren. 3 übergehen. 4 handeln, verfahren. **procedure** n 1 Verfahren, Vorgehen neu. 2 Prozedur f.

process ('prouses) n 1 Vorgang m. 2 Verfahren neu. Prozeß m. **in process** im Gang. ~vt 1 behandeln, verarbeiten. 2 law prozessieren, gerichtlich belangen.

procession (prəˈseʃən) n Prozession f. Umzug. (Fest)Zug m.

proclaim (prəˈkleim) vt proklamieren, verkünden.

procreate (ˈproukrieit) vt 1 erzeugen. 2 hervorbringen.

procure (prəˈkjuə) vt 1 verschaffen, anschaffen, besorgen. 2 zustandebringen, bewirken. vi Kuppelei betreiben. **procurer** n Kuppler m.

prod (prɒd) n 1 Stich m. 2 Stoß m. vt 1 stechen. 2 stoßen.

prodigal (ˈprɒdigəl) adj verschwenderisch.

prodigy (ˈprɒdidʒi) n Wunder neu. **child prodigy** Wunderkind neu.

produce (v prəˈdjuːs; n ˈprɒdjuːs) vt 1 herstellen, erzeugen, produzieren. 2 vorzeigen. 3 veranlassen, bewirken. n Ertrag. Frucht f. Produkt neu. **product** n 1 Erzeugnis, Produkt neu. 2 Ergebnis neu. 3 math Resultat neu. **production** n Erzeugung, Produktion f.

profane (prəˈfein) vt entweihen, profanieren. adj 1 weltlich, profan. 2 gottlos.

profess (prəˈfes) vt 1 gestehen, bekennen. 2 erklären. vi ein Bekenntnis ablegen. **profession** n 1 Beruf m. 2 Bekenntnis neu.

professor (prəˈfesə) n Professor m.

proficient (prəˈfiʃənt) adj 1 geübt, erfahren. 2 tüchtig.

profile (ˈproufail) n Profil neu. Querschnitt m.

profit (ˈprɒfit) n Gewinn, Profit m. vi profitieren, Nutzen ziehen.

profound (prəˈfaund) adj 1 (tief)liegend. 2 tiefsinnig, gründlich, profund.

profuse (prəˈfjuːs) adj 1 überreichlich. 2 verschwenderisch.

programme (ˈprougræm) n 1 Programm neu. 2 Sendung f. **program** (computers) n Programm neu. vt programmieren.

progress (n ˈprougres; v prəˈgres) n Fortgang, Fortschritt m. vi fortschreiten, Fortschritte machen. **progression** n 1 Fortschreiten neu. Fortschritt m. 2 Progression f. **progressive** adj 1 fortschreitend. 2 fortschrittlich.

prohibit (prəˈhibit) vt verbieten, verhindern.

project (n ˈprɒdʒekt; v prəˈdʒekt) n 1 Projekt neu. Plan m. 1 schleudern. 2 werfen. 3 projizieren. 4 entwerfen. **projectile** n Projektil, (Wurf)Geschoß neu. **projection** n 1 Wurf m. 2 Entwurf, Plan m. 3 Projektion f. **projector** n Projektionsapparat m.

proletariat (prouliˈtɛəriət) n Proletariat neu.

proliferate (prəˈlifəreit) vi 1 sprossen. 2 med wuchern.

prolific (prəˈlifik) adj 1 fruchtbar. 2 reich.

prologue (ˈproulɒg) n Prolog m. Einleitung f.

prolong (prəˈlɒg) vt verlängern.

promenade (prɒmiˈnɑːd) n 1 Promenade f. Spaziergang m. vi spazierengehen.

prominent (ˈprɒminənt) adj 1 hervorragend. 2 berühmt, prominent.

promiscuous (prəˈmiskjuəs) adj 1 unterschiedslos. 2 gemeinsam. 3 vermischt.

promise (ˈprɒmis) n Versprechen neu. Zusage f. vt versprechen, zusagen.

promote (prəˈmout) vt 1 begünstigen, fördern. 2 erheben, befördern. 3 anpreisen. **promotion** n 1 Förderung f. 2 Beförderung f. 3 Werbung f.

prompt (prɒmpt) adj schnell, rasch, prompt. vt anspornen, veranlassen.

prone (proun) adj 1 geneigt, neigend. 2 auf dem Gesicht liegend.

prong (prɒg) n Zinke, Spitze f.

pronoun (ˈprounaun) n gram Pronomen, Fürwort neu.

pronounce (prəˈnauns) vt 1 aussprechen. 2 verkünden. vi sich aussprechen. **pronunciation** n Aussprache f.

proof (pruːf) n 1 Beweis, Nachweis m. 2 Abzug m. 3 Probe f. adj fest, sicher, undurchdringlich. vt imprägnieren. **proofread** vt korrigieren.

prop[1] (prɒp) n Stütze, Strebe f. vt stützen.

prop[2] (prɒp) n Th (Bühnen)Requisit neu.

propaganda (prɒpəˈgændə) n Propaganda f.

propagate (ˈprɒpəgeit) vt 1 fortpflanzen, übertragen. 2 ausbreiten.

propel (prəˈpel) vt vorwärtsstreiben. **propeller** n Propeller m.

proper (ˈprɒpə) adj 1 passend, angebracht. 2 eigen(tlich). 3 richtig, korrekt. 4 ordnungsgemäß. **proper noun** n Eigenname m.

property (ˈprɒpəti) n 1 Eigentum neu. Besitz m. 2 Eigenschaft, Eigentümlichkeit f. 3 Grundbesitz m. Immobilien pl.

prophecy (ˈprɒfisi) n Prophezeiung, Weissagung f. **prophesy** vt prophezeien, weissagen.

prophet (ˈprɒfit) n Prophet m.

proportion (prəˈpɔːʃən) n 1 Proportion f. Verhältnis neu. 2 Maß neu. 3 pl Ausmaß neu.

propose (prəˈpouz) vt 1 vorschlagen. 2 (a toast) ausbringen. vi 1 beabsichtigen. 2 einen Heiratsantrag machen. **proposal** n 1 Vorschlag m. 2 (Heirats)Antrag m. **proposition** n 1 Vorschlag, Antrag m. 2 Behauptung f.

proprietor (prə'praiətə) *n* Besitzer, Eigentümer *m*.

propriety (prə'praiəti) *n* Anstand *m*. Angemessenheit *f*.

propulsion (prə'pʌlʃən) *n* Antrieb *m*.

prose (prouz) *n* Prosa *f*. *adj* Prosa—, prosaisch. **prosaic** *adj* prosaisch, alltäglich.

prosecute ('prɔsikju:t) *vt* 1 *law* strafrechtlich verfolgen. 2 verfolgen. 3 betreiben. *vi law* Klage erheben.

prospect ('prɔspekt) *n* 1 Aussicht *f*. 2 Erwartung, Voraussicht *f*. **prospective** *adj* voraussichtlich, künftig. **prospectus** *n* Prospekt *m*.

prosper ('prɔspə) *vi* gedeihen. *vt* begünstigen. **prosperity** *n* Wohlstand *m*. **prosperous** *adj* 1 erfolgreich, gedeihend. 2 wohlhabend.

prostitute ('prɔstitju:t) *n* Prostituierte, Dirne *f*. *vt* 1 prostituieren. 2 entehren. **prostitution** *n* Prostitution *f*.

prostrate (*v* prɔs'treit; *adj* 'prɔstreit) *vt* 1 niederwerfen. 2 entkräften. 3 demütigen. *adj* 1 auf der Erde hingestreckt. 2 unterwürfig. 3 kraftlos.

protagonist (prə'tægənist) *n lit* Held *m*. Hauptperson *f*. Verfechter *m*.

protect (prə'tekt) *vt* (be)schützen, bewahren. **protection** *n* Schutz *m*. Beschützung *f*.

protégé ('prɔtiʒei) *n* Schützling *m*.

protein ('prouti:n) *n* Protein, Eiweiß *neu*.

protest (*n* 'proutest; *v* prə'test) *n* Protest, Einspruch *m*. *vt* 1 beteuern. 2 protestieren gegen. *vi* protestieren, Einspruch erheben.

Protestant ('prɔtistənt) *adj* protestantisch. *n* Protestant *m*.

protocol ('proutəkɔl) *n* Protokoll *neu*.

prototype ('proutətaip) *n* Prototyp, Urtyp *m*.

protractor (prə'træktə) *n* Winkelmesser *m*.

protrude (prə'tru:d) *vi* (her)vorragen, (her)vorstehen. *vt* (her)vortreten lassen.

proud (praud) *adj* 1 stolz. 2 hochmütig. 3 stattlich, prächtig.

prove (pru:v) *vt* 1 beweisen, erweisen. 2 bestätigen. *vi* sich herausstellen. **proven** *adj* 1 bewiesen. 2 bewährt.

proverb ('prɔvə:b) *n* Sprichwort *neu*.

provide (prə'vaid) *vt* 1 beschaffen, versorgen. 2 bereitstellen. *vi* Vorkehrungen treffen. **provision** *n* 1 Vorsorge, Vorkehrung *f*. 2 Bestimmung *f*. 3 *pl* Proviant *m*. *vt* mit Proviant versorgen. **provisonal** *adj* provisorisch.

province ('prɔvins) *n* 1 Provinz *f*. 2 (Arbeits)-

Gebiet *neu*. **provincial** *adj* 1 provinziell. 2 engstirnig, beschränkt. *n* Provinzbewohner *m*.

proviso (prə'vaizou) *n law* Klausel *f*. Vorbehalt *m*.

provoke (prə'vouk) *vt* 1 provozieren, reizen. 2 hervorrufen. 3 veranlassen. **provocation** *n* 1 Provokation *f*. 2 Aufreizung *f*. 3 Anlaß *m*. **provocative** *adj* provozierend.

prow (prau) *n naut* Bug *m*.

prowess ('prauis) *n* 1 Geschicklichkeit *f*. Können *neu*. 2 Tapferkeit *f*.

prowl (praul) *vt* durchstreifen. *vi* umherstreifen. *n* Umherstreifen *neu*. **be on the prowl** umherstreifen.

proximity (prɔk'simiti) *n* Nähe *f*.

proxy ('prɔksi) *n* 1 Vollmacht *f*. 2 Bevollmächtigte(r) *m*. 3 (Stell)Vertreter *m*.

prude (pru:d) *n* Spröde, Prüde *f*. **prudish** *adj* prüde, zimperlich.

prudent ('pru:dnt) *adj* 1 klug, weis. 2 vorsichtig. 3 sparsam.

prune[1] (pru:n) *n* (Dörr)Pflaume *f*.

prune[2] (pru:n) *vt* beschneiden, (zu)stutzen.

Prussia ('prʌʃə) *n* Preußen *neu*. **Prussian** *adj* preußisch. *n* Preuße *m*.

pry (prai) *vi* neugierig schauen, spähen. **pry into** seine Nase stecken in.

psalm (sɑ:m) *n* Psalm *m*.

pseudonym ('sju:dənim) *n* Pseudonym *neu*.

psychedelic (saiki'delik) *adj* psychedelisch.

psychiatry (sai'kaiətri) *n* Psychiatrie *f*. **psychiatric** *adj* psychiatrisch. **psychiatrist** *n* Psychiater *m*.

psychic ('saikik) *adj* 1 psychisch, seelisch. 2 übersinnlich.

psychoanalysis (saikouə'næləsis) *n* Psychoanalyse *f*. **psychoanalyst** *n* Psychoanalytiker *m*.

psychology (sai'kɔlədʒi) *n* Psychologie *f*. **psychological** *adj* psychologisch. **psychologist** *n* Psychologe *m*.

psychopathic (saikə'pæθik) *adj med* psychopathisch.

psychosomatic (saikousə'mætik) *adj* psychosomatisch.

pub (pʌb) *n inf* Kneipe *f*. Lokal, Wirtshaus *neu*.

puberty ('pju:bəti) *n* Pubertät *f*.

public ('pʌblik) *adj* 1 öffentlich, allgemein. 2 national, Volks—. 3 bekannt. *n* 1 Publikum *neu*. 2 Öffentlichkeit *f*. **in public** öffentlich. **public house** *n* Wirtshaus *neu*. Gaststätte *f*. **public relations** *n* öffentliche Meinungspflege *f*. Public Relations *pl*. **public school** *n* Internat *neu*. Privatschule *f*.

publication (pʌbli'keiʃən) n 1 Veröffentlichung f. 2 Publikation, Druckschrift f.

publicity (pʌb'lisiti) n 1 Öffentlichkeit, Publizität f. 2 Reklame f.

publicize ('pʌblisaiz) vt bekanntmachen, publizieren.

publish ('pʌbliʃ) vt 1 herausgeben, verlegen, veröffentlichen. 2 bekanntmachen.

pucker ('pʌkə) (vi),vt (sich) falten, (sich) runzeln. n Falte, Runzel f.

pudding ('pudiŋ) n Pudding m. Süßspeise f. **black pudding** Blutwurst f.

puddle ('pʌdl) n Pfütze, Lache f.

puff (pʌf) n 1 Windstoß m. 2 Hauch m. 3 Zug m. Paffen neu. vi 1 puffen, blasen. 2 schnaufen, keuchen. **puff up** or **out** aufblasen, schwellen. **puff pastry** n Blätterteig m.

pull (pul) vt 1 ziehen. 2 zerren. 3 schleppen. vi ziehen, zerren. **pull down** niederreißen, abreißen. **pull oneself together** sich zusammenreißen. **pull through** inf durchkommen. ~n 1 Zug, Ruck m. 2 Anziehungskraft f. **pullover** n Pullover m.

pulley ('puli) n (Riemen)Scheibe, Rolle f.

pulp (pʌlp) n 1 Brei m. 2 Fruchtfleisch neu. 3 Pulpe f. Papierbrei m. vt in Brei verwandeln.

pulpit ('pulpit) n Kanzel f. Katheder neu.

pulsate (pʌl'seit) vi pulsieren, pochen.

pulse (pʌls) n Puls(schlag) m.

pulverize ('pʌlvəraiz) vt pulverisieren, zermahlen. vi zu Staub zerfallen.

pump (pʌmp) n Pumpe f. vt 1 pumpen. 2 ausfragen, ausholen.

pumpkin ('pʌmpkin) n Kürbis m.

pun (pʌn) n Wortspiel neu. vi ein Wortspiel machen, witzeln.

punch[1] (pʌntʃ) vt (mit der Faust) schlagen. n Faustschlag, Knuff m.

punch[2] (pʌntʃ) vt 1 lochen. 2 stempeln. n 1 Locheisen neu. 2 Locher m. 3 Stempel m.

punch[3] (pʌntʃ) n Punsch m. Bowle f.

punctual ('pʌŋktʃuəl) adj pünktlich. **punctuality** n Pünktlichkeit f.

punctuate ('pʌŋktʃueit) vt 1 interpunktieren. 2 unterbrechen. **punctuation** n Interpunktion f.

puncture ('pʌŋktʃə) n 1 Loch neu. Stich m. 2 mot Reifenpanne f. 3 med Punktur f. vt 1 durchstechen, perforieren. 2 med punktieren. vi (of a tyre) ein Loch bekommen.

pungent ('pʌndʒənt) adj scharf, beißend.

punish ('pʌniʃ) vt (be)strafen, züchtigen.

punt[1] (pʌnt) n 1 Punt, Flachboot neu. 2 sport Fallstoß m. vt 1 staken. 2 stoßen.

punt[2] (pʌnt) vi wetten.

pupil[1] ('pju:pəl) n Schüler m. Schülerin f.

pupil[2] ('pju:pəl) n anat Pupille f.

puppet ('pʌpit) n Puppe, Marionette f.

puppy ('pʌpi) n junger Hund, Welpe m.

purchase ('pə:tʃis) vt kaufen. n Kauf m.

pure (pjuə) adj 1 rein, sauber. 2 unberührt.
purify vt 1 reinigen. 2 klären.

purgatory ('pə:gətri) n Fegefeuer neu.

purge (pə:dʒ) vt 1 reinigen. 2 pol säubern. n 1 Reinigung f. 2 pol Säuberung f.

Puritan ('pjuəritən) n Puritaner m. adj also **puritanical** puritanisch.

purl (pə:l) vt linksstricken.

purple ('pə:pəl) adj purpurn. n Purpur m.

purpose ('pə:pəs) n Absicht f. Zweck m. **purposeful** adj 1 entschlossen. 2 zweckmäßig.

purr (pə:) vi schnurren.

purse (pə:s) n Geldbeutel m. Portemonnaie neu.

pursue (pə'sju:) vt 1 verfolgen. 2 fortsetzen. 3 betreiben. **pursuit** n Verfolgung f.

pus (pʌs) n Eiter m.

push (puʃ) vt 1 schieben, stoßen. 2 drängen. 3 treiben. **push off** 1 abstoßen. 2 inf abhauen. **push on** vordringen. **push through** durchsetzen. ~n 1 Stoß m. 2 Drang m. Energie f. **pushbike** n inf Fahrrad neu. **pushchair** n (leichter) Kinderwagen m.

pussy ('pusi) n inf Kätzchen neu. Mieze f.

put[*] (put) vt 1 setzen, stellen, legen. 2 ausdrücken. 3 richten, tun. 4 sport schleudern, werfen. **put away** 1 weglegen. 2 sparen. **put by** zurücklegen. **put down** 1 niedersetzen. 2 unterdrücken. 3 demütigen. 4 töten. **put forward** 1 vorschlagen. 2 vorbringen. **put off** 1 verschieben. 2 abhalten. **put on** 1 anziehen. 2 herausbringen. 3 zunehmen. 4 vorgeben. **put through** 1 durchführen. 2 verbinden. **put up** 1 errichten, erhöhen. 2 unterbringen.

putrid ('pju:trid) adj verfault, verwest.

putt (pʌt) vt sport putten. n Putten neu.

putty ('pʌti) n (Fenster)Kitt m.

puzzle ('pʌzəl) n Rätsel neu. vt verwirren.

PVC n PVC neu.

Pygmy ('pigmi) n Pygmäe, Zwerg m.

pyjamas (pə'dʒɑ:məz) n pl Schlafanzug, Pyjama m.

pylon ('pailən) n Leitungsmast m.

pyramid ('pirəmid) n Pyramide f.

Pyrenees (pirə'ni:z) n pl Pyrenäen pl.

quote

Pyrex (ˈpaireks) n Tdmk Jenaer Glas Tdmk neu.
python (ˈpaiθən) n Pythonschlange f.

Q

quack[1] (kwæk) vi (of a duck, etc.) quaken.
quack[2] (kwæk) n Quacksalber, Kurpfuscher m.
quadrangle (ˈkwodræŋgəl) n 1 Viereck neu. 2 Hof m.
quadrant (ˈkwodrənt) n Quadrant m.
quadrilateral (kwodriˈlætərəl) adj vierseitig. n Viereck neu.
quadruped (ˈkwodruped) n Vierfüßer m.
quadruple (ˈkwodrupəl) adj vierfach. **quadruplet** n Vierling m.
quail (kweil) n Wachtel f.
quaint (kweint) adj malerisch, kurios.
quake (kweik) vi zittern, beben. n 1 Zittern neu. 2 Erdbeben neu.
Quaker (ˈkweikə) n Quäker m.
qualify (ˈkwolifai) vt 1 befähigen, qualifizieren. 2 einschränken. vi sich eignen. **qualification** n 1 Qualifikation, Befähigung f. 2 Voraussetzung f. 3 Einschränkung f.
quality (ˈkwoliti) n 1 Eigenschaft f. 2 Qualität f.
qualm (kwɑːm) n 1 Skrupel, Zweifel m. 2 Übelkeit f.
quandary (ˈkwondəri) n Verlegenheit f.
quantify (ˈkwontifai) vt quantitativ bestimmen, messen.
quantity (ˈkwontiti) n Menge, Größe, Quantität f.
quarantine (ˈkworəntiːn) n Quarantäne f. vt isolieren.
quarrel (ˈkworəl) n Streit, Zank m. vi streiten, zanken.
quarry[1] (ˈkwori) n 1 Steinbruch m. 2 Quelle f. vt 1 brechen. 2 ausgraben.
quarry[2] (ˈkwori) n (verfolgtes) Wild neu. Beute f.
quart (kwɔːt) n Quart neu.
quarter (ˈkwɔːtə) n 1 Viertel neu. 2 pl Unterkunft f. Quartier neu. vt 1 vierteln. 2 einquartieren. **quarterdeck** n Achterdeck neu. **quartermaster** n 1 mil Quartiermeister m. 2 naut Steuerer m.
quartet (kwɔːˈtet) n Quartett neu.
quartz (kwɔːts) n Quarz m.
quash[1] (kwoʃ) vt unterdrücken, vernichten.
quash[2] (kwoʃ) vt law annullieren, abweisen, niederschlagen.

quaver (ˈkweivə) vi 1 zittern. 2 trillern. n mus Achtelnote f.
quay (kiː) n Kai m.
queasy (ˈkwiːzi) adj unwohl.
queen (kwiːn) n Königin f.
queer (kwiə) adj 1 wunderlich, sonderbar. 2 komisch, kurios. 3 sl schwul, homosexuell.
quell (kwel) vt unterdrücken, bezwingen.
quench (kwentʃ) vt löschen.
query (ˈkwiəri) n Frage, Erkundigung f. vt (be)fragen, sich erkundigen.
quest (kwest) n Suche f.
question (ˈkwestʃən) n 1 Frage f. 2 Problem neu. vt 1 (be)fragen. 2 bezweifeln. **question mark** n Fragezeichen neu. **questionnaire** n Fragebogen m.
queue (kjuː) n Schlange, Reihe f. vi Schlange stehen.
quibble (ˈkwibəl) n Spitzfindigkeit f. vi spitzfindig sein, Haarspalterei betreiben.
quick (kwik) adj 1 schnell, rasch, geschwind. 2 flink. 3 scharf. 4 lebend. **quicken** (vi),vt 1 (sich) beschleunigen. 2 (sich) beleben. **quicksand** n Treibsand m. **quicksilver** n Quecksilber neu. **quickstep** n Quickstep m. **quick-tempered** adj jähzornig, reizbar. **quick-witted** adj schlagfertig.
quid (kwid) n sl Pfund (sterling) neu.
quiet[1] (ˈkwaiət) n Stille, Ruhe f. Frieden m. **quieten** vt beruhigen.
quiet[2] (ˈkwaiət) adj still, ruhig. **quietness** n Ruhe, Stille f.
quill (kwil) adj Feder f.
quilt (kwilt) n Steppdecke f. vt 1 steppen. 2 wattieren.
quinine (kwiˈniːn) n Chinin neu.
quintessence (kwinˈtesəns) n Quintessenz f.
quintet (kwinˈtet) n Quintett neu.
quirk (kwɜːk) n Eigenart, Verschrobenheit f.
quit (kwit) vi inf seine Stelle aufgeben. vt 1 aufgeben. 2 verlassen.
quite (kwait) adv 1 ziemlich. 2 ganz, durchaus, völlig.
quiver[1] (ˈkwivə) vi zittern, beben n. Zittern, Beben neu.
quiver[2] (ˈkwivə) n Köcher m.
quiz (kwiz) n, pl quizzes Quiz neu.
quizzical (ˈkwizikəl) adj 1 seltsam, komisch. 2 spöttisch.
quota (ˈkwoutə) n Anteil m. Quote f.
quote (kwout) vt 1 anführen, zitieren. 2 angeben. n Zitat neu. **quotation** n 1 Zitat neu. 2

257

comm (Kurs)Notierung *f.* **quotation marks** *n pl* Anführungszeichen *neu pl.*

R

rabbi (´ræbai) *n* Rabbiner *m.*

rabbit (´ræbit) *n* Kaninchen *neu.*

rabble (´ræbəl) *n* Pöbel, Mob *m.*

rabies (´reibi:z) *n* Tollwut *f.* **rabid** *adj* 1 tollwütig. 2 wütend, rasend. 3 fanatisch.

race[1] (reis) *vi* rennen. *n.* (Wett)Rennen *neu.* **racecourse** *n* Rennbahn *f.* **racehorse** *n* Rennpferd *neu.*

race[2] (reis) *n* Rasse *f.* **race relations** *n pl* Rassenbeziehungen *f pl.* **racial** *adj* rassisch, Rassen–. **racialism** *n* Rassenvorurteil *neu.*

rack (ræk) *n* 1 Gestell *neu.* 2 Ständer *m.* 3 Gepäcknetz *neu.* 4 Folterbank *f.*

racket[1] (´rækit) *n* 1 Lärm *m.* 2 Gaunerei *f.*

racket[2] (´rækit) *n* Schläger *m.* Rakett *neu.*

radar (´reidə:) *n* Radar *neu.*

radial (´reidiəl) *adj* radial.

radiant (´reidiənt) *adj* strahlend, glänzend.

radiate (´reidieit) *vt,vi* ausstrahlen. **radiation** *n* (Aus)Strahlung *f.* Strahlen *m pl.* **radiator** *n* 1 Heizkörper *m.* 2 *mot* Kühler *m.*

radical (´rædikəl) *adj* 1 *pol* radikal. 2 gründlich.

radio (´reidiou) *n* Radio *neu.* Rundfunk *m.*

radioactive (reidiouæk´tiv) *adj* radioaktiv. **radioactivity** *n* Radioaktivität *f.*

radish (´rædiʃ) *n* Radieschen *neu.* Rettich *m.*

radium (´reidiəm) *n* Radium *neu.*

radius (´reidiəs) *n, pl* **radii** 1 Halbmesser, Radius *m.* 2 Bereich *m.*

raffia (´ræfiə) *n* Raffiabast *m.*

raffle (´ræfəl) *n* Verlosung *f.* *vt* verlosen.

raft (rɑ:ft) *n* Floß *neu.*

rafter (´rɑ:ftə) *n* Dachbalken *m.*

rag[1] (ræg) *n* 1 Fetzen, Lumpen, Lappen *m.* 2 Schundblatt *neu.* **ragged** *adj* zerlumpt.

rag[2] (ræg) *vt* 1 anschnauzen. 2 aufziehen. *n* Streich, Ulk, Unfug *m.*

rage (reidʒ) *n* Wut *f.* *vi* wüten.

raid (reid) *n* 1 Überfall, Angriff *m.* 2 (by the police) Razzia *f.*

rail (reil) *n* 1 Riegel *m.* 2 Geländer *neu.* **by rail** mit der Eisenbahn. **railway** *n* Eisenbahn *f.*

rain (rein) *n* Regen *m.* *vi* regnen. **rainbow** *n* Regenbogen *m.* **rainfall** *n* Niederschlagsmenge *f.*

raise (reiz) *vt* 1 (auf-, er-)heben. 2 errichten. 3 erhöhen, steigern. 4 aufbringen.

raisin (´reizən) *n* Rosine *f.*

rake (reik) *n* Rechen *m.* *vt* rechen.

rally (´ræli) *n* 1 Versammlung *f.* 2 *mot* Sternfahrt *f.* 3 *sport* Schlagwechsel *m.* *vt* 1 wieder sammeln. 2 aufmuntern. *vi* 1 sich wieder sammeln. 2 sich erholen. **rally round** sich scharen um.

ram (ræm) *n* 1 *zool* Widder *m.* 2 Ramme *f.* Rammbock *m.* *vt* rammen.

ramble (´ræmbəl) *vi* 1 wandern. 2 umherschweifen. *n* Wanderung *f.*

ramp (ræmp) *n* Rampe *f.*

rampage (´ræmpeidʒ) *vi* (herum)toben.

rampant (´ræmpənt) *adj* 1 zügellos. 2 wuchernd.

rampart (´ræmpɑ:t) *n* (Schutz)Wall *m.*

ramshackle (´ræmʃækəl) *adj* baufällig.

ran (ræn) *v* see **run.**

ranch (rɑ:ntʃ) *n* Ranch, Viehfarm *f.*

rancid (´rænsid) *adj* ranzig.

rancour (´ræŋkə) *n* Groll *m.* Erbitterung *f.*

random (´rændəm) *adj* zufällig, planlos. **at random** aufs Geratewohl.

rang (ræŋ) *v* see **ring**[2].

range (reindʒ) *n* 1 Reihe *f.* 2 *geog* Kette *f.* 3 Reichweite *f.* 4 Kollektion *f.* 5 Herd *m.* *vt* 1 einreihen. 2 durchstreifen. *vi* 1 sich erstrecken. 2 reichen. 3 streifen.

rank[1] (ræŋk) *n* 1 Reihe *f.* 2 Rang *m.* 3 Stand *m.* Klasse *f.* *vt* 1 einordnen. 2 rangieren. *vi* gehören. **rank and file** *n* 1 Mannschaftstand *m.* 2 die Masse *f.*

rank[2] (ræŋk) *adj* 1 üppig, überwuchert. 2 stinkend. 3 unanständig. 4 rein, kraß.

rankle (´ræŋkəl) *vi* nagen, wühlen.

ransack (´rænsæk) *vt* durchwühlen, plündern.

ransom (´rænsəm) *n* Lösegeld *neu.* *vt* loskaufen.

rap (ræp) *vi* klopfen. *n* Klopfen *neu.*

rape (reip) *vt* vergewaltigen. *n* Vergewaltigung, Notzucht *f.*

rapid (´ræpid) *adj* schnell, eilig, rapid.

rapier (´reipiə) *n* Rapier *neu.* (Stoß)Degen *m.*

rapture (´ræptʃə) *n* Entzücken *neu.* Verzückung *f.*

rare[1] (rɛə) *adj* selten, rar.

rare[2] (rɛə) *adj* nicht durchgebraten.

rascal (rɑ:skəl) *n* 1 Schurke *m.* 2 Spitzbube *m.*

rash[1] (ræʃ) *adj* 1 übereilt. 2 tollkühn.

rash[2] (ræʃ) *n* Hautausschlag *m.*

rasher (´ræʃə) *n* Speckschnitte *f.*

raspberry (´rɑ:zbri) *n* Himbeere *f.*

rat (ræt) *n* Ratte *f.*

rate (reit) *n* 1 Grad *m.* 2 Verhältnis *neu.* Maßstab *m.* 3 Geschwindigkeit *f.* 4 *comm*

recoil

Kurs m. 5 Gebühr f. 6 pl Gemeindesteuer f. at any rate auf jeden Fall. vt einschätzen.
rather ('rɑ:ðə) adv 1 eher, lieber. 2 ziemlich.
ratio ('reiʃiou) n Verhältnis neu.
ration ('ræʃən) n Ration f. vt rationieren.
rational ('ræʃənəl) adj rational, vernünftig. **rationalize** vt 1 rational erklären. 2 rationalisieren.
rattle ('rætl) vt,vi rasseln, klappern. n 1 Gerassel neu. 2 Klapper f.
raucous ('rɔ:kəs) adj heiser, rauh.
ravage ('rævidʒ) vt verwüsten, verheeren.
rave (reiv) vi rasen, toben, wüten. **rave about** schwärmen für.
raven ('reivən) n Rabe m. **ravenous** adj gefräßig, heißhungrig.
ravine (rə'vi:n) n (Berg)Schlucht f.
ravish ('ræviʃ) vt 1 entzücken, hinreißen. 2 vergewaltigen. 3 fortraffen.
raw (rɔ:) adj 1 rauh. 2 roh. 3 unreif, unerfahren.
ray (rei) n Strahl m.
rayon ('reiən) n Kunstseide f. Rayon neu.
razor ('reizə) n Rasiermesser neu. **electric razor** elektrischer Rasierapparat m. **safety razor** Rasierapparat m. **razor blade** Rasierklinge f.
reach (ri:tʃ) vt (er)reichen. vi reichen. 1 Reichweite f. 2 Bereich m.
react (ri'ækt) vi reagieren. **reaction** n 1 Reaktion f. 2 Rückwirkung f. **reactionary** adj reaktionär. n Reaktionär m.
read* (ri:d) vt,vi lesen.
readjust (ri:ə'dʒʌst) vt wieder anpassen, einstellen. vi sich umorientieren, sich wieder anpassen.
ready ('redi) adj 1 bereit, fertig. 2 schnell. **readily** adv bereitwillig, ohne weiteres.
real (riəl) adj 1 wirklich, tatsächlich. 2 echt, wahr. **real estate** n Grundbesitz m. **really** adv wirklich, tatsächlich. **realism** n Realismus m. **realize** vt 1 verwirklichen. 2 sich vorstellen. 3 begreifen. 4 comm realisieren.
realm (relm) n 1 Reich neu. 2 Bereich m.
reap (ri:p) vt 1 ernten. 2 mähen, schneiden.
reappear (ri:ə'piə) vi wieder erscheinen.
rear¹ (riə) n 1 Rückseite f. 2 Hintergrund m. adj hinterst. **rear admiral** n Konteradmiral m. **rearguard** n Nachhut f.
rear² (riə) vt 1 züchten, (er)ziehen. 2 erheben. vi 1 sich (auf)bäumen. 2 hochfahren.
rearrange (riə'reindʒ) vt neuordnen.
reason ('ri:zən) n 1 Vernunft f. 2 Grund, Anlaß

m. vi vernünftig denken. **reasonable** adj 1 vernünftig. 2 angemessen, annehmbar.
reassure (ri:ə'ʃuə) vt 1 beruhigen. 2 wieder beteuern.
rebate ('ri:beit) n 1 Rabatt m. 2 Zurückzahlung f.
rebel (n,adj 'rebəl; v ri'bel) n Rebell m. adj aufrührerisch. vi sich empören, sich auflehnen.
rebound (v ri'baund; n 'ri:baund) vi zurückprallen. n 1 Rückprall m. 2 Rückschlag m.
rebuff (ri'bʌf) n Abweisung f. vt abweisen.
rebuild* (ri:'bild) vt wiederaufbauen.
rebuke (ri'bju:k) vt tadeln. n Tadel m.
recall (ri'kɔ:l) vt 1 zurückrufen. 2 sich erinnern an. n Widerruf m.
recede (ri'si:d) vi zurückweichen, zurückgehen.
receipt (ri'si:t) n 1 Quittung f. 2 Empfang m.
receive (ri'si:v) vt 1 empfangen. 2 erhalten. 3 annehmen. **receiver** n 1 Empfänger m. 2 comm Konkursverwalter m. 3 (telephone) Hörer m.
recent ('ri:sənt) adj letzt, neu, jung. **recently** adv kürzlich, in letzter Zeit, neulich.
receptacle (ri'septəkəl) n Behälter m.
reception (ri'sepʃən) n 1 Empfang m. 2 Aufnahme f. **receptive** adj empfänglich, aufnahmebereit.
recess (ri'ses) n 1 Pause f. Ferien pl. 2 Nische f. vt einsenken.
recession (ri'seʃən) n 1 Rezession f. Konjunkturrückgang m. 2 Zurücktreten neu.
recipe ('resipi) n Rezept neu.
recipient (ri'sipiənt) n Empfänger m. adj empfänglich.
reciprocate (ri'siprəkeit) vi einen Gegendienst leisten. vt 1 erwidern. 2 austauschen. **reciprocal** adj gegenseitig, wechselseitig.
recite (ri'sait) vt 1 vortragen. 2 Aufzählung f. 3 Bericht m.
reckless ('rekləs) adj 1 unbekümmert. 2 rücksichtslos. 3 fahrlässig.
reckon ('rekən) vt 1 zählen, rechnen. 2 inf meinen, glauben.
reclaim (ri'kleim) vt 1 zurückfordern. 2 urbar machen.
recline (ri'klain) vi sich zurücklehnen.
recluse (ri'klu:s) n 1 Einsiedler m. adj 1 abgeschieden. 2 einsiedlerisch.
recognize ('rekəgnaiz) vt 1 wiedererkennen. 2 (an)erkennen. 3 zugeben. **recognition** 1 Erkenntnis f. 2 Anerkennung f.
recoil (ri'kɔil) vi vt 1 zurückschrecken, zurückfahren. 2 zurückweichen. n Rückstoß m.

259

recollect (rekə'lekt) vt sich erinnern an.

recommence (ri:kə'mens) vt,vi wieder beginnen or anfangen.

recommend n (rekə'mend) vt empfehlen. **recommendation** n Empfehlung f. Vorschlag m.

recompense ('rekəmpəns) vt 1 entschädigen, belohnen. 2 wiedergutmachen. n 1 Entschädigung, Belohnung f. 2 Rückerstattung f.

reconcile ('rekənsail) vt versöhnen.

reconstruct (ri:kən'strʌkt) vt 1 wiederaufbauen. 2 rekonstruieren.

record (v ri'kɔ:d; n,adj 'rekɔ:d) vt 1 aufzeichnen. 2 tech aufnehmen. 3 eintragen. n 1 Niederschrift f. Bericht m. 2 Schallplatte f. 3 sport Rekord m. adj Rekord—. **recording** n Aufnahme f. **record-player** n Plattenspieler m.

recount (ri'kaunt) vt erzählen.

recover (ri'kʌvə) vt 1 wiederfinden, zurückgewinnen. vi sich erholen. **recovery** n 1 Rettung f. 2 Erholung f.

recreation (rekri'eiʃən) n Erholung f. **recreation ground** Sportplatz, Spielplatz m.

recruit (ri'kru:t) vt rekrutieren, anwerben. n Rekrut m. **recruitment** n Rekrutierung f.

rectangle ('rektæŋgəl) n Rechteck neu. **rectangular** adj rechteckig.

rectify ('rektifai) vt berichtigen, korrigieren.

recuperate (ri'kju:pəreit) vi sich erholen. **recuperation** n Erholung f.

recur (ri'kə:) vi wiederkehren, zurückkehren.

red (red) adj rot. n Rot neu. **caught red-handed** auf frischer Tat ertappt. **redcurrant** n Rote Johannisbeere f. **redden** vi 1 erröten. 2 rot werden.

redeem (ri'di:m) vt 1 zurückkaufen. 2 einlösen. 3 wiedergutmachen. 4 (er)retten. 5 rel erlösen. **redemption** n 1 Rückkauf m. 2 Einlösung f. 3 Wiedergutmachung f. 4 (Er)-Rettung f. 5 rel Erlösung f.

redevelop (ri:di'veləp) vt,vi neu entwickeln.

Red Indian n Indianer m.

redress (ri'dres) vt 1 abhelfen, beseitigen. 2 wiederherstellen. n Abhilfe, Behebung f.

reduce (ri'dju:s) vt 1 vermindern. 2 erniedrigen. 3 verwandeln. 4 zwingen. vi abnehmen. **reduction** n 1 Verminderung f. 2 Abnahme f.

redundant (ri'dʌndənt) adj 1 überflüssig. 2 übermäßig. **make redundant** entlassen. **redundancy** n 1 Entlassung f. 2 Überfluß m.

reed (ri:d) n 1 Rohr neu. 2 mus (Rohr)Blatt neu.

reef (ri:f) n (Felsen)Riff m.

reek (ri:k) vi stinken. n Gestank m.

reel[1] (ri:l) n Spule, Rolle f. vt spulen.

reel[2] (ri:l) vi 1 taumeln. 2 schwanken.

re-establish (ri:i'stæbliʃ) vt wiederherstellen.

refectory (ri'fektəri) n 1 Speisesaal m. 2 Mensa f.

refer (ri'fə:) vt verweisen. vi 1 sich beziehen. 2 hinweisen. **referee** n Schiedsrichter m. **reference** n 1 Hinweis m. 2 Bezugnahme f. 3 Quellenangabe f. 4 Zeugnis neu. **referendum** n, pl **-da** Volksabstimmung f. Referendum neu.

refill (v ri:'fil; n 'ri:fil) vt nachfüllen, auffüllen. n Nachfüllung f. Ersatzfüllung f.

refine (ri'fain) vt 1 läutern, raffinieren. 2 verfeinern. **refined** adj 1 raffiniert. 2 kultiviert. **refinement** n 1 Feinheit, Kultiviertheit f. 2 Raffinierung f. **refinery** n Raffinerie f.

reflation (ri'fleiʃən) n Wirtschaftsbelebung f. Reflation f.

reflect (ri'flekt) vt wiederspiegeln. vi 1 zurückstrahlen, reflektieren. 2 nachdenken. **reflection** n 1 Rückstrahlung, Reflexion f. 2 Spiegelbild neu. 3 Überlegung f. **reflector** n 1 Reflektor m. 2 mot Rückstrahler m.

reflex (adj,n 'ri:fleks) adj 1 rückwirkend. 2 Reflex—. n Reflex m. **reflexive** adj gram rückbezüglich, reflexiv.

reform (ri'fɔ:m) n Reform, Verbesserung f. vt reformieren. vi sich bessern. **reformation** n 1 Umgestaltung f. 2 cap rel Reformation f.

refract (ri'frækt) vt brechen.

refrain[1] (ri'frein) vi sich enthalten, unterlassen.

refrain[2] (ri'frein) n mus Refrain, Kehrreim m.

refresh (ri'freʃ) vt 1 erfrischen. 2 erneuern. **refreshment** n Erfrischung f.

refrigerator (ri'fridʒəreitə) n Kühlschrank m.

refuel (ri:'fju:əl) vt,vi (auf)tanken.

refuge ('refju:dʒ) n Zuflucht f. Zufluchtsort m. **refugee** n Flüchtling m.

refund (v ri'fʌnd; n 'ri:fʌnd) vt zurückzahlen. n Rückzahlung f.

refuse[1] (ri'fju:z) vt 1 ablehnen. 2 verweigern. vi sich weigern.

refuse[2] ('refju:s) n Abfall, Müll m.

refute (ri'fju:t) vt widerlegen.

regain (ri'gein) vt wiedergewinnen.

regal ('ri:gəl) adj 1 königlich. 2 prunkvoll.

regard (ri'ga:d) vt 1 ansehen, betrachten. 2 berücksichtigen. n 1 Rücksicht f. 2 Achtung f. **regardless** adj, adv ohne Rücksicht.

regatta (ri'gɑ:tə) n Regatta f.

regent ('ri:dʒənt) n Regent m.

regime (rei'ʒi:m) n Regime neu.

regiment ('redʒimənt) n Regiment neu. vt reglementieren. **regimental** adj Regiments—.

region ('ri:dʒən) n Gegend f. Gebiet neu. Bereich m. **in the region of** ungefähr.

register ('redʒistə) n 1 Liste f. Verzeichnis neu. 2 mus,lit Register neu. vt 1 eintragen. 2 zeigen. vi sich eintragen, sich (an)melden. **registrar** n Standesbeamte(r) m.

regress (ri'gres) vi zurückgehen. n Rückschritt m.

regret (ri'gret) vt bedauern. n Bedauern neu. **regrettable** adj bedauerlich.

regular ('regjulə) adj 1 regelmäßig. 2 ordentlich. 3 gewöhnlich. **regularity** n Regelmäßigkeit f.

regulate ('regjuleit) vt regeln, ordnen, regulieren. **regulation** n 1 Vorschrift f. 2 Regelung f.

rehabilitate (ri:ə'biliteit) vt rehabilitieren.

rehearse (ri'hə:s) Th vt,vi proben. **rehearsal** n Probe f.

reign (rein) n Regierung(szeit) f. vi regieren.

reimburse (ri:im'bə:s) vt 1 entschädigen. 2 zurückzahlen.

rein (rein) n Zügel m. vt zügeln.

reincarnation (ri:inka:'neiʃən) n 1 Wiedergeburt f. 2 (Wieder)Verkörperung f.

reindeer ('reindiə) n Renntier, Ren neu.

reinforce (ri:in'fɔ:s) vt 1 verstärken. 2 bewehren. **reinforced concrete** n Eisenbeton m.

reinstate (ri:in'steit) vt wiedereinsetzen.

reinvest (ri:in'vest) vt wieder anlegen.

reissue (ri:'iʃu:) vt wieder ausgeben. n Neuausgabe f.

reject (v ri'dʒekt; n 'ri:dʒekt) vt 1 zurückweisen, ablehnen. 2 abstoßen. n Ausschußartikel m. **rejection** n Zurückweisung, Ablehnung f.

rejoice (ri'dʒɔis) vi sich freuen.

rejoin (ri'dʒɔin) vi erwidern.

rejuvenate (ri'dʒu:vəneit) vt verjüngen.

relapse (ri'læps) n Rückfall m. vi wieder verfallen, rückfällig werden.

relate (ri'leit) vt 1 berichten, erzählen. 2 verbinden. vi sich beziehen. **relation** n 1 Verwandte(r) m. 2 Verhältnis neu. Beziehung f. **relationship** n 1 Verwandtschaft f. 2 Verbindung f. Verhältnis neu.

relative (relativ) adj 1 bezüglich, relativ. 2 verhältnismäßig. n Verwandte(r) m. **relatively** adv verhältnismäßig. **relativity** n Relativität f.

relax (ri'læks) vi 1 sich entspannen. 2 sich lockern. 3 nachlassen. vt 1 lockern. 2 entspannen. 3 abschwächen. **relaxation** n 1 Entspannung f. 2 Lockerung f. 3 Nachlassen neu.

relay (n 'ri:lei; v ri'lei) n 1 sport Staffel f. 2 tech Relais neu. vt 1 übertragen. 2 weitergeben. **relay race** Staffellauf m.

release (ri'li:s) vt 1 freilassen, loslassen. 2 aufgeben. 3 freigeben. n 1 Entlassung, Befreiung f. 2 Aufgabe f.

relent (ri'lent) vi sich erweichen lassen. **relentless** adj unbarmherzig.

relevant ('relavant) adj relevant, belangvoll. **relevance** n Relevanz, Bedeutung f.

reliable ('laiabal) adj zuverlässig, verläßlich. **reliability** n Zuverlässigkeit f.

relic ('relik) n 1 rel Reliquie f. 2 Überbleibsel neu.

relief (ri'li:f) n 1 Erleichterung f. 2 Ablösung f. 3 Entlastung f.

relieve (ri'li:v) vt 1 erleichtern. 2 entlasten. 3 entheben. 4 ablösen.

religion (ri'lidʒən) n Religion f. Glaube m. **religious** adj 1 religiös. 2 fromm.

relinquish (ri'liŋkwiʃ) vt aufgeben, loslassen.

relish ('reliʃ) vt genießen. n 1 pikante Würze f. 2 Geschmack m.

relive (ri:'liv) vt wieder erleben.

reluctant (ri'lʌktənt) adj widerwillig, ungern. **reluctance** n Abneigung f. Widerwille m.

rely (ri'lai) vi **rely on** sich verlassen auf.

remain (ri'mein) vi 1 bleiben. 2 übrigbleiben. **remains** n pl Reste m pl. **remainder** n Rest m.

remand (ri'ma:nd) vt in die Untersuchungshaft zurückschicken. n Untersuchungshaft f.

remark (ri'ma:k) vt 1 bemerken. n Bemerkung f. **remarkable** adj bemerkenswert.

remarry (ri:'mæri) vi (sich) wieder (ver)heiraten.

remedy ('remədi) n 1 Heilmittel neu. 2 Gegenmittel neu. vt 1 abhelfen. 2 in Ordnung bringen.

remember (ri'membə) vt 1 sich erinnern an. 2 sich merken. 3 grüßen. **remembrance** n 1 Erinnerung f. 2 Gedenken neu.

remind (ri'maind) vt erinnern, mahnen.

reminiscence (remi'nisəns) n Erinnerung f. **reminiscent** adj (sich) erinnernd.

remiss (ri'mis) adj nachlässig, säumig. **remission** n Erlaß m. Ermäßigung f.

remit (ri'mit) vt 1 überweisen. 2 erlassen. **remittance** n (Geld)Sendung. Überweisung f.

remnant ('remnənt) n 1 Überrest m. 2 Spur f.

261

remorse (ri'mɔ:s) n Reue f.

remote (ri'mout) adj entfernt, abgelegen.

remove (ri'mu:v) vt 1 entfernen, beseitigen. 2 zurückziehen, wegnehmen. 3 ausziehen. vi umziehen. **removal** n 1 Entfernung f. 2 Abhebung f. 3 Umzug m.

remunerate (ri'mju:nəreit) vt 1 belohnen. 2 vergüten. **remuneration** n 1 Lohn m. Honorar neu. 2 Belohnung f.

renaissance (ri'neisəns) n 1 Wiedergeburt f. 2 cap Renaissance f.

rename (ri:'neim) vt umbenennen.

render ('rendə) vt 1 übergeben. 2 leisten, erweisen. 3 machen. 4 interpretieren, darstellen. 5 übertragen.

rendezvous ('rɒndivu:) n 1 Treffpunkt m. 2 Verabredung f. **rendezvous** neu.

renew (ri'nju:) vt 1 erneuern. 2 wieder aufnehmen.

renounce (ri'nauns) vt verzichten auf, entsagen, ablehnen.

renovate ('renəveit) vt renovieren, erneuern.

renown (ri'naun) n Ruhm, Ruf m. Ansehen neu. **renowned** adj berühmt, renommiert.

rent (rent) n Miete f. vt 1 mieten. 2 vermieten. **rental** n Mietbetrag m.

reopen (ri:'oupən) vt,vi wieder (er)öffnen.

reorganize (ri:'ɔ:gənaiz) vt reorganisieren.

repair (ri'pɛə) vt reparieren, ausbessern. n Reparatur, Ausbesserung f.

repartee (repɑ:'ti:) n 1 Schlagfertigkeit f. 2 schlagfertige Antwort f.

repatriate (ri'pætrieit) vt repatriieren.

repay (ri'pei) vt 1 zurückzahlen. 2 erwidern.

repeal (ri'pi:l) vt aufheben. n Aufhebung f.

repeat (ri'pi:t) vt 1 wiederholen. 2 nachsagen. n Wiederholung f.

repel (ri'pel) vt 1 zurücktreiben, zurückschlagen. 2 abweisen, abstoßen, zuwider sein.

repent (ri'pent) vt bereuen. vi Reue empfinden. **repent** of bereuen.

repercussion (ri:pə'kʌʃən) n Rückwirkung f.

repertoire ('repətwɑ:) n Spielplan m. Repertoire neu.

repetition (repə'tiʃən) n Wiederholung f.

replace (ri'pleis) vt 1 ersetzen. 2 wieder hinstellen.

replay ('ri:plei) n sport Wiederholungsspiel neu.

replenish (ri'pleniʃ) vt (wieder) auffüllen.

replica ('replikə) n 1 Kopie f. 2 Ebenbild neu.

reply (ri'plai) vi antworten, erwidern. n Antwort, Erwiderung f.

report (re'pɔ:t) n 1 Bericht m. 2 Gerücht neu. 3 Knall m. vt 1 berichten. 2 melden. vi 1 berichten. 2 sich melden. **reporter** n Reporter, Berichterstatter m.

repose (ri'pouz) n Ruhe f. vi ruhen.

represent (repri'zent) vt 1 vertreten, repräsentieren. 2 darstellen. 3 bedeuten. **representation** n 1 Vertretung, Repräsentation f. 2 Darstellung f. 3 Vorstellung, Aufführung f. **representative** adj 1 darstellend. 2 (stell-) vertretend. 3 typisch. n 1 Vertreter, Repräsentant m. 2 Beauftragte(r) m.

repress (ri'pres) vt 1 unterdrücken. 2 verdrängen. **repression** n 1 Unterdrückung f. 2 Verdrängung f.

reprieve (ri'pri:v) vt begnadigen. n Begnadigung, Gnadenfrist f.

reprimand (repri'mɑ:nd) n Verweis m. vt einen Verweis erteilen.

reprint (v ri:'print; n 'ri:print) vt neu auflegen or drucken. n Neudruck m.

reprisal (ri'praizəl) n Repressalie f.

reproach (ri'proutʃ) vt vorwerfen. n Vorwurf m. **reproachful** adj vorwurfsvoll.

reproduce (ri:prə'dju:s) vt 1 (wieder) hervorbringen. 2 wiedergeben. 3 erzeugen. 4 kopieren. vi sich fortpflanzen. **reproduction** n 1 Wiedergabe f. 2 Kopie, Nachbildung f. 3 Fortpflanzung, Vermehrung f.

reptile ('reptail) n Kriechtier, Reptil neu.

republic (ri'pʌblik) n Republik f.

repudiate (ri'pju:dieit) vt 1 nicht anerkennen. 2 ablehnen, abweisen.

repugnant (ri'pʌgnənt) adj zuwider, widerlich.

repulsion (ri'pʌlʃən) n 1 Widerwille m. Abscheu f. 2 Abstoßung f. **repulsive** adj 1 widerwärtig. 2 abstoßend.

repute (ri'pju:t) n Ruf m. vt halten für. **reputed** adj angeblich. **reputable** adj 1 angesehen. 2 geachtet. **reputation** n 1 Ruf m. 2 Ansehen neu.

request (ri'kwest) n Bitte f. Gesuch, Verlangen neu. vt 1 bitten. 2 beantragen.

requiem ('rekwiəm) n Requiem neu.

require (ri'kwaiə) vt 1 verlangen. 2 erfordern.

re-route (ri:'ru:t) vt umleiten.

resale (ri:'seil) n Weiterverkauf m.

rescue ('reskju:) vt 1 retten. 2 befreien. n 1 Rettung f. 2 Befreiung f.

research (ri'sə:tʃ) n 1 Forschung f. 2 Untersuchung f.

resell (ri:'sel) vt weiterverkaufen.

resemble (ri'zembəl) vt ähnlich sein, gleichen. **resemblance** n Ähnlichkeit f.

retrogress

resent (ri'zent) vt übelnehmen. **resentful** adj ärgerlich, aufgebracht. **resentment** n Ressentiment neu.

reserve (ri'zə:v) vt 1 aufbewahren. 2 reservieren. 3 sich vorbehalten. n 1 Reserve f. 2 Zurückhaltung f. **reservation** n 1 Vorbestellung, Reservierung f. 2 Vorbehalt m. **reserved** adj 1 reserviert, zurückgelegt. 2 zurückhaltend.

reservoir ('rezəvwa:) n 1 Reservoir neu. 2 Staubecken neu.

reside (ri'zaid) vi wohnen, leben. **residence** n 1 Wohnsitz m. 2 Aufenthalt m. **resident** adj wohnhaft, ansässig. n Einwohner m.

residue ('rezidju:) n Rest m.

resign (ri'zain) vi zurücktreten. vt 1 aufgeben. 2 niederlegen. **resign oneself to** sich versöhnen mit. **resignation** n 1 Rücktritt m. 2 Resignation f.

resilient (ri'ziliənt) adj 1 federnd. 2 elastisch. 3 nicht unterzukriegen.

resin ('rezin) n Harz neu.

resist (ri'zist) vt 1 sich widersetzen. 2 widerstehen. vi sich widersetzen. **resistance** n Widerstand m.

resit (ri:'sit) vt (an exam) wiederholen.

resolve (ri'zɔlv) vt 1 auflösen. 2 lösen. 3 beschließen. vi 1 sich auflösen. 2 sich entschließen. **resolute** adj entschlossen. **resolution** n 1 Beschluß m. Resolution f. 2 Lösung f. 3 Entschlossenheit f.

resonant ('rezənənt) adj 1 widerhallend. 2 mitschwingend.

resort (ri'zɔ:t) vi **resort to** 1 sich begeben nach. 2 zurückgreifen auf. ~n 1 Mittel neu. 2 Ferienort m. **last resort** letzter Ausweg m.

resound (ri'zaund) vi widerhallen.

resource (ri'zɔ:s) n 1 Hilfsquelle f. 2 Findigkeit f. 3 pl Rohstoffquellen. 4 pl Bodenschätze m pl. **resourceful** adj findig, einfallsreich.

respect (ri'spekt) n 1 Respekt m. Achtung f. 2 Rücksicht f. 3 Hinsicht f. 4 pl Grüße m pl. vt 1 achten. 2 respektieren. **respectable** anständig, respektabel. **respective** adj jeweilig. **respectively** adv beziehungsweise.

respite ('respit) n 1 Frist f. Aufschub m. 2 Ruhepause f.

respond (ri'spɔnd) vi 1 antworten. 2 entgegenkommen. 3 reagieren. **response** n 1 Antwort f. 2 Reaktion f. **responsibility** n 1 Verantwortlichkeit f. 2 Verantwortung f. 3 pl Verpflichtungen f pl. **responsible** adj 1 verantwortlich. 2 verantwortungsbewußt. **respon-**

-sive adj 1 empfänglich. 2 zugänglich. 3 entgegenkommend.

rest¹ (rest) n 1 Ruhe f. 2 Rast f. 3 Pause f. 4 Stütze f. vi 1 ruhen. 2 sich verlassen. vt 1 stützen. 2 begründen. **restless** adj 1 unruhig. 2 ruhelos.

rest² (rest) n 1 Rest m. 2 das Übrige.

restaurant ('restərɔnt) n Restaurant neu.

restore (ri'stɔ:) vt 1 zurückgeben. 2 wiederherstellen. 3 restaurieren. **restoration** n 1 Wiederherstellung f. 2 Rückerstattung f. 3 cap Restauration f.

restrain (ri'strein) vt 1 zurückhalten. 2 hindern. 3 einschränken. **restraint** n 1 Zurückhaltung f. 2 Zwang m.

restrict (ri'strikt) vt einschränken, beschränken.

result (ri'zʌlt) n Ergebnis neu. Folge f. vi 1 sich ergeben. 2 zur Folge haben.

resume (ri'zju:m) vt 1 wiederaufnehmen. 2 zurücknehmen.

résumé ('rezumei) n Zusammenfassung f. Resümee neu.

resurrect (rezə'rekt) vt 1 ausgraben. 2 wieder aufleben lassen. **resurrection** n Auferstehung f.

retail ('ri:teil) n Kleinhandel m. adj Einzelhandels—. vt im kleinen verkaufen. adv en detail.

retain (ri'tein) vt 1 bewahren. 2 zurückhalten.

retaliate (ri'tælieit) vi sich rächen, Vergeltung üben. **retaliation** n Vergeltung f.

retard (ri'ta:d) vt 1 verzögern, verlangsamen. **retarded** adj med zurückgeblieben.

reticent ('retisənt) adj verschwiegen, zurückhaltend.

retina ('retinə) n Netzhaut, Retina f.

retire (ri'taiə) vi 1 in den Ruhestand treten. 2 sich zurückziehen. vt 1 in den Ruhestand versetzen.

retort¹ (ri'tɔ:t) vi erwidern. n Erwiderung f.

retort² (ri'tɔ:t) n sci Retorte f.

retrace (ri'treis) vt zurückverfolgen.

retract (ri'trækt) vt 1 zurücknehmen. 2 widerrufen. 3 einziehen.

retreat (ri'tri:t) n 1 Rückzug m. 2 Zurückweichen neu. 3 Zuflucht f. vi 1 sich zurückziehen. 2 zurückweichen.

retrieve (ri'tri:v) vt 1 wiederbekommen. 2 wiedergewinnen.

retrograde ('retrəgreid) adj 1 rückläufig. 2 rückschrittlich. 3 retrograd.

retrogress (retrə'gres) vi zurückgehen, sich verschlechtern.

retrospect ('retrəspekt) n Rückblick m. **in retrospect** rückblickend.

return (ri'tə:n) vi 1 zurückkehren. vt 1 zurückgeben. 2 erwidern. n 1 Rückkehr f. 2 Rückgabe f. 3 comm Umsatz m. 4 Bericht m.

reunite (ri:ju:'nait) vt wiedervereinigen.

reveal (ri'vi:l) vi 1 offenbaren, enthüllen. 2 zeigen. **revelation** n Offenbarung, Enthüllung f.

revel ('revəl) vi sich weiden an.

revenge (ri'vendʒ) n Rache f. vt (sich) rächen.

revenue ('revənju:) n Einkommen neu. Einnahmen f pl.

reverberate (ri'və:bəreit) vi widerhallen, reflektiert werden.

reverence ('revərəns) n 1 Ehrfurcht f. 2 Verehrung f.

reverse (ri'və:s) adj umgekehrt. n 1 Gegenteil neu. 2 Rückseite f. 3 Rückschlag m. 4 tech,mot Rückwärtsgang m. vt 1 umkehren, umdrehen. 2 rückwärts fahren. vi rückwärts fahren.

revert (ri'və:t) vi 1 zurückfallen. 2 sich zurückverwandeln.

review (ri'vju:) n 1 Überblick m. 2 Nachprüfung f. 3 Rezension, Besprechung f. 4 Rundschau f. vt 1 nachprüfen. 2 überblicken. 3 rezensieren.

revise (ri'vaiz) vt 1 überprüfen. 2 verbessern, bearbeiten. vi studieren.

revive (ri'vaiv) vt wiederbeleben.

revoke (ri'vouk) vt widerrufen, aufheben.

revolt (ri'voult) vi sich erheben, rebellieren. vt abstoßen. n Revolte f. Aufstand m. **revolting** adj abstoßend.

revolution (revə'lu:ʃən) n 1 pol Revolution f. 2 Umdrehung f.

revolve (ri'volv) vi sich drehen. vt kreisen. **revolver** n Revolver m.

revue (ri'vju:) n Revue f.

revulsion (ri'vʌlʃən) n Abscheu m. Ekel m.

reward (ri'wɔ:d) n Belohnung f. vt belohnen.

rhetoric ('retarik) n Rhetorik, Redekunst f. **rhetorical** adj rhetorisch.

rheumatism ('ru:matizəm) n Rheumatismus m.

Rhine (rain) n Rhein m. **Rhineland-Palatinate** n Rheinland-Pfalz neu.

rhinoceros (rai'nɔsərəs) n Nashorn neu.

Rhodesia (rou'di:ʃə) n Rhodesien f. **Rhodesian** adj rhodesisch. n Rhodesier m.

rhododendron (roudə'dendrən) n Rhododendron m,neu.

rhubarb ('ru:ba:b) n Rhabarber m.

rhyme (raim) n Reim m. vt,vi reimen.

rhythm ('riðəm) n Rhythmus m.

rib (rib) n Rippe f.

ribbon ('ribən) n Band neu. Streifen m.

rice (rais) n Reis m.

rich (ritʃ) adj 1 reich. 2 fett. 3 voll. 4 kräftig.

rickety ('rikiti) adj wackelig, baufällig.

rid (rid) vt befreien. adj los, frei. **get rid of** los werden.

riddance ('ridns) n Loswerden neu. Befreiung f. **good riddance** den wäre ich glücklich los.

riddle¹ ('ridl) n Rätsel neu.

riddle² ('ridl) vt 1 durchlöchern. 2 durchsieben.

ride (raid) vt,vi 1 reiten. 2 fahren. n 1 Ritt m. 2 Fahrt f.

ridge (ridʒ) n 1 geog Kamm m. 2 Rücken m.

ridicule ('ridikju:l) n Spott m. Verspottung f. vt verspotten, lächerlich machen. **ridiculous** adj lächerlich.

rife (raif) adj 1 weit verbreitet. 2 zahlreich. 3 voll von.

rifle¹ ('raifəl) n mil Gewehr neu. Büchse f.

rifle² ('raifəl) vt plündern, berauben.

rift (rift) n 1 Spalt m. 2 Riß m.

rig (rig) n 1 naut Takelwerk neu. 2 Ausrüstung f. vt 1 einrichten. 2 (auf)takeln.

right (rait) adj 1 richtig. 2 recht. n 1 Recht neu. 2 Rechte f. adv 1 richtig. 2 rechts. 3 sehr, ganz. vt 1 aufrichten. 2 in Ordnung bringen. **right angle** n rechter Winkel m. **right-hand** adj recht. **right-handed** adj rechtshändig. **right of way** n 1 Vorfahrtsrecht neu. 2 Wegerecht neu. **right wing** n rechter Flügel m. adj Rechts—, rechtradikal.

righteous ('raitʃəs) adj gerecht, rechtschaffen.

rigid ('ridʒid) adj 1 steif. 2 unbeugsam.

rigour ('rigə) n 1 Strenge f. 2 Härte f.

rim (rim) n Rand m. Kante f.

rind (raind) n Rinde, Schale f.

ring¹ (riŋ) n 1 Ring m. 2 Kreis m. 3 Bande f. vt einkreisen. **ringleader** n Rädelsführer m. **ringroad** n Ringstraße f.

ring² (riŋ) vt 1 läuten. 2 erklingen. 3 anrufen. vi läuten, klingeln, ertönen. **ring up** anrufen. ~n 1 Klingeln, Geklingel neu. 2 Klang m. 3 inf Anruf m.

rink (riŋk) n Eisbahn f.

rinse (rins) vt (aus)spülen.

riot ('raiət) n Aufruhr, Tumult m. vi an einem Aufruhr teilnehmen. **run riot** 1 sich austoben. 2 umherschwärmen.

rip (rip) vt (zer)reißen. vi reißen. n Riß m.

ripe (raip) adj reif. **ripen** vi reifen, reif werden. vt reifen lassen.

ripple ('ripəl) *n* kleine Welle *f*. *(vi)*,*vt* (sich) kräuseln.

rise (raiz) *vi* 1 aufstehen. 2 sich erheben. 3 sich empören. 4 aufgehen. 5 (an)steigen. *n* 1 Steigen *neu*. 2 Erhebung *f*. 3 Aufstieg *m*. 4 Erhöhung *f*.

risk (risk) *n* Risiko *neu*. *vt* riskieren, wagen.

rissole ('risoul) *n cul* Frikadelle *f*.

rite (rait) *n* Ritus *m*. Zeremonie *f*.

ritual ('ritjuəl) *adj* feierlich. *n* Ritual *neu*.

rival ('raivəl) *n* Rivale, Nebenbuhler *m*. *adj* rivalisierend, wetteifernd. *vt* wetteifern mit, rivalisieren mit. **rivalry** *n* Rivalität, Wetteifer *m*.

river ('rivə) *n* Fluß, Strom *m*. **riverbed** *n* Flußbett *neu*. **riverside** *n* Flußufer *neu*.

rivet ('rivit) *n* Niet *m*. Niete *f*. *vt* 1 (ver)nieten. 2 (attention) fesseln.

road (roud) *n* 1 (Land)Straße *f*. 2 Weg *m*. **roadblock** *n* Straßensperre *f*. **roadside** *n* Straßenrand *m*.

roam (roum) *vi* umherstreifen. *vt* durchstreifen.

roar (rɔː) *vi* brüllen. *n* Gebrüll *neu*.

roast (roust) *vt* braten, rösten. *n* Braten *m*. *adj* gebraten, geröstet.

rob (rɔb) *vt* (be)rauben. **robber** *n* Räuber *m*.

robe (roub) *n* 1 Gewand, Kleid *neu*. 2 *rel*,*law* Talar *m*.

robin ('rɔbin) *n* Rotkehlchen *neu*.

robot ('roubɔt) *n* Roboter *m*.

robust (rou'bʌst) *adj* stark, kräftig, robust.

rock[1] (rɔk) *n* 1 Gestein *neu*. 2 Fels(en) *m*. **rock-bottom** *adj* allerniedrigst. **rockery** *n* Steingarten *m*.

rock[2] (rɔk) *vt*,*vi* schaukeln. **rocker** *n* 1 Kufe *f*. 2 *tech* Wippe *f*. **rocking-chair** *n* Schaukelstuhl *m*. **rocking-horse** *n* Schaukelpferd *neu*.

rocket ('rɔkit) *n* Rakete *f*. *vi* hochschießen.

rod (rɔd) *n* 1 Rute *f*. 2 Stange *f*.

rode (roud) *v* see **ride**.

rodent ('roudnt) *n* Nagetier *neu*.

roe (rou) *n* Fischlaich, Rogen *m*.

rogue (roug) *n* Schurke, Schelm *m*.

role (roul) *n* Rolle *f*.

roll (roul) *vi* 1 rollen. 2 schwanken. 3 sich wälzen. *vt* 1 rollen, wälzen. 2 walzen. 3 zusammenrollen. *n* 1 Rolle *f*. 2 Verzeichnis *neu*. 3 Brötchen *neu*. 4 Rollen *neu*. **rollcall** *n* 1 Namensaufruf *m*. 2 *mil* Appell *m*. **roller** *n* Rolle, Walze *f*. **roller-skate** *n* Rollschuh *m*. *vi* Rollschuh laufen. **rolling pin** *n* Teigrolle *f*.

Roman Catholic *adj* (römisch-)katholisch. *n* Römisch-Katholische(r), Katholik *m*.

romance ('roumæns) *n* 1 *lit* Romanze *f*. 2 Liebschaft *f*. 3 Übertreibung *f*. **romantic** *adj* romantisch. *n* Romantiker *m*. **romanticize** *vt* romantisch darstellen, romantisieren.

Rome (roum) *n* Rom *neu*. **Roman** *adj* römisch. *n* Römer *m*.

romp (rɔmp) *vi* herumspielen, balgen. *n* Balgerei *f*. **rompers** *n pl* Spielanzug *m*.

roof (ruːf) *n* Dach *neu*. *vt* bedachen.

rook (ruk) *n* Saatkrähe *f*. *vt sl* betrügen.

room (ruːm) *n* 1 Zimmer *neu*. Stube *f*. 2 Raum, Platz *m*.

roost (ruːst) *n* 1 auf der Stange sitzen. 2 schlafen. *n* 1 Hühnerstange *f*. 2 Ruheplatz *m*.

root[1] (ruːt) *n* 1 Wurzel *f*. 2 Quelle *f*. Kern *m*. *vi* einwurzeln. **take root** Wurzel schlagen.

root[2] (ruːt) *vi* wühlen. *vt* durchwühlen.

rope (roup) *n* Seil, Tau *neu*. *vt* anseilen.

rosary ('rouzəri) *n rel* Rosenkranz *m*.

rose[1] (rouz) *n* 1 Rose *f*. *adj* rosa. **rosette** *n* Rosette *f*. **rosy** *adj* rosig.

rose[2] (rouz) *v* see **rise**.

rosemary ('rouzməri) *n* Rosmarin *m*.

rot (rɔt) *vi* verfaulen. *n* 1 Fäulnis *f*. 2 *inf* Unsinn, Quatsch *m*. **rotten** *adj* 1 faul, verfault, zersetzt. 2 verdorben. 3 *sl* gemein.

rota ('routə) *n* Dienstturnus *m*. Dienstliste *f*. **rotary** *adj* (sich) drehend. **rotate** *vi* sich drehen. *vt* 1 drehen. 2 wechseln. **rotation** *n* 1 Umdrehung *f*. 2 Abwechselung *f*.

rouge (ruːʒ) *n* (rote) Schminke *f*. Rouge *neu*.

rough (rʌf) *adj* 1 rauh. 2 roh, grob. 3 wild. **roughly** *adv* ungefähr.

roulette (ruː'let) *n* Roulett *neu*.

round (raund) *adj* rund, kreisförmig. *adv* herum, rundum. *n* 1 Runde *f*. 2 Serie *f*. *vt* runden. *prep* um. **roundabout** *adj* indirekt, umständlich, weitschweifig. *n* 1 Kreisverkehr *m*. 2 Karussell *neu*.

rouse (rauz) *vt* (auf)wecken, erregen.

route (ruːt) *n* Route *f*. Weg *m*. *vt* leiten, senden.

routine (ruː'tiːn) *n* Routine *f*. *adj* üblich, Routine—

rove (rouv) *vi* umherschweifen.

row[1] (rou) *n* Reihe, Zeile *f*.

row[2] (rou) *vi*,*vt* rudern.

row[3] (rau) *n inf* Krach, Streit *m*. *vi* streiten.

rowdy ('raudi) *n* Raufbold, Rowdy *m*. *adj* rauflustig.

royal ('rɔiəl) *adj* königlich. **royalty** *n* 1 könig-

rub

licher Rang m. 2 Mitglieder der königlichen Familie pl. 3 Verfasserhonorar neu.
rub (rʌb) vt,vi reiben.
rubber (ˈrʌbə) n 1 Gummi neu. 2 Radiergummi neu. **rubber band** n Gummiband neu.
rubbish (ˈrʌbiʃ) n 1 Müll, Abfall m. 2 inf Quatsch m.
rubble (ˈrʌbəl) n Bauschutt m.
ruby (ˈruːbi) n Rubin m.
rucksack (ˈrʌksæk) n Rucksack m.
rudder (ˈrʌdə) n (Steuer)Ruder neu.
rude (ruːd) adj 1 unhöflich. 2 roh. 3 rauh.
rudiment (ˈruːdimənt) n 1 Rudiment neu. 2 pl Rudimente neu pl. Grundlagen f pl.
rueful (ˈruːfəl) adj kummervoll, reumütig.
ruff (rʌf) n Halskrause f.
ruffian (ˈrʌfiən) n Raufbold m.
ruffle (ˈrʌfəl) vt 1 kräuseln. 2 sträuben. 3 verärgern. n 1 Kräuselung f. 2 Kräuseln neu.
rug (rʌg) n 1 Decke f. 2 Vorleger m. kleiner Teppich m.
rugby (ˈrʌgbi) n Rugby neu.
rugged (ˈrʌgid) adj uneben, rauh, derb.
ruin (ˈruːin) n 1 Ruine f. 2 Verfall m. 3 Trümmer m pl. vt 1 verderben. 2 zugrunde richten, ruinieren.
rule (ruːl) n 1 Regel f. 2 Gewohnheit f. 3 Herrschaft f. 4 Lineal neu. vt 1 regeln, bestimmen. 2 regieren, beherrschen. 3 ziehen. **ruler** n 1 Herrscher m. 2 Lineal neu.
rum (rʌm) n Rum m.
Rumania (ruːˈmeiniə) n Rumänien neu. **Rumanian** adj rumänisch. n 1 Rumäne m. 2 (language) Rumänisch neu.
rumble (ˈrʌmbəl) vi rumpeln. n Rumpeln neu.
rummage (ˈrʌmidʒ) vi (herum)stöbern. **rummage through** durchstöbern.
rumour (ˈruːmə) n Gerücht neu. **rumour has it** es geht das Gerücht.
rump (rʌmp) n Steiß m. **rump steak** n Rumpsteak neu.
run* (rʌn) vi 1 rennen, laufen. 2 fließen. 3 lauten. 4 im Gang sein. vt 1 betreiben. 2 rennen, laufen. 3 in Gang halten. 4 befördern. **run away** davonlaufen. **run out** 1 hinauslaufen. 2 zu Ende gehen. **run over** überfahren. ~n 1 Lauf m. Rennen neu. 2 Zustrom neu. 3 comm Zulauf m. **runner** n 1 Läufer m. 2 Bote m. **runner bean** n Stangenbohne f. **runner-up** n Zweitbeste(r) m. **running** n 1 Laufen, Rennen neu. 2 Betrieb m. **runway** n aviat Startbahn, Landebahn f.
rung¹ (rʌŋ) v see ring².

rung² (rʌŋ) n 1 (of a ladder) Sprosse f. 2 Stufe f.
rupture (ˈrʌptʃə) n Bruch, Riß m. vt sprengen, brechen, (zer)reißen. vi einen Bruch or Riß bekommen.
rural (ˈruərəl) adj ländlich, Land—.
rush¹ (rʌʃ) vi (sich) stürzen, stürmen. vt 1 drängen, hetzen. 2 sich stürzen auf. n 1 Hast f. 2 Andrang m. **rush hour** Hauptverkehrszeit f.
rush² (rʌʃ) n bot Binse f.
Russia (ˈrʌʃə) n Rußland neu. **Russian** adj russisch. n 1 Russe m. 2 (language) Russisch neu.
rust (rʌst) n Rost m. vi (ver)rosten. **rusty** adj 1 verrostet. 2 außer Übung.
rustic (ˈrʌstik) adj 1 bäuerisch. 2 ländlich, rustikal.
rustle (ˈrʌsəl) vi,(vt) rascheln (mit). n Geraschel neu.
rut (rʌt) n 1 Furche f. 2 (Rad)Spur f. **be in a rut** stagnieren.
ruthless (ˈruːθləs) adj 1 erbarmungslos. 2 rücksichtslos.
rye (rai) n Roggen m.

S

Sabbath (ˈsæbəθ) n Sabbat m.
sable (ˈseibəl) n Zobel m.
sabotage (ˈsæbətɑːʒ) n Sabotage f. vt sabotieren.
sabre (ˈseibə) n Säbel m.
saccharin (ˈsækərin) n Saccharin neu.
sachet (ˈsæʃei) n 1. Sachet neu. 2 Schampoobeutel m. 3 Duftkissen neu.
sack (sæk) n Sack m. **get the sack** sl entlassen werden. ~vt sl entlassen.
sacrament (ˈsækrəmənt) n Sakrament neu.
sacred (ˈseikrid) adj heilig, geweiht.
sacrifice (ˈsækrifais) n 1 Opfer neu. 2 Verlust m. vt opfern.
sacrilege (ˈsækrilidʒ) n Sakrileg neu. Entweihung, Kirchenschändung f.
sad (sæd) adj 1 traurig. 2 ernst, schlimm. 3 düster. **sadden** vt betrüben, traurig machen. vi traurig werden.
saddle (ˈsædl) n 1 Sattel m. vt satteln.
sadism (ˈseidizəm) n Sadismus m. **sadist** n Sadist m. **sadistic** adj sadistisch.
safari (səˈfɑːri) n Safari f.
safe (seif) adj 1 sicher. 2 heil. 3 vorsichtig. **play**

266

safe kein Risiko eingehen. ~*n* Geldschrank, Safe *m*. **safeguard** *n* Vorsichtsmaßnahme *f*. Schutz *m*. *vt* 1 schützen. 2 sichern. **safety** *n* Sicherheit *f*. **safety belt** *n* Sicherheitsgürtel *m*. **safety pin** *n* Sicherheitsnadel *f*.

saffron ('sæfrən) *n* Safran *m*. *adj* safrangelb.

sag (sæg) *vi* 1 sacken. 2 nachlassen.

saga ('sɑːgə) *n* Saga *f*.

sage[1] (seidʒ) *n* Weise(r) *m*. *adj* weise.

sage[2] (seidʒ) *n* Salbei *m*,*f*.

Sagittarius (sædʒi'tɛəriəs) *n* Schütze *m*.

sago ('seigou) *n* Sago *m*.

said (sed) *v* see **say**.

sail (seil) *n* 1 Segel *neu*. 2 Seefahrt *f*. *vi*,*vt* segeln, fahren. **sailor** *n* Matrose, Seemann *m*.

saint (seint) *n* Heilige(r) *m*.

sake (seik) *n* **for the sake of** um...willen. **for my sake** um meinetwillen.

salad ('sæləd) *n* Salat *m*. **salad dressing** *n* Salatsoße *f*.

salami (sə'lɑːmi) *n* Salami *f*.

salary ('sæləri) *n* Gehalt *neu*. *vt* besolden.

sale (seil) *n* 1 Verkauf *m*. 2 Ausverkauf *m*. 3 Absatz *m*. **salesman** *n* Verkäufer *m*.

saliva (sə'laivə) *n* Speichel *m*. **salivate** *vi* Speichel absondern.

sallow ('sælou) *adj* bläßlich, gelblich.

salmon ('sæmən) *n* Lachs *m*.

salon ('sælɔn) *n* Salon *m*.

saloon (sə'luːn) *n* Salon, Saal *m*. **saloon car** *n* Limousine *f*.

salt (sɔːlt) *n* Salz *neu*. *adj* salzig, Salz— *vt* (ein)salzen. **salt-cellar** *n* Salzfäßchen *neu*. **salty** *adj* salzig.

salute (sə'luːt) *n* 1 Gruß *m*. 2 *mil* Ehrenbezeichnung *f*. *vi* grüßen. *vt* 1 (be)grüßen. 2 *mil* salutieren vor.

salvage ('sælvidʒ) *n* Bergung *f*. *vt* bergen.

salvation (sæl'veiʃən) *n* 1 *rel* Erlösung *f*. 2 (Er)Rettung *f*.

same (seim) *adj*,*pron* derselbe, der gleiche. *adv* ebenso. **all the same** trotzdem.

sample ('sɑːmpəl) *n* 1 Probe *f*. 2 Auswahl *f*. 3 Muster *neu*. *vt* (aus)probieren.

sanatorium (sænə'tɔːriəm) *n*, *pl* **-iums** *or* **-ia** Sanatorium *neu*. Heilanstalt *f*.

sanction ('sæŋkʃən) *n* 1 Sanktion, Billigung *f*. 2 Zwangsmaßnahme *f*. *vt* billigen, gutheißen.

sanctity ('sæŋktiti) *n* Heiligkeit *f*.

sanctuary ('sæŋktʃuəri) *n* 1 Asyl *neu*. 2 *rel* Heiligtum *neu*.

sand (sænd) *n* 1 Sand *m*. 2 *pl* Sandfläche *f*. Strand *m*.

sandal ('sændl) *n* Sandale *f*.

sandwich ('sænwidʒ) *n* Sandwich, belegtes Brot, Butterbrot *neu*.

sane (sein) *adj* 1 geistig gesund. 2 vernünftig.

sang (sæŋ) *v* see **sing**.

sanitary ('sænitri) *adj* gesundheitlich, hygienisch. **sanitary towel** *n* Damenbinde *f*.

sank (sæŋk) *v* see **sink**.

sap (sæp) *n bot* Saft *m*.

sapphire ('sæfaiə) *n* Saphir *m*.

sarcasm ('sɑːkæzəm) *n* Sarkasmus, bitterer Hohn *m*. **sarcastic** *adj* sarkastisch.

sardine (sɑː'diːn) *n* Sardine *f*.

Sardinia (sɑː'diniə) *n* Sardinien *neu*.

sardonic (sɑː'dɔnik) *adj* höhnisch, sardonisch.

sash[1] (sæʃ) *n* Schärpe *f*.

sash[2] (sæʃ) *n* Fensterrahmen *m*. **sash-window** *n* Schiebefenster *neu*.

sat (sæt) *v* see **sit**.

Satan ('seitn) *n* Satan *m*.

satchel ('sætʃəl) *n* Schultasche *f*.

satellite ('sætəlait) *n* Satellit *m*.

satin ('sætin) *n* Atlas, Satin *m*.

satire ('sætaiə) *n* 1 Satire *f*. 2 Spott *m*. **satirical** *adj* satirisch.

satisfy ('sætisfai) *vt* 1 zufriedenstellen, befriedigen. 2 genügen. 3 überzeugen. **satisfaction** *n* 1 Zufriedenheit *f*. 2 Genugtuung *f*.

saturate ('sætʃəreit) *vt* sättigen.

Saturday ('sætədi) *n* Sonnabend, Samstag *m*.

Saturn ('sætən) *n* Saturn *m*.

sauce (sɔːs) *n* 1 Soße *f*. 2 *inf* Frechheit *f*. **saucepan** *n* Kochtopf *m*. **saucer** *n* Untertasse *f*. **saucy** *adj* frech.

Saudi Arabia ('saudi) *n* Saudi-Arabien *neu*.

sauna ('sɔːnə) *n* Sauna *f*.

saunter ('sɔːntə) *vi* schlendern. *n* Schlendern *neu*.

sausage ('sɔsidʒ) *n* Wurst *f*.

savage ('sævidʒ) *adj* wild. *n* Wilde(r) *m*.

save[1] (seiv) *vt* 1 (er)retten. 2 bewahren. 3 (money) sparen. **savings** *n pl* Ersparnisse *f pl*.

save[2] (seiv) *prep* außer, ausgenommen.

saviour ('seiviə) *n* 1 *rel* Erlöser, Heiland *m*. 2 Retter *m*.

savoury ('seivəri) *adj* 1 schmackhaft. 2 würzig. *n* pikantes Gericht *neu*.

saw[1] (sɔː) *n* Säge *f*. *vi*,*vt* sägen. **sawdust** *n* Sägemehl *neu*.

saw[2] (sɔː) *v* see **see**[1].

Saxon ('sæksən) *adj* 1 sächsisch. 2 angelsächsisch. *n* 1 Sachse *m.* 2 Angelsachse *m.*

saxophone ('sæksəfoun) *n* Saxophon *neu.*

say* (sei) *vt, vi* 1 sagen. 2 sprechen. 3 äußern. 4 heißen, bedeuten. *n* Wort *neu.* Rede *f.* **saying** *n* 1 Sprichwort *neu.* 2 Redensart *f.*

scab (skæb) *n* Schorf *m.* Krätze *f.*

scaffold ('skæfəld) *n* 1 (Bau)Gerüst *neu.* 2 Schafott *neu.* **scaffolding** *n* Gerüst *neu.*

scald (skɔ:ld) *vt* 1 (ver)brühen. *n* Verbrühung *f.* **scalding** *adj* 1 brühend. 2 brühheiß.

scale¹ (skeil) *n* 1 *zool* Schuppe *f.* 2 Kesselstein *m. vt* abschuppen.

scale² (skeil) *n* 1 Waagschale *f.* 2 *pl* Waage *f.*

scale³ (skeil) *n* 1 Maßstab *m.* 2 Skala *f.* 3 Ausmaß *neu.* 4 *mus* Tonleiter *f. vt* ersteigen.

scallop ('skɔləp) *n* Kammuschel *f.*

scalp (skælp) *n* Kopfhaut *f.*

scalpel ('skælpəl) *n* Skalpell *neu.*

scampi ('skæmpi) *n* Kaiserhummer *m.*

scan (skæn) *vt* 1 untersuchen, prüfen. 2 abtasten. 3 *lit* skandieren.

scandal ('skændl) *n* 1 Skandal *m.* 2 Verleumdung *f.* **scandalous** *adj* skandalös.

Scandinavia (skændi'neiviə) *n* Skandinavien *neu.* **Scandinavian** *adj* skandinavisch. *n* Skandinavier *m.*

scapegoat ('skeipgout) *n* Sündenbock *m.*

scar (skɑ:) *n* Narbe, Schramme *f. vt* 1 schrammen. 2 entstellen. *vi* vernarben.

scarce (skɛəs) *adj* 1 knapp. 2 spärlich. **scarcely** *adv* kaum.

scare (skɛə) *vt* erschrecken. *n* Schreck(en) *m.*

scarf (skɑ:f) *n* Schal *m.* Halstuch *neu.*

scarlet ('skɑ:lit) *adj* scharlachrot. **scarlet fever** *n* Scharlachfieber *neu.*

scathing ('skeiðiŋ) *adj* scharf, beißend, ätzend.

scatter ('skætə) *vt* 1 (ver)streuen. 2 zerstreuen. *vi* sich zerstreuen.

scavenge ('skævindʒ) *vt* reinigen. *vi* Nährung suchen. **scavenger** *n* 1 Aasgeier *m.* 2 Straßenkehrer *m.*

scene (si:n) *n* 1 Szene *f.* 2 Schauplatz *m.* 3 Bild *neu.* **behind the scenes** hinter den Kulissen.

scenery ('si:nəri) *n* 1 Bühnenbild *neu.* 2 Landschaft *f.*

scent (sent) *n* 1 Geruch, Duft *m.* 2 Parfüm *neu.* 3 Spur *f. vt* 1 riechen. 2 parfümieren.

sceptic ('skeptik) *n* Skeptiker *m.* **sceptical** *adj* skeptisch. **scepticism** *n* Skeptizismus *m.*

sceptre ('septə) *n* Zepter *neu.*

schedule ('ʃedju:l) *n* 1 Arbeitsplan *m.* 2

Fahrplan *m.* 3 Liste *f. vt* 1 aufzeichnen. 2 planen.

scheme (ski:m) *n* 1 Plan *m.* 2 Intrige *f.* 3 Schema *neu. vi* Ränke schmieden, intrigieren.

schizophrenia (skitsou'fri:niə) *n* Schizophrenie *f.* **schizophrenic** *adj* schizophren. *n* Schizophrene(r) *m.*

scholar ('skɔlə) *n* 1 Gelehrte(r) *m.* 2 Studierende(r) *m. f.* 3 Stipendiat *m.* **scholarship** *n* 1 Stipendium *neu.* 2 Gelehrsamkeit *f.*

scholastic (skə'læstik) *adj* 1 akademisch. 2 Schul—, schulisch.

school¹ (sku:l) *n* 1 Schule *f. vt* schulen. **schoolboy** *n* Schüler *m.* **schoolgirl** *n* Schülerin *f.* **schoolmaster** *n* Lehrer, Schulleiter *m.* **schoolmistress** *n* Lehrerin *f.*

school² (sku:l) *n* *zool* Schule *f.* Schwarm *m.*

schooner ('sku:nə) *n* 1 *naut* Schoner *m.* 2 (hohes) Bierglas *or* Weinglas *neu.*

science ('saiəns) *n* 1 Wissenschaft *f.* 2 Naturwissenschaft *f.* **science fiction** *n* Zukunftsroman *m.* **scientific** *adj* wissenschaftlich. **scientist** *n* (Natur)Wissenschaftler *m.*

scissors ('sizəz) *n pl* Schere *f.*

scoff¹ (skɔf) *vi* spotten. *n* Spott *m.*

scoff² (skɔf) *vt sl* fressen.

scold (skould) *vt* ausschimpfen. *vi* schimpfen.

scone (skoun) *n* (flaches) Teegebäck *neu.*

scoop (sku:p) *n* 1 Schaufel *f.* 2 Schöpfkelle *f.* 3 Schub. 4 Erstmeldung *f. vt* schaufeln, schöpfen.

scooter ('sku:tə) *n* (Motor)Roller *m.*

scope (skoup) *n* 1 Spielraum *m.* 2 Gebiet *neu.* Bereich *m.*

scorch (skɔ:tʃ) *vt* 1 versengen. 2 verbrennen. *vi* verbrennen.

score (skɔ:) *n* 1 *sport* (Punkt)Zahl *f.* 2 Rechnung *f.* 4 *mus* Partitur *f.* 5 Kerbe *f. vt* 1 gewinnen. 2 einkerben. 3 (a goal) schießen. *vi* Punkte gewinnen. **scoreboard** *n* Anschreibetafel *f.*

scorn (skɔ:n) *n* Hohn *m.* Verachtung *f. vt* verachten. **scornful** *adj* verächtlich.

Scorpio ('skɔ:piou) *n* Skorpion *m.*

scorpion ('skɔ:piən) *n* Skorpion *m.*

Scotland ('skɔtlənd) *n* Schottland *neu.* **Scot** *n* Schotte *m.* **Scotch** *adj* schottisch. *n* (schottischer) Whisky *m.* **Scots** *n* schottischer Dialekt. *adj* schottisch. **Scottish** *adj* schottisch.

scoundrel ('skaundrəl) *n* Schurke, Schuft *m.*

scour¹ ('skauə) *vt* 1 scheuern. 2 wegwischen.

scour² ('skauə) *vt* durchsuchen, durchstreifen.

scout (skaut) *n* 1 Späher, Kundschafter *m.* 2 Pfadfinder *m. vi, vt* kundschaften, spähen.

scowl (skaul) vi finster blicken. n finsterer Blick m.

scramble ('skræmbəl) vi 1 krabbeln. 2 sich balgen. n 1 Krabbelei f. 2 Balgerei f.

scrap (skræp) n 1 Stückchen neu. 2 Brocken m. Schrott m. vt 1 wegwerfen. 2 verzichten auf. 3 verschrotten. adj Schrott—. **scrapbook** n Einklebebuch neu.

scrape (skreip) vt 1 kratzen, schaben. vi kratzen. n 1 Kratzen neu. 2 Klemme f.

scratch (skrætʃ) vt kratzen. n 1 Kratzen neu. 2 Schramme f. Riß m.

scrawl (skrɔ:l) vt,vi kritzeln. n Gekritzel neu.

scream (skri:m) vi,vt schreien. n Schrei m.

screech (skri:tʃ) vi,vt kreischen, schreien. n Kreischen neu.

screen (skri:n) n 1 Schirm m. 2 (Lein)Wand f. vt 1 (ab)schirmen. 2 überprüfen. 3 (a film) vorführen.

screw (skru:) n Schraube f. vt schrauben. **screwdriver** n Schraubenzieher m.

scribble ('skribəl) vt,vi kritzeln. n Gekritzel neu.

script (skript) n 1 Th Manuskript neu. 2 (of a film) Drehbuch neu. 3 Schrift f.

Scripture ('skriptʃə) n Heilige Schrift f.

scroll (skroul) n 1 Schriftrolle f. 2 Schnörkel m.

scrounge (skraundʒ) vt,vi schnorren, klauen.

scrub[1] (skrʌb) vi,vt schrubben, scheuern. n Schrubben neu. **scrubbing brush** n Scheuerbürste f.

scrub[2] (skrʌb) n Gestrüpp neu. Busch m.

scruffy ('skrʌfi) adj inf schäbig.

scruple ('skru:pəl) n Skrupel m. Bedenken neu. **have scruples** sich ein Gewissen machen. **scrupulous** adj gewissenhaft.

scrutiny ('skru:tini) n 1 Untersuchung f. 2 prüfender Blick m. **scrutinize** vt 1 (genau) prüfen, untersuchen. 2 genau ansehen.

scuffle ('skʌfəl) n Balgerei, Schlägerei f. vi sich balgen, raufen.

scullery ('skʌləri) n Spülküche f.

sculpt (skʌlpt) vt (heraus)meißeln, schnitzen. vi bildhauern. **sculptor** n Bildhauer m. **sculpture** n Bildhauerei, Skulptur f.

scum (skʌm) n 1 Schaum m. 2 Abschaum m.

scurf (skə:f) n 1 Schuppen f pl. 2 Schorf m.

scythe (saið) n Sense f. vt (ab)mähen.

sea (si:) n 1 See f. Meer neu. **by the sea** an der See.

seabed ('si:bed) n Meeresgrund m.

seafront ('si:frʌnt) n Strandpromenade f.

seagull ('si:gʌl) n Möwe f.

seal[1] (si:l) n 1 Siegel neu. 2 Stempel m. 3 Dichtung f. vt 1 (ver)siegeln. 2 bestätigen. 3 abdichten.

seal[2] (si:l) n Seehund m. Robbe f. **sealskin** n Seehundfell neu.

sea-level n Meeresspiegel m. Meereshöhe f.

sea-lion n Seelöwe m.

seam (si:m) n 1 Saum m. Naht f. 2 Spalt m. Schicht f. vt säumen.

seaman ('si:mən) n Seemann, Matrose m.

search (sə:tʃ) vt durchsuchen. 2 erforschen. vi suchen, forschen. n Suche f. **searchlight** n Scheinwerfer f.

seashore ('si:ʃɔ:) n Seeküste f.

seasick ('si:sik) adj seekrank.

seaside ('si:said) n Seeküste f. **go to the seaside** an die See fahren. ~adj See—. **seaside resort** n Seebad neu.

season ('si:zən) n 1 Jahreszeit f. 2 Saison f. **season ticket** n Dauerkarte f. vt 1 cul würzen. 2 ausreifen lassen. **seasoning** n Würze f.

seat (si:t) n 1 Sitz, Platz m. 2 Bank f. 3 Wohnsitz m. 3 Gesäß neu. vt 1 setzen. 2 Raum haben für. **seat-belt** n Sitzgurt m.

seaweed ('si:wi:d) n Alge f.

secluded (si'klu:did) adj abgelegen, abgeschlossen.

second[1] ('sekənd) adj 1 zweite. 2 nächst. **second best** adj zweitbest. **second-class** adj,adv zweiter Klasse. adj zweitrangig. **second-hand** adj aus zweiter Hand, gebraucht. **secondly** adv zweitens. **second-rate** adj zweitrangig, minderwertig. **secondary** adj 1 untergeordnet. 2 sekundär. 3 Neben—. **secondary school** n Oberschule f.

second[2] ('sekənd) n Sekunde f.

secret ('si:krət) n Geheimnis neu. adj geheim, heimlich. **secrecy** n Geheimhaltung, Verschwiegenheit f. **secretive** adj geheimtuerisch.

secretary ('sekrətri) n 1 Sekretär m. Sekretärin f. 2 Schriftführer m. 3 Schreibtisch m.

secrete (si'kri:t) vt 1 verbergen, verheimlichen. 2 anat absondern.

sect (sekt) n Sekte f. **sectarian** adj sektiererisch.

section ('sekʃən) n 1 Abschnitt, Teil m. 2 Abteilung f. 3 Schnitt m. 4 Sektion f.

sector ('sektə) n 1 Abschnitt m. 2 math Sektor m.

secular ('sekjulə) adj weltlich, säkular.

secure (si'kjuə) adj 1 sicher. 2 fest. vt 1 sichern.

2 sicherstellen. 3 festbinden, festmachen. **security** n Sicherheit f.

sedate (si'deit) adj gesetzt, ernst, ruhig. **sedation** n Beruhigung f. **sedative** adj beruhigend, stillend. n Beruhigungsmittel neu.

sediment ('sedimənt) n 1 Satz m. 2 Sediment neu. 3 Ablagerung f.

seduce (si'dju:s) vt verführen. **seduction** n Verführung f.

see*¹ (si:) vt,vi 1 sehen. 2 verstehen. 3 besichtigen, ansehen. 4 besuchen. **see off** fortbegleiten. **see out** hinausbegleiten. **see through** 1 durchschauen. 2 durchführen.

see ² (si:) n Bischofssitz m.

seed (si:d) n 1 Same(n) m. Saat f. 2 Keim m. vi keimen n Sämling neu. **seedy** adj schäbig, mies.

seek* (si:k) vt,vi suchen.

seem (si:m) vi 1 (er)scheinen. 2 aussehen. **seeming** adj anscheinend.

seep (si:p) vi sickern.

seesaw ('si:sɔ:) n Wippe f. vi wippen.

seethe (si:ð) vi 1 sieden, kochen. 2 brodeln.

segment ('segmənt) n Abschnitt m.

segregate ('segrigeit) vt absondern, trennen. vi sich absondern.

seize (si:z) vt 1 ergreifen, packen. 2 an sich reißen. 3 begreifen.

seldom ('seldəm) adv selten.

select (si'lekt) vt aussuchen, auswählen. adj ausgewählt. **selection** n Auswahl f. **selective** adj auswählend, selektiv.

self (self) n, pl **selves** Selbst, Ich neu. pron selbst.

self-assured adj selbstsicher.

self-aware adj selbstbewußt.

self-centred adj egozentrisch, ichbezogen.

self-confident adj selbstsicher.

self-conscious adj 1 befangen. 2 selbstbewußt.

self-contained adj 1 selbständig. 2 zurückhaltend. 3 (in sich) geschlossen.

self-defence n Notwehr, Selbstverteidigung f.

self-discipline n Selbstdisziplin f.

self-employed adj selbständig.

self-expression n Ausdruck der eigenen Persönlichkeit m.

self-indulgent adj schwächlich, genußsüchtig.

self-interest n Eigennutz m.

selfish ('selfiʃ) adj selbstsüchtig, eigennützig. **selfishness** n Selbstsucht f.

self-pity n Selbstbemitleidung f.

self-portrait n Selbstporträt neu.

self-respect n Selbstachtung f.

self-righteous adj selbstgerecht, pharisäisch.

self-sacrifice n Selbstaufopferung f.

selfsame ('selfseim) adj eben derselbe.

self-satisfied adj selbstzufrieden.

self-service n Selbstbedienung f.

self-sufficient adj unabhängig, selbständig.

self-will n Eigensinn m.

sell* (sel) vt verkaufen. vi handeln. **sell out** or **up** ausverkaufen.

Sellotape ('seləteip) n Tdmk Klebestreifen m.

semantic (si'mæntik) adj semantisch. **semantics** n Semantik f.

semaphore ('seməfɔ:) n Semaphor m.

semibreve ('semibri:v) n mus ganze Note f.

semicircle ('semisə:kəl) n Halbkreis m.

semicolon (semi'koulən) n Strichpunkt m.

semidetached (semidi'tætʃt) adj halb freistehend.

semifinal (semi'fainl) n Vorschlußrunde f. Semifinale neu.

seminar ('seminɑ:) n Seminar neu.

semiprecious (semi'preʃəs) adj Halbedel—.

semiquaver (semi'kweivə) n mus Sechzehntelnote f.

semivowel ('semivauəl) n Halbvokal m.

semolina (seməli:nə) n Grieß m.

senate ('senət) n Senat m. **Senator** n Senator m.

send* (send) vt 1 schicken, (ab)senden. **send for** kommen lassen. **send word** mitteilen. **sender** n (Ab)Sender m.

senile ('si:nail) adj altersschwach.

senior ('si:niə) adj 1 älter. 2 Senior—. n 1 Ältere(r) m. 2 Senior m.

sensation (sen'seiʃən) n 1 Empfindung f. 2 Sensation f. **sensational** adj sensationell.

sense (sens) n 1 Sinn m. 2 Empfindung f. 3 Vernunft f. 4 Bedeutung f. **talk sense** vernünftig reden. ~vt empfinden, spüren, fühlen. **senseless** adj 1 sinnlos. 2 bewußtlos.

sensible ('sensəbl) adj 1 verständig, vernünftig. 2 fühlbar. 3 empfänglich. **sensibility** n 1 Empfindungsvermögen neu. 2 Empfindlichkeit f.

sensitive ('sensitiv) adj 1 empfindlich, sensibel, feinfühlig. **sensitivity** n 1 Empfindlichkeit f. 2 Empfindungsvermögen neu. 3 Feingefühl neu.

sensual ('senʃuəl) adj sinnlich. **sensuality** n Sinnlichkeit f.

sensuous ('senʃuəs) adj sinnenfreudig, sinnlich.

sentence ('sentəns) n 1 Satz m. 2 Urteil neu. vt verurteilen.

sentiment ('sentimənt) n 1 Gefühl neu. Empfindung f. 2 pl Gesinnung f. **sentimental** adj sentimental. **sentimentality** n Sentimentalität f.

sentry ('sentri) n Wache f.

separate (v 'sepəreit; adj 'seprit) (vi),vt (sich) trennen, (sich) scheiden. adj getrennt, gesondert. **separation** n Trennung, Scheidung f.

September (sep'tembə) n September m.

septic ('septik) adj septisch, eitrig.

sequel ('si:kwəl) n 1 Folge f. 2 Fortsetzung f.

sequence ('si:kwəns) n 1 (Reihen)Folge f. 2 Szene f.

sequin ('si:kwin) n Zechine f.

serenade (serə'neid) n Ständchen neu. Serenade f. vt ein Ständchen bringen.

serene (si'ri:n) adj 1 heiter. 2 ruhig. **serenity** n 1 Heiterkeit f. 2 Ruhe f.

serf (sə:f) n 1 Leibeigene(r) m. 2 Sklave m.

sergeant ('sa:dʒənt) n 1 mil Feldwebel m. 2 (Polizei)Sergeant m. **sergeant-major** n mil Hauptfeldwebel m.

serial ('siəriəl) adj 1 Fortsetzungs—. 2 serienmäßig. n Fortsetzungsroman m. **serialize** vt in Fortsetzungen veröffentlichen.

series ('siəri:z) n 1 Reihe f. 2 Serie f. 3 Folge f.

serious ('siəriəs) adj ernst, ernsthaft. **seriousness** n Ernst m. Ernsthaftigkeit f.

sermon ('sə:mən) n Predigt f.

serpent ('sə:pənt) n Schlange f.

servant ('sə:vənt) n Diener m.

serve (sə:v) vt,vi 1 (be)dienen. 2 erfüllen. 3 nützen. 4 sport aufschlagen. **it serves him right** das geschieht ihm recht. n sport Aufschlag m.

service ('sə:vis) n 1 Dienst m. 2 Bedienung f. 3 sport Aufschlag m. 4 rel Gottesdienst m. 5 Kundendienst m. 6 mot Service m. **serviceable** adj 1 dienlich. 2 betriebsfähig. **service station** n Tankstelle f.

serviette (sə:vi'et) n Serviette f.

servile ('sə:vail) adj 1 unterwürfig, servil. 2 sklavisch.

session ('seʃən) n Sitzung f. **be in session** tagen.

set (set) vt 1 setzen. 2 stellen. 3 legen. 4 (ein)richten. vi 1 (of the sun) untergehen. 2 cul gerinnen. **set an example** ein Beispiel geben. **set off** sich auf den Weg machen. ~adj 1 fest. 2 bestimmt. 3 vorgeschrieben. n 1 Satz m. Sammlung f. 2 Serie f. **setback** n Rückschlag m. **setting** n 1 Setzen neu. 2 (of a gem) Fassung f. 3 Bühnenausstattung f.

settee (se'ti:) n Sofa neu.

settle ('setl) vt 1 (fest)setzen. 2 erledigen. 3 entscheiden. 4 beruhigen. vi 1 sich ansiedeln. 2 (of the weather) beständig werden. **settle down** sich niederlassen. **settle with** sich begnügen mit. **settlement** n 1 Regelung f. 2 (Be)Siedlung f. **settler** n Siedler m.

seven ('sevən) adj sieben. n Sieben f. **seventh** adj siebente, siebte.

seventeen (sevən'ti:n) adj siebzehn. n Siebzehn f. **seventeenth** adj siebzehnte.

seventy ('sevənti) adj siebzig. n Siebzig f. **seventieth** adj siebzigste.

several ('sevrəl) adj 1 mehrere. 2 einige. 3 besonder, eigen. **several times** mehrmals.

severe (si'viə) adj 1 streng, hart. 2 schwer. 3 heftig. **severity** n 1 Strenge, Härte f. 2 Schwere f.

sew (sou) vt,vi nähen. **sew up** zunähen. **sewing** n Nähen neu. **sewing machine** n Nähmaschine f.

sewage ('su:idʒ) n Abwasser neu.

sewer ('su:ə) n Abwasserkanal m. Kloake f.

sex (seks) n Geschlecht neu. adj Geschlechts—. **sexual** adj geschlechtlich, Geschlechts—, sexuell, Sexual—. **sexual intercourse** n Geschlechtsverkehr neu. **sexy** adj sexy.

sextet (seks'tet) n Sextett neu.

shabby ('ʃæbi) adj schäbig.

shack (ʃæk) n Hütte f.

shade (ʃeid) n 1 Schatten m. Spur f. 3 (of a lamp, etc.) Schirm m. vt 1 beschatten. 2 abschirmen. 3 schattieren. **shady** adj 1 schattig. 2 anrüchig, fragwürdig.

shadow ('ʃædou) n 1 Schatten m. 2 Phantom neu. 3 Spur f. vt 1 beschatten. 2 verfolgen. **shadow cabinet** n Schattenkabinett neu.

shaft (ʃa:ft) n 1 Schaft m. 2 tech Welle f. 3 (of light) Strahl m.

shaggy ('ʃægi) adj zottig.

shake (ʃeik) vt 1 schütteln. 2 erschüttern. vi zittern, wackeln. **shake hands with someone** jemandem die Hand geben. ~n 1 Schütteln neu. 2 Erschütterung f. 3 Beben neu. **shaky** adj 1 wacklig. 2 zitterig.

shall (ʃəl; stressed ʃæl) v mod aux 1 werden. 2 wollen. 3 sollen.

shallot (ʃə'lɔt) n Schalotte f.

shallow ('ʃælou) adj seicht. n Untiefe f.

sham (ʃæm) adj 1 falsch. 2 Schein—. vt vortäuschen, vorgeben. n Täuschung f.

shame (ʃeim) n 1 Scham f. 2 Schamgefühl neu. 3 Schande f. **what a shame!** wie schade! ~vt beschämen. **shamefaced** adj schamhaft, verschämt. **shameful** adj schändlich, schmächlich. **shameless** adj schamlos.

shampoo (ʃæm'pu:) n Shampoo, Haarwaschmittel neu. vt schampunieren.

shamrock ('ʃæmrɔk) n 1 Feldklee m. 2 (Irish emblem) Kleeblatt neu.

shanty[1] ('ʃænti) n Matrosenlied neu.

shanty[2] ('ʃænti) n Bude f. **shanty town** n Elendsviertel neu. schäbige Vorstadt f.

shape (ʃeip) n Gestalt, Form f. **in good shape** in gutem Zustand. ~vt gestalten, formen, bilden. vi sich entwickeln. **shapely** adj wohlgestaltet.

share (ʃɛə) n 1 Anteil m. 2 Beitrag m. 3 comm Aktie f. **have a share in** teilhaben an. **shareholder** n Aktionär m. vt teilen. **share out** verteilen.

shark (ʃɑ:k) n 1 Hai(fisch) m. 2 Gauner m.

sharp (ʃɑ:p) adj 1 scharf. 2 spitz. 3 schrill. n mus Kreuz neu. **sharp-sighted** adj scharfsichtig. **sharpen** vt 1 (ver)schärfen. 2 (a pencil) spitzen. **sharpener** n 1 Schärfer m. 2 Spitzer m. **sharpness** n Schärfe f.

shatter ('ʃætə) vt zerschmettern, zerbrechen. **shattered** adj 1 erschüttert. 2 erschöpft.

shave (ʃeiv) vt 1 rasieren. 2 (wood) (ab)schälen. vi sich rasieren. n Rasieren neu. **have a close shave** knapp davonkommen.

shawl (ʃɔ:l) n Schal m.

she (ʃi:) pron 3rd pers s sie.

sheaf (ʃi:f) n 1 Garbe f. 2 Bündel neu.

shear[*] (ʃiə) vt scheren. **shears** n pl (große) Schere f.

sheath (ʃi:θ) n Scheide f. **sheathe** vt 1 in die Scheide stecken. 2 umhüllen.

shed[1] (ʃed) n Hütte f. Schuppen m.

shed[*2] (ʃed) vt 1 vergießen. 2 verbreiten. 3 abwerfen.

sheen (ʃi:n) n Glanz m.

sheep (ʃi:p) n, pl **sheep** Schaf m. **sheepdog** n Schäferhund m. **sheepskin** n 1 Schaffell neu. 2 Schafleder neu. **sheepish** adj blöd.

sheer[1] (ʃiə) adj 1 steil. 2 rein, bloß.

sheer[2] (ʃiə) vi naut abscheren.

sheet (ʃi:t) n 1 Bettuch neu. 2 Platte f. 3 Blatt neu. 4 (of water) Fläche f.

shelf (ʃelf) n, pl **shelves** 1 Brett neu. 2 Regal neu. 3 geog Riff m.

shell (ʃel) n 1 Muschel f. 2 Schale f. 3 (of a building) Gerippe neu. 4 Granate f. vt 1 schälen. 2 beschießen, bombardieren. **shellfish** n Schalentier neu.

shelter ('ʃeltə) n 1 Obdach neu. Schutz m. 2

Schirm m. vt 1 (be)schützen. 2 Zuflucht gewähren. vi Schutz suchen.

shelve (ʃelv) vt 1 auf ein Brett stellen. 2 beiseite legen. 3 aufschieben.

shepherd ('ʃepəd) n Hirt, Schäfer m. vt 1 hüten. 2 geleiten, (an)führen.

sheriff ('ʃerif) n Sheriff m.

sherry ('ʃeri) n Sherry m.

shield (ʃi:ld) n 1 Schild neu. 2 Schutz, Schirm m. vt (be)schirmen.

shift (ʃift) vt 1 (ver-, weg-)schieben. 2 umlegen. 3 wechseln. 4 verändern. vi sich bewegen. n 1 Wechsel m. 2 Arbeitsschicht f. **shifty** adj schlau, raffiniert. **shiftwork** n Schichtarbeit f.

shilling ('ʃiliŋ) n Schilling m.

shimmer ('ʃimə) vi schimmern. n Schimmer m.

shin (ʃin) n Schienbein neu.

shine[*] (ʃain) vi scheinen, leuchten. 2 glänzen. vt polieren. n 1 Schein m. 2 Glanz m.

ship (ʃip) n Schiff neu. vt 1 an Bord nehmen. 2 verschiffen. **shipment** n 1 Verschiffung f. 2 Ladung f. **shipshape** adj ordentlich. **shipwreck** n Schiffbruch m. vi scheitern, Schiffbruch leiden. **shipyard** n Schiffswerft f.

shirk (ʃə:k) vt sich drücken, vermeiden. **shirker** n Drückeberger m.

shirt (ʃə:t) n Hemd neu.

shit (ʃit) n tab Kot m. Exkremente pl.

shiver ('ʃivə) n Schauer m. vi 1 schauern. 2 frösteln.

shock[1] (ʃɔk) n 1 (An)Stoß m. 2 Erschütterung f. vt 1 (an)stoßen. 2 erschüttern, schockieren. **shock absorber** n Stoßdämpfer m.

shock[2] (ʃɔk) n (Haar)Schopf m.

shoddy ('ʃɔdi) adj minderwertig, schlecht.

shoe[*] (ʃu:) n 1 Schuh m. 2 (of a horse) Hufeisen neu. vt (a horse) beschlagen. **shoelace** n Schnürsenkel m.

shone (ʃɔn) v see **shine**.

shook (ʃuk) v see **shake**.

shoot[*] (ʃu:t) n 1 bot Sproß m. 2 Jagdgesellschaft f. vt 1 schießen. 2 erschießen. 3 (a film) drehen. vi schießen.

shop (ʃɔp) n 1 Laden m. Geschäft neu. 2 Fabrik, Werkstatt f. vi einkaufen gehen. **shop assistant** n Verkäufer m. **shop floor** 1 Werkstatt f. 2 Arbeiter m pl. **shopkeeper** n Ladeninhaber m. **shoplifter** n Ladendieb m. **shop steward** n Betriebsrat m. **shopwindow** n Schaufenster neu. **shopping** n 1 Einkaufen neu. 2 Einkäufe m pl. adj Einkaufs—.

shore[1] (ʃɔ:) n 1 Strand m. 2 Küste f.

shore[2] (ʃɔ:) n Stütze f. v **shore up** stützen.

shorn (ʃɔːn) *v* see **shear**.

short (ʃɔːt) *adj* 1 kurz. 2 klein. 3 knapp. **short cut** *n* Abkürzung *f*. **shorts** *n pl* kurze Hose *f*. **shorten** *vt* (ab-, ver-)kürzen. *vi* kürzer werden.

shortage (ˈʃɔːtidʒ) *n* Mangel *m*. Knappheit *f*.

shortbread (ˈʃɔːtbred) *n* Mürbekuchen *m*.

shortcoming (ˈʃɔːtkʌmiŋ) *n* Unzulänglichkeit *f*.

shorthand (ˈʃɔːthænd) *n* Stenographie *f*. **shorthand typist** *n* Stenotypistin *f*.

shortlived (ˈʃɔːtlivd) *adj* kurzlebig.

short-sighted *adj* kurzsichtig.

short-tempered *adj* reizbar, leicht aufgebracht.

short-term *adj* kurzfristig.

short-wave *adj* Kurzwellen—.

shot[1] (ʃɔt) *n* 1 Schuß *m*. 2 Kugel *f*. 3 Schütze *m*. 4 *sport* Stoß *m*. 5 *phot* Aufnahme *f*. 6 Schrotkugel *f*. **have a shot at** *inf* versuchen. **like a shot** wie der Blitz. **shotgun** *n* Schrotflinte *f*.

shot[2] (ʃɔt) *v* see **shoot**.

should (ʃəd; *stressed* ʃud) *v* see **shall**.

shoulder (ˈʃouldə) *n* Schulter *f*. *vt* auf sich nehmen. **shoulder-blade** *n* Schulterblatt *neu*.

shout (ʃaut) *vi* 1 (laut) schreien. 2 jauchzen. *n* (lauter) Schrei *m*.

shove (ʃʌv) *n* Schub *m*. *vt* schieben.

shovel (ˈʃʌvəl) *n* Schaufel *f*. *vt* schaufeln.

show[*] (ʃou) *vt* 1 zeigen. 2 ausstellen. 3 erweisen. *vi* erscheinen. **show off** angeben, sich aufspielen. ~*n* 1 Schau *f*. 2 Ausstellung *f*. 3 Anschein *m*. 4 *Th* Aufführung *f*. **show business** *n* Unterhaltungsindustrie *f*. **showcase** *n* Schaukasten *m*. **show-jumping** *n* Schauspringen *neu*. **showroom** *n* Ausstellungsraum *m*.

shower (ˈʃauə) *n* 1 (Regen)Schauer *m*. 2 Dusche *f*. 3 Fülle *f*. *vt* 1 herabschütten. 2 übergießen. *vi* sich duschen. **showerproof** *adj* wasserdicht.

shrank (ʃræŋk) *v* see **shrink**.

shred (ʃred) *n* 1 Schnitzel *m*. 2 Fetzen *m*. *vt* 1 (zer)schnitzeln. 2 zerfetzen. 3 reißen.

shrew (ʃruː) *n* 1 *zool* Spitzmaus *f*. 2 *inf* Kratzbürste *f*.

shrewd (ʃruːd) *adj* scharfsinnig.

shriek (ʃriːk) *vi* schreien, kreischen. *n* (greller) Schrei *m*.

shrill (ʃril) *adj* 1 schrill, gellend. 2 grell. *vi* schrillen, gellen.

shrimp (ʃrimp) *n* 1 Garnele *f*. 2 Knirps *m*.

shrine (ʃrain) *n* 1 Reliquienschrein *m*. 2 Altar *m*.

shrink[*] (ʃriŋk) *vi* 1 (ein-, zusammen-)schrumpfen. 2 sich zurückziehen. *vt* einschrumpfen lassen.

shrivel (ˈʃrivəl) *vi,(vt)* schrumpfen (lassen).

shroud (ʃraud) *n* 1 Leichentuch *neu*. 2 Umhüllung *f*. *vt* 1 in ein Leichentuch einhüllen. 2 (ein)hüllen.

Shrove Tuesday (ʃrouv) *n* Fastnachtsdienstag *m*.

shrub (ʃrʌb) *n* Strauch, Busch *m*. **shrubbery** *n* Strauchpflanzung *f*. Strauchwerk *neu*.

shrug (ʃrʌg) *(vi),vt* (die Achseln) zucken. **shrug off** abtun. *n* (Achsel)Zucken *neu*.

shrunk (ʃrʌŋk) *v* see **shrink**. *adj* 1 eingeschrumpft. 2 eingefallen.

shudder (ˈʃʌdə) *vi* 1 schaudern. 2 erbeben. *n* 1 Schauder *m*. 2 Erbeben *neu*.

shuffle (ˈʃʌfəl) *vt* 1 *game* mischen. 2 hin und herschieben. *vi* schlurfen. *n* 1 Mischen *neu*. 2 Schlurfen *neu*. 3 Schiebung *f*.

shun (ʃʌn) *vt* (ver)meiden.

shunt (ʃʌnt) *vt* rangieren. *n* Rangieren *neu*.

shut[*] (ʃʌt) *vt* (ver)schließen, zumachen. *vi* (sich) schließen, zugehen. **shut out** ausschließen. **shut up!** *inf* halt den Mund! ~*adj* zu, geschlossen.

shutter (ˈʃʌtə) *n* 1 Rolladen *m*. 2 *phot* Verschluß *m*.

shuttlecock (ˈʃʌtəlkɔk) *n* Federball *m*.

shy (ʃai) *adj* 1 scheu. 2 schüchtern. *vi* scheuen.

Sicily (ˈsisəli) *n* Sizilien *neu*. **Sicilian** *adj* sizilianisch *n* Sizilianer *m*.

sick (sik) *adj* 1 krank. 2 übel. 3 überdrüssig. 4 *inf* (of humour) schwarz. **be sick** sich erbrechen. **be sick of** satt haben. **sicken** *vi* krank werden. *vt* anekeln. **sickening** *adj* ekelhaft. **sickness** *n* 1 Krankheit *f*. 2 Übelkeit *f*.

sickle (ˈsikəl) *n* Sichel *f*.

side (said) *n* 1 Seite *f*. 2 Flanke *f*. 3 Partei *f*. *adj* Seiten—, Neben—. *v* **side with** Partei ergreifen für. **sideboard** *n* Büffett *neu*. Anrichte *f*. **side effect** *n* Nebenwirkung *f*. **sidelight** *n* Seitenlampe *f*. **sideline** *n* Nebenbeschäftigung, Seitenlinie *f*. **sideshow** *n* Nebenvorstellung *f*. **sidestep** *vi* beiseite treten. **sidetrack** *vt inf* 1 ablenken. 2 abschieben. **sideways** *adv* seitwärts. **siding** *n* Nebengleis *neu*.

sidle (ˈsaidl) *vi* **sidle up to** sich heranschleichen an.

siege (siːdʒ) *n* Belagerung *f*. **lay siege to** belagern.

sieve (siv) n Sieb neu. vt sieben.

sift (sift) vt 1 sieben. 2 prüfen.

sigh (sai) vi seufzen. n Seufzer m.

sight (sait) n 1 Sehkraft f. 2 Anblick m. 3 Sicht f. 4 pl Sehenswürdigkeiten f pl. **catch sight of** erblicken. **know by sight** vom Sehen kennen. ~vt sichten. **sightread** vt vom Blatt singen or spielen. **sightseeing** n Besichtigung von Sehenswürdigkeiten f.

sign (sain) n 1 Zeichen neu. 2 Schild neu. 3 Wink m. vi winken. vt unterschreiben. **signpost** n Wegweiser m.

signal ('sign̩) n 1 Signal neu. 2 Zeichen neu. vi,vt signalisieren.

signature ('signətʃə) n Unterschrift f.

signify ('signifai) vt 1 bedeuten. 2 bezeichnen. **significant** adj 1 bedeutsam. 2 bezeichnend. **significance** n 1 Bedeutsamkeit f. 2 Bedeutung f.

silence ('sailəns) n 1 Schweigen neu. 2 Ruhe f. vt zum Schweigen bringen. **silencer** n 1 Schalldämpfer m. 2 mot Auspufftopf m.

silent ('sailənt) adj 1 still. 2 ruhig. 3 schweigsam. 4 stumm.

Silesia (sai'li:ziə) n Schlesien neu.

silhouette (silu:'et) n Silhouette f. **be silhouetted against** sich abheben gegen.

silk (silk) n Seide f. adj Seiden—. **silkworm** n Seidenraupe f.

sill (sil) n 1 Fensterbrett neu. 2 Schwelle f.

silly ('sili) adj albern, dumm.

silt (silt) n Schlamm m.

silver ('silvə) n 1 Silber neu. adj silbern, Silber—. vt versilbern. vi silberweiß werden.

similar ('similə) adj ähnlich. **similarity** n Ähnlichkeit f.

simile ('simili) n Gleichnis, Simile neu.

simmer ('simə) vi,(vt) sieden (lassen).

simple ('simpəl) adj 1 einfach. 2 einfältig. **simply** adv einfach, nur. **simplify** vt vereinfachen.

simultaneous (siməl'teiniəs) adj gleichzeitig.

sin (sin) n Sünde f. vi sündigen.

since (sins) prep seit. adv seitdem, seither. conj 1 seitdem. 2 da, weil.

sincere (sin'siə) adj aufrichtig, ehrlich. **yours sincerely** Ihr ergebener. **sincerity** n Aufrichtigkeit f.

sinew ('sinju:) n Sehne f.

sing* (siŋ) vt 1 singen. 2 summen. **singer** n Sänger m. Sängerin f.

singe (sindʒ) vt (ver)sengen.

single ('siŋgəl) adj 1 einzig. 2 einzeln. 3 ledig. 4

einfach. v **single out** auswählen. **single file** n Gänsemarsch m. **single-handed** adj,adv allein, eigenhändig. **single-minded** adj 1 zielbewußt. 2 aufrichtig.

singular ('siŋgjulə) adj 1 einzigartig. 2 sonderbar. n gram Singular m. Einzahl f.

sinister ('sinistə) adj unheilvoll, finster.

sink* (siŋk) vi 1 sinken. 2 sich senken. 3 eindringen. vt versenken. n Spülbecken neu.

sinner ('sinə) n Sünder m.

sinus ('sainəs) n (Neben)Höhle f. Sinus m.

sip (sip) n Schlückchen neu. vt nippen.

siphon ('saifən) n 1 Siphon m. 2 Siphonflasche f. vt absaugen.

sir (sə:) n 1 Herr m. 2 cap Sir m.

siren ('sairən) n Sirene f.

sirloin ('sə:lɔin) n cul Lendenstück neu.

sister ('sistə) n 1 Schwester f. 2 med Oberschwester f. **sisterhood** n rel Schwesternschaft f. **sister-in-law** n Schwägerin f.

sit* (sit) vi 1 sitzen. 2 tagen. **sit down** sich (hin)setzen. **sit-in** n Sitzstreik m. **sitting** n Sitzung f. **sitting room** n Wohnzimmer neu.

site (sait) n 1 Lage f. 2 Bauplatz m. 3 Gelände neu.

situation (sitju'eiʃən) n 1 Lage f. 2 Stellung f. **be situated** liegen, sich befinden.

six (siks) adj sechs. n Sechs f. **sixth** adj sechste.

sixteen (siks'ti:n) adj sechzehn. n Sechzehn f. **sixteenth** adj sechzehnte.

sixty ('siksti) adj sechzig. n Sechzig f. **sixtieth** adj sechzigste.

size (saiz) n 1 Größe f. 2 Maß neu. v **size up** inf einschätzen.

sizzle ('sizəl) vi zischen. n Zischen neu.

skate¹ (skeit) n Schlittschuh m. vi Schlittschuh laufen.

skate² (skeit) n Rochen m.

skeleton ('skelətn̩) n 1 Skelett neu. 2 Gerippe neu.

sketch (sketʃ) n 1 Skizze f. 2 Entwurf m. vt 1 skizzieren. 2 entwerfen.

skewer ('skjuə) n Fleischspieß m. vt spießen.

ski (ski:) n Schi or Ski m. vi Schi or Ski laufen. **ski-lift** n Schilift m.

skid (skid) n 1 Rutschen neu. 2 mot Schleudern neu. vi 1 ausrutschen. 2 schleudern.

skill (skil) n Geschicklichkeit f. **skilful** adj geschickt. **skilled** adj gelernt, Fach—.

skim (skim) vt entrahmen. **skim over** dahingleiten über. **skim through** durchblättern.

skimp (skimp) vi knapp halten. **skimpy** adj knapp.

skin (skin) n 1 Haut f. 2 Fell n. 3 Schale f. vt 1 enthäuten. 2 schälen. **skin-diving** n Sporttauchen neu. **skin-tight** adj hauteng. **skinny** adj mager.

skip (skip) vi 1 hüpfen. 2 seilhüpfen. n Sprung m. **skipping-rope** n Springseil neu.

skipper ('skipə) n Schiffsherr, Kapitän m.

skirmish ('skə:miʃ) n Scharmützel neu. vi plänkeln.

skirt (skə:t) n Rock m. vt entlangfahren. **skirting board** n Scheuerleiste f.

skittle ('skitl) n Kegel m.

skull (skʌl) n Schädel m. **skull and crossbones** n Totenkopf m.

skunk (skʌŋk) n Stinktier neu. Skunk m.

sky (skai) n Himmel m. **sky-high** adj himmelhoch. **skylark** n Feldlerche f. **skyline** n Horizont m. **skyscraper** n Wolkenkratzer m.

slab (slæb) n 1 Platte, Tafel f. 2 Holzschwarte f.

slack (slæk) adj 1 schlaff. 2 lose. 3 nachlässig. **slacken** vi 1 schlaff werden. 2 nachlassen. vt 1 schlaff machen. 2 nachlassen.

slacks (slæks) n pl Damenhose f.

slalom ('slɑ:ləm) n Slalom m.

slam (slæm) vt 1 zuschlagen. 2 knallen. vi zuschlagen. n 1 Zuschlagen neu. 2 Knall m.

slander ('slændə) n Verleumdung f. vt verleumden.

slang (slæŋ) n Slang, Jargon m.

slant (slɑ:nt) n Schräge, Neigung f. vi schräg liegen. **slanting** adj schräg, schief.

slap (slæp) n Klaps, Schlag m. vt klapsen, schlagen. **slapdash** adj 1 hastig, übereilt. 2 unbekümmert. **slapstick** n Schwank m.

slash (slæʃ) vt 1 (auf)schlitzen. 2 inf drastisch kürzen. n Schnitt m.

slat (slæt) n Lamelle f. Streifen m.

slate (sleit) n 1 Schiefer m. 2 Schiefertafel f.

slaughter ('slɔ:tə) n 1 Schlachten neu. 2 Blutbad neu. vt 1 schlachten. 2 niedermetzeln. **slaughterhouse** n Schlachthaus neu.

slave (sleiv) n Sklave m. vi inf schuften. **slavery** n Sklaverei f.

sledge (sledʒ) n Schlitten m. vi Schlitten fahren.

sledgehammer ('sledʒhæmə) n Schmiedehammer m.

sleek (sli:k) adj geschmeidig, glatt.

sleep (sli:p) vi schlafen. n Schlaf m. **go to sleep** einschlafen. **sleeper** n 1 Schläfer m. 2 (railway) Schwelle f. **sleeping-bag** n Schlafsack m. **sleeping-car** n Schlafwagen m. **sleeping-pill** n Schlafmittel neu. **sleepwalk** vi nachtwandeln. **sleepy** adj schläfrig.

sleet (sli:t) n Graupelregen m. vi graupeln.

sleeve (sli:v) n Ärmel m. **have something up one's sleeve** etwas im Schilde führen.

sleigh (slei) n Schlitten m.

slender ('slendə) adj 1 schlank. 2 gering.

slept (slept) v see **sleep**.

slice (slais) n 1 Scheibe f. Schnitte f. 2 Kelle f. vt in Scheiben schneiden.

slick (slik) adj 1 glatt. 2 raffiniert.

slide (slaid) vi,(vt) gleiten (lassen). n 1 Gleiten neu. 2 phot Dia(positiv) neu. 3 Schlittenbahn f. **slide-rule** n Rechenschieber m.

slight (slait) adj 1 schmächtig. 2 gering. n Geringschätzung f. vt geringschätzig behandeln. **slightly** adv etwas mehr.

slim (slim) adj 1 schlank. 2 dürftig. vi Schlankheitskur machen, abnehmen.

slime (slaim) n Schlamm m. **slimy** adj schlammig.

sling (sliŋ) n 1 Schleuder f. 2 med Schlinge f. vt 1 schleudern. 2 umhängen.

slink* (sliŋk) vi schleichen. **slink off** sich wegschleichen.

slip[1] (slip) vi rutschen, schlüpfen. vt schlüpfen lassen. **slip on/off** überstreifen/abstreifen. 1 (Aus)Rutschen neu. 2 Fehltritt m. 3 Fehler m. **slippery** adj schlüpfrig, glitschig.

slip[2] (slip) n Zettel m.

slipper ('slipə) n Pantoffel, Hausschuh m.

slippery ('slipri) adj schlüpfrig, glitschig.

slit* (slit) n Schlitz m. Spalte f. vt,vi (zer-, auf-)splittern.

slobber ('slɔbə) vi sabbern. n Sabber m.

sloe (slou) n Schlehe f. 2 Schlehdorn m.

slog (slɔg) vt (heftig) schlagen. vi inf schuften. n 1 Hieb m. 2 Plackerei f.

slogan ('slougən) n 1 Schlagwort neu. 2 Werbeslogan m.

slop (slɔp) vt verschütten. **sloppy** adj 1 labberig. 2 schlampig. **slops** n pl Spülicht neu.

slope (sloup) n 1 Abhang m. 2 Neigung f. vi 1 abfallen. 2 sich neigen. vt abschrägen. **sloping** adj schräg.

slot (slɔt) n Schlitz m. **slot-machine** n 1 Warenautomat m. 2 Spielautomat m.

slouch (slautʃ) vi latschig gehen or sitzen.

slovenly ('slʌvənli) adj schlampig.

slow (slou) adj 1 langsam. 2 schwerfällig. 3 langweilig. vt verlangsamen. vi langsamer werden or gehen.

slug¹ (slʌg) n 1 Schnecke f. 2 Kugel f. **sluggish** adj 1 träge. 2 faul.

slug² (slʌg) vt (mit dem Faust) heftig schlagen. n heftiger Schlag m.

sluice (slu:s) n Schleuse f. vt (aus)spülen.

slumber ('slʌmbə) n Schlummer m. vi schlummern.

slump (slʌmp) n 1 (Preis)Sturz m. 2 Tiefstand, Rückgang m. vi 1 stürzen. 2 hinplumpsen.

slums (slʌmz) n pl Elendsviertel neu.

slung (slʌŋ) v see **sling**.

slur (slə:) vt verschlucken. 2 mus binden. n 1 Fleck, Tadel m. 2 mus Bindebogen neu.

slush (slʌʃ) n 1 Matsch m. 2 inf Kitsch m.

sly (slai) adj schlau. **on the sly** heimlich.

smack¹ (smæk) n (Bei)Geschmack m. v **smack of** schmecken nach.

smack² (smæk) n 1 Klatsch, Klaps m. 2 Schmatz m. vt klatschen, jemandem einen Klaps geben. **smack the lips** mit den Lippen schmatzen.

small (smɔ:l) adj 1 klein. 2 gering. **in a small way** bescheiden. **make someone feel small** einen beschämen. **smallholding** n Kleinbauernbesitz m. **small-minded** adj kleinlich, engstirnig. **smallpox** n Pocken f pl.

smart (smɑ:t) adj 1 heftig. 2 adrett. 3 fein. 4 gescheit. n Schmerz m. vi schmerzen. **smarten up** vt herausputzen. vi sich schön machen.

smash (smæʃ) vt 1 zerbrechen. 2 vernichtend schlagen. vi 1 zerbrechen. 2 zusammenstoßen. 3 krachen. n 1 Krach m. 2 Zusammenbruch m. 3 Zusammenstoß m.

smear (smiə) vt 1 beschmieren. 2 verleumden. n 1 Schmiere f. 2 Fleck m.

smell* (smel) n Geruch m. vt riechen. **smelly** adj übelriechend.

smile (smail) vi lächeln. n Lächeln neu.

smirk (smə:k) vi grinsen. n Grinsen neu.

smog (smɔg) n Smog, rauchiger Nebel neu.

smoke (smouk) n Rauch m. vt 1 rauchen. 2 cul räuchern. vi rauchen.

smooth (smu:ð) adj 1 glatt. 2 fließend. 3 sanft. 4 gewandt. **smoothen** vt also **smooth** 1 glätten. 2 ebnen. **smoothly** adv reibungslos, glatt.

smother ('smʌðə) vt,vi ersticken.

smoulder ('smouldə) vi 1 glimmen, schwelen. 2 glühen.

smudge (smʌdʒ) vt beschmieren. n Klecks m.

smug (smʌg) adj selbstgefällig, überheblich.

smuggle ('smʌgəl) vt schmuggeln. **smuggler** n Schmuggler m. **smuggling** n Schmuggel m.

snack (snæk) n Imbiß m. **snack-bar** n Imbißstube f.

snag (snæg) n 1 Aststumpf m. 2 Schwierigkeit f. Haken m. 3 Nachteil m.

snail (sneil) n Schnecke f.

snake (sneik) n Schlange f. vi sich schlängeln.

snap (snæp) vt 1 schnappen. 2 phot knipsen. 3 knicken. vi 1 (zu)schnappen. 2 knacken. **snap at** anschnauzen. ~n 1 Schnappen neu. 2 Knacks m. **snapshot** n Schnappschuß m.

snarl (snɑ:l) vi,vt knurren. n Knurren neu.

snatch (snætʃ) vt 1 haschen, packen. 2 ergreifen. n 1 Haschen neu. Griff m. 2 Stückchen neu.

sneak (sni:k) vi 1 schleichen. 2 sl petzen. n 1 Schleicher, Kriecher m. 2 sl Petzer m.

sneer (sniə) vi 1 hohnlächeln. 2 spotten. n 1 Hohnlächeln neu. 2 Spott m.

sneeze (sni:z) vi niesen. n Niesen neu.

sniff (snif) vt riechen. vi schnüffeln. **sniff at** die Nase rümpfen über. ~n 1 Schnüffeln neu. 2 Naserümpfen neu.

snip (snip) vt schnipseln. n Schnipsel m.

snipe (snaip) n zool Schnepfe f. vt,vi aus dem Hinterhalt schießen. **sniper** n Heckenschütze m.

snivel ('snivəl) vi 1 aus der Nase triefen. 2 wimmern, schnüffeln, heulen.

snob (snɔb) n Snob, Vornehmtuer m.

snooker ('snu:kə) n eine Art Billardspiel neu.

snoop (snu:p) vi (herum)schnüffeln.

snooty ('snu:ti) adj hochnäsig, arrogant.

snooze (snu:z) vi ein Schläfchen machen. n Schläfchen neu.

snore (snɔ:) vi schnarchen. n Schnarchen neu.

snort (snɔ:t) vi schnauben. n Schnauben neu.

snout (snaut) n 1 Schnauze f. 2 (of a pig) Rüssel m.

snow (snou) n Schnee m. vi schneien. **snowball** n Schneeball m. vt mit Schneebällen bewerfen. **snowdrift** n Schneewehe f. **snowdrop** n Schneeglöckchen neu. **snowflake** n Schneeflocke f. **snowman** n Schneemann m. **snowplough** n Schneepflug m.

snub (snʌb) vt (kurz) abweisen, zurückweisen. n Zurückweisung, Abfertigung f.

snuff (snʌf) n Schnupftabak m. **take snuff** schnupfen.

snug (snʌg) adj 1 behaglich. 2 eng.

snuggle ('snʌgəl) vi **snuggle up to** sich schmiegen an.

so (sou) *adv* so. *conj* deshalb, so. **so that** damit ~ *interj* so, also. **and so on** und so weiter. **so-and-so** *n* so und so. **so-called** *adj* sogenannt. **so-so** *adj,adv* so so.

soak (souk) *vt* 1 durchnässen. 2 durchtränken. *vi* 1 einweichen. 2 durchsickern. **soak up** aufsaugen.

soap (soup) *n* Seife *f*. *vt* einseifen. **soap-powder** *n* Seifenpulver *neu*. **soapy** *adj* seifig.

soar (sɔ:) *vi* 1 sich erheben. 2 sich aufschwingen. 3 schweben. 4 (auf)steigen. 5 *comm* in die Höhe schießen.

sob (sɔb) *vi* schluchzen. *n* Schluchzen *neu*.

sober ('soubə) *adj* nüchtern. *vt* ernüchtern. **sober up** nüchtern werden.

social ('souʃəl) *adj* 1 gesellschaftlich. 2 sozial, Sozial—. **Social Services** *n pl* soziale Einrichtungen *f pl*. **sociable** *adj* gesellig, gemütlich. **socialism** *n* Sozialismus *m*. **socialist** *n* Sozialist *m*. *adj* sozialistisch.

society (sə'saiəti) *n* 1 Gesellschaft *f*. 2 Verein, Verband *m*.

sociology (sousi'ɔlədʒi) *n* Sozialwissenschaft, Soziologie *f*. **sociological** *adj* soziologisch. **sociologist** *n* Soziologe *m*.

sock[1] (sɔk) *n* Socke *f*.

sock[2] (sɔk) *sl vt* (ver)hauen. *n* Schlag *m*.

socket ('sɔkit) *n* 1 *anat* Höhle, Pfanne *f*. 2 *tech* Muffe *f*. 3 (electrical) Steckdose *f*.

soda ('soudə) *n* Soda *f,neu*. **soda-water** *n* Sodawasser, Mineralwasser *neu*.

sofa ('soufə) *n* Sofa *neu*.

soft (sɔft) *adj* 1 weich. 2 leise. 3 weichlich. **soft drink** *n* alkoholfreies Getränk *neu*. **soft-hearted** *adj* weichherzig. **soften** *vt* weich machen. *vi* 1 (sich) erweichen. 2 mildern.

soggy ('sɔgi) *adj* durchnäßt, feucht.

soil[1] (sɔil) *n* Boden *m*. Erde *f*.

soil[2] (sɔil) *vt* 1 beschmutzen. 2 beflecken.

solar ('soulə) *adj* Sonnen—.

sold (sould) *v* see **sell**.

solder ('sɔldə) *vt* löten. *n* Lötmetall *neu*.

soldier ('souldʒə) *n* Soldat *m*.

sole[1] (soul) *adj* einzig, Allein—. **solely** *adv* allein, ausschließlich.

sole[2] (soul) *n* Sohle *f*. *vt* besohlen.

sole[3] (soul) *n* Seezunge *f*.

solemn ('sɔləm) *adj* 1 feierlich. 2 ernst. **solemnity** *n* Feierlichkeit *f*.

solicitor (sə'lisitə) *n* Anwalt *m*.

solid ('sɔlid) *adj* 1 fest. 2 dauerhaft. 3 kräftig. *n* Körper *m*. **solidarity** *n* Solidarität *f*. **solidify** (*vi*), *vt* (sich) verfestigen.

solitary ('sɔlitri) *adj* 1 einsam. 2 einzeln, allein. **solitary confinement** *n* Einzelhaft *f*.

solitude ('sɔlitju:d) *n* Einsamkeit *f*.

solo ('soulou) *n mus* Solo *neu*. *adj* Allein—, Einzel—.

solstice ('sɔlstis) *n* Sonnenwende *f*.

soluble ('sɔljubəl) *adj* 1 löslich. 2 (auf)lösbar.

solution (sə'lu:ʃən) *n* 1 Lösung *f*. 2 *sci* (Auf)-Lösung *f*.

solve (sɔlv) *vt* (auf)lösen. **solvent** *adj* 1 (auf)lösend. 2 *comm* zahlungsfähig. *n* Lösungsmittel *neu*.

sombre ('sɔmbə) *adj* düster, trübe.

some (sʌm) *adj* 1 irgendein, irgendwelche. 2 einige. 3 etwas. 4 gewisse. 5 manche. 6 etwa, ungefähr. **somebody** *pron also* **someone** jemand. **somehow** *adv* irgendwie. **something** *pron* 1 etwas. 2 irgendetwas. **sometime** *adv* irgendwann, eines Tages. **sometimes** *adv* manchmal. **somewhat** *adv* etwas, ziemlich. **somewhere** *adv* irgendwo(hin).

somersault ('sʌməsɔːlt) *n* Purzelbaum *m*. **turn a somersault** einen Purzelbaum schlagen.

son (sʌn) *n* Sohn *m*. **son-in-law** *n* Schwiegersohn *m*.

sonata (sə'nɑːtə) *n* Sonate *f*.

song (sɔŋ) *n* 1 Lied *neu*. 2 Gesang *m*.

sonic ('sɔnik) *adj* Schall—.

sonnet ('sɔnit) *n* Sonett *neu*.

soon (suːn) *adv* 1 bald. 2 gern. **as soon as** sobald wie. **sooner** *adv* 1 früher. **no sooner than** kaum...als. **no sooner said than done** gesagt, getan.

soot (sut) *n* Ruß *m*. *vt* verrußen.

soothe (suːð) *vt* 1 beruhigen. 2 lindern.

sophisticated (sə'fistikeitid) *adj* 1 verfeinert. 2 hochentwickelt. 3 kultiviert.

soprano (sə'prɑːnou) *n* Sopran *m*.

sordid ('sɔːdid) *adj* schmutzig, gemein.

sore (sɔː) *adj* 1 wund, weh. 2 schlimm. 3 verletzt. *n* wunde Stelle *f*.

sorrow ('sɔrou) *n* 1 Trauer *f*. 2 Kummer *m*. Leid *neu*. *vi* trauern. **sorrowful** *adj* 1 traurig, betrübt. 2 elend.

sorry ('sɔri) *adj* 1 bekümmert. 2 erbärmlich. *interj* Verzeihung! **I am sorry** es tut mir leid.

sort (sɔːt) *n* Sorte, Art *f*. **what sort of** was für. *vt* sortieren. **sort out** 1 aussortieren. 2 *inf* erledigen.

soufflé (suː'flei) *n* Soufflé *neu*. Auflauf *m*.

sought (sɔːt) *v* see **seek**. **sought-after** *adj* gesucht, begehrt.

soul (soul) *n* Seele *f*. **soul-destroying** *adj*

seelentötend, bedrückend. **soulful** adj seelenvoll. **soulless** adj seelenlos.

sound[1] (saund) n 1 Ton, Laut m. 2 Klang m. 3 Geräusch neu. vi 1 klingen. 2 tönen, lauten. vt ertönen or erklingen lassen.

sound[2] (saund) adj 1 gesund. 2 ganz. 3 fest. 4 vernünftig. 5 kräftig.

sound[3] (saund) vt 1 naut loten. 2 sondieren.

soup (su:p) n Suppe f.

sour (sauə) adj 1 sauer, scharf. 2 bitter, mürrisch. vi sauer or bitter werden. vt 1 säuern. 2 erbittern.

source (sɔ:s) n 1 Quelle f. 2 Ursprung m.

south (sauθ) n Süd(en) m. adj Süd—, südlich. adv südwärts, nach Süden. **south-east** n Südosten m. **south-eastern** adj südöstlich. **southerly** adj südlich. **southern** adj Süd—, südlich. **southwards** adv südwärts, nach Süden. **south-west** n Südwesten m. **south-western** adj südwestlich.

South Africa n Südafrika neu.

South America n Südamerika neu.

South Pole n Südpol m.

souvenir (su:və'nia) n Andenken neu.

sovereign ('sovrin) adj 1 souverän. 2 höchst. n Souverän, Monarch m.

Soviet Union ('souviət) n Sowjetunion f.

sow[1] (sou) vt 1 (aus)säen. 2 besäen.

sow[2] (sau) n zool Sau f.

soya bean ('sɔiə) n Sojabohne f.

spa (spɑ:) n Kurort m. Bad neu.

space (speis) n 1 Weltraum m. 2 Platz m. 3 Zwischenraum m. 4 Zeitraum m. vt 1 einteilen. 2 sperren. **spaceship** n Raumschiff m. **spacious** adj 1 geräumig. 2 weit.

spade[1] (speid) n Spaten m. vt graben.

spade[2] (speid) n game Pik neu.

Spain (spein) n Spanien neu. **Spaniard** n Spanier m. **Spanish** adj spanisch. n (language) Spanisch neu.

span (spæn) n 1 (Zeit)Spanne f. 2 Spannweite f. vt 1 (um-, über-)spannen. 2 (aus)messen.

spank (spæŋk) vt schlagen. n Schlag m.

spanner ('spænə) n Schraubenschlüssel m.

spare (spɛə) adj 1 spärlich. 2 mager. 3 übrig. 4 Ersatz—. n Ersatzteil neu. vt 1 (ver)schonen. 2 übrig haben für. **sparing** adj sparsam.

spark (spɑ:k) n Funken m. **spark plug** n Zündkerze f. ~vi Funken sprühen. **spark off** auslösen.

sparkle ('spɑ:kəl) vi 1 funkeln. 2 sprühen. 3 schäumen. n Funkeln neu.

sparrow ('spærou) n Sperling, Spatz m.

sparse (spɑ:s) adj spärlich, dünn.

spasm ('spæzəm) n Krampf m. **spasmodic** adj 1 krampfhaft. 2 unregelmäßig. **spastic** adj spastisch, krampfhaft.

spat (spæt) v see **spit**.

spatial ('speiʃəl) adj räumlich, Raum—.

spatula ('spætjulə) n Spatel m. Spachtel f.

spawn (spɔ:n) n Laich m. vi laichen. vt hervorbringen.

speak[*] (spi:k) vi sprechen, reden. vt (aus)sprechen, äußern. **speaking!** am Apparat!

spear (spiə) n Speer, Spieß m. vt (auf)spießen.

special ('speʃəl) adj 1 besonder. 2 Sonder—, speziell, Spezial—, extra. **specialist** n 1 Spezialist, Fachmann m. 2 med Facharzt m. **speciality** n 1 Besonderheit f. 2 Spezialfach neu. 3 Spezialität f. **specialize** vi sich spezialisieren.

species ('spi:ʃi:z) n, pl **species** Art, Spezies f.

specify ('spesifai) vt spezifizieren. **specific** adj 1 spezifisch. 2 bestimmt. **specification** n Spezifizierung f.

specimen ('spesimən) n Muster, Exemplar neu.

speck (spek) n Fleck m. vt flecken.

spectacle ('spektəkəl) n 1 Schauspiel neu. 2 Schau f. 3 pl Brille f. **spectacular** adj 1 auffallend, spektakulär. 2 eindrücksvoll.

spectator (spek'teitə) n Zuschauer m.

spectrum ('spektrəm) n Spektrum neu.

speculate ('spekjuleit) vi 1 nachsinnen. 2 comm spekulieren. **speculation** n 1 (theoretische) Betrachtung f. 2 comm Spekulation f.

speech (spi:tʃ) n 1 Sprache f. 2 Rede f. **speechless** adj sprachlos.

speed[*] (spi:d) n 1 Geschwindigkeit f. 2 Eile f. 3 phot Lichtempfindlichkeit f. **speed-boat** n Rennboot neu. **speedometer** n Geschwindigkeitsmesser neu. ~vi schnell fahren. **speed up** beschleunigen. **speedy** adj geschwind.

spell[1] (spel) vt 1 buchstabieren. 2 inf bedeuten. vi richtig schreiben. **spelling** n Rechtschreibung f.

spell[2] (spel) n Zauber(spruch), Bann m. **spellbound** adj gebannt.

spell[3] (spel) n 1 Schicht f. 2 Weilchen neu.

spend[*] (spend) vt 1 (money) ausgeben. 2 (time) verbringen. 3 (energy) verwenden. **spendthrift** n Verschwender m. adj verschwenderisch.

spent (spent) v see **spend**. adj erschöpft, matt.

sperm (spɑ:m) n Same m. Sperma neu.

sphere (sfiə) n 1 Kugel f. 2 Sphäre f. Bereich m. **spherical** adj kugelförmig.

spice (spais) n Gewürz neu. Würze f. vt würzen. **spicy** adj pikant, würzig.

spider ('spaidə) n Spinne f.

spike (spaik) n Spitze f. vt 1 festnageln. 2 aufspießen. **spiky** adj spitzig.

spill[1] (spil) vt 1 verschütten. 2 vergießen. vi 1 verschüttet werden. 2 überlaufen.

spin[*] (spin) vi,vt 1 spinnen. 2 wirbeln. 3 (a coin) hochwerfen. 4 (a tale) ausdenken. n Wirbeln neu. **spin-dry** vt schleudern. **spin-dryer** n Wäscheschleuder f.

spinach ('spinidʒ) n Spinat m.

spindle ('spindl) n Spindel f. **spindly** adj spindeldürr.

spine (spain) n 1 Rückgrat neu. Wirbelsäule f. 2 Stachel m.

spinster ('spinstə) n 1 unverheiratete Frau, Junggesellin f. 2 alte Jungfer f.

spiral ('spairəl) n 1 Spirale f. 2 Wirbel m. adj 1 spiralig. 2 schraubenförmig. vi sich schrauben.

spire (spaiə) n Turmspitze f. Kirchturm m.

spirit ('spirit) n 1 Geist m. 2 Temperament neu. 3 Mut m. 4 Spiritus m. 5 pl Stimmung f. 6 pl Spirituosen pl. v **spirit away** wegzaubern. **spirited** adj lebhaft. **spiritual** adj 1 geistig. 2 geistlich.

spit[1] (spit) vi 1 spucken. 2 (of rain) sprühen. **spit out** ausspucken. n Spucke f.

spit[2] (spit) n 1 Bratspieß m. 2 Landzunge f.

spite (spait) n Bosheit, Gehässigkeit f. **in spite of** trotz. ~vt ärgern. **spiteful** adj boshaft, gehässig.

splash (splæʃ) n 1 Spritzfleck m. 2 Patschen neu. vt (be)spritzen. vi patschen.

splendid ('splendid) adj 1 herrlich. 2 großartig. **splendour** n Herrlichkeit, Pracht f.

splint (splint) n med Schiene f. vt schienen. **splinter** n Splitter m. vi,vt (zer)splittern.

split[*] (split) n 1 (zer)spalten. 2 teilen. vi 1 sich spalten. 2 sich entzweien. **split hairs** Haarspalterei treiben. ~n 1 Spalt, Riß m. 2 Spaltung f.

splutter ('splʌtə) vi 1 spritzen. 2 stottern, plappern. n 1 Spritzen neu. 2 Geplapper neu.

spoil[*] (spoil) vt 1 verderben. 2 (a child) verwöhnen. 3 plündern. vi schlecht werden. **spoils** n pl Beute f. Gewinn neu. **spoil-sport** n Spielverderber m.

spoke[1] (spouk) v see **speak**.

spoke[2] (spouk) n Speiche f.

spoken ('spoukən) v see **speak**.

spokesman ('spouksmən) n Wortführer m.

sponge (spʌndʒ) n Schwamm m. vt mit einem Schwamm (ab)wischen. vi schmarotzen.

sponsor ('sponsə) n 1 Pate m. 2 Bürge m. 3 Förderer m. vt 1 fördern. 2 finanzieren.

spontaneous (spon'teiniəs) adj 1 spontan. 2 freiwillig. 3 tech Selbst—. **spontaneity** n 1 Spontaneität f. 2 Freiwilligkeit f.

spool (spu:l) n Spule f.

spoon (spu:n) n Löffel m. vt löffeln. **spoonfed** adj verhätschelt.

sport (spo:t) n 1 Sport m. 2 Scherz m. **a good sport** n feiner Kerl m. **do** or **play sport** Sport treiben. **sportsman** n Sportler m. ~vi scherzen. vt zur Schau tragen.

spot (spot) n 1 Fleck m. 2 Stelle f. 3 Pickel m. **be on the spot** zur Stelle sein. **spotlight** n Scheinwerfer m. vt 1 beflecken. 2 bemerken. **spotless** adj fleckenlos.

spouse (spaus) n Gatte m. Gattin f.

spout (spaut) n 1 Schnauze f. 2 Ausgußröhre f. 3 Wasserstrahl m. vt (heraus)spritzen.

sprain (sprein) vt verrenken. n Verrenkung f.

sprang (spræŋ) v see **spring**.

sprawl (spro:l) vi 1 sich rekeln. 2 bot wuchern.

spray[1] (sprei) n 1 Gischt m. 2 Spray m. vt besprühen, spritzen.

spray[2] (sprei) n 1 Zweig m. 2 Blütenzweig m.

spread[*] (spred) vt 1 (aus-, ver-)breiten. 2 **aufstreichen** vi sich verbreiten. n 1 Verbreitung f. 2 Spanne f. 3 Brotaufstrich m.

spree (spri:) n 1 Jux m. 2 Orgie f.

sprig (sprig) n 1 Sproß m. 2 Sprößling m.

sprightly ('spraitli) adj lebhaft, munter.

spring[*] (spriŋ) vi 1 springen. 2 entstehen. vt sprengen. **spring a leak** leck werden. ~n 1 Sprung m. 2 Sprungkraft f. 3 Triebfeder f. 4 Quelle f. Brunnen m. 5 Frühling m. **springboard** n Sprungbrett neu. **spring-cleaning** n Frühjahrsputz m.

sprinkle ('spriŋkəl) vt (be)streuen. vi sprühen.

sprint (sprint) vi sprinten. n Sprint m.

sprout (spraut) vi sprießen. n Sproß m.

sprung (sprʌŋ) v see **spring**.

spun (spʌn) v see **spin**.

spur (spə:) n 1 Reitsporn m. 2 Ansporn m. vt (an)spornen.

spurt (spə:t) vi 1 sport spurten. 2 herausspritzen. n 1 Spurt m. 2 Wasserstrahl m.

spy (spai) vi,vt 1 spähen. vt n (er)spähen. vi spionieren. **spy on someone** jemandem nachspionieren.

squabble ('skwɔbəl) vi sich zanken. n Zank m.

squad (skwɔd) n Gruppe f. Trupp m. Kommando neu.

squadron ('skwɔdrən) n 1 mil Schwadron f. 2 aviat Staffel f. 3 naut Geschwader neu.

squalid ('skwɔlid) adj armselig, verwahrlost. **squalor** n Schmutz m. Verwahrlosung f.

squander ('skwɔndə) vt verschwenden.

square (skwɛə) adj 1 viereckig. 2 quadratisch. 3 ehrlich. 4 quitt. n 1 Viereck neu. 2 Quadrat neu. 3 (in a town) Platz m. vt 1 viereckig machen. 2 quadrieren. 3 (an account) ausgleichen. vi passen.

squash (skwɔʃ) n 1 Gedränge neu. 2 Fruchtgetränk neu. 3 sport Squash neu. vt 1 (zer)quetschen. 2 (er)drücken, zerdrücken.

squat (skwɔt) vi 1 kauern, hocken. 2 unbefugt besetzen. adj 1 kauernd. 2 untersetzt. **squatter** n Siedler ohne Rechtstitel, Squatter m.

squawk (skwɔ:k) vi kreischen. n Kreischen neu.

squeak (skwi:k) vi 1 quietschen. 2 knarren. n 1 Gequieke, Quietschen neu. 2 Knarren neu.

squeal (skwi:l) vi 1 quieken, quietschen. 2 inf verpfeifen. n Quieken, Quietschen neu.

squeamish ('skwi:miʃ) adj 1 überempfindlich. 2 heikel.

squeeze (skwi:z) vt 1 drücken, pressen. 2 bedrängen. vi dringen, drängen. n 1 Druck m. 2 inf Gedränge. **squeezer** n Presse f.

squid (skwid) n Tintenfisch m.

squiggle ('skwigəl) n Kritzelei f. Schnörkel m. vi kritzeln.

squint (skwint) vi schielen. n Schielen neu.

squire ('skwaiə) n Landjunker, Gutsherr m.

squirm (skwə:m) vi sich winden, sich krümmen.

squirrel ('skwirl) n Eichhörnchen neu.

squirt (skwə:t) vt spritzen. n Spritze f.

Sri Lanka (sri:'læŋkə) n Sri Lanka neu.

stab (stæb) n Stich m. **stab in the back** hinterlistiger Angriff m. ~vt erstechen. vi stechen.

stabilize ('steibəlaiz) vt stabilisieren. **stability** n 1 Stabilität f. 2 Festigkeit f.

stable [1] ('steibəl) n Stall m. vt einstallen.

stable [2] ('steibəl) adj 1 stabil. 2 beständig.

stack (stæk) n 1 Schober m. 2 Schornstein m. 3 Stapel m. vt (auf)stapeln.

stadium ('steidiəm) n Stadion neu.

staff (stɑ:f) n 1 Stab m. 2 Personal neu. Belegschaft f. vt (mit Personal) besetzen.

stag (stæg) n Hirsch m.

stage (steidʒ) n 1 Bühne f. 2 Schauplatz m. 3 Stufe f. 4 Teilstrecke f. **stage manager** n Regisseur m. ~vt inszenieren, vorführen.

stagger ('stægə) vi taumeln, schwanken. vt 1 verblüffen. 2 staffeln. n Schwanken neu.

stagnant ('stægnənt) adj 1 stagnierend 2 träge. **stagnate** vi stocken, stagnieren.

stain (stein) n 1 Flecken m. 2 Makel m. 3 Beize f. vt 1 beflecken. 2 beizen. **stained glass** n buntes Glas neu. **stainless** adj 1 fleckenlos. 2 (of steel) rostfrei.

stair (stɛə) n 1 Stufe f. 2 pl Treppe f. **staircase** n Treppenhaus neu.

stake [1] (steik) n Pfahl m.

stake [2] (steik) n game, sport Einsatz m. **be at stake** auf dem Spiele stehen.

stale (steil) adj 1 alt, schal. 2 fad.

stalemate ('steilmeit) n 1 game Patt neu. 2 Stillstand m.

stalk [1] (stɔ:k) n 1 Stiel m. 2 (of corn) Halm m.

stalk [2] (stɔ:k) vt beschleichen. vi stolzieren.

stall [1] (stɔ:l) n 1 Pferdebox f. 2 (Markt)Bude f. 3 pl Th Parkett neu. 4 Chorstuhl m. vt einstallen. vi mot aussetzen, stehenbleiben.

stall [2] (stɔ:l) n inf Verwand m. Ausflucht f. vt ausweichen. vi Ausflüchte machen.

stallion ('stæliən) n Hengst m.

stamina ('stæminə) n Ausdauer, Vitalität f.

stammer ('stæmə) vi stammeln. n Stammeln neu.

stamp (stæmp) n 1 Stempel m. 2 (Brief)Marke f. 3 Gepräge neu. vt 1 stempeln. 2 frankieren. 3 prägen. vi stampfen.

stampede (stæm'pi:d) n Panik f. wilde Flucht f. vi flüchten, durchgehen.

stand (stænd) vi stehen. **stand by** 1 treu bleiben. 2 in Bereitschaft halten. **stand-by** n Beistand m. **stand for** 1 bedeuten. 2 ertragen. 3 kandidieren für. **stand up** aufstehen. ~n 1 Stand m. 2 Standpunkt m. 3 Bude f. **standing** adj 1 stehend. 2 (be)ständig. n 1 Stellung f. 2 Ruf m. **standstill** n Stillstand m. **come to a standstill** zum Stehen kommen.

standard ('stændəd) n 1 Standarte f. 2 Standard m. Norm f. 3 Stufe f. adj maßgebend, Normal—, Standard—.

stank (stæŋk) v see stink.

stanza ('stænzə) n Strophe, Stanze f.

staple [1] ('steipəl) n 1 Krampe f. 2 Heftklammer f. **stapler** n Heftmaschine f.

staple [2] ('steipəl) adj Haupt—, Stapel—. n 1 Haupterzeugnis neu. 2 Hauptgegenstand m.

star (sta:) n 1 Stern m. 2 Star m. vi die Hauptrolle spielen. **starfish** n Seestern m.

starboard ('sta:bəd) n Steuerbord neu.

starch (sta:tʃ) n (Wäsche)Stärke f. vt stärken. **starchy** adj inf steif.

stare (stɛə) vi große Augen machen, starren. **stare** at anstarren. ~n 1 Starren neu. 2 starrer Blick m.

stark (sta:k) adj 1 steif, starr. 2 völlig. **stark naked** adj splitternackt.

starling ('sta:liŋ) n Star m.

start (sta:t) vi 1 anfangen. 2 starten. 3 abgehen, abfahren. 4 auffahren. vt 1 in Gang bringen. 2 starten lassen. 3 anfangen. n 1 Auffahren neu. 2 Anfang, Beginn m. 3 sport Start m.

startle ('sta:tl) vt erschrecken.

starve (sta:v) vi,(vt) verhungern (lassen). **starvation** n (Ver)Hungern neu. adj Hunger—.

state (steit) n 1 pol Staat m. 2 Zustand m. **get into a state** inf sich aufregen. ~vt 1 angeben. 2 darlegen. 3 feststellen. 4 aufstellen. adj Staats—. **stately** adj 1 stattlich. 2 prächtig. 3 erhaben. **statement** n 1 Angabe f. 2 Darlegung f. 3 Kontoauszug m. 5 Behauptung f. **statesman** n Staatsmann m.

static ('stætik) adj statisch.

station ('steiʃən) n 1 (railway) Bahnhof m. 2 (Polizei)Wache f. 3 Platz m. 4 Station f. vt mil stationieren. **station-master** n Stationsvorsteher m.

stationary ('steiʃənri) adj 1 stillstehend. 2 stationär.

stationer ('steiʃənə) n Schreibwarenhändler m. **stationery** n Schreibwaren f pl.

statistics (stə'tistiks) n pl Statistik f.

statue ('stætju:) n Statue f. Standbild neu.

stature ('stætʃə) n 1 Statur f. Gestalt f. 2 Größe f.

status ('steitəs) n 1 Rang m. 2 Status m.

statute ('stætju:t) n 1 Statut, (Landes)Gesetz neu. 2 Satzung f. **statutory** adj gesetzlich.

stay¹ (stei) vi 1 (sich) aufhalten. 2 bleiben. 3 wohnen. n Aufenthalt m.

stay² (stei) n Stütze f.

steadfast ('stedfa:st) adj 1 fest. 2 (of a look) unverwandt. 3 standhaft.

steady ('stedi) adj 1 (be)ständig. 2 sicher. 3 fest. 4 ruhig. vt 1 sicher machen. 2 (sich) festigen. 3 (sich) beruhigen.

steak (steik) n 1 Steak neu. 2 (Fisch)Filet neu.

steal (sti:l) vt,vi stehlen.

steam (sti:m) n 1 Dampf m. 2 Dunst m. vi dampfen. vt cul dünsten. **steam-engine** n

Dampfmaschine f. **steam-roller** n Dampfwalze f. **steamer** n 1 Dampfer m. Dampfschiff neu. 2 Dampfkochtopf m.

steel (sti:l) n Stahl m. adj stählern, Stahl—. vt stählen.

steep¹ (sti:p) adj 1 steil, jäh. 2 inf stark.

steep² (sti:p) vt 1 einweichen. 2 versenken.

steeple ('sti:pəl) n Kirchturm m. **steeplechase** n Hindernisrennen neu.

steer (stiə) vt steuern. **steer clear of** vermeiden. **steering-wheel** n Steuerrad neu.

stem¹ (stem) n 1 Stamm m. 2 Stengel m. v **stem from** stammen von.

stem² (stem) vt eindämmen.

stencil ('stensəl) n 1 Schablone f. 2 Matrize f. vt schablonieren.

step (step) n 1 Schritt m. 2 (Fuß)Tritt m. 3 Stufe f. 4 Maßnahme f. vi 1 schreiten. 2 treten, gehen. **stepladder** n Trittleiter f.

stepbrother ('stepbrʌðə) n Stiefbruder m.

stepdaughter ('stepdɔ:tə) n Stieftochter f.

stepfather ('stepfa:ðə) n Stiefvater m.

stepmother ('stepmʌðə) n Stiefmutter f.

stepsister ('stepsistə) n Stiefschwester f.

stepson ('stepsʌn) n Stiefsohn m.

stereo ('steriou) adj Stereo—. n Stereoanlage f. **stereophonic** adj stereophonisch.

stereotype ('steriətaip) n Stereotype f. vt stereotypieren. **stereotyped** adj stereotyp.

sterile ('sterail) adj 1 steril. 2 unfruchtbar. **sterilize** vt 1 sterilisieren. 2 unfruchtbar machen. **sterilization** n Sterilisierung f.

sterling ('stə:liŋ) adj 1 gediegen. 2 Sterling—. n Sterling m-s.

stern¹ (stə:n) adj streng, hart.

stern² (stə:n) n naut Heck neu. Spiegel m.

stethoscope ('steθəskoup) n Stethoskop neu.

stew (stju:) n Schmorgericht neu. vt schmoren.

steward ('stju:əd) n 1 Steward m. 2 Verwalter m. 3 Ordner m. **stewardess** n Stewardeß f.

stick¹ (stik) n Stock m. **get hold of the wrong end of the stick** die Geschichte in den falschen Hals kriegen.

stick²(stik) vt 1 ankleben. 2 stecken. vi 1 kleben. 2 steckenbleiben. **sticker** n Klebzettel m. **sticky** adj klebrig. **come to a sticky end** ein schlimmes Ende nehmen.

stiff (stif) adj 1 steif. 2 starr. 3 (of a drink) stark. **stiffen** vt steifen. vi 1 sich versteifen. 2 erstarren.

stifle ('staifəl) vt ersticken.

stigma ('stigmə) n Stigma neu.

stile (stail) n Zauntritt m. Steige f.

still

still[1] (stil) *adj* still. *adv* **1** immer noch. **2** noch, immer. *conj* doch, dennoch. *vt* **1** stillen. **2** beruhigen. *n* Photographie *f.* **stillborn** *adj* totgeboren. **still life** *n* Stilleben *neu.*

still[2] (stil) *n* Destillierapparat *m.*

stilt (stilt) *n* Stelze *f.* **stilted** *adj* gespreizt, geschraubt.

stimulus ('stimjuləs) *n* **1** Antrieb *m.* **2** Reizmittel *neu.* **stimulate** *vt* anreizen, stimulieren.

sting (stiŋ) *vi,vt* **1** stechen. **2** schmerzen. *n* **1** (of an insect) Stachel *m.* **2** Stich *m.*

stink (stiŋk) *vi* stinken. *n* Gestank *m.*

stint (stint) *vt* einschränken. *n* **1** Einschränkung *f.* **2** Schicht *f.*

stipulate ('stipjuleit) *vt* festsetzen, vereinbaren. **stipulation** *n* **1** Festsetzung *f.* **2** Bedingung *f.*

stir (stə:) *vt* **1** rühren. **2** aufregen. *vi* sich rühren. *n* **1** Rühren *neu.* **2** (Auf)Regung *f.*

stirrup ('stirəp) *n* Steigbügel *m.*

stitch (stitʃ) *n* **1** Stich *m.* **2** Masche *f.* *vt* nähen, heften.

stoat (stout) *n* Hermelin *neu.*

stock (stɔk) *n* **1** Vorrat *m.* **2** Stamm *m.* **3** Stock *m.* **4** *pl* Aktien *f pl.* **5** *cul* Brühe *f.* **take stock of** abschätzen. ~*adj* **1** Standard—. **2** stereotyp. *vt* **1** versehen. **2** vorrätig haben. **stockbreeding** *n* Viehzucht *f.* **stockbroker** *n* Börsenmakler *m.* **stock exchange** *n* Börse *f.* **stockpile** *n* Vorrat *m.* *vt* aufstapeln. **stocktaking** *n* Inventur *f.*

stocking ('stɔkiŋ) *n* Strumpf *m.*

stocky ('stɔki) *adj* untersetzt.

stodge (stɔdʒ) *n* schwerverdauliches Essen *neu.* **stodgy** *adj* **1** schwer. **2** schwerfällig.

stoical ('stouikl) *adj* stoisch.

stoke (stouk) *vt* (an)schüren.

stole[1] (stoul) *v see* **steal.**

stole[2] (stoul) *n* Pelzkragen *m.* Stola *f.*

stolen ('stoulən) *v see* **steal.**

stomach ('stʌmək) *n* Magen *m.* *vt* **1** verdauen. **2** ertragen. **stomach-ache** *n* Magenschmerzen *m pl.*

stone (stoun) *n* **1** Stein *m.* **2** Kern *m.* *vt* **1** steinigen. **2** (fruit) entsteinen. **stony** *adj* **1** steinig. **2** stainern.

stood (stud) *v see* **stand.**

stool (stu:l) *n* Hocker *m.*

stoop (stu:p) *vi* **1** sich bücken. **2** sich erniedrigen. **3** krumm gehen.

stop (stɔp) *vt* **1** (an)halten. **2** hindern. **3** aufhören. **4** verstopfen. *vi* **1** anhalten. **2** aufhören. **3** stehenbleiben. *n* **1** Halt *m.* **2** Pause *f.* **3** Hemmung *f.* **4** (Bus)Haltestelle *f.* **5**

Punkt *m.* **stopgap** *n* Notbehelf *m.* **stopwatch** *n* Stoppuhr *f.* **stoppage** *n* **1** Stockung *f.* **2** Einstellung *f.* **3** Sperrung *f.* **stopper** *n* Stöpsel *m.* *vt* zustöpseln.

store (stɔ:) *n* **1** Vorrat *m.* **2** Lagerhaus *neu.* **3** Fülle *f.* **4** *pl* Kaufhaus *neu.* **5** Schiffsbedarf *m.* *vt* lagern, aufbewahren. **set store by** Wert legen auf. **storage** *n* **1** Aufbewahrung, Lagerung *f.* **2** (of electricity) Speicherung *f.*

storey ('stɔ:ri) *n* Stock *m.* Stockwerk, Geschoß *neu.*

stork (stɔ:k) *n* Storch *m.*

storm (stɔ:m) *n* Sturm *m.* *vt* stürmen. *vi* toben. **stormy** *adj* stürmisch.

story ('stɔ:ri) *n* **1** Geschichte *f.* **2** Erzählung *f.* **3** Handlung *f.*

stout (staut) *adj* **1** stark. **2** dick. **3** tapfer. *n* Starkbier *neu.*

stove (stouv) *n* **1** Ofen *m.* **2** (for cooking) Herd *m.*

stow (stou) *vt* verstauen. **stowaway** *n* blinder Passagier *m.*

straddle ('strædl) *vi* breitbeinig gehen *or* stehen. *vt* spreizen.

straggle ('strægəl) *vi* **1** verstreut liegen. **2** umherschweifen. **3** wuchern. **straggling** *adj* weitläufig, lose.

straight (streit) *adj* **1** gerade. **2** aufrichtig. **3** glatt. **get straight** klarmachen. **put straight** in Ordnung bringen. **straight ahead** *adv* geradeaus. **straight away** *adv* sofort, unmittelbar. **straighten** *vt* gerademachen. *vi* gerade werden. **straightforward** *adj* **1** gerade. **2** redlich.

strain[1] (strein) *n* **1** Anstrengung *f.* **2** Druck *m.* **3** *med* Zerrung *f.* *vt* **1** anstrengen. **2** zerren. **3** (durch)seihen. *vi* sich anstrengen. **strainer** *n* Seiher *m.* Sieb *neu.*

strain[2] (strein) *n* Abstammung, Rasse *f.*

strand[1] (strænd) *vi,(vt)* stranden (lassen).

strand[2] (strænd) *n* Strähne *f.*

strange (streindʒ) *adj* **1** fremd. **2** seltsam. **stranger** *n* **1** Fremde(r) *m.* **2** Neuling *m.*

strangle ('stræŋgəl) *vt* **1** erwürgen. **2** unterdrücken.

strap (stræp) *n* **1** Riemen *m.* **2** Träger *m.* *vt* festschnallen.

strategy ('strætidʒi) *n* Strategie *f.* **strategic** *adj* strategisch.

straw (strɔ:) *n* **1** Stroh *neu.* **2** Strohhalm *m.* *adj* Stroh—. **strawberry** *n* Erdbeere *f.*

stray (strei) *vi* **1** sich verirren. **2** abirren. *adj* verirrt. *n* verirrtes Tier *neu.*

streak (stri:k) n 1 Streifen m. 2 Spur f. vt streifen. **streaky** adj 1 streifig. 2 (of bacon) durchwachsen.

stream (stri:m) n 1 Bach m. 2 Strom m. vi 1 strömen. 2 flattern. **streamer** n Papierschlange f. **streamline** n Stromlinie f. vt modernisieren.

street (stri:t) n Straße f.

strength (streŋθ) n Kraft, Stärke f. **on the strength of** aufgrund. **strengthen** vt (be)kräftigen, (be)stärken. vi erstärken.

strenuous ('strenjuəs) adj 1 emsig. 2 eifrig. 3 anstrengend.

stress (stres) n 1 Ton m. Betonung f. 2 Nachdruck m. Gewicht neu. 3 med Streß m. vt 1 betonen. 2 unterstreichen.

stretch (stretʃ) vt 1 strecken. 2 (aus)dehnen. 3 anspannen. vi 1 sich erstrecken. 2 sich dehnen. n 1 Strecke f. 2 Dehnung f. **at a stretch** in einem Zug. **stretcher** n Tragbahre f.

strict (strikt) adj 1 streng. 2 genau. **strictly speaking** streng genommen.

stride (straid) vi schreiten. n (langer) Schritt m.

strike* (straik) vt 1 schlagen. 2 treffen. 3 auffallen. 4 anzünden. vi 1 schlagen. 2 streiken. n Streik m.

string* (striŋ) n 1 Schnur f. 2 mus Saite f. 3 Reihe f. vt 1 aufreihen. 2 mus besaiten. **stringed instruments** n pl Saiteninstrumente neu pl.

stringent ('strindʒənt) adj 1 streng. 2 fest. knapp. **stringency** n 1 Strenge f. 2 Härte f. 3 Knappheit f.

strip¹ (strip) vi sich ausziehen. vt 1 entkleiden. 2 entblößen. 3 abreißen. **striptease** n Striptease neu.

strip² (strip) n (schmaler) Streifen m.

stripe (straip) n Streifen m. **striped** adj gestreift.

strive* (straiv) vi 1 streben. 2 ringen.

stroke¹ (strouk) n 1 Schlag, Hieb m. 2 Streich m. 3 Strich m. **stroke of luck** m glücklicher Zufall m.

stroke² (strouk) vt streicheln.

stroll (stroul) vi bummeln, schlendern. 2 spazierengehen. n 1 Bummel m. 2 Spaziergang m.

strong (strɔŋ) adj 1 stark. 2 kräftig. 3 fest. **stronghold** n Festung f. **strong-minded** adj willenstark.

struck (strʌk) v see **strike.**

structure ('strʌktʃə) n 1 Bau m. 2 Struktur f. **structural** adj 1 Bau—. 2 strukturell.

struggle ('strʌgəl) vi 1 sich (ab)mühen. 2 kämpfen, ringen. 3 zappeln. n 1 Kampf m. 2 Ringen neu.

strum (strʌm) vi,(vt) klimpern (auf).

strung (strʌŋ) v see **string.**

strut¹ (strʌt) vi stolzieren. n Stolzieren neu.

strut² (strʌt) n Strebe, Stütze f.

stub (stʌb) n 1 Stumpf m. 2 Stummel m, vt stoßen. **stub out** ausdrücken.

stubborn ('stʌbən) adj 1 hartnäckig. 2 halsstarrig. **stubbornness** n Hartnäckigkeit f.

stud¹ (stʌd) n 1 Beschlagnagel m. 2 Kragenknopf m. vt 1 beschlagen. 2 bestreuen.

stud² (stʌd) n Gestüt neu.

student ('stju:dənt) n Student m. Studentin f.

studio ('stju:diou) n 1 Atelier neu. 2 Senderaum m. 3 Studio neu.

study ('stʌdi) n 1 Studium neu. 2 Studierzimmer neu. 3 Art Studie f. vt 1 studieren. 2 genau beobachten. vi studieren. **studious** adj 1 fleißig. 2 beflissen.

stuff (stʌf) n 1 Stoff m. 2 Zeug neu. vt 1 (voll-, aus-)stopfen. 2 cul füllen. **stuffing** n 1 cul Füllung f. 2 Polsterung f. **stuffy** adj 1 muffig. 2 inf spießig.

stumble ('stʌmbəl) vi stolpern. **stumble upon** stoßen auf. ~n Stolpern neu. **stumbling block** n Stein des Anstoßes m.

stump (stʌmp) n 1 Stumpf m. 2 sport Stab m. vt inf verblüffen. vi stapfen.

stun (stʌn) vt betäuben. **stunning** adj 1 betäubend. 2 inf sagenhaft, toll.

stung (stʌŋ) v see **sting.**

stunk (stʌŋk) v see **stink.**

stunt¹ (stʌnt) vt im Wachstum hindern.

stunt² (stʌnt) n 1 Kunststück neu. 2 Trick m.

stupid ('stju:pid) adj 1 dumm. 2 blöd. **stupidity** n Dummheit f.

sturdy ('stə:di) adj 1 derb. 2 stämmig.

stutter ('stʌtə) vi stottern. n Stottern neu.

sty (stai) n 1 Schweinestall m. 2 med Gerstenkorn neu.

style (stail) n Stil m. **in style** adv vornehm. **stylish** adj 1 stilvoll. 2 elegant.

stylus ('stailəs) n 1 Griffel m. 2 Grammophonnadel f.

subconscious (sʌb'kɔnʃəs) adj unterbewußt. n Unterbewußte neu.

subcontract (sʌbkən'trækt) n Nebenvertrag m.

subdue (səb'dju:) vt 1 unterwerfen. 2 dämpfen.

subject (n,adj 'sʌbdʒikt; v səb'dʒekt) n 1 pol

subjunctive

Untertan, Staatsangehörige(r) m. 2 Thema neu. 3 Fach neu. 4 Subjekt neu. adj 1 unterworfen. 2 abhängig. **subject to** vorbehaltlich. ~vt 1 unterwerfen. 2 unterziehen. 3 aussetzen. **subjective** adj subjektiv.

subjunctive (səb'dʒʌŋktiv) n Konjunktiv m. adj konjunktivisch.

sublime (sə'blaim) adj 1 erhaben. 2 inf großartig.

submachine-gun (sʌbmə'ʃi:ngʌn) n Maschinenpistole f.

submarine (sʌbmə'ri:n) n Unterseeboot neu. adj Untersee—.

submerge (səb'mə:dʒ) vt 1 untertauchen. 2 überschwemmen. vi untertauchen.

submit (səb'mit) vt 1 vorlegen. vi 1 sich unterwerfen. 2 sich ergeben. **submission** n 1 Vorlage f. 2 Unterwerfung f. **submissive** adj unterwürfig.

subnormal (sʌb'nɔ:məl) adj unternormal, subnormal.

subordinate (sə'bɔ:dinət) adj 1 untergeordnet. 2 Neben—. n Untergebene(r) m. vt 1 unterordnen. 2 unterwerfen. **subordination** n Unterordnung f.

subscribe (səb'skraib) vt 1 unterschreiben (mit). 2 (money) zeichnen. vi 1 abonnieren. 2 zustimmen. **subscriber** n Abonnent m. **subscription** n 1 Unterzeichnung f. 2 Abonnement n. 3 Mitgliedsbeitrag m.

subsequent ('sʌbsikwint) adj folgend. **subsequently** adv 1 hinterher. 2 anschließend.

subservient (səb'sə:viənt) adj 1 unterwürfig. 2 dienlich.

subside (səb'said) vi 1 sich senken. 2 sich legen. **subside into** verfallen in. **subsidence** n Senkung f.

subsidiary (səb'sidiəri) adj Hilfs—, Neben—.

subsidize ('sʌbsidaiz) vt (mit Geld) unterstützen, subventionieren. **subsidy** n 1 Beihilfe f. 2 Subvention f.

subsist (səb'sist) vi 1 leben. 2 bestehen. vt unterhalten. **subsistence** n 1 Lebensunterhalt m. 2 Dasein neu.

substance ('sʌbstəns) n 1 Substanz f. 2 Wesen neu. 3 Inhalt m. 4 Wirklichkeit f. **substantial** adj 1 wesentlich. 2 wirklich. 3 solid. **substantive** adj 1 gram substantivisch. 2 selbständig. 3 fest. n Substantiv neu.

substitute ('sʌbstitju:t) vt ersetzen. vi vertreten. n 1 Ersatz m. 2 Stellvertreter m. adj Ersatz—.

subtitle ('sʌbtait|) n Untertitel m.

subtle ('sʌt|) adj 1 fein(sinnig). 2 spitzfindig. **subtlety** n 1 Feinheit f. 2 Spitzfindigkeit f.

subtract (səb'trækt) vt subtrahieren, abziehen. **subtraction** n Subtraktion f. Abzug m.

suburb ('sʌbə:b) n Vorstadt f. Vorort m. **suburban** adj vorstädtisch, Vorstadt—.

subvert (sʌb'və:t) vt umstürzen. **subversive** adj umstürzlerisch, subversiv.

subway ('sʌbwei) n Fußgängerunterführung f.

succeed (sək'si:d) vi 1 Erfolg haben. 2 gelingen. 3 (nach)folgen. vt (nach)folgen. **success** n Erfolg m. **successful** adj erfolgreich. **be successful** Erfolg haben. **succession** 1 Nachfolge, Reihenfolge f. 2 Erbfolge f. 3 Thronfolge f. **in succession** adv nacheinander. **successive** adj aufeinanderfolgend.

succulent ('sʌkjulənt) adj 1 saftig. 2 fleischig.

succumb (sə'kʌm) vi 1 unterliegen. 2 sich ergeben.

such (sʌtʃ) adj 1 solch. 2 derartig. 3 so. pron solch. **suchlike** adj dergleichen.

suck (sʌk) vt 1 saugen. 2 ansaugen. 3 (sweets, etc.) lutschen. **suck up to** sl sich einschmeicheln. **sucker** ('sʌkə) n 1 Sauger m. 2 bot Sprößling m. **suckle** vt säugen, nähren.

suction ('sʌkʃən) n 1 Saugen neu. 2 Ansaugung f. adj Saug—.

Sudan (su:'dæn) n Sudan m. **Sudanese** adj sudanesisch. n Sudanese m.

sudden ('sʌdn) adj plötzlich.

suds (sʌdz) n pl (Seifen)Lauge f.

sue (su:) vt verklagen. vi klagen.

suede (sweid) n Wildleder neu. adj Wildleder—.

suet ('su:it) n 1 Nierenfett neu. 2 Talg m.

suffer ('sʌfə) vi leiden. vt erdulden, erleiden. **suffering** n Leiden neu.

sufficient (sə'fiʃənt) adj genug, genügend. **be sufficient** genügen.

suffix ('sʌfiks) n Nachsilbe f. Suffix neu.

suffocate ('sʌfəkeit) vi,vt ersticken. **suffocation** n Erstickung f.

sugar ('ʃugə) n Zucker m. vt 1 zuckern. 2 versüßen. **sugar beet** n Zuckerrübe f. **sugar cane** n Zuckerrohr neu. **sugary** adj 1 zuckerig. 2 zuckersüß.

suggest (sə'dʒest) vt 1 vorschlagen. 2 andeuten. 3 eingeben. **suggestion** n 1 Vorschlag m. 2 Andeutung f. 3 Eingebung f. **suggestive** adj 1 andeutend. 2 zweideutig.

suicide ('su:isaid) n 1 Selbstmord m. 2 Selbstmörder m. **suicidal** adj selbstmörderisch.

suit (sju:t) n 1 (Herren)Anzug m. 2 (Damen)-Kostüm neu. 3 Bitte f. 4 game Farbe f. vi,vt passen. **suit oneself** tun, was einem beliebt. **suitcase** n (Hand)Koffer m. **suitable** adj passend, geeignet.

suite (swi:t) n 1 Gefolge neu. 2 Garnitur f. 3 mus Suite f. **suite of rooms** Zimmerflucht f.

sulk (sʌlk) vi schmollen. **sulky** adj 1 schmollend. 2 mürrisch, launisch.

sullen ('sʌlən) adj verdrossen.

sulphur ('sʌlfə) n Schwefel m. **sulphuric** adj Schwefel–.

sultana (sʌl'tɑ:nə) n cul Sultanine f.

sultry ('sʌltri) adj 1 schwül. 2 stechend heiß.

sum (sʌm) n 1 Summe f. 2 Rechenaufgabe f. **do sums** rechnen. v **sum up** zusammenfassen.

summarize ('sʌməraiz) vt zusammenfassen. **summary** n Zusammenfassung f.

summer ('sʌmə) n Sommer m. **summertime** n Sommerzeit f.

summit ('sʌmit) n Gipfel m. **summit conference** n Gipfelkonferenz f.

summon ('sʌmən) vt 1 auffordern. 2 rufen. 3 vorladen. **summon up** aufbieten. **summons** n 1 Aufforderung f. 2 gerichtliche Vorladung f.

sun (sʌn) n Sonne f. **sunny** adj sonnig. v **sun oneself** sich sonnen.

sunbathe ('sʌnbeið) vi ein Sonnenbad nehmen.

sunburn ('sʌnbə:n) n Sonnenbrand m.

Sunday ('sʌndi) n Sonntag m.

sundial ('sʌndaiəl) n Sonnenuhr f.

sundry ('sʌndri) adj verschieden. n pl Verschiedenes neu.

sunflower ('sʌnflauə) n Sonnenblume f.

sung (sʌŋ) v see **sing**.

sunglasses ('sʌnglɑ:siz) n pl Sonnenbrille f.

sunk (sʌŋk) v see **sink**.

sunlight ('sʌnlait) n Sonnenlicht neu.

sunrise ('sʌnraiz) n Sonnenaufgang m.

sunset ('sʌnset) n Sonnenuntergang m.

sunshine ('sʌnʃain) n Sonnenschein m.

sunstroke ('sʌnstrouk) n Sonnenstich m.

suntan ('sʌntæn) n Sonnenbräune f.

super ('su:pə) adj inf prima, erstklassig.

superannuation (su:pərænju'eiʃən) n 1 Pensionierung f. 2 Ruhegehalt neu. Pension f.

superb (su:'pə:b) adj 1 prächtig. 2 herrlich.

superficial (su:pə'fiʃəl) adj oberflächlich.

superfluous (su:'pə:fluəs) adj überflüssig.

superhuman (su:pə'hju:mən) adj übermenschlich.

superimpose (su:pərim'pouz) vt auflegen.

superintendent (su:pərin'tendənt) n 1 Aufseher m. 2 Inspektor m. adj aufsichtführend.

superior (su'piəriə) adj 1 ober. 2 höher. 3 besser, überlegen. n 1 höherer Offizier m. 2 Vorgesetzte(r) m. 3 rel Superior m. **superiority** n Überlegenheit f.

superlative (su'pə:lətiv) adj 1 höchst. 2 gram superlativisch. n Superlativ m.

supermarket ('su:pəmɑ:kit) n Supermarkt m.

supernatural (su:pə'nætʃrəl) adj übernatürlich.

supersede (su:pə'si:d) vt 1 ersetzen. 2 verdrängen. 3 überholen.

supersonic (su:pə'sɔnik) adj Überschall—.

superstition (su:pə'stiʃən) n Aberglaube m. **superstitious** adj abergläubisch.

supervise ('su:pəvaiz) vt beaufsichtigen. **supervision** n 1 Beaufsichtigung f. 2 Aufsicht f. **supervisor** n Aufseher m.

supper ('sʌpə) n Abendessen, Abendbrot neu.

supple ('sʌpəl) adj biegsam, geschmeidig.

supplement ('sʌplimənt) n 1 Ergänzung f. 2 Nachtrag m. 3 Beilage f. vt ergänzen. **supplementary** adj 1 Ergänzungs—. 2 Nachtrags—.

supply (sə'plai) vt 1 (be)liefern, versorgen, besorgen. 2 decken. n 1 Versorgung f. 2 Vorrat m. 3 Angebot neu. 4 pl Vorräte m pl. **supply and demand** Angebot und Nachfrage. **supplier** n Lieferant m.

support (sə'pɔ:t) vt 1 (unter)stützen. 2 tragen. n 1 Unterstützung f. 2 Stütze f. Träger m.

suppose (sə'pouz) vt 1 annehmen. 2 voraussetzen. vi vermuten, glauben.

suppress (sə'pres) vt 1 unterdrücken. 2 hemmen. **suppression** n Unterdrückung f.

supreme (sə'pri:m) adj höchst, oberst.

surcharge ('sə:tʃɑ:dʒ) n Zuschlag m. vt mit Zuschlag belegen.

sure (ʃuə) adj 1 sicher, gewiß. 2 zuverlässig. **surely** adv 1 gewiß, sicherlich. 2 vermutlich. **surety** n 1 Bürge f. 2 Sicherheit f.

surf (sə:f) n Brandung f.

surface ('sə:fis) n 1 Oberfläche f. 2 Äußere neu. vi auftauchen. adj oberflächlich.

surfeit ('sə:fit) n 1 Übermaß neu. vt übersättigen.

surge (sə:dʒ) vi 1 branden. 2 aufwallen. 3 vorwärtsdrängen. n 1 Brandung f. 2 Flut f.

surgeon ('sə:dʒən) n Chirurg m. **surgery** n 1 Chirurgie f. 2 Sprechzimmer neu. 3 Sprechstunde f.

surly ('sə:li) adj mürrisch.

surmount (sə'maunt) vt 1 übersteigen. 2 überwinden.

surname ('sɔːneim) n Zuname, Familienname m.

surpass (sɔ'pɑːs) vt übertreffen.

surplus ('sɔːpləs) n Überschuß m. adj überschüssig.

surprise (sɔ'praiz) vt 1 überraschen. 2 ertappen. n Überraschung f. **surprised** adj überrascht, verblüfft.

surrealism (sɔ'riəlizəm) n Surrealismus m.

surrender (sɔ'rendə) vt 1 übergeben. 2 aufgeben. vi sich ergeben. n Übergabe f.

surreptitious (sʌrəp'tiʃəs) adj heimlich, verstohlen.

surround (sɔ'raund) vt 1 umgeben. 2 umzingeln, einschließen. **surrounding** adj umgebend. **surroundings** pl n Umgebung f.

survey (sɔ'vei) n 1 Überprüfung f. 2 Überblick m. 3 Landvermessung f. vt 1 (über)prüfen. 2 überblicken. 3 vermessen.

surveyor (sɔ'veiə) n 1 Feldmesser, Geometer m. 2 Aufseher m.

survive (sɔ'vaiv) vt,vi überleben. **survivor** n Überlebende(r) m.

susceptible (sɔ'septəbəl) adj empfänglich, anfällig.

suspect (v sɔ'spekt; n,adj 'sʌspekt) vt 1 verdächtigen. 2 vermuten. 3 mißtrauen. n Verdächtigte(r) m. adj verdächtig.

suspend (sɔ'spend) vt 1 aufhängen. 2 verschieben. 3 einstellen. 4 unterbrechen. **suspense** n 1 Spannung f. 2 Ungewißheit f. **suspension** n 1 Aufhängung f. 2 mot Federung f. 3 Verschiebung f. 4 Einstellung f.

suspicion (sɔ'spiʃən) n 1 Verdacht m. 2 Vermutung f. 3 Spur f. **suspicious** adj 1 verdächtig. 2 mißtrauisch.

sustain (sɔ'stein) vt 1 aushalten. 2 unterstützen.

swab (swɔb) n 1 Tupfer m. 2 Scheuerlappen m. vt 1 aufwischen, scheuern. 2 betupfen.

Swabia ('sweibiə) n Schwaben neu. **Swabian** adj schwäbisch. n Schwabe m.

swagger ('swægə) vi 1 stolzieren. 2 prahlen. n 1 stolzierender Gang m. 2 Prahlerei f.

swallow[1] ('swɔlou) vt 1 (ver)schlucken, verschlingen. vi schlucken. n Schluck m.

swallow[2] ('swɔlou) n zool Schwalbe f.

swam (swæm) v see **swim.**

swamp (swɔmp) n Sumpf m. vt überschwemmen.

swan (swɔn) n Schwan m.

swank (swæŋk) n inf Prahlerei, Angeberei f. vi inf aufschneiden, prahlen.

swap (swɔp) vt also **swop** (aus)tauschen. n Tausch m.

swarm (swɔːm) n Schwarm m. vi 1 schwärmen. 2 wimmeln.

swastika ('swɔstikə) n Hakenkreuz neu.

swat (swɔt) vt zerquetschen, schlagen.

sway (swei) vi schwanken, schaukeln. vt 1 beeinflussen. 2 mitreißen. n 1 Herrschaft f. 2 Einfluß m.

swear[*] (swɛə) vi 1 fluchen. 2 schwören. vt (be)schwören. **swearword** n Fluchwort neu.

sweat (swet) vi,vt schwitzen. n 1 Schweiß m. 2 inf Plackerei f. **sweater** n Pullover m.

swede (swiːd) n Steckrübe f.

Sweden ('swiːdn) n Schweden neu. **Swede** n Schwede m. **Swedish** ('swiːdiʃ) adj schwedisch. n (language) Schwedisch neu.

sweep[*] (swiːp) vt 1 fegen, kehren. 2 durchstreifen. vi vorbeirauschen. n 1 Schornsteinfeger m. 2 Fegen neu.

sweet (swiːt) adj süß. n 1 Bonbon m. Süßigkeit f. 2 Nachtisch m. **sweetbread** n Bries m. **sweet corn** n Zuckermais m. **sweetheart** n Liebchen neu. Liebste(r) m. **sweet pea** n Wicke f. **sweeten** vt 1 süßen. 2 versüßen.

swell[*] (swel) vi (an)schwellen. adj sl 1 prima. 2 vornehm.

swelter ('sweltə) vi vor Hitze umkommen.

swept (swept) v see **sweep.**

swerve (swɔːv) vi 1 (plötzlich) abbiegen. 2 ausweichen.

swift (swift) adj schnell, rasch.

swig (swig) inf n Schluck, Zug m. vt saufen, hinunterschlucken.

swill (swil) n 1 Schweinefutter neu. 2 Spülwasser neu. vt spülen.

swim[*] (swim) vi 1 schwimmen. vt durchschwimmen. n Schwimmen neu. **swimming** n Schwimmen neu. **swimming costume** n Badeanzug m. **swimming pool** n Schwimmbad neu. **indoor swimming pool** n Hallenbad neu.

swindle ('swindl) vt betrügen, beschwindeln. n Schwindel, Betrug m.

swine (swain) n Schwein neu.

swing[*] (swiŋ) vi,vt schwingen, schaukeln. n 1 Schwung m. 2 Schaukel f.

swipe (swaip) vi,vt 1 hauen. n wilder Schlag m.

swirl (swɔːl) vi,vt (herum)wirbeln. n Wirbel m.

swish (swiʃ) vi 1 schwirren. 2 rascheln. vt schwirren lassen. adj schick, elegant.

Swiss (swis) adj schweizerisch. n Schweizer m.

switch (switʃ) n 1 Schalter m. 2 Umstellung f.

Wechsel *m*. 3 Rute *f*. *vt* 1 wechseln, tauschen. 2 umstellen. *vi* umstellen. **switch off** ausschalten. **switch on** anschalten. **switchboard** *n* Schalttafel *f*.

Switzerland ('switsələnd) *n* Schweiz *f*.

swivel ('swivəl) (*vi*,)*vt* (sich) drehen.

swollen ('swoulən) *adj* geschwollen.

swoop (swu:p) *vi* sich stürzen, herabschießen. *n* plötzlicher Angriff, Sturz *m*.

swop (swɔ:) *v* see **swap**.

sword (sɔ:d) *n* Schwert *neu*. **swordfish** *n* Schwertfisch *m*. **swordsman** *n* Fechter *m*.

swore (swɔ:) *v* see **swear**.

sworn (swɔ:n) *adj* 1 eidlich. 2 geschworen.

swot (swɔt) *vi inf* pauken. *n* Streber *m*.

swum (swʌm) *v* see **swim**.

swung (swʌŋ) *v* see **swing**.

sycamore ('sikəmɔ:) *n bot* Bergahorn *m*.

syllable ('siləbəl) *n* Silbe *f*.

syllabus ('siləbəs) *n* 1 Lehrplan *m*. 2 Verzeichnis *neu*.

symbol ('simbəl) *n* Symbol, Sinnbild *neu*. **symbolism** *n* 1 Symbolismus *m*. 2 Symbolik *f*. **symbolize** *vt* symbolisieren.

symmetry ('simitri) *n* Symmetrie *f*. Ebenmaß *neu*. **symmetrical** *adj* symmetrisch.

sympathy ('simpəθi) *n* 1 Mitgefühl, Mitleid *neu*. 2 Sympathie *f*. **sympathetic** *adj* 1 mitfühlend. 2 verständnisvoll. 3 wohlwollend. **sympathize** *vi* 1 mitfühlen, Mitleid haben. 2 übereinstimmen.

symphony ('simfəni) *n* Sinfonie, Symphonie *f*.

symposium (sim'pouziəm) *n* 1 Konferenz *f*. Symposion *neu*. 2 Tagungsbericht *m*.

symptom ('simptəm) *n* Symptom, Anzeichen *neu*. **symptomatic** *adj* symptomatisch.

synagogue ('sinəgɔg) *n* Synagoge *f*.

synchronize ('siŋkrənaiz) *vt* synchronisieren.

syndicate (*n* 'sindikət; *v* 'sindikeit) *n* Syndikat, Kartell *neu*. *vt* zu einem Syndikat vereinigen.

syndrome ('sindroum) *n* Syndrom *neu*.

synonym ('sinənim) *n* Synonym *neu*.

synopsis (si'nɔpsis) *n* Übersicht *f*. Abriß *m*.

syntax ('sintæks) *n* Syntax *f*. Satzbau *m*.

synthesis ('sinθəsis) *n* Synthese, Zusammensetzung *f*. **synthetic** *adj* synthetisch.

syphilis ('sifilis) *n* Syphilis *f*.

Syria ('siriə) *n* Syrien *neu*. **Syrian** *adj* syrisch. *n* Syrier *m*.

syringe (si'rindʒ) *n* Spritze *f*.

syrup ('sirəp) *n* Sirup *m*.

system ('sistəm) *n* 1 System *neu*. 2 Verfahren *neu*. Methode *f*. **systematic** *adj* systematisch, methodisch.

T

tab (tæb) *n* Aufhänger *m*. Etikett *neu*. **keep tabs on** kontrollieren.

tabby ('tæbi) *n* getigerte Katze *f*.

table ('teibəl) *n* 1 Tisch *m*. 2 Tafel *f*. 3 Liste *f*. **tablecloth** *n* Tischtuch *neu*. **tablemat** *n* Untersatz *m*. **tablespoon** *n* Eßlöffel *m*. **table tennis** *n* Tischtennis *neu*.

tablet ('tæblət) *n* 1 *med* Tablette *f*. 2 Tafel *f*.

taboo (tə'bu:) *n* Tabu *neu*. *adj* tabu, verboten.

tack (tæk) *n* 1 Zwecke *f*. 2 Heftstich *m*. 3 *naut* Lavieren *neu*. *vi naut* lavieren. *vt* (an)heften, befestigen.

tackle ('tækəl) *n* 1 Gerät *neu*. Ausrüstung *f*. 2 *naut* Takelwerk. 3 *sport* Angreifen *neu*. *vt* 1 angreifen. 2 angehen.

tact (tækt) *n* 1 Takt *m*. 2 Feingefühl *neu*. **tactful** *adj* taktvoll.

tactics ('tæktiks) *n pl* Taktik *f*. **tactical** *adj* taktisch.

tadpole ('tædpoul) *n* Kaulquappe *f*.

taffeta ('tæfitə) *n* Taft, Taffet *m*.

tag (tæg) *n* 1 Etikett *neu*. Anhängezettel *m*. 2 Stift *m*. *vt* anheften. **tag along** hinterherlaufen.

tail (teil) *n* 1 Schwanz *m*. 2 Ende *neu*. *vt* beschatten, verfolgen.

tailor ('teilə) *n* Schneider *m*. *vt* schneidern.

taint (teint) *vt* 1 beflecken. 2 verderben. *n* Makel, Fleck *m*.

take* (teik) *vt* 1 nehmen. 2 bringen. 3 ergreifen. 4 gewinnen. 5 fangen. 6 halten. **take in** 1 aufnehmen 2 einschließen. **take off** *vi* abfliegen. *vt* ausziehen, abnehmen. **take-off** *n aviat* Abflug *m*. **take-over** *n* Übernahme *f*. **take place** stattfinden.

talcum powder ('tælkəm) *n* Talkpuder *m*.

tale (teil) *n* 1 Erzählung *f*. 2 Lüge *f*.

talent ('tælənt) *n* Begabung, Talent *neu*.

talk (tɔ:k) *vi* reden, sprechen. *n* 1 Rede *f*. 2 Gespräch *neu*. 3 Gerede, Geschwätz *neu*. **talkative** *adj* geschwätzig, gesprächig.

tall (tɔ:l) *adj* 1 groß. 2 hoch. 3 lang. **tall story** *n* Spinnerei, unglaubliche Geschichte *f*.

tally ('tæli) *n* Rechnung *f*. *vi* übereinstimmen.

talon ('tælən) *n* Kralle, Klaue *f*.

tambourine (tæmbə'ri:n) *n* Tamburin *neu*.

tame (teim) *adj* zahm, gezähmt. *vt* zähmen.

tamper

tamper ('tæmpə) vi **tamper with** 1 sich einmischen in. 2 herumbasteln an.

tampon ('tæmpɔn) n Wattebausch, Tampon m.

tan (tæn) n 1 Lohe f. 2 Bräune f. adj gelbbraun. vt 1 gerben. 2 braun werden.

tangent ('tændʒənt) n Tangente f.

tangerine ('tændʒə'ri:n) n Mandarine f.

tangible ('tændʒəbəl) adj 1 greifbar. 2 fühlbar.

Tangier (tæn'dʒiə) n Tanger neu.

tangle ('tæŋgəl) n Wirrwarr m. Verwirrung f. vt 1 verwirren, verwickeln. 2 verknoten.

tank (tæŋk) n 1 Zisterne f. 2 Tank m. 3 mil Panzer m. v **tank up** tanken. **tanker** n Tanker m.

tankard ('tæŋkəd) n Kanne f. Bierkrug m.

tantalize ('tæntəlaiz) vt quälen.

tantrum ('tæntrəm) n Wutanfall m.

tap[1] (tæp) vt,vi klopfen. n Klopfen neu.

tap[2] (tæp) n Hahn, Zapfen m. vt 1 anzapfen. 2 (a telephone) anzapfen.

tape (teip) n 1 Band neu. 2 Tonband m. vt 1 auf Band aufnehmen. 2 mit einem Band befestigen. **tape measure** n Maßband neu. **tape-recorder** n Tonbandgerät neu.

taper ('teipə) vi,(vt) spitz zulaufen (lassen). n dünne Kerze f.

tapestry ('tæpistri) n Wandteppich m.

tapioca (tæpi'oukə) n Tapioka f.

tar (tɑ:) n Teer m. vt teeren.

tarantula (tə'ræntjulə) n Tarantel f.

target ('tɑ:git) n 1 Zielscheibe f. 2 Ziel neu.

tariff ('tærif) n 1 Zolltarif m. 2 Preisliste f.

Tarmac ('tɑ:mæk) n Tdmk Asphalt m.

tarnish ('tɑ:niʃ) vt 1 trüben. 2 beflecken. vi sich trüben.

tarragon ('tærəgən) n Estragon m.

tart[1] (tɑ:t) adj 1 sauer, herb. 2 beißend.

tart[2] (tæt) n 1 (Obst)Torte f. 2 sl Dirne f.

tartan ('tɑ:tn) n 1 karierter Wollstoff m. 2 kariertes Schottenmuster neu.

task (tɑ:sk) n Aufgabe f. **take someone to task** jemanden zur Rede stellen.

Tasmania (tæz'meiniə) n Tasmanien neu.

tassel ('tæsəl) n Quaste f.

taste (teist) vt 1 schmecken. 2 kosten. vi schmecken. n 1 Geschmack m. 2 Kostprobe f. **tasty** adj schmackhaft.

tattoo[1] (tə'tu:) n mil Zapfenstreich m.

tattoo[2] (tə'tu:) vt tätowieren. n Tätowierung f.

taught (tɔ:t) v see **teach**.

taunt (tɔ:nt) vt sticheln. n Stichelei f.

Taurus ('tɔ:rəs) n Stier m.

taut (tɔ:t) adj 1 gespannt, straff. 2 steif.

tautology (tɔ:'tɔlədʒi) n Tautologie f.

tavern ('tævən) n Schenke, Kneipe f.

tax (tæks) n Steuer f. vt 1 besteuern. 2 anstrengen. **income tax** Einkommensteuer f. **tax evasion** n Steuerhinterziehung f.

taxi (tæksi) n Taxi neu. vi aviat rollen.

tea (ti:) n 1 Tee m. 2 Teemahlzeit f. **high tea** n Abendbrot neu. **tea-bag** n Teebeutel m. **tea-break** n Teepause f. **tea-cloth** n Geschirrtuch neu. **teacup** n Teetasse f. **tea-leaves** n pl Teesatz m. **teapot** n Teekanne f. **teaspoon** n Teelöffel m.

teach[*] (ti:tʃ) vt lehren, unterrichten. vi unterrichten. **teacher** n Lehrer m. Lehrerin f. **teacher training college** n pädagogische Hochschule f.

teak (ti:k) n 1 Tiekbaum m. 2 Tiekholz neu.

team (ti:m) n 1 sport Mannschaft f. 2 (of horses) Gespann neu. 3 Team neu. v **team up** sich zusammentun.

tear[1] (tiə) n Träne f. **tear-gas** n Tränengas neu.

tear[2] (tɛə) vt (zer)reißen. vi 1 (zer)reißen. 2 zerren. 3 inf rasen. n Riß m.

tease (ti:z) vt 1 necken, ärgern, quälen. 2 tech (aus)zupfen, kämmen.

teat (ti:t) n 1 Brustwarze, Zitze f. 2 Lutscher m.

technical ('teknikəl) adj 1 technisch. 2 fachlich. **technician** n Techniker m. **technique** n Technik f. Verfahren neu. **technology** n 1 Technologie. 2 Gewerbekunde f.

tedious ('ti:diəs) adj langweilig, ermüdend.

tee[1] (ti:) n tech T-Stück neu.

tee[2] (ti:) n sport Abschlagstelle f. v **tee off** den Ball abschlagen.

teenage ('ti:neidʒ) adj jugendlich, Teenager—. **teenager** n Teenager m.

teetotal (ti:'toutl) adj antialkoholisch, abstinent. **teetotaller** n Abstinenzler m.

telegram ('teligræm) n Telegramm neu.

telegraph ('teligrɑ:f) vt telegraphieren. n Telegraph m. **telegraph pole** n Telegraphenstange f.

telepathy (ti'lepəθi) n Telepathie f.

telephone ('telifoun) n Telephon neu. Fernsprecher m. vt,vi telephonieren, anrufen. **telephone box** Telephonzelle f. **telephone call** Anruf m.

telescope ('teliskoup) n Fernrohr, Teleskop neu.

televise ('telivaiz) vt im Fernsehen übertragen. **television** n Fernsehen neu. **television (set)** n Fernsehapparat m.

telex ('teleks) n Fernschreibnetz neu.

tell (tel) vt 1 sagen, erzählen. 2 mitteilen. 3 erkennen. 4 unterscheiden. vi 1 erzählen. 2 Wirkung haben. **telltale** adj verräterisch. n Zuträger m.

temper ('tempə) n 1 Laune f. 2 Wut f. 3 tech Härtegrad m. vt 1 mildern. 2 tech härten. **temperament** n Temperament neu. **temperamental** adj temperamentvoll. **temperate** adj 1 mäßig. 2 mild. **temperature** n Temperatur f. **have a temperature** Fieber haben.

tempestuous (tem'pestjuəs) adj stürmisch.

temple[1] ('tempəl) n rel Tempel m.

temple[2] ('tempəl) n anat Schläfe f.

tempo ('tempou) n Tempo neu.

temporal ('tempərəl) adj 1 weltlich. 2 zeitlich. **temporary** adj vorübergehend, vorläufig.

tempt (tempt) vt 1 versuchen. 2 verlocken. **temptation** n 1 Versuchung f. 2 Anreiz m.

ten (ten) adj zehn. n Zehn f. **tenth** adj zehnte.

tenacious (tə'neiʃəs) adj beharrlich, zäh.

tenant ('tenənt) n Mieter, Pächter m. **tenancy** n Mietverhältnis neu.

tend[1] (tend) vi 1 neigen. 2 führen, gehen.

tend[2] (tend) vt 1 pflegen, hüten. 2 bedienen.

tendency ('tendənsi) n Neigung, Tendenz f.

tender[1] ('tendə) adj 1 weich, zart. 2 empfindlich. **tenderness** n Zartheit f.

tender[2] ('tendə) vt anbieten. n Angebot neu.

tendon ('tendən) n Sehne f.

tendril ('tendril) n Ranke f.

tenement ('tenəmənt) n 1 Mietwohnung f. 2 Miethaus neu.

tennis ('tenis) n Tennis neu. **tennis court** n Tennisplatz m.

tenor ('tenə) n 1 mus Tenor m. 2 Sinn m.

tense[1] (tens) adj gespannt, straff. (vi).vt (sich) anspannen. **tension** n Spannung f.

tense[2] (tens) n gram Zeit(form) f.

tent (tent) n Zelt neu.

tentacle ('tentəkəl) n Fühler m.

tentative ('tentətiv) adj 1 Versuchs—. 2 zögernd. **tentatively** adv versuchsweise.

tenuous ('tenjuəs) adj 1 dürftig. 2 dünn.

tepid ('tepid) adj (lau)warm.

term (tə:m) n 1 Termin m. 2 educ Trimester, Semester neu. 3 Ausdruck m. 4 pl Bedingungen f pl. 5 pl (persönliche) Beziehungen f pl. 6 pl Zahlungsforderungen f pl. vt (be)nennen.

terminal ('tə:minl) adj letzt, End—. n 1 Endstation f. 2 (electricity) Pol m. 3 Flughafengebäude neu.

terminate ('tə:mineit) vt 1 (be)endigen. 2 kündigen. vi aufhören, zu Ende kommen.

terminology (tə:mi'nolədʒi) n Terminologie f.

terminus ('tə:minəs) n 1 Endpunkt m. 2 Endstation f.

terrace ('terəs) n 1 Terrasse f. 2 Häuserreihe f.

terrestrial (tə'restriəl) adj irdisch, Erd—.

terrible ('teribəl) adj schrecklich, furchtbar.

terrier ('teriə) n Terrier m.

terrify ('terifai) vt erschrecken. **terrific** adj 1 fürchterlich. 2 inf großartig.

territory ('teritri) n Gebiet neu.

terror ('terə) n 1 Entsetzen neu. Schrecken m. 2 pol Terror m. **terrorist** n Terrorist m. **terrorize** vt terrorisieren.

Terylene ('terili:n) n Tdmk Terylene neu.

test (test) vt 1 prüfen, testen. 2 untersuchen. n 1 Prüfung, Probe f. 2 Test m. **test-tube** n Reagenzglas neu.

testament ('testəmənt) n Testament neu.

testicle ('testikəl) n Hoden m.

testify ('testifai) vt bezeugen. vi Zeugnis ablegen.

testimony ('testiməni) n 1 Zeugenaussage f. 2 Beweis m. **testimonial** n 1 Empfehlungsschreiben neu. 2 Gedenkzeichen neu.

tether ('teðə) n Haltestrick m. **be at the end of one's tether** nicht mehr weiter wissen. ~vt anbinden.

Teutonic (tju:'tonik) adj teutonisch.

text (tekst) n Text, Wortlaut m. **textbook** n Lehrbuch neu.

textile ('tekstail) n 1 Webstoff m. 2 pl Textilien pl. adj gewebt, Textil—. Web—.

texture ('tekstʃə) n 1 Gewebe neu. 2 Struktur f.

Thames (temz) n Themse f.

than (ðən; stressed ðæn) conj,prep als.

thank (θæŋk) vt danken. **thanks** n Dank m. interj also **thank you** danke (schön), vielen Dank. **thankful** adj dankbar.

that (ðæt) adj,pron jener, jene, jenes, der, die, das. pron der, die, das, welch. conj 1 daß. 2 daß, damit. **in that** insofern als. **so that** so daß.

thatch (θætʃ) n Dachstroh neu. vi mit Stroh decken.

thaw (θɔ:) vt,vi (auf)tauen. n Tauwetter neu.

the (ðə; stressed ði:) def art 1 der, die, das. 2 pl die. **the...the** je...desto.

theatre ('θiətə) n 1 Theater, Schauspielhaus neu. 2 med Operationssaal m. **theatrical** adj 1 bühnenmäßig. 2 theatralisch.

theft (θeft) n Diebstahl m.

their (ðɛə) poss adj 3rd pers pl ihr.

theirs (ðɛəz) poss pron 3rd pers pl ihrer, der ihre or ihrige.

them (ðəm; stressed ðem) pron 3rd pers pl 1 sie. 2 ihnen. **themselves** pron 3rd pers pl 1 sich. 2 sich selbst. 3 sie selbst.

theme (θi:m) n Thema neu. **thematic** adj thematisch.

then (ðen; stressed ðen) adv 1 dann, da, darauf, damals. 2 dann, demnach, weiter. conj also, dann. **until then** bis dahin.

theology (θi'ɔlədʒi) n Theologie f. **theologian** n Theologe m. **theological** adj theologisch.

theorem ('θiərəm) n Lehrsatz m. Theorem neu.

theory ('θiəri) n Theorie f. **theoretical** adj theoretisch. **theorize** vi Theorien aufstellen.

therapy ('θerəpi) n Therapie f. Heilverfahren neu. **therapeutic** adj therapeutisch.

there (ðɛə) adv dort(hin), da(rin). interj na nu! na also! **over there** dort drüben. **there is** es gibt, es ist. **there are** es gibt, es sind. **thereabouts** adv 1 da herum, in der Gegend. 2 so etwa, ungefähr. **thereafter** adv danach. **thereby** adv dadurch. **therefore** adv deshalb, deswegen, infolgedessen. **thereupon** adv darauf, danach. **therewith** adv damit.

thermal ('θə:məl) adj also **thermic** 1 thermisch. 2 warm.

thermodynamics (θə:moudai'næmiks) n Thermodynamik f.

thermometer (θə'mɔmitə) n Thermometer neu. Temperaturmesser m.

thermonuclear (θə:mou'nju:kliə) adj thermonuklear.

Thermos ('θə:məs) n Tdmk also **thermos flask** Thermosflasche f.

thermostat ('θə:məstæt) n Thermostat m.

these (ði:z) adj,pron pl diese, die.

thesis ('θi:sis) n, pl **-ses** 1 These, Behauptung f. 2 Dissertation f.

they (ðei) pron 3rd pers pl sie. **they say** man sagt.

thick (θik) adj 1 dick, dicht. 2 sl dumm. **thick-skinned** adj dickfellig. **thicken** vt 1 dick machen. 2 eindicken. vi 1 dick werden. 2 sich verdichten. **thickness** n 1 Dicke f 2 Dichtheit f.

thief (θi:f) n, pl **thieves** Dieb m. **stop thief!** haltet den Dieb!

thigh (θai) n (Ober)Schenkel m. **thigh-bone** n Oberschenkelknochen m.

thimble ('θimbəl) n Fingerhut m.

thin (θin) adj 1 dünn, mager. 2 spärlich. vt 1 dünn machen. 2 verdünnen. **thin-skinned** adj empfindlich. **thinness** n 1 Dünnheit f. 2 Dürftigkeit f.

thing (θiŋ) n 1 Ding neu. Sache f. 2 Geschöpf neu. **among other things** unter anderem. **no such thing** nichts dergleichen. **the very thing** genau das.

think* (θiŋk) vt,vi 1 denken. 2 sich vorstellen. 3 überlegen. **think of/about** denken an/über, halten von. **I think** so ich denke schon.

third (θə:d) adj dritte. n Drittel neu. **third party** n Dritte(r) m. **third-party insurance** n Haftpflichtversicherung f. **third person** n dritte Person f. **third-rate** adj drittrangig.

thirst (θə:st) n 1 Durst m. 2 Sehnsucht f. vi also **be thirsty** dürsten, Durst haben. **thirsty** adj 1 durstig. 2 begierig.

thirteen (θə:'ti:n) adj dreizehn. n Dreizehn f. **thirteenth** adj dreizehnte.

thirty ('θə:ti) adj dreißig. n Dreißig f. **thirtieth** adj dreißigste.

this (ðis) adj,pron dieser, diese, dies(es). **this minute** augenblicklich. **this morning** heute morgen.

thistle ('θisəl) n Distel f.

thorn (θɔ:n) n Dorn m. **thorny** adj dornig.

thorough ('θʌrə) adj 1 vollständig. 2 gründlich. **thoroughbred** n Vollblüter m. adj Vollblut--. **thoroughfare** n 1 Verkehrsader f. 2 Durchfahrt f. **thoroughly** adv 1 gründlich. 2 höchst.

those (ðouz) adj,pron pl jene, diejenigen.

though (ðou) conj 1 obgleich, obschon. 2 zwar. **as though** als ob.

thought[1] (θɔ:t) n 1 Denken neu. 2 Gedanke m. 3 Überlegung f. 4 Rücksicht f. **thoughtful** adj 1 rücksichtsvoll. 2 gedankenvoll. **thoughtless** adj 1 rücksichtslos. 2 gedankenlos. 3 unbesonnen.

thought[2] (θɔ:t) v see **think**.

thousand ('θauzənd) adj tausend. n Tausend neu. **thousandth** adj tausendste.

thrash (θræʃ) vt 1 prügeln. 2 besiegen.

thread (θred) n 1 Faden m. 2 tech Gewinde neu. vt einfädeln. vi sich durchziehen. **threadbare** adj fadenscheinig, abgedroschen.

threat (θret) n Drohung f. **threaten** (vt),vi (be)drohen.

three (θri:) adj drei. n Drei f. **three-cornered** adj dreieckig. **three-dimensional** adj dreidimensional. **threequarters** adj dreiviertel. **threesome** n Dreier neu. Dreiergruppe f.

thresh (θreʃ) vt (aus)dreschen.

threshold ('θreʃhould) n Schwelle f.

throw (θru:) v see **throw**.

thrift (θrift) n Sparsamkeit f. **thrifty** adj sparsam.

thrill (θril) n 1 Schauer m. 2 Sensation f. vt 1 erregen, 2 durchschauern. vi beben. **thriller** n 1 Sensationsfilm m. 2 Sensationsroman.

thrive (θraiv) vi gedeihen.

throat (θrout) n Kehle f. Schlund m.

throb (θrob) vi pochen, klopfen. n 1 Klopfen, Pochen neu. 2 Erregung f.

throne (θroun) n Thron m.

throng (θrɔŋ) n 1 Gedränge neu. Andrang m. 2 Menge f. vi (sich) drängen. vt bedrängen.

throttle (ˈθrɔtl) n Drosselventil neu. vt 1 erdrosseln. 2 ersticken.

through (θru:) prep 1 durch. 2 mit Hilfe (von). adv durch. **throughout** prep 1 überall in. 2 während. adv 1 überall. 2 durchaus.

throw* (θrou) vt werfen, schleudern. n Wurf m. **throw away** wegwerfen. **throw off** abwerfen. **throw out** hinauswerfen. **throw up** inf kotzen.

thrush (θrʌʃ) n zool Drossel f.

thrust* (θrʌst) vt 1 stoßen. 2 stecken. vi stoßen. n Stoß m.

thud (θʌd) n dumpfer Schlag m. vi dumpf aufschlagen.

thumb (θʌm) n Daumen m. vt durchblättern. **well-thumbed** adj (of a book) abgegriffen.

thump (θʌmp) n (dumpfer) Schlag, Puff m. vt schlagen. vi klopfen.

thunder (ˈθʌndə) n Donner m. vi donnern. **thunderstorm** n Gewitter neu.

Thuringia (θjuˈrindʒiə) n Thüringen neu.

Thursday (ˈθəːzdi) n Donnerstag m.

thus (ðʌs) adv so, also, auf diese Weise.

thwart (θwɔːt) vt durchkreuzen, vereiteln.

thyme (taim) n Thymian m.

thyroid (ˈθairɔid) adj 1 Schilddrüsen—. 2 Schildknorpel—. n 1 Schilddrüse f. 2 Schildknorpel m.

tiara (tiˈɑːrə) n Tiara f. Stirnreif m.

tick[1] (tik) vi 1 ticken. 2 inf funktionieren. vt abhaken. n 1 Ticken neu. 2 Häckchen neu.

tick[2] (tik) n zool Zecke f.

ticket (ˈtikit) n 1 Karte f. 2 Fahrschein m. Fahrkarte f. 3 Zettel m. **return ticket** Rückfahrkarte f. **season ticket** Zeitkarte f. **single ticket** einfache Fahrkarte f. **ticket collector** n Bahnsteigschaffner m. **ticket-office** n Fahrkartenschalter m.

tickle (ˈtikəl) vt,vi kitzeln. **ticklish** adj 1 kitz(e)lig. 2 heikel.

tide (taid) n 1 Ebbe und Flut f. 2 Strom m. **high tide** Flut f. **low tide** Ebbe f. **tidemark** n Gezeitenmarke f.

tidy (ˈtaidi) adj ordentlich, sauber. vt also **tidy up** aufräumen.

tie (tai) vt (ver)binden, schnüren. n 1 Schlips m. 2 Band neu. 3 sport Unentschieden neu.

tier (tiə) n Reihe f. Rang m.

tiger (ˈtaigə) n Tiger m.

tight (tait) adj 1 fest. 2 dicht. 3 eng, knapp. 4 straff, gespannt. 5 sl beschwipst. **tight-fisted** adj knauserig. **tightrope** n Drahtseil neu. **tights** n pl Strumpfhose f. **tighten** vt 1 straff spannen. 2 enger machen. 3 zusammenziehen.

tile (tail) n 1 Dachziegel m. 2 Fliese f. vt mit Ziegeln or Fliesen decken.

till[1] (til) prep,conj bis.

till[2] (til) vt bebauen, bearbeiten.

till[3] (til) n Kasse, Geldschublade f.

tiller (ˈtilə) n Ruderpinne, Steuerstange f.

tilt (tilt) (vi,)vt (sich) kippen, (sich) neigen. n Neigung f. Hang m.

timber (ˈtimbə) n 1 Bauholz, Nutzholz neu. 2 Balken m. adj hölzern.

time (taim) n 1 Zeit f. 2 Mal neu. 3 mus Takt m. 4 pl Zeitalter neu. vi 1 die Zeit bestimmen. 2 die Zeit messen von. **time bomb** n Zeitbombe f. **timetable** n 1 Stundenplan m. 2 Fahrplan m.

timid (ˈtimid) adj 1 furchtsam. 2 scheu.

tin (tin) n 1 Zinn, (Weiß)Blech neu. 2 Dose, Büchse f. adj zinnern. vt 1 konservieren. 2 verzinnen. **tin-opener** n Büchsenöffner m.

tinge (tindʒ) n 1 Färbung f. 2 Anhauch m. vt 1 färben. 2 einen Anhauch geben.

tingle (ˈtiŋgəl) vi 1 prickeln. 2 klingen. n 1 Klingen neu. 2 Prickeln neu.

tinker (ˈtiŋkə) n Kesselflicker m. vi basteln.

tinkle (ˈtiŋkəl) vi klingeln. n Geklingel neu.

tinsel (ˈtinsəl) n 1 Flitter m. 2 Lametta neu.

tint (tint) n Tönung f. vt leicht tönen.

tiny (ˈtaini) adj winzig.

tip[1] (tip) n Spitze f. vt mit einer Spitze versehen. **tiptoe** vi auf Zehenspitzen gehen.

tip[2] (tip) vt,vi umkippen. n Abladeplatz m.

tip[3] (tip) n 1 Trinkgeld neu. 2 Wink, Tip m. vt 1 ein Trinkgeld geben. 2 einen Wink geben.

tipsy (ˈtipsi) adj beschwipst.

tire (ˈtaiə) vt 1 müde machen. 2 erschöpfen. vi müde werden. **tired** adj 1 müde. 2 erschöpft. **be tired of something** etwas satt haben.

tissue ('tiʃuː) n 1 (feines) Gewebe neu. 2 Papiertaschentuch neu.

title ('taitl) n Titel m. vt betiteln.

to (tə; stressed tuː) prep 1 zu. 2 vor. 3 nach. 4 an. 5 gegen. 6 zugleich. conj um zu. to and fro adv hin und her. **to-do** n Getue neu.

toad (toud) n Kröte f. **toadstool** n Giftpilz m.

toast[1] (toust) n Toast m. vt 1 toasten, rösten. 2 wärmen.

toast[2] (toust) n Trinkspruch m. vt trinken auf.

tobacco (tə'bækou) n Tabak m. **tobacconist** n Tabakhändler m.

toboggan (tə'bɔgən) n Rodelschlitten m. vi rodeln.

today (tə'dei) adv heute, heutzutage.

toddler ('tɔdlə) n kleines Kind neu.

toe (tou) n Zehe f. **toenail** n Zehennagel m.

toffee ('tɔfi) n Karamelle f. Toffee neu.

together (tə'geðə) adv 1 zusammen, miteinander. 2 zugleich.

toil (tɔil) vi arbeiten, sich mühen. n Mühe, Plackerei f.

toilet ('tɔilət) n 1 Toilette f. 2 Klo(sett) neu. **toilet paper** n Klosettpapier neu.

token ('toukən) n 1 Zeichen neu. 2 Andenken neu. 3 Gutschein m.

told (tould) v see **tell**.

tolerate ('tɔləreit) vt 1 dulden. 2 aushalten. 3 tolerieren. **tolerance** n Duldsamkeit, Toleranz f. **tolerant** adj tolerant.

toll[1] (toul) vt,vi läuten, schlagen.

toll[2] (toul) n 1 Wegegeld neu. Zoll m. Tribut m. **tollgate** n Schlagbaum m.

tomato (tə'maːtou) n, pl **-oes** Tomate f.

tomb (tuːm) n Grab(mal) neu.

tomorrow (tə'mɔrou) adv morgen. **the day after tomorrow** übermorgen. **tomorrow morning** morgen früh. **tomorrow week** morgen in acht Tagen.

ton (tʌn) n Tonne f.

tone (toun) n 1 Ton m. 2 Tönung f. vt abtönen.

tongs (tɔŋz) n pl Zange f.

tongue (tʌŋ) n 1 anat Zunge f. 2 Sprache f. **hold one's tongue** den Mund halten. **tongue in cheek** ironisch. **tongue-tied** adj stumm. **tongue-twister** n Zungenbrecher m.

tonic ('tɔnik) adj 1 tonisch, stärkend. 2 mus Grundton—. n 1 Stärkungsmittel neu. 2 mus Grundton m. **tonic water** n Sprudel(wasser) m, neu.

tonight (tə'nait) adv heute abend or nacht.

tonsil ('tɔnsəl) n Mandel f. **tonsilitis** n Mandelentzündung f.

too (tuː) adv 1 (all)zu. 2 sehr. 3 auch, dazu. **all too** viel zu, allzu.

took (tuk) v see **take**.

tool (tuːl) n Werkzeug, Gerät neu.

tooth (tuːθ) n, pl **teeth** Zahn m. **toothache** n Zahnweh neu. Zahnschmerzen m pl. **toothbrush** n Zahnbürste f. **toothpaste** n Zahnpasta f. **toothpick** n Zahnstocher m.

top[1] (tɔp) n 1 Spitze f. Wipfel, Gipfel m. 2 Oberfläche f. Oberteil m. 3 Deckel m. adj 1 oberst, höchst. 2 best. vt 1 übertreffen. 2 köpfen. 3 anführen. **top hat** n Zylinder m. **top-heavy** adj kopflastig.

top[2] (tɔp) n Kreisel m.

topaz ('toupæz) n Topaz m.

topic ('tɔpik) n Gegenstand m. Thema neu. **topical** adj 1 aktuell. 2 med örtlich.

topography (tə'pɔgrəfi) n Topographie f.

topple ('tɔpəl) vi kippen, stürzen. **topple down** or **over** umkippen, niederstürzen.

topsoil ('tɔpsɔil) n Ackerkrume f.

topsy-turvy (tɔpsi'təːvi) adj,adv inf das Oberste zuunterst, drunter und drüber.

torch (tɔːtʃ) n 1 Taschenlampe f. 2 Fackel f.

tore (tɔː) v see **tear**.

torment (n 'tɔːment) n Qual f. vt quälen.

torn (tɔːn) v see **tear**.

tornado (tɔː'neidou) n Tornado, Wirbelsturm m.

torpedo (tɔː'piːdou) n Torpedo m. vt torpedieren.

torrent ('tɔrənt) n 1 Sturzbach m. 2 Wolkenbruch m. 3 Strom m. 4 Wortschwall m.

torso ('tɔːsou) n Torso m.

tortoise ('tɔːtəs) n Schildkröte f.

tortuous ('tɔːtʃuəs) adj gewunden, krumm.

torture ('tɔːtʃə) n Folter, Marter, Qual f. vt foltern, martern, quälen.

Tory ('tɔːri) n britische(r) Konservative(r) m.

toss (tɔs) vt 1 (hoch)werfen. 2 schütteln. vi 1 sich unruhig bewegen. 2 schlingern. n Wurf m.

tot[1] (tɔt) n Schluck m.

tot[2] (tɔt) vt **tot up** zusammenrechnen.

total ('toutl) adj 1 gesamt. 2 ganz, völlig, total. n 1 Ganze f. 2 Summe f. Gesamtbetrag m. vi sich belaufen auf. **totalitarian** adj totalitär.

totem ('toutəm) n Totem neu. **totem pole** n Totempfahl m.

totter ('tɔtə) vi schwanken, wanken.

touch (tʌtʃ) vt (an-, be-)rühren. vi in Berührung kommen, berühren. **touch down** aviat landen. **touch up** auffrischen. ~n 1 Berührung

f. **2** Tastsinn m. **3** Spur f. Hauch m. **4** Hand f. **touchy** adj reizbar, überempfindlich.

tough (tʌf) adj **1** zäh. **2** hart. **toughen** vt zäh(er) machen, abhärten.

toupee ('tu:pei) n Toupet neu.

tour (tuə) n Tour, Reise, Rundfahrt f. Rundgang m. vt bereisen, besuchen. vi reisen. **tourism** n Fremdenverkehr, Tourismus m. **tourist** n Tourist m.

tournament ('tuənəmənt) n Tournier neu.

tow (tou) vt **1** (ab)schleppen. **2** bugsieren. **towrope** n Schlepptau neu.

towards (tə'wɔːdz) prep also **toward 1** gegen. **2** nach (...zu), auf...zu or hin. **3** entgegen.

towel ('tauəl) n Handtuch, Badetuch neu.

tower ('tauə) n Turm m. vi sich erheben, emporragen. **tower-block** n Hochhaus neu.

town (taun) n Stadt f. **town clerk** n Stadtsyndikus m. **town hall** n Rathaus neu. **town-planning** n Städteplanung f.

toxic ('tɔksik) adj giftig, toxisch.

toy (tɔi) n Spielzeug neu. v **toy with** spielen mit.

trace (treis) n Spur f. vt **1** folgen, nachgehen. **2** zurückverfolgen. **3** durchzeichnen.

track (træk) n **1** Weg, Pfad m. **2** (of a railway) Gleis neu. **3** Spur f. **4** sport Bahn f. vt (ver)folgen, nachspüren. **tracksuit** n Trainingsanzug m.

tract[1] (trækt) n **1** Strecke f. **2** anat System neu. **3** Zeitraum m.

tract[2] (trækt) n rel Traktat m,neu.

tractor ('træktə) n Schlepper, Traktor m.

trade (treid) n **1** Handel m. **2** Gewerbe f. Geschäft neu. vi handeln. vt austauschen. **trademark** n Schutzmarke f. **tradesman** n Ladenbesitzer, Händler m. **trade union** n Gewerkschaft f.

tradition (trə'diʃən) n **1** Tradition, Überlieferung f. **2** Brauch m. **traditional** adj traditionell.

traffic ('træfik) n **1** Verkehr m. **2** comm Handel m. **traffic jam** n Verkehrsstockung f. **traffic lights** n pl Verkehrsampel f. **traffic warden** n Verkehrsaufseher m.

tragedy ('trædʒədi) n Trauerspiel neu. Tragödie f. **tragic** adj tragisch.

trail (treil) n **1** Spur f. **2** Schweif m. vt **1** nachschleppen. **2** verfolgen. vi schleifen. **trailer** n **1** mot Anhänger m. **2** (of a film) Vorschau f.

train (trein) n **1** Zug m. **2** Reihe f. **3** Gefolge neu. vt **1** schulen, ausbilden. **2** sport trainie-

ren. vi sport trainieren. **trainee** n Lehrling, Praktikant m.

traitor ('treitə) n Verräter m.

tram (træm) n Straßenbahn f.

tramp (træmp) vi **1** wandern. **2** trampeln, treten. n **1** Landstreicher m. **2** Wanderung f.

trample ('træmpəl) vt zertrampeln. vi herumtreten.

trampoline ('træmpəli:n) n Trampoline f.

trance (trɑːns) n **1** Verzückung f. **2** Trance f.

tranquil ('træŋkwil) adj still, ruhig, gelassen. **tranquillity** n **1** Ruhe f. **2** Gelassenheit f. **tranquillizer** n Beruhigungsmittel neu.

transact (træn'zækt) vt durchführen. **transaction** n Geschäft neu. Verhandlung f.

transatlantic (trænzət'læntik) adj transatlantisch.

transcend (træn'send) vt übersteigen, überschreiten.

transcribe (træn'skraib) vt **1** umschreiben. **2** mus umsetzen.

transfer (v træns'fəː; n 'trænsfəː) vt **1** übertragen. **2** versetzen. **3** (money) überweisen. n **1** Übertragung f. **2** Versetzung f. **3** Überweisung f. **4** Versand m. **5** Abziehbild neu.

transform (træns'fɔːm) vt verwandeln, umformen. **transformation** n Verwandlung f. **transformer** n tech Transformator m.

transfuse (træns'fjuːz) vt **1** med übertragen. **2** durchtränken. **transfusion** n **1** med Blutübertragung f. **2** Durchtränkung f.

transistor (træn'zistə) n Transistor m. **transistor (radio)** Transistorradio neu.

transit ('trænsit) n **1** Durchgang m. **2** Durchgangsverkehr m. **in transit** unterwegs.

transition (træn'ziʃən) n Übergang m.

transitive ('trænsitiv) adj transitiv.

translate (trænz'leit) vt übersetzen, übertragen.

translucent (trænz'luːsənt) adj **1** nicht ganz durchsichtig. **2** lichtdurchlässig.

transmit (trænz'mit) vt **1** (by radio, etc.) (über)senden, übertragen. **2** überliefern. **transmitter** n Sender m. **transmission** n **1** (by radio, etc.) Sendung f. **2** tech Getriebe neu. **3** Übersendung m.

transparent (trænz'pɛərənt) adj durchsichtig.

transplant (v trænz'plɑːnt; n 'trænsplɑːnt) vt **1** umpflanzen. **2** med transplantieren. n **1** Umpflanzung f. **2** Transplantation f.

transport (v 'trænspɔːt; n,adj 'trænspɔːt) vt befördern, transportieren. n **1** Beförderung, Spedition f. Transport m. Versand m. **2** Begeisterung f. adj Transport—.

293

transpose (træns'pouz) vt 1 umsetzen. 2 mus transponieren.

trap (træp) n Falle f. vt (ein)fangen, erwischen. **trapdoor** n Falltür f.

trapeze (trə'piːz) n 1 Trapez neu.

trash (træʃ) n 1 wertloses Zeug neu. Kitsch m. 2 Unsinn m. 3 Abfall m.

trauma ('trɔːmə) n Trauma neu.

travel ('trævəl) vi reisen. vt bereisen. n 1 Reise f. Reisen neu. 2 pl Reisen f pl. **travel agency** n Reisebüro n. **traveller** n Reisende(r) m. **traveller's cheque** n Reisescheck m.

trawl (trɔːl) n Schleppnetz neu. vi mit dem Schleppnetz fischen. **trawler** n Schleppnetzfischerboot neu. Trawler m.

tray (trei) n Tablett, Servierbrett neu.

treachery ('tretʃəri) n Verrat m. Untreue f. **treacherous** adj 1 verräterisch. 2 gefährlich.

treacle ('triːkəl) n Sirup m. Melasse f.

tread (tred) vi treten. vt betreten. n 1 Schritt, Tritt m. 2 mot Reifenprofil neu.

treason ('triːzən) n Verrat m. **high treason** Hochverrat m.

treasure ('treʒə) n Schatz m. vt 1 (hoch)schätzen. 2 anhäufen. **treasurer** n Schatzmeister, Kassenwart m. **treasury** n 1 Schatzkammer f. 2 Finanzministerium neu.

treat (triːt) vt 1 behandeln. 2 freihalten. n Genuß m. Vergnügen neu. **treatment** n Behandlung f.

treatise ('triːtiz) n Abhandlung f.

treaty ('triːti) n Vertrag m. Abkommen neu.

treble ('trebəl) adj 1 dreifach. 2 mus Sopran—. n mus Sopran, Diskant m.

tree (triː) n Baum m.

trek (trek) vi trecken. n lange Reise f. Treck m.

trellis ('trelis) n 1 Gitter neu. 2 Spalier neu.

tremble ('trembəl) vi zittern, beben.

tremendous (tri'mendəs) adj 1 furchtbar. 2 inf riesig, gewaltig.

tremor ('tremə) n Zittern, Beben neu.

trench (trentʃ) n Graben m. vt mit Gräben durchziehen.

trend (trend) n 1 Neigung, Tendenz f. Trend m. 2 Mode f.

trespass ('trespəs) n 1 unerlaubtes Betreten neu. 2 Vergehen neu. vi 1 widerrechtlich betreten. 2 verstoßen.

trestle ('tresəl) n Bock m. Gestell neu.

trial ('traiəl) n 1 Gerichtsverfahren neu. Prozeß m. 2 Versuch m. Probe f. 3 Prüfung f.

triangle ('traiæŋgəl) n 1 Dreieck neu. 2 mus Triangel m. **triangular** adj dreieckig.

tribe (traib) n (Volks)Stamm m. **tribesman** n Stammesangehörige(r).

tribunal (trai'bjuːnl) n 1 Gericht, Tribunal neu. 2 Gerichtshof m.

tributary ('tribjutəri) adj 1 zinspflichtig. 2 zufließend. n Nebenfluß m.

tribute ('tribjuːt) n 1 Tribut m. 2 Lob neu.

trick (trik) n 1 Streich m. 2 Trick, Kniff m. 3 game Stich m. vt überlisten, betrügen. **tricky** adj 1 schlau. 2 verwickelt, heikel.

trickle ('trikəl) vi tröpfeln. n Tröpfeln neu.

tricycle ('traisikəl) n Dreirad neu.

tried (traid) adj erprobt.

trifle ('traifəl) n 1 Kleinigkeit f. 2 cul (süßer) Auflauf m. v **trifle with** tändeln, spielen.

trigger ('trigə) n Abzug, Drücker m. vt auslösen.

trill (tril) vi trillern. n Triller m.

trim (trim) adj 1 nett, hübsch. 2 ordentlich, in Ordnung. vt 1 beschneiden. 2 garnieren. 3 naut trimmen. n 1 Schmuck m. 2 Ordnung f.

trio ('triou) n Trio neu.

trip (trip) n 1 Reise f. 2 Ausflug m. vi stolpern. vt ein Bein stellen.

tripe (traip) n 1 cul Kaldaunen f pl. 2 inf Quatsch m.

triple ('tripəl) adj dreifach. (vi).vt (sich) verdreifachen. **triplet** n 1 lit Dreireim m. 2 Dreiergruppe f. 3 Drilling m.

tripod ('traipɔd) n Dreifuß m.

trite (trait) adj abgedroschen, platt.

triumph ('traiʌmf) n Triumph m. vi triumphieren, siegen. **triumphant** adj triumphierend, jubelnd.

trivial ('triviəl) adj trivial, unbedeutend.

trod (trɔd) v see **tread.**

trodden ('trɔdn) v see **tread.**

trolley ('trɔli) n 1 (Hand)Karren m. 2 Kontaktrolle f. **trolley bus** n Obus m.

trombone (trɔm'boun) n Posaune f.

troop (truːp) n 1 Truppe f. 2 Trupp m. Schar f. vi sich sammeln, sich scharen.

trophy ('troufi) n Trophäe f. Siegeszeichen neu. Preis m.

tropic ('trɔpik) n 1 Wendekreis m. 2 pl Tropen pl.

trot (trɔt) vi traben, trotten. n Trab m. **trotter** n 1 Traber m. 2 pl cul Hammelfüße, Schweinsfüße m pl.

trouble ('trʌbəl) n 1 Unruhe, Schwierigkeit f. 2 Kummer m. Unglück neu. 3 tech Störung f. **in trouble** in Verlegenheit or Not. ~vt 1 beunruhigen, stören. 2 belästigen. *vi* sich bemühen. **troublemaker** *n* Unruhestifter. Störenfried *m*. **troublesome** *adj* lästig, störend.

trough (trɔf) *n* Mulde *f*. Trog *m*.

troupe (tru:p) *n* (Theater)Truppe *f*.

trousers ('trauzəz) *n pl* Hose *f*. Hosen *f pl*.

trout (traut) *n* Forelle *f*.

trowel ('trauəl) *n* 1 Maurerkelle *f*. 2 Ausheber *m*.

truant ('truənt) *n* 1 Schulschwänzer *m*. 2 Müßiggänger *m*. *adj* 1 schulschwänzend. 2 müßig. **play truant** (die Schule) schwänzen.

truce (tru:s) *n* Waffenstillstand *m*.

truck (trʌk) *n* 1 Güterwagen *m*. 2 Lastkraftwagen *m*.

trudge (trʌdʒ) *vi* sich (mühsam) schleppen.

true (tru:) *adj* 1 wahr, richtig. 2 echt, wirklich. 3 treu. **truly** *adv* 1 wirklich, tatsächlich. 2 aufrichtig. **yours truly** Hochachtungsvoll.

truffle ('trʌfəl) *n* Trüffel *f*.

trump (trʌmp) *n* Trumpf *m*. *vt* stechen.

trumpet ('trʌmpit) *n* Trompete *f*.

truncheon ('trʌntʃən) *n* Knüttel, Knüppel *m*.

trunk (trʌŋk) *n* 1 *bot* Stamm *m*. 2 *anat* Rumpf *m*. 3 *zool* Rüssel *m*. 4 (Schrank)Koffer *m*. 5 *pl* Badehose *f*.

trust (trʌst) *vt* (ver)trauen, sich verlassen auf. *vi* 1 vertrauen, sich verlassen. 2 (zuversichtlich) hoffen. *n* 1 Vertrauen *neu*. 2 *comm* Kartell *neu*. 3 *law* Pflegschaft *f*. **trustworthy** *adj* zuverlässig, vertrauenswürdig. **trustee** *n* Treuhänder, Vermögensverwalter *m*.

truth (tru:θ) *n* Wahrheit *f*. **truthful** *adj* 1 ehrlich, wahrhaftig. 2 wahrheitsgemäß.

try (trai) *vt* 1 versuchen, probieren. 2 *law* verhören. 3 proben. *n* Versuch *m*. **trying** *adj* 1 unangenehm, lästig. 2 anstrengend.

tsar (tsa:) *n* Zar *m*.

T-shirt *n* Trikot, Sporthemd *neu*.

tub (tʌb) *n* 1 Faß *neu*. 2 (Bade)Wanne *f*. **tubby** *adj inf* rundlich, dickbauchig.

tuba ('tju:bə) *n* Tuba *f*.

tube (tju:b) *n* 1 Rohr *neu*. 2 Schlauch *m*. 3 Tube *f*. 4 Untergrundbahn, U-Bahn *f*.

tuber ('tju:bə) *n bot* Knolle *f*.

tuberculosis (tju:bə:kju'lousis) *n* Tuberkulose *f*.

tuck (tʌk) *n* 1 Falte *f*. Umschlag *m*. 2 *sl* Süßigkeiten *f pl*. *vt* 1 falten. 2 einschlagen. **tuck away** wegstecken. **tuck in** *inf* zugreifen, einhauen.

Tuesday ('tju:zdi) *n* Dienstag *m*.

tuft (tʌft) *n* Büschel *neu*.

tug (tʌg) *vt* 1 zerren, ziehen. 2 *naut* schleppen. *vi* ziehen. *n* 1 Ruck *m*. 2 *naut* Schlepper *m*. **tug of war** *n* Tauziehen *neu*.

tuition (tju:'iʃən) *n* Unterricht *m*.

tulip ('tu:lip) *n* Tulpe *f*.

tumble ('tʌmbəl) *vi* 1 (hin)fallen. 2 purzeln. *vt* (um)stürzen. *n* Sturz, Fall *m*. **tumbler** *n* Becher *m*. Trinkglas *neu*.

tummy ('tʌmi) *n inf* Magen, Bauch *m*.

tumour ('tju:mə) *n* Geschwulst *f*. Tumor *m*.

tumult ('tumʌlt) *n* Tumult *m*. Getümmel *neu*. Aufruhr *m*.

tuna ('tju:nə) *n* Thunfisch *m*.

tune (tju:n) *n* 1 Melodie *f*. 2 Stimmung *f*. *vt* stimmen. **in tune** (gut) gestimmt. **out of tune** verstimmt. **tuneful** *adj* melodisch.

tunic ('tju:nik) *n* 1 Bluse *f*. Überkleid *neu*. 2 Soldatenrock *m*.

Tunisia (tju:'nizia) *n* Tunesien *neu*.

tunnel ('tʌnl) *n* Tunnel *m*.

tunny ('tʌni) *n* see **tuna.**

turbine ('tə:bain) *n* Turbine *f*.

turbot ('tə:bət) *n* Steinbutt *m*.

turbulent ('tə:bjulənt) *adj* 1 unruhig. 2 aufgeregt, stürmisch, turbulent.

turf (tə:f) *n* 1 Rasen *m*. 2 Torf *m*. 3 Pferderennen *neu*. *vt* mit Rasen belegen. **turf accountant** *n sport* Buchmacher *m*.

Turk (tə:k) *n* Türke *m*.

turkey ('tə:ki) *n* Truthahn *m*. Pute *f*.

Turkey ('tə:ki) *n* Türkei *f*. **Turkish** *adj* türkisch. *n* (language) Türkisch *neu*. **Turkish bath** *n* Schwitzbad *neu*.

turmeric ('tə:mərik) *n* Gelbwurz *f*.

turmoil ('tə:moil) *n* Aufruhr, Tumult *m*.

turn (tə:n) *vt* 1 drehen. 2 machen, verwandeln. 3 (um)wenden. 4 lenken, abbringen. 5 werden. *vi* 1 sich drehen. 2 werden. 3 sich umwenden. 4 gehen. **turn down** ablehnen. **turn off** abbiegen. 2 abstellen, abdrehen. **turn on** anstellen, einschalten. **turn up** auftauchen. ~*n* 1 Drehung *f*. 2 Wendung *f*. 3 Runde *f*. 4 Versuch *m*. 5 Veränderung *f*. **turning** *n* 1 Drehen *neu*. 2 Kurve *f*. 3 Ecke *f*. 4 Querstraße *f*. **turnover** *n* 1 Umschwung *f*. 2 *comm* Umsatz *m*. 3 *cul* (Apfel)Tasche *f*. **turnstile** *n* Drehkreuz *neu*. **turntable** *n* Plattenteller *m*.

turnip ('tə:nip) *n* (weiße) Rübe *f*.

turpentine ('tə:pəntain) *n* Terpentin *m*.

turquoise ('tə:kwoiz) *n* Türkis *m*.

turret ('tʌrət) *n* Türmchen *neu*. Turm *m*.

turtle ('tə:tl) *n* Schildkröte *f*.

tusk (tʌsk) n Stoßzahn m.

tussle ('tʌsəl) n Kampf m. Balgerei f. vi kämpfen, sich balgen.

tutor ('tjuːtə) n 1 law Vormund m. 2 (at a university) Tutor m. 3 Privatlehrer m. vt Unterricht geben.

tweed (twiːd) n Tweed m.

tweezers ('twiːzəz) n pl Pinzette f.

twelve (twelv) adj zwölf. n Zwölf f. **twelfth** adj zwölfte.

twenty ('twenti) adj zwanzig. n Zwanzig f. **twentieth** adj zwanzigste.

twice (twais) adv zweimal.

twiddle ('twidʒl) vt müßig herumdrehen, spielen mit.

twig (twig) n Zweig m.

twilight ('twailait) n Zwielicht neu. Dämmerung f.

twin (twin) n Zwilling m. adj doppelt, Zwillings—.

twine (twain) n Bindfaden m. Zwirn m. vt (ineinander) verflechten, winden. vi sich winden, sich verflechten.

twinge (twindʒ) n 1 (stechender) Schmerz m. 2 Gewissensbiß m.

twinkle ('twiŋkəl) vi blinken, funkeln. n Blinzeln, Funkeln neu.

twirl (twəːl) vi,vt zwirbeln, herumwirbeln. n Wirbel m.

twist (twist) vt 1 (zusammen)drehen, winden. 2 verdrehen. 3 biegen. vi sich drehen, sich winden. n 1 Drehung, Windung f. 2 Biegung f. 3 Verdrehung f.

twitch (twitʃ) vi zucken. vt zwicken. n Ruck m. Zucken neu.

twitter ('twitə) vi zwitschern. n Gezwitscher neu.

two (tuː) adj 1 zwei. 2 beide. n Zwei f. **in twos** zu zweit. **in two** entzwei. **two-faced** adj 1 doppelgesichtig. 2 heuchlerisch. **twosome** n Paar, Pärchen neu. **two-way** adj 1 Doppel—. 2 Gegen—.

tycoon (tai'kuːn) n inf Industriekapitän m.

type (taip) n 1 Typ m. Art, Sorte f. 2 Klasse, Kategorie f. 3 Muster neu. 4 Type f. vi,vt tippen, mit der Maschine schreiben. **typewriter** n Schreibmaschine f. **typical** adj typisch, kennzeichnend. **typify** vt verkörpern, typisch sein für. **typist** n Maschinenschreiberin f.

typhoid ('taifoid) n Typhus m.

typhoon (tai'fuːn) n Taifun m.

tyrant ('taiərənt) n Tyrann m. **tyranny** n Tyrannei f.

tyre ('taiə) n Reifen m.

Tyrol (ti'roul) n Tirol neu.

U

ubiquitous (juː'bikwitəs) adj allgegenwärtig.

udder ('ʌdə) n Euter neu.

ugly ('ʌgli) adj häßlich. **ugliness** n Häßlichkeit f.

ukulele (juːkə'leːli) n Ukulele neu.

ulcer ('ʌlsə) n Geschwür neu.

ulterior (ʌl'tiəriə) adj 1 jenseitig. 2 verborgen.

ultimate ('ʌltimət) adj 1 äußerst. 2 letzt. **ultimatum** n Ultimatum neu.

ultraviolet (ʌltrə'vaiələt) adj ultraviolett.

umbrella (ʌm'brelə) n Regenschirm m.

umlaut ('umlaut) n Umlaut m.

umpire ('ʌmpaiə) n Schiedsrichter m.

umpteen (ʌmp'tiːn) adj inf zahllos. **umpteen times** x-mal.

unable (ʌn'eibəl) adj unfähig.

unacceptable (ʌnək'septəbəl) adj unannehmbar, nicht akzeptabel.

unaccompanied (ʌnə'kʌmpnid) adj unbegleitet.

unanimous (juː'næniməs) adj einstimmig.

unarmed (ʌn'ɑːmd) adj unbewaffnet.

unattractive (ʌnə'træktiv) adj reizlos.

unavoidable (ʌnə'vɔidəbəl) adj unvermeidlich.

unaware (ʌnə'wɛə) adj 1 nicht bewußt. 2 ahnungslos. **unawares** adv unversehens, unerwartet. **catch unawares** überraschen.

unbalanced (ʌn'bælənst) adj 1 unausgeglichen, unstet. 2 (of mind) gestört.

unbearable (ʌn'bɛərəbəl) adj unerträglich.

unbelievable (ʌnbi'liːvəbəl) adj unglaublich, unglaubhaft.

unbend (ʌn'bend) vi 1 sich entspannen. 2 gerade werden. vt entspannen, losmachen. **unbending** adj unnachgiebig.

unbreakable (ʌn'breikəbəl) adj unzerbrechlich.

unbridled (ʌn'braidld) adj zügellos.

uncalled-for (ʌn'kɔːld-) adj unnötig, unangebracht.

uncanny (ʌn'kæni) adj unheimlich.

uncertain (ʌn'səːtn) adj 1 unbestimmt. 2 ungewiß. 3 unzuverlässig.

uncle ('ʌŋkəl) n Onkel m.

uncomfortable (ʌn'kʌmftəbəl) adj 1 unbequem. 2 unbehaglich.

unconscious (ʌn'kɔnʃəs) adj 1 bewußtlos, ohnmächtig. 2 unbewußt. n Unbewußte neu.

unconventional (ʌnkən'venʃənəl) adj unkonventionell, ungezwungen.

uncooked (ʌn'kukt) adj ungekocht, roh.

uncouth (ʌn'ku:θ) adj grob, roh, ungebildet.

uncover (ʌn'kʌvə) vt 1 aufdecken. 2 bloßlegen.

uncut (ʌn'kʌt) adj 1 ungeschnitten. 2 (of a gem) ungeschliffen.

undecided (ʌndi'saidid) adj unentschlossen.

undeniable (ʌndi'naiəbəl) adj unleugbar.

under (ʌndə) prep unter. adv (nach) unten.

under age adj,adv minderjährig.

undercharge (ʌndə'tʃɑːdʒ) vt,vi zu wenig berechnen.

undercoat (ʌndəkout) n (of paint) Untergrund, Grundanstrich m.

undercover (ʌndəkʌvə) adj Geheim—.

undercut (ʌndə'kʌt) vt comm unterbieten.

underdeveloped (ʌndədi'veləpd) adj unterentwickelt.

underdone (ʌndə'dʌn) adj nicht gargekocht.

underestimate (ʌndər'estimeit) vt unterschätzen.

underfoot (ʌndə'fut) adv unter den Füßen.

undergo* (ʌndə'gou) vt 1 erleben. 2 erdulden. 3 sich unterziehen.

undergraduate (ʌndə'grædjuət) n Student m. Studentin f. Nichtgraduierter m.

underground (adv ʌndə'graund; adj,n 'ʌndəgraund) adv,adj 1 unterirdisch. 2 geheim. n Untergrund m. **underground (railway)** n Untergrundbahn, U-Bahn f.

undergrowth ('ʌndəgrouθ) n Unterholz neu.

underhand (ʌndə'hænd) adj hinterlistig.

underline (ʌndə'lain) vt unterstreichen.

undermine (ʌndə'main) vt untergraben.

underneath (ʌndə'ni:θ) adv unten, darunter. prep unter(halb).

underpants ('ʌndəpænts) n pl Unterhose f.

underpass ('ʌndəpɑːs) n Unterführung f.

underprivileged (ʌndə'privilidʒd) adj benachteiligt, unterprivilegiert.

understand* (ʌndə'stænd) vt verstehen, begreifen. **understanding** n Verständnis neu. Verstand m. adj verständnisvoll.

understate (ʌndə'steit) vt untertreiben.

understudy ('ʌndəstʌdi) n 1 Ersatzschauspieler m. 2 Ersatzmann m.

undertake* (ʌndə'teik) vt 1 unternehmen. 2 zusagen. **undertaker** n Leichenbestatter m. **undertaking** n 1 Unternehmen neu. 2 Versprechen neu.

undertone ('ʌndətoun) n 1 gedämpfte Stimme f. 2 Unterton m.

underwear ('ʌndəwɛə) n Unterwäsche f.

underworld ('ʌndəwə:ld) n Unterwelt f.

underwrite* ('ʌndərait) vt 1 unterschreiben. 2 comm versichern, übernehmen.

undesirable (ʌndi'zaiərəbəl) adj unerwünscht.

undo* (ʌn'du:) vt 1 aufmachen. 2 aufknöpfen, losbinden. 3 rückgängig machen. 4 ruinieren.

undoubted (ʌn'dautid) adj unbezweifelt.

undress (ʌn'dres) (vi,) vr (sich) ausziehen.

undue ('ʌndju:) adj 1 unangemessen, ungebührlich. 2 unnötig. 3 unzulässig.

undulate ('ʌndjuleit) vi wogen, wellen.

unearth (ʌn'ə:θ) vt 1 ausgraben. 2 ans Licht bringen. **unearthly** adj 1 unirdisch. 2 unheimlich.

uneasy (ʌn'iːzi) adj unruhig, ängstlich.

uneducated (ʌn'edjukeitid) adj ungebildet.

unemployed (ʌnim'plɔid) adj 1 arbeitslos. 2 unbeschäftigt. **the unemployed** n die Arbeitslosen pl. **unemployment** n Arbeitslosigkeit f.

unequal (ʌn'iːkwəl) adj ungleich.

uneven (ʌn'iːvən) adj 1 uneben. 2 unausgeglichen.

unfair (ʌn'fɛə) adj unfair, ungerecht.

unfaithful (ʌn'feiθfəl) adj treulos, untreu.

unfamiliar (ʌnfə'miliə) adj nicht vertraut.

unfit (ʌn'fit) adj 1 untauglich. 2 unfähig.

unfold (ʌn'fould) (vi,) vr (sich) entfalten.

unfortunate (ʌn'fɔːtʃunət) adj unglücklich.

unfurnished (ʌn'fəːniʃt) adj 1 nicht ausgerüstet. 2 unmöbliert.

ungrateful (ʌn'greitfəl) adj undankbar.

unhappy (ʌn'hæpi) adj unglücklich.

unhealthy (ʌn'helθi) adj ungesund.

unicorn ('juːnikɔːn) n Einhorn neu.

uniform ('juːnifɔːm) adj gleich(förmig), einförmig. n Uniform f.

unify ('juːnifai) vt vereinheitlichen, vereinigen.

unilateral (juːni'lætərəl) adj einseitig.

uninhabited (ʌnin'hæbitid) adj unbewohnt.

uninterested (ʌn'intrəstid) adj uninteressiert.

union ('juːniən) n 1 Vereinigung, Verbindung f. 2 Union f. 3 Verein m. 4 Einheit f.

Union Jack n britische Nationalflagge f.

unique (juː'niːk) adj 1 einzigartig, einmalig. 2 einzig.

unison ('juːnizən) n 1 Einklang m. 2 mus Unisono neu.

unit ('juːnit) n Einheit f.

unite (juː'nait) (vi,) vt (sich) vereinigen or vereinen. **unity** n 1 Einheit f. 2 Einigkeit f.

United Kingdom n das Vereinigte Königreich neu.

United States of America n die Vereinigten Staaten m pl.

universe ('ju:nivə:s) n Weltall, Universum neu. **universal** adj 1 allgemein, universal. 2 allumfassend.

university (ju:ni'və:siti) n Universität, Hochschule f.

unjust (ʌn'dʒʌst) adj ungerecht.

unkempt (ʌn'kempt) adj zerzaust, ungepflegt.

unkind (ʌn'kaind) adj unfreundlich, herzlos.

unknown (ʌn'noun) adj unbekannt.

unlawful (ʌn'lɔ:fəl) adj ungesetzlich.

unless (ən'les) conj 1 es sei denn, daß. 2 wenn...nicht.

unlike (ʌn'laik) adj unähnlich, ungleich. prep im Gegensatz zu. **unlikely** adj,adv unwahrscheinlich.

unload (ʌn'loud) vt ausladen, entladen.

unlock (ʌn'lɔk) vt aufschließen.

unlucky (ʌn'lʌki) adj unglücklich.

unnatural (ʌn'nætʃərəl) adj unnatürlich.

unnecessary (ʌn'nesəsri) adj unnötig.

unofficial (ʌnə'fiʃəl) adj nicht amtlich, inoffiziell.

unorthodox (ʌn'ɔ:θədɔks) adj unorthodox.

unpack (ʌn'pæk) vt,vi auspacken.

unpleasant (ʌn'plezənt) adj 1 unangenehm. 2 unfreundlich.

unpopular (ʌn'pɔpjulə) adj unbeliebt.

unprecedented (ʌn'presidentid) adj einmalig, unerhört, beispiellos.

unravel (ʌnrævəl) vt entwirren.

unreasonable (ʌn'ri:zənəbəl) adj unvernünftig, unsinnig.

unrelenting (ʌnri'lentiŋ) adj unerbittlich.

unreliable (ʌnri'laiəbəl) adj unzuverlässig.

unrest (ʌn'rest) n Unruhe f.

unruly (ʌn'ru:li) adj unbändig, ungestüm.

unscrew (ʌn'skru:) vt abschrauben, losschrauben.

unsettle (ʌn'setl) vt verwirren, durcheinanderbringen, ins Wanken bringen.

unsightly (ʌn'saitli) adj unansehnlich.

unsound (ʌn'saund) adj 1 ungesund. 2 unsicher. 3 unsolid(e). 4 falsch.

unsteady (ʌn'stedi) adj 1 wackelig. 2 unstet, unbeständig.

unsuccessful (ʌnsək'sesfəl) adj erfolglos.

untangle (ʌn'tæŋgəl) vt entwirren.

untidy (ʌn'taidi) adj unordentlich.

untie (ʌn'tai) vt aufbinden, auflösen.

until (ʌn'til) prep,conj bis. **not until** nicht vor, erst.

untrue (ʌn'tru:) adj falsch, unwahr.

unusual (ʌn'ju:ʒuəl) adj ungewöhnlich, seltsam.

unwell (ʌn'wel) adj unwohl.

unwind (ʌn'waind) vt abwinden. vi 1 sich abwickeln. 2 inf sich entspannen.

unwrap (ʌn'ræp) vt auswickeln.

up (ʌp) adv 1 auf(wärts). 2 hinauf. 3 empor. 4 nach oben. 5 oben, hoch. prep auf. **be up against** gegenüberstehen. **what's up?** inf was ist los?

upbringing ('ʌpbriŋiŋ) n Erziehung f.

upheaval (ʌp'hi:vəl) n Erhebung f. Umsturz m.

uphill (ʌp'hil) adv bergauf. adj 1 ansteigend. 2 anstrengend.

uphold (ʌp'hould) vt aufrecht(er)halten.

upholster (ʌp'houlstə) vt polstern. **upholstery** n Polsterung f.

upkeep ('ʌpki:p) n Instandhaltung f.

uplift (v ʌp'lift; n 'ʌplift) vt emporheben. n Hebung f.

upon (ə'pɔn) prep auf.

upper ('ʌpə) adj ober, höher. **upper class** n Oberklasse f. **upper house** n Oberhaus neu. **uppermost** adj oberst, höchst. adv am höchsten.

upright ('ʌprait) adj 1 aufrecht. 2 aufrichtig.

uprising ('ʌpraiziŋ) n Aufstand m. Erhebung f.

uproar ('ʌprɔ:) n Aufruhr, Lärm m.

uproot (ʌp'ru:t) vt entwurzeln.

upset (v, adj ʌp'set; n 'ʌpset) vt 1 umkippen. 2 (um)stürzen. 3 bestürzen. adj 1 umgekippt. 2 außer Fassung. n 1 Umsturz m. 2 Verstimmung f.

upshot ('ʌpʃɔt) n (End)Ergebnis neu. **in the upshot** am Ende.

upside down (ʌpsaid 'daun) adv 1 mit dem Kopf nach unten. 2 drunter und drüber.

upstairs (ʌp'stɛəz) adv 1 (nach) oben. 2 die Treppe hinauf. adj ober.

upstream (ʌp'stri:m) adv stromaufwärts.

upward ('ʌpwəd) adj ansteigend. adv aufwärts. **upwards** adv aufwärts.

uranium (ju'reiniəm) n Uran neu.

Uranus (ju'reinəs) n Uranus m.

urban ('ə:bən) adj städtisch.

urge (ə:dʒ) vt 1 (auf)drängen. 2 dringend bitten. n Drang m.

urgent ('ə:dʒənt) adj dringend.

urine ('juərin) n Urin, Harn m. **urinate** vi urinieren.

urn (ə:n) n Urne f.

us (ʌs) pron 1st pers pl uns.
usage ('juːsidʒ) n 1 Brauch m. 2 Gebrauch m.
use (vt juːz; vi,n juːs) vt 1 benutzen, gebrauchen. 2 anwenden. 3 ausnutzen. vi pflegen. n 1 Gebrauch m. 2 Anwendung f. 3 Nutzen neu. **useful** adj nützlich, brauchbar. **useless** adj 1 nutzlos. 2 unbrauchbar.
usher ('ʌʃə) n Platzanweiser m. vt (her-, hin)einführen. **usherette** n Platzanweiserin f.
usual ('juːʒuəl) adj gewöhnlich, üblich.
usurp (juːzɔːp) vt an sich reißen. vi sich widerrechtlich bemächtigen. **usurper** n 1 Usurpator, Thronräuber m. 2 Eindringling m.
utensil (juːtensəl) n Gerät neu.
uterus ('juːtərəs) n Gebärmutter f.
utility (juːtiliti) n Nützlichkeit f.
utmost ('ʌtməust) adj also **uttermost** äußerst, höchst. n Äußerste neu.
utter[1] ('ʌtə) vt äußern, sagen.
utter[2] ('ʌtə) adj 1 äußerst. 2 endgültig. 3 vollkommen.

V

vacant ('veikənt) adj 1 leer. 2 frei. 3 unbewohnt. 4 ausdruckslos. **vacancy** n 1 freie or offene Stelle f. 2 Leere f. **vacate** vt 1 räumen. 2 niederlegen. **vacation** n Ferien pl.
vaccine ('væksiːn) n Impfstoff neu. **vaccinate** vt impfen.
vacillate ('væsəleit) vi 1 schwanken. 2 zaudern.
vacuum ('vækjuəm) n 1 Vakuum neu. **vacuum cleaner** n Staubsauger m. **vacuum flask** n Thermosflasche f.
vagina (vəˈdʒainə) n anat Scheide f.
vagrant ('veigrənt) n Landstreicher m. adj wandernd.
vague (veig) adj vage, ungenau, undeutlich.
vain (vein) adj 1 eitel. 2 leer. **in vain** umsonst.
valiant ('væliənt) adj tapfer, mutig.
valid ('vælid) adj gültig. **validity** n Gültigkeit f.
valley ('væli) n Tal neu.
value ('væljuː) n Wert m. vt 1 bewerten. 2 (hoch)schätzen. **valuable** adj wertvoll. **valuables** n pl Wertsachen f pl.
valve (vælv) n 1 Ventil neu. 2 Klappe f.
vampire ('væmpaiə) n Vampir, Blutsauger m.
van (væn) n Lieferwagen, Lastwagen m.
vandal ('vændl) n Vandale m. **vandalism** n Vandalismus m.
vanilla (vəˈnilə) n Vanille f.
vanish ('væniʃ) vi verschwinden.

vanity ('væniti) n Eitelkeit f.
vapour ('veipə) n Dunst, Dampf m.
variety (vəˈraiəti) n 1 Vielfalt, Auswahl f. 2 Art f. **variety show** n Varietévorstellung f.
various ('veəriəs) adj verschieden(artig).
varnish ('vɑːniʃ) n 1 Firnis m. 2 Politur f. 3 Lack m. vt 1 firnissen. 2 polieren. 3 lackieren.
vary ('veəri) vt 1 (ab-, ver-)ändern. 2 wechseln. vi variieren. **variable** adj 1 veränderlich, wechselnd. 2 tech regelbar, variabel. **variant** adj abweichend. **variation** n 1 Veränderung f. Wechsel m. 2 Variation f.
vase (vɑːz) n Vase f.
vasectomy (væˈsektəmi) n Vasektomie f.
vast (vɑːst) adj 1 riesig. 2 ausgedehnt.
vat (væt) n Faß neu. Bottich m.
Vatican ('vætikən) n Vatikan m.
vault[1] (vɔːlt) n 1 Gewölbe neu. 2 Stahlkammer f. 3 Grabgewölbe neu. Gruft f.
vault[2] (vɔːlt) vi springen. vt überspringen.
veal (viːl) n Kalbfleisch neu.
veer (viə) (vi),vt (sich) drehen, (sich) wenden. vi umschwenken.
vegetable ('vedʒtəbəl) n 1 Gemüse neu. 2 Pflanze f. **vegetarian** n Vegetarier m. adj vegetarisch. **vegetation** n Vegetation f.
vehement ('viːimənt) adj heftig, vehement.
vehicle ('viːikəl) n 1 Fahrzeug neu. 2 Vehikel neu.
veil (veil) n Schleier m. vt verschleiern.
vein (vein) n 1 anat Vene f. 2 Ader f.
velocity (vəˈlɔsiti) n Geschwindigkeit f.
velvet ('velvit) n Samt m. adj 1 samtartig. 2 sanft.
vendetta (venˈdetə) n Blutrache f.
veneer (viˈniə) n Furnier neu. vt furnieren.
venerate ('venəreit) vt (ver)ehren, hochachten.
venereal disease (viˈniəriəl) n Geschlechtskrankheit f.
Venetian (viˈniːʃən) adj venezianisch. **Venetian blind** n Jalousie f.
vengeance ('vendʒəns) n Rache f.
Venice ('venis) n Venedig neu.
venison ('venisən) n Wildbret, Rehfleisch neu.
venom ('venəm) n Gift neu.
vent[1] (vent) n 1 Luftloch neu. 2 Öffnung f.
vent[2] (vent) vt freien Lauf lassen, auslassen.
ventilate ('ventileit) vt (durch)lüften.
venture ('ventʃə) n 1 Wagnis neu. 2 Unternehmen neu. vt wagen.
Venus ('viːnəs) n Venus f.
verb (vəːb) n Zeitwort, Verb(um) neu.

verdict ('və:dikt) n 1 law Urteilsspruch, Wahrspruch m. 2 Urteil neu.

verge (və:dʒ) n Rand m. vi grenzen.

verify ('verifai) vt 1 prüfen. 2 bestätigen. 3 beglaubigen.

vermin ('və:min) n Ungeziefer neu.

vermouth (və:məθ) n Wermut m.

vernacular (və'nækjulə) n 1 Landessprache f. 2 Umgangssprache f. 3 Jargon m.

versatile ('və:sətail) adj 1 vielseitig, wendig. 2 wandelbar.

verse (və:s) n 1 Vers m. Strophe f. 2 Poesie f.

version ('və:ʃən) n 1 Gestaltung f. 2 Auffassung, Version f.

vertebrate ('və:tibreit) n Wirbeltier neu.

vertical ('və:tikəl) adj senkrecht, vertikal.

verve (və:v) n Begeisterung f. Feuer neu.

very ('veri) adv sehr. adj 1 genau. 2 bloß. 3 derselbe.

vessel ('vesəl) n 1 naut Schiff neu. 2 Gefäß neu.

vest (vest) n Unterhemd neu.

vestment ('vestmənt) n Gewand neu.

vestry ('vestri) n Sakristei f.

vet (vet) inf n Tierarzt m. vt untersuchen.

veteran ('vetərən) n Veteran m.

veterinary surgeon ('vetrinəri) n Tierarzt m.

veto ('vi:tou) n 1 Veto neu. Einspruch m. 2 Einspruchsrecht neu. vt verbieten.

vex (veks) vt ärgern, plagen. **vexation** n 1 Ärger m. 2 Belästigung f.

via ('vaiə) prep über, via.

viable ('vaiəbəl) adj 1 lebensfähig. 2 praktisch, ausführbar.

viaduct ('vaiədʌkt) n Viadukt m. Brücke f.

vibrate (vai'breit) vi schwingen, vibrieren. **vibration** n Schwingung, Vibration f.

vicar ('vikə) n Vikar, Pfarrer m.

vicarious (vi'kɛəriəs) adj 1 aus zweiter Hand. 2 stellvertretend.

vice[1] (vais) n 1 Laster neu. 2 Fehler m.

vice[2] (vais) n Schraubstock m.

vice-chancellor n Vizekanzler m.

vice-president n Vizepräsident m.

vice versa ('və:sə) adj umgekehrt.

vicinity (vi'sinəti) n Nähe, Nachbarschaft f.

vicious ('viʃəs) adj 1 bösartig. 2 lasterhaft.

victim ('viktim) n Opfer neu. **victimize** vt 1 (auf)opfern. 2 quälen, belästigen.

Victorian (vik'tɔ:riən) adj 1 viktorianisch. 2 prüde. n Viktorianer m.

victory ('viktri) n Sieg m. **victorious** adj siegreich.

video-tape ('vidiouteip) n Magnetbildband neu.

Vienna (vi'enə) n Wien neu. **Viennese** adj wienerisch. n Wiener m.

Vietnam (viet'næm) n Vietnam neu. **Vietnamese** adj vietnamesisch. n Vietnamese m.

view (vju:) n 1 Aussicht f. 2 Ansicht f. 3 Einstellung f. **with a view to** zu dem Zweck. **view-finder** n Sucher m. ~vt 1 anschauen. 2 besichtigen.

vigil ('vidʒil) n Nachtwache f. **vigilant** adj wachsam.

vigour ('vigə) n 1 Kraft, Lebenskraft f. 2 Intensität f. **vigorous** adj 1 kräftig. 2 lebhaft.

vile (vail) adj 1 widerlich. 2 gemein.

villa ('vilə) n 1 Landhaus neu. 2 Villa f.

village ('vilidʒ) n Dorf neu. **villager** n Dorfbewohner m.

villain ('vilən) n Schurke m.

vindictive (vin'diktiv) adj rachsüchtig.

vine (vain) n 1 Rebe f. 2 Weinstock m. **vineyard** n Weinberg m.

vinegar ('vinigə) n Essig m.

vintage ('vintidʒ) n Lese f. adj hervorragend.

vinyl ('vainil) n Vinyl neu.

viola (vi'oulə) n Viola f.

violate ('vaiəleit) vt 1 verletzen, brechen. 2 schänden.

violence ('vaiələns) n 1 Gewalt(tätigkeit) f. 2 Heftigkeit f. **violent** adj 1 gewalttätig, gewaltsam. 2 heftig.

violet ('vaiəlit) adj violett. n 1 bot Veilchen neu. 2 Violett neu.

violin (vaiə'lin) n Violine, Geige f. **violinist** n Violinist m.

viper ('vaipə) n Viper, Natter f.

virgin ('və:dʒin) n Jungfrau f. adj also **virginal** jungfräulich.

Virgo ('və:gou) n Jungfrau f.

virile ('virail) adj männlich.

virtue ('və:tju:) n 1 Tugend f. 2 Vorzug m. **by virtue of** kraft. **virtual** adj eigentlich, tatsächlich. **virtuous** adj tugendhaft.

virus ('vaiərəs) n Virus m, neu.

visa ('vi:zə) n Visum neu. Einreisebewilligung f.

viscount ('vaikaunt) n Vicomte m.

vision ('viʒən) n 1 Sehvermögen neu. 2 Erscheinung f. 3 Anblick m. **visible** adj 1 sichtbar. 2 offensichtlich.

visit ('vizit) vt besuchen. n Besuch m.

visual ('vizjuəl) adj visuell, Seh—. **visualize** vt sich (klar) vorstellen.

vital ('vaitļ) adj 1 lebenswichtig. 2 Lebens—. 3 vital. **vitality** n Lebenskraft f.

vitamin ('vitəmin) n Vitamin neu.

vivacious (vai'veiʃəs) adj lebhaft, munter.

vivid ('vivid) adj lebhaft, deutlich.

vixen ('viksən) n zool Füchsin f.

vocabulary (və'kæbjuləri) n 1 Wortschatz m. Vokabular neu. 2 Wörterverzeichnis neu.

vocal ('voukəl) adj 1 mündlich, stimmlich. 2 stimmhaft. **vocal chords** n pl Stimmbänder neu pl.

vocation (vou'keiʃən) n 1 Berufung f. 2 Beruf neu.

vodka ('vodkə) n Wodka m.

voice (vois) n Stimme f. vt äußern.

void (void) adj 1 leer. 2 unwirksam. 3 ungültig. n 1 Leere f. 2 Lücke f.

volatile ('volətail) adj 1 flüchtig. 2 vorübergehend. 3 unbeständig. 4 lebhaft.

volcano (vol'keinou) n, pl -oes Vulkan m.

volley ('voli) n 1 mil Salve f. Hagel m. 2 sport Flugball m.

volt (voult) n Volt neu.

volume ('volju:m) n 1 Umfang m. 2 Inhalt m. Volumen neu. 3 Lautstärke f. 4 Band m.

volunteer (volən'tiə) n Freiwillige(r) m. vi sich freiwillig melden. vt freiwillig anbieten. **voluntary** adj freiwillig.

voluptuous (və'lʌptʃuəs) adj 1 wollüstig. 2 sinnlich.

vomit ('vomit) vi sich erbrechen or übergeben. vt auswerfen, ausspeien. n Erbrochene neu.

voodoo ('vu:du:) n Wodu, Wudu m.

vote (vout) n 1 Stimme f. 2 Stimmrecht neu. 3 Wahl f. vi abstimmen, wählen.

vouch (vautʃ) vi **vouch for** bürgen für.

voucher ('vautʃə) n 1 Gutschein m. 2 Unterlage f.

vow (vau) n Gelübde neu. vt geloben.

vowel ('vauəl) n Vokal m.

voyage ('voiidʒ) n (See)Reise f. vi reisen.

vulgar ('vʌlgə) adj 1 gemein, vulgär. 2 unanständig. 3 gewöhnlich.

vulnerable ('vʌlnrəbl) adj 1 verwundbar. 2 anfällig.

vulture ('vʌltʃə) n Geier m.

W

wad (wod) n 1 Bündel neu. Stoß m. 2 Bausch m. **wadding** n Watte, Wattierung f.

waddle ('wodl) vi watscheln. n Watscheln neu.

wade (weid) vi waten. **wade through** sich durcharbeiten durch.

wafer ('weifə) n 1 Waffel f. 2 rel Oblate f.

waft (woft) vt,vi wehen. n Wehen neu.

wag (wæg) vt 1 schütteln. 2 (a tail) wedeln.

waggle ('wægəl) vt wackeln.

wagon ('wægən) n 1 Lastwagen m. 2 Güterwaggon neu.

waif (weif) n verwahrlostes Kind neu.

wail (weil) vi wehklagen. n Klagen. neu.

waist (weist) n Taille f. **waistband** n Bund m. **waistcoat** n Weste f.

wait (weit) vi 1 warten. 2 bedienen. **wait for** erwarten, warten auf. **waiting list** n Warteliste f. **waiting room** n Wartezimmer neu. 2 (of a station) Wartesaal m. **waiter** n Kellner m. **waitress** n Kellnerin f.

waive (weiv) vt verzichten auf.

wake* (weik) also **wake up** vt (auf-, er-) wecken. vi erwachen, aufwachen. **waken** vi erwachen, aufwachen. vt (auf-, er-)wecken.

Wales ('weilz) n Wales neu.

walk (wo:k) vi 1 laufen, (zu Fuß) gehen. 2 wandern. n 1 Spaziergang m. 2 Gang m. **go for a walk** spazierengehen. **walking stick** n Spazierstock m. **walkout** n Streik m. **walkover** ('wo:kouvə) n leichter Sieg m.

wall (wo:l) n 1 Mauer f. 2 Wand f. **wallflower** n 1 bot Goldlack m. 2 inf Mauerblümchen neu. **wallpaper** n Tapete f.

wallet ('wolit) n Brieftasche f.

wallop ('woləp) inf vt prügeln, (heftig) schlagen. n (heftiger) Schlag m.

wallow ('wolou) vi sich wälzen.

walnut ('wo:lnʌt) n Walnuß f.

walrus ('wo:lrəs) n Walroß neu.

waltz (wo:ls) n Walzer m. vi Walzer tanzen.

wand (wond) n 1 (Zauber)Stab m. 2 mus Taktstock m.

wander ('wondə) vi 1 wandern. 2 irregehen. 3 abbiegen.

wane (wein) vi 1 (of the moon) abnehmen. 2 nachlassen, schwächer werden.

wangle ('wæŋgəl) vt sl 1 hinkriegen, organisieren. 2 abluchsen.

want (wont) vt 1 wollen. 2 benötigen. vi mangeln. n 1 Bedürfnis neu. 2 Not f. 3 Begierde f.

wanton ('wontən) adj 1 mutwillig. 2 geil.

war (wo:) n Krieg m. **wage war** Krieg führen. **warfare** n Kriegsführung f. Krieg m.

warble ('wo:bəl) vt,vi trillern, singen.

ward (wo:d) n 1 Abteilung f. 2 med Station f. 3 law Mündel neu. v **ward off** abwehren.

warden n 1 Vorsteher. m. 2 Jugendherbergsvater m. **warder** n (Gefängnis)Wärter m.

wardrobe ('wɔ:droub) n 1 Kleiderschrank m. 2 Garderobe f.

warehouse ('wɛəhaus) n Lagerhaus neu.

warm (wɔ:m) adj warm. vt (er)wärmen. vi sich erwärmen. **warm-blooded** adj warmblütig. **warm-hearted** adj warmherzig.

warn (wɔ:n) vt warnen. **warning** n Warnung f. adj warnend.

warp (wɔ:p) (vi),vt (sich) werfen, (sich) verziehen. n Verwerfung, Verkrümmung f.

warrant ('wɔrənt) n 1 Vollmacht f. 2 Rechtfertigung f. 3 Haftbefehl. m. vt 1 rechtfertigen. 2 haften für. **warrant officer** n 1 Stabsfeldwebel m. 2 Stabsbootsmann m.

warren ('wɔrən) n Gehege neu.

warrior ('wɔriə) n Krieger m.

wart (wɔ:t) n Warze f.

wary ('wɛəri) adj vorsichtig, behutsam.

was (wəz; stressed wɔz) v see be.

wash (wɔʃ) vt 1 waschen. 2 spülen. vi (sich) waschen. **wash up** spülen. ~n 1 Waschen neu. 2 Wäsche f. 3 naut Kielwasser neu. **washbasin** n Waschbecken neu. **washer** n tech Dichtungsring m. **washing** n 1 Wäsche f. 2 Waschen neu. **washing machine** n Waschmaschine f. **wash-out** n s/ Fiasko neu. **washroom** n Toilette f.

wasp (wɔsp) n Wespe f.

waste (weist) vt 1 verschwenden. 2 verwüsten. vi also **waste away** abnehmen, schwinden. ~adj 1 wüst. 2 unnütz. 3 Ab—. n 1 Müll, Abfall m. 2 Öde f. 3 Verschwendung f. **wastepaper basket** Papierkorb m.

watch (wɔtʃ) vt 1 bewachen. 2 beobachten. 3 zusehen. vi 1 aufpassen. 2 zuschauen. 3 wachen. **watch television** fernsehen. ~n 1 Armbanduhr f. 2 Taschenuhr f. 3 Wache f. **watchdog** n Wachhund m. **watchful** adj aufmerksam, wachsam.

water ('wɔ:tə) n Wasser neu. **drinking water** Trinkwasser neu. ~vt (be)wässern, (be)gießen. **water down** verwässern. **watering-can** n Gießkanne f.

water-closet n Klosett neu.

watercolour ('wɔ:təkʌlə) n 1 Aquarell neu. 2 Wasserfarbe f.

watercress ('wɔ:təkres) n Brunnenkresse f.

waterfall ('wɔ:təfɔ:l) n Wasserfall m.

waterlily ('wɔ:təlili) n Seerose f.

waterlogged ('wɔ:təlɔgd) adj vollgesogen.

watermill ('wɔ:təmil) n Wassermühle f.

waterproof ('wɔ:təpru:f) adj wasserdicht. n Regenmantel m. vt imprägnieren.

water-ski n Wasserschi m. vi Wasserschi fahren.

watertight ('wɔ:tətait) adj wasserdicht.

waterway ('wɔ:təwei) n Wasserweg m.

waterworks ('wɔ:təwɜ:ks) n pl Wasserwerk neu.

watery ('wɔ:təri) adj wässerig.

watt (wɔt) n Watt neu.

wave (weiv) n 1 Welle f. vi 1 winken. 2 wehen. vt 1 winken. 2 schwingen. 3 wellen. **waveband** n Frequenzband neu. **wavelength** n Wellenlänge f. **wavy** adj wellig, gewellt.

waver ('weivə) vi schwanken, zittern.

wax [1] (wæks) n Wachs neu. vt bohnern, wachsen. adj also **waxen** or **waxy** wächsern.

wax [2] (wæks) vi 1 wachsen, zunehmen. 2 werden.

way (wei) n 1 Weg m. 2 Mittel neu. 3 Richtung f. 4 Weise f. **by the way** übrigens, nebenbei. **under way** 1 unterwegs. 2 im Gange. **way in** Eingang m. **way out** Ausgang m.

waylay (wei'lei) vt auflauern.

wayward ('weiwəd) adj 1 widerspenstig. 2 launisch.

we (wi:) pron 1st pers pl wir.

weak (wi:k) adj schwach. **weak-minded** adj 1 schwachsinnig. 2 charakterschwach. **weak-willed** adj willensschwach. **weaken** vt 1 schwächen. 2 verdünnen. vi schwächer werden. **weakling** n Schwächling m.

wealth (welθ) n Reichtum m. **wealthy** adj wohlhabend, reich.

weapon ('wepən) n Waffe f.

wear* (wɛə) vt tragen. vi haltbar sein. **wear out** 1 abtragen, abnutzen. 2 ermüden.

weary ('wiəri) adj erschöpft, müde. vt 1 ermüden. 2 langweilen.

weasel ('wi:zəl) n Wiesel neu.

weather ('weðə) n Wetter neu. vt überstehen.

weave* (wi:v) vt 1 weben, wirken. 2 (ver)flechten. vi 1 weben. 2 sich verflechten.

web (web) n 1 Gewebe neu. 2 Netz neu.

wedding ('wediŋ) n Hochzeit f. **wedding anniversary** n Hochzeitstag m. **wedding ring** n Trauring m.

wedge (wedʒ) n Keil m. vt verkeilen.

Wednesday ('wenzdi) n Mittwoch m.

weed (wi:d) n Unkraut neu. vt jäten. **weed out** aussondern.

week (wi:k) n Woche f. **weekday** n Wochentag m. **weekend** n Wochenende neu.

weekly adj,adv wöchentlich. n Wochenzeitung f.

weep* (wi:p) vt,vi weinen.

weigh (wei) vt (ab)wiegen, abwägen. vi wiegen. **weighbridge** n Brückenwaage f. **weight** n 1 Gewicht neu. 2 Last f. **weightlifting** n Gewichtheben neu.

weird (wiad) adj 1 unheimlich. 2 inf ulkig.

welcome ('welkəm) adj,interj willkommen. vt willkommen heißen, begrüßen. n Willkommen neu.

weld (weld) vt schweißen.

welfare ('welfɛə) n Wohlfahrt f.

well¹ (wel) n Brunnen m. vi quellen. **well up** hervorquellen.

well² (wel) adv 1 gut. 2 wohl. adj gesund. interj also, na. **as well** auch. **do well** 1 gut tun. 2 wohlauf sein. 3 Erfolg haben. **feel good** wohlauf sein. **just as well** ebenso gut.

well-bred adj wohlerzogen.

well-built adj gut gebaut.

well-known adj (wohl)bekannt.

well-off adj wohlhabend.

well-paid adj wohlbezahlt.

well-spoken adj redegewandt.

well-worn adj abgenutzt.

Welsh (welʃ) adj walisisch. n (language) Walisisch neu. **Welshman** n Waliser m.

went (went) v see **go.**

wept (wept) v see **weep.**

were (wə:) v see **be.**

west (west) n 1 West(en) m. 2 cap Westen m. Abendland neu. adj westlich. adv westwärts, nach Westen. **westerly** adj westlich. n Westwind m. **western** adj westlich. n Wildwestfilm m. **westward** adj nach Westen. **westwards** adv westwärts.

West Indies ('indiz) n pl Westindien neu. **West Indian** adj westindisch. n Westindier m.

Westphalia (west'feilia) n Westfalen neu.

wet (wet) adj naß, feucht. n Nässe f. vt naßmachen, nässen.

whack (wæk) inf vt schlagen. n 1 heftiger Schlag m. 2 Anteil m.

whale (weil) n Wal(fisch) m.

wharf (wɔ:f) n Kai m. Landungsbrücke f.

what (wɔt) pron,interj was, wie. adj welch, was für ein. **what for?** wozu? **what sort of?** was für? **whatever** pron was auch immer, alles was. adj 1 welch auch immer. 2 überhaupt.

wheat (wi:t) n Weizen m.

wheedle ('wi:dl) vt beschwatzen, überreden. vi schmeicheln.

wheel (wi:l) n Rad neu. vt 1 rollen. 2 drehen. vi rollen. **wheelbarrow** n Schubkarren m. **wheelchair** n Rollstuhl m.

wheeze (wi:z) vi keuchen. n Keuchen neu.

whelk (welk) n Wellhornschnecke f.

when (wen) adv wann, zu welcher Zeit. conj als, wenn. **whenever** adv wann auch immer. conj wenn (immer), so oft als.

where (wɛə) adv,conj wo, wohin, woher. **whereabouts** n pl 1 Aufenthalt(sort) m. 2 Verbleib m. adv wo herum. **whereas** conj während. **whereby** adv,conj wodurch, wie. **whereupon** adv,conj worauf. **wherever** adv wo(hin) auch immer.

whether ('weðə) conj ob.

which (witʃ) pron 1 welch. 2 der. 3 was. adj welch. **whichever** pron welcher auch immer.

whiff (wif) n Hauch m. vt,vi paffen.

while (wail) conj also **whilst** während, solange. n Weile f.

whim (wim) n Laune, Grille f.

whimper ('wimpə) vi,vt wimmern.

whimsical ('wimzikəl) adj wunderlich.

whine (wain) vi wimmern, winseln.

whip (wip) n Peitsche f. vt 1 peitschen, schlagen. 2 reißen.

whippet ('wipit) n Whippet m.

whirl (wə:l) vi,vt wirbeln. n 1 Wirbeln neu. 2 Wirbel m. **whirlwind** n Wirbel(wind) m.

whirr (wə:) vi,(vt) schwirren (lassen). n Schwirren neu.

whisk¹ (wisk) vt 1 fegen. 2 rasch wegnehmen.

whisk² (wisk) cul vt schlagen. n Schneebesen m.

whiskers ('wiskəz) n pl 1 Backenbart m. 2 zool Schnurrhaare neu pl.

whisky ('wiski) n Whisky m.

whisper ('wispə) vi flüstern. n Geflüster neu.

whistle ('wisəl) vi,vt pfeifen. n 1 Pfeife f. 2 Pfiff m.

white (wait) adj weiß. n 1 Weiß neu. 2 Weiße(r) m. **whitewash** n (weiße) Tünche f. vt 1 tünchen, weißen. 2 reinwaschen. **whiting** n Weißfisch m.

Whitsun ('witsən) n Pfingsten neu.

whiz (wiz) vi sausen. n Sausen neu.

who (hu:) pron 1 wer. 2 der, welch. **whoever** pron 1 wer auch immer. 2 jeder der.

whole (houl) adj ganz, vollständig. n Ganze neu. Gesamtheit f. **wholehearted** adj rückhaltslos. **wholemeal** adj Vollkorn—. **wholesale** n Großhandel m. adj 1 Großhandels—. 2 vollständig. adv 1 im großen. 2 en gros

wholesome adj gesund, heilvoll. **wholly** adv ganz, völlig.

whom (hu:m) pron 1 wen, wem. 2 den, welchen.

whooping cough ('hu:piŋ) n Keuchhusten m.

whore (hɔ:) n Hure f. vi huren.

whose (hu:z) pron 1 wessen. 2 dessen.

why (wai) adv, conj warum, weshalb, wozu. interj nun, doch.

wick (wik) n Docht m.

wicked ('wikid) adj böse, boshaft.

wicket ('wikit) n sport Tor neu. Dreistab m.

wide (waid) adj breit, weit. **widely** adv 1 weit, breit. 2 in hohem Maße. **widen** vt erweitern. **widespread** adj weit verbreitet.

widow ('widou) n Witwe f. **widower** n Witwer m.

width (widθ) n Breite, Weite f.

wield (wi:ld) vt 1 handhaben. 2 ausüben.

wife (waif) n, pl **wives** (Ehe)Frau f.

wig (wig) n Perücke f.

wiggle ('wigəl) vi,(vt) wackeln mit.

wigwam ('wigwæm) n Wigwam m.

wild (waild) adj wild. **run wild** 1 sich austoben. 2 wild wachsen. **wildlife** n Wild neu.

wilderness ('wildənəs) n Wildnis, Wüste f.

wilful ('wilfəl) adj 1 eigensinnig. 2 absichtlich.

will[1] (wil) v mod aux 1 werden. 2 wollen. 3 sollen.

will[2] (wil) n 1 Wille f. 2 Testament neu. **willpower** n Willenskraft f.

willing ('wiliŋ) adj (bereit)willig.

willow ('wilou) n Weide f.

wilt (wilt) vi (ver)welken.

win[*] (win) vt 1 gewinnen. 2 erlangen. vi gewinnen, siegen. n Sieg m.

wince (wins) vi zusammenzucken.

winch (wintʃ) n Winde, Kurbel f.

wind[1] (wind) n Wind m. **windbag** n Windbeutel m. **windfall** n 1 Glücksfall m. 2 Fallobst m. **wind instrument** n Blasinstrument neu. **windmill** n Windmühle f. **windpipe** n Luftröhre f. **windscreen** n Windschutzscheibe f. **windscreen wipers** n pl Scheibenwischer m. **windswept** adj sturmgepeitscht. **windy** adj windig.

wind[2] (waind) vt 1 winden, wickeln. 2 drehen. vi sich winden.

windlass ('windləs) n Winde, Haspel f.

window ('windou) n Fenster neu. **window box** n Blumenkasten m. **window-shop** vi einen Schaufensterbummel machen.

wine (wain) n Wein m.

wing (wiŋ) n 1 Flügel m. 2 aviat Tragfläche f. 3 Gruppe f. vi fliegen. **wing commander** n Oberstleutnant der britischen Luftwaffe m.

wink (wiŋk) vi,vt blinzeln. n Blinzeln neu.

winkle ('wiŋkəl) n Strandschnecke f.

winter ('wintə) n Winter m. vi,vt überwintern.

wipe (waip) vt (ab)wischen. n Wischen neu.

wire (waiə) n 1 Draht m. 2 Telegramm neu. vt 1 telegrafieren. 2 mit Draht versehen.

wise (waiz) adj weise, klug.

wish (wiʃ) vt,vi wünschen. n Wunsch m.

wisp (wisp) n 1 Wisch m. 2 Streifen m.

wisteria (wis'tiəriə) n Glyzine f.

wistful ('wistfəl) adj sehnsüchtig.

wit (wit) n 1 Witz, Esprit m. 2 Verstand m.

witch (witʃ) n Hexe f. **witchcraft** n Hexerei f.

with (wið) prep mit, bei.

withdraw (wið'drɔ:) vi sich zurückziehen, ausscheiden. vt zurückziehen.

wither ('wiðə) vi (ver)welken, vertrocknen.

withhold (wið'hould) vt 1 zurückhalten. 2 vorenthalten.

within (wið'in) prep in, innerhalb, binnen. adv drinnen.

without (wið'aut) prep ohne. adv (dr)außen.

withstand (wið'stænd) vt widerstehen.

witness ('witnəs) n Zeuge m. vt 1 bezeugen. 2 Zeuge sein von.

witty ('witi) adj geistreich, witzig.

wizard ('wizəd) n Zauberer, Hexenmeister m.

wobble ('wɔbəl) vi wackeln.

woke (wouk) v see **wake**.

woken ('woukən) v see **wake**.

wolf (wulf) n Wolf m.

woman ('wumən) n 1 Frau f. 2 Weib neu.

womb (wu:m) n Gebärmutter f.

wonder ('wʌndə) n 1 Wunder neu. 2 Verwunderung f. vi 1 sich fragen. 2 sich wundern. **wonderful** adj wunderbar.

wonky ('wɔŋki) adj inf schwankend, wackelig.

wood (wud) n 1 Holz neu. 2 Wald m. **woodcock** n Waldschnepfe f. **wooden** adj 1 hölzern. 2 ausdruckslos, steif. **woodland** n Wald m. Waldland neu. **woodpecker** n Specht m. **woodpigeon** n Ringeltaube f. **woodwind** n Holzblasinstrument neu. **woodwork** n Holzwerk neu. **woodworm** n Holzwurm m.

wool (wul) n Wolle f. **woollen** adj wollen, Woll—. **woolly** adj 1 wollen. 2 wollig. 3 verschwommen.

word (wə:d) n Wort neu. vt ausdrücken.

wore (wɔ:) v see **wear**.

work (wəːk) n 1 Arbeit f. 2 Werk neu. 3 pl Werk neu. Betrieb m. vi 1 arbeiten. 2 funktionieren. vt 1 bearbeiten. 2 betätigen, bedienen. 3 min ausbeuten. **worker** n 1 Arbeiter m. 2 pl Arbeiterschaft f. **working class** n Arbeiterklasse f. **workman** n Arbeiter, Handwerker m. **workmanship** n 1 Kunstfertigkeit f. 2 Arbeit f.

world (wəːld) n Welt f. adj Welt—. **not for the world** um keinen Preis. **man/woman of the world** n Weltmann, Weltdame m,f. **worldly** adj weltlich. **worldwide** adj weltweit.

worm (wəːm) n Wurm m.

wormwood ('wəːmwud) n Wermut m.

worn (wɔːn) adj abgenutzt.

worry ('wʌri) vi sich sorgen or beunruhigen. vt 1 beunruhigen. 2 plagen. n 1 Sorge f. Kummer m. 2 Ärger m.

worse (wəːs) adj,adv schlechter, schlimmer. **worsen** (vi),vt (sich) verschlechtern, (sich) verschlimmern.

worship ('wəːʃip) vt anbeten, verehren. vi beten. n Anbetung, Verehrung f.

worst (wəːst) adj schlechtest, schlimmst. adv am schlimmsten. vt überwältigen.

worth (wəːθ) n Wert m. adj wert. **it is worth doing** es lohnt sich, es zu tun. **worthwhile** adj der Mühe wert. **worthy** adj würdig, wert.

would (wud; stressed wud) v see **will**[1].

wound[1] (wuːnd) n Wunde, Verletzung f. vt verwunden, verletzen.

wound[2] (waund) v see **wind**[2].

wove (wouv) v see **weave.**

wrangle ('ræŋgəl) vi zanken. n Zank m.

wrap (ræp) vt (um-, ein-)wickeln. n 1 Hülle f. 2 Schal m. **wrapper** n Hülle f. Umschlag m. **wrapping** n Hülle, Verpackung f. **wrapping paper** n Packpapier neu.

wreath (riːθ) n 1 Kranz m. 2 Gewinde f.

wreathe (riːð) vt 1 winden. 2 bekränzen. vi sich winden or kräuseln.

wreck (rek) n 1 Wrack m. 2 Schiffbruch m. vt 1 zertrümmern. 2 zerstören. **wreckage** n Trümmer.

wren (ren) n Zaunkönig m.

wrench (rentʃ) vt verrenken, verdrehen. n 1 (heftiger) Ruck m. 2 tech Schraubenschlüssel m.

wrestle ('resəl) vi ringen, kämpfen mit. vt ringen n Ringkampf m.

wretch (retʃ) n Elende(r) m. **wretched** adj elend, unglücklich.

wriggle ('rigəl) vi sich winden. n Winden neu.

wring* (riŋ) vt 1 (aus)wringen. 2 (an animal's neck) abdrehen. 3 (one's hands) ringen.

wrinkle ('riŋkəl) n Runzel, Falte. f. (vi),vt (sich) falten, (sich) runzeln.

wrist (rist) n Handgelenk neu. **wristwatch** n Armbanduhr f.

writ (rit) n 1 Erlaß m. 2 law Vorladung f.

write* (rait) vt,vi schreiben. **write down** aufschreiben, niederschreiben. **write off** abschreiben. **write up** (ausführlich) beschreiben. **writer** n 1 Verfasser m. 2 Schriftsteller m. **writing paper** n Schreibpapier neu.

writhe (raið) vi sich krümmen, sich winden.

wrong (rɔŋ) adj 1 verkehrt, falsch. 2 unrecht. 3 irrtümlich. adv falsch, verkehrt. **be wrong** unrecht haben. **go wrong** schiefgehen. **something is wrong** etwas stimmt nicht. **what is wrong?** was ist los?

wrote (rout) v see **write.**

wrought iron (rɔːt) n Schmiedeeisen neu.

wrung (rʌŋ) v see **wring.**

wry (rai) adj schief, verzogen.

X

xenophobia (zenə'foubiə) n Fremdenhaß m.

Xerox ('ziərɔks) Tdmk n Photokopiergerät neu. vt photokopieren.

X-ray n Röntgenstrahl m. vt röntgen.

xylophone ('zailəfoun) n Xylophon neu.

Y

yacht (jɔt) n Jacht f. vi segeln. **yachtsman** n 1 Jachtsegler. 2 Jachtbesitzer m.

yank (jæŋk) vi,vt inf heftig ziehen.

yap (jæp) vi kläffen.

yard[1] (jɑːd) n Yard neu. **yardstick** n Maßstab m.

yard[2] (jɑːd) n Hof m.

yarn (jɑːn) n 1 Garn neu. Faden m. 2 Erzählung f. **spin a yarn** ein Seemannsgarn spinnen.

yawn (jɔːn) vi gähnen. n Gähnen neu.

year (jiə) n Jahr neu. **yearly** adj,adv jährlich.

yearn (jəːn) vi sich sehnen. **yearning** n Sehnsucht f. Sehnen neu.

yeast (jiːst) n Hefe f.

yell (jel) vi,vt (gellend) schreien. n gellende(r) Schrei m.

yellow ('jelou) adj gelb. n Gelb neu.

yelp (jelp) vi kläffen.

yes (jes) *adv* ja, jawohl. *n* Ja *neu*.

yesterday ('jestədi) *adv* gestern. *n* der gestrige Tag *m*. **the day before yesterday** vorgestern. **yesterday's** *adj* gestrig.

yet (jet) *adv* 1 (schon) noch. 2 sogar. 3 schon. 4 bis jetzt. *conj* jedoch. **not yet** noch nicht.

yew (ju:) *n* Eibe *f*.

Yiddish ('jidiʃ) *n* Jiddisch *neu*.

yield (ji:ld) *vt* 1 hervorbringen, einbringen. 2 hergeben. 3 tragen. *vi* 1 nachgeben. 2 sich ergeben. 3 tragen. *n* Ertrag *m*.

yodel ('joudl) *vi* jodeln.

yoga ('jougə) *n* Joga *m*.

yoghurt ('jɔgət) *n* Joghurt *m*.

yoke (jouk) *n* Joch *neu*. *vt* anjochen.

yolk (jouk) *n* Dotter *m*. Eigelb *neu*.

yonder ('jɔndə) *adv* dort drüben. *adj* jener.

you (ju:) *pron 2nd pers* 1 *fam* du, dich, dir. 2 *fml* Sie, Ihnen. 3 *pl fam* ihr, euch. 4 *pl fml* Sie, Ihnen. 5 *imp* man, einen, einem.

young (jʌŋ) *adj* jung. **youngster** *n* Junge *m*.

your (jɔ:, juə) *poss adj 2nd pers* 1 *fam* dein. 2 *fml* Ihr. 3 *pl fam* euer. 4 *pl fml* Ihr. **yours** *poss pron 2nd pers* 1 *fam* deiner, der deine or deinige. 2 *fml* Ihrer, der Ihre or Ihrige. 3 *pl fam* eurer, der eure or eurige. 4 *pl fml* Ihrer, der Ihre or Ihrige. **yourself** *pron 2nd pers s* 1 *fam* dich, dich selbst, du selbst. 2 *fml* sich, sich selbst, Sie selbst. **yourselves** *pron 2nd pers pl* 1 *fam* euch, euch selbst, ihr selbst. 2 *fml* sich, sich selbst, Sie selbst.

youth (ju:θ) *n* 1 Jugend *f*. 2 Jüngling *m*. **youth hostel** *n* Jugendherberge *f*.

Yugoslavia (ju:gou'slɑ:viə) *n* Jugoslawien *neu*. **Yugoslav** *n* Jugoslawe *m*. *adj* jugoslawisch.

Z

Zambia ('zæmbiə) *n* Sambia *neu*.

zeal (zi:l) *n* Eifer *m*.

zebra ('zebrə) *n* Zebra *neu*. **zebra crossing** *n* Zebrastreifen *m pl*.

zero ('ziərou) *n* 1 Null *f*. 2 Gefrierpunkt *m*.

zest (zest) *n* Begeisterung *f*. Reiz *m*.

zigzag ('zigzæg) *n* Zickzack *m*. *adj, adv* im Zickzack.

zinc (ziŋk) *n* Zink *neu*.

Zionism ('zaiənizəm) *n* Zionismus *m*.

zip (zip) *n* Zischen *neu*. *vi* sausen. *vt* mit einem Reißverschluß schließen. **zip (fastener)** *n* Reißverschluß *m*.

zodiac ('zoudiæk) *n* Tierkreis *m*.

zone (zoun) *n* 1 Zone *f*. 2 Erdgürtel *m*.

zoo (zu:) *n* Zoo *m*. **zoology** *n* Zoologie *f*. **zoological** *adj* zoologisch. **zoologist** *n* Zoologe *m*.

zoom (zu:m) *vi* 1 summen. 2 *aviat* hochschnellen.

Zurich ('zjuərik) *n* Zürich *neu*.